Audio Processes

Audio Processes

Musical Analysis, Modification, Synthesis, and Control

David Creasey

NEW YORK AND LONDON

First published 2017
by Routledge
711 Third Avenue, New York, NY 10017

and by Routledge
2 Park Square, Milton Park, Abingdon, Oxon OX14 4RN

Routledge is an imprint of the Taylor & Francis Group, an informa business

Library of Congress Cataloging in Publication Data
Names: Creasey, D. P. (David P.), author.
Title: Audio processes : musical analysis, modification, synthesis, and control / David Creasey.
Description: New York ; London : Routledge, 2017. | ©2017
Identifiers: LCCN 2016012376 | ISBN 9781138100138 (hardback) | ISBN 9781138100114 (paperback) | ISBN 9781315657813 (ebook)
Subjects: LCSH: Computer sound processing. | Music–Computer programs.
Classification: LCC MT723 .C72 2017 | DDC 786.7–dc23
LC record available at http://lccn.loc.gov/2016012376

ISBN: 978-1-138-10013-8 (hbk)
ISBN: 978-1-138-10011-4 (pbk)
ISBN: 978-1-315-65781-3 (ebk)

Typeset in URW Palladio L by the author
Printed and bound by CPI Group (UK) Ltd, Croydon, CR0 4YY

Contents

Part III — Synthesis

Appendices

Key Data Resources

Abbreviations

AD	Attack-Decay
ADC	Analogue-to-Digital Converter
ADR	Attack-Decay-Release
ADSR	Attack-Decay-Sustain-Release
AHDSR	Attack-Hold-Decay-Sustain-Release
AM	Amplitude Modulation
AR	Attack-Release
ASR	Attack-Sustain-Release
BPF	Bandpass Filter
BPM	Beats Per Minute
BRF	Bandreject Filter
DAC	Digital-to-Analogue Converter
DAW	Digital Audio Workstation
DC	Direct Current (0Hz)
DFT	Discrete Fourier Transform
EG	Envelope Generator
EQ	Equaliser/Equalisation
FDN	Feedback Delay Network
FFT	Fast Fourier Transform
FIR	Finite Impulse Response
FM	Frequency Modulation
HPF	Highpass Filter

HF	High Frequency
HMF	High-Mid Frequency
IFFT	Inverse Fast Fourier Transform
IIR	Infinite Impulse Response
LF	Low Frequency
LMF	Low-Mid Frequency
LPF	Lowpass Filter
MF	Mid-range Frequency
MIDI	Musical Instrument Digital Interface
PWM	Pulse-Width Modulation
RMS	Root Mean Square
SPL	Sound Pressure Level
STFT	Short Time Fourier Transform

Preface

The Power of Audio Processes

Digital audio processes are algorithmic forms that generate, modify, and analyse audio data. They dominate the landscape of audio recording and production, deeply affecting the way in which music is originated, performed, edited, and consumed. Audio processes enable the exploration of obscure hidden features within sounds, the radical transformation of tonality, the generation of instrument sounds with wild new characteristics, and the potential to all be controlled with natural and expressive human gestures. They also allow great subtlety and precision; slightly changing individual frequencies and amplitudes, accurately synthesising the character of acoustic instruments, and gently massaging a track to fit better in a mix.

The potential is vast, but the basic principles of audio processes are within the grasp of novices and enthusiasts. This is aided by the fact that the quantity of key element types is relatively modest. Figure 1 illustrates the most common process elements that appear in this book. Audio processes are often based on simple forms that are gradually expanded into larger structures. Where the expansion ends depends on the complexity that is desired and how much computational power is available. But even simple forms can have sufficient capacity to provide hours of pleasure. A simple monophonic synthesizer, a distortion effect, and some imagination is sufficient for creating superb musical results.

Exploring the potential of audio processes can take a lifetime. Not only is there the opportunity to build bigger and bigger structures, but also the depth to dig down to the underlying construction of elements and their relationship to the way in which humans perceive sound. This book covers a wide range of topics and provides many routes to explore the world of audio analysis, modification, synthesis, and control. All of them build from decades of work by dedicated individuals, and there are a huge number of books, journal papers, and other sources of information for those who want to learn more. The journey starts here.

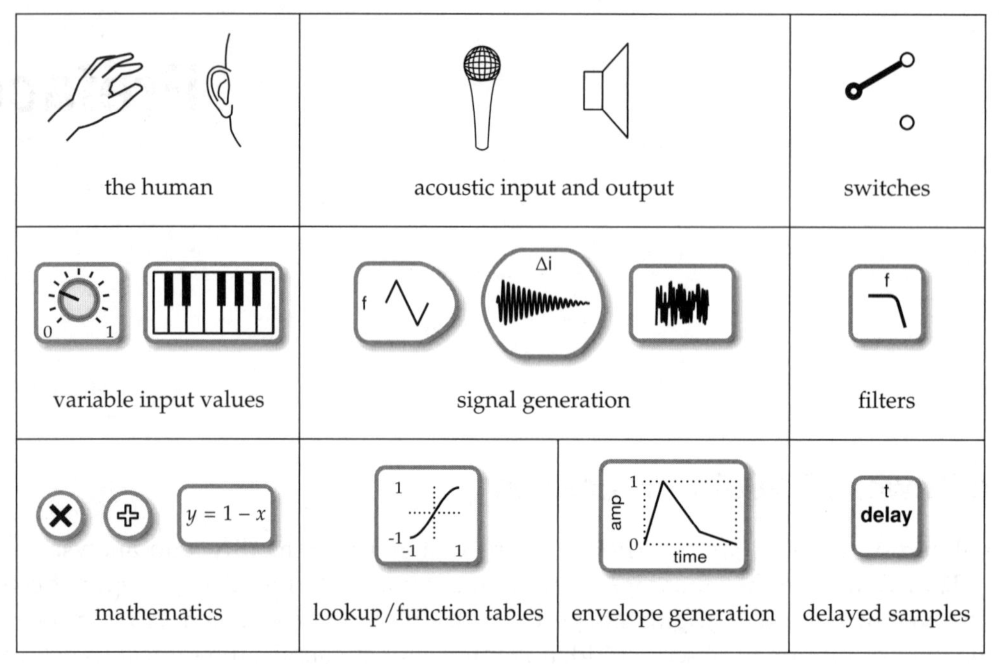

Figure 1 Common process elements

How to Use this Book

This book is about the practical design of audio processes for musical applications. Computer software for making and recording music is the main application being considered, but the principles are also applicable to other situations. This is not a book that teaches programming nor how to use commercial effects and synthesizers; there are many other books in those areas. Rather, the information here is about the insides of audio processes; understanding how they work, and creating new designs.

This book can be read in different ways depending on prior understanding and the topics of interest. For someone who is new to audio processes and needs a comprehensive grounding in the subject, such as an undergraduate university student, the expectation is that it will be read from the start to the end. The chapters of this book are ordered to aid in the progressive accumulation of understanding. The early chapters introduce fundamental ideas and processes, which later chapters build into more complex arrangements. Care has been taken in sequencing the topics to reduce the need to understand everything at once.

Those with prior experience might choose to read individual chapters, as efforts have been made to contain related methods together, rather than spreading them across the book. Inevitably there are many overlaps between techniques, however, and it is often possible to combine approaches to achieve more sophisticated results. Cross-references are provided where possible to direct the reader to related chapters and methods, rather than repeating basic ideas in every chapter. Notations specific to particular programming languages are avoided where possible.

The aim of the book is to explain the key techniques for each topic. From the fundamentals it is usually possible to achieve sophistication by expanding and combining ideas. Although it is not always the case, a simple process with a small number of elements will tend to produce an unsophisticated result. Professional systems build on basic ideas to create more naturalistic, tonally-interesting or target-specific results.

Digital audio processes are implemented as computer software within different types of environment:

- **Conventional text-based general purpose programming languages**. For conventional languages libraries of functions exist to provide audio and control input and output, and often complete objects such as filters, oscillators, and envelope generators. The power of conventional languages can be in the access to low-level data and associated structures, which allow more compact and effective coding by moving beyond simple linking of standard process elements. The issue for many people is the time taken to learn the programming language, in order to then apply it to audio process development.
- **Graphical/visual dataflow programming environments**. In these environments audio process objects are provided to the user in their finished form, ready to be configured and linked together as required. This can make it easy to rapidly develop a prototype, as well as construct larger processes. The visual environment can often make the nature of signal flows clearer than in text-based programming languages. However, organising the process for greatest clarity and efficiency can be a challenge. There are usually ways of extending the functionality with custom objects, which might be programmed by third parties or users themselves, in order to overcome limitations with the standard elements.
- **Text-based audio-specific programming languages**. These have rapid prototyping characteristics that are similar to graphical dataflow environments, but a visual form more similar to text-based general purpose languages.

Many people find it helpful to learn through practice, and methods are presented in this book to encourage this. However, this book does not assume that a particular programming language or environment is being used. There is no perfect choice that can be recommended, so personal preference will affect the selection. It is often the case that there is a balance to be chosen between initial learning curve and ultimate flexibility. Different environments, toolkits, and libraries have different strengths, and so sometimes the choice can affect the ease with which certain processes can be created. However, common elements sufficient for the majority of process types tend to be available in all standard audio programming environments.

The audio processes in this book are applicable to a wide range of software implementations. There are three major representations that are used:

- Block diagrams are the main tool for explaining how process elements are linked together to achieve particular results. It is normally easy to translate from a block diagram to the on-screen representations in a graphical programming environment. In text-based programming languages, the data flow through a complex process element is typically implemented as a function call, and the links between elements are variables.
- Text-based algorithmic forms are used where a block diagram is unable to express a process elegantly or clearly. They are designed for readability and to allow easy translation into conventional programming languages. Conventions are as follows:
  - Assignment is with "=" but equality is tested with "==". For example:

    ```
    if x == 1 then
    └ out = in * 2
    ```

  - Inequality is tested with "!=" (meaning "not equal to"). For example:

    ```
    if x != 2 then
    └ y = x + 6
    ```

  - Comments are from a double-slash to the end of the line. For example:

    ```
    position = position + 1     // move to next position
    ```

  - Arrays are accessed with an index in square brackets and the first element is index 0. For example, to store the value 7 in the first element of an array called *buffer*:

    ```
    buffer[0] = 7
    ```

- Mathematical equations are used for compactness and clarity when the alternative would be a long algorithm or a messy block diagram. Angles are expressed in radians (and therefore trigonometric function arguments as well). See Appendix A for further help in understanding the mathematical forms in this book.

Additional supporting materials for this book can be found on the companion website (www.routledge.com/cw/creasey).

Acknowledgements

This book is dedicated to my Dad, John Creasey, and the memory of my Mum, Gwenn.

Many thanks to all those who have supported the production of this book, directly or indirectly, including:

★ The Music Technology staff at the University of the West of England, Bristol (Stephen Allan, Zak Baracskai, Rich Brown, Lukas Greiwe, Martyn Harries, Adrian Hull, Gethin John, Liz Lane, Marcus Lynch, Tom Mitchell, Chris Nash, Phill Phelps, Alan Price, Martin Robinson, Matt Welch), and all my other colleagues past and present.

★ The students I have taught at UWE, whose demands for greater clarity have helped me to develop new explanations and examples whenever I thought that things were obvious.

★ Martyn Harries for playing the trumpet, and Linda Allan for helping with vocal recordings.

★ Ian Holmes and the UWE Centre for Performing Arts for providing a number of instruments for recording.

★ Purton Methodist Church for allowing their vintage organ to be recorded.

★ Chris Nash for being technical editor, counsellor, and for providing suggestions for improvements.

★ Everyone at Routledge/Focal Press for dealing with my many questions and complex requirements.

★ Anne Collie, John Collie, and Jude Sullivan for their encouragement and interest in the project.

★ Saskia, Lily, and Poppy for help and company in the office.

★ My brother, Steve.

Finally I want to thank my wife, Emma, for her musical talents, emotional support, English language skills, and endless patience in coping with what seemed like a never-ending project.

1

Introduction

1.1 The Nature of Audio Processes

1.1.1 Introducing Audio Processes

Audio processes are at the heart of common musical software such as effects and synthesizers. Fundamentally they are algorithmic forms that generate, modify, and analyse audio data. Their design is not driven by simple rules, but rather through the requirements of musical practice and their relationship to the human auditory system. In one musical context a particular effect might be regarded as enhancing the result, in another it might be regarded as completely inappropriate. The configuration of that effect can depend on the combination of notes being played, and the role of a particular instrument within the overall mix.

There is endless scope for developing novel versions of audio processes to match the variety and context-specific requirements of the target applications. The subject would not be as interesting if there were a single method that was always applied in the same way for a particular problem. There are, however, common principles and techniques that enable the novice to start from the fundamentals and work gradually towards more complex forms. This is one of the key roles of this book.

1.1.2 Constructing an Audio Process

These are some of the significant features that influence audio process design, implementation, and configuration:

- There is substantial scope for varying the designs of audio processes to fit the context and the artistic desires of the user. The wide range of commercial implementations of audio processes demonstrates the range of possibilities for tonal variation and control style, and the many possible situations to which the processes could be applied.
- Available computation and storage has always had a strong influence on the development of digital audio process implementations. The extensibility of audio processes means that gains in computational capabilities always appear to be matched by increases in algorithmic complexity to take advantage of the additional processing power. If there are restrictions within which an audio process must work, there will be influences on the tonal character produced.
- Fashion and novelty can cause certain ideas to receive more attention than others, such as a fashion for vocoding and pitch correction, or a desire for warm or dirty-sounding compression, or sample-based synthesis. As research progresses, new methods and new associated sound characters add to the available palette.

- Control characteristics, accessibility, and learning time are all important. A process is more than just the underlying computation and audio output, as its usefulness depends on the nature of the mapping from the user to the system. The idea is to optimise the relationship, such that the quantity of control parameters is not excessive, that a synthesizer can be played in an expressive manner, that the reaction of a modifier to change of control values is progressive and natural, and so on.

A wide variety of audio processes exist:

- Some processes are so common that they are regarded as standard technology. These can be found in such places as on mixing consoles and effects racks in the studio. Many are based on requirements that have not changed fundamentally in many years.
- Some processes are well known, but often seen as less mainstream, or suitable for more experimental composers or producers, or only the domain of specialists such as synthesizer programmers. Some have been around for many years, but the average home studio musician is less likely to have any direct experience of them.
- Some processes are created as custom one-off solutions to particular problems. This might be a tool that is needed in a particular studio for a particular session, or an art installation with very particular requirements.

Although the capability exists to produce any possible sound, there is the issue of how to get from an idea to an implementation. One way of starting is to recognise that many people want to produce systems that relate in some way to the world around us, such as a realistic cathedral-like reverberation, or synthesis of a percussive instrument, or a performance interface that utilises arm gestures.

It is often harder to achieve audio processes that fit naturally into the sound world than it is to create "unnatural" sounds. For example, creating a sound that has never been heard before might be achieved by sketching and synthesising an arbitrary waveform. Synthesising a sound that convincingly could have come from an acoustic source (an animal, an instrument), yet actually does not exist outside the computer, is a rather more complex task. It is necessary to understand the nature of sounds from acoustic sources; how they start, how they develop over time, how the sound character can be altered by physical interaction, and so on. In that way, an audio process can convince the listener that the result should fit in the soundscape being created.

Although it can appear daunting to have many possibilities, there is a fairly logical progression in how a fundamental method can be enhanced or extended. For example, a parallel set of bandpass filters can be added to many modification and synthesis processes to add tonal shaping. A distortion method can be applied to synthesis outputs in the same way that it is applied to a guitar signal. A varying blend of multiple oscillators can be used in place of a single oscillator in a synthesis scheme. This book explains not only the fundamental toolkit of audio process structures, but also suggests ways in which the parts can be used to build more sophisticated forms.

1.1.3 Real-Time and Non-Real-Time Systems

A typical audio process has some means by which current or past outputs are used to inform future action. For example, the value on a mixing console level meter reflects the recent audio signal level, such that the engineer can adjust the amplitude gain. Likewise the sound of an instrument will be used by the performer to adjust their control of the instrument, and so the future audible results. If the output of a system is occurring at the same time as the inputs are affecting those results, then the system is working in a *real-time* (or performance) mode. Playing an instrument is usually a real-time process.

However, some tasks are performed where there is no real-time performance interaction. This can be called a *non-real-time* (or editing) mode. In these cases the output is not being produced continuously in response to the control inputs, such as when a system is being configured in preparation for a performance. Computer-based tasks have historically been orientated around an editing-type mode, with often only one parameter being affected at once, such as when adjusting a setting in a popup window accessed from a menu. In those cases there is a series of separate steps performed in sequence towards an end, rather than a performance interaction.

Some typical non-real-time tasks are:

- Non-linear audio editing where a portion of a sound file is cut from one position in time and pasted at another. It would be possible to do this by selecting the portion while the sound is playing, and pasting it as the relevant position is reached during playback. For purposes of precise control, however, it is far more desirable to make this edit graphically, and then play back the result as a separate step.
- Arranging music for an orchestra. It would be enormously time-consuming to try arranging music while the whole orchestra were present, attempting to direct each player individually as to the composer's intentions. The normal method is to write the score in an editing stage beforehand, using knowledge of instrument ranges and sound characters, and an understanding of harmony and so forth. Individual parts might be tested on another instrument such as a piano or synthesizer, but the full effect is only achieved in the performance stage when the score is used by the orchestra.
- Complex computer-based sound processing. There are tasks for which real-time operation is beyond the state of the art. If the system is not fast enough, it can be necessary to let the computer generate a result (such as a sound file), and then to play that back when the task has been completed. Historically this has been a major problem, but has become less so as technology has progressed.

The conditions for real-time operation in digital audio systems can be viewed from two key perspectives:

- A digital audio system must operate at the sample rate. For example, at a sample rate of 96kHz there are 96000 audio output samples per second, so it must produce a new output every $1/96000^{th}$ of a second. If it cannot achieve that because the processing task is too complex for the available computing power, then gaps will occur in the output.
- Another constraint is the acceptable delay (or *latency*) between an event occurring and the system output demonstrating a response to that event. For example, if a key is pressed on a musical keyboard, what is the longest acceptable delay before a synthesizer produces an output? Similarly if a guitar signal is passing through a computer to add a flanging effect, how quickly must the output reflect a change in input to be acceptable? In general such latency need only be a few milliseconds before the delay is perceptible. Delays are often due to the operation of hardware interfaces, operating systems, communication mechanisms, and block-based processing.

It is possible for an audio system to be able to operate consistently at the sample rate, yet have a latency in response to events that makes it impractical to use the system in performance.

While real-time performance operation is often associated with placing high load on a computing system, that is not always the case. A digital room thermostat is a real-time electronic device, but uses very limited processing power. Similarly, many processing tasks can be completed faster than required for real-time performance. For example, creating a data compressed audio file, or bouncing audio tracks from a Digital Audio Workstation (DAW) can typically be completed faster than the time taken to play the whole audio file through from beginning to end.

1.1.4 Audio Process Themes

This book is organised around four themes; analysis, modification, synthesis, and control:

Analysis

Humans *analyse* sound constantly, looking for patterns in the stream of information reaching the ears, in order to gain understanding of what is going on in the environment. In musical terms, certain patterns are important, such as those that identify a particular type of instrument, or characteristics like pitch. When playing an instrument, analysis helps the performer to adjust their physical inputs to achieve the desired pitch, loudness, and tonal character. When mixing a recorded track, analysis helps the engineer to vary process controls to achieve different sound modifications.

Turning the concept around, the information that is important to the human auditory system is also important to the audio process designer. For example, to synthesize a percussive sound means generating the sonic cues that a human recognises as reflecting acoustic percussive sound sources. Similarly, a noise gate must analyse its input in order to recognise the difference between noise and non-noise in a similar way to a human.

As part of the audio process control loop, the human brain is often used to analyse information (such as audio signals, visual displays, and tactile and kinaesthetic feedback) and then produce a control output (such as moving the fingers) to alter the behaviour of the system. Therefore, the brain can be represented in block diagram terms as follows:

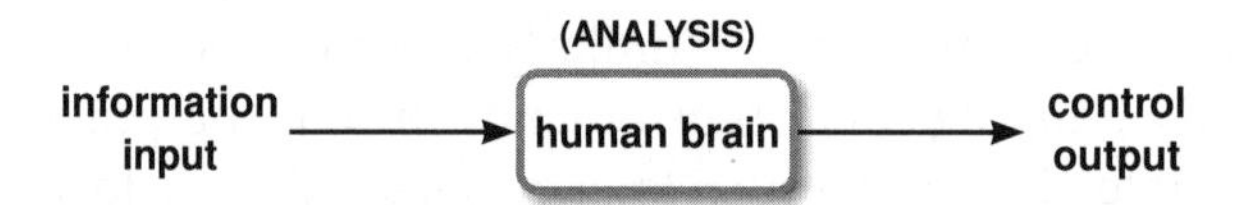

Software or electronic process elements that perform an analysis role have a similar form to the brain in a block diagram, where they take an input (such as an audio or control signal) and produce a control output.

Modification

Many of the most common audio processes are concerned with *modification* of existing sounds. This can be as simple as changing the amplitude of a signal or attenuating high frequencies, all the way through to complex effects processes such as chorus and reverberation. Most sounds encounter some modification from source to ear, either in software, electronically, or acoustically. The recording studio contains many sound modifiers that can take a source sound and change it such that it has the desired character. Even listening to a recording in a living room causes modification of sound, as the characteristics of the room are superimposed on the aural result.

Modifiers are not necessarily specific to a particular instrument, and usually work independently. For example, a tremolo effect might be used with an electric guitar, a synthesizer, or the sound of a clarinet recorded using a microphone. In a block diagram a typical modifier will take an audio input and produce an audio output. Consider a distortion effect, for example:

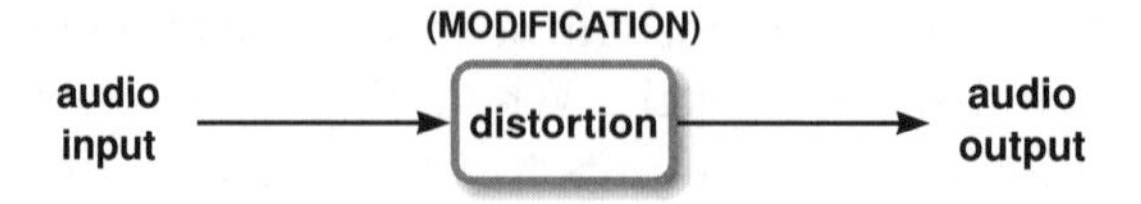

Synthesis

Audio *synthesis* can be defined as the generation of sound from scratch. Synthesis is often derived, at least in part, from understanding the characteristics of existing sounds and replicating them in some way. The important feature is that synthesis is the source of sound, without needing a continual audio input from elsewhere (as modifiers must have). A simple example of a synthesizer is an instrument such as an electronic piano. It does not have an audio input like the modifier, but instead has a control input (the hands and feet determining the sound that is produced):

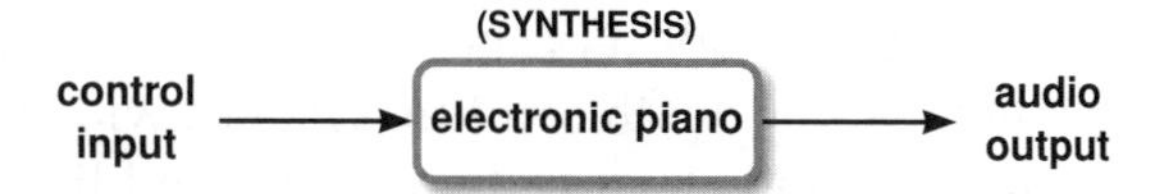

In audio process terms, a synthesizer often incorporates fundamental modification elements within its design, such as amplitude gain control, mixing, and filtering.

Control

The nature of the *control* system has a significant effect on the results produced. It might be assumed that certain tasks are always controlled in the same way, such as a musical keyboard being the input to a synthesizer. However, synthesizers can be controlled by a wide variety of sources, from a simple computer mouse to a guitar. A different technique will produce a different sonic result, as the ergonomics of interfaces provide different styles of control. For example, a guitar provides the opportunity for rapid and precise positioning of many fingers in different positions, whereas a computer mouse provides two linked dimensions of control and a small number of switch inputs.

Parameter control is an important feature of both modifiers and synthesizers. This is found both in setup stages, as well as in performance. Therefore, it is typically the case that there will be more than one input to a process. For example:

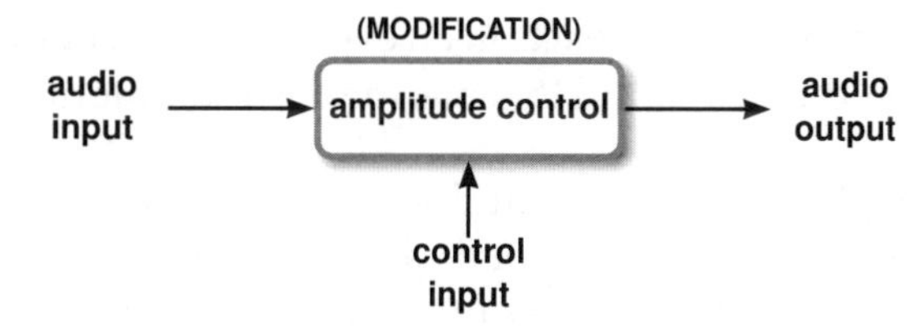

The later chapters in this book will examine the techniques used to achieve effective control.

All four themes are discussed in depth through the chapters of this book in terms of:

- The underlying technologies, and the forms used in real systems. The basic structures and techniques are expanded to help the reader understand how to construct more complex real-world systems.
- The response that a human has when interacting with those systems; both aurally and using other senses. An audio process is most useful when it provides a result that is controllable in a way that the human finds natural and suitable.

There are many ways in which this information can be applied, but one of the points of learning about audio processes in all its aspects is to understand the benefits and limitations of existing technologies. From this, future systems will be developed that will produce new understanding of sound, creative techniques, and listening experiences. It is not the case that audio processes are always tied to particular musical styles. In fact, the result might not be classed as musical at all. A science fiction sound effect, a slowly changing electroacoustic sonic landscape, and a rock track are equally valid contexts for understanding the elements of interest.

1.2 Example Audio Process Systems

This section introduces some typical arrangements of audio process elements, to illustrate how they are combined to form working systems.

1.2.1 Playing an Acoustic Instrument

Imagine a musician playing an acoustic instrument. Although this scenario includes no electronic components, it is worth considering in terms of audio processes. Figure 1.1 shows how playing an instrument requires some kind of control input, to which the instrument reacts and synthesizes an output sound. Any instrument can be considered to have those two elements, whether electronic or acoustic. The challenge when creating an instrument is designing it such that it reacts in an expressive and natural way to the human input, and such that it produces a sound that has the desired timbral (tonal) characteristics.

When an instrument is played, there is aural feedback to the performer. Therefore, figure 1.1 can be extended to include that path as shown in figure 1.2. The performer's brain analyses the sound in order to appropriately adjust control of the instrument and so achieve variations of pitch, amplitude, and tonality. A feedback path is important in the operation of most audio systems. For example, a recording engineer uses aural information to adjust the controls of a mixing console and balance the relative amplitudes of different instruments.

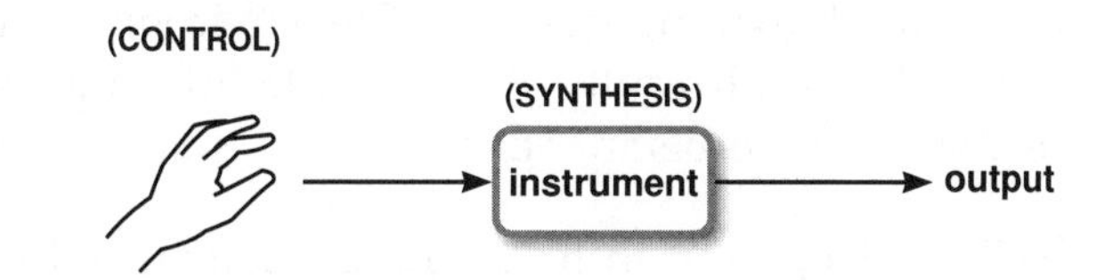

Figure 1.1 Playing an acoustic instrument (simplest form)

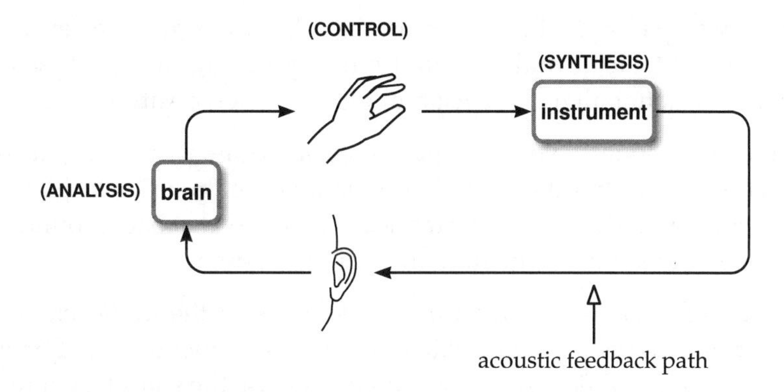

Figure 1.2 Playing an acoustic instrument (including aural feedback)

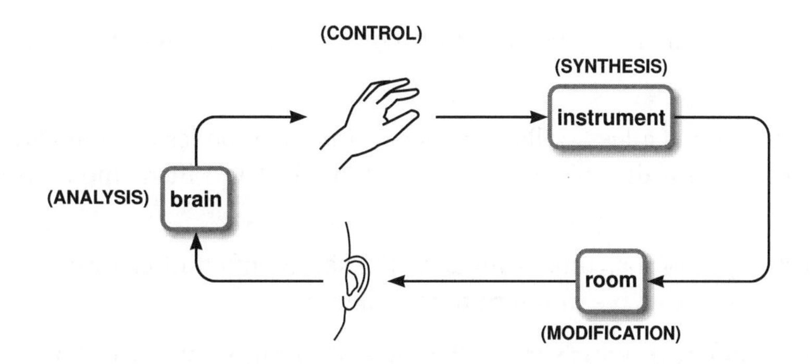

Figure 1.3 Playing an acoustic instrument (including room acoustics)

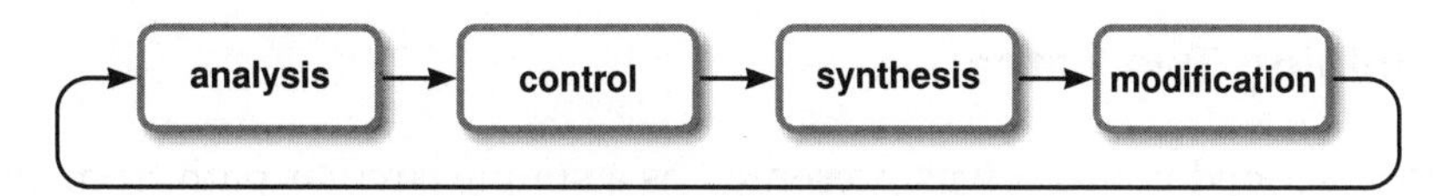

Figure 1.4 An audio process feedback loop

Another element that can be added to the model is the effect of the room in which the instrument is being played, as shown in figure 1.3. The environment in which a sound exists can radically change the aural result. For example, playing an instrument in a cathedral produces a very strong reverberant effect.

The structure of the feedback loop seen in figure 1.3 is summarised in figure 1.4. This feedback loop has an arrangement of parts that is found in a number of audio process systems. It is possible to extend the loop with further elements:

- Other feedback paths used by the musician. For example, the sense of touch that helps a guitarist to achieve the desired tone, by feeling the response of the strings. Or visual information that a musician might use when positioning their fingers.
- Other sources of sound. For example, other instruments playing at the same time that produce sound that the musician must analyse, in order to play in synchrony and to interact with them in performance. There are also background noise sources that must be filtered out by the human auditory system.
- Other modifiers. There are often many elements in the audio chain between the instrument and the ear, some deliberate and some incidental. For example, if a microphone and amplifier are being used to increase the sound level for an audience then they will also have an effect on the tonality of the sound that is heard. Similarly an acoustic guitar recorded with a pickup will sound different to when a microphone is used.

Changing any one element of the structure will produce a different audible result. For example:

- If the performer is a less skilled musician, they will be less able to produce control inputs that realise the full expressive potential of the instrument, compared to a virtuoso.
- Even if the type of instrument remains the same, different examples from different manufacturers will have different tonal qualities.
- The environment in which the instrument is being played can have a large effect not only on the sound character, but also on the style of music that can be clearly conveyed. A complex high-tempo tune will be unclear in a cathedral, for example.

1.2.2 Combining Two Paths

The scenario described in §1.2.1 was presented as a simple circular path from analysis, to control, to synthesis, to modification, and back to analysis. In most cases there will be multiple signal paths within an audio process.

Imagine that a musician carefully tips a large bucket of marbles onto an electronic drum pad to cause a rapid series of triggered sound events. The drum pad is connected to a synthesizer, and then to an amplifier and loudspeaker. However, as the marbles fall off the drum pad and onto the floor, that will also create sound. Figure 1.5 shows how this situation might be represented as a block diagram.

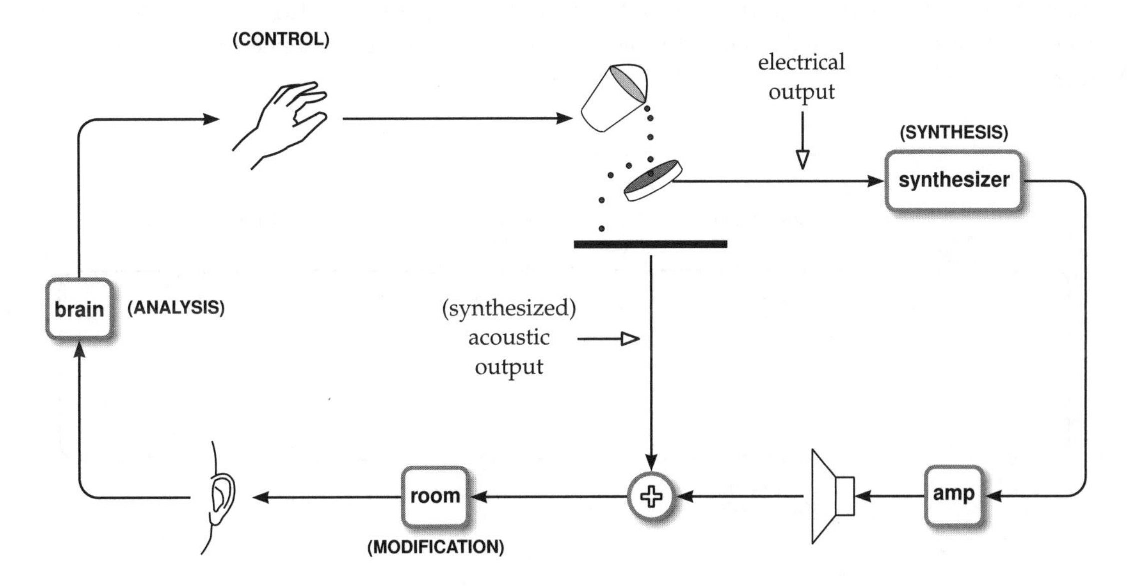

Figure 1.5 Playing a drum pad with marbles

In the diagram, there are two types of synthesis; acoustic generation of sound as the marbles hit the floor, and electronic synthesis. These two separate signals are mixed together (in the adder block) to create the signal that is modified by the room acoustics and heard by the person creating the effect. This feedback allows the person to adjust the tilt of the bucket to control the audible result.

Transducers (such as microphones, headphones, and loudspeakers) and amplifiers can be regarded as signal modifiers as well. For example, a microphone's electrical output is not a completely accurate representation of the corresponding variation in sound pressure. In many cases transducers and amplifiers are quite subtle modifiers, however.

1.2.3 Automated Analysis

It is not only humans that can perform audio analysis. With some audio processes there is a computer algorithm or electronic circuit that is responsible for analysing the content of a signal, and producing a suitable effect based upon the results. Automation is commonly used where a task is boring or repetitive, or where a human is unable to react quickly or accurately enough.

Figure 1.6 shows an example use of an automated analysis process. This represents a system that might be used in an audio artwork at a public exhibition, where the computer is responsible for controlling the audible results. The computer analyses the audio signal from the microphone, and produces a control signal that depends upon the nature of that signal. For example, it might detect the footsteps of the humans in the room, or whether they are talking, or try to gauge the number of people present. This information is then used to create a particular sound character that reacts to the presence of humans in the room.

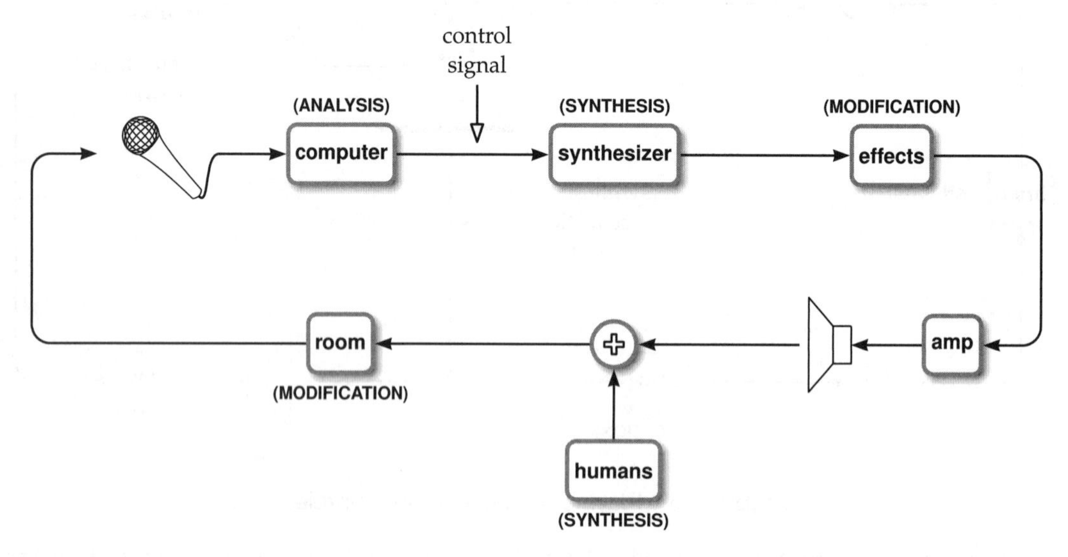

Figure 1.6 Processing loop for an audio artwork

In the figure there are two principal sound creation (synthesis) blocks (the synthesizer and the humans), and two principal modifier blocks (the effects unit and the room). There are some fairly complex elements to this arrangement:

- A computer does not have the experience or imagination of a human, which means that when the system is programmed it must be given a set of rules with which to work. Such rules can be very difficult to specify in order to achieve an appropriate result. For example, it might be desirable to achieve a musical character that is increasingly harsh and tense as the number of human visitors to the room increases. Such instructions are fairly easy for a human musician to interpret, but it is less clear how to translate these into a computer algorithm.
- Humans can easily recognise the difference between footsteps and voices, even when they are occurring simultaneously. Achieving this with a computer algorithm is a challenge.

- There are two principal audio sources that are received as a combined signal at the microphone. The computer must not only distinguish between different human sounds, but also between the human sounds and those produced by the synthesizer. Due to the modifications created by the effects unit and the room, this is not a trivial task.
- Finally, it is important to remember that part of the complexity of these systems is that previous outputs affect the current input. With positive feedback, this can lead to an unstable system (or at least one that has quite dramatic behaviour). For example, imagine that the computer algorithm has a rule that the louder the humans talk, the louder the synthesizer should become. Of course, if the synthesizer becomes louder, the humans are likely to talk more loudly in order to be heard, causing the synthesizer to become louder, and so on in an escalating fashion.

1.2.4 Two Humans Working Together

Figure 1.7 shows the signal flows in a studio session where two instrumentalists are separated by an acoustic partition, but are recording their parts simultaneously. It is assumed that the studio acoustic is dead and so there is minimal modification due to the acoustic environment. One performer is playing an electric guitar plugged into a guitar amplifier simulator (which models the behaviour of different amplifier and loudspeaker combinations). The other performer is playing a pair of conga drums, using one hand per drum.

Each performer is listening on headphones to a mix of their own instrument and the other performer, such that they can play in time with each other. There is a split in the electrical signal from both the amplifier simulator output and the microphone output that feed the adders either side of the acoustic partition. Each performer has their own amplitude gain control such that the level of the signal from the other performer can be tailored for personal preference. For example, they might want to hear their own output signal slightly higher in level than the other performer's output.

There are a number of ways in which the diagram could be extended to represent other features of the studio recording scenario. For example, the output from the amplifier simulator and the microphone will be connected to a mixing console and an audio recorder. Similarly, there are likely to be paths back from the recorder to the performers such that they can hear previously recorded parts, or a click track. The guitarist might well have a control path to the amplifier simulator (as well as to the guitar) such as a foot pedal or expression pedal in order to change parameter settings while playing. The recording engineer in the control room will also be analysing the signals, and applying suitable modification processes.

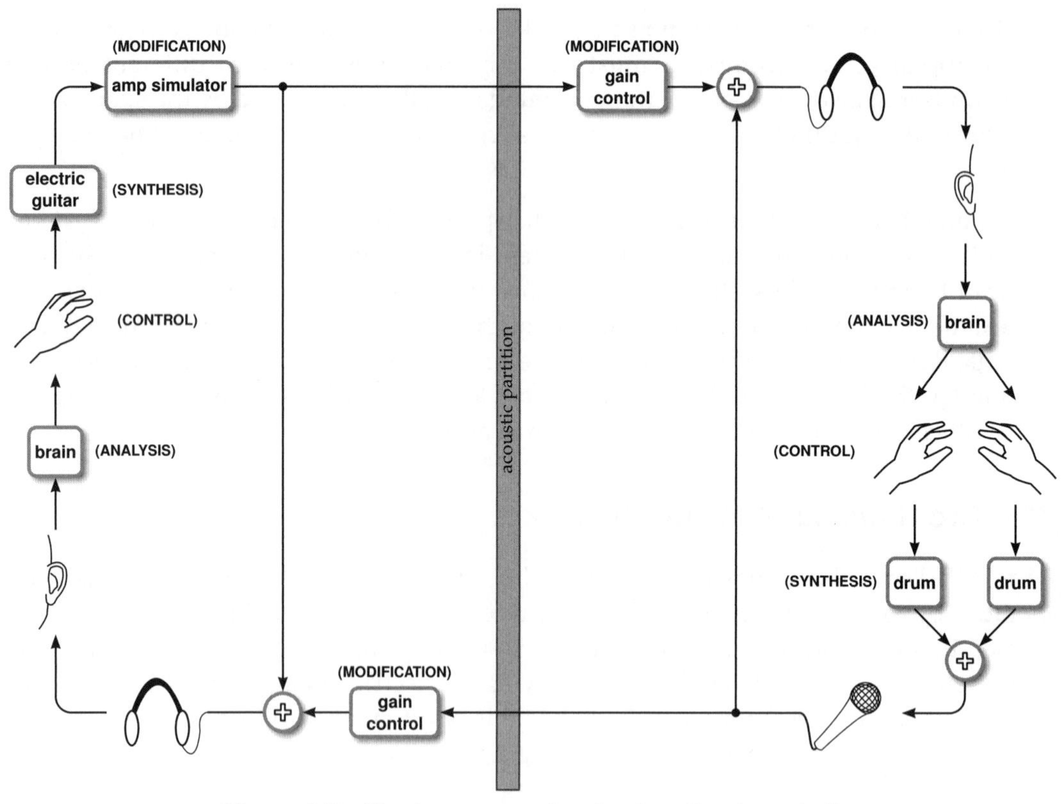

Figure 1.7 Two humans performing together in a studio

The examples above illustrate the typical roles of analysis, modification, synthesis, and control. Practical audio systems often combine processes from different areas to achieve the required results. Subsequent chapters will explore each area in detail.

Part I
Analysis

2

Audio Data Fundamentals

2.1 The Nature of Sound

2.1.1 Sound in the Time Domain

The acoustic form of sound is varying air pressure, which is sensed by the human auditory system and interpreted as audio information. An audio process deals with an information form that is analogous to these air pressure variations, such as voltages or numerical data streams. The conversion between these forms is considered later, but first it is worth examining the basic characteristics of sound waveforms.

Audio information is conveyed in the variation of signal magnitude over time, which is known as the *waveform*. When this is plotted it is a *time domain* form. The waveform magnitude is called the *amplitude*, which can relate to air pressure, a voltage, or numerical values in a digital system. Because it is assumed that the voltages and numerical data are completely analogous to air pressure variation, they will look the same when plotted. Figure 2.1 shows two example sound waves in the time domain:

- Figure 2.1a shows a simple waveform (a sinusoidal wave). It has a regular repeating pattern, a lack of sharp edges, and a very plain sound character.
- Figure 2.1b shows a more complex waveform. It is very difficult to spot repeating patterns by visual examination of the plot, and it displays a considerable range of different shapes. It sounds less plain than the sinusoid.

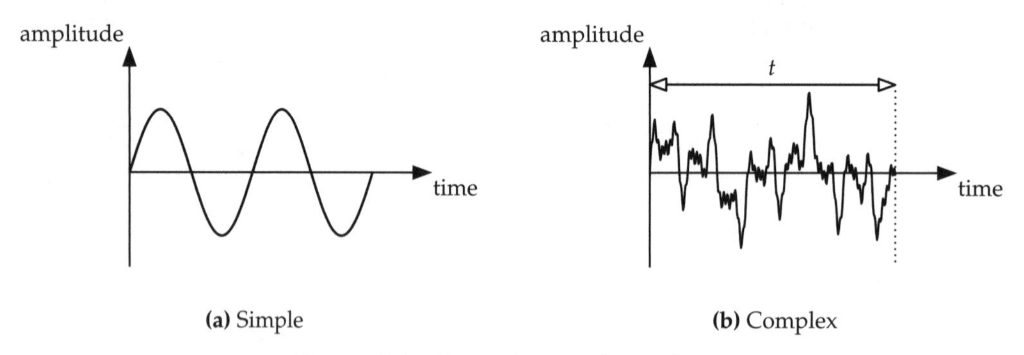

Figure 2.1 Example sound waveforms

It is often the case that the visual representation of sound in the time domain will be complex. Examining the waveform plot of an acoustic instrument recording in a Digital Audio Workstation (DAW) shows that sounds in the real world are usually more like figure 2.1b than 2.1a. Just because a signal is complex does not imply that it is random, however. Humans are able to interpret very complex aural information that might be visually impenetrable when plotted.

The reasons for this are as follows:

- The human auditory system is very sophisticated. Its job is to identify features in sounds, some of which might be beyond visual acuity when examining a time domain plot. Humans are capable of distinguishing between such things as different quality violins, even when played identically.
- The information in the waveform must be viewed in the right manner. The resolution of a computer screen, or the format in which the data is displayed, or the way in which the waveform is zoomed are all important. Figure 2.2 shows how varying the way in which the waveform in figure 2.1b is viewed can cause it to appear very different.

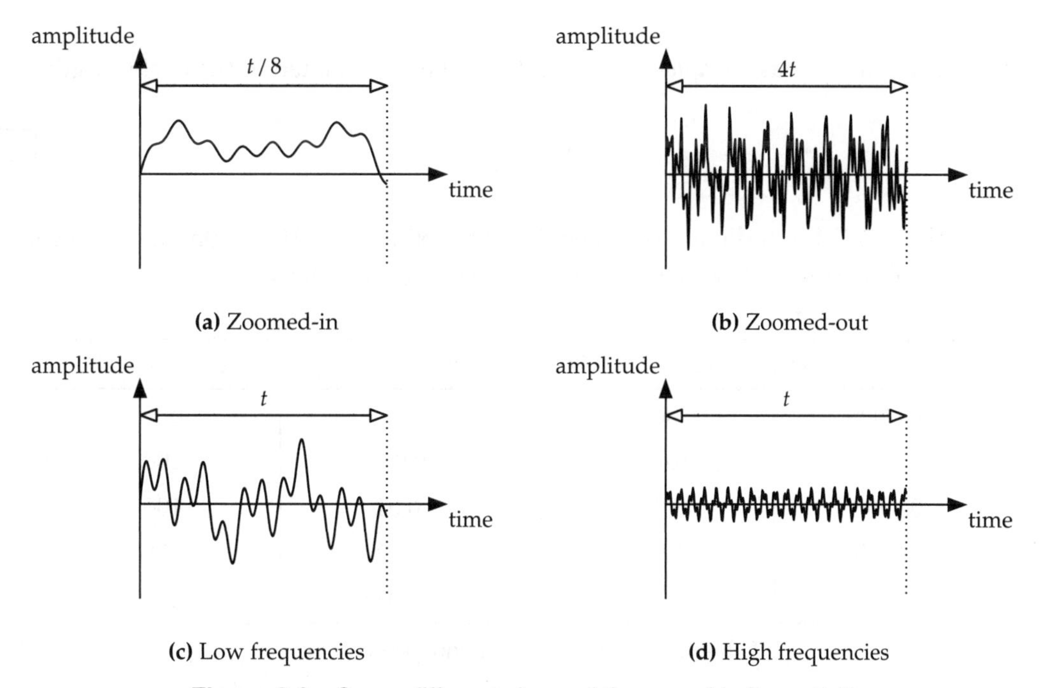

(a) Zoomed-in **(b)** Zoomed-out

(c) Low frequencies **(d)** High frequencies

Figure 2.2 Some different views of the sound in figure 2.1b

2.1.2 Cycle Length, Frequency, and Amplitude

Precise analysis of the time domain form is considered in more detail in Chapter 3. To begin with it is necessary to examine the basic elements of a waveform. The conventional building block for audio is the *sinusoidal wave* (figure 2.3). These are produced by the sine and cosine functions in mathematics. The wave has a cyclical (periodic) form that repeats every T seconds (T is called the *cycle length* or *period*). It has a peak positive amplitude of A and a peak negative amplitude of $-A$.

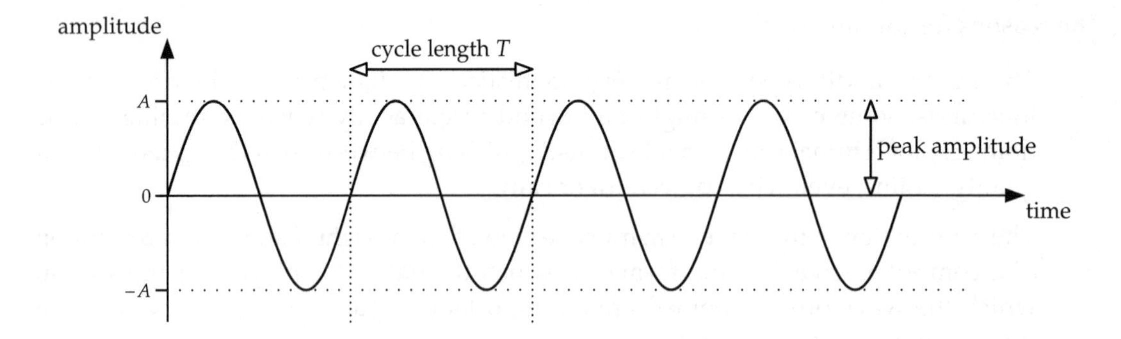

Figure 2.3 Sinusoidal form

A periodic oscillation has a *frequency* F in hertz (Hz) that is related to the cycle length by:

$$F = \frac{1}{T} \tag{2.1}$$

Typical values of T for audio are between 0.00005s (50μs) and 0.05s (50ms), which correspond to F values of 20000Hz (20kHz) to 20Hz as shown in table 2.1.

Cycle length T (s)	Frequency F (Hz)
0.00005	20000
0.0001	10000
0.0002	5000
0.0005	2000
0.001	1000

Cycle length T (s)	Frequency F (Hz)
0.002	500
0.005	200
0.01	100
0.02	50
0.05	20

Table 2.1 Cycle lengths and frequencies

High frequencies are associated with such words as brightness, whistling, hissing, and treble. Low frequencies have more in common with rumbling, grumbling, thumping, bass, and similar words. Frequencies less than 20Hz are also found in audio applications, such as the rate of a tremolo or vibrato modulation. Such low frequencies are heard as a pulsing or slow movement of an audible characteristic rather than a pitched tone.

A special case is a frequency of 0Hz, also known as *DC*. This has no variation over time, but rather is a flat line at a fixed amplitude value. When this is added to an oscillation it is offset vertically on the amplitude axis. This might be deliberate as part of a process such as modulation (described in Chapter 9). Alternatively a DC offset might be an unwanted

byproduct of a process that must be removed, or it can cause a thump in the output when the process terminates.

It is normal to consider sounds to be composed of a number of sinusoidal waves. Because sinusoids are the component parts in more complex sounds, they are commonly known as *partials* (or frequency partials). There are infinite shades of tonal character that are achieved with combinations of partials at different frequencies and amplitudes in a sound. The novice audio process engineer must learn through experience to associate particular characters of sound with particular characteristic features in terms of partials. This is very useful when trying to create a modification process or a synthesized result as it indicates what is happening in different parts of the sound.

When a sound contains harmonically-related sinusoidal partials (described in Chapter 3) then it produces a sensation of *pitch*. Pitch is a sound's perceived point on the musical scale (a note on the stave in the Western musical tradition) corresponding to a frequency. Increasing pitch is associated with fret positions moving towards the body from the head-stock on a guitar, or moving from left to right on a piano keyboard. Higher pitches tend to be associated with smaller vibrating object sizes (short strings, small bars on a glock-enspiel, smaller diameter drum heads) and smaller sound-producing objects in general (a domestic cat compared to a lion, a violin compared to a double bass) to accommodate those vibrating objects.

The principal vibrating (or *fundamental*) frequencies of the notes on a piano are shown in figure 2.4. Notes with the same name (A, B, C etc.) are referred to as being an *octave* apart, which corresponds to a doubling or halving of fundamental frequency. The numerical suffix indicates the octave in which the note is located. The suffix changes between notes B and C. Notes are spaced by a *semitone* on a piano keyboard. There are 12 semitone steps in an octave.

From a given note, it is possible to calculate another note's fundamental frequency with the following equation:

$$f_2 = f_1 \times 2^{s/12} \tag{2.2}$$

where f_1 is the starting note's fundamental frequency, f_2 is the note frequency to be found, and s is the number of semitone steps separating them (which is negative if note 2 is lower than note 1). The modern standard is to have note A4 tuned to a fundamental frequency of 440Hz (called *concert pitch*). From this note, the fundamental frequencies of other notes can be calculated using equation 2.2. For example, starting at note A4 (440Hz), note C5 is 3 semitone steps above, which gives a frequency:

$$f_{C5} = 440 \times 2^{3/12} \approx 523.25\text{Hz}$$

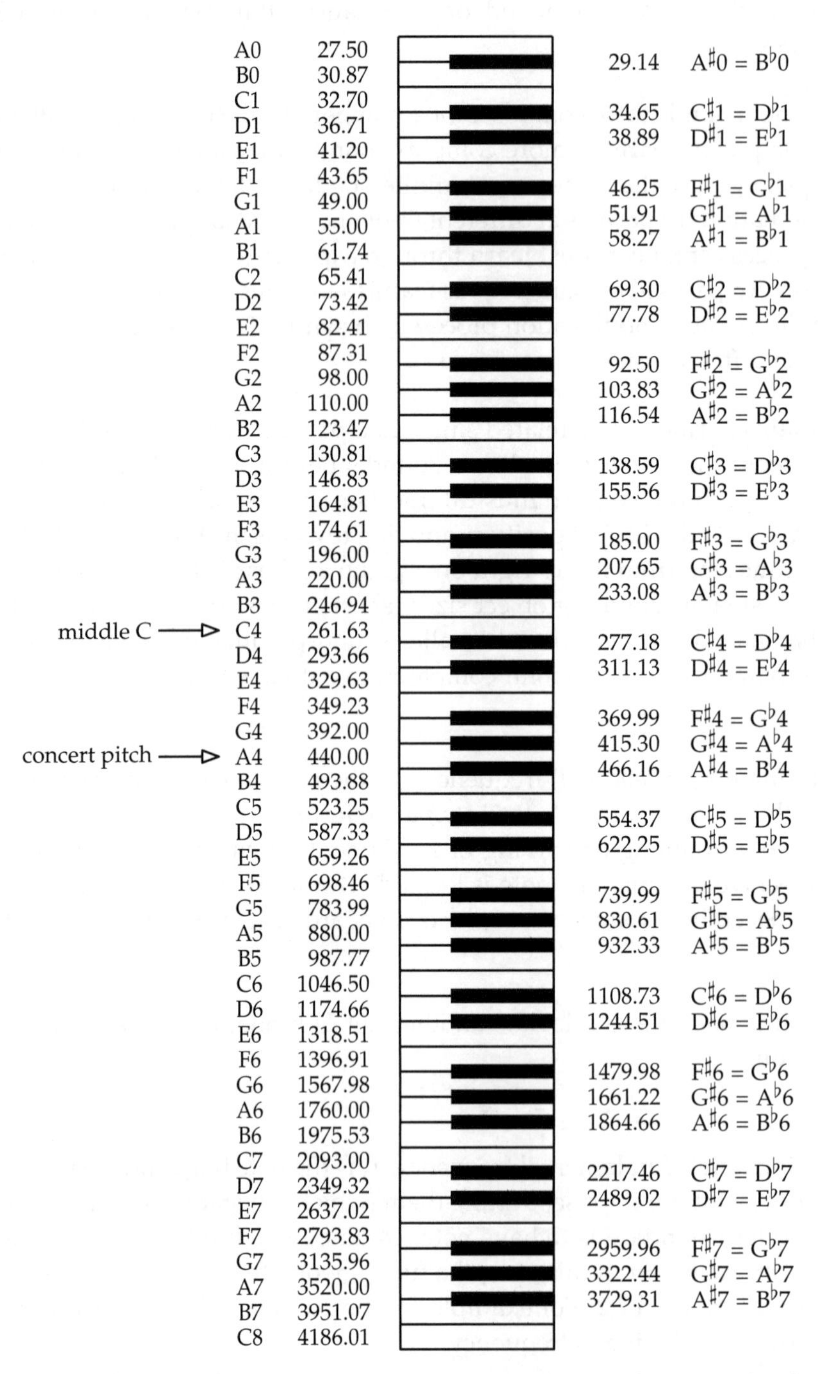

Figure 2.4 Piano note names and fundamental frequencies (in hertz)

It is also sometimes useful to consider very small changes in pitch, which are described in terms of *cents*. There are 100 cents to a semitone, so 1 cent means a 0.01 semitone change. Table 2.2 shows the conversion between some common pitch changes and equivalent frequency multipliers.

Pitch change	Difference in semitones	Frequency multiplier $2^{S/12}$
+3 octaves	36	8
+2 octaves	24	4
+1 octave	12	2
+perfect fifth	7	1.498307
+1 tone	2	1.122462
+1 semitone	1	1.059463
+1 cent	0.01	1.000578
unison	0	1
−1 cent	−0.01	0.999423
−1 semitone	−1	0.943874
−1 tone	−2	0.890899
−perfect fifth	−7	0.66742
−1 octave	−12	0.5
−2 octaves	−24	0.25
−3 octaves	−36	0.125

Table 2.2 Common pitch change frequency multipliers

It is important to appreciate that fundamental frequency and perceived pitch do not have a linear relationship. It is apparent from figure 2.4 that equal steps in pitch (such as increasing or decreasing pitch by octaves) do not lead to equal steps in frequency (in hertz). For example, the semitone step B1 to C2 is a difference in fundamental frequency of approximately 3.67Hz, but B7 to C8 is a difference of 234.94Hz. These are **perceived** as equal steps in pitch, despite being different steps in frequency, because the human auditory system perceives frequency on a logarithmic scale rather than a linear scale.

Figure 2.5a illustrates the relationship between notes (pitch) and fundamental frequency. The frequency rises exponentially with pitch. This relationship is important for calculating oscillator frequencies for a particular note on a synthesizer (as described in §13.1.3, p.399). It is also important when creating frequency controls in a process such as an equaliser

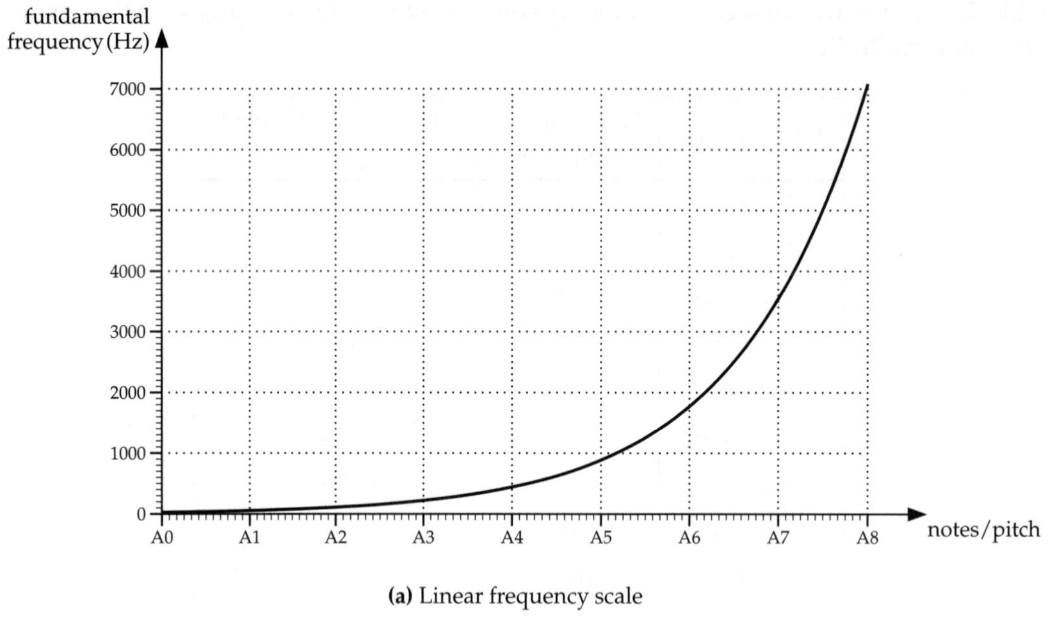

(a) Linear frequency scale

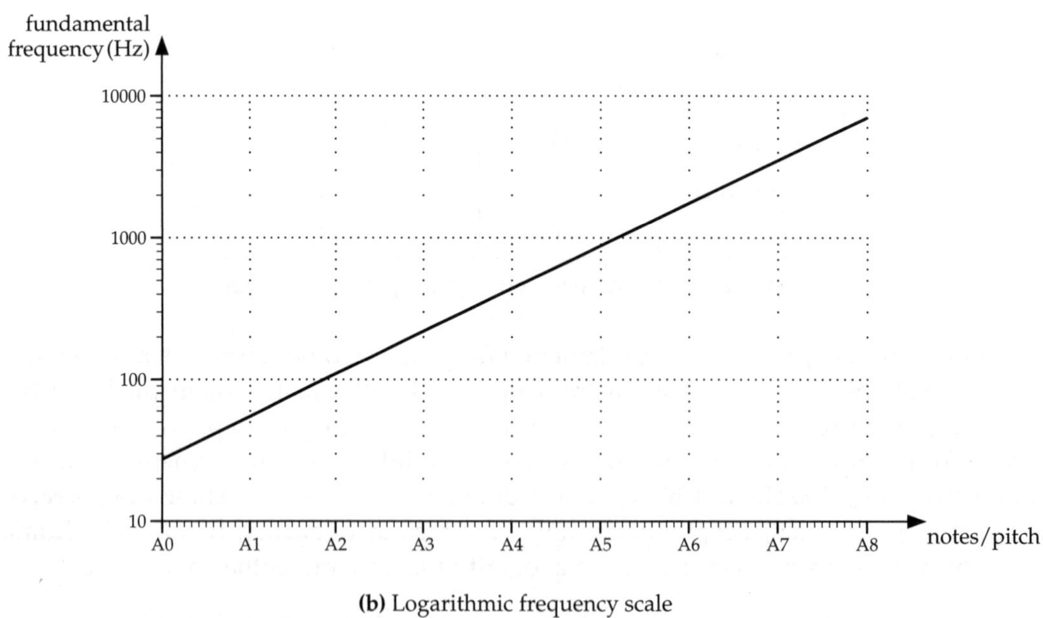

(b) Logarithmic frequency scale

Figure 2.5 Relationship between notes/pitch and fundamental frequency

(EQ), where a non-linear change in frequency should result when a linear change in the position of a control occurs, in order that the perceived change is also linear (as described in §24.1.1, p.656). Figure 2.5b shows the same relationship as figure 2.5a but using a logarithmic frequency axis (where the major marks are spaced by a factor of 10). When using this scale the result is a straight line.

As well as frequency, amplitude is also perceived in a non-linear manner. Figure 2.6 illustrates the relationship between *Sound Pressure Level (SPL)* in decibels (dB) and air pressure (the acoustic form of sound wave magnitude) in pascals (Pa). A sound pressure level of 0dB is regarded as the lower limit of audibility under perfect conditions, 60dB is the level of normal conversation at about 1m from the person speaking, and 120dB is the level when very close to a loud instrument. The vertical axis on the graph has a logarithmic scale, which produces a straight line relationship with sound pressure level. This indicates the non-linear way that the human auditory system reacts to air pressure.

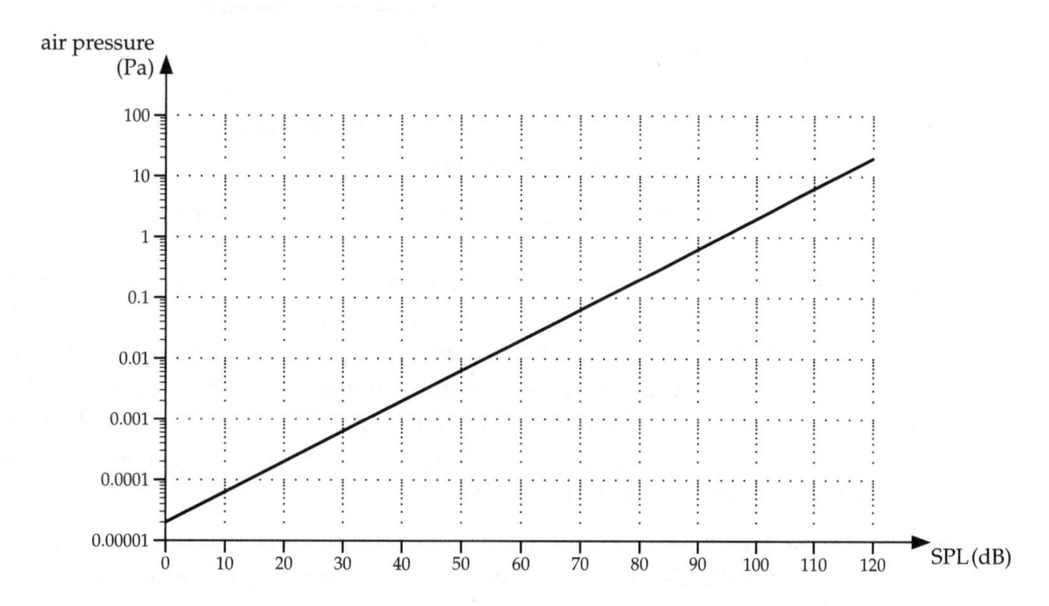

Figure 2.6 Relationship between sound pressure level and air pressure

Sound pressure level is not the same as *loudness* (perceived amplitude level), as loudness is a complex characteristic that depends on a number of factors such as frequency content and duration of a sound. However, figure 2.6 does indicate that amplitude should be controlled in a non-linear manner in order to achieve suitable control over air pressure variation. For example, an amplitude control fader on a mixing console is designed for a fairly even distribution of gain values along its length in decibels, rather than linear gain factors (as described in §5.3.3, p.109).

2.1.3 Construction and Deconstruction with Sinusoids

It is common to model complex sounds as a combination of a number of simpler elements (figure 2.7a). Similarly, an existing complex sound might be broken into simpler component parts by a separation process (figure 2.7b). This allows sounds to be viewed as a collection of parts that have individual characteristics.

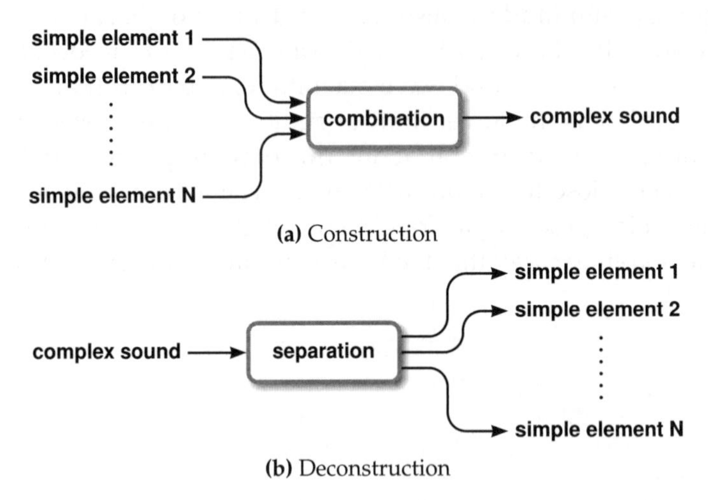

Figure 2.7 Complex sounds as a combination of simpler elements

The sinusoid is a natural periodic form that can be regarded as a pure tone. A deviation from that shape will make the tone more complex. It is conventional to use sinusoidal waves as the element from which sounds are considered to be constructed, and into which they can be deconstructed in analysis. Natural sounds, such as those produced by an acoustic instrument, can be a combination of huge numbers of partials with different frequencies and amplitudes. As an example of construction and deconstruction that can occur with sinusoidal partials, consider figure 2.8:

- Starting at the top left of the diagram, there are two sinusoids; one with a frequency of 600Hz with an amplitude of 0.25, and one of 200Hz with an amplitude of 0.75.
- The two waves are blended by summation, resulting in a combined waveform as shown.
- It is possible to split the combined waveform again using lowpass and highpass filters. The lowpass filter attenuates partials above a *cutoff* frequency and keeps those below. The cutoff value is connected to the "f" input of the filter. In this case, the cutoff is set at 400Hz, so the 200Hz wave is extracted from the combined signal. The highpass filter has the opposite effect to the lowpass, and is configured to attenuate frequency partials below 400Hz and keep those above. Thus it extracts the 600Hz wave from the combined signal.

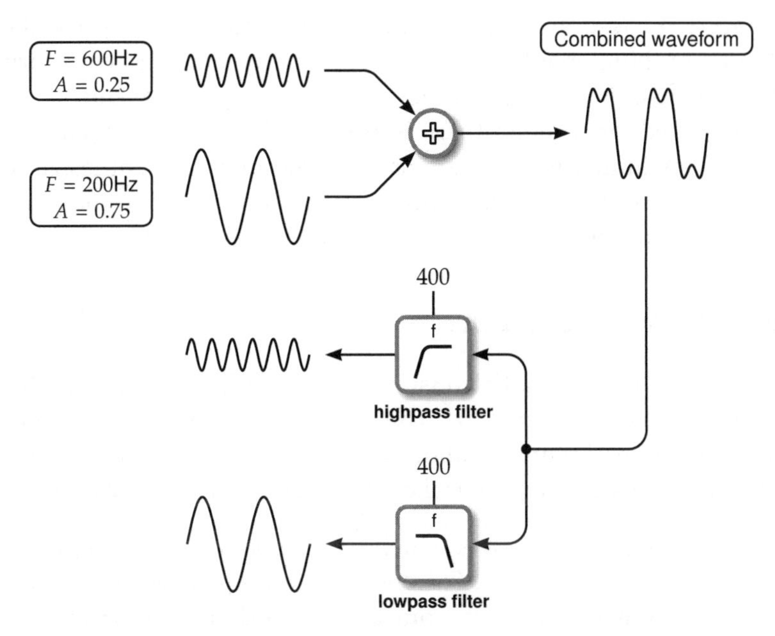

Figure 2.8 Construction and deconstruction with sinusoids

Combining through summation, and splitting though filtering, are two key elements in audio processes. At present this might appear to have limited use, but this is the basis on which many subsequent ideas are built.

2.2 Sound as Numbers

2.2.1 Overview

Acoustic sound waves can be represented accurately by numerical values inside a digital audio system. For example, it is possible to record the output of a microphone into a digital system and then play it back at a later stage in such a manner that there is no significant difference in perceived sound quality. There are two particular questions that must concern the audio process engineer:

- How is an accurate digital representation achieved?
- What do the numbers mean?

The first question is about achieving an effective translation between the acoustic domain and the digital domain (and vice versa). Once that has been achieved, it is not a great step to being able to store and retrieve the audio data. After all, storing and retrieving numerical data is a task at which computers excel.

In terms of the second question, being able to achieve a numerical representation of audio does not indicate anything about what it means. There is no explicit information in the translation from acoustic waves to numbers and back again that indicates what instruments are being played, or whether there is any reverberation, or what words are being sung. To construct an audio process that analyses, modifies, or synthesizes digital audio, it is necessary to understand what the patterns of numbers within the stream represent. Chapters 3 and 4 consider that in depth.

2.2.2 Sampling Continuous Data

An acoustic waveform is time-continuous; it is an unbroken line, even when zoomed to very small lengths of time (figure 2.9). This would suggest a level of precision that is difficult to match in a digital representation of that signal, but it is not necessarily the case that the very smallest details in a practical continuous signal are of value. For example:

- The shorter the length of time over which a variation occurs, the higher the frequency it represents (equation 2.1, p.20). Extremely high frequencies (say, 500kHz) might be present in the acoustic waveform, but are not audible to humans. Including that information can be a waste of processing power and storage space.
- There are limits to the frequency range of analogue audio equipment (such as microphones, preamplifiers, and equalisers). Very high frequencies might not actually be present in the signal that reaches the digital system.
- The details of the signal with the very smallest amplitude are likely to be background noise. There are many sources of this, such as acoustic background noise, and noise added by electronic components in circuits. There comes a point at which increasing the resolution with which the continuous signal is represented means that the noise is represented with increasing accuracy, rather than the sound source that is of interest.

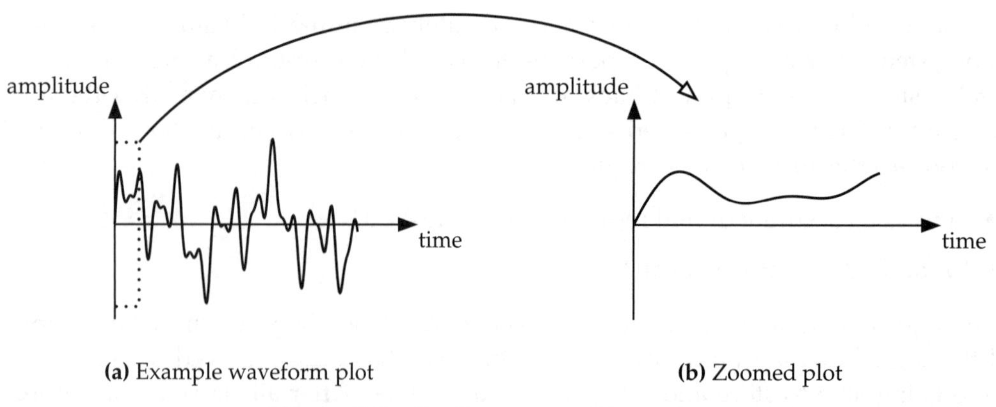

(a) Example waveform plot **(b)** Zoomed plot

Figure 2.9 Continuous sound waveform

A digital system represents the continuous signal as a set of numerical values that are the amplitude of the waveform at particular points in time. It is necessary to establish how many numbers are necessary to accurately describe the continuous signal. Clearly the aim is to use enough values that a human cannot tell the difference between a digitised (and restored) version, and the original acoustic waveform.

Measuring the acoustic waveform is known as *sampling*. The major elements for converting from air pressure variations to digital audio are shown in figure 2.10:

- A microphone converts acoustic air pressure variations to (continuous analogue) variations in voltage.
- An Analogue-to-Digital Converter (ADC) converts voltage to digital values by repeatedly measuring the instantaneous voltage and producing a binary numerical equivalent.

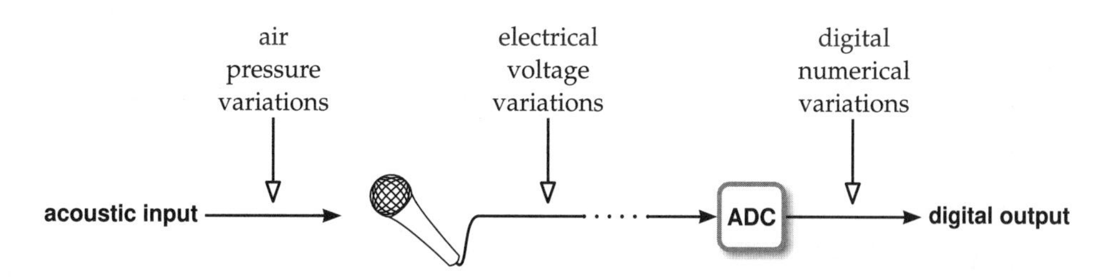

Figure 2.10 Three forms of sonic information

Some more parts will be required to link these together, as described later. The intention is that the three time-varying forms (air pressure, voltage, digital values) represent the same sonic information. The ADC operates by sampling the input at regular points in time, creating a stream of numbers that represent the continuous input. The rate of sampling must be sufficient that the variations in the input are captured by the process. Unless the input has a constant amplitude, there is a danger of failing to sample sufficiently often to represent the changing input.

In figure 2.11 the continuous input on the left has an amplitude that changes over time. The sampled measurement points are shown as dots on the right of the figure, with increasing frequency of sampling between cases 1 and 4. The number of (equally spaced) sample points per second is called the *sample rate* (a frequency in hertz).

In the first case in the figure, the sample points are too widely spaced to follow the shape of the continuous input accurately. As the sample rate increases, the spacing between the points decreases, and the original shape becomes more apparent. As a first approximation it is possible to say that the higher the sample rate, the greater the number of measurement points per second, and the more the digitised result will be like the original input.

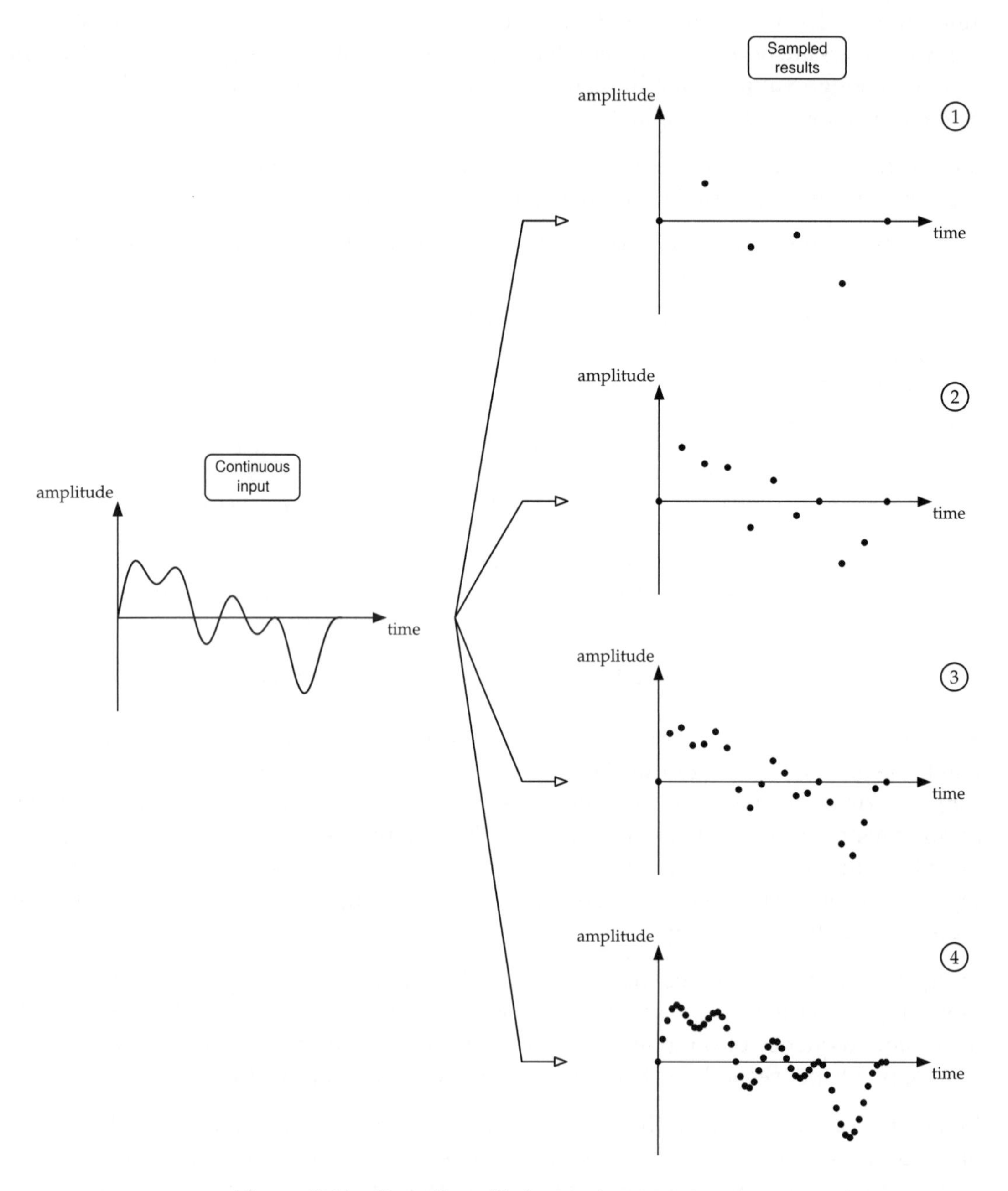

Figure 2.11 Sampling with increasing sample rate

There are two issues with this basic idea:

- A law of diminishing returns applies. There is a point where increasing the number of measurement points on the line has little effect on the audible result. While a sample rate of 48kHz produces a much better audible result than a rate of 12kHz, the audible difference between sample rates of 48kHz and 96kHz is much less.
- The digital representation is smoothed when it is converted back to an analogue signal. The appearance as a set of individual points is something of an illusion. The sampled data values are converted back from that representation into a continuous signal at the output, so the discrete nature of the samples is not present in the analogue voltage or acoustic forms.

Knowing that increasing sample rate generally increases perceived accuracy is useful, but it does not indicate a sufficient standard for high quality audio. The answer relates to the rate of variation in the input. Figure 2.12 illustrates the effect of sampling four sinusoids that all have different frequencies. As with figure 2.11, the sampled points are shown as dots in the second column. The sample rate is the same in all four cases, so the measurement points are at the same points in time. The third column illustrates what will happen when the sampled data becomes a continuous signal at the output of the digital sampled system (called *reconstruction*). Considering the different cases in the figure:

- The measurement points are the same distance apart in time because the sample rate is the same for all the cases. So the number of sample points per cycle decreases as the input frequency increases, as shown in cases 1 to 3. The resulting sample points do, however, still follow the same shape as the input, although in a visually increasingly coarse manner. The output remains exactly the same as the input.
- Case 4 shows a condition where there are exactly two sample points per cycle of the input wave and those sample points are positioned at the positive and negative peaks of the sinusoidal wave. This represents a theoretical limit at which there are just enough samples per cycle for the resulting frequency to be the same as the input.

Figure 2.13 shows a case where there is only one sample point for every 0.9 cycles of the input. The result is a sampled wave with a **lower** frequency than the input (unlike the examples in figure 2.12). This condition is known as *aliasing* (or *foldover*). That means that the conversion to and from the digital representation has failed and it will sound different. Aliasing cannot be removed once it has occurred.

As sounds can be considered to be constructed from a combination of sinusoidal waves (§2.1.3, p.26) the test for accurate sampling is whether the highest frequency sinusoidal partial contained in the sound is being sampled often enough to avoid aliasing. Figure 2.14 illustrates a waveform broken into its constituent sinusoidal frequency partials. For compatibility and simplicity the sample rate will be a fixed value, rather than varying over time. Therefore it is chosen such that it is sufficient for all likely inputs.

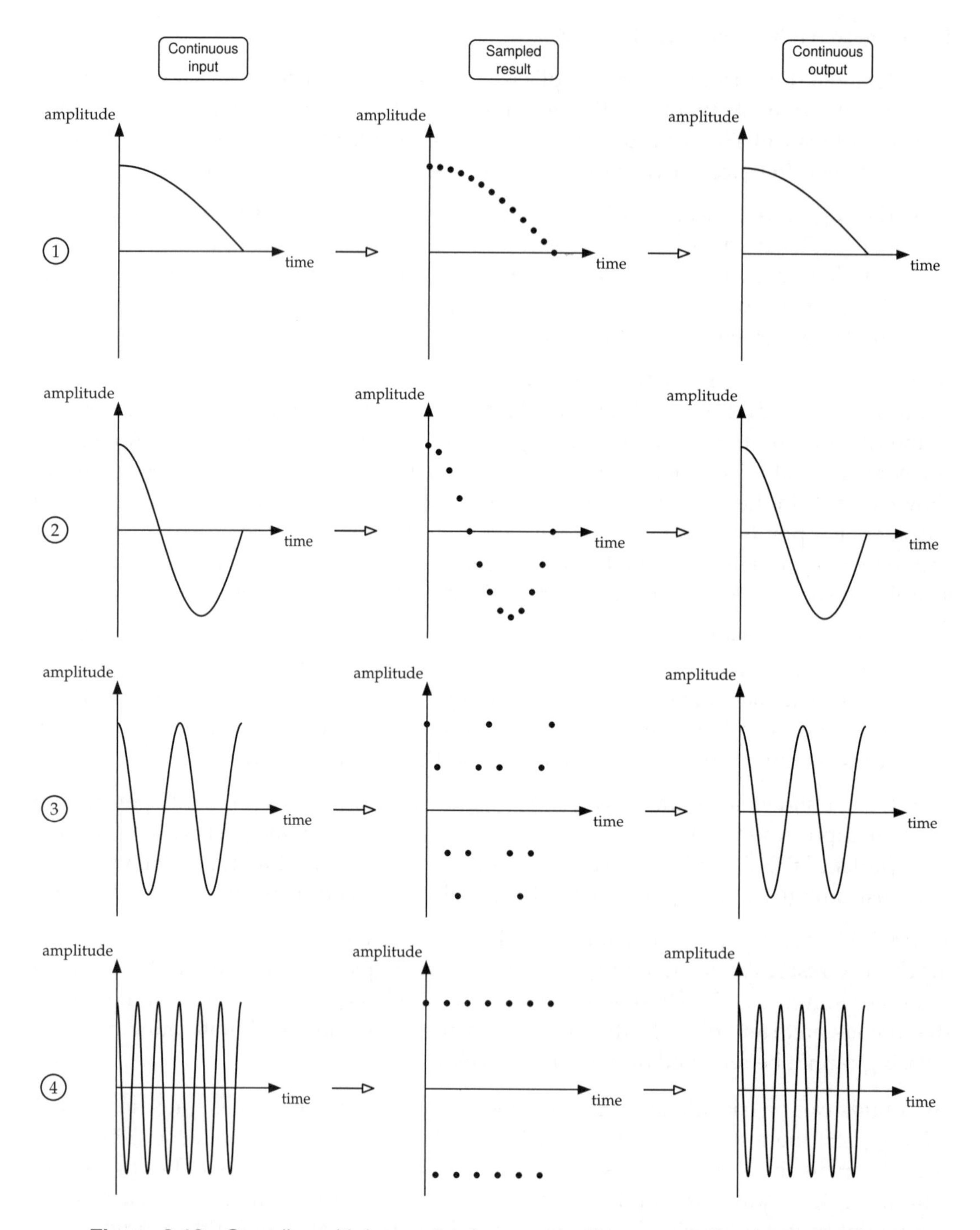

Figure 2.12 Sampling with increasing frequency of input wave (fixed sample rate)

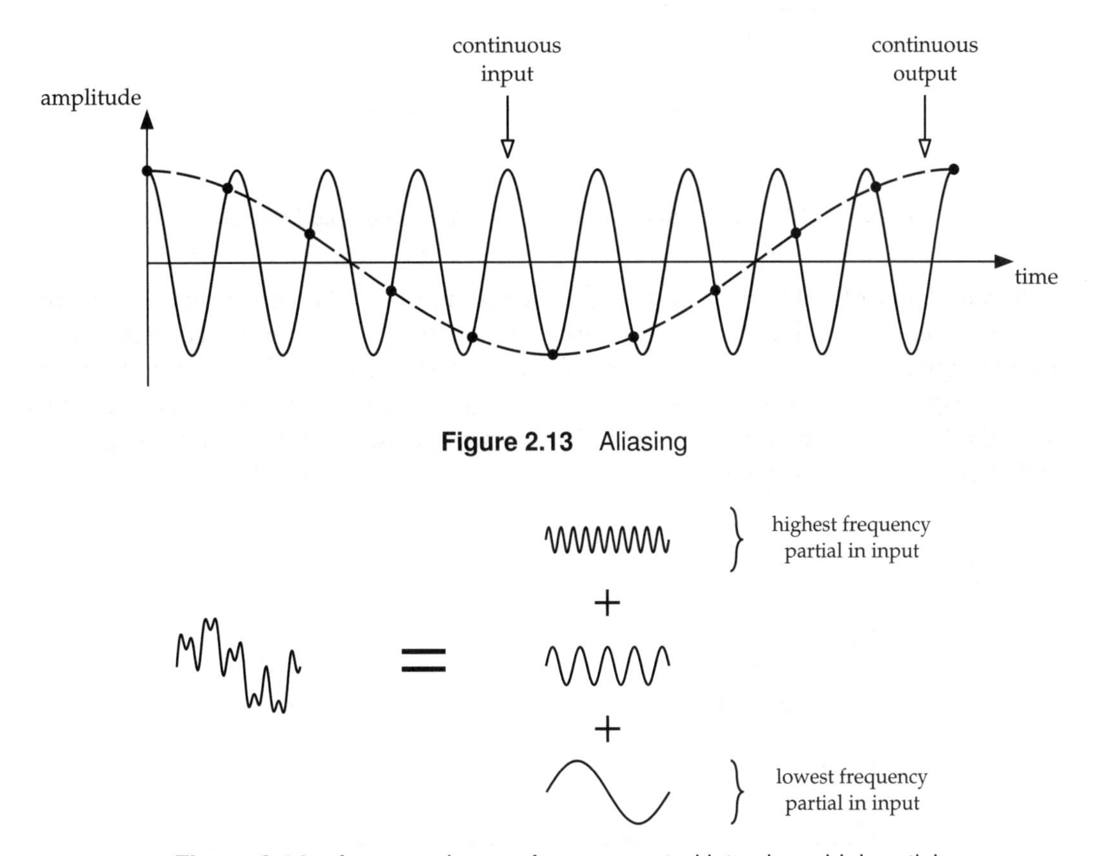

Figure 2.13 Aliasing

Figure 2.14 An example waveform separated into sinusoidal partials

The *sampling theorem* says that there must be more than two sample points per cycle of a sinusoidal frequency partial to enable accurate reconstruction of that wave at the output of the digital system. That is, the sample rate must be more than twice the highest frequency that will occur in the input. In mathematical terms:

$$f_S > 2f_B \qquad \text{or} \qquad f_B < \frac{f_S}{2} \tag{2.3}$$

where f_S is the sample rate and f_B the highest frequency of a sinusoidal partial that can occur in the input signal. Figure 2.15 illustrates the position of the key frequency values in a digital sampled system. Frequency $f_S/2$ is known as the *Nyquist frequency*. For practical reasons (described later) it is desirable to have a significant gap between f_B and $f_S/2$.

Measures must be taken to prevent aliasing. Partials at frequencies above the Nyquist frequency must be blocked before the ADC. However, the frequency limit imposed by the

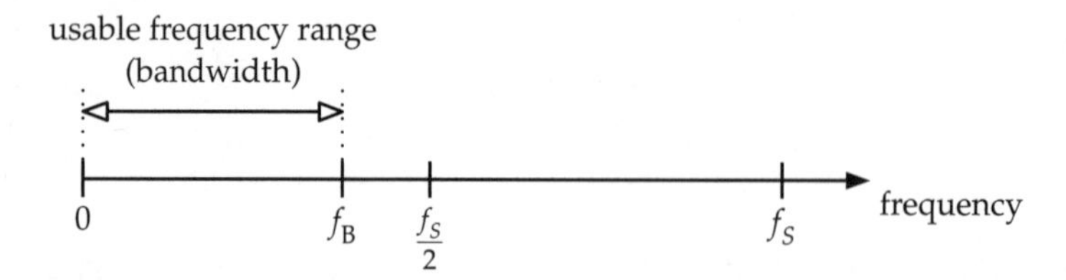

Figure 2.15 Key frequency values in a digital sampled system

sample rate does not only affect digitised analogue inputs. When creating an oscillator inside the digital system it is necessary to prevent the attempted generation of frequencies above the limit imposed by the sample rate. Figure 2.16 shows the audible output frequencies that occur when a sinusoidal wave is digitally generated with oscillation frequencies beyond the Nyquist frequency. A constantly increasing generation frequency leads to an audible frequency that rises and falls, as it reflects back and forth at $f_S/2$ and 0Hz.

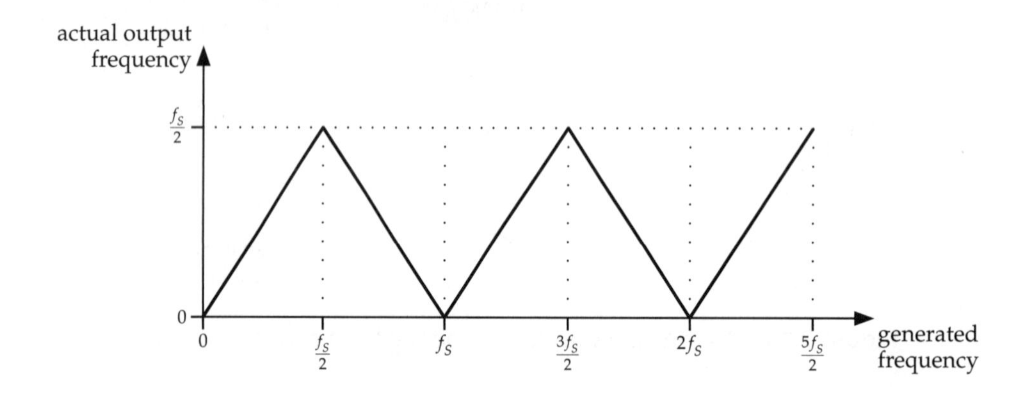

Figure 2.16 Aliasing from a digital sinusoidal oscillator

2.2.3 A Complete Digital Audio System

Figure 2.17 shows the key parts of a general digital audio system including input, processing, and output stages:

- The microphone converts acoustic air pressure variations to variations in voltage. The small signal produced by the microphone is amplified to a level suitable for subsequent stages.
- The *antialiasing* lowpass filter has a cutoff set such that frequency partials above f_B are heavily attenuated. That is, it limits the frequency range (or *bandwidth*). If the input filter were not present, there might be partials of a frequency high enough that less than two samples per cycle would exist (above $f_S/2$) and aliasing would occur.

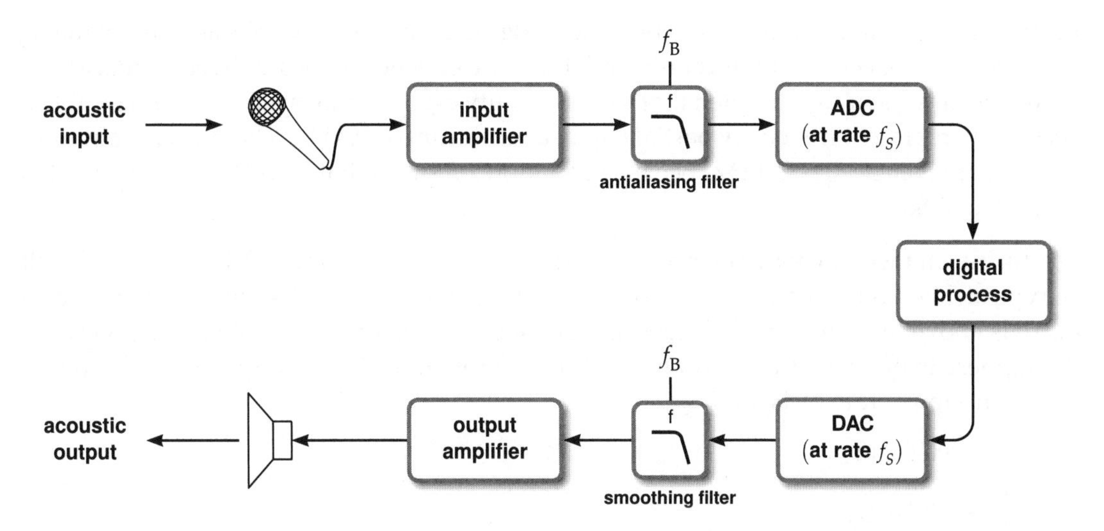

Figure 2.17 Complete digital audio system

- The *Analogue-to-Digital Converter (ADC)* converts continuous voltage to digital values by repeatedly measuring the instantaneous voltage and producing a binary numerical equivalent at sample rate f_S (which is greater than $2f_B$).
- The numerical representation is stored, or analysed, or manipulated in some manner in the digital process. An output stream of numerical values is produced by replaying stored data, or synthesising, or outputting the manipulated input stream.
- The *Digital-to-Analogue Converter (DAC)* converts digital values to voltages at sample rate f_S.
- The lowpass *smoothing* filter has a cutoff at f_B. This is the final step in creating the continuous output signal. The smoothing filter is also known as an anti-imaging, or reconstruction, filter.
- The output amplifier produces sufficient electrical power to drive the loudspeaker, which converts voltage to air pressure variations.

2.2.4 Choosing a Sample Rate

So far the process and rules of sampling have been described, but not any numerical values for parameters f_S (the sample rate) and f_B (the highest frequency partial in the input signal). Suitable choices relate to both the response of the human auditory system at very high frequency values, and practical considerations in the design and implementation of audio processes.

Partials at very high frequencies become progressively less audible as the frequency increases. The decrease in audibility relative to frequency varies between individuals. However, it is generally accepted that a good quality digital audio system should be able to accurately represent frequency partials up to a **minimum** of 20kHz. Therefore, a minimum value of frequency f_B is 20kHz. Because equation 2.3 states that $f_S > 2f_B$ then f_S must be more than 40kHz.

Producing an ideal lowpass filter to use in the arrangement in figure 2.17 is very difficult. A typical lowpass filter with a cutoff at f_B does not remove absolutely all frequency partials above that limit (as described in Chapter 6). As such there will be a gap between the highest frequency of interest and half the sample rate. For example, considering the common sample rate of 44.1kHz:

- f_S = 44100Hz.
- $\frac{f_S}{2}$ = 22050Hz.
- f_B = 20000Hz.

Sample rates of 44.1kHz or 48kHz are often regarded as adequate. There are a number of reasons for using higher sample rates (such as 96kHz and 192kHz):

- A higher value of $f_S/2$ means that f_B can be above 20kHz. Some studies indicate that frequencies above 20kHz might contribute to the perceived nature of sounds. If audible, the effects of those frequencies are very subtle. In some cases the non-linear nature of audio systems can cause audible artefacts from those very high frequencies; in other words, a byproduct of the imperfections of the system rather than people being sensitive to those frequencies directly.
- The lowpass filters in figure 2.17 must be designed to keep frequencies of f_B and below, and completely reject those above $f_S/2$. Producing a filter that does this without causing audible effects below f_B is not trivial. This is particularly true when the difference between $f_S/2$ and f_B (known as the transition band) is small. At higher sample rates, it can be easier to produce a lowpass filter that avoids creating audible effects below 20kHz. Filters are described further in Chapter 6.
- The digital process in figure 2.17 can benefit from having more high frequency "headroom" for its operation. For example, a clipping distortion process (described in Chapter 7) will usually create amplitude at frequencies above those in the input signal. Such frequencies might well be above the Nyquist frequency $f_S/2$, leading to aliasing. The higher the sample rate, the less likely it is that clipping distortion will have unintentional audible effects. Similarly, a synthesis process producing harmonic frequency partials at f, $2f$, $3f$, $4f$, and so on (relative to a fundamental frequency of f) will produce aliasing if any of those frequencies accidentally fall above $f_S/2$. One technique is to use a high sample rate internally within a digital

process, but a standard (lower) sample rate for the ADC and DAC. This is achieved by processes called *upsampling* and *downsampling*.

- Related to the previous point is that some processes can have operational inconsistencies as signals approach the Nyquist frequency, or parameter limitations relative to the sample rate. Some of these are found in the filter designs described in §6.4 (p.164). Using a higher sample rate can produce more consistent behaviour within the range of 0 to 20kHz.

There are certain consequences to choosing higher sample rates in order to achieve better audio quality, however:

- The higher the sample rate, the more computation and storage will be required for the same length of sound. If a computer is required to produce digital audio samples 96000 times a second (a sample rate of 96kHz), it is likely to require twice as much computation as when the sample rate is 48kHz. This can have consequences elsewhere; an audio workstation might only be able to play half as many tracks at once, or run half as many effects.
- The sample rate is not the only determinant of audio quality. If a high sample rate is used in order to accurately input, manipulate, and output a wide frequency range, then the whole audio system should be of an appropriate standard in order to benefit. For example, the specification of microphones, analogue amplifiers, headphones, loudspeakers, and other component parts must be examined to establish their frequency bandwidth, noise performance, and linearity (whether there is a directly proportional relationship between input and output). At an even finer level, the design of antialiasing and smoothing filters, and ADC and DAC parts will affect the result in subtle ways.
- The type of audio and listening context should be taken into consideration. An industrial audio alarm system might be more expensive to manufacture with a 96kHz sample rate than if 44.1kHz were used, but the higher rate would be unlikely to benefit the user. Studio recordings typically use higher sample rates, because the results will be heard under carefully controlled listening conditions.

2.2.5 Amplitude

In the preceding discussions it has been assumed that the amplitude of sampled data is always represented perfectly. In reality there are some limits to the representation. The first is *quantization*, which is the process of using discrete (stepped) values to express the continuous voltage found on the analogue side of figure 2.17. A key characteristic of ADCs and DACs is how many binary digits (bits) are used to represent the range of voltage values.

The number of bits (sometimes called *bit depth*) is associated with a range of integer number values:

- 1 bit can represent 2 values.
- 8 bits can represent 256 values.
- 16 bits can represent 65536 values.
- 24 bits can represent 16777216 values.
- 32 bits can represent 4294967296 values.

The maximum input or output voltage range is divided by the binary number range to work out the smallest step in voltage that can be expressed. 16-bit resolution is often regarded as the minimum appropriate for ADC and DACs in good quality digital audio. Commonly resolutions of at least 24 bits are used, which allow very small amplitude details to be represented and subsequently amplified. As the number of bits per sample increases, the representation theoretically becomes more accurate. However, there are a range of sources of noise and distortion in the audio chain, such as background noise in the acoustic environment, electrical noise in the analogue circuitry, and inaccuracies within the operation of the ADC and DAC components. The result is that the noise is often larger than the smallest signal variations that a large bit depth suggests could be captured and generated.

Considering the digital audio process itself (between the ADC and DAC in figure 2.17) it is desirable to have numerical values that are easy to manipulate. The integer value ranges associated with the ADC and DAC will typically be converted to, and from, real values (with a fractional/decimal part) between −1 and +1. A floating-point data type will normally be used, for ease of writing software. Floating-point representations often include good numerical precision (such as 23 or 52 bits dedicated to the fractional part of the number). High precision is needed for maintaining accuracy of internal calculations, and so the least unintentional distortion through accumulation of small errors.

There is a trade-off between cost and the quality of amplitude representation. To reduce electrical noise requires more expensive hardware components and improved construction techniques. To maintain accuracy in calculations requires data types that consume more storage space and require more computation.

3

Time Domain Analysis

3.1 Basic Concepts

The time domain form is the variation of signal amplitude over time, as described in Chapter 2. Complex sounds can be modelled as a combination of sinusoidal elements of different amplitudes and frequencies. This chapter delves more deeply into the form of sounds in the time domain and the characteristic features that give rise to particular perceptual effects. This information is useful when developing audio processes that relate to those features.

Particular waveforms are interpreted by the human auditory system as representing particular sounds. For example, some shapes will indicate that a cello is playing, some that an alarm is sounding, and some that rain is falling. The human auditory system responds to patterns in sound and is able to consider many levels of detail at once. There are certain features that can be found in the time domain that indicate the way in which instruments are played and how they respond physically to energy input. The characteristics of common acoustic instrument sounds are a useful reference for creating similar sounds, and also suggest how new or contrasting characteristics can be achieved.

3.1.1 Continuum of Sound Character

Figure 3.1 shows two extreme waveforms; *sinusoidal* oscillation and *white noise*. These have the following key features:

Sinusoid	White noise
Periodic and unchanging; repeats in exactly the same way every cycle	Irregular vibration; each value is random and has no relationship to those before or afterwards
Pure tone; perceived as having a neutral character	Impure; a dense noise effect
Has a single frequency determined by its cycle length	Composed of all audible frequencies; effectively composed of an infinite number of sinusoidal partials

The sinusoid and white noise represent two ends of a continuum, from the elemental sinusoid at one end, to the completely random white noise at the other (figure 3.2). It is possible to imagine that a typical acoustic sound has some position between the two, depending upon how noisy or pure it is. In fact, many sounds have a character that develops over time. It might start at one point on the continuum and end up somewhere else. The exact nature of this development is discussed later in this chapter.

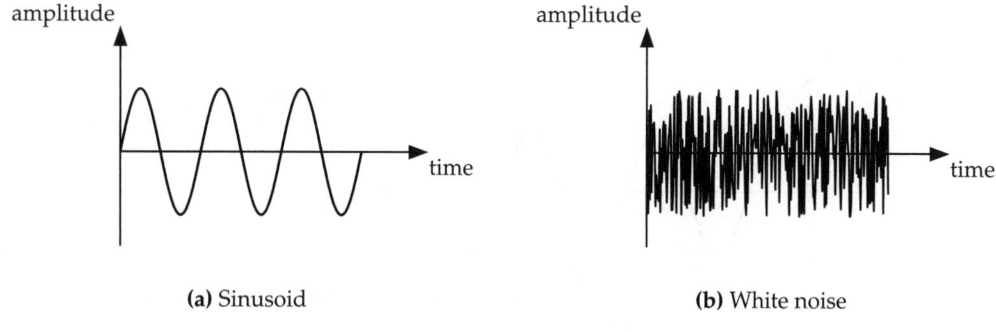

(a) Sinusoid

(b) White noise

Figure 3.1 Extreme waveforms

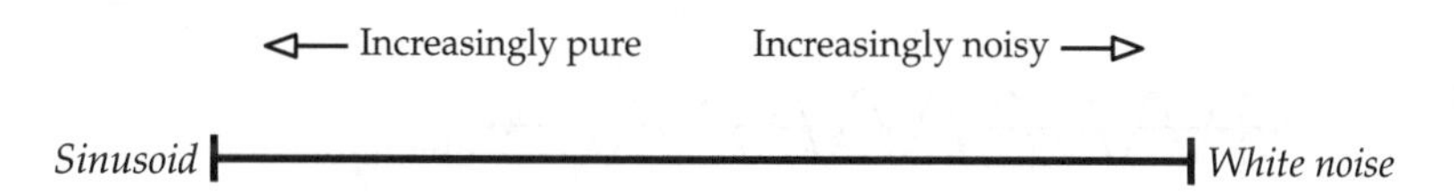

Figure 3.2 Continuum of sound character

3.1.2 Harmonic Sounds

It is possible to combine sinusoidal partials of different frequencies and amplitudes, in order to create more complex sounds (as described in §2.1.3, p.26). Consider the combination in figure 3.3. The result is achieved by the addition of two sinusoids that have frequencies f_1 and f_2 with amplitudes a_1 and a_2.

The combined waveform displays characteristics of both its constituent partials:

- The principal cycle length (0.01 seconds) is the same as the first sine wave (as 100Hz gives a cycle length of $1/100 = 0.01$s).
- The 300Hz sinusoid is superimposed on the 100Hz variation. Figure 3.4 shows how the waveform features combine over a single cycle length. Notice how the peaks of the 300Hz wave have pulled the 100Hz wave up and down to achieve the combined shape.
- The combined wave has steeper slopes than the 100Hz wave. Although it is not always the case, a steep gradient often indicates high frequency content, as the high frequency partials contribute that effect to the combined waveform.

One of the features of the combined waveform in figure 3.3 is that it repeats exactly every 0.01 seconds (the cycle length of the 100Hz sinusoid). This is because the other constituent partial has a frequency that is an integer multiple of 100Hz. This means that there are an integer number of 300Hz cycle lengths that fit within one cycle of the 100Hz wave.

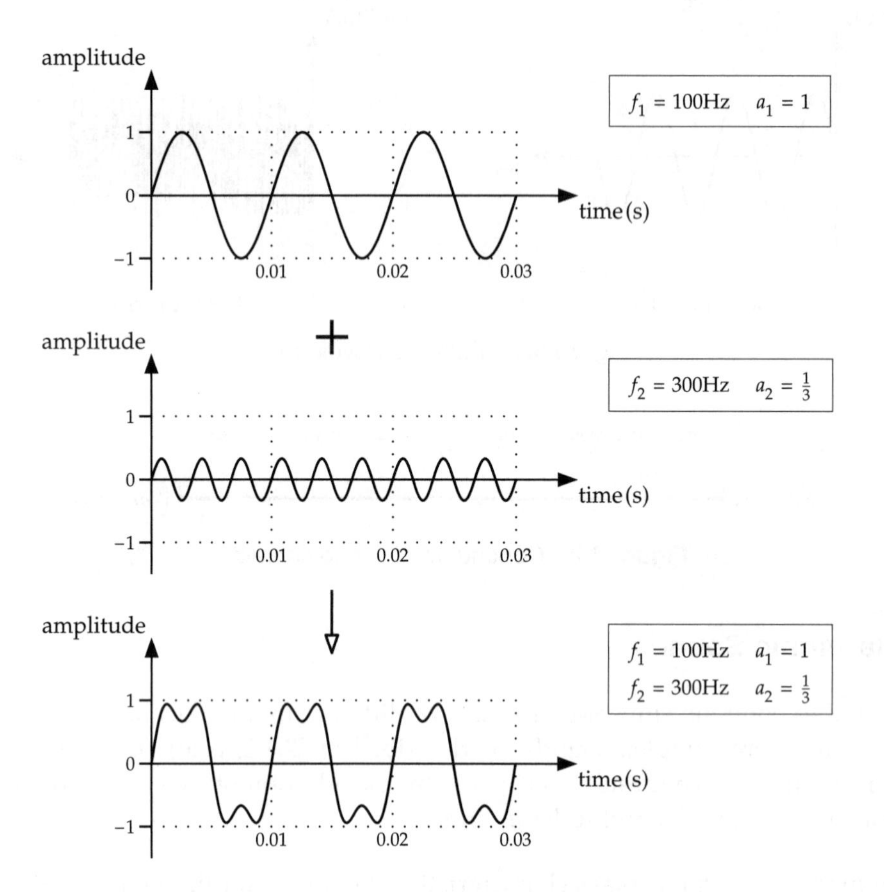

Figure 3.3 Addition of two sinusoidal partials

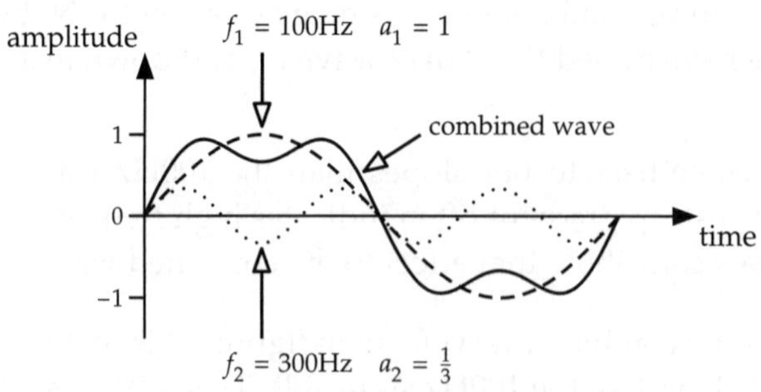

Figure 3.4 Combination effect from figure 3.3

Figure 3.5 shows another example of summing sinusoidal partials (three in this case). Because 200Hz and 400Hz are integer multiples of 100Hz, it is again apparent that the wave repeats exactly every 0.01 seconds. Where sinusoidal waves are summed whose frequencies are integer multiples of a common frequency (the *fundamental frequency*), the result is *harmonic*. In such cases, the waveform repeats in exactly the same way for every cycle length of the fundamental.

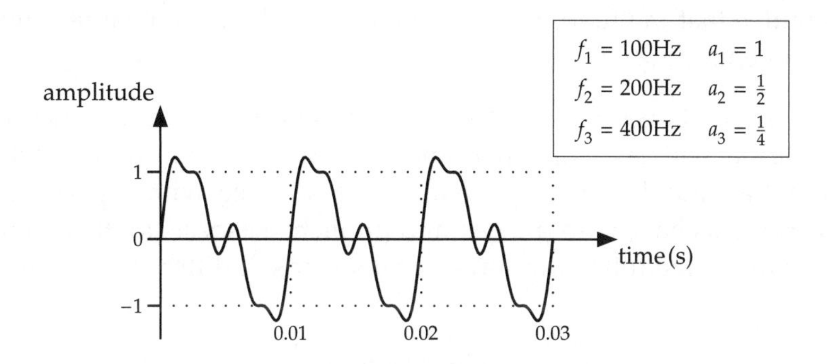

Figure 3.5 Addition of three sinusoidal partials

The partial whose frequency is n times the fundamental frequency is known as the nth *harmonic* (where n is an integer). That is, if the fundamental frequency is F:

frequency	F	$2F$	$3F$	$4F$	$5F$	$6F$	...
harmonic	1st	2nd	3rd	4th	5th	6th	...

However, it is not always the case that consecutive harmonics have significant amplitude. For example, a sound could be composed of 100Hz, 200Hz, and 500Hz frequency partials, where the 3rd and 4th harmonics have zero amplitude:

frequency(Hz)	100	200	—	—	500	—	...
harmonic	1st	2nd	3rd	4th	5th	6th	...

It is also possible to have a harmonic sound where the fundamental frequency partial is missing (has no amplitude). For example, if a sound is composed of partials at 150Hz, 225Hz, and 375Hz, then the fundamental frequency is 75Hz (as the partials are all at integer multiples of 75Hz):

frequency(Hz)	—	150	225	—	375	—	...
harmonic	1st	2nd	3rd	4th	5th	6th	...

A harmonic sound (which consistently repeats from cycle to cycle) produces a *pitched* sensation. Harmonic forms tend to lead to a perceived pitch at the fundamental frequency. However, the relative amplitude emphasis of different partials affects this. For example, if partials are at 500Hz and 600Hz only, the pitch does not appear to be at 100Hz. Adding a partial at the fundamental frequency enhances the pitch sensation at that frequency. Many harmonic sounds from acoustic instruments have significant amplitude emphasis on the lower harmonics, but there is no universal pattern of harmonic amplitudes. For example, there is no guarantee that the fundamental frequency will have the largest amplitude in an acoustic instrument sound.

The less periodic a sound becomes, the less clear the sense of pitch. A tuned instrument like a guitar or clarinet will have some periodic characteristics in its output, while a noisy sound (like the vocal sound "f") cannot really be associated with a particular musical pitch. Many instruments have both pitched and unpitched aspects to their sounds. As an example, trying singing the following three vocal sounds at different notes on a musical scale:

"ur" as in "purpose"
"s" as in "saline"
"z" as in "zygote"

It is possible to pitch "ur" and "z", but not "s". Notice that "ur" has a largely noise-free sound, "s" is clearly noisy, and "z" has both pitched and noisy aspects. The relationship between noisy sources and pitch is described further in §18.3.3 (p.535).

The relationship between harmonic amplitudes is an important contributor to the *sound character* (also known as the *timbre* or *tonal character*). The amplitudes provide a pattern that helps the human auditory system to identify a sound source; for example, whether a sound might be from a clarinet rather than a flute, even if other aspects of the sound are similar. Consider the waveforms in figure 3.6:

- Figure 3.6a illustrates a waveform composed of even-numbered integer multiples of the fundamental frequency (even harmonics). It has something of a church organ-like tone.
- Figure 3.6b illustrates a waveform composed of odd-numbered integer multiples of the fundamental frequency (odd harmonics). It has a more hollow tone.

Although the harmonic amplitudes affect the visual and audible results, the time domain plot of the waveform has a complex relationship to tonality. Even to the trained eye, many waveform shapes do not directly suggest what they might sound like. There is also the problem that the fundamental frequency has an effect on the tonal character; for example, the same waveform at 100Hz and 2kHz usually conveys a different impression.

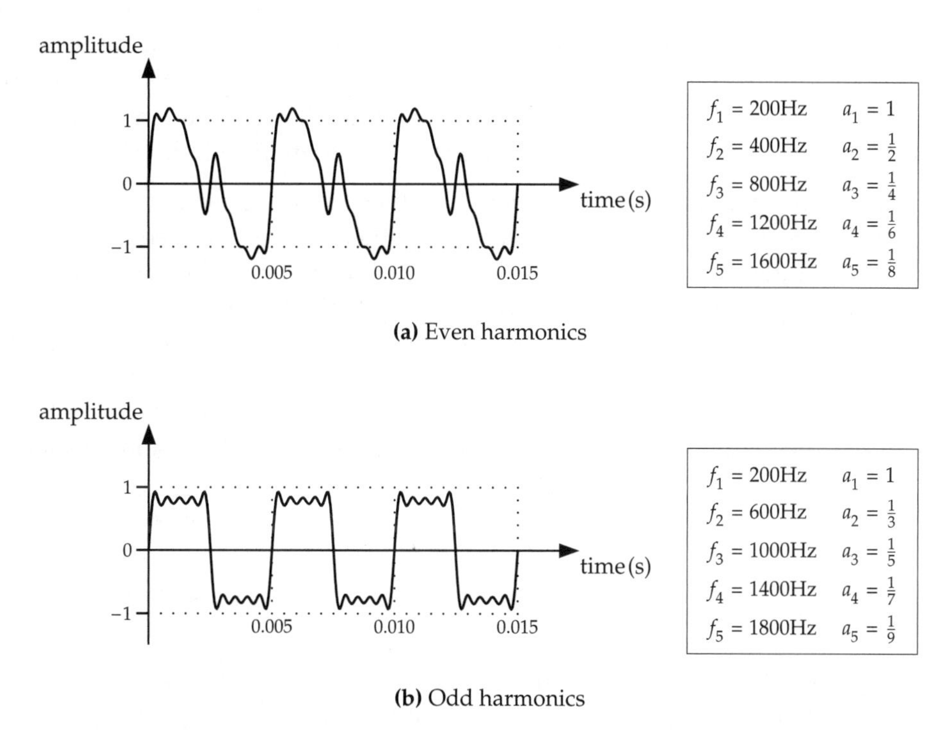

(a) Even harmonics

(b) Odd harmonics

Figure 3.6 Waveforms with different harmonic balance

3.1.3 Inharmonic Sounds

A sound that is a sum of sinusoids and whose frequencies are integer multiples of the fundamental frequency, has a periodic waveform shape that causes a pitched sensation. At the other end of the scale, a noisy sound does not have that clear form and pitched result. Many sounds exist between the two. With a harmonic form the frequencies are known, and variation is achieved through the relative balance of partial amplitudes. With an inharmonic form (where some frequencies are not integer multiples of a fundamental frequency) the number of possibilities is vastly expanded. It is worth noting that:

- If frequencies of partials are not at integer multiples of the fundamental, there is likely to be some loss of clarity or increase in roughness in the sound. White noise could be considered all roughness and no clarity.
- Inharmonics are likely to reduce the sensation of a clear pitch, towards something more ambiguous or unpitched. For example, a crash cymbal has many partials with complex non-integer frequency relationships, and tends to produce a very vague sense of pitch.

- If two partial frequencies are within about 20Hz of each other, they tend to introduce a beating or pulsing sensation. For example, simultaneous partials at 200Hz and 207Hz will appear to pulse at 7Hz. For increasing frequency difference the sound has some element of roughness or dissonance. With enough difference, the result is a clearer chord-like sensation. This is explored further in §16.1.2 (p.483).

Figure 3.7 illustrates two inharmonic sounds. Neither has the clear periodic form seen previously with harmonic sounds. In figure 3.7a, there is no one frequency that can be multiplied by integers to achieve f_1, f_2, and f_3. In figure 3.7b the three partials' frequencies **are** integer multiples of another frequency (25Hz), so the wave repeats every $1/25 = 0.04$ seconds. However, 25Hz is a very low frequency and the low harmonics (25, 50, 75, 100, 125, 150, 175) are not present. As such, a listener does not hear a 25Hz fundamental frequency, but rather a tone in the region of 200Hz. Because 225 and 300 are not integer multiples of 200, the effect is not a completely clear pitch, but slightly dissonant sounding.

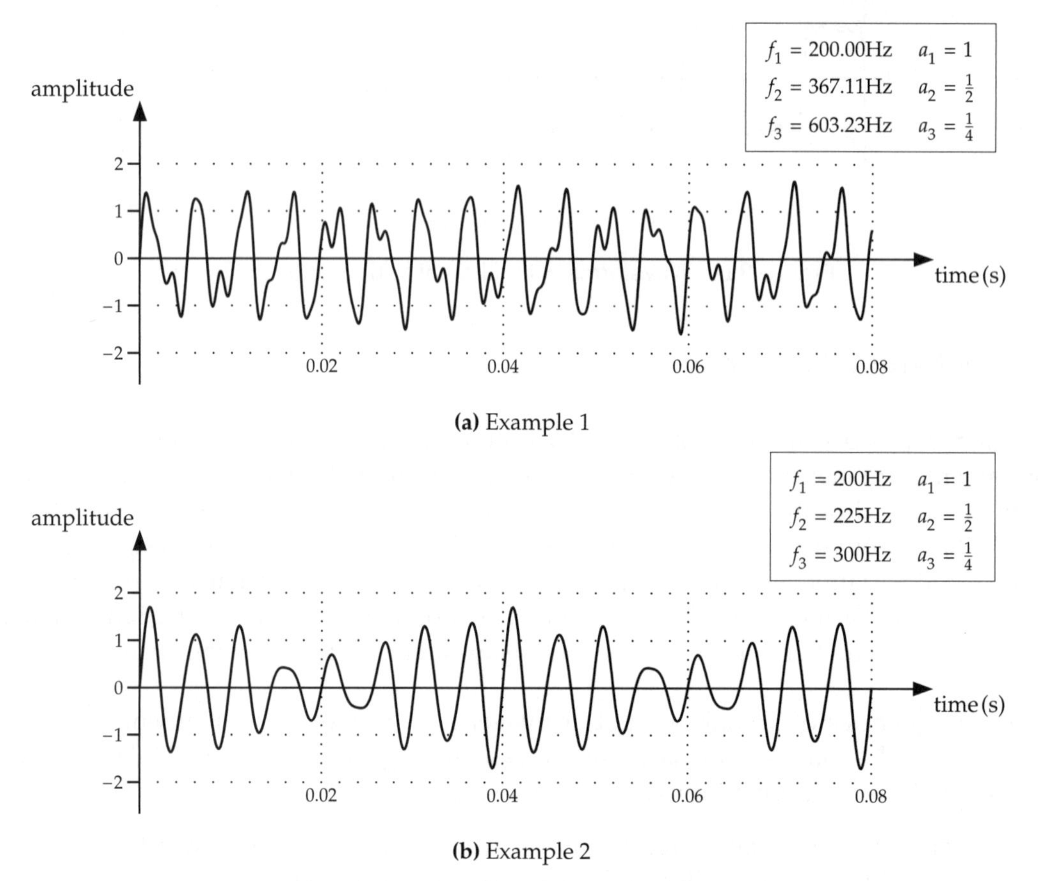

Figure 3.7 Example inharmonic combinations of sinusoidal partials

3.1.4 Phase Effects

The visual character of waveforms that result from the combination of sinusoids seen in §3.1.2 and §3.1.3 depends not only on the frequencies and amplitudes of the partials, but also on their *phases*. Phase means the position in the waveform cycle at a particular point in time.

Figure 3.8 shows what happens when combined partials have different starting phases. The first partial is the same in the two combinations. The second partial has the same frequency and amplitude in both combinations, but different phase, so the resulting waveforms look different. Differences in starting phase are apparent where the waveforms meet the amplitude axes.

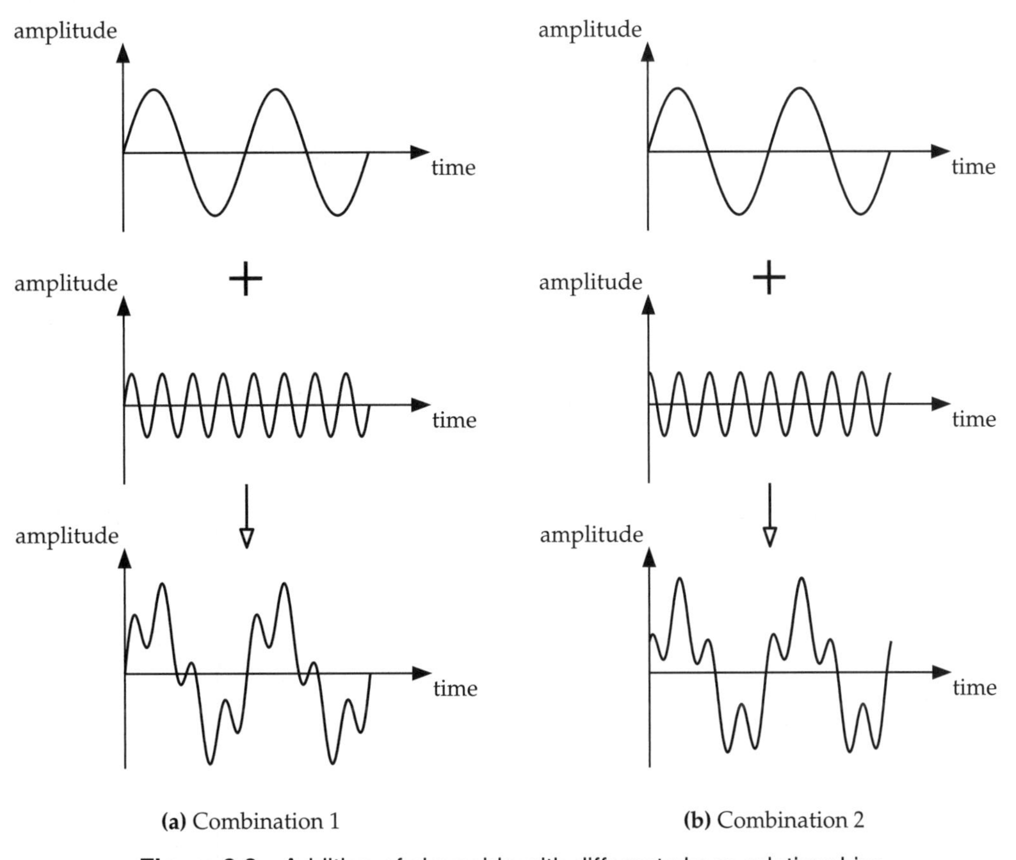

(a) Combination 1 **(b)** Combination 2

Figure 3.8 Addition of sinusoids with different phase relationships

There are two important points here:

- The resulting time domain waveform is different for the two combinations. Although they clearly have some similarities, they do not rise and fall in quite the same way.
- The timbral (tonal) difference between the two combinations is not very significant. In general, the human auditory system is much more concerned with the amplitudes and frequencies of the partials than their relative phases. This is the case so long as the phase relationships between the partials are constant (as in figure 3.8), not changing over time.

As well as the effect on the visual shape of the waveform for partials with different frequencies, it is also worth noting the effect of phase when combining partials of the **same** frequency. Figure 3.9 shows what happens when two partials are combined that have the same frequency, but different starting phase.

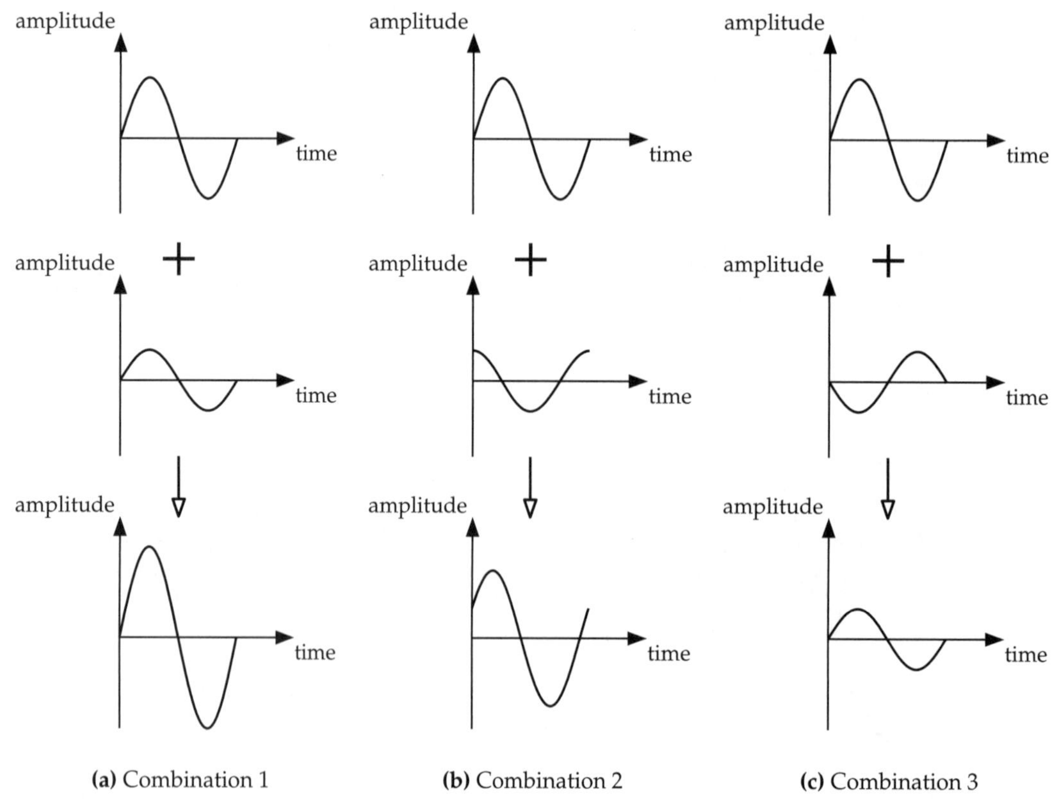

(a) Combination 1 **(b)** Combination 2 **(c)** Combination 3

Figure 3.9 Addition of sinusoids with the same frequency, but different phase relationships

The results in figure 3.9 are sinusoids of the same frequency, but with varying amplitudes:

- If the partials are in phase (figure 3.9a) then the amplitudes add together.
- If the partials are in antiphase (180° or π radians difference, figure 3.9c) then one sinusoid has negative values while the other has positive, so amplitude is subtracted.
- In between (figure 3.9b) the partials are out of phase, and there is a peak amplitude between the two extremes.

If the two input partials have the same amplitude, then the summed amplitude is double when they are in phase, and zero when in antiphase.

3.2 Dynamic Sound Character

The previous section considered sounds that are unchanging in character, which use fixed combinations of sinusoids to achieve particular tonal results. Musical instrument sounds usually develop over time; for example, starting in an inconsistent or noisy fashion and becoming more sinusoidal later, or starting loudly and fading away. This can be termed *dynamic sound character*, and often makes a sound more interesting and musically useful.

3.2.1 Chime Bar

A whole note of an instrument often lasts for several seconds. As such, when talking about dynamic changes to sound character it is necessary to consider longer lengths of time than the individual cycles of sound seen in the previous section. Figure 3.10 shows the time domain form of a note played on a chime bar. This instrument consists of a wooden xylophone bar mounted on a resonator box, which produces a similar tonal result to a xylophone or marimba when struck. There are two features of the way in which the sound develops over time that are of interest:

- The waveform does not have constant peak amplitude over the whole note. The overall level rises within the first 50ms and then decays gradually towards the end of the sound.
- The waveform shape is not consistent throughout the sound. This variation is not visually clear when viewing a zoomed-out time domain plot, but it is audible as a change of tonal character over time.

The long-term variation in peak amplitude over the length of the sound event is called the *amplitude envelope*. It is audible as a changing level, which is interpreted as the sound getting louder and quieter. The underlying waveform is also rising and falling in value, but it is changing too quickly for that rise and fall to be audible directly as an overall level variation.

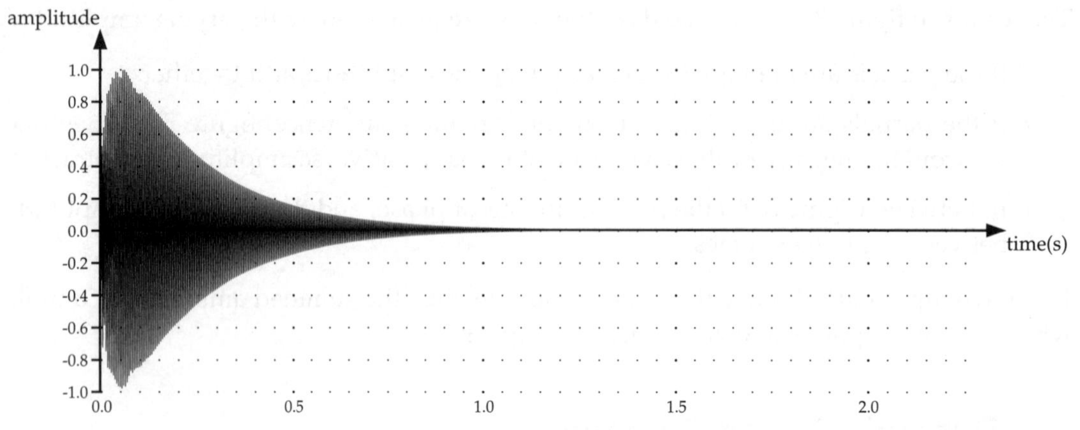

Figure 3.10 Chime bar waveform plot

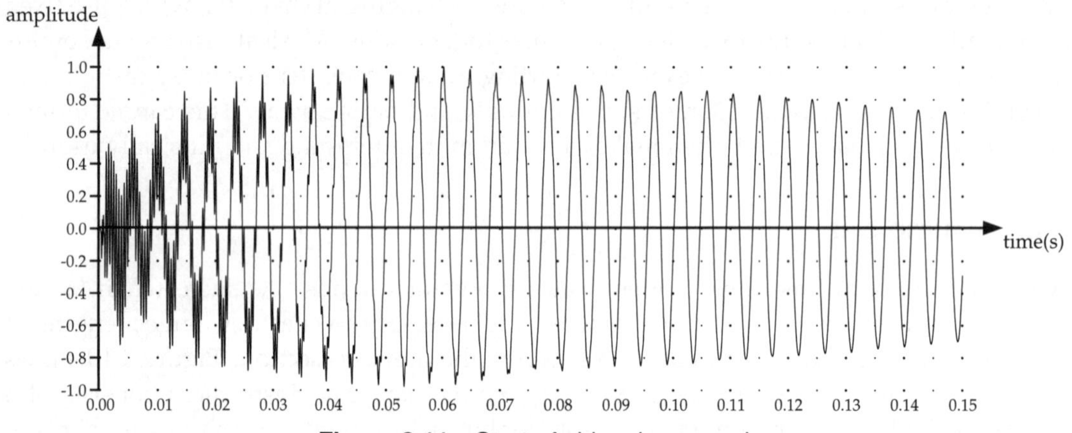

Figure 3.11 Start of chime bar sound

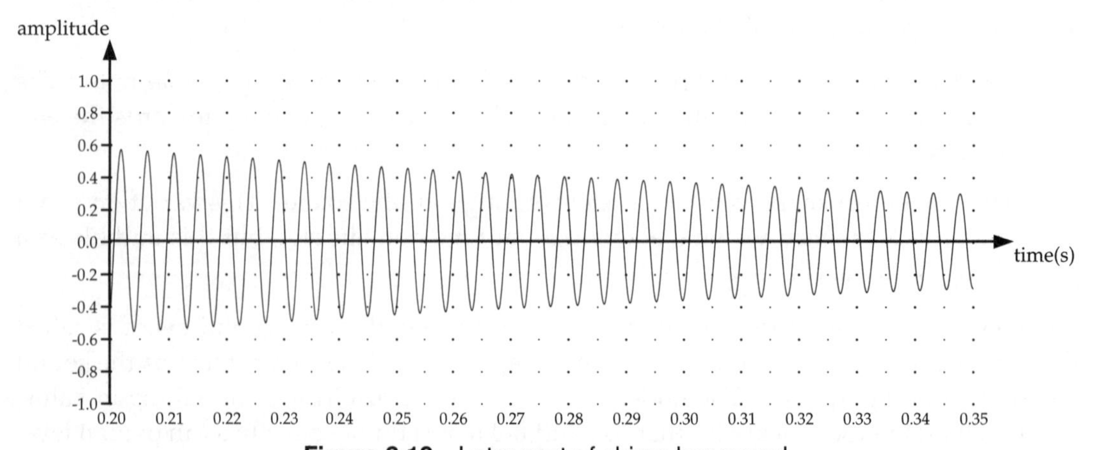

Figure 3.12 Later part of chime bar sound

It is unwise to infer too much about the detail of a waveform over a short length of time from a visual plot of the whole sound. The limited resolution of a computer screen or a printer means that it is easy to be fooled into thinking that an effect is occurring when it is not. It is necessary to zoom into a time domain plot to fully understand the waveform details. In particular, it often seems on a computer display that there are strange oscillating patterns within the sound that are visible when zoomed-out. This is due to an effect called visual aliasing (which is closely related to the audio aliasing described in Chapter 2).

Figure 3.11 shows the first 150ms of the chime bar sound:

- The more the plot is zoomed-in, the harder it is to make out the overall amplitude envelope.
- The waveform is not repeating exactly from cycle to cycle in the way that it does in, say, figure 3.5 (p.43). As the signal develops over the length of the plot, it is becoming more regular and consistent.
- At the start of the sound, it appears noisy and irregular. This is due to the injection of many frequency partials into the system by the beater striking the instrument and forcing it to make a sound. The instrument is losing more and more of those frequency partials over time, however, as it settles down into a repeating (and so pitched) waveform.

To emphasise what is happening as the sound progresses, examine figure 3.12, which shows a zoomed-in section of the chime bar sound from 200ms to 350ms. It is apparent how regular the waveform has become and how much more like a sine wave. It is not actually perfectly sinusoidal, but it is clearly much more so than at the beginning of the sound. The changing visual character is reflected in the audible result.

An amplitude envelope that rises rapidly and then decays, and a waveform that starts inconsistently and gradually simplifies to a more regular form, are typical of a simple percussive sound. Not all percussive sounds work in this way, but this is information that could be used in a synthesizer or a modification system. It is now necessary to investigate dynamic changes in amplitude and waveform in more detail.

3.2.2 Amplitude Envelopes

Amplitude envelopes are an important contributor to sound character. The human auditory system can infer certain things about the nature of a sound source from the shape and duration of the amplitude envelope. For example:

- An object that is struck or plucked will tend to have a rapid onset, indicating the rapid energy input to the sound source.

- A consistent level of amplitude over several seconds indicates constant energy input (such as blowing into a wind instrument, or bowing a stringed instrument) rather than a brief energy input, such as a string being plucked.
- A sound source that decays slowly after the energy input has ended (such as a bell) has less damping than a sound that decays more quickly (such as a knock on a wooden door).

There is some common terminology used when describing the different parts (or *segments*) of an amplitude envelope:

- The *onset* or *attack* occurs when the sound begins. In a number of instruments this is related to a *transient*, where a rapid rise in amplitude is typically coupled with a rapid change in the underlying waveform as well. In terms of acoustic sound sources, the onset is often an important indicator to the human auditory system of the excitation technique employed (how energy is applied to the object), such as how it is struck, plucked, bowed, blown, or rubbed.
- A *swell* is an increase in amplitude envelope level over time. This term is generally applied to more gradual variations than are found in a transient or rapid attack. In acoustic sound sources a swell is normally associated with continuous control over the amplitude of the instrument. For example, an oboe player can gradually increase amplitude over time through breath control. However, the amplitude of a single piano note is determined at the start of the sound, and the player cannot change its level half way through the note, so a swell is not possible with that instrument for a single note event.
- A *sustain* is where the level of the amplitude envelope is maintained at a somewhat consistent value. This is generally associated with a constant input of energy into a sound-producing object (a sustained excitation). As with the swell, a sustain is possible with an oboe, but not with a piano (as the energy input only occurs during the onset). Note that in this book the term *sustain* is used to mean a consistent level rather than the length of a decay.
- A *tremolo* occurs when the envelope has a low-frequency periodic (or semi-periodic) rise-and-fall in amplitude. This is sometimes produced automatically (mechanically or electronically) by the instrument, and sometimes is created by the player having direct control over amplitude and causing it to vary.
- A *decay* is a reduction in amplitude envelope level over time. With the chime bar example seen earlier, the whole of the sound from the onset onwards is a long decay (there is no swell, and no sustain). In that case the decay represents the dissipation of energy over time as the instrument resonates. Other instruments display more complex behaviour. A piano has a gradual decay after the onset, and then a more rapid decay when the key is released. With an instrument such as a flute, the shape

and length of the decay can be controlled directly by the player. If a decay occurs at the end of a sound, it is often called a *release*, particularly when triggered by the performer.

The features described above can be found in different quantities, sizes, and shapes in the output from different sound sources. There are some well known envelope styles traditionally associated with synthesizers, such as those shown in figure 13.13 (p.411). However, there are huge variations found in the complexity and nature of amplitude envelopes from different acoustic and synthetic sources.

Although some amplitude envelopes are fairly consistent between notes, such as the attack and decay form of a chime bar, with some instruments there can be large differences between notes, such as with a wind instrument. This reflects the variations that occur in control mechanisms. The following amplitude envelope examples illustrate the range of results that are possible. It should not be considered, however, that these are the only amplitude envelopes possible with these particular instruments.

The amplitude envelope of the chime bar sound seen previously can be separated from the underlying waveform and plotted as shown in figure 3.13. When plotting the envelope it is only shown with positive values.

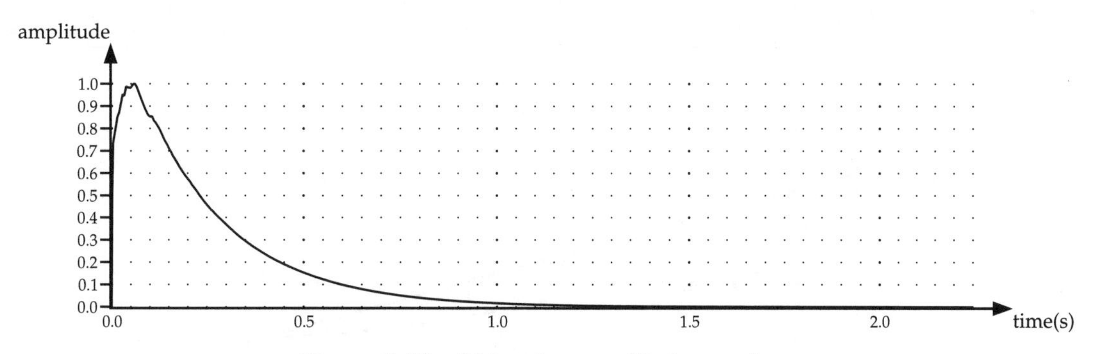

Figure 3.13 Chime bar amplitude envelope

The first important thing to notice is that there are two major sections to the envelope:

- The onset is when the instrument initially reacts to the injection of energy from the beater onto the wooden bar. The amplitude envelope rises to a peak level during this attack section. The shape of the onset and how quickly it rises depends upon the nature of the stimulation and the reaction of the object. The chime bar has an onset time of about 50ms. Some percussive instruments have an even shorter onset, which is perceived to be sharper or more forceful. If it had been longer (say 500ms), it might be perceived as a swell rather than a sharp injection of energy.

- The decay is from the end of the onset to the end of the sound. Because no more energy is being injected into the instrument, the energy will gradually dissipate. Again, the shape and rate of decay depends on the nature of the object, and how it reacts to the energy input. A pillow will react very differently when struck compared to a bell. Many percussive objects designed for musical use have a long decay.

The second important thing to notice is that the chime bar envelope lacks any straight line features. Amplitude envelopes of acoustic sound sources generally display non-linear shapes. It is important when attempting to synthesize natural-sounding results that the curves found in acoustic instrument envelopes are replicated appropriately in simulations, or there will be audible differences.

The decay of the chime bar amplitude envelope illustrates a very important characteristic of many acoustic instruments, which is a somewhat *exponential decay*. A linearly-decaying envelope is achieved by subtracting a fixed amount at each step in time, whereas exponential decay is achieved by removing a **proportion** of the current amplitude each time. To understand the relationship between linear and exponential decay, examine the following table and the plot in figure 3.14:

Time step	0	1	2	3	4	5	6	7	8	9	10
Linear decay	1.000	0.910	0.820	0.730	0.640	0.550	0.460	0.370	0.280	0.190	0.100
Exponential decay	1.000	0.800	0.640	0.512	0.410	0.328	0.262	0.210	0.168	0.134	0.107

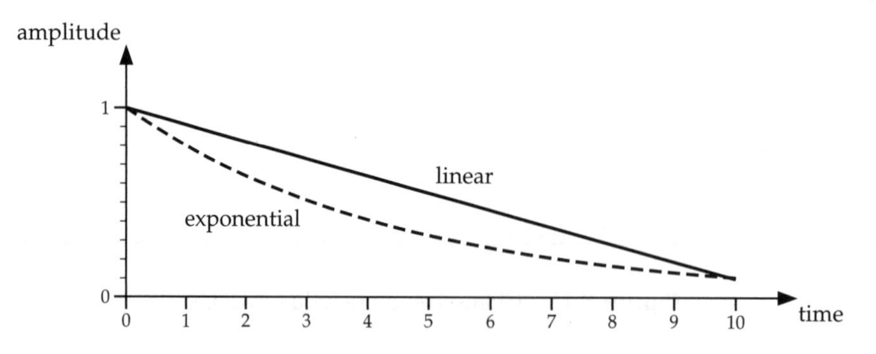

Figure 3.14 Linear and exponential decays

The table compares subtracting 0.09 at each time step (an example of a linear decay), with multiplying the previous value by 0.8 (removing 20% of the value each time, an example of an exponential decay). In figure 3.14 it is apparent that the exponential line initially drops more rapidly than the linear example, but levels out towards the bottom. There is an audible difference between amplitude decays that are linear and those that are exponential.

There are two reasons why an exponential curve should be expected with a decaying acoustic effect:

- When a sound source is resonating, it is more likely to follow an exponential (proportional) decay, which corresponds with the physics of sound-producing objects.
- Humans **perceive** an exponential decay as being a consistent linear decay. That is, the exponential decay in figure 3.14 sounds like a straight line reduction in amplitude to the human auditory system.

A truly exponential decay appears as a straight line on a plot with a decibel amplitude axis. To convert from linear to decibel amplitude the following equation is used:

$$\text{amplitude}_{\text{dB}} = 20\log_{10}(\text{amplitude}) \tag{3.1}$$

Figure 3.15 shows that the chime bar exhibits a fairly straight decay line when plotted with decibel amplitude values, reflecting its somewhat exponential decay. Notice that there are some wobbles in the line at very low amplitude values. These are due to background noise in the recording room, and noise added by the recording equipment (such as the microphone and preamplifier).

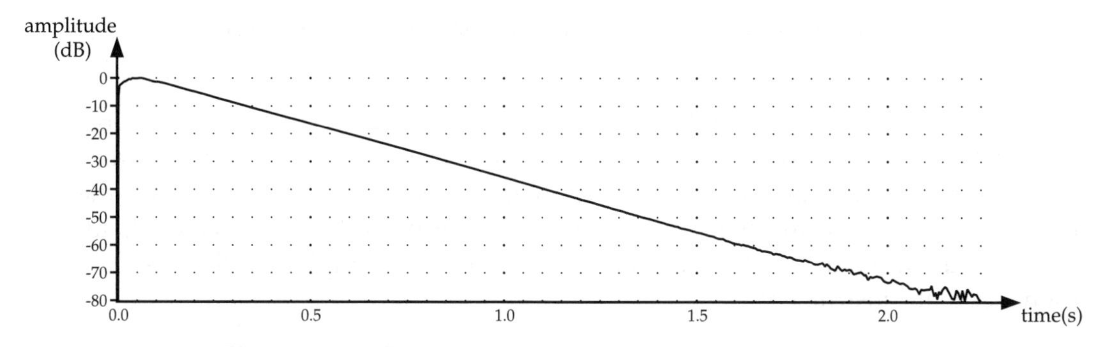

Figure 3.15 Chime bar (decibel scale) amplitude envelope

Most acoustic sound sources produce amplitude envelopes that are more complex than that of the chime bar. The subtle variations in acoustic instrument envelope shapes are one way in which they are audibly distinguished from simple synthesized tones. A number of examples follow to illustrate the range of typical shapes.

Figure 3.16 illustrates the decibel scale amplitude envelope for a solid-bodied electric guitar note recorded using pickups. There are some broad similarities in shape with the envelope for the chime bar. They both have a sharp injection of energy into the instrument at the beginning of the sound (striking or plucking), followed by a resonance that causes a gentle decay over a number of seconds as the energy is dissipated. For that reason, plucking an electric guitar can be regarded as having a percussive quality. Although the decay in decibels is not as close to a straight line as that seen in figure 3.15, the general trend is still somewhat towards an exponential decay.

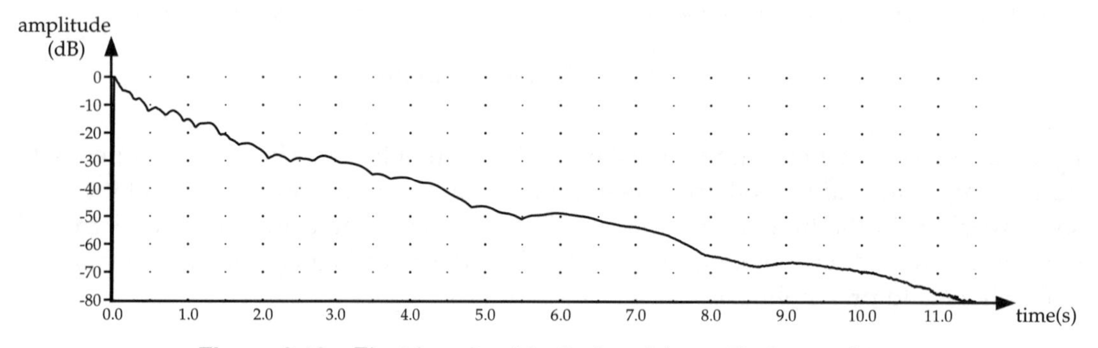

Figure 3.16 Electric guitar (decibel scale) amplitude envelope

Figure 3.17 illustrates a different type of percussive instrument amplitude envelope; that of a plastic egg-shaped shaker. The first important feature is the very short time scale compared to the previous sounds. Secondly, there are two parts to the envelope; the first occurs when the beads inside hit the top of the shaker when the object is lifted, and the second occurs when they fall again. The rise and fall is quite rapid and there is not much resonance in the instrument.

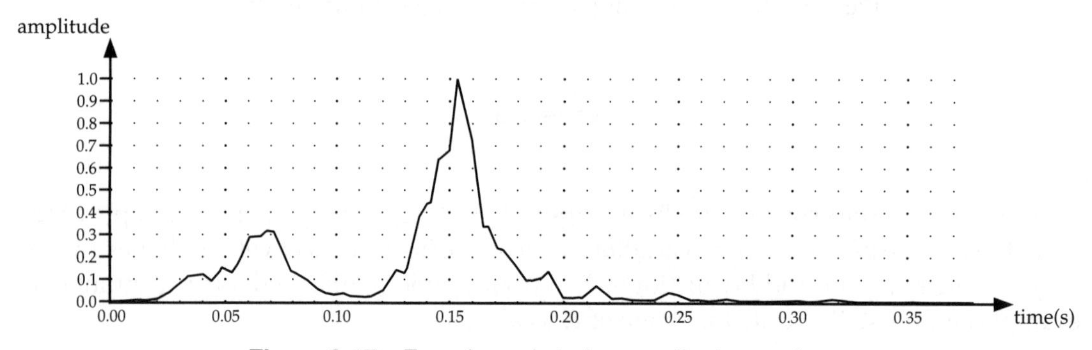

Figure 3.17 Egg-shaped shaker amplitude envelope

Figure 3.18 illustrates two amplitude envelopes from an ocarina, which is a small keyless wind instrument. The chime bar and electric guitar seen previously have a sharp injection of energy at the start of the note, and little control over the shape of the decay (other than deliberate damping). An ocarina allows the player to vary the amplitude of the sound constantly, and extend the length of the note as long as they have breath.

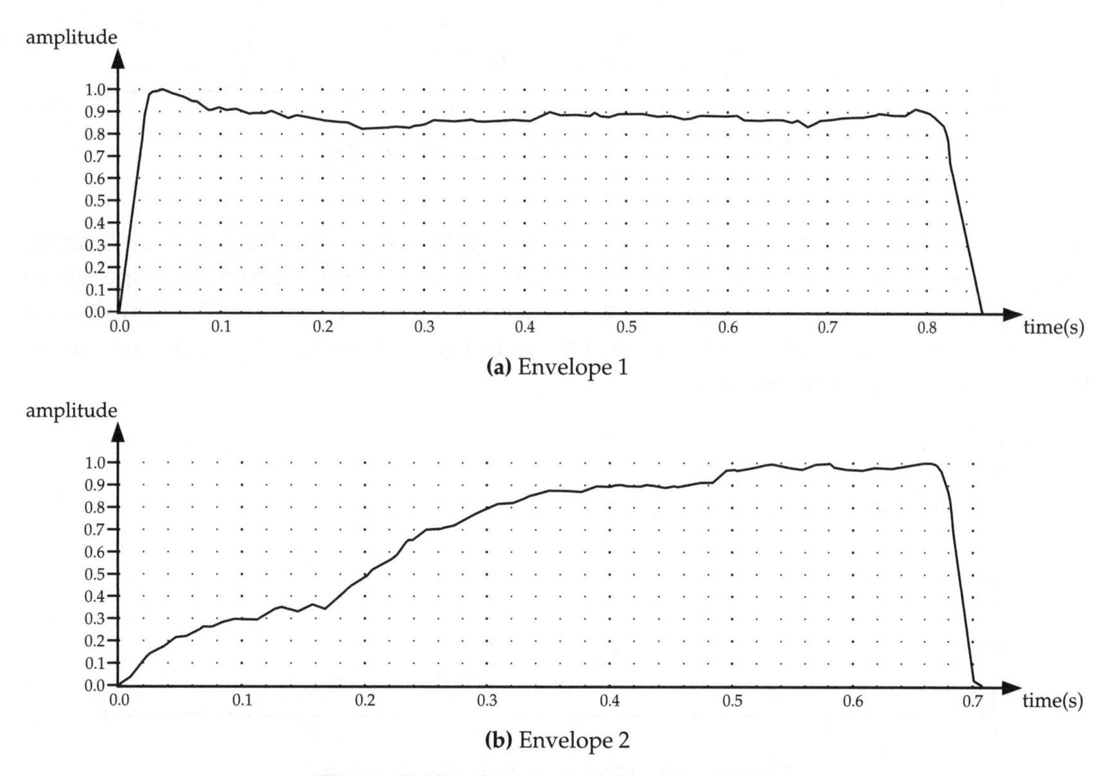

(a) Envelope 1

(b) Envelope 2

Figure 3.18 Ocarina amplitude envelopes

Figure 3.18a shows a clear onset as the player starts the sound, a small decay to a slightly inconsistent sustaining level, and then a final decay at the end. Figure 3.18b, on the other hand, is a swell followed by a rapid release at the end of the sound. The ocarina allows the performer to create a wide range of amplitude envelope shapes due to the continuous input of energy through their breath.

Figure 3.19 shows an example amplitude envelope produced by a cabasa. The cabasa is a percussion instrument with a steel bead chain wrapped around a textured steel cylinder. This enables the creation of sounds with unusual envelopes such as that in the figure, where the sound swells and then stops abruptly. This time the control over amplitude is provided by the hands of the player.

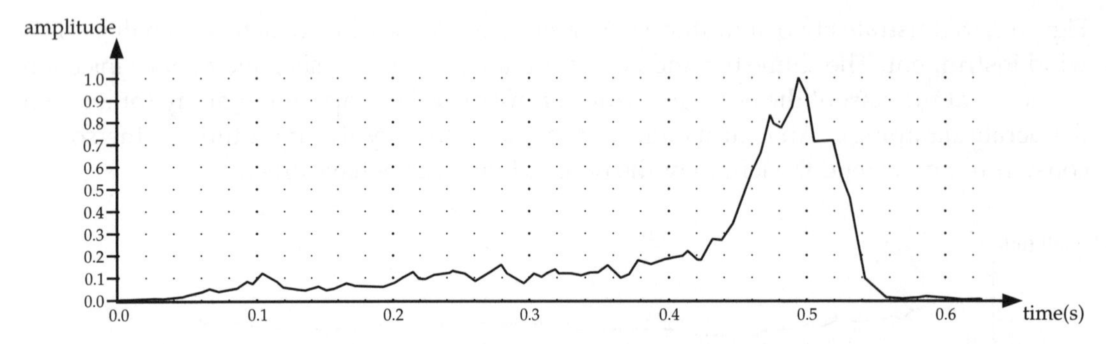

Figure 3.19 Cabasa amplitude envelope

A clarinet provides the opportunity to control the amplitude in a similar way to an ocarina, because it is a wind instrument. Figure 3.20 illustrates an example clarinet envelope where the player has created a fairly rapid onset and swell at the start of the sound, followed by a decay with noticeable tremolo variations. The tremolo is created by the player modulating the flow of air into the instrument.

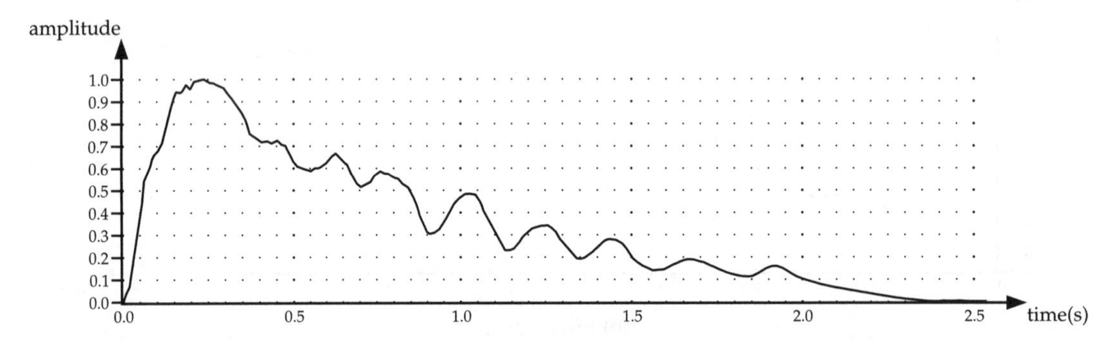

Figure 3.20 Clarinet amplitude envelope

Figure 3.21 shows an example bowed cello envelope. It has an initial onset as the note starts and the string begins to vibrate, followed by a swell up to the condition where the sound is being maintained at a somewhat consistent average amplitude on which a tremolo effect is imposed, before the amplitude gradually decays to zero. The tremolo (amplitude modulation) is a side effect of the player rocking their finger back and forth on the fingerboard to create a vibrato (frequency modulation).

As with the ocarina, cabasa, and clarinet, there is continuous control of amplitude over the duration of the sound. The cello player can control such elements as the rate at which the sound swells, the rate and depth of the vibrato and tremolo, and how aggressive the initial onset segment will be. It is also the case that every note will be different in its development, even if the player intends it to sound the same, as the continuous control

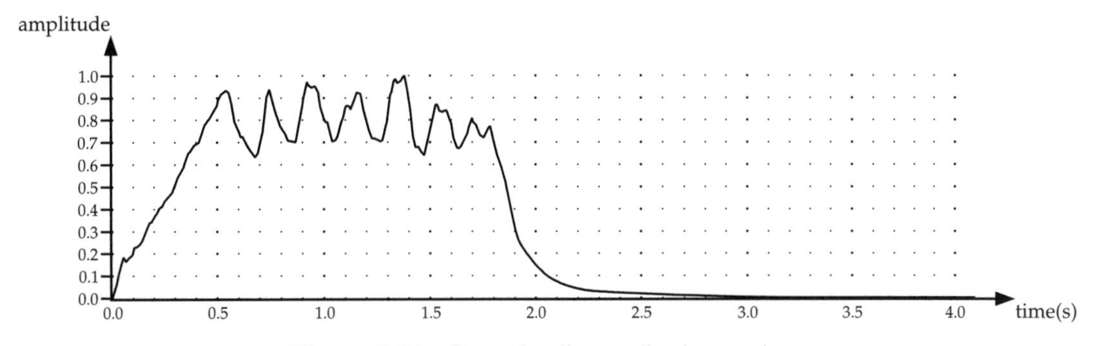

Figure 3.21 Bowed cello amplitude envelope

method responds to every subtle variation of player input and it can be very difficult to achieve exact control.

Figure 3.22 illustrates an amplitude envelope example for a güiro. The güiro has a hollow wooden body with parallel ridges on the surface, across which a stick is dragged to create sounds. The effect is to produce a series of peaks in the amplitude envelope that could either be described as a set of many individual attacks and decays, or an overall envelope with a very large tremolo. The performer has some control over the rate at which the peaks occur.

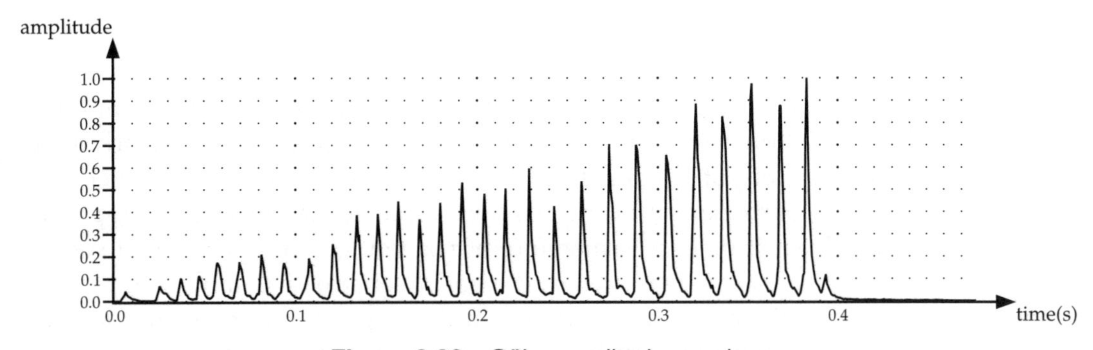

Figure 3.22 Güiro amplitude envelope

Figure 3.23a shows an amplitude envelope produced by a Hammond organ. Keys on this organ have a simple switch-like effect. When the key is depressed there is a rapid onset, followed by a sustaining level. When the key is released, there is a rapid decay at the end of the sound. The sustain includes subtle envelope variations throughout that contribute to the character. Figure 3.23b shows another Hammond organ envelope, but this time with a very large amount of tremolo variation. This has changed the overall shape quite dramatically compared to figure 3.23a, as the tremolo effect is superimposed on top of the simple underlying envelope.

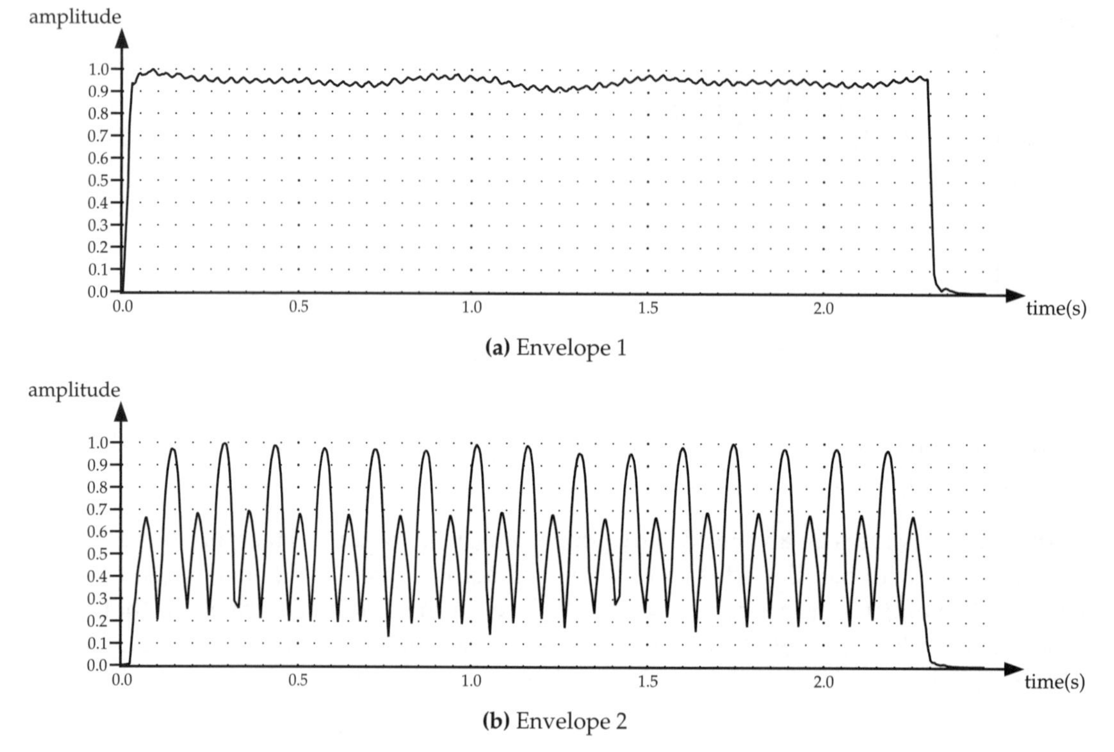

(a) Envelope 1

(b) Envelope 2

Figure 3.23 Hammond organ amplitude envelopes

These examples demonstrate the types of features that are typically found in amplitude envelopes, reflecting the physical nature of the sound-producing object. Clearly there is an almost endless variety of shapes that are possible, and a single instrument can generate different types of shape depending on how it is played. Analysing the amplitude envelopes produced by instruments is therefore of use both in the synthesis of sounds designed to have similar sonic character, and also in constructing modifiers that are supposed to respond to the amplitude envelope in their operation. It also helps in the consideration of how instrument controllers relate to the underlying sonic form.

3.2.3 Dynamic Waveform Changes

The overall amplitude envelope indicates much about the nature of the sound source, but the underlying waveform and its development over time is also important. The chime bar example in figures 3.11 and 3.12 (p.50) showed how the underlying waveform might change through a sound. With the chime bar, there is a fairly clear movement from the inconsistent/noisy character at the beginning, to a simpler form as the sound decays.

Many instrument sounds start in an inconsistent or noisy fashion, as the process of starting an object resonating can involve some forceful energy input, which often produces a wide range of frequencies. Whether that changes quickly to a smoother, resonant oscillation depends on how the object reacts to the input. For example, a chime bar settles quickly to a simple waveform shape, whereas a crash cymbal is more inconsistent for much longer. There are two elements that are important here:

- If the sound source has a clear pitch, the output will tend towards a repeating (harmonic) waveform.
- If the sound source receives constant input (say, blowing a clarinet or bowing a cello), then the player can impart changes to the sound as it progresses.

The following sections describe some different examples of changing waveforms found in acoustic instruments. It is important to remember that most instruments can produce a considerable range of results, and these are just a snapshot of the sound output under particular playing conditions.

3.2.4 Oboe

The oboe is a member of the woodwind family of instruments. Its principal resonant medium is a column of air in a wooden tube, which resonates due to the input from a vibrating reed. A constant flow of air is required to maintain the sound, by which the player can control the development of the sound. After energy input ceases, the output ends abruptly.

Figure 3.24 shows the amplitude envelope of an oboe tone. It has a fairly clear attack, decay, sustain, and release character. Because the oboe is an instrument with constant input from the performer, some of these features could have been different; for example, a more rapid release, or adding a swell or tremolo modulation. The length of the note also depends on the performer, who could make it very short, or as long as their breath allows.

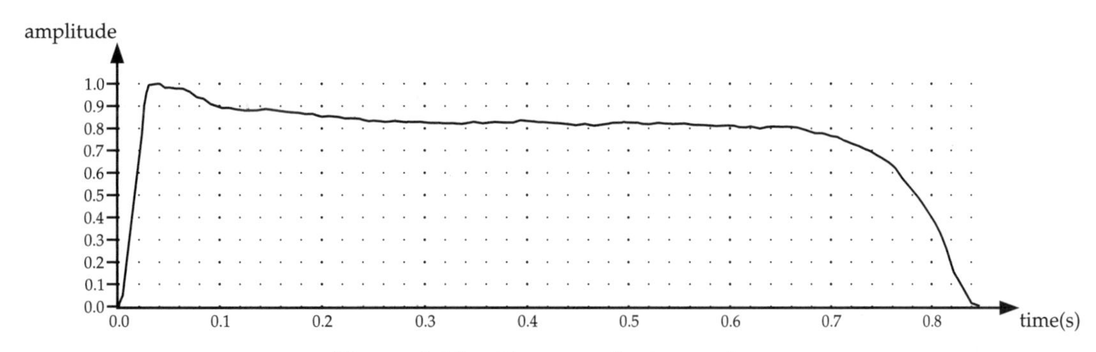

Figure 3.24 Oboe amplitude envelope

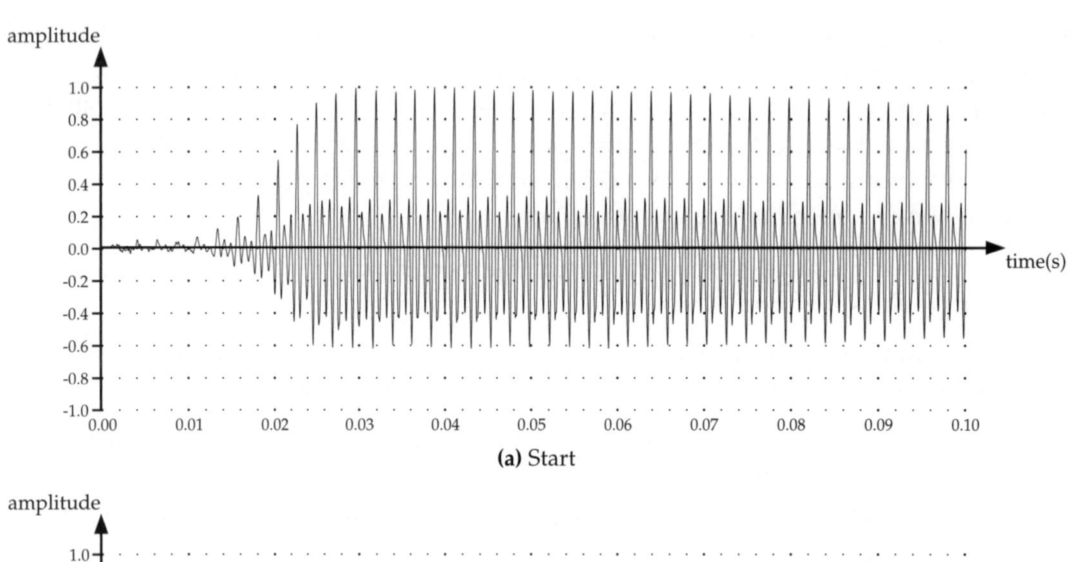

(a) Start

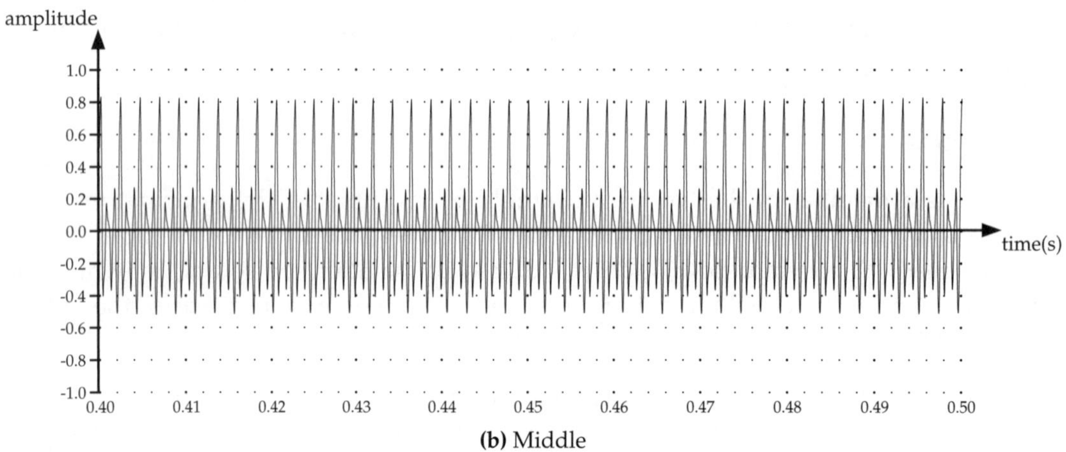

(b) Middle

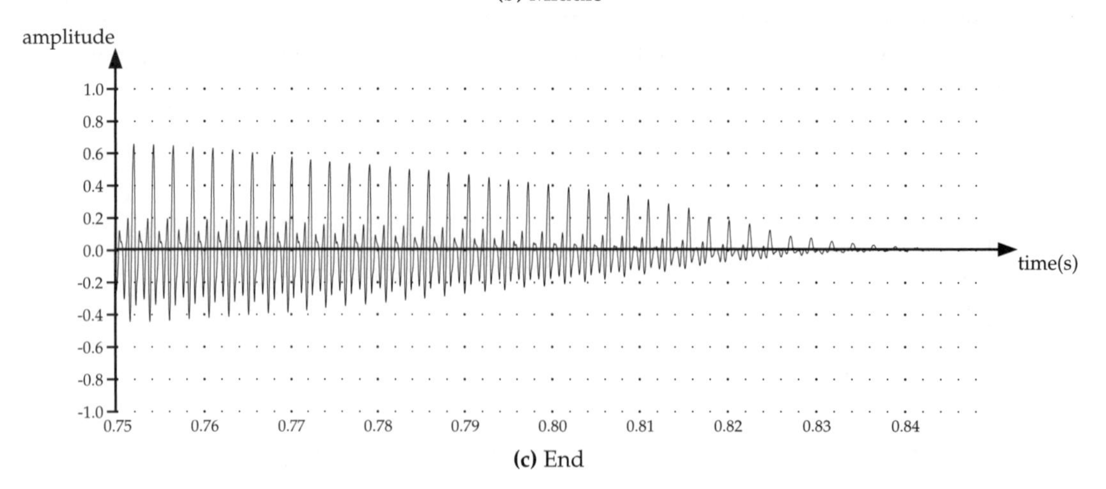

(c) End

Figure 3.25 Oboe waveform plots

Figure 3.25 shows three sections of the oboe tone; at the start, in the middle and near the end. What is noticeable is how similar the waveform is in each case (but with a different amplitude). That is, the performer has produced a tone with little timbral change from beginning to end. It is far less inconsistent at the start than the chime bar sound shown in figure 3.11 (p.50). It is also apparent that the sound is highly periodic (and harmonic), which gives a clear sense of pitch.

3.2.5 Vibraphone

The vibraphone is a percussion instrument similar to a marimba, but with metal bars and where the resonators have vanes (flat disks) inside that can optionally be made to revolve with a motor, causing the sound to gently pulse. Figure 3.26 illustrates two amplitude envelopes from the same note of the same instrument, one produced by striking the bar softly with a beater, and one by bowing the bar. In both cases the motor was switched off. The onset portions of the two notes reflect the different methods of excitation. However, the decays have a more similar appearance.

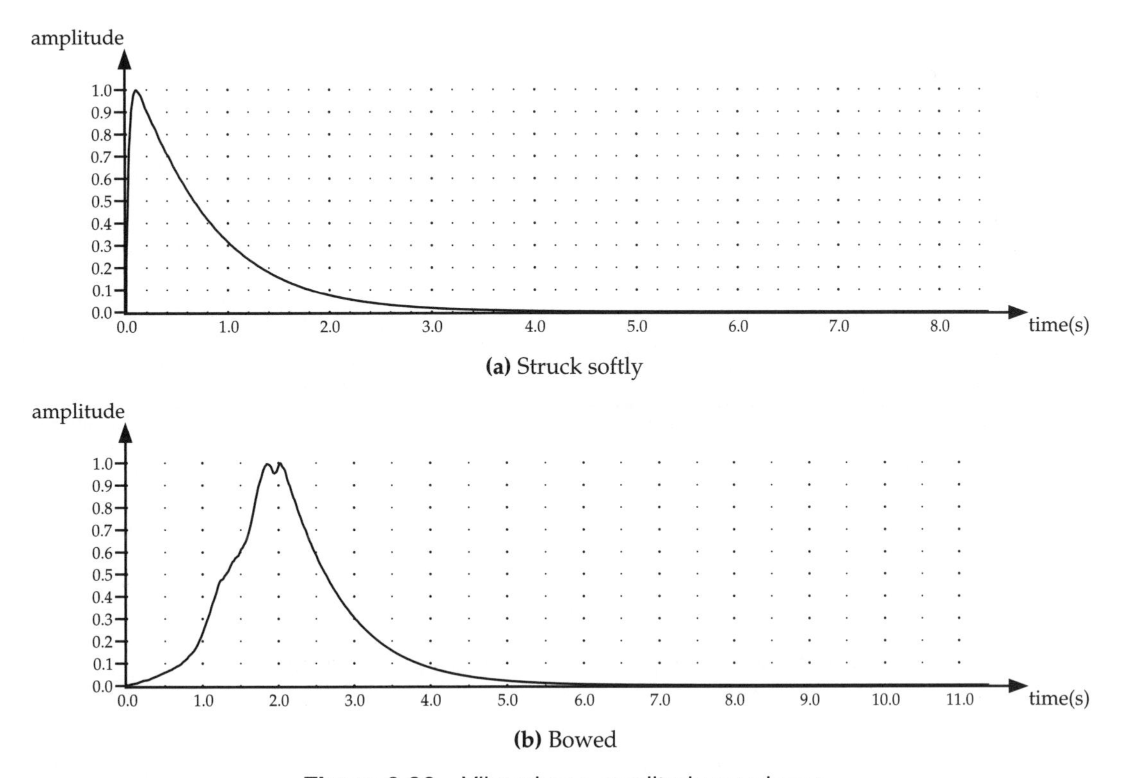

Figure 3.26 Vibraphone amplitude envelopes

Figure 3.27 shows waveform plots from the vibraphone sounds at the point where the energy input has ended and the decay is occurring. That is, after the beater has struck, and after the bowing has ended. The waveforms are remarkably similar, despite the different ways in which the sounds started. This reflects the nature of the instrument, where the differences in excitation are attenuated by the time the resonant decay is reached. If the two sounds are played from the start of the decay onwards they do sound very similar. The similarities are less obvious when the entire sounds are played, as the onset is very important to the human auditory system.

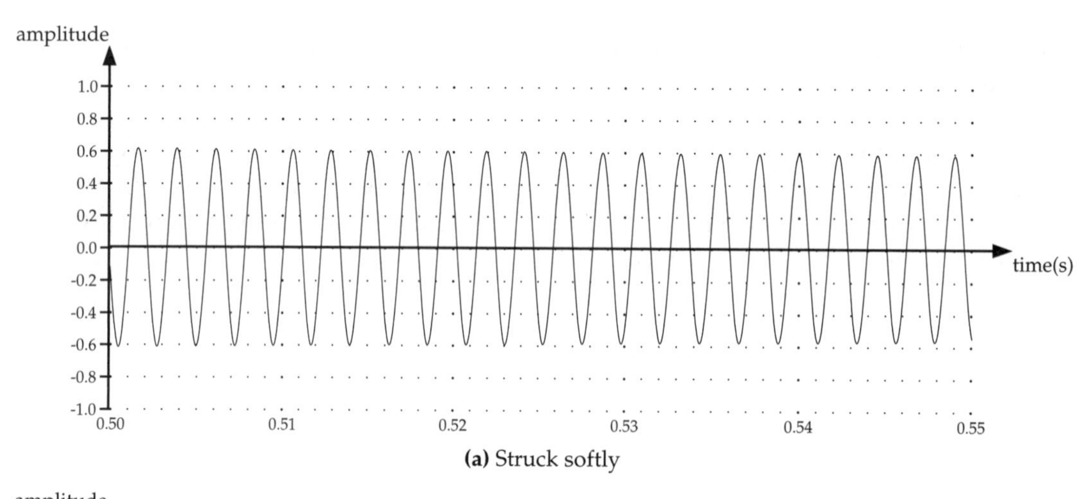

(a) Struck softly

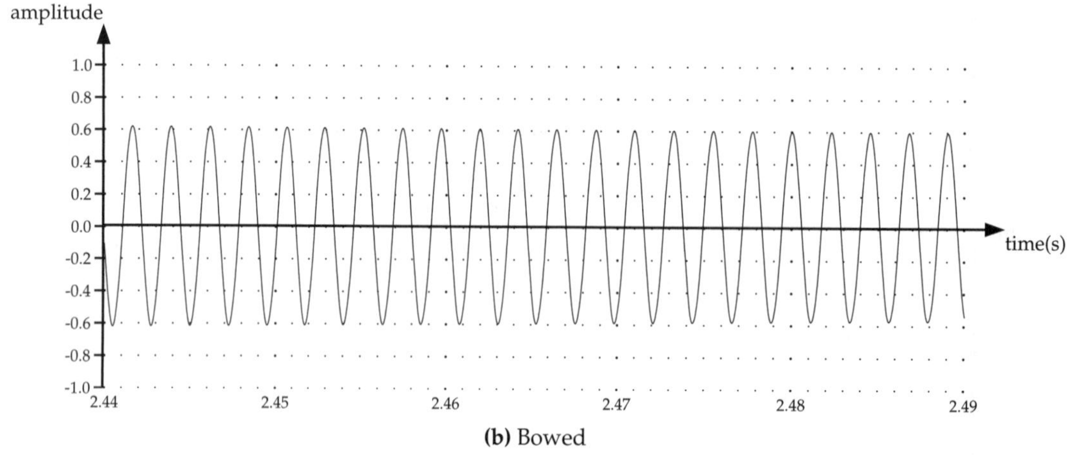

(b) Bowed

Figure 3.27 Vibraphone waveform plots (from decays)

Figure 3.28 illustrates two examples of the onset of the vibraphone when struck with the same beater, but with different amounts of force. The amount of force used affects the strength of upper frequency partials at the start of the sound, changing the tonal characteristic. The plots have been normalised for amplitude to make the differences more apparent.

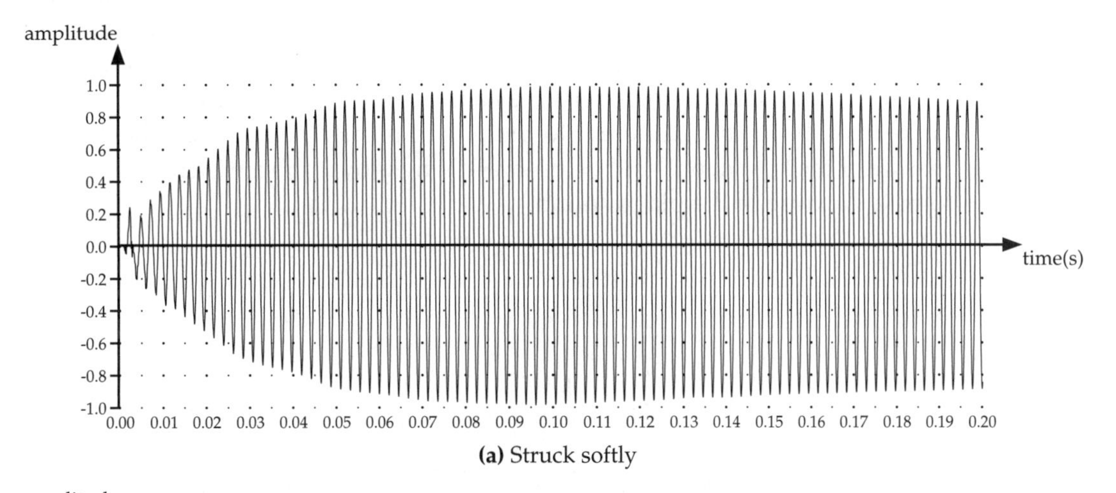

(a) Struck softly

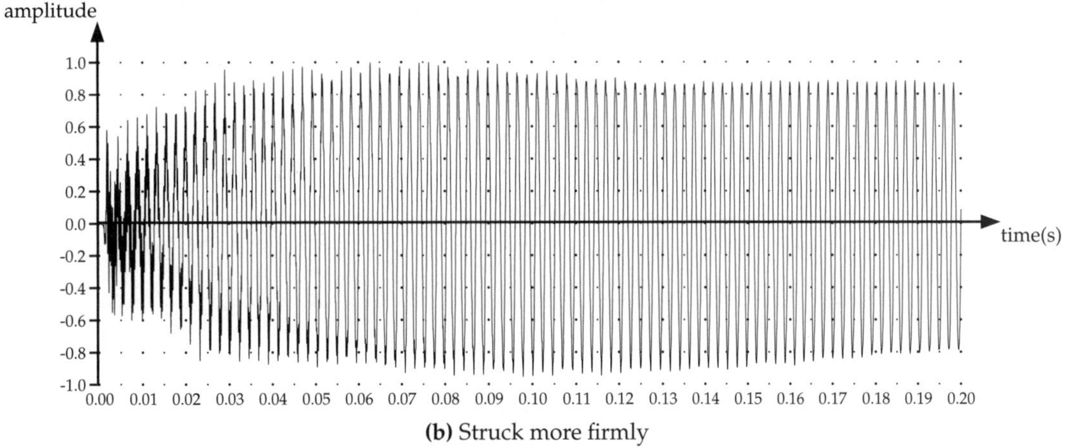

(b) Struck more firmly

Figure 3.28 Vibraphone waveform plots (part of onset)

With many sound sources, the onset is important in indicating the nature of acoustic excitation (the cause of the sound event) to the human auditory system. The latter parts of sounds will often indicate how the sound source reacts to the excitation; for example, if it settles to a harmonic (pitched) form after beginning in an irregular manner, or whether it continues in a similar way to that in which it started, or whether there is control from the performer such that the sound can be changed over the length of the note.

3.2.6 Piano

The piano creates sound when keys cause felt hammers to strike metal strings. The player cannot change the timbre after the note has begun, other than to dampen it by releasing the key. However, it is possible to achieve different tonalities by changing the force with which the string is struck, much like the vibraphone. Figure 3.29 shows waveform plots from different points in a piano tone. The waveform does have a cyclical component (it is a pitched instrument), but it is apparent that the shape is neither as simple and regular as the oboe, nor as clearly simplifying over time as the chime bar or vibraphone. In fact, every cycle appears to be slightly different to the previous one. This reflects the slightly inharmonic nature of the sound, with subtle timbral changes over time, which adds a great deal to the complex texture of the piano sound.

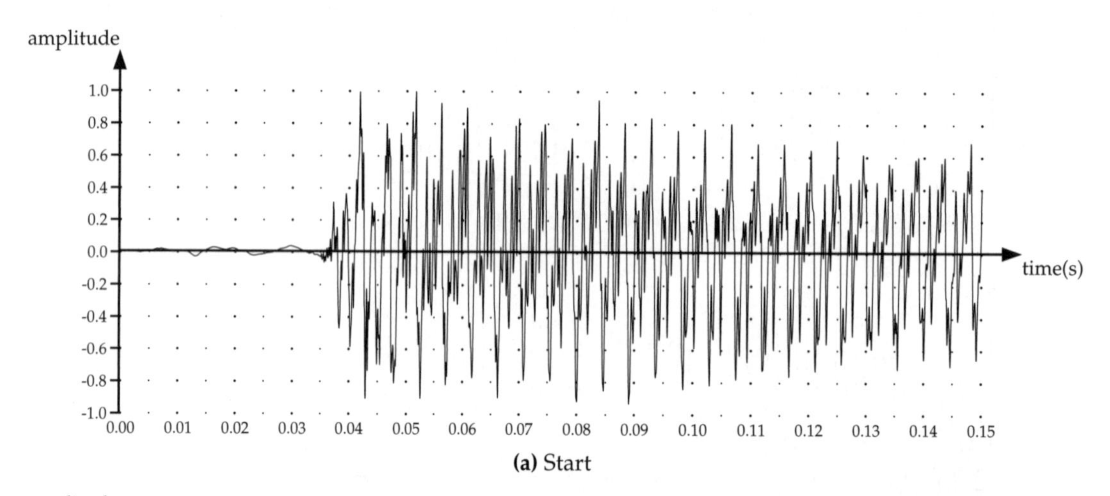

(a) Start

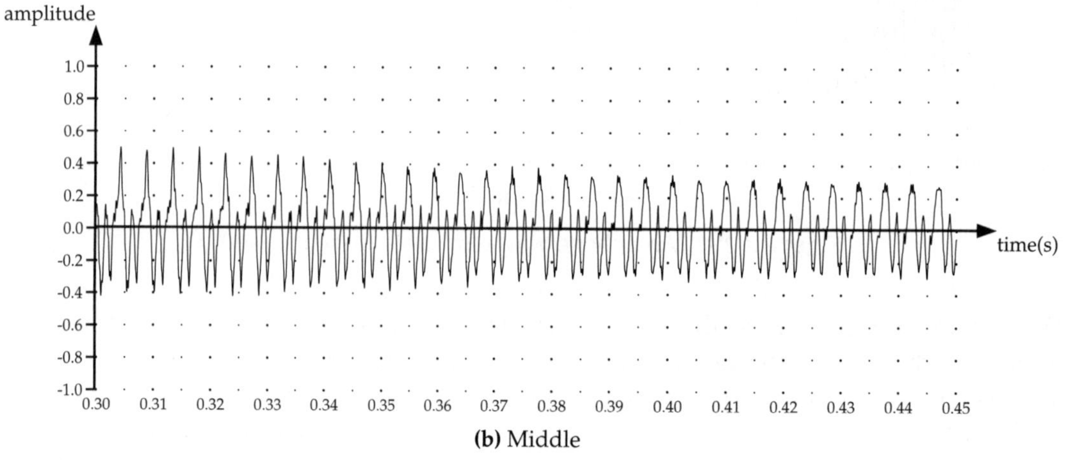

(b) Middle

Figure 3.29 Piano waveform plots

3.2.7 Tubular Bell

The tubular bell is a suspended tube of metal that is struck with a hammer. Figure 3.30 shows waveform plots from different points in a tubular bell tone. While the piano waveform has some cyclical aspects with subtle inharmonics causing variation over time, the tubular bell is an instrument with strong inharmonic partials and so the waveform is quite irregular. It does have a pitch, but it is a little less definite than that of a more harmonic instrument. As with the piano, the waveform shape changes over time as the energy put into the instrument is dissipated. However, while there is a fairly clear attenuation of high frequencies over time in figure 3.29, the nature of the variation in frequency content is less obvious in figure 3.30.

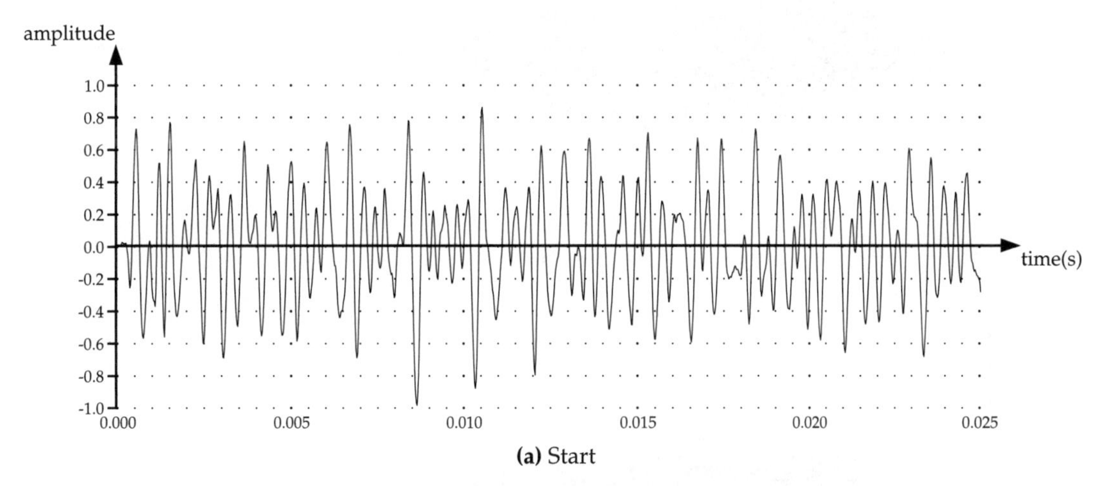

(a) Start

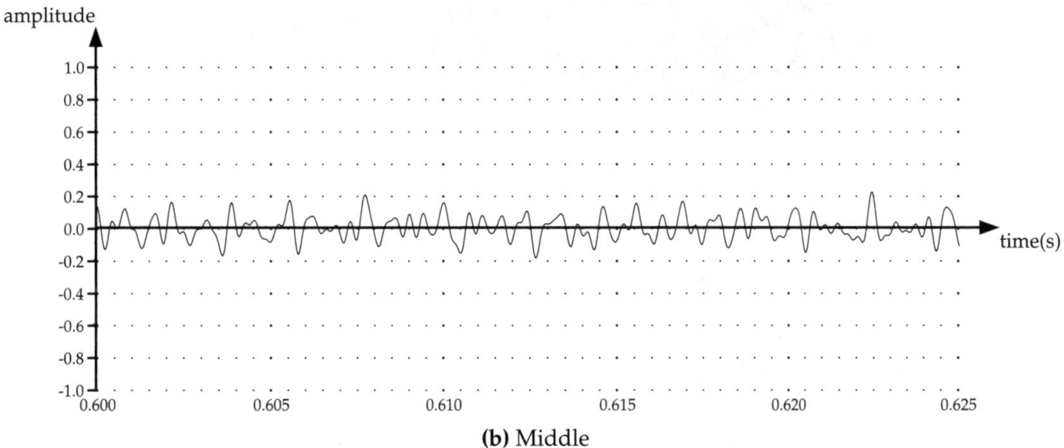

(b) Middle

Figure 3.30 Tubular bell waveform plots

3.2.8 Vocal "sh" and "f" Sounds

Sounds with a significant periodic element are important for creating a tune, but there are many sounds that do not have a clear pitch. Figure 3.31 shows the time domain forms of vocal "sh" and "f" sounds, which have a noisy nature. The sounds have been performed with a swell effect in the amplitude envelopes.

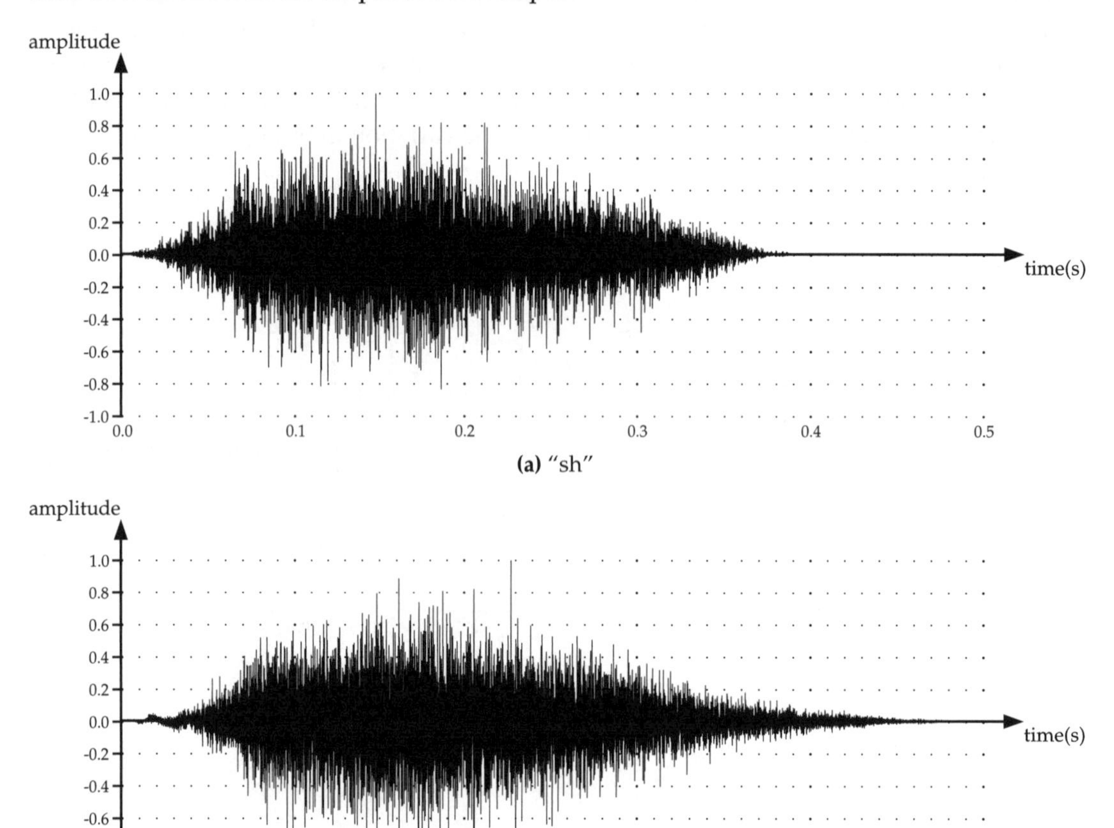

Figure 3.31 Vocal waveform plots (whole sound)

The plots in figure 3.31 look fairly similar, but there is a clear audible difference between them. Figure 3.32 illustrates the waveforms for a shorter length of time. While there are visible differences in the waveforms, the patterns are very complex and irregular. There is more high frequency emphasis in the "f" sound than the "sh", as indicated by the rapidity of waveform variation over the same length of time. However, it is not possible to precisely describe the amplitudes at different frequencies.

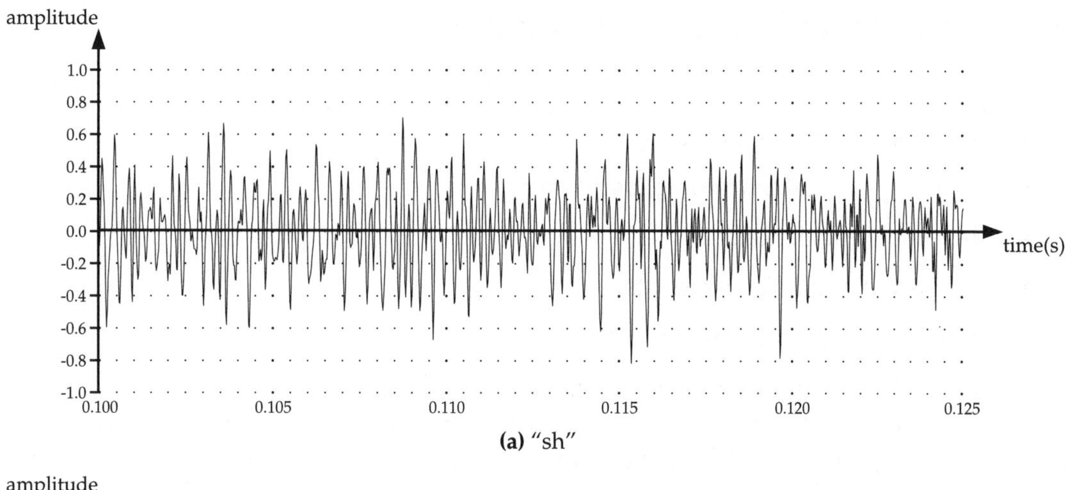

(a) "sh"

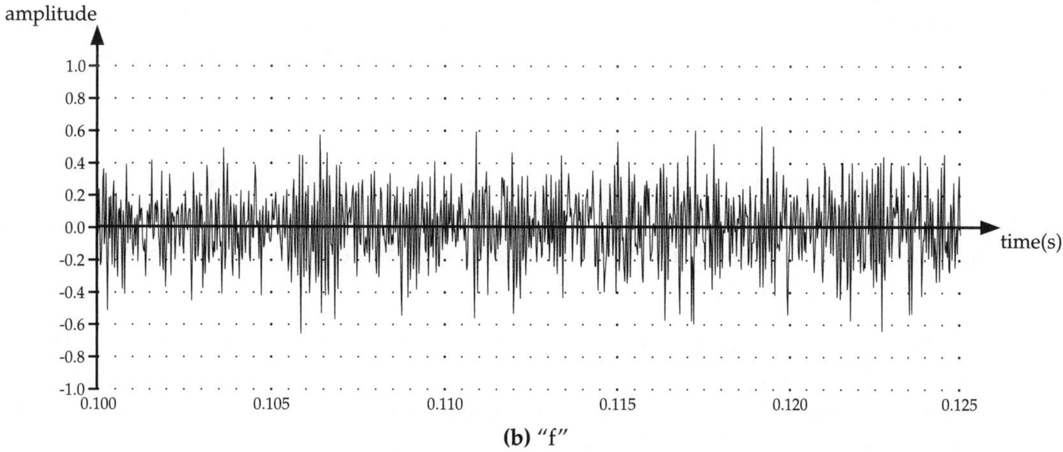

(b) "f"

Figure 3.32 Vocal waveform plots (zoomed-in)

A time domain waveform plot is analogous to the air pressure variation that arrives at the human ear. It is a neutral representation, as it makes no assumptions about the processing that occurs inside the human auditory system. When plotted, it is possible to distinguish certain features, particularly those of amplitude envelope and changes in periodic forms. However, a time domain plot is insufficient for examining the finer details of timbral form. Chapter 4 describes frequency domain techniques that are used to supplement time domain analysis.

3.3 Using Time Domain Information

Different elements of the time domain form have been examined in this chapter, such as:

- The amplitude envelope shape.
- Consistent cyclical (harmonic) oscillation.
- Inharmonic oscillation.
- Inconsistent and noisy elements.
- Changing waveform shape over time.

These reflect the underlying physics of the sound-producing object, and are used by the human auditory system to aid in understanding the nature of the sound source. Later chapters will explain how this information is relevant to modification and synthesis processes. In both modification and synthesis, if a result is to appear natural it must take account of the characteristic features of acoustic sounds. Alternatively, if an unnatural or synthetic sound character is required, one might deliberately avoid recreation of those features.

Consider the simple synthesized test tone in figure 3.33. A test tone such as this is used to examine the behaviour of a system, and so has a very consistent waveform and an unchanging peak amplitude. It is worth contrasting how such a sound differs from the instrument sounds seen so far:

- The amplitude envelope of the test tone is completely rectangular; it starts immediately, holds exactly the same amplitude level throughout the sound, and ends without a decay. This switch-like (on-off) character sounds unlike most acoustic instruments.

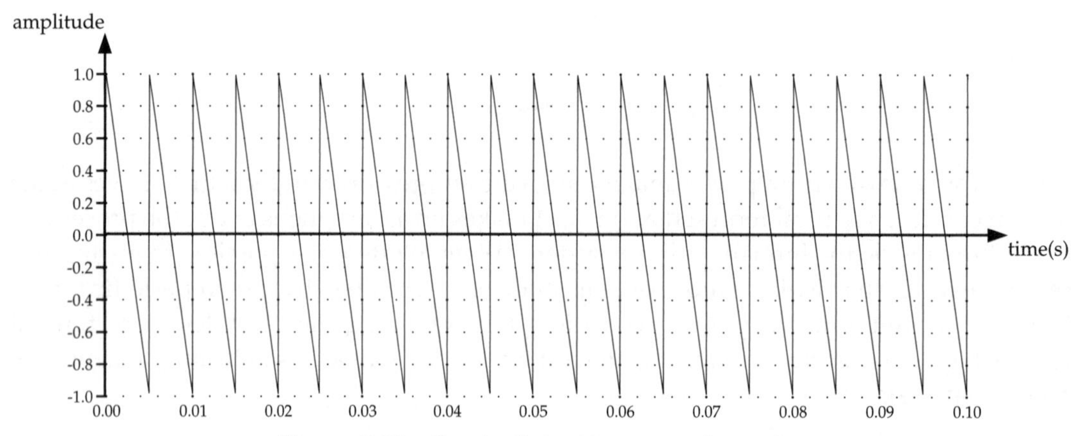

Figure 3.33 Sawtooth test tone waveform plot

- Most acoustic instruments have a waveform that changes over the length of the sound. To synthesize a sound that appears less synthetic to the human auditory system, it is necessary to include waveform variation.
- The waveform has precisely straight edges, and no hint of any inharmonic or noisy elements. Again, this is different to that of most acoustic sound sources.

It is often desirable to create natural effects; for example, to convince the listener that they could be listening to a sort of drum they have not heard before, rather than a synthesizer. Or that a large hall reverberation process creates an accurate impression of a sound source being in that space. It is often possible to identify the important features of acoustic phenomena in recorded sounds, and then replicate them in audio processes.

It is also possible to turn the logic around and create a result that stands out as being unusual. A simple time domain effect is to reverse a sound as shown in figure 3.34. The reversed sound is unusual primarily because the amplitude and frequency partial content both increase over time, in a way that does not happen in most acoustic instruments. The second element that is unusual is how abruptly it ends, disturbing the typical acoustic form of cause and effect.

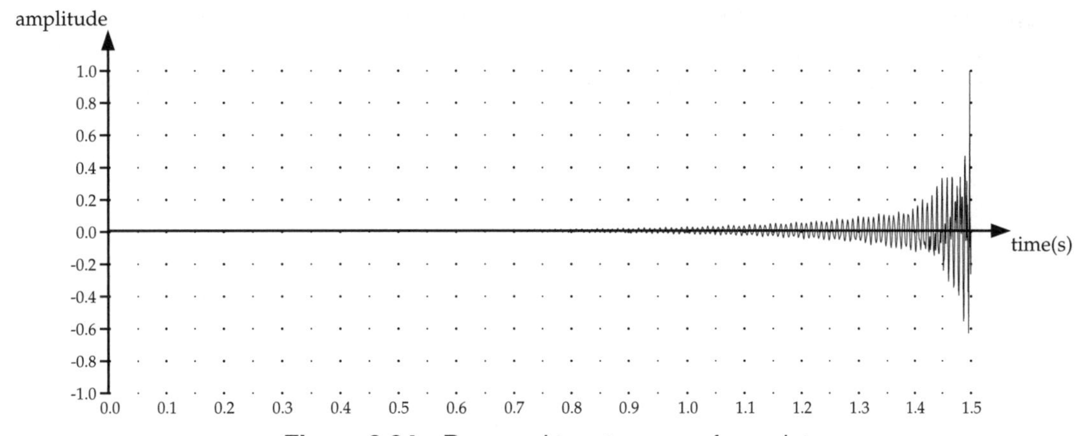

Figure 3.34 Reversed tom-tom waveform plot

It is worth remembering that what is "normal" or "common" is constantly changing. Certain common sounds created on synthesizers or through modification of acoustic sources would have been regarded as very unusual and distinctive a few decades ago. As people become immersed in particular sorts of sounds, they begin to regard them as normal.

3.4 Learning More

Understanding the nature of instrument sounds in the time domain is vital to the art of developing and configuring modification and synthesis processes. Understanding amplitude envelopes is key to creating a dynamics process (described in Chapter 11). The variation in the underlying waveform of acoustic sounds is mirrored in synthesis processes that vary parameters over time to achieve similar interesting tonal variations (as described in Chapter 13).

While there are quite a few examples in this chapter, it is possible to learn more by examining sounds in a waveform editor or analysis program. It is easiest to examine the nature of the waveform if the sound events being considered are isolated and monophonic. Notes that overlap in time, chords, and multiple sounds mixed together are much more challenging. Suitable material can be recorded with a Digital Audio Workstation (DAW) or obtained from sound libraries or online sources. Sounds that are not created by the typical range of acoustic instruments used in classical and popular music are also interesting to examine, such as synthesized sounds that are not simulating acoustic instruments, and those produced by the many everyday objects in the environment around us.

The character of an instrument is not defined comprehensively by a single recorded sound, but varies considerably with playing style. Different excitation force, length of note, pitch, and damping can all be significant. Understanding such variations is necessary when it comes to trying to develop a similar synthesized instrument. It can be a valuable learning experience to analyse different sound events from the same instrument to understand their similarities and differences.

4

Frequency Domain Analysis

4.1 Introduction

The *frequency domain* describes a signal with respect to the frequencies and amplitudes of the sinusoidal partials of which it is composed. A range of techniques for examining the tonal characteristics of a sound are associated with frequency domain analysis, as will be described later in this chapter. These techniques help to inform the development of modification and synthesis processes.

Frequency domain analysis is complementary to time domain analysis (described in Chapter 3). There are some things that are clear in the time domain, such as the amplitude envelope. However, the principal problem with understanding the time domain form is the lack of a clear link between waveform shape and perception. The time domain signal is effectively a highly compressed bundle of information that must be deconstructed to understand what is going on inside. To achieve this, Fourier Transform methods are used, which transform the sound from the time domain to the frequency domain. The properties of the Fourier Transform are described in more detail in §12.1.2 (p.371).

Frequency domain analysis techniques require suitable configuration to highlight the details of interest. Similarly to time domain analysis, it is necessary to look for patterns of information in the frequency domain that indicate particular characteristics. Features of interest include harmonics, inharmonics, noisy elements, transient effects, the spectral envelope, and the trajectories of partials over time. All of these are examined in this chapter.

4.2 Static and Average Sound Character

4.2.1 Spectral Form

A frequency domain plot (or frequency spectrum plot, or spectral plot) describes sounds as a set of sinusoidal components. This is very useful for seeing the waveform composition at a glance. As was seen in §2.1.3 (p.26), it is possible to deconstruct waveforms into a set of sinusoidal partials. The Fourier Transform technique that is used to generate the plots in this chapter takes a large number of time domain input samples and generates a set of amplitude values corresponding to different frequencies, which can then be displayed in a graphical form.

The simplest frequency domain example is as shown in figure 4.1. The time domain waveform is a sinusoid with a cycle length of 0.01 seconds, so it has a frequency of 100Hz. It has a peak amplitude of ±1. Both of these pieces of information are elegantly summarised in the frequency domain spectral plot.

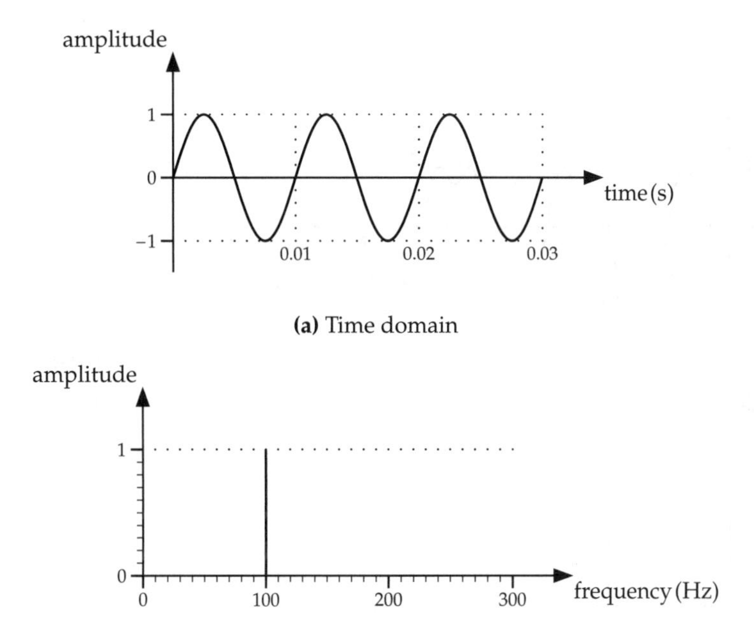

Figure 4.1 Sinusoidal form

Because the waveform in figure 4.1 is a sinusoid, it appears as a single thin spike in the spectral plot. If a sound is composed of N sinusoids, then the frequency domain form will have N peaks in it. Consider figure 4.2, which is a combination of two sinusoids first seen in §3.1.2 (p.41). The two partials that compose the sound have frequencies f_1 and f_2 with amplitudes a_1 and a_2. The transformation from time to frequency domain splits apart the components that were originally combined to make the waveform.

When a waveform repeats exactly every cycle, it has a harmonic composition (as described in §3.1.2, p.41). That is, the frequency partials are at frequencies that are integer multiples of the fundamental frequency ($F, 2F, 3F, 4F$, and so on). The exact amplitude weighting of the harmonics is difficult to work out by examination of the time domain form. Comparing figures 4.2 and 4.3, it is apparent that as the number of partials increases, the time domain becomes more complex to interpret, but the frequency domain form is clear.

When there are several harmonic partials, a pattern emerges in the spectral form, as harmonics have equal spacing in frequency (although some might have zero amplitude). This pattern is important to both the timbre of the sound (through the relative amplitude balance) and its pitch (through the fact that it causes cyclical repetition at the fundamental frequency), as described in Chapter 3. As such, it is an important characteristic to identify when analysing sounds.

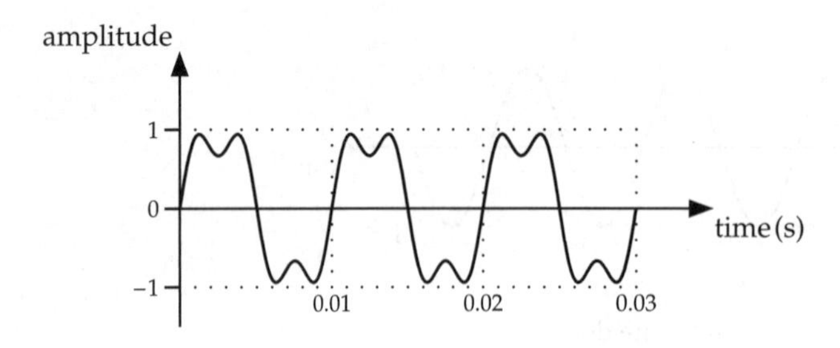

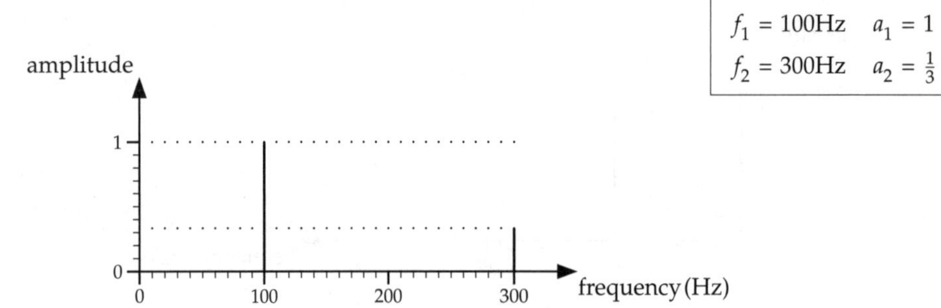

Figure 4.2 Two sinusoidal partials

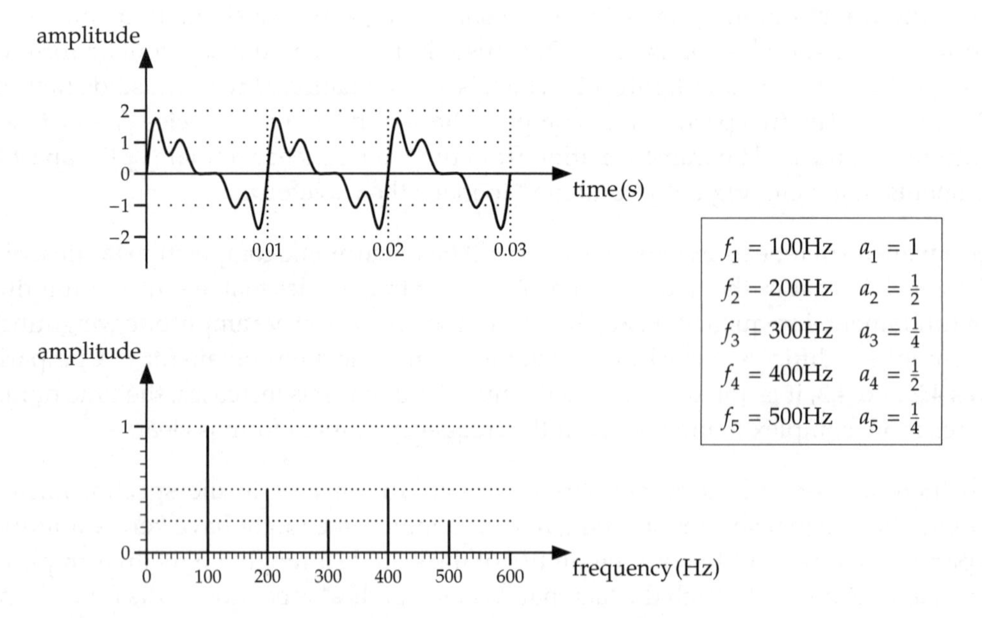

Figure 4.3 Five sinusoidal partials

Figure 4.4 shows two views of the same harmonic sound with a 200Hz fundamental frequency. With a linear frequency axis the partials are spaced evenly, so it is visually clear that they are harmonic. However, with a logarithmic frequency scale there is the same physical length on the axis between frequencies that are an octave apart (such as 500Hz, 1kHz, 2kHz, 4kHz, and 8kHz). Figure 4.4b therefore gives an impression of the **perceived** proximity of the different harmonics. Partials that are close together will audibly interact, which is explored further in §16.1.2 (p.483).

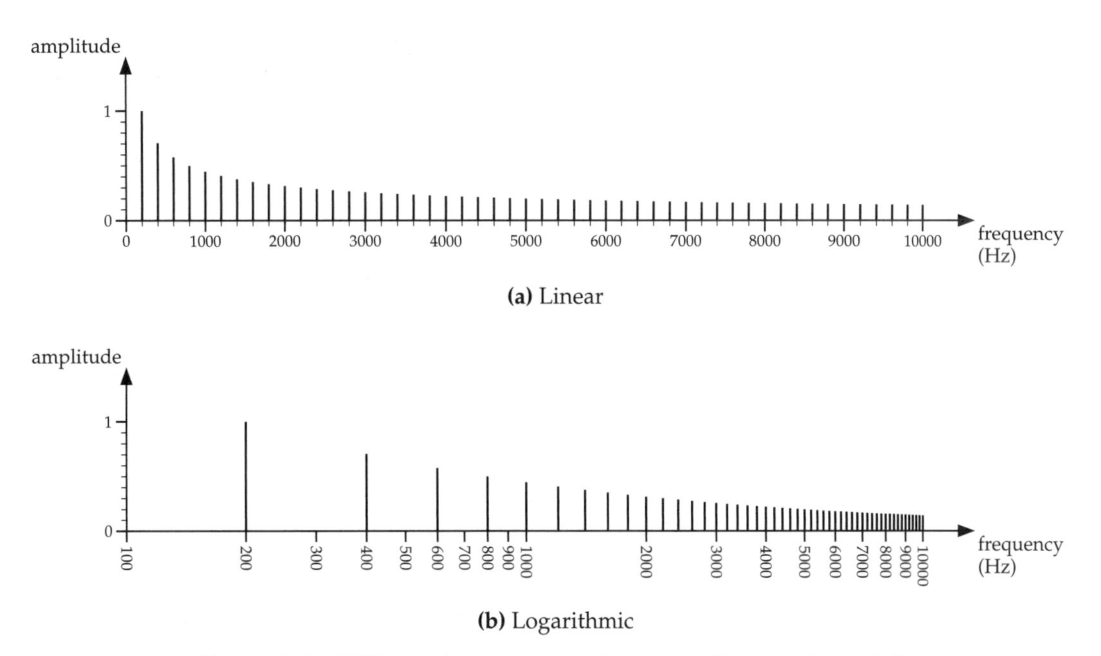

Figure 4.4 Different frequency scale views of harmonic partials

Figure 4.5 shows two views of a harmonic sound with a 200Hz fundamental frequency, but with a different amplitude pattern to figure 4.4. With a linear amplitude axis the amplitude of the upper partials is small and unclear; in some cases it will be hard to decide whether partials actually exist. With a decibel (logarithmic) scale (using equation 3.1, p.55) those partials are clearer. Human amplitude perception is not linear, and the decibel scale helps when examining the contribution of the lower amplitude partials to the result.

Inharmonic combinations are particularly difficult to follow in the time domain, as they do not result in the simple cyclical patterns that harmonics produce. The frequency domain form is useful in this regard as it makes it much easier to establish the composition of the waveform. Figure 4.6 shows a combination of non-harmonically-related sinusoids. Knowing that certain inharmonic patterns lead to rough or dissonant sounds (see §3.1.3, p.45), the frequency plot can be used to explain some of the characteristics that are heard.

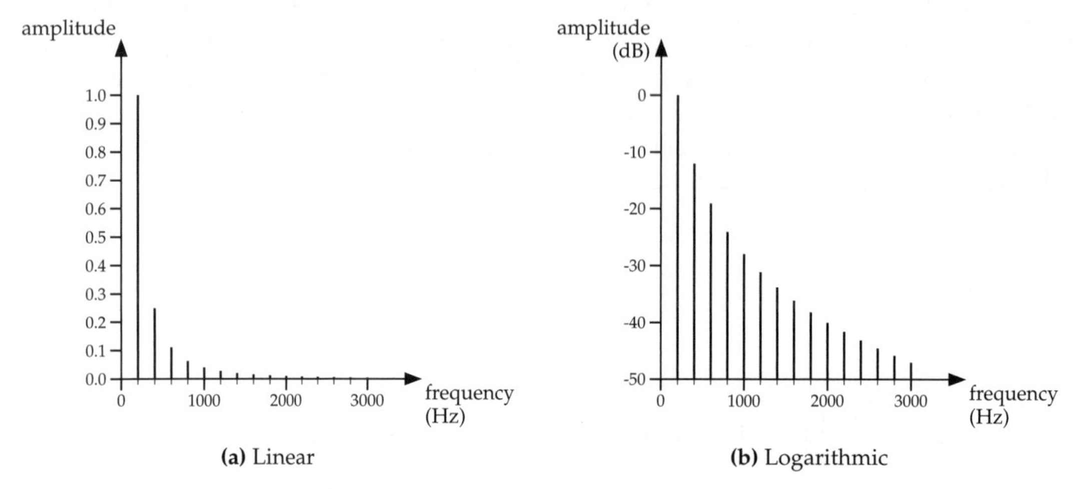

(a) Linear **(b)** Logarithmic

Figure 4.5 Different amplitude scale views of harmonic partials

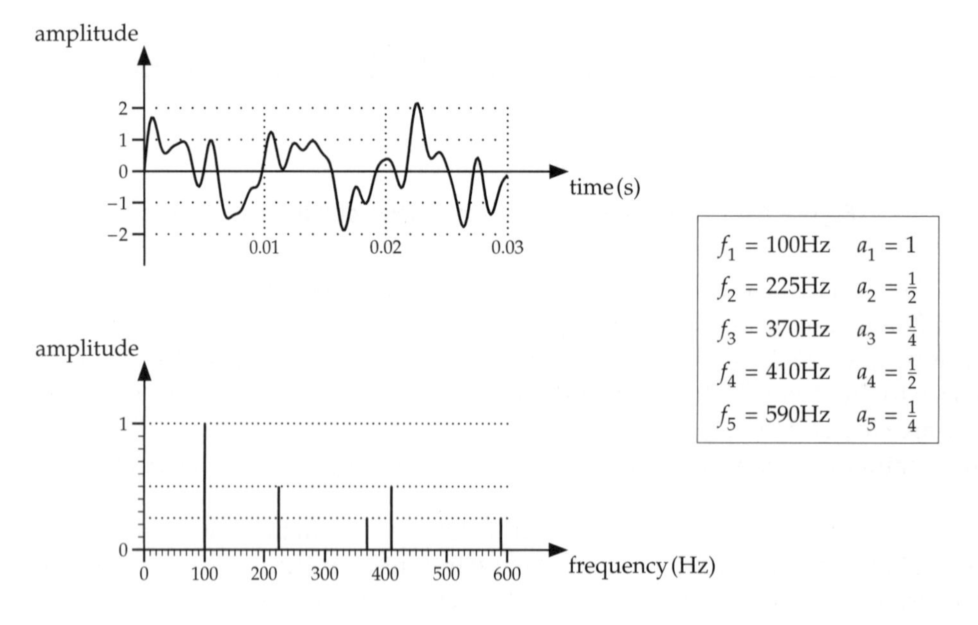

Figure 4.6 Inharmonic combination of five sinusoidal partials

As the number of partials composing a sound increases, the density of lines in the spectrum plot increases. The extreme case is white noise, where the signal is completely random. In the theoretical case, this gives a completely flat spectral profile, as all frequencies have equal amplitude. This could be plotted as a dense mass of partials in the frequency domain, but the alternative is to draw the *spectral envelope* of the sound as shown in figure 4.7. $f_S/2$ is the Nyquist frequency (as described in §2.2.2, p.28).

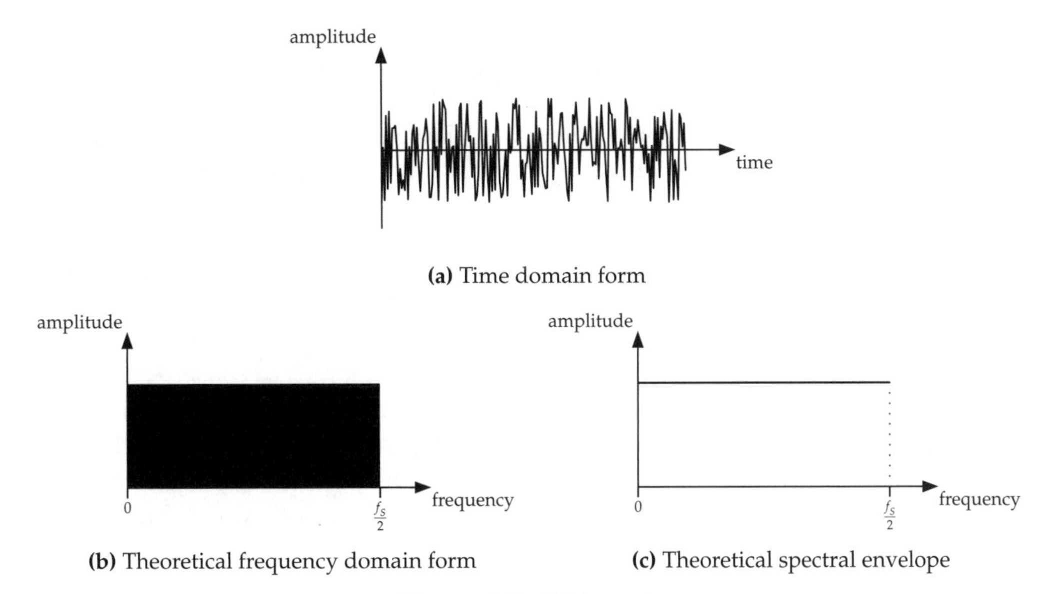

(b) Theoretical frequency domain form **(c)** Theoretical spectral envelope

Figure 4.7 White noise

4.2.2 Frequency Domain Analysis of Simple Waveform Shapes

Certain waveform shapes are seen regularly in audio processes. Sinusoidal waves and white noise have already been considered, but *sawtooth*, *square/pulse/rectangular*, and *triangle* waves are also encountered on a regular basis. They are simple waveforms that do not sound very similar to acoustic instrument sounds, and can sound a little unpleasant in their raw forms, but they are a standard part of the audio process toolkit. These waveform shapes are important for the following reasons:

- They are easy to generate with minimal electronic circuitry and quite simple computer algorithms. This has made them popular historically, particularly in early analogue synthesizers (where maximum effect for simplest circuitry was important).
- The amplitudes of their frequency partials can be determined by Fourier series mathematical techniques, producing a simple set of rules that describe their frequency domain forms.

- They are useful test tones, as they have very well understood time and frequency behaviour. If an examination of the response of a system to a simple input is needed, then it is often the case that a test tone will reveal the behaviour of a system in a clearer manner than, say, a complex tone produced by an acoustic instrument.
- The waveforms repeat in exactly the same wave every cycle, so they are harmonic and have a clear pitch. This is useful for testing a system where the effect on pitch and harmonic balance is required.
- They can be used for tasks requiring a simple oscillation (as shown in Chapter 9).

The properties of the sawtooth, square, pulse, and triangle waveform shapes are described below. In each case the fundamental frequency is F, and value a_i is the relative amplitude of harmonic i (at frequency $i \times F$).

Figure 4.8 illustrates a sawtooth wave in time and frequency domains. The frequency domain form of a sawtooth wave is composed of an infinite set of sinusoidal harmonic partials, with **all** harmonics present, and $a_i = 1/i$.

Figure 4.9 illustrates a square wave in time and frequency domains. The frequency domain form of a square wave is composed of an infinite set of sinusoidal harmonic partials, with only **odd-numbered** harmonics present, and $a_i = 1/i$. Note how the harmonic amplitudes of the partials in the square wave are the same as the sawtooth wave, but the even-numbered harmonics are missing.

The pulse (or rectangular) wave alternates between amplitudes $+c$ and $-c$. A parameter called the *duty cycle* (d) corresponds to the proportion of the output cycle that is positive, and has a value between 0 and 1. When $d = 0.5$ a pulse wave is the same as a square wave. Varying the duty cycle varies the harmonic amplitude balance (and so the tonal character), as shown in figure 4.10. The amplitudes are calculated with $a_i = (1/i)\sin(\pi i d)$, where i is the harmonic number, d is the duty cycle, and the sine function takes an argument in radians.

Figure 4.11 illustrates a triangle wave in time and frequency domains. The frequency domain form of a triangle wave is composed of an infinite set of sinusoidal harmonic partials, with only **odd-numbered** harmonics present, and $a_i = 1/i^2$. As with the square wave, the triangle wave is missing the even-numbered harmonics, but this time the amplitudes relate to $1/i^2$ instead of $1/i$.

The following features are of note:

- Although the frequency domain plots for sawtooth, square, and triangle waves only show the first eight harmonics for clarity, the sequence continues onward.

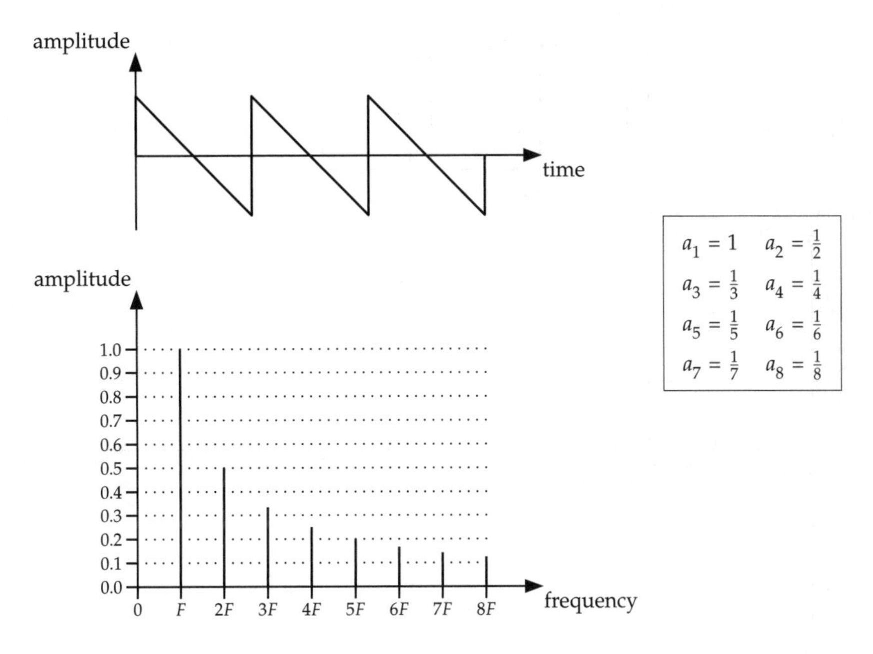

$a_1 = 1$	$a_2 = \frac{1}{2}$
$a_3 = \frac{1}{3}$	$a_4 = \frac{1}{4}$
$a_5 = \frac{1}{5}$	$a_6 = \frac{1}{6}$
$a_7 = \frac{1}{7}$	$a_8 = \frac{1}{8}$

Figure 4.8 Sawtooth wave

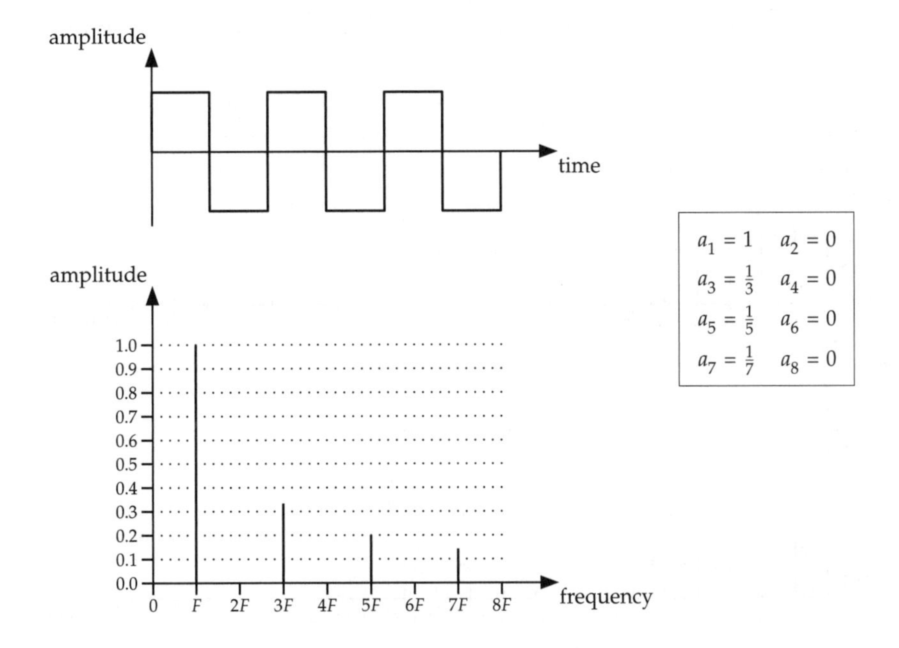

$a_1 = 1$	$a_2 = 0$
$a_3 = \frac{1}{3}$	$a_4 = 0$
$a_5 = \frac{1}{5}$	$a_6 = 0$
$a_7 = \frac{1}{7}$	$a_8 = 0$

Figure 4.9 Square wave

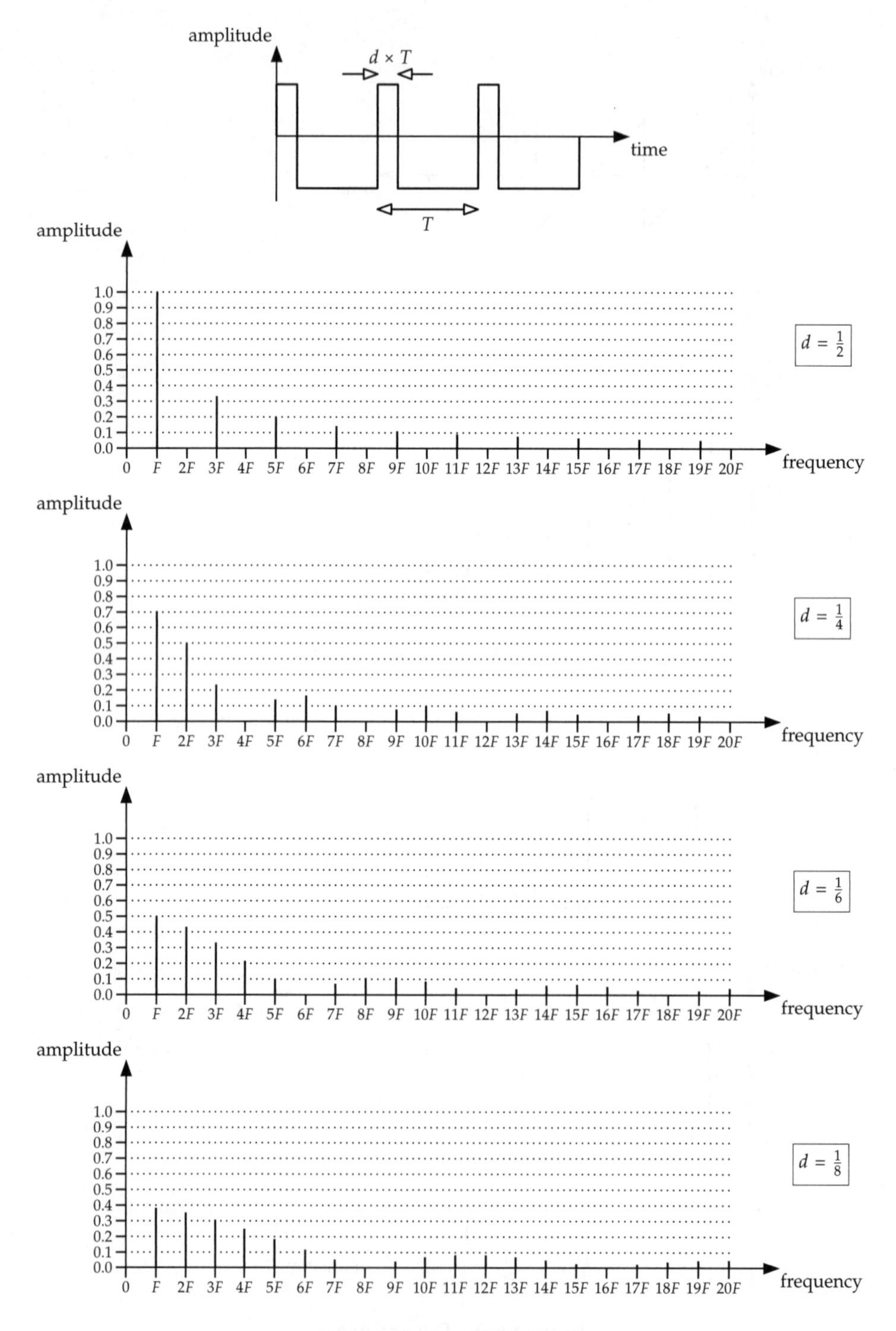

Figure 4.10 Pulse wave

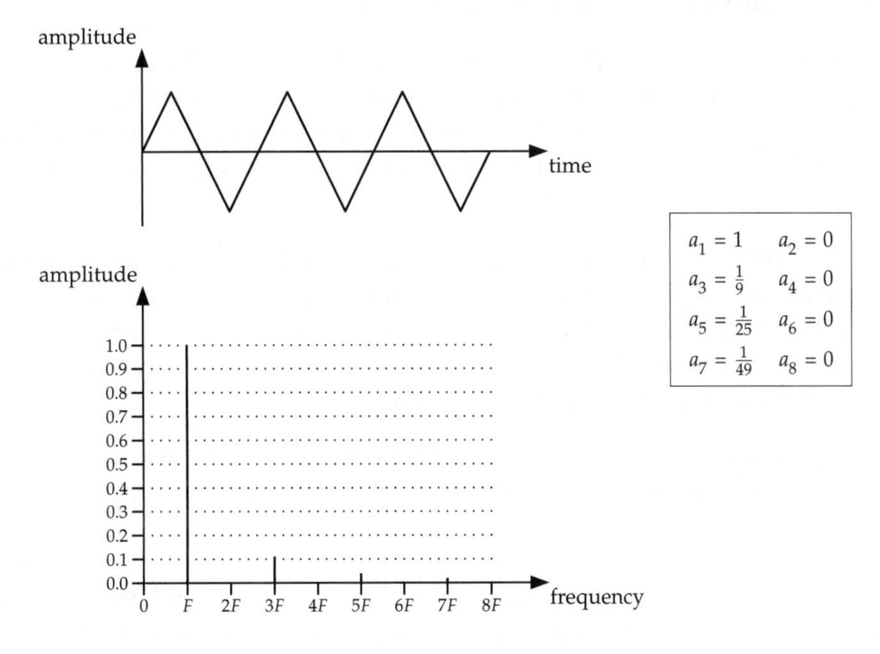

Figure 4.11 Triangle wave

- Although theoretically there are an infinite number of harmonic partials that compose the waveforms above, in practice the highest frequency partial that exists is limited by the available frequency bandwidth in the system (f_B as described in §2.2.2, p.28).

- The amplitudes of the harmonics (a_i) in the description are relative to each other (often to achieve a fundamental frequency amplitude of 1). It is possible to have results of any size by scaling the partial amplitudes. For example, if the amplitude of the fundamental frequency of a sawtooth wave were 0.3, then the amplitudes of the harmonics would be:

$$a_1 = 0.3 \quad a_2 = \frac{0.3}{2} \quad a_3 = \frac{0.3}{3} \quad a_4 = \frac{0.3}{4} \quad a_5 = \frac{0.3}{5} \quad a_6 = \frac{0.3}{6} \quad a_7 = \frac{0.3}{7} \quad a_8 = \frac{0.3}{8}$$

- Averaging the values over a cycle of a sawtooth, square, or triangle wave produces a result of 0, as the positive and negative values cancel out. However, that is not the case for pulse waves with duty cycle values other than 0.5. The non-zero average manifests itself as a DC offset (0Hz component) that varies with the duty cycle. For clarity this is not shown in figure 4.10, but it will appear in frequency domain analysis plots in practical circumstances and in the output of pulse wave synthesizers.

4.2.3 Average Spectrum Analysis Examples

The sounds that have been considered so far have had a static timbre. They start with a particular character and continue in the same manner for as long as the sound lasts. This allows the frequency spectrum to be plotted as amplitude against frequency (without any reference to time). Acoustic sound sources, on the other hand, produce sounds that change over time.

If a source is producing a fairly consistent sound character, it is useful to *average* the frequency domain description through all (or a portion) of the sound. The averaging technique works well for sounds with strong, steady frequency components. Averaging attenuates short (transient) details and the development of the sound over time in general. This leaves the consistent core structure of the sound.

The average spectrum plot of an acoustic instrument sound generally displays a more complex combination of partials than those shown in the previous examples. Analysing the pattern of partials in terms of the relative frequencies and amplitudes is key to understanding how the tonal character of the instrument is achieved. While the sawtooth, square, and triangle waves have a constantly decreasing amplitude with frequency, acoustic instrument sounds can have a more uneven amplitude profile. Sounds can often be a combination of harmonics and inharmonics, rather than just being one or the other. Most acoustic instruments can have a variation in character depending on how they are played. Therefore it should not be assumed that the following plots are a definitive template for the instrument, but rather an example of a typical characteristic.

The chime bar was illustrated in figures 3.10, 3.11, and 3.12 (p.50). It was noted in Chapter 3 that the sound starts with an amount of inconsistency, but rapidly becomes periodic and gradually tends towards a somewhat sinusoidal shape. An average spectrum plot of the sound is shown in figure 4.12. Remember that this is the averaged effect over the entire sound, so represents the principal long-term character. Note the following points:

- The plot has been maximised such that the highest peak fills the display. The frequency labels at the top of the peaks have been automatically detected by the analysis tool and are only accurate to the nearest 1 or 2Hz. It is also the case that real instruments are not necessarily perfectly tuned.
- The highest peak is shown as being at 219Hz (close to note A3 at 220Hz, as shown in figure 2.4, p.22), which in this case is the fundamental frequency and perceived pitch of the tone.
- Compared to the theoretical examples described previously, the peaks in the spectrum plot are not as neat and precise. There are two reasons for this:
    - The sounds produced by acoustic instruments are often complex and inconsistent.

- The Fourier Transform used to generate the spectrum plot does not necessarily produce a representation that shows all the features perfectly clearly.

It is often appropriate to use a decibel amplitude scale with a frequency domain plot to examine the contribution of the lower amplitude details to the overall tonality. Comparing figures 4.12 and 4.13:

- The use of an amplitude axis in decibels makes the smaller details clearer. Many of these partials are present in the attack, but less so later in the sound. Because this is an average spectrum over the length of the sound, only the most consistent features will have large amplitude in the plot.
- There are clear peaks in figure 4.13 that are only just visible in figure 4.12. The largest is at 2212Hz, which is the 10th harmonic. As well as harmonics there are also inharmonic partials, which are often a characteristic of percussion instrument sounds.

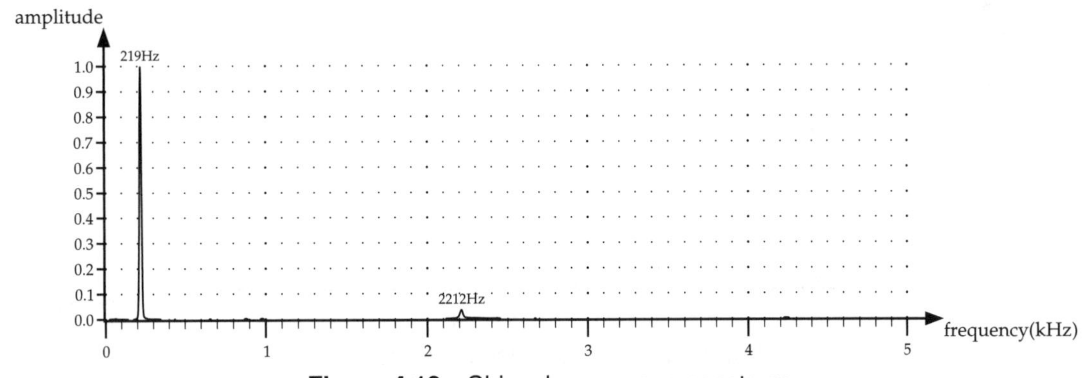

Figure 4.12 Chime bar average spectrum

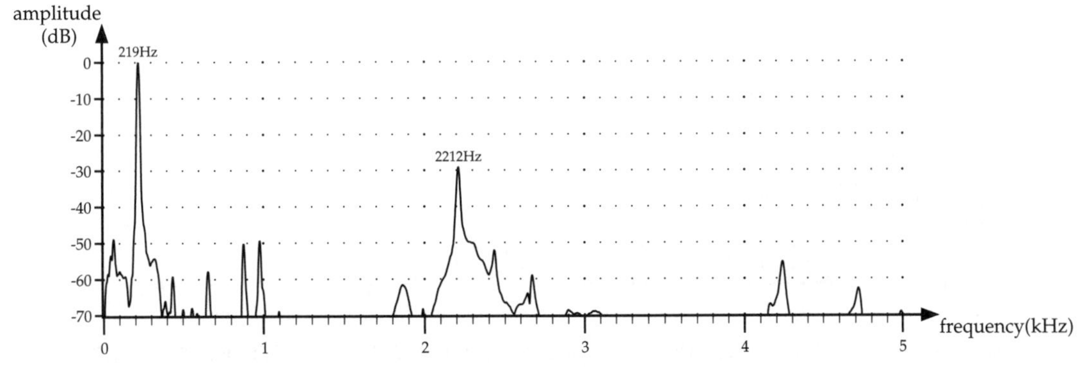

Figure 4.13 Chime bar average spectrum (decibel amplitude scale)

Figure 4.14 shows the average spectrum plot of an oboe tone at note A4 (440Hz). The peaks are positioned at harmonic intervals, as shown on the plot at approximately integer multiples of 440Hz, which gives a strong pitched sensation. The fundamental frequency partial is large, but not the largest component visible in the frequency spectrum. This illustrates that it is not necessarily the case that there is a consistent decrease in amplitude from the first harmonic partial upwards. Figure 4.15 shows the same sound, but with a frequency range up to 22kHz and a decibel amplitude axis to emphasise the lower amplitude details. The equally-spaced pattern of partials continues up to the 44th harmonic.

The amplitudes of the harmonics do not have random values, but rather have a particular pattern. This is known as the *spectral envelope* and is indicated by the dashed line in figure 4.15. The shape of an instrument and the materials used in its construction determine its resonances and tonal character, which affect the spectral envelope. A sound source that has a character such as heavy bass, or sparkling treble, will have that reflected in the balance of amplitude within the frequency spectrum.

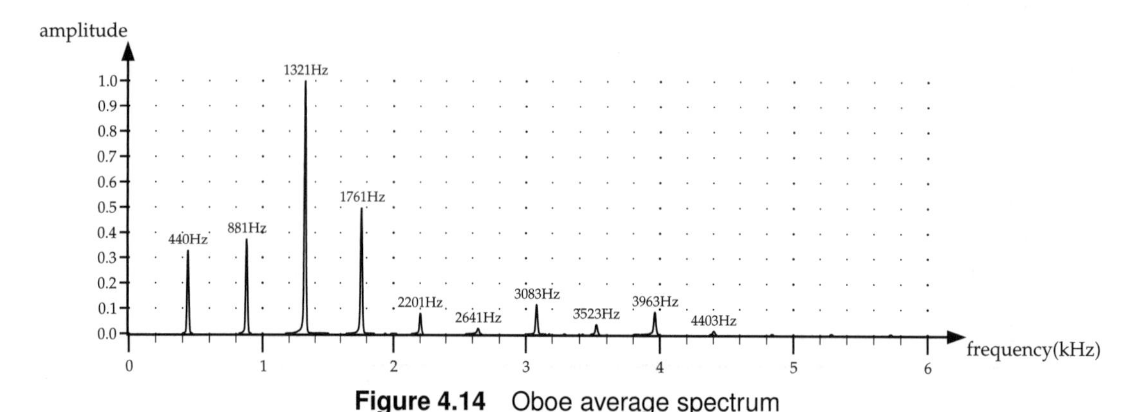

Figure 4.14 Oboe average spectrum

Figure 4.15 Oboe average spectrum (decibel amplitude scale, with spectral envelope marked)

Figure 4.16 shows the average spectrum plot for a melodica tone at a fundamental frequency of 880Hz (note A5). This again is a wind instrument, but the spectral envelope is different to the oboe, producing a different tonality. One feature is that the lower frequency even harmonics (1760Hz, 3520Hz, 5280Hz) have a lower amplitude than the neighbouring odd harmonics (880Hz, 2640Hz, 4400Hz, 6160Hz). This is also a characteristic associated with clarinet sounds.

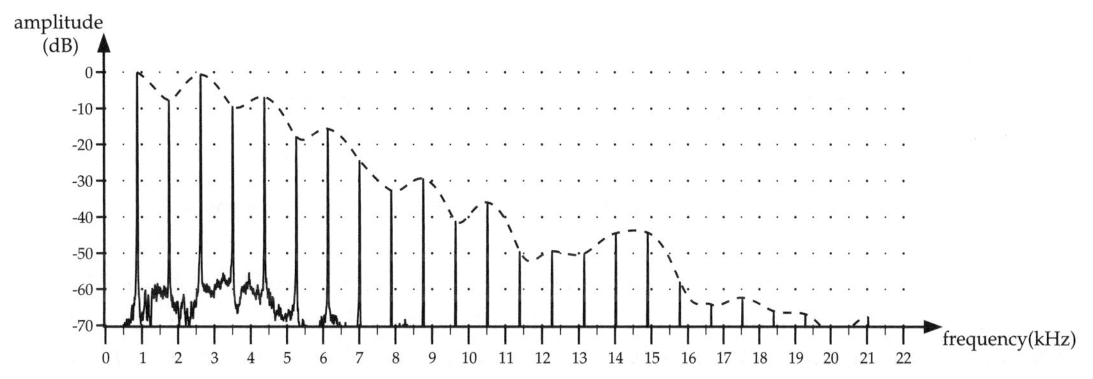

Figure 4.16 Melodica average spectrum (decibel amplitude scale, with spectral envelope marked)

Figure 4.17 shows the average spectrum plot for the first 10 seconds of a tubular bell sound. As can be seen from the frequency labels on the peaks, the largest amplitude partials are positioned in quite an unusual pattern relative to the harmonics of 440Hz (the perceived pitch, note A4). Bells tend to be instruments that produce strong inharmonic partials, and it is difficult to tune them such that they produce a harmonic series of partials. This contributes greatly to their character. Note that the plot in figure 4.17 has significant partials at frequencies below the fundamental frequency (440Hz).

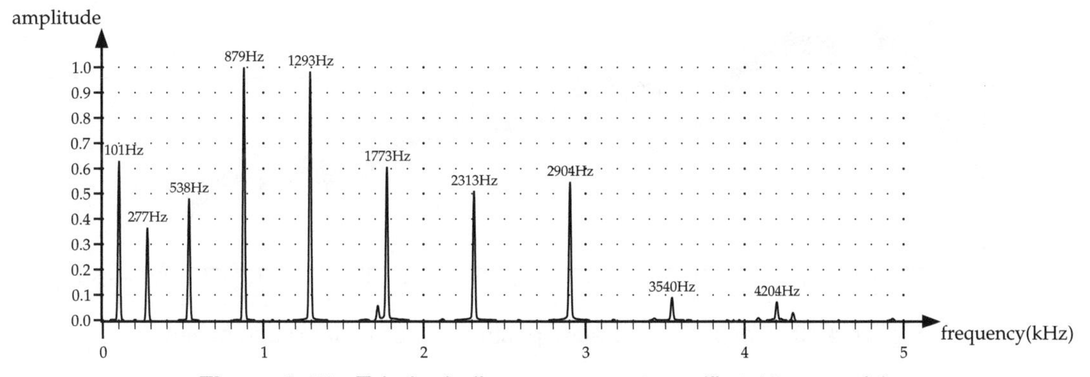

Figure 4.17 Tubular bell average spectrum (first 10 seconds)

Figure 4.18 compares the positions of the tubular bell partials with high amplitude, to the harmonic positions for a fundamental frequency of 440Hz. Some of the partials are quite close to the harmonic frequencies. There is no fundamental frequency partial at 440Hz in the sound and significant inharmonics, but the human auditory system can detect a pitch at 440Hz from the almost-harmonic partials. The sense of pitch is not as strong as with sounds produced by the oboe and melodica, however.

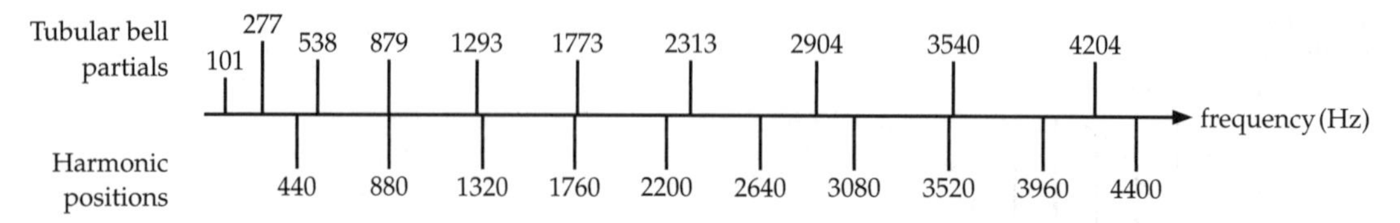

Figure 4.18 Tubular bell partials relative to harmonics of 440Hz

Figures 4.19 and 4.20 illustrate average spectrum plots for vocal sounds "sh" and "f". The plots are a demonstration of the noisy character of the sounds, with a very large number of frequency partials, in contrast to the clear harmonic and inharmonic tones seen so far.

In the time domain, it is difficult to quantify the differences between such sounds due to their lack of consistent stable waveform shape, as previously described in §3.2.8 (p.68). However, in the frequency domain, there are some clear differences. The average spectrum shows a spectral envelope that has shaped the noise in the frequency domain. If the sounds were pure white noise, then the partial amplitudes would be very consistent. There are large lumps (known as formants) in the spectrum, which reflect how the vocal tract has shaped the noisy sound, and make it possible for listeners to identify which phoneme is being spoken.

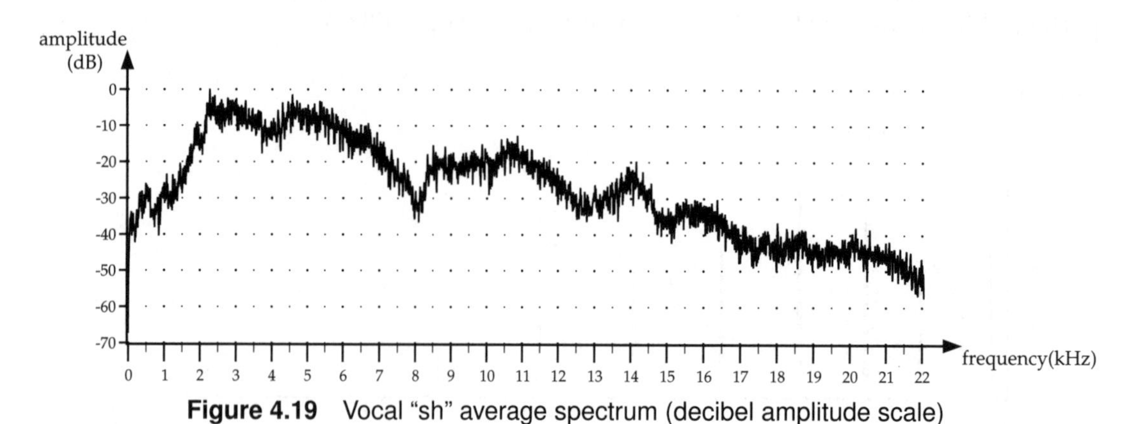

Figure 4.19 Vocal "sh" average spectrum (decibel amplitude scale)

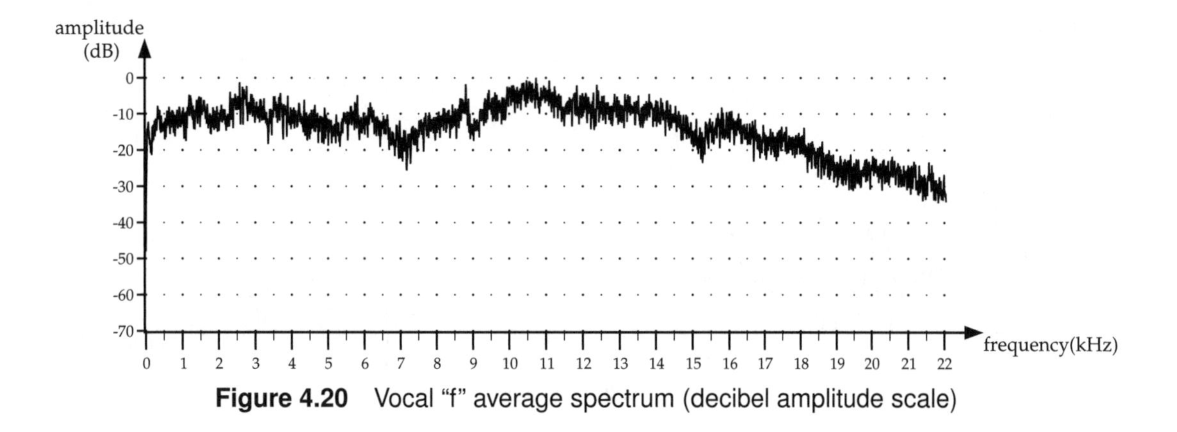

Figure 4.20 Vocal "f" average spectrum (decibel amplitude scale)

4.3 Dynamic Sound Character

4.3.1 Representing Three Dimensions

The techniques described in this chapter so far have removed the dynamic elements by presenting averaged amplitude against frequency. However, variations are important in the character of sounds. One way of representing time-varying sound data is a series of average spectrum plots that relate to particular parts of the sound. Figure 4.21 shows the difference between an average spectrum of the beginning of the chime bar sound seen earlier, and a section later on. There is clearly a difference in the relative balance of the strong partials and the amount of lower amplitude partials. Both plots have been normalised to the amplitude of the largest partial to make the comparison clearer.

The problem with multiple average spectrum plots is that it is difficult to follow the changes occurring to particular partials over time. There are a number of techniques that allow frequency, amplitude, and time to be viewed at the same time. The three-dimensional spectrum plot in figure 4.22 gives a good impression of the shape of partial amplitude variations. Determining values of frequency, amplitude, and time manually from a printed three-dimensional plot is not too difficult where the partials meet the axes, but can be harder for data points away from the edges. The other problem is that it is hard to achieve a perfect angle of view, where all axes are clear and no details are hidden.

An alternative to plotting three dimensions as separate orthogonal axes is the *spectrogram* (also known as a sonogram), with axes of frequency (vertically) and time (horizontally), and amplitude on a colour scale (such as white to black). This method gives an ability to read frequency and time values quite accurately, with a general impression of the shape of amplitude variations. The disadvantage is the limited ability to determine exact amplitude information. Some analysis examples with this plotting technique follow.

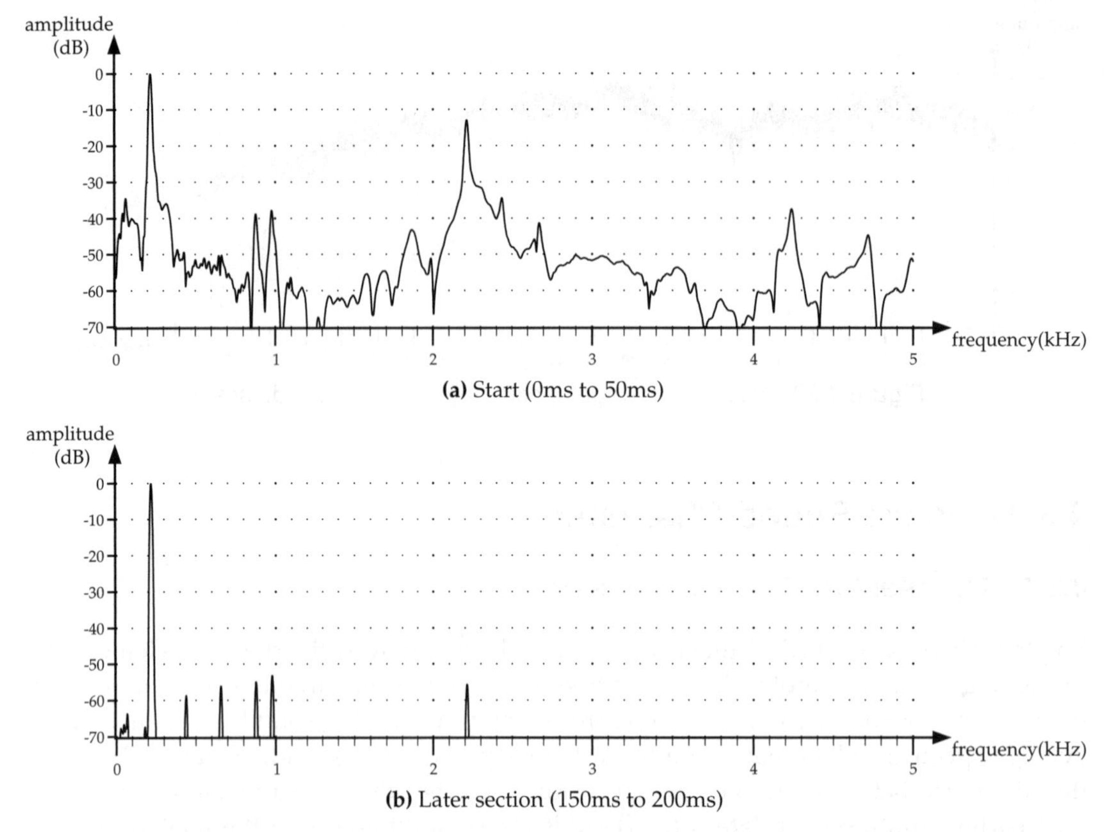

Figure 4.21 Chime bar average spectrum plots (short sections, decibel amplitude scale)

4.3.2 Simple Spectrogram Examples

Figure 4.23 shows the spectrogram of a constant amplitude sinusoid with a frequency of 100Hz that lasts for 3 seconds. This is about the most simple spectrogram form possible. Figure 4.24 shows a simple harmonic sound in three forms; as time domain, average spectrum, and spectrogram plots. Because the sound does not change over time, the average spectrum plot is most useful as it shows the precise harmonic amplitudes. The spectrogram shows the frequency information and the length of the sound clearly, but the precise amplitudes are unclear.

Figure 4.25 shows a more effective use of a spectrogram. It shows a sinusoid that rises steadily in frequency from 0 to 400Hz over a period of 3 seconds. A rising frequency sinusoidal tone is known as a *chirp*. This sort of signal is not well represented by an average spectrum, as the frequency is constantly changing, meaning that (on average) all frequencies are present equally. An average spectrum cannot express **when** those frequencies are occurring nor the trajectory of the partial.

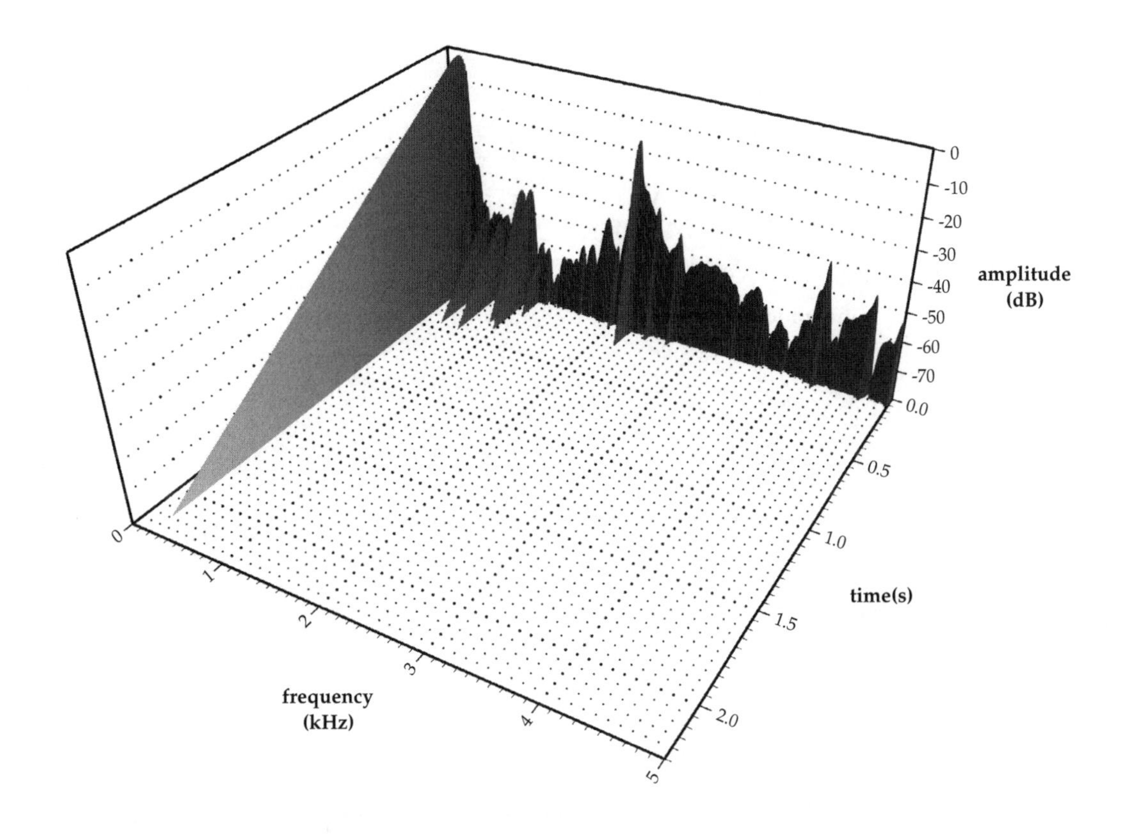

Figure 4.22 Chime bar 3D spectrum plot

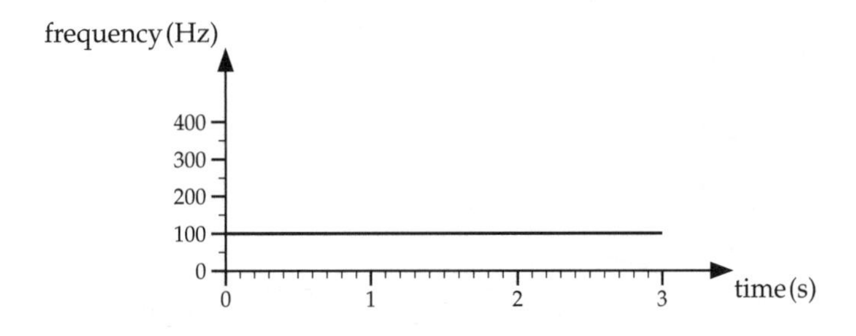

Figure 4.23 Constant sinusoid spectrogram

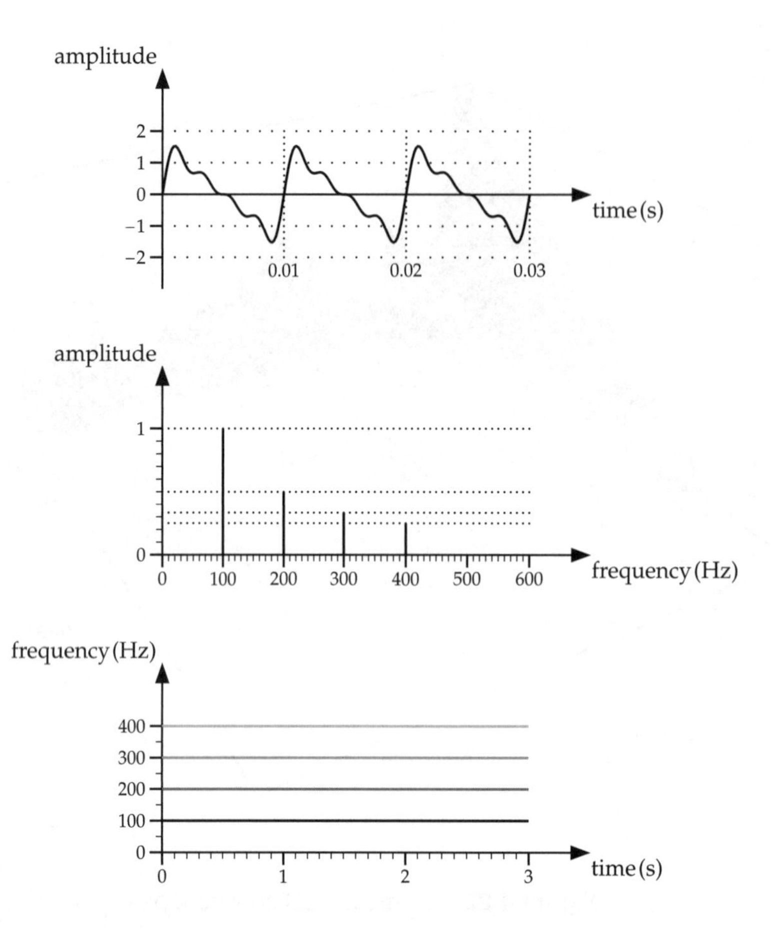

Figure 4.24 Harmonic sound; time domain, average spectrum, and spectrogram plots

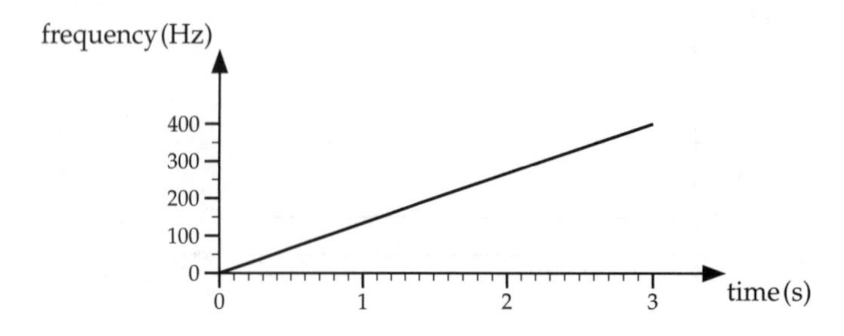

Figure 4.25 Chirp spectrogram

Figure 4.26 shows a spectrogram of four harmonics of 100Hz, which have different amplitudes and are fading over time. As with the static spectrum plots, it is very simple to see a harmonic pattern, due to the equal spacing along the frequency axis. The partials' amplitudes are indicated by the colour of the line. This allows the audio process engineer to see that different parts of the frequency spectrum have different relative amplitudes and how they are changing over time. The plot indicates a decreasing amplitude with increasing frequency, and that the upper harmonics are fading away before the fundamental does. However, it is very difficult to precisely quantify those amplitudes.

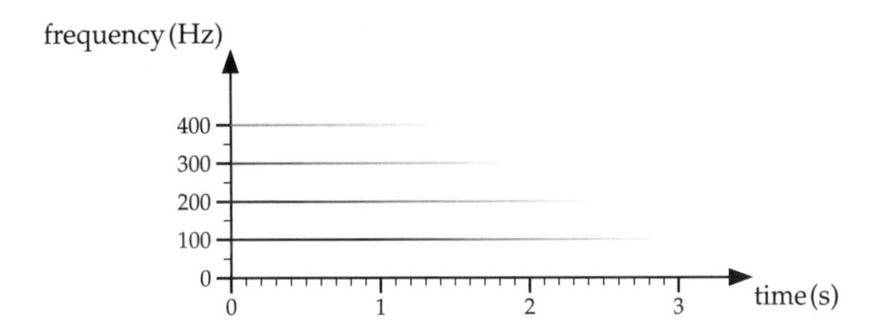

Figure 4.26 Fading harmonics spectrogram

The chirp and the fading harmonics examples have a set of partials that demonstrate a clear trajectory through the sound. Something else that is difficult to see on an average spectrum plot is transients. Transients occur for a short period of time and have an important perceptual effect, but not such a large effect on the average spectrum. They typically occur in the onset portion of a sound, when energy is being put into a percussion instrument like a xylophone, for example. This causes *wideband* effects (many partials over a wide range of frequencies). For example, figure 4.27 illustrates a brief burst of wideband sound that settles rapidly to a simpler form.

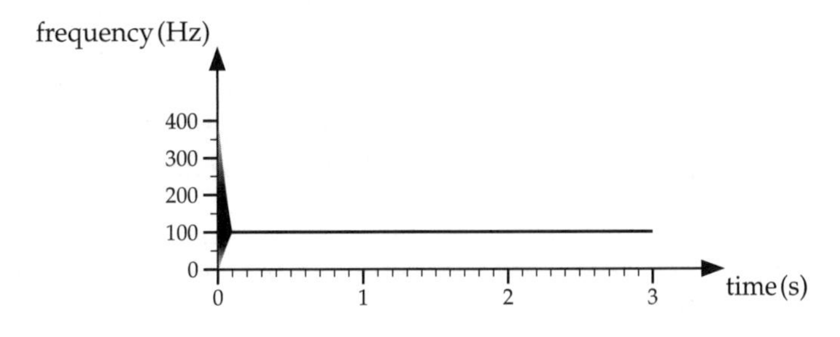

Figure 4.27 Spectrogram showing transient information

4.3.3 More Complex Spectrogram Examples

Figure 4.28 shows the spectrogram of the first 5kHz of the chime bar tone. Several features that have been explained already are visible:

- The major peaks in figure 4.13 (p.85) are visible as high amplitude horizontal lines with consistent frequencies in the spectrogram.
- The major partials fade away at different rates and positions in time. This has similarities to the form shown in figure 4.26. There is a correspondence between figure 4.28 and those in figure 4.21 (p.90), in that the start of the sound demonstrates a different balance of frequency partial amplitudes to that further into the sound.
- There is also strong evidence of a transient/attack portion with wideband noise that fades away in a somewhat similar way to figure 4.27.

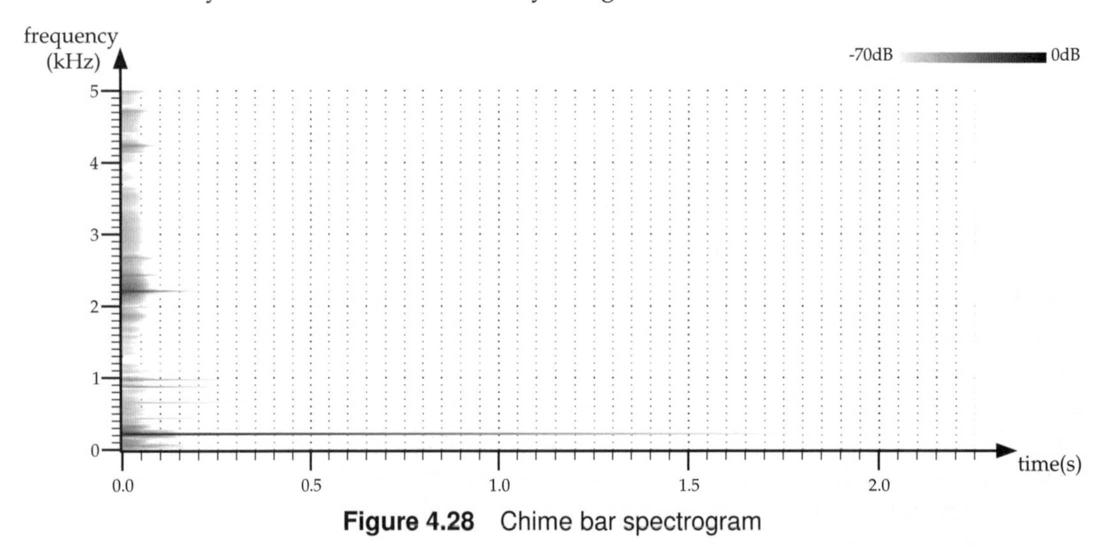

Figure 4.28 Chime bar spectrogram

Figure 4.28 illustrates the difference between noise and strong inharmonics. Noise is many frequency partials occurring together, often associated with irregular or inconsistent vibration. The majority of noise partials will not be at integer multiples of the main fundamental frequency, and so are not harmonic. A strong inharmonic, however, is a partial where there is consistent prolonged vibration for a significant length of time, at a frequency that is not an integer multiple of the fundamental frequency (such as the partial at 977Hz in the chime bar plots).

A partial such as that at 977Hz in the example chime bar tone is located at a frequency determined by the physical form of the instrument, just as the harmonics fall at particular frequencies due to the way the instrument is constructed and tuned. Therefore 977Hz is not a random frequency. It is possible to change the amplitudes and frequencies of the partials by reshaping the bar.

Figure 4.29 shows the spectrogram of a bowed cello playing note A3 (with a fundamental frequency of 220Hz). An important feature that is visible in the spectrogram is the vibrato (cyclical variation in pitch). This occurs in the central portion of the sound, rather than in the onset where the sound is being established or in the release where the tone dies away, due to the playing technique employed by the performer. Careful examination also shows that there are slight variations in the frequency partial amplitudes throughout the length of the sound; a natural acoustic tone is rarely completely consistent even when the performer is attempting to maintain a constant sound character.

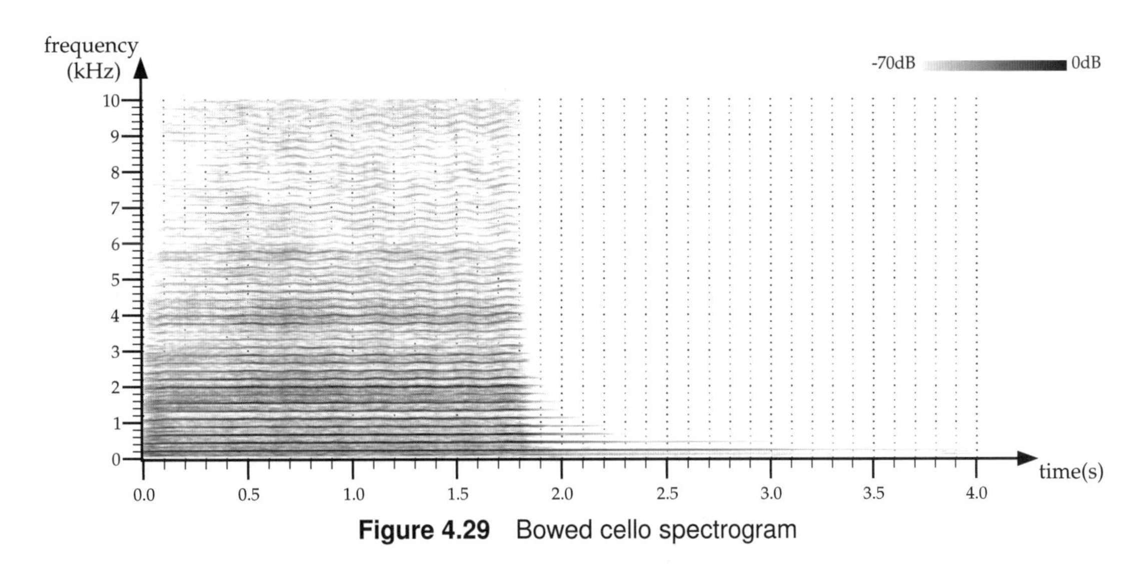

Figure 4.29 Bowed cello spectrogram

Figure 4.30 illustrates the combination of noisy and harmonic components found in a vocal "z" sound. It is a voiced fricative, which means that there are both pitched and noisy elements present. The harmonic partials in the lower half of the plot have varying frequencies as the performer changes the pitch over the length of the sound. At higher frequencies there are noisy partials. There are regions of amplitude emphasis present with fairly consistent frequencies, which are the vocal formants. Inconsistencies in amplitude over time are again apparent, even when the intention was only to have varying pitch.

Bar chimes (not to be confused with chime bars) are an array of small metal bars of different lengths hung from a horizontal rail. They are played by running a finger or similar object along the row, causing them to knock into each other and create a descending (or ascending) series of pitches. This produces a complex spectrogram plot, as shown in figure 4.31. There are multiple sound events in quick succession, each of which has resonances at multiple frequencies. It is difficult to visually distinguish the partials that are associated with the individual sound events.

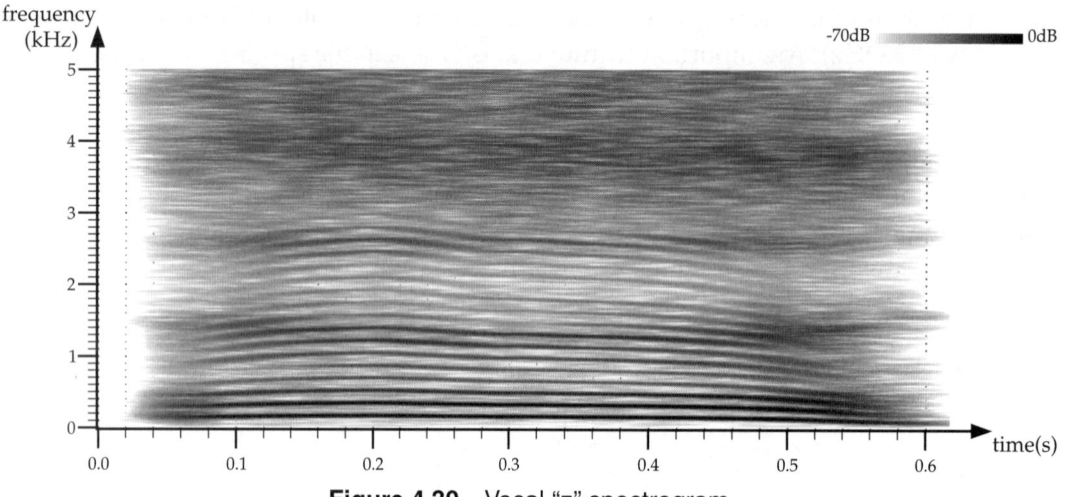

Figure 4.30 Vocal "z" spectrogram

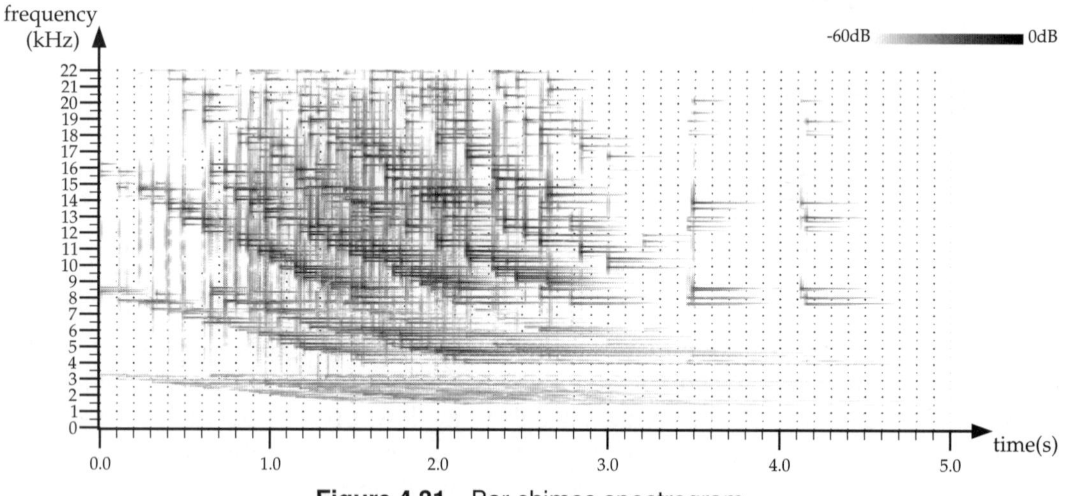

Figure 4.31 Bar chimes spectrogram

4.4 Using Frequency Domain Information

This chapter has examined elements of the frequency domain form, such as:

- Harmonic and inharmonic partials.
- Amplitude patterns of partials, and the spectral envelope.
- Noisy elements within sounds.
- Transient effects.
- Changing spectral composition over time.

Just like features in the time domain, these reflect the underlying physics of the sound-producing object, and are used by the human auditory system to aid in identifying the nature of the sound source.

Frequency domain representations provide an insight into the composition of sounds. Such information can be used to identify the frequency partials that are causing a particular tonal effect. This can be used in turn to inform the development of new modification and synthesis processes. The problems of interpreting a frequency domain plot are also apparent. In particular, the human auditory system is so effective in analysing sounds and picking out features that the visual forms are often lacking in clarity by comparison.

It is important to remember that a single recorded sound is not a description of the sound source in its entirety. For example, one recorded clarinet note does not represent every possible sound a clarinet can produce. However, the human auditory system is able to pick out the relevant features that represent clarinet character. This might seem like an impossible problem to deal with, but if a listener can hear those features in the audio signal, then there is the potential for an audio process to relate to them as well:

- Although human auditory perception is exceedingly complex, it reacts predictably when presented with sonic information. For example, a new form of drum is recognised as a percussion instrument when it is first heard. This means that the auditory system is locating the common percussive features that have already been discussed such as a noisy attack, simplifying form, and patterns of harmonics and inharmonics.
- Similarly, multiple instances of a sound source that have never been heard before are recognised as being from the same source, which indicates that there is common information in the sounds that links them together. Although different notes from the same instrument have differences, they also have similarities such that it is heard as a single sound source.
- When creating an audio process it is rarely necessary to analyse absolutely everything presented by the time and frequency domain forms. For example, if trying to automatically find the pitch of a note it is not necessary to be concerned with nuances of playing style or timbral development. The technique is adapted to cope with the problem at hand.

The Fourier Transform process used in producing average spectrum and spectrogram plots does not automatically separate or identify features within the frequency spectrum. It is the job of the audio process engineer to configure the process appropriately and isolate the features of interest. Finding those features aurally or visually can be easier than designing an automatic process to do so. This can be significant when trying to design a system to, say, extend a recorded instrument sample in a naturalistic manner (as described in Chapter 15).

The frequency domain representation is not only of use in analysis, but also can be used for direct modification of the sound character. For example, it might be desirable to increase the amplitude of particular harmonics, or change frequencies to make a sound more inharmonic. Further information on this topic can be found in Chapter 12.

4.5 Learning More

As with time domain analysis, understanding the nature of instrument sounds in the frequency domain is vital to the art of developing and configuring modification and synthesis processes. It provides further information on the composition of a sound from frequency partials that is hard to establish in the time domain. For example, a waveform might look sinusoidal in the time domain, but frequency domain analysis can be used to establish whether there is only one partial or not. Spectral relationships are particularly significant for developing synthesized versions of sounds (as described in Chapter 16). But frequency domain analysis is also significant in understanding how modification processes such as flanging (§9.2.4, p.279) are producing their audible effects.

Frequency domain analysis programs are very useful for developing understanding. However, there tend to be many more configuration parameters than those in time domain waveform analysis. Ineffective configuration can lead to visual representations that are not as revealing as expected. Humans are far more effective at identifying sonic features than a simple software analysis system, so it is important to listen for key characteristics and adjust the parameters to highlight them. There is a trade-off between time and frequency resolution in Fourier Transform-based analysis techniques (as described further in Chapter 12). Therefore a sound characteristic such as vibrato, or a chirp, might require a reduction in frequency resolution to be clearly visible as a variation over time. When trying to identify the exact frequencies of steady harmonics, then a higher frequency resolution might be used.

Some of the limitations of frequency domain analysis have already been described in this chapter; for example, that exact amplitudes in a spectrogram can be hard to identify, but average spectrum plots lose information on variation over time. In some cases the data can become clearer by limiting analysis to a particular length of time or frequency range. Some analysis tools allow parameter changes such as the window that is used (described further in Appendix B), colour schemes, or gain ranges. It can be a valuable experience to vary configuration parameters and learn how they affect the visual representation of different sound events.

PART II
MODIFICATION

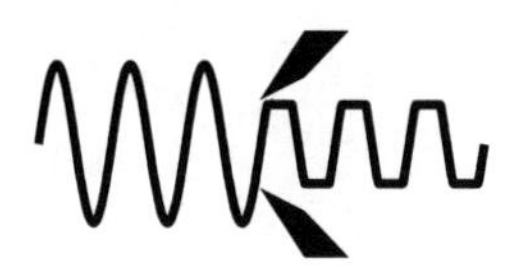

5

Basic Modifications

5.1 Introduction

A number of fundamental operations occur regularly in audio processes:

- Signals can be routed to particular destinations. This might be selecting from a number of input sources, or sending a signal to one of several possible outputs. Alternatively, a signal might be copied and sent to multiple destinations simultaneously.
- The amplitude of a signal can be changed, such as adjusting the level of a particular input, or the amount of a signal fed to a reverberation effect.
- Signals can be mixed. This might be where several channels are mixed onto a stereo bus, or where some amount of reverberant signal is added to the unprocessed signal.
- Signals can be positioned in a soundfield, such as using a pan control to position a monophonic input signal in a stereophonic output, or balancing a stereo input signal to one side or the other.

These operations are very apparent in mixing consoles. However, they are also found in many other systems, such as effects units and synthesizers, as will be seen in later chapters. The following sections describe the design of each of the process elements listed above.

5.2 Signal Flow Control

The ability to select one output signal from two or more inputs, and switching an input path between two or more destinations, are about the most simple elements in an audio process. Figure 5.1 shows examples of how these appear in block diagram form. The switch symbols have a contact arm that is always connected to a common terminal, but which can pivot in order to connect the common terminal to one of the others. The diagram shows which connection is made by default. Switching is useful for such tasks as bypassing an effect, or routing to a particular bus on a mixing console.

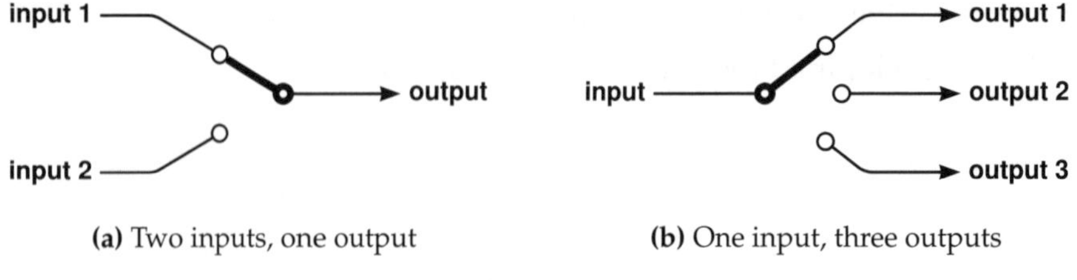

(a) Two inputs, one output　　**(b)** One input, three outputs

Figure 5.1 Switching

It is possible to express a switching operation as an algorithm suitable for converting into a text-based programming language. Algorithms 5.1 and 5.2 correspond to figures 5.1a and 5.1b (respectively).

Algorithm 5.1 – Switch function; two inputs, one output

```
input  : input signals in1 and in2
       : switch position x (1 or 2)
output : output signal out

if x == 1 then
|  out = in1
else
L  out = in2
```

Algorithm 5.2 – Switch function; one input, three outputs

```
input  : input signal in
       : switch position x (1, 2 or 3)
output : output signals out1, out2, out3

out1 = out2 = out3 = 0
if x == 1 then out1 = in
if x == 2 then out2 = in
if x == 3 then out3 = in
```

Figure 5.2 shows how multiple signal paths can be switched together. Each input has two signals associated with it (L and R). There are a pair of switches that are ganged together (shown with a dashed line) such that they operate at the same time, but the signal paths themselves are kept separate (called a two-pole or double-pole switch). When the switches are up then the outputs are taken from input 1. When the switches are down, then the outputs are taken from input 2. It is possible to extend this idea to larger numbers of inputs, or to turn the switches around to select between multiple two channel outputs.

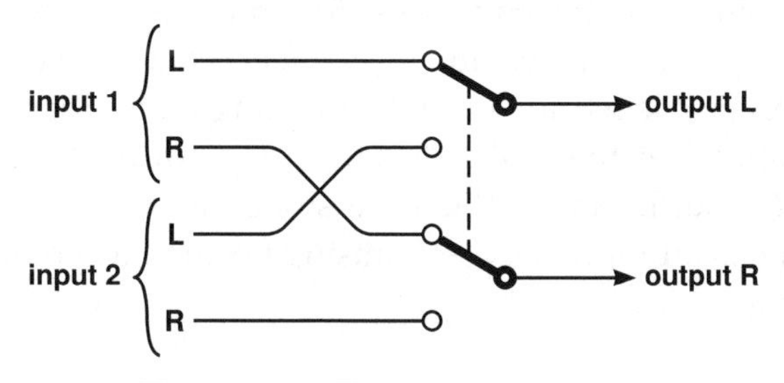

Figure 5.2 Two channel switching

Splitting a signal at a common point means that the same signal will be present on all the wires connected to the junction (figure 5.3a). This is useful when one signal needs to be sent to multiple destinations, such as routing the same signal to three parallel effects. For clarity, it is important to use a dot to signify a junction, and no dot when signal paths are crossing over without interacting (figure 5.3b).

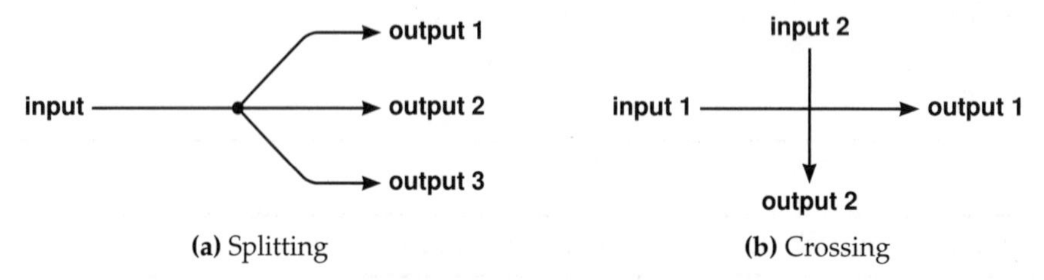

Figure 5.3 Junctions

Splitting and switching can be combined to allow selection between different processes acting on the same input signal, as shown in figure 5.4. For example, on a guitar amplifier it is often desirable to be able to switch between multiple gain levels or tonal characters with a switch. In that case the settings for the processes are set up in advance, and it is possible to switch between them instantly.

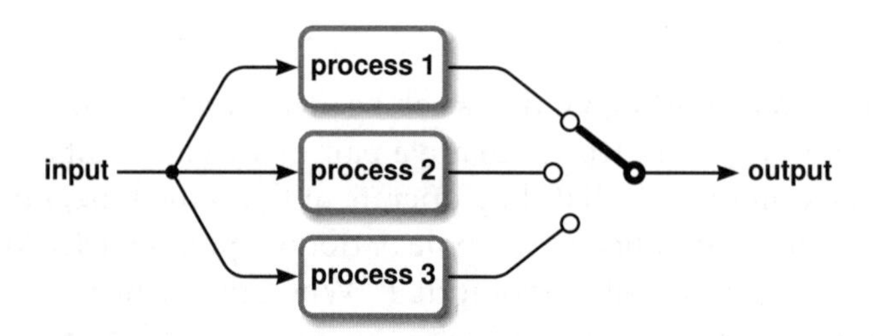

Figure 5.4 Switching between processes

Figure 5.5 illustrates a simple switched process found on most mixing consoles, called a *polarity/phase reverse* (or polarity/phase invert) switch. This can be useful when dealing with phase cancellation problems, such as when mixing microphone signals from above and below a snare drum. When the switch is in the first position, the input passes through to the output without modification. When the switch is in the second position, every sample passing through is multiplied by −1, causing positive waveform values to become negative, and vice versa.

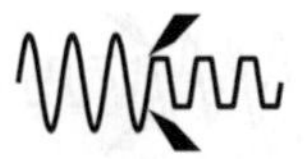

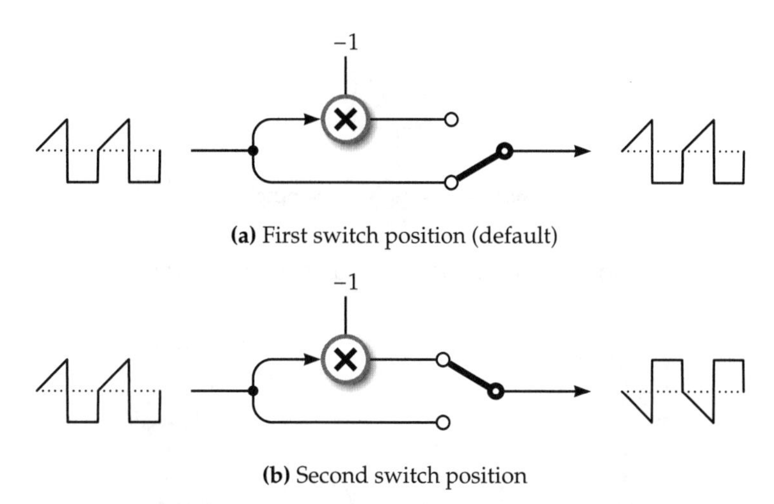

(a) First switch position (default)

(b) Second switch position

Figure 5.5 Polarity/phase reverse switch

5.3 Amplitude Control

5.3.1 Simple Amplitude Control

Changing signal amplitude is achieved by multiplication, as illustrated in figure 5.6. The rotary control produces an output known as the *gain* value. There is a linear relationship between the control position and its output. The input audio signal is multiplied by the gain value, so the time domain form is scaled in the vertical dimension. This gives a simple mapping between control position and output amplitude, as shown in figure 5.7. This demonstrates *attenuation*, as there is a variation between no output (when the gain is 0), and the same amount of output as input (when the gain is 1).

The amplitude control process can be described by algorithm 5.3. Each input sample is multiplied individually by the control value, and then fed to the output. This needs to occur at the sample rate. For example, at a sample rate of 96kHz there must be 96000 multiplications per second to apply the gain value to the signal. While the audio input signal is at the sample rate, the gain value will typically be fixed or varying slowly.

Algorithm 5.3 – Monophonic amplitude control function

input : input signal `in`
: control value `x` (between 0 and 1)
output: output signal `out`

```
out = in * x
```

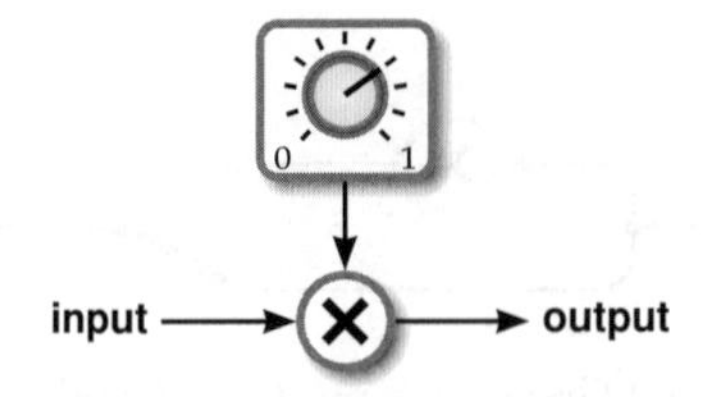

Figure 5.6 Monophonic amplitude control

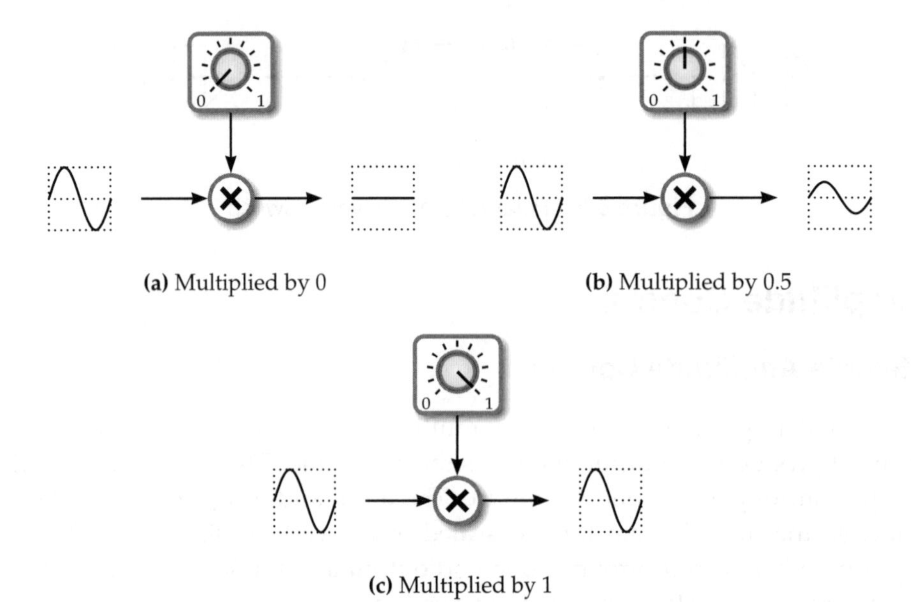

(a) Multiplied by 0

(b) Multiplied by 0.5

(c) Multiplied by 1

Figure 5.7 Monophonic amplitude control results

Rather than attenuating, amplitude control often involves being able to increase the size of a small signal to make it louder, which implies the use of multiplication by values greater than 1. Figure 5.8 shows a control that allows both attenuation (gain values between 0 and 1) and amplification (gain values between 1 and 4).

Amplification by gain values greater than 1 requires a process that can cope with output values that are larger than the input values. Computer software can represent a huge range of values internally using floating-point numbers. However, when the signal is fed to the final output it will be restricted to range limits. A typical maximum output amplitude range for a software audio system is −1.0 to +1.0. Attempting to exceed the value range imposed by a system will cause distortion of the signal (known as *clipping*). If gain values greater than 1 are used with a large amplitude input, then a signal that is within range at the input could be amplified to one that is out of range at the output.

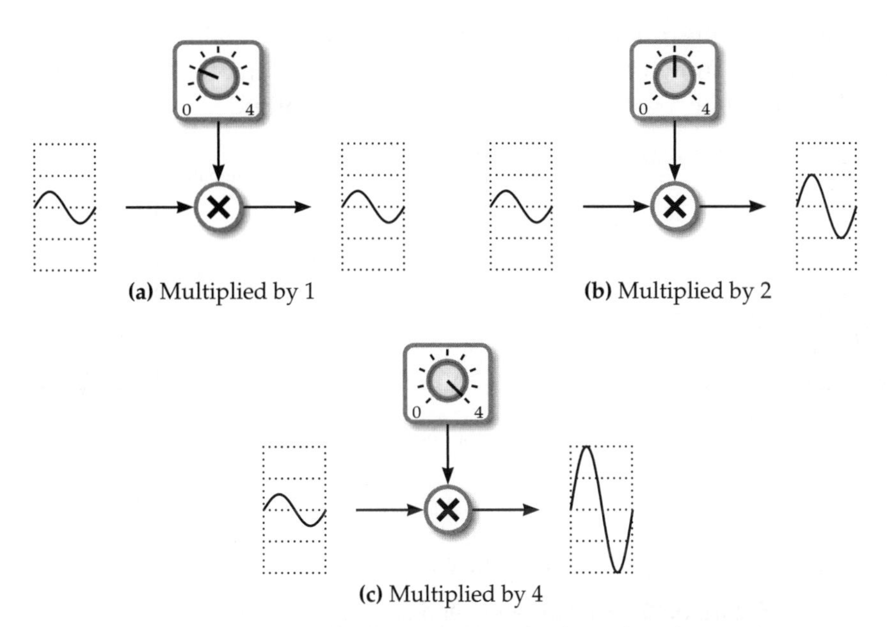

Figure 5.8 Amplitude control results for gain values ⩾ 1

An example of signal clipping is shown in figure 5.9 where a sinusoidal signal has been amplified beyond the output range of the system. It is not always certain what amplitude the input signal will have, and so what a safe multiplication factor will be. This is why audio equipment and software will often have a clip indicator, to show when the signal is exceeding the available output range.

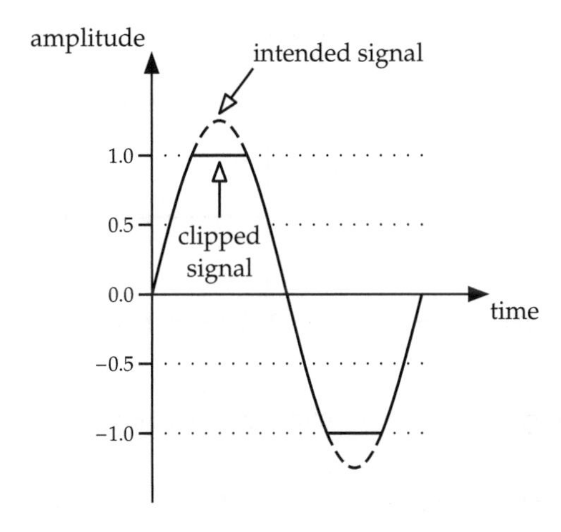

Figure 5.9 Sinusoidal signal amplified beyond the limits of the system (±1.0)

It is worth comparing the difference between multiplying by a gain value, and adding that value to the signal, as shown in figure 5.10. Addition causes an offset in the signal position relative to the amplitude axis, rather than a scaling of amplitude.

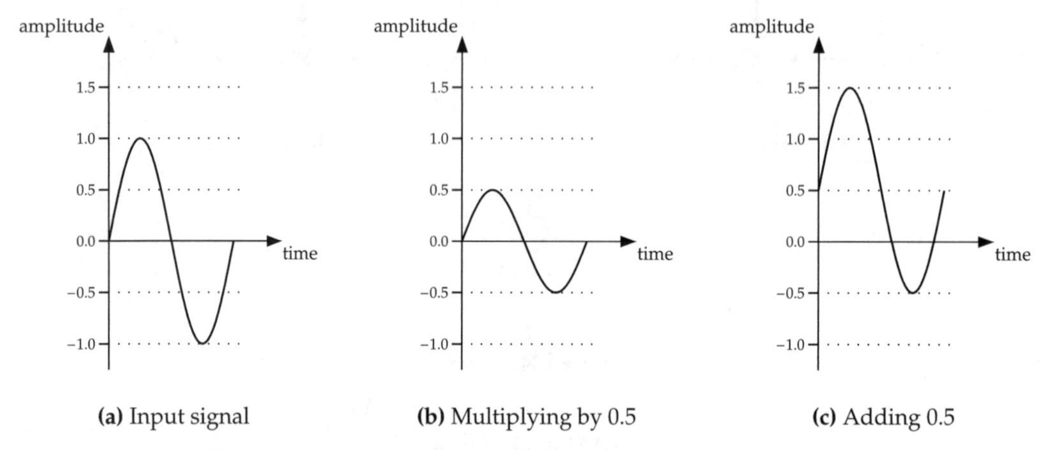

(a) Input signal **(b)** Multiplying by 0.5 **(c)** Adding 0.5

Figure 5.10 Multiplication and addition with a fixed value

5.3.2 Two Channel Amplitude Control

In many cases more than one channel must be affected by the same gain control, such as the master fader on a mixing console. This can be achieved by parallel multiplication paths as shown in figure 5.11 and algorithm 5.4.

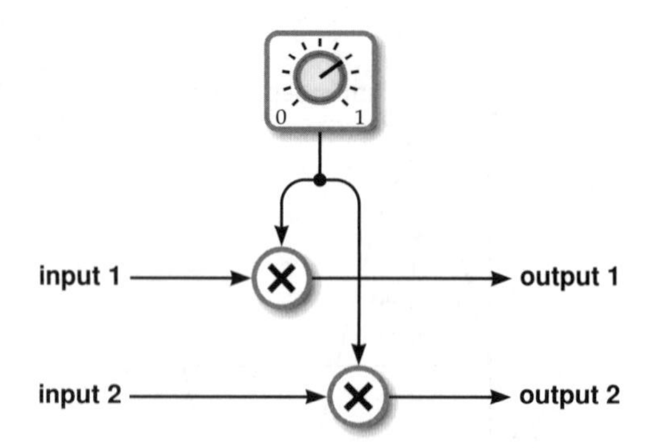

Figure 5.11 Two channel amplitude control

The signal paths are completely separate so there is no interference between them, but the same control is used to affect the amplitude of both. This style can be extended to any number of channels.

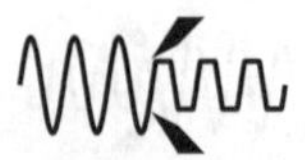

Algorithm 5.4 – Two channel amplitude control function

---

input : input signals `in1` and `in2`
: control value `x` (between 0 and 1)
output: output signals `out1` and `out2`

```
out1 = in1 * x
out2 = in2 * x
```

5.3.3 Naturalistic Amplitude Control

The amplitude of a signal is a measurement of magnitude, as described in Chapter 2. However, the perceived loudness of a sound is not the same as the amplitude. It is desirable to control amplitude in a naturalistic way such that it relates well to perception. This requires some adjustment of gain values along the control range.

As described in §2.1.2 (p.19), the human auditory system reacts in a non-linear manner to the magnitude of air pressure variation. Decibel (dB) values are a better representation of the perceived effects of gain variations than linear values. Gain in decibels can be calculated using the equation $\text{gain}_{\text{dB}} = 20\log_{10}(\text{gain})$. Figure 5.12a illustrates how the position of the control in figure 5.6 (p.106) relates to the gain values produced. When those values are expressed in decibels (figure 5.12b) it is apparent that the spacing is not consistent. Half of the scale relates to a fairly small range of values (−6dB to 0dB), and much of the decibel range is over a tenth of the scale (−∞dB to −20dB).

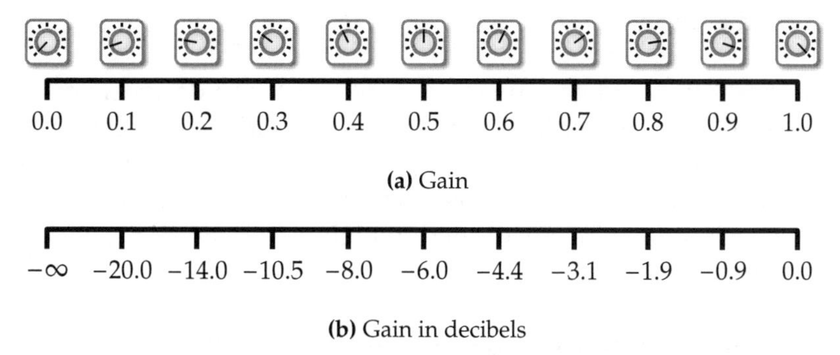

(a) Gain

(b) Gain in decibels

Figure 5.12 Linear scale of gain values

To achieve more naturalistic gain control requires a non-linear mapping between control values and gain values. Some improvement can be achieved by cubing the control values using the following equation, where x is the output from the linear control, and y is the gain value fed to the multiplier:

$$y = x^3$$

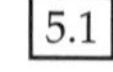

Two ways of expressing the cubic mapping in block diagram form are shown in figure 5.13. The style in figure 5.13b is generally easier to read, and also easier to adapt to alternative mappings using different equations.

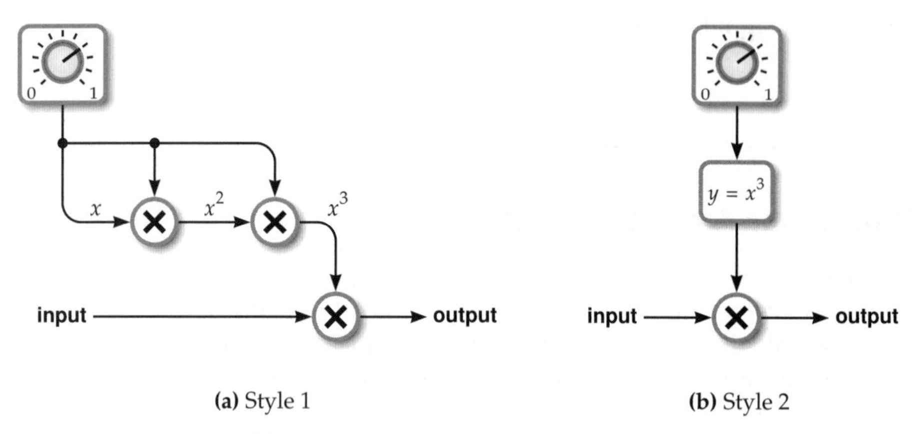

(a) Style 1 **(b)** Style 2

Figure 5.13 Cubic amplitude control

Figure 5.14 illustrates the difference between a linear control value, and cubing the control value first. If the control value is cubed, then the gain value fed to the multiplier will be lower for smaller control values. It then rises more rapidly as the control value becomes larger. Cubing the values creates a scale as shown in figure 5.15. Comparing this to figure 5.12 demonstrates how more of the scale is now used for small gain values and less for larger ones, which provides a fairly good balance of control. Algorithm 5.5 shows the cubic effect in another form.

There is no universal standard gain function (fader law), and designers choose different characteristics for different examples of Digital Audio Workstation (DAW) software and mixing consoles. For practical purposes, some more control is desired at the high gain range (towards 0dB) than at very low gains (towards $-\infty$dB). However, the linear control ($y = x$) has too much of the range dedicated to high gain. Gain functions are discussed further in §24.1.2 (p.658).

The previous examples produce a range of gain values from 0 to 1 ($-\infty$dB to 0dB). If maximum gain values greater than 1 are required (as described in §5.3.1) and a non-linear mapping function is being used, then it is easiest to scale up to greater gain values **after** mapping (figure 5.16). If scaling of gain values occurs **before** a cubic mapping function, then the range relates to the cubed value of the factor employed ($4^3 = 64$ in the case of figure 5.17).

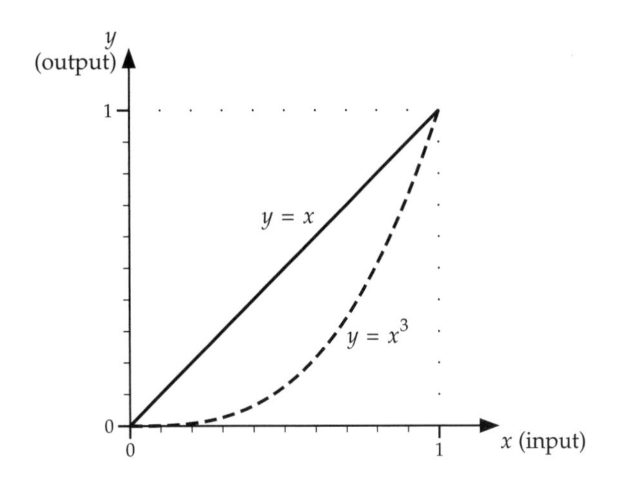

Figure 5.14 Linear and cubic functions

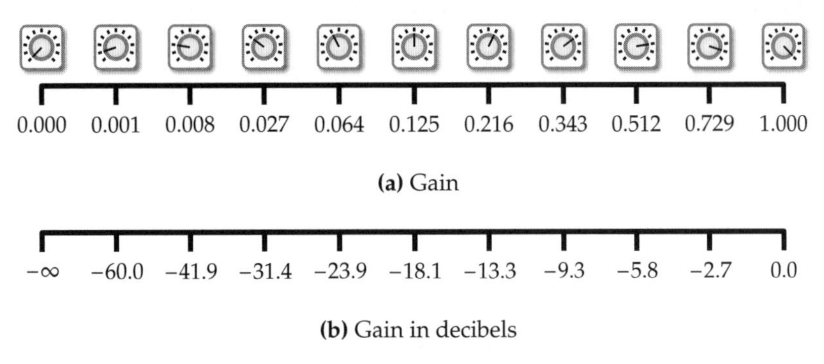

Figure 5.15 Cubic scale of gain values

Algorithm 5.5 – Cubic amplitude control function

---

input : input signal `in`
: control value `x` (between 0 and 1)
output: output signal `out`

```
out = in ∗ (x ∗ x ∗ x)
```

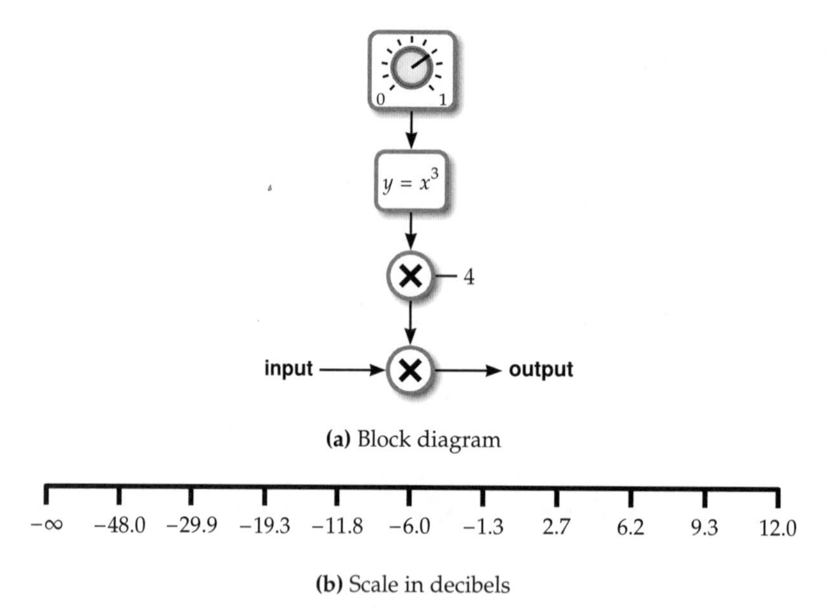

(a) Block diagram

(b) Scale in decibels

Figure 5.16 Cubic amplitude control with gain from 0 to 4 (−∞dB to +12dB)

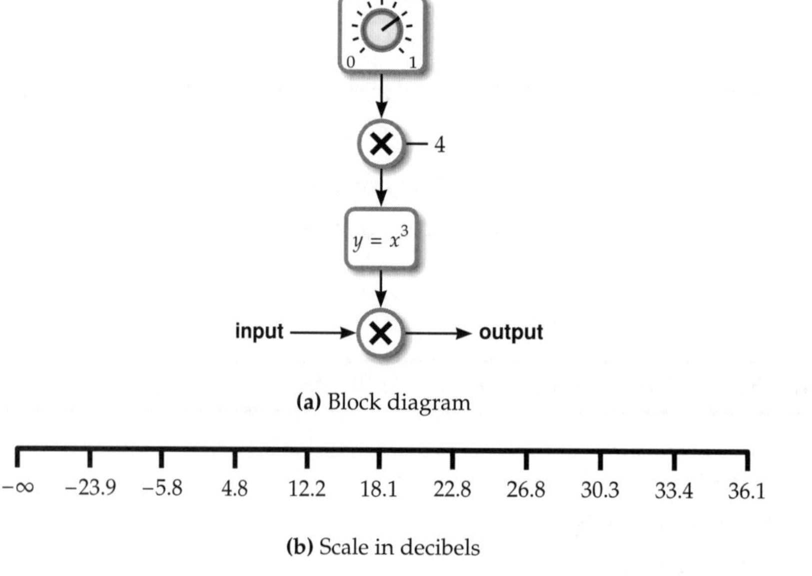

(a) Block diagram

(b) Scale in decibels

Figure 5.17 Cubic amplitude control with gain from 0 to 64 (−∞dB to +36.1dB)

5.3.4 Working with Decibels

It is common to use decibels to express amplitude gain in many audio processes to reflect the nature of the human auditory system. However, linear units are required when applying a gain value to a signal. The following conversion functions are used:

$$F_{a \to dB}: \quad \text{value}_{\text{dB}} = 20 \log_{10}(\text{value}_{\text{linear}}) \qquad [5.2]$$

$$F_{dB \to a}: \quad \text{value}_{\text{linear}} = 10^{\text{value}_{\text{dB}}/20} \qquad [5.3]$$

Figure 5.18 is an example of how a control can be based on decibel units and then be converted to linear units when it is applied to the signal through multiplication. The decibel gain range has been chosen in this example to achieve a range of linear unit multipliers from 0 to 1. It is also important to understand how gain factors are combined. Figure 5.19 shows a simple cascade of three gain controls.

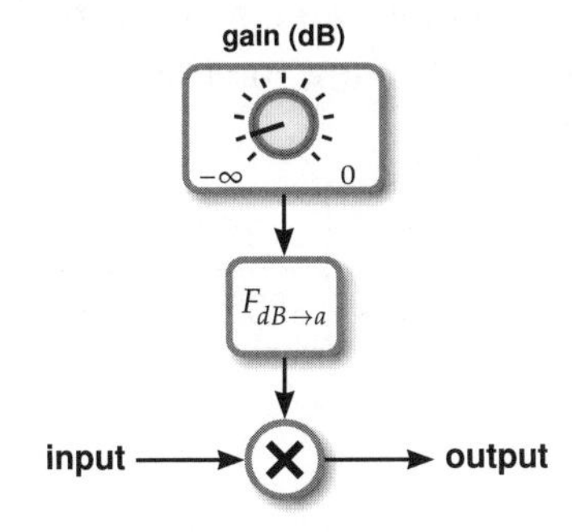

Figure 5.18 Monophonic amplitude control (decibel control values)

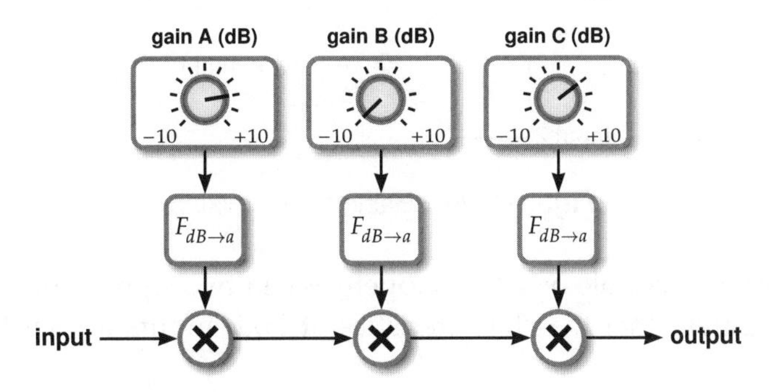

Figure 5.19 Cascaded monophonic amplitude controls (decibel control values)

An interesting mathematical property of the cascaded form in figure 5.19, is that the total linear gain can be calculated by multiplying the three numbers together, but the decibel values are summed to calculate the overall effect. It is possible to see how this works by taking three example decibel gain values and converting to linear units with equation 5.3, as shown in this table:

	gain A	gain B	gain C	overall gain
decibels	+6	−10	+4	6 − 10 + 4 = 0dB
linear units	1.995	0.316	1.585	1.995 × 0.316 × 1.585 = 1

The following table shows another example of how adding or subtracting decibel values is equivalent to multiplying in linear units:

decibels	−80	−60	−40	−20	0	20	40	60	80
linear units	0.0001	0.001	0.01	0.1	1	10	100	1000	10000

Adding 20dB to the decibel value is the same as multiplying the linear value by 10, and subtracting 20dB is the same as multiplying the linear value by 0.1. This works from any starting position. For example:

decibels	−25.4	−5.4
linear units	0.0537	0.5370

5.4 Mixing

Adding two signals together is used to create a single *mix* signal, as shown in figure 5.20.

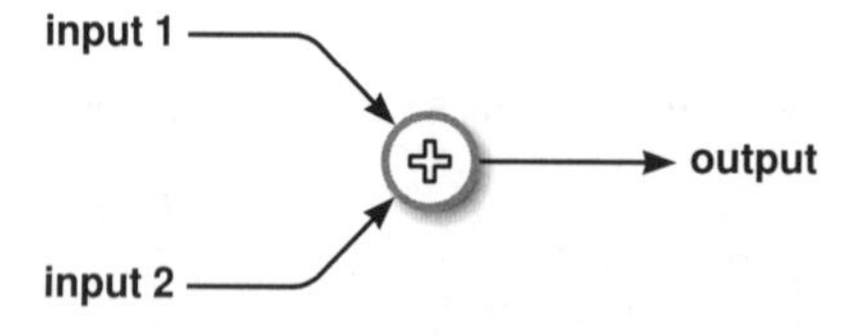

Figure 5.20 Basic signal mixing

Figure 5.21 shows an example of what happens when two signals are mixed in the time domain. It is apparent that the characteristics of both inputs are visible in the output signal.

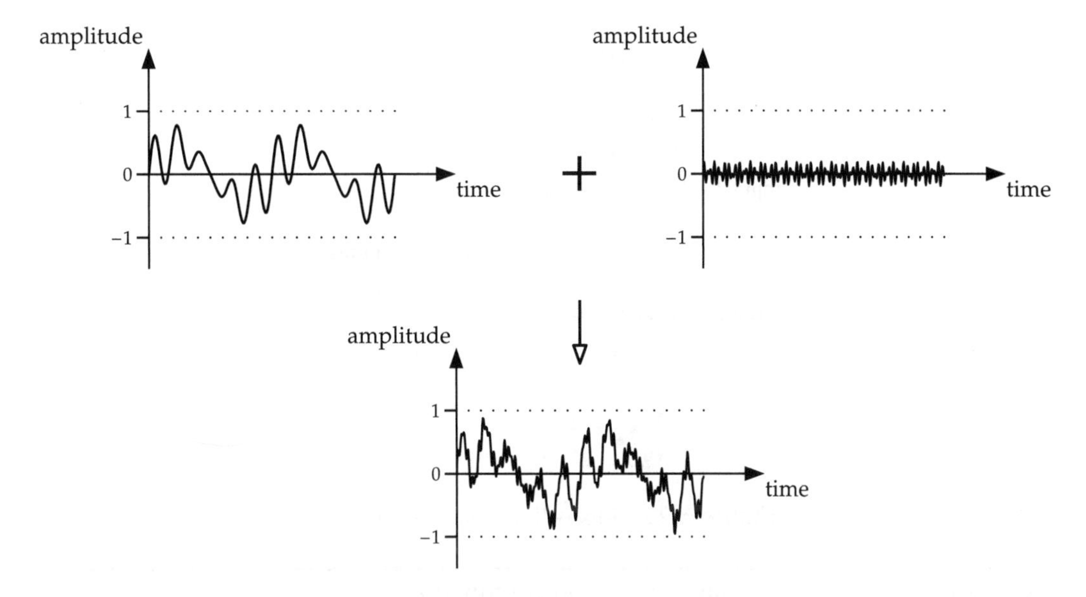

Figure 5.21 Signal mix example

It is possible to mix more than two signals, such as where multiple channels are mixed on a bus in a mixing console. This can be represented by a single summation block as shown in figure 5.22a. In a computer program this translates into:

```
out = in1 + in2 + in3 + in4
```

Therefore, mixing four signals requires three additions. A more explicit (although less elegant) block diagram representation of this process is shown in figure 5.22b.

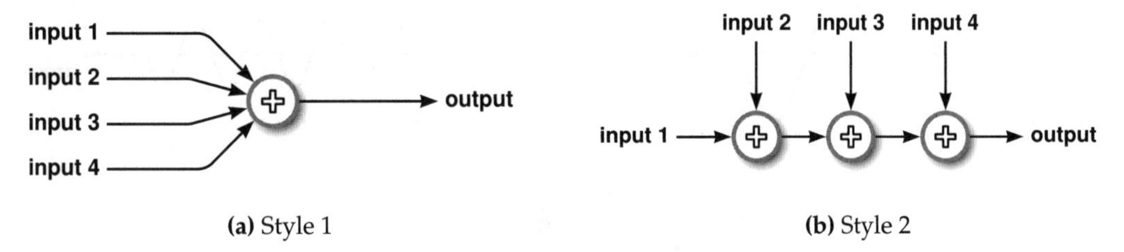

(a) Style 1

(b) Style 2

Figure 5.22 Mixing four signals

Mixing can be combined with amplitude control as shown in figure 5.23 and algorithm 5.6. This is a fairly simple effect, but note that it can potentially suffer from the output exceeding the amplitude limitations of the system (figure 5.24). While the input signals might not individually exceed the limits of the system, it is possible for the total mixed signal to do so.

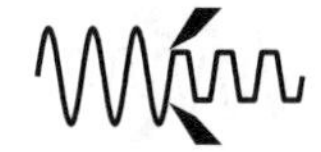

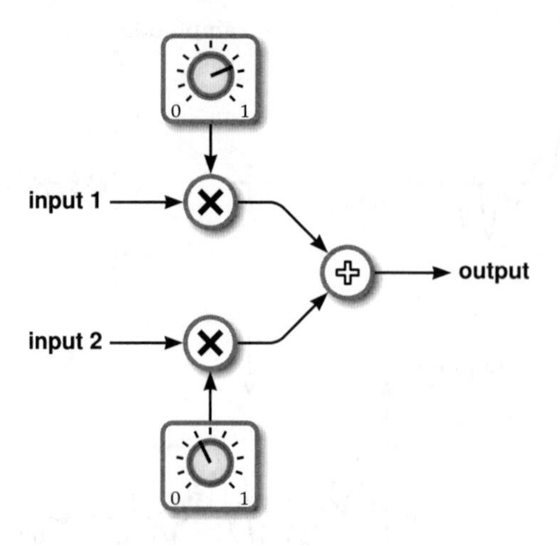

Figure 5.23 Mix with amplitude control

Algorithm 5.6 – Mix with amplitude control function

---

input : input signals `in1` and `in2`
: amplitude control values `x1` and `x2` (between 0 and 1)
output: output signal `out`

`out = (in1 * x1) + (in2 * x2)`

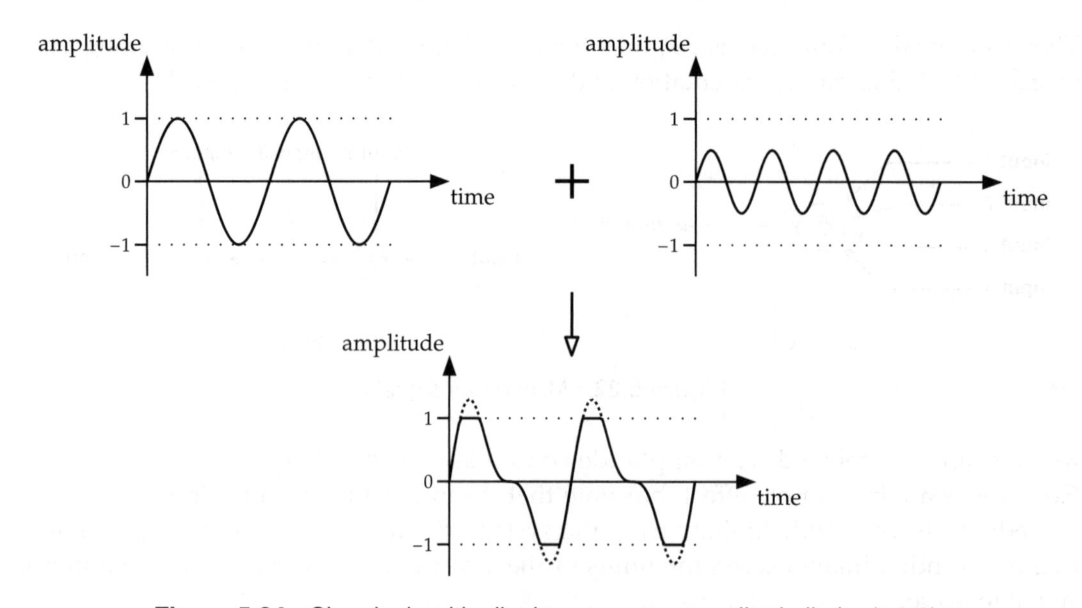

Figure 5.24 Signal mix with clipping at system amplitude limits (±1.0)

Where mixing occurs, there are two common tactics for dealing with the issue of the output signal potentially being too large:

- A fixed-value attenuator can be positioned to ensure that the output cannot become too large. For example, figure 5.25 uses a factor of 1/3 to ensure that even if all three signals' amplitudes are already at the clipping limit, the output will not exceed it. However, input signals will often be considerably less than their maximum levels. If only one signal is present and the other two are not, then the output will be a third of the size of the original input if a fixed attenuator is used.
- The second method, therefore, is to provide the user with a visual indication that clipping is occurring. This is the method that is usually found on mixing consoles. The user is responsible for reducing the amplitude of the input or output signals when the sum becomes too great and clipping is indicated.

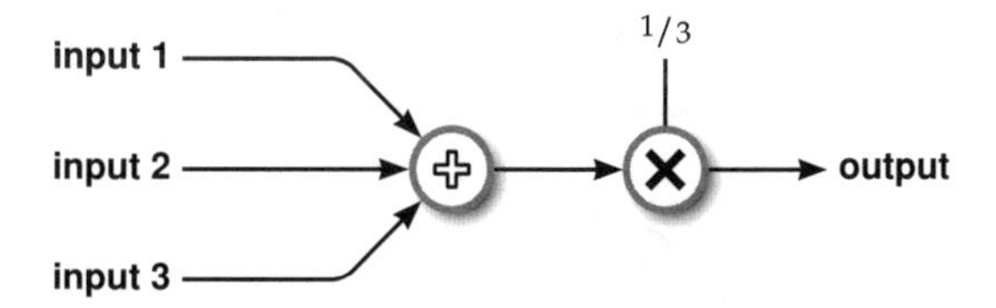

Figure 5.25 Mix with fixed-value attenuator

It is worth noting that with a computer program, the clipping problem only usually occurs at the final output. In the middle of the algorithm it is fine to have large amplitudes, but when that signal is passed to the audio output, then the clipping limits are enforced. That means that it is possible to use an attenuator on the output to correct the level, without needing to worry that signals elsewhere are exceeding the limits.

It is often necessary to mix stereo pairs of signals. This can be achieved in much the same way as a mono mix, but by having parallel paths and pairing left and right signals (as shown in figure 5.26).

5.5 Pan Control and Stereo Balance

5.5.1 Monophonic and Stereophonic Signals

With monophonic (mono) reproduction of sound, the listener hears a single audio channel. A simple case occurs when a microphone converts air pressure variations to an electrical signal, and that signal is then converted back into air pressure variations at the listening position with one loudspeaker (figure 5.27). From the perspective of the listener, this copies the sound from one acoustic space to another.

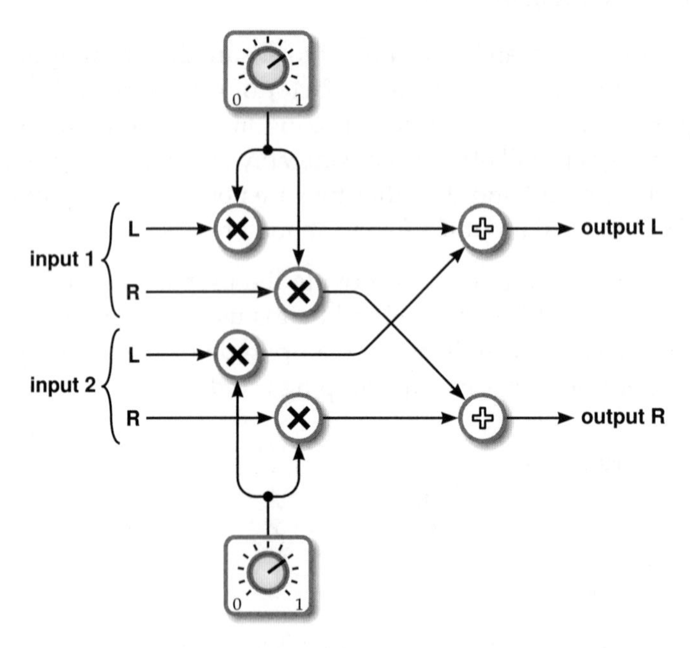

Figure 5.26 Two channel stereo mix with input amplitude controls

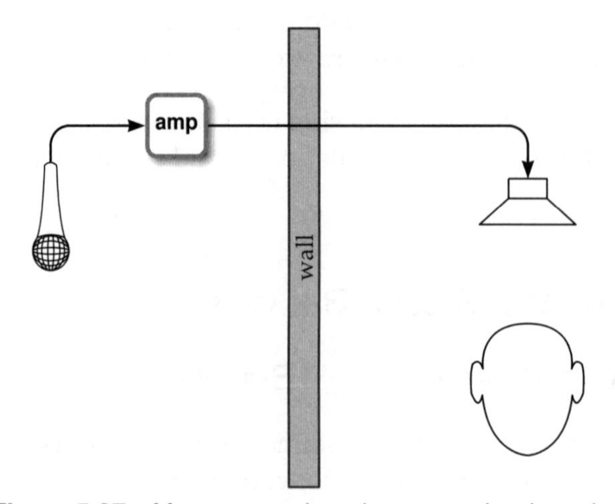

Figure 5.27 Mono; one microphone, one loudspeaker

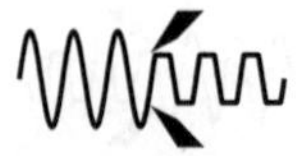

Mono reproduction loses a lot of information about sound source direction. For example, if a person is standing in a wooden-floored room with their eyes closed, and another person is walking across the floor from left to right, then the difference between sounds received at the left and right ears can be used to determine the position of the walker. If the arrangement in figure 5.27 is used and a person is walking left to right in front of the microphone, then the effect is similar to the listener only having one ear. Certain information will still be apparent such as the differences in amplitude and reverberation between near and far sources, but the directional information will be largely missing.

In figure 5.28 there are two loudspeakers that are both carrying the same signal from a single microphone. This is **not** stereophonic sound. It is still mono because there is no left-right difference in output signal, and no sound source directional information that is captured and reproduced. This is true no matter how many loudspeakers are used.

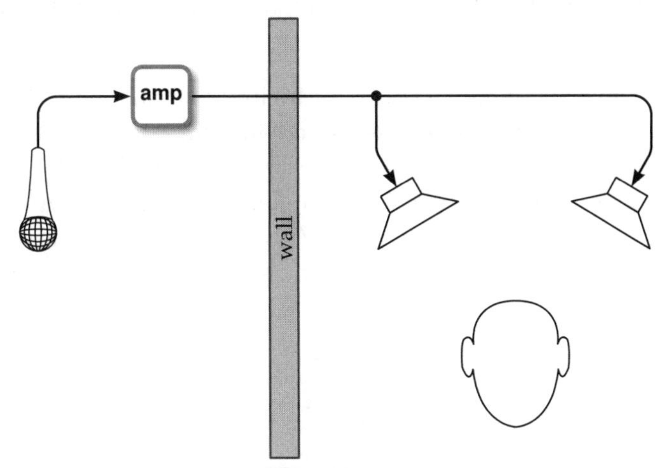

Figure 5.28 Mono; one microphone, two loudspeakers

True stereophonic (stereo) reproduction requires the sound to be captured with two microphones and reproduced with two loudspeakers (figure 5.29). This uses the microphones as substitutes for the two human ears in the recording space, and then relocates that sound to the listening space where the two signals are recreated as air pressure variations. It is still the case that the idea is to copy the sound from the position of the microphone to the equivalent position of the loudspeaker.

Although the process is not perfect, much of the spatial positioning information is preserved. This is true of both clear effects (such as the person walking left to right as described earlier) and in subtle terms (such as the differences in reverberation received on the left-hand and right-hand sides of the body). It is possible to extend this arrangement to more than two microphones and more than two loudspeakers (as commonly found in surround sound systems).

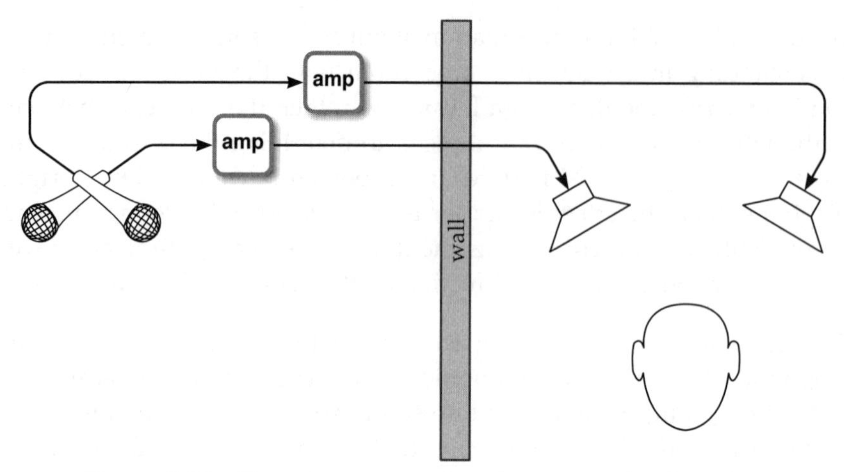

Figure 5.29 True stereo; two microphones, two loudspeakers

It is often desirable, however, to take a single audio input signal and create a stereophonic result. In this case, audio processes are used to create different signals for two (or more) loudspeakers, such that different signals arrive at each ear. This is often used where the source of the signal is monophonic (say, an electric guitar pickup), or a potentially stereophonic source has been recorded in mono (say, a piano), and it is desirable to create a spatial positioning effect from that monophonic signal. This arrangement is shown in figure 5.30.

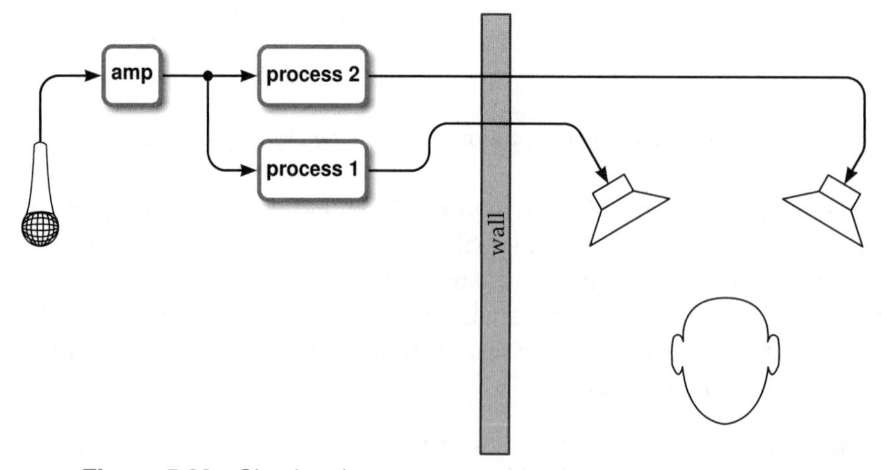

Figure 5.30 Simulated stereo; one microphone, two loudspeakers

In the figure process 1 and process 2 will be very similar, but configured in a different way such that the two resulting signals are different. Such processes can be quite complex, such as a reverberation effect that produces a different signal for left and right ears.

5.5.2 Panning

Humans use a number of cues to determine the location of a sound source, including differences in amplitude and arrival time of sounds that originate closer to one ear than the other. There are also cues that relate to the filtering associated with the human body when a sound arrives from different directions (such as from behind, in front, above, or below). It is possible to achieve a reasonable localisation effect by only using a relative amplitude effect, which is implemented in the *pan* (panoramic) controls found in mixing consoles and DAW software.

A panning process takes a single input signal and produces a stereo output such that the sound appears to be located at a chosen spatial position. The basic arrangement of the process is shown in figure 5.31, where gain factors a_L and a_R control the signal to left and right outputs. The amplitude-based panning principle is that a human will perceive a source signal to have a left-to-right position depending upon the relative amplitude of that signal from the left and right loudspeakers. When a sound source appears to be located in a position somewhere between the two loudspeakers it is often called a *phantom image*.

Panning can be expressed in general terms as follows:

left level	right level	perceived spatial position
maximum	zero	fully to the left
high	low	left of centre
medium	medium	in the centre
low	high	right of centre
zero	maximum	fully to the right

The simplest way of achieving this result is shown in figure 5.32. Gain values for both outputs are derived from a single rotary control with a range of 0 to 1. The value from the control is used directly as the gain value for the right channel output. However, the function $y = 1 - x$ is used to change the right channel gain values into those used on the left. This causes the left gain to decrease as the right gain increases, and vice versa.

The level of the gain values at points L and R in the block diagram are shown in figure 5.33. This is known as a *linear pan law*. As the control position (from the rotary control) moves from 0 to 1, the relative amplitude on each side is changed and the perceived spatial position moves from left to right. Notice that when the control is in the centre position, both channels are subject to a gain value of 0.5.

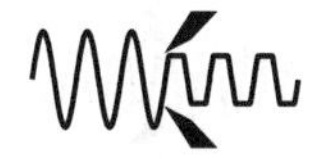

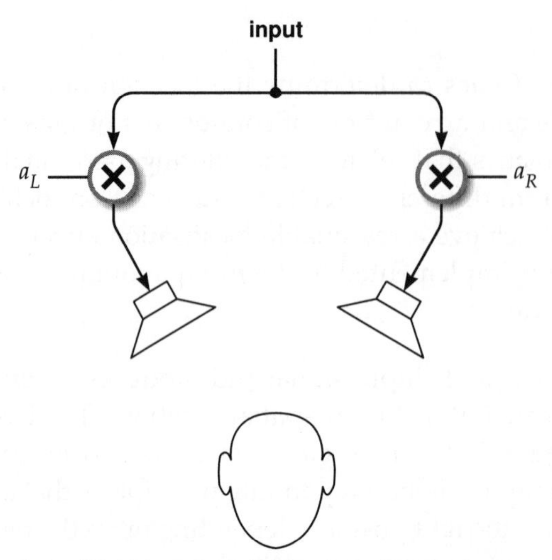

Figure 5.31 Basic panning form

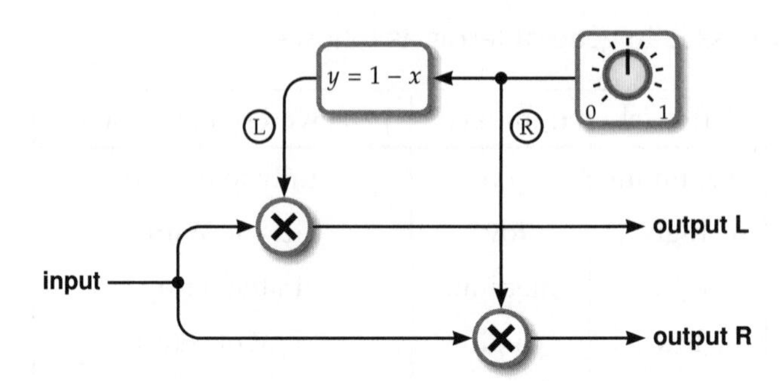

Figure 5.32 Linear pan

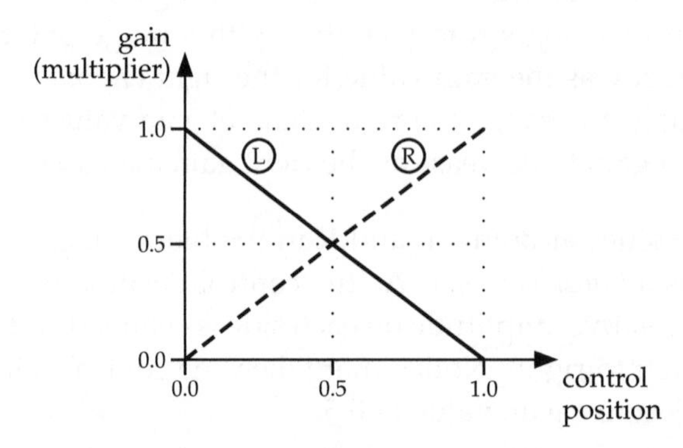

Figure 5.33 Linear pan gain control values

The main advantage of the linear panning technique is that it is fully *mono compatible*. That is, it is possible to sum the left and right output signals to achieve a correct monophonic signal suitable for, say, AM radio, or small portable televisions with a single loudspeaker. Mathematically, it is as if the pan process never existed:

$$\begin{aligned}
\text{output}_{\text{mono}} &= \text{output}_{\text{L}} + \text{output}_{\text{R}} \\
&= ((1 - x) \times \text{input}) + (x \times \text{input}) \\
&= \text{input} - (x \times \text{input}) + (x \times \text{input}) \\
&= \text{input}
\end{aligned}$$

This means that it is possible to create a stereo mix from mono sources for a stereo playback system, but that the stereo result can also be mixed down to mono if required with complete consistency. A linear pan law is sometimes called a −6dB law, which is the attenuation applied to each of the channels when the control is in the centre position.

The problem with the linear pan law is that when listening in stereo there is a slight perceived dip in level as the pan position moves towards the centre. For this reason, a number of non-linear pan laws exist to counteract the perceived dip. The non-linear pan is achieved using the form shown in figure 5.34, where a mapping function is used to convert from linear to non-linear control values. The nature of the mapping function is to take input values between 0 and 1 and translate those into output values. Figure 5.35 illustrates how a linear change in pan control will map to non-linear gain results. The same mapping function is used for left and right sides, but the $y = 1 - x$ function reverses the effect.

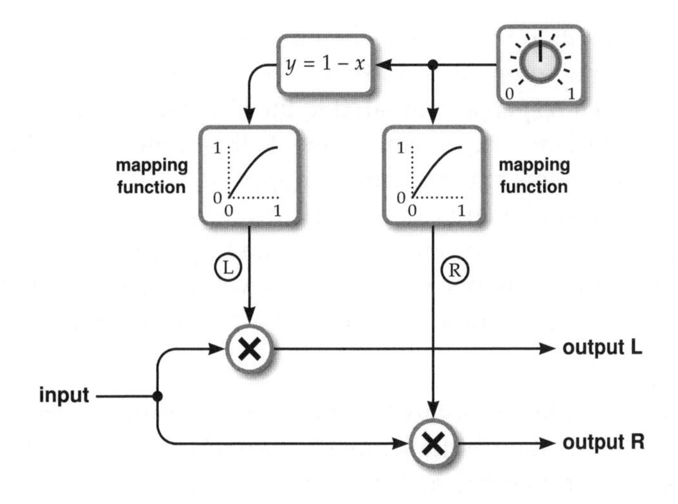

Figure 5.34 Non-linear pan

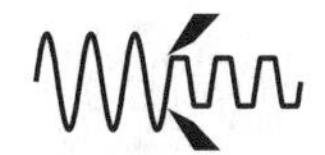

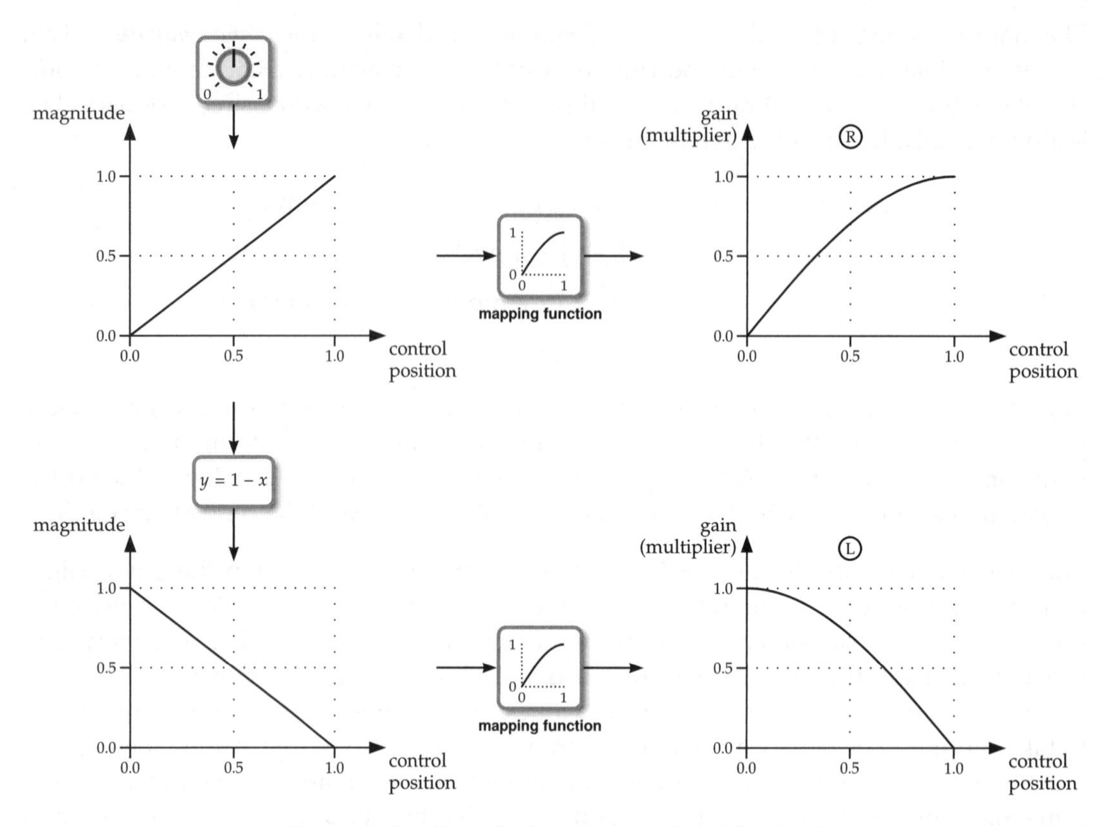

Figure 5.35 Non-linear pan mapping (sine law)

A typical non-linear pan mapping uses a sine function, as shown in algorithm 5.7 (where the sine function takes an argument in radians). The sine function pan law tends to give a more perceptually even response compared to the linear law when the signal is panned from one side to the other in a stereo environment. It is sometimes called a −3dB law or *constant power law*. −3dB refers to the attenuation applied to each of the channels when the control is in the centre position. It is a constant power law as squaring the left and right gains and adding them together produces a constant sum whatever the control position. Although this law counters the perceived dip in level in stereo, if the panned result is mixed to create a mono signal, then the level will increase as the pan position moves to the centre.

DAW software often provides the ability to switch between different pan laws. This allows different amounts of attenuation in the centre position relative to the fully left or fully right positions. A range of non-linear function shapes is possible. Different mixing consoles have different shaped functions, depending on what the designer considered to be the most natural effect.

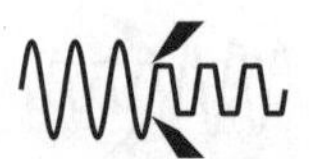

Algorithm 5.7 – Non-linear (sine) pan mapping function

input : pan control value x (between 0 and 1)
output: value to multiplier y

$y = \sin(0.5 * \pi * x)$

Recording projects often consist of multiple channels that are positioned in different places in the stereo soundfield. Therefore, each channel on a mixing console or DAW has its own pan block. The outputs of the pan blocks are mixed onto a stereo bus to create the overall two-channel result, as shown in figure 5.36.

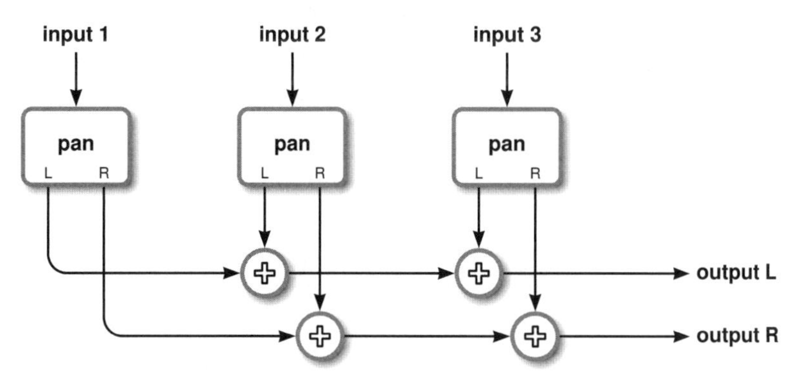

Figure 5.36 Panning and mixing channels to a stereo bus

5.5.3 Stereo Balance

A pan process takes a single input signal and creates a two channel output. By contrast, a *balance* control takes two input signals (left and right) and varies the relative amplitudes on either side, producing a two channel output. The basic purpose of this is to allow adjustment of the relative amplification of a two channel stereo source. A typical approach to creating the balance process is to adapt the non-linear pan form of figure 5.34, as shown in figure 5.37. The first difference from the pan method is that there are now two inputs that are varied in amplitude. The second difference is that the mapping function is a different shape (but again, the same function for left and right).

Figure 5.38 illustrates the gain functions used for left and right channels at points L and R in figure 5.37. When the control is in the centre position (rotary control value 0.5) then both left and right channels are multiplied by a value of 1, so the output is the same as the input. When the control is moved away from the centre position, the gain is decreased on one side, while it is held constant at a value of 1 on the other side.

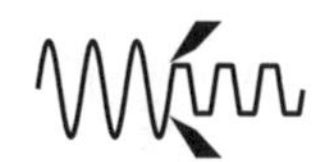

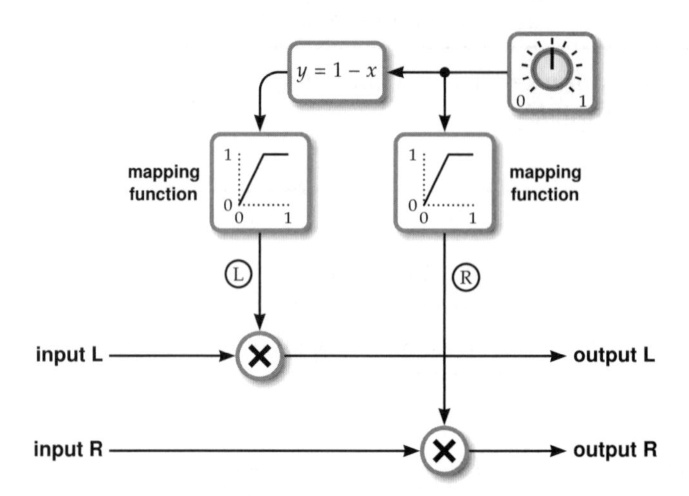

Figure 5.37 Balance

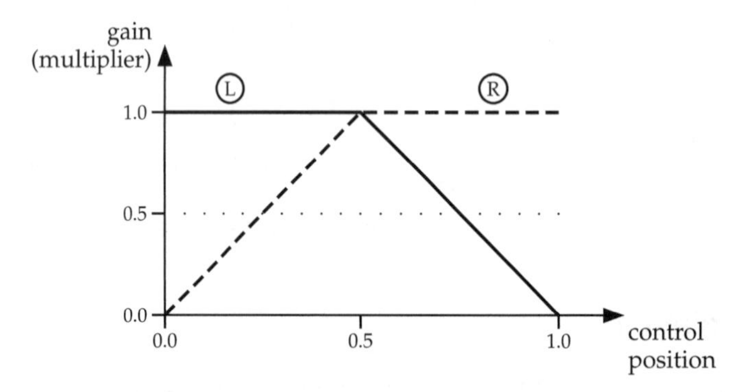

Figure 5.38 Balance gain control values

Algorithm 5.8 – Balance mapping function

---

input : balance control value x (between 0 and 1)
output: value to multiplier y

if x < 0.5 **then**
  y = 2 ∗ x
else
  y = 1

The left-hand gain shape is again the reverse of the right, so a $y = 1 - x$ function is used to invert the control values, followed by the same mapping function (algorithm 5.8). As with pan laws, different shapes of balance mapping function can be used to achieve the amplitude gain style desired by the designer.

5.6 Combination of Elements

5.6.1 Ordering

The more complex a system becomes, the more design decisions need to be made about the way in which an audio process will be structured. Sometimes the ordering of process elements will have no effect on the result, such as the two cases in figure 5.39. In the second example, the delay block causes all samples to be delayed by the same length of time (0.1s) before reaching the output (see Chapter 8). It does not matter if those samples are modified by the multiplier beforehand or afterwards.

There are also cases where reordering has no effect on the audible result, but **does** have an effect on the efficiency of computation. Figure 5.40 illustrates the case where three signals need to be amplified by a factor of 3 because they are insufficiently loud, and then mixed together. Because they are all amplified by the same amount, the multiplication can be performed after the addition as $(3a + 3b + 3c) \equiv 3 \times (a + b + c)$. Using one multiplier rather than three is more computationally-efficient.

Reordering does not necessarily mean that the configuration values remain the same. Mathematically, $(5x + 2) \equiv 5(x + 0.4)$, so the two forms in figure 5.41a produce the same result. Similarly $27(x^3) \equiv (3x)^3$, so the two forms in figure 5.41b are equivalent.

Not all elements can be reordered as easily as these examples. It is important to carefully consider the effects of different elements when ordering them. In particular there is a difference between *linear* and *non-linear* processes. A linear process has an output proportional to the input. These are generally easier to reorder without having an effect on the audible result. Some example linear audio process elements are multipliers and simple filters (see Chapter 6). However, other elements such as distortion (Chapter 7) and noise gates (Chapter 11) are non-linear.

The examples in figure 5.42 include two elements; an echo that repeats the input with decreasing output level over time, and a noise gate that removes all signals below a certain amplitude threshold level. The blocks are configured in the same way in both cases, and the inputs are the same. The echo block in figure 5.42a takes a single impulsive input and produces multiple decaying copies of the input at its output. The noise gate then removes the echoes below the threshold (set to half the peak amplitude in this case). The output is different in figure 5.42b, where the blocks are reordered, because the noise gate is applied to the input (which is above the threshold) and the result is echoed.

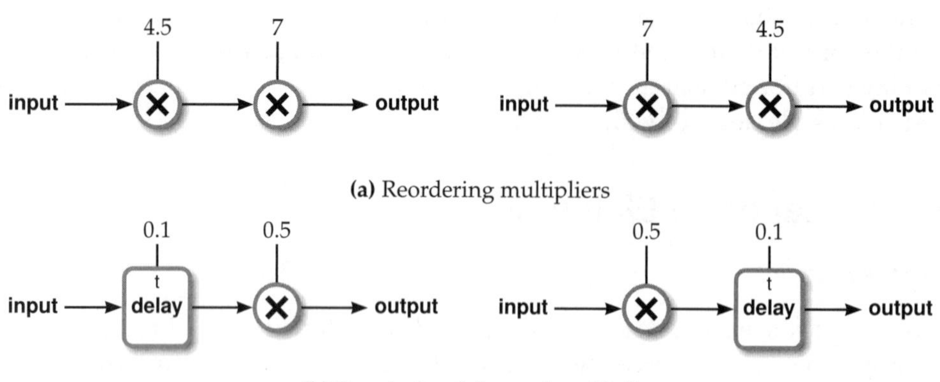

Figure 5.39 Reordering without affecting the result

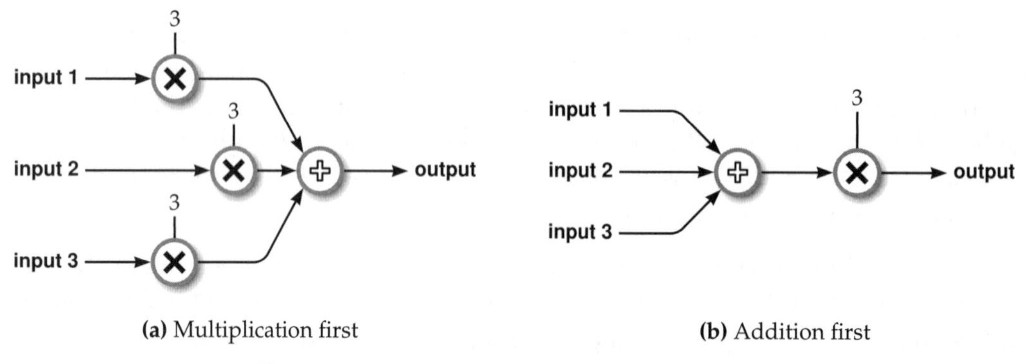

Figure 5.40 Reordering affecting computation

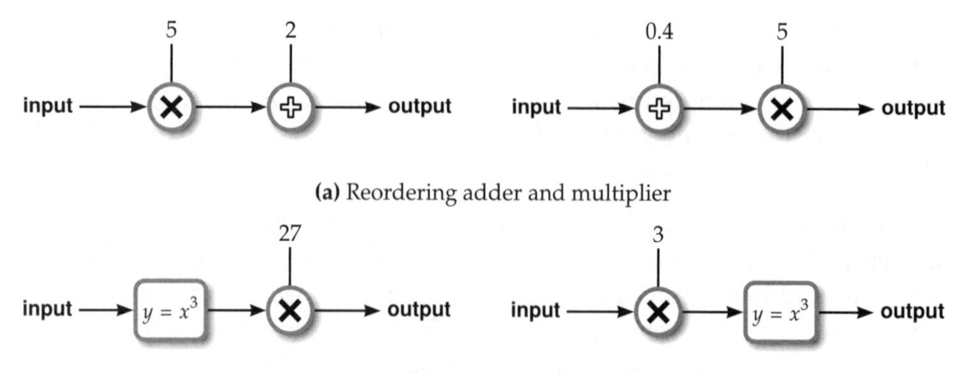

Figure 5.41 Reordering requiring reconfiguration

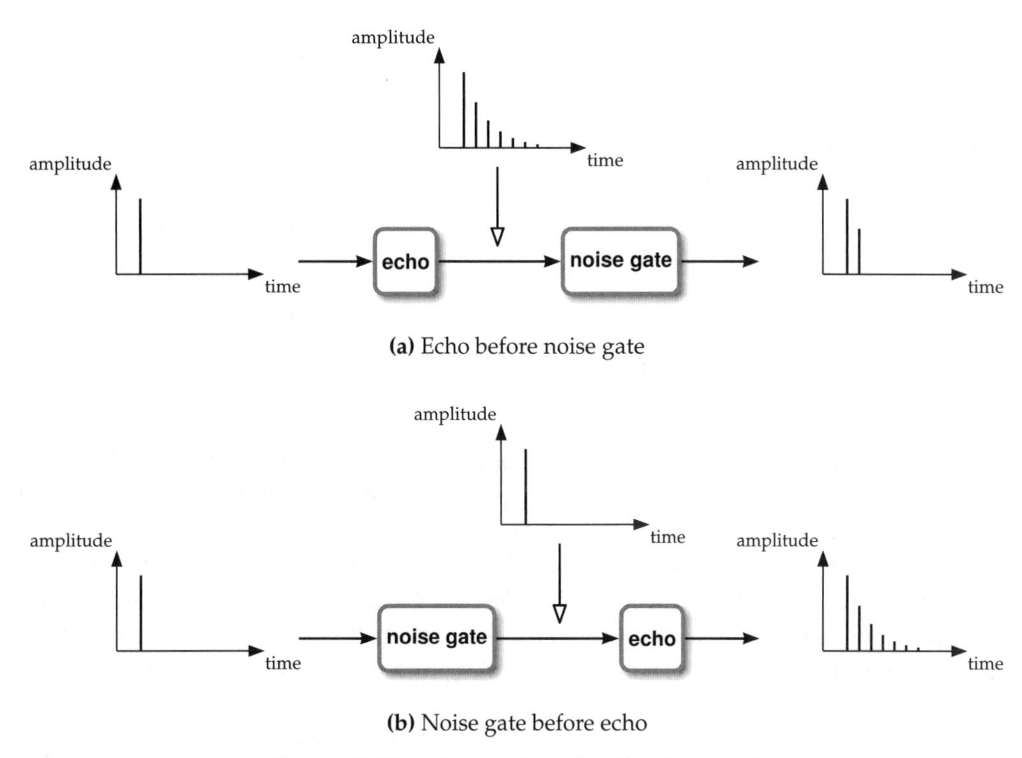

(a) Echo before noise gate

(b) Noise gate before echo

Figure 5.42 Reordering affecting the result

5.6.2 Series and Parallel Forms

Figure 5.43 illustrates two standard ways in which a modifier is applied to a signal; often called *insert* (or *inline*) and *send* (or *additive*) styles. In the insert style, the modifier is positioned such that all inputs pass through it. The input is the *dry* signal, and the processed output is *wet*. However, there are times when it is desirable to maintain some amount of the dry signal, and add an amount of wet result to it, which is the send style.

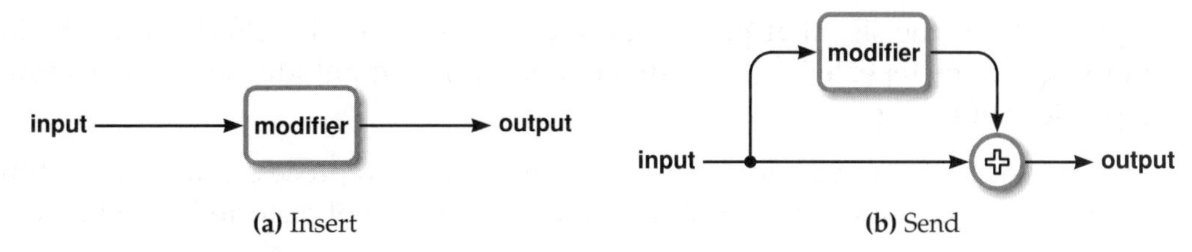

(a) Insert **(b)** Send

Figure 5.43 Insert and send style uses of modifiers

It is possible to generalise the insert and send techniques to any number of modifiers. Figure 5.44 shows these two forms, which are known as *series* (or *cascade*) and *parallel*

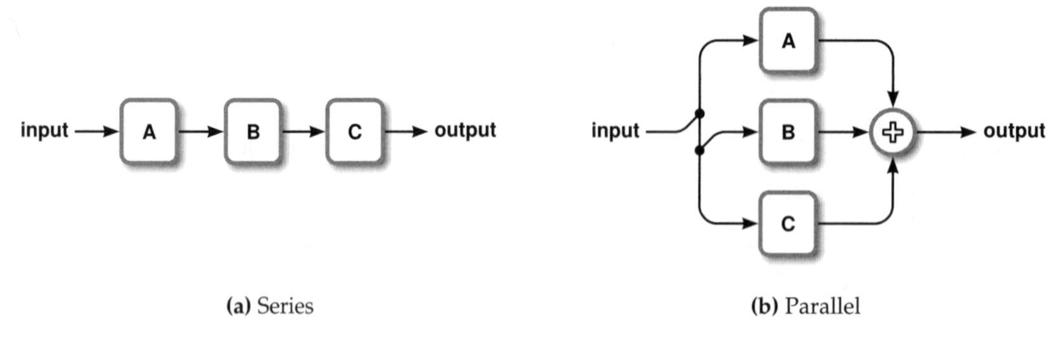

(a) Series (b) Parallel

Figure 5.44 Series and parallel combination

combinations. The series technique builds one process on top of another; the input is processed by block A, the output of which is processed by block B, the output of which is processed by block C. The parallel technique feeds the input to all three blocks, and then mixes their outputs. One of those blocks might not alter the sound at all, providing a dry signal in the same way as the simple send style. At a basic level, both forms are taking the input signal and creating an output that is the effect of A, B, and C on that input. The way the results from the processes A, B, and C combine, however, is different in the two forms.

As an example of the difference between series and parallel combination, consider figure 5.45. Point D in both diagrams is the same signal (the distorted version of the input). To show the difference in output for the same input, consider the example stylised time domain forms in figure 5.46:

- Figure 5.46a shows a single instance of a decaying sound, which is the input signal for both series and parallel forms.
- Figure 5.46b is a representation of that input when it has been distorted (coloured black to make it apparent that it is a modified version of the input sound). This is the signal found at point D in figures 5.45a and 5.45b.
- Figure 5.46c is the signal at point E in figure 5.45b. An echo effect causes the input signal to be repeated with gradually decreasing amplitude, so the plot shows repetitions of the input signal.
- Figure 5.46d is the output from the series form. The echo process causes the output of the distortion block to be repeated, so the result is a set of distorted sound echoes.
- Figure 5.46e is the output from the parallel form. This is a mix of the signals at point D (figure 5.46b) and point E (figure 5.46c). The result is that the first sound instance is a blend of the distorted sound and non-distorted sound. The subsequent echoes are those of the non-distorted sound.

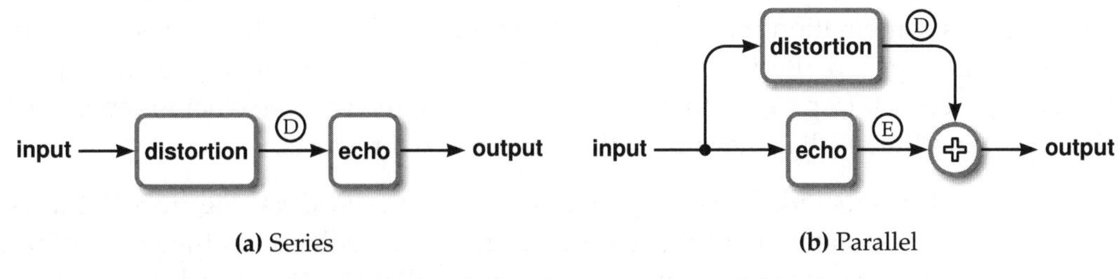

(a) Series **(b)** Parallel

Figure 5.45 Distortion and echo combination

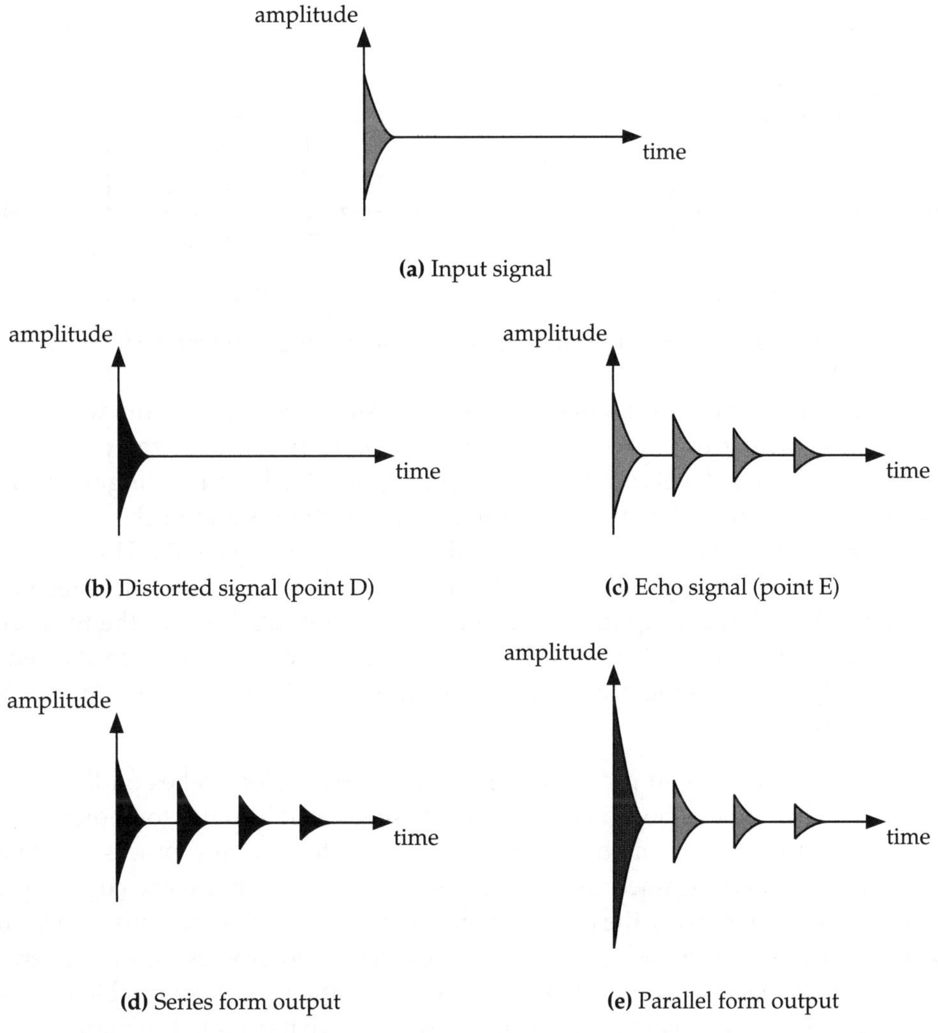

(a) Input signal

(b) Distorted signal (point D)

(c) Echo signal (point E)

(d) Series form output

(e) Parallel form output

Figure 5.46 Distortion and echo combination example for figure 5.45

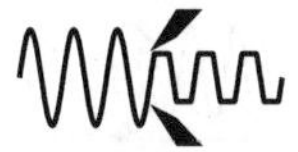

It is important to think about the appropriate form of combination to achieve the desired results. In series combination each stage builds on top of what has already been achieved in the previous stage, so altering the first process in the series form affects the input to subsequent processes. In parallel combination, however, the processes act independently on the input, and the result is the sum of those independent effects.

Some audio processes include looped signal flows, known as *feedback*. Figure 5.47 shows a pair of arrangements, one without feedback and one with feedback. In the non-feedback form the current input is processed in two ways in parallel (A and B) and the results are then mixed. The feedback form is different, in that the signal from the feedback path (through block A) is mixed with the current input, before being processed by block B to produce the output.

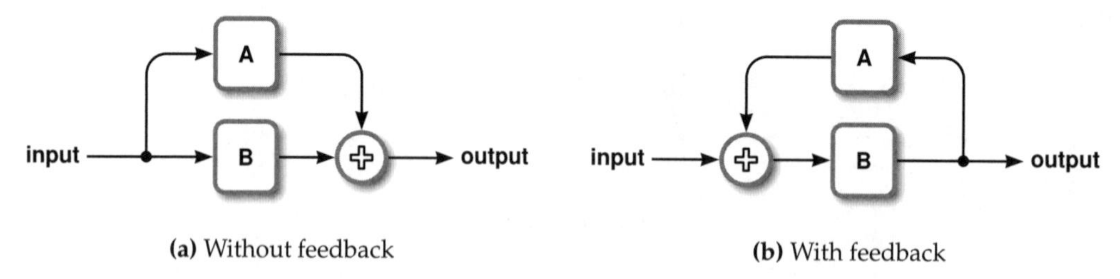

(a) Without feedback

(b) With feedback

Figure 5.47 Example arrangements without and with feedback

Feedback is often described as *positive* or *negative*. Positive feedback occurs when the fed-back signal (the output of block A in figure 5.47b) is in phase with the process input, leading to an increase in level compared to having no feedback. Depending on the nature of the process, if the overall loop gain (through block B then A and back to the input) is sufficiently large then a continual increase in the signal level can result. This is generally undesirable. However, many audio processes use a small amount of positive feedback to create results where future outputs derive from current outputs (such as the recirculating echo effects described in §10.3.2, p.315). Negative feedback occurs when the fed-back signal is in antiphase with the process input, leading to a decrease in level compared to having no feedback.

The nature of feedback is that processing the input to each block relies on the output of another block in an endless loop. This can be confusing when it comes to implementation. It is necessary to choose a suitable point on the loop to start the process calculation. Typically a feedback arrangement is using old signal values to influence current process behaviour. In the simplest case the output sample calculated at the previous step in time is used as the input to the feedback path to start the calculation process for the current step. Alternatively if blocks A or B include an explicit delay line then it is possible to read old sample values out of that delay before writing new values to its input. The implementation of delay lines is discussed further in Chapter 8.

5.6.3 Practical Combination Examples

This section describes some typical series and parallel combinations that are found in a wide range of audio processes. Figure 5.48 shows a set of three modifiers, each of which has an ability to be *bypassed* with a switch. This is a typical construction for guitar effects units, or a series of insert effects in a DAW. The bypass switches allow individual modifiers to be instantly removed from (or added to) the signal chain without having to change the parameter settings inside the modifier block.

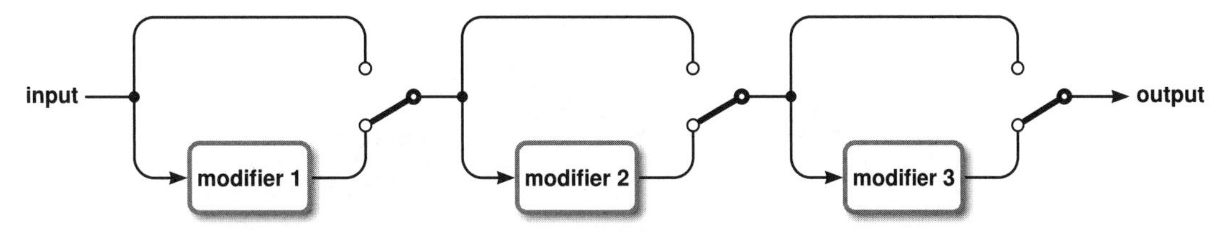

Figure 5.48 Multiple series modifiers with bypass switches

The form shown in figure 5.49 achieves a *wet/dry mix*. The dry signal is the unprocessed input that is mixed into the output. The wet signal is that which is produced by the modifier block. The two rotary controls affect the blend of the two signals. The output can be all dry, or all wet, or anything in between. This is a good way of controlling how much reverberation to add to the original signal to simulate the effect of playing in a large room.

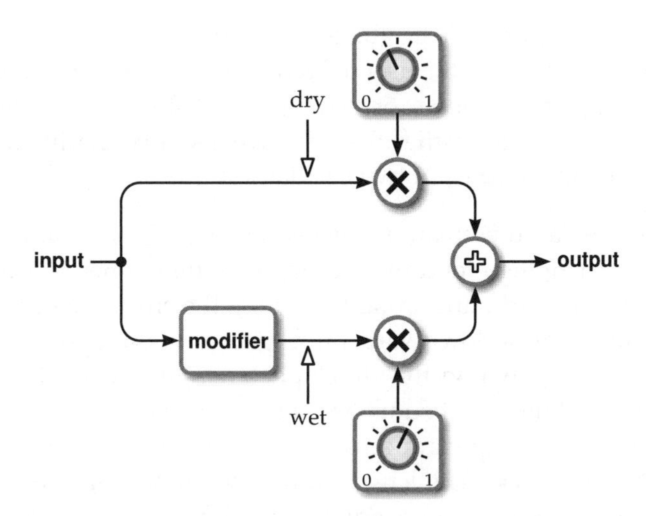

Figure 5.49 Wet/dry mix

An issue with the form in figure 5.49 is that the blend of wet and dry signals and the overall output gain are coupled together. When both controls are at their maximum the

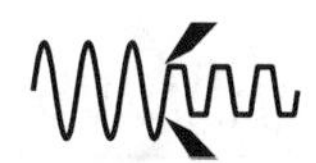

overall gain will be 2 (assuming that the wet signal is the same amplitude as the dry). But when the signal is all dry (wet gain is 0, dry gain is 1) the overall gain will be 1. Thus to maintain a consistent output level one control must be decreased as the other is increased. Figure 5.50 illustrates an alternative arrangement where the wet and dry blend ratio is determined by a single control, and the output gain is varied separately. The equation $y = 1 - x$ is used to invert the control value in the same way as in figure 5.32 (p.122). The output can still be all dry, or all wet, or anything in between. This time, however, the overall gain is not changed by the blend, and the maximum gain is always 1.

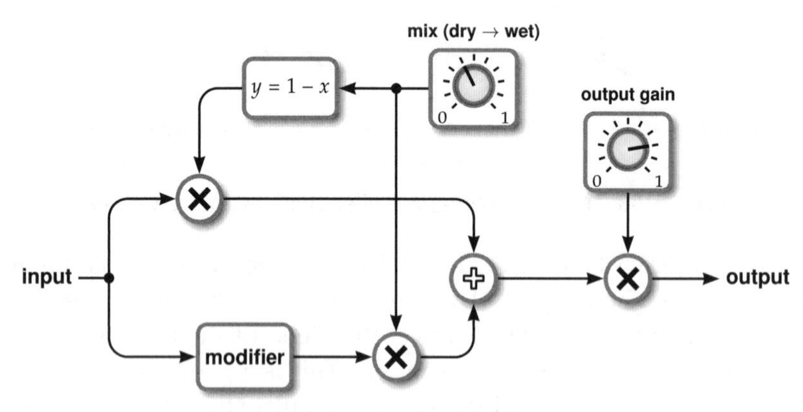

Figure 5.50 Wet/dry ratio mix

The wet/dry ratio mix in figure 5.50 can be easily adapted to the related forms shown in figure 5.51. The *wet/wet mix* allows the user to blend between two different modifiers, such as two different filtering arrangements, or two types of distortion. The *cross-fade mix* is for two independent signal sources (rather than the same source modified in two different ways), such as blending the outputs of two oscillators.

The manual control is replaced with an *envelope generator (EG)* in the automated cross-fade mix. This achieves a changing blend over a length of time when a *gate* signal causes a transition to occur. An upward ramp from 0 to 1 from the envelope generator cross-fades from input 1 to input 2, and a downward ramp produces the opposite cross-fade. The shape of the transition is shown on the envelope generator block. A simple use of this form is to achieve a switching effect similar to figure 5.1a (p.102), but avoiding a sudden jump in output value. The jump can occur due to differences in the two input signals, which can be audible as a click. The length of the transition might be about 50ms. The uses and designs of envelope generators are discussed further in Chapters 13 and 14.

Rather than blending between two signals (as in figure 5.51), there are cases where it is useful to be able to blend between parameter (control) values as shown in figure 5.52. The idea is that the end point values (A and B) for each parameter are specified with the

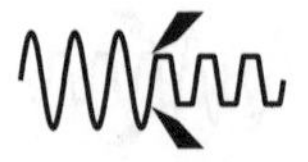

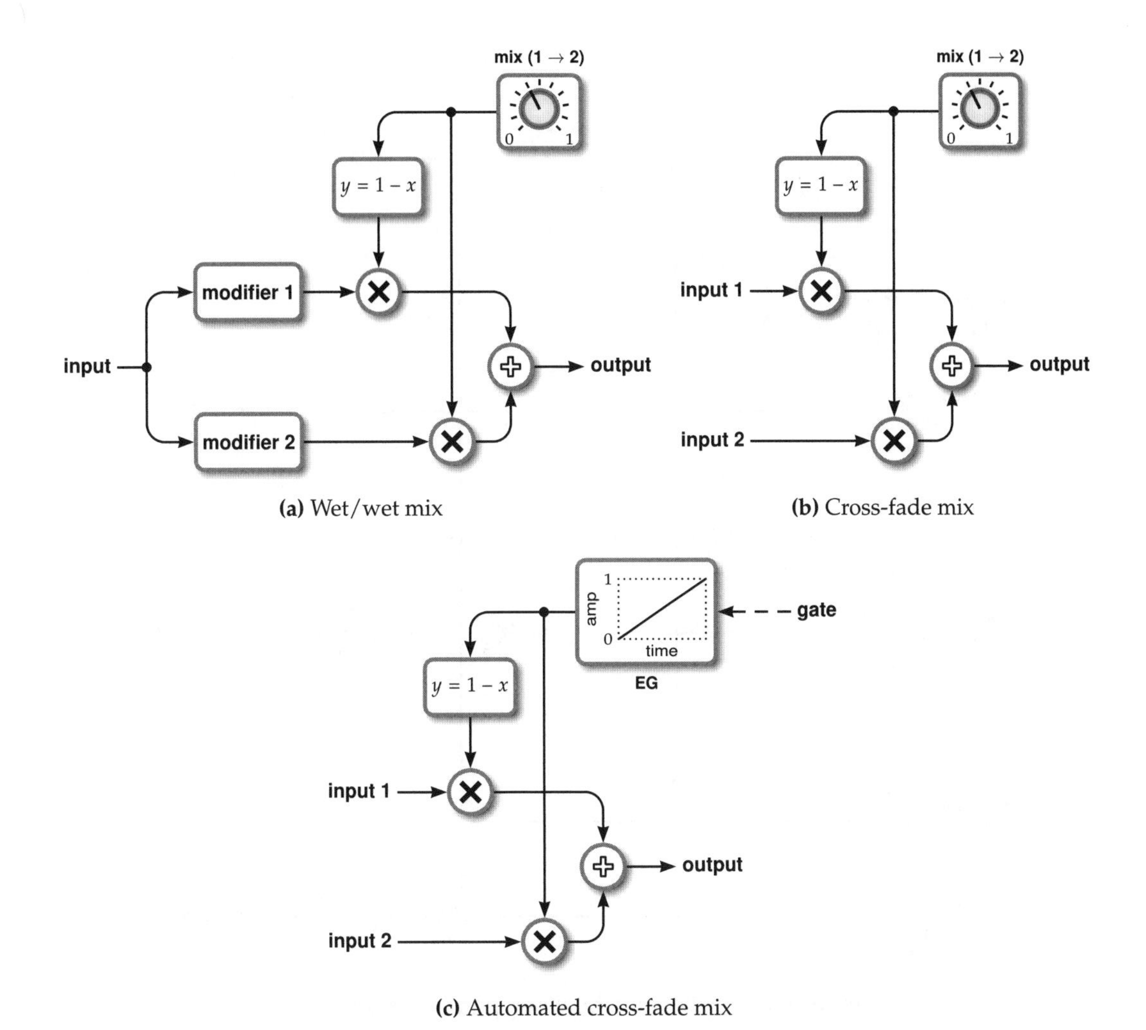

(a) Wet/wet mix

(b) Cross-fade mix

(c) Automated cross-fade mix

Figure 5.51 Wet/wet and cross-fade mix forms

controls on the left of the diagram, and then a single blend control can select a position between the two end points for all the parameters. The parameter output values are then used to control such things as gain values for different audio channels, or bandpass filter centre frequencies (Chapter 6), or synthesizer control parameters. The result is an ability to create continuous variations between two tonal characters.

The parameter ranges for the controls on the left of the diagram depend on the parameter type (such as gain, frequency, or time values). They can represent presets that are stored in the system, such that the blend control is the only one needed in performance. The form can be extended to as many parameters as required. Blending between parameter values

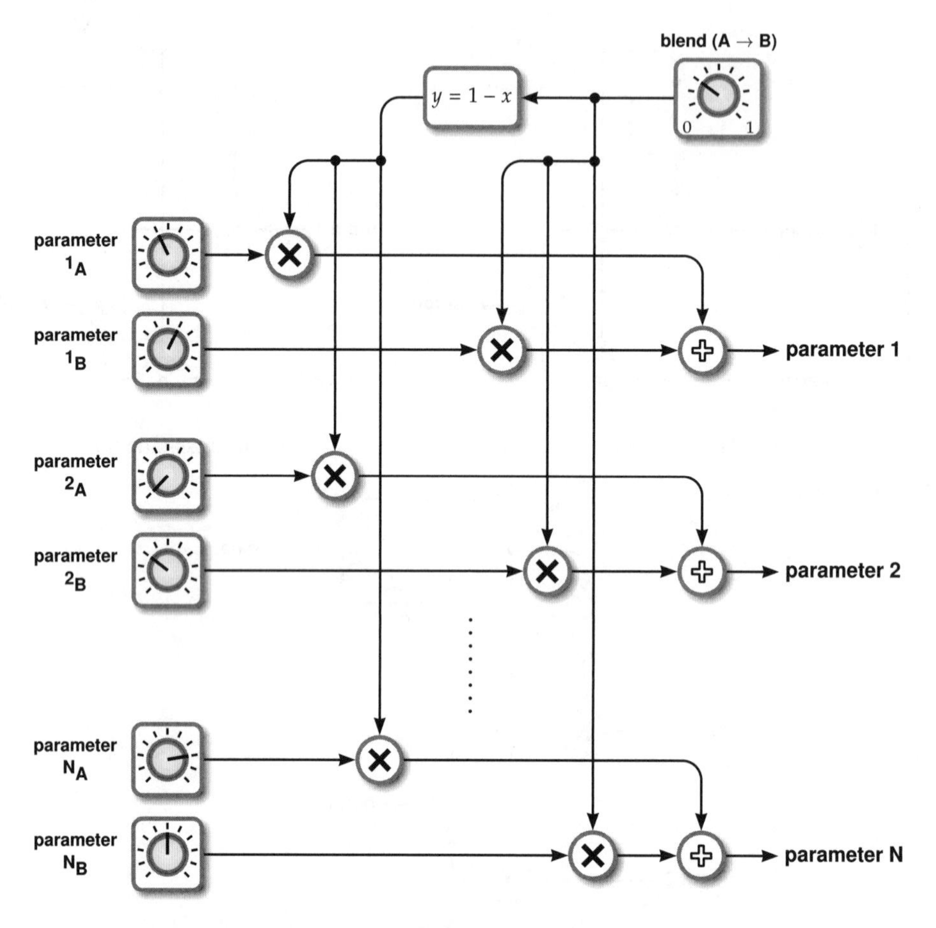

Figure 5.52 Blending between parameter values

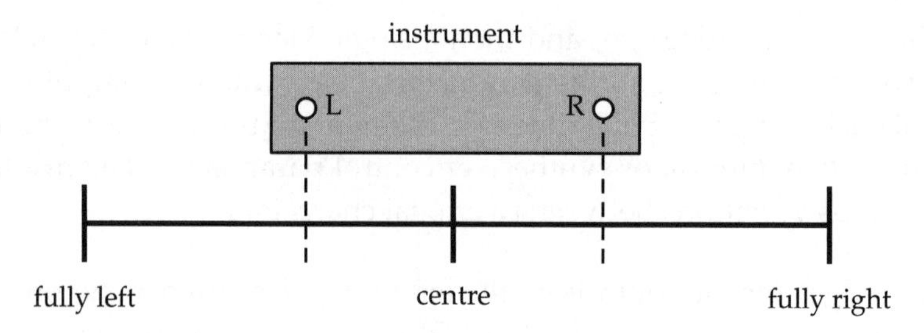

Figure 5.53 Controlling stereo width for an instrument

can sometimes be more efficient than a wet/wet blend between modifiers (figure 5.51a) as it is not necessary to duplicate the process elements (such as filters, oscillators, and so on) in two paths, and parameter values are usually calculated at a lower rate than audio samples. However, if the two modifiers in the wet/wet mix are quite different in terms of type or quantity of process elements, then the parameter blend is not as appropriate.

Instruments are often recorded in stereo, such as a pair of microphones above a drum kit. When creating a stereo output mix the channels must be suitably positioned in the soundfield to achieve the desired image. This is often achieved by panning one channel to the left and another to the right. It often produces an unnaturally wide image if the panning is too far to the extremes. Figure 5.53 shows how the two channels of an instrument recording might be positioned over a more limited width. After panning the two signals, the results are then summed as shown previously in figure 5.36 (p.125).

Rather than having separate controls to pan left and right signals, it is possible to use a single parameter to control *stereo width* as shown in figure 5.54. Both outputs are a mono mix of the two inputs when the width parameter is 0. As the value is increased, the image widens until (when it is 1) the outputs are the same as the inputs. The process is mathematically equivalent to a pair of summed linear pan processes and is mono compatible.

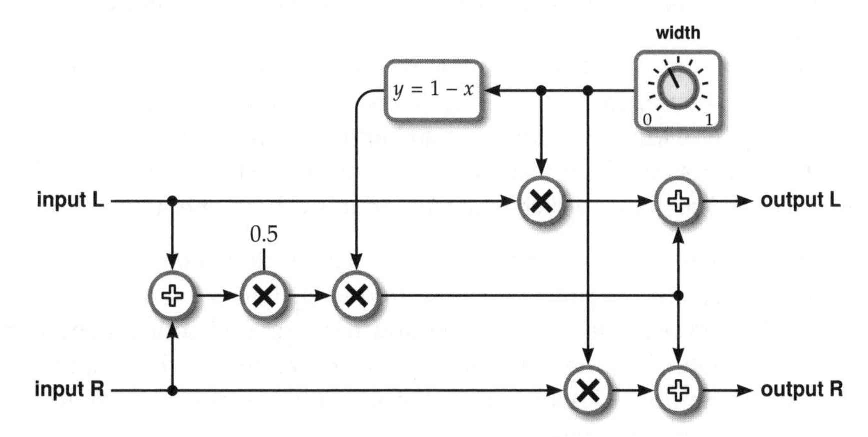

Figure 5.54 Stereo width control

5.7 Developing Processes and Learning More

Techniques such as switching, splitting, amplitude control, mixing, and series and parallel combination are part of many audio processes. The forms in this chapter are found as core elements within a mixing console. Learning about the structure and signal flows within a hardware mixing console is a good way of appreciating the use of the process elements for managing and combining multiple signal paths. Owner's manuals often

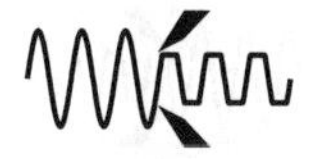

include a graphical summary of the entire system as a block diagram that allows the recording engineer to understand the routing and modification at a glance. One limitation of such diagrams is that they can be rather vague in terms of the underlying processes; for example, summation of signals might be represented as a simple joining of lines, and polarity/phase reverse as a block marked ϕ. It is also difficult to graphically represent more complex options such as multichannel techniques (like the use of solo buttons).

One interesting characteristic of mixing consoles and DAWs is the inconsistency between manufacturers in terms of control ranges and mapping; for example, different spacing of decibel values along gain controls, and different non-linear pan mapping laws. In software it is sometimes possible to switch the behaviour to different modes. There are a wide range of opinions on how best to control the processes for best effect.

The processes in this chapter are developed from an understanding of how the human auditory system interprets sound; for example, perception of sound level relates to the use of non-linear gain control, and how humans localise sound relates to the design of pan processes. Information on these topics, and the principles and operation of mixing consoles can be found in the following book:

> Rumsey, Francis, and Tim McCormick. 2014. *Sound and Recording: Applications and Theory (Seventh Edition)*. Burlington, MA: Focal Press.

It is possible to have more than two channels in the output, such as different surround sound formats; for example, controlling six channels from a single gain control is very similar to controlling two. Mixing multiple four channel inputs onto a four channel output bus is also just an extension of the technique seen before. More complex is the idea of multichannel surround panning, which is discussed in the book mentioned above.

The forms in this chapter are the foundation for processes that achieve more substantial modifications to sounds; for example, changing frequency balance with filters (discussed in Chapter 6), distortion (Chapter 7), delayed and reverberated sound (Chapters 8 and 10), periodic modulations (Chapter 9), noise gates and compressors (Chapter 11), and frequency domain techniques (Chapter 12). Modification techniques are also used extensively when creating synthesizers.

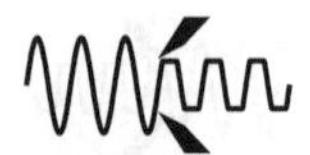

6

Filtering

6.1 Introduction

6.1.1 Filters and Audio Processes

Filters are used in a wide range of audio processes to shape spectral envelopes. At the simplest level, filters are characterised by the amount of attenuation that they apply at particular frequencies. This enables a signal path to relate primarily to a restricted band (or bands) of frequencies. This is useful for tonal shaping because changing gain makes it possible to emphasise or deemphasise particular frequency ranges. It is also useful to isolate a range such that the signal reaching a subsequent process block is targeted on a certain area of the frequency spectrum.

Using filters to change the amplitude of ranges of frequency partials has quite a clear relationship to perceived tonality. Changes in the frequency domain necessarily also change how a signal varies in the time domain. The particular filter design used will determine how control variations relate to the results in both domains, which can sometimes have unexpected consequences (as described in §6.4, p.164).

The range of possibilities for filter designs in terms of their frequency and time effects is very wide. However, audio filtering is often achieved through the combination of a relatively small number of standard filtering styles. This chapter covers the fundamental filter techniques and designs necessary to support the other processes described in this book.

6.1.2 Filtering and Acoustic Sound Sources

The physical shape of an acoustic instrument and the materials used in its construction clearly have a strong influence on the end result. If the body of a drum is made of plastic it sounds different to one made of wood. Similarly, making a violin body much larger changes its tonality. Such features relate to filtering; they change the time and frequency character of the sound source in a particular way. This filtering is of interest in synthesis in terms of recreating particular instrument characteristics. It is also possible to imagine changing or hybridising instruments electronically, such as changing the filtering of a guitar synthesizer such that it sounds more like a mandolin, or a more radical change to the body to have similarities to a drum.

The spectral envelope of a sound relates to the regions of frequency emphasis that result from the nature of the sound-producing object. A clear example of this is the human voice, as discussed in §17.3 (p.509). However the spectral envelope is apparent in the frequency domain plots of many instruments, as shown in Chapter 4. The resonant peaks within the spectral envelope can be related to a filtering operation in synthesis, in terms of having particular centre frequency, amplitude, and bandwidth.

An example of spectral envelope modification is found in the use of brass instrument mutes, which fit in (or on) the bell of the instrument. They change the spectral balance, and can achieve a range of effects depending upon their shape and materials. Sometimes the mute position can be altered during playing to add dynamic control over the effect on frequency and amplitude. Figure 6.1 illustrates average spectrum plots of three trumpet sounds that have been played in the same manner, but with different muting. When a mute is applied it significantly alters the spectral envelope shape (indicated by the dashed line) compared to the sound without a mute. It is also apparent that the two mutes have quite different effects on the spectrum. The results are such that, without prior experience, a listener might suppose that they were different brass instruments, as opposed to being the same instrument modified in different ways.

6.1.3 Musical Frequency Ranges

It is common to divide the range of frequencies that are audible to humans into smaller regions for purposes of description or user control. A typical set of classifications is low frequencies (LF, or bass), mid-range frequencies (MF), and high frequencies (HF, or treble). Regions of frequency associated with those words are only approximate, due to the subjective nature of description. There is nothing in the human auditory system that creates a fixed boundary that determines when a frequency is too high to be classified as bass, for example.

Table 6.1 indicates some example frequency ranges for filter controls split into four sections that might be found in equaliser (EQ) software or on analogue mixing consoles. The ranges overlap and can vary considerably between different commercial systems, but they give a general idea of the relationship between the names and frequencies. Many digital filters on commercial equipment have no restrictions on frequency parameters, such that they can be varied to any frequency that is appropriate for a particular application or musical situation. It is convenient for users, however, if the frequencies for, say, a mixer EQ are in useful default positions when the system is reset (such as those shown in the f_{typical} column in the table).

Name	f_{min} (Hz)	f_{max} (Hz)	f_{typical} (Hz)
LF (low)	20	500	100
LMF (low-mid)	100	1500	500
HMF (high-mid)	500	8000	2500
HF (high)	1500	20000	10000

Table 6.1 Example frequency ranges for filter controls

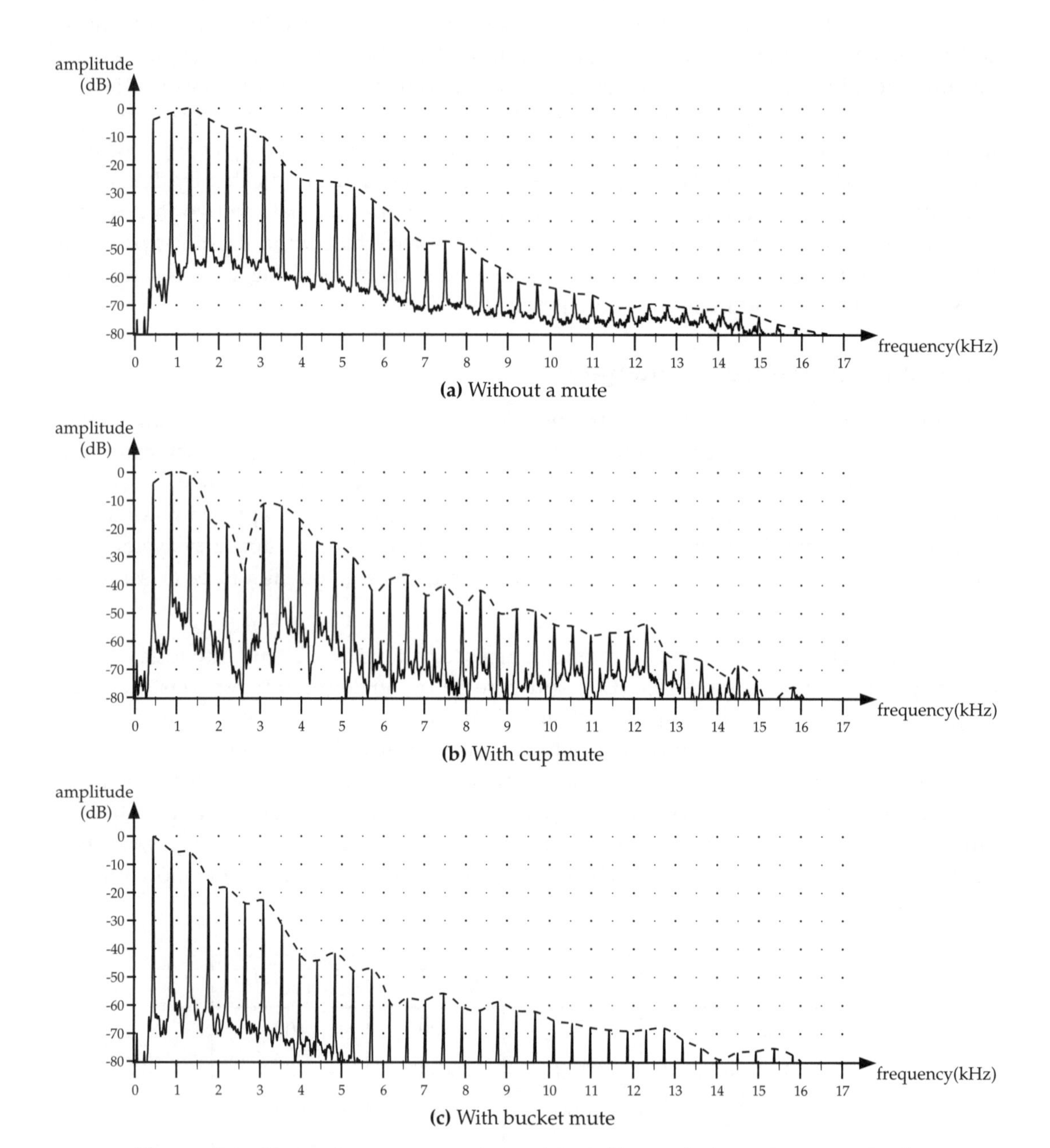

Figure 6.1 Trumpet average spectrum plots (with spectral envelopes marked)

It is important to remember that humans perceive frequency on a logarithmic scale, as described in §2.1.2 (p.19). Figure 6.2 shows that typical control ranges are therefore chosen to be reasonably evenly spread across the frequency range when the axis is logarithmic. This also implies that control relates to a widening numerical range higher up the frequency scale; for example, table 6.1 suggests a control range of 480Hz for LF but 18.5kHz for HF. Similarly filter parameter values are not usually linearly controlled, which is discussed in more detail in §24.1.1 (p.656).

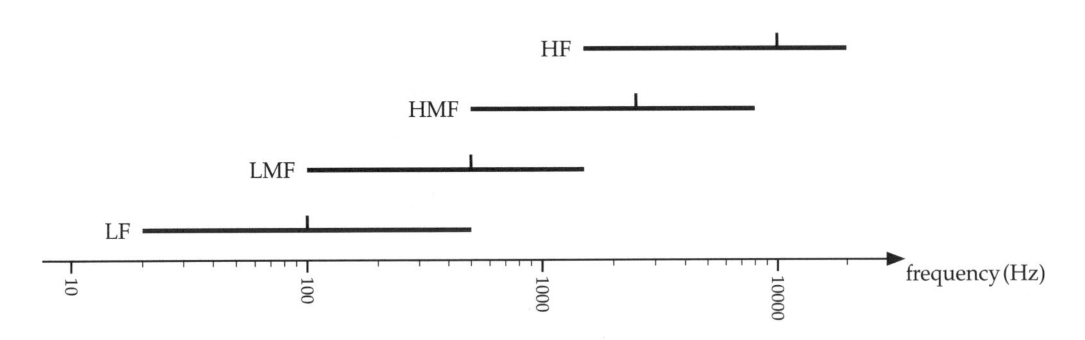

Figure 6.2 Example frequency ranges for filter controls (from table 6.1, typical frequencies marked)

6.1.4 Frequency (Magnitude) Responses

The most important characteristic of a filter is the frequency (magnitude) response (often just called the *frequency response*), which indicates the gain applied at different frequencies. As a very simple example, consider figure 6.3a, which is the linear amplifier first seen in §5.3.1 (p.105). Every input sample is treated the same as every other (output = gain × input), so **all** partials will be attenuated by the same amount whatever their frequencies.

In figure 6.3a, the control is set to a value of 0.5, so the frequency response in figure 6.3b shows a gain value of 0.5 at all frequencies. It is more usual to express gain in terms of decibels in frequency response plots, as in figure 6.3c. Some important values for linear gain converted into decibels (using equation 5.2, p.113) are described in table 6.2. The half-power gain value (≈ -3dB) is often used to indicate the boundary between significant, and less significant, gain regions.

Figure 6.4a illustrates a frequency response where there is increasing attenuation at frequencies above 500Hz. The gain is 0dB at 500Hz and below, −6.02dB at 1kHz, and −12.04dB at 2kHz. When plotting the linear gain version of the frequency response (figure 6.4b), those key values are converted as described in table 6.2. Note that a linear gain change on a decibel scale is curved on a linear scale.

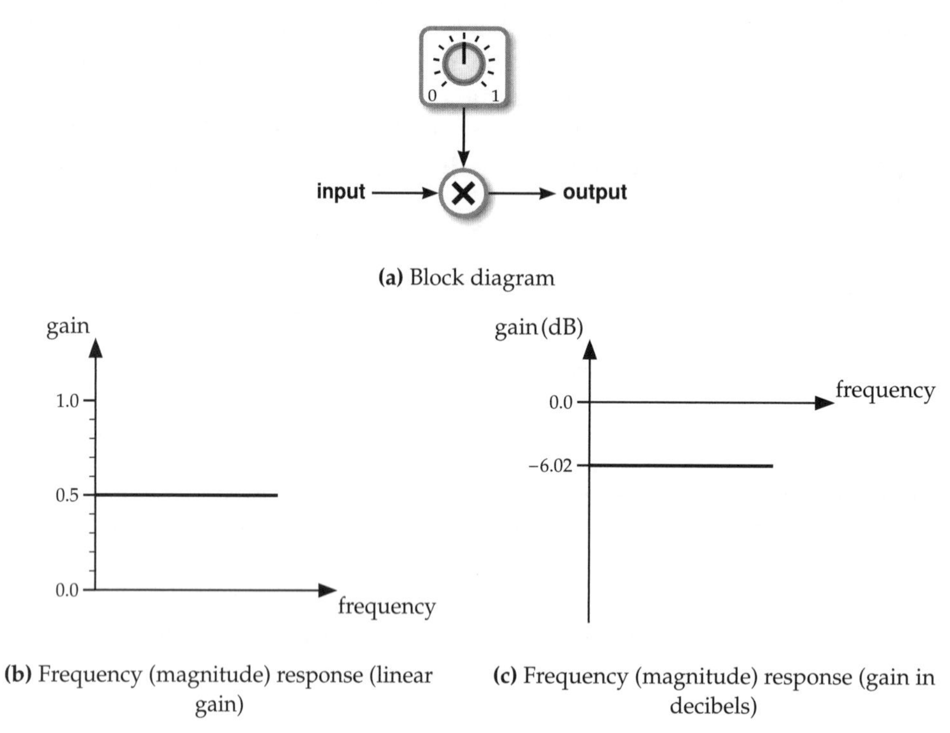

(a) Block diagram

(b) Frequency (magnitude) response (linear gain)

(c) Frequency (magnitude) response (gain in decibels)

Figure 6.3 Linear amplifier

Most sounds consist of multiple frequency partials. When these pass through a filter, different frequencies will have different gain applied, as described by the frequency response. Therefore a filter is likely to change the amplitude balance of frequency partials and so the overall tonality. Figure 6.5 illustrates the effect of passing a sound with three partials with equal amplitude through a filter with the frequency response shown in figure 6.4. In the frequency domain the amplitude of the partials are multiplied by the linear gain values that correspond to their frequencies. In the example the linear gain values are 1 at 250Hz, 0.5 at 1kHz and 0.25 at 2kHz. In the time domain plots it is also apparent that the higher frequency partials have been attenuated.

In figure 6.5 the effect is fairly clear, as the output partial amplitudes follow the shape of the frequency response (with linear axes). However, in most circumstances partials do not have equal amplitude at the input to the filter. Figure 6.6 illustrates the effect of passing a sound with unequal partial amplitudes through a filter with the frequency response shown in figure 6.4. The principles are the same as the simpler example, in that linear gain values of 1, 0.5 and 0.25 are multiplied by the corresponding input amplitudes at frequencies 250Hz, 1kHz, and 2kHz.

	gain	gain (dB)
Unity gain	1	0
Half-power gain	$\sqrt{0.5} \approx 0.707$	−3.01
Half-amplitude gain	0.5	−6.02
Quarter-amplitude gain	0.25	−12.04
Zero gain	0	$-\infty$

Table 6.2 Important gain values

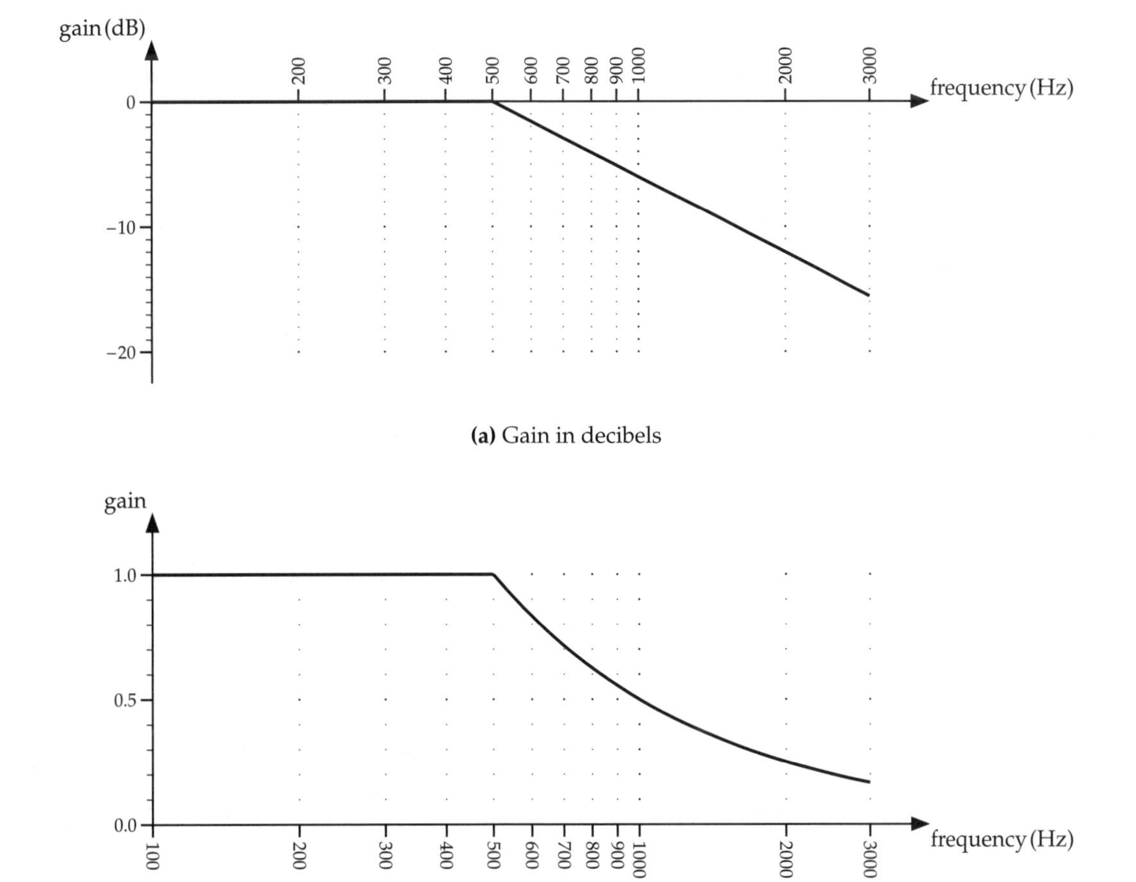

(a) Gain in decibels

(b) Linear gain

Figure 6.4 Example filter frequency (magnitude) response

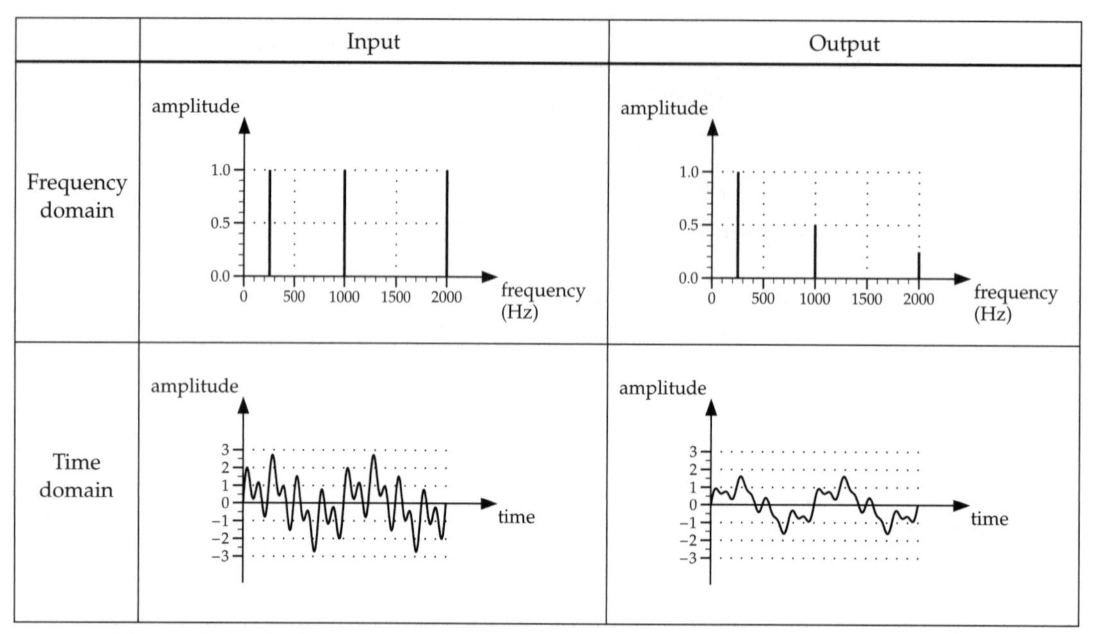

Figure 6.5 Application of example filter to three partials with equal amplitude

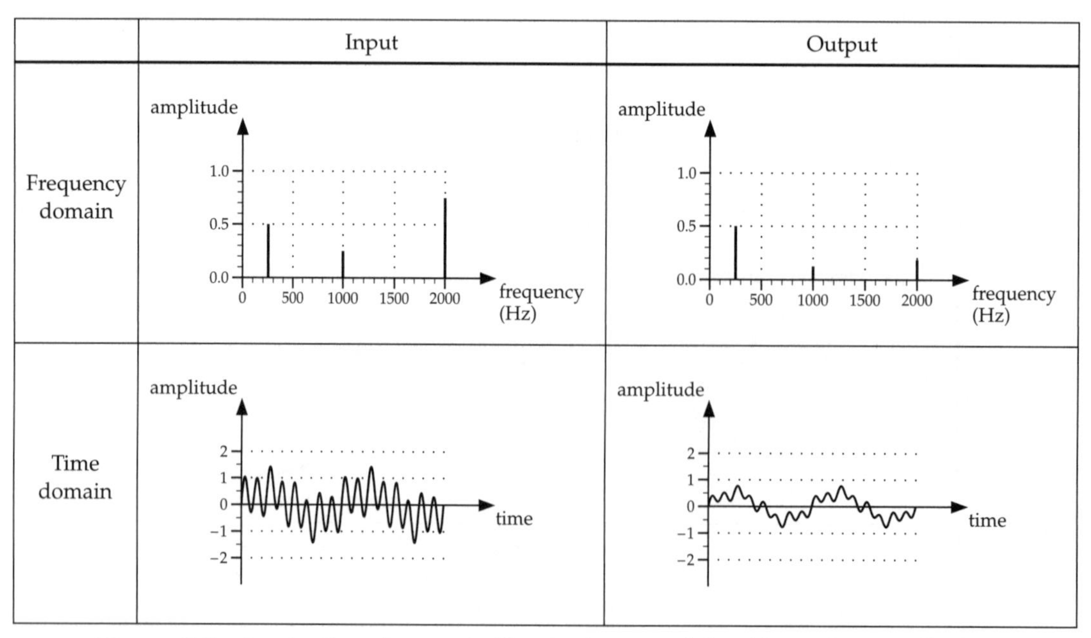

Figure 6.6 Application of example filter to three partials with varying amplitudes

Figure 6.7 illustrates what happens when a more complex pattern of partials is passed through a filter with the frequency response shown in figure 6.4. Note that the application of the filter does not replace the spectral envelope of the input with the frequency response, but rather the two are combined such that some of the input envelope variations are visible in the output.

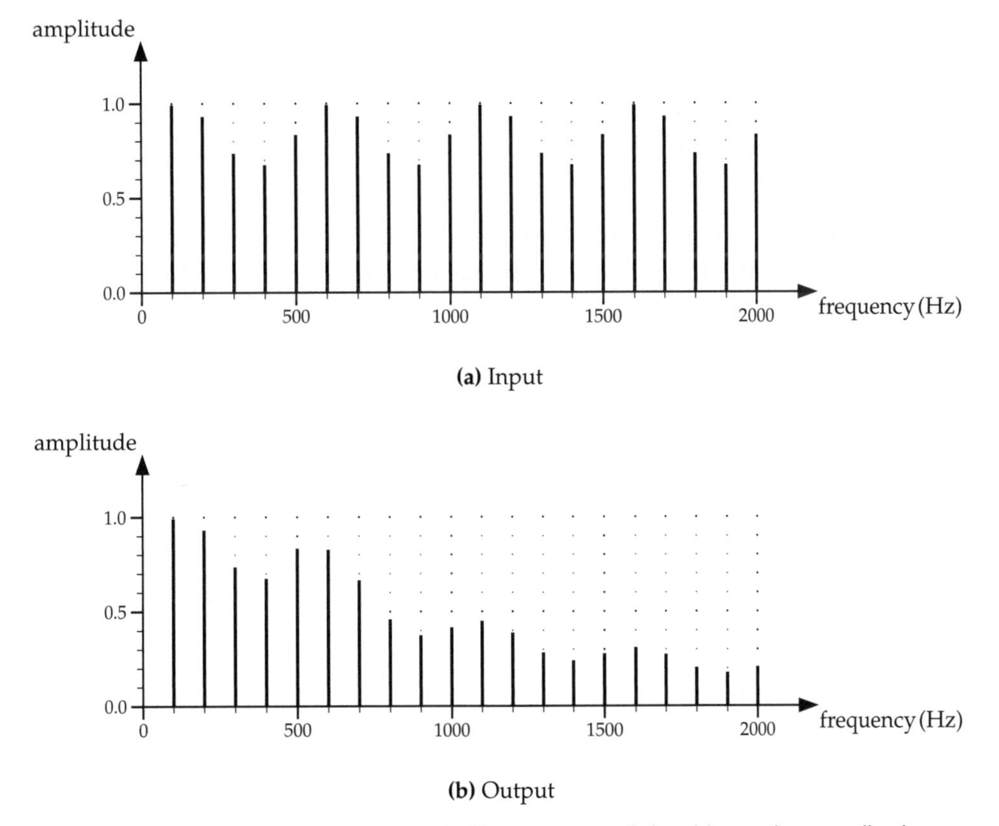

(a) Input

(b) Output

Figure 6.7 Application of example filter to 20 partials with varying amplitudes

As can be seen from the examples above, a simple filter will affect partials by attenuating their amplitudes by different amounts. However, that process does not create new partials. Therefore if a partial is not present in the input, it is not present in the output. The tonal effects of a filter are due to the differences in response at different frequencies causing a rebalancing of the amplitude of partials. Note that if the input is a single sinusoidal partial, then the output is also a single sinusoidal partial (with potentially a change in amplitude), which means that the result has the same tonality.

6.2 Standard Filters

Four types of filter (lowpass, highpass, bandpass, and bandreject) are sufficient for the majority of tasks within audio processes. The following text describes the fundamental characteristics that define those types. Two more specialised filters are also introduced (comb and allpass).

6.2.1 Lowpass and Highpass Filters

The purpose of a *lowpass filter* (LPF) is to allow low frequency partials to pass through with minimal change in amplitude, but to progressively attenuate higher frequency partials. The *cutoff frequency* separates the two regions. This is also known as the corner, breakpoint, break, half-power, or turnover frequency.

A typical lowpass filter frequency response is shown in figure 6.8. Remember from previously that 0dB is a linear gain of 1 (i.e. no change in amplitude). The cutoff frequency (f_c) corresponds to a point where the curve reaches −3dB down from the unity gain level. The *passband* is the region of maximum gain (least attenuation) that has a frequency range or *bandwidth* of f_c Hz. If the cutoff frequency is controllable manually by a user, then a non-linear mapping is appropriate to reflect the nature of human hearing. This is discussed further in §24.1.1 (p.656).

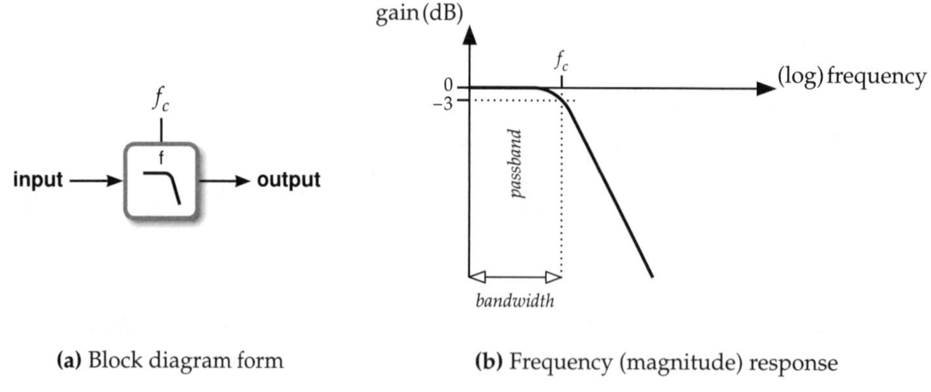

(a) Block diagram form

(b) Frequency (magnitude) response

Figure 6.8 Lowpass filter

It might be imagined that the frequency response of a lowpass filter should have 0dB gain throughout the passband, and $-\infty$ dB gain outside (sometimes called a *brickwall* response). In practice, a filter used in an audio process is often employed to modify the sound in a moderately subtle manner, rather than to completely remove frequency partials outside of the passband. The result is that the transitions between high and low gain regions in audio filter responses are usually quite progressive. There is a curve through the region of the cutoff frequency, meaning that some attenuation occurs within the passband.

A *highpass filter* (HPF) has a complementary effect to a lowpass filter. It allows high frequency partials to pass through with minimal change in amplitude, but progressively attenuates lower frequencies (figure 6.9). Once again the cutoff frequency (f_c) separates the two regions of the response. The passband continues to the upper frequency limit of the system.

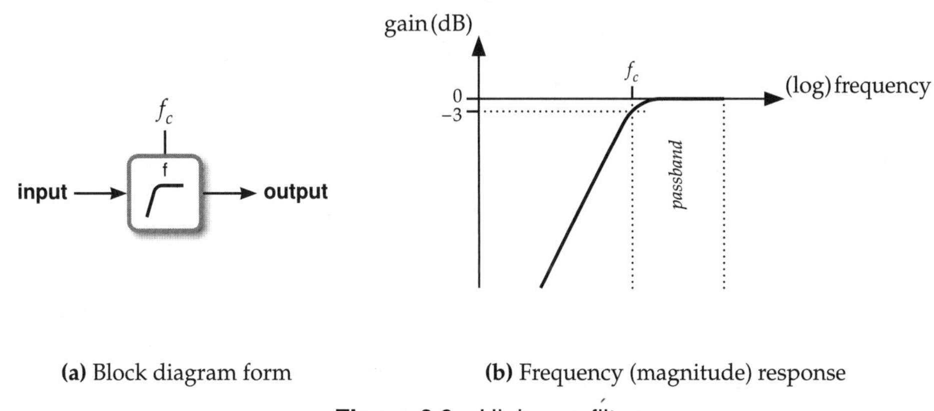

(a) Block diagram form **(b)** Frequency (magnitude) response

Figure 6.9 Highpass filter

6.2.2 Bandpass and Bandreject Filters

A *bandpass filter* (BPF) has a passband around a *centre frequency* (f_c) with a bandwidth as illustrated in figure 6.10. Outside the passband there is progressive attenuation towards lower and higher frequencies. Sometimes the bandwidth is specified directly (in hertz). However, with many audio filters the bandwidth is specified indirectly through a parameter called Q, as shown on the block diagram form. The filter parameters are related as follows, where f_{bw} is the bandwidth:

$$Q = \frac{f_c}{f_{\text{bw}}} \qquad \boxed{6.1}$$

Rearranging the previous equation:

$$f_{\text{bw}} = \frac{f_c}{Q} \qquad \boxed{6.2}$$

This means that if a constant value is specified for Q then the bandwidth will increase proportionally with the centre frequency. This suits the nature of the human auditory system, where frequency is perceived on a logarithmic scale (as described in §6.1.3, p.141). Figure 6.11 illustrates this effect in graphical form. If bandwidth is constant, then increasing centre frequency produces a bandpass effect that has a decreasing size on the logarithmic

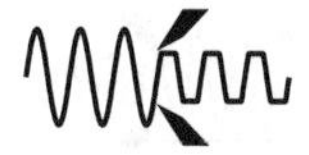

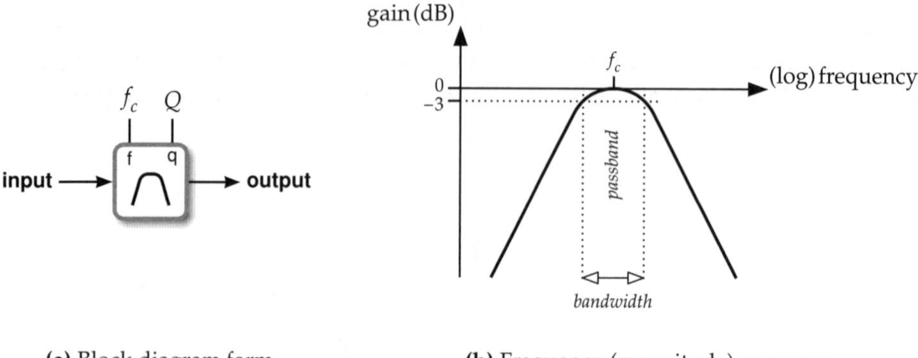

(a) Block diagram form **(b)** Frequency (magnitude) response

Figure 6.10 Bandpass filter

frequency scale. However, with a constant Q the bandwidth is automatically adjusted. In terms of user control, this means that the centre frequency can be changed without having to simultaneously worry about changing the bandwidth to maintain consistency of result.

Note that equation 6.2 can lead to some confusion as f_{bw} is inversely proportional to Q. That is, increasing Q produces a decreasing bandwidth for a fixed value of centre frequency. Increasing Q can be equated to an increasing "peakiness" of the frequency response. For example, if Q is 1, then the bandwidth is the same value as the centre frequency (from equation 6.2). If Q is 2, then the bandwidth is half the centre frequency.

It is sometimes useful to be able to specify the passband width of a bandpass filter in terms of octaves. This can be achieved by setting the Q using the following equation, where "oct" is the number of octaves that the passband should cover:

$$Q = \frac{2^{\text{oct}/2}}{2^{\text{oct}} - 1} \tag{6.3}$$

For example, 1 octave corresponds to a Q of $\sqrt{2}$ (≈ 1.414), and 2 octaves corresponds to $\frac{2}{3}$ (≈ 0.667).

A *bandreject filter* (BRF, also known as a notch filter or bandstop filter, BSF) attenuates frequency partials in a particular band around a centre frequency (figure 6.12). It therefore has some properties that are the reverse of the bandpass filter. It has two passbands (either side of the attenuated bandwidth), rather than a passband around the centre frequency (as with a bandpass filter). More process examples in this book use a bandpass than a bandreject filter. A bandreject filter is often used in a more subtle way, such as attenuating a particular narrow range of frequency partials.

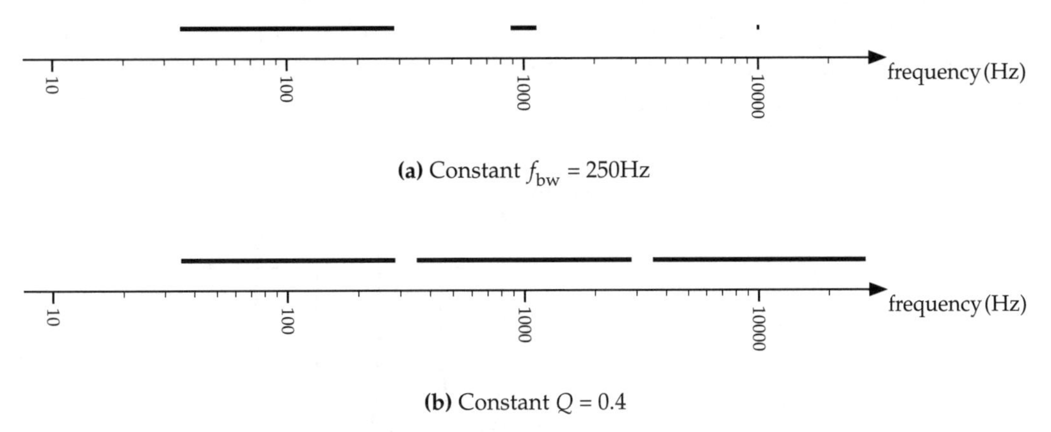

(a) Constant f_{bw} = 250Hz

(b) Constant Q = 0.4

Figure 6.11 Filter passband extents for constant bandwidth and constant Q (f_c = 100Hz, 1kHz, 10kHz)

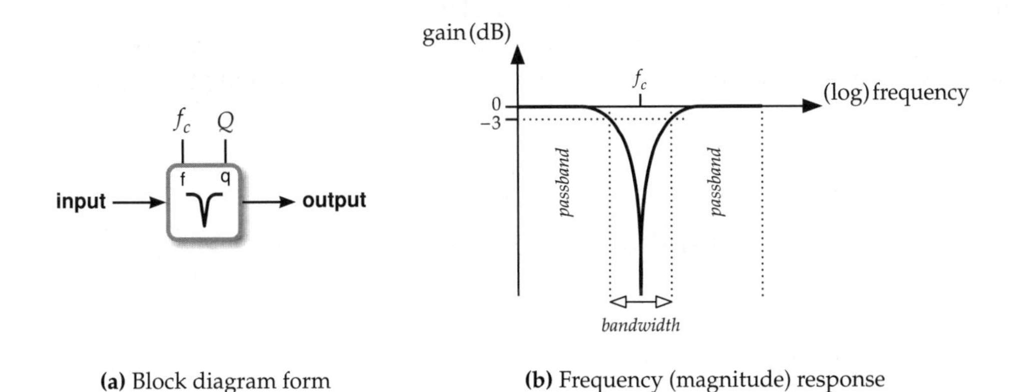

(a) Block diagram form

(b) Frequency (magnitude) response

Figure 6.12 Bandreject filter

6.2.3 Comb and Allpass Filters

A *comb filter* has multiple passbands spaced at integer multiples of a fundamental frequency (f_c). In figure 6.13 the passbands have a small bandwidth, but that characteristic depends on the nature of the underlying design as described in §6.4.4 (p.183). The spacing of the passbands relates naturally to harmonic forms, which is a property that can be used in subtractive synthesis (Chapter 17).

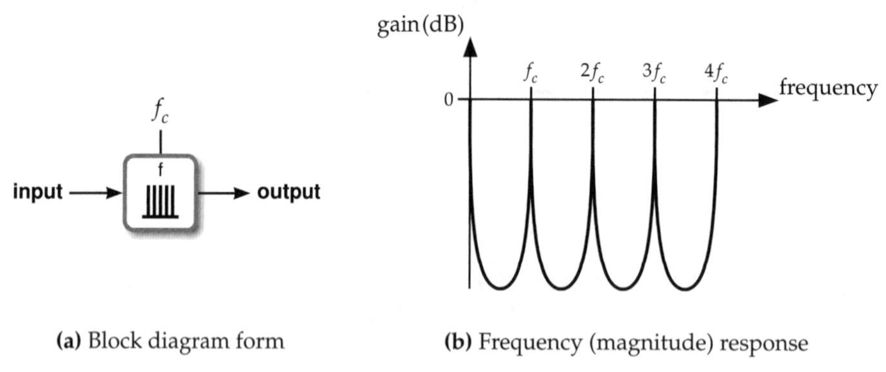

(a) Block diagram form **(b)** Frequency (magnitude) response

Figure 6.13 Comb filter

An *allpass filter* has a response (figure 6.14) where all frequencies are subject to the same amplitude gain. This would initially appear to have no benefit, but the allpass filter produces a modification in terms of delaying different frequencies by different amounts, and so an effect in the time domain on phase. This specialised behaviour is used in such applications as phasers (described in §9.2.4, p.279) and in creating inharmonicity in a waveguide physical model synthesizer (§21.2.4, p.592). It is represented in block diagrams in one of two ways depending on how it is configured, as explained in §6.4.4 (p.183).

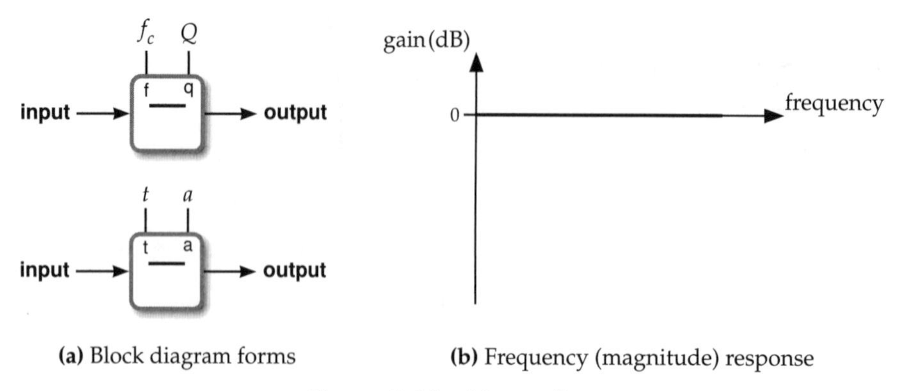

(a) Block diagram forms **(b)** Frequency (magnitude) response

Figure 6.14 Allpass filter

6.2.4 Variations in Filter Responses

In practical situations filters display variations in response from the basic patterns detailed so far. There are a wide range of possible filter designs. This means that two filters of the same general type (such as a lowpass form, for example) might produce an audibly different result when used in the same situation with the same control parameter values. Selection of an appropriate filter design is influenced by a number of factors:

- A particular application or audio programming library is likely to be supplied with a limited selection of filters. Designing and implementing new filters is not simple, so the output of many audio processes will be tonally influenced by the range of filters that are available as standard.
- Different designs require different amounts of computation, sometimes radically so. If an audio process has many hundreds or thousands of filters then it might not be practical to use a filter design that is computationally-intensive, even if it has more desirable sonic characteristics.
- A filter might be selected for its particular behaviour or configuration capabilities, such as its resonance or roll-off (discussed below). The tonal characteristics of a particular filter might be hard to define in scientific terms. For example, the filters of a particular analogue synthesizer might be appreciated for the way in which the sonic character of the sound is modified to appear more "warm" or "fat".

The gradient of a filter frequency response function outside the passband is known as the *roll-off*. This is specified in terms of both logarithmic gain variation (in decibels) and logarithmic frequency (in octaves). For example, a decrease in gain of 6dB when a frequency doubles is a roll-off of *6dB per octave*. Figure 6.15 shows an example lowpass filter frequency response with a 12dB per octave roll-off that is apparent for each octave increase between 1kHz, 2kHz, 4kHz, and 8kHz. In practical situations a roll-off is not perfectly consistent over the entirety of a function outside the passband, but rather is the tendency of the slope.

Filters used in audio often have a roll-off that tends towards 6dB, 12dB, 18dB, or 24dB per octave. It might be imagined that a very high roll-off (say 60dB per octave) would always be used in preference to a lower value. However, the choice of roll-off depends on context. For EQ purposes a very high roll-off might produce an inappropriately obvious transition between the passband and other frequencies, or unintended audible artefacts (such as those due to phase changes). A high roll-off might be chosen in a synthesis context to aggressively modify the sound character, however.

The *order* of the filter relates to its internal construction, as described in §6.4 (p.164). Filters can be described as first order, second order, third order, and so on. Increasing order is often related to increasing roll-off. For a lowpass design, a first order filter is

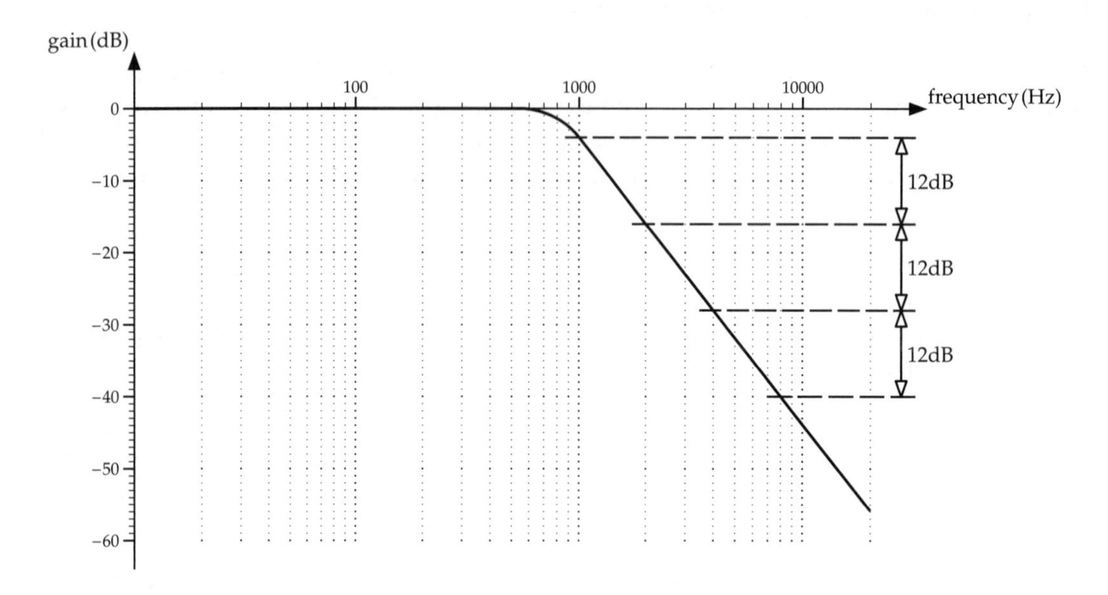

Figure 6.15 Example LPF frequency (magnitude) response with 12dB per octave roll-off

normally associated with a 6dB per octave roll-off, and a second order with 12dB per octave. Sometimes filters are cascaded in series to achieve a greater roll-off (see §6.3.1, p.155)

As well as variations in roll-off, there can be other variations in frequency response. The standard filters described so far are characterised by attenuation outside the passband. Sometimes it is more useful to have a filter which can boost (amplify) in a particular region, rather than attenuate outside that region. A *peaking filter* is a type of bandpass filter where the passband gain can be varied to achieve symmetric boost or cut, and the gain is 0dB at low and high frequencies (no attenuation). See figure 6.53 (p.183) for some example frequency responses. This style is useful in equaliser (EQ) processes. A similar scheme for lowpass or highpass cases is called a *shelving filter*.

The discussion of filters so far has focused mainly on the frequency domain effects, but these are inseparable from those in the time domain. In the simplest sense, a filter will change the shape of a waveform (as illustrated in figure 6.5, p.146). But filters can also cause significant phase changes and delays that vary with frequency, and *resonant* (ringing) behaviour (described in §6.4, p.164). Of particular interest in subtractive synthesis techniques (Chapter 17) is the use of resonant filter designs that can be configured with a high Q value leading to a high gain peak at f_c and an output that resonates at that frequency considerably beyond the point at which the input has stopped. This behaviour has some similarity to resonance in acoustic instruments.

6.3 Filter Combinations

It is sometimes possible to select a filter from a standard library that has the desired characteristics for a particular process. However, in many cases the required filtering is not as simple as that achieved with a single filter. In some circumstances it is appropriate to implement a filter design from scratch to achieve the required result (some of which are described in §6.4, p.164). However, it can often be quicker to combine standard filters to achieve a frequency response that suits the situation.

6.3.1 Common Series and Parallel Forms

Figure 6.16 illustrates a simple series arrangement of two lowpass filters. They share a common cutoff frequency value, such that the amount of attenuation at particular frequencies is the same for both filters (if they are of the same internal design). The attenuation achieved by the first filter is increased by the second stage, causing a more rapid roll-off (as shown in figure 6.17). Using series filter stages configured with the same parameters can be useful for producing a more severe effect than is achieved by a single filter.

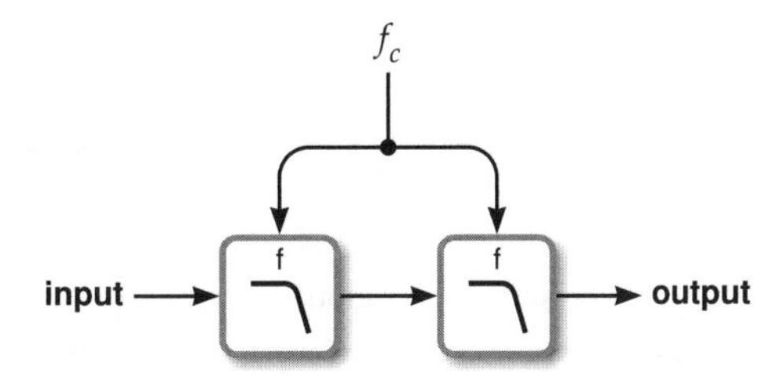

Figure 6.16 Series lowpass filters (same cutoff frequency)

It is not necessarily the case that the series form has the same effect as a single filter that has been designed with a higher roll-off. Firstly, figure 6.17 shows that the attenuation at frequency f_c is approximately −6dB at 1kHz for the series combination. A single filter with a higher roll-off is expected typically to have −3dB gain at that frequency. Filters also have associated phase effects (described in §6.4, p.164) that might be different for the two methods.

Series filters can have different configurations rather than needing to be identical, as shown in figure 6.18. The advantage of this is that a more complex reshaping of the frequency response is possible. Figure 6.19 shows the result of two lowpass filters in series with cutoff frequencies of 1kHz and 5kHz. The attenuation is similar to the 1kHz cutoff for lower frequencies, but the 5kHz cutoff filter causes higher attenuation for upper frequencies. The frequencies might be controlled independently (figure 6.18a). Alternatively there might be a multiplier m that links the filters parameters together, as shown in figure

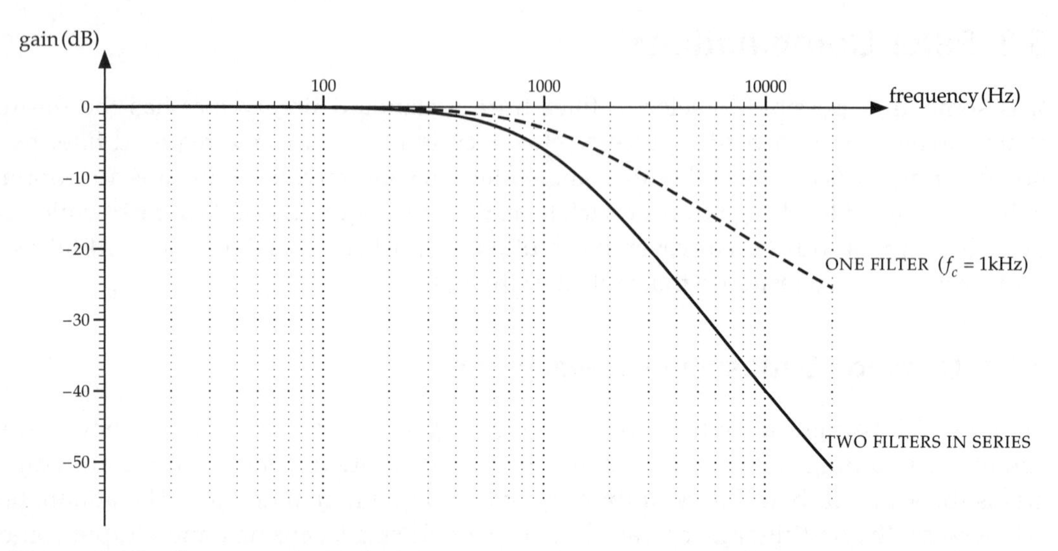

Figure 6.17 Frequency (magnitude) response plots comparing a single one pole lowpass filter with two in series (same cutoff, f_S = 96kHz)

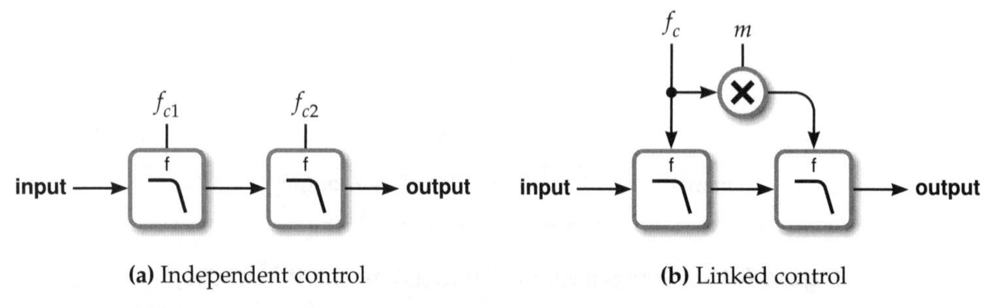

Figure 6.18 Series lowpass filters (different cutoff frequencies)

6.18b, such that it is possible to maintain a constant value for m while changing the value of f_c, and both filters maintain their frequency relationship.

Series combination is not restricted to lowpass filters, nor does it have to be limited to two cascaded filters. The complexity when dealing with series forms is that each stage builds on the result produced by the previous one. For example, if the first filter has heavily attenuated a frequency region, a subsequent filter that has a passband in that region has no significant partial amplitude with which to work.

Figure 6.20 illustrates a parallel bank of bandpass filters, which is a useful tonal shaping tool. Each path adds a region of emphasis to the frequency response whose magnitude can be controlled by a gain value (a_i). This can be viewed as each filter selecting part of

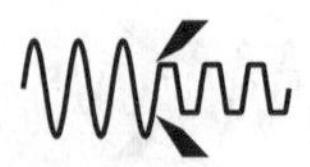

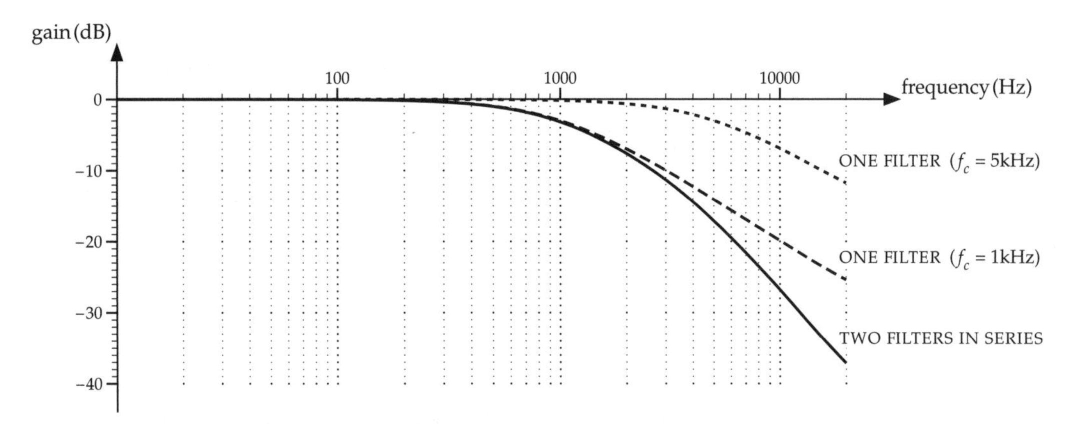

Figure 6.19 Frequency (magnitude) response plots comparing single one pole lowpass filters with two in series (different cutoff, f_S = 96kHz)

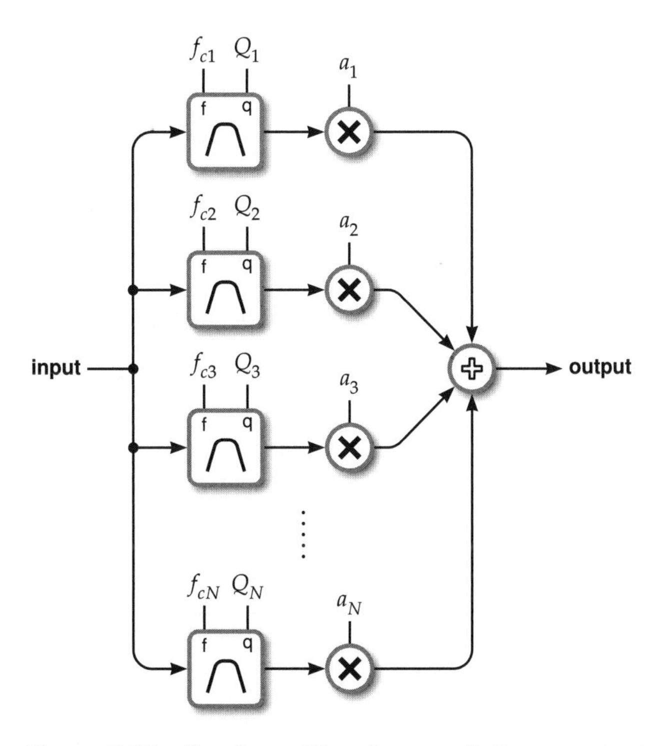

Figure 6.20 Bandpass filters in a parallel arrangement

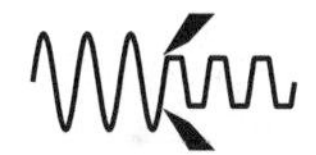

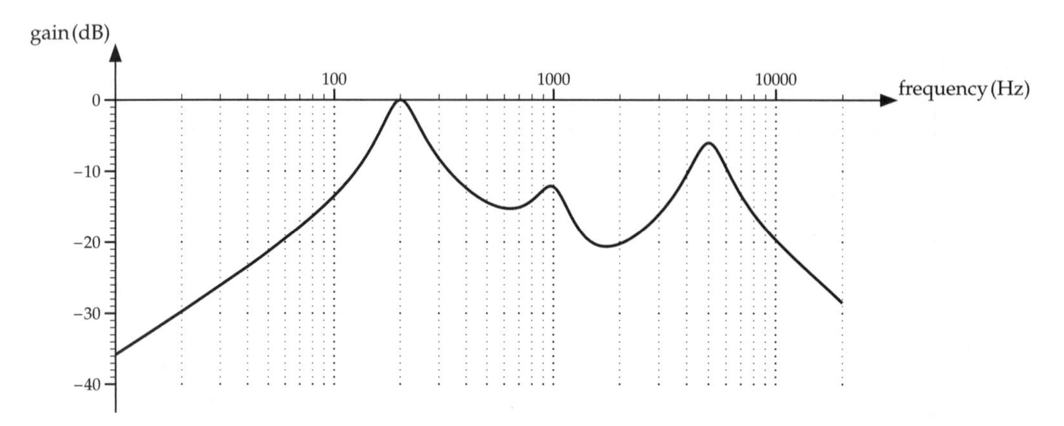

Figure 6.21 Frequency (magnitude) response plot of three parallel second order bandpass filters (f_c = 200Hz / 1kHz / 5kHz, Q = 3, a = 1 / −0.25 / 0.5, f_S = 96kHz)

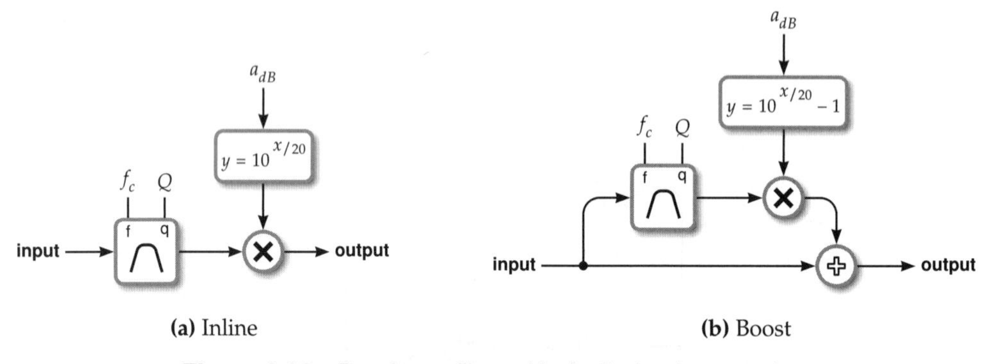

Figure 6.22 Bandpass filter with decibel gain control

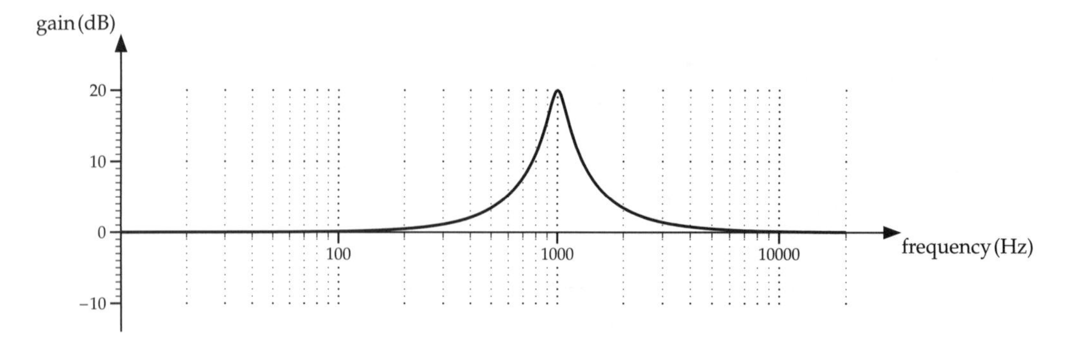

Figure 6.23 Frequency (magnitude) response plot of second order bandpass boost (f_c = 1kHz, Q = 6, a_{dB} = 20, f_S = 96kHz)

the input sound to be summed into the output. The number of filters used depends on how many contributions are required to achieve the desired shape. With a suitable input this might be used to create a spectral envelope similar to those of the muted trumpet in figure 6.1 (p.142). Figure 6.21 shows an example frequency response for a parallel set of three bandpass filters.

Linear gain values are used in figure 6.20 for simplicity. It is often appropriate to provide a gain control in decibels, to reflect the nature of the human auditory system. In that case, a conversion to a linear factor is required, as shown in figure 6.22a. Another possible extension is to link control parameters together such that multiple values can be controlled with a single input and maintaining a particular configuration relationship. An example of this is shown in figure 17.7 (p.509).

An alternative parallel scheme is to use an unfiltered (dry) path as shown in figure 6.22b. Variable a_{dB} is an amplitude gain value in decibels. When a_{dB} is 0 the filter has no effect on the output, and positive values boost the passband of the filter response. The effect is illustrated in figure 6.23. Notice that low and high frequencies have a gain close to 0dB. This is closely related to peaking filters, which allow a cut with a frequency response that is the symmetric complement to the boost. A design for this is described in §6.4.3 (p.180). Attempting a cut effect with the form in figure 6.22b (using negative values of a_{dB}) does not produce a symmetric result.

Several boost processes can be cascaded in series (potentially with different filter types) allowing multiple frequency ranges to be boosted in different ways, while also allowing individual filter effects (or all of them) to be removed entirely by setting a_{dB} values to 0. Figure 6.24 illustrates two cascaded boost processes, one with a lowpass filter and the other with a bandpass filter.

6.3.2 Subtractive Techniques

Figure 6.25 uses a single lowpass filter to create a split lowpass/highpass output. It uses the simple logic that subtracting a lowpass signal from the original input will leave the remainder, which is the rest of the frequency spectrum. One possible use for this form is if a lowpass filter is available but a highpass is not. Figure 6.26 shows an example pair of output frequency responses.

The idea in figure 6.25 can be extended to multiple cascaded sections as shown in figure 6.27. The highpass output from each section itself is split at a higher frequency producing a bandpass and another highpass output. An example result is illustrated in figure 6.28. One use for splitting the frequency range into multiple outputs is to allow each range to be processed in a different way (such as different amounts of distortion) and then mixed to create the final output (sometimes called a *multi-band process*).

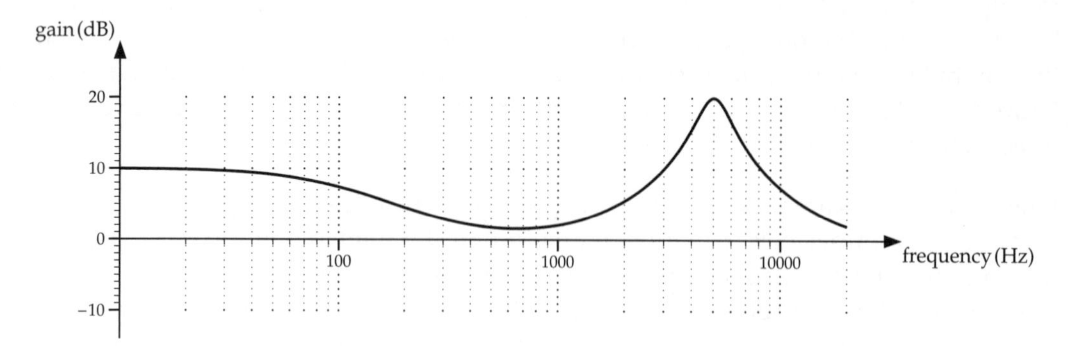

Figure 6.24 Frequency (magnitude) response plot of cascaded first order lowpass and second order bandpass boost (f_c = 100Hz / 5kHz, Q = 3, a_{dB} = 10 / 20, f_S = 96kHz)

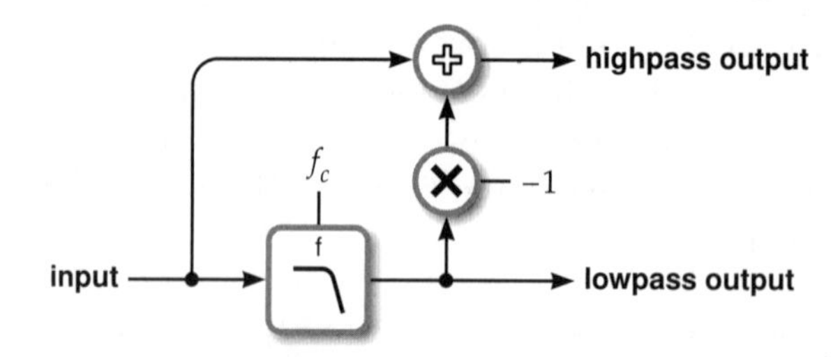

Figure 6.25 Splitting into two frequency bands

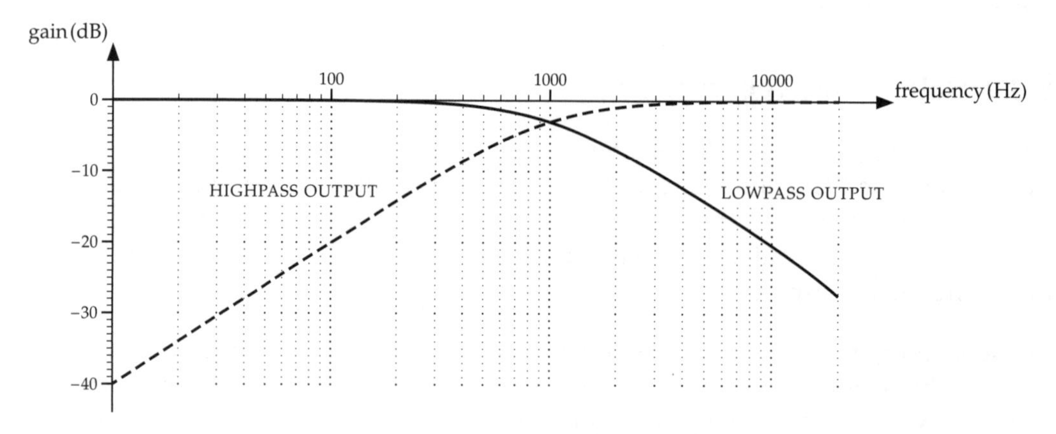

Figure 6.26 Frequency (magnitude) response plots for two band split with first order LPF (f_c = 1kHz, f_S = 96kHz)

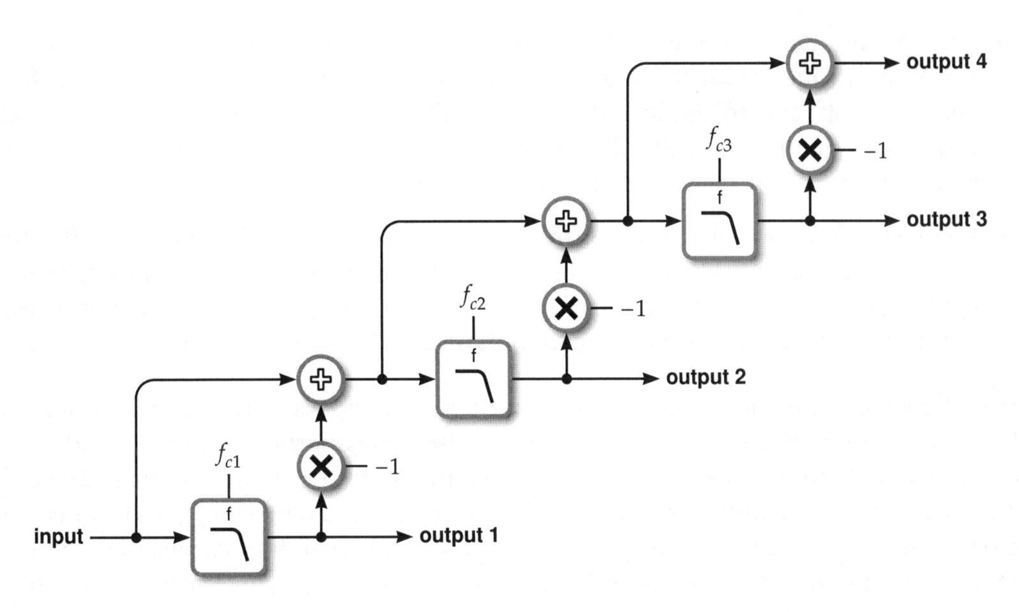

Figure 6.27 Splitting into four frequency bands

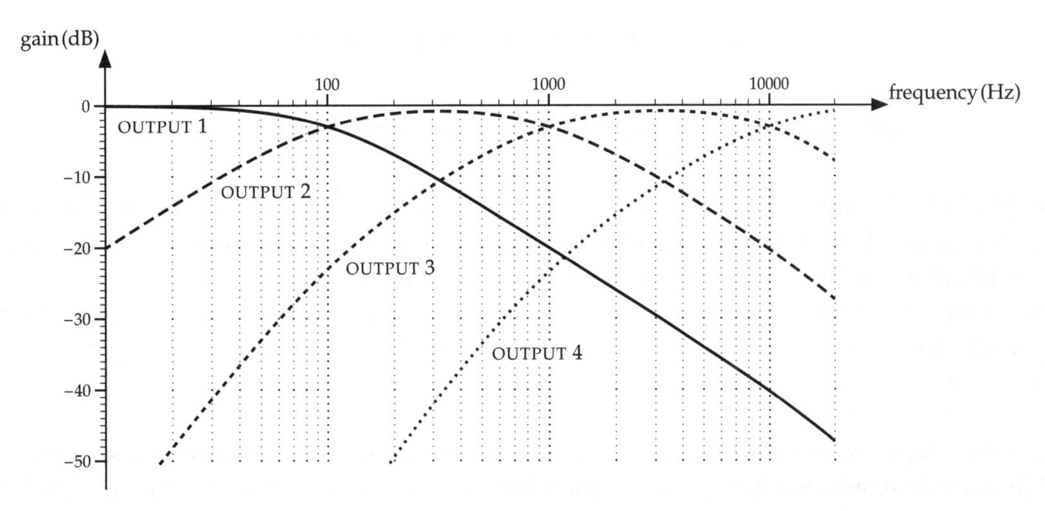

Figure 6.28 Frequency (magnitude) response plots for four band split with first order LPF (f_{c1} = 100Hz, f_{c2} = 1kHz, f_{c3} = 10kHz, f_S = 96kHz)

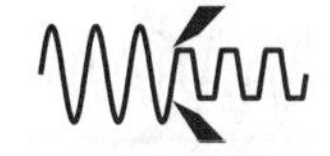

There are some practical issues in using this splitting technique:

- The type of filter chosen will affect the amount of attenuation outside the passband for each output. With the first order filters used for figure 6.28 there is a fairly gentle roll-off, and so significant overlap in the upper gain regions. In many audio processes a gentle filter roll-off is appropriate, but it is worth remembering that the split outputs do not relate to completely separate sets of frequency partials.
- Lowpass filters not only have a frequency response, but also effects in the time domain in terms of delay and phase (as described in §6.4, p.164). This means that the splitting effect (and so the shapes of highpass and bandpass frequency responses) is not necessarily as neat as that shown in figures 6.26 and 6.28 for all filter designs.

Figure 6.29 illustrates how a series combination of lowpass and highpass filters can achieve a bandpass result. The highpass filter attenuates partials below f_{c1} and passes those above that cutoff. The lowpass filter then attenuates frequency partials above f_{c2}, with those below that cutoff being passed. Therefore the band between f_{c1} and f_{c2} becomes the passband. It is necessary that $f_{c2} > f_{c1}$. If $f_{c2} < f_{c1}$ then all the partials passed by the first filter are attenuated by the second, which is not the desired effect. An example result is shown in figure 6.30.

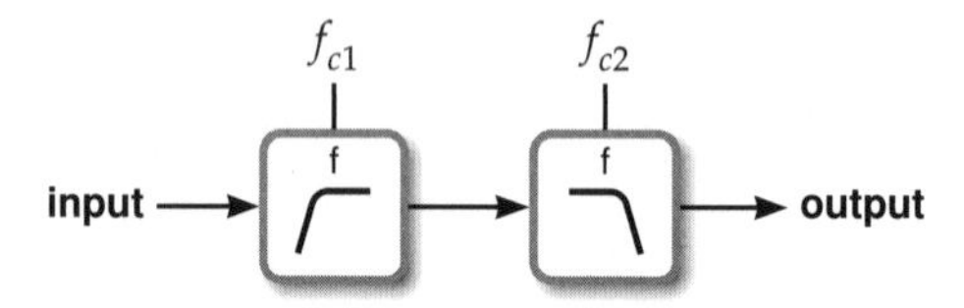

Figure 6.29 Series combination of LPF and HPF to achieve BPF result

Figure 6.31 illustrates how a parallel combination of lowpass and highpass filters can achieve a bandreject result. The filter effects are similar to those seen in the bandpass combination, but this time the two passbands are added together leaving a notch in between. It is necessary that $f_{c2} > f_{c1}$. If $f_{c2} < f_{c1}$, then all the partials attenuated by one filter are restored by the other, which is not the desired effect. An example result is shown in figure 6.32.

The techniques shown in figures 6.29 and 6.31 can be used when lowpass and highpass filters are available, but bandpass or bandreject are not. It is also the case that being able to adjust the two edge cutoff frequencies is sometimes more useful than specifying a centre frequency and Q. For example, when an engineer wishes to adjust the low and high cutoff frequencies independently for a recorded instrument, it can be easier to use figure 6.29 rather than a single bandpass filter.

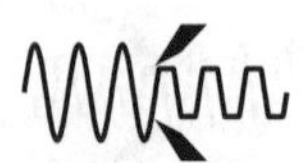

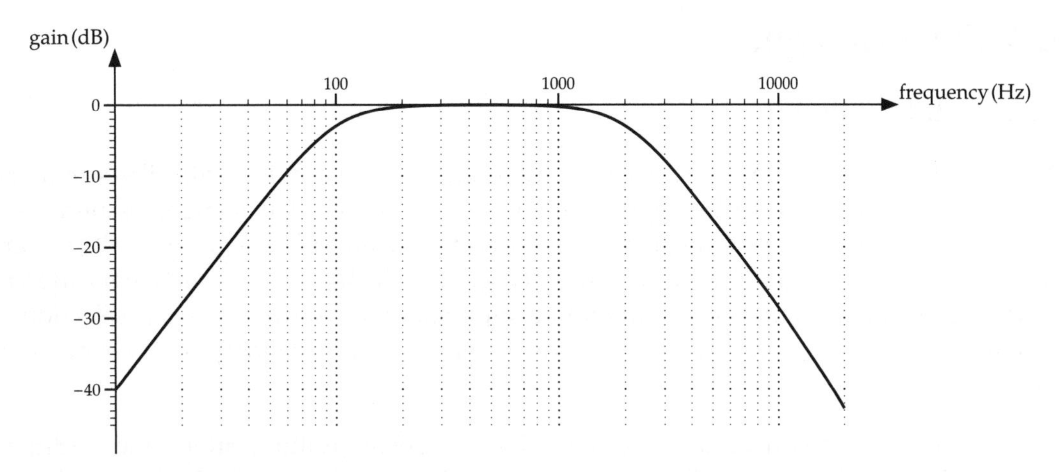

Figure 6.30 Frequency (magnitude) response plot for combination of second order LPF and HPF to achieve BPF result (f_{c1} = 100Hz, f_{c2} = 2kHz, f_S = 96kHz)

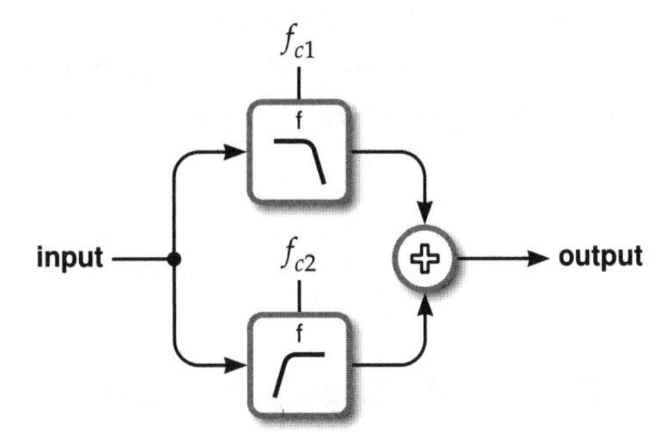

Figure 6.31 Parallel combination of LPF and HPF to achieve BRF result

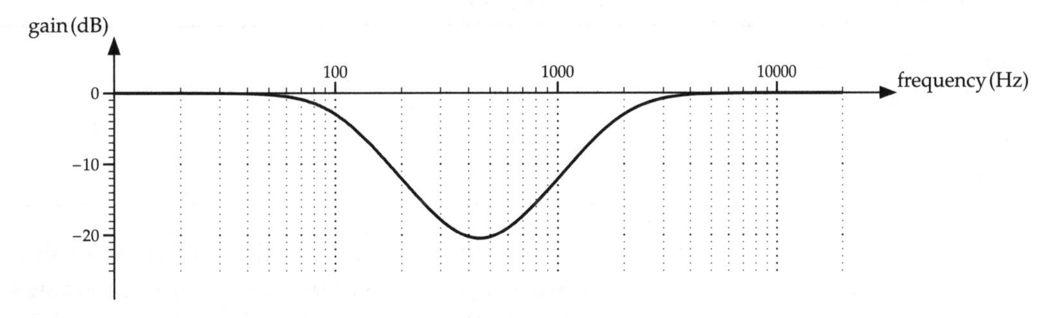

Figure 6.32 Frequency (magnitude) response plot for combination of second order LPF and HPF to achieve BRF result (f_{c1} = 100Hz, f_{c2} = 2kHz, f_S = 96kHz)

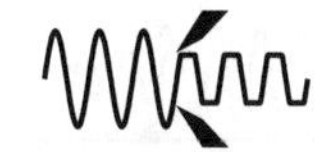

6.4 Filter Designs

6.4.1 Introduction

Many audio programming libraries and environments are supplied with filters that can be used in the ways described within this book. However, it is sometimes necessary to implement filters from scratch, or to modify an existing filter algorithm. There are many ways of designing filters of the same type, but which produce somewhat different tonal characteristics. Filters have common component parts, however, so the selection of examples in this section are a useful starting point for understanding a wider range of designs.

Filter designs are based around the operations of delay, multiplication, and addition. Figure 6.33 shows the block diagram form for a single (or unit) sample delay (labelled z^{-1}), which is key to the construction of filters. It stores and delays the input such that the output is one sample old. For example, if the sample rate is 96kHz, then the delay is $1/96000^{\text{th}}$ of a second. Algorithm 6.1 demonstrates how this is achieved. The value of variable *lastvalue* is maintained between calls to the function and initially it has a value of 0. The function is called once per sample at the sample rate.

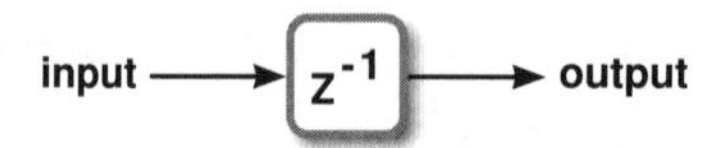

Figure 6.33 Single sample delay

Algorithm 6.1 – Single sample delay function

---

input : input signal in
output: output signal out

out = lastvalue
lastvalue = in

Filter designs often involve cascaded unit sample delays, such that values at multiple delay amounts can be incorporated into the output calculation. Figure 6.34 illustrates a two sample delay, and algorithm 6.2 achieves the same result. The value of variables *lastvalue1* and *lastvalue2* are maintained between calls to the function and initially both have a value of 0. The function is called once per sample at the sample rate. In both algorithms 6.1 and 6.2 the ordering of the lines is important to the result, where variables are updated from the output back to the input rather than the other way around.

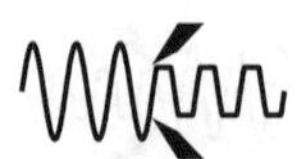

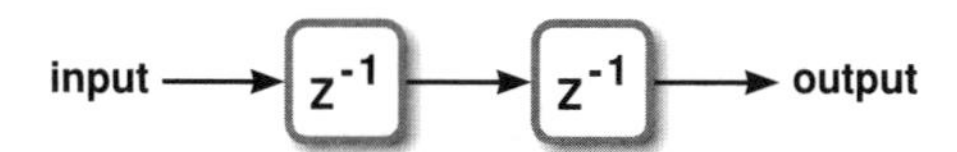

Figure 6.34 Two sample delay

Algorithm 6.2 – Two sample delay function

---

input : input signal `in`
output: output signal `out`

`out` = lastvalue2
lastvalue2 = lastvalue1
lastvalue1 = `in`

Filters are usually expressed in a mathematical form called a *difference equation* using variables $x[n-i]$ and $y[n-i]$, where x values are input samples, y values are output samples and i is the number of samples of delay. Therefore $x[n]$ is the current input sample, $y[n]$ is the current output sample and $y[n-4]$ is the output delayed by 4 samples. Therefore, the form in figure 6.34 can be expressed as:

$$y[n] = x[n-2] \tag{6.4}$$

The advantage of the mathematical form is that it translates well into a conventional programming language. It should be apparent that there is a relationship between equation 6.4 and the line "`out` = lastvalue2" in algorithm 6.2.

Filters are based on a weighted sum of delayed sample values. A simple example of filtering is calculating the mean average of the current and last two input samples, which can be expressed mathematically like this:

$$y[n] = \frac{1}{3}x[n] + \frac{1}{3}x[n-1] + \frac{1}{3}x[n-2] \tag{6.5}$$

This difference equation can be represented in block diagram form as shown in figure 6.35. It is also possible to rewrite the equation in a more compact form using the summation symbol Σ (sigma) like this:

$$y[n] = \sum_{i=0}^{2} \frac{1}{3}x[n-i] \tag{6.6}$$

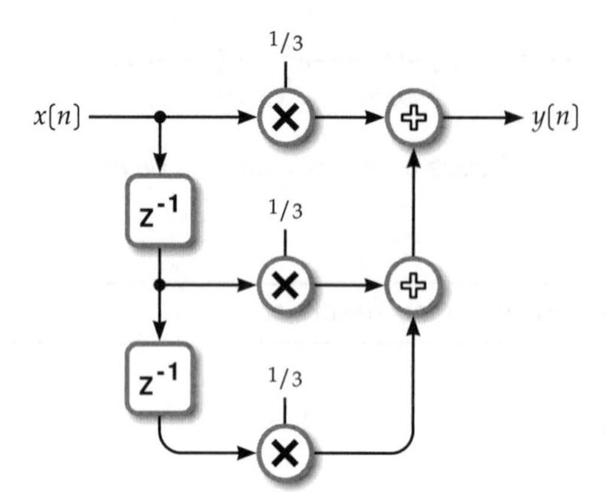

Figure 6.35 Three sample mean average

Some filters use delayed output samples, such as the following equation, which is called an *integrator*:

$$y(n) = x(n) + y(n-1) \tag{6.7}$$

The equation means that each new input sample value is added to the previous output value, creating a running total. It is assumed that the output is initially 0. Figure 6.36 shows the equation in block diagram form.

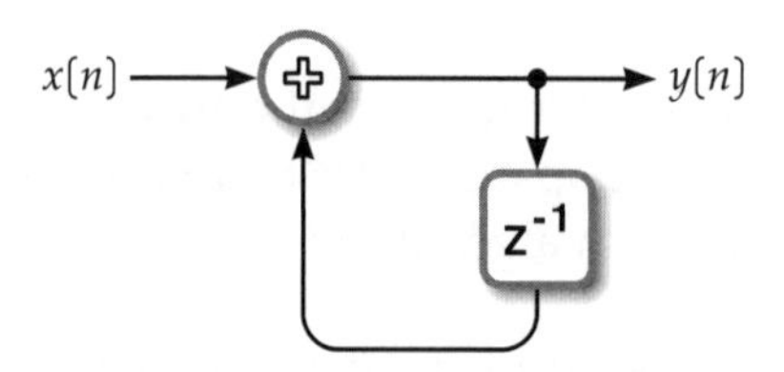

Figure 6.36 Integrator

The general mathematical form of a filter is as follows:

$$y(n) = \sum_{i=0}^{N} a_i x(n-i) - \sum_{i=1}^{M} b_i y(n-i) \tag{6.8}$$

There are a number of significant features in the equation:

- The current output $y(n)$ is a weighted sum of current and previous inputs ($i = 0, 1, 2, 3$, and so on), from which the weighted sum of previous outputs ($i = 1, 2, 3$, and so on) is subtracted. Note the different starting values of i in each summation, as the

output can include an amount of the current input $a_0x[n]$ but only **previous** outputs, starting with $b_1y[n-1]$. It is not possible to know the value of the next output until it is calculated, so $y[n]$ does not appear on the right-hand side of the equation.

- The number of terms in each sum can be different, as controlled by values N and M. The oldest samples being included are $x[n-N]$ and $y[n-M]$. The largest value of N or M describes the *order* of the filter.
- The multipliers a_i and b_i are called *filter coefficients*. The current and previous samples can all be multiplied by different values (including negative numbers and zero). Those values are calculated to achieve the desired frequency response. Note that the labels a and b are used the other way around in some published texts, with b coefficients multiplied by x values, and a by y values.
- If previous output values are not used (b_i is always zero), then it is called a *Finite Impulse Response (FIR)* filter (such as equation 6.5). If previous output values are used, then it is called an *Infinite Impulse Response (IIR)* filter (such as equation 6.7). The terms FIR and IIR relate to the feedback (recursion) associated with reusing old output values, and so whether the filter has the potential to produce an infinite output when stimulated by an impulse input. This idea is explored further in Chapter 10.

It is very important to maintain precision when calculating filter equations in order that the output meets the required specification. Using double-precision floating-point variables in a computer program is often appropriate.

There are a number of ways of characterising the behaviour of a filter. Figure 6.37 illustrates four ways of describing the effect of the simple two sample delay of figure 6.34. The plots would be more sophisticated for a practical filter, but they indicate the different ways in which the behaviour of a filter can be examined:

- The *impulse response* indicates how the process responds to an input of a single sample of amplitude 1 followed by silence. In the case of a two sample delay the input emerges after two samples, as might be expected. In a practical filter there is a more complex pattern of different values that emerge over time, reflecting the delay, multiplication, and addition that occur inside. This is relevant when wishing to understand how the filter causes an extension or smearing of data over time, such as with a resonant filter.
- The *frequency (magnitude) response* shows how gain varies with frequency. This is the response seen in the examples in §6.2. As might be expected for this simple example there is a constant gain of 0dB at all frequencies, as the signal is delayed by two samples but otherwise not changed in value.

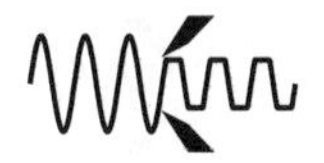

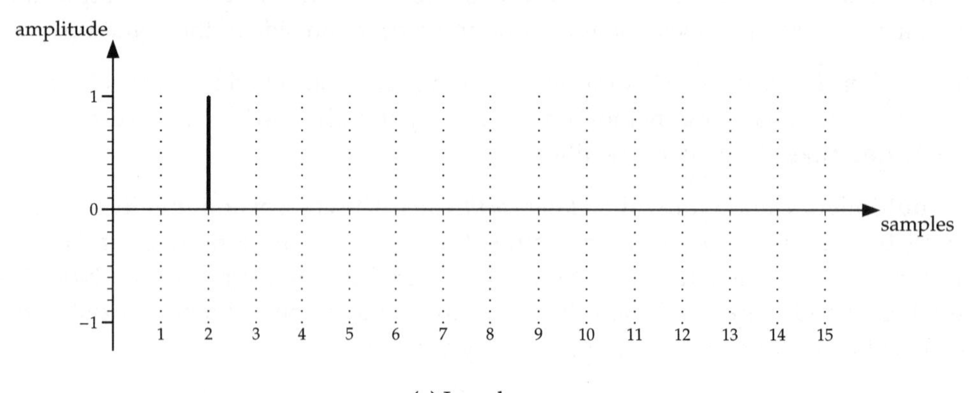

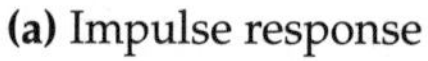
(a) Impulse response

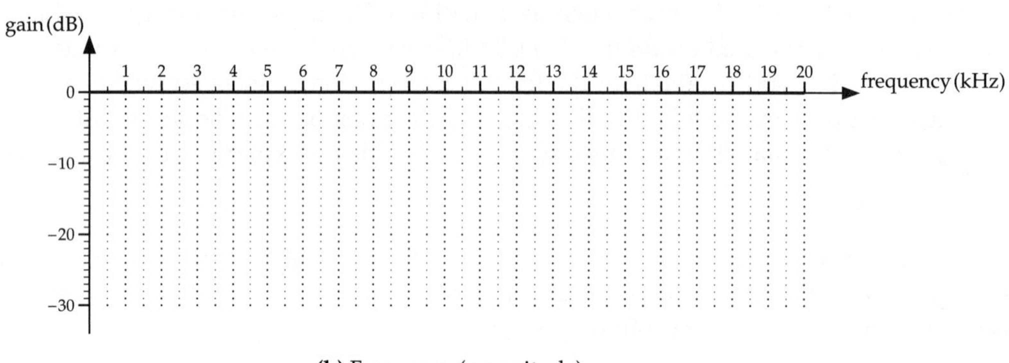

(b) Frequency (magnitude) response

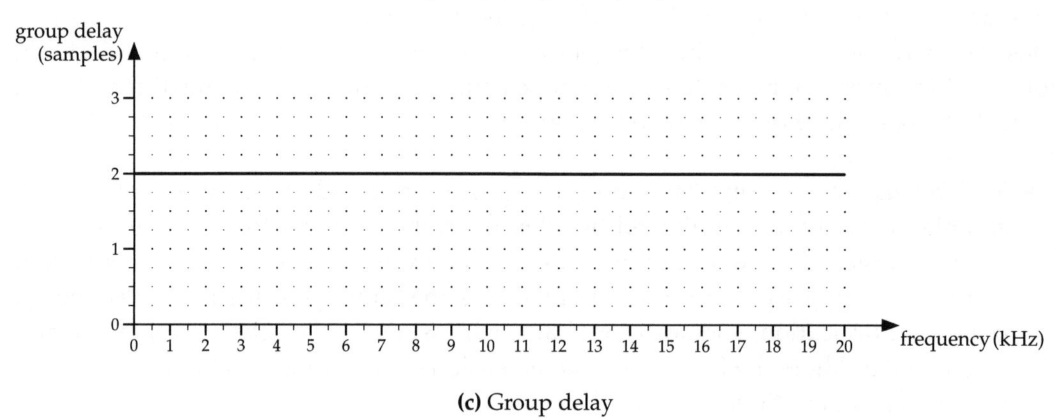

(c) Group delay

Figure 6.37 Response plots for a two sample delay (f_S = 40kHz, continued on the next page)

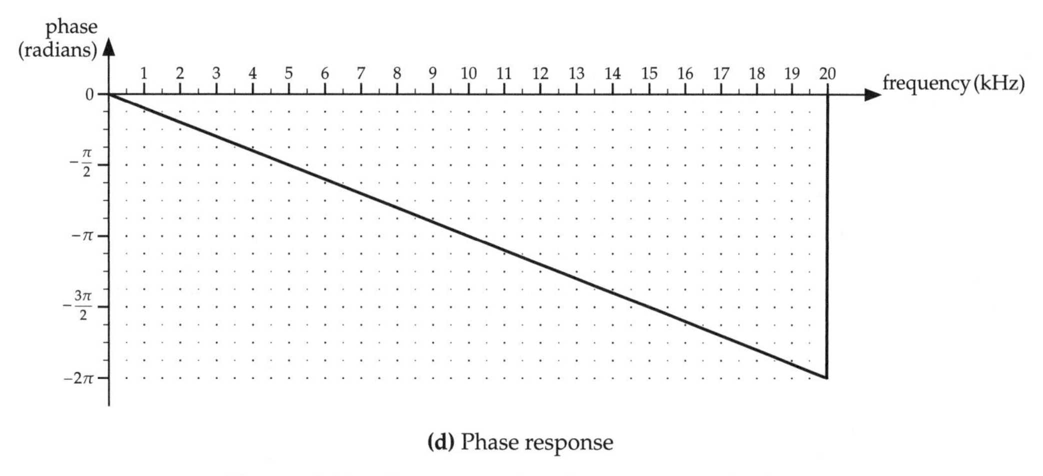

(d) Phase response

Figure 6.37 Response plots for a two sample delay (f_S = 40kHz, continued from the previous page)

- The *group delay* is the number of samples of delay at different frequencies. For the two sample delay this is consistent for all frequencies, but this is not necessarily the case for practical filters. The significance of group delay depends on how the filter is used. For example, the total delay in a waveguide resonator affects the tuning of the synthesizer, requiring suitable compensation (as described in §21.2.1, p.584).
- The *phase response* indicates the relative positions in the waveform cycle in the output compared to the input at different frequencies. Phase effects can lead to subtle audible changes, or they can be significant (such as in a phaser process, described in §9.2.4, p.279).

To understand how the phase response in figure 6.37d arises, consider a situation where the sample rate (f_S) is 40kHz. In that case a two sample length delay corresponds to 50μs. Figure 6.38 shows the effect of delaying 5kHz and 10kHz partials by 50μs. The two frequencies have different cycle lengths (200μs and 100μs respectively). 50μs corresponds to a quarter cycle ($\pi/2$ radians) at 5kHz and a half cycle (π radians) at 10kHz. This shows how different frequencies can have a different phase difference between input and output. These effects are shown in the phase response plot as a phase lag in radians. A value of 0 or -2π indicates that the input and output are in phase.

The frequency (magnitude) response is the characteristic that is typically used when selecting a filter. The filter icon in a block diagram gives a general indication of the required response, but does not specify aspects such as the roll-off. The other responses in figure 6.37 can also be important in understanding how a filter will affect the results of an audio process, such as resonant characteristics and the delays that occur. As a process is developed and refined, the selection of particular characteristics becomes more important.

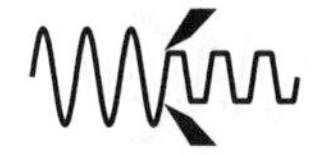

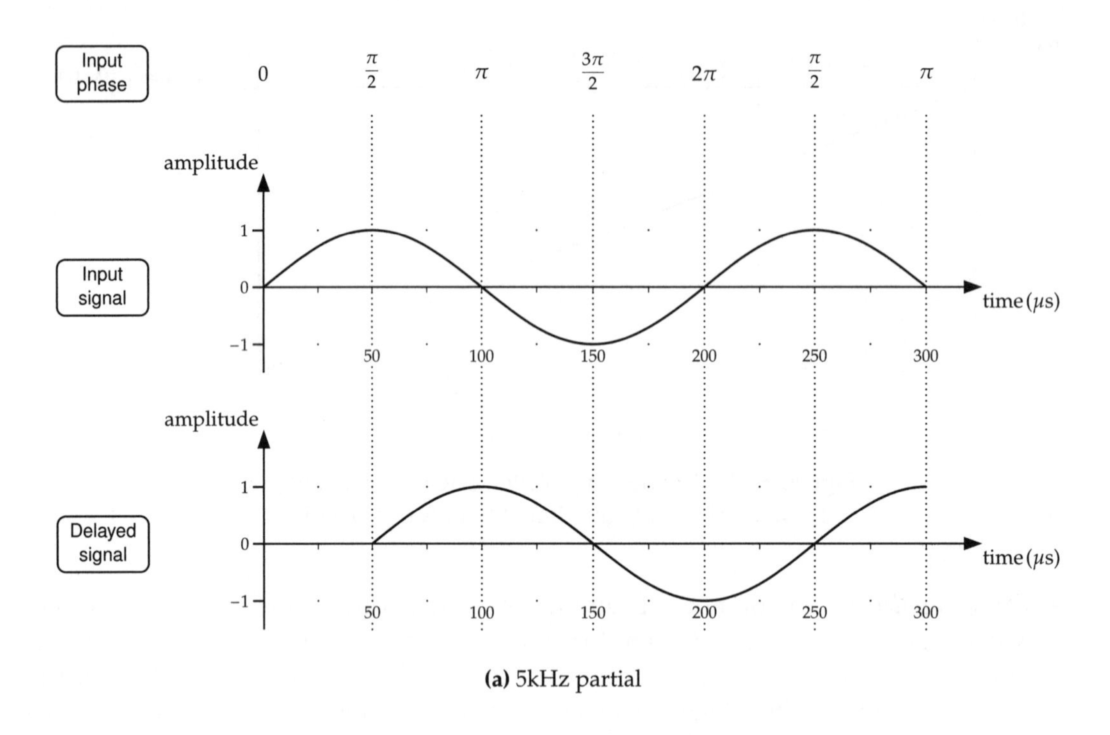

(a) 5kHz partial

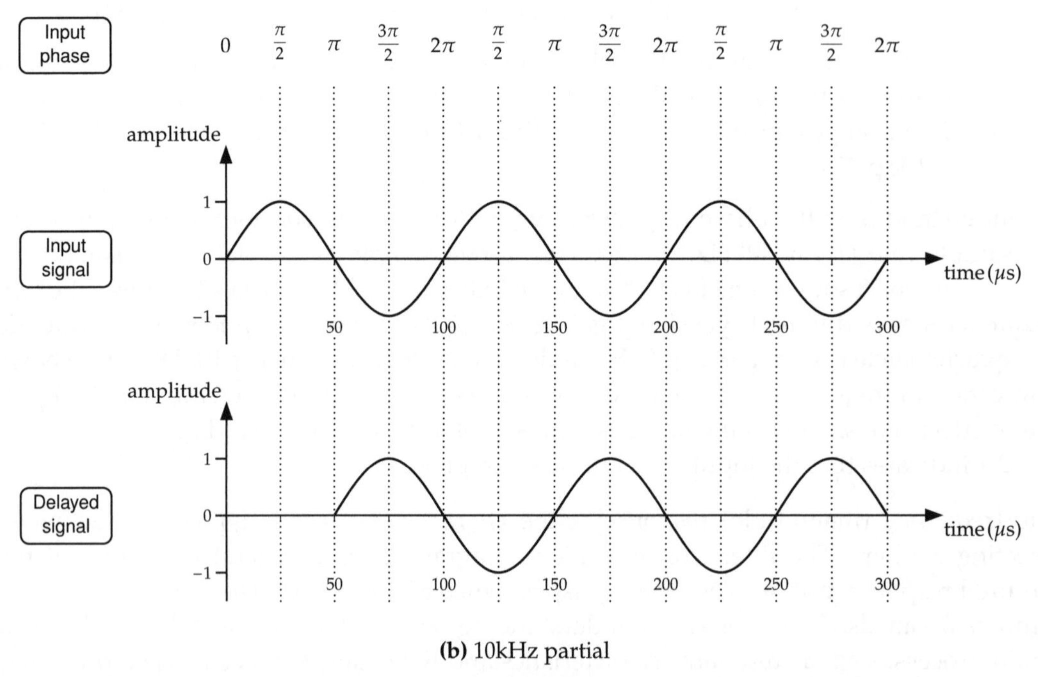

(b) 10kHz partial

Figure 6.38 Phase effects of delaying different frequency partials by two samples (f_S = 40kHz)

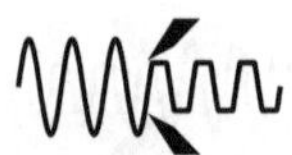

6.4.2 Lowpass and Highpass Designs

The *one pole* first order lowpass (IIR) filter uses a small number of component parts, as shown in figure 6.39.

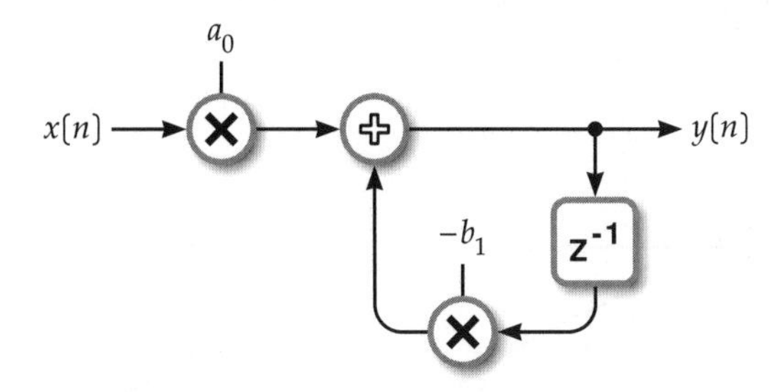

Figure 6.39 One pole first order lowpass filter

The block diagram translates into the following difference equation:

$$y(n) = a_0 x(n) - b_1 y(n-1) \tag{6.9}$$

The filter can be expressed as shown in algorithm 6.3. Variable *y1* is the output from the unit delay whose value must be maintained between calls to the function and initially has a value of 0. The order of updating variables is important.

Algorithm 6.3 – One pole first order lowpass filter function

input : input signal x0
output: output signal y0

```
y0 = (a0 * x0) - (b1 * y1)
y1 = y0
```

The filter coefficients are calculated from the cutoff frequency f_c and the sample rate f_S as follows:

$$\begin{aligned} c &= 2 - \cos\left(\frac{2\pi f_c}{f_S}\right) \quad \text{where} \quad 0 < f_c < \frac{f_S}{2} \\ b_1 &= \sqrt{c^2 - 1} - c \\ a_0 &= 1 + b_1 \end{aligned} \tag{6.10}$$

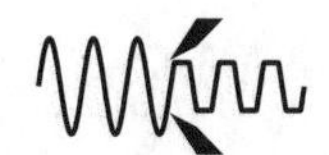

The cosine function takes an argument in radians (as do all trigonometric functions in this book). Note that when coefficient b_1 is used in equation 6.9 or the block diagram then it is multiplied by −1. Varying the value of f_c has the expected effect on the frequency response as shown in figure 6.40. Using a logarithmic frequency axis and gain in decibels gives a good impression of how the effect of the filter will be perceived. Frequencies an octave apart are equally-spaced on a logarithmic frequency axis (such as 500Hz, 1kHz, 2kHz, 4kHz, and 8kHz).

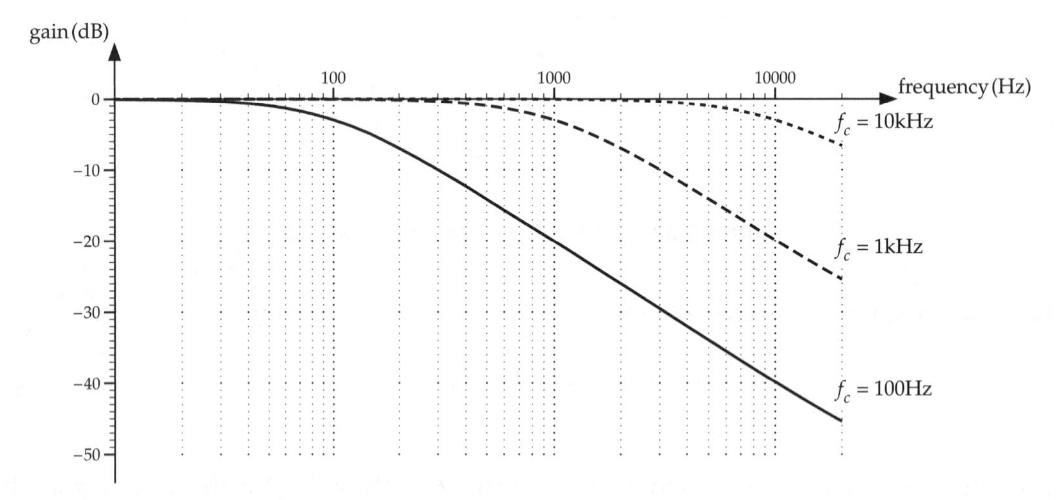

Figure 6.40 Frequency (magnitude) response plots for one pole LPF (f_S = 96kHz)

Some key features of the plots are as follows:

- The gain at the cutoff frequency is −3dB.
- The roll-off beyond the cutoff frequency is approximately 6dB per octave, which is standard for a first order lowpass filter. This is particularly apparent when f_c is 100Hz, such as between 1kHz (−20dB) and 2kHz (−26dB).
- It is important to appreciate that there is attenuation below the cutoff frequency and that the roll-off varies somewhat above the cutoff. It should not be assumed that a practical filter conforms to an idealised shape.

A development of the one pole filter is the first order filter shown in figure 6.41. The block diagram translates into the following difference equation:

$$y[n] = a_0 x[n] + a_1 x[n-1] - b_1 y[n-1] \quad \boxed{6.11}$$

The filter can be expressed as shown in algorithm 6.4. The values of variables *x1* and *y1* must be maintained between calls to the function, and both have the value 0 initially.

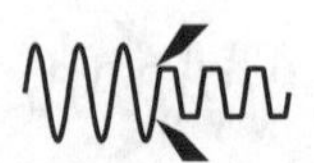

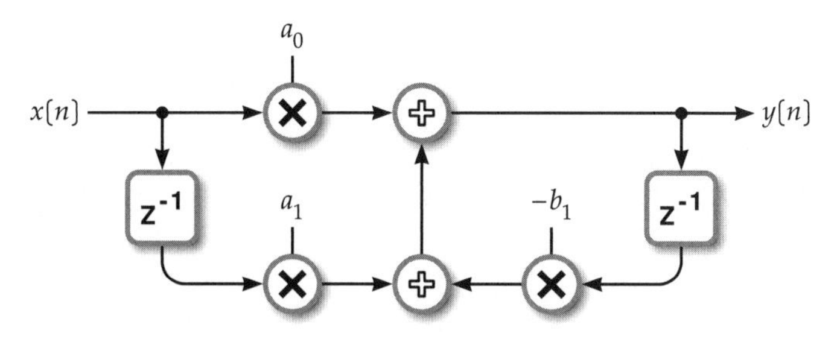

Figure 6.41 More advanced first order filter

Algorithm 6.4 – More advanced first order filter function

---

input : input signal x0
output: output signal y0

```
y0 = (a0 * x0) + (a1 * x1) - (b1 * y1)
x1 = x0
y1 = y0
```

The filter coefficients for lowpass and highpass filters are calculated from the cutoff frequency f_c and the sample rate f_S as follows:

$$b_1 = \frac{-\cos(\phi)}{1+\sin(\phi)} \quad \text{where} \quad \phi = \frac{2\pi f_c}{f_S} \quad \text{and} \quad 0 < f_c < \frac{f_S}{2}$$

lowpass	**highpass**
$a_0 = 0.5\,(1 + b_1)$	$a_0 = 0.5\,(1 - b_1)$
$a_1 = a_0$	$a_1 = -a_0$

(6.12)

Note that there are a number of negative signs in equations 6.11 and 6.12 that must be included correctly. Varying the value of f_c has the expected effect on the frequency response as shown in figures 6.42 and 6.43. The roll-off is again approximately 6dB per octave, as is expected with a first order design.

The more advanced first order filter requires more computation than the one pole form, but has the advantage of a complementary highpass design. Figures 6.40 and 6.42 (generated with a sample rate of 96kHz) are quite similar, but there are differences when the response approaches $f_S/2$. This is demonstrated in figure 6.44 with a sample rate of 40kHz, where one response flattens out, but the other heads towards a gain of $-\infty$dB.

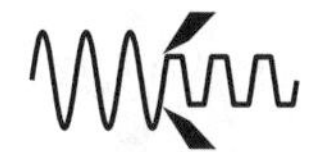

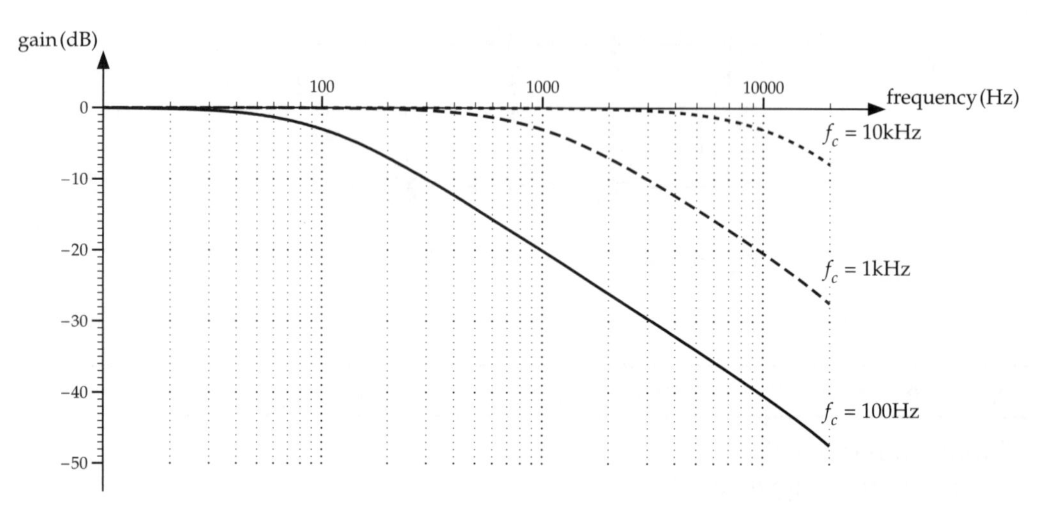

Figure 6.42 Frequency (magnitude) response plots for more advanced first order LPF (f_S = 96kHz)

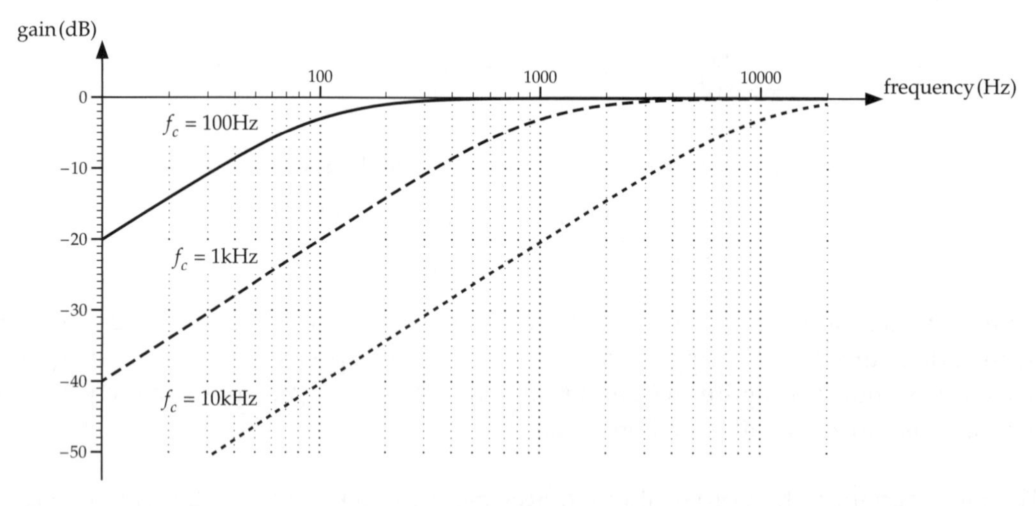

Figure 6.43 Frequency (magnitude) response plots for more advanced first order HPF (f_S = 96kHz)

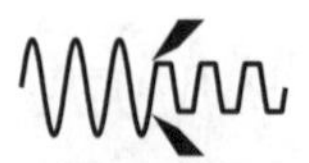

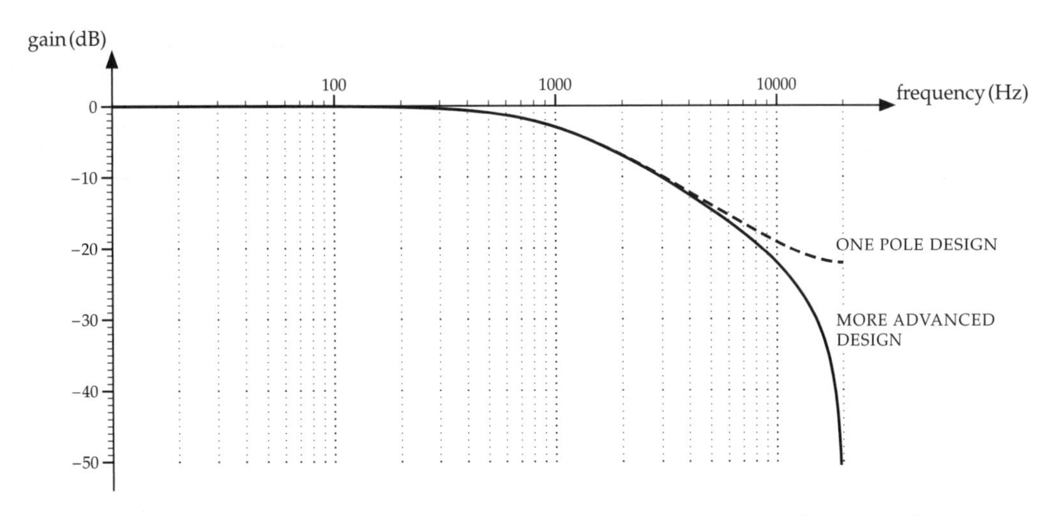

Figure 6.44 Frequency (magnitude) response plots comparing first order filters (f_c = 1kHz, f_S = 40kHz)

Figure 6.45 illustrates a second order filter, commonly known as a *biquad* form. It is very flexible, and can be configured to produce a range of different filter responses, such as lowpass, highpass, bandpass, and bandreject. Note that if coefficients a_2 and b_2 are 0 it is identical in effect to figure 6.41, so it is possible to produce both first and second order results with the same process.

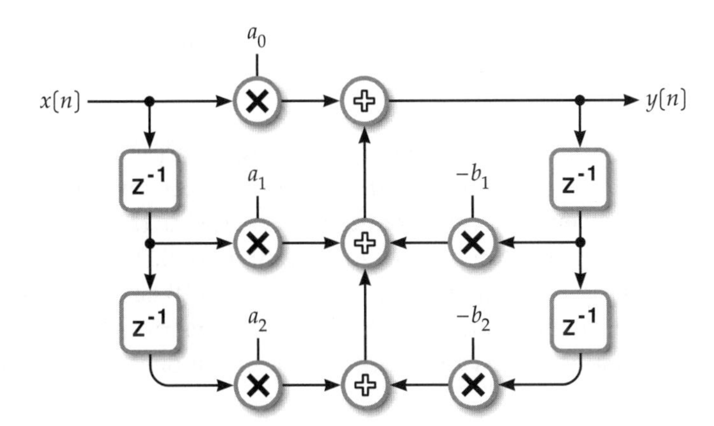

Figure 6.45 Second order (biquad) filter

The block diagram translates into the following difference equation:

$$y(n) = a_0x(n) + a_1x(n-1) + a_2x(n-2) - b_1y(n-1) - b_2y(n-2) \tag{6.13}$$

The filter can be expressed as shown in algorithm 6.5. The values of variables *x1, x2, y1,* and *y2* must be maintained between calls to the function, and all have the value 0 initially.

Algorithm 6.5 – Second order filter function

input : input signal x0
output: output signal y0

```
y0 = (a0 ∗ x0) + (a1 ∗ x1) + (a2 ∗ x2) − (b1 ∗ y1) − (b2 ∗ y2)
x2 = x1
x1 = x0
y2 = y1
y1 = y0
```

The filter coefficients for lowpass and highpass filters are calculated from the cutoff frequency f_c, Q value, and the sample rate f_S as follows:

$$b_2 = \frac{2Q - \sin(\phi)}{2Q + \sin(\phi)} \qquad \text{where} \quad \phi = \frac{2\pi f_c}{f_S} \quad \text{and} \quad 0 < f_c < \frac{f_S}{2}$$

$$b_1 = -\left(1 + b_2\right)\cos(\phi) \qquad Q \geqslant \sqrt{0.5}$$

6.14

lowpass

$$a_0 = 0.25\left(1 + b_1 + b_2\right)$$
$$a_1 = 2a_0$$
$$a_2 = a_0$$

highpass

$$a_0 = 0.25\left(1 - b_1 + b_2\right)$$
$$a_1 = -2a_0$$
$$a_2 = a_0$$

Figures 6.46 and 6.47 show some example frequency response plots. The roll-off is approximately 12dB per octave, as is expected with a second order lowpass/highpass design. The sharper roll-off clearly enables greater attenuation outside the passband than the first order designs. When Q has a value of $\sqrt{0.5}$ (approximately 0.7071), the filter produces a "normal" lowpass or highpass frequency response with −3dB gain at the cutoff frequency (also known as a Butterworth response). For larger values of Q the filter gains a resonant peak. This combination of lowpass and bandpass response is useful for subtractive synthesis (Chapter 17).

Figure 6.48 illustrates a group delay plot for the second order lowpass filter. Although a delay of less than 0.3ms is not significant in many cases, it is important in a waveguide resonator such as figure 21.2 (p.584) where it will affect the tuning of the synthesizer. The group delay will vary with f_c and Q. However, without a suitable mathematical simulation it is not easy to predict how the parameters of different designs will affect the

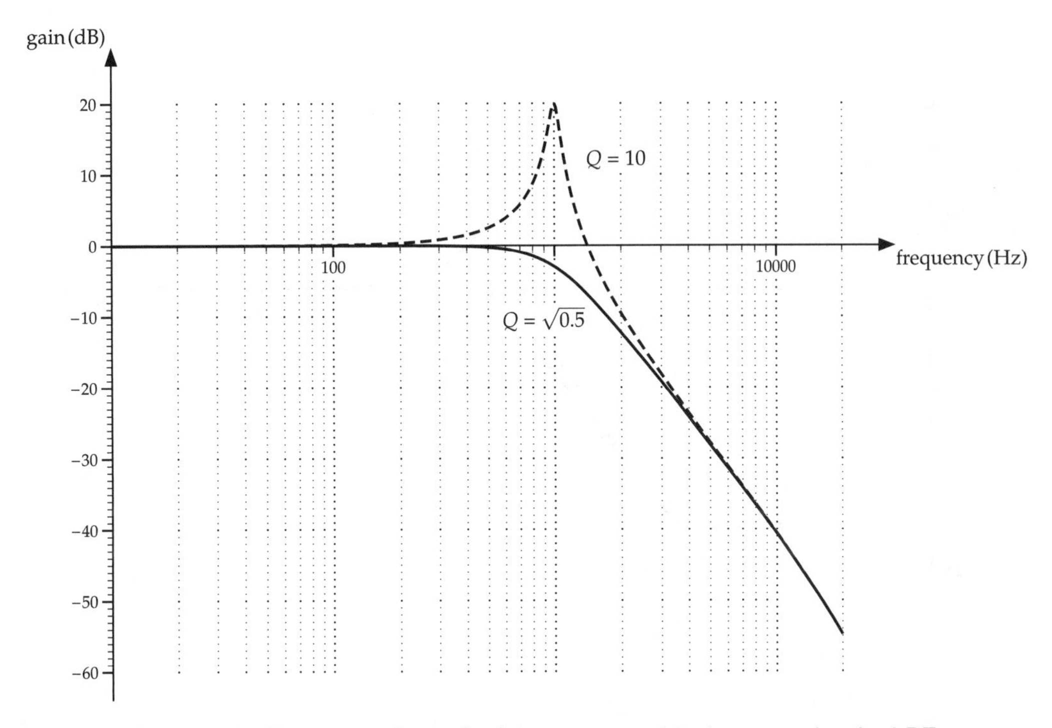

Figure 6.46 Frequency (magnitude) response plots for second order LPF (f_c = 1kHz, f_S = 96kHz)

resulting group delay, so a certain amount of adjusting a process through trial-and-error might be required.

Figure 6.49 demonstrates how varying the Q value in the second order lowpass filter relates to resonance in the time domain. The impulse response plots indicate how the process responds to an input of a single sample of amplitude 1 followed by silence. When Q has a value of $\sqrt{0.5}$ the output quickly settles, but for high values the output "rings" at the resonant frequency (a frequency of 1kHz corresponds to a cycle length of 1ms). The resonance can be exploited in synthesis to create partials that decay exponentially over a long period of time (§17.4, p.517).

The group delay and impulse response plots help in appreciating that a filter is not a process element that acts purely in terms of attenuation at different frequencies. It depends on the process being considered, but selecting a particular filter design can make a subtle tonal difference due to these characteristics. Other filter designs than those detailed in this book are available that have different responses in the time and frequency domains.

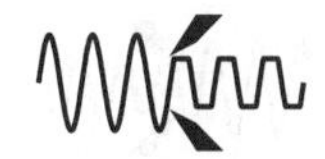

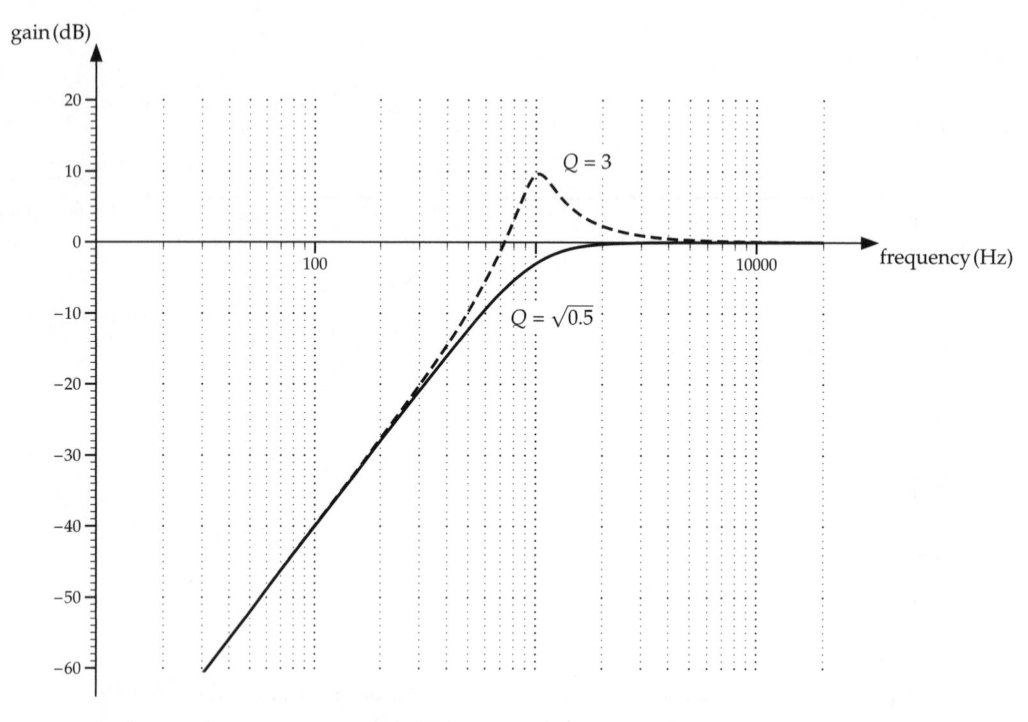

Figure 6.47 Frequency (magnitude) response plots for second order HPF (f_c = 1kHz, f_S = 96kHz)

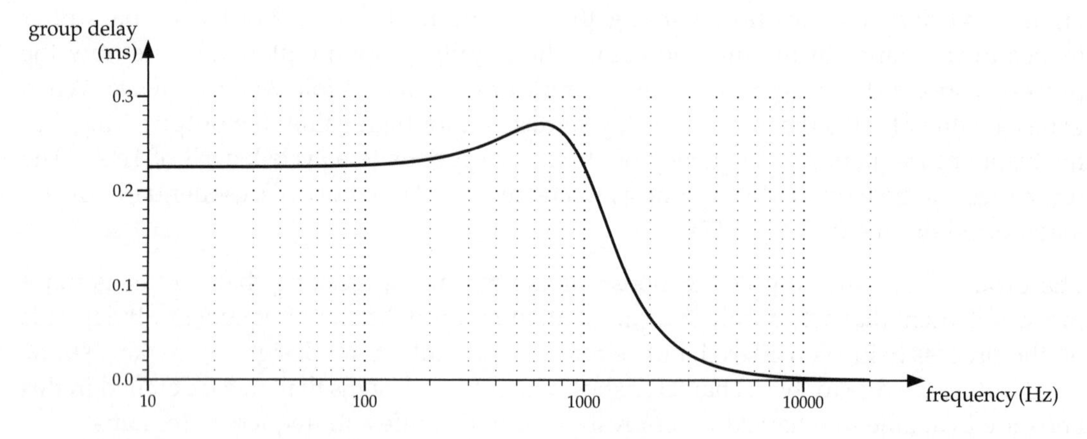

Figure 6.48 Group delay plot for second order LPF (f_c = 1kHz, $Q = \sqrt{0.5}$, f_S = 96kHz)

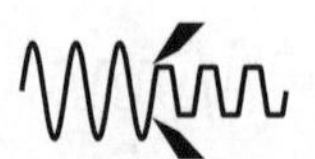

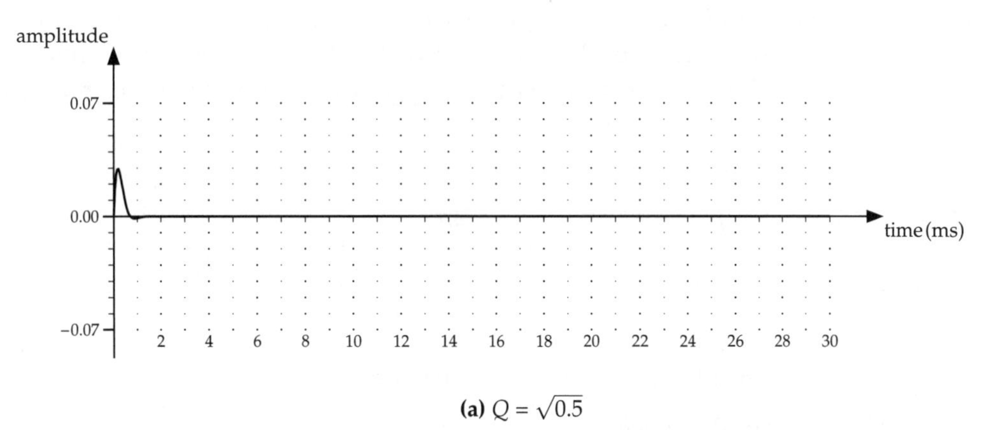

(a) $Q = \sqrt{0.5}$

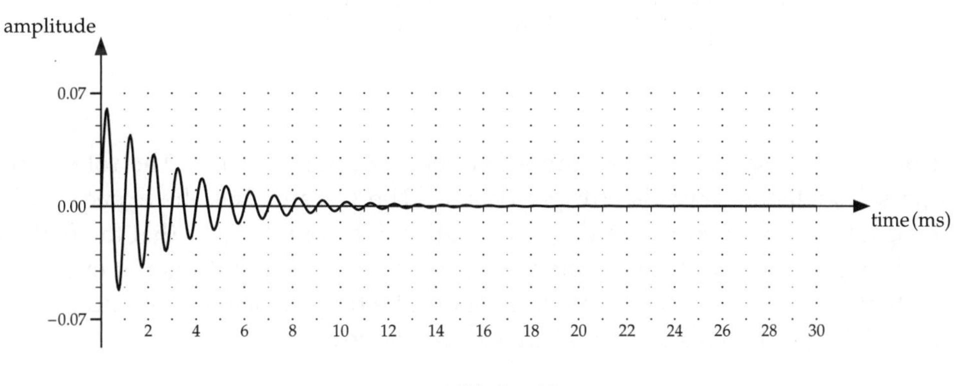

(b) $Q = 10$

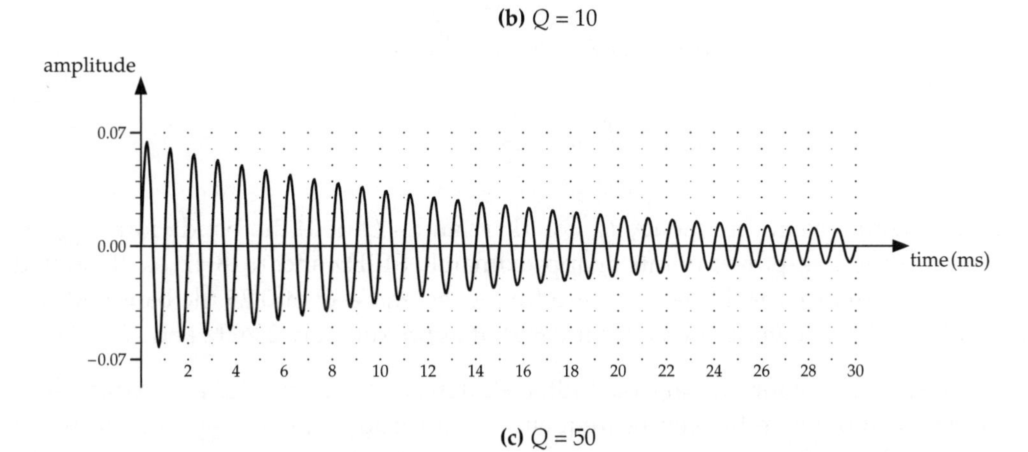

(c) $Q = 50$

Figure 6.49 Impulse response plots for second order LPF (f_c = 1kHz, f_S = 96kHz)

6.4.3 Bandpass and Bandreject Designs

Second order bandpass and bandreject filters are achieved with the same form as shown in figure 6.45 (p.175) and equation 6.13 (p.175), but with different filter coefficients. The coefficients are calculated from the centre frequency f_c, Q value, and the sample rate f_S as follows:

$$b_2 = \tan\left(\frac{\pi}{4} - \frac{\phi}{2Q}\right) \qquad \text{where} \quad \phi = \frac{2\pi f_c}{f_S} \quad \text{and} \quad 0 < f_c < \frac{Qf_S}{4}$$

$$b_1 = -(1 + b_2)\cos(\phi) \qquad\qquad f_c < \frac{f_S}{2}$$

bandpass

$$a_0 = 0.5\,(1 - b_2) \qquad a_1 = 0 \qquad a_2 = -a_0$$

bandreject

$$a_0 = 0.5\,(1 + b_2) \qquad a_1 = b_1 \qquad a_2 = a_0 \tag{6.15}$$

Figures 6.50 and 6.51 show some example frequency response plots. The roll-off with the bandpass filter tends towards 6dB per octave. The Q value has the expected effect of producing a bandwidth corresponding to equation 6.2 (p.149). Note that the response is symmetric with respect to logarithmic frequency, so the bandwidth is not evenly distributed in hertz either side of the centre frequency. The frequencies corresponding to the half-power (−3dB gain) points can be calculated as follows:

$$f_{\text{min}} = \frac{f_c}{2Q}\left(\sqrt{1 + 4Q^2} - 1\right)$$

$$f_{\text{max}} = f_{\text{min}} + \frac{f_c}{Q} \tag{6.16}$$

For example, with a centre frequency (f_c) of 1kHz and a Q of 1, the bandwidth (f_{bw}) is 1kHz. This leads to half-power points of approximately 618Hz and 1618Hz, as illustrated in figure 6.50. Similarly for the same centre frequency and a Q of 0.25 the bandwidth is 4kHz, leading to half-power points in figure 6.51 at approximately 236Hz and 4236Hz.

The phase response plot for the bandpass filter is interesting (figure 6.52) as the difference in phase below and above the centre frequency could lead to phase cancellation when filters are combined. For example, greater attenuation might occur between two peaks using the form in figure 6.20 (p.157) than might be expected. With a high Q value the second order bandpass filter design will display a resonant characteristic, which is useful for synthesis in a similar manner to a resonant lowpass filter (§17.4, p.517).

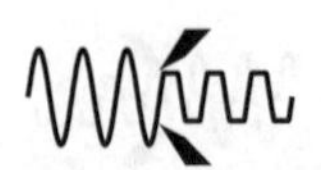

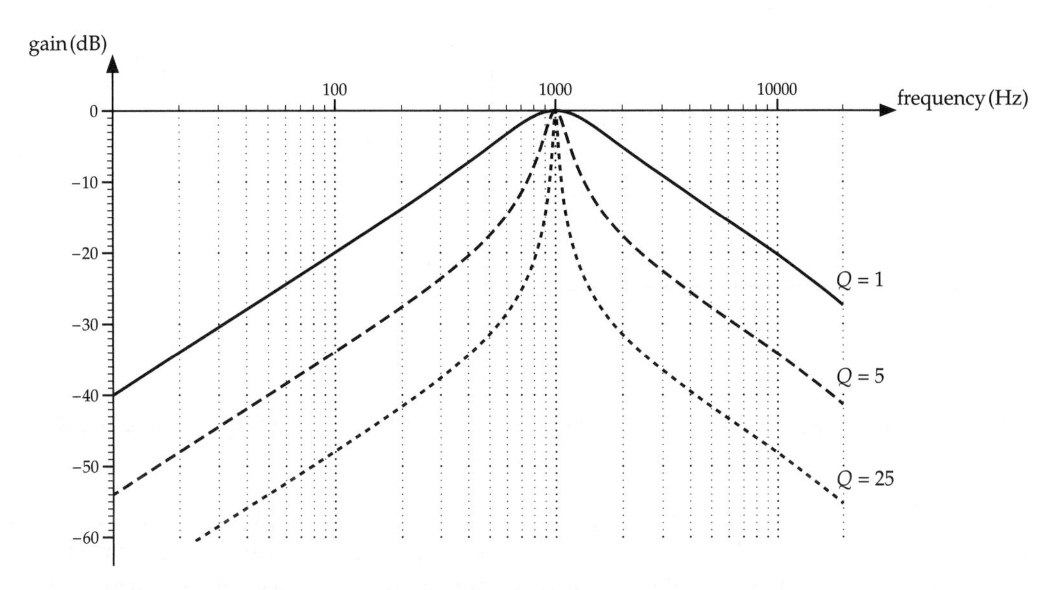

Figure 6.50 Frequency (magnitude) response plots for second order BPF (f_c = 1kHz, f_S = 96kHz)

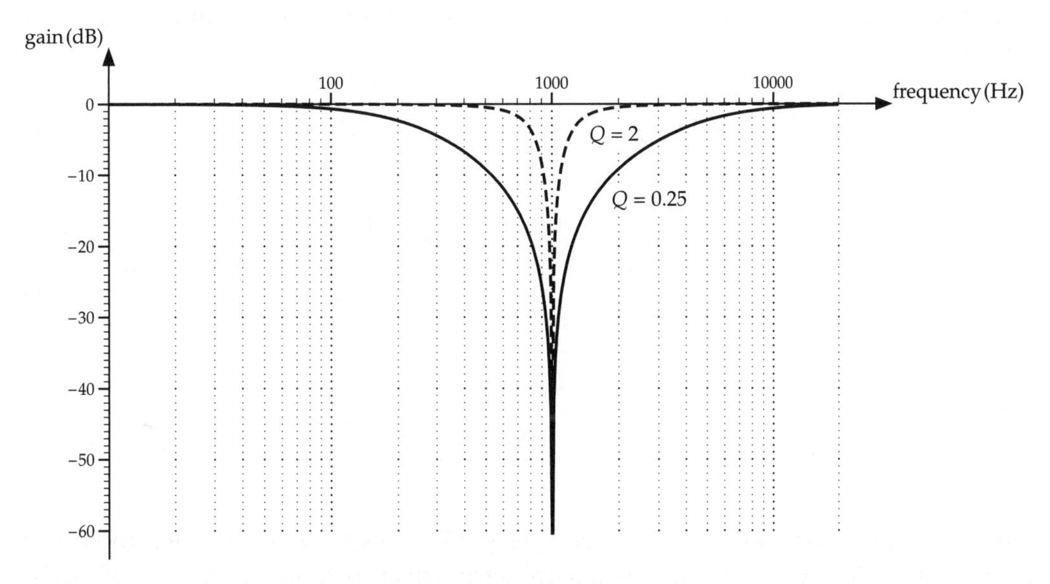

Figure 6.51 Frequency (magnitude) response plots for second order BRF (f_c = 1kHz, f_S = 96kHz)

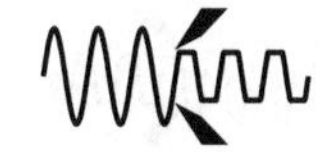

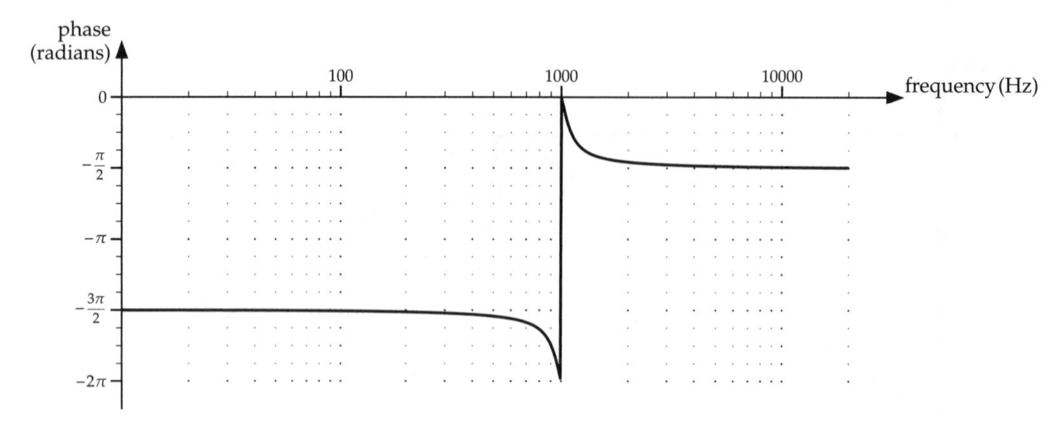

Figure 6.52 Phase response plot for second order BPF (f_c = 1kHz, Q = 5, f_S = 96kHz)

A peaking filter has a controllable gain parameter that allows it to either produce a positive decibel bandpass gain peak, or a negative decibel bandreject response. It is related to the form in figure 6.22b (p.158). However, it is designed such that it produces symmetric boost and cut responses, which makes it useful for such tasks as creating parametric equalisers.

The second order peaking filter is achieved with the same form as shown in figure 6.45 (p.175) and equation 6.13 (p.175), but with different filter coefficients. The coefficients are calculated from the centre frequency f_c, Q value, gain in decibels a_{dB}, and the sample rate f_S as follows:

$$
\begin{aligned}
b_2 &= \frac{1 - g_1 \tan\left(\frac{\phi}{2Q}\right)}{1 + g_1 \tan\left(\frac{\phi}{2Q}\right)} & \phi &= \frac{2\pi f_c}{f_S} \\
b_1 &= -(1 + b_2)\cos(\phi) \qquad \text{where} & g_0 &= 0.5\left(10^{a_{dB}/20} - 1\right) \\
a_0 &= 1 + g_0(1 - b_2) & g_1 &= \frac{2}{1 + g_0} \\
a_1 &= b_1 \\
a_2 &= 1 + (b_2 - a_0) \qquad \text{and} & 0 &< f_c < \frac{Qf_S}{4}, \quad f_c < \frac{f_S}{2}
\end{aligned}
\tag{6.17}
$$

Figure 6.53 shows some example frequency response plots for a Q value of 2 and different values of a_{dB}. As expected, there is a symmetric effect in terms of gain in decibels for equivalent positive and negative values of a_{dB}. Something that is apparent with this peaking filter, however, is that the response changes width with varying a_{dB} values, which is known as a non-constant-Q or proportional-Q design. In practical circumstances this

is a useful characteristic in terms of usability for achieving modifications. However, it means that equation 6.16 (p.180) cannot be used to predict the extents of −3dB response (bandwidth) relative to the peak value.

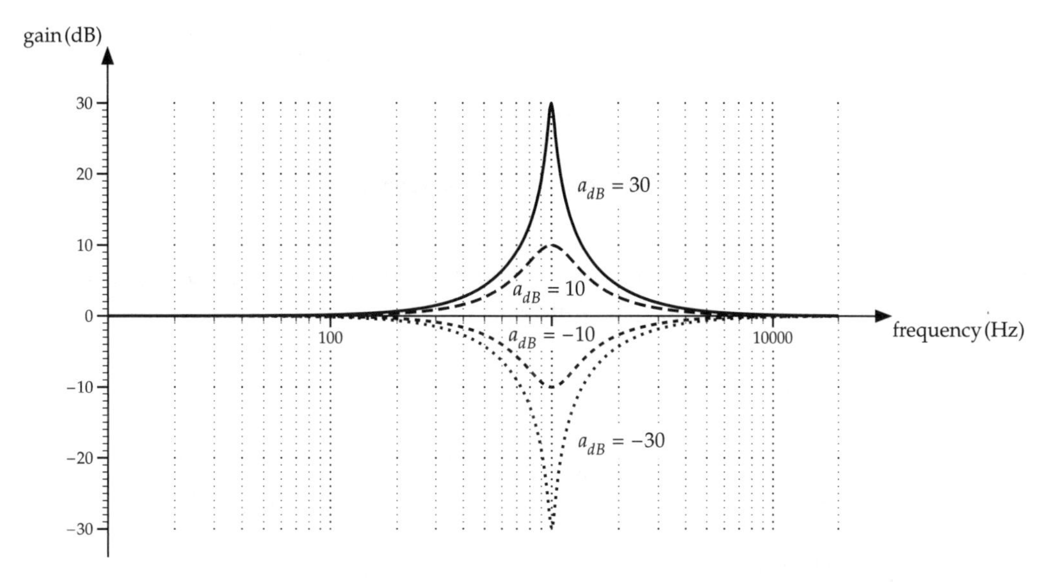

Figure 6.53 Frequency (magnitude) response plots for peaking filter (f_c = 1kHz, Q = 2, f_S = 96kHz)

Multiple peaking filters can be cascaded in series to provide a user with an ability to boost and cut multiple frequency bands for equalisation (EQ) purposes. When a_{dB} is zero, the filter produces a flat response at 0dB and so is transparent. This means that it is possible to set up multiple filters in series (initially all producing a flat response), from which the user can select the quantity necessary to emphasise or attenuate particular frequency ranges when required.

6.4.4 Comb and Allpass Designs

Figure 6.54 shows an FIR comb filter form. A new feature is the z^{-d} block, which indicates a delay of d samples. Previous filter designs always used single sample delays (z^{-1}). The value of d varies as the comb filter parameters are changed. This necessitates a general solution to creating delays of an arbitrary length called a circular buffer, which is described in detail in §8.1.3 (p.225).

The block diagram translates into the following difference equation:

$$y(n) = a_0 x(n) + a_d x(n-d) \quad \boxed{6.18}$$

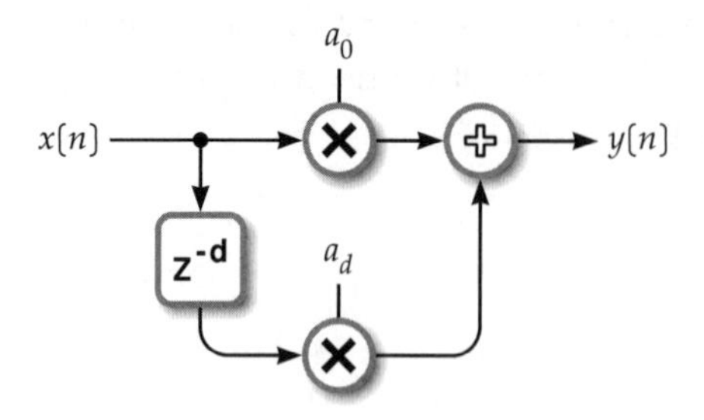

Figure 6.54 FIR comb filter

The filter coefficients are calculated from the comb frequency f_c, minimum gain value g_{dB} (in decibels), and the sample rate f_S as follows:

$$
\begin{aligned}
d &= \frac{f_S}{f_c} \\
a_d &= \pm 0.5\left(1 - 10^{g_{dB}/20}\right) \quad \text{where} \quad \begin{array}{c} 0 < f_c \leqslant f_S \\ -\infty \leqslant g_{dB} \leqslant 0 \end{array} \\
a_0 &= 1 - |a_d|
\end{aligned}
\qquad \boxed{6.19}
$$

There are a number of important features in the equations. Firstly, d might be a fractional number, which means that a fractional delay is required. Suitable techniques are described in §8.2 (p.237). Another feature is that there is a ± symbol in the calculation for a_d, which allows two choices of frequency response shape. When a positive prefix is used for a_d the peaks occur at integer multiples of f_c, as shown in figure 6.55. When a negative prefix is used for a_d the value is multiplied by -1 and the troughs (dips) occur at integer multiples of f_c, as shown in figure 6.56. Finally, a_0 is calculated using $|a_d|$, which means that the negative sign is removed (if present) from a_d before the subtraction occurs (known as taking the absolute value).

Unlike most of the other frequency response plots previously, figures 6.55 and 6.56 have linear frequency axes, to illustrate the fact that the comb filtering occurs at integer multiples of f_c. This effect could be used to produce filtering at harmonics of particular frequency.

It is useful to consider how the comb filtering occurs. Examining the block diagram in figure 6.54 it is apparent that the output is a weighted sum of the input with a delayed copy of the input. Imagine that the input is a sinusoid with a cycle length T, which corresponds to $T \times f_S$ samples. Figure 6.57 illustrates the output of the comb filter, when $a_0 = a_d = 0.5$ and the delay in samples (d) is varied. If there is no delay between the two, then the waveforms are synchronised and the output is the same as the input. If the delay is exactly

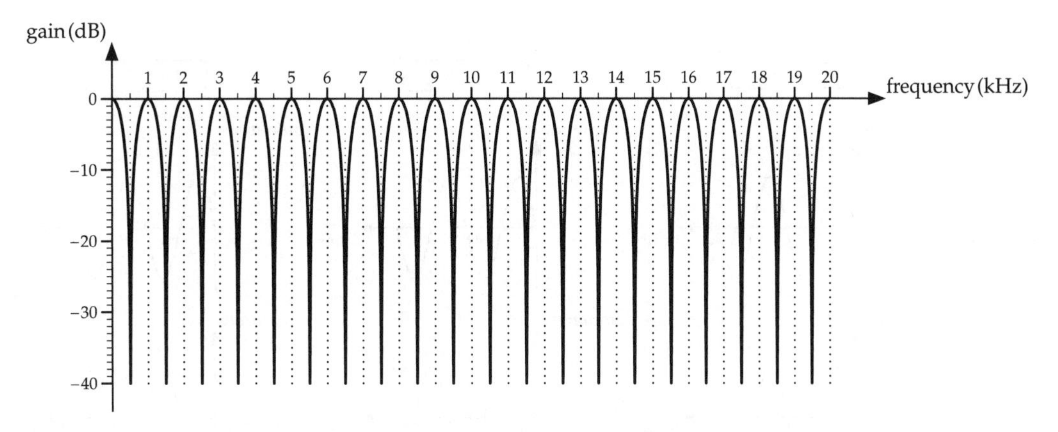

Figure 6.55 Frequency (magnitude) response plots for FIR comb filter with positive a_d prefix (g_{dB} = −40, f_c = 1kHz, f_S = 96kHz)

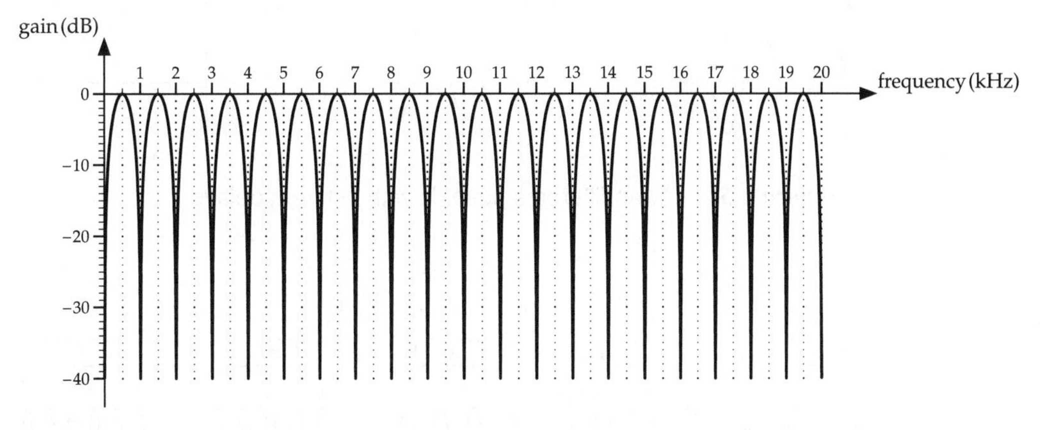

Figure 6.56 Frequency (magnitude) response plots for FIR comb filter with negative a_d prefix (g_{dB} = −40, f_c = 1kHz, f_S = 96kHz)

half a cycle length, then complete cancellation occurs, as the positive and negative halves of the cycles are added together. If the delay is part way between these extremes, then part-cancellation occurs.

The repetition in the comb filter frequency response arises from the fact that integer multiples of frequencies sum and cancel in the same way for a particular delay time. For example, figure 6.58 shows how a delay of one cycle length of frequency F affects harmonics of that frequency and those half way in between (again with $a_0 = a_d = 0.5$). Comparing to figure 6.55 it should be apparent how that translates into a frequency response.

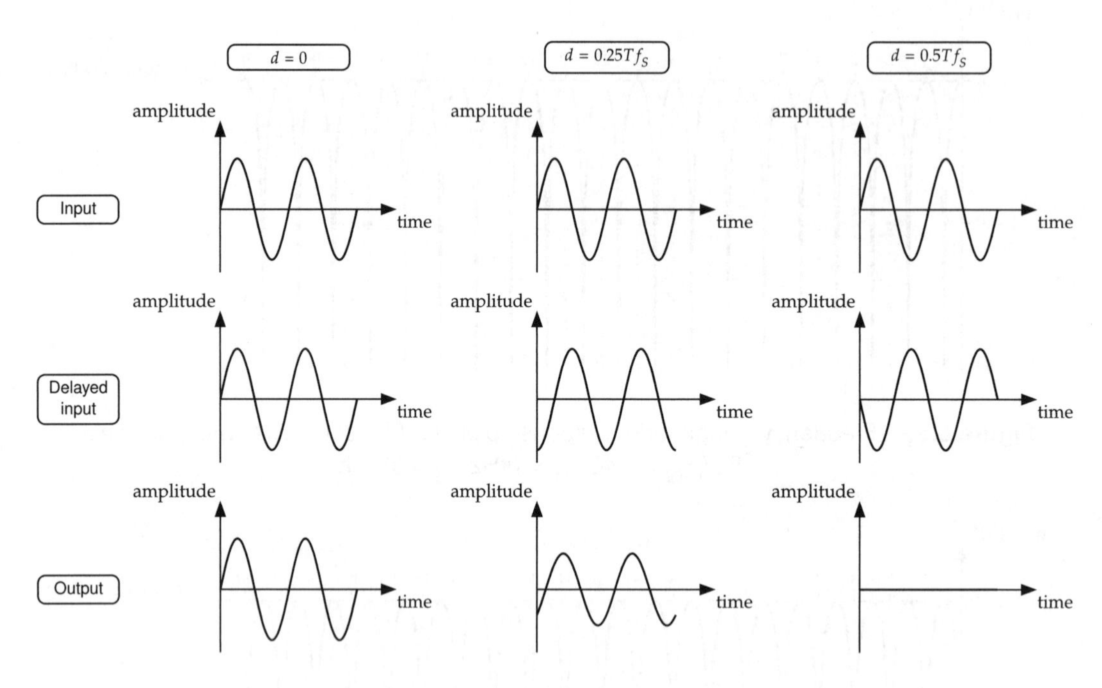

Figure 6.57 Comb filtered sinusoids with different delays

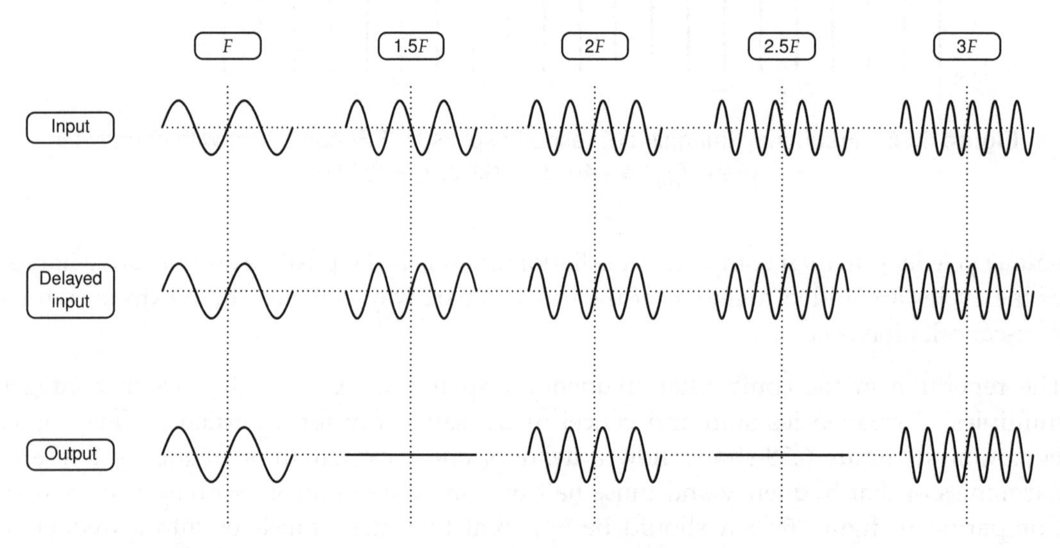

Figure 6.58 Comb filtered sinusoids with a delay of one cycle of frequency F

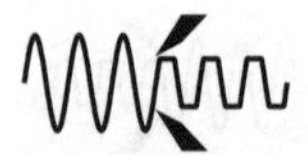

Figure 6.59 shows an IIR comb filter form.

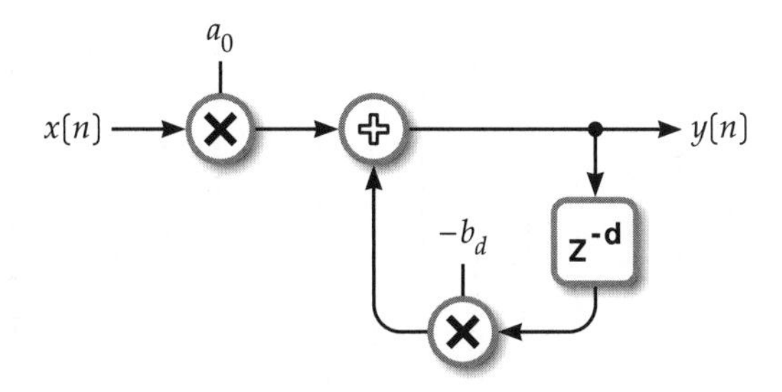

Figure 6.59 IIR comb filter

The block diagram translates into the following difference equation:

$$y(n) = a_0 x(n) - b_d y(n - d) \tag{6.20}$$

The filter coefficients are calculated from the comb frequency f_c, minimum gain value g_{dB} (in decibels), and the sample rate f_S as follows:

$$\begin{aligned} d &= \frac{f_S}{f_c} \\ b_d &= \pm\left(\frac{10^{g_{dB}/20} - 1}{10^{g_{dB}/20} + 1}\right) \quad \text{where} \quad \begin{aligned} 0 < f_c \leqslant f_S \\ -\infty < g_{dB} \leqslant 0 \end{aligned} \\ a_0 &= 1 - |b_d| \end{aligned} \tag{6.21}$$

Notice that the equation for b_d includes a $\pm$ symbol. This allows two choices of frequency response shape (in a similar way to the FIR comb filter) depending on whether the value is multiplied by $+1$ or -1.

Figures 6.60 and 6.61 show some example frequency response plots. Comparing to the FIR comb filter result the position of the peaks is the same, but the peaks are narrow and the troughs are wide. Changing g_{dB} for the IIR form allows some control over the bandwidth of the peaks, as illustrated by comparing figures 6.61 and 6.62.

With a short delay time, the effect of a comb filter is perceived as a frequency domain effect, as described so far. However, a comb filter can also be used with long delay times to create echo and reverberation effects as described in Chapter 10.

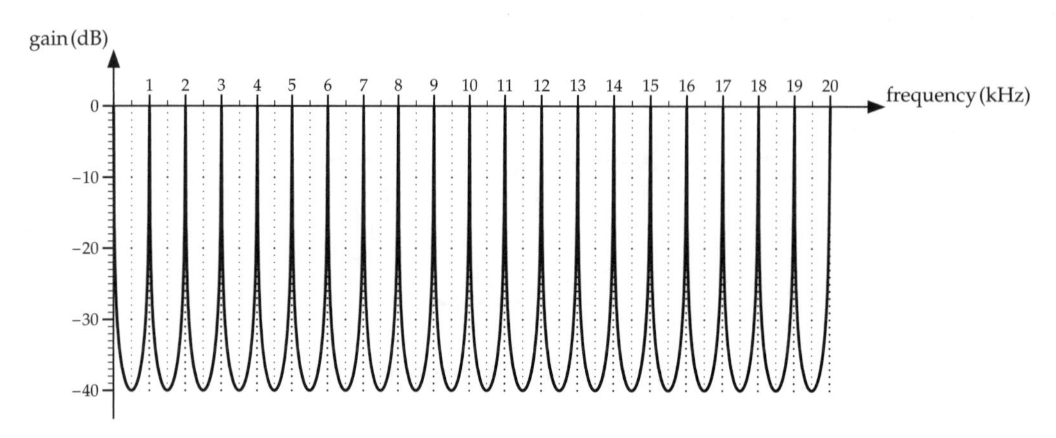

Figure 6.60 Frequency (magnitude) response plots for IIR comb filter with positive b_d prefix (g_{dB} = −40, f_c = 1kHz, f_S = 96kHz)

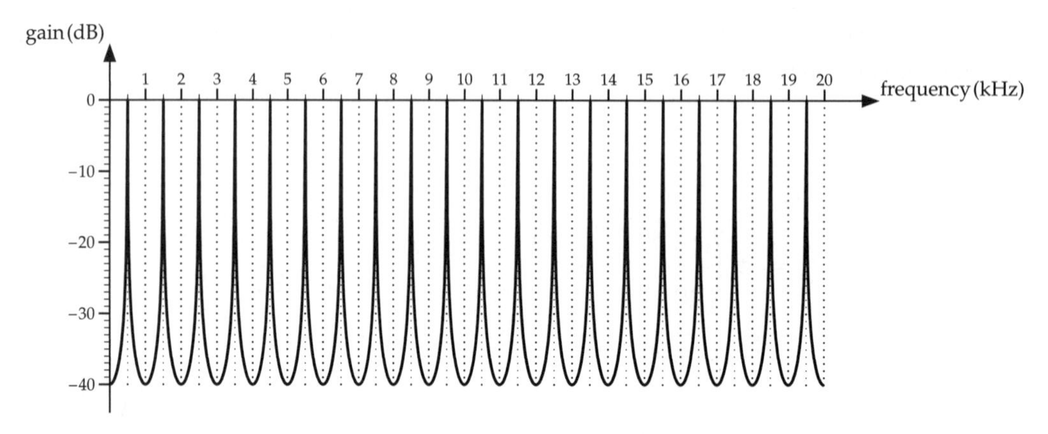

Figure 6.61 Frequency (magnitude) response plots for IIR comb filter with negative b_d prefix (g_{dB} = −40, f_c = 1kHz, f_S = 96kHz)

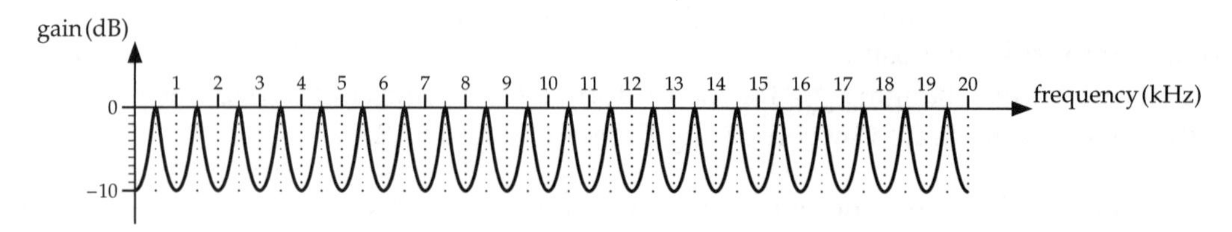

Figure 6.62 Frequency (magnitude) response plots for IIR comb filter with negative b_d prefix (g_{dB} = −10, f_c = 1kHz, f_S = 96kHz)

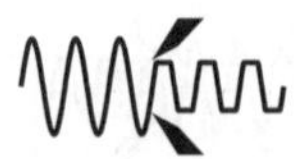

Figure 6.63 shows a pair of simple allpass designs. They both produce the same results. Figure 6.63a has some similarities to figure 6.41 (p.173), but with a variable delay of d samples.

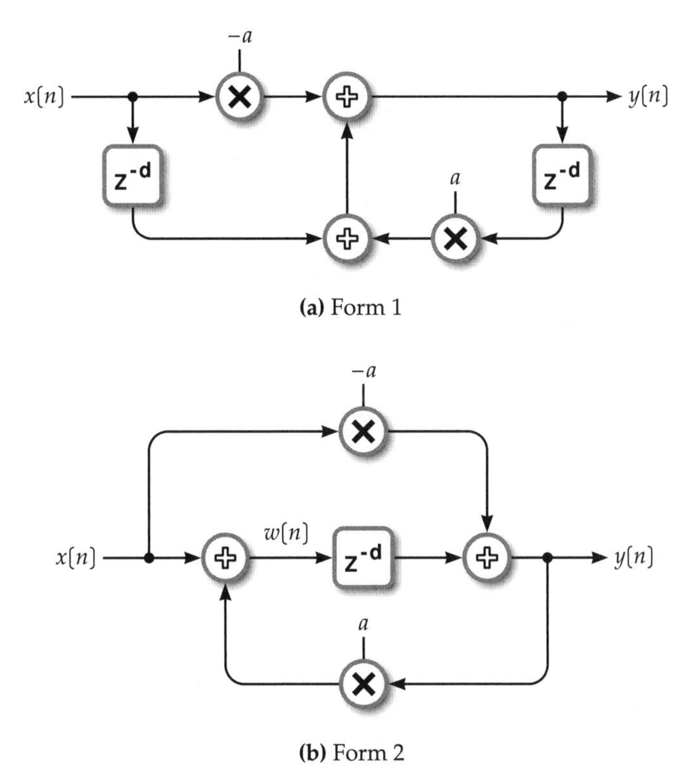

Figure 6.63 Simple allpass filters

The block diagrams translate into the following difference equation:

$$y[n] = -ax[n] + x[n-d] + ay[n-d] \qquad \boxed{6.22}$$

Figure 6.63b is more efficient than the first form, as it only uses a single delay, and so a single circular buffer when implemented. Its equations are as follows:

$$\begin{aligned} y[n] &= -ax[n] + w[n-d] \\ w[n] &= x[n] + ay[n] \end{aligned} \qquad \boxed{6.23}$$

which is completely equivalent to the previous equation. Note in equation 6.23 that it is necessary to calculate the value of $y[n]$ first, whose value can subsequently be used to calculate $w[n]$ (the value stored into the delay buffer).

In terms of configuration, the delay in samples might typically be configured in terms of a required delay time t or a frequency f_c, relative to the sample rate f_S, as follows:

$$d = tf_S \quad \text{or} \quad d = \frac{f_S}{f_c} \quad \text{and} \quad \begin{matrix} 0 < f_c \leqslant f_S \\ -1 < a < 1 \end{matrix} \tag{6.24}$$

As expected with an allpass filter, a flat magnitude response is produced (figure 6.64). The interesting effect is in terms of phase, as shown in figure 6.65. The phase variation repeats at multiples of f_c (which is related to the delay in samples as described in equation 6.24). When gain coefficient a is zero, the filter reduces to a simple delay of d samples, so the phase response is a straight line (as previously seen in figure 6.37d, p.169). If a is a value other than zero it changes the curvature of the phase response.

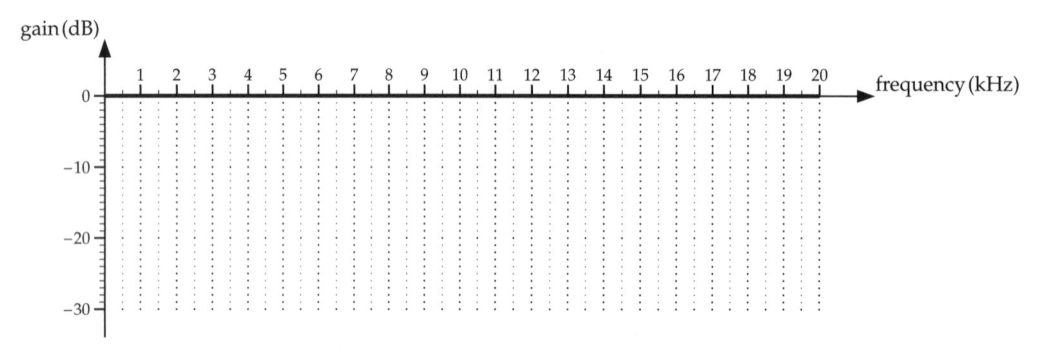

Figure 6.64 Frequency (magnitude) response plot for simple allpass filter

The changing phase response affects the group delay, as shown in figure 6.66. The further a deviates from zero, the higher the gradient of the phase response curve becomes, which translates to a larger peak in the group delay. This is significant as it means that it is possible to control the variation in delay with frequency.

It is also possible to create an allpass filter with somewhat different characteristics using the second order form of figure 6.45 (p.175) and equation 6.13 (p.175). The coefficients are calculated from the centre frequency f_c, Q value, and the sample rate f_S as follows:

$$\begin{aligned} b_2 &= \tan\left(\frac{\pi}{4} - \frac{\phi}{2Q}\right) \\ b_1 &= -(1 + b_2)\cos(\phi) \end{aligned} \quad \text{where} \quad \phi = \frac{2\pi f_c}{f_S} \quad \text{and} \quad \begin{matrix} 0 < f_c < \dfrac{Qf_S}{4} \\ f_c < \dfrac{f_S}{2} \end{matrix} \tag{6.25}$$

$$a_0 = b_2 \qquad a_1 = b_1 \qquad a_2 = 1$$

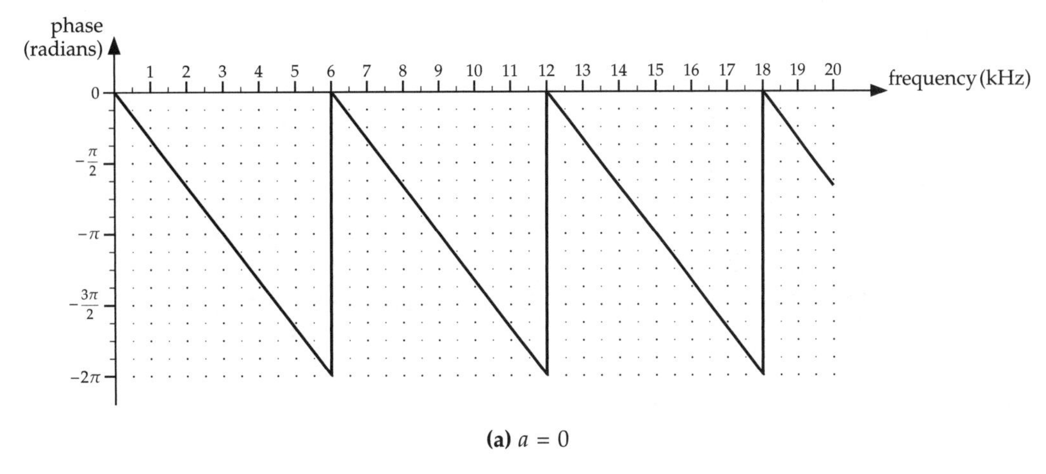

(a) $a = 0$

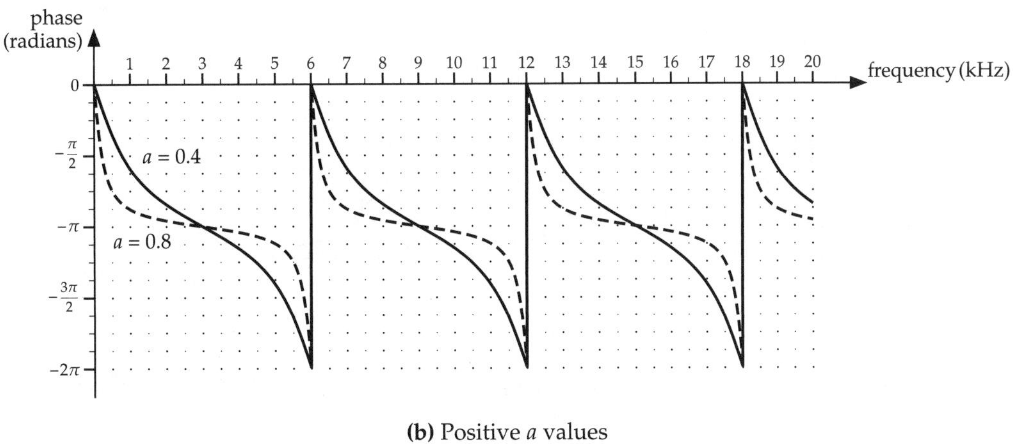

(b) Positive a values

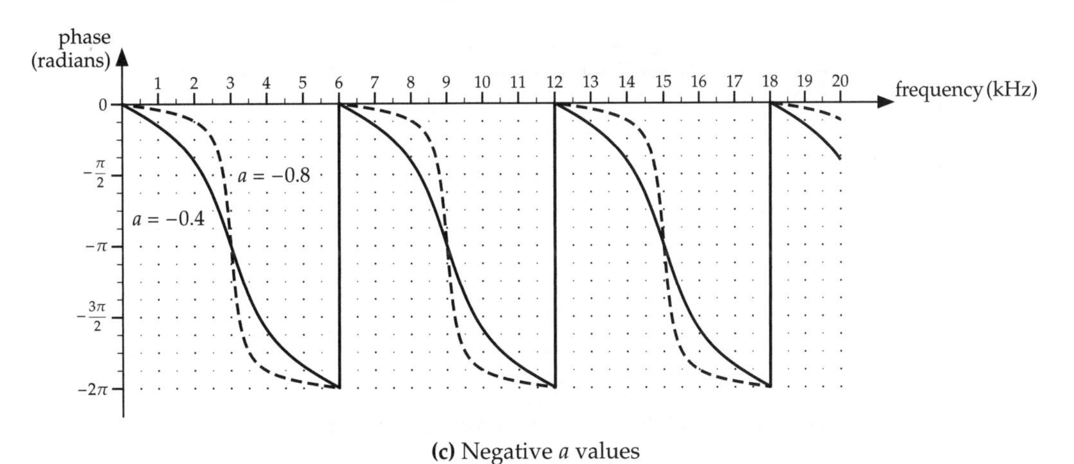

(c) Negative a values

Figure 6.65 Phase response plots for simple allpass filter (f_c = 6kHz, f_S = 96kHz)

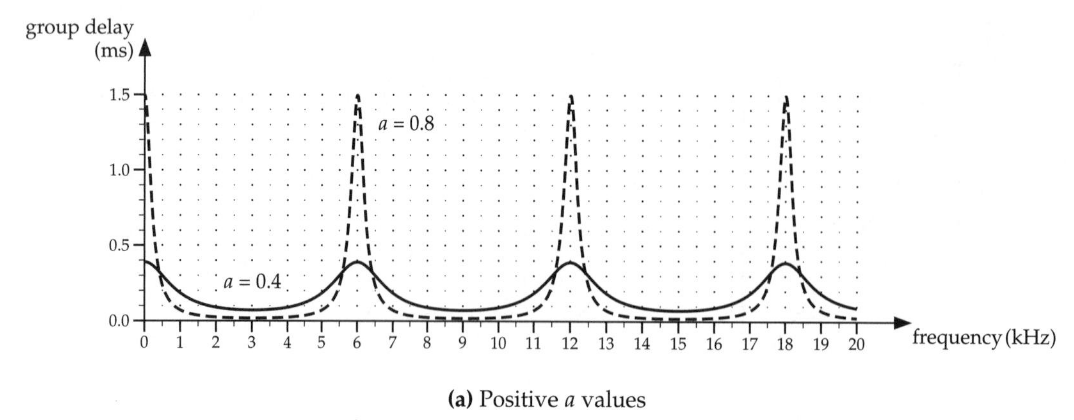

(a) Positive a values

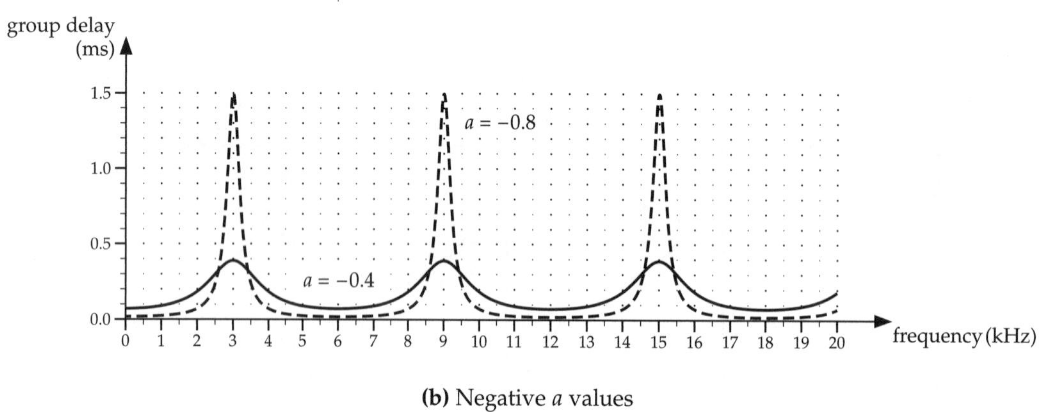

(b) Negative a values

Figure 6.66 Group delay plots for simple allpass filter (f_c = 6kHz, f_S = 96kHz)

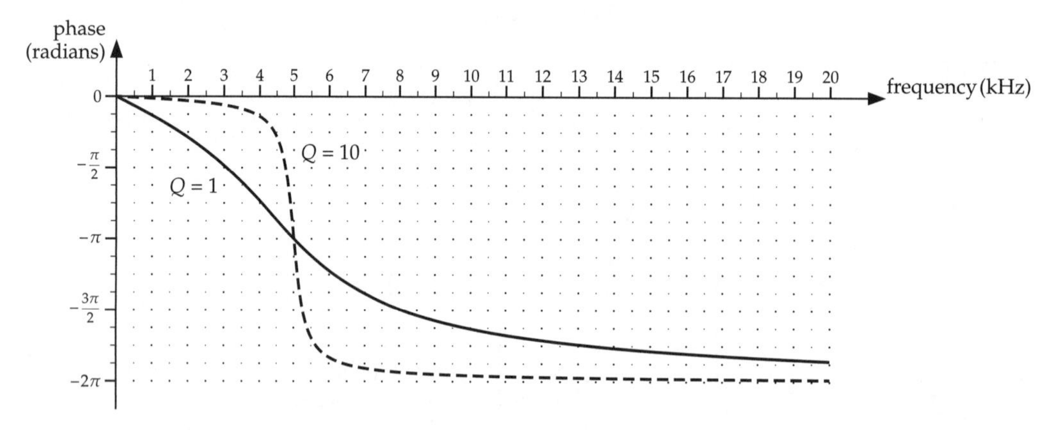

Figure 6.67 Phase response plots for second order allpass filter (f_c = 5kHz, f_S = 96kHz)

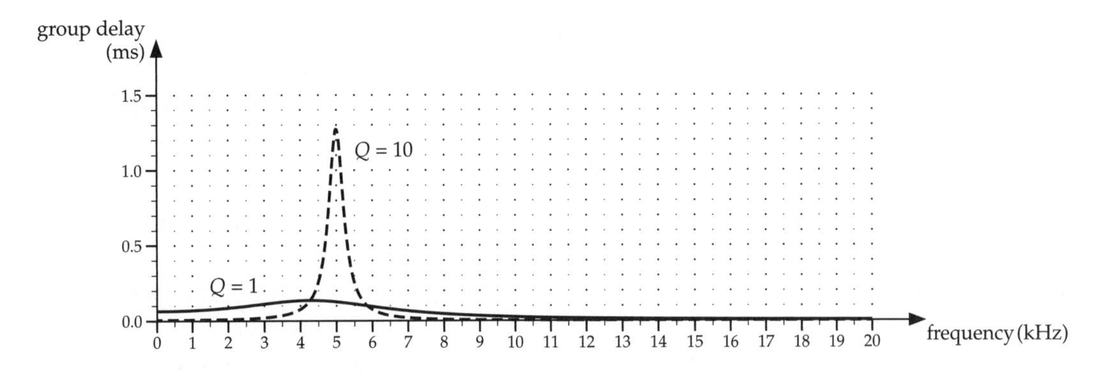

Figure 6.68 Group delay plots for second order allpass filter (f_c = 5kHz, f_S = 96kHz)

The second order allpass filter has the same magnitude response to the simple allpass form seen previously. However, it displays different phase and group delay responses, as shown in figures 6.67 and 6.68. Frequency f_c determines the point at which the phase response passes through $-\pi$. The slope of the line is determined by the value of Q. This form of allpass filter is used in a phaser effect (as described in §9.2.4, p.279) and in creating inharmonicity in a waveguide physical model synthesizer (§21.2.4, p.592).

6.5 Developing Processes and Learning More

Filters are a core tonal shaping element in a wide range of modification and synthesis processes. There is a clear relationship between filter configuration and perceived effect in many cases. For example, the form in figure 6.20 (p.157) can be used in different modifiers and synthesizers to allow a spectral envelope to be shaped. This might be applied at the end of a process to adjust the tonality of the output. In practical circumstances, filters are often adjusted by listening to the effect and modifying the control parameters appropriately.

In a number of cases the filter is not an ancillary tonal shaping element, but rather is the focus of the modification or synthesis technique. For example, a filter is the central element in the phaser (as described in §9.2.4, p.279) and the high resonance subtractive synthesizer (§17.4, p.517). Filters also have a role in selecting frequency ranges for further processing. For example, it might be desirable for a compressor sidechain to only react to a limited range of frequencies (as described in §11.4.2, p.364). Similarly, it is not always musically desirable that a modification effect (say, distortion or reverberation) is applied in the same way to all frequencies in the input. Splitting the frequency range using the techniques in §6.3.2 (p.159) can allow different frequency ranges to be processed in different ways.

Analogue and older audio systems often display characteristic filtering that might be simulated in the digital domain; for example, a traditional analogue telephone system, a guitar loudspeaker and cabinet, or an early phonograph/gramophone horn. Digital simulation for musical or sound effect purposes is both convenient to use and also provides the opportunity to modify the effect to suit a particular situation.

Many audio programming environments are supplied with filter implementations that allow the development of processes without having to start from scratch. A set of filters composed of lowpass, highpass, bandpass, bandreject, comb, and allpass types is sufficient for creating the audio processes in this book. There are, however, a wide range of filter designs that have subtle differences in their tonal characteristics. For example, the tonality of classic analogue synthesizers owes much to the nature of the filter designs that are used. It is useful, therefore, to have software simulations of those analogue filters, in order to achieve similar sounding results.

As an audio process becomes more sophisticated it can be desirable to select from a range of different filters to achieve particular tonal qualities. The following books describe a number of different filter designs that can help with this:

Pirkle, Will. 2013. *Designing Audio Effect Plug-Ins in C++: With Digital Audio Signal Processing Theory*. Burlington, MA: Focal Press.

Pirkle, Will. 2015. *Designing Software Synthesizer Plug-Ins in C++: For RackAFX, VST3, and Audio Units*. Burlington, MA: Focal Press.

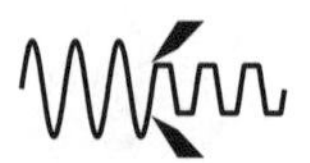

7

Distortion

7.1 Introduction

7.1.1 Avoiding and Creating Distortion

Distortion is defined as the deformation of a signal in some way as it passes through a system. Most electronic and computer systems attempt to avoid this such that the signal character is preserved. For example, a video system will usually attempt to create a visual output that matches the original input as accurately as possible. In such cases increased quality involves minimising distortion.

For musical applications the desirability of distortion depends on context. When recording classical music, microphones and preamplifiers will be chosen that have the most transparent and accurate character. However, an electric guitar amplifier might deliberately distort the signal for use in rock music. There are a wide range of analogue circuits and systems whose results include some amount of distortion, such as:

- Amplifiers.
- Loudspeakers.
- Communication links (such as analogue telephone lines, AM radio, submarine communications).
- Magnetic tape audio recorders.

Distortions such as those in the above circuits can be musically useful. Simulating them in digital form is convenient, and avoids the dangers of damaging equipment when used at the limits of operation.

It is very difficult to objectively measure whether a particular type of distortion is of higher or lower quality than another, as it depends on the desired musical results. One of the most common types of distortion is that associated with *non-linear amplification*, which is the focus of much of this chapter. Non-linear amplification means that the gain applied to a signal is not constant with input amplitude. This is closely related to waveshaping synthesis (described in §14.5.3, p.452). The general intention is to maintain some of the character of the original signal, while adding a controllable amount of distortion to make it less pure and more rough, trashy, fuzzy, or gritty.

7.1.2 Hard Clipping

In an ideal amplifier the signal is simply multiplied by a gain factor. For a preamplifier the maximum gain factor can be considerably larger than 1, in order to significantly increase the size of a small signal (such as from a guitar or microphone). In practical circumstances there are limits to how large the output signal can become when amplified before a *clipping* effect will occur (as described in §5.3.1, p.105). Figure 7.1 is a basic model of a practical amplifier where the gain and clipping functions are combined.

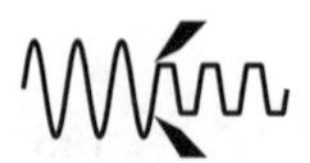

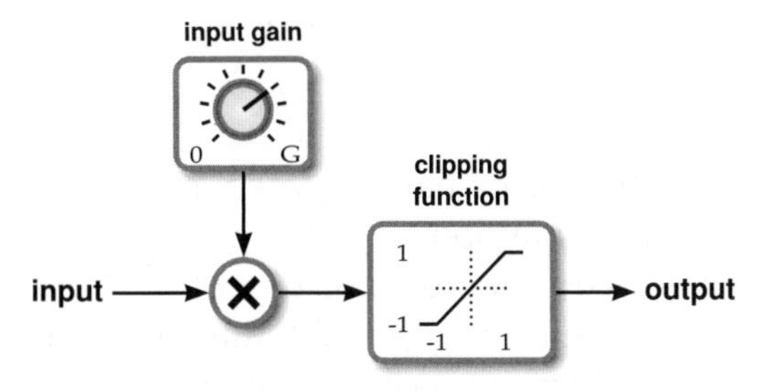

Figure 7.1 Basic practical amplifier form

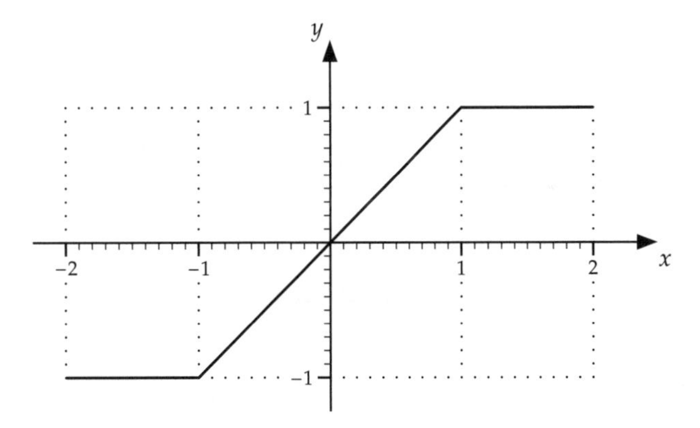

Figure 7.2 Hard clipping transfer function

Clipping is described by an input/output characteristic or *transfer function* where each input signal value (x) is mapped to an output value (y). Figure 7.2 shows the simplest of these, which is a *hard clipping* transfer function. The clipping limits (or thresholds) are at input values of −1 and +1. In between the limits there is a gradient of 1 such that output values are the same as the input ($y = x$). Beyond the limits the input values all map to the clipped values. For example:

input value x	-2.0	-1.5	-1.0	-0.5	0.0	0.5	1.0	1.5	2.0
output value y	-1.0	-1.0	-1.0	-0.5	0.0	0.5	1.0	1.0	1.0

The hard clipping function can be described by the following equation:

$$y = \begin{cases} 1 & \text{if} \quad x > 1 \\ x & \text{if} \quad -1 \leqslant x \leqslant 1 \\ -1 & \text{if} \quad x < -1 \end{cases} \tag{7.1}$$

Algorithm 7.1 expresses equation 7.1 in a form that could be implemented in a computer program.

The effect of amplification followed by hard clipping is illustrated in figure 7.3. At each point in time the input value is multiplied by the gain value (2 in this example). The result is then mapped using the transfer function described above. Notice that the parts of the amplified signal that fall within the clipping limits retain the sinusoidal shape of the input. However, the clipped values produce flat waveform regions and a change of tonal character.

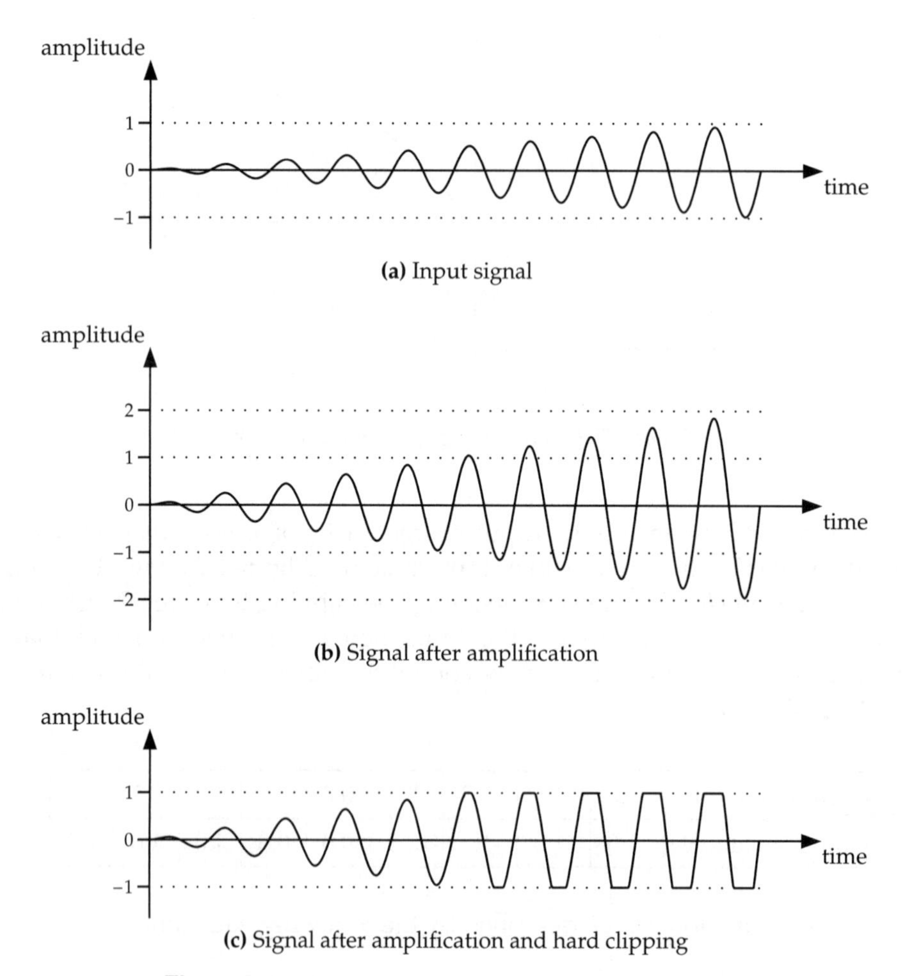

Figure 7.3 Amplification ×2 and hard clipping at ±1

Algorithm 7.1 – Hard clipping function

input : input signal `in`
output: output signal `out`

```
out = in
if out > 1 then
  out = 1
if out < −1 then
  out = −1
```

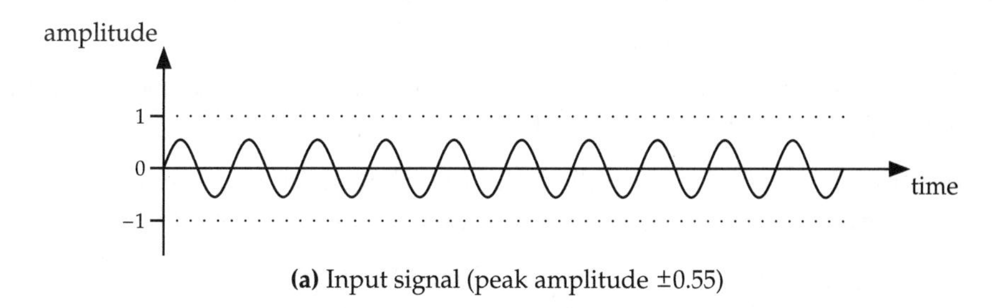

(a) Input signal (peak amplitude ±0.55)

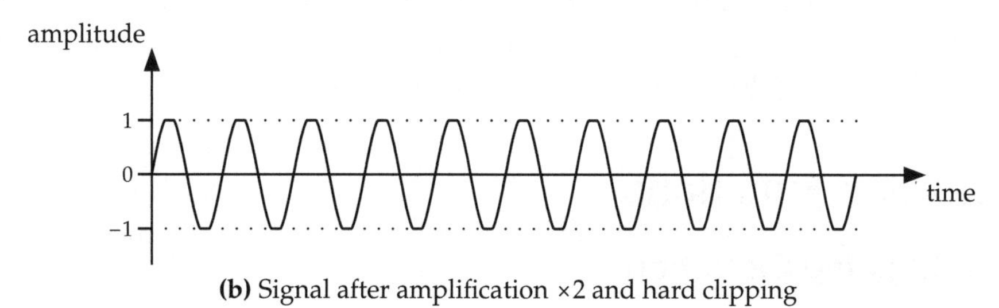

(b) Signal after amplification ×2 and hard clipping

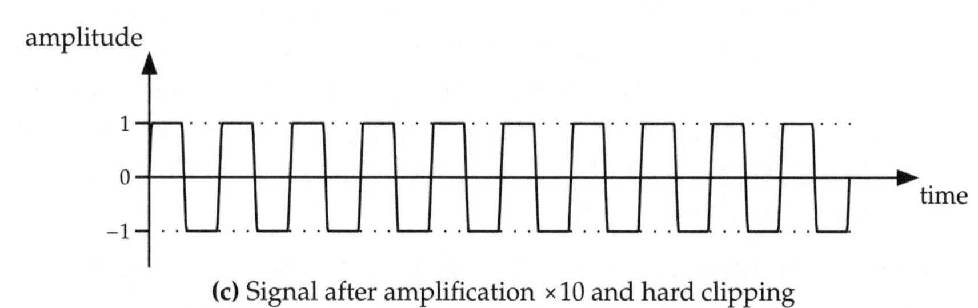

(c) Signal after amplification ×10 and hard clipping

Figure 7.4 Amplification by different factors, hard clipping at ±1

The gain value controls how much of the signal is beyond the clipping limits, and therefore the resulting tonal character. Figure 7.4 shows the effect of hard clipping with variable amplification of the input signal. Notice how the output waveform has larger flattened regions with greater amplification, increasing the similarity to a square wave. However the part of the signal that is not clipped actually retains its original (sinusoidal) shape as it is linearly amplified.

Figure 7.5 shows three average spectrum plots which correspond to the time domain plots in figure 7.4. A logarithmic amplitude scale has been chosen to make small amplitude details more apparent, and the largest partial has been normalised to 0dB. Note the following points:

- A sinusoid is a single peak in the frequency domain. As such, if a modification to the frequency content of the input occurs due to the distortion, then it is clearly apparent.
- As the amplitude multiplier increases, the amount of clipping increases. This is reflected in the increasing amplitude of the additional partials added to the signal.
- The additional components are odd-numbered harmonics of the 250Hz fundamental frequency (750Hz, 1250Hz, 1750Hz etc).
- The spectral envelope shapes in the latter two plots exhibit rising and falling values that are characteristic of rectangular pulse waveforms (as shown in figure 4.10, p.82).

The overall perceptual effect of hard clipping distortion is that it produces a fairly harsh, fuzzy tone due to the high frequency partials that are added by the process. The character is controllable to an extent by varying the amplification, which might include a large range of gain values (such as up to a factor of 30, or even more).

7.2 Distortion Functions

7.2.1 Soft Clipping Distortion

Hard clipping distortion is not progressive with increasing input signal amplitude, as shown by the transfer function in figure 7.2 (p.197). This means that distortion only occurs when parts of the signal are beyond the clipping limits. Many musical signals have significant dynamic variation in amplitude, so the loudest parts are distorted, but quiet note events and the latter part of decaying sounds are not. Hard clipping distortion therefore has the following characteristics:

- At moderate gains, there is a marked audible difference between the parts of the signal that retain their original shape and those that are clipped.
- High gains are required to amplify a significant proportion of the signal values beyond the clipping limits, and so achieve significant distortion.

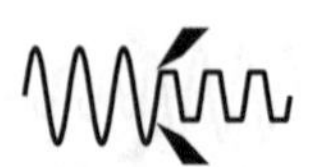

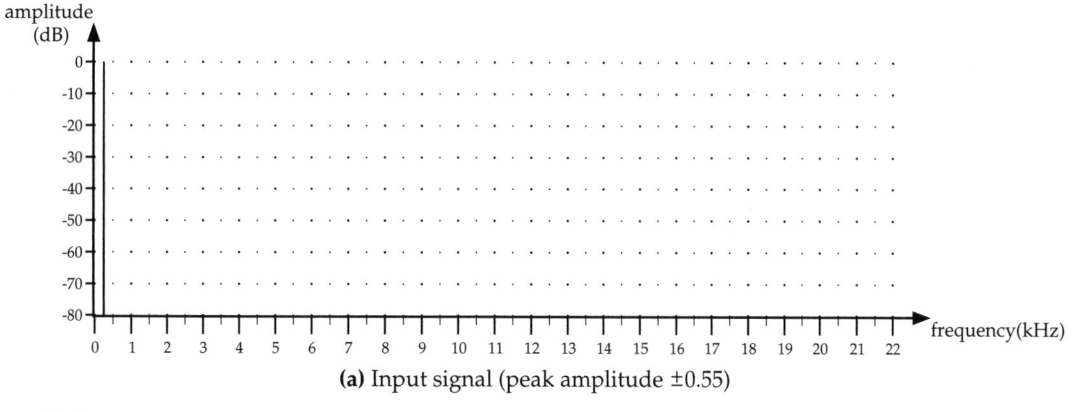

(a) Input signal (peak amplitude ±0.55)

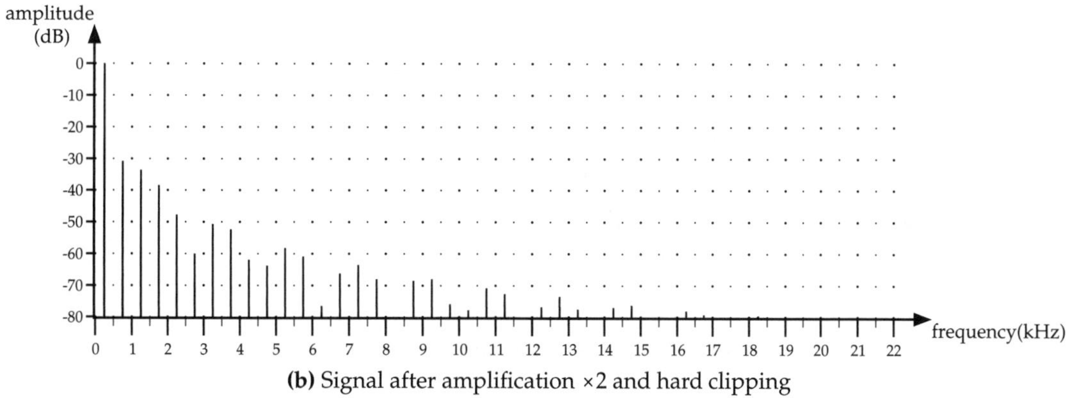

(b) Signal after amplification ×2 and hard clipping

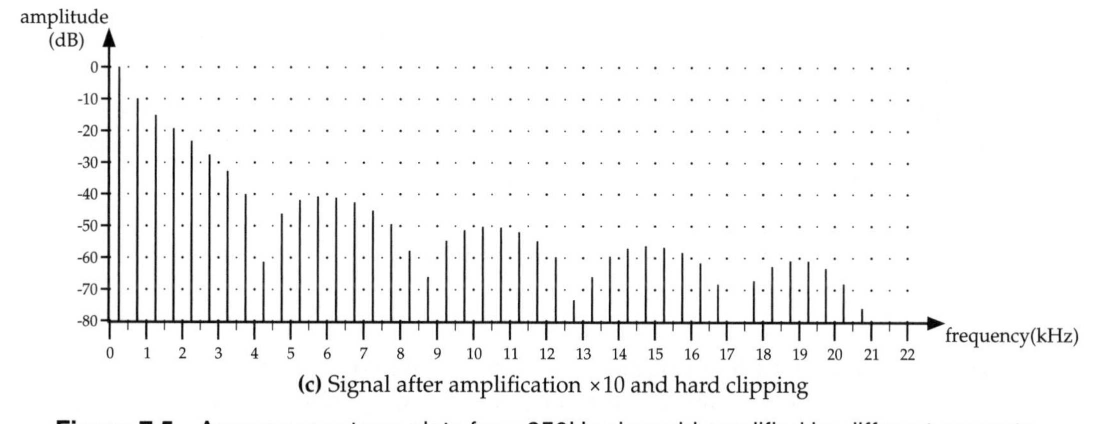

(c) Signal after amplification ×10 and hard clipping

Figure 7.5 Average spectrum plots for a 250Hz sinusoid amplified by different amounts, hard clipping at ±1

- Signal variations that fall beyond the clipping limits are completely removed and changed into a flat line.

To make distortion more controllable in musical contexts it is desirable to have transfer functions that allow progressive distortion with amplitude gain, or input amplitude (for example, depending on the force with which a guitar is plucked). Figure 7.6 shows a *soft clipping* transfer function. The function includes a shaped region in between the linear amplification and hard clipping regions seen before. This sigmoid (s-shaped) form has some similarities to the amplification associated with guitar amplifiers and distortion circuits.

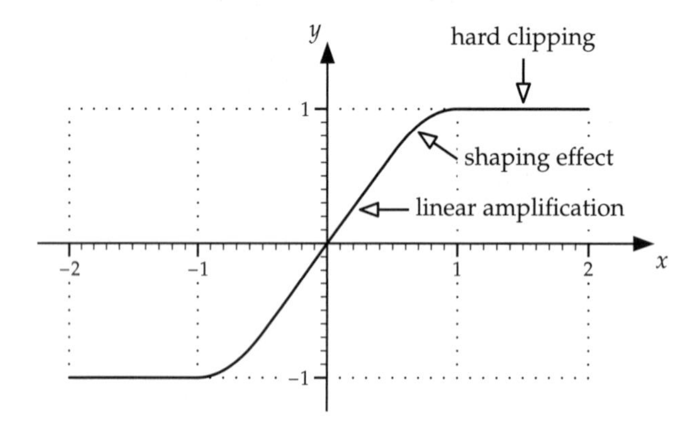

Figure 7.6 Example soft clipping transfer function

The result of soft clipping is that increasing input amplitude relates to gradually increasing distortion, due to increasing deviation of the shape compared to the original input. With suitable input gain this can produce a less harsh result than hard clipping alone. There is also the potential to change the shape of the soft clipping transfer function shape to achieve a range of slightly different distortion characters.

Figure 7.7 extends the form in figure 7.1 (p.197) to include a shaping function to achieve soft clipping effects. Note the following:

- The intention is that the input signal will be amplified to achieve progressive distortion with increasing amplitude (using the shaping effect region of the transfer function). This is sometimes called *overdrive distortion*. If too much input gain is used, then most of the signal will fall in the hard clipping region and the tonal effect of the shaping function will be less significant. Generally, much less input gain will be used than with figure 7.1.

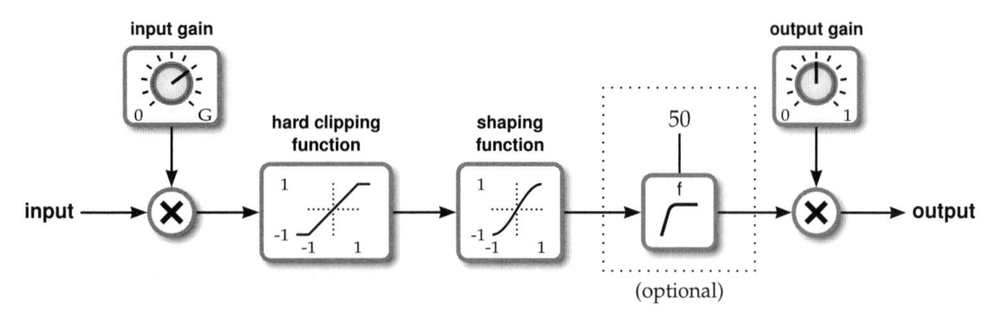

Figure 7.7 Shaped distortion form

- The hard clipping transfer function is the same as that shown in figure 7.2 (p.197). Positioning the clipping function before the shaping function ensures that only values between −1 and +1 reach the shaping effect. This often makes it easier to specify the equation for the shaping function, as there is only a limited range of input values.
- In some cases the shaping function will be asymmetric and create an offset in the average amplitude of the waveform (often known as a DC offset). The highpass filter is employed in these circumstances to address this issue.
- The output gain control is useful to control the final level, as the previous stages can increase the amplitude considerably.

Figure 7.8 describes a range of equations that can be used in the shaping function block in figure 7.7. The first equation is a simple sine function (which takes an argument in radians). The limitation with that equation is that there is no control over the curvature of the function. The other equations include a shaping parameter c that allows the function to be reshaped from a straight line with a gradient of 1 (like simple hard clipping) through to lines with significant curvatures. The plots show multiple examples for each equation depending on the value of c. Note the following:

- The subtle differences between the shapes of the functions are audible when careful process configuration is used.
- The character of the effect is controlled by a combination of the input gain and the shaping parameter c.
- As the value of c is increased, the gradient of the line for low input values also increases, which means that the shaping function applies more gain to those values.
- The range of c values appropriate to each equation is different, as shown by the example values in the plots. To achieve a progressive change in tonality requires some suitable mapping of the non-linear control values (some related mapping techniques are described in Chapter 24).

Function 1

$$y = \sin(0.5\pi x) \quad \text{where} \quad -1 \leqslant x \leqslant 1$$

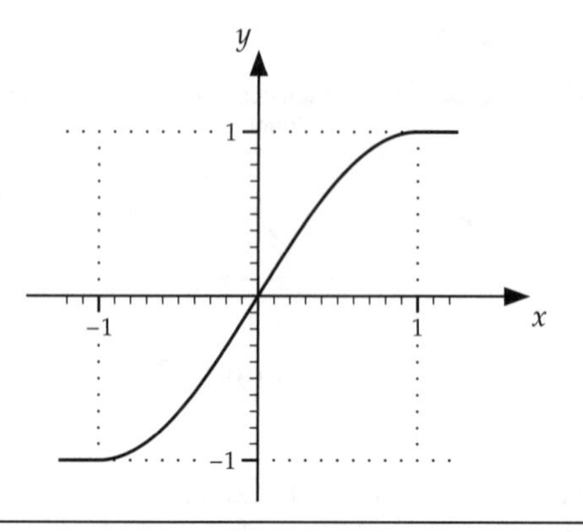

Function 2

$$y = \begin{cases} \dfrac{x^2 - 2x + (c-1)^2}{c(c-2)} & \text{if} \quad k < x \leqslant 1 \\ \dfrac{2}{2-c}x & \text{if} \quad -k < x \leqslant k \\ \dfrac{x^2 + 2x + (c-1)^2}{c(2-c)} & \text{if} \quad -1 \leqslant x \leqslant -k \end{cases}$$

$$\text{where} \quad k = 1 - c \quad \text{and} \quad 0 < c \leqslant 1$$

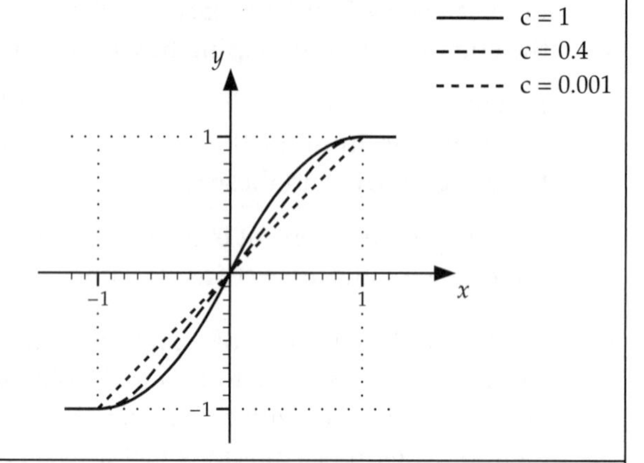

Function 3

$$y = \frac{\tanh(cx)}{\tanh(c)} \quad \text{where} \quad -1 \leqslant x \leqslant 1$$

$$\text{and} \quad c > 0$$

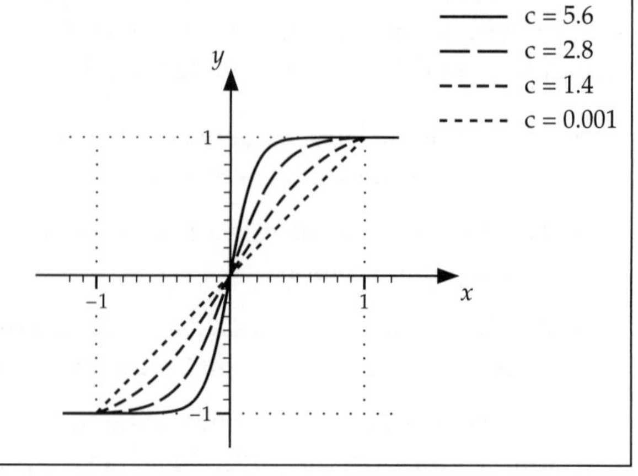

Figure 7.8 Soft clipping shaping functions (continued on the next page)

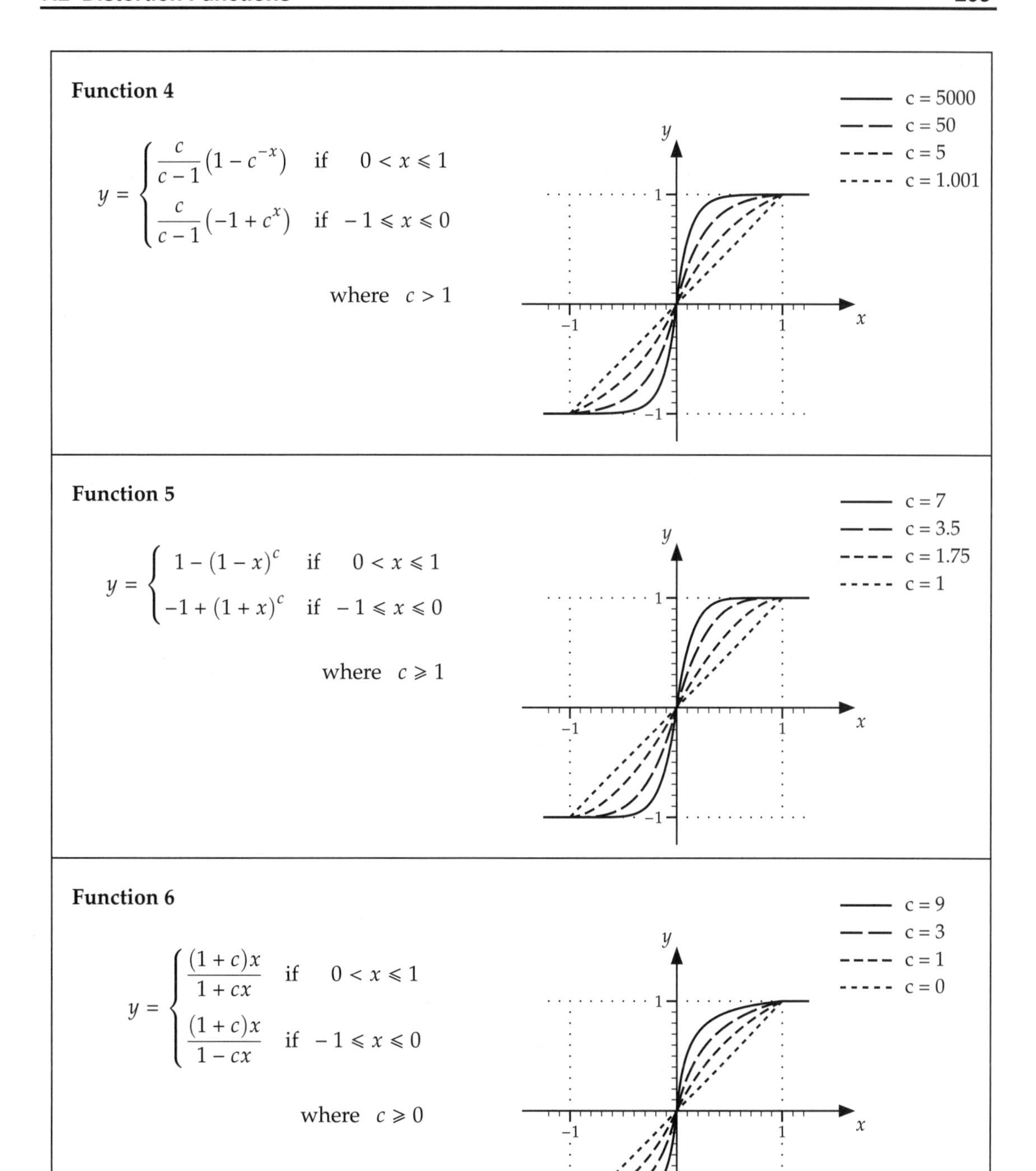

Figure 7.8 Soft clipping shaping functions (continued from the previous page)

The best way of selecting between the functions is to test them with suitable musical input material. The differences might be too subtle for the choice to be significant, or it might be that a very particular character is required in a particular context.

Figure 7.9b shows an example of soft clipping using the tanh-based function from figure 7.8, which illustrates both the amplification of small signals and the reshaping of the sinusoidal input waveform that is produced by the transfer function.

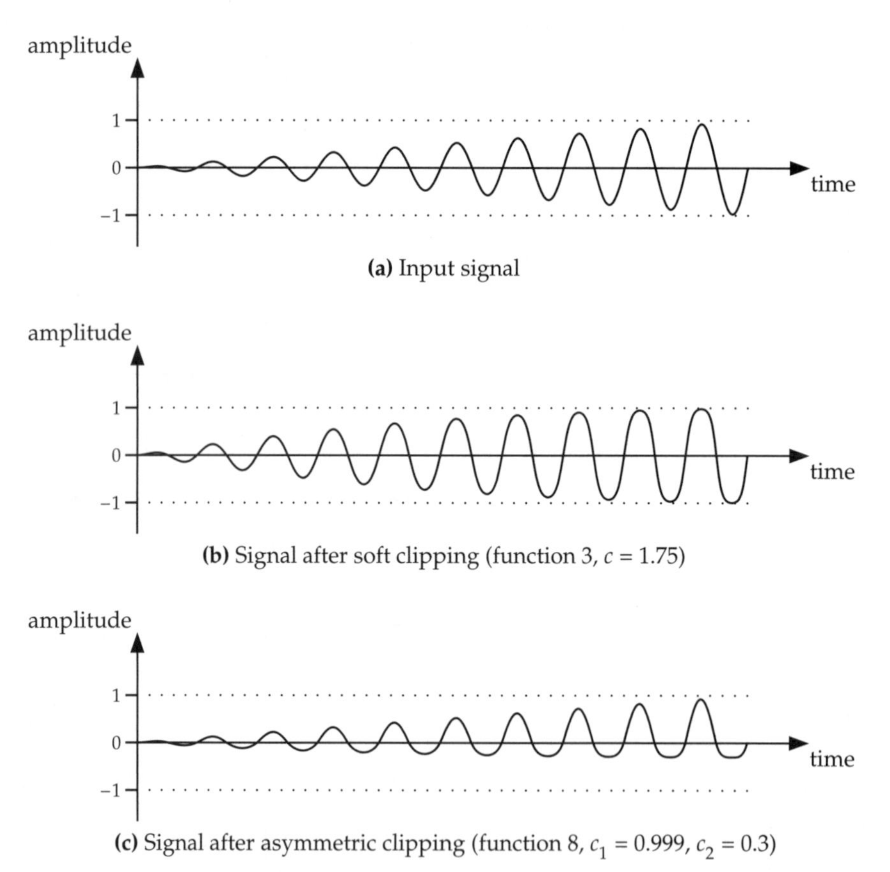

Figure 7.9 Shaping function examples (input gain = 1, no filter, output gain = 1)

The functions in figure 7.8 have a symmetric mapping characteristic for positive and negative values. An interesting tonal variation can be achieved by distorting positive and negative values in different ways. Figure 7.10 describes functions that can achieve this. The control parameters c_1 and c_2 relate to the y value that the function reaches at $x = 1$ and $x = -1$ respectively. As the control values become smaller the distortion becomes more severe (unlike the functions in figure 7.8). Choosing different values for c_1 and c_2 produces asymmetric results.

Figure 7.9c shows an example asymmetric clipping result. Notice how the output waveform is now offset vertically in terms of its average level, which means that a very low frequency component has been added. This can cause problems in subsequent processing, which means that the highpass filter in figure 7.7 (p.203) should be included. It is possible to apply asymmetric shaping after one of the functions in figure 7.8 is applied, such that the two are combined. Further ways of combining distortions are described in §7.2.3 (p.208).

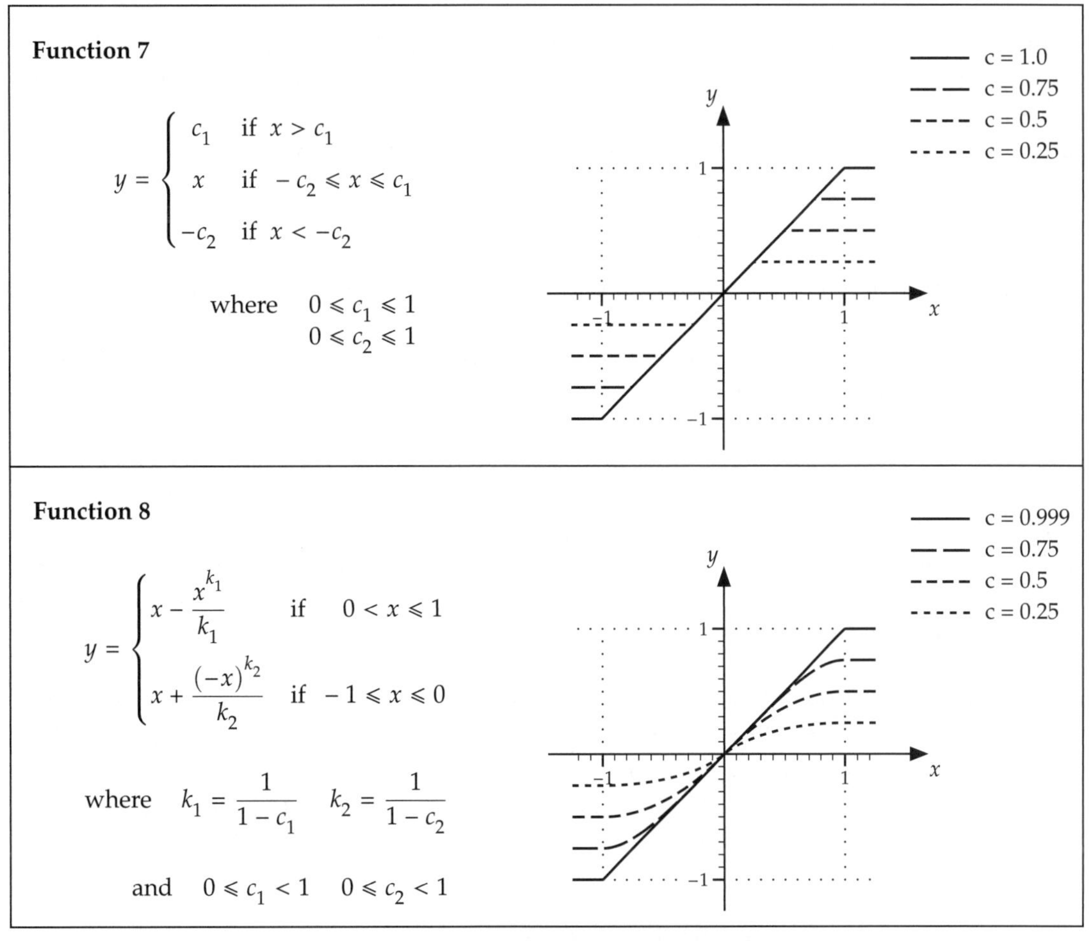

Figure 7.10 Asymmetric shaping functions

7.2.2 Other Distortion Transfer Functions

The functions in §7.2.1 tend towards the typical soft clipping shape in figure 7.6 (p.202) with its regions of linear amplification, shaping, and hard clipping. As the shaping effect deviates further from that pattern, the relationship between input and output character can become less clear. However, such shaping can still have interesting tonal characteristics. Figure 7.11 illustrates mapping functions that can be used in the shaping function block in figure 7.7 (p.203). Figure 7.12 shows some example results for those functions in the time domain.

Function 9 has a quarter circle shape, which produces significant distortion at a wide range of input signal amplitudes. There is large gain at low amplitudes, so only a modest input gain is required before the shaping function. It is possible for background noise to be amplified too much, which might necessitate the use of a noise gate (described in Chapter 11).

Function 10 with a control parameter $c = 0$ is called taking the absolute value (or full wave rectification), where negative values are made positive. This is quite a strong distortion effect that often results in audible octave intervals from the original pitch of the input. A range of related distortions are achieved with c values other than 0, and the strength of the effect decreases as c increases.

Function 11 achieves amplitude quantization, which is sometimes called *bitcrushing*. The effect has some similarities to the characteristics of early home computer audio systems, which had limited bit depth to represent audio samples (bit depth is discussed in §2.2.5, p.37). Parameter c controls the number of steps in the output, and as c decreases the distortion becomes stronger. If c is not an integer value then the output of this function should be hard clipped with equation 7.1 (p.197).

There are endless possibilities for creating different distortion transfer function shapes. The potential exists for using a graphical system to draw and modify a function. It is then necessary to have a mechanism for mapping input values through the function to output values. One method is to store the y axis values for a graphical line in a lookup table, and access them with algorithm 14.14 (p.448), as described in §14.4.2, p.445.

7.2.3 Controlling Distortion Character

Distortion character can be changed by varying the input gain, function type, and control parameter values described previously. Control over distortion can be extended by use of other modification and combination techniques, in order to achieve a particular desired tonality.

Function 9

$$y = \begin{cases} \sqrt{1-(x-1)^2} & \text{if} \quad 0 < x \leqslant 1 \\ -\sqrt{1-(x+1)^2} & \text{if} \quad -1 \leqslant x \leqslant 0 \end{cases}$$

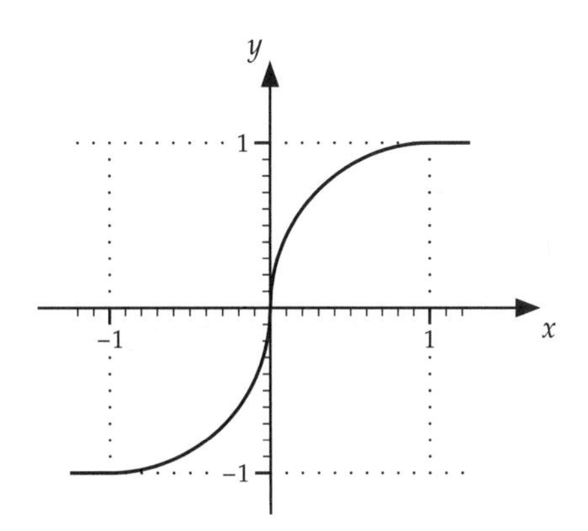

Function 10

$$y = \begin{cases} x & \text{if} \quad -c < x \leqslant 1 \\ -2c - x & \text{if} \quad -1 \leqslant x \leqslant -c \end{cases}$$

$$\text{where} \quad 0 \leqslant c \leqslant 1$$

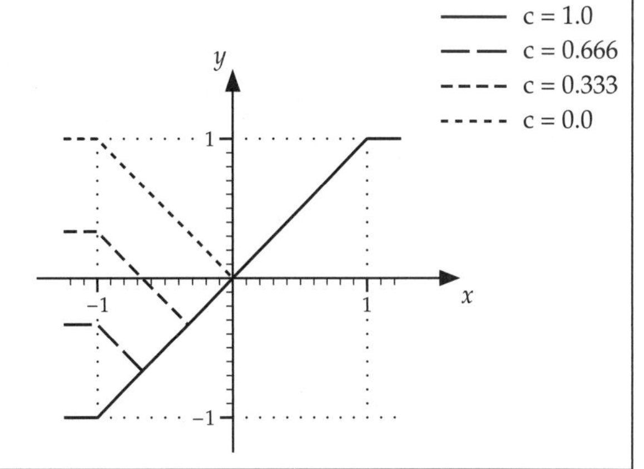

Function 11

$$y = \frac{R(cx)}{c} \quad \text{if} \quad -1 \leqslant x \leqslant 1$$

where $R()$ is a rounding function and $c \geqslant 1$

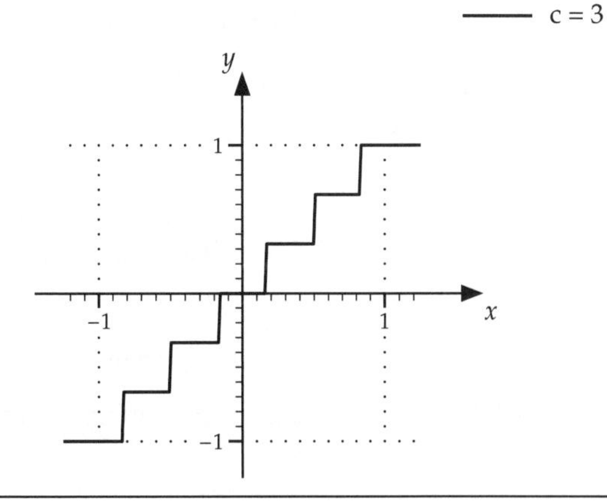

Figure 7.11 Other shaping functions

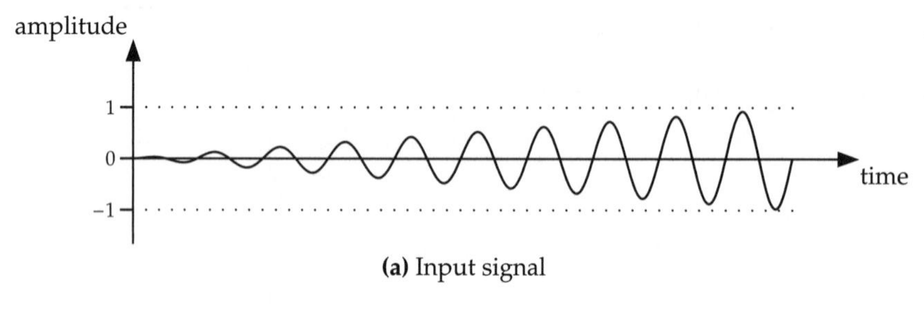

(a) Input signal

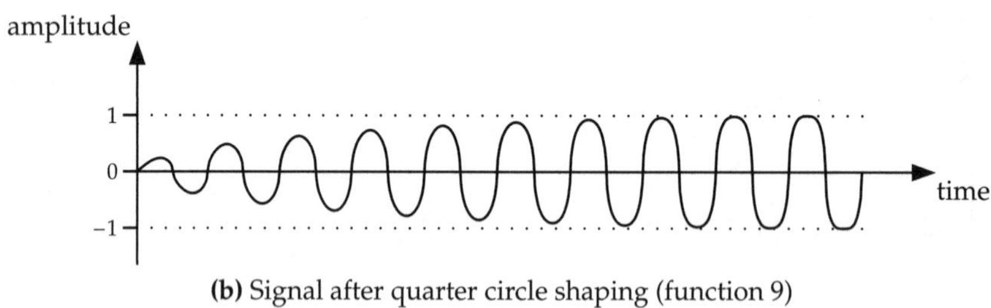

(b) Signal after quarter circle shaping (function 9)

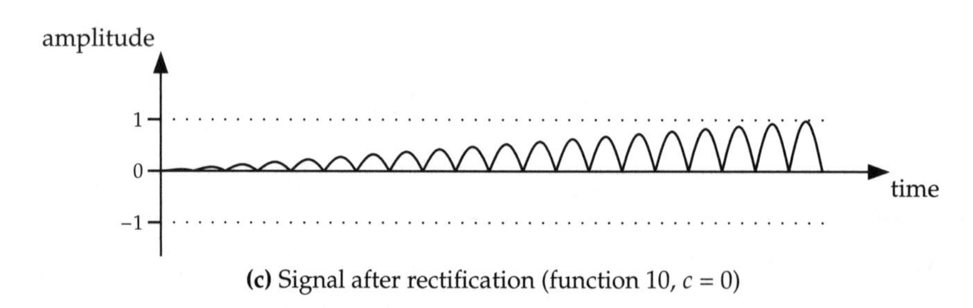

(c) Signal after rectification (function 10, $c = 0$)

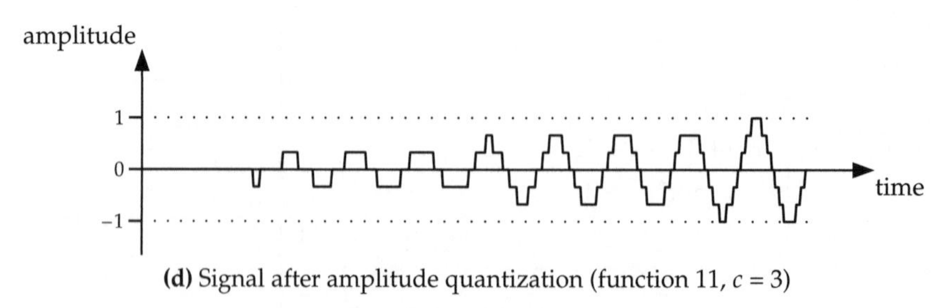

(d) Signal after amplitude quantization (function 11, $c = 3$)

Figure 7.12 Other shaping function examples (input gain = 1, no filter, output gain = 1)

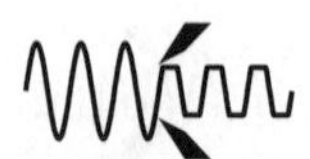

Series and Parallel Combination

If two distortion functions exist but neither achieve the required result on their own, then it can be appropriate to combine them in series or parallel. A series (cascade) combination means that each function builds on that produced by the previous shaping effect (as described in §5.6.2, p.129). For example, a symmetric shaping function from figure 7.8 (p.204) might be followed by an asymmetric function from figure 7.10 (p.207). Cascaded functions are likely to require less input gain than when a single function is used, because samples are distorted twice, making the effect more severe.

Parallel combination is not the same effect as series combination as the distortions do not build on each other, but retain some independence. Blending a dry path with a distorted path (a wet/dry ratio mix, figure 5.50, p.134) or two different distortions (a wet/wet mix, figure 5.51a, p.135) allows the relative amount of each signal to be balanced in the required manner.

Sample Rate Considerations

Transfer function clipping distortion typically adds frequency partials to the signal that are above those in the original input, as demonstrated in figure 7.5 (p.201). This gives the potential for partials being created above the Nyquist frequency, which will cause aliasing (see §2.2.2, p.28). Whether this is a significant contributor to the sound character will depend on the frequencies of the input partials, the severity of the distortion, the sample rate chosen, and whether the required part of the sound masks the audibility of the aliased partials. Using a higher sample rate will reduce the aliasing, as described in §23.1.3 (p.637).

Pre- and Post-Distortion Filtering

Filtering is often used to control distortion character. A simple technique is to use a lowpass filter in series after the distortion, where increasing the cutoff frequency generally relates to increasing brightness and harshness. A more sophisticated method is to use a parallel set of bandpass filters (figure 6.20, p.157) to modify the spectral envelope. This has some similarities to the nature of a guitar "combo" amplifier where the loudspeaker and cabinet modify the character of the signal produced by the amplifier.

Filtering that occurs before the distortion function produces different results to that which occurs afterwards. Attenuating high frequencies before distortion with a lowpass filter can sometimes be used to reduce aliasing, as fewer high frequency partials are created. With a pre-distortion lowpass filter it is still possible to have output partials at frequencies well above the filter cutoff with significant amplitude, due to the nature of the distortion process. This is in contrast to the same filter used after the distortion. One technique is to use series lowpass and highpass filters (figure 6.29, p.162) before the distortion to allow control of the range of frequencies that are distorted.

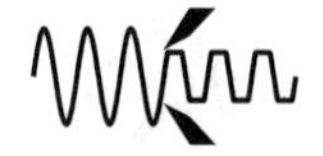

Multi-Band Techniques

Figure 7.13 illustrates the process of using filters to separate an input signal into multiple frequency bands, distort them in different ways and then mix the results. This allows a balance of distortion characteristics across the frequency spectrum. Having more distortion of low frequencies than of high frequencies can be used to reduce the harshness and aliasing that might occur when distorting the whole frequency spectrum at once. Distorting within frequency bands will reduce *intermodulation distortion*, which can mean that the output has greater clarity.

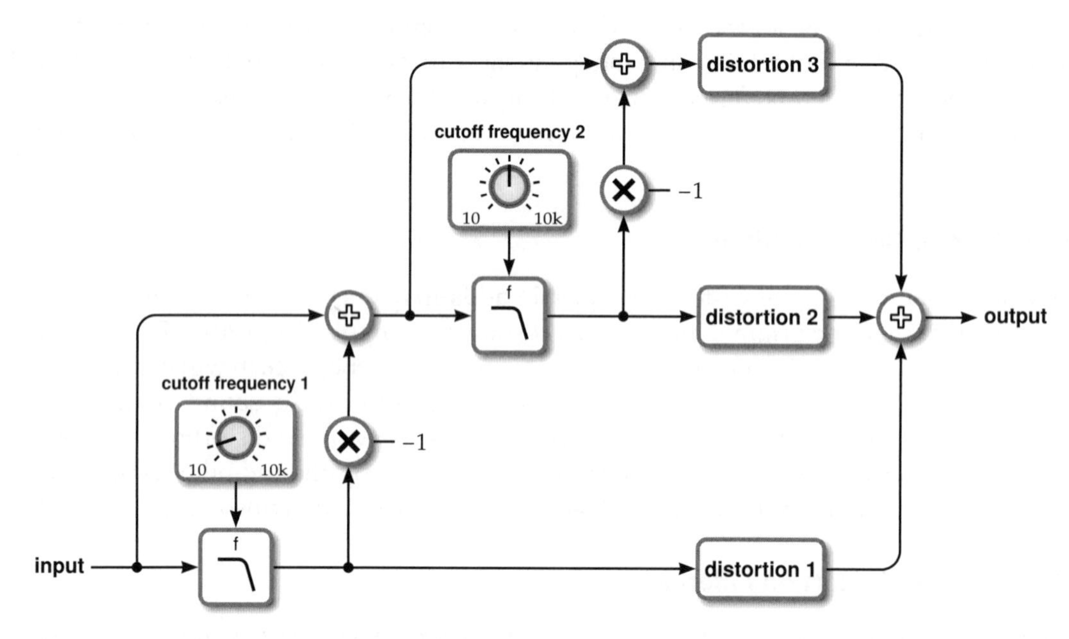

Figure 7.13 Multi-band distortion

The figure uses a similar form to that in figure 6.27 (p.161) to create three frequency bands. The splitting technique can be extended to more bands, or reduced to fewer if required. First order filters are suitable. Example values for cutoff frequencies 1 and 2 are 250Hz and 2.5kHz respectively, to achieve bands from 0 to 250Hz, 250Hz to 2.5kHz, and above 2.5kHz. These can be adjusted to suit the material and desired effect.

The three frequency bands are each distorted using a process such as figure 7.7 (p.203). It is important that every distortion path has its own input and output gain controls. Typical musical sounds have more amplitude at lower frequencies, so if all the input gains are the same then different amounts of distortion will occur in each path. Having less distortion with increasing frequency will often be desirable, but input gains might be adjusted for different results. The output gains can be used to compensate for different signal gain in different paths and to achieve the desired spectral balance.

The audible differences between full-band and multi-band techniques can sometimes be subtle. When configuring the process it is often useful to listen to each distortion path output individually before mixing them together. This can make it easier to set the filter frequencies and distortion parameters.

7.3 Distortion of Complex Signals

It is difficult to predict the tonal character effect of a distortion process on a practical musical input due to the non-linear nature of transfer function-based distortion. Two key considerations are as follows:

- Typical musical signals have many frequency partials, rather than a single sinusoid as was used to illustrate distortion effects in §7.1 and §7.2.
- The amplitude envelope of musical signals changes over time, such as while a note is decaying or if different notes are played with different force. This means that different parts of the distortion transfer function are used at different times.

Figure 7.14a shows the results of hard clipping a sinusoid. The shape is unaltered when the peak amplitude is below the clipping limit, but there is a waveform (and so tonal) modification when the amplitude is greater. The square wave examples in figure 7.14b show a different effect, where there is no difference in waveform shape when clipping, and so no tonal change (although there is an amplitude change). This is a simple example of how a distortion process can produce different results with different inputs.

Figure 7.15 illustrates clipping effects on a signal with multiple frequency partials. In the hard clipping case the signal variations above the clipping limit are removed from the output. Below the clipping limit there is a difference between hard and soft clipping. While the hard clipping preserves the original variations, with soft clipping the variations at high amplitude are progressively reduced in height as the peak approaches the hard clipping limit.

Both types of clipping can reduce the amplitude difference between the largest and smallest variations. This is a type of instantaneous dynamic range compression, which is related to the processes described in Chapter 11. However the compressors described in that chapter analyse longer-term amplitude envelope variations, and attempt to avoid distortion effects.

The non-linearity of distortion is also apparent in the frequency domain:

- Figure 7.16a shows a pair of partials at 100Hz and 400Hz which are mixed together, but with no other processing.

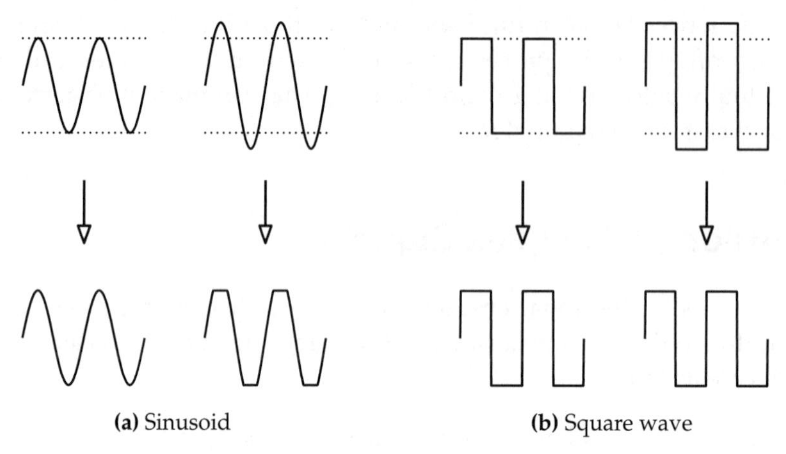

Figure 7.14 Hard clipping examples

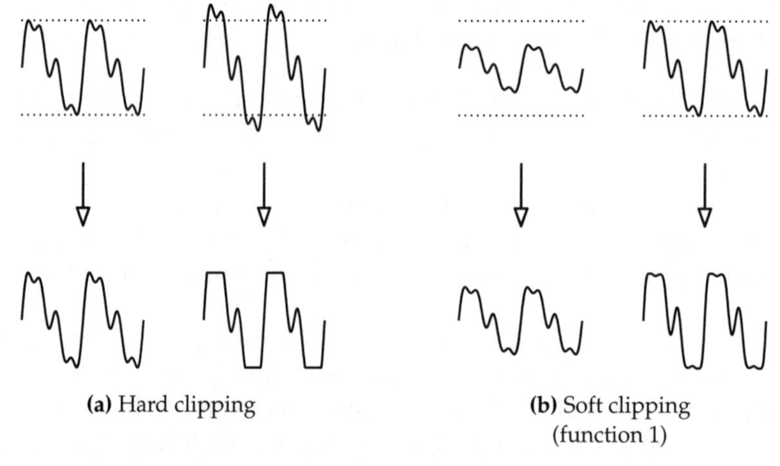

Figure 7.15 Hard and soft clipping comparisons

- Figure 7.16b shows what happens if each partial is separately hard clipped, and then the two results are mixed together. As might be expected with a clipped sinusoid, odd harmonics of each partial are present; 300Hz, 500Hz, 700Hz, and so on for the 100Hz partial; 1.2kHz, 2kHz, 2.8kHz, and so on for the 400Hz partial.

- Figure 7.16c shows the effect of mixing the two partials first, and then hard clipping the combination. The result is significantly different from figure 7.16b. There are now **even** harmonics of 100Hz present, and a pattern of amplitudes that is not as obvious as that in figure 7.16b.

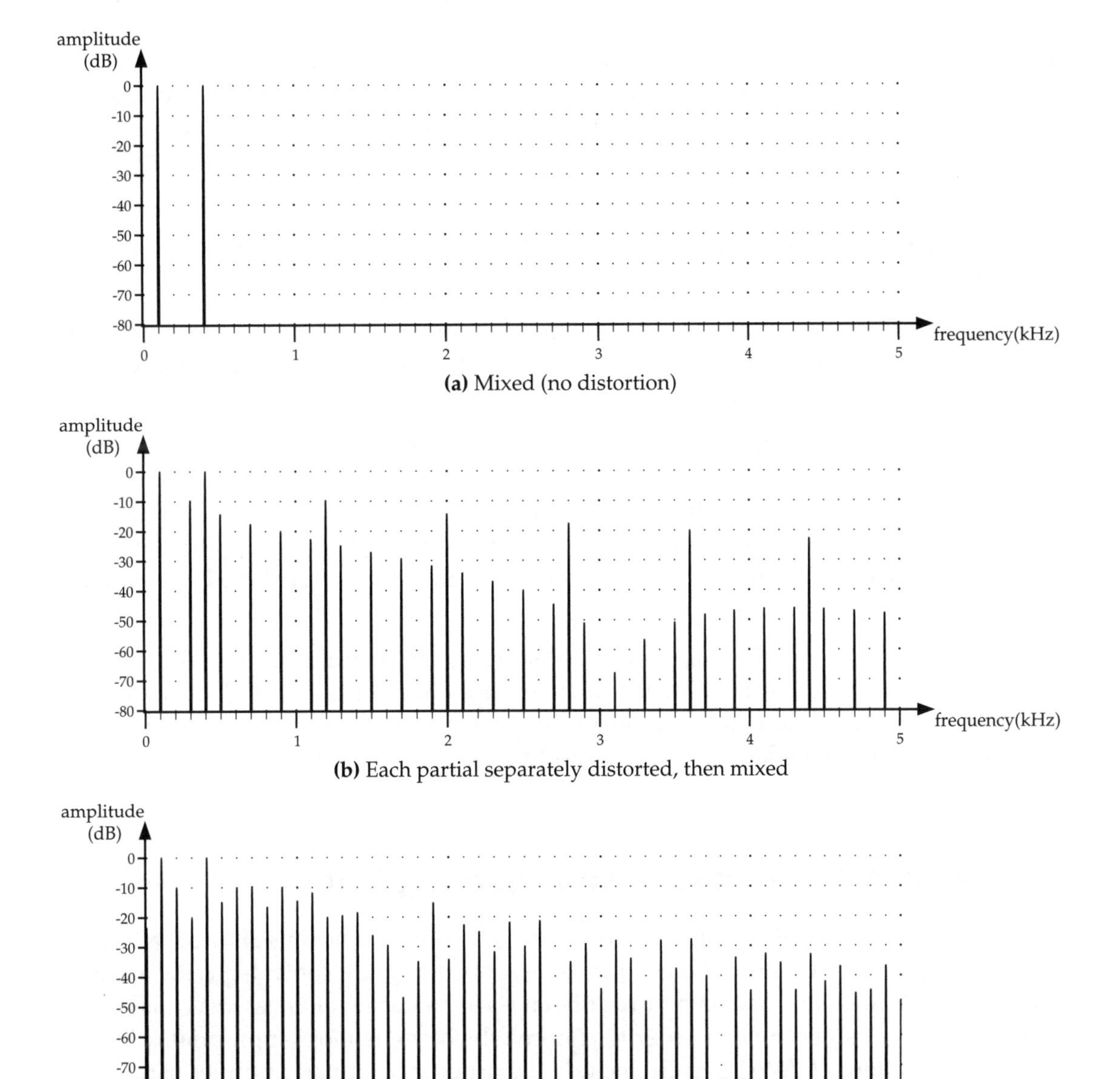

(a) Mixed (no distortion)

(b) Each partial separately distorted, then mixed

(c) Partials mixed, then distorted

Figure 7.16 Average spectrum plots for a pair of partials distorted in different ways

If distortion were a linear process then figures 7.16b and 7.16c would be the same. However, non-linearity means that the order in which processing occurs is important. Distorting each partial in a sound individually is not the same as distorting them all together. This means that the frequency domain output when a signal composed of many partials (such as an electric guitar output) is distorted will not be as simple as that with a single sinusoid. Similarly there can be a different character when a chord is distorted compared to a single note. However the general characteristics in terms of tonality described in §7.1 and §7.2 are still applicable.

It is also interesting to examine complex sounds that change over time in the frequency domain:

- Figure 7.17a shows the spectrogram plot of an unprocessed guitar chord. It starts with a wide range of frequency partials as the strings are initially caused to vibrate, which then smoothly fade away in amplitude and frequency range over time.
- Figure 7.17b shows the effect of hard clipping distortion. The input signal is multiplied by 10 and then clipped at the limits of the system range. The effect is to create a significant density of inharmonic frequency partials that create a rough, harsh sounding effect. As the chord fades away, it drops below the clipping threshold and is only linearly amplified. Thus the latter part of the sound is unaltered in frequency content compared to the input sound.
- Figure 7.17c shows the quarter-circle distortion effect (function 9). The shaping function is non-linear over a wide range of input amplitudes, so it does not matter how much the input fades, it is always being distorted. This is demonstrated in the spectrogram by the large number of additional partials continuing throughout the sound.

7.4 Developing Processes and Learning More

Distortion based on non-linear amplification through transfer functions allows many variations in result. The non-linear behaviour (as described in §7.3), context-specific application, and the difficulty in describing the differences in character, all mean that it is best to audition different algorithms in order to choose which one is most appropriate. Digital Audio Workstations (DAWs) usually include distortion and guitar amplifier simulation plugins that can be useful for experiencing the range of possible effects.

The differences between the different distortion functions can be quite subtle. Some care is required in configuration to hear these differences and achieve the best result. The input gain (figure 7.7, p.203) should be adjusted to ensure that the amplitude of the signal is neither too small to be significantly distorted, nor so large that the majority always falls in the hard clipping region. The intention is that the shaping region of soft clipping functions

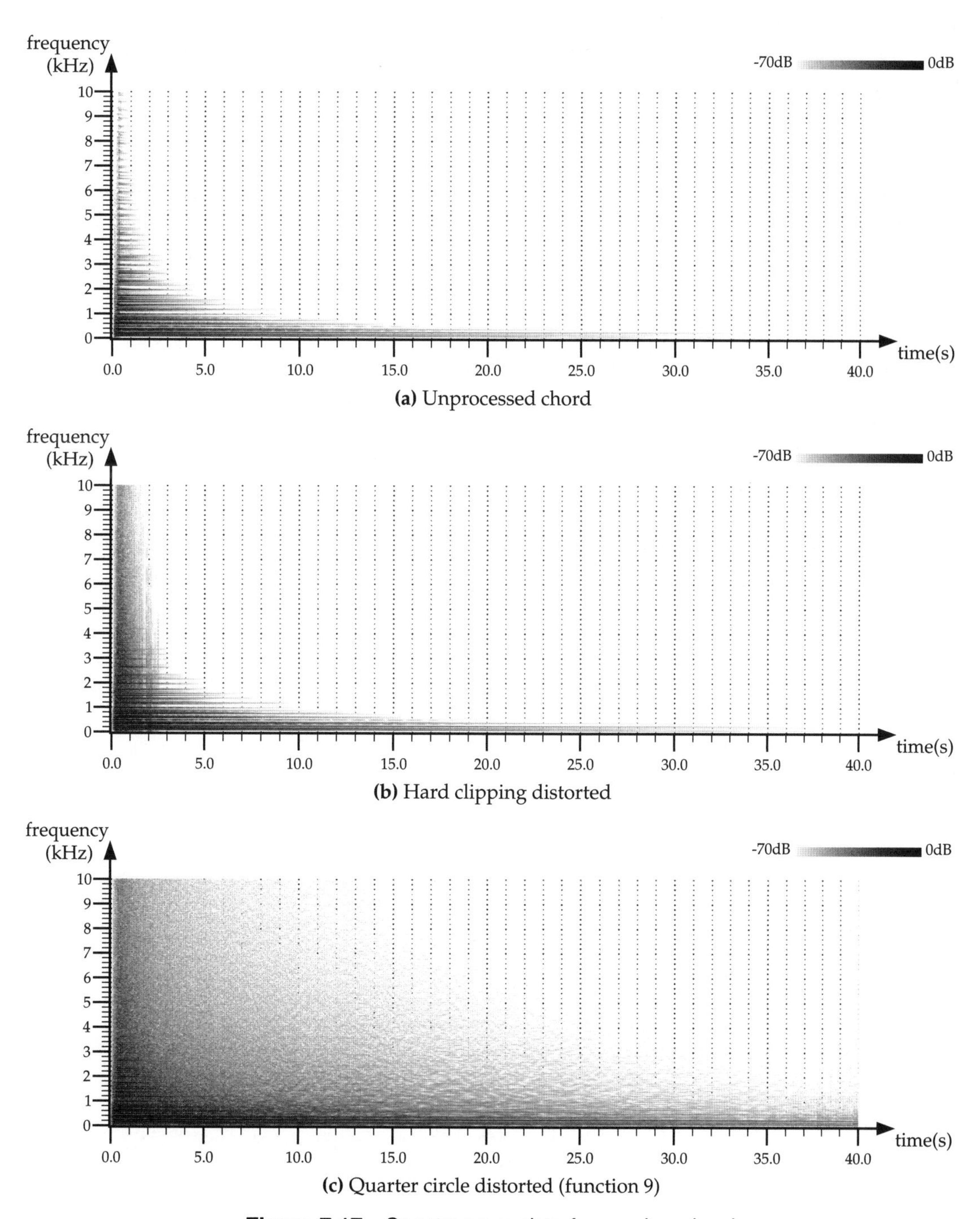

(a) Unprocessed chord

(b) Hard clipping distorted

(c) Quarter circle distorted (function 9)

Figure 7.17 Spectrogram plots for a guitar chord

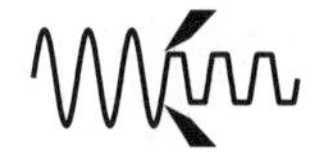

affects a significant proportion of the input signal. Parameters other than input gain are also important in shaping the tonality, such as the shaping parameter value and filtering that is applied. It can therefore take quite a lot of effort to achieve the most desirable result in a particular context.

Care is required when implementing the shaping functions, as some have an amount of mathematical complexity. The input ranges must be correctly implemented, such as using appropriate *if* statements in a conventional programming language. The control variables must also be kept within range. For example, if the equation states that $0 < c \leqslant 1$, then c must not be allowed to reach 0, nor exceed the value 1.

The following sources provide some further background to the topics discussed in this chapter, and the scientific characteristics of different distortions:

Enderby, Sean, and Zlatko Baracskai. 2012. "Harmonic Instability of Digital Soft Clipping Algorithms." Paper presented at the 15th International Conference on Digital Audio Effects (DAFx-12), York, UK, September 17–21.

Pakarinen, Jyri, and David T. Yeh. 2009. "A Review of Digital Techniques for Modeling Vacuum-Tube Guitar Amplifiers." *Computer Music Journal* 33:2:85–100.

Rutt, T.E. 1984. "Vacuum Tube Triode Nonlinearity as Part of the Electric Guitar Sound." Paper presented at the 76th Convention of the Audio Engineering Society, New York, October 8–11.

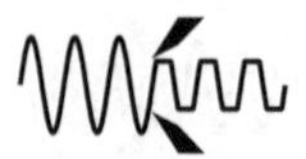

8

Audio Data Techniques

8.1 Storing and Accessing Audio Data

8.1.1 Storage and Processing Requirements

Time domain sound data inside a digital audio process is a set of numerical values spaced at regular intervals. Each value represents the amplitude of the signal at a particular point in time, as described in Chapter 2. At a sample rate f_S, each sample lasts $1/f_S$ seconds. It is possible to convert between lengths of time and numbers of samples as follows:

$$\begin{aligned}
\text{length of time (in seconds) equivalent to 1 sample} &= \frac{1}{f_S} \\
\text{length of time equivalent to } i \text{ samples} &= \frac{i}{f_S} \\
\text{number of samples equivalent to } T \text{ seconds} &= T \times f_S
\end{aligned} \tag{8.1}$$

It is useful to be able to calculate the total data size for a particular length of time, using an equation like this:

$$\begin{aligned}
\text{total data (bytes)} &= T \times f_S \times C \times B \\
\text{where} \quad T &= \text{time in seconds} \\
f_S &= \text{sample rate} \\
C &= \text{number of channels} \\
B &= \text{bytes to store 1 sample}
\end{aligned} \tag{8.2}$$

The trend in process implementations over time is towards higher sample rates, larger numbers of channels, and higher precision data representations (and thus the size in bytes of each sample). The variables in the equation above not only affect the amount of storage required (such as for an audio recorder), but also the computational power required to process this data in real-time. For example, increasing the sample rate from 48kHz to 96kHz requires a doubling of the amount of data processed per second.

There are three main storage techniques that are commonly encountered in audio processes:

- Storage of the entire set of audio data items (such as a whole song).
- Temporary storage of a small amount of audio while it is being processed (known as *buffering*).
- Processing the current incoming sample immediately, rather than explicitly storing the data.

Systems often have a combination of techniques at different stages. In particular, almost every system has some kind of buffering, even those that are primarily concerned with either of the other types of operation (large amounts of storage, or no storage). The reasons for this will be explained later.

8.1.2 Simple Buffering

Buffering is essentially about keeping a set of audio samples in memory locations (an *array*) in order to process it as a block. Figure 8.1 illustrates storing a sequence of data items (0.3, −0.1, 0.8, 0.7, 0.2, 0.1), known as a *data stream*, into a buffer with 6 elements. The previous values are kept in their memory locations unless overwritten. The arrow indicates the *write pointer* position where the value is being written.

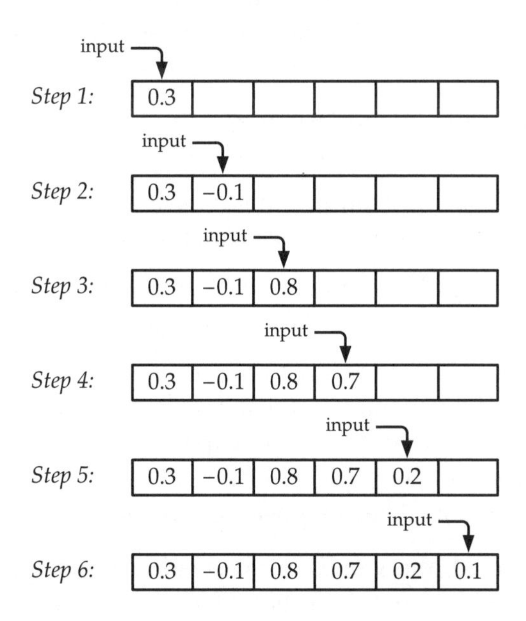

Figure 8.1 Writing values to a buffer sequentially

Each number is spaced from its neighbour by a sample length in time. Therefore at step 6, 0.1 is the current sample value, and 0.3 is 5 samples older. Each sample lasts for $1/f_S$ seconds. For example, at a sample rate of 10kHz, the entire buffer of 6 samples represents a total of $6/10000$ seconds = 0.6ms in time.

The method of writing values into a buffer sequentially is described by algorithm 8.1. The function is called each time a new input value is available. This might be audio samples from a live input in order to store the data for later playback, for example. The buffer is an array of memory locations from index 0 to index N−1 where N is the length of the array. Variable *writeposition* is the index of the next position to be written, which is initialised to 0

Algorithm 8.1 – Sequential buffer write function

```
input : new input value in
if writeposition < N then
    buffer[writeposition] = in                    // store new value
    writeposition = writeposition + 1             // move to next position
```

before the writing process starts. It is also assumed that the states of *buffer* and *writeposition* are maintained between calls to the function.

There are further points to consider before the algorithm can work in practical situations. Firstly, in many programming systems it is necessary to specify the size of the array (N) in advance of writing the data to it. These are some typical situations:

- If audio data is being passed in blocks between two software processes, then the size of the buffer will be specified in advance (say, 512 samples at a time).
- If an entire audio file is being read into memory then there are methods for determining the number of samples that the file contains and so the array size.
- If storing a live sound input and a maximum of T seconds needs to be stored at a sample rate of f_S, then the buffer needs to be (at least) $T \times f_S$ samples long.

The final step in the sequential writing function is to move the *writeposition* to the **next** position to which a value will be written in the array, so the recently recorded values are at array index positions 0 to (*writeposition* − 1). Variable *writeposition* is also the number of values that have been stored. Typically a buffer will be filled with zero values before writing audio data, such that unused array positions are blank.

Once the buffer has been filled, the values can be read out in sequence by use of a *read pointer* as shown in figure 8.2. A function that achieves this behaviour is described by algorithm 8.2. The function is called each time a new output value is required. This might be once for every sample at the sample rate in order to playback a previously stored sound. Once again the buffer is an array of memory locations from index 0 to index N−1 where N is the length of the array. Variable *readposition* is the index of the next position to be read, which is initialised to 0 before the reading process starts. It is also assumed that the states of *buffer* and *readposition* are maintained between calls to the function.

Sequential writing and reading of buffers is a regular operation in digital audio systems. Once information is stored in a buffer it can be passed as a block to another part of the system. It is common to store a set of samples, and then pass that set onto the next part of the processing system, which then operates on all those samples, then passes them on, and so on. It might appear easier to process one sample at a time, which should be less

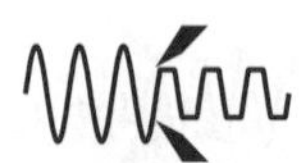

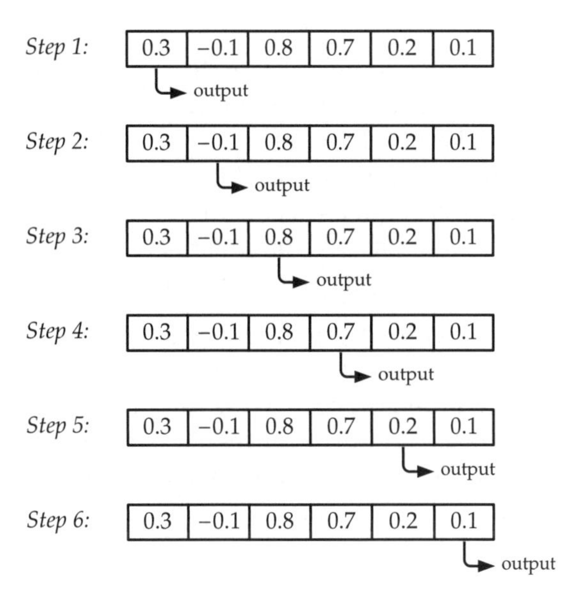

Figure 8.2 Sequentially reading values from a buffer

Algorithm 8.2 – Sequential buffer read function

```
output: output signal out
if readposition < N then
    out = buffer[readposition]
    readposition = readposition + 1        // move to next position
else
    out = 0
```

complex to manage. However, there are three good reasons why it is appropriate to use buffers, which are the desirability of process optimisation, the requirement for consistent output, and the need to process using many samples at once:

Optimisation

It is generally more efficient to perform an operation on a block of data rather than processing one item at a time. A number of activities such as data processing, communication, and storage can often be optimised with multiple items. In some cases there can be a setup overhead for operations, which can be minimised by processing a larger number of data items at once.

Consistent Output

General purpose computers and operating systems have not usually been designed for the efficient and regular throughput of real-time audio data. The problem is that tasks such as updating the display and background housekeeping are liable to use the same resources as audio tasks. This can reduce the power available for audio processes at different times. There are also other elements of digital systems that can reduce the timeliness of audio data items, such as the use of long-distance computer networks. The result is that different output samples can take different lengths of time to produce.

If each sample is processed individually, some will be done quickly, but some will take too long and cause a click or glitch in the output. Figure 8.3 shows how the sample output positions are regularly spaced (determined by the sample rate), but the processing time per sample is variable. In this just-in-time processing method, there is always a danger that a sample will take a little too long to process and miss the output position. The result will be an audible anomaly.

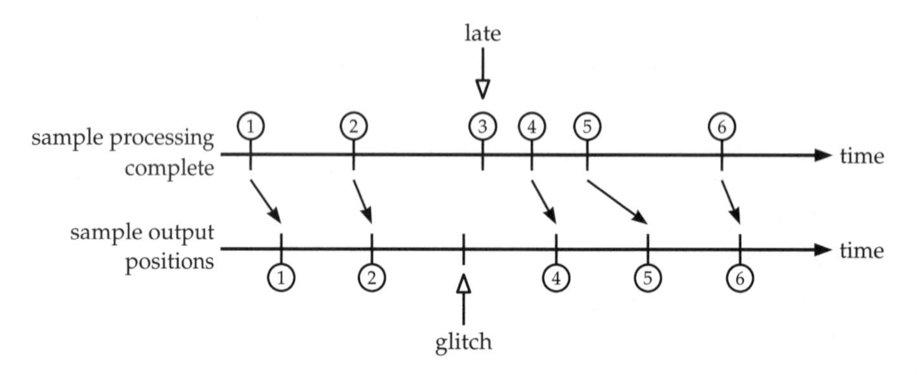

Figure 8.3 Processing samples individually

The alternative to the just-in-time technique is to buffer the data, and then only output the set of samples after they have all been processed. This enables the variability of processing to be smoothed over. Figure 8.4 demonstrates a form where the current buffer is being processed, while the previously processed buffer is being outputted. Although some samples take longer than others to be completed, buffering provides time for long delays to be absorbed. For example, when buffer A is processed, the delay between completing samples 4 and 5 is balanced by the rapid processing of other samples, such that all are ready when the buffer is to be output. This takes advantage of the fact that some samples can be processed more quickly than the sample rate, providing extra time for others.

The compromise with this type of processing is that there is a buffer-length delay before output occurs. A small buffer size is desirable to minimise the delay, but it must also be large enough to avoid the problem of glitches.

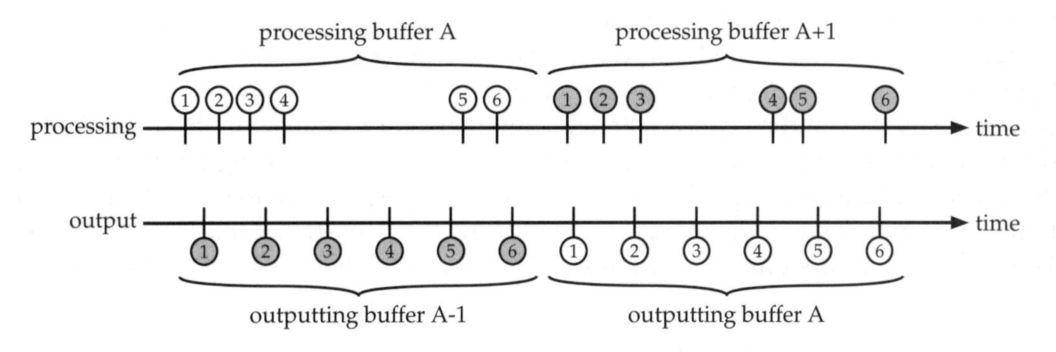

Figure 8.4 Processing samples with buffers

Processing Using Many Samples

Sometimes more samples than the current value are required in order to perform an audio process task. Some typical examples include:

- Storing recent sound in order to create an echo a short time later.
- Implementing a filter design from low-level components.
- Measuring recent signal levels to create an amplitude display.
- Frequency domain analysis using Discrete Fourier Transforms.

A consideration for real-time audio systems is whether the delay imparted by the buffering process is acceptable. The transfer of audio data from an interface, through the operating system, to a piece of software, and back again can introduce an unpleasant latency. As processing power and operating system designs improve, some of these problems become less apparent. With some other cases (such as measuring the peak amplitude level of a low frequency, or encoding a block of audio data) it is not possible to produce a result until a certain amount of input data has arrived, which imposes a delay that cannot be avoided.

8.1.3 Shift Registers and Circular Buffers

The basic sequential writing and reading of values with a buffer as described in §8.1.2 is easy to imagine when a finite amount of data is to be buffered; for example, storing a 10 second long piano note and then playing it back later. In many cases, however, it is necessary to operate on a continuous stream of data. In those circumstances buffering is a process of creating a *moving window* on the data, where the buffer contents is constantly being updated to reflect the latest input data.

Figure 8.5 illustrates two different moving window methods, which shows how the buffer contents relates to the audio input data. The equivalent process styles are described in figure 8.6. The non-overlapping method is typically the way in which audio data is passed between hardware and software within a computer. For example, an input block of 512 samples might be copied from the audio hardware, passed to a program that processes the sound, and then an output block of 512 samples is passed back to the audio hardware. In the overlapping method, the buffer moves along the data stream one sample at a time. This method is used within algorithms such as filters, reverberators, and compressors.

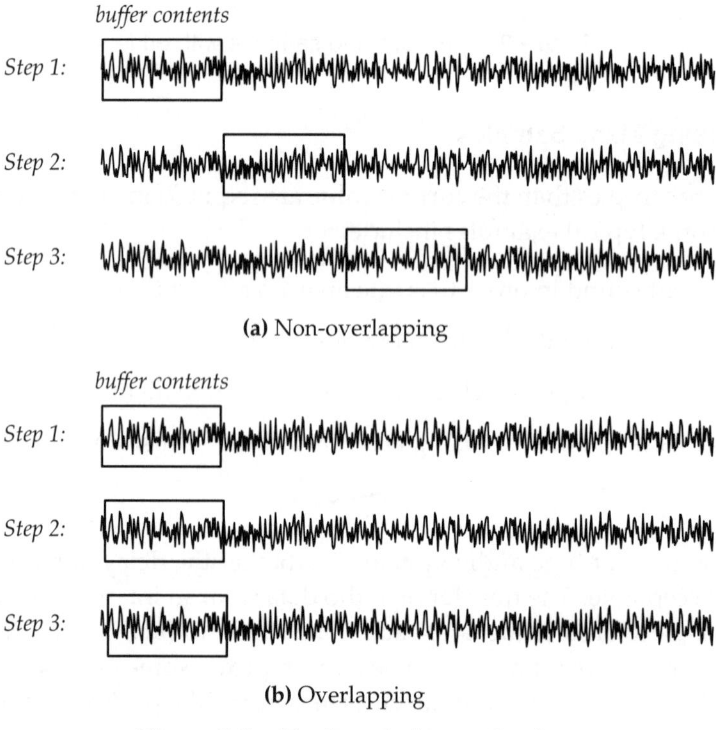

Figure 8.5 Moving window methods

Figure 8.7 shows an example of data processed in non-overlapping and overlapping windows. In both cases a simple mean average has been taken within the window (known as a *moving average*). In the non-overlapping case, there are only a few output data points, as the window hops along the data a large chunk at a time. However, in the overlapping case, the hop size is only 1 sample and there are as many output data points as input data points. The window size is the same in both cases. The output from the overlapping method is smoother, but requires much more computation. A mean average in an overlapping window is a type of lowpass filter; the higher frequency component in the original data is attenuated, as shown in the figure.

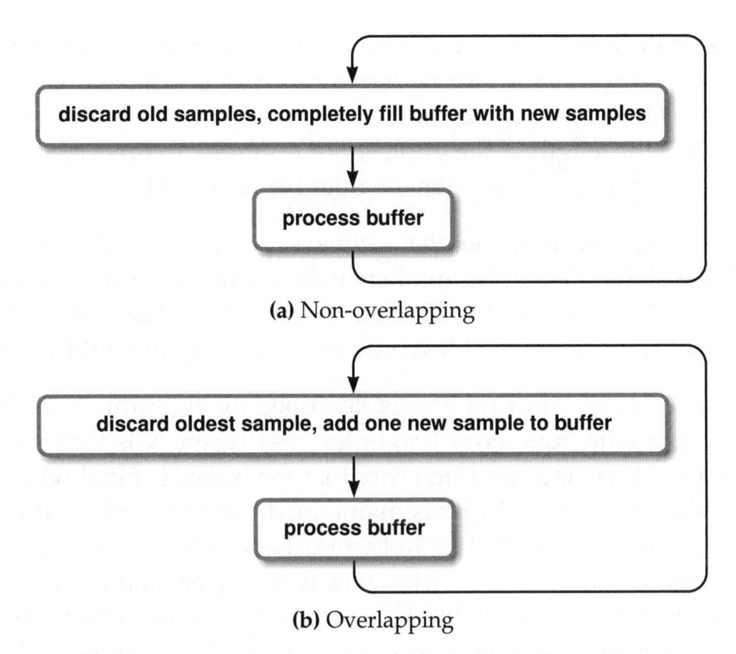

(a) Non-overlapping

(b) Overlapping

Figure 8.6 Processing to achieve a moving window

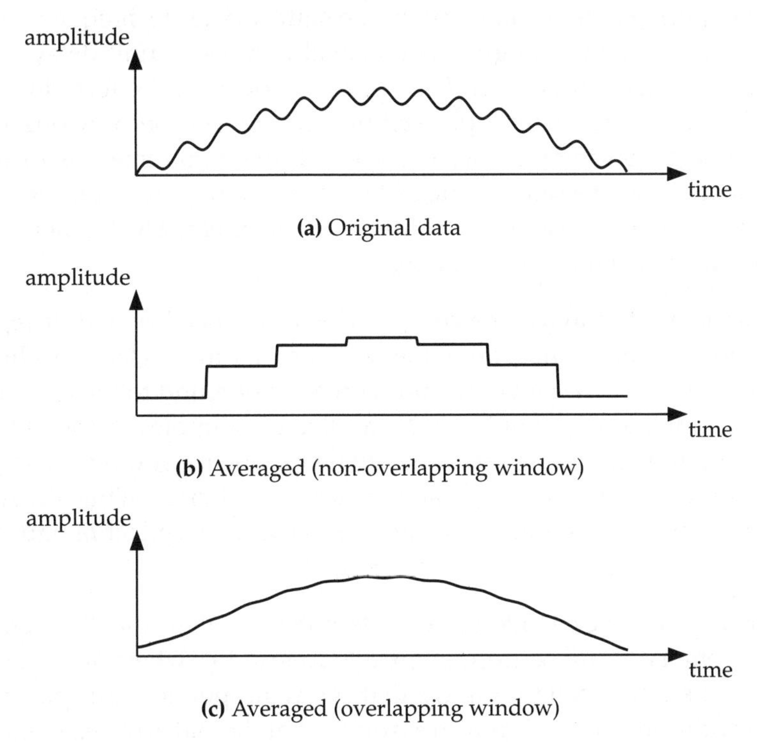

(a) Original data

(b) Averaged (non-overlapping window)

(c) Averaged (overlapping window)

Figure 8.7 Example of data processed in non-overlapping and overlapping windows

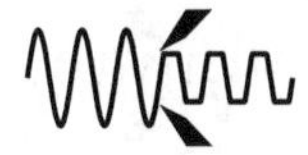

A *shift register* is an example of a technique that can achieve an overlapping moving window. With this form, at each sample step a new value is moved into the buffer, and the oldest one is discarded. This means that the buffer always holds the most recent N samples (where N is the length of the buffer). For example, figure 8.8 shows a buffer of 6 elements with a sequence of 9 audio signal values being shifted into it.

In the shift register form, the write pointer is always positioned on the left-hand end. Each time a new value is shifted in, all the numbers move along one place and the oldest value drops out of the right-hand edge of the buffer. As such, the value in the left-most element is the current signal value, and the oldest buffered value is in the right-most element.

The process of updating the shift register is described by algorithm 8.3. The buffer is an array of memory locations from index 0 to index N−1 where N is the length of the array (figure 8.9). The initial starting conditions are that the buffer is filled with zero values. It is also assumed that the state of *buffer* is maintained between calls to the function. The algorithm starts at the end of the buffer and works back to the beginning, copying values between array positions. It is necessary to work that way around in order to ensure that values are overwritten correctly. Finally the new input value is written into the first array position. This function must be called every time a new value is added to the shift register.

For processes requiring a very small buffer, the shift register technique is easy to understand and implement. Filter designs with a small number of unit delay elements use a type of shift register (as described in §6.4, p.164). However, the technique is inefficient for large buffer sizes. Each new input sample requires all the previous samples to be copied into the neighbouring memory positions. If the requirement is to store the most recent 1 second of sound at a sample rate of 44.1kHz, that requires a buffer length of 44100 elements. Thus every time 1 sample is shifted into the buffer, 44099 other values must be copied into neighbouring memory locations.

A *circular buffer* is used to avoid the computational overhead of a shift register. In this case, the data does not move, but rather the write pointer moves left to right in the buffer. When the pointer reaches the end of the buffer it wraps around to the first position again. In this way, the buffer always holds the N most recent samples as the oldest values are automatically overwritten. Using the same number sequence and buffer length as for the shift register, figure 8.10 shows the operation of a circular buffer. While the set of numbers stored in the circular buffer is exactly the same as in the shift register in figure 8.8 for every step, they are not in the same order in the buffer.

The process of updating the circular buffer is described by algorithm 8.4. Again, the buffer is an array of memory locations from index 0 to index N−1 where N is the length of the array. The initial starting conditions are that the write pointer is at position 0 and the buffer is filled with zero values. It is also assumed that the states of *buffer* and *writeposition* are maintained between calls to the function.

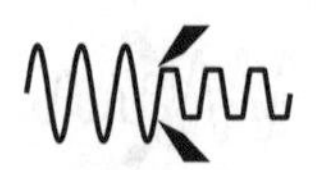

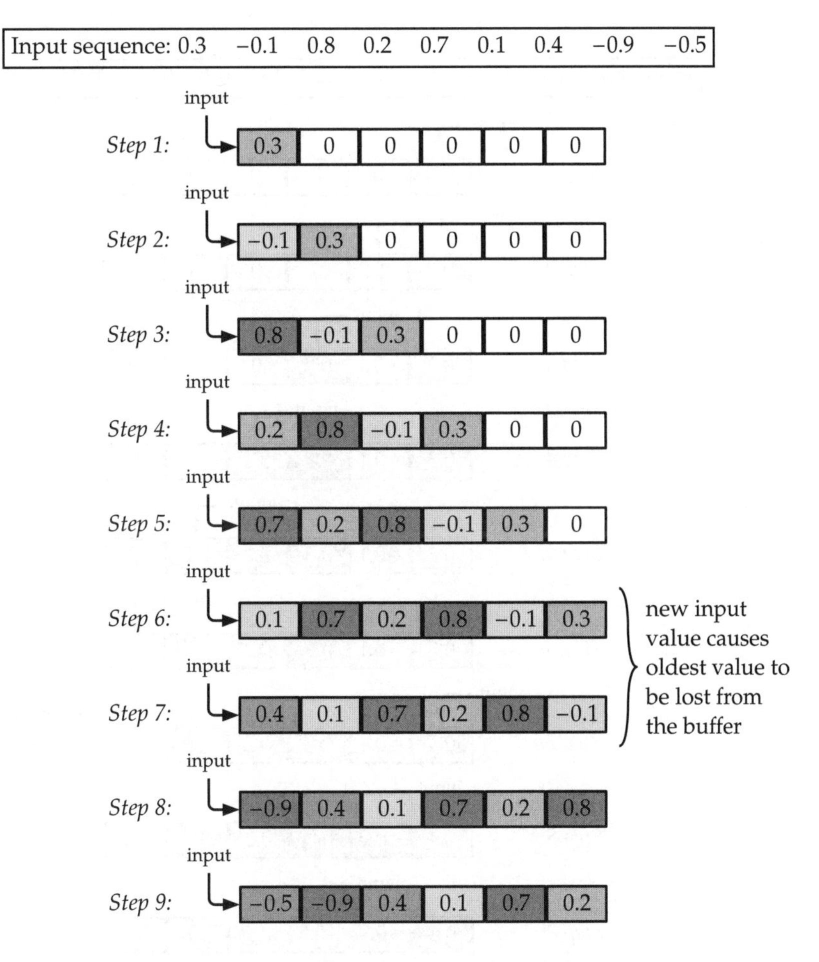

Figure 8.8 Shift register operation example

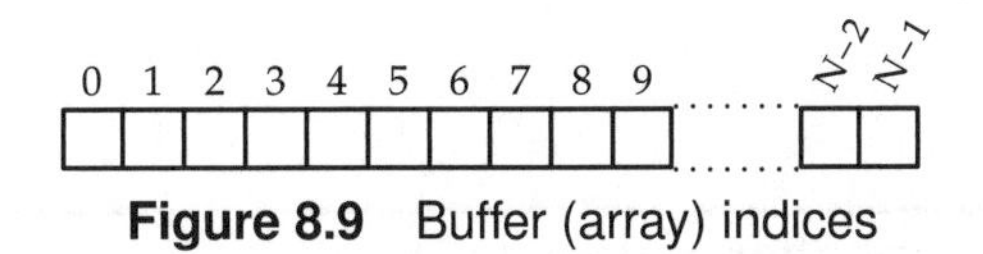

Figure 8.9 Buffer (array) indices

Algorithm 8.3 – Shift register update function

---

input : new input value `in`

for storeposition = N−1 **downto** 1 **do**
  buffer[storeposition] = buffer[storeposition − 1]

buffer[0] = `in` `// store new value`

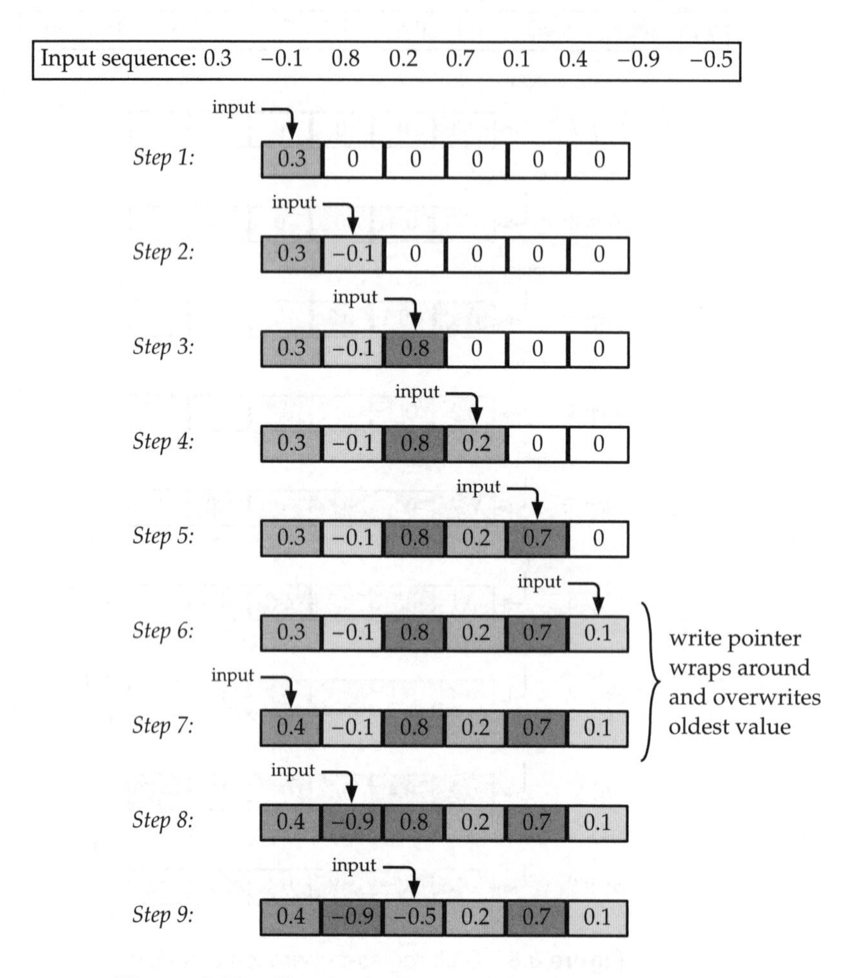

Figure 8.10 Circular buffer operation example

Algorithm 8.4 – Circular buffer update function

input : new input value `in`

writeposition = writeposition + 1 `// move to next position`
if writeposition == N **then**
  writeposition = 0 `// wrap around`
buffer[writeposition] = `in` `// store new value`

Each time the buffer is updated, it is necessary to move *writeposition* one position forwards. If this new position is beyond the end of the buffer, then *writeposition* is returned to the first array position. Note that the last array index is N−1, so index N is just beyond the end of the array. When the new input value is stored, it overwrites the oldest value in the buffer. After the function has been called, *writeposition* is at the location of the most recent value that was written.

The update function will be called for each new sample (or 44100 times per second at a sample rate of 44.1kHz). Because there is no shuffling of values with the circular buffer, there is no *for* loop in the algorithm (as there is with the shift register). Thus the computation required to update the buffer is always the same with the circular buffer no matter how long the array. The circular buffer is far more efficient than a shift register when the buffer size is significant.

With the shift register, the most recent stored value is always in the first array position (0), and the oldest value is always in the last array position (N−1). With a circular buffer, these positions change at every step. The current value is at the write pointer position and the oldest value is one position to the right of the write pointer. This can be confusing as the write pointer is constantly moving, and it is necessary to wrap around the end of the buffer.

Figure 8.11 shows three examples of how the positions of samples relate to each other in the circular buffer. In the first example, the current sample is just to the right of the previously stored sample, and just to the left of the oldest sample in the buffer. The other two examples show that when the write pointer is at the edges of the buffer, that the previous and oldest samples wrap around the edges of the buffer in the same way that the write pointer does. In the second example the oldest sample is one place to the right, which means it wraps to the beginning of the buffer. In the third example the previous sample is one place to the left, which means it wraps around to the end of the buffer. It can take some time to become familiar with these position relationships.

Knowing the current write pointer position, it is possible to locate stored values that are a certain number of samples older than the present one. This is very useful for being able to construct such things as filter algorithms and echo effects. Figure 8.12 shows a circular buffer of 9 elements where the filled boxes show the four most recently written samples. The sample at index 2 is the latest, array index 1 holds the value that is one sample old, array index 0 is two samples old, and array index 8 is three samples old. Another way of imagining the circular buffer is to draw it with the ends joined together as shown in figure 8.13.

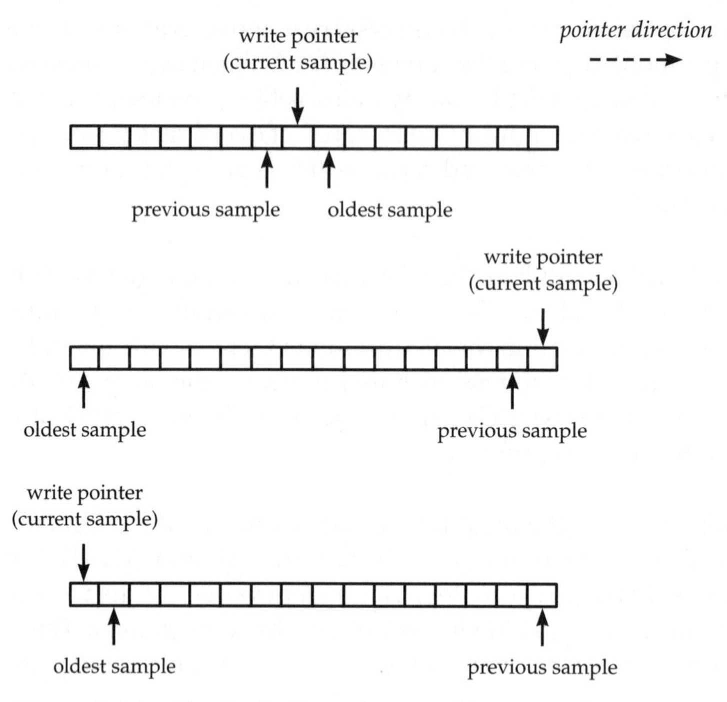

Figure 8.11 Circular buffer pointer position examples

8.1.4 Delayed Sound

Delayed audio data samples are the basis of a number of interesting effects, such as reverberation, echo, and other environmental sound modifications. These are described in more detail in Chapter 10, but this section will describe a basic *delay* (also known as a delay line) process.

Figure 8.14a shows the block diagram form for a delay. The delay time (T) is set by the rotary control connected to the "t" input of the delay block. Each sample that enters the delay block on the left will emerge T seconds later on the right. The delay is the same for every sample, so the output is in the same order as the input, but delayed in time.

Figure 8.14b shows how a circular buffer can be used as the delay block. In the diagram, the input is connected to the write pointer, and the read pointer is connected to the output. The arrows with dashed lines have been used to indicate that the pointers are moving to the right at each sample step and wrap to the beginning of the buffer when they reach the end. At a sample rate of 44.1kHz, the write and read pointers will move one sample to the right 44100 times per second. The read pointer is d samples behind the write pointer, such that it is reading out a value a set distance in samples before the current input sample.

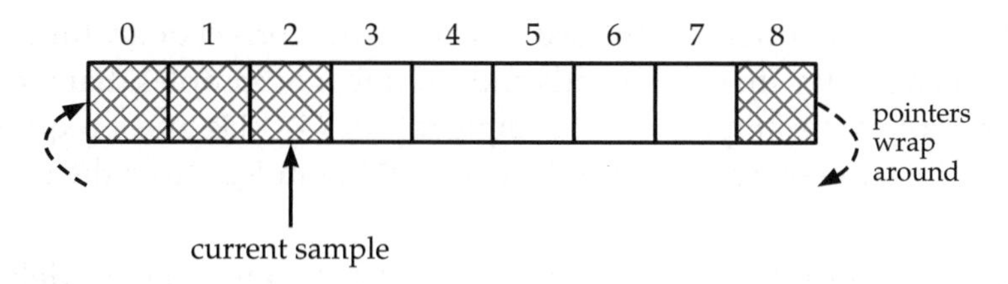

Figure 8.12 Recent samples in a circular buffer

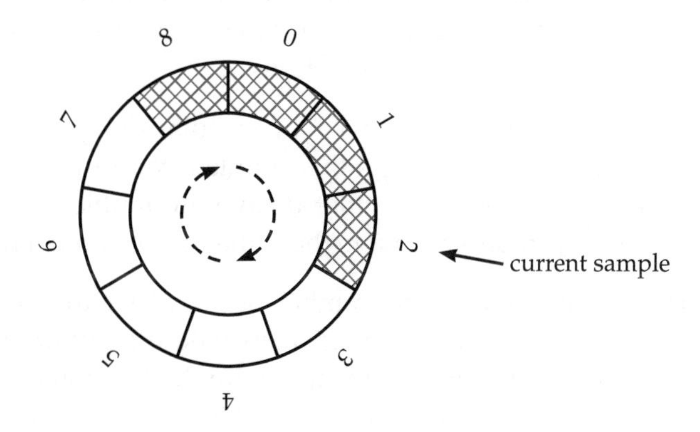

Figure 8.13 Recent samples in a circular buffer (alternative representation)

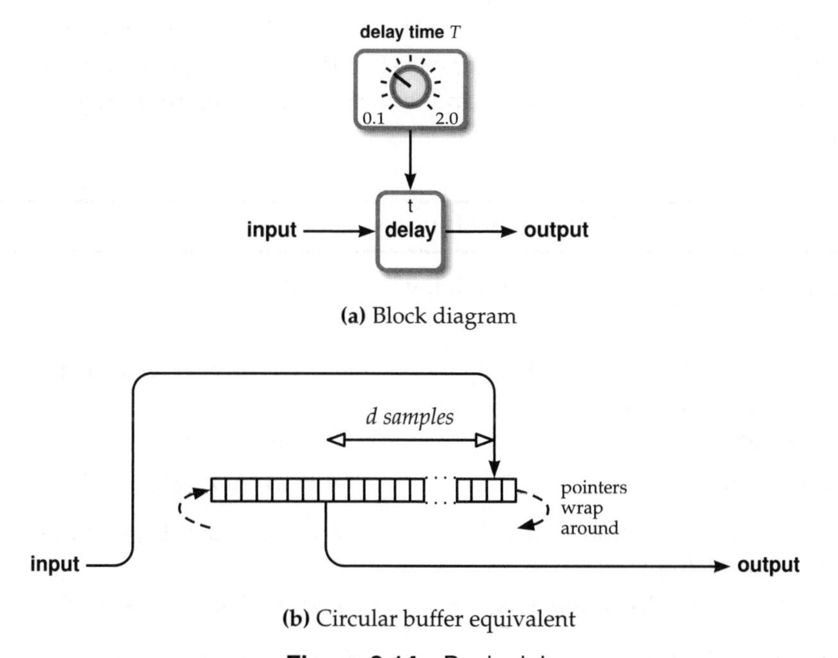

(a) Block diagram

(b) Circular buffer equivalent

Figure 8.14 Basic delay

In order that the circular buffer can be used to achieve the correct delay time, it is necessary to convert between a delay time in seconds and a number of samples that is equivalent (see equation 8.1, p.220). For example, with a sample rate of 44.1kHz and a required delay time of 0.12 seconds, it is necessary to have a delay of 5292 samples. Note the following:

- The circular buffer length must be more samples than the longest delay required. If the range on the rotary control in figure 8.14a is to be used, then the longest delay is going to be 2 seconds, or 88200 samples if the sample rate is 44.1kHz. In that case the buffer must be at least 88201 samples long in order to accommodate a **difference** of 88200 between the two pointer positions.
- The number of samples to achieve a particular delay time depends on the current sample rate. If the user changes the sample rate from 44.1kHz to 88.2kHz, then the number of samples for a particular delay will double, and the length of the buffer must also double in order to have the same maximum delay time.
- There is a possibility that the number of samples equivalent to the required delay time might be a fractional number. However, the buffer only has values at integer positions. The simplest method is to ignore the fractional part, but this might cause audible effects. This problem is discussed further in §8.2 (p.237).

The delay function is described by algorithm 8.5. As usual, the buffer is an array of memory locations from index 0 to index N−1 where N is the length of the array. The initial starting conditions are that *writeposition* is 0 and the buffer is filled with zero values. It is also assumed that the states of *buffer* and *writeposition* are maintained between calls to the function.

Algorithm 8.5 – Circular buffer delay function

```
input : current input signal value in, delay in samples del
output: output signal out

writeposition = writeposition + 1            // move to next position
if writeposition == N then
  writeposition = 0                          // wrap around
buffer[writeposition] = in                   // store new value

readposition = writeposition − del           // offset to delayed sample
if readposition < 0 then
  readposition = readposition + N            // wrap around to end of buffer

out = buffer[readposition]                   // read delayed value
```

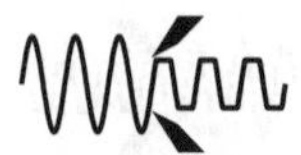

The algorithm starts with the code seen in the circular buffer update function (algorithm 8.4, p.230). The *readposition* is offset by the required number of samples from the *writeposition*. There is a possibility that this will be positioned at negative index values. If that occurs, it is necessary to add the length of the buffer, to wrap around to the end of the buffer. For example, if *writeposition* is 0 and the delay is 1 sample then the *readposition* is −1. Adding N produces the correct value of position N−1. The output value is then read from the *readposition* to obtain the delayed sample value.

An echo occurs when the listener hears a sound, and then a copy of that sound is replayed a short time later. In the natural world, this occurs when sound reflects from a distant surface and arrives at the listener some time after the original sound is heard. A simple echo form is shown in figure 8.15:

- The lower path from input to output is the direct sound from source to listener. The upper path passes through a delay that simulates the sound travelling some significant distance from the source, reflecting from a surface and then returning to the listener some time later.
- The two sound paths are mixed with an adder. This is because the listener hears a combination of the direct path and the delayed sound.

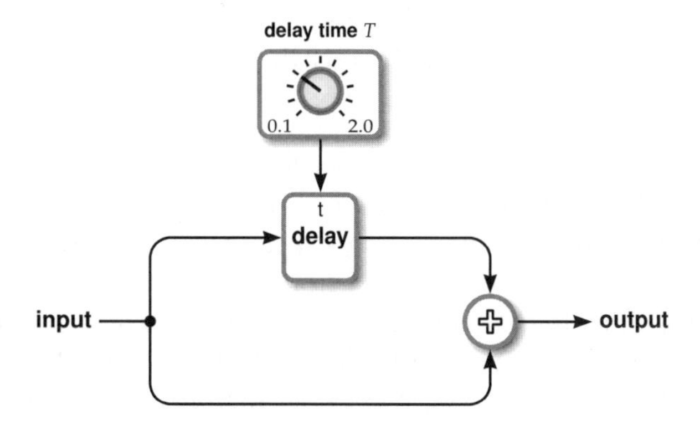

Figure 8.15 Simple echo

8.1.5 Pointer Position Considerations

In cases such as the delay example in §8.1.4, there is a simple relationship between the read and write pointers. That is, there is a constant offset between their positions and both move forward in the buffer at the same rate, which is one index increment per sample period. There is the option, however, to have more sophisticated relationships to achieve different results.

There is a danger when constructing a process based on circular buffers that the limits of the buffer and algorithm are forgotten. The value of *del* in algorithm 8.5 cannot become larger than N−1 samples or less than 0. The former can occur, for example, when multiple delay values are accumulated:

$$\begin{aligned} \text{delay2} &= \text{delay1} + \text{offset1} \\ \text{delay3} &= \text{delay2} + \text{offset2} \\ \text{delay4} &= \text{delay3} + \text{offset3} \end{aligned}$$

The *delay1*, *offset1*, *offset2* and *offset3* values might be derived from user controls with ranges within the length of the buffer. However, *delay4* corresponds to *delay1* + *offset1* + *offset2* + *offset3* whose value might be too large for the buffer.

Attempting to access at negative delay times is a possible mistake when programming. For example, when constructing an oscillating delay time it is possible to forget the range of values being produced. With a flanger (described in §9.2.4, p.279) it is necessary to configure the process to ensure that the depth cannot be more than the offset parameter. In some cases it might be appropriate to add checks to an algorithm to ensure that mistakes are caught, like this:

```
if del < 0 then
  └ del = 0
if del >= N then
  └ del = N−1
```

Another buffer technique is for the read pointer to travel in the opposite direction to the write pointer (figure 8.16). This implies that the output is played backwards compared to the input. This can produce some interesting effects, but consideration must be given to the way in which data is written to, and read from, the buffer. If the reversing process is not being used in real-time, then it is possible to store an entire recording and then play back the buffer in reverse from the end back to the start. This allows such techniques as adding a reverberation to a reversed recording, then reversing the result to achieve a reverb that builds before the start of each sound event.

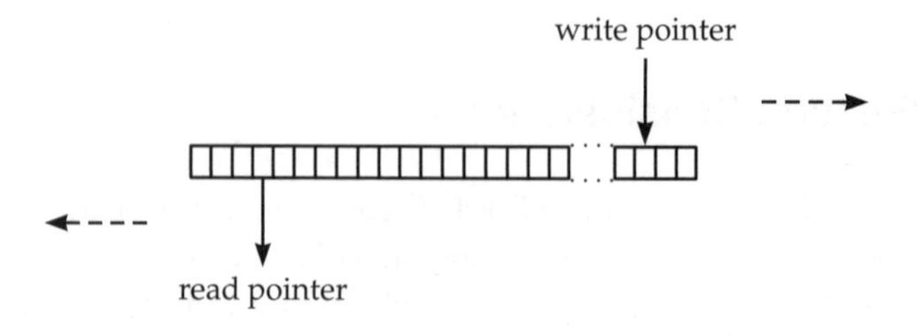

Figure 8.16 Reversed read pointer direction

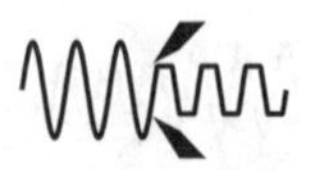

If reversing is to occur in real-time, then certain issues occur:

- It is not possible to play a complete sound event in reverse until the sound has been recorded all the way to the end.
- If a circular buffer is being used then the synchronisation of read and write pointers is important. If the pointers are constantly moving in opposite directions (and wrapping around the ends of the buffer), then sometimes the read pointer will be near to the write pointer (and the reverse output will occur close to the input), and sometimes they will be further apart (and there will be a greater delay between input and output).
- There is a possibility of a significant discontinuity in value between the current input value (at the write pointer position), and the oldest value in the buffer. Thus when the read pointer position crosses over with the write pointer position there is a possibility of a click occurring. This might require a suitable smoothing of values to mask the join.

As well as changing direction, it is also possible to vary the rate at which data is read from the buffer. This is found in such processes as time domain sample pitch changing (§15.3.1, p.473). With slower read pointer than write pointer movement the stored waveform is stretched out in time (producing a lower pitch), and with faster read pointer movement it is compressed (producing a higher pitch).

In a non-real-time process where all the data is stored in the buffer in advance these effects are fairly easy to manage. However, with a real-time process there are pointer position considerations. If the read pointer is moving more slowly than the write pointer and with constant speed, then eventually the write pointer will catch up with the read pointer. If the read pointer is moving more quickly than the write pointer and with constant speed, then the reading process runs out of data more quickly than it arrives, requiring some kind of looping. As with reverse playback a decision must be made about how resulting signal discontinuities will be handled. Granular techniques (Chapter 22) can address some of these issues.

8.2 Selecting and Interpolating Values

8.2.1 Introduction

It is often the case in audio processes that a value is required from a position **between** two stored values. When storing samples into a buffer at sample rate f_S, the samples are stored at intervals of $1/f_S$ seconds. For example, at a sample rate of 44.1kHz the interval between samples is approximately 22.68μs. If a buffer is used to create a delay, and the data values are read from it with a steadily increasing delay time, there will be steps in the actual delay time achieved, as shown in figure 8.17.

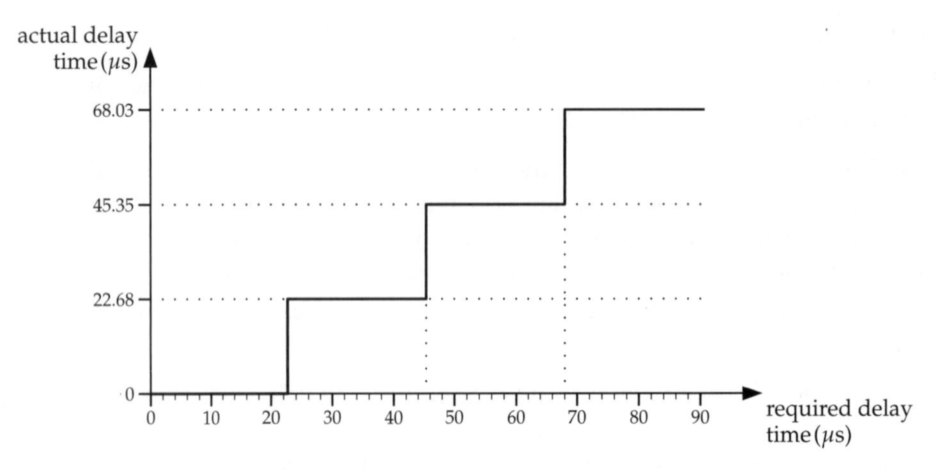

Figure 8.17 Stepped delay effect (samples stored at 44.1kHz)

A step size of 22.68μs might seem insignificant, but it is large enough to be a problem in some circumstances. In effects such as flanging (§9.2.4, p.279), a steadily changing delay time is used when reading values from a buffer. With a simple delay function (such as algorithm 8.5, p.234) the output will jump at the boundary between stored sample values, as shown in figure 8.18. These signal discontinuities are likely to produce audible stepping, clicking, or "zipper noise". Interpolating to create a *fractional delay* result will achieve a smoother transition between values.

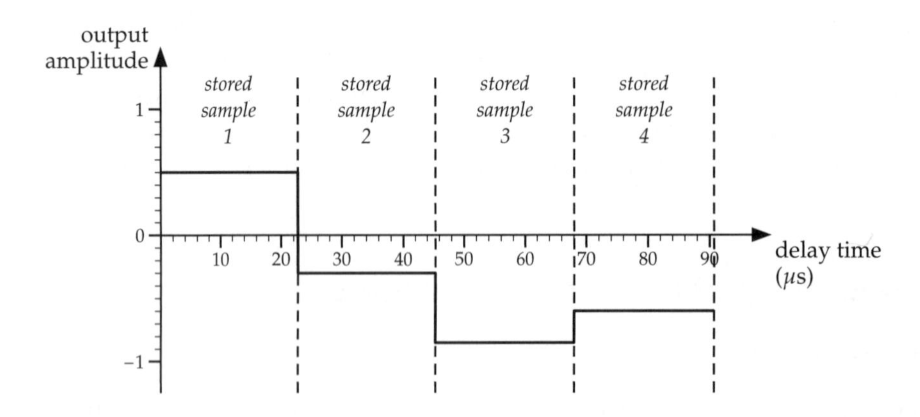

Figure 8.18 Example stepped output with increasing delay time (samples stored at 44.1kHz)

Delays can also be used in generating pitched tones, such as in a waveguide instrument, where the delay time corresponds to the cycle length of a generated oscillation (§21.2.1, p.584). Inaccuracies in delay will lead to errors in pitch, which become more apparent as the pitch increases.

A similar situation occurs when values are required more frequently than they are available. This can happen when storing a waveform and then playing it back at a different speed (§14.4, p.444). For example, if every fourth output sample is a stored value, then it is necessary to decide what values are produced in between (figure 8.19). In a digital sampled system it is not possible to just ignore the intermediate samples, as a suitable value must be produced for every sample period. The easiest choice is to output the previous known value, but this will lead to distortions in the output. A number of processes have a similar problem, such as when a hardware control provides updated values infrequently, which can cause audible jumps in a controlled parameter (say, a frequency or amplitude value).

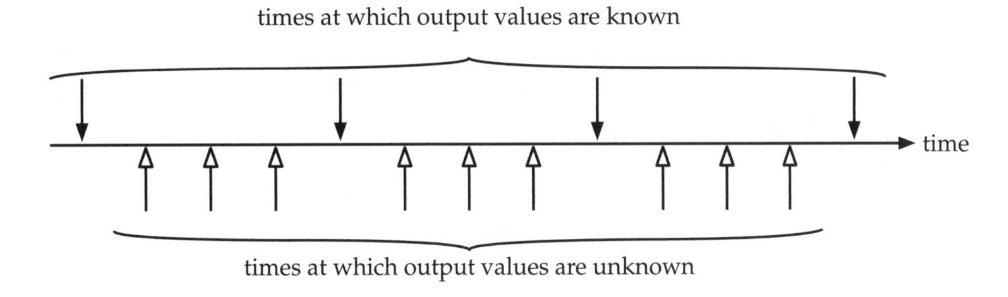

Figure 8.19 Intermediate values between known data points

In these types of cases, a suitable mechanism for determining the output value is required. Many possible methods exist, and selecting an appropriate method depends on a consideration of the computational overhead and the audible improvement achieved. The following text describes some typical approaches.

8.2.2 Truncation and Rounding

Figure 8.20 illustrates the case where values v_1 and v_2 are stored at positions p_1 and p_2 (which are consecutive positions in the buffer). The position of interest is p_d. The simplest technique is to select value v_1 when p_d is between p_1 and p_2. This is known as *truncating* (removing the fractional part of the read position).

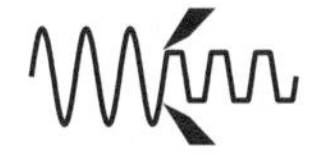

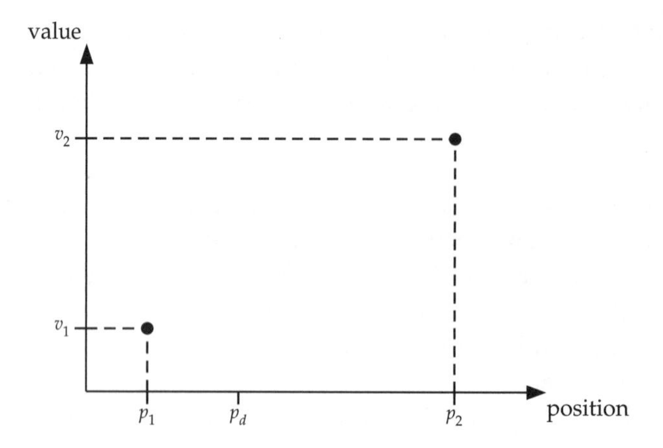

Figure 8.20 Selecting output values

A slightly more sophisticated method is to *round* to the nearest stored position. That is, select value v_1 when p_d is closer to p_1, and v_2 when closer to p_2. Using this technique can reduce error (and so distortion in the output) compared to truncating, although it often takes slightly more computation. Programming languages and environments usually include a rounding function as standard.

Algorithm 8.5 (p.234) is a case where a technique such as truncation or rounding is required. The last line of that algorithm assumes that *readposition* is an integer value:

out = buffer[readposition]

When *readposition* has been a calculated as a fractional value, then truncation (using a function called *trunc*) could be applied like this:

out = buffer[trunc(readposition)]

With the rounding technique it is necessary to consider what happens at the upper end of index values. For example, if p_1 happens to coincide with the last sample in a circular buffer, then finding value v_2 at position p_2 will require wrapping around the end of the array. In which case the last line of algorithm 8.5 is replaced by this (using a rounding function called *round*):

```
indexposition = round(readposition)
if indexposition > N−1 then
    indexposition = indexposition − N
out = buffer[indexposition]
```

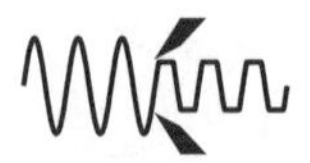

8.2.3 Linear Interpolation

Rounding often reduces error compared to truncation, but it can be even more effective to estimate an intermediate value between known points. The simplest way of doing this is *linear interpolation*. This is equivalent to drawing a line between the two known points and finding a point on that line corresponding to intermediate position p_d (figure 8.21).

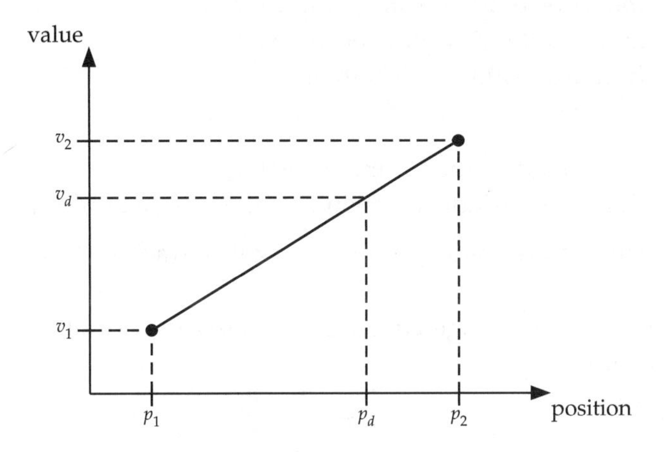

Figure 8.21 Linear interpolation

The output value v_d is calculated as follows:

$$v_d = v_1 + \left[(v_2 - v_1) \times \left(\frac{p_d - p_1}{p_2 - p_1} \right) \right] \tag{8.3}$$

The fraction $(p_d - p_1)/(p_2 - p_1)$ is the proportion of the distance along the line (with a value between 0 and 1) at which to find v_d. For clarity this fraction can be called p_{frac}, which means that equation 8.3 can be rewritten:

$$v_d = v_1 + \left[(v_2 - v_1) \times p_{\text{frac}} \right] \tag{8.4}$$

In a typical situation, p_1 and p_2 will be integer locations in memory and spaced by 1. In that case p_{frac} is just the fractional part of p_d. For example, if $p_1 = 35$, $p_d = 35.72$, and $p_2 = 36$, the fraction becomes:

$$p_{\text{frac}} = \frac{p_d - p_1}{p_2 - p_1} = \frac{35.72 - 35}{36 - 35} = \frac{0.72}{1} = 0.72 \tag{8.5}$$

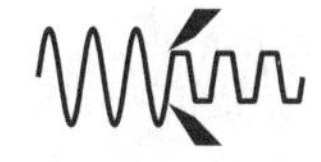

Linear interpolation is sufficient to reduce error and distortion in a wide range of cases. However, it takes more computation than rounding and truncation. Remember when using a circular buffer that finding value v_2 at position p_2 will require wrapping around the end of the buffer if p_1 is the last sample in the array. Linear interpolation can be used in place of the last line of algorithm 8.5 (p.234) as follows:

```
indexposition1 = trunc(readposition)
indexposition2 = indexposition1 + 1
if indexposition2 == N then
    indexposition2 = 0

frac = readposition − indexposition1
diff = buffer[indexposition2] − buffer[indexposition1];

out = buffer[indexposition1] + (diff * frac)
```

Sometimes it is useful to rearrange equation 8.4 to derive a position from values rather than the other way around:

$$p_{\text{frac}} = \frac{v_d - v_1}{v_2 - v_1} \tag{8.6}$$

This might be used for estimating the position of a zero crossing. For example, if v_1 is negative, and v_2 is positive, then setting v_d to zero in the equation will produce a value of p_{frac} where the line passes through zero. This can be useful when trying to determine the length of a waveform cycle, for instance.

8.2.4 Non-linear Interpolation

There are many ways of interpolating between stored values in order to achieve estimates of intermediate values. With additional computation (compared to the previous methods) it is possible to generate estimates that follow curves. *Cosine interpolation* (figure 8.22) is a way of creating curved transitions between the data points. In this technique the values of p_{frac} are mapped through the following equation (where the cosine function takes an argument in radians):

$$p_{\text{frac}} = 0.5\left[1 - \cos\left(\pi p_{\text{frac}}\right)\right] \tag{8.7}$$

The mapped value is then used in equation 8.4. Figure 8.23 shows a comparison of linear and cosine methods when used to estimate the values between multiple points. Linear interpolation can result in more sharp angles at the points where two lines meet.

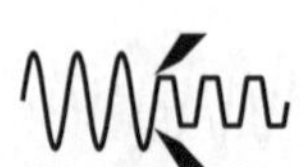

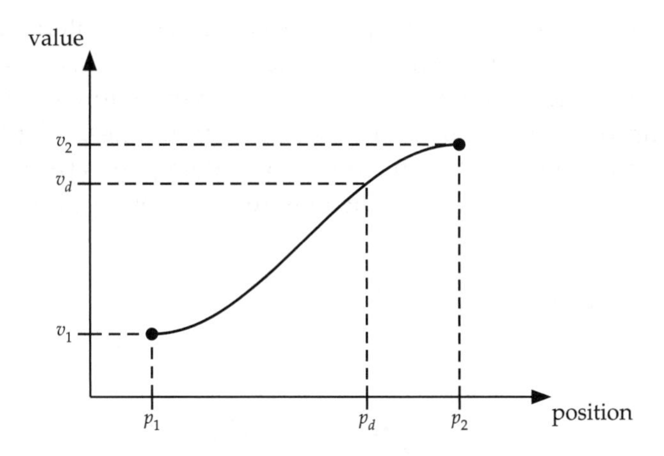

Figure 8.22 Cosine interpolation

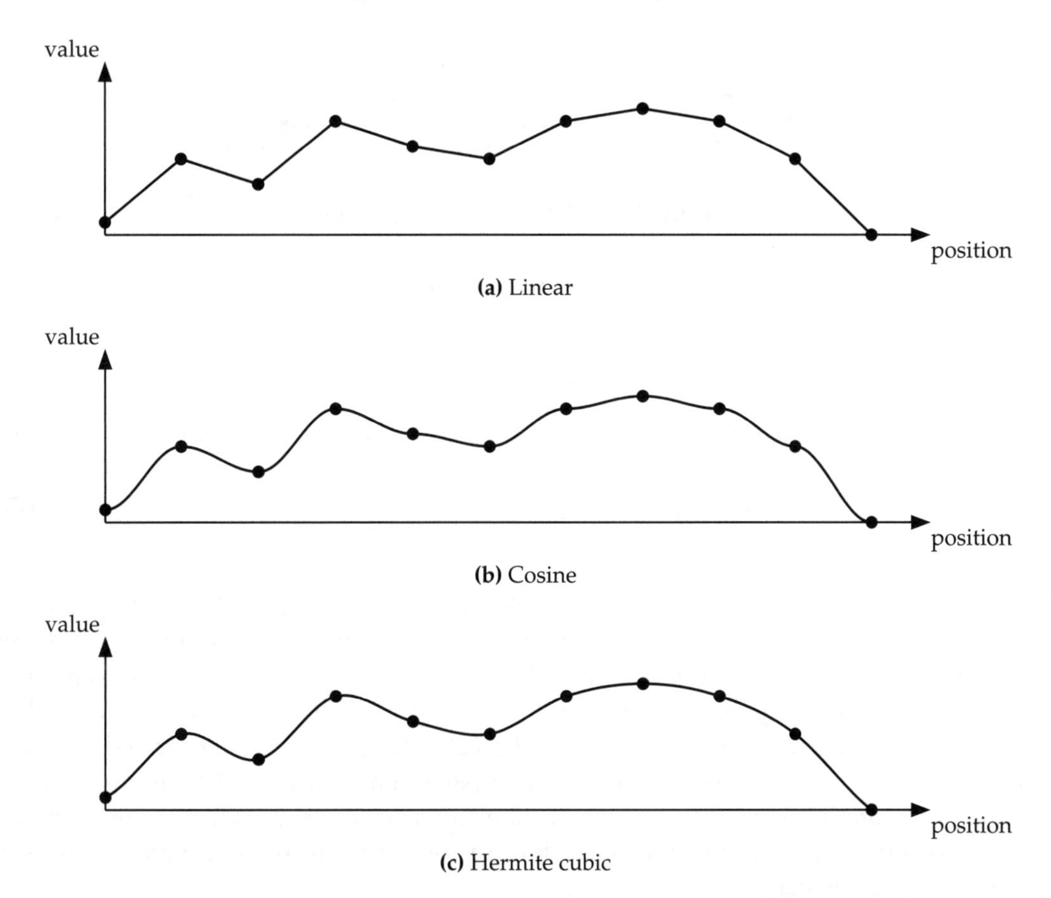

Figure 8.23 Comparison of interpolations over multiple data points

Linear and cosine interpolation methods produce an estimate of intermediate values based on two neighbouring data points. More sophisticated methods use more points, in order that the interpolation takes the surrounding signal shape into consideration. This can create audible improvements, particularly at high frequencies. Figure 8.24 illustrates interpolation based on four points. The four known data points (p_0 to p_3) are uniformly spaced. As with the previous examples, the required position (p_d) is between p_1 and p_2.

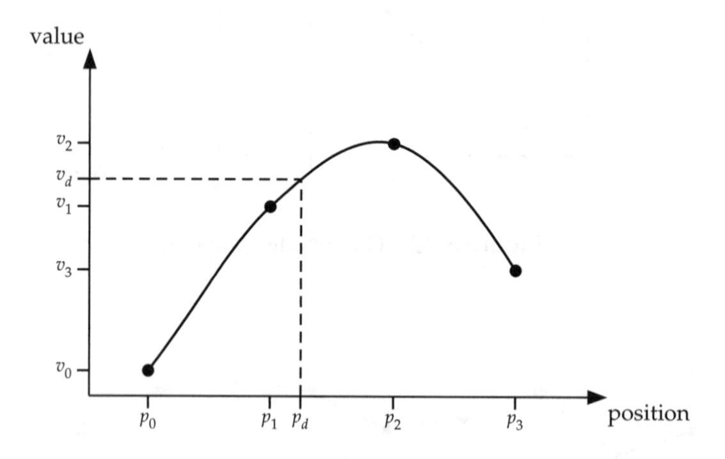

Figure 8.24 Four point interpolation

A typical way of calculating value v_d is with *Hermite cubic polynomial interpolation*, which is calculated as follows:

$$a_0 = v_1 \qquad a_2 = v_0 - 2.5v_1 + 2v_2 - 0.5v_3$$

$$a_1 = 0.5(v_2 - v_0) \qquad a_3 = 0.5(v_3 - v_0) + 1.5(v_1 - v_2)$$

$$v_d = a_3 p_{\text{frac}}^3 + a_2 p_{\text{frac}}^2 + a_1 p_{\text{frac}} + a_0 \tag{8.8}$$

Value p_{frac} is calculated in the same way as before, as the fractional distance of p_d between p_1 and p_2 (a value between 0 and 1). It is important to remember that four data points are required for this method; there is the potential for this to cause issues. For example, if generating a delay where the delay time is less than one sample (very close to zero), then position p_2 is the current input sample and the value for p_3 has not yet arrived. In these cases it is either necessary to restrict the range (such that delay must be more than one sample), or to predict a suitable value v_3 for the equation to work. When using a circular buffer, the implementation must also check if it is necessary to wrap around the ends of the array to find the values.

It is apparent in figure 8.23c that the additional sophistication of the Hermite method produces a result that follows the wider contours of the data points more smoothly than either the linear or cosine methods, as it takes into account the values of four points rather than just two.

8.3 Level Measurement

8.3.1 Introduction

Level measurement is used in a range of different audio processes. A simple case involves finding the peak sample value in an entire audio file, such that the whole data set can be normalised. For example, if the largest absolute sample value (ignoring the negative sign if present) in an audio file is 0.8, and the data is required to peak at a maximum value of ± 1, then multiplying all the sample values in the file by $1/0.8 = 1.25$ will achieve the required normalisation.

Many level measurement tasks are about extracting the amplitude envelope (whose characteristics are discussed in §3.2, p.49). Figure 8.25 shows an example waveform and its amplitude envelope. The aim in level measurement is following the long-term envelope level, rather than the underlying oscillating waveform, for such purposes as:

- Measuring the level for display on a mixing console meter.
- Judging whether the input is background noise or the wanted signal in a simple noise gate.
- Extracting the envelope to apply it to another sound in a synthesizer.
- Finding the start of sonic events when measuring the tempo.

An algorithm that can extract the envelope automatically is called an amplitude *envelope follower* (or envelope detector, or level detector). While the amplitude envelope is often clear to the human eye, there are a number of significant challenges in constructing and configuring an envelope follower algorithm that can perform the task in the required manner. Different envelope followers produce different results, which can affect the audible results of a process.

The two most common measurement standards are *peak* and *RMS* (Root Mean Square). Peak measurement is the idea of finding the largest values and so tracing the outline of the input (as shown in figure 8.25). Measuring the peak level is important when trying to prevent a signal going outside the maximum signal range and distorting. The purpose of the RMS technique is to provide a better indication of loudness (perceived amplitude) by calculating an average level over time. Figure 8.26 illustrates the differences between peak and RMS levels for some simple constant test tones. The equation for calculating an RMS value will be described later.

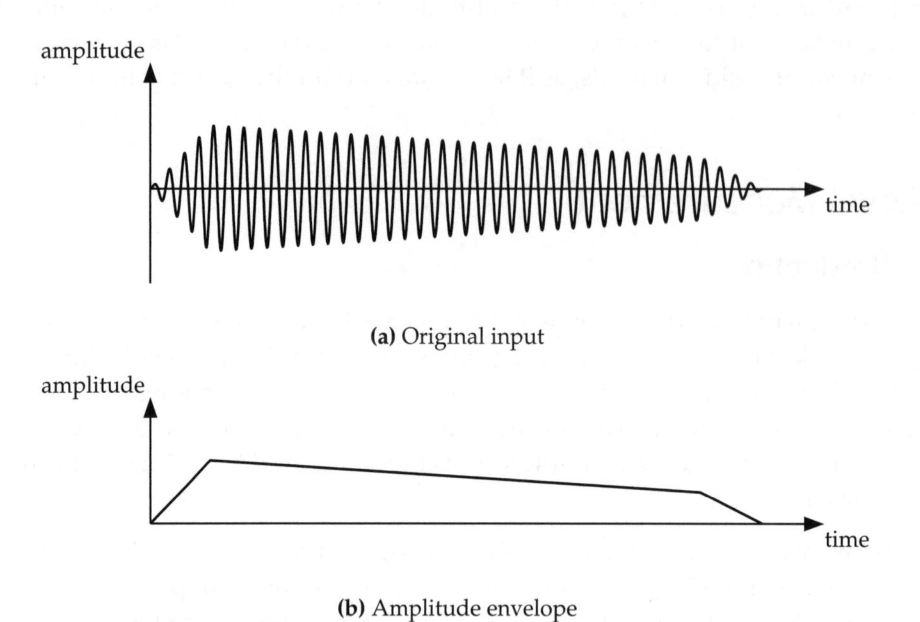

Figure 8.25 A waveform and its amplitude envelope

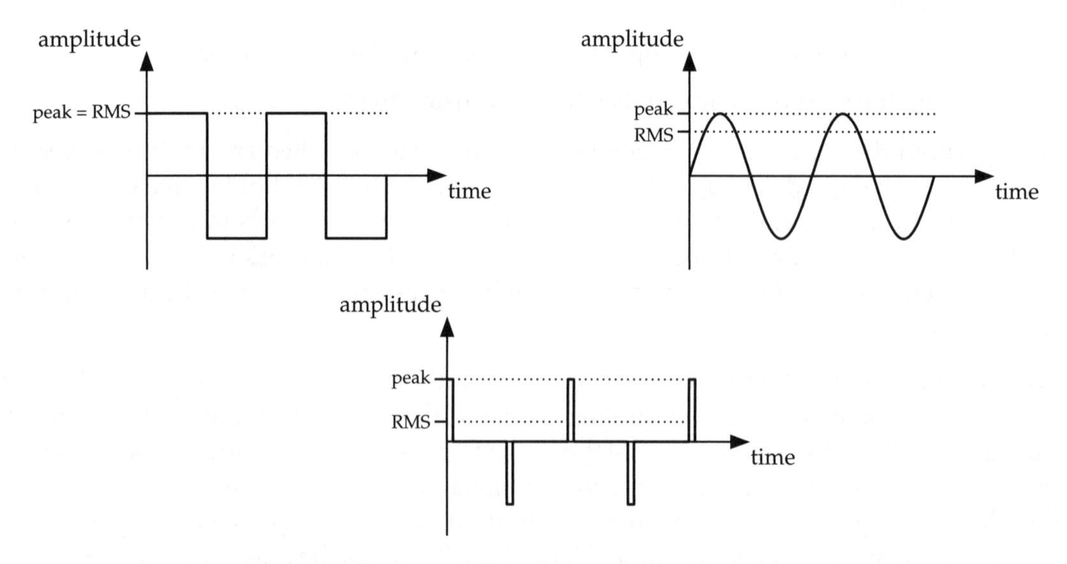

Figure 8.26 Peak and RMS levels for different waveforms

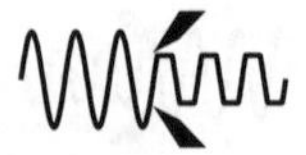

The following sections describe a number of envelope following techniques, which each have different properties, and different complexities of implementation.

8.3.2 Accurate Peak Measurement

Algorithm 8.6 is a peak level envelope follower. It utilises an overlapping window (as per figure 8.5, p.226) such that an updated output is produced for every sample.

Algorithm 8.6 – Peak envelope follower function

```
input  : current signal value in
output: envelope value out

writeposition = writeposition + 1                        // increment position
if writeposition == N then
    writeposition = 0                                    // wrap around
buffer[writeposition] = |in|                             // store new value
if writeposition == peakposition then
    // overwriting previous peak position; search for a new one
    maximumvalue = 0                                     // reset largest value
    for readposition = 0 to N−1 do
        if buffer[readposition] > maximumvalue then
            maximumvalue = buffer[readposition]          // update largest value
            peakposition = readposition
else if buffer[writeposition] > buffer[peakposition] then
    // latest input is the new peak value
    peakposition = writeposition
out = buffer[peakposition]
```

The algorithm has the following important features:

- The buffer is an array of at least length N, where N corresponds to the window length over which the peak value will be found. The initial starting conditions are that *writeposition* is 0, *peakposition* is 0, and *buffer* is filled with zero values. The states of *writeposition*, *peakposition*, and *buffer* are maintained between calls to the function. The function is called once for each new input sample.
- The initial part works in a similar way to the standard circular buffer update function. The difference is that the buffer stores the absolute values of the input samples (removing the negative sign if present, expressed as mathematical form $|x|$). This ensures that the algorithm finds the largest positive or negative value.

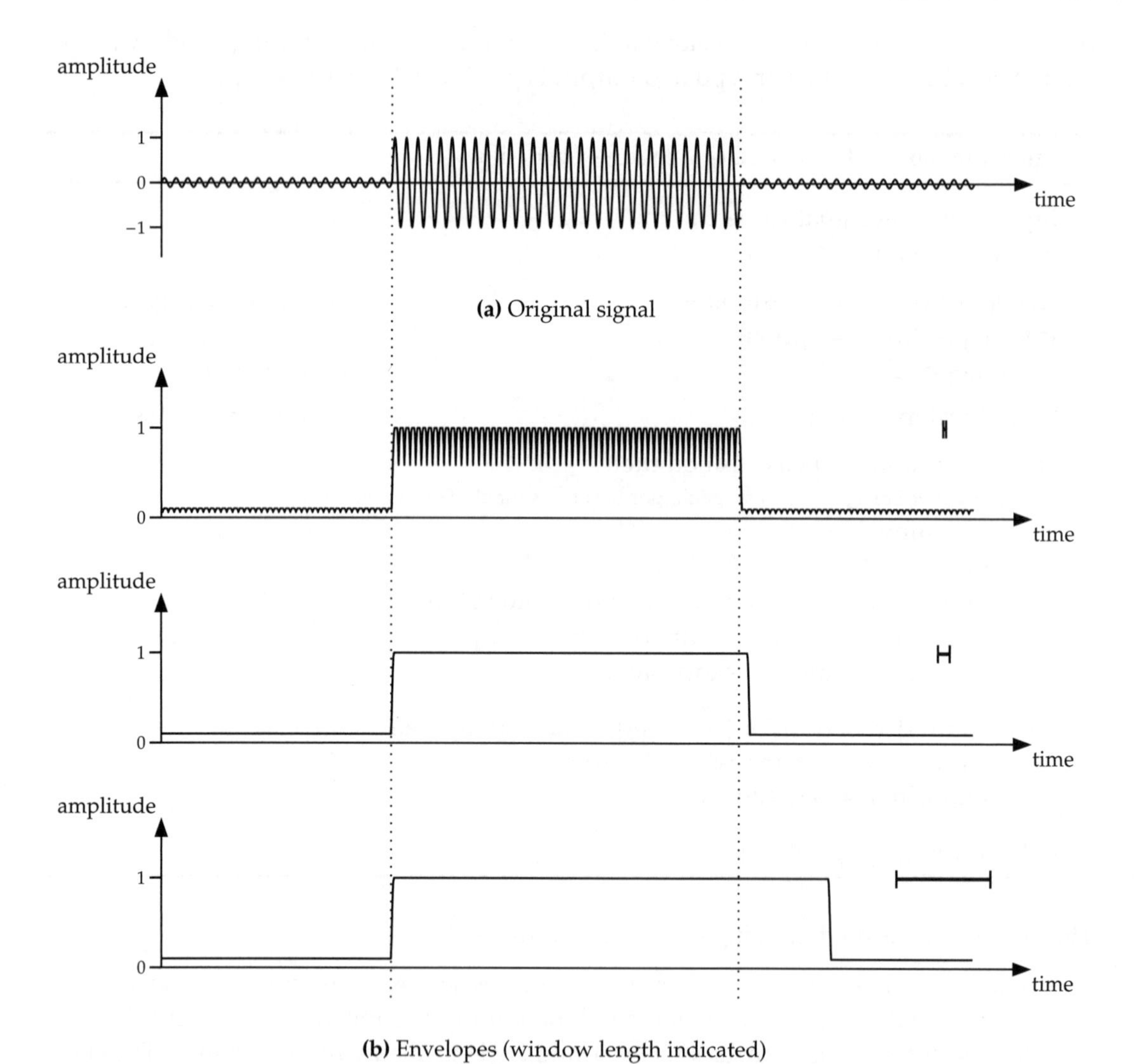

(a) Original signal

(b) Envelopes (window length indicated)

Figure 8.27 Peak envelope follower response

- It would be very inefficient to scan the entire buffer for the peak amplitude for each new input sample. As such, *peakposition* (the position in the array where the largest value is stored) is only updated when necessary. There are two update conditions that can occur:
  - If the previous known peak has just been overwritten with a new value, it is necessary to do a complete search of the buffer for the new peak.
  - If the most recent input sample is larger than the previous peak value, then the current position is the new peak position.

Figure 8.27 shows the peak envelope follower response to a signal with steps in its amplitude envelope. Three window lengths are demonstrated. When the window length is less than the distance between peaks in the input (absolute values), the envelope output moves up and down with the waveform. This *ripple* is removed as the window length gets longer, but also reduces how rapidly the follower responds to the downward step in amplitude envelope.

8.3.3 Accurate RMS Measurement

The RMS measurement technique is a type of averaging process. Mathematically it is expressed as follows:

$$\text{RMS average} = \sqrt{\frac{1}{N}\sum_{i=0}^{N-1} x_i^2} \qquad \boxed{8.9}$$

where N is the number of samples being considered, and x_i is the value of the ith input sample. Algorithm 8.7 is an RMS envelope follower. Like the peak follower before, it utilises an overlapping window.

The algorithm has the following important features:

- The buffer is an array of at least length N, where N corresponds to the window length over which the RMS value will be found. The initial starting conditions are that *writeposition* is 0, *runningtotal* is 0, and *buffer* is filled with zero values. The states of *writeposition*, *runningtotal*, and *buffer* are maintained between calls to the function. The function is called once for each new input sample.
- It would be very inefficient to calculate equation 8.9 from scratch for all N recent input values every time a new input sample is processed. A more efficient arrangement is used instead. The squared values of the input samples are stored in the buffer such that it is not necessary to square each value more than once. A running total of the N most recent squared values is kept by subtracting the oldest stored value in the buffer and then adding the newest at each step.

Algorithm 8.7 – RMS envelope follower function

```
input : current signal value in
output: envelope value out

writeposition = writeposition + 1                          // increment position
if writeposition == N then
    writeposition = 0                                      // wrap around

runningtotal = runningtotal – buffer[writeposition]        // subtract oldest value
buffer[writeposition] = in * in                            // store new value
runningtotal = runningtotal + buffer[writeposition]        // add newest value

if runningtotal < 0 then
    runningtotal = 0                                       // correct calculation

out = √(runningtotal / N)                                  // finish calculation
```

- A check is included to avoid trying to calculate the square root of a negative number. If the calculations are always performed perfectly, then *runningtotal* will never be negative. However, inaccuracies associated with floating-point number representations can produce tiny errors.

The response of the RMS technique has a dependency on window length (in a similar way to the peak follower method) as shown in figure 8.28. Note that the rise and fall of the envelope follower output is different for the peak and RMS methods.

An envelope following technique that has a similar algorithmic form to the RMS method is an absolute value average, which is based on the following equation:

$$\text{Absolute value average} = \frac{1}{N}\sum_{i=0}^{N-1} |x_i| \qquad \boxed{8.10}$$

The equation is similar to a normal arithmetic mean, but absolute values of the input are taken. An arithmetic mean will often result in 0 for audio signals, which tend to have as much positive as negative amplitude deviation. The envelope is different from that calculated with an RMS method, but can be used for similar purposes and takes a little less computation. The RMS envelope follower algorithm can be adapted to achieve an absolute value average. The first step is to change the line where new values are stored to this:

```
buffer[writeposition] = |in|
```

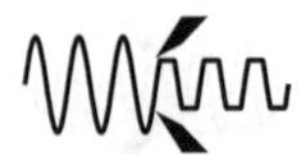

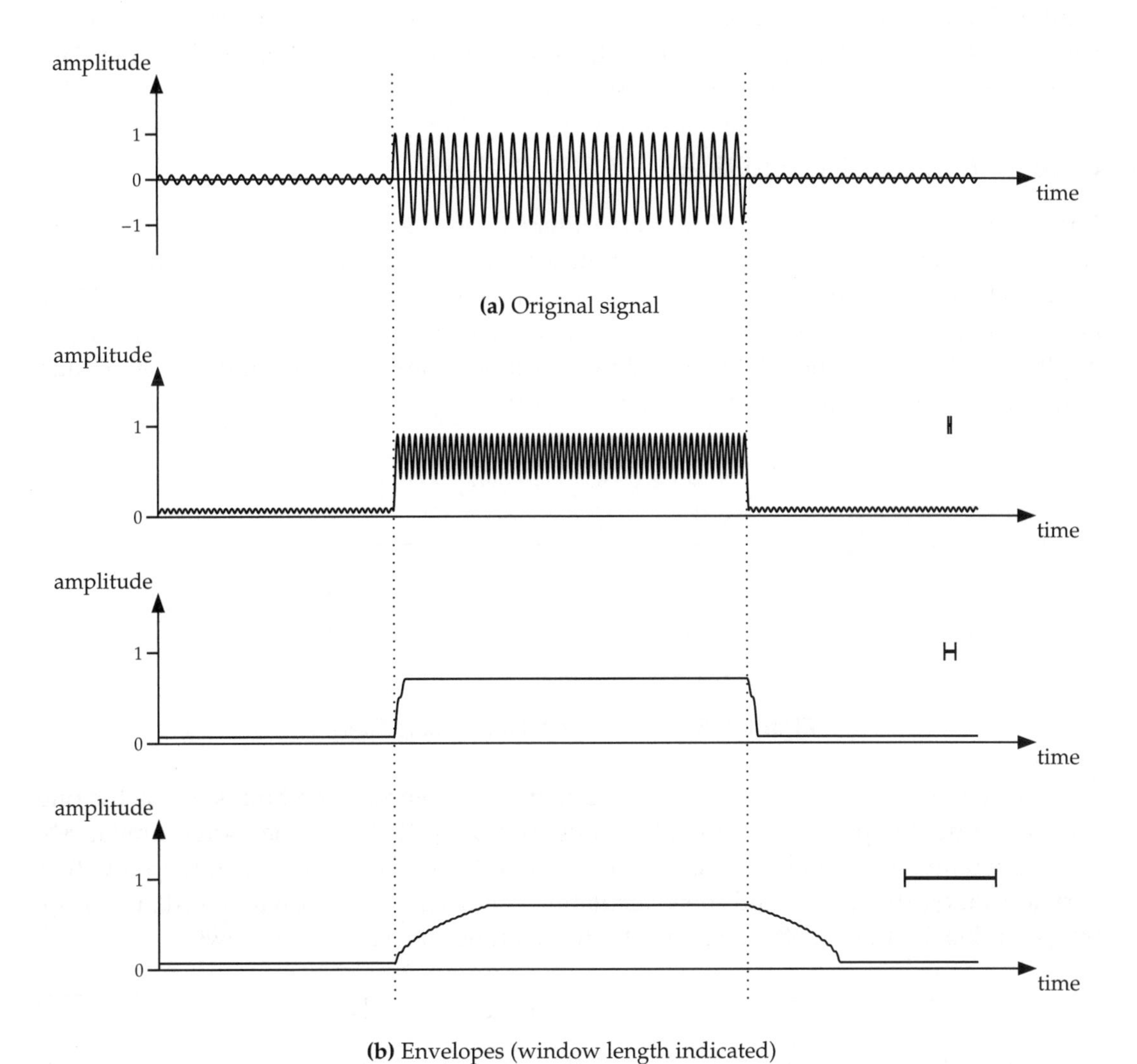

(a) Original signal

(b) Envelopes (window length indicated)

Figure 8.28 RMS envelope follower response

The second step is to change the final line to this:

out = runningtotal / N

The methods described above assume an overlapping window such that an output is produced for each new input sample. If a result is required less frequently, such as for a graphical meter display, then it is possible to create related algorithms for peak and RMS level detection with a non-overlapping window.

8.3.4 Filter-Based Techniques

Envelope following is related to lowpass filtering, as it is attenuating high frequencies while retaining the lower frequency amplitude variation. A general arrangement using lowpass filtering is shown in figure 8.29. The first step is to take the absolute value. There are then two controls over behaviour; the cutoff frequency (f_c) and the number of stages of filtering. The more filters that are included in series, the greater the attenuation of high frequencies, as previously described in §6.3.1 (p.155).

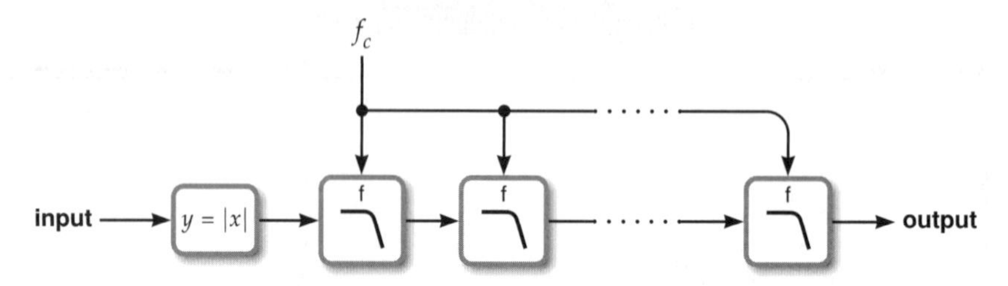

Figure 8.29 Envelope follower using filters

Using a single simple filter uses least computation. A common method is to use the one pole first order lowpass filter illustrated in figure 6.39 (p.171). This has some similarities to the operation of an analogue peak detector circuit. The filter can be configured with a very low cutoff frequency (and then calculating coefficients with equation 6.10, p.171) or by specifying the filter coefficients directly from a time constant T as follows:

$$g = k^{-1/(Tf_S)} \qquad a_0 = 1 - g \qquad -b_1 = g \tag{8.11}$$

where f_S is the sample rate, T is a length of time, and k controls the rate of change. A typical value of k is 9. Variable g determines how rapidly the envelope output moves from its current value to the latest input value. If g is 0, then the output is always the latest (absolute) input value. If g is 1, then the output never changes from its previous value (at the last sample step). For values in between some of the previous output value and some of the latest (absolute) input value are used to create the output. This causes the signal to be smoothed, as the output cannot change as rapidly as the input.

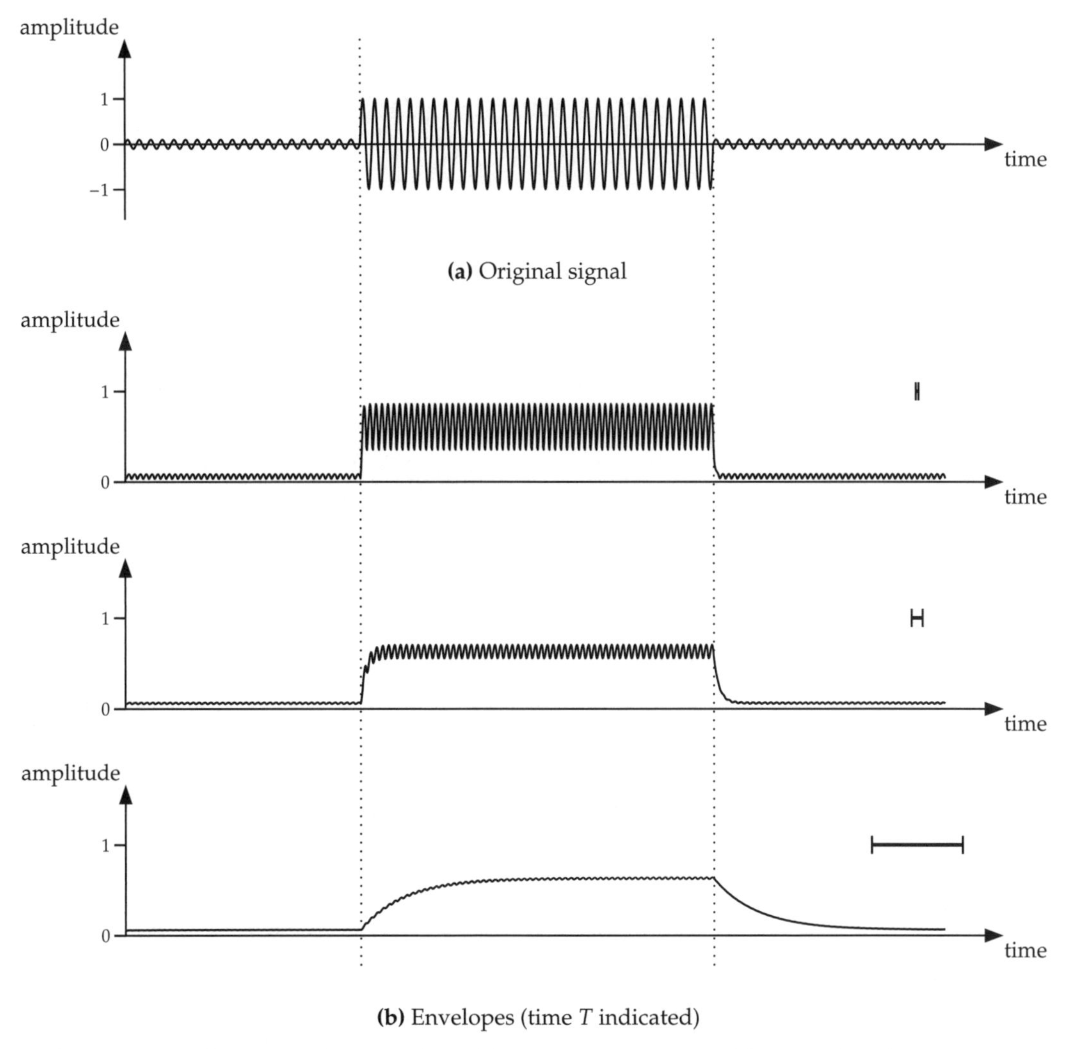

Figure 8.30 One pole filter envelope follower response; one filter, varying time constant

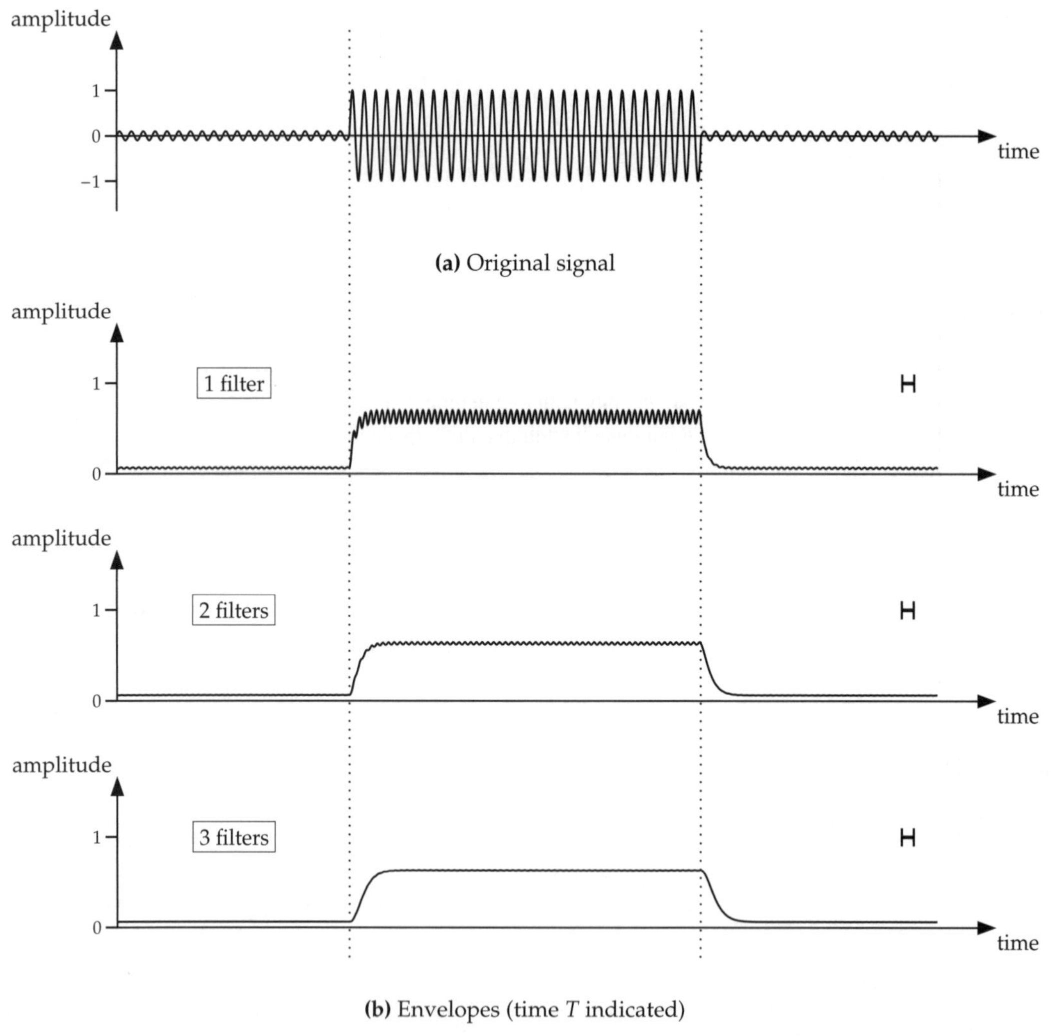

Figure 8.31 One pole filter envelope follower response; series filters, fixed time constant

Figure 8.30 shows how increasing time constant T (for a k value of 9) reduces the amount of ripple in the output, but also reduces the speed of response to the input level variation. In figure 8.31 the number of series filter stages is varied while the value of T remains the same. The higher frequencies become more attenuated as the roll-off increases.

A feature of the one pole filter envelope follower is that it is possible to choose a different value of g for when the (absolute) input is above the current output envelope level and when it is below. Normally this is termed *attack* and *release* behaviour, which is explored further in Chapter 11. Typically, the desirable behaviour is a rapid attack (smaller value of T) to follow the input upwards, but a slower release (larger value of T).

Figure 8.32 shows example results corresponding to one pole filter-based algorithms 8.8 and 8.9 incorporating attack and release behaviour. The algorithms produce slightly different results for the same settings, which can result in audible differences under some circumstances. Note the following:

- Circular buffers are not required for these algorithms, but it is necessary to maintain the values of *output* and *outputrel* between calls to the functions. These values are initialised to 0 when the program starts.
- The values of *gattack* and *grelease* are calculated before the function is called, using equation 8.11 (p.252) and appropriate values for attack and release time constants.

Algorithm 8.8 – One pole filter-based envelope follower function A

```
input  : current signal value in
output: envelope value out

newval = |in|                                  // new absolute value

if newval > output then
|  g = gattack
else
L  g = grelease

output = newval + g * (output − newval)
out = output                                   // output result
```

8.3.5 Ramping Techniques

A third type of envelope following technique is to use a ramping method where the output envelope increases and decreases at particular gradients (change of level per second). If the ramping is slower than the higher frequency variations in the original waveform, then the output follows the envelope shape.

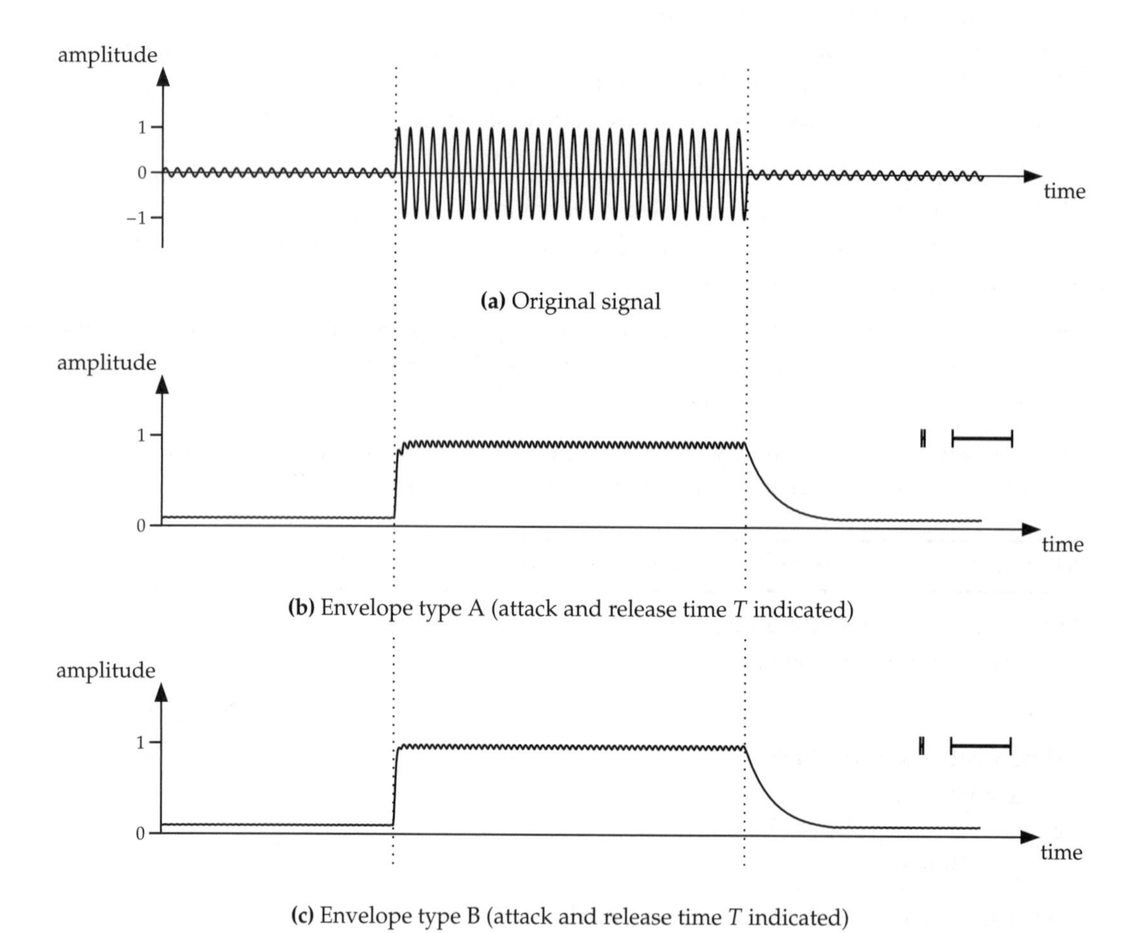

(c) Envelope type B (attack and release time *T* indicated)

Figure 8.32 One pole filter envelope follower response; one filter, attack faster than release

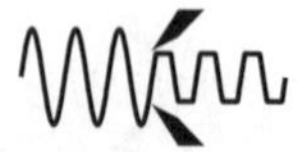

Algorithm 8.9 – One pole filter-based envelope follower function B

```
input : current signal value in
output: envelope value out

newval = |in|                                              // new absolute value
outputrel = newval + grelease * (outputrel − newval)

if newval > outputrel then
    outputrel = newval

output = gattack * output + (1 − gattack) * outputrel
out = output                                               // output result
```

Algorithm 8.10 describes a linear ramping envelope follower:

- A circular buffer is not required for this algorithm, but it is necessary to maintain the value of *output* between calls to the function. This value is initialised to 0 when the program starts.
- The values of *attackstep* and *releasestep* are calculated before the function is called, and are the maximum rates at which the output value can increase and decrease per sample. From equation 8.1 (p.220) it is possible to say that the step size required to move from an output value of 0 to 1 (or 1 to 0) in T seconds can be calculated like this:

$$\text{step size} = \frac{1}{T f_S} \tag{8.12}$$

It is also possible to have a ramp that works in decibels, as achieved by algorithm 8.11. This is similar to algorithm 8.10, but uses equations 5.2 and 5.3 (p.113) to make conversions:

- It is necessary to maintain the value of *output* between calls to the function. This value is initialised to −80 when the program starts, which is the lower limit of the envelope output in decibels (equivalent to a linear amplitude of 0.0001).
- The values of *attackstep* and *releasestep* are again calculated before the function is called, but are in terms of decibels for this algorithm. For example, the step size required to vary by 20dB in T seconds can be calculated like this:

$$\text{step size (dB)} = \frac{20}{T f_S} \tag{8.13}$$

Figure 8.33 shows the ramping envelope follower outputs. It is apparent that the ripple and the response to steps in input amplitude are different from both the accurate (peak and RMS) techniques as well as the one pole filter method.

Algorithm 8.10 – Linear ramping envelope follower function

```
input  : current signal value in
output: envelope value out

newval = |in|                                  // new absolute value

if newval > output then
    output = output + attackstep
    if output > newval then
        output = newval                        // prevent overshoot
else if newval < output then
    output = output – releasestep
    if output < newval then
        output = newval                        // prevent overshoot
out = output                                   // output result
```

Algorithm 8.11 – Decibel ramping envelope follower function

```
input  : current signal value in
output: envelope value out

newval = |in|                                  // new absolute value
if newval < 0.0001 then
    newval = 0.0001                            // clamp at lower limit (-80dB)
newval = 20 * log10(newval)

if newval > output then
    output = output + attackstep
    if output > newval then
        output = newval                        // prevent overshoot
else if newval < output then
    output = output – releasestep
    if output < newval then
        output = newval                        // prevent overshoot

out = 10^(output/20)                           // output result
```

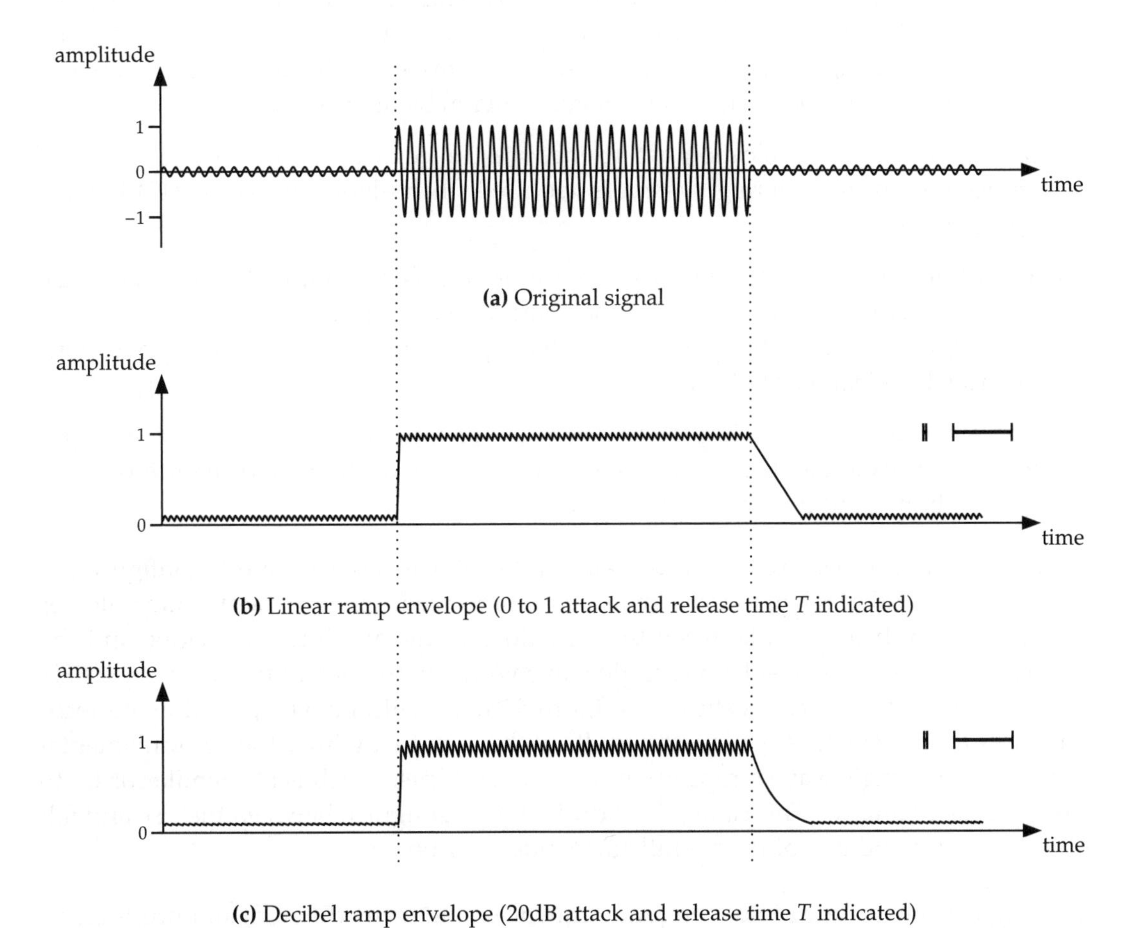

(a) Original signal

(b) Linear ramp envelope (0 to 1 attack and release time T indicated)

(c) Decibel ramp envelope (20dB attack and release time T indicated)

Figure 8.33 Ramping envelope follower response; attack faster than release

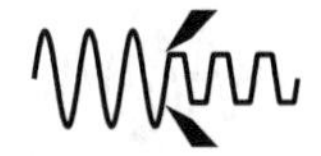

8.3.6 Selecting and Configuring Envelope Followers

The envelope follower techniques all have a different balance of performance characteristics, which affect the choice of method for particular applications:

- The algorithms produce different outputs for the same step change in amplitude envelope, as seen in the response plots previously. These can produce subtle differences in the audible results of a process, such as a noise gate or compressor (which are described in Chapter 11). Some commercial systems allow the user to select between measurement techniques to suit the sonic material being processed.
- In some cases the application determines the choice of technique. For example, if an accurate peak metering system is required, then algorithm 8.6 (p.247) is most appropriate.
- The flexibility of configuration can be important. For example, the accurate peak and RMS algorithms do not have attack and release controls, but the one pole filter-based and ramping techniques do. This has significance in some of the applications described in Chapter 11.
- The algorithms vary in implementation complexity, and computational requirements. For example, the accurate peak and RMS algorithms both require use of a circular buffer, but the other techniques do not.

As well as the performance characteristics described above, there are subtle configuration issues to consider that relate to the signals being processed. Firstly, an envelope follower must attempt to distinguish between the variations in the amplitude envelope and the underlying waveform. Consider a triangle wave with a fundamental frequency of 100Hz and a cycle length of 10ms, as shown in figure 8.34. A typical envelope following technique uses absolute values of waveforms. It can be seen that with a 100Hz fundamental frequency, the triangle wave ramps up or down over 2.5ms, which is of a similar order to some percussive attacks. This can make it difficult to distinguish between the rise and fall of the waveform and that of the overall amplitude envelope.

Audio signals can include a wide range of frequencies and many different amplitude envelope shapes. A low frequency tone whose amplitude rises slowly and stops abruptly might require a different envelope analysis technique or configuration to a high frequency sound with a typical percussive envelope. Generally it is harder to distinguish the envelope from the underlying waveform as the cycle lengths of the waveform approach the length of the variations in the envelope (i.e. with decreasing waveform oscillation frequency). For example, with a 20Hz sinusoid the cycle length is 50ms, and peaks occur every 25ms, which is slower than some envelope variations.

Consider figure 8.35, where the original signal is fairly complex. Underneath the original signal plot are three amplitude envelopes that have been created with the RMS measurement technique. They have been configured with different window lengths such that different amounts of signal are used in the measurement. When the shortest length is used the measured envelope tends to follow short term variations. With the longest window the output fails to respond to more rapid changes. The intermediate window length, however, has highlighted the gentle oscillatory component in the original signal.

An appropriate response time of an envelope follower to signal variations depends on the context. For example, graphical level meters are unlikely to be updated very frequently, so finding the peak or RMS value in a 25ms or longer window is likely to be appropriate. If the envelope follower is to be used with short attack times found in compressors (discussed in §11.3, p.353) then much shorter lengths of time could be required. It might be necessary for the user of the process to choose an appropriate value.

8.4 Developing Processes and Learning More

The techniques described in this chapter are important for implementing more sophisticated modifiers such as vibrato, flanger, phaser, and chorus effects (described in Chapter 9), echo and reverberation processes (Chapter 10), and noise gates and compressors (Chapter 11). Elements such as buffers, delays, and envelope followers are provided as standard in some programming environments. In those cases configuring them to achieve the desired results is important, such as a particular style of interpolation or envelope smoothing. Reading the relevant manuals needs to be combined with suitable trial-and-error configuration to achieve the required results.

In cases where the audio data techniques are implemented from scratch, there are a number of pitfalls to be considered. A particular issue when dealing with buffers is ensuring that elements are only accessed within the boundaries of the array. This is made more complex in the circular buffer form by the movement of the write and read pointers over time. Although it can take some time to learn how to implement circular buffers, they are a very powerful tool in audio process implementation.

Interpolation and level measurement techniques present the audio process engineer with a range of implementation choices. One consideration is the computational complexity of the different algorithms, which affects the processing power consumed. Related to algorithmic complexity is the difficulty for novices in understanding how to implement the more complex schemes (such as the four point Hermite cubic polynomial interpolation in §8.2.4, p.242). Another consideration is the audible differences between different algorithms. These can be subtle tonal differences which suit particular contexts, rather than one technique being clearly better or worse than another. For example, the envelope follower techniques in §8.3 (p.245) each produce a different response to a step in amplitude

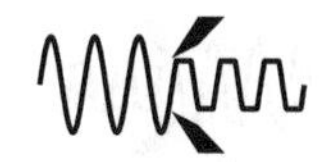

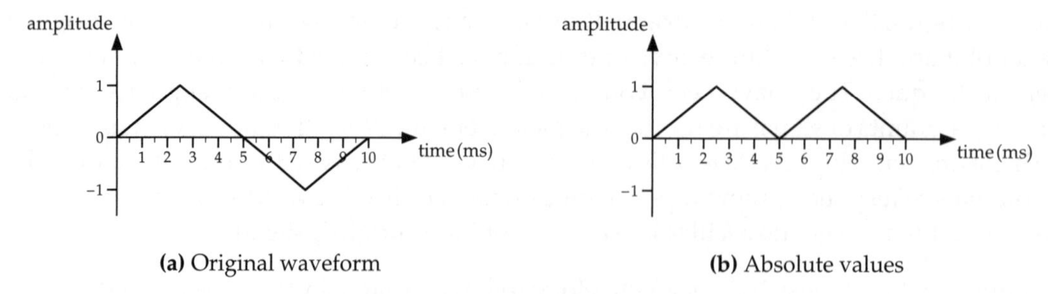

(a) Original waveform **(b)** Absolute values

Figure 8.34 100Hz triangle waveform

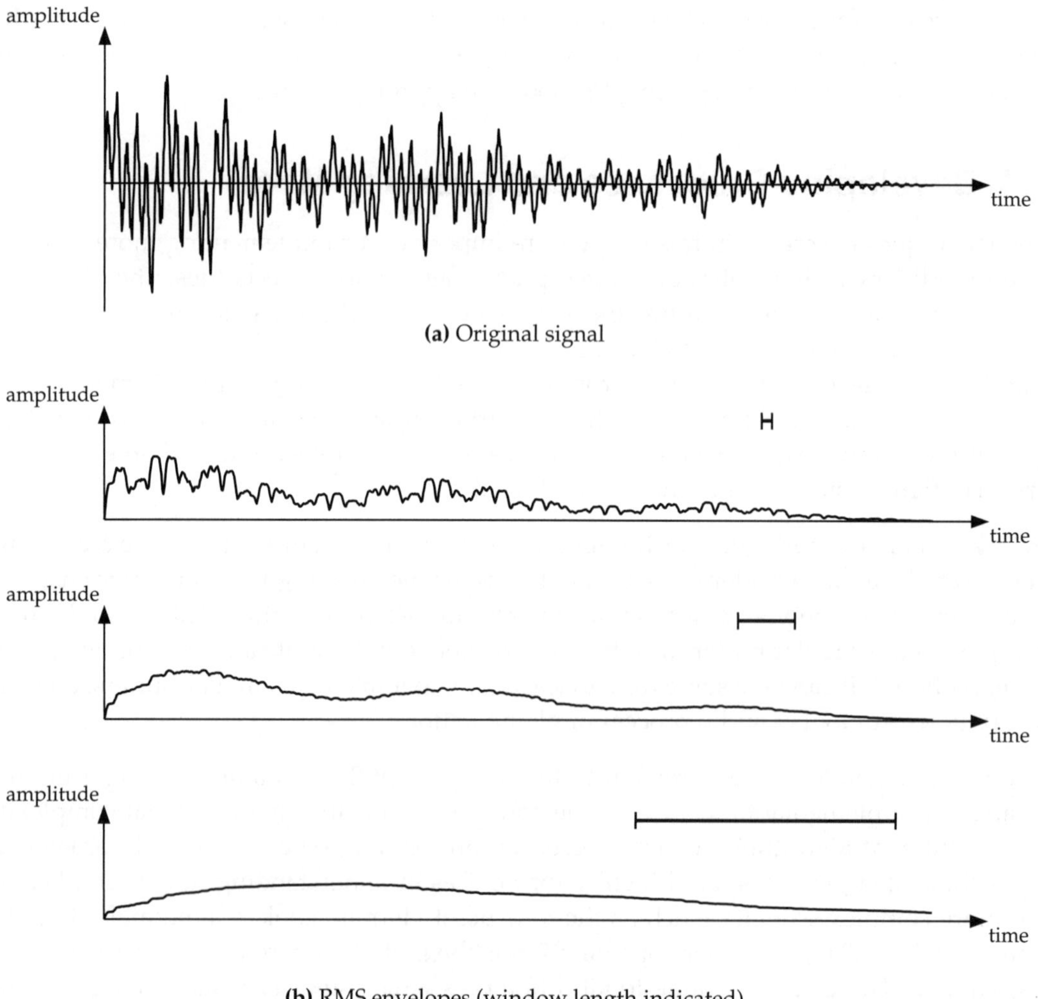

(a) Original signal

(b) RMS envelopes (window length indicated)

Figure 8.35 Envelope follower response

envelope level, which will produce subtle differences in the results of processes that use envelope followers, such as compressors.

The following sources provide some further details on the topics discussed in this chapter:

Boulanger, Richard, and Victor Lazzarini, eds. 2011. *The Audio Programming Book*. Cambridge, MA: The MIT Press.

Giannoulis, Dimitrios, Michael Massberg, and Joshua D. Reiss. 2012. "Digital Dynamic Range Compressor Design – A Tutorial and Analysis." *Journal of the Audio Engineering Society* 60:6:399–408.

Pirkle, Will. 2013. *Designing Audio Effect Plug-Ins in C++: With Digital Audio Signal Processing Theory*. Burlington, MA: Focal Press.

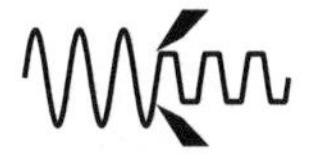

9

Modulated Modifiers

9.1 Introduction

9.1.1 Variation over Time

Previous chapters have been concerned mainly with static parameters. The position of a pan control (§5.5.2, p.121), the parameters of a distortion transfer function (Chapter 7), and the centre frequency of a bandpass filter (§6.2.2, p.149) are often consistent once they have been configured. However, a manual control input can be replaced by an automatically-generated value that changes over time, producing a different style of modification effect.

Figure 9.1 shows an example situation where a manual control could be replaced by a signal generator. There are a couple of good reasons to use a signal generator rather than (or in addition to) a manual control:

- Sometimes it is desirable to record variations to a control over time, and then replay them at a later stage. This is the idea behind mix automation. It is not possible for one person to vary the parameters of all tracks simultaneously, so mix automation allows the engineer to program the variations to one control at once. These changes are stored, and then replayed together for the final mix.
- Sometimes a continuous variation to a parameter produces an interesting sonic character. The nature of sonic variation is important to perception, as described in Chapters 3 and 4. Modifiers that generate periodic variation (such as tremolo) are used widely.

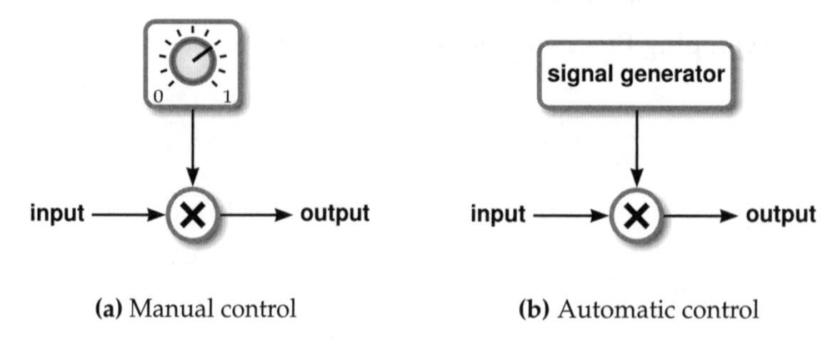

(a) Manual control **(b)** Automatic control

Figure 9.1 Monophonic amplitude control

Modulation is the process of varying one aspect of a signal, using another signal, over a length of time. This chapter concentrates on typical modifiers that use periodic modulation. This is also discussed in Chapter 20, which considers its application in synthesis and with higher rates of modulation. Chapter 11 discusses how envelope following can be used to modulate parameters.

9.1.2 Oscillators

An *oscillator* is the signal generator that is used when creating periodic variation. It produces a repeating waveform at a particular frequency and amplitude. Figure 9.2 illustrates three oscillator configurations and their outputs:

- The oscillator has a fundamental frequency input in hertz (marked "f"). This produces a waveform of cycle length T, where frequency and cycle length are related by $T = 1/F$. The three examples in the figure have frequencies of 10Hz, 1Hz, and 4Hz (which have cycle lengths of 0.1s, 1s, and 0.25s).
- For the purposes of this book, the oscillator block will always produce a waveform with a ±1 peak amplitude. This makes it easy to scale the output subsequently.
- Finally, the oscillator has a waveform shape. A single cycle is illustrated on the block diagram symbol. This might be a standard shape (previously described in §4.2.2, p.79) or something more unusual, depending on the required result.

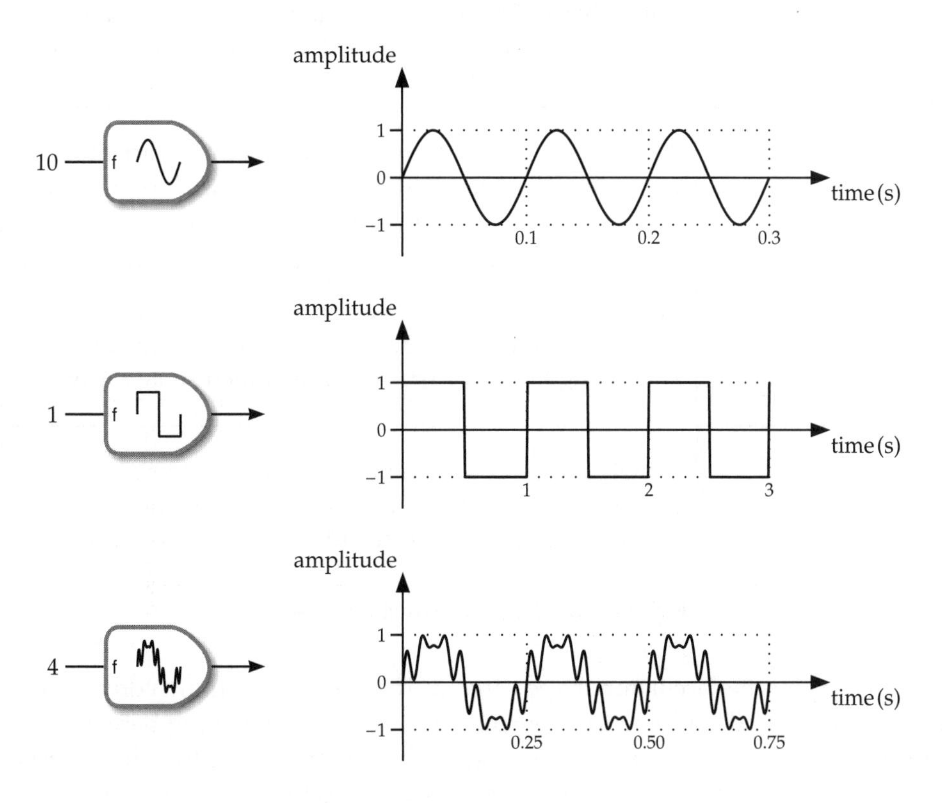

Figure 9.2 Oscillator examples

The construction of oscillator algorithms is discussed in Chapter 14. The choice of oscillator waveform depends on the parameter being modulated and the sonic situation in which it is used. It is important to consider the implications of the choice of shape, as illustrated in figure 9.3.

Shape	Characteristics
	The sinusoid has a smooth variation, but the rate of change slows down towards the maximum and minimum values.
	The triangular shape has a constant rate of change (but changing direction every half cycle).
	The sawtooth shape mostly has a constant rate of change but with a sudden jump in value at the end. The ramp could be upward or downward depending on the desired result.
	This shape shows a decreasing amplitude of variation over time. Non-standard shapes can be used to produce a result that is tailored for a particular situation.
	Vertical lines tend to produce clicks in the output when used in a modulating effect, which can be avoided by smoothing the shape (such as a smoothed square wave).
	A high frequency variation can be too rapid to be perceived as a clear shaped parameter variation in a modulating effect, and can add roughness to the result.

Figure 9.3 Example oscillator shapes

Instead of changing the oscillator shape directly, it is sometimes more convenient to take existing oscillators and combine their outputs; for example, switching between two oscillator outputs as shown in figure 9.4. Note that both oscillators have the same fundamental frequency value at their inputs. Alternatively, oscillator outputs might be blended (figure 9.5) to provide the user with continuous control over shape. The figure uses a cross-fade

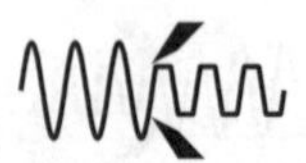

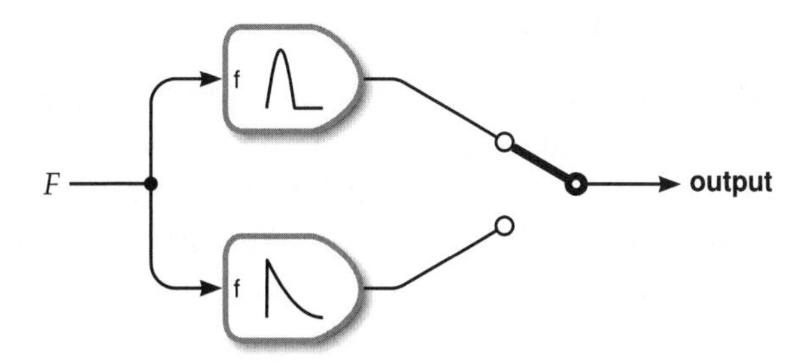

Figure 9.4 Switching oscillator outputs

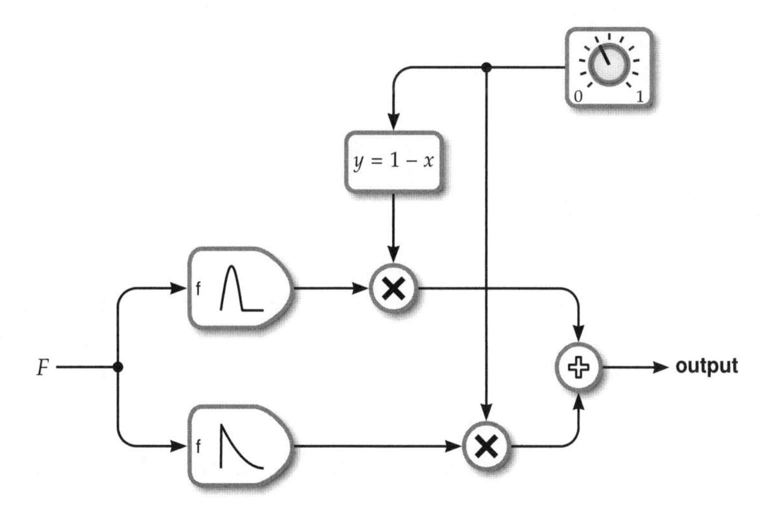

Figure 9.5 Blending oscillator outputs

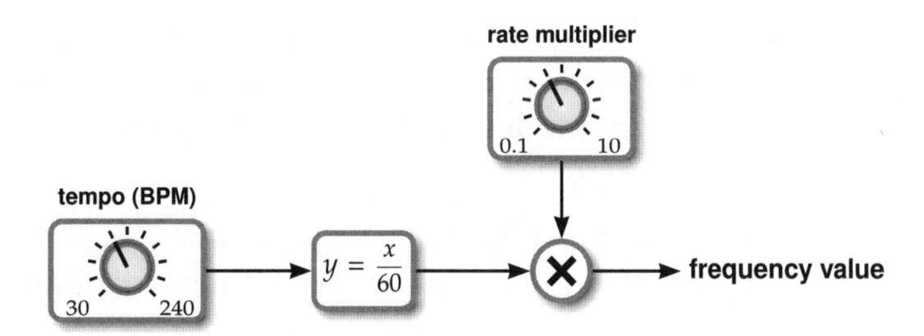

Figure 9.6 Tempo to frequency conversion

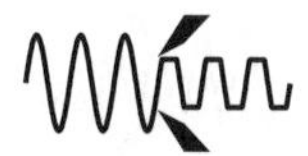

technique as seen previously in figure 5.51b (p.135). The two oscillators are synchronised in phase such that they always rise and fall together.

The oscillator frequency might be set directly, or it might be determined from other parameters. For example, figure 9.6 shows how a tempo in beats per minute (BPM) can be converted to a frequency for an oscillator. The BPM value might be provided by a master clock (such as from a sequencer or Digital Audio Workstation), and the rate multiplier makes it easy to make a change relative to the base tempo, such as being able to specify 2 oscillator cycles per beat, or 0.25 to achieve 1 cycle every 4 beats.

An advantage of the oscillator producing an output with a ±1 peak amplitude, is that multiplying by a fixed value will scale the amplitude of the signal to that value, as shown in figure 9.7. This is very useful for achieving an oscillation to suit a particular parameter range, such as for an amplitude gain value, or a filter frequency, which is a technique that is used in the following section.

9.2 Examples of Periodic Modulation

9.2.1 Tremolo and Autopan

One of the most common types of periodic modulation is *tremolo*, where the amplitude of the sound is varied to achieve a wobbling or pulsing effect. This is similar to moving a mixer fader up and down cyclically as the sound is playing. The difference is that an electronic system can do this with great accuracy of frequency, amplitude, and waveform shape.

Figure 9.8 shows the general form of a tremolo effect. It has the following features:

- **Shape**. The oscillator can have any required waveform function. If the shape is smooth, such as a sinusoidal function, it will result in a smooth perceived variation in amplitude. However, if the shape has sharp edges, then they will be audible as sudden variations in output amplitude.
- **Rate**. The rate at which the cyclical form repeats is determined by frequency f_d. If it is a low frequency, such as 0.5Hz (a cycle every 2 seconds), then the sound appears to wander up and down in amplitude. With a higher frequency, such as 15Hz, the output gains a rapid pulsing quality.
- **Depth**. The amount of variation in amplitude, or modulation depth, determines the perceived magnitude of the effect. This is parameter a_d in the diagram.
- **Offset**. The offset a_0 is the central value of amplitude to which the oscillation is applied. The larger this value, the higher the average amplitude.

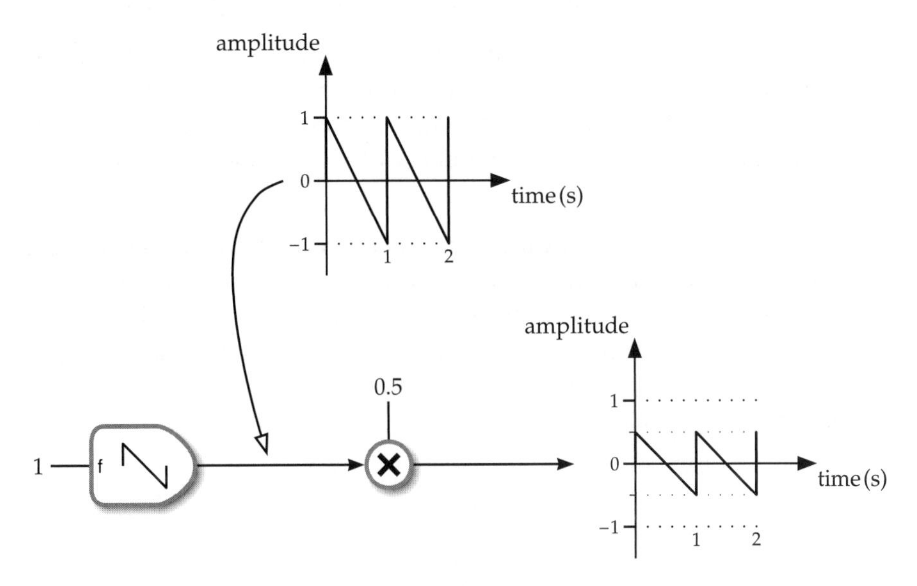

Figure 9.7 Oscillator with scaled output amplitude

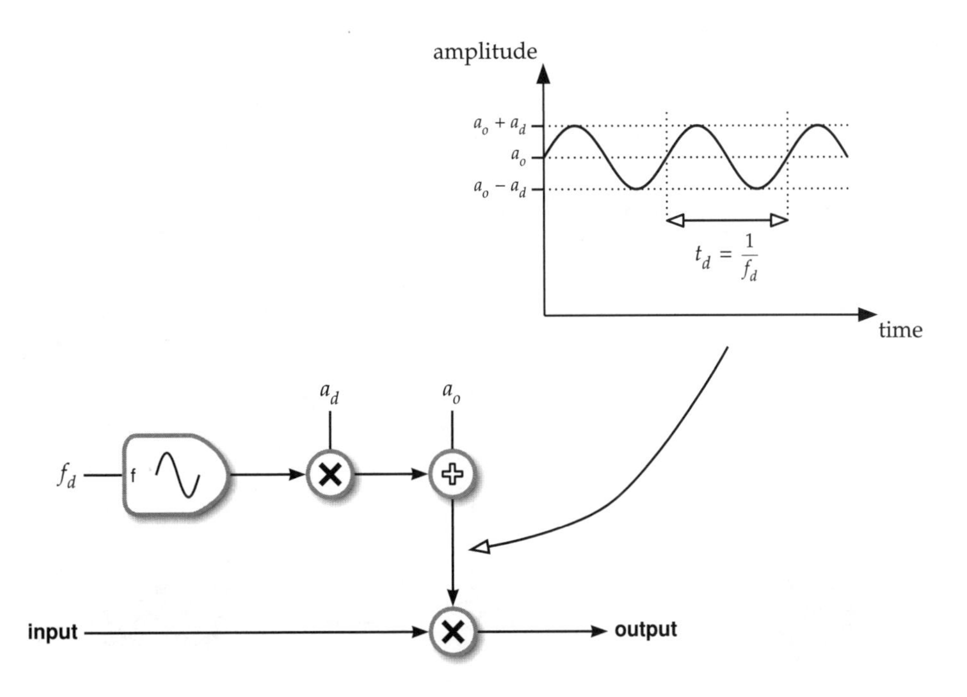

Figure 9.8 Tremolo

Figure 9.9 illustrates an example tremolo effect applied to a simple input signal:

- The rate (frequency) of the modulating oscillator is much lower than that of the signal being modulated. Typical tremolo rates are in the range 0.1Hz to 20Hz. As rates increase beyond 20Hz the effect tends towards one that is gritty or rough, rather than a clear pulsing amplitude. The effect of amplitude modulation frequency is explored further in §20.2 (p.561).
- The depth and offset of the modulating signal determine the range and centre value of the effect. In the figure, the oscillator output varies between −1 and +1. After the multiplier, the variation is between −0.2 and +0.2. When added to an offset of 0.5, this produces a waveform that varies between 0.3 (0.5 – 0.2) and 0.7 (0.5 + 0.2). This is in the range 0 to 1, suitable for an amplitude multiplier value, as originally described in §5.3.1 (p.105).

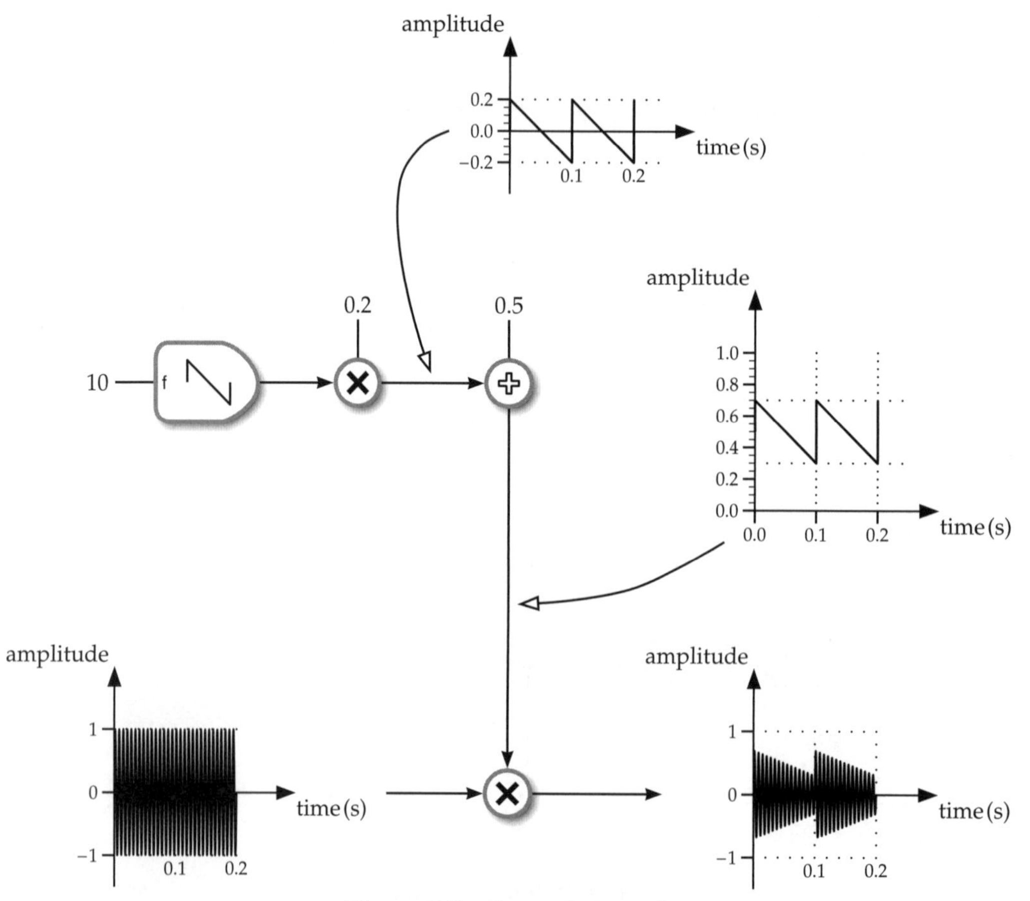

Figure 9.9 Example tremolo

- The sawtooth shape used in the example has significant jumps in amplitude that are audible in the output. In some circumstances this will be a useful audible effect, but alternatively a different shape might be more appropriate for the musical context.

Figure 9.10 illustrates the effects of varying the rate and depth of a tremolo modulation. It is always necessary to think about the context when selecting rate, depth, offset, and shape. A modulation rate will often be set to synchronise with the tempo of the music being modified.

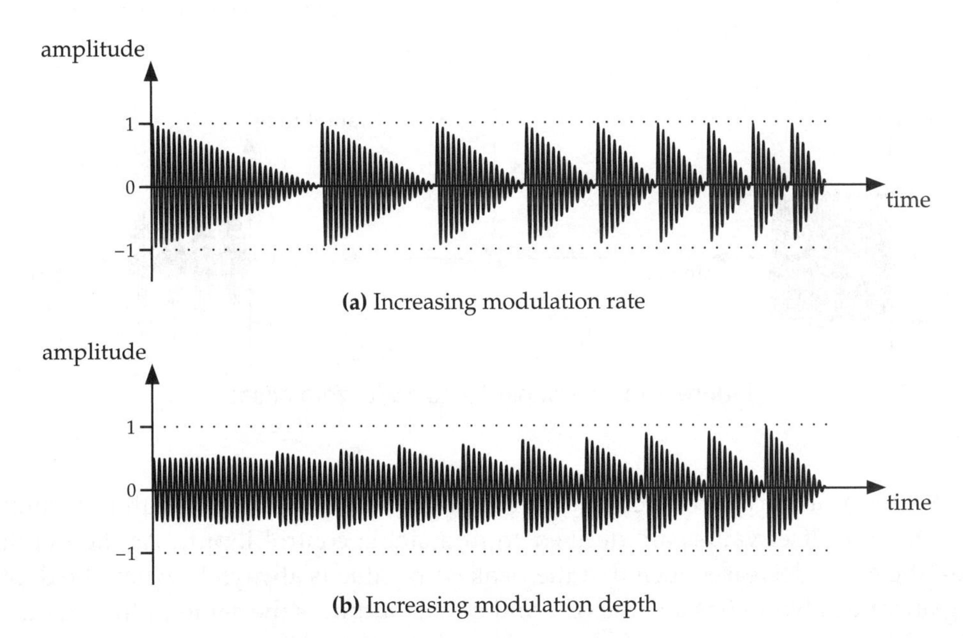

Figure 9.10 Parameter effects for tremolo

The offset in figure 9.9 ensures that the modulating waveform applied to the multiplier does not include values below zero. Without the offset, unexpected results can occur. Figure 9.11 illustrates what happens with a zero offset:

- Each cycle of the modulating sinusoid appears as two in the output wave. In the figure, the modulating oscillator is set to 4Hz, but the output will appear to pulse at 8Hz.
- When the modulating waveform moves between positive and negative values a phase shift will occur in the output.

With a zero offset the negative values in the modulating waveform effectively create the same shape as if they were positive. Generally zero offsets should be avoided.

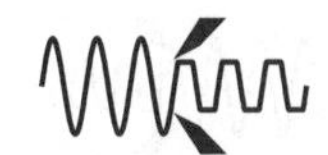

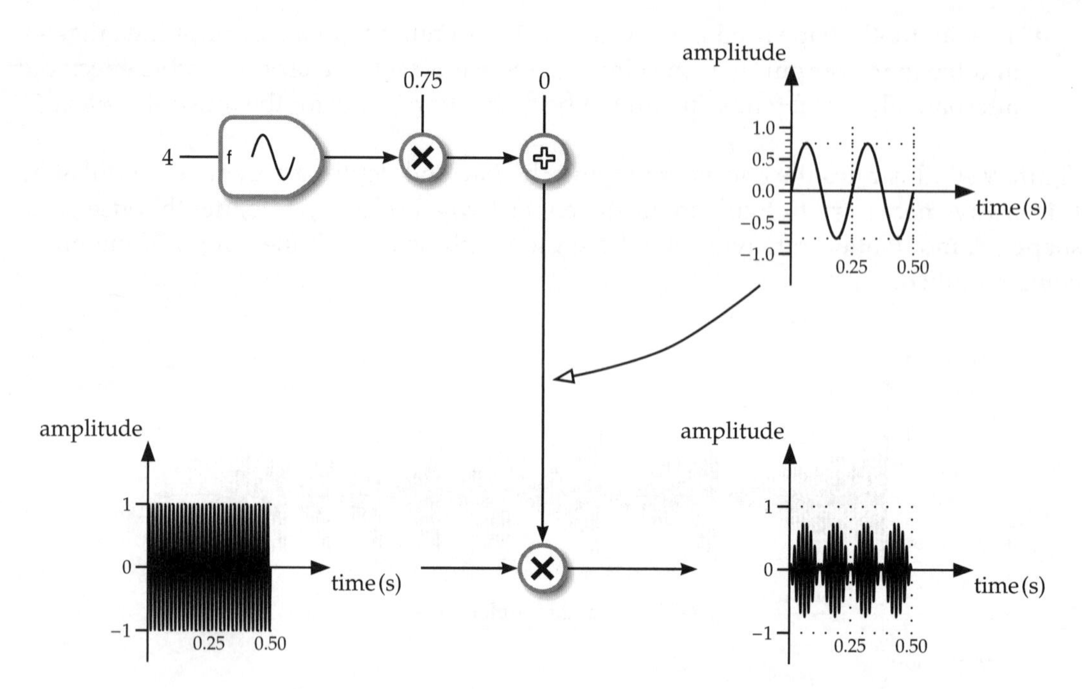

Figure 9.11 Example tremolo with zero offset

Figure 9.12 is a practical arrangement for controlling a tremolo effect with two controls. The depth and offset values are derived from a single control input. As the depth increases, the offset decreases such that the peak gain value is always 1. When the depth is 0 the gain value always has a value of 1 and so the output is the same as the input. At a depth of 0.5, the gain variation is between 0 and 1.

Figure 9.13 illustrates an *autopan* process, which achieves an output where the sound moves left and right in the stereo soundfield over time. It extends the tremolo process by incorporating the equation $y = 1 - x$ to calculate a second gain value (for the left output channel). This is the same technique as seen in figure 5.32 (p.122). An offset of 0.5 means that the effect is centred, and the depth controls the amount of left-right variation. The figure uses a triangle waveform, with a rate of 1Hz and depth of 0.5, to achieve an effect that oscillates fully between left and right loudspeakers. Lower values of depth achieve a more subtle effect.

As with the tremolo, different waveforms will produce different types of effects with an autopan. A triangle wave will have a constant rate of movement. A sawtooth, however, will appear to jump at the end of a cycle from one side to the other.

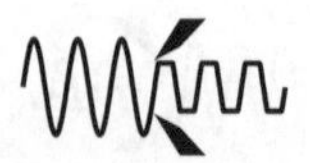

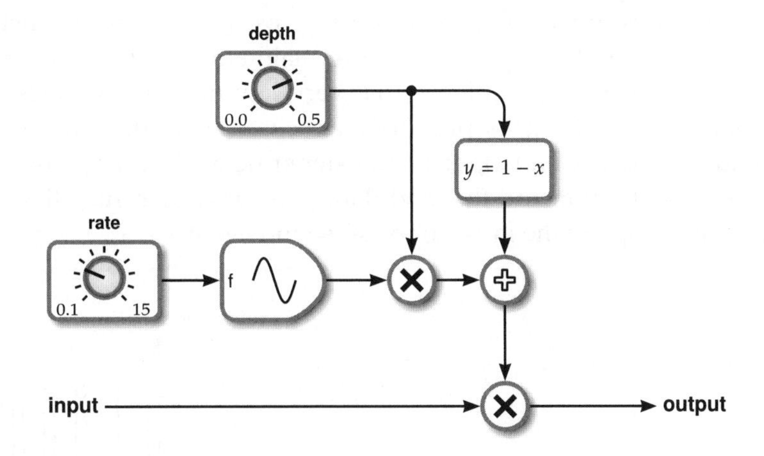

Figure 9.12 Practical tremolo

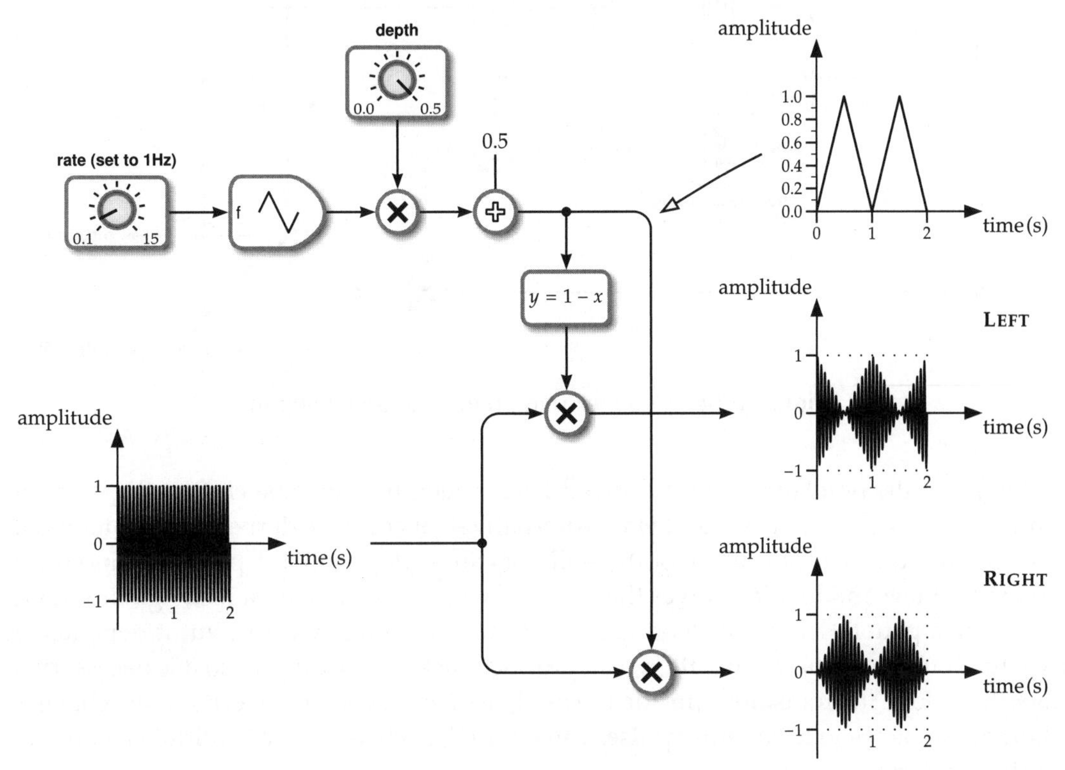

Figure 9.13 Example autopan

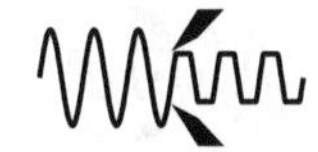

Figure 9.14 shows a way of combining tremolo and pan effects. As with the oscillator blend example in figure 9.5 (p.269) there are two oscillators that are using the same fundamental frequency, and are synchronised to maintain their phase relationship. The difference from the previous examples is that very low modulation rates and complex oscillation patterns are used. This produces a cyclical effect that causes the audio to be chopped and moved left and right in the stereo field. The patterns are chosen to complement the type of input, and the modulation rate is chosen such that the repetitive pattern fits with the tempo of the music or other sound event.

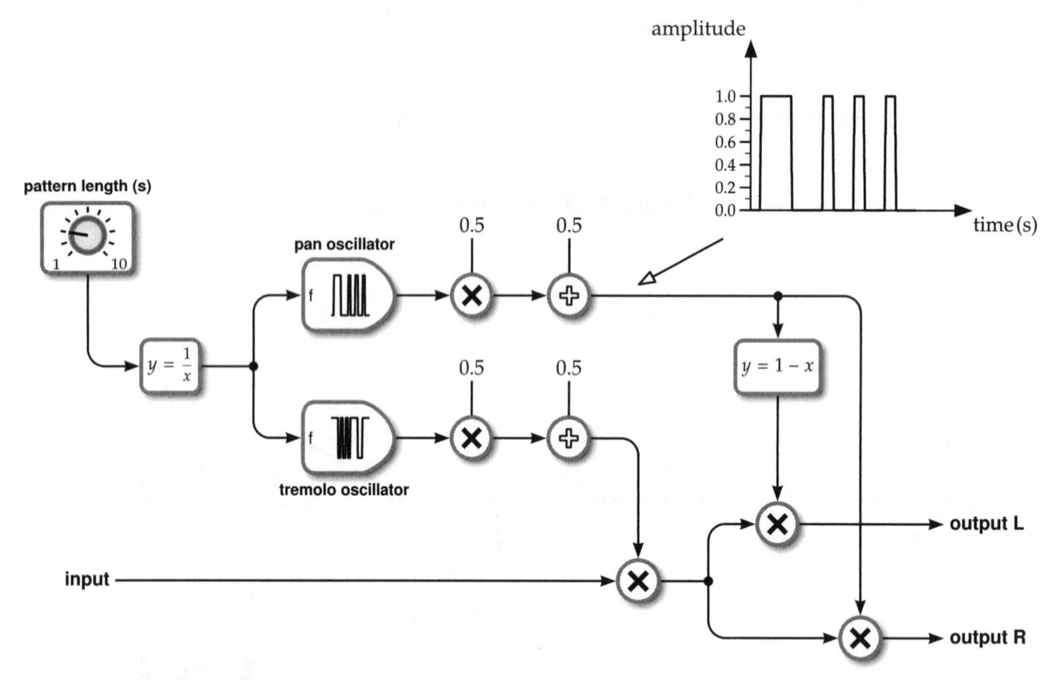

Figure 9.14 Complex pattern tremolo and autopan

In the figure the oscillation rate is derived from a length in time, such that the user can control the effect in a more natural way. Alternatively it could be derived from a tempo in beats per minute. The outputs of both oscillators are scaled with a depth of 0.5 and offset by 0.5 to achieve modulating waves that vary between 0 and 1. With a rectangular pattern as shown, a pattern length of 16 or 32 steps is suitable in many cases, but it depends on the situation. The rectangular pattern can produce clicks in the output, so it is necessary to smooth or slope the transitions (inside the oscillator) to reduce the severity of the changes. Alternative shapes to rectangular pulses can be used, such as steps at multiple levels, or a gently wandering pattern.

9.2.2 Filter Modulation

All types of parameters can be modulated, not just amplitude. Figure 9.15 shows one way of modulating the centre frequency of a bandpass filter. Typical parameter ranges are shown.

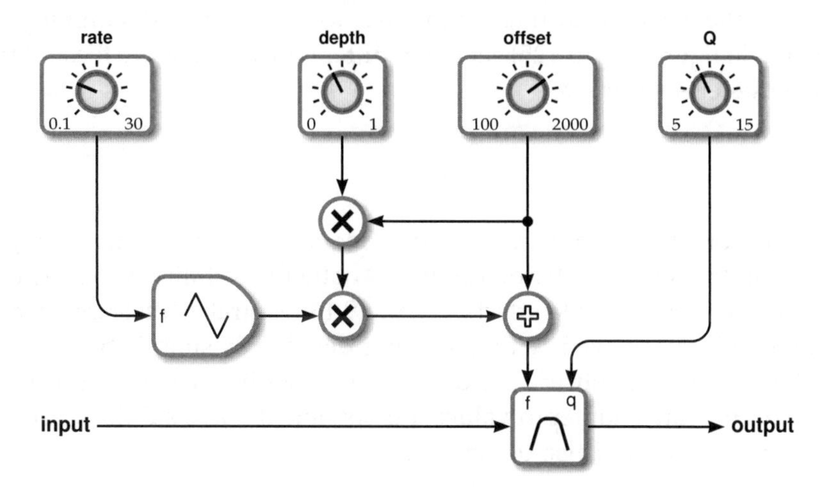

Figure 9.15 Modulating filter centre frequency

The rate chosen produces a number of effects:

- With a low rate (say, 0.5 to 3Hz), the result has a wah-wah character.
- Higher rates (say, 10Hz) could not be created manually with any kind of precision. This can produce a bubbling character.
- High rates (say, 30Hz) cause the sound to have a slightly coarse quality.

The offset is the centre of the frequency range, and the depth is calculated as a proportion of that frequency, which ensures that the value reaching the bandpass filter cannot be negative. The input signal is important in determining the output effect, as it depends on whether frequency partials exist in the input sound that correspond with the range of effect of the modulated filter.

The form in figure 9.15 can be extended to a number of parallel paths, similar to figure 6.20 (p.157) but with an individual modulator for each filter. Because a single bandpass filter only emphasises a single range of partials, using multiple filters allows different regions of frequency to be emphasised simultaneously. With separate modulators it is possible to create different but complementary modulations; for example, the rates might be the same, but with different offsets. Alternatively the rates might be different integer multiples of a base frequency.

Parallel modulated paths do not have to be configured with uniform spacing in frequency or consistent depth; for example, frequency ranges might overlap. One variation is to invert the shape of the oscillation (or multiply the oscillator output by −1) for one path, such that the modulated frequency is rising on one path while falling on another, if the modulation rates are the same and the oscillators are synchronised. It is also possible to extend the parallel form by adding a pan effect to each path and summing to a stereo output as shown in figure 5.36 (p.125) such that different variations are located in different positions in the stereo soundfield.

9.2.3 Vibrato

Cyclical variation of amplitude gain and filter frequency are fairly clear ways of using modulation to modify the character of a sound. Another possibility is to use periodically-varying delays to achieve audible effects. Figure 9.16 illustrates a *vibrato* effect (periodic frequency modulation) achieved with a varying delay. For simplicity, a single control provides both the depth and offset. The delay time varies between 0 and twice the depth value. More extreme rate and depth values are possible if a less subtle effect is required. Other waveform shapes could also be considered.

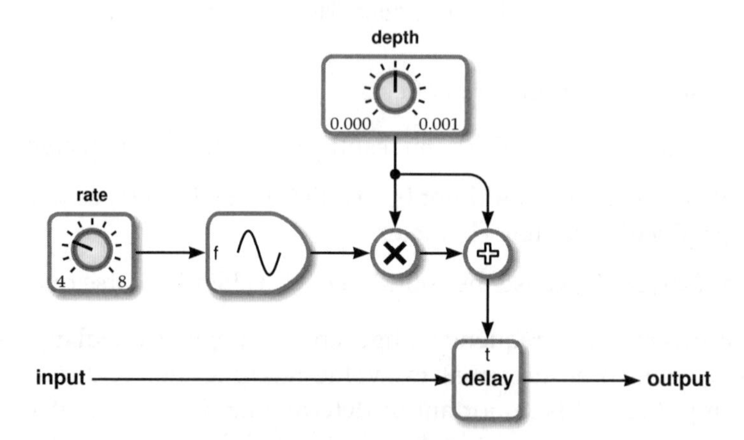

Figure 9.16 Vibrato

To understand how a varying delay modifies the input, it is necessary to consider the relationship between the read and write pointers in a delay buffer (see §8.1.4, p.232). With a constant delay time both pointers are moving at the same constant rate through the buffer, so the output is a delayed identical copy of the input. However, if the read pointer is moving through the buffer faster or slower than the write pointer then it changes the playback speed, and so increases or decreases the fundamental frequency of the output relative to the input.

A cyclically-varying delay implies that the read pointer is not a fixed distance behind the write pointer, but is periodically getting further away and closer (figure 9.17a). If the delay is increasing, the pointers are moving further apart, so the read pointer is travelling more slowly than the write pointer, and the cycles are read out at a slower rate than they are written. If the delay is decreasing, the pointers are moving closer together, so the read pointer is travelling faster than the write pointer, and the cycles are read out at a faster rate than they are written. As the delay time varies, therefore, the cycles are stretched and squashed, changing the cycle length, and so changing the fundamental frequency over time (figure 9.17b).

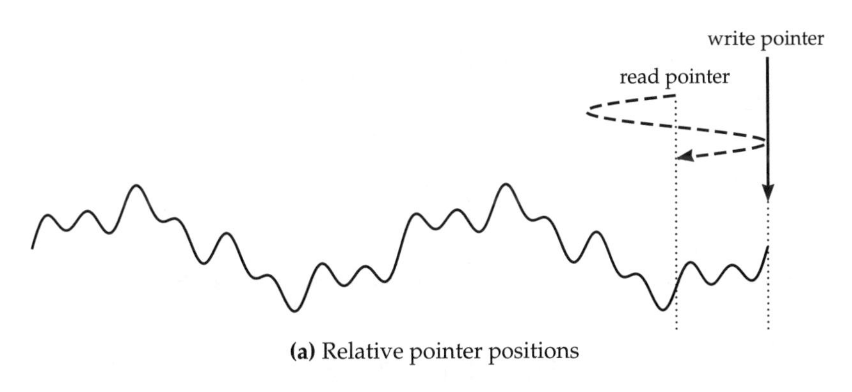

(a) Relative pointer positions

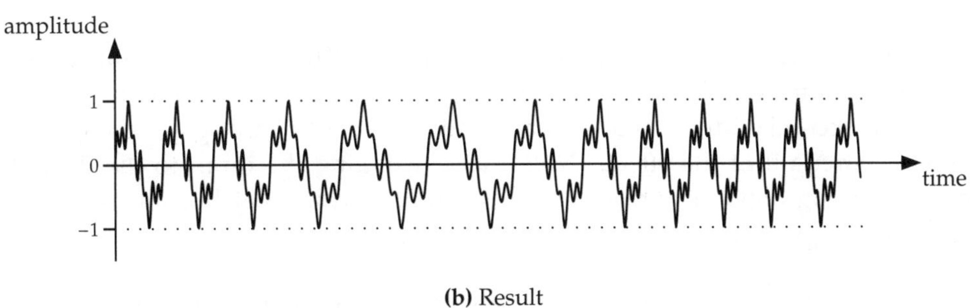

(b) Result

Figure 9.17 Vibrato example

9.2.4 Flanger and Phaser

Flanging is based on adding a signal to a fractionally-delayed copy of that signal, where the length of the delay is varying over time (as shown in figure 9.18). This is a time-varying comb filter (§6.4.4, p.183). In the block diagram, the depth is the same as the offset, which means that the effect always varies between a delay of zero, and a maximum of twice the depth. A triangle wave is used to achieve a steady variation in delay, but other waveform shapes can give interesting results. It is sometimes worth experimenting with higher rates and depths than those shown in the diagram, which produce quite strange

sound characters. The delay algorithm used in the flanger should use interpolation to remove stepping, clicking, or zipper sounds if the delay time changes slowly. Interpolation methods are described in §8.2 (p.237).

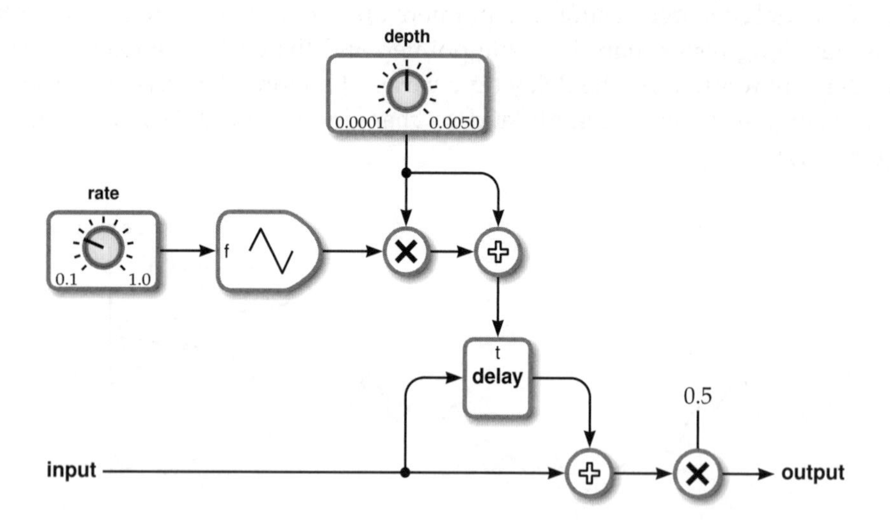

Figure 9.18 Flanger

Figure 9.19 illustrates two extensions to the basic flanger. The first is a separate control for minimum delay time, which can be useful for fine tuning the range, and so the character of the effect. The second addition is a feedback path with controllable gain. Using feedback increases the strength of the effect. Note that calculating the input to the delay block depends on having previously read a value from its output, which is an issue explored further in §10.3.2 (p.315).

The sonic results of a *phaser* have similar aspects to those of a flanger. However, the phaser uses a set of cascaded second order allpass filters (§6.4.4, p.183) rather than a delay block, as shown in figure 9.20. The phaser produces cancellation and summation at frequencies where the allpass filters produce phase shifts, as the filtered result is summed with the dry signal.

The modulation of filter frequency in figure 9.20 is a similar arrangement to figure 9.15 (p.277). The quantity of allpass filter stages generally relates to the strength of the effect, so up to 12 stages are used in typical implementations. The frequency multipliers m_2 to m_N might be set to 1 such that all filters are configured in the same way, or have different values (for example, exponentially increasing) to spread out the frequencies affected.

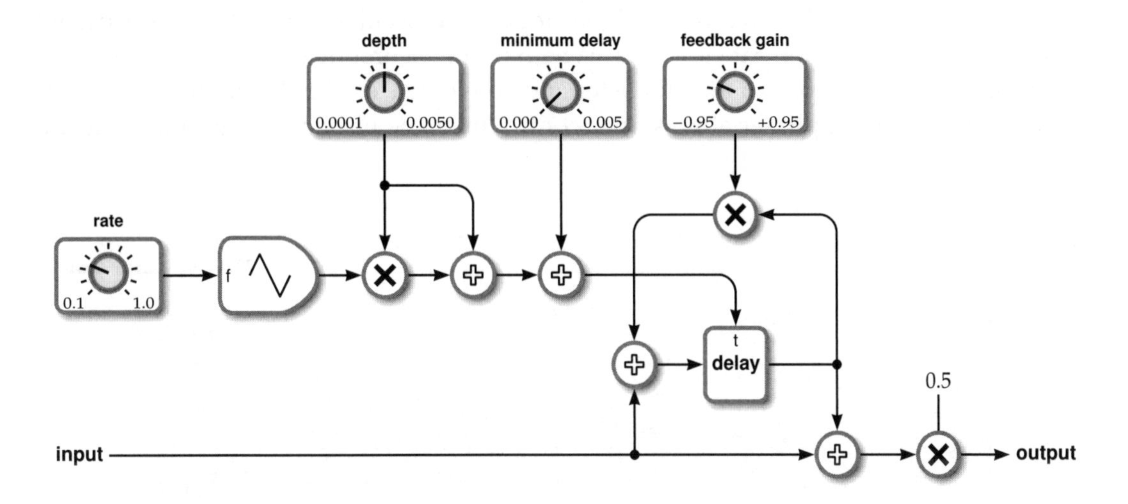

Figure 9.19 Extended flanger

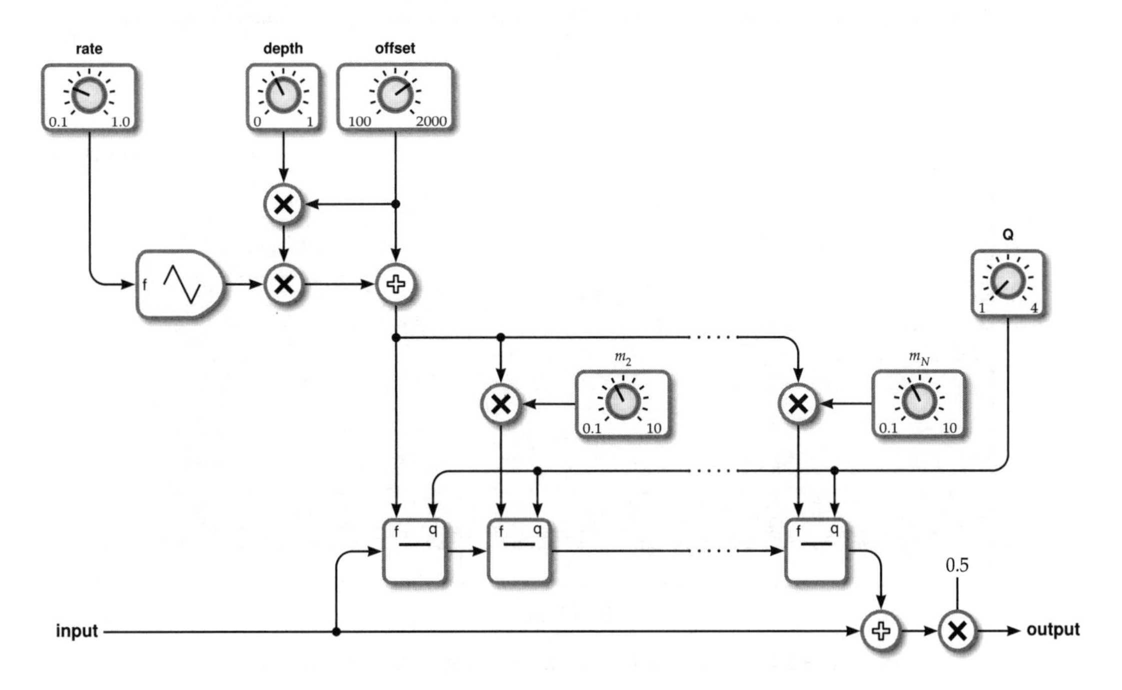

Figure 9.20 Phaser

Figure 9.21 shows typical flanger and phaser results in the frequency domain. In both cases a 110Hz sawtooth wave is the signal input, the oscillator waveform is a triangle wave, and the modulation rate is 0.5Hz. Whether one technique or the other is chosen is determined by the desired sound character and convenience. The flanger has fewer component parts, and the phaser allows finer control over the effects through the frequency multipliers.

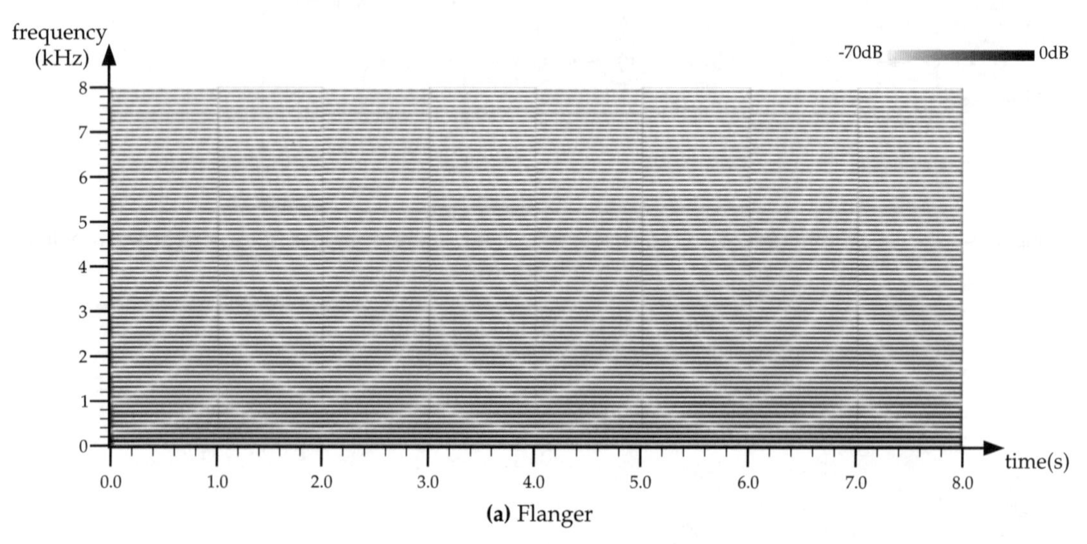

(a) Flanger

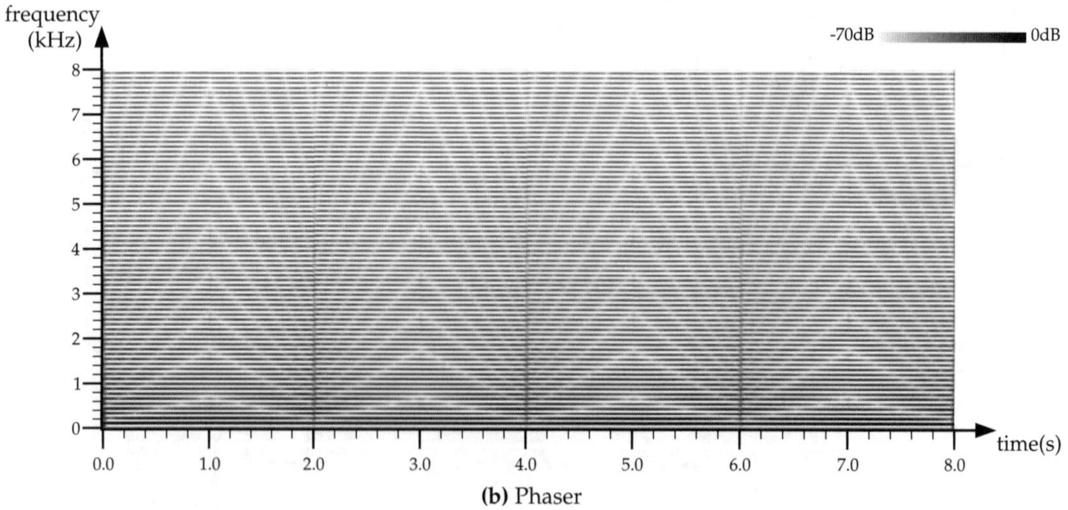

(b) Phaser

Figure 9.21 Example flanger and phaser spectrogram plots

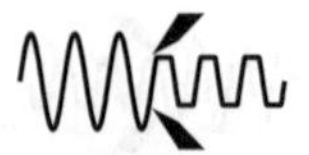

9.2.5 Chorus

Chorus effects are designed to modify signals to give the impression of additional sound sources. For example, a single instrument signal could be modified to appear as if there are several instruments playing in unison. In practice, simple chorus effects are more about broadening the sound character, rather than being a convincing impression of multiple sound sources. The concept behind a chorus effect is delaying the input signal by different amounts, varying those delays, and summing the results together. This loosely models how multiple players who are not perfectly synchronised produce slight time-varying differences in timing and pitch.

Figure 9.22 illustrates an example chorus effect. The top path is the dry non-delayed signal. There are three delay paths illustrated, but as many as desired can be used. Each path has a gain factor g_i. The chorus has some similarities to a flanger (figure 9.18) with additional delay paths and differences in the parameter values. Typical values are as follows:

- The gains g_0 to g_N have values between 0 and 1 and are used to balance the different signal paths. More active delay paths allow a more complex sound character to be created, as different modulation settings can be used on each one. However, sometimes it can be desirable to have only a small number of paths with non-zero gain, in order to have a less dense effect.
- If the intention is to simulate multiple players, then each path should have different settings for f_{di}, a_{di}, and a_{oi}. Subtle effects are achieved with f_{di} (modulation rate) values of 0 to 2Hz, a_{di} (modulation depth) values of 0 to 6ms, and a range of values of a_{oi} such that each path has a different time offset from the others (0 to 30ms). Ensure that $a_{oi} \geqslant a_{di}$, such that there cannot be negative delay times.
- Waveform function W_i might typically be sinusoidal or triangular. However, an alternative is to use rate-controlled interpolated noise generators (described in §18.2.2, p.529) rather than oscillators. Noise generators produce a random (unpredictable) variation in the delays between the different paths, which might be regarded as a better model of the effects with a real ensemble of instruments.
- More extreme values of f_{di} and a_{di} can be used to achieve anything from a light vibrato to bizarre wobbling effects. Larger values of a_{oi} produce reverberation and echo effects (discussed further in Chapter 10).

The parallel delay paths can be implemented as a multitap scheme with a single buffer, as described in §10.2.3 (p.303). It is also possible to extend the parallel form by adding a pan process to each path and summing to a stereo output (figure 5.36, p.125), such that different delayed signals are located in different positions in the stereo soundfield.

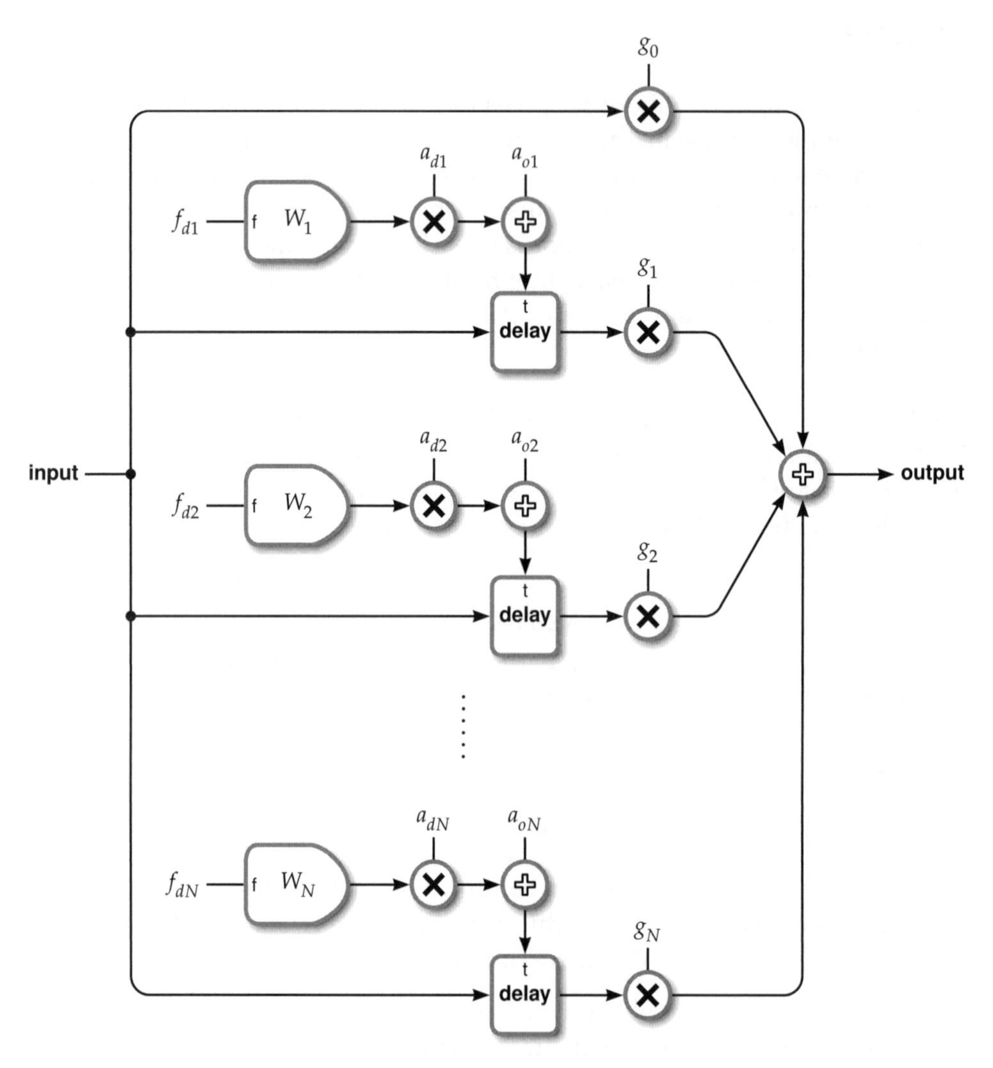

Figure 9.22 Chorus

9.2.6 Modulated Modulators

Just as a modulating oscillator can be used to vary parameters such as amplitude gain, filter frequency, or delay time, the control parameters of the modulator itself can be modulated. That is, the shape, rate, depth, and offset do not have to be fixed values. This enables the character of the modulation to vary over time, in order to add further complexity and interest. It is likely that the variations to the modulator parameters will be at a lower rate than the principal modulation rate, such that there is an audible trend that occurs over the long term.

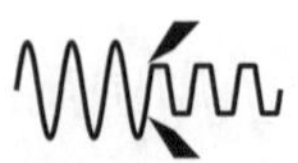

Figure 9.23 shows how tremolo depth can be modulated. Oscillator 1 modulates the depth of oscillator 2, which in turn modulates the amplitude of the input signal. When depth 1 is 0, a constant value of 1 occurs at point A and the lower part of the diagram acts as a standard tremolo (like figure 9.8, p.271). As depth 1 increases, the variation at point A also increases. The control ranges have been chosen such that oscillator 1 creates slower variations than oscillator 2. In a musical context, both might be synchronised to the tempo of the music, but at different numbers of beats per cycle. As usual, it is possible to change the ranges and waveform shapes for different results.

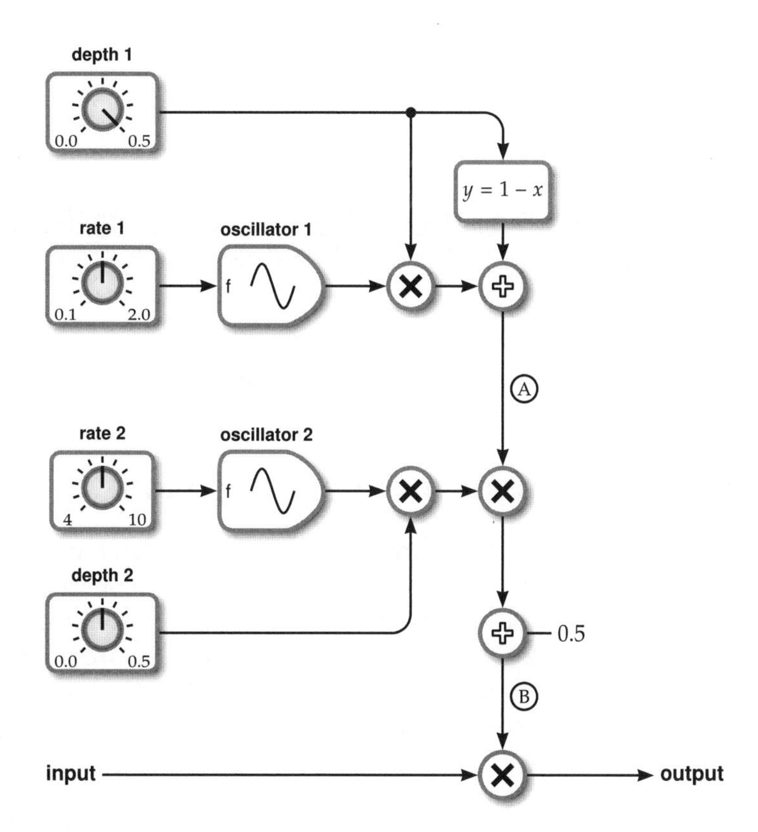

Figure 9.23 Modulated tremolo depth

Figure 9.24 shows some typical results for figure 9.23, where depth 1 is 0.5, depth 2 is 0.25 and the input is a constant tone with a peak amplitude of ±1. The same principles can be applied to parameters other than tremolo depth.

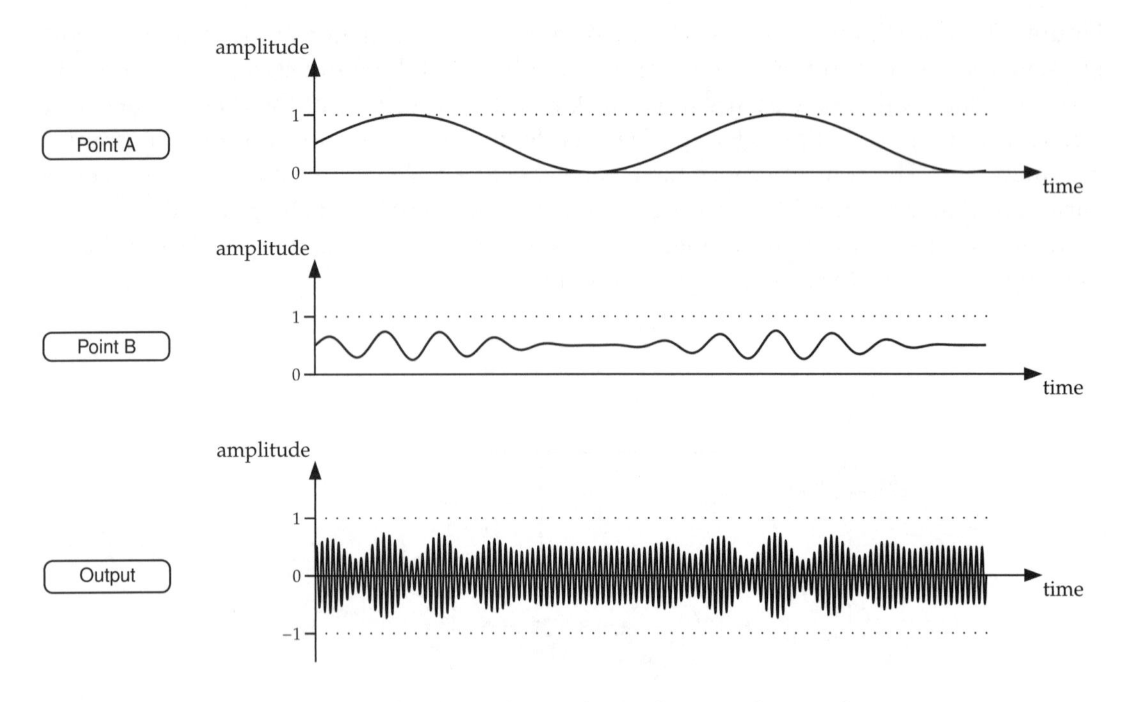

Figure 9.24 Modulated tremolo depth example waveforms

9.3 Developing Processes and Learning More

The processes described in this chapter are achieved with a relatively small number of standard elements. The oscillators, filters, and delays are combined with quite similar mathematical operations. If those core elements are in place through preprogrammed functions or objects, then it is fairly straightforward to extend a program progressively from a simple form like a tremolo to the more sophisticated examples such as a chorus. Otherwise it will be necessary to consider the design and implementation of those blocks, as found in Chapters 6, 8, and 14.

There is generally a clear relationship between modulated modifier parameters and audible effects, which is not necessarily the case with some other processes. This makes it easier to work out when the process is working as expected, or if there is a mistake in the programming. Some consideration of the ranges of parameters is required to achieve a particular style of result. Modulation rates between 0 and 1Hz produce a very different character to those of 20Hz and more. Many users will require moderately limited parameter ranges in order to achieve a standard effect, whereas experimental styles might require more extreme values. Digital Audio Workstations (DAWs) usually include a set of modulation effects with presets, which can be useful for learning about typical parameter

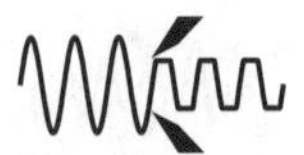

ranges and audible effects. There is also advice available in terms of configuration and creative methods in sources such as the following book:

> Case, Alexander U. 2007. *Sound FX: Unlocking the Creative Potential of Recording Studio Effects*. Burlington, MA: Focal Press.

The techniques in this chapter can be creatively applied to other processes, as static parameters can usually be replaced with those that vary over time. The sophistication of the modulated modifiers can also be extended. Using more than one instance of the process would allow a stereo version to be created. The examples in this chapter generally have fairly simple oscillator waveform shapes, but exploration of more unusual shapes can lead to some interesting results. As demonstrated in figure 9.14 (p.276), it is also possible to combine modulator processes to achieve multiple simultaneous variations.

The following paper provides some more advanced material that relates to this chapter, which can be used for further study:

> Dattorro, Jon. 1997. "Effect Design Part 2: Delay-Line Modulation and Chorus." *Journal of the Audio Engineering Society* 45:10:764–788.

10

Acoustic Environment

10.1 Basic Concepts

10.1.1 Types of Environmental Effects

Most sounds are heard in an *acoustic environment* of some description, such as in a living room, an office, a concert hall, or outside. It is often desirable to be able to apply an acoustic effect that is different from where a sound was originally recorded. In particular, reverberation and echo effects are widely used to change the perceived sonic character from the actual recording space (such as an acoustically-controlled studio environment) to a virtual space that is more acoustically reflective or live.

Environmental effects that are used with audio and music have a wide range of characteristics. An appropriate audio process technique must be chosen in order to create the desired style of result. Some typical types of effects are as follows:

- **Accurate models**. It is possible to faithfully reproduce the effect that an environment has on a sound. Techniques exist to capture the characteristic of a particular space, such as a concert hall, and automatically turn it into an effect to be used in the studio. A common application of an accurate model is to create the effect of performing in a particular environment without having the difficulties of going to the venue in order to record. There are also more subtle advantages such as being able to overdub a part on a previously recorded live performance with a realistic reverberation, without having to return to the venue and record that one part. Such models tend to be the most computationally-expensive methods of creating acoustic environment effects.
- **Convincing simulations**. It is possible to produce computationally-efficient systems that simulate the effects associated with an acoustic environment, without accurately copying a real acoustic space; for example, creating the general effect of a large hall rather than a specific hall in a particular town. In terms of using an effect for musical purposes, it is desirable to be able to fit the environmental effect to the context by modifying its particular characteristics. It is often easier to vary the characteristics of these simulations than those of an accurate model. However, such a system is not necessarily a complete representation of an environment that exists in the real world.
- **Unnatural effects**. It is possible to use the methods associated with creating environment effects and use them to create unrealistic or unusual results; for example, an echo that bounces cleanly between left and right loudspeakers exactly six times, where the echoes are all of the same amplitude. The human auditory system is stimulated in a similar way to that which occurs with convincing simulations or accurate models, so the perceptual effects are similar. However, there are endless possibilities in terms of the character and progression of the effect over time. This is a very powerful musical tool.

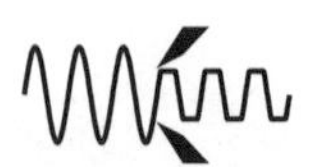

Context will determine the type of effect that is used. In the studio, it is often desirable to be able to specify the acoustic environment effect to fit the musical context, rather than adapting the music to fit a particular room response. It is also quite common for a combination of effect types to be present. For example, an unusual rhythmical echo effect might be used as a musical feature, the result of which is processed by a convincing simulation of stadium acoustics.

10.1.2 Fundamentals of Sound in Enclosed Spaces

Sound waves propagate through the air from the source of sound to the listener. Sound not only travels along the *direct path* between the two, but also spreads out from the source into the acoustic space, as shown in figure 10.1. Therefore, sound can reach the listener indirectly by reflecting from surfaces (such as the walls, floor, and ceiling). Figure 10.2 shows an example of how a sound wave might propagate from one point in a room to another via reflections.

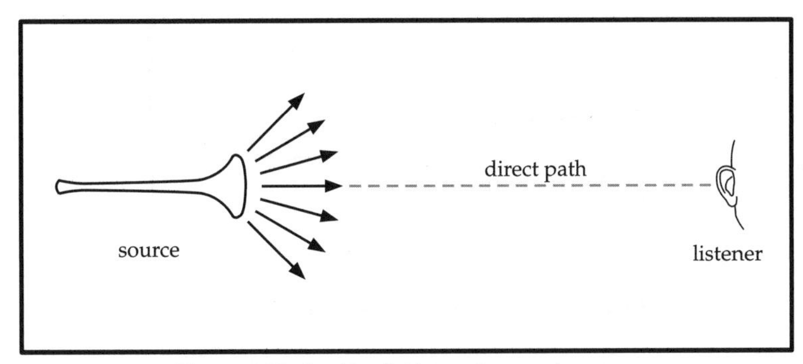

Figure 10.1 Radiation of sound energy

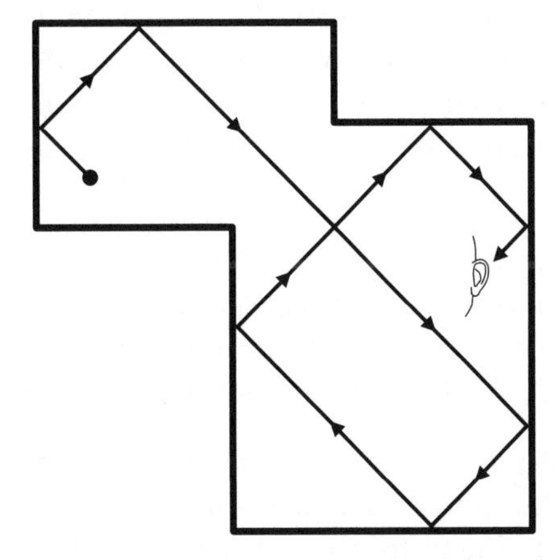

Figure 10.2 Example indirect path from source to listener

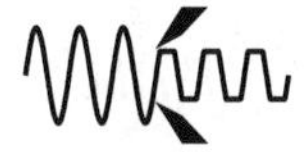

The speed of sound is typically about 340m/s in air. The longer the path from source to listener, the longer the sound will take to arrive, as determined by the following equation (where time t is in seconds and distance d is in metres):

$$t = \frac{d}{340} \quad (10.1)$$

Sound pressure waves travelling by different length routes from source to listener can produce a perceptible difference in arrival time. Figure 10.3 illustrates a very simple theoretical situation. The dot represents the source of an *impulse*. A practical impulse is a maximum amplitude, minimum duration sonic event (an abrupt burst of sound), which can be created by something like a gunshot, or a spark generator. It is assumed that the impulse source radiates sound in all directions, and with sufficient energy at all frequencies, that the reflections that arrive at the microphone are representative of the room response at all frequencies of interest.

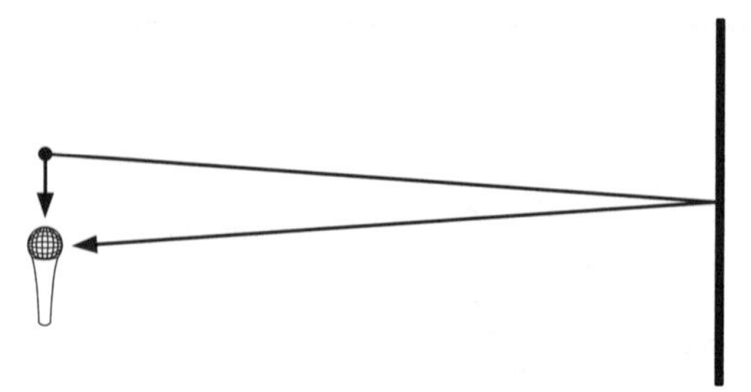

Figure 10.3 Two paths from source to listener

In the simple case shown in figure 10.3, it is imagined that there are only two paths from source to microphone. When the impulse is generated, the sound travels the short distance to the microphone (the direct path), but also travels a longer distance via a reflection from the wall. The time taken for each sound wave to reach the microphone is proportional to the distance travelled (as described by equation 10.1). This results in spaced peaks in the *impulse response*, as shown in figure 10.4. The peaks occur at times t_1 (the direct sound) and t_2 (the indirect sound).

As well as the spacing between the peaks in the output, there is also a difference in amplitude. When sound reflects from a surface some of the energy is absorbed and some is reflected. Therefore the sound arriving from the shorter path will have a larger amplitude (a_1) than the longer path (a_2). Absorption effects will be explored in more detail later.

Figure 10.5a shows a slightly more complex two-dimensional example with four walls. Four of the possible paths are shown by which sound might reach a microphone from the source position. Figure 10.5b illustrates the impulse response where the walls absorb half of the amplitude on each reflection. The sound arrives at the listener at a range of times

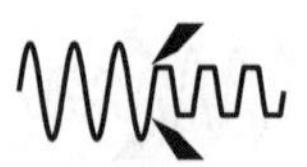

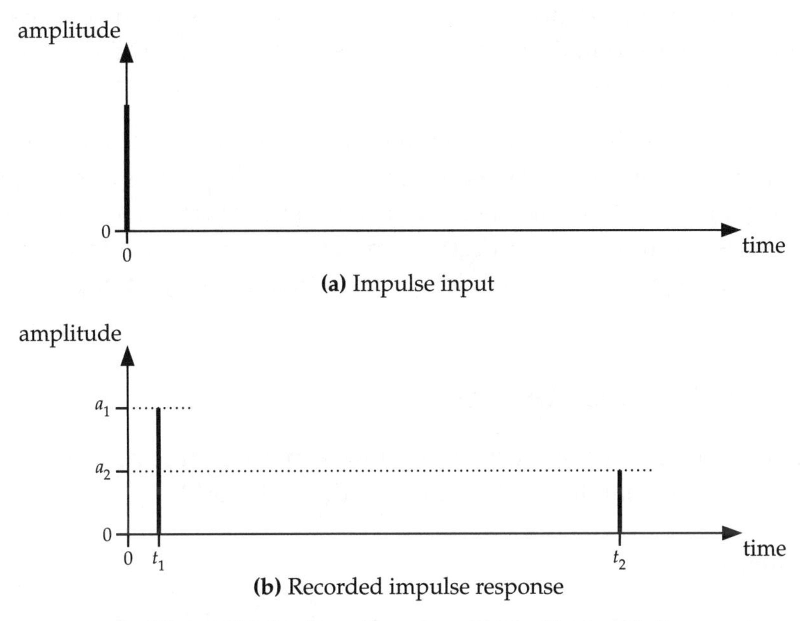

(b) Recorded impulse response

Figure 10.4 Impulse response for figure 10.3

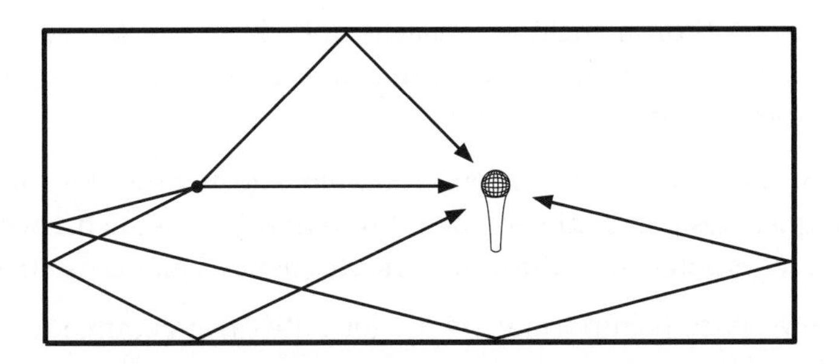

(a) Example paths from impulse source to recording position

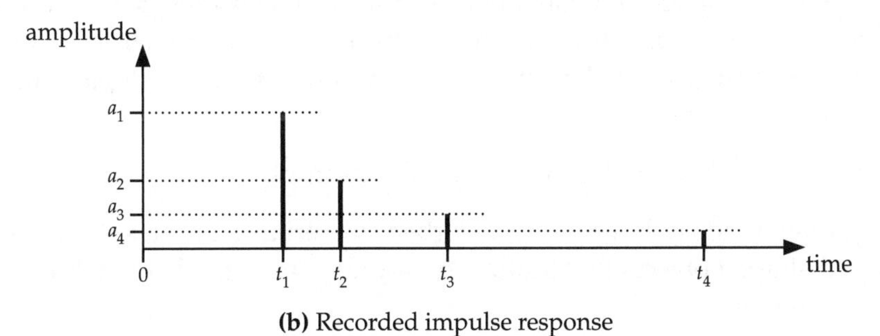

(b) Recorded impulse response

Figure 10.5 Slightly more complex impulse response

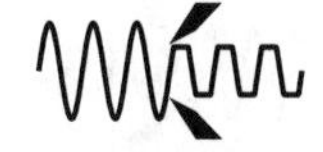

with different amplitudes, extending the sound in time relative to its original length. In effect, the sound is smeared in time by the response of the room. The multiple reflections are perceived as reverberation and echoes.

These ideas can be extended to a three-dimensional environment with any number of reflections. A practical impulse response is usually very complex, as a result of the sound waves travelling along the huge number of paths from the source to the microphone. Such impulse responses are modelled in digital simulations, such that the individual audio sample values are subject to the same delays and attenuations that apply to an acoustic impulse.

10.1.3 Practical Enclosed Spaces

The previous text described some trivial impulse responses. It is now necessary to consider how those ideas extend to practical cases in the real world.

General Features

When a sound is generated in an enclosed space, the sound waves will keep reflecting around the room until all the energy is dissipated as heat. The wide dispersion of sound waves from the source means that there are usually many thousands of routes from the source to the listener. A typical enclosed space is not empty, but rather includes all kinds of objects that can absorb and reflect sound (such as chairs, tables, and people). There are three principal factors that affect the results:

- The nature of the materials in the environment affects how the sound is absorbed. Different frequencies will be absorbed at different rates. As such, each time the sound is reflected it loses some amplitude and the frequency balance is affected.
- The size of the space is important, as longer paths from source to listener relate to longer lengths of time.
- The shape of the space controls the direction in which reflected sound will travel. Curved walls will cause different effects to flat walls, for example. In particular, hard parallel walls can lead to standing waves that emphasise particular resonant frequencies.

These three factors combine in different ways. For example:

- A living room tends to have many absorbent materials (carpet, soft furnishings) and many odd shaped objects that scatter the sound. There tends to be little reverberant sound as a result.
- A bathroom has small dimensions and many hard surfaces. These combine to produce a brief but strong reverberation.

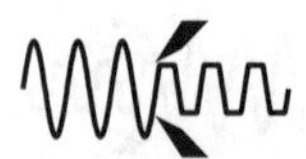

- A cathedral has hard surfaces, but very large dimensions. This means long delays between reflections and a long reverberation time.

This information can be used by an audio process designer to simulate acoustic characteristics that create a perception of a sound source being played in a particular environment.

Typical Reverberant Patterns

Figure 10.6 shows an impulse response that illustrates features that might be found in a practical acoustic environment:

- Direct sound is the sound travelling by the shortest path from source to listener.
- *Early reflections* are those where there are only a couple of reflections of the sound from walls and other surfaces.
- As sound waves travel along increasingly long paths from source to listener, the *later reverberation* is formed with a far less distinct pattern of reflections.

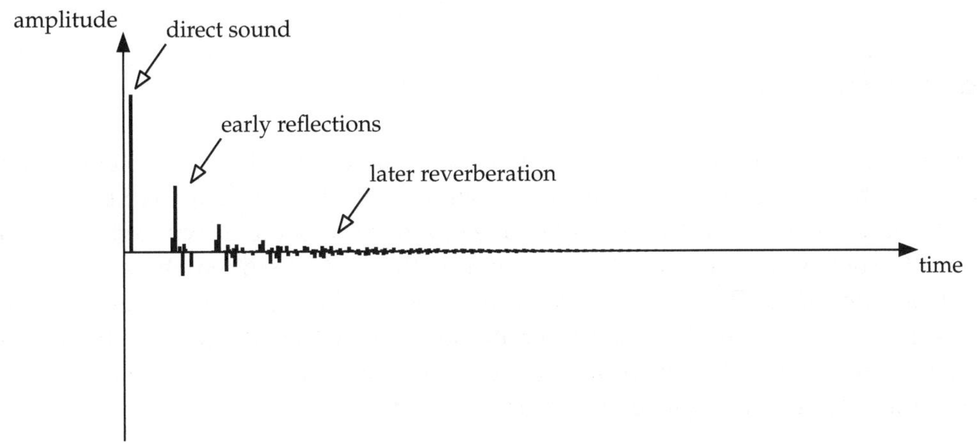

Figure 10.6 Example practical impulse response

Figure 10.6 is only a simplified example of what happens in a real room. It is useful to break down the problem in these terms, however, when considering how reverberant effects might be simulated. Some features to consider are as follows:

- The amount of delay between the direct sound and the reverberation that follows varies between acoustic environments. In some cases the early reflections and later reverberation follow immediately after the direct sound, and sometimes there is more of a gap.

- As a sound is reflected around an acoustic environment, an increasing number of paths contribute to the result, and a greater number of reflections alter the characteristics of the sound. This will lead generally to an increase over time in the density and lack of clarity of the reflected sound reaching the listener.
- Acoustic environment processes will not necessarily be realistic. For example, there are artificial echo effects where there is deliberately no increase in density over time, which can be musically useful.

An *echo* is a delayed sound that is heard as a distinct aural event. Such events generally have a significant length of time between them (usually at least 50ms) and are louder than the surrounding sound. *Reverberation* on the other hand, is often more of an extension of the sound decay involving a complex series of reflections at short time intervals.

Small spaces or those with a diffuse sonic environment (many complex reflections) will generally only produce reverberation, whereas large and non-diffuse spaces will have both echoes and reverberation. Using equation 10.1 (p.292), a 50ms delay means a distance of 17m from source to reflective surface and back again. This suggests that echoes are not likely in small spaces, which is confirmed by experience.

Absorption and Decay

Each time sound is reflected at a surface (whether wall, ceiling, floor, or an object within the room such as a chair) part of the energy will be reflected and part will be absorbed. With repeated reflections the amplitude envelope of reverberation will tend towards a somewhat exponential decay as shown in figure 10.7. This is often characterised by a *reverberation time* (RT or RT_{60}), which is the time taken for the sound level to decay by 60dB from its initial peak value. A typical reverberation time for a small room with absorbent materials is likely to be less than 0.5 seconds, a concert hall is likely to be less than 3 seconds, but a cathedral might be more than 5 seconds.

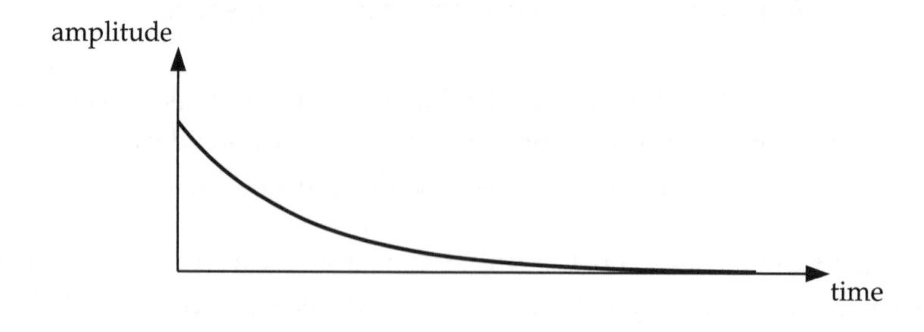

Figure 10.7 Exponential decay

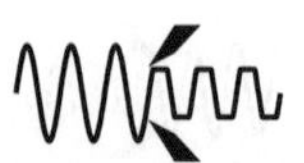

An exponential decay sounds smooth and linear to the human auditory system, as described in §3.2.2 (p.51). Many environments will not produce a perfectly exponential decay, due to the complex combination of materials and surfaces that they contain. Alternatively the designer of an acoustic environment effect might desire an artificial sounding result where the decay deliberately does not conform to natural patterns.

Absorption of materials varies with frequency, meaning that there are filtering effects as sound is reflected. Those effects vary between materials. Concrete and stone are highly reflective at most frequencies, whereas a thick carpet absorbs high frequencies well, and humans are quite effective absorbers over a wide range of frequencies. Air itself also absorbs a small proportion of the sound, particularly at high frequencies, so the further the sound travels the more amplitude is lost.

An additional feature of enclosed spaces is that there are often paths that can support cyclical reflections. These occur when an integer number of half-wavelengths fit along a consistent cyclical path causing standing wave resonant modes. Necessarily, because an exact multiple of a half wavelengths is involved, this relates to particular frequencies. If those frequencies are present in the sound source, the room will resonate (ring). These can cause peaks or troughs in the frequency response.

10.2 Non-Recirculating Echo and Reverberation Forms

10.2.1 A Simple Model

A simple way of expressing the effect that an environment has on a sound is shown in figure 10.8. Each path from source to listener is modelled as a delay and a filter. The delay represents the time taken for the sound to travel the path around the room, and the corresponding filter is the absorption that occurs at different frequencies on the way. The sound waves travel along all paths in the acoustic environment simultaneously, so the delay and filter pairs are in parallel and the results are summed together at the output.

The form shown in figure 10.8 is known as *non-recirculating* (or non-recursive), because there are no feedback paths within the process (from the output back to an earlier stage, for example). This is also known as a Finite Impulse Response (FIR) form, because if a single impulse is used as the input sound, then the output will cease after it has passed through the path with the longest delay in the model.

There are different ways of using the simple model as a basis for the creation of acoustic environment processes:

- The most practical way of using the model is to have a small number of delay paths, which are easy to configure by hand. Although this might not produce results

that are similar to a real room, it is a particularly good way of creating effects for musical purposes, such as strong rhythmical echo patterns. Small numbers of delay paths can achieve quite radical changes to sound character while being relatively computationally-efficient.

- It is possible to adapt the model such that it can be automatically configured. This is achieved by a process that derives the characteristics of a real room, and applies them to the model. This can produce very realistic results, as described in §10.2.6 (p.310).

- It is not generally practical to create a realistic reverberant room effect (such as a concert hall) with this model if the delay and filter parameters are configured by hand. A very large number of these would have to be individually specified, corresponding to all the routes from source to listener. It is not easy to specify an overall character (such as room size, room type, or decay time) when there are so many individual paths to be configured.

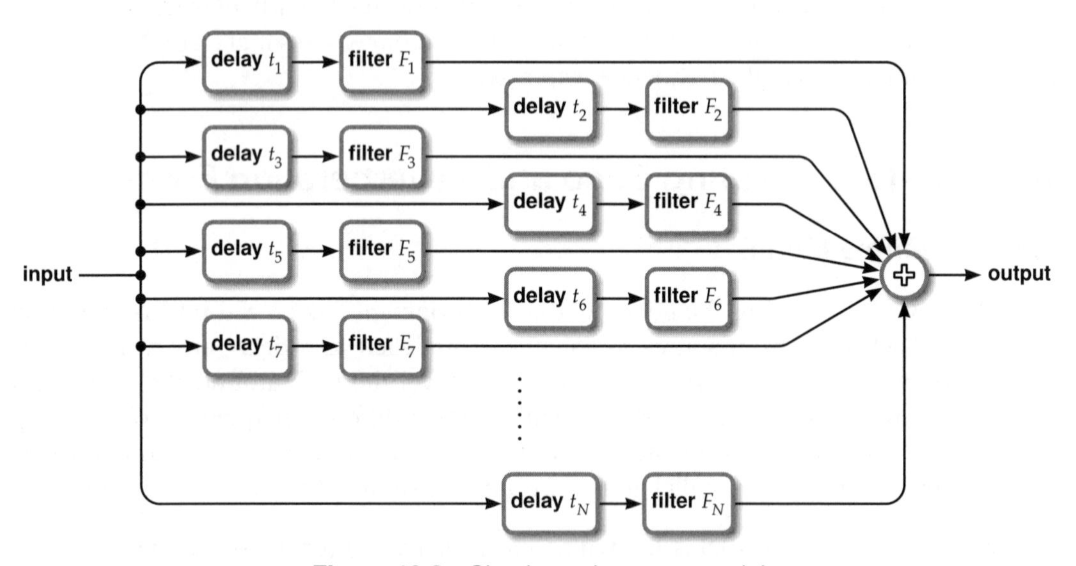

Figure 10.8 Simple environment model

10.2.2 Echo Effects

Figure 10.9 is an adaption of the model in figure 10.8. It has a non-delayed dry path that allows the original input to be heard in the output, and five delay paths to provide echoes at different times. There could be more or fewer delay paths depending upon the desired effect. The form is useful for creating rhythmical effects.

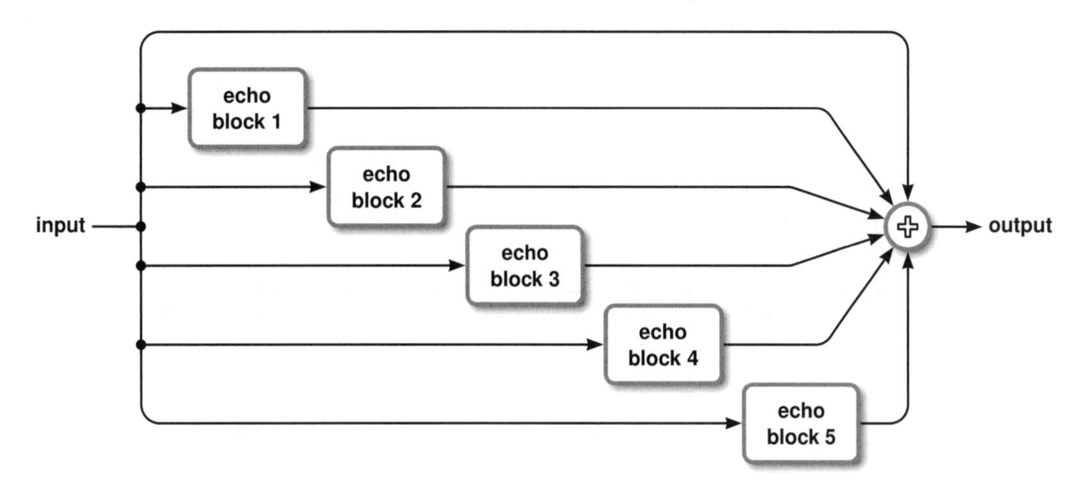

Figure 10.9 Non-recirculating echo

A suitable echo block to fit in the five positions in figure 10.9 is shown in figure 10.10. Control over delay time and gain factor is provided. The delay block is implemented in the manner described in §8.1.4 (p.232) with a "t" input to control delay time. The delay time range is suitable for an echo effect (50ms to 2s) and the gain range is from 0 to 1. In acoustic terms, each delayed path represents a sound travelling from the source to a surface, reflecting and losing amplitude, and then reaching the listener. A principal difference from a real acoustic environment is that there will only be six paths.

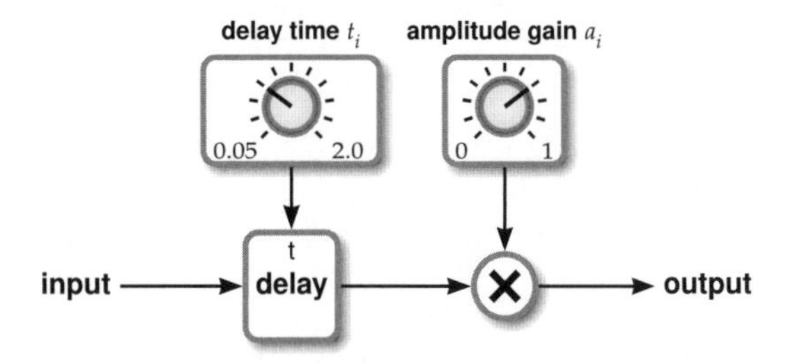

Figure 10.10 Echo block with gain control

Figure 10.11 shows some example impulse responses for different configurations of delay times and amplitude gains using the echo block in figure 10.10 with figure 10.9. The variable subscripts refer to the appropriate numbered block. The input is a single impulse with an amplitude of 1. The output in each case consists of the original impulse at 0 seconds that is from the non-delayed path, followed by up to five delayed copies via the echo blocks.

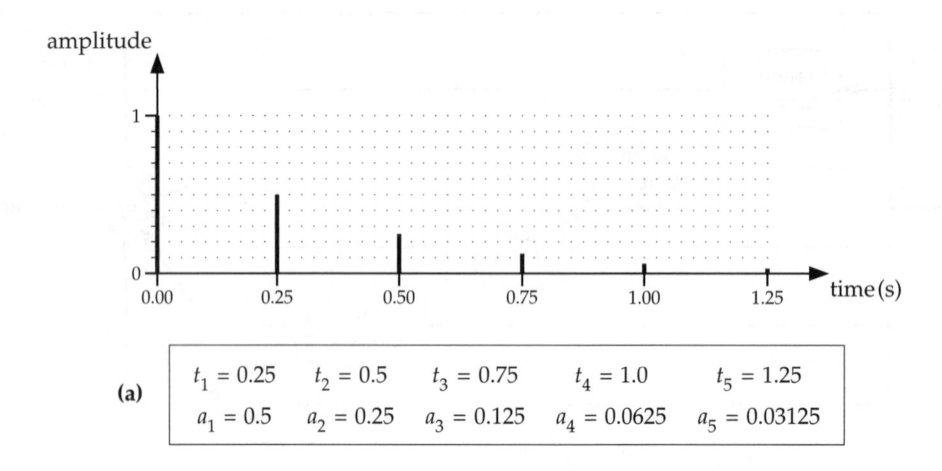

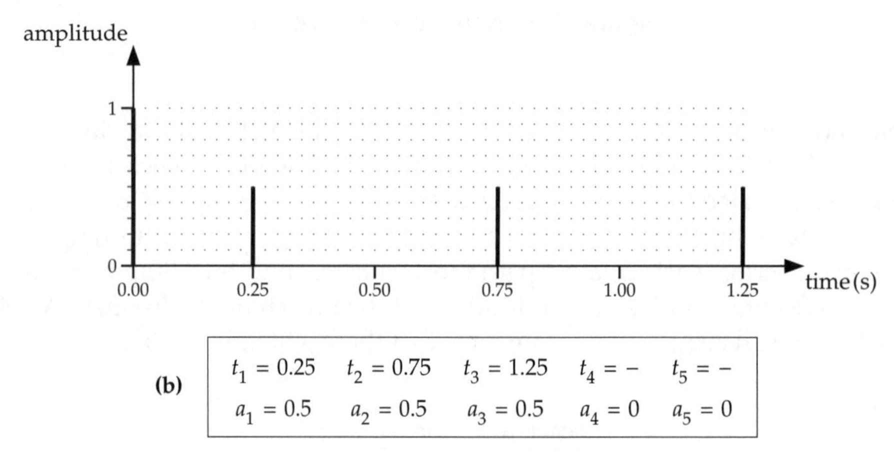

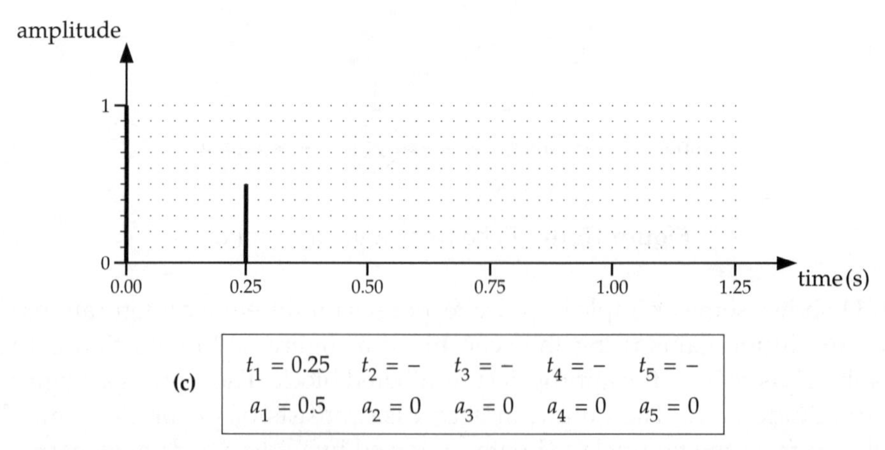

Figure 10.11 Example non-recirculating echo impulse responses

The parameter configuration in figure 10.11a achieves an exponential decay with delays spaced by 0.25 seconds. The decay shape is natural, but the neat spaced peaks do not display a typical build up of density as seen in figure 10.6 (p.295), nor an endless decay pattern as found with physical acoustic environments.

It might be appropriate in a particular musical situation to have an irregular spacing of impulse response peaks, and non-exponential decay. Figure 10.11b illustrates a pattern with two different sized gaps, and where the delayed peaks all have the same amplitude gain. Figure 10.11c is even simpler, where there is a single echo. It should be apparent that there is no end to the number of different patterns in time and amplitude that could be developed for rhythmical effects in musical contexts.

In terms of the effect on musical sounds, the impulse response indicates the effect on each sample value within the input. To take figure 10.11c as an example, every sample value will appear twice in the output, once at its original amplitude, and once 250ms later at half its original amplitude. The more delay paths with non-zero gain, the more times each input sample will appear in the output.

Short sounds, such as brief percussive sounds with a clearly defined attack, are good test sounds for acoustic environment effects, as the results corresponding to particular paths are distinctly audible. Figure 10.12 illustrates a single tom-tom strike that has been processed with the echo effect configured with parameters from figure 10.11a. The tom-tom sound appears six times, corresponding to the non-delayed and five delayed paths. The attack phases within the plot can be seen to be spaced at 0, 0.25, 0.5, 0.75, 1, and 1.25 seconds from the start. The gain effects for the different paths are also apparent. In effect, the entire sound has been copied five times, displaced in time and multiplied by different factors, and the results are summed together. The tom-tom sound is long enough that there is an overlap between the delayed copies. For example, the input sound has not finished emerging from the first delay path before the next copy starts emerging from the second delay path.

Figure 10.13 is the same as figure 10.10 but with an added switch. This allows the gain values to be set up for all delay paths, and then different numbers of paths can be switched in and out of operation instantly (without having to change the gain values). For example, a stepped rotary control might be used to progressively switch in more paths so that there are increasing numbers of echoes of the original sound.

Figure 10.14 is another echo block that can be used in figure 10.9. This illustrates a more radical departure from the simple echo effect, where each delayed path can have different tonal manipulation to create a shifting timbre over time. Quite unusual effects can be achieved using this form. Chapter 7 describes a number of possible distortion effects that could be used. The wet/dry ratio mix allows the amount of clean and distorted sound to be varied (similarly to figure 5.50, p.134).

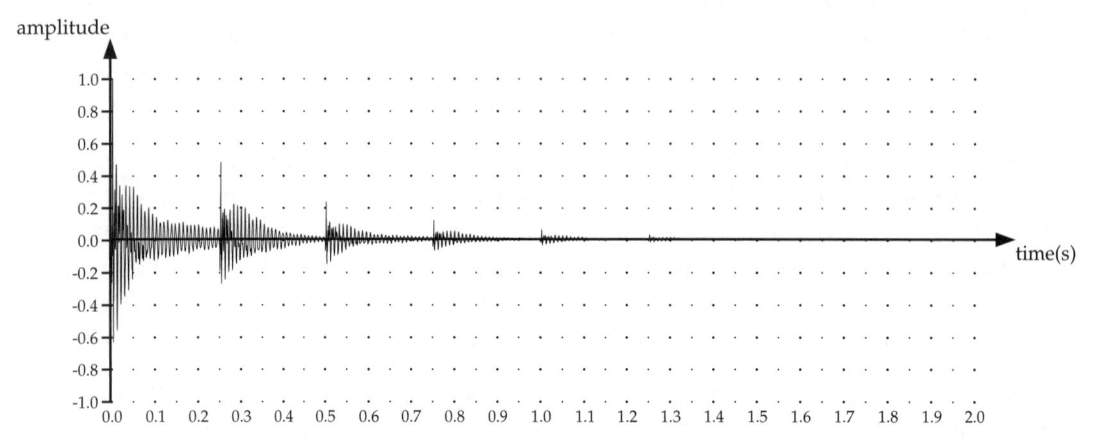

Figure 10.12 Tom-tom through echo effect

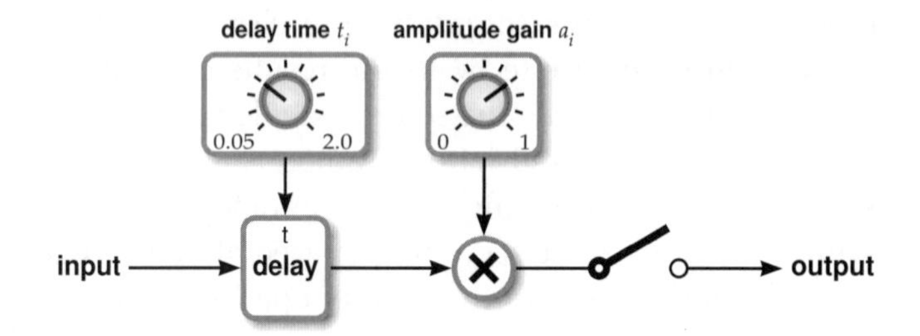

Figure 10.13 Echo block with switching

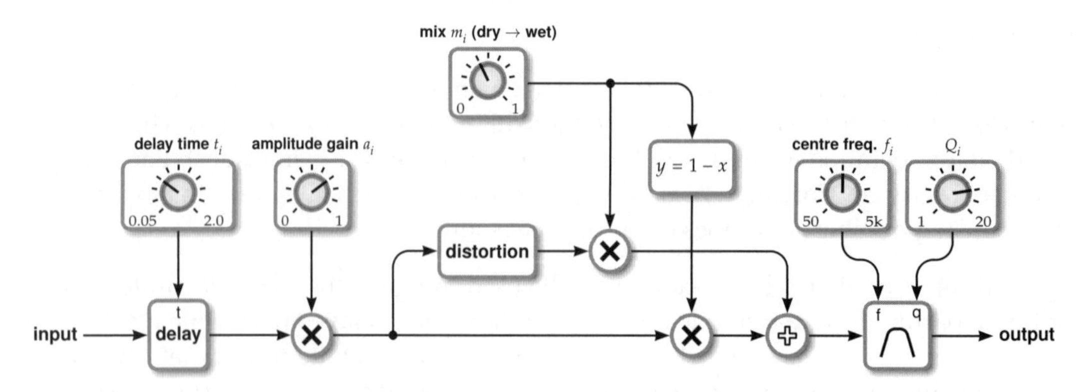

Figure 10.14 Echo block with distortion and filtering

There are a large number of possible ways of using the echo block in figure 10.14. For example, between the shortest and longest delay there might be:

- Progressively increasing filter centre frequency.
- Alternating distorted and dry sounds.
- Decreasing Q value to create wider filter bandwidth.

It is possible to extend the form seen in figure 10.9 to a two channel stereo output as shown in figure 10.15. Figure 10.16 illustrates an example echo block to use with this arrangement, which is similar to figure 10.10 but adds a simple linear pan effect to each delayed path (similarly to figure 5.32, p.122). The left and right signals are summed into the corresponding outputs (similarly to figure 5.36, p.125). The non-delayed direct path also has a pan control (which corresponds to the form in figure 5.32, p.122). The position of the source sound can vary over time, such as jumping left and right, or steadily moving across the soundfield.

10.2.3 Multitap Implementation

When implementing the non-recirculating echo effects one method is to have a separate buffer for each echo block. That would mean using five buffers (for the examples seen so far) implemented using the techniques seen in §8.1.3 (p.225). However, in figures 10.9 and 10.15 the delays are in parallel and are fed by the same input signal. This means that if five separate buffers are used, the data values in all the buffers are identical. The only difference between them is the read pointer position for each path. In these circumstances it is possible to use multiple read pointers in a single buffer, which is known as a *multitap delay*.

The circular buffer form first seen in §8.1.3 (p.225) is ideally suited to implementing a multitap delay. Figure 10.17 shows the equivalence between a set of three parallel delays fed by the same input signal, and a single circular buffer with three taps (read pointers) and one write pointer. At each sample step in time, the pointers all move one position to the right, wrapping around the end of the buffer as necessary. The write pointer writes the current sample value and the three values are read at the read positions. The number of samples between the pointers determines the length of the delays (as described in §8.1.4, p.232).

If `delay[i]` is the number of samples equivalent to time t_i in seconds, and f_S is the sample rate, then:

$$\texttt{delay[i]} = t_i \times f_S$$

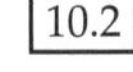

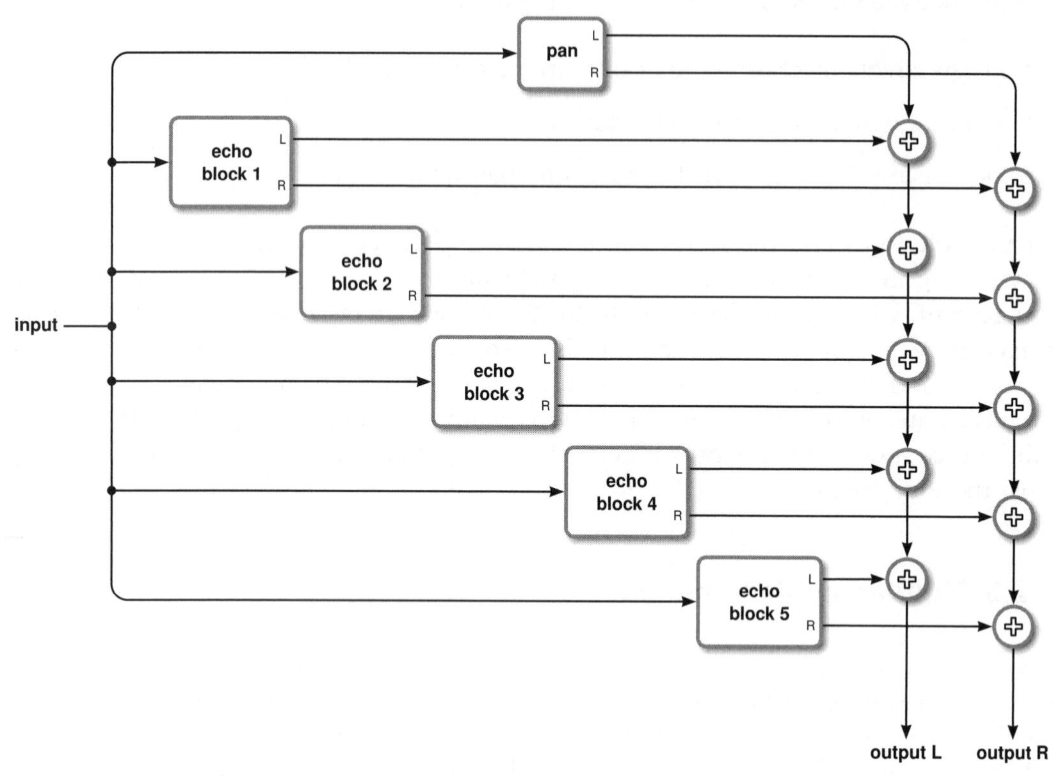

Figure 10.15 Non-recirculating echo with two channel output

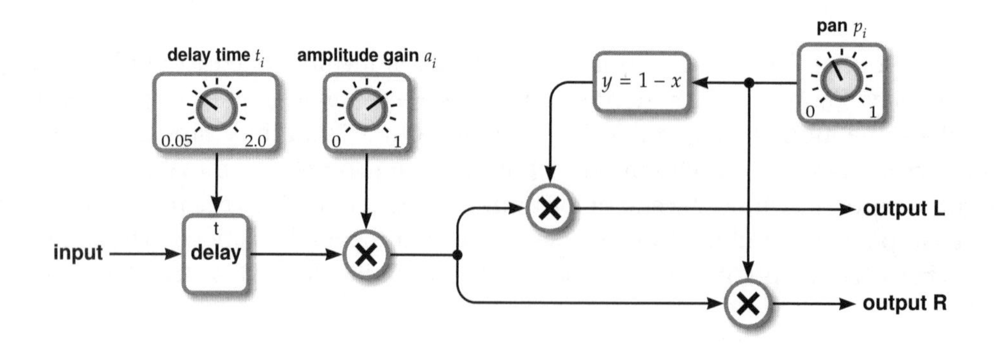

Figure 10.16 Echo block with pan

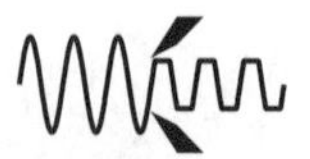

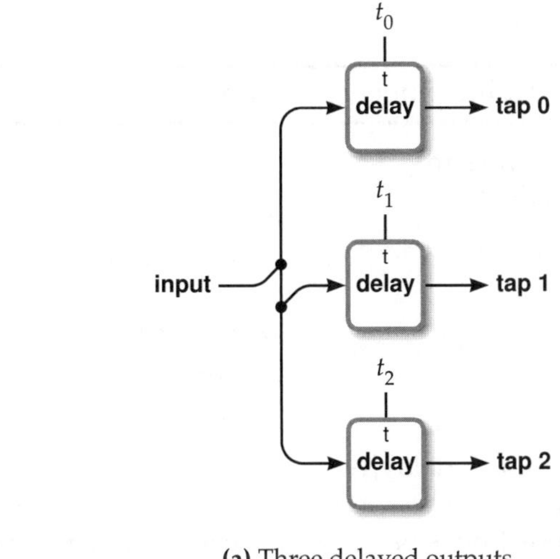

(a) Three delayed outputs

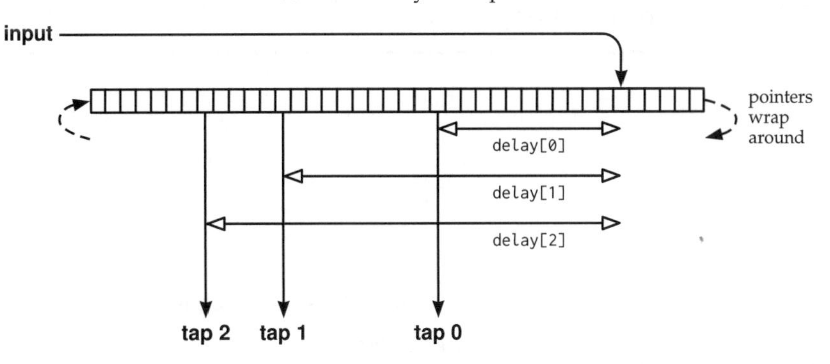

(b) Equivalent buffer form

Figure 10.17 Multitap circular buffer

The form seen in figure 10.17 can be described by algorithm 10.1 where *delay[]* is an array holding the delay in samples for the three taps, and N is the length of the buffer. The initial starting conditions are that *writeposition* is 0 and the buffer is filled with zero values. It is also assumed that the states of *buffer* and *writeposition* are maintained between calls to the function. The buffer size must be sufficient to achieve the longest required delay.

Representing multiple delay blocks with a single multitap circular buffer depends on the input to the delays. Figure 10.17a has three delays with exactly the same input, so the delay buffers contain the same data. In the series form in figure 10.18a, the two delays could also be realised with a single circular buffer, with two taps at times t_a (to feed the filter) and $t_a + t_b$ (for output B). Figure 10.18b cannot be treated in that manner, however, as the signal into the second delay is not the same as the output from the first delay.

Algorithm 10.1 – Three tap multitap delay function

input : current input signal value `in`
output: output value array `tap[]`

```
writeposition = writeposition + 1            // move to next position
if writeposition == N then
    writeposition = 0                        // wrap around
buffer[writeposition] = in                   // store new value

for i = 0 to 2 do
    readposition = writeposition − delay[i]
    if readposition < 0 then
        readposition = readposition + N      // wrap around to end of buffer
    tap[i] = buffer[readposition]
```

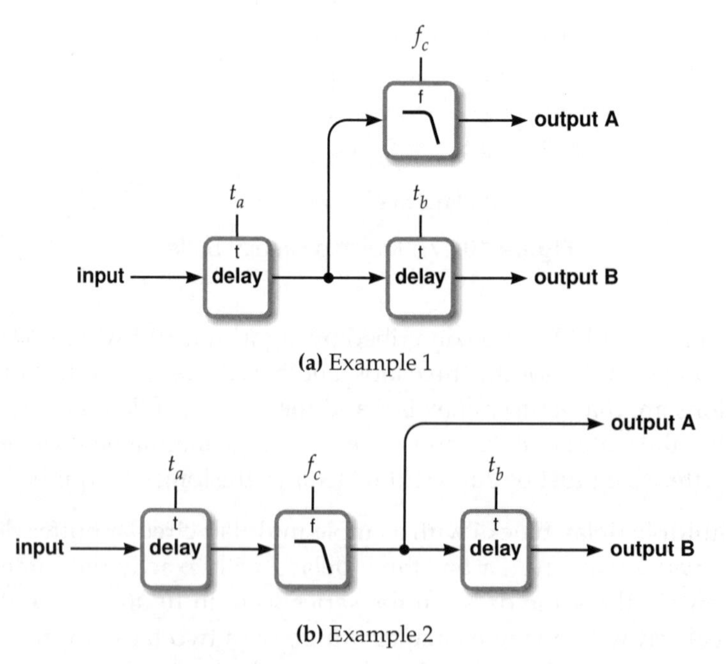

Figure 10.18 Series arrangements

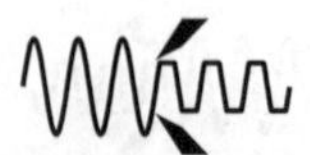

10.2.4 Improvements to Echo Effects

The echo effects seen so far have individual controls for parameters such as times and amplitude gain values. Improvements can be made to achieve a more sophisticated design, such that the effect is easier to use, or faster to configure.

Wet/Dry Mix

One simple improvement over figure 10.9 (p.299) is to have an overall wet/dry mix control between the direct (non-delayed) path and the delayed signals, as shown in figure 10.19. The delayed path outputs are summed together inside the relevant block. Having such an overall control makes it easier to affect the relative levels than having to change all the amplitude gain factors in the delayed paths.

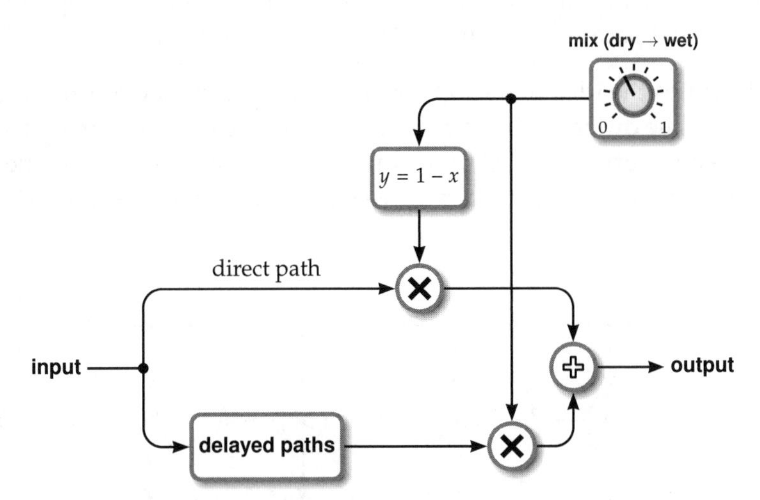

Figure 10.19 Wet/dry ratio mix (non-recirculating)

Tempo-Based Time Controls

Although specifying delay times in seconds is useful, it is often the case that echoes should synchronise with the tempo of a piece of music. One way of achieving that is a tap-tempo facility, where the user presses a switch in time with the beats in a piece of music, and the system calculates the parameters based on the time between tapped beats. Another method is to specify a BPM (beats per minute) value that can be converted into the length of time equivalent to a crotchet (quarter note), quaver (eighth note), semiquaver (sixteenth note) and so on. Those values can then be used to configure the echo time parameters. Figure 10.20 shows an example tempo (BPM) to time (seconds) conversion.

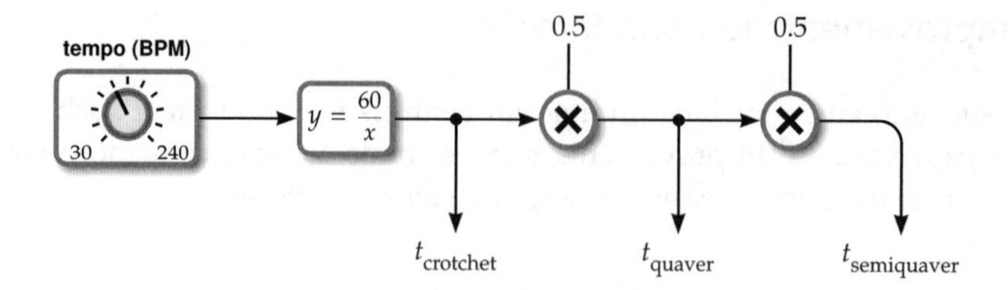

Figure 10.20 Tempo to time conversion

Multiple Parameter Control

Sometimes it is desirable to be able to configure each path individually within an echo effect. However, in commercial products it is often the case that a small set of controls is used to configure many internal parameters, making it quicker to set up. To achieve this requires the individual parameter values to be automatically derived from global values.

Figure 10.21 illustrates the idea of a single overall time parameter control from which the individual times for the different delay paths are automatically calculated. The idea is that factors d_1 to d_5 are a pattern that is set up in advance (such as a preset). As the overall time control is changed, the same relationship between the delay times is maintained.

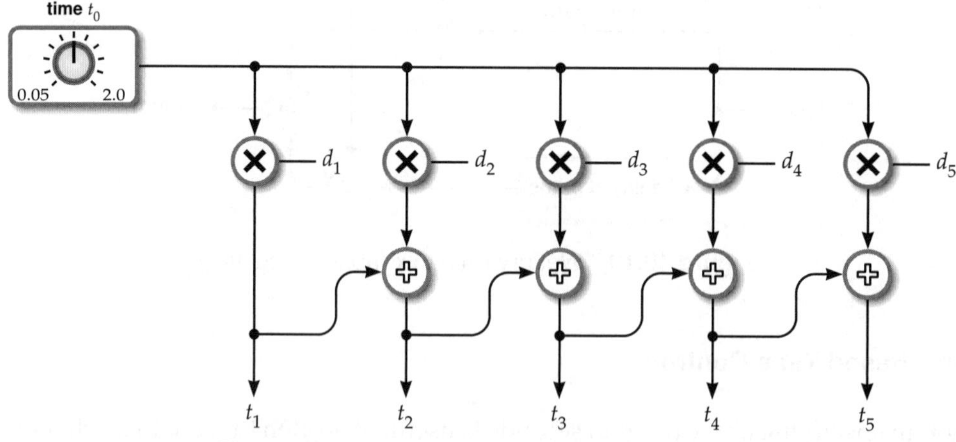

Figure 10.21 Overall time parameter control

Each of the time values is calculated by adding a multiple of time t_0 to the previous delay value. Consider the following example, where t_0 = 0.1s and all the factors are 1:

$d_1 = 1$	$d_2 = 1$	$d_3 = 1$	$d_4 = 1$	$d_5 = 1$
$t_1 = 0.1$	$t_2 = 0.2$	$t_3 = 0.3$	$t_4 = 0.4$	$t_5 = 0.5$

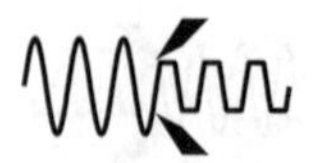

If the value of t_0 is changed to 0.2s, then the outputs automatically update to achieve the same time relationship:

$d_1 = 1$	$d_2 = 1$	$d_3 = 1$	$d_4 = 1$	$d_5 = 1$
$t_1 = 0.2$	$t_2 = 0.4$	$t_3 = 0.6$	$t_4 = 0.8$	$t_5 = 1.0$

It is possible to change the delay factors (say, by selecting another preset pattern) and achieve a different rhythmical pattern, without having to change the principal time unit. For example, keeping $t_0 = 0.2$s:

$d_1 = 0.5$	$d_2 = 1.5$	$d_3 = 0.5$	$d_4 = 1.5$	$d_5 = 0.5$
$t_1 = 0.1$	$t_2 = 0.4$	$t_3 = 0.5$	$t_4 = 0.8$	$t_5 = 0.9$

Two Channel Input

In the examples seen so far, there has always been one input channel to the process. In some cases there will be a two channel input (or more channels in a surround sound system). If the input channels are mixed before passing through the echo effect, then the stereo characteristics are lost. If they are to be maintained, then it is necessary to have a separate echo process for each input channel. For an echo effect where there is intended to be a consistent impulse response pattern, the parallel effects would likely be configured in exactly the same way, using the same parameter values.

In the simplest case, each channel has its own input and feeds its own output. In the case where each input channel results in a two channel output, then a decision must be made about how to combine the process outputs, such that a sound on one side of the input soundstage appears to still be on that side after the effect. This might be achieved by panning the outputs corresponding to left and right inputs differently before mixing.

10.2.5 Reverberation Effects

The main differences between echo and reverberation effects are as follows:

- Shorter times between reflections are usually found in reverberation (typically 0 to 50ms).
- To achieve more realistic reverberation, complex irregular relationships between delay times are necessary. A very regular set of delay times for different paths will tend to produce gritty or metallic results. In some circumstances that is a desirable effect, but typically a more subtle or smooth reverberation is required.
- Similarly, the smoothness and realism of reverberation can be related to the density of reflections, and so the quantity of delay paths is likely to be higher in a reverberator compared to an echo effect.

- If the reverberation is supposed to be realistic, then a somewhat exponential decay of amplitude envelope with time is expected, whereas some of the echo effects seen so far have patterns designed more for musical effect.

It is difficult to achieve a long realistic reverberation with a modest number of delay paths in a non-recirculating form. It is possible, however, to construct realistic early reflections. These model reflections at the start of a room response. Although this is not usually the basis for a powerful reverberation sound, it is useful for subtly thickening the sound character.

Early reflections reverberation can follow a similar pattern to figures 10.9 (p.299) and 10.10, but with the changes described in the list above. More complex forms of reverberation process are considered later in the chapter.

10.2.6 Convolution with Impulse Responses

The number of delay paths considered so far has been small enough to allow configuration of parameters by hand, the creation of non-realistic echo effects, and early reflections of reverberation. An alternative approach to the non-recirculating model of figure 10.8 (p.298) is to consider how it might be adapted to create a form that can realistically model an acoustic environment through automatic configuration of parameter values.

Modelling an environment accurately is useful for such things as:

- Investigating the sonic behaviour of a hall through simulation, in order to work out how to improve it acoustically.
- Reproducing the effect of a particular venue in the studio, without a musician having to travel to the venue to record their instrument.

One way of finding an acoustic response is to use an algorithm to trace the paths of sound waves around a three-dimensional model of the space. Although complex, this can be useful for simulating the acoustics of a building before it is constructed, saving on costly remedial work after it has been built. Another common technique, especially when the building already exists, is to construct an effect using the impulse response of the environment.

The idea of characterising an environment with an impulse response was discussed in §10.1.2 (p.291). The important benefit from doing so is that the impulse response can be used to apply the acoustic environmental characteristic of a particular room to **any** input sound. The implementation of a process with a particular impulse response will achieve delayed sounds at the positions in time and with amplitudes described by that response. This principle extends to any complexity of impulse response, with the additional feature that filtering occurs as well as amplitude and time effects in a real acoustic environment.

The technique for creating a suitable process to model a real environment is as follows. Firstly an impulse is created in the acoustic environment of interest, such as with a gunshot or a spark generator, and the impulse response of a room is recorded. This can also be derived from the response of the environment to a sinusoidal tone that sweeps across the entire audible frequency range. The result is a large number of data points similar to figure 10.22.

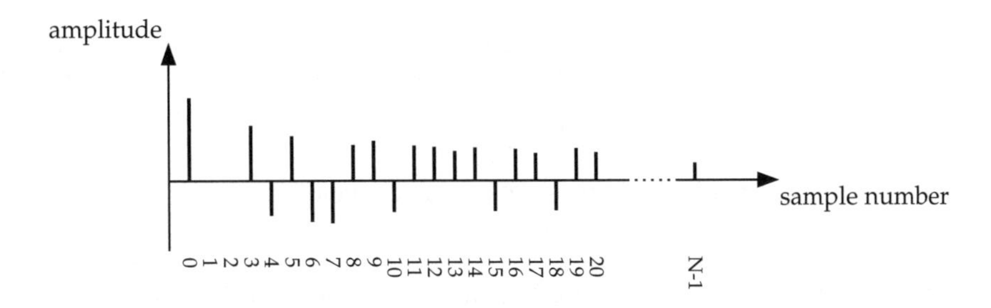

Figure 10.22 Digitised impulse response

The pattern of data values can be complex, due to the combination of reflections from many paths around the environment. The amplitude trend is a gradual decay to zero as the sound energy is absorbed. For a living room the decay time is likely to be less than a second, but for a cathedral it might be 10 seconds. This length of time (t) determines the number of data points (N) at sample rate f_S:

$$N = t \times f_S \tag{10.3}$$

The number of impulse response samples could be very large; for example, 960000 for a 10 second impulse response at a sample rate of 96kHz. Figure 10.23 shows the block diagram of the *convolution filter* required to apply the impulse response to an input sound. The process is composed of delays, multiplications, and additions in a similar way to the filter designs described in §6.4 (p.164):

- The block labelled z^{-1} is a single sample delay. If the sample rate is 96kHz, each of these blocks delay for $1/96000^{\text{th}}$ of a second.
- $x[n]$ is the current input sample value, $x[n-1]$ is the previous input sample, $x[n-2]$ is the next oldest input sample, and so on.
- a_i is the multiplier corresponding to sample value $x[n-i]$.

The block diagram can be translated into the following mathematical equation:

$$y[n] = \sum_{i=0}^{N-1} a_i x[n-i] \tag{10.4}$$

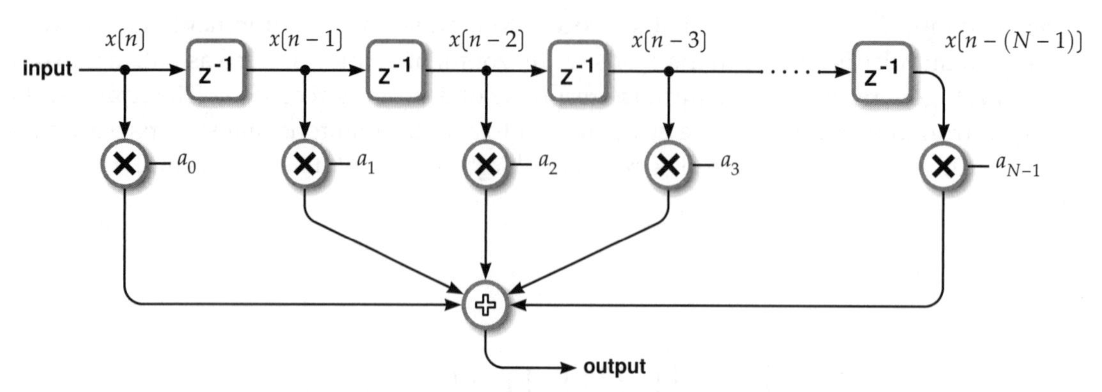

Figure 10.23 Impulse response convolution filter

There are as many multipliers as there are impulse response samples. Each multiplication factor a_i corresponds to the recorded sample at position i. So the amplitude value at position 0 in figure 10.22 becomes multiplier value a_0 in figure 10.23, and so on. This means that the longer the impulse response, the larger the filter becomes.

At each sample step the sample values shuffle down the row of unit delays. Figure 10.24 illustrates the signal sequence *0.1 0.2 0.3 0.4 0.5 0.6* passing through the first part of the filter (assuming that the filter is initially filled with zero values). It should be apparent that figure 10.24 could be implemented with a shift register or an efficient circular buffer as described in §8.1.3 (p.225).

A major consideration with this process is the number of calculations involved. All the $x[n-i]$ values are individually multiplied by the impulse response coefficients a_i, and the results of the multiplications are then added together. This must happen for **every** input sample. For example, if the impulse response is 960000 samples long (10 seconds at a sample rate of 96kHz), then the filter must have the same length, so there must be 960000 × 96000 = 92.16 billion multiplication and addition (multiply-accumulate) operations per second. There are more efficient fast convolution techniques that are used in preference to the basic algorithm described above, but the details of those is beyond the scope of this book. All convolution techniques require considerable computation, however, compared to the simpler simulation techniques seen elsewhere in this chapter.

Another feature is that the impulse response filter is a compact combination of all the delays and filters in the simple model shown in figure 10.8 (p.298). Where separate delay and filter elements exist (as in the other examples in this chapter) it is easy to change characteristics of individual paths. With the convolution filter it is more difficult, although with a suitable editor the impulse response amplitude envelope could be reshaped, or filtering applied to the response to change the tonality.

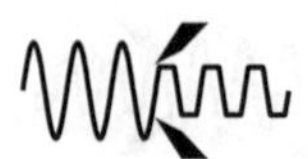

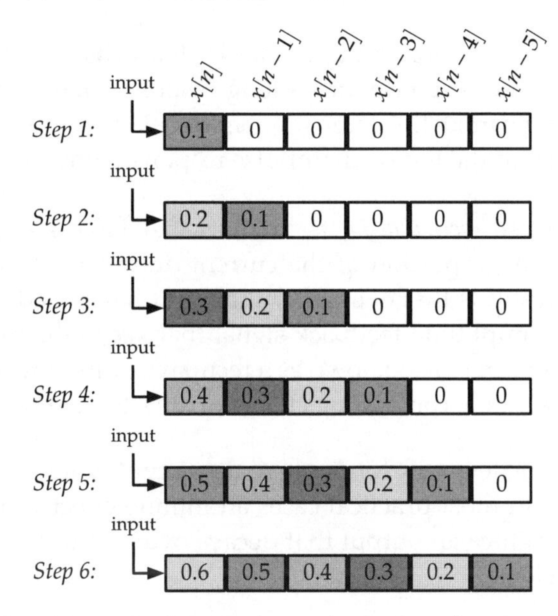

Figure 10.24 Example data sequence in the impulse response filter

Despite these issues, this system allows the environmental response of any space to be captured, and then applied accurately to any desired sound in the studio, which is very useful.

10.3 Recirculating Echo Forms

10.3.1 Basic Concepts

The techniques in §10.2 are derived from the non-recirculating model of figure 10.8 (p.298). A key feature of that form is the lack of feedback paths (a non-recursive or Finite Impulse Response (FIR) form). This has two important characteristics:

- Once an input sample or impulse has passed through the longest delay path in the model, it no longer contributes to the output. Therefore, after the input sound has ended, there is a finite time before the output will be silent.
- The FIR form is normally stable. For example, a brief input sound is not going to produce a never-ending output with a constantly increasing amplitude. The only way that will happen is if one of the blocks within the form (such as a filter) is realised with a non-FIR technique (which has a feedback loop).

The limitation of the non-recirculating model is that achieving both a high density of peaks within the impulse response **and** a long response, requires a very large number of delay paths within the model. A large number of delay paths implies a large amount of configuration by hand, or the use of an impulse response convolution technique.

The alternative is to use *recirculating* techniques that have feedback paths within the model. For example, a proportion of the current output might be added to the input of the process. The result is that even after the input has ended, the output can still be providing a non-zero amplitude feedback signal that keeps the process producing more output values. Such a form is also known as a recursive or Infinite Impulse Response (IIR) form. The IIR form has some contrasting characteristics to the FIR:

- It is possible to create an IIR form where the output will never become silent due to feedback paths. In most practical cases an infinite effect is avoided, as the form is configured to produce an output that decays over a significant length of time to an inaudibly small level.
- The IIR form can become unstable. For example, the output can become larger and larger until it reaches the amplitude limits of the system, and will not stop producing values. This means that careful design and configuration is required to ensure reliable operation of the process.

There are different ways of using recirculating forms as a basis for the creation of acoustic environment processes:

- As with the non-recirculating form, a small number of delay paths can be used to produce unnatural effects, such as strong echo patterns as an obvious feature in a musical piece.
- It is possible to use recirculating forms to create acoustic-like models, such as a fairly realistic generic reverberant room model. Quite a large number of parameters are often required to produce convincing and natural-sounding results. However, an advantage of this over impulse response convolution methods (described in §10.2.6, p.310) is the ability to more easily tailor the result to the musical situation in terms of tonal character, reflection pattern, decay time, and so on. The second advantage is that these methods can be very computationally-efficient compared to an equivalent FIR realisation.
- It is not generally practical to try to create an exact model of an actual acoustic environment with a recirculating form. In those cases it is more appropriate to use the impulse response convolution method.

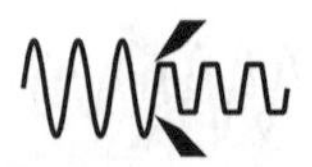

10.3.2 Echo Effects

Figure 10.25 shows the simplest recirculating echo form. This is a complete effect in itself, and does not need to be used in parallel in a form like figure 10.9 (p.299). As with the non-recirculating examples there is a delay block and a gain control. The significant difference from the non-recirculating examples is the presence of a signal flow from output back to the input. Each output sample is delayed, attenuated, and then added to the current input, such that it in turn is delayed, attenuated, added to the input, and so on. The recursion mirrors the natural effect where a sound repeatedly bounces between surfaces, losing a proportion of its amplitude each time, and so decays exponentially.

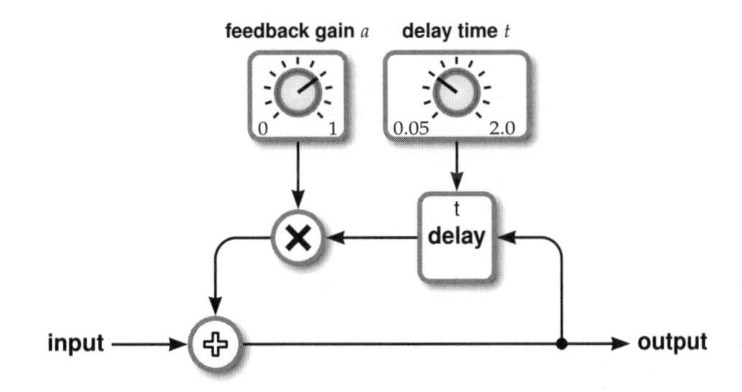

Figure 10.25 Simplest recirculating echo

Figure 10.26 shows some example impulse responses for different values of delay time t and feedback gain a using the form in figure 10.25. As usual, the input to the system is a single impulse with an amplitude of 1. The first thing of note is that there are multiple peaks despite there only being a single delay block, due to the recirculating effect. This is different from the non-recirculating forms where a delay path is required for each reflection. There are two important features:

- For simple exponentially decaying echo results, the recirculating form in figure 10.25 is more computationally-efficient than the non-recirculating in figure 10.9. However, the non-recirculating method allows any desired decay shape, whereas the recirculating is more limited.
- The reflections will continue forever (until the amplitude is insignificant) with the recirculating form, as the output is constantly fed back to the input. This is in contrast to the non-recirculating form, where the impulse response will end after the path with the longest delay has produced its output.

The decay is exponential because the sound is multiplied by the same factor between 0 and 1 on each loop. Both the delay time t and feedback gain a affect the decay time, as shown in

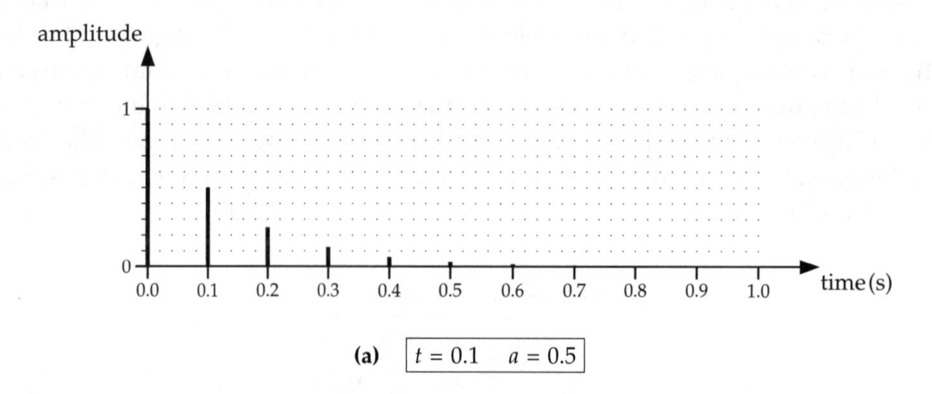

(a) $t = 0.1 \quad a = 0.5$

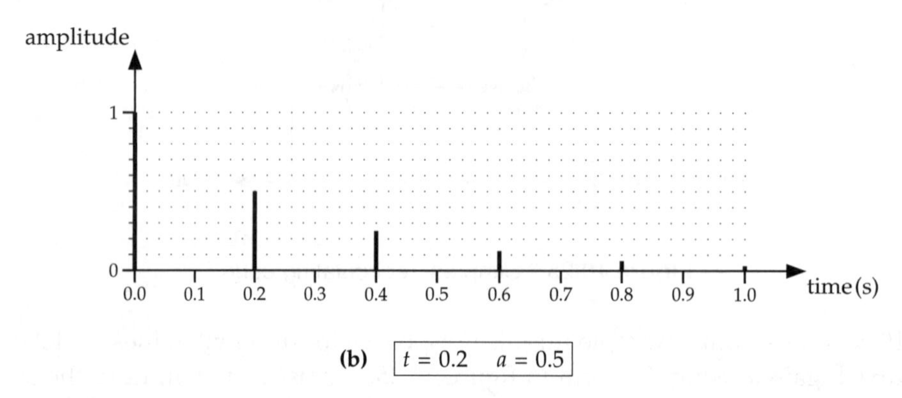

(b) $t = 0.2 \quad a = 0.5$

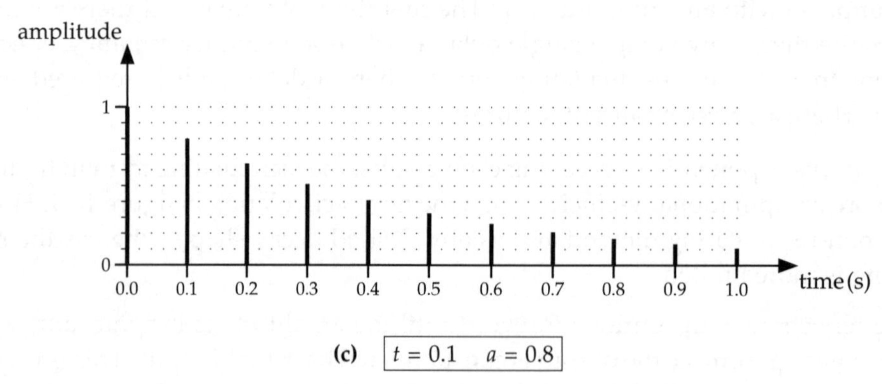

(c) $t = 0.1 \quad a = 0.8$

Figure 10.26 Example recirculating echo impulse responses (first 1 second)

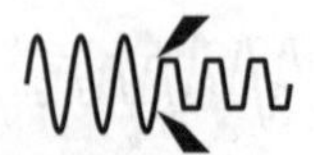

figure 10.26. If t increases, then it takes longer for each reflection to pass through the delay, and then be attenuated, increasing the decay time. If a increases, then less amplitude is lost on each loop, and so the decay time increases.

With an impulse input, the results are fairly clear, as the input only lasts for a single sample. With a musical input, the situation becomes more complex as musical sounds have significant length, or are continuous. This means that input values with non-zero amplitude are likely to be present when the samples that have passed through the feedback path arrive and are added to the input. It is likely that the summed result will be larger than the input alone.

If the value of feedback gain a is too high, there is a potential that too much amplitude will build up through repeated summation, causing the system to become unstable (the output amplitude becoming larger and larger until the amplitude limits of the system are reached). This results in clipping distortion and "howl". Generally the value of a must be considerably less than 1 for this to be avoided.

In terms of acoustics the effect of the simple recirculating echo is rather unnatural as it does not gain reflection density and become a reverberation, as it would in a cathedral, for example. However, it is musically useful and creates a clean and manipulable set of decaying echoes.

Comparing figure 10.25 with figure 6.59 (p.187) it can be seen that the simplest recirculating echo effect is a type of comb filter. It can be implemented using algorithm 10.2, where *delay* is the delay in samples (from equation 10.2, p.303), *gain* is the feedback gain value, and N is the length of the buffer in samples. It is assumed that the states of *buffer* and *writeposition* are maintained between calls to the function.

Algorithm 10.2 – Simplest recirculating echo function

```
input : current input signal value in
output: output value out

writeposition = writeposition + 1                  // move to next position
if writeposition == N then
    writeposition = 0                              // wrap around

readposition = writeposition − delay
if readposition < 0 then
    readposition = readposition + N                // wrap around to end of buffer

out = in + (gain ∗ buffer[readposition])

buffer[writeposition] = out                        // store new value
```

Writing the latest value to the circular buffer must occur as the **last** step in the process, after the output value has been calculated. The minimum delay time possible with the algorithm is one sample, although that is not an issue in most cases (such as in figure 10.25 with a minimum delay time of 50ms).

Figure 10.27 extends the block diagram in figure 10.25 such that a mono-to-stereo echo effect is created. The single channel input is processed in exactly the same way for the left output as figure 10.25. The right output is a delayed version of the left. That means that when the echoes appear on the left channel, a corresponding echo occurs some time later with the same amplitude on the right channel.

The relationship between the delay times determines the rhythmical pattern of the echoes. For example, if t_2 is set to half the value of t_1, the right-hand response peaks are half way between the left-hand ones (as shown in figure 10.28). In a practical system, the relationship between the times might be determined by a preset multiplier, allowing a single delay time control to affect both delays.

Figure 10.29 illustrates a stereo *ping-pong echo* effect. The input could be either stereo material, or monophonic material that is panned beforehand. There is a delayed cross-feed between the channels, such that delayed sound moves from side to side while the amplitude is attenuated. If the delay times and feedback gains are the same then monophonic input material that is panned to the centre position before the process will produce centre-panned echoes, as the two channels will produce the same results. However, with different delay times (such as $t_2 = 0.5t_1$) a clear side-to-side effect is produced.

Figure 10.30 illustrates a cascaded non-recirculating and recirculating echo effect. The first half has a direct path added to a delayed and attenuated path. The second half is the same as figure 10.25. The result is that the non-recirculating part produces two peaks in the impulse response; one at zero delay, and one at delay t_1 attenuated by factor a_1. These then feed the recirculating effect, causing a repeat of the two peaks every t_2 seconds, with decreasing amplitude due to multiplying by a_2. An example impulse response is shown in figure 10.31.

When implementing the forms in figures 10.29 and 10.30 it is necessary to have separate buffers for the two delays, as they are not fed by the same signal. That is, it is **not** possible to use a single multitap buffer.

A simple extension to the cascaded form is to add more delay paths to the non-recirculating part, giving a more complex set of reflections. For example, having four paths (including the direct path) in the non-recirculating half would produce sets of four reflections that repeat at the regularity determined by the delay time in the recirculating part. Another possible extension is to add another recirculating section (like figure 10.25) on the end of the process. That would allow the first recirculating effect to create fast repeats, and the second to create multiple repetitions of the result with a slow repeat, for example.

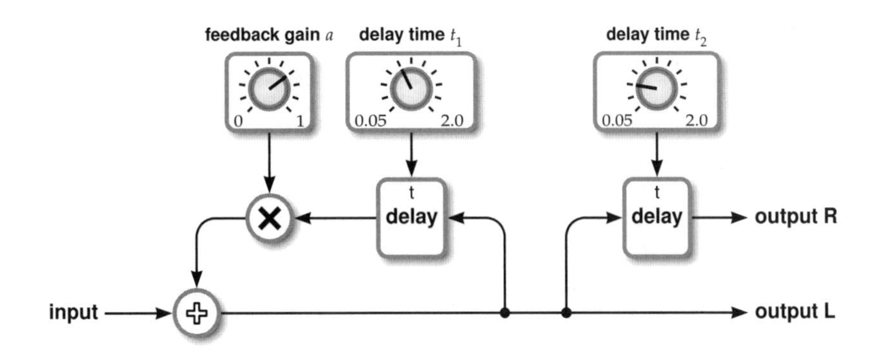

Figure 10.27 Mono-to-stereo recirculating echo

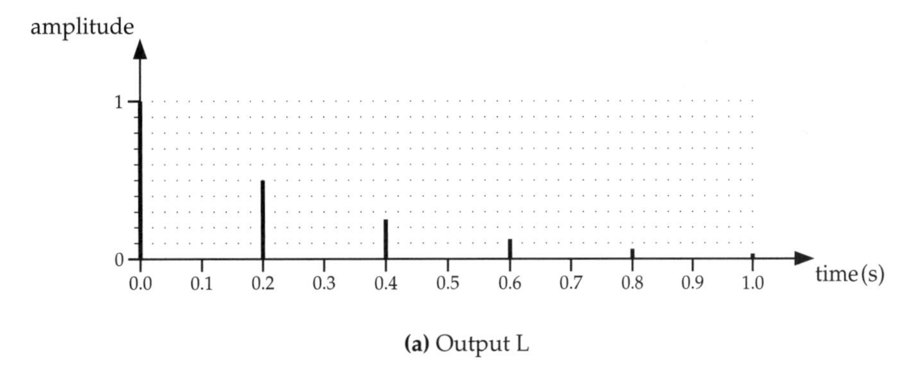

(a) Output L

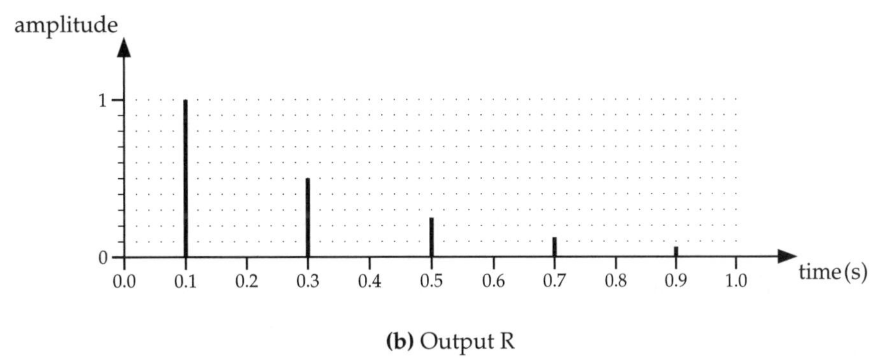

(b) Output R

Figure 10.28 Example mono-to-stereo echo impulse response (first 1 second, $t_1 = 0.2$, $a = 0.5$, $t_2 = 0.1$)

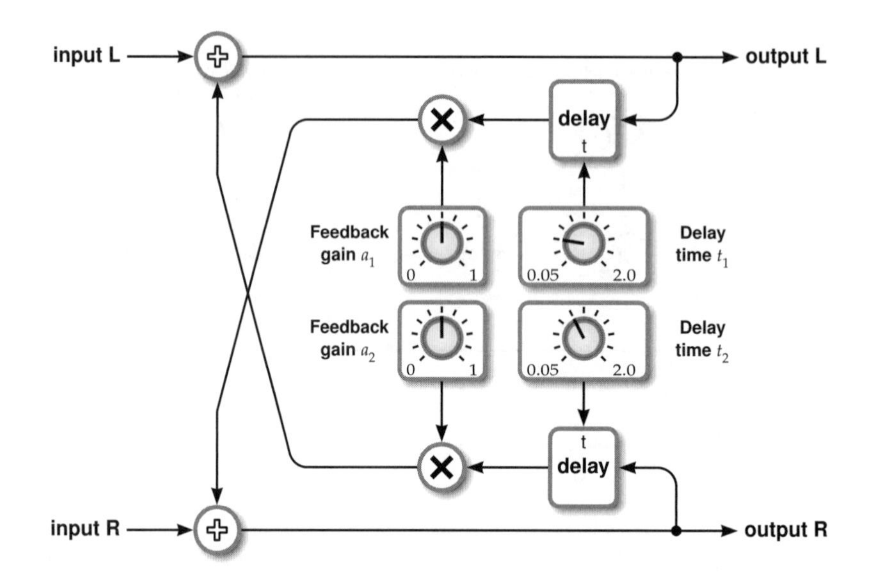

Figure 10.29 Ping-pong recirculating echo

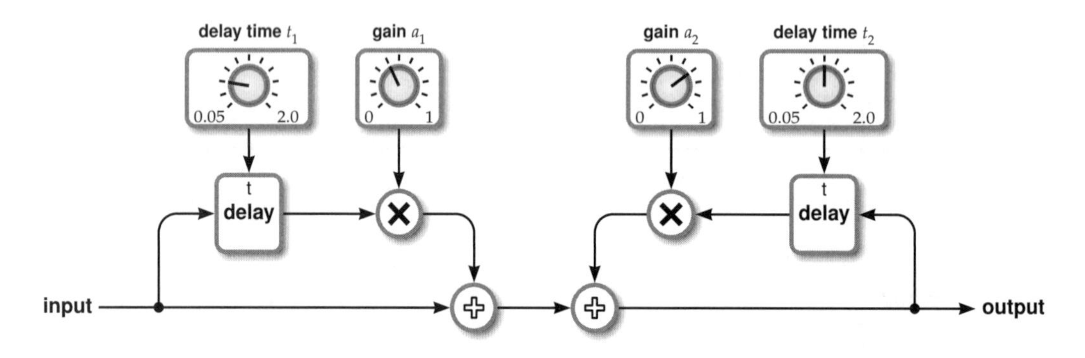

Figure 10.30 Cascaded non-recirculating and recirculating echo

Figure 10.32 illustrates two delay paths in a recirculating loop. Each output sample produces two delayed samples fed back to the adder. That is, each output sample is delayed by t_1 and t_2 seconds, producing two results, both of which are subsequently delayed by t_1 and t_2 seconds (producing delayed sounds at $2t_1$, $t_1 + t_2$, $t_2 + t_1$, and $2t_2$), and so on. In fact, reflections will occur at times $nt_1 + mt_2$ where n and m are integers that are $\geqslant 0$.

As long as t_1 and t_2 are not related as a simple integer multiple of a common factor (such as 0.1 and 0.2), then the reflections can form more irregular patterns, as shown in figure 10.33.

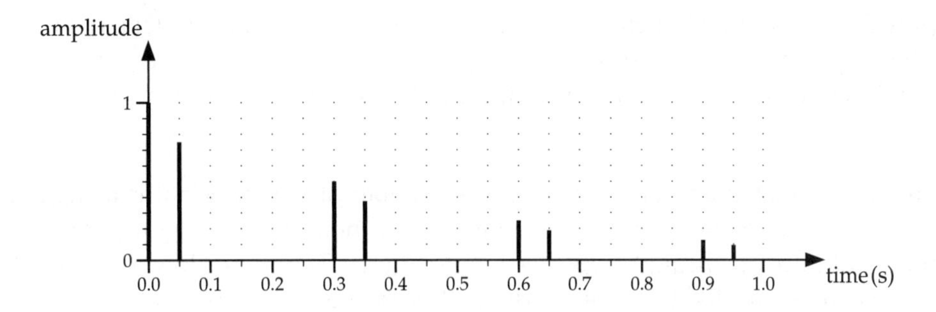

Figure 10.31 Example cascaded echo impulse response (first 1 second, $t_1 = 0.05$, $a_1 = 0.75$, $t_2 = 0.3$, $a_2 = 0.5$)

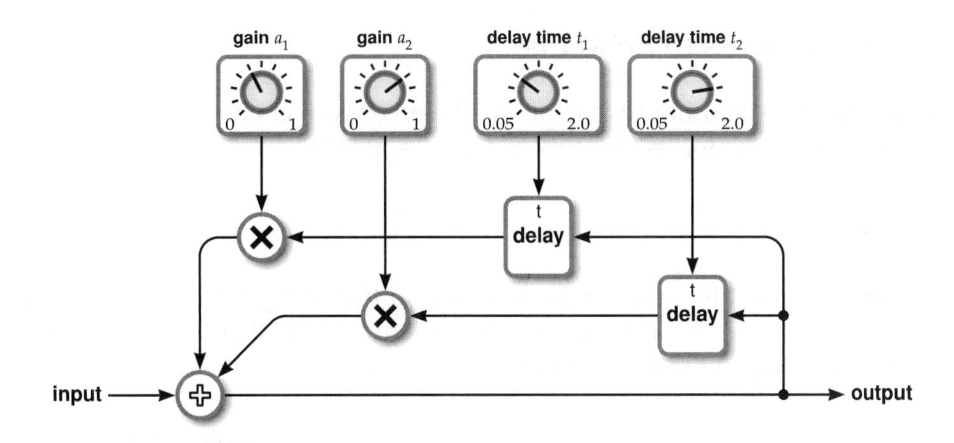

Figure 10.32 Two feedback path recirculating echo

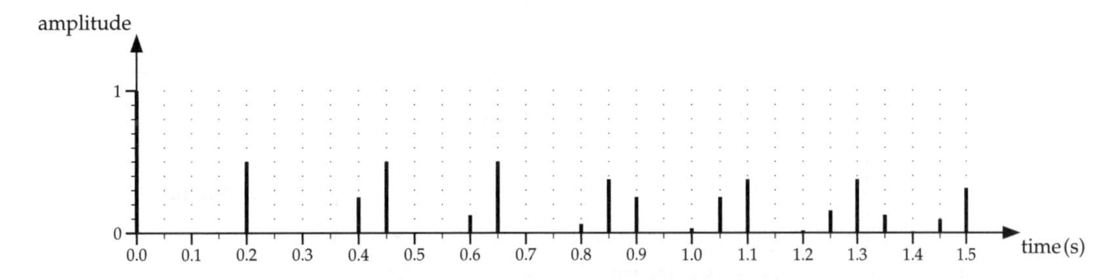

Figure 10.33 Example two feedback path echo impulse response (first 1.5 seconds, $t_1 = 0.2$, $a_1 = 0.5$, $t_2 = 0.45$, $a_2 = 0.5$)

Sometimes different combinations of delay time will be the same, leading to a summation of amplitude at that point. There is often an audible increase of echo density in the early part of the impulse response. For musical applications, the results of the process in figure 10.32 are different from the regular repeating outputs of the previous recirculating echo examples.

The potential for instability increases with the number of feedback paths being summed together. If the values of a_1 and a_2 are both large, there is the potential for too much amplitude to build up through repeated summation. Therefore, lower values than in previous examples are likely to be needed. It is simple to extend the form and make the patterns more complex by adding further feedback delay paths, although reducing the feedback gain values will be necessary. It is possible to use a single multitap buffer for this form, as all the delays have the same input signal.

10.3.3 Improvements to Echo Effects

Similar modifications and improvements can be made to recirculating echo processes as for the non-recirculating forms (described in §10.2.4, p.307).

Wet/Dry Mix

The wet/dry mix effect in figure 10.34 is similar to that in figure 10.19 (p.307). Having an overall control makes it easier to affect the relative levels than having to change the amplitude gain factors in the delayed paths.

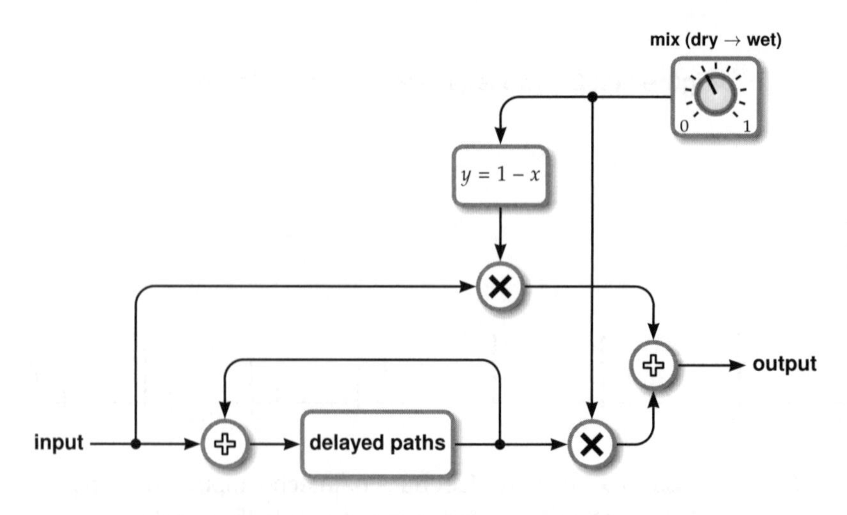

Figure 10.34 Wet/dry ratio mix (recirculating)

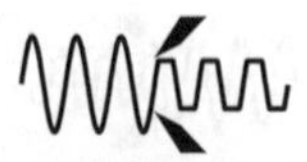

Controls

It is often useful to have a small set of controls for most adjustments, with automatically derived internal parameter values. Preset relationships between values might be provided to achieve particular patterns. With the recirculating forms it is also important to consider stability issues. Commercial products protect the user from unstable conditions by limiting the ranges of gain parameters.

Sound Character

Similarly to figure 10.14 (p.302), modifiers such as distortion and filtering can be used to change the character of the results. With such effects in the feedback loop, the sound modifications will accumulate over time, as the sample values repeatedly loop. This is useful for creating gradually degrading sounds, which have some similarities to analogue technologies such as tape loops.

It is possible to impart subtle modulations to the delay time using the form shown in figure 10.35. This can also give the impression of imperfect processes, such as a slightly varying analogue tape loop speed. It has similarities to the examples in Chapter 9.

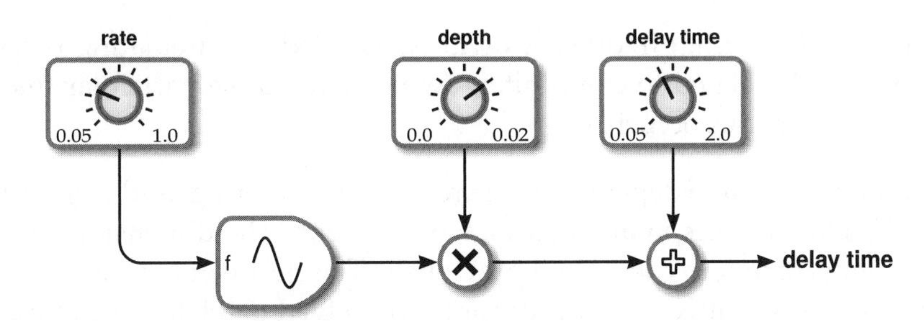

Figure 10.35 Modulated delay time

10.4 Recirculating Reverberation Forms

10.4.1 Basic Concepts

The basic requirements for naturalistic reverberation effects are described in §10.2.5 (p.309):

- There are short delays between reflections.
- Complex irregular relationships between delay times are necessary to avoid grainy and metallic sounds.
- The smoothness and realism of a reverberation can be improved with a greater density of reflections.

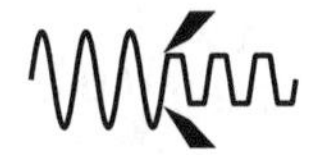

- A somewhat exponential decay of amplitude envelope with time is expected.

With a non-recirculating reverberation process the impulse response is unlikely to last very long, unless there are very large numbers of delay paths to achieve a naturalistic density. With a recirculating effect, however, there is the opportunity to create long decaying effects with moderate computation. While they might only approximate the effect of a real acoustic environment, they stimulate the same areas of perception, can be convincing, and can be configurable to the musical context.

These are the targets for a smooth and natural-sounding reverberation:

- The density of delayed sounds reaching the listener will increase over time. This was first seen in the impulse response of figure 10.6 (p.295). The result is that more overlapping of delayed sounds occurs as the sound progresses, leading to a loss of clarity.
- The spectral envelope will change over time. Typically, this means a progressive attenuation of higher frequency partials over time. However, different environments will have different characteristics, such as the loss of low frequencies, or the emphasis of particular frequency bands.
- Strong resonant (ringing) frequencies will be avoided. Recirculating reverberation effects are closely related to comb filters (which emphasise particular frequencies), so there is a risk of this occurring.

Tonal development over time depends on the reflection, scattering, and absorption properties of the different surfaces in an acoustic environment. The dimensions of the space also relate to lengths of time, as described previously. The choice of parameters within the reverberation process will affect how the output is perceived to relate to a natural acoustic environment.

As with recirculating echo effects, there is a danger of producing an unstable process where the output becomes larger and larger until it reaches the amplitude limits of the system. With the short delay times associated with reverberation, this can happen very quickly and requires care when configuring parameters.

10.4.2 Reverberator with Comb and Allpass Filters

Figure 10.36 shows a reverberator that has some similarities to the forms devised by Schroeder and Moorer. The first part is a parallel set of recirculating feedback loops with delays, lowpass filters, and attenuators. These are related to the simplest recirculating echo effect (a comb filter, figure 10.25, p.315), with the addition of a lowpass filter, and shorter delay times.

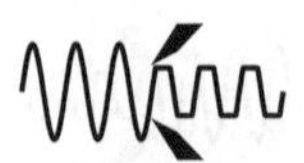

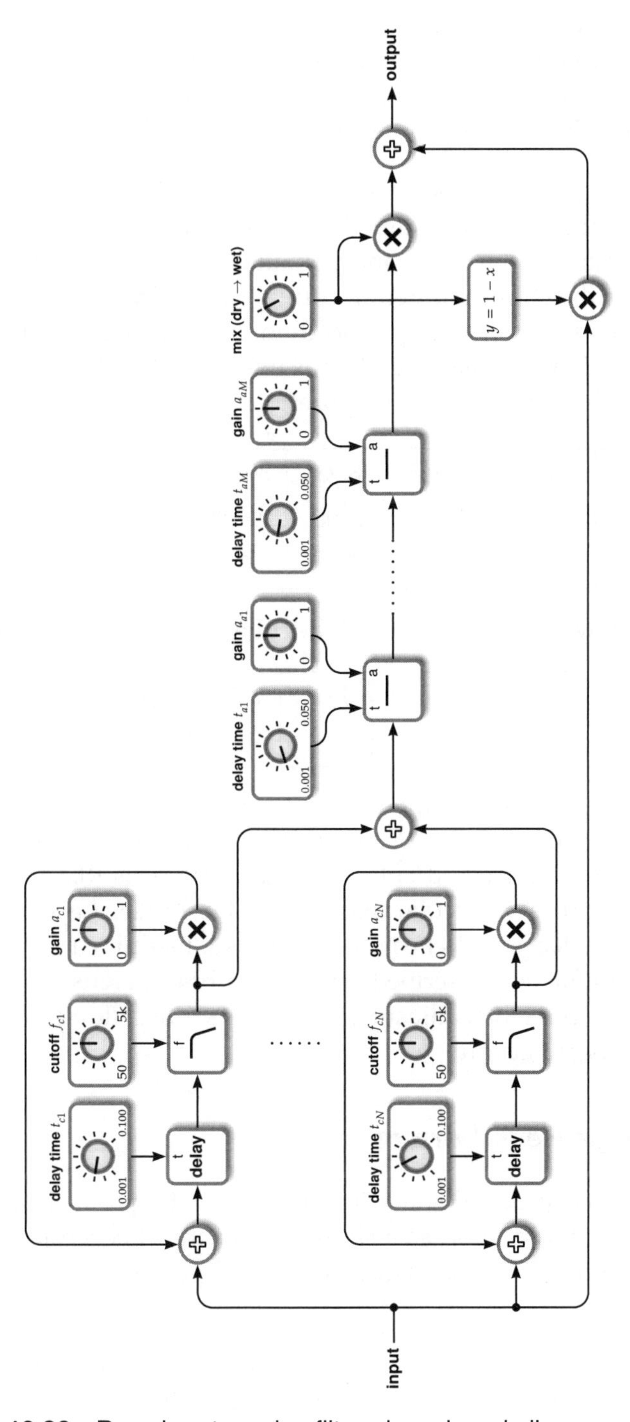

Figure 10.36 Reverberator using filtered comb and allpass sections

The second part is a cascaded set of allpass filters of the type shown in figure 6.63 (p.189). The allpass filters increase the complexity of the impulse response output, by multiplying the number of reflections resulting from the parallel section. Finally there is a control to mix the ratio of the original (dry) and effected (wet) signals.

The reason for employing multiple parallel and cascaded sections is to achieve a complex set of overlapping, decaying, and filtered sounds. Increasing the number of sections can increase the complexity of the result and potentially reduces the artificiality of the effect, but it also increases the effort required in configuration. Typically the aim is to achieve a set of delay times that are not evenly spaced nor related to a common factor, in order to reduce regularity and grainy character. For example, the first (parallel) part might consist of eight sections with the following configuration:

Delay time t_{ci} (ms)	21.884	25.885	28.934	30.739	32.229	33.829	35.329	37.017
Cutoff f_{ci} (Hz)	2500	2500	2500	2500	2500	2500	2500	2500
Gain a_{ci}	0.5	0.5	0.5	0.5	0.5	0.5	0.5	0.5

These might be followed by four series allpass filters configured as follows:

Delay time t_{ai} (ms)	5.118	7.762	9.957	12.402
Gain a_{ai}	0.5	0.5	0.5	0.5

The cutoff frequencies and gain values do not have to be the same for all paths, and can be adjusted to change the tonality of the result or change the length of the reverberant decay. The danger with increased cutoff and gain values is that the sound can become gritty or metallic, or ring at particular frequencies. Of course, it is not always the case that a reverberation-type effect should be naturalistic, as sometimes a grainy or metallic sound can be musically useful. As described on p.301, a brief percussive sound with a sharp attack is a good test input when adjusting parameters. This allows the development of the reverberation to be heard clearly.

10.4.3 Multi-Stage Reverberator

While figure 10.36 can produce some useful results, the parallel loops with consistent repetition can be improved upon as a simulation of the effects found in typical acoustic environments. Figure 10.37 is a cascaded multi-stage reverberator with the following features:

- The early reflections generator is a non-recirculating stage that creates a fairly complex pattern of initial reflections. This achieves the part of the impulse response between the direct sound and the later reverberation in figure 10.6 (p.295).

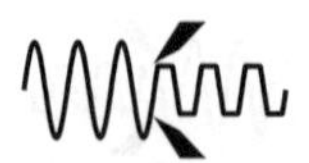

- The later reflections generators are recirculating stages. The first causes the pattern generated by the early reflections generator to be repeated, which has similarities to figure 10.30 (p.320). The second recirculating stage creates further repetition, but at different time intervals. Both stages are about creating complexity, an increased density of delayed sounds, and a gradually decaying reverberation.
- Each stage has its own gain control, to allow the different parts of the reverberation to be balanced as appropriate for the musical context. The weighted signals are summed to create the output. Some ways of using these controls are:
  - Emphasising the later reflections over the direct sound and early reflections to give an impression of distance from the sound source.
  - Setting the direct sound gain to 0 if the reverberator is to be used as a send rather than an insert effect with a mixing console (figure 5.43, p.129).
  - Setting the later reflection gains to 0 to allow a thickening effect rather than an obvious reverberation (as described previously in §10.2.5, p.309).

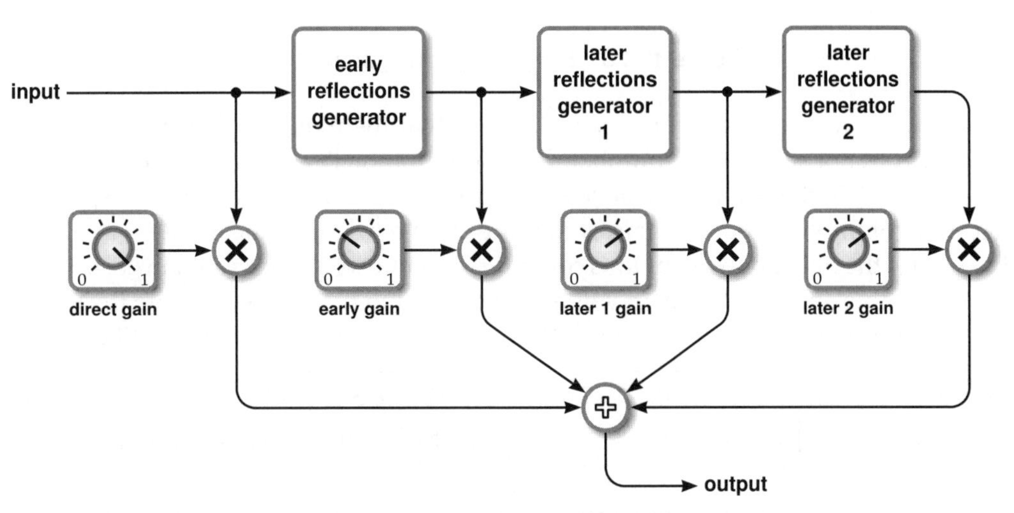

Figure 10.37 Multi-stage reverberator

There are some similarities between figure 10.37 and the impulse response convolution filter in figure 10.23 (p.312). Both have cascaded sections which are amplitude weighted into the output. However, the multi-stage reverberator is far more computationally-efficient as it utilises the recirculating blocks to create a large density of reflections with a relatively small number of delay paths.

Figure 10.38 illustrates an early reflections generator suitable for use in the multi-stage reverberator. The filters represent the absorption of low and high frequencies of materials from which sound is reflected. Frequency f_{c1} can be increased to counter any undesired boomy quality, and f_{c2} can be decreased from 20kHz to help reduce grainy character.

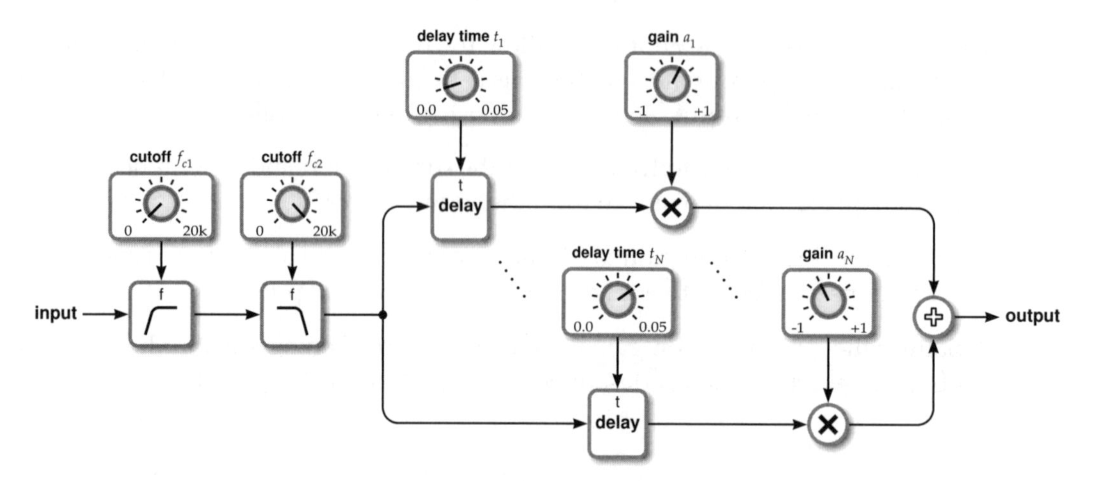

Figure 10.38 Early reflections generator

As many delay paths as necessary are used, such that the required density of reflections is achieved, but not such a large number that configuration becomes too difficult. As with figure 10.36 (p.325) the aim is to achieve a set of delay times that are not evenly spaced nor related to a common factor. The gain values are chosen to mimic inconsistent absorption, and to reduce the likelihood of obvious comb filtering effects (as described in §6.4.4, p.183). A mix of positive and negative gain values can be used to further decorrelate the different paths. For example, a set of eight early reflection paths might be configured like this:

Delay time t_i (ms)	2.078	5.154	5.947	7.544	8.878	10.422	13.938	17.140
Gain a_i	0.609	0.262	−0.360	−0.470	0.290	−0.423	0.100	0.200

The time values correspond to moderately small distances associated with reflections from nearby surfaces. On their own the early reflections will not produce a long reverberation, but when fed to the subsequent stages their effect will be more significant. A single multitap buffer could be used to implement the early reflections stage, as all the delays are in parallel and fed from the same input signal. For accuracy it is appropriate to use interpolated fractional delays. Interpolation methods are described in §8.2 (p.237).

Figure 10.39 illustrates a later reflections generator suitable for use in the multi-stage reverberator. It is a four delay path recirculating form known as a *Feedback Delay Network (FDN)*. The output from each delay path block is summed into the output (much like

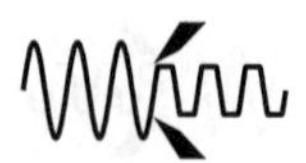

the early reflections form). However, the outputs also pass through the feedback matrix multiplier whose outputs are summed with the input to create the recirculating effect. It is important to note that each output of the feedback matrix multiplier will be different, and so the input to each delay path block is different. This is more sophisticated than all the delayed feedback paths summing together (as is the case in figure 10.32, p.321), as it is possible to control which delay outputs contribute to each of the parallel paths on the next loop.

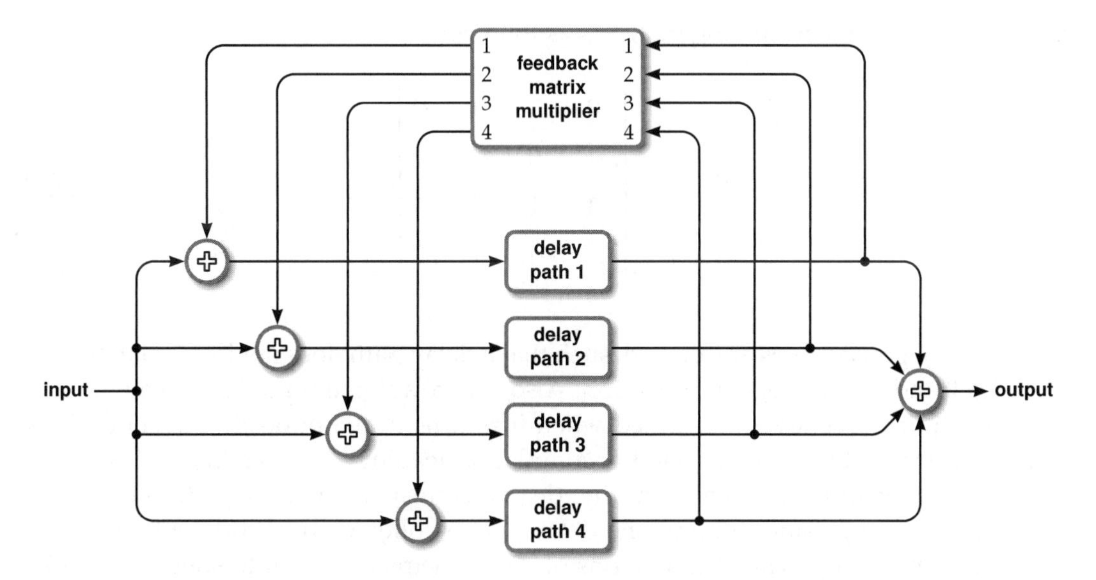

Figure 10.39 Later reflections generator

The feedback matrix multiplier in figure 10.39 creates sums of the different delay paths using the following matrix operation:

$$\begin{matrix} \boldsymbol{O} & = & \boldsymbol{A} & \boldsymbol{I} \end{matrix}$$

$$\begin{bmatrix} o_1 \\ o_2 \\ o_3 \\ o_4 \end{bmatrix} = \begin{bmatrix} a_{11} & a_{12} & a_{13} & a_{14} \\ a_{21} & a_{22} & a_{23} & a_{24} \\ a_{31} & a_{32} & a_{33} & a_{34} \\ a_{41} & a_{42} & a_{43} & a_{44} \end{bmatrix} \begin{bmatrix} i_1 \\ i_2 \\ i_3 \\ i_4 \end{bmatrix} \tag{10.5}$$

In the matrix multiplication, i_1 to i_4 are the four input signals, o_1 to o_4 are the four output signals, and amplitude weights a_{11} to a_{44} control the amount of each input signal that reaches each output.

Writing out the matrix operation in full produces the following:

$$\begin{array}{lllllllll} o_1 & = & a_{11}i_1 & + & a_{12}i_2 & + & a_{13}i_3 & + & a_{14}i_4 \\ o_2 & = & a_{21}i_1 & + & a_{22}i_2 & + & a_{23}i_3 & + & a_{24}i_4 \\ o_3 & = & a_{31}i_1 & + & a_{32}i_2 & + & a_{33}i_3 & + & a_{34}i_4 \\ o_4 & = & a_{41}i_1 & + & a_{42}i_2 & + & a_{43}i_3 & + & a_{44}i_4 \end{array} \tag{10.6}$$

An example amplitude weighting matrix is as follows:

$$A = \begin{bmatrix} 0 & 1 & 1 & -1 \\ -1 & 0 & -1 & 1 \\ -1 & 1 & 0 & -1 \\ 1 & -1 & 1 & 0 \end{bmatrix} \tag{10.7}$$

The leading diagonal values are all zero, such that a delay path does not immediately feed back to itself and create a regular repetition. Also, where a signal is positively weighted in one direction, it is negatively weighted when it returns in the opposite direction. This helps to reduce problems of repeated accumulation leading to instability. All sorts of different matrix values could be used; the idea is to create a complex pattern of delays where each sample passing through one delay path is followed by a different pattern of delays on the next loop. The combinations of delays helps the result to sound more like a natural environment with its complex reflection, scattering, and absorption patterns. Feedback Delay Networks are very useful, therefore, for creating convincing artificial reverberation.

Figure 10.40 shows the delay path block for figure 10.39. Each path has a delay, a lowpass filter to simulate the attenuation of higher frequency partials as the sound is reflected, and an overall attenuation factor. A separate buffer, filter, and multiplier set is required for each path, as each is processing a different signal.

As with the early reflection delay paths, there needs to be a spread of delay time values with an unusual relationship between them to achieve a non-grainy and smoothly-decaying sound. The two later reflections generator stages have the role of creating complex overlapping repetitions of the early reflections pattern, in order to create the later reverberation seen in figure 10.6 (p.295). The time delay values will range from a few milliseconds to hundreds of milliseconds in order to achieve this effect. The first later reflections generator is likely to use lower values than the second to achieve a shorter repetition that is then repeated over longer delays.

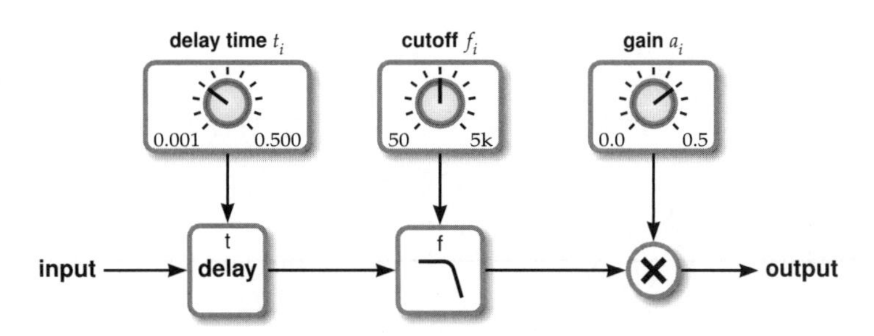

Figure 10.40 Delay path block for figure 10.39

As with the configuration of figure 10.36 (p.325), the lowpass filter cutoff and gain factor for the delay paths should be set high enough to achieve a long reverberation, but without an unstable, metallic, or ringing character. For example, the later reflection generator paths might be configured like this:

	Later reflections generator 1				Later reflections generator 2			
Delay time t_i (ms)	6.040	8.868	17.390	48.870	34.270	61.720	74.603	96.130
Cutoff f_i (Hz)	4000	4000	4000	4000	900	900	900	900
Gain a_i	0.25	0.25	0.25	0.25	0.35	0.35	0.35	0.30

It is impossible to state values that are suitable for all cases. Not only do they depend on the tonality of reverberation required, they must also be adjusted to reflect the response of the chosen filter implementation (as described in §6.4, p.164). A good technique is to develop and test one stage at a time; starting with early reflections, then adding later reflections 1, then later reflections 2. This can be more effective than trying to configure all stages from scratch simultaneously.

Figure 10.41 illustrates the result of passing a snare drum sound through the multi-stage reverberator when configured to achieve a large room type of effect. The reverberation causes the sound to be extended in time.

10.4.4 Improvements to the Multi-Stage Reverberator

Increasing Complexity

Making the output of a reverberation process convincing and natural-sounding often relates to the complexity of the structure that is used. The aim is to create a density and randomness to the reflections such that they appear to be the result of an enclosed space with many objects and surfaces creating different reflections, scattering, and absorption at different frequencies.

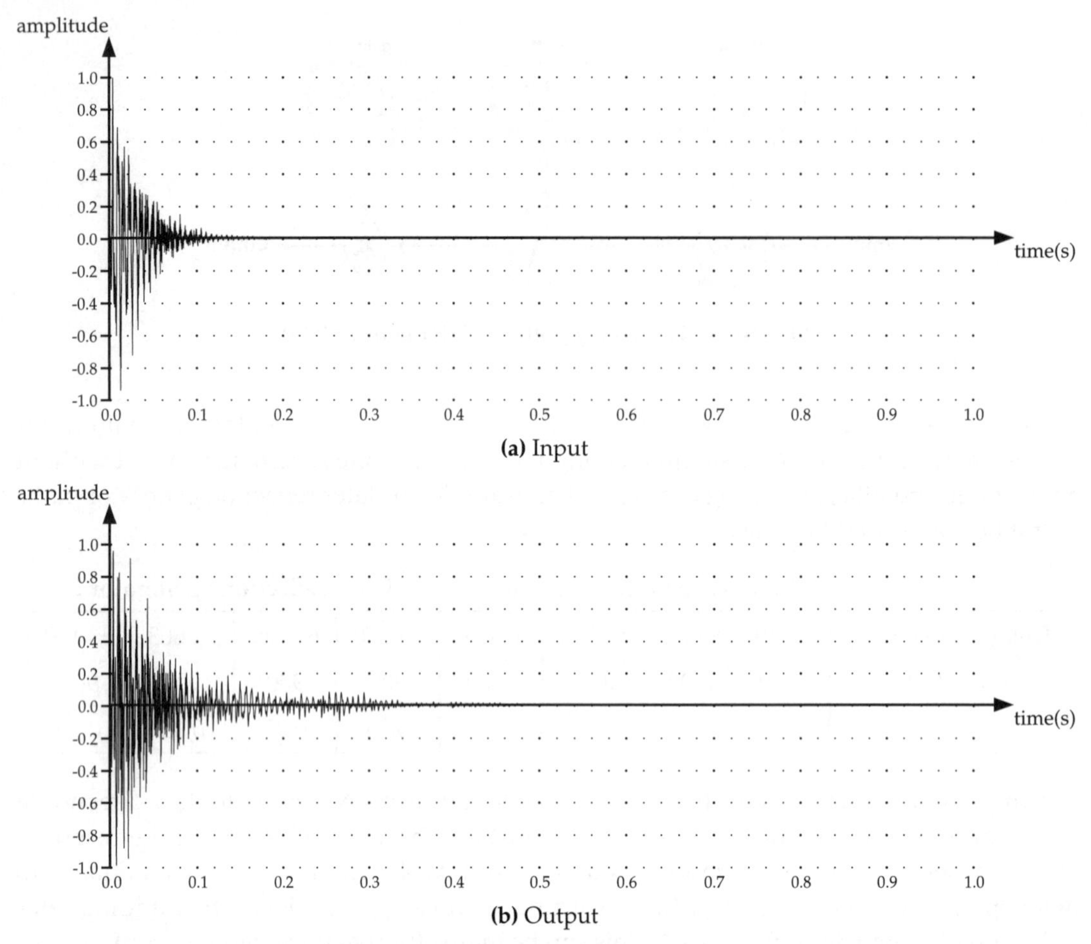

Figure 10.41 Snare drum through multi-stage reverberator waveform plots

Some ways of achieving this are as follows:

- An initial delay might be inserted just before the early reflections generator (often called a predelay), such that there is a single control for the amount of time between the direct sound and the start of the reverberant sound. This is a common feature on commercial reverberators. It can affect the perception of distance from the reflecting surfaces and so reflects the room size. Musically, it can be used to create subtle separation between direct and reverberant sound (with small values), or a very obvious echo (with larger values).
- Adding more delay paths in the non-recirculating and recirculating stages can increase the density of delayed sounds.

- More complex filtering might be used to adjust the tonal characteristics.
- More stages might be added to figure 10.37 (p.327). The advantages of having separate stages is that they can be configured and enabled individually, and that it is easier to prevent instability if the recirculation loops are fairly small.

Multiple Parameter Control

Large numbers of configuration parameters are present in a complex system such as the multi-stage reverberator. Most users will not be interested in detailed control, especially over such things as the individual weights in the recirculating feedback matrix. It is typical to provide users with preset configurations and then an ability to modify high-level parameters to change the nature of the effect (within certain boundaries). Typically this means providing a small set of user controls that are automatically mapped to a larger set of internal parameters. Some typical user parameters that might be found in commercial products are as follows:

- **Room size**. This will affect the decay time and the spacing of reflections (or the rate of buildup of reflections). Therefore, the control should couple to the delay times, and also to the feedback gain factors.
- **Diffusion**. This relates to the density of reflections, particularly in the initial part of the sound, and so the delay times and amplitudes of the early reflections.
- **Reverb time** or **Decay time**. If this is provided separately to the size parameter, it controls the feedback gain factors.
- **Tone**. This reflects the nature of the materials of which the acoustic environment is composed. It relates to filter controls, either in the recirculating loop, or applied to the output of the reverberator. It might apply to specific parts of the sound such as early reflections.

In most cases it is necessary to have mappings from a single input control to multiple internal parameters (in a similar manner to figure 10.21, p.308). In some cases internal parameter values might work in opposition. For example, increasing the cutoff frequency of a filter might necessitate the reduction of a feedback gain value, in order to change the tonal character but maintain the same decay time. Control mapping is discussed further in Chapter 24.

10.4.5 Stereo Reverberation

To maintain stereo separation with more than one input channel it is necessary to have separate process paths. Figure 10.42 illustrates a simple parallel arrangement for two channels. The direct paths have the same gain. It is also possible to have the same

parameter controls for the two reverberators. If the configuration is the same for the two sets of indirect paths then there are two notable features of this arrangement:

- Monophonic input material that is panned to the centre position before the process will produce centre-panned reverberation, as the two channels will produce the same results.
- Monophonic input material that is panned fully to one side will only produce reverberation on that side and silence on the other.

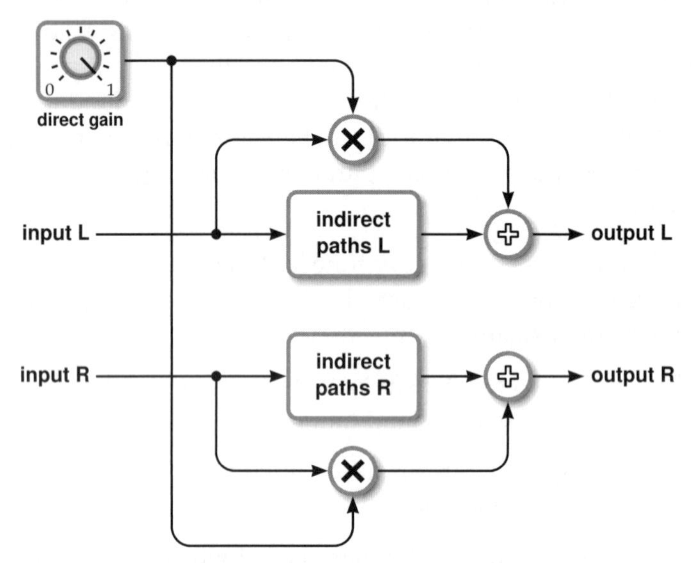

Figure 10.42 Stereo form 1

It is often desirable that panned monophonic source material has more stereo width at the output of the reverberator. The first step is to configure the two sets of indirect paths differently, as if the sound reaching the listener has taken different paths to arrive at left and right ears (which is likely in practical acoustic environments). To give the impression that the two ears are in the same environment the general tonality and decay time will still need to be very similar. One way of creating a subtle difference is to make the delay times for one channel similar, but with small variations from those for the other. The other parameters can be the same for both channels.

The second variation is to add an ability to cross-feed the output from one channel to the other, as shown in figure 10.43. This has similarities to the ping-pong echo form in figure 10.29 (p.320). The cross-feed means that a sound that is panned to one side also generates some reverberation on the other. This reflects the fact that a sound source on one side of a human will also generate reverberation that reaches the ear on the other side.

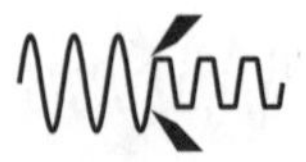

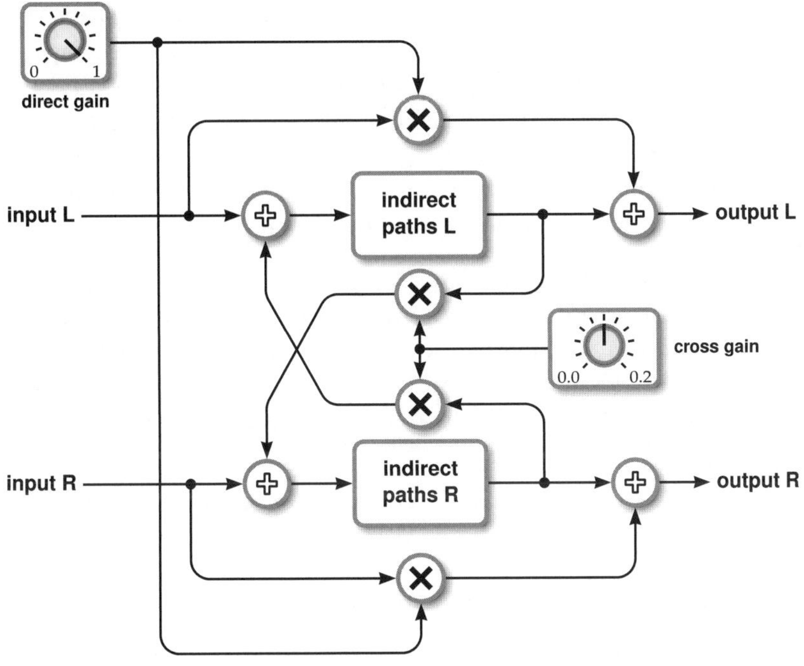

Figure 10.43 Stereo form 2

10.5 Developing Processes and Learning More

Acoustic environment processes can be produced with various complexities; from the single delay element design in figure 10.25 (p.315), through to the multi-stage reverberator in §10.4.3 (p.326). They are mainly achieved with a relatively small set of standard elements such as delays, multipliers, and filters. If those core elements are in place through preprogrammed functions or objects, then it is possible to achieve results relatively quickly. Alternatively, it might be necessary to consider the design and implementation of those blocks, as found in Chapters 6 and 8.

Constructing and configuring echo effects is generally easier than with reverberators. The difficulty is that the character of reverberation depends on creating a dense set of reflections whose relationships in time and tonality need to be suitable to achieve a result that does not appear grainy or metallic. The parameter suggestions in §10.4 (p.323) provide some pointers. By contrast, the spacing between delayed sounds in an echo process means that the relationship between changes in design or parameter values and audible results is more obvious.

With recirculating forms there is the issue of maintaining the stability of the process through suitable control of feedback gain. Sometimes when trying to achieve a long decaying effect it is possible to accidentally create an unstable (rapidly increasing amplitude) output. Wearing headphones and using a significant output gain is not advised in the early development stages. Another feature of feedback loops is that the order of computation can be more confusing than usual. Algorithm 10.2 (p.317, corresponding to figure 10.25, p.315) is an example of how it can be appropriate to start from the output of a delay block and work towards the current value to be written as its input.

Because acoustic environment effects relate closely to everyday acoustic experiences, they are used in many musical recording and production situations. Digital Audio Workstations normally include reverberation, delay, and echo effects, which are useful for learning about the parameters that are appropriate for end users and the results that can be achieved. There is also advice available in terms of configuration and creative methods in sources such as the following book:

> Case, Alexander U. 2007. *Sound FX: Unlocking the Creative Potential of Recording Studio Effects*. Burlington, MA: Focal Press.

The following sources provide some more advanced material that relates to this chapter, which can be used for further study:

> Moorer, James A. 1979. "About This Reverberation Business." *Computer Music Journal* 3:2:13–28.

> Pirkle, Will. 2013. *Designing Audio Effect Plug-Ins in C++: With Digital Audio Signal Processing Theory*. Burlington, MA: Focal Press.

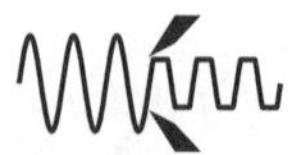

11

Dynamics Processes

11.1 Introduction

11.1.1 Manual and Automated Control Loops

The modification processes seen in previous chapters (such as distortion and reverberation) have no analysis component within them. Those processes take an input, apply a function, and produce an output from it. They will apply the function in the same way whatever the nature of the input signal. The configuration of those modifiers depends on the analysis performed by the user. Figure 11.1 shows a control arrangement where the user changes the parameters of a modifier to achieve the required result.

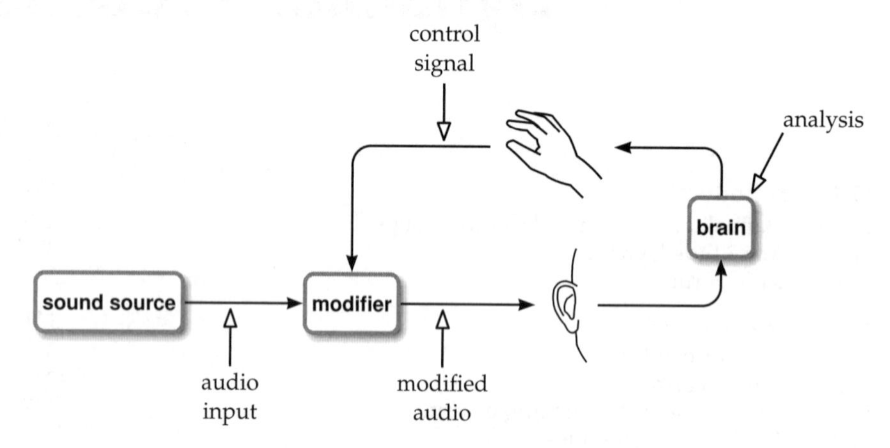

Figure 11.1 Modification control loop

This arrangement can be found in both of the following cases:

- **Performance**. For example, a guitarist might change a wah-wah effect with a foot control while playing.
- **Editing**. For example, a recording engineer might change the tonal balance of a track or the trajectory of an amplitude fade in the mix long after the performance has finished.

In both of the cases above, the user interacts with the modifier as a control loop external to the modification process. The alternative is that the process itself adapts to the nature of the signal arriving at the input using an internal control loop. This often approximates the behaviour of a human in the same situation. The automatic adaption of behaviour will usually be based on some parameters set by the user, which configure the operating characteristics in advance of the process being used.

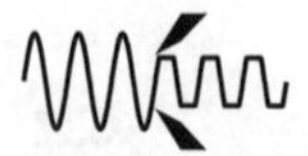

There are a number of situations where automating processes is useful:

- If the user is unable to react quickly enough and with sufficient precision to control the system in real-time. The alternative is non-real-time editing, where the slow feedback cycle can reduce the efficiency of the control process.
- If the nature of control involves too many dimensions of adjustment for the user to manage the relationship between parameters sufficiently well.
- If the task is boring or repetitive, or requires highly consistent application.

To automate a control process requires an ability for the system to mimic human behaviour. There are many tasks that might be appropriate for some form of automated control, but are very difficult to realise as an algorithm. Describing the analysis part is a particular problem. It is necessary to identify the relevant sonic features, and how that information is used to change the parameters of the modifier.

11.1.2 Amplitude Dynamics

Dynamic range refers to the amount of amplitude envelope level variation found in an audio signal. This might be considered over a relatively short length of time, such as the difference in amplitude between the attack peak and a sustain level of an instrument note. Alternatively it might be over a longer period, such as the difference between loud and quiet notes in a musical passage. Studio mixing practice often involves either increasing or reducing dynamic range in different circumstances, known as *expansion* and *compression* respectively. For example:

- Reducing amplitude levels below a threshold, but leaving those above unchanged, in order to attenuate background sounds or shorten an amplitude envelope decay. This increases (expands) the dynamic range.
- Reducing peak amplitude levels relative to the body of the sound, such that the signal can be amplified subsequently without it exceeding the maximum amplitude limits of the system (see figure 11.2). This reduces (compresses) the dynamic range.

The key to dynamic range control is calculating an amplitude gain value that varies over time. The gain value is multiplied by the input signal to change the amplitude envelope in the desired manner. The process which achieves this is commonly called a *dynamics processor*.

Sometimes these techniques are applied in a subtle way, and the effects might not be obvious to a casual listener. At other times they are used to create significant tonal modifications. The musical aspects of manipulation of dynamic range can be a complex topic, but understanding the process designs and their typical uses makes employing them appropriately in a musical context easier to achieve.

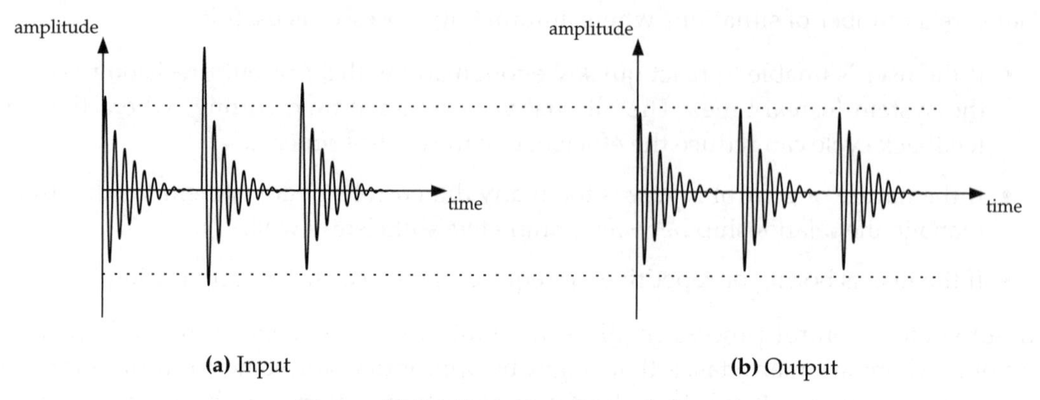

(a) Input **(b)** Output

Figure 11.2 Reducing dynamic range

11.1.3 Basic Forms

Figure 11.3 shows the two main structural forms that are used in dynamics processors:

- A *feedback* arrangement uses the **output** signal from the modifier as the input to the analysis block. Humans often use a feedback form, analysing whether the output has the desired characteristics and, if not, changing the modifier controls until it does.
- A *feedforward* arrangement controls the modification process from an analysis of the **input** signal.

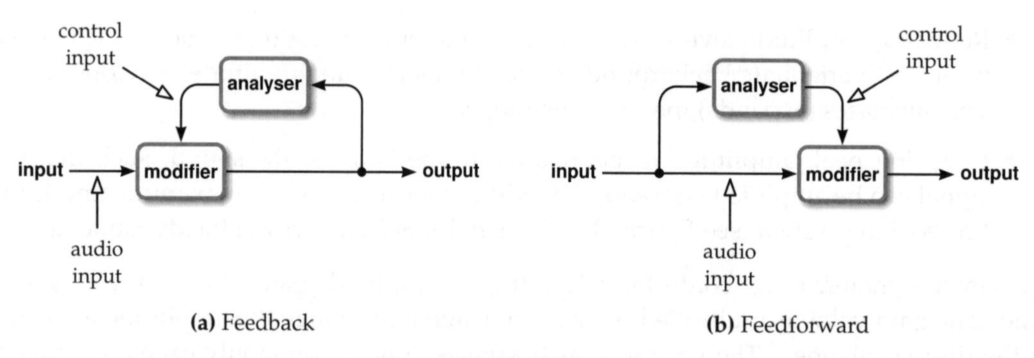

(a) Feedback **(b)** Feedforward

Figure 11.3 Basic forms

The choice of arrangement depends on whether the analysis task is described in terms of the input, or the output signal. In a feedback form the output is the source of information, and the results of analysis will be applied to **future** input signals, as the current signal has already passed through. In a feedforward form, however, the current input signal determines the effect that is applied.

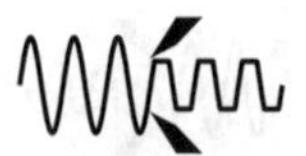

Figure 11.4 shows a dynamics process with manual control. The switch allows the user to listen to either the input signal (feedforward) or output signal (feedback). The user's brain analyses the signal and an appropriate change is made to the gain value, which is multiplied by the input signal to produce the output. The input signal is likely to be changing over time, so the user must continually adjust the gain value to achieve the desired results.

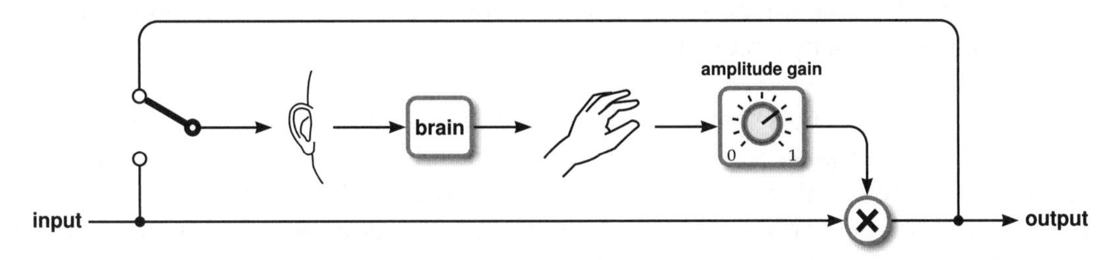

Figure 11.4 Manual dynamics control

The basic automatic form equivalent to figure 11.4 is illustrated in figure 11.5. The ear and brain have been replaced by an automatic analysis process, and the control of gain value is now a mapping from the analysed value. The mapping uses the same principles as a transfer function seen in Chapter 7, where an input value is mapped to an output value through the function line. The nature of the analysis and mappings will be described in more detail later.

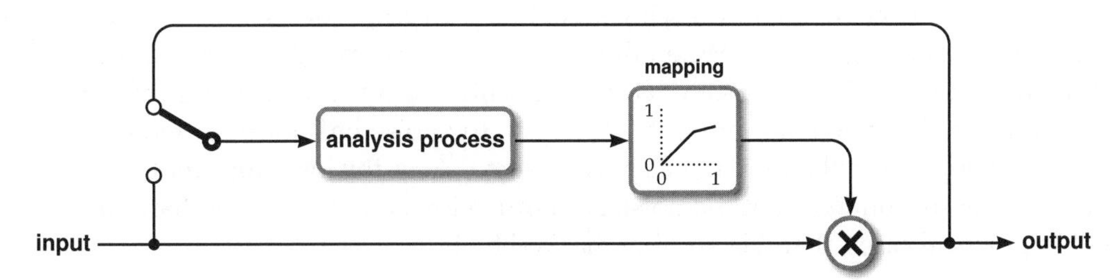

Figure 11.5 Automatic dynamics control

11.2 Noise Gates

11.2.1 Main Principles

The main purpose of a *noise gate* is to attenuate unwanted background noise in a signal while leaving the wanted signal in place. To put it another way, much of the noise is blocked, but the wanted signal is allowed through the open gate. Noise gates can also be used as a deliberate sound manipulation effect (such as shortening the decay of a sound).

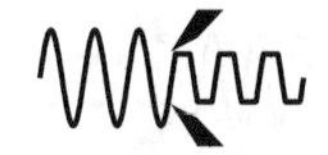

A principle of basic noise gate design is that background noise is not as audible when the wanted signal is present. For example, a constant background hiss might only be audible between passages of notes on an old tape recording. This principle means that a noise gate must determine when the wanted signal is present and when it is not. This leads to a second simple concept, that background noise usually has far less amplitude than the wanted signal. Thus if the signal has high amplitude, it is the wanted signal, and low amplitude indicates background noise. These two principles do not always hold true, but they are adequate in many circumstances.

Figure 11.6 illustrates a noise gating effect. Signal A is what the signal would have been if noise had not been present; a short burst of sinusoidal oscillation with silence either side. Signal B is the signal with lower amplitude noise added. The amplitude envelope of signal B is the level of the noise when the wanted signal is not present, but rises to a much higher value when the wanted signal is present.

A *threshold* is set by the user that is positioned between low (noise only) and high (wanted signal present) amplitude envelope levels. When the envelope level is above the threshold, the gate is opened and the signal is allowed through. When the level is below the threshold, the gate is closed and the signal is blocked. Therefore, once the threshold has been set, the system can automatically determine whether the input is classed as noise or wanted signal, and act appropriately.

An open gate corresponds to multiplying signal B by an amplitude gain of 1, and a closed gate corresponds to a gain of 0. When the gating effect is applied to signal B it results in the final plot in figure 11.6. The gate has successfully removed the noise from the output when the wanted signal is not present. However, the noise has not been removed when the gate is open; the oscillation is not as pure as signal A, as the low amplitude noise is still present. The assumption is that the noise is so much lower in amplitude than the wanted signal in practical cases, that it is audibly masked by it.

The noise gating operation could be performed by a person listening to the sound and rapidly moving a gain fader (as in figure 11.4). However, a noise gate satisfies two of the reasons for automating processes described in §11.1.1; firstly that a human would struggle to react as quickly and as accurately as an automated system, and secondly that the task is both boring and repetitive.

Figure 11.7 illustrates a noise gating effect where the wanted signal is a decaying sinusoidal oscillation. Again, signal A is what the signal would have been if noise had not been present, and signal B is the signal with lower amplitude noise added. The amplitude envelope of signal B is not as clearly divided into regions as it was in figure 11.6. As such the positioning of the threshold is much more difficult.

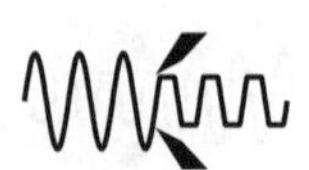

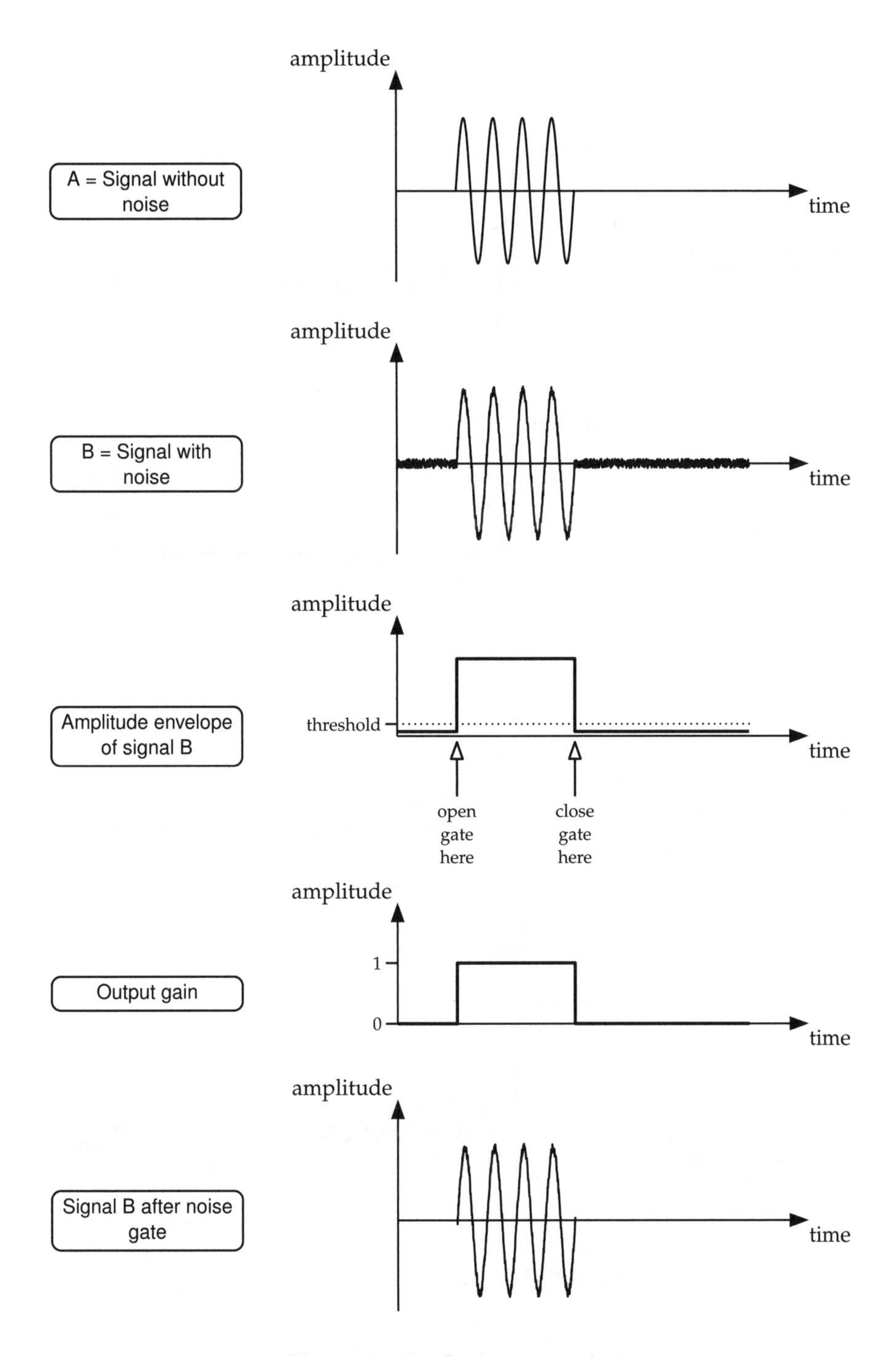

Figure 11.6 Gating example 1

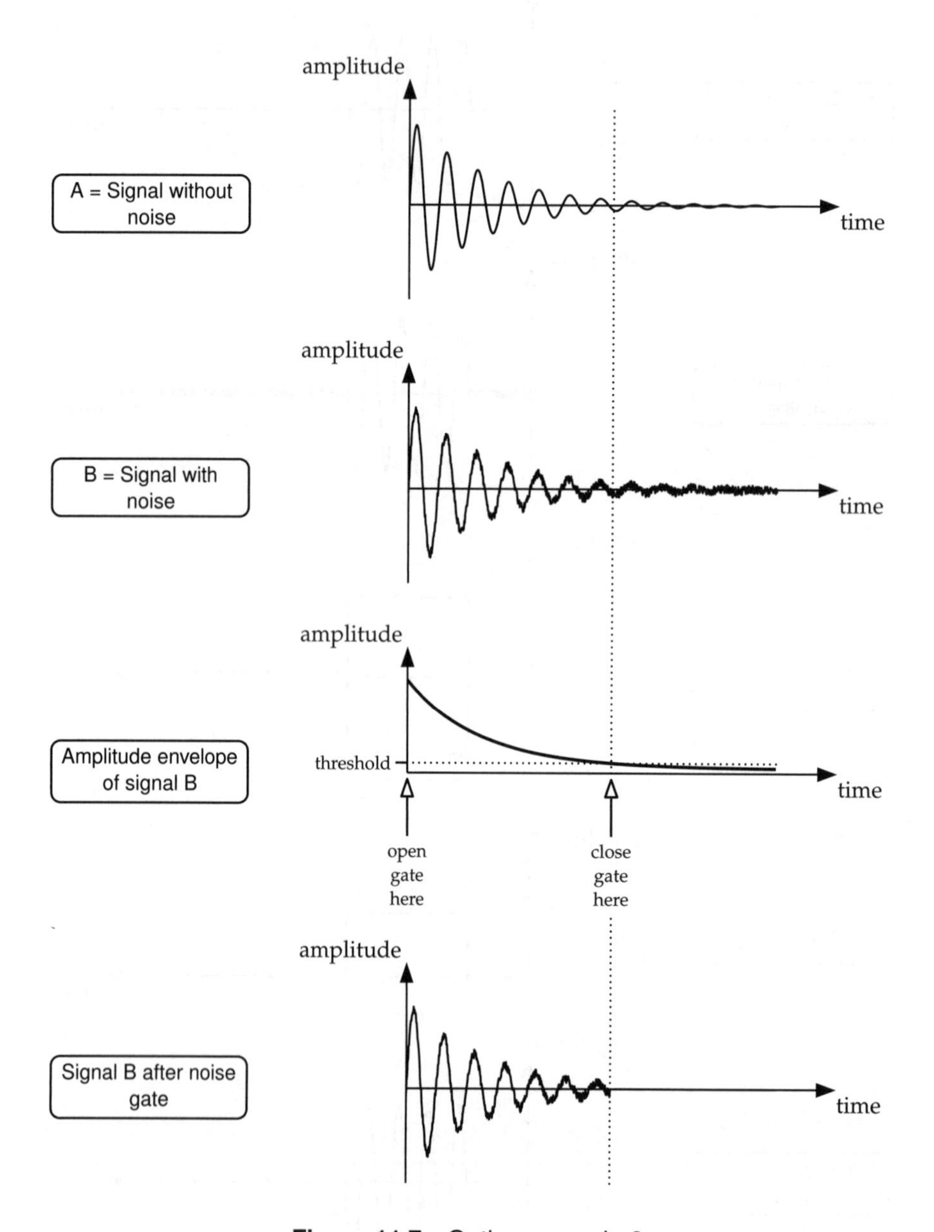

Figure 11.7 Gating example 2

The result of gating signal B is illustrated at the bottom of the figure. The problem is that the end of the wanted sound has been removed from the output due to the position of the threshold being higher than the smallest wanted signal level. However, if the threshold were set lower, more of the noise would be audible in the output, defeating the purpose of the noise gate. This is a common problem when configuring a noise gate, particularly where the wanted signal is decaying slowly and meeting the level of the background noise. The threshold is normally set manually, and the user must decide the best compromise position for a particular musical context. More advanced features such as attack and release time, and downward expansion (which are covered later) can help with this problem.

11.2.2 Simple Form

Figure 11.8 shows the block diagram form of a simple noise gate. A feedforward form has been used. The path through the envelope follower and mapping block is commonly known as the *sidechain*. The envelope follower determines the amplitude envelope of the input signal. The result of this is fed through a gain mapping function whose threshold can be set by the user, the output of which is a gain value fed to the multiplier. The gain value is multiplied by the input signal to produce the output.

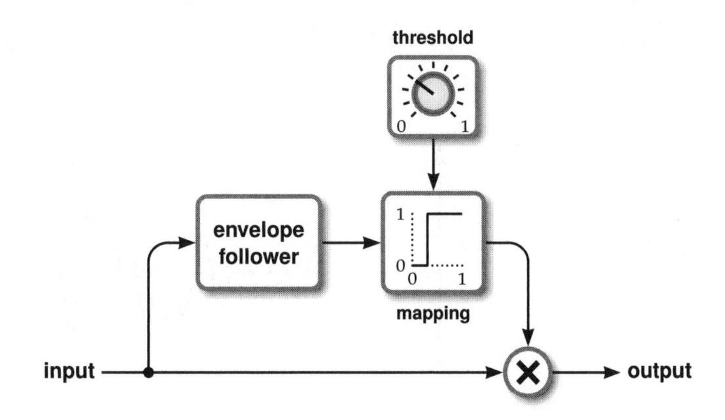

Figure 11.8 Simple noise gate form

Measurement of the long-term amplitude envelope level is discussed in §8.3 (p.245). It is vital that the envelope is measured, **not** the instantaneous amplitude, or signals will be clipped in the lower part of the cycle, which will cause distortion in the output. The difference is illustrated in figure 11.9. If the instantaneous amplitude value of the input is used for judgement it is constantly moving above and below the threshold on each cycle of the input waveform. The envelope, however, describes the long term trend, so the required gating of low signal levels is achieved.

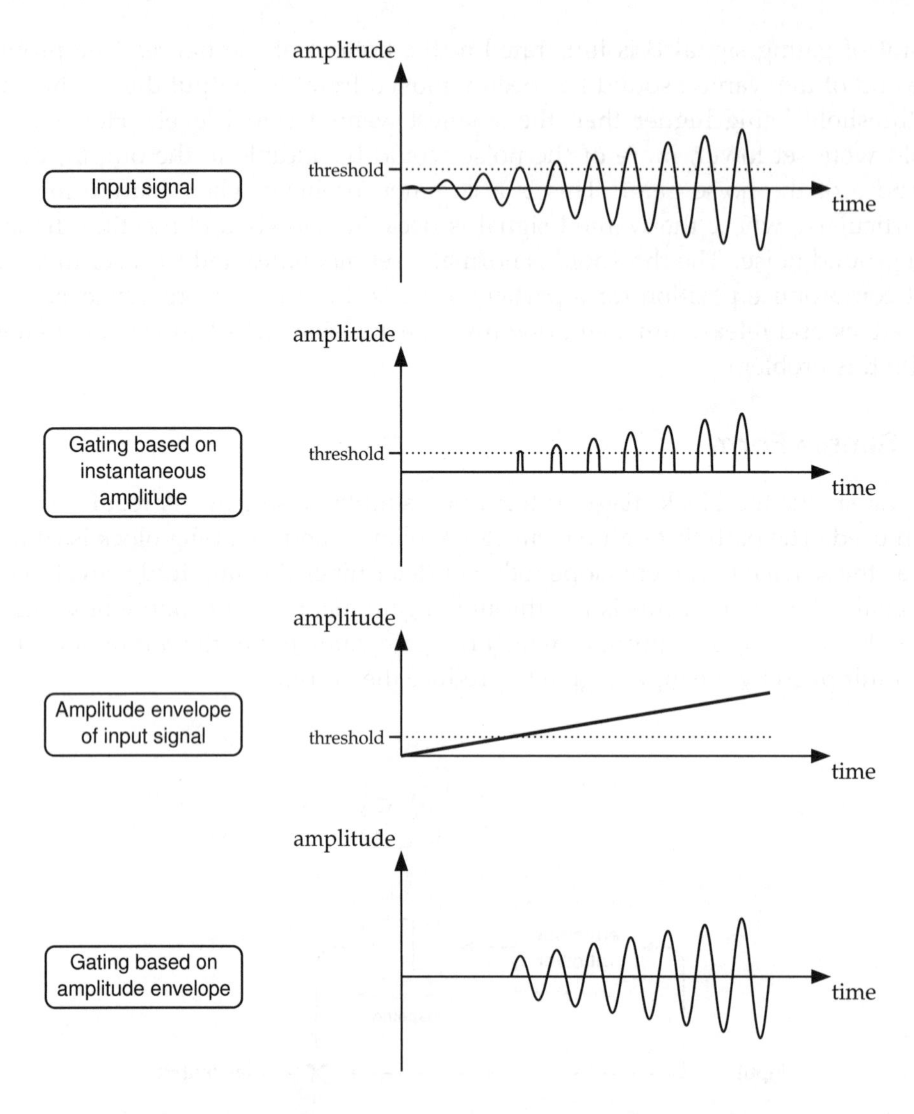

Figure 11.9 Instantaneous value versus envelope-based gating

The action of the noise gate can be expressed in two different ways (figure 11.10):

- The *input/output characteristic* (transfer function) is the most common way of expressing the effect of dynamics processors (as found in equipment manuals and graphical software interfaces). It describes the behaviour of the whole process in terms of amplitude envelope levels. Figure 11.10a shows that for input envelope amplitudes below the threshold level, the output amplitude is 0. Above the threshold the output amplitude envelope level is the same as the input.

- The *gain mapping function* describes the effect of the mapping block in figure 11.8, which maps from input amplitude envelope level to a gain value used by the multiplier. Figure 11.10b shows that for envelope levels below the threshold level, the output gain is 0. Above the threshold, the output gain is 1 (i.e. the output signal is the same as the input signal).

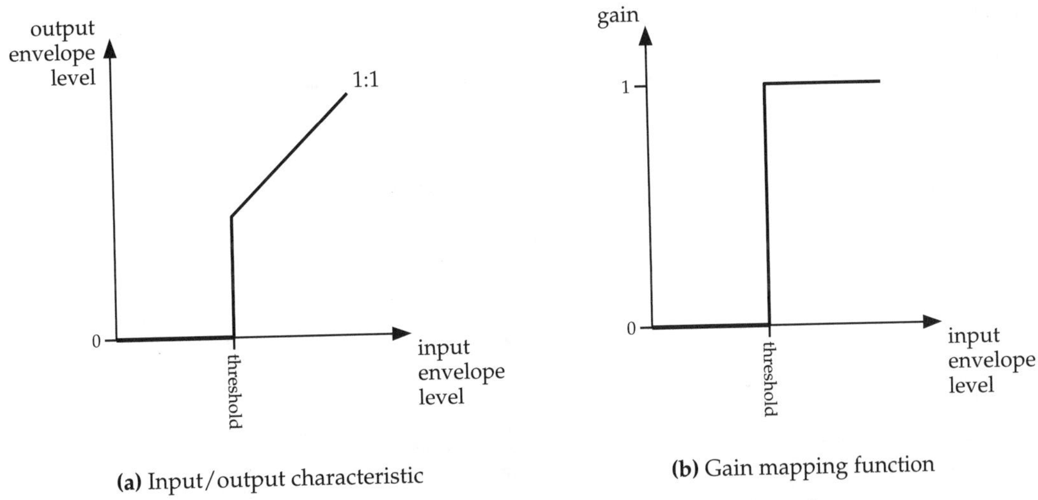

(a) Input/output characteristic

(b) Gain mapping function

Figure 11.10 Simple noise gate functions (linear)

This achieves the desired effect of allowing large signals through the gate, but blocking those with an input envelope level below the threshold value. The gain mapping function for the simple gate can be described by algorithm 11.1.

11.2.3 Improvements to the Simple Form

Figure 11.8 is fairly unsophisticated and can produce quite coarse results. A number of improvements can be made to the technique.

Decibel Conversion and Gate Range Control

It is common for dynamics processors to work in decibels rather than linear units. This relates more appropriately to the way in which humans perceive amplitude. Figure 11.11 illustrates an extended version of figure 11.8, with conversions to and from decibels either side of the mapping function in the sidechain. The conversion functions are those described in equations 5.2 and 5.3 (p.113).

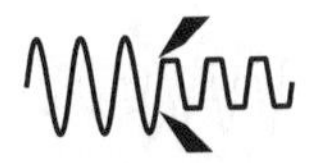

Algorithm 11.1 – Simple noise gate gain mapping function

input : envelope level x (⩾ 0)
output: output gain y

if x > threshold **then**
  y = 1
else
  y = 0

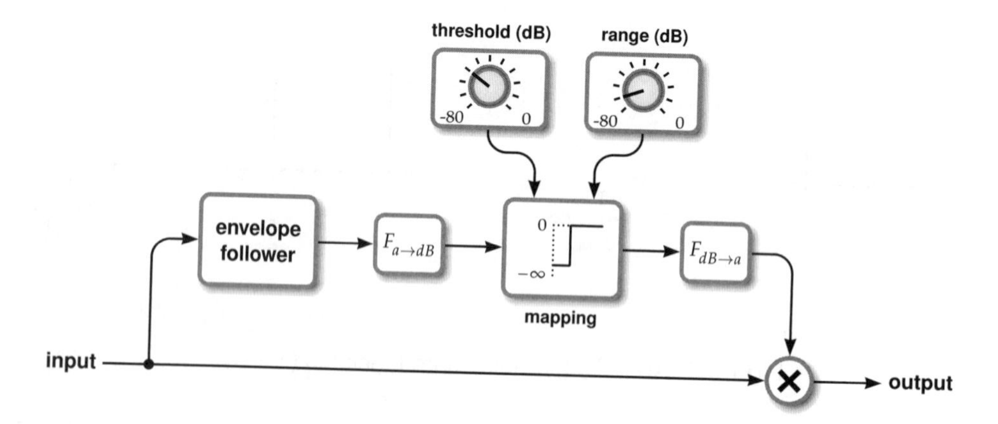

Figure 11.11 Noise gate form with decibel conversion and gate range control

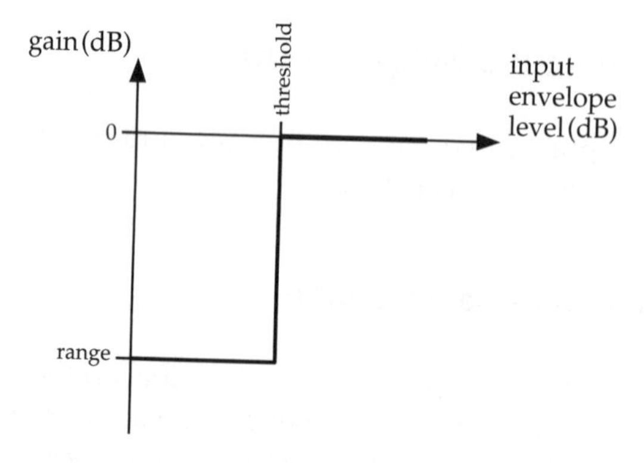

Figure 11.12 Noise gate gain mapping function (in decibels)

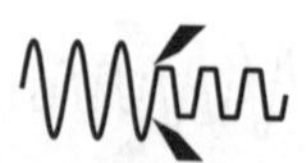

The decibel conversions mean that the mapping function uses values from $-\infty$dB (equivalent to a linear value of 0) to 0dB (equivalent to a linear value of 1). The additional feature in figure 11.11 is the *range* control, which determines the gain value when the gate is closed. This is a useful adjustment, as completely zeroing the signal can sound less natural than merely reducing its amplitude. Figure 11.12 and algorithm 11.2 illustrate the gain mapping function in decibels with a gate range control.

Algorithm 11.2 – Noise gate gain mapping function in decibels with range

input : envelope level (dB) x
output: output gain (dB) y

if x > threshold **then**
  y = 0
else
  y = range

Envelope Followers and Fine Tuning

Figure 11.13 includes a second envelope follower to add flexibility compared to the previous designs. The two envelope followers have different roles in achieving the desired variation in the gain factor multiplied into the output. Envelope follower 1 must be configured to achieve a clean transition across the threshold level. If there is insufficient smoothing at that stage then the gate will open and close multiple times in quick succession, causing audible "crackling" in the output, which is illustrated in figure 11.14.

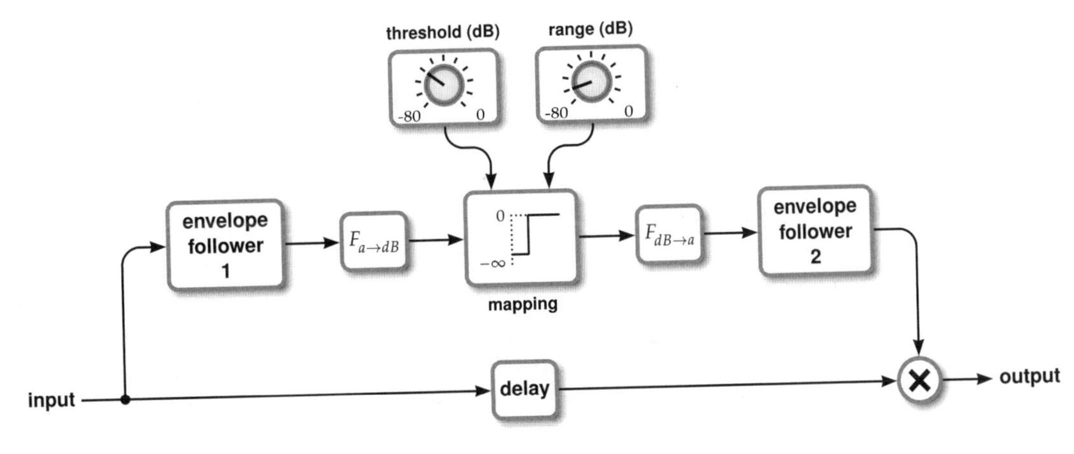

Figure 11.13 Noise gate form with two envelope followers

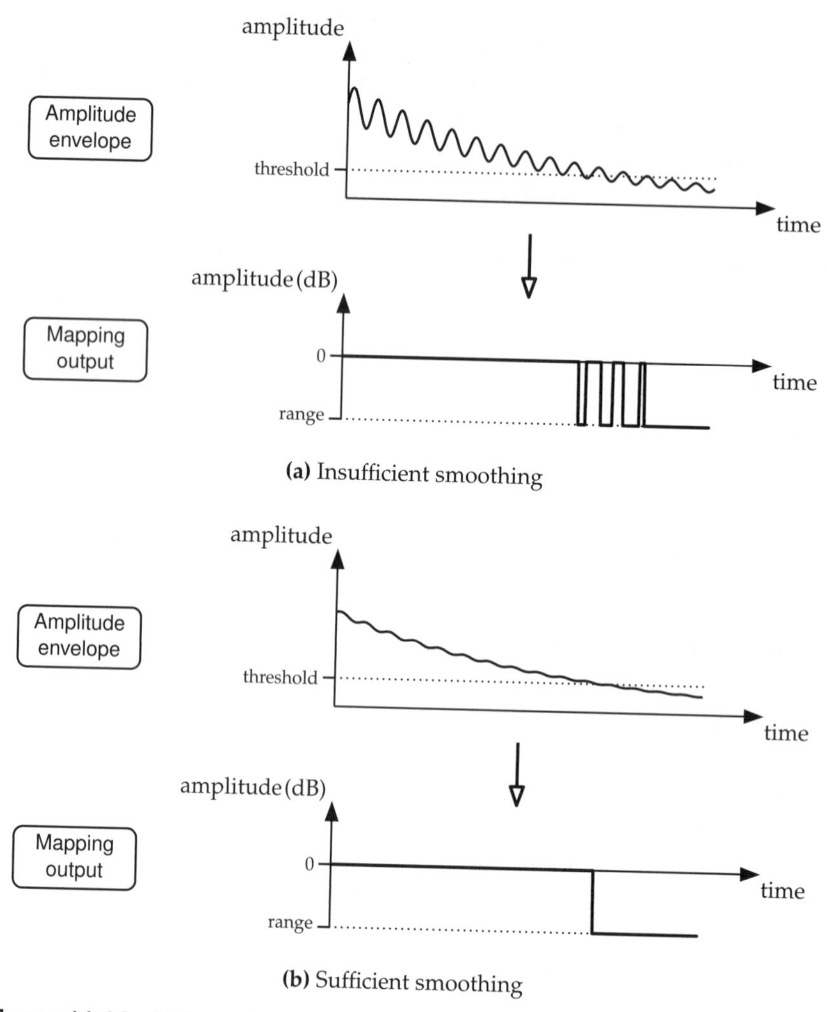

Figure 11.14 Noise gate operation with different input envelope smoothing

Increased smoothing of the amplitude envelope can be associated with slower reaction to changes of input level, as described in §8.3 (p.245). For example, if envelope follower 1 responds too slowly to changes in the input signal, then the gate might fail to open sufficiently quickly for a percussive sound to pass through the process without part of the attack portion being removed. It is also the case that different designs of envelope follower produce different output levels for the same input (such as the difference between peak and RMS levels), which might affect the choice of threshold.

No matter how much the input amplitude envelope is smoothed by envelope follower 1, the mapping function will always produce sharp edges in the gain function when the gate opens and closes, which can produce audible clicks. The role of envelope follower 2 is to allow control over the rate of change. Typically a gate will be configured to open (*attack*) rapidly and close (*release*) more slowly, such that percussive onsets are allowed through unchanged and decays fade away rather than being cut-off suddenly. Alternatively, a gate that opens slowly will allow reshaping of the onset portion of a sound. To achieve this control implies choosing a design for envelope follower 2 that allows separate control of attack and release times. The minimum required values of attack or release time are likely to be 1ms or less. The maximum values could be 1 second or more.

A further element included in figure 11.13 is a delay in the main signal path that compensates for the response time of the sidechain, and is sometimes called a *lookahead* feature. Without this delay it is possible that the gate will not open sufficiently early that the whole of a percussive attack will reach the output. Generally a very short delay (a few milliseconds or less) is sufficient, and can be adjusted by ear for best effect.

Different envelope followers respond in slightly different ways to a step change in the input (as considered in §8.3, p.245) and so influence the audible results of a dynamics process. With a delay in the main signal path and two envelope followers, there are quite a few underlying process parameters that most users will not wish to adjust individually. It might be appropriate to select suitable fixed values, therefore, or create mappings from a pair of attack and release controls to multiple underlying parameters.

Another possible improvement is to use filtering in the sidechain before envelope follower 1. This can be used to tune the response of the gate to a particular part of the input sound (such as the low frequencies associated with a kick drum) and reduce the influence of other instruments that are also in the signal (such as spill picked up by a microphone). See §11.4.2 (p.364) for an example of how this can be achieved.

11.2.4 Additional Techniques

There are a number of ways of adapting the noise gate technique to achieve results that are not necessarily to do with the attenuation of background noise.

Envelope Modification

A noise gate allows the amplitude envelope of a sound to be modified. Varying the attack time causes the gate to open at different rates. For example, a long attack time will soften the attack portion of the envelope by reshaping the onset at the start of the sound. This is particularly clear with percussive sounds. Alternatively, a high threshold and a short release time can be used to shorten the decay of a percussive sound.

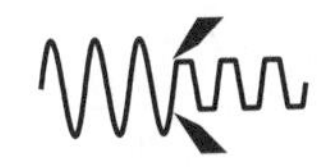

A related effect is *gated reverb*, which is achieved by applying a noise gate after a strong reverberation effect. This allows a powerful wash of reverberant sound that ends suddenly, rather than decaying slowly (as might be expected with a very reverberant acoustic space). This has often been used as a musical effect.

Separate Keying

Figure 11.15 illustrates a noise gate where the sidechain and main signal path have been split. The sidechain processing is the same as seen in previous examples, and input B (the sidechain signal) is often known as the *key input*.

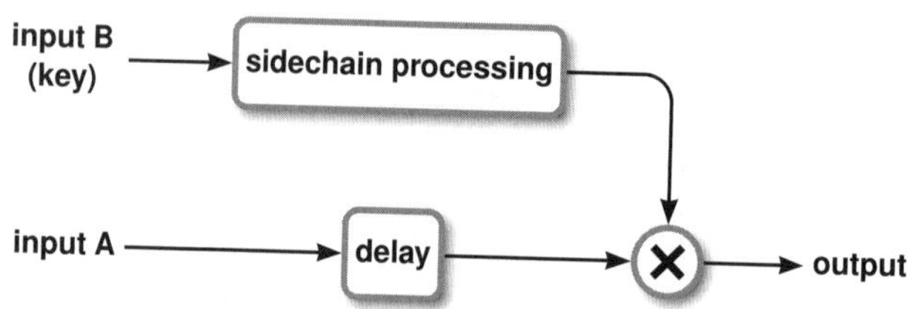

Figure 11.15 Separately keyed noise gate

The purpose of this form is to use one sound to control the amplitude of another. For example, a real snare might be used as input B, and a synthesized continuous noise sound as input A, allowing a burst of noise to be produced in time with the snare sound, which could be mixed with the actual snare afterwards to produce a modified sound character. Alternatively, it might be used to emphasise one sound (say a bass guitar) when another is present (say a kick drum). The range control determines the depth of the gating effect, and so the amount of attenuation of input A when the gate is closed.

Ducking

Ducking uses the same structural form as a noise gate, but a reversed gain mapping function, as shown in figure 11.16. The mapping means that low input envelope levels produce 0dB gain (output the same as the input). Above the threshold the ducker closes and the gain is set to the range level. This function will normally be used with separate signal keying (figure 11.15).

Ducking allows the presence of one sound (input B in figure 11.15) to reduce the level of another (input A). For example, in a radio broadcast it is conventional that the music level is attenuated when the presenter is speaking. By making the presenter's voice input B and the music input A, this will happen automatically. Again, a suitable range setting is required; the music should be moderately attenuated, rather than disappearing entirely. Radio broadcasts are usually two channel stereo, so two input A paths controlled by a single gain value from the sidechain will be required. The problem with this technique

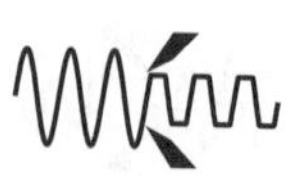

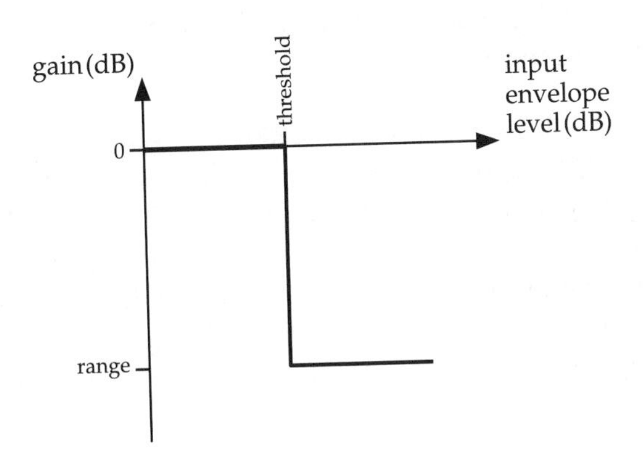

Figure 11.16 Ducking gain mapping function

is that unintentional sound in the presenter's microphone (a cough, or an off-microphone conversation) will cause the ducking to occur. As such, manual control of faders or a more complex scheme might be preferable.

11.3 Compressors

11.3.1 Main Principles

A *compressor* is designed to reduce the dynamic range of a signal, by attenuating the input signal when its amplitude envelope is above a threshold, but leaving the signal unchanged when the amplitude envelope is below the threshold (sometimes called *downward* compression). As with the noise gate, it achieves this by analysing the input signal and mapping to a varying gain value that is multiplied by the input. Uses of compressors are varied and their configuration depends on context and input material. Some typical uses of a compressor include:

- Attenuating amplitude peaks such that the signal can subsequently be amplified to a higher average level (without clipping).
- Reducing the amplitude variation in an uneven musical performance.
- Deliberately manipulating the character of a sound as it changes over time.

Like the noise gate, the compression process could be achieved by a human manually adjusting the gain of the signal (figure 11.4, p.341). The compressor also satisfies two of the reasons for automating processes described in §11.1.1; firstly that a human would struggle to react as quickly and as accurately as an automated system, and secondly that the task is both boring and repetitive. It is worth noting that what is being discussed in this

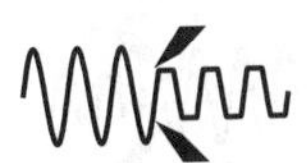

section is audio **dynamic range** compression, which should not be confused with audio **data** compression (data rate reduction).

Compression uses amplitude envelope-based gain reduction to reduce the overall amplitude of the signal. Clipping distortion (as described in Chapter 7) and compression have the common property of affecting dynamic range. However, the results are usually different, as illustrated in figure 11.17. The figure shows an input signal whose amplitude envelope ramps up to a maximum and down to zero again. Hard clipping prevents the signal exceeding a certain value by setting all sample values beyond the clipping point to that value, distorting the waveform. However, compression generally preserves the original waveform shape.

The strongest example of standard compression is *limiting*, where the output amplitude envelope is prevented from exceeding the threshold. The further the input envelope rises above the threshold, the lower the gain value must become to keep the resulting output at that level. Table 11.1 shows example gain values that reduce amplitude levels such that they do not exceed a threshold value of 0.125. Figure 11.18 shows a corresponding plot of gain values with varying input level.

Input amplitude envelope level	Linear gain value to keep at the threshold or below	Envelope level after gain applied
0.0625	1	$0.0625 \times 1 = 0.0625$
0.125	1	$0.125 \times 1 = 0.125$
0.25	$0.125/0.25 = 0.5$	$0.25 \times 0.5 = 0.125$
0.5	$0.125/0.5 = 0.25$	$0.5 \times 0.25 = 0.125$
1	$0.125/1 = 0.125$	$1 \times 0.125 = 0.125$

Table 11.1 Linear gain values to achieve limiting (threshold = 0.125)

The *compression ratio* describes how the output envelope changes relative to the input envelope. With a ratio of 2:1, each 2dB increase in input amplitude envelope level above the threshold produces a 1dB increase in output amplitude level. Similarly, at a ratio of 5:1, a 5dB increase in input level above the threshold will result in a 1dB increase in output level. Limiting is theoretically a ratio of ∞:1, although a ratio of at least 10:1 is severe enough to be regarded as a limiter in many circumstances. Figure 11.17 shows the difference between limiting and 2:1 compression applied to the simple input signal.

The larger the compression ratio, the more obvious the audible effect will be. However, it also depends on the position of the threshold. Limiting is often used with a high threshold, such that only the most extreme amplitude envelope peaks will be caught. This is useful for preventing amplitudes reaching the signal limits of the system. A more subtle

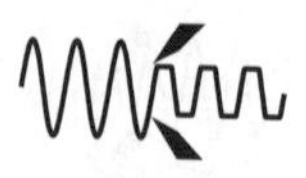

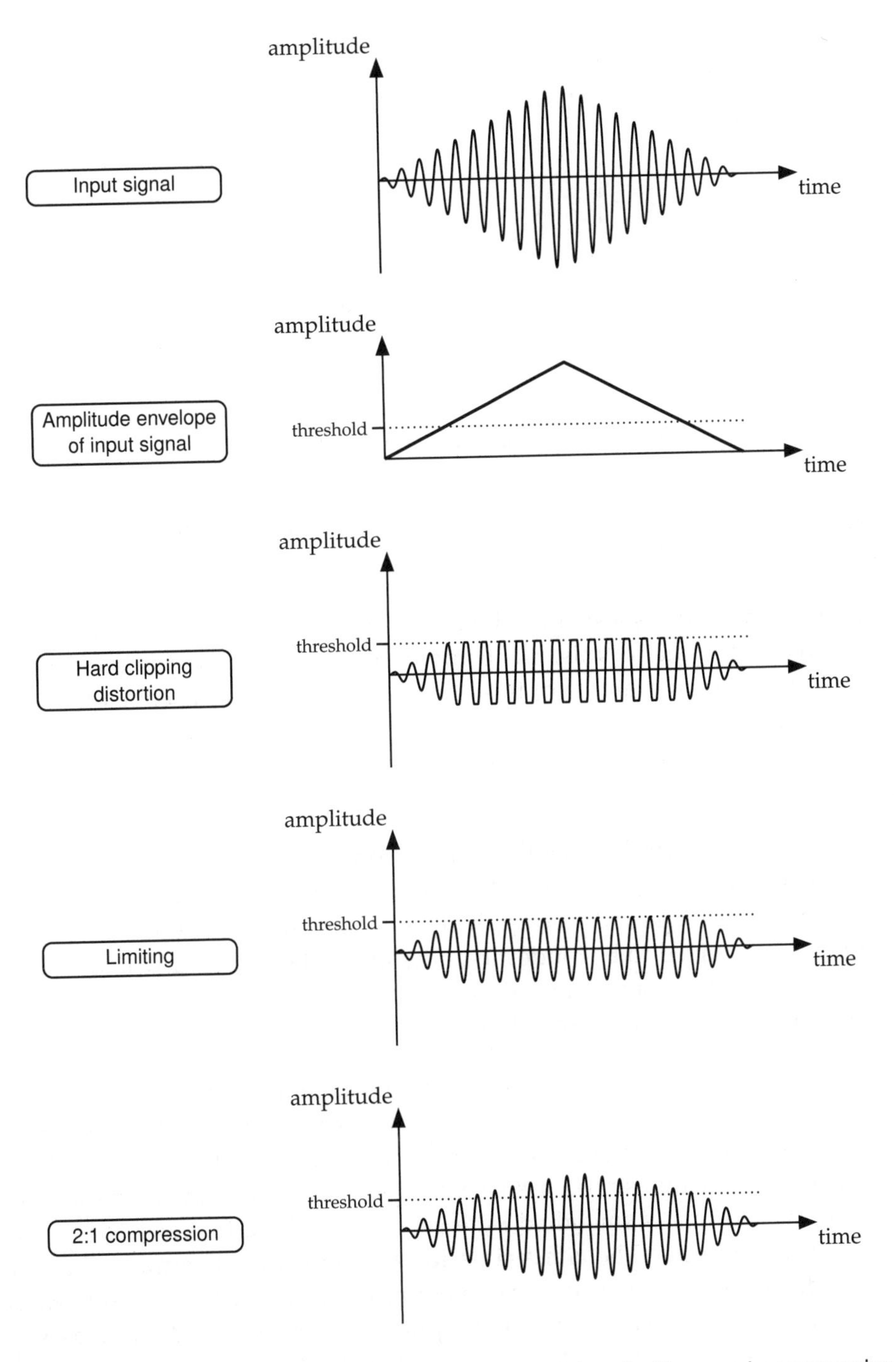

Figure 11.17 Comparison of hard clipping distortion, limiting, and compression

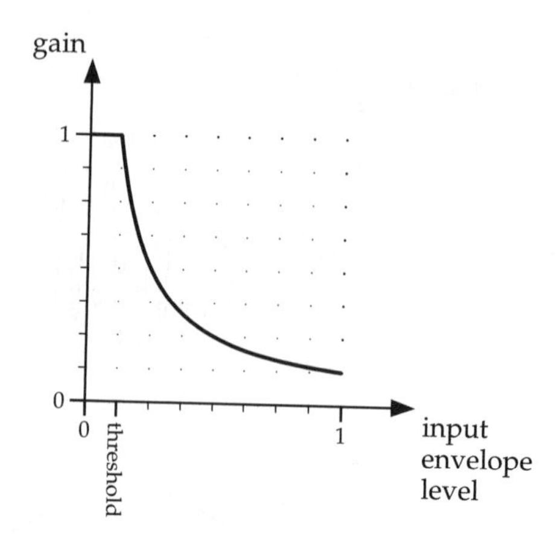

Figure 11.18 Limiter gain function (linear)

compression ratio, such as 2:1 can be used at lower threshold values without the effect being as audibly severe. A low threshold and high ratio will lead to heavy compression.

The result of compression is a smaller dynamic range, and also a lower overall average amplitude. To compensate for this, it is common to apply *makeup gain* after the process. Figure 11.19 illustrates an example of this. As usual, the amplitude envelope level of the input sound is determined, and compression is applied above the threshold (at a ratio of 4:1 in this example). Afterwards the signal is multiplied by a value greater than 1, in order to restore the original peak amplitude.

Although the peak amplitude after the application of makeup gain is the same as it was originally, the average amplitude afterwards is greater than in the original signal. Reducing the dynamic range and then applying makeup gain is therefore likely to produce an output that is perceived to be louder than the input. However, it will also reduce the dynamic variation in the sound, amplify the background noise (as well as the wanted signal), and reshape the amplitude envelope.

In a similar manner to the noise gate, the mapping function can produce sharp edges in the output gain values. A second envelope follower can again be employed to smooth the transitions in gain value in order to minimise audible anomalies (or to create musical effects). Figure 11.20 demonstrates a sharp stepped envelope that results in a stepped gain function. When this is smoothed by a second envelope follower the output gain transitions are less abrupt. The *attack* time for a compressor determines how quickly the gain is reduced when the input envelope amplitude increases, and the *release* time is how quickly the gain increases when the input envelope amplitude decreases. This is the opposite way around to the gate attack/release effect. The shape of the attack and release depends on the chosen envelope follower algorithm.

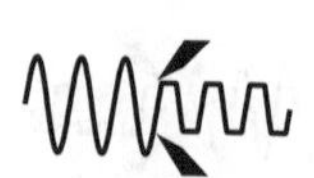

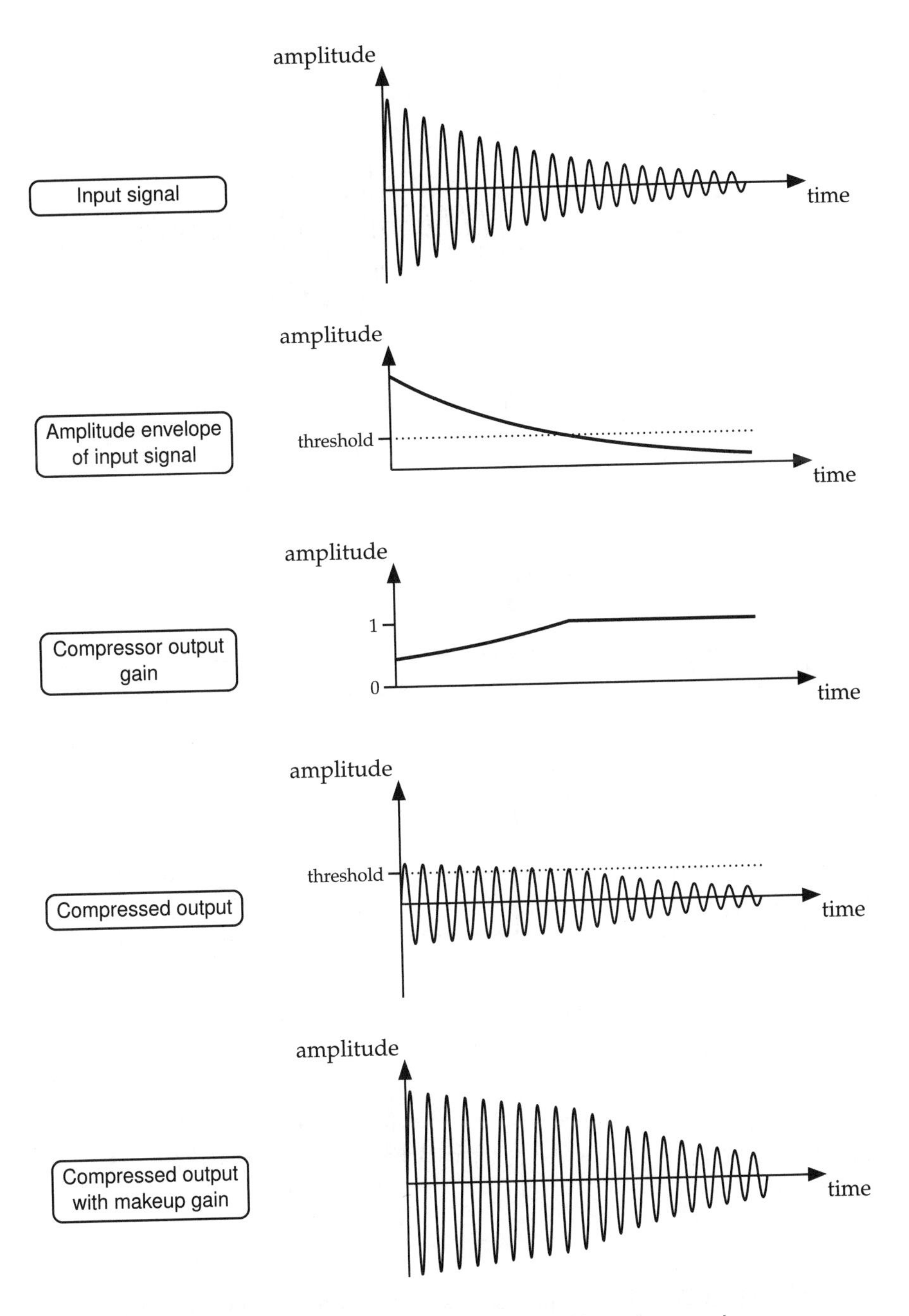

Figure 11.19 4:1 compression with makeup gain

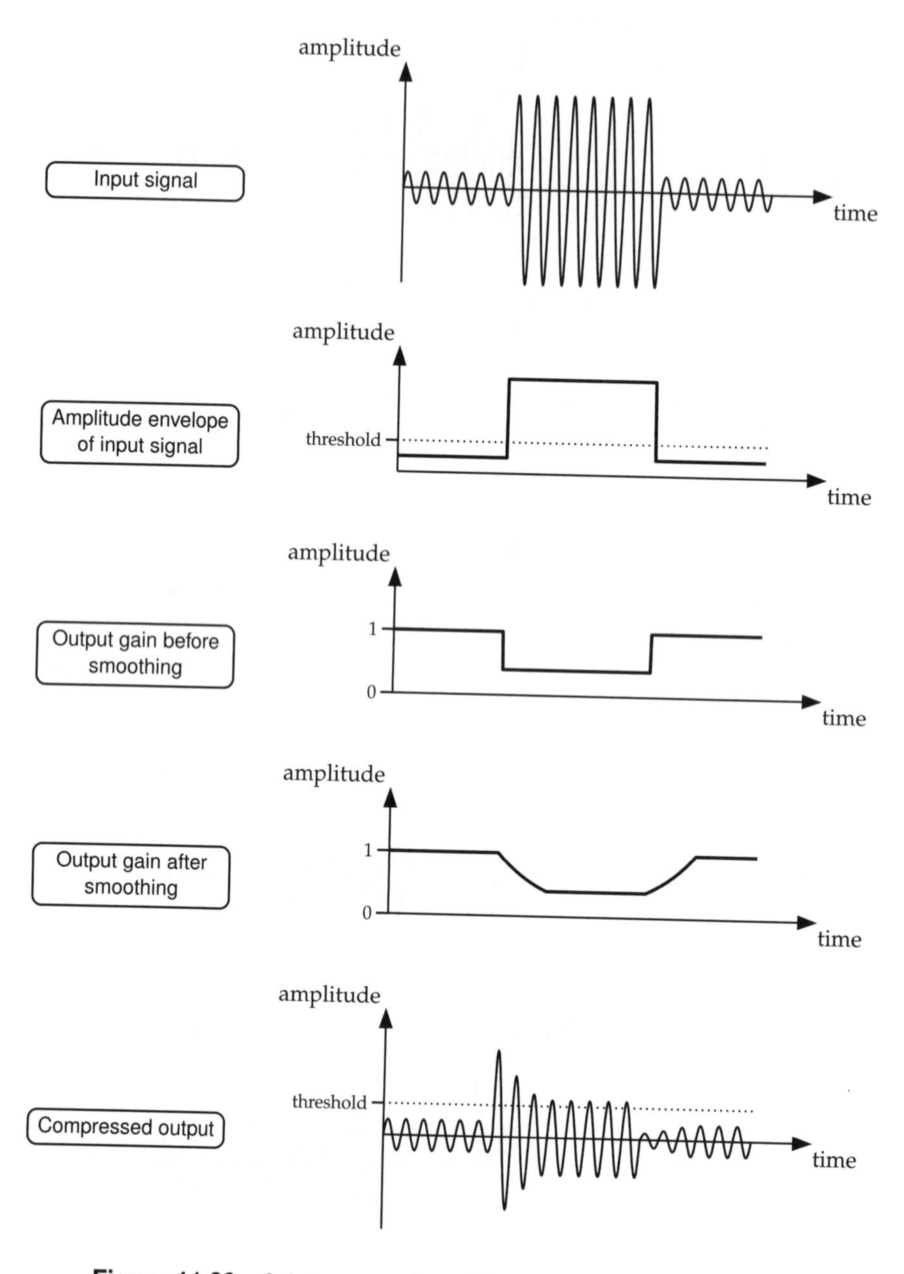

Figure 11.20 6:1 compression with attack and release effects

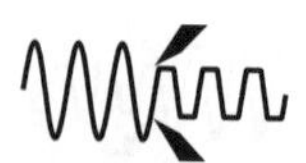

In terms of using attack and release controls, a short attack time is useful for catching peaks that might cause overload. A longer attack time can be used to prevent the attack portion of highly dynamic sounds being over-dampened. Similarly, the release time can be used to prevent overly rapid changes from compressed to uncompressed states. Typical attack times are from 1ms to 100ms, typical release times are from 10ms to 1s.

11.3.2 Compressor Form

Figure 11.21 shows the block diagram form of a compressor. This has similarities to the noise gate shown in figure 11.13 (p.349):

- The first envelope follower measures the amplitude level of the input.
- The result is converted to decibels as described by equation 5.2 (p.113).
- The mapping block produces a gain value (in decibels) from the envelope level. The main differences from the noise gate are that the mapping function is a different shape, and it has a ratio control as well as a threshold.
- The result is converted from decibels to linear units as described by equation 5.3 (p.113).
- The second envelope follower is used to smooth variations in gain value, with suitable control of attack and release.
- The resulting gain value is multiplied into the signal path, followed by the application of the makeup gain.

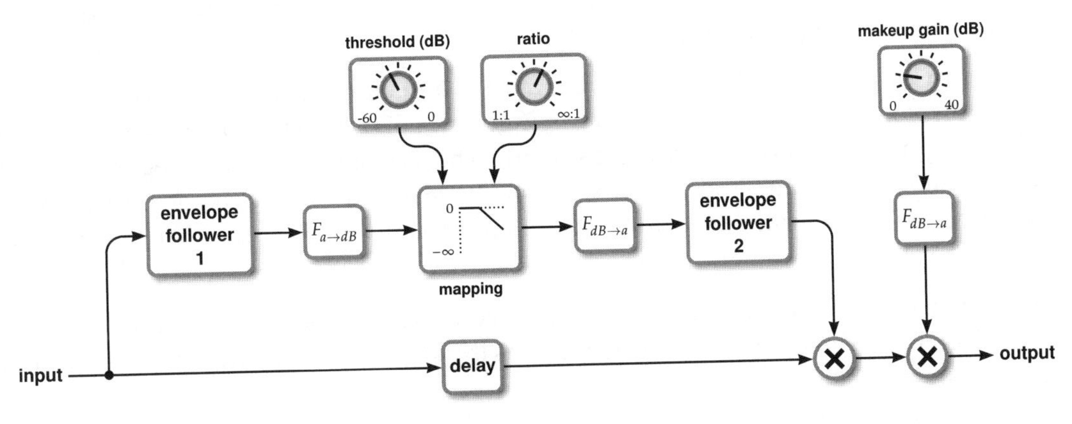

Figure 11.21 Compressor form

Similarly to the noise gate, the compressor input/output characteristics express the behaviour of the whole process (excluding the makeup gain) in terms of amplitude envelope levels. There are multiple lines to illustrate different values of the ratio parameter.

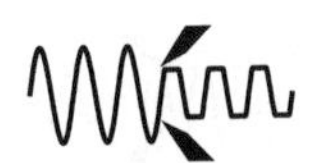

Figure 11.22a shows the simplest form, known as a *hard knee* style, with two linear regions:

- For input envelope amplitudes below the threshold level, the output envelope level is the same as the input. When the input envelope level is at the threshold, then so is the output, as the gradient of the line is 1.
- For input levels above the threshold, the gradient of the line determines how rapidly the output level increases as the input level increases. When the ratio is set to ∞:1 (limiting), then the output envelope level is prevented from exceeding the threshold level. When the ratio is set to 1:1, then the output envelope level is the same as the input. When the ratio is R:1, then (above the threshold) an increase of R decibels in input envelope level results in an increase of 1dB in output envelope level.

The input/output characteristic must be converted to a gain mapping function for use in the mapping block in figure 11.21. The two functions are related by the following equation:

$$\text{gain}_{\text{dB}} = \text{output}_{\text{dB}} - \text{input}_{\text{dB}} \tag{11.1}$$

As shown in figure 11.23a, there are two linear regions in the hard knee gain mapping function:

- For input envelope amplitudes below the threshold level, the output gain is 0dB (which translates to a linear multiplier value of 1).
- Above the threshold there is a gradual decrease in gain as the input envelope level increases (for ratios other than 1:1). The most rapid fall is the limiting (∞:1) case, where each 1dB increase in input level above the threshold produces a 1dB decrease in gain (a 45 degree downward angle).

In many cases it is desirable to have a less abrupt transition between the two regions of the compressor functions. The *soft knee* form (figures 11.22b and 11.23b) achieves a gradual change of gradient that is audibly more smooth. The size of the transition region is called the *knee width*, which can be adjusted to achieve the required audible characteristics. Note that with a soft knee form there will be an amount of compression below the threshold as well as above it.

The following equation is the gain function for a compressor, where x is the input envelope level, T is the threshold, the ratio is R:1, and W is the knee width. All quantities apart from the ratio are in decibels:

$$g = \begin{cases} 0 & \text{if} \quad x \leqslant \left(T - \frac{W}{2}\right) \\ \frac{1}{2W}\left(\frac{1}{R} - 1\right)\left(x - T + \frac{W}{2}\right)^2 & \text{if} \quad \left(T - \frac{W}{2}\right) < x \leqslant \left(T + \frac{W}{2}\right) \\ \left(\frac{1}{R} - 1\right)(x - T) & \text{if} \quad x > \left(T + \frac{W}{2}\right) \end{cases} \tag{11.2}$$

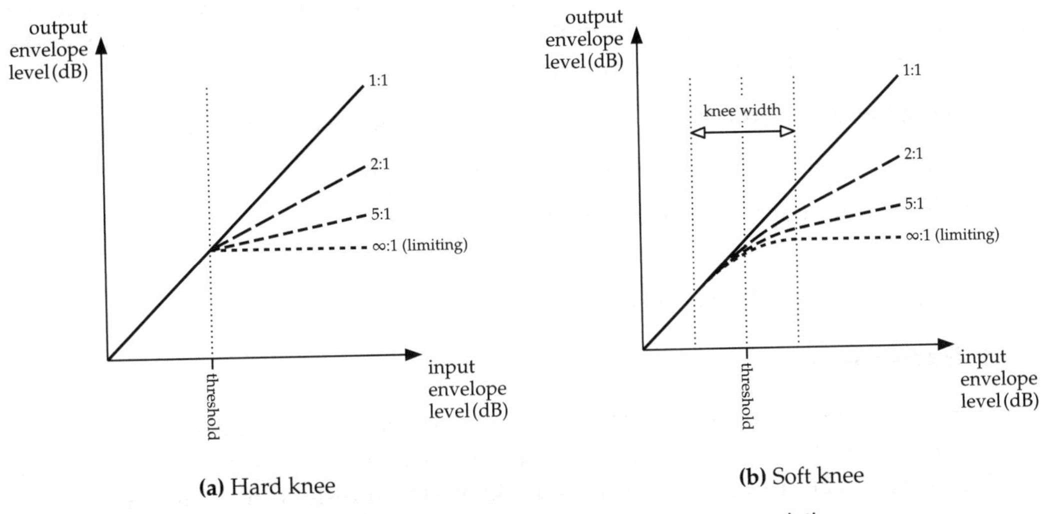

(a) Hard knee

(b) Soft knee

Figure 11.22 Compressor input/output characteristics

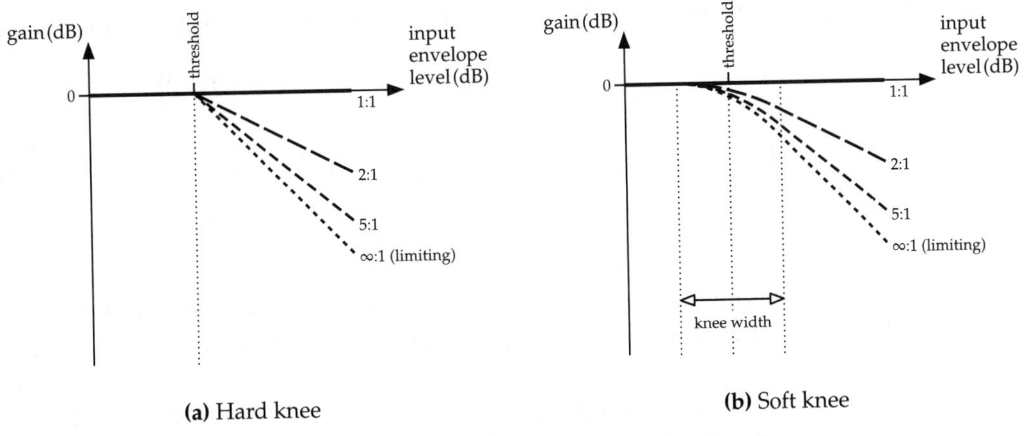

(a) Hard knee

(b) Soft knee

Figure 11.23 Compressor gain mapping functions

Reducing the knee width (W) to 0dB removes the middle line of the equation and produces a hard knee result.

As well as changing the threshold, ratio, and knee width parameters, there is considerable potential for modifying the behaviour of the different elements of the compressor, and so the audible results of the process. For example:

- Varying the attack and release time parameters for the envelope followers.
- Changing the algorithms used for the envelope followers.
- Modifying the shape of the mapping function.

11.4 Further Techniques

11.4.1 Expanders

Expanders are used to increase dynamic range, whereas a compressor is used to decrease it. An *upward expander* has the opposite effect to a compressor, as shown by the input/output characteristics in figure 11.24a. Below the threshold, the ratio is 1:1 so the output is the same as the input. Above the threshold the ratio is 1:R, where a 1dB increase in the input envelope level results in an R decibel increase in output level. Upward expansion is not a common studio technique, but with care (values of R close to 1) can be used to increase the dynamic variation in a sound. If the peak signal level is already high, then it is necessary to attenuate the signal before applying this technique.

Figure 11.25a shows the gain mapping function for an upward expander. This can be described by the following equation, where x is the input envelope level, T is the threshold, the ratio is 1:R, and W is the knee width. All quantities apart from the ratio are in decibels:

$$g = \begin{cases} 0 & \text{if} \quad x \leqslant \left(T - \frac{W}{2}\right) \\ \frac{1}{2W}(R-1)\left(x - T + \frac{W}{2}\right)^2 & \text{if} \quad \left(T - \frac{W}{2}\right) < x \leqslant \left(T + \frac{W}{2}\right) \\ (R-1)(x-T) & \text{if} \quad x > \left(T + \frac{W}{2}\right) \end{cases} \tag{11.3}$$

A *downward expander* is more common than the upward form, and is often simply called an "expander". Figure 11.24b shows some example input/output characteristics. Above the threshold the ratio is 1:1, so the output is the same as the input. Below the threshold the ratio is 1:R, where a 1dB decrease in input envelope level results in an R decibel decrease in output level. A downward expander is, in effect, a progressive version of a noise gate. A gate is a downward expander with a ratio of 1:∞ and a knee width of 0dB. A downward expander can be useful for gradually attenuating the signal as the amplitude decreases. In some cases that can be more effective than an abrupt gate effect.

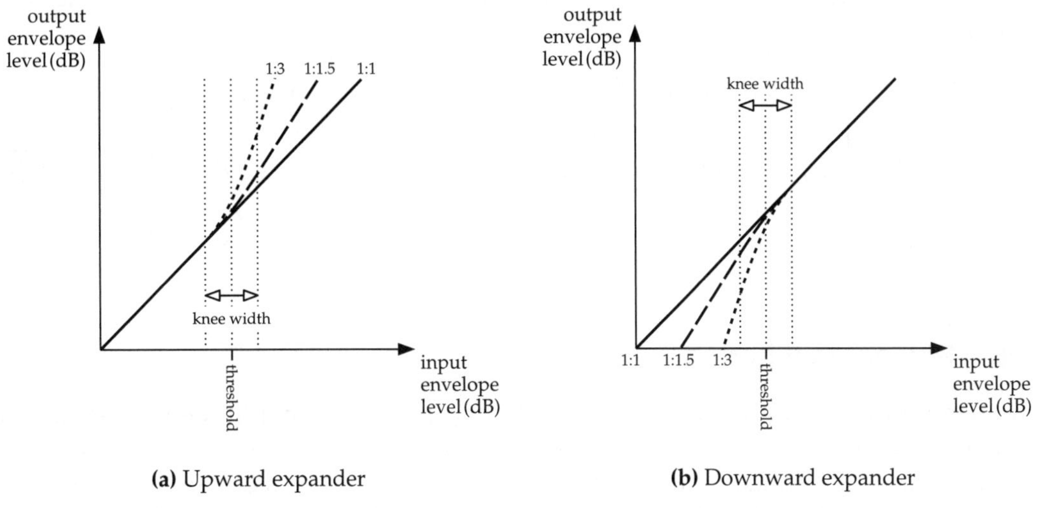

Figure 11.24 Expander input/output characteristics

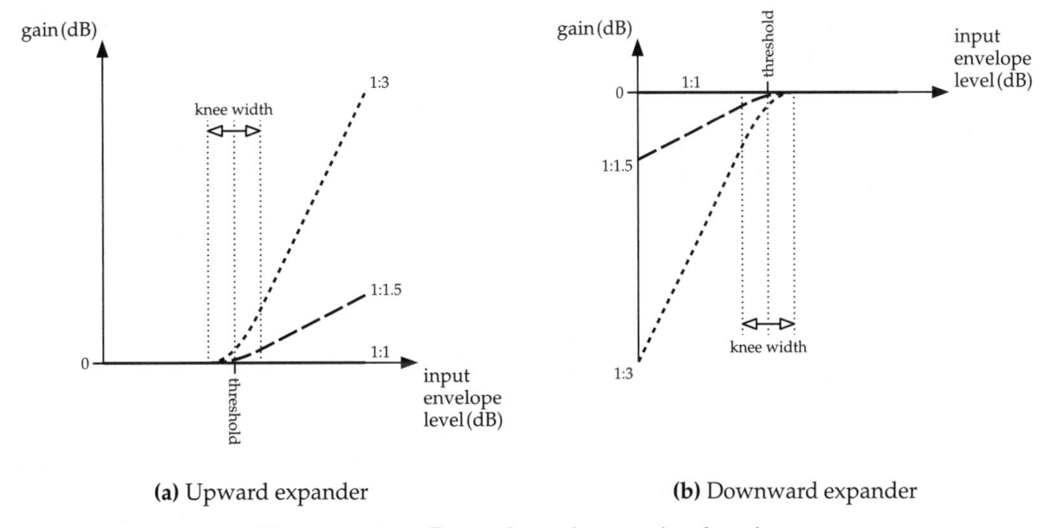

Figure 11.25 Expander gain mapping functions

Figure 11.25b shows the gain mapping function for a downward expander. This can be described by the following equation, where x is the input envelope level, T is the threshold, the ratio is 1:R, and W is the knee width. All quantities apart from the ratio are in decibels:

$$g = \begin{cases} (1-R)(T-x) & \text{if} \quad x \leqslant \left(T - \frac{W}{2}\right) \\ \frac{1}{2W}(1-R)\left(T - x + \frac{W}{2}\right)^2 & \text{if} \quad \left(T - \frac{W}{2}\right) < x \leqslant \left(T + \frac{W}{2}\right) \\ 0 & \text{if} \quad x > \left(T + \frac{W}{2}\right) \end{cases} \tag{11.4}$$

11.4.2 Sidechain Filtering

It is often desirable for a dynamics process to respond to the amplitude of partials in a particular frequency range. To achieve this it is appropriate to use bandpass filtering in the sidechain, as illustrated in figure 11.26. Alternative filter types can also be used, such as a highpass filter. Note that the filtering does not affect the main signal path (through the delay block). The output switch allows three different signals to be heard at the output:

- The signal used in the sidechain (key listen position), such that the filter can be tuned by ear to the frequency region of interest.
- The processed signal.
- The original input signal (bypass position), such that it can be compared to the processed signal.

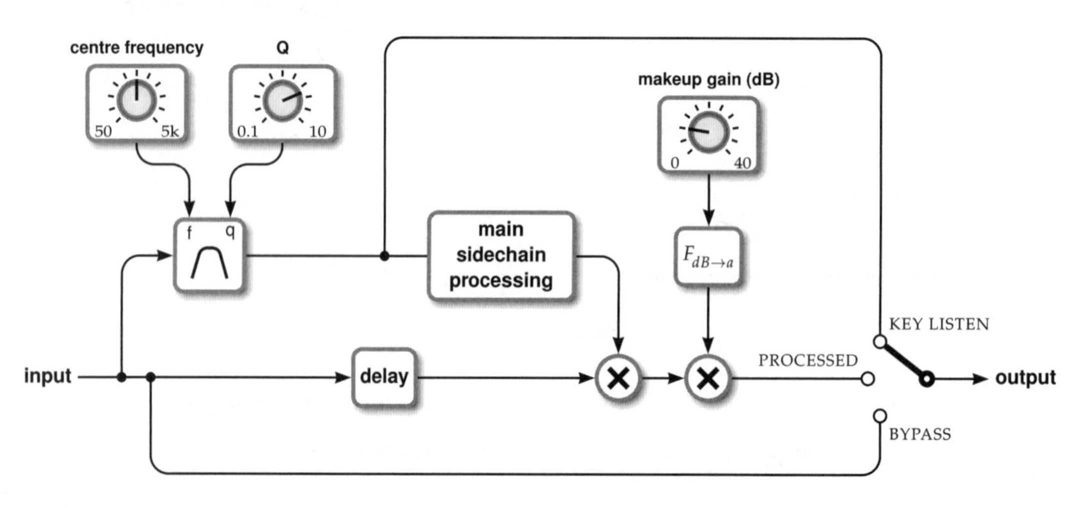

Figure 11.26 Dynamics process with sidechain filtering

Filtering in the sidechain is particularly useful where the input signal is not a single sound but a mix. In those cases certain parts of the signal can have an unwanted effect on the result. For example, when compressing a mixed rock or pop track, a loud kick drum sound can cause the entire mix to modulate up and down in amplitude. By tuning the filter away from the problem frequencies, this effect can be reduced.

Another use for sidechain filtering is to make the compressor act as a simple *de-esser*. A de-esser is designed to compress the output by a couple of decibels when sounds such as "s", "sh", and "f" are overly-prominent in a vocal signal. The sidechain filter can be tuned to the problematical frequency range and then used to cause a little compression when the relevant phonemes appear in the vocal signal. It can also be used to process other overly-prominent sounds in a similar way.

11.4.3 Combinations

Sometimes it is useful to employ multiple compressors in series or parallel, or multiple signal paths in a compression scheme, in order to achieve a blended effect. Figure 11.27 shows a simple *parallel compression* scheme. A typical configuration is heavy compression blended with the dry path to achieve a balance of the original dynamics with the processed character. The delay in the dry path is necessary to match any delay in the compressor, and so avoid comb filtering (as described in §6.4.4, p.183).

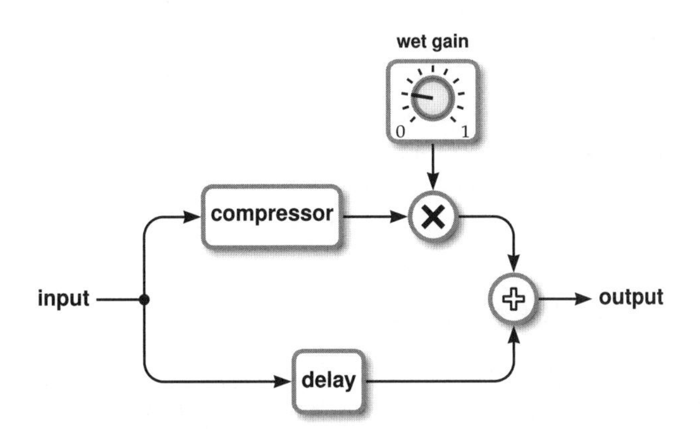

Figure 11.27 Simple parallel compression

Multi-band techniques use filters to separate the input signal into separate frequency bands that can be processed in different ways. For example, low and high frequencies could be processed by different compressors with different configurations, which enables optimum dynamic range to be achieved in each area of the frequency spectrum. It also addresses problems of interactions between the different frequency ranges, such as a high amplitude kick drum sound causing a whole mix to be affected. Some associated filtering techniques are described in §6.3.2 (p.159).

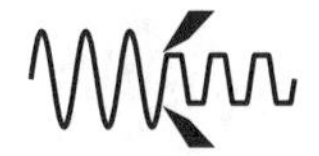

Dynamics processors such as noise gates and compressors are sometimes used in situations with multiple input channels. There are different ways of processing the signals in these cases:

- With different signals on each channel, such as a guitar on one and a snare drum on another, they might be processed independently. Separate processes with different configurations are used in order to achieve different results for each.
- Sometimes the channels can carry closely-related signals such as a stereo mix, or left and right microphone signals for a piano. If the channels are processed independently then an unstable stereo image might occur, as the gain values could be different on different channels. Therefore a common processing arrangement is required with the same control parameters and a common output gain value.

The idea in the second case is to derive a single gain value that can be multiplied by all of the channel signals. Typically there is a single sidechain whose input is a sum of the original input signals, or a sum of the envelope values for the input signals (from separate envelope followers), or by choosing the largest of the current envelope values for all the inputs.

11.4.4 Other Modifications

Dynamics processes create a gain value that is multiplied by the main signal path. It is possible to derive other control values from the amplitude envelope. For example, figure 11.28 modifies the centre frequency of a bandpass filter, achieving a region of frequency emphasis that follows the rise and fall of the amplitude envelope. The main sidechain processing is assumed to work in a similar way to the previous examples, creating a value between 0 and 1, which can then be scaled and offset to a range suitable for the filter. The form has similarities to figure 9.15 (p.277), but is controlled by the amplitude envelope rather than an oscillator.

There are several ways in which this form can be modified:

- The shape of the mapping function can be changed in the sidechain. This might produce either an upward or downward change of centre frequency with amplitude. It can also be shaped to give a progressive or a sudden change in frequency as the amplitude increases. The frequency change might be linear, or logarithmic with amplitude.
- Envelope follower attack and release effects might be used to create slower, or more rapid changes.
- A more complex filter arrangement might be used; for example, a parallel bank of filters whose centre frequencies are related to the master control signal by suitable multipliers.

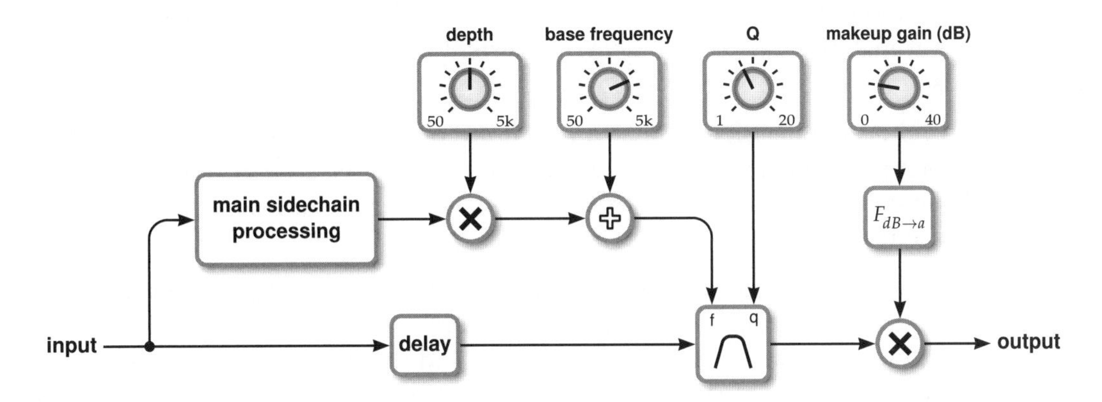

Figure 11.28 Envelope-controlled filter

It should be apparent that the ideas discussed in this chapter can be extended to any other analysis and modification process. The analysis results can be mapped to the control parameters associated with different modifiers, such as delay times, modulation depths, transfer function shape, and so on.

11.5 Developing Processes and Learning More

Of all the modifiers used commonly in music production and recording, dynamics processors are the ones that usually cause greatest confusion for novices. Confusion can occur in understanding the internal designs of the processes, and also their application and configuration in musical contexts. The concept of controlling dynamic range is quite straightforward, but there are a number of additional complicating factors:

- The processes can cause significant tonal changes, as well as changing amplitude dynamics.
- Dynamics processes can have long term effects (over many notes), and short term effects (such as affecting part of the onset of a sound event, or causing a decay to be modified), depending upon their configuration.
- Professional recording engineers often configure dynamics processes to achieve subtle changes that might not be instantly apparent to the casual listener, but which are very important to the overall character in the mix.
- The relationships between process parameters and perceived effects are not necessarily obvious.

- Configuration of control parameters depends greatly on the dynamic properties of the input material, rather than being consistent in effect when applied to different sounds.
- Low-level design decisions, such as the choice of envelope follower and curvature of the mapping function, can have an effect on the results. That means that different implementations can have quite different results when the user-level parameters are configured in the same way.

There are no obvious shortcuts in terms of learning how to use these processes. However, developing understanding of the use of noise gates and downward expanders is generally more straightforward than with compressors. A wide variety of standard and third-party dynamics processor plugins are available for Digital Audio Workstations. Once an understanding of their configuration has been gained and the subtle audible effects can be identified, it is useful to examine the results of different designs. For example, it can be interesting to compare a compressor that is designed to be precise and transparent against one that models an analogue circuit design. The latter implementation will usually create significant tonal change and deviate from standard theoretical behaviour. In terms of configuration and creative methods, advice is available in the following books:

Case, Alexander U. 2007. *Sound FX: Unlocking the Creative Potential of Recording Studio Effects*. Burlington, MA: Focal Press.

Katz, Bob. 2015. *Mastering Audio: The Art and the Science (Third Edition)*. Burlington, MA: Focal Press.

The following sources provide some more advanced material that relates to this chapter, which can be used for further study:

Giannoulis, Dimitrios, Michael Massberg, and Joshua D. Reiss. 2012. "Digital Dynamic Range Compressor Design – A Tutorial and Analysis." *Journal of the Audio Engineering Society* 60:6:399–408.

McNally, G.W. 1984. "Dynamic Range Control of Digital Audio Signals." *Journal of the Audio Engineering Society* 32:5:316–327.

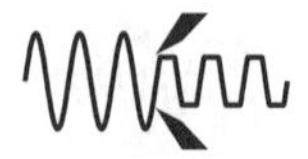

12

Frequency Domain Methods

12.1 Time Domain and Frequency Domain Processes

12.1.1 Introduction

The majority of audio processes are constructed to modify and synthesize audio data in terms of time domain signals (amplitude varying over time). This form of audio data is analogous to the variations in air pressure that are received by the human auditory system. The human auditory system, however, is sensitive to the nature of the frequency domain partials that compose the time domain signal (as described in Chapters 3 and 4). In some cases it can be useful to directly manipulate the frequency domain form of sounds, when a time domain approach would be awkward, or produce side effects.

Changes to signals in the time domain often have consequences in the frequency domain. A typical distortion effect based on a transfer function (as described in Chapter 7) takes a time domain input and produces a time domain output, but has an effect on the amplitude of partials in the frequency spectrum. It is not the case that each partial in the frequency domain is identified and processed individually in a typical distortion effect. Similarly, amplitude modulation (Chapter 20) can change the frequency domain form of a sound, but the process itself is based on time domain process blocks.

The principal advantage of processing in the frequency domain is the ability to control the dimensions of frequency, time, and amplitude separately. This can provide more control than other process techniques. For example, changing the pitch of signals in the time domain can cause side effects, as described in §15.3.1 (p.473) and §22.2.2 (p.620). Figure 12.1 shows two examples of how independent control of frequency and time can allow frequency partials to be scaled in one dimension without affecting the other. The figure illustrates scaling applied consistently across each dimension. There is also the potential for more sophisticated and non-linear operations.

There are two significant issues with frequency domain methods:

- There is often a significant computational load associated with them. Audio data at the input or output of an audio process is most likely to be in the time domain. Transformation between the time and frequency domains is required to directly manipulate frequency partials, as shown in figure 12.2.
- The process of transforming into the frequency domain, manipulating the data, and transforming back to the time domain can add unintended audible artefacts and some delay to the signal (latency). Care is required in configuring the processes to minimise these issues.

The advantages of frequency domain methods outweigh the issues in many of the examples described later.

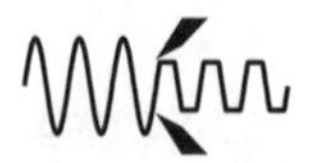

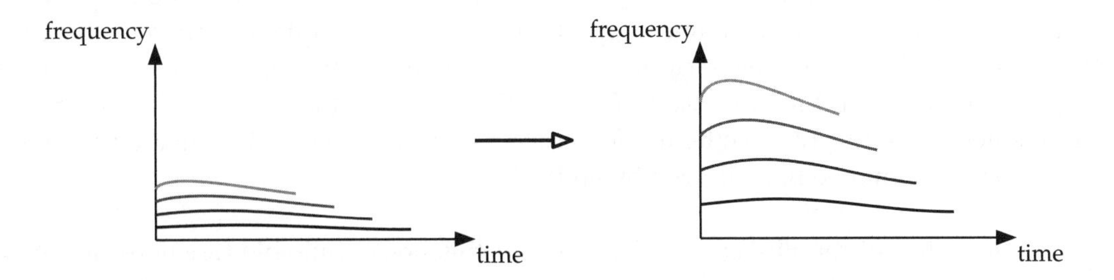

(a) Scaling frequencies without changing location in time

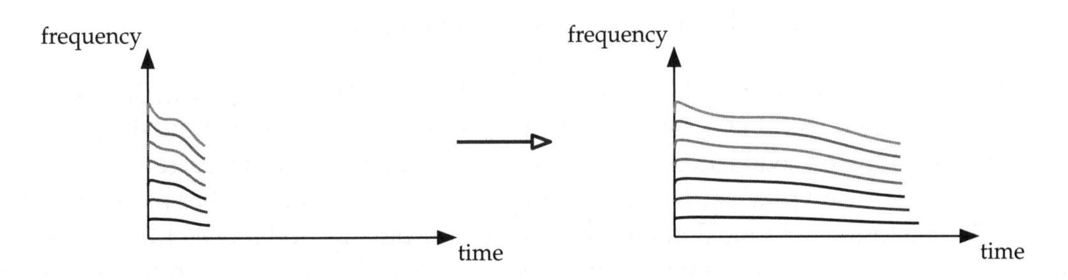

(b) Scaling development over time without changing frequencies

Figure 12.1 Modifying partials in the frequency domain (spectrogram plots)

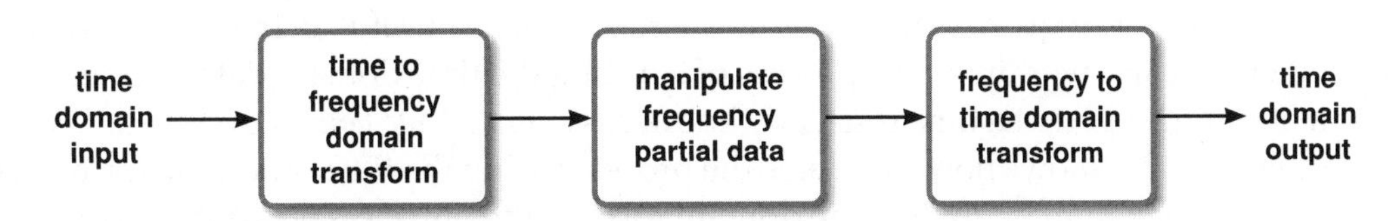

Figure 12.2 Frequency domain basic method

12.1.2 Fourier Transform Basics

Any periodic function can be expressed as a summation of harmonically-related sinusoids (sine and cosine terms) of appropriate frequencies and amplitudes. It is possible to use Fourier series mathematical techniques to establish this information. This can be used, for example, to calculate the frequency domain form of standard waveform shapes such as sawtooth, square, and triangle (§4.2.2, p.79).

Rather than working with mathematical functions, a normal audio process will deal with time-varying discrete sample values. In those cases the *Discrete Fourier Transform (DFT)* is used, which is the class of methods most commonly associated with transforming between

time and frequency domains. The type of DFT used most regularly is the *Fast Fourier Transform (FFT)*, which (as its name suggests) is an efficient implementation of the DFT. There are two related mathematical forms; the FFT that transforms from the time to the frequency domain, and the Inverse FFT (IFFT) that achieves the opposite. Therefore the arrangement in figure 12.2 can be implemented as an FFT, followed by manipulation of the frequency domain data, followed by an IFFT.

The mathematics of the FFT and IFFT is beyond this book. Suitable functions are often provided in libraries or as standard objects in programming languages, so it is not necessary for those creating frequency domain audio processes to have to implement them from scratch. It is important, however, to understand the configuration, limitations, and side effects of the FFT and IFFT in order to use them properly.

Figure 12.3 illustrates how the FFT might typically be used. The time domain data is stored in a buffer (as described in Chapter 8). The reason for buffering is that the time domain data must be transformed in sections. The number of samples considered at once is called the *window size* (also known as the transform size, or FFT size, or number of FFT points). The FFT transforms the time domain data into an output spectral *frame* of the same size as the input window. This frame is composed of a set of *bins* that contain the frequency domain data (splitting up the frequency range into parts).

The process of taking a window of samples and transforming into the frequency domain must occur for successive sections of the time domain data, as shown in figure 12.3. This produces a series of frequency domain data frames, which is useful as frequency domain data is likely to vary over time. The process of splitting the time domain data into sections and transforming a part at a time is usually known as a *Short Time Fourier Transform (STFT)* method. Figure 12.4 shows how to reverse the process (using the IFFT) and transform back from the frequency domain to the time domain form in the output stage of the process.

These are some of the key characteristics of this arrangement:

- It is necessary to buffer a significant number of samples before the FFT process can occur. Therefore there will be a delay between audio input and output (latency). The larger the window size, the more significant this will be.
- The window (transform) size for an FFT (and IFFT) must be a power of 2, such as $2^9 = 512$, $2^{10} = 1024$, $2^{11} = 2048$, $2^{12} = 4096$, and $2^{13} = 8192$.
- There are the same number of bins in a frequency domain frame as there are time domain samples used in the input window. The bins segment the frequency spectrum up to the sample rate. With a window size of 16, the bins are positioned as shown in figure 12.5, where f_S is the sample rate and the Nyquist frequency is $f_S/2$.

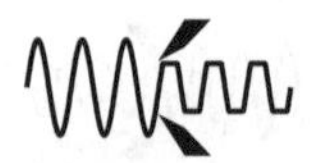

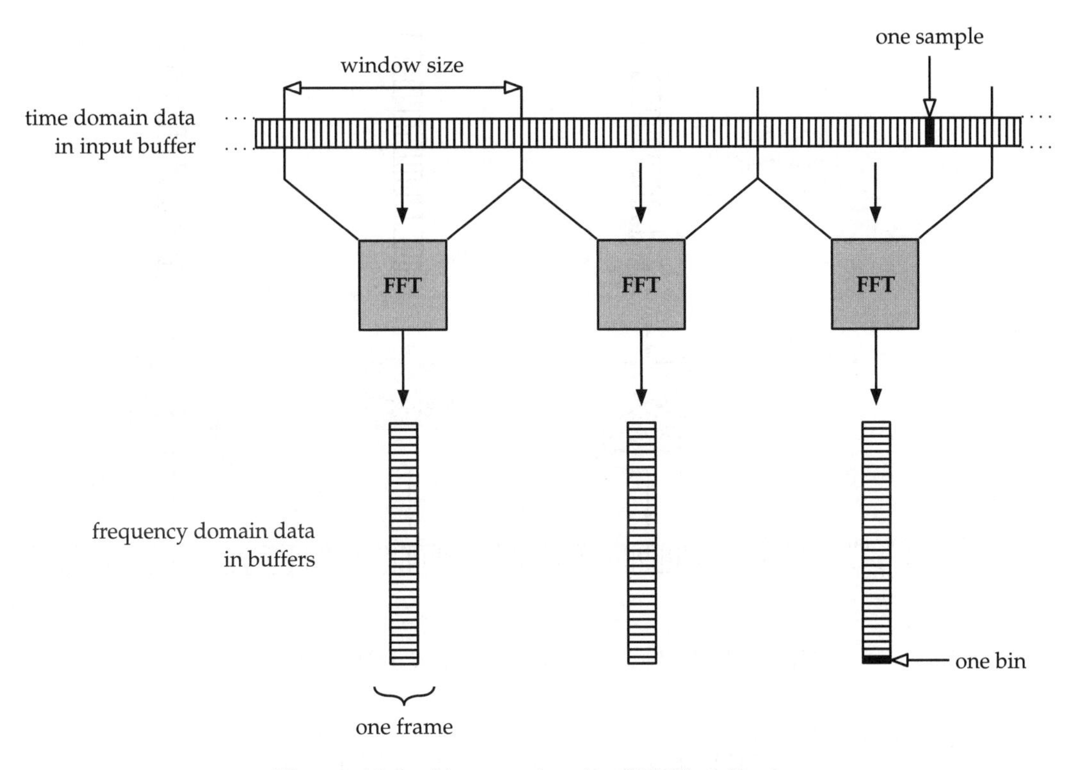

Figure 12.3 Non-overlapping STFT method

The bin size is calculated as follows:

$$\text{bin size (Hz)} = \frac{\text{sample rate}}{\text{window size}} \qquad \boxed{12.1}$$

and also

$$\text{bin centre frequency (Hz)} = \frac{(\text{bin number}) \times (\text{sample rate})}{\text{window size}} \qquad \boxed{12.2}$$

- The bins are of equal size in hertz. However, the perception of frequency is non-linear (as illustrated in figure 2.5, p.24), so a bin size that equates to an octave at low frequencies can equate to less than a semitone at very high frequencies.
- As is shown in figure 12.5, half the bins are positioned at or above the Nyquist frequency. Only the bins up to the Nyquist frequency represent usable frequencies (as described in §2.2.2, p.28). The bins above the Nyquist frequency hold data that is a mirror of those below.
- The larger the window size, the more frequency bins exist, and so each bin relates to a smaller range of frequencies. However, if the window size increases, it also means

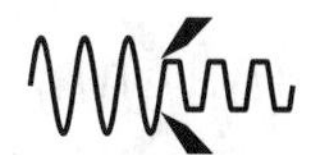

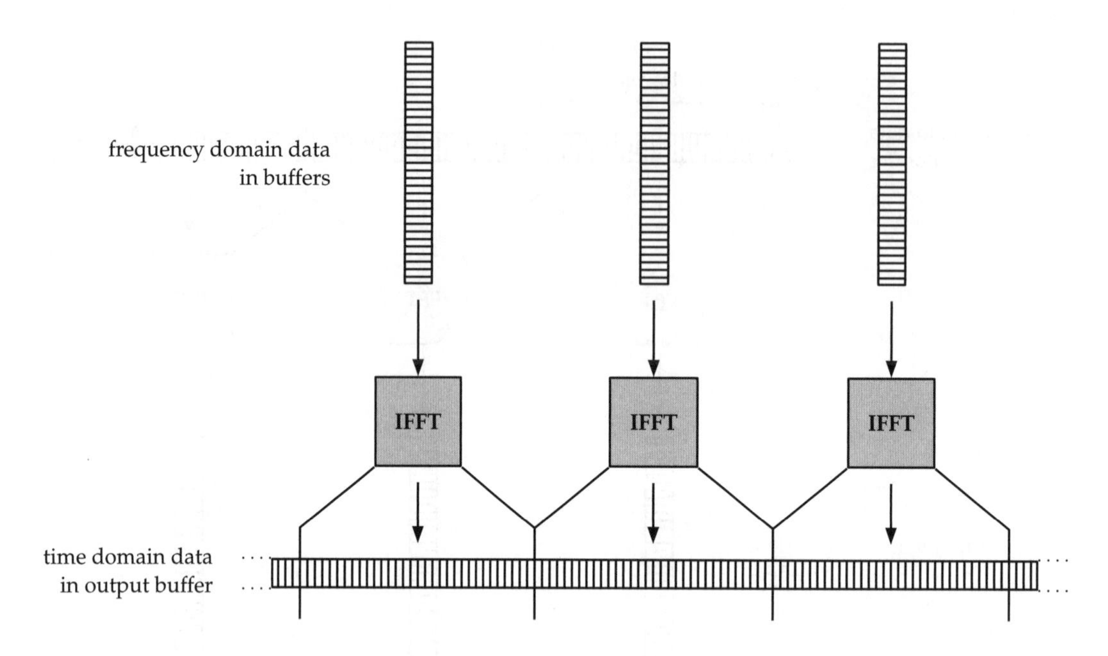

Figure 12.4 Non-overlapping inverse STFT method

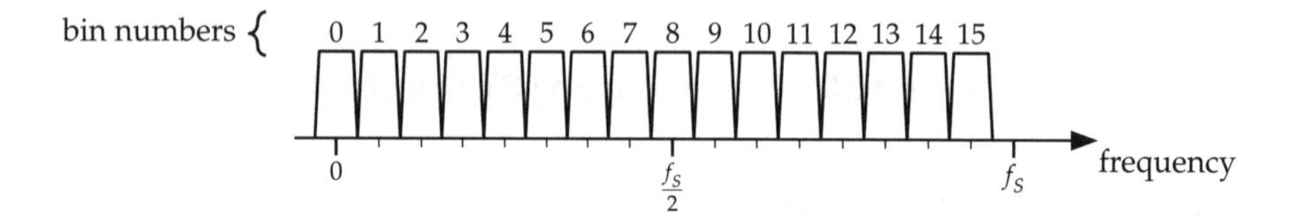

Figure 12.5 Bin positions with a window size of 16

that the spectral frame relates to a greater length in the time domain:

$$\text{window length (s)} = \frac{\text{window size}}{\text{sample rate}} \tag{12.3}$$

If the window is too long then the processing can cause the resulting sound to be smeared in time. If it is too short, then the resolution in frequency will be too low to be of use. This issue is known as a *time-frequency resolution trade-off*. Figure 12.6 illustrates the same sound analysed with three different window sizes. The sound is harmonic but modulated with a square wave tremolo such that there are sharp changes of amplitude at the edges of the bursts of sound (wide frequency range transient effects). As the window size increases the frequency resolution of the harmonics increases but the time resolution decreases, making the edges of the bursts less clear.

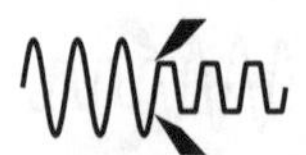

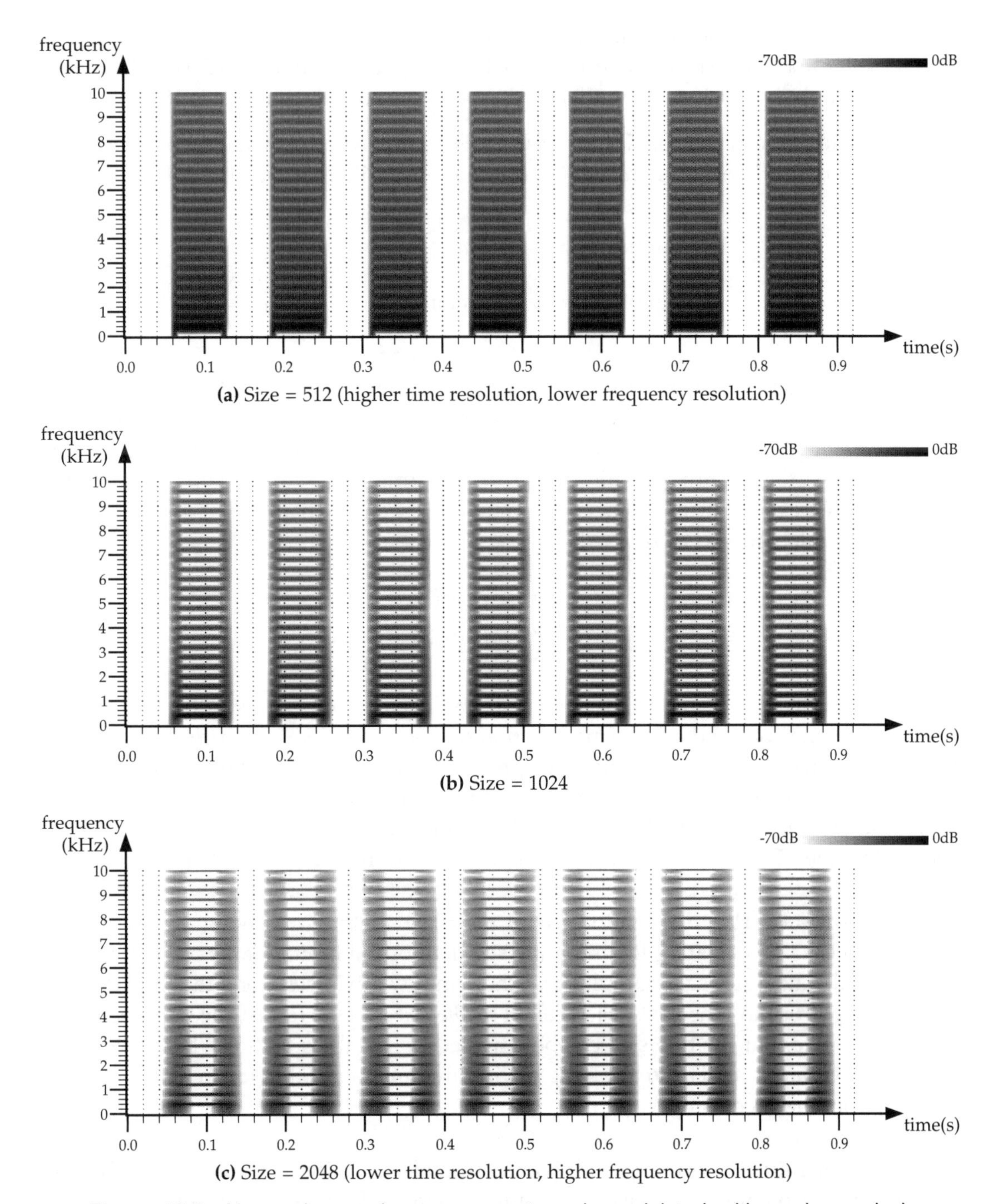

(a) Size = 512 (higher time resolution, lower frequency resolution)

(b) Size = 1024

(c) Size = 2048 (lower time resolution, higher frequency resolution)

Figure 12.6 Harmonic sound, square wave tremolo modulated, with varying analysis window size (spectrogram plots)

- The bin size depends on the chosen sample rate. For example, at a sample rate of 44.1kHz and a window size of 1024, the bin size is approximately 43.1Hz. However, at a sample rate of 192kHz with the same window size, the bin size is 187.5Hz.
- The data value in each bin is a *complex number* $a + jb$ where a is the *real* part and b the *imaginary* part. This is often converted into more easily manipulable data as follows:

$$\text{bin amplitude} = r = \sqrt{a^2 + b^2} \tag{12.4}$$

$$\text{bin phase} = \phi = \arctan\left(\frac{b}{a}\right) = \tan^{-1}\left(\frac{b}{a}\right) \tag{12.5}$$

  This is called converting from *cartesian* (or rectangular) coordinates to *polar coordinates*. IEEE standard 754 defines functions *hypot* (for calculating amplitude) and *atan2* (for phase) that cope appropriately with all input values. These functions are available in many programming libraries. The amplitude data is commonly plotted on an average spectrum or spectrogram plot (as seen in Chapter 4). For the IFFT, the inverse calculations can be used:

$$a = r\cos(\phi) \tag{12.6}$$

$$b = r\sin(\phi) \tag{12.7}$$

An additional feature of the STFT method is the need to apply a window function to smooth the edges of the data. A small section of a sound is likely to include significant amplitude values at the ends, which can produce odd artefacts in the transformed frequency domain data. The corrective measure is to multiply the time domain data items by values that tend towards 1 in the centre of the window and taper to 0 at the edges. This is done before the FFT occurs. Window functions are described further in Appendix B.

It is common to overlap the windows with the STFT method, as shown in figure 12.7. Rather than each FFT relating to a separate segment of the input data, overlapping data sets are used. The number of samples that the window advances along the time domain data before performing the next FFT is called the *hop size*. In the figure, the hop size is half the window size, but the hop size can be adjusted to suit the situation. The purpose of having an overlap is similar to applying a window function in that it can help to reduce artefacts from the processing.

One of the difficulties in working with Fourier Transform methods is establishing how to set the different parameters to achieve a suitable effect. In general, the configuration is a matter of compromise achieved through experimentation, in order to produce a result with the minimum of audible oddities.

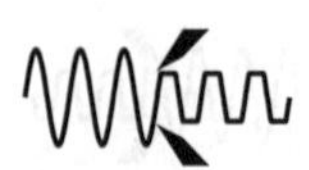

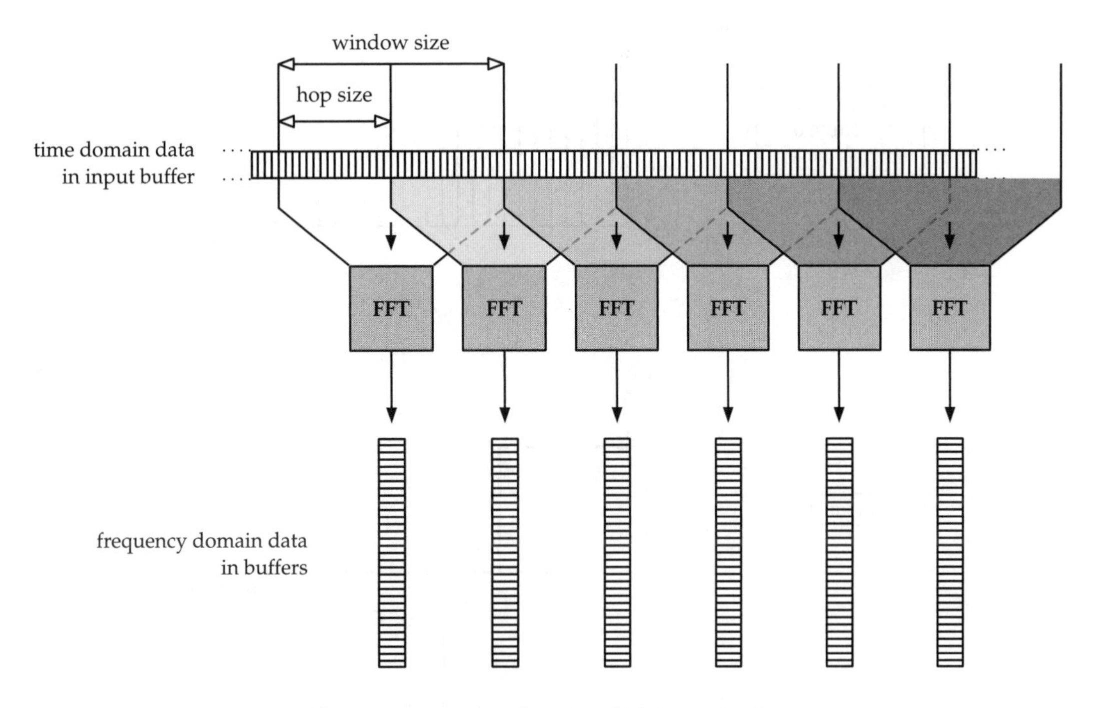

Figure 12.7 Overlapping STFT method

12.2 General Techniques

The STFT method makes it possible to transform to the frequency domain, modify the data, and then (inverse) transform back to the time domain. This enables quite complex filter effects to be achieved without resorting to a large number of individual filters.

12.2.1 Filtering

Figure 12.8 shows how a brickwall type lowpass filter can be created in the frequency domain. The overall process is as follows:

- A set of input time domain samples is transformed into a frequency domain frame.
- The data for each bin is multiplied by the corresponding value in the gain function (either 1 or 0 in this example). This can be achieved by multiplying both the real and imaginary components of the bin data by the gain value.
- The frequency domain frame is transformed back into time domain data and passed to the output.
- The process is repeated for every subsequent frame of data.

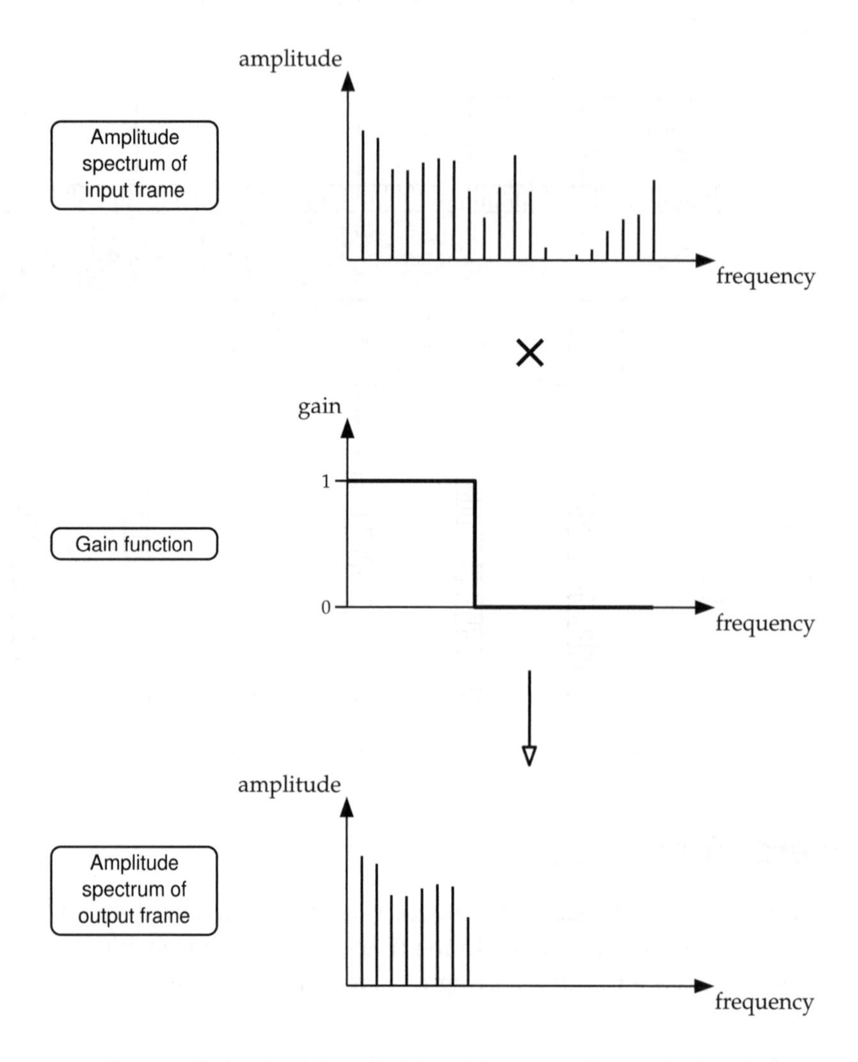

Figure 12.8 Applying a brickwall lowpass filter gain function

This is a fairly crude effect, but it shows the general method. In terms of configuration, then a reasonable starting point is a window size of 1024 at a sample rate of 44.1kHz. This and other parameters of the STFT process must be adjusted to minimise artefacts from processing.

Figure 12.9 shows a more advanced use of the frequency domain form than the previous example. It illustrates how a complex shape described in terms of gain against frequency can be used as a filter frequency response. With a graphical user interface a complex shape can be drawn that is hard to specify with conventional filter parameters. The resolution of such a shape can be as precise as specifying gain for individual bins.

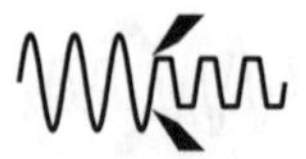

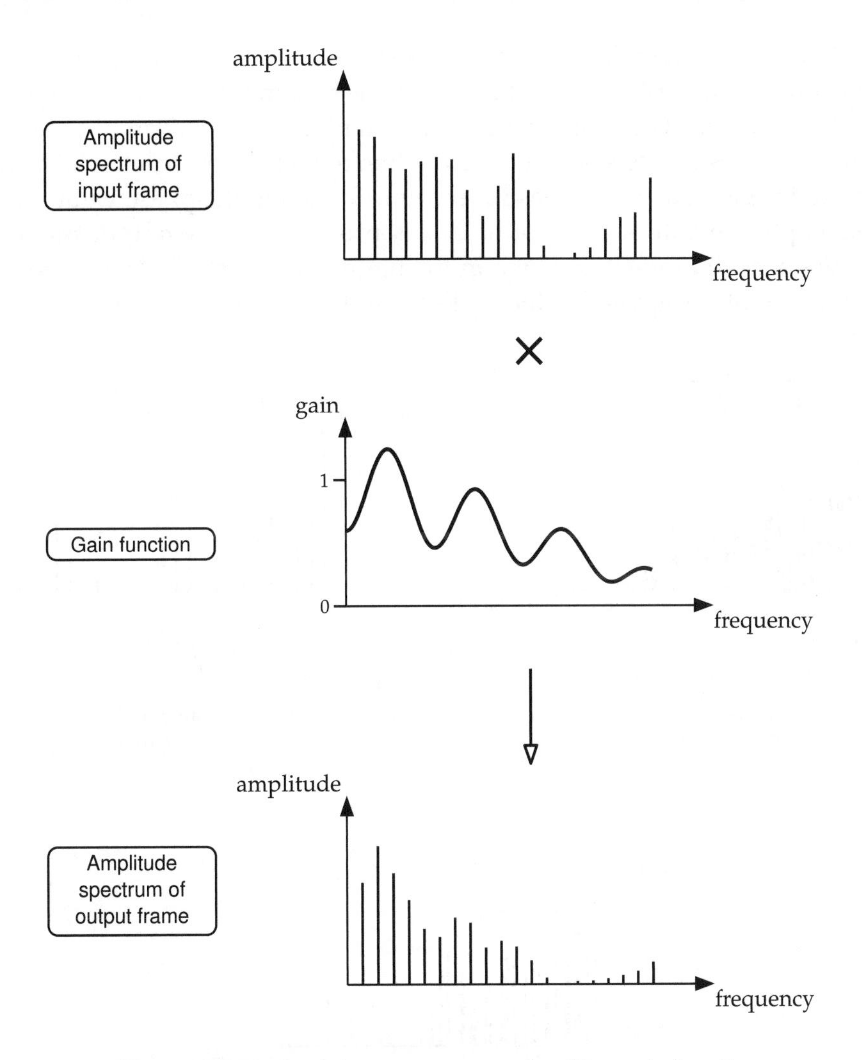

Figure 12.9 Applying a more complex filter gain function

12.2.2 Vocoding and Application of Spectral Envelopes

The term *vocoder* is applied to a range of techniques that involve the automatic extraction of the spectral envelope from one signal, and the application of that envelope to another signal. Vocoders were originally developed as a method for encoding the fundamental characteristics of a vocal input sound, transmitting over a limited bandwidth connection, and *resynthesizing* the voice at the other end. In modern musical contexts, however, vocoding is more usually associated with the idea of blending the characteristics of two sounds in interesting ways.

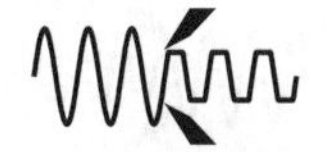

Figure 12.10 shows an example technique for performing vocoding-type operations using an STFT method. As described in §12.1.2 (p.371), the bins in the frequency domain frames hold complex numbers. The complex numbers can be converted to amplitude and phase values. This produces two sets of values across the frequency spectrum, which are known as an amplitude spectrum and a phase spectrum. By taking the phase values from input 1, and the amplitude values from input 2, this produces a new output frame that has characteristics of both inputs (as shown in the figure). In effect, the (amplitude) spectral envelope from input 2 is applied to the underlying partials from input 1.

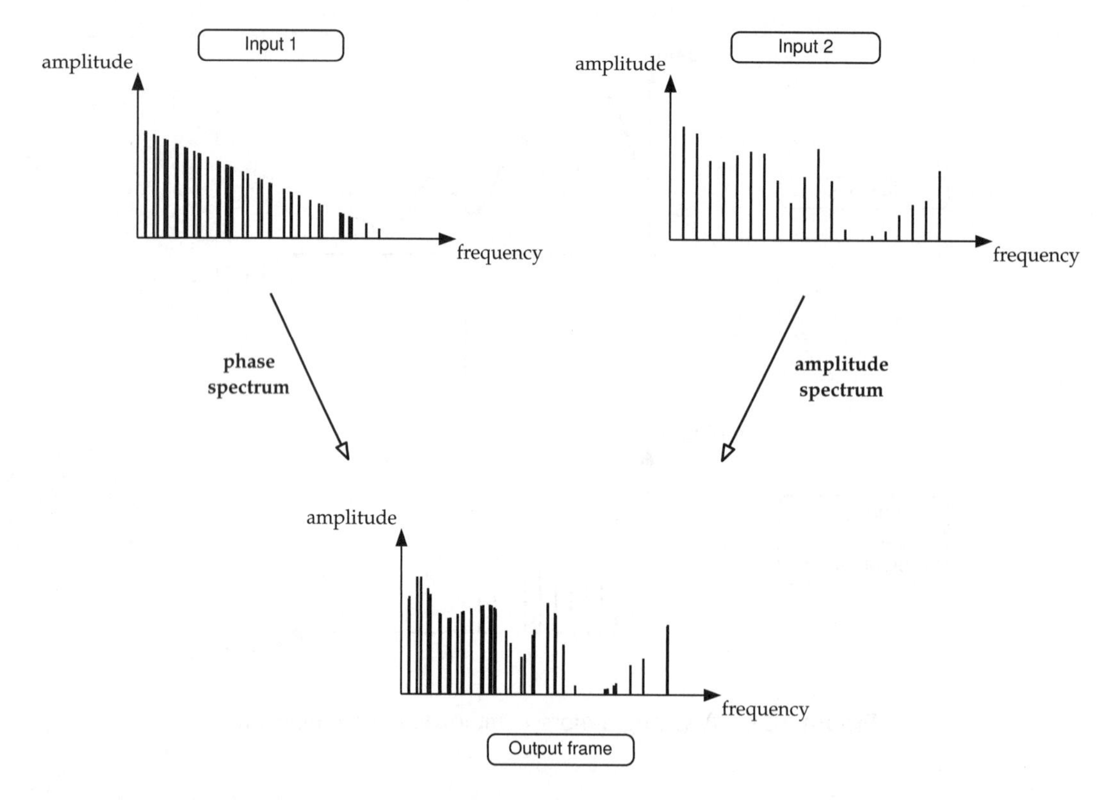

Figure 12.10 Applying a spectral envelope from one sound to another

The process requires two time domain inputs to be transformed into the frequency domain, combined, and then transformed back into the time domain. As with the filtering examples, the process must occur for every frame. The two input sounds can vary in character over time, so the combination will be slightly different for each frame. A typical effect is using a synthesized tone for input 1 and a voice for input 2. This achieves a synthesizer that has some recognisable speech characteristics, because much of the information content of a voice is in the amplitude spectrum.

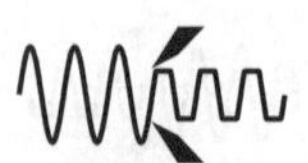

The pitch of the combined sound will be determined by input 1 (if it has harmonic content). If the pitch of input 1 is varying over time, then it is possible to play a different tune to that which might originally have existed in input 2. This is not the same, however, as pitch changing or pitch correction, where the underlying partials of the voice are preserved. Note that these techniques do not have to be restricted to voices combined with simple synthesized tones. It is possible to create interesting hybrid characters with a wide range of sound sources.

In terms of configuration, if the window size (and so the number of frequency bins) is too small then the amplitude spectral envelope will be too coarse for a good effect. If it is too large then the individual partials (and so pitch) of input 2 can be evident in the output. A reasonable starting point is a window size of 512 at a sample rate of 44.1kHz. As with the filter examples, this and other parameters of the STFT process must be adjusted to minimise artefacts from processing.

12.2.3 Delay

With the STFT approach it is possible to offset the position of partials in time by applying different delays to different frequency bins. This can be used to creatively reshape the development of sounds over time. An example of this is shown in figure 12.11. When applied to a percussive sound the different frequencies in the onset will no longer have a common start time and will be spread out. Percussive type sounds usually have many partials starting almost together, so spreading the start times will have a significant effect on the way in which the sound appears to have been created. The delays can be in any desired pattern; they do not have to increase linearly with frequency.

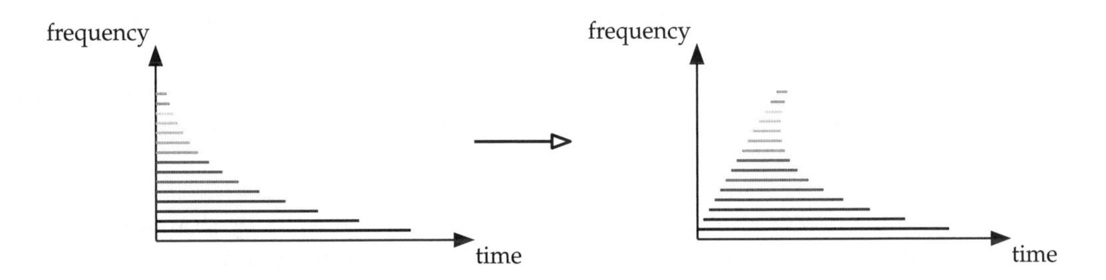

Figure 12.11 Applying different delays at different frequencies (spectrogram plots)

In terms of implementation each bin must have its own delay buffer. Each has a similar form to that seen in §8.1.4 (p.232), but the buffer stores pairs of values (a complex number). The time spacing of values in the buffers equates to the hop size of the STFT (figure 12.7, p.377). A window size of 1024 and a hop size of 128 at a sample rate of 44.1kHz is a

reasonable starting point. A range of delays from 0 to 50 frames often produces a clear effect with a percussive sound.

Once buffers have been implemented for each bin, it is possible to use them for other effects. For example, a recirculating form such as figure 10.25 (p.315) can be used to extend the frequency partials in time, but with different delay times for different bins. The real and imaginary parts of the delayed and new input complex numbers are summed independently.

12.3 More Sophisticated Techniques

The techniques described in §12.2 use the data in STFT frequency domain bins in either the original complex number form, or in terms of amplitude and phase values. In more sophisticated frequency domain methods, more precise control over individual partials is required. The problem with the basic STFT technique described in §12.1.2 (p.371) is that regularly-spaced frames of bin data are quite a coarse representation. For example, with a sample rate of 44.1kHz and a window size of 1024, the frequency bins are about 43.1Hz wide. It is possible to move that bin data into the adjacent bin (and so add or subtract 43.1Hz from the partial frequencies). However, adding 5Hz to the frequency of a partial is not such a clear operation.

There are a number of ways of improving on the data representation produced by the STFT. A particularly useful method is to analyse the input data frames and convert to a data set composed of individual partials. The analysis tracks information from frame-to-frame and calculates the time-varying frequencies and amplitudes of the underlying partials. The McAulay-Quatieri technique is an example of this. A more sophisticated alternative is the Reassigned Bandwidth-Enhanced Additive Sound Model, which represents spectral components with a noise bandwidth as well as frequency and amplitude. Having accurate control over spectral components is enormously powerful, as it is possible to individually modify their parameters over time. The results are then resynthesized with a bank of oscillators (one for each component). Programming libraries exist to support these techniques.

Both real-time and non-real-time approaches are used with frequency domain methods. In real-time, only current or past information is available to make a modification to the sound. However, with some modifications it is appropriate to record the whole sound, then analyse characteristics such as the overall length, or the pitch reached in a stable region towards the end of the sound. Once that information is established it is possible to make a modification to the whole sound. Similarly if a sound is to be made shorter by progressing through the sound faster than the original speed, then that is only possible if the sound has been recorded first. Applications include modifications in Digital Audio Workstation software, and advanced approaches to sample-based synthesis (Chapter 15).

12.3.1 Time-Stretching

Frequency domain methods where there is separation between the time and frequency dimensions enable sounds to be stretched or squashed in time without it moving the positions of the partials in frequency (and so without changing pitch). Related time domain methods and their audible effects are described in §15.3.1 (p.473) and §22.2.2 (p.620).

Time-stretching involves moving through the data at a different speed to the original sound, either increasing the number of output samples, or skipping over the input data at a faster speed. This is achieved by interpolating frequency and amplitude values for the individual partials. Interpolation is described in §8.2 (p.237). With a long recorded passage (such as a drum loop or a guitar riff) it is possible to achieve changes of tempo without pitch changes. Modest changes of tempo can be accommodated without difficulties. More extreme variations can produce odd artefacts as changes to the length of individual notes become more noticeable, and artefacts of the frequency domain transform and analysis process become apparent.

Individual note events can be treated in a similar way to a longer loop, but it is useful to modify the character of different parts of the event with an envelope. Figure 12.12a illustrates what can happen when a note event is lengthened. The partials (and so the pitch) remain the same as in the original sound because the process is performed in the frequency domain. However, with a consistent playback speed the amplitude envelope of the sound is stretched out.

It might be desirable to keep the attack portion of the sound the same as the input, but lengthen the decay. As shown in figure 12.12b, the technique is to have two speeds; playing the attack at the original speed, and the decay portion more slowly. Playing back different portions at different speeds will not affect the pitch, as it would with a time domain method. However, it will affect the rate of any tremolo that might be present, and the speed of development of tonal character over time. Another technique is to create a sustaining section, but keep the attack and final release the same as the original sound (figure 12.12c).

12.3.2 Changing Pitch

As well as being able to change the length of a sound without changing the pitch, it is possible to change the pitch without changing the length. The basic operation for pitch changing in the frequency domain is to multiply the frequencies of all partials by $2^{s/12}$ to achieve an s semitone pitch variation (as per equation 2.2, p.21). The value of s does not have to be an integer.

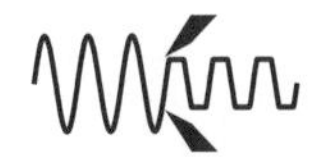

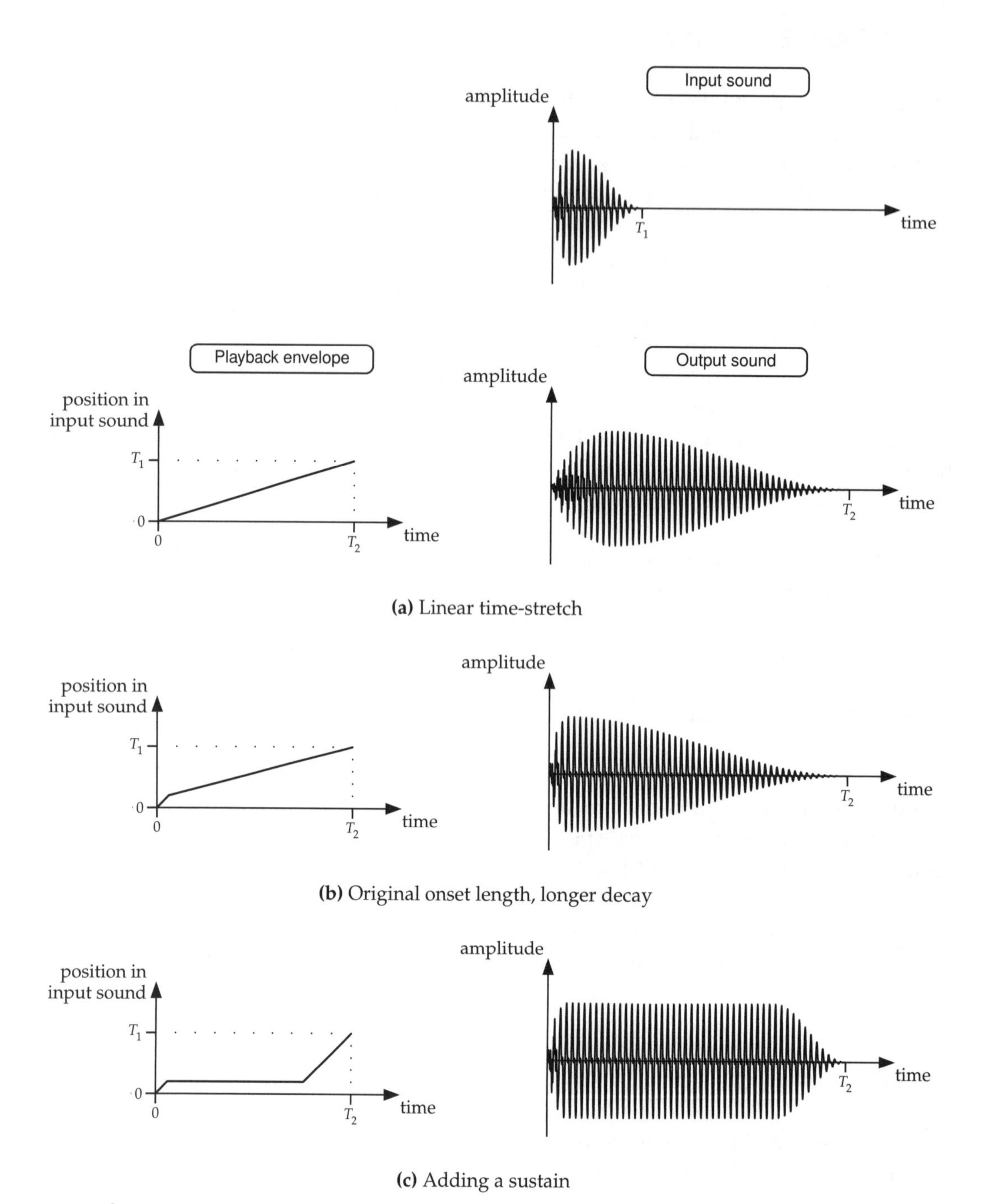

Figure 12.12 Time-stretching an individual note event

It is not necessarily the case that it is desirable to change the frequency of all partials by the same amount to achieve a pitch change. For example, if the main pitched tone of a snare drum sound is to be reduced by an octave, then reducing the frequencies of the high frequency partials associated with the snare wires might create quite a dull and unrealistic tone. If the fundamental frequency is known (or can be derived automatically) then it is possible to identify which partials are associated with the principal harmonics of the sound (and so the main pitch) and which are not.

Figure 12.13 compares the effect of reducing the frequency of **all** partials against reducing the harmonics of the fundamental frequency only. It is often appropriate to use an amount of tolerance when identifying harmonics, to reflect slight inharmonicity or variations in tuning; for example, identifying partials of interest as those within 2% of the predicted harmonic frequencies. It can also be useful to consider harmonics below a frequency limit, such that high frequencies that are less associated with the pitched tone are not modified.

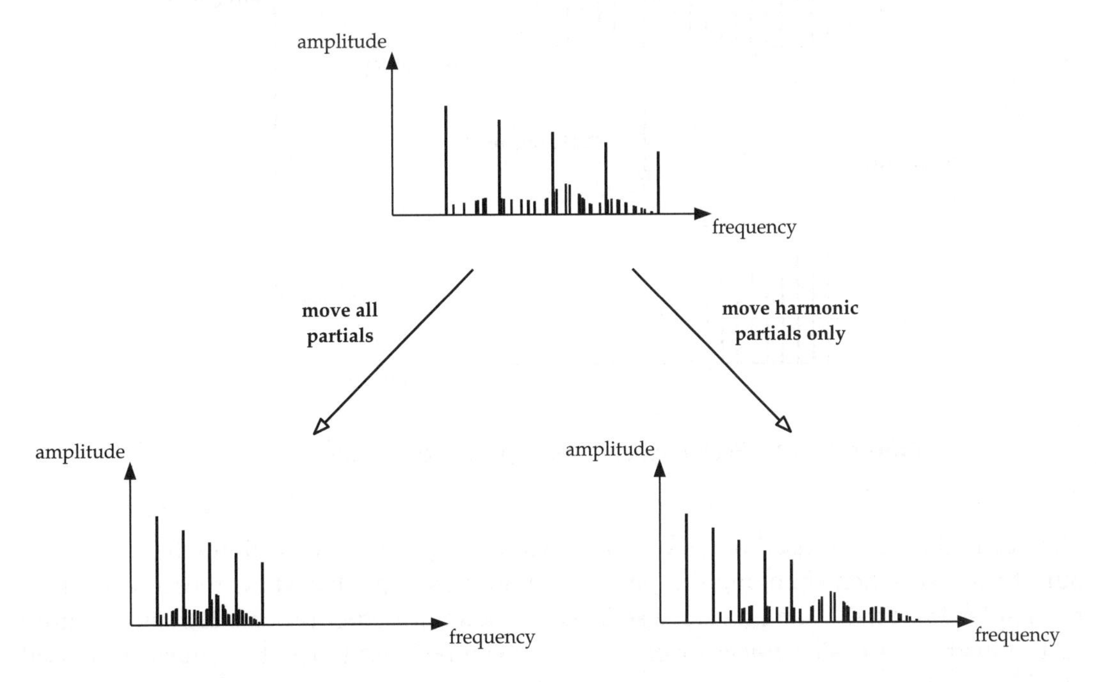

Figure 12.13 Changing frequency of all partials or a harmonic subset

One side effect of pitch changing is that the spectral envelope is stretched when the partials are moved. If this is not a desirable change then it is possible to reapply the original spectral envelope (known as *spectral envelope preservation* or formant preservation) as demonstrated in figure 12.14. This can improve the tonality of pitch changed vocal sounds. However, it requires some careful configuration and works better at moderate pitch changes than more extreme ones.

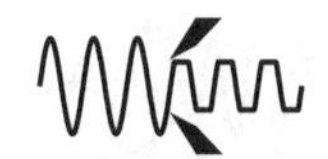

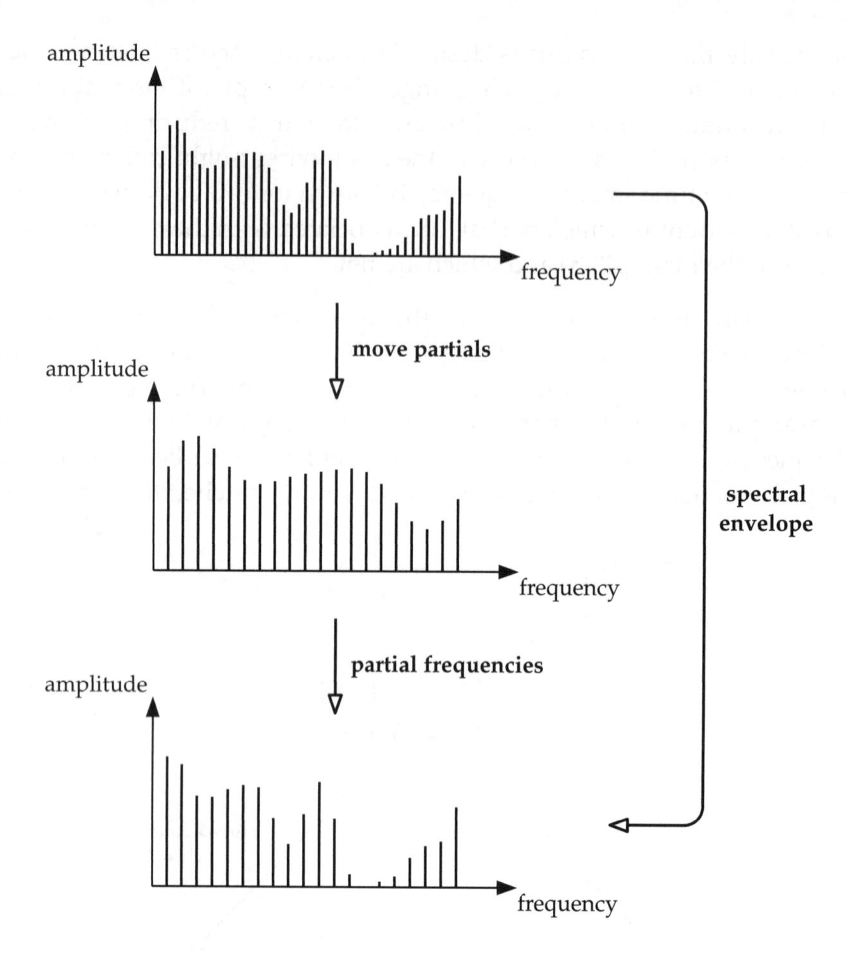

Figure 12.14 Pitch changing with spectral envelope preservation

Pitch changing can be used on its own for such tasks as pitch correction where a note is out of tune, or when changing the pitch of a note in sample-based synthesis (discussed in Chapter 15). Pitch changing can also be combined with other process elements. Figure 12.15 illustrates a basic *harmoniser* effect, which can be used to create a musical interval from a single source input. The original pitched sound is added to a version with a changed pitch, including control over the amplitude gains of the two paths.

The delay in the figure can be used to compensate for the time taken to transform into the frequency domain, make the pitch change and transform back to the time domain, such that the two versions remain in synchrony. The delay time therefore depends on the technique used. However, it might also be desirable to use the delay to slightly mis-synchronise the signals such that it appears that two independent sound sources are

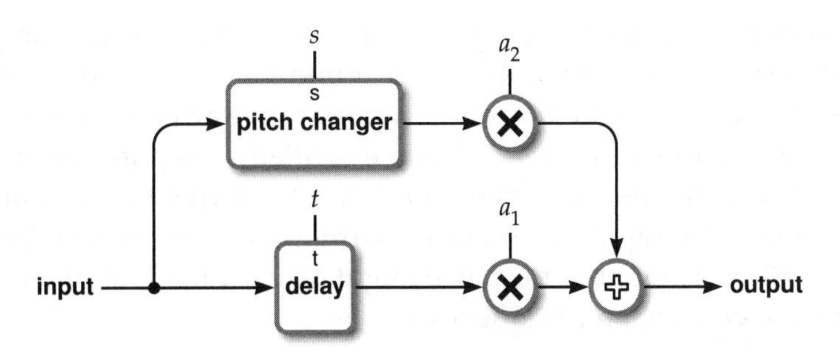

Figure 12.15 Basic harmoniser effect

producing the notes rather than one. There are possibilities for automating the amount of pitch change (s), the amount of delay(t) and relative amplitudes (a_1 and a_2) over time, to achieve varying harmonising.

Another modifier based on pitch change is shown in figure 12.16. The intention is to create a variation in pitch over time that is not part of the original input signal. A feedback loop is used that has similarities to a recirculating echo or reverberation effect (figure 10.25, p.315). The recirculation causes the signal to gradually change in pitch (either increasing or decreasing), be filtered, and attenuated over time. Time t is not the only delay, as it is also introduced by the pitch changer and filter blocks. The intention is that the overall feedback delay will be small enough such that the result is a sliding pitch rather than a series of echoes. The amount of pitch change heard not only depends on the value of s, but also how rapidly amplitude and high frequencies are lost in the attenuator (a values between 0 and 1) and filter (a cutoff f_c around 1kHz).

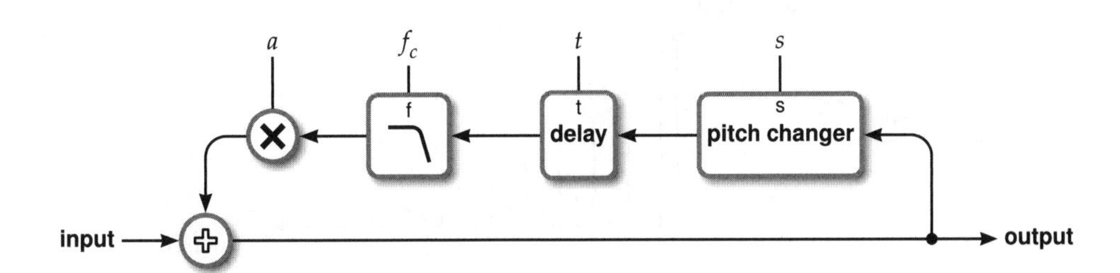

Figure 12.16 Sliding pitch effect

12.3.3 Modifying Amplitude and Frequency Relationships

Control over individual partials is a powerful tool. A frequency domain sample editor allows the user to change the frequencies and amplitudes of partials, and add partials to the sound. Automatically modifying partials based on a mapping function is also possible.

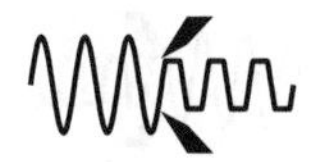

Figure 12.17 shows how an amplitude gain function can be used to change amplitudes on a per-partial basis. In the figure, the input sound has steadily decreasing harmonic amplitudes, but the output sound has more emphasis on low odd harmonics, which will significantly change the tonal character. This is essentially a sophisticated filtering effect, but if the fundamental frequency is known (or can be derived automatically) then the amplitude variations can be applied to specific harmonics rather than at fixed frequencies. As with figure 12.13, an amount of tolerance might be used to identify partials of interest relative to the predicted harmonic frequencies.

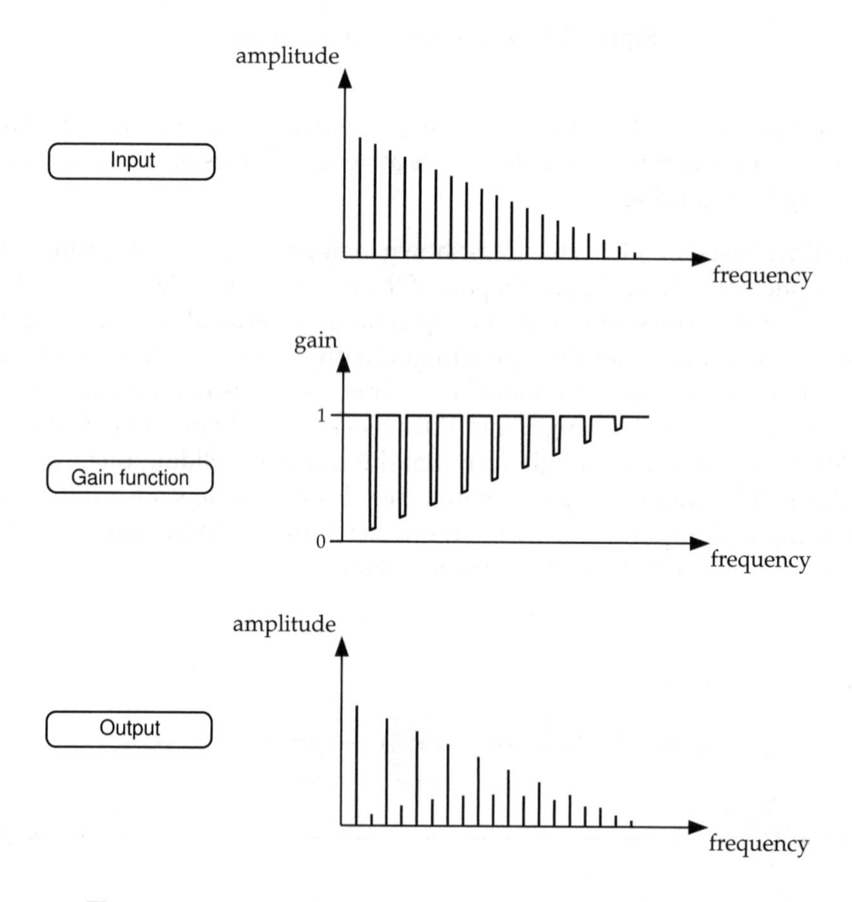

Figure 12.17 Changing partial amplitudes with a gain function

Figure 12.18 shows how a frequency multiplier function can be used to change partial frequencies. The input sound is harmonic in the figure, but the output sound is inharmonic as the partials have been multiplied by different scaling factors. This is a fairly simple modification, but the process of changing partial characteristics can be as sophisticated as required.

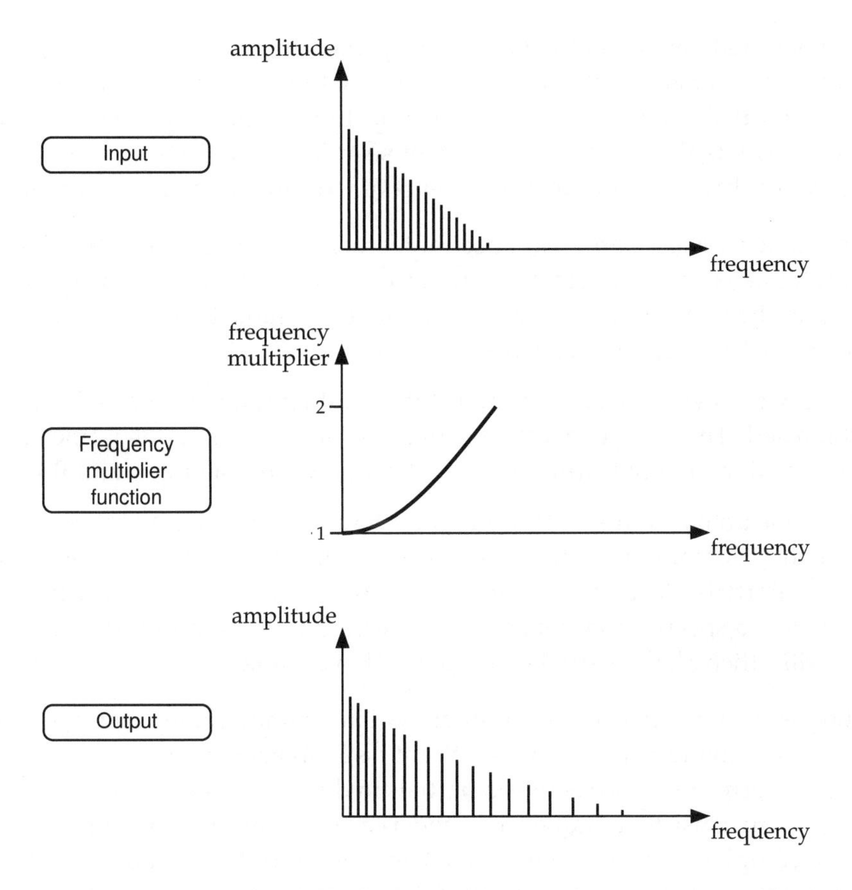

Figure 12.18 Changing partial frequencies with a frequency multiplier function

12.3.4 Blending and Morphing

Figure 12.19 shows an example of combining characteristics from two different sounds by blending the lower harmonics from one sound with the upper harmonics from another. It is important to consider whether the two source sounds are sufficiently compatible that the result will be a coherent or convincing blend; for example, whether the pitches and lengths are the same, such that the features line up. This might be achieved by using time-stretching and pitch changing as described in §12.3.1 and §12.3.2.

In simple cases where pitch and length are compatible between the two sounds it can be possible to use simple filtering instead of a more sophisticated technique in the frequency domain. The effect in the figure might be achieved by use of lowpass and highpass filters on the two sounds respectively, and then mixing the results. However, access to individual partials in the frequency domain allows complex combinations, such as interleaving sets of harmonics and inharmonics, or selection based on partial amplitudes.

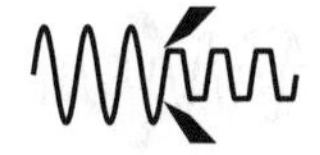

A more sophisticated version of blending is *morphing* (timbral interpolation), which produces intermediate versions between two sounds with weighted characteristics of both; for example, gradually changing from one sound to another over time. This has some similarities to cross-fading in the time domain seen in figure 5.51b (p.135) and in §19.4 (p.553). However, there are a number of benefits of working in the frequency domain:

- It is possible to select particular spectral features that will be affected; for example, to morph the harmonics from one sound to another, but leave other components the same as in the first sound. Similarly it might be desirable to morph different parts of the sound with different envelope shapes.
- As described previously, pitches and lengths could be adjusted such that features are synchronised. This might be a change over the entire sound, or specifically targeted to achieve alignment of features such as the attack, tremolo rates, and final decay.
- While a time domain cross-fade technique attenuates one sound as another increases, in frequency domain morphing it is possible to interpolate the frequencies of corresponding partials. A simple example of this is shown in figure 12.20. In a representation where a spectral component has three parameters (amplitude, frequency, and bandwidth) then all three can be interpolated over time.

The intention is to produce convincing intermediate sounds rather than the impression of there being two sound sources. A significant issue in achieving effective morphing is establishing the correspondence between partials in the two sounds. With two simple harmonic sounds with consistent frequencies there is a clear pattern that matches. As sounds become more complex and change more over the length of the sounds then there is less certainty over correspondence. It is useful if the correspondence between partials can be established automatically, but in more complex cases it can require manual configuration. It is not necessarily the case that a linear change from one sound to the other over the sound duration is appropriate.

12.4 Developing Processes and Learning More

Frequency domain modifications are computationally-expensive, which has limited their practicality in mainstream real-time applications in the past. The complexity of the underlying transformation processes makes these techniques difficult to implement from scratch. Audible artefacts and processing delays are also issues that must be addressed in order to achieve high quality results. However, there is significant potential for achieving sophisticated sound modification through access to individual frequency partials. As computing power and the sophistication of frequency domain tools and libraries continues to improve, that potential is realised more and more.

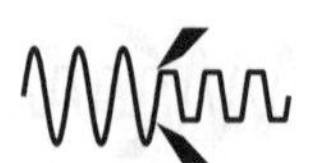

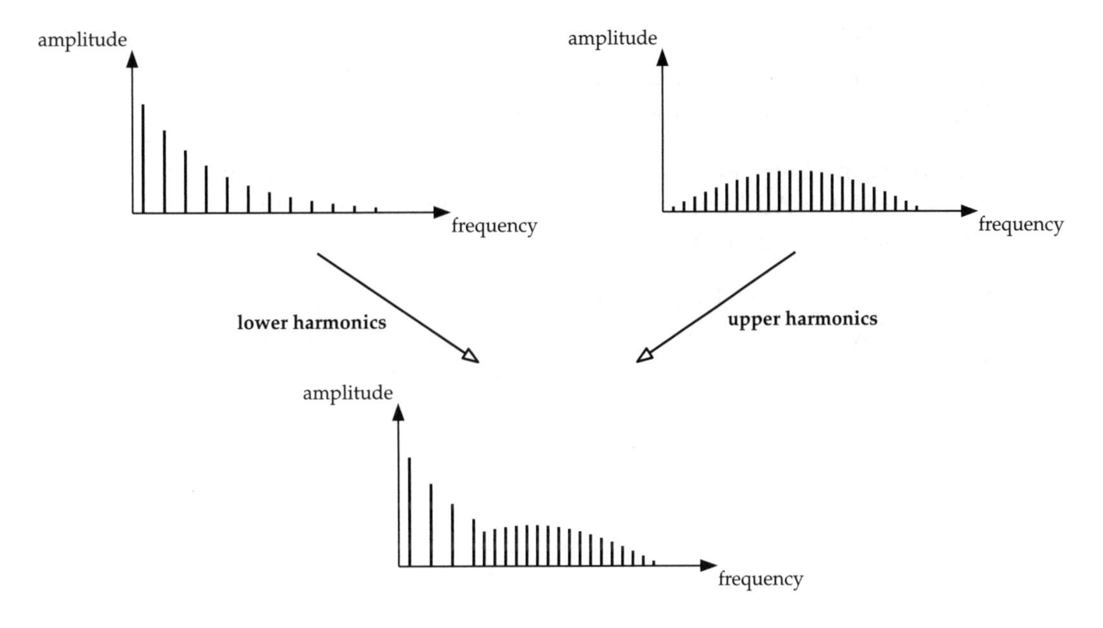

Figure 12.19 Combining harmonics from two sounds

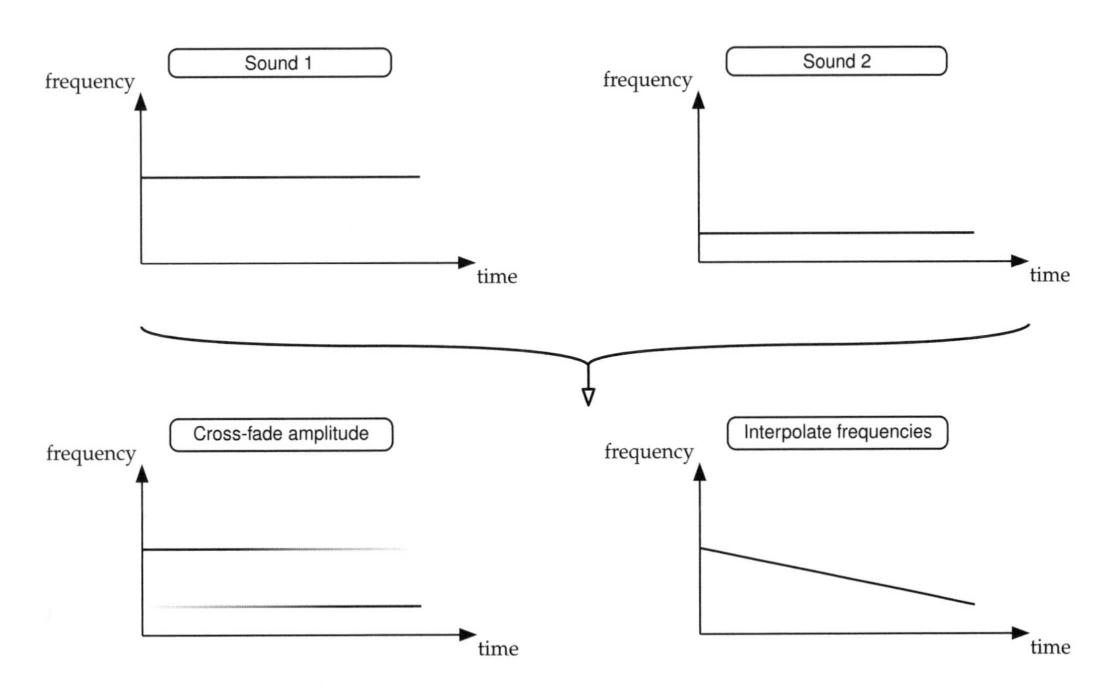

Figure 12.20 Comparison of cross-fading amplitude and interpolating frequency over time (spectrogram plots)

The following sources provide some further details on the topics discussed in this chapter:

Boulanger, Richard, and Victor Lazzarini, eds. 2011. *The Audio Programming Book*. Cambridge, MA: The MIT Press.

Fitz, Kelly, and Lippold Haken. 2002. "On the Use of Time-Frequency Reassignment in Additive Sound Modeling." *Journal of the Audio Engineering Society* 50:11:879–893.

McAulay, Robert J., and Thomas F. Quatieri. 1986. "Speech Analysis/Synthesis Based on a Sinusoidal Representation." *IEEE Transactions on Acoustics, Speech, and Signal Processing* 34:4:744–754.

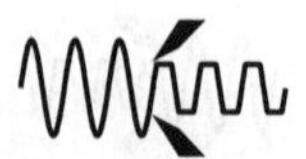

PART III
SYNTHESIS

13

Basic Synthesis

13.1 Basic Concepts

13.1.1 From Modifiers to Synthesizers

Audio synthesis is the generation of sound from scratch. Many of the elements associated with synthesis (such as gain control, mixing, filtering, mapping, and delays) have been seen previously in chapters concerned with the modification of sound. In addition, synthesizers also incorporate significant use of oscillators and envelope generators that are driven by a control input such as a keyboard, as described later in this chapter.

Distortion, flanging, noise gates, and other modifiers use process designs that each achieve a relatively well-defined range of effects. Synthesizers have a rather different style, as each technique lends itself to creating a large number of different sonic characters. For example, there are multiple ways to synthesize a bell-like sound, and no single method that is best in all circumstances.

A considerable range of synthesis techniques exist, as described in the chapters that follow, each with its own strengths and weaknesses. Typically a synthesis technique is selected based on the following criteria:

- Whether it has the capability to create a specific type of sound character, such as the generation of a realistic acoustic instrument sound, or a sound associated with a certain musical style or era, or a synthetic sound that stands out against other tonal colours, or a sound effect.
- Whether it has efficiency of control for achieving a specific target sound. A synthesis technique might be capable of creating a certain type of sound, but that does not necessarily mean that it is easy to do so. Once the synthesizer has been programmed to achieve a sound character, it is likely that tonal variations will be required in performance, and the synthesizer must also be able to achieve those changes in the desired manner.
- Whether it is computationally-efficient. A particular synthesis technique will tend to produce certain types of results when using a limited number of elements in its structure. Processing a small number of elements that are quite efficient has been of great importance historically. However, it also means that creating radically different results might require a much larger structure, compared to a synthesis technique that is more naturally adapted to the tonal characteristic of interest.

The creation of a specific sound character often starts from an analysis of the properties of similar sounds in the time and frequency domains (see Chapters 3 and 4). This gives an idea of the characteristics that must be created, which in turn points to the required features of the synthesizer. However, synthesis techniques also lend themselves to an iterative process of manipulation towards a desired tonality. For example, exploring

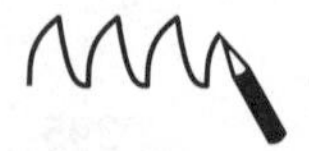

typical structures of subtractive synthesis can lead to musically useful results, even if there was not an intention to match a particular template sound at the beginning.

The choice of synthesis technique affects the ease of achieving a particular sonic result. For example, creating an analogue synthesizer-style filter sweep is easier with subtractive methods than with granular. Granular synthesis is more suited to creating audience applause. However, synthesis techniques are not constrained within one small region of tonal character. The overlaps in the capabilities of different techniques mean that there are usually several ways of achieving a similar result.

Despite their structural and control differences, there are certain common approaches to extending synthesizers. Most synthesis techniques have extensibility that enables an increase in the sophistication of the sonic result. The enhancements do not all have to be of a similar magnitude. A suitable development might be adding a subtle variation over time to a parameter that otherwise is static, or a low amplitude inharmonic aspect where the main bulk of the sound is harmonic, or a contrasting element that only emerges in the latter part of the sound. More broadly, there are standard techniques for building up multiple synthesis structures with different configurations and blending the results to achieve composite sound characters (as described in Chapter 19).

A synthesizer produces a sound that develops over time in most cases, either automatically or due to changes of input parameters. The way in which control links to synthesis affects the nature of the result. A typical control device is a piano-style keyboard, which is the input element shown in many synthesizer diagrams in this book. However, the control device can equally well be a drum pad, an infra-red distance sensor, a foot-controlled expression pedal, a breath sensor, or note data derived from an acoustic instrument source. Other means of control value generation are also possible, such as from a sequencer, arpeggiator, or algorithmic composition. The designs in this book can use any of these, assuming that there is a suitable mapping to the synthesis parameters.

Modifier processes can be applied to synthesized sounds to enhance the character. For example, parallel bandpass filtering might be used to reshape the spectral envelope (figure 6.20, p.157). Stereo techniques can be used, such as slightly different filtering, timings, and panning (§5.5.2, p.121) for the parts of a design that produce the left and right outputs. More complex modifiers such as reverberation (Chapter 10) are also often used.

In a computer-based system, the elements used to create a synthesizer are sometimes known as *unit generators* or *objects*. The programming technique depends on the system being used, but the elements and their connections are similar. The presentation of designs in this book does not assume a particular implementation style. The designs are not tied to a specific control device, protocol (such as MIDI), or programming language or environment. They are sufficiently flexible that they work in a wide variety of contexts, although the implementation might impose limitations on the results that can be achieved.

13.1.2 Oscillators

The basic building block of most traditional synthesis is some form of oscillator, which produces a repeating (harmonic) waveform with a particular fundamental frequency and peak amplitude. Modulation techniques such as tremolo and vibrato (described in Chapter 9 and §13.3, p.418) are usually configured with low frequencies (typically less than 20Hz). In synthesis the oscillator is used with a much wider frequency range. In particular, an oscillator is often used as the source of a pitched tone (typically frequencies in the range 20Hz to 20kHz) as an element in the construction of a new sound. Oscillator designs are described in more detail in Chapter 14.

The three properties associated with an oscillator introduced in Chapter 9 are also applicable here:

- **Frequency**. The repetition of a cyclical waveform is perceived as a pitch by the human auditory system. If several waveforms are combined together, then the frequency relationships of the partials within that combination are important.
- **Amplitude**. For purposes of this book the oscillator block will always produce a waveform with a ± 1 peak amplitude. However, that amplitude is likely to be varied by scaling the oscillator output, in order to produce enveloped amplitude effects, or to weight the output of different oscillators before mixing the signals, for example.
- **Waveform shape**. An oscillator waveform can be any shape. For example, it might be a simple elemental sine wave with a very plain character, or it might be a complex shape that has a timbral character determined by the frequencies and amplitudes of the partials of which it is composed.

Figure 13.1a shows the simplest oscillator form where fundamental frequency (F), peak amplitude (A) and waveform shape (W) can all be specified. A possible variation is to offset the signal through addition of a fixed value to the output (figure 13.1b). This enables a signal to be produced that has an oscillation that is not centred on a value of zero (originally seen in figure 9.8, p.271). Through the use of scaling and an offset, a signal can be produced that is suitable for cyclically modulating another quantity in the system, such as frequency or amplitude parameters (discussed in Chapter 20).

As well as adding fixed values to the output of an oscillator, signals are often mixed together with an adder element to create a composite sound (as seen in §5.4, p.114). This is used in most synthesis techniques as the simplest means of combining sound qualities. Figure 13.2 shows an example of mixing two sinusoids at different frequencies and amplitudes. Oscillators might also be configured with a non-integer relationship between their fundamental frequencies in order to produce an inharmonic mixed result.

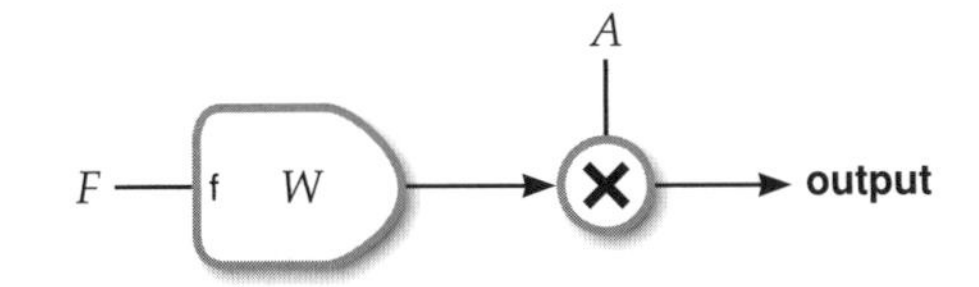

(a) With amplitude scaling

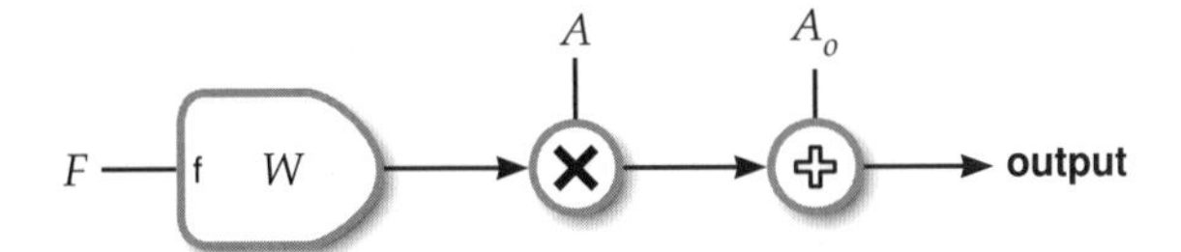

(b) With amplitude scaling and offset

Figure 13.1 Basic oscillator forms

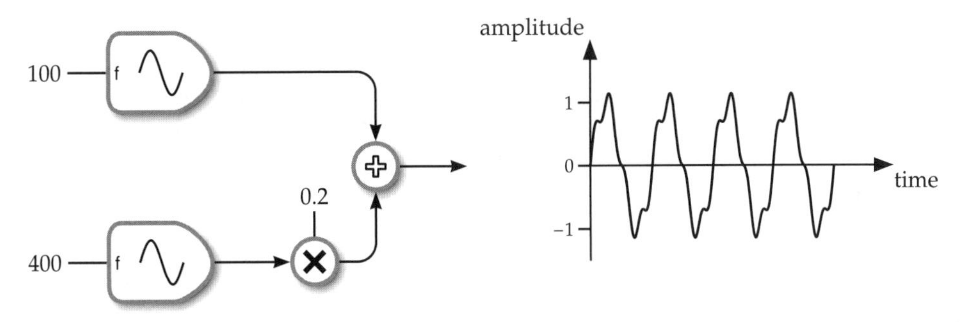

Figure 13.2 Mixing oscillator outputs

13.1.3 Note Numbers and Frequency Values

In many cases, it is desirable to be able to change the pitch of a synthesized sound with an input control device. The most common of these is the piano-style keyboard controller. Such a device will normally produce a linear scale of note numbers (such as 60 for note C4, 61 for note C♯4, 62 for note D4, and so on). Alternatively, it might produce a frequency output in hertz (such as 261.63 for note C4, 277.18 for note C♯4, 293.66 for note D4, and so on).

Table 13.1 illustrates the relationship between note numbers and corresponding fundamental frequencies. The note numbers are the same as those used in the MIDI control standard. In terms of note numbers, a semitone increase corresponds to adding 1, a half-semitone decrease corresponds to subtracting 0.5, and so on. As described by equation 2.2 (p.21), a change of s semitones is equivalent to multiplying a frequency by $2^{s/12}$.

Note number	Note name	Fundamental frequency (Hz)
0	C-1	8.18
1	C♯-1 = D♭-1	8.66
2	D-1	9.18
3	D♯-1 = E♭-1	9.72
4	E-1	10.30
5	F-1	10.91
6	F♯-1 = G♭-1	11.56
7	G-1	12.25
8	G♯-1 = A♭-1	12.98
9	A-1	13.75
10	A♯-1 = B♭-1	14.57
11	B-1	15.43
12	C0	16.35
13	C♯0 = D♭0	17.32
14	D0	18.35
15	D♯0 = E♭0	19.45
16	E0	20.60
17	F0	21.83
18	F♯0 = G♭0	23.12
19	G0	24.50
20	G♯0 = A♭0	25.96
21	A0	27.50
22	A♯0 = B♭0	29.14
23	B0	30.87
24	C1	32.70
25	C♯1 = D♭1	34.65
26	D1	36.71
27	D♯1 = E♭1	38.89
28	E1	41.20
29	F1	43.65
30	F♯1 = G♭1	46.25
31	G1	49.00
32	G♯1 = A♭1	51.91
33	A1	55.00
34	A♯1 = B♭1	58.27
35	B1	61.74
36	C2	65.41
37	C♯2 = D♭2	69.30
38	D2	73.42
39	D♯2 = E♭2	77.78
40	E2	82.41
41	F2	87.31
42	F♯2 = G♭2	92.50
43	G2	98.00
44	G♯2 = A♭2	103.83
45	A2	110.00
46	A♯2 = B♭2	116.54
47	B2	123.47
48	C3	130.81
49	C♯3 = D♭3	138.59
50	D3	146.83
51	D♯3 = E♭3	155.56
52	E3	164.81
53	F3	174.61
54	F♯3 = G♭3	185.00
55	G3	196.00
56	G♯3 = A♭3	207.65
57	A3	220.00
58	A♯3 = B♭3	233.08
59	B3	246.94
60	C4	261.63
61	C♯4 = D♭4	277.18
62	D4	293.66
63	D♯4 = E♭4	311.13
64	E4	329.63
65	F4	349.23
66	F♯4 = G♭4	369.99
67	G4	392.00
68	G♯4 = A♭4	415.30
69	A4	440.00
70	A♯4 = B♭4	466.16
71	B4	493.88
72	C5	523.25
73	C♯5 = D♭5	554.37
74	D5	587.33
75	D♯5 = E♭5	622.25
76	E5	659.26
77	F5	698.46
78	F♯5 = G♭5	739.99
79	G5	783.99
80	G♯5 = A♭5	830.61
81	A5	880.00
82	A♯5 = B♭5	932.33
83	B5	987.77
84	C6	1046.50
85	C♯6 = D♭6	1108.73
86	D6	1174.66
87	D♯6 = E♭6	1244.51
88	E6	1318.51
89	F6	1396.91
90	F♯6 = G♭6	1479.98
91	G6	1567.98
92	G♯6 = A♭6	1661.22
93	A6	1760.00
94	A♯6 = B♭6	1864.66
95	B6	1975.53
96	C7	2093.00
97	C♯7 = D♭7	2217.46
98	D7	2349.32
99	D♯7 = E♭7	2489.02
100	E7	2637.02
101	F7	2793.83
102	F♯7 = G♭7	2959.96
103	G7	3135.96
104	G♯7 = A♭7	3322.44
105	A7	3520.00
106	A♯7 = B♭7	3729.31
107	B7	3951.07
108	C8	4186.01
109	C♯8 = D♭8	4434.92
110	D8	4698.64
111	D♯8 = E♭8	4978.03
112	E8	5274.04
113	F8	5587.65
114	F♯8 = G♭8	5919.91
115	G8	6271.93
116	G♯8 = A♭8	6644.88
117	A8	7040.00
118	A♯8 = B♭8	7458.62
119	B8	7902.13
120	C9	8372.02
121	C♯9 = D♭9	8869.84
122	D9	9397.27
123	D♯9 = E♭9	9956.06
124	E9	10548.08
125	F9	11175.30
126	F♯9 = G♭9	11839.82
127	G9	12543.85

Table 13.1 Note numbers, note names, and fundamental frequencies

Note numbers and frequencies are useful in different circumstances. A frequency value is necessary for providing the input to an oscillator. However, note numbers are easier to manipulate to achieve linear changes in perceived pitch. The following equation converts from note number n to a fundamental frequency f:

$$F_{n \to f}: \qquad f = 440 \times 2^{(n-69)/12} \tag{13.1}$$

The following equation converts from fundamental frequency f to note number n:

$$F_{f \to n}: \qquad n = 69 + 12 \log_2 \left(\frac{f}{440} \right) \tag{13.2}$$

Equation 13.2 can be useful in designing an instrument tuner, where a detected fundamental frequency needs to be converted to a note number to see how far the instrument is in error in terms of semitones or cents from the desired pitch.

It is common in music to combine notes in intervals, chords, scales, and arpeggios, so it is useful to know the number of semitones separating notes in those combinations. Knowing a root or starting note, it is possible to work out the offset to the other notes. This allows a synthesizer to be programmed to generate chords, arpeggios, and algorithmic music based in a particular key. Table 13.2 illustrates some common intervals, chords, and scales. As an example, creating a minor triad chord starting at note A1 requires notes at an offset of 0, 3, and 7 semitones, which corresponds to notes A1, C2, and E2.

Name	Semitone offsets from root/starting note
Minor third	0, 3
Major third	0, 4
(Perfect) fourth	0, 5
(Perfect) fifth	0, 7
Minor sixth	0, 8
Major sixth	0, 9
Octave	0, 12
Major triad	0, 4, 7
Minor triad	0, 3, 7
Major scale	0, 2, 4, 5, 7, 9, 11, 12
Minor scale	0, 2, 3, 5, 7, 8, 10 (or 11), 12

Table 13.2 Common intervals, chords, and scales

Figure 13.3 compares the use of note number and frequency inputs. Both block diagrams produce two oscillations at an interval of s semitones when a single key is pressed on the keyboard. If the keyboard device produces note number information, then creating an offset requires **adding** s to the number. It is then necessary to convert to frequency information afterwards to use the oscillators (with function $F_{n \to f}$, from equation 13.1). If the keyboard device produces frequency information, then it is necessary to **multiply** by $2^{s/12}$, and there is no need for a conversion to frequency afterwards.

It is often easier to think in terms of note numbers when manipulating pitch information. For example, to transpose a piece of music up a semitone, add 1 to all the values. It is also the case that achieving a linear change in pitch requires a linear change in note numbers, but a non-linear change in frequency. Figure 13.4 illustrates *pitch-bend* techniques with a range of $\pm s$ semitones, where the centre position of the rotary control is no pitch change. When using note numbers the method is to add an offset. When using frequency values the bend value has to be converted into a multiplying factor.

13.1.4 Parameter Variation

Chapters 3 and 4 described how typical acoustic instruments produce sounds that vary over time. Examining the characteristics of existing sounds is useful for understanding how to construct and configure a synthesizer. The character of a sound source and its control are conveyed by such time-varying physical properties as:

- The overall amplitude envelope.
- Periodic features such as vibrato and tremolo.
- The composition of the sound in terms of the frequency and amplitude of partials, and how they change between the beginning and end of a sound event.

It is common to include these and other variations when synthesising sounds, to avoid producing a sterile or test tone type of sound. If a sound is changing its characteristics over time, it will generally be more musically interesting than one that is not varying. This might happen because the performer manually changes an input control, or because the synthesized character is programmed to modulate parameters automatically.

It is important that synthesizers produce variations of an appropriate length in time, to reflect both acoustic sound production mechanisms and the region of sensitivity of the human auditory system. For example, a typical tune might be played at a tempo of 120 beats per minute. If, however, it is played at 1 beat per minute, it is very difficult to follow the pattern and recognise the tune. Similarly, if it is played at 12000 beats per minute, it is over too quickly to pick up the note pattern.

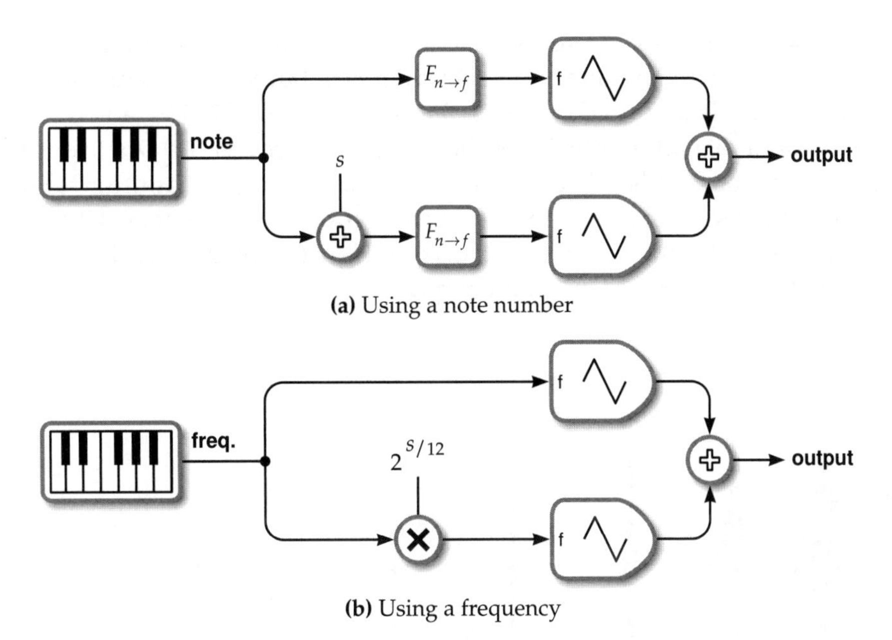

(a) Using a note number

(b) Using a frequency

Figure 13.3 Note number and frequency control inputs

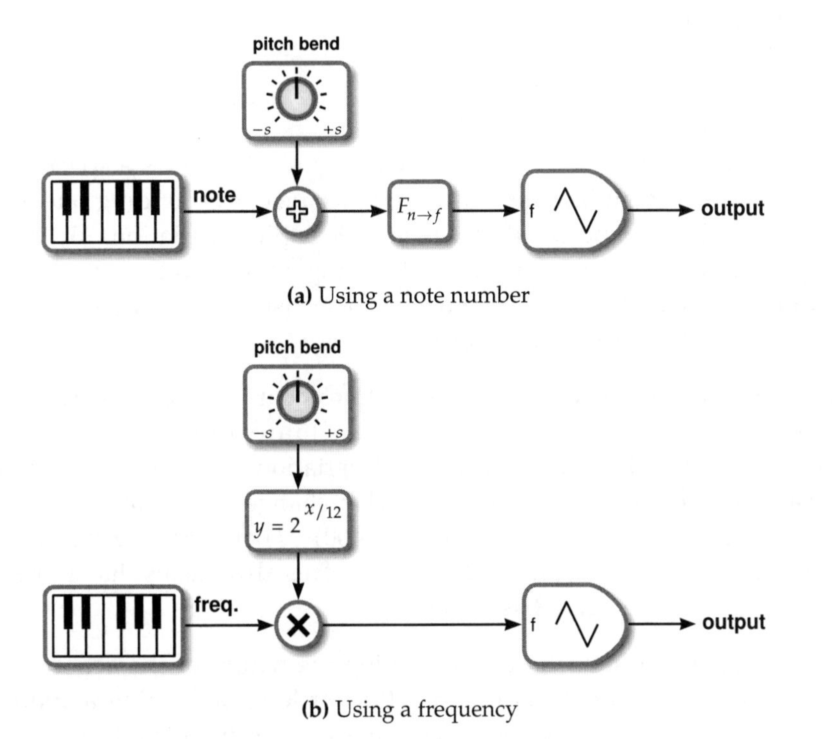

(a) Using a note number

(b) Using a frequency

Figure 13.4 Pitch-bend techniques

Figure 13.5 shows a series of 1kHz sinusoidal tones with exponential amplitude envelopes. The envelopes have matching attack and decay times, but with decreasing length over time. The events have lengths in the order 1, 0.5, 0.2, 0.1, 0.05, 0.02, 0.01, and 0.005 seconds. The last event has a total of five cycles of the waveform, because 1kHz equates to a cycle length of 0.001 seconds. When listening to these there is a gradual progression from a clear audible variation in time with the 1 second event, to a transient click with the 0.005 second version. By about the fourth event (0.1s) the sense of pitch starts to disappear and the transient nature starts to become more important.

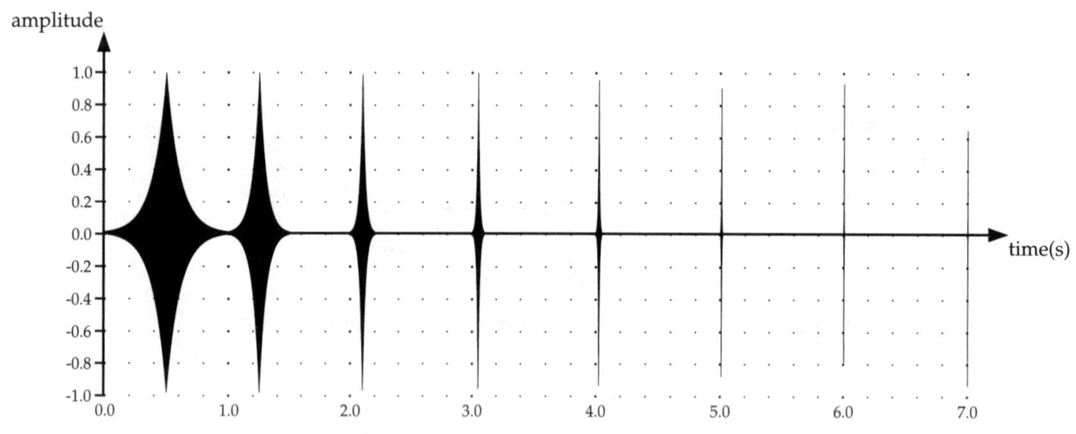

Figure 13.5 Amplitude-enveloped 1kHz sinusoidal test tones

A similar effect occurs when modulating pitch. Figure 13.6 shows a spectrogram plot of pitch variations. Each event has the same length as the corresponding one in figure 13.5. The first event (1s long) is perceived to have a clear pitch variation. By the fifth event (0.05s) the pitch change is starting to fuse into a single timbre rather than being heard to vary over time. By the end it is a transient click. The visual representation in both figures mirrors the audible one in some key respects.

As well as the length of time over which a variation occurs, it is also necessary to consider the shape of the variation and its magnitude. The nature of different amplitude envelopes is discussed in §3.2.2 (p.51), where shaping of variation is important to the end result. Another example is frequency variation. A 1Hz change is a different proportion of a semitone at different frequencies (table 13.1, p.400). Therefore 1Hz will have different significance depending on the starting frequency. This also means that a linear variation in frequency will not be **perceived** as linear.

The onset region is often important in indicating the nature of the action that caused a sonic event. Many onsets are brief (often 100ms or less), indicating a sudden input of energy. The length and shape of the onset variation can be related to figures 13.5 and 13.6 in terms of how short variations are perceived. In a synthesized sound it is common

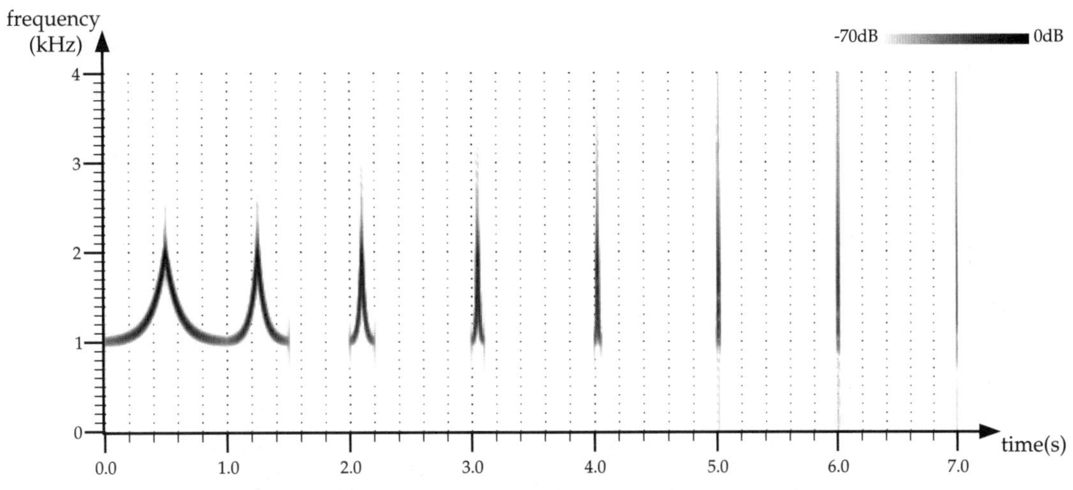

Figure 13.6 Spectrogram of pitch-enveloped sinusoidal test tones

to have both a significant amplitude variation and underlying tonal change at the start, which relates to the nature of acoustic instruments and the importance of those variations to the human auditory system. However, that is not the only way of developing a sound over time. Variations can be placed anywhere in the sound event to add interest.

Sounds that have been generated acoustically are a useful source of information. Figure 13.7 shows a spectrogram plot of the word "far" sung by a male voice. Some features are as follows:

- The composition of the sound is constantly changing over its length.
- At the start of the sound there is the noisy "f", which subsequently blends into the rest of the sound in a transition region at around 0.45s. The change of character is not instantaneous, and the harmonics in the "ah" part of the sound do not emerge at exactly the same time.
- In the "ah" part of the sound there is a clear vibrato modulation that affects the frequencies of the harmonic partials. The vibrato does not begin immediately after the transition from "f" to "ah", as there is a more stable region first.
- At the end of the sound, the frequency partials do not all fade simultaneously.

Mechanisms are required to incorporate variations in synthesis, in order to generate a sound that has similar interest and depth of tonality to the "far" example. These mechanisms can control characteristics from the overall amplitude envelope down to individual frequency partials.

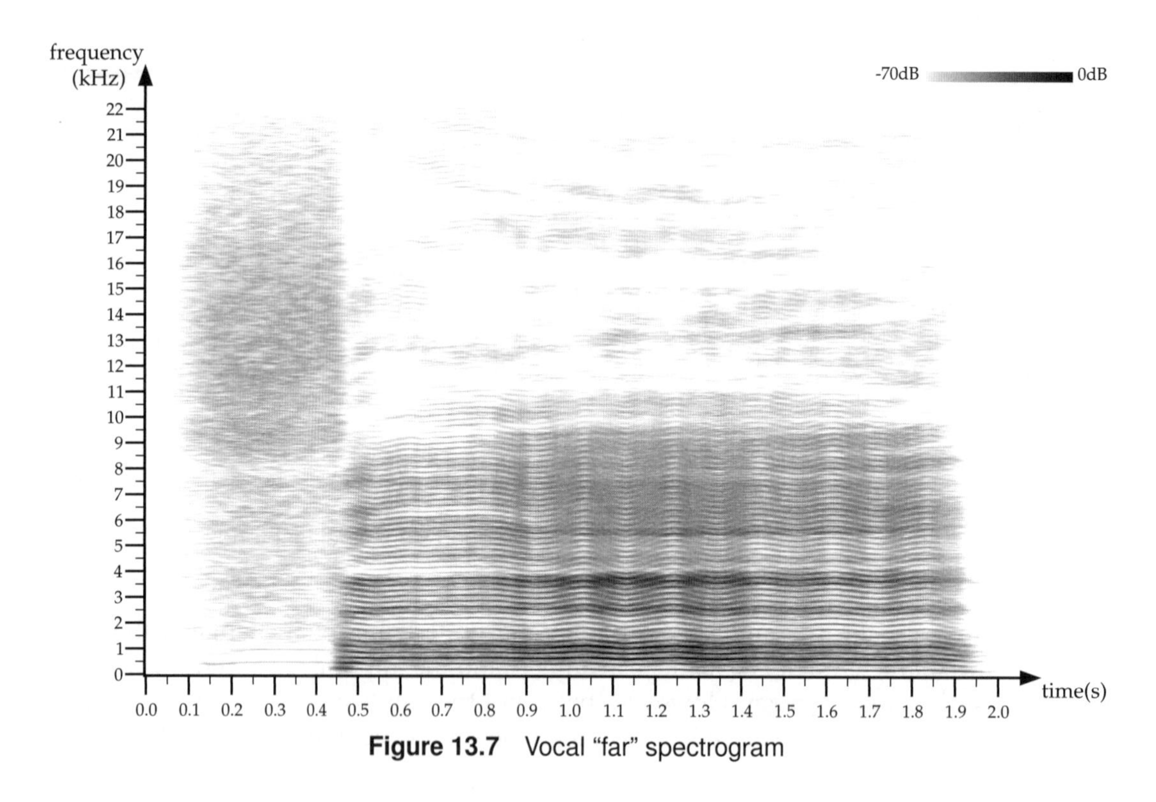

Figure 13.7 Vocal "far" spectrogram

13.2 Gate and Envelope Methods

13.2.1 Basic Methods

Most synthesis is driven directly from some kind of user input to cause individual sound events. A synthesizer requires a suitable set of signals from the control device to create the desired result. Figure 13.8 shows a basic keyboard-controlled synthesizer. The keyboard produces a fundamental frequency value (corresponding to the note selected) and a *gate* signal (which indicates *note-on* and *note-off* events). The fundamental frequency is fed to an oscillator, and the gate signal is used as the input to an *envelope generator (EG)*. The symbol on the envelope generator block indicates how its output will vary over time when a note event occurs. The envelope generator output is used as a gain value to create an amplitude envelope.

Figure 13.9 shows one way in which the note-on and note-off events can be used by the envelope generator. When a note-on event occurs (a key is depressed) the attack (onset) part of the note begins, followed by a gradual decay of amplitude. After the note-off event there is a release with a more rapid decay. This has something in common with a piano,

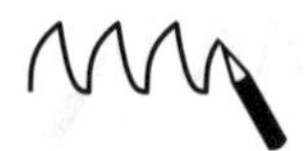

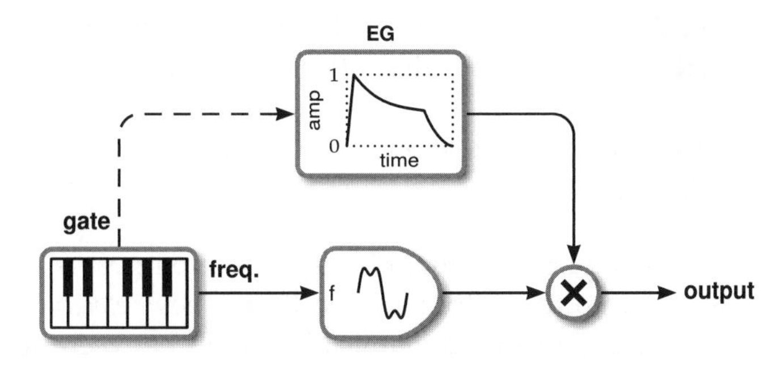

Figure 13.8 Basic keyboard-controlled synthesizer

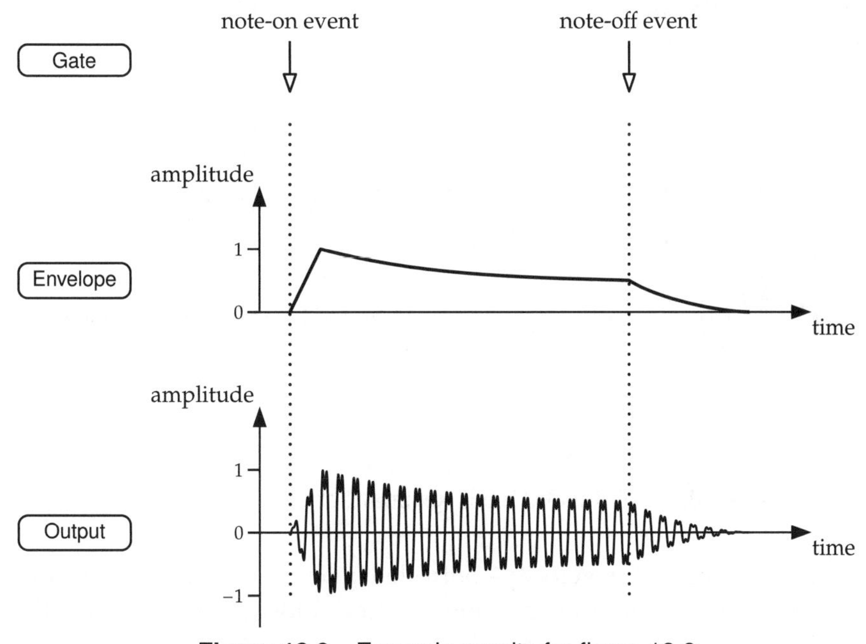

Figure 13.9 Example results for figure 13.8

where the note attacks as the key is depressed, then begins to gradually decay. If the key is lifted before the decay finishes, a faster fade occurs as the strings are damped.

In the example, the envelope generator is programmed to respond to note-off events. In some cases the note-off event will be ignored. This is because instruments such as a crash cymbal, snare drum, and xylophone have an envelope that is started by an input of energy, after which there is not usually an end of note damping effect. In some cases it is possible to end the sound rapidly by way of deliberately damping the resonance, but that is not the principal way of playing the instrument.

An important feature of figures 13.8 and 13.9 is that the frequency value provided to the oscillator and the oscillator output must both continue after the note-off event in order that the output can have an appropriate release. This is also a monophonic arrangement, as a single oscillator can only produce a single output at once. Synthesis control is discussed in more detail in §23.2 (p.644).

Figure 13.10 illustrates how figure 13.8 might be extended to increase usability. Firstly a master gain control is added to the output. Secondly the key *velocity* is used to control gain such that peak amplitude can be dynamically varied between notes (greater key velocity leading to a louder result). Key velocity in many systems has a range of 0 to 127. Velocity information is provided at the note-on event, reflecting how quickly the key was depressed. The scaling of velocity can be made more sophisticated, as described in §24.1.3 (p.661).

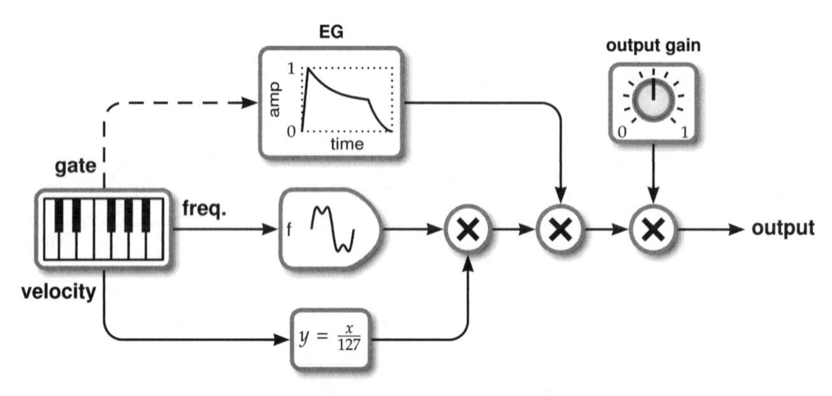

Figure 13.10 Extended basic keyboard-controlled synthesizer

An output gain control and a velocity-controlled gain are standard features of many synthesizers. For visual clarity they are omitted from most of the diagrams that follow, but they are easy to include if required.

13.2.2 Envelope Shapes and Applications

The shape produced by an envelope generator is often chosen to match an existing sound, or adjusted by ear to have the desired characteristics. For example, attack length can be changed between indicating a sudden input of energy or a more gentle swell to maximum level over a long period of time. Similarly the shape might be fairly simple (such as an attack and decay) or a complex series of different variations.

What happens if the key is held down indefinitely (rather than released) is not necessarily clear in figure 13.9. With a basic arrangement there are two common amplitude envelope effects after the onset when a key is held down:

- The amplitude steadily decays to zero (similar to a piano).
- The amplitude settles to a somewhat steady level that continues until the key is released (similar to a pipe organ).

These are illustrated in figure 13.11. The difference is whether the instrument sound being synthesized is associated with an instrument that is excited and then allowed to resonate and decay (like a xylophone, cymbal, or piano), or whether there is a continual excitation that maintains the amplitude level (like an organ, clarinet, or bowed violin).

There are many possibilities with envelopes other than the short attack followed by a fade seen previously. Figure 13.12a shows an example of a gentle swell with some superimposed variations. This is the sort of shape that can be created with a wind or bowed string instrument where there is continuous control over amplitude. Figure 13.12b is a more unusual characteristic where the accelerating rise and rapid release is the reverse of a shape such as figure 13.11a. As well as copying a typical acoustic instrument shape, it is equally valid to choose an envelope characteristic that stands out due to its atypical style.

It is necessary to consider the technique by which envelopes are configured, such that users can achieve the desired effect easily. Some traditional envelope forms are shown in figure 13.13. The envelopes are described as a series of line segments between breakpoint positions. *Attack-Decay-Sustain-Release (ADSR)* is the most common form, and is typically configured with four controls; attack time (to reach the maximum level), decay time, sustain level, and release time. The sustain segment will normally last as long as a key is held, and when the key is lifted the release will occur. The AD, ADR, and ASR/AR shapes can be achieved by zeroing or removing segments from the ADSR form.

The traditional envelope styles have the following useful features:

- They can be configured very quickly with a small number of parameters.
- Because only a small number of parameters are required, they are cheap to implement on a hardware control device.
- A fair amount of flexibility is present to allow shape variations.
- A simple on-off key control style can be used to drive the envelope generator.

A significant issue with the traditional envelope shapes is whether they can be adapted to achieve all desired shapes. It is apparent in §3.2.2 (p.51) that many interesting sounds have a much more complex amplitude variation than those shown in figure 13.13.

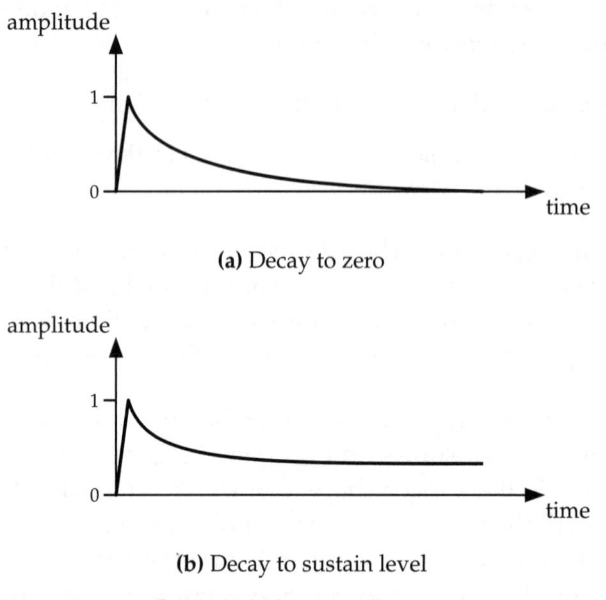

(a) Decay to zero

(b) Decay to sustain level

Figure 13.11 Basic held key amplitude envelope effects

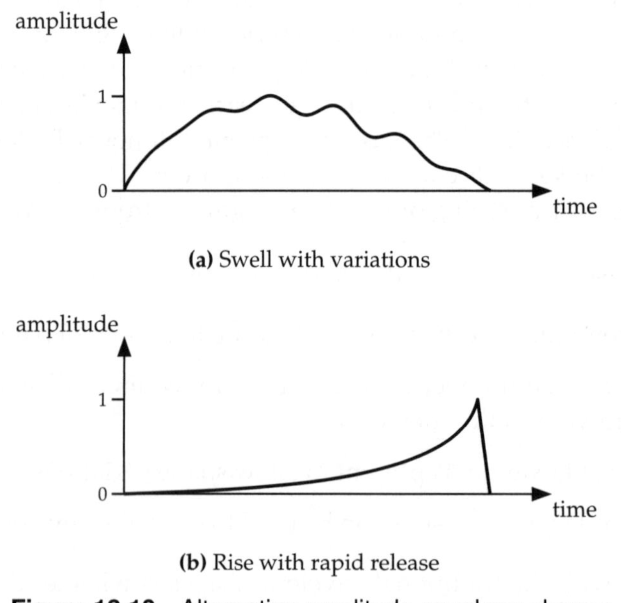

(a) Swell with variations

(b) Rise with rapid release

Figure 13.12 Alternative amplitude envelope shapes

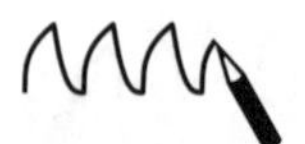

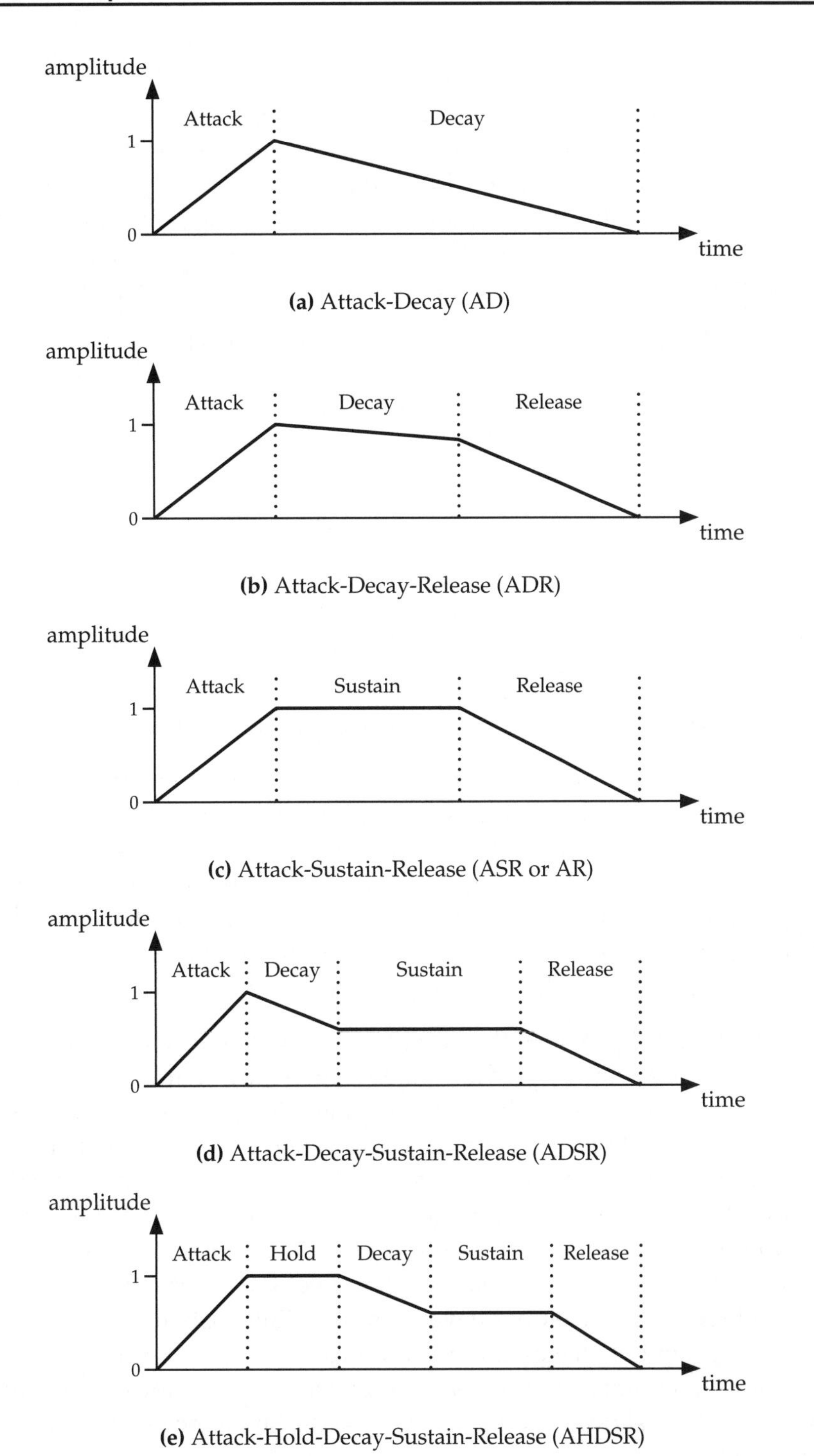

Figure 13.13 Traditional envelope styles

There are two key ways in which envelope control can be made more flexible:

- It is possible to add additional segments of similar types. For example, ADDSR would have two decay segments before the sustain in order to allow more control over the shaping in that region. In a graphical system it is possible to create an interface that allows the manipulation of a series of breakpoints that can exist in any desired quantity and positions. This allows the creation of an arbitrarily complex shape, rather than being restricted to a particular pattern of segments.
- Linear envelope segments are not necessarily most appropriate to achieve amplitude variation that has similarities to acoustic sources. It is possible to use curves to link the breakpoints together as shown in figure 13.14.

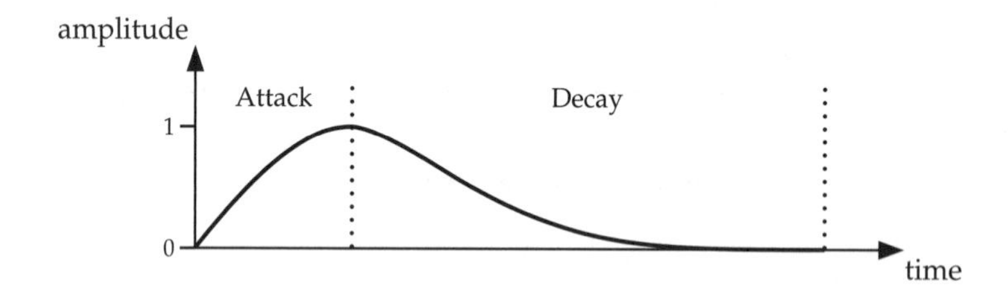

Figure 13.14 Attack-decay envelope with non-linear segments

The advantage of having a sustain segment in an envelope generator shape is that the output can continue at a non-zero value for as long as the key is held down, and then enter the final stages at a time determined by the performer. The issue is that if the output is constant then there is no associated sound development. This can mean that the beginning and end of the sound has interest, but it is plain in the middle. One technique for avoiding this problem is to impose an enveloped oscillation on the main envelope, such that the sound continues to develop while sustaining, as shown in figure 13.15.

In the figure, oscillator 2 provides the amplitude envelope variation effect. The rate of oscillation might be very low to provide a slowly evolving character over a long period of time, or faster to provide more obvious wobbling effects. Its waveform might be more complex to provide an interesting variation. The gate input to the oscillator is to reset it to a zero phase position when the note starts. This ensures that the oscillation pattern is synchronised to the main amplitude envelope, otherwise with a low rate there is a possibility of oscillator 2 being at a different part of its cycle for each note. Envelope generator 1 controls the depth of oscillation and envelope generator 2 provides the main amplitude envelope. Both envelopes have corresponding sustaining portions. Note that the two envelope generators have different amplitude ranges. Another way of producing a variation over a long period of time is as an envelope generator that includes internal looping, for example as shown in figure 14.11 (p.442). Envelope generation processes are discussed in more detail in Chapter 14.

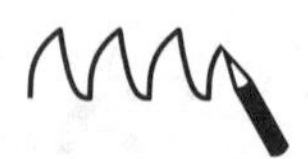

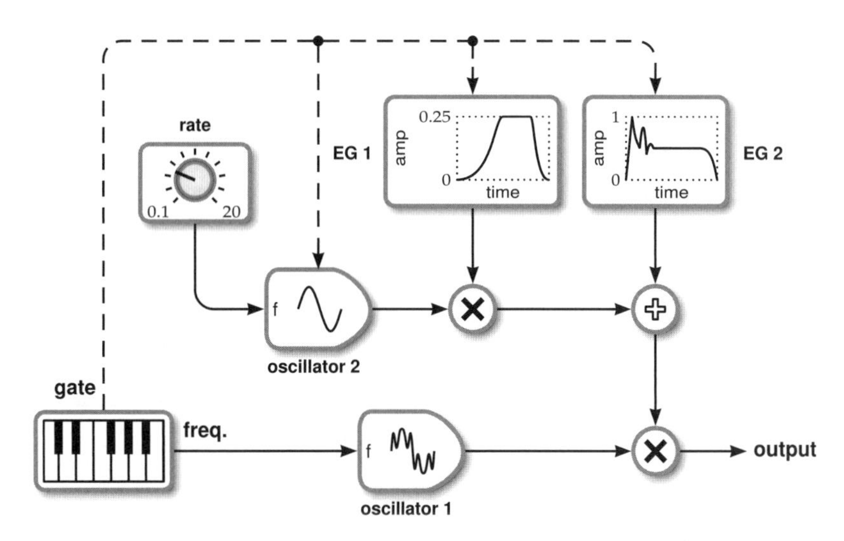

Figure 13.15 Amplitude envelope with oscillator modulation

Creating an overall amplitude envelope is a typical use of an envelope generator, but more sophisticated synthesis uses envelope generators to control many different parameters within the system. Sounds produced by acoustic sources tend to have significant variation in multiple aspects of sound character over time. The synthesis of variations needs to be tailored to the type of sound being produced. If a sound is to appear similar to that of an acoustic instrument, then it is necessary to analyse the time and frequency domain behaviour of recorded sounds and then apply those features to synthesis. However, if it is to appear unlike acoustic sources, then there are fewer constraints on behaviour.

Many parameters can be controlled using envelope generators, including filter frequency values, waveform shapes, and sample playback positions. The output range of the envelope generator must be adjusted to suit the controlled parameter; it will not always be between 0 and 1. Figure 13.16 illustrates a synthesizer with two envelope generators, where generator 1 controls a fundamental frequency variation and generator 2 controls the output amplitude envelope. The pitch variation is specified in terms of semitones, so is converted to a frequency multiple using the same method as figure 13.4b (p.403). An envelope value of 0 means that the oscillator will have the same fundamental frequency as produced from the input device. The figure also demonstrates that envelopes produced within a single synthesis structure can have significantly different shapes.

There are a number of ways of configuring the pitch envelope. Firstly, the time duration of the two envelopes does not have to be the same. For example, the pitch envelope might be very short (say 10ms) compared to the amplitude envelope, such that the variation is concentrated in the attack portion of the sound. It is quite common for sounds to have

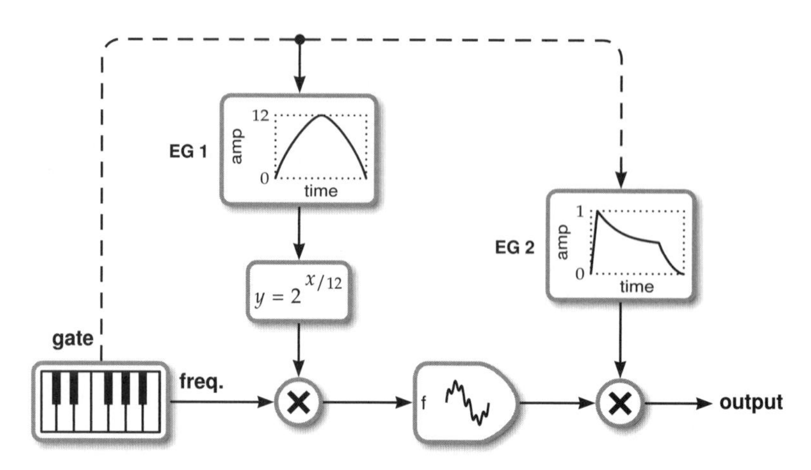

Figure 13.16 Creating a pitch envelope

a character variation in the attack, and pitch variation can be part of that. Alternatively, there might be a longer term trend such as a gentle decrease of a few semitones in pitch over the early stages, which is associated with sounds such as a tom-tom. Sometimes the pitch effect can be more extreme in range, complexity, or length in order to create a variation over time that will make it stand out.

Figure 13.17 shows an example of how an envelope generator can be used to control filter cutoff frequencies. The synthesizer has a two channel output where the filtering is applied at related, but different, cutoff frequencies such that a stereo effect is achieved. The output of envelope generator 2 has been chosen to have a falling and rising shape, which is quite different from the amplitude envelope shapes seen previously. The oscillator produces a wide range of frequency partials such that the filtering effect is clear. This is an example of subtractive synthesis, which is explored further in Chapter 17.

The diagrams above show a piano-style keyboard controlling the synthesizer, but this could be replaced with other control inputs such as another physical controller, or a sequencer. Different devices produce different control information. For example, a breath sensor will produce a value that varies continuously, which could be used as an amplitude gain factor instead of employing an envelope generator. It is also possible to derive information from an audio source such as the amplitude envelope and pitch of a guitar, and use that to control the synthesizer.

13.2.3 Audio Input Methods

Figure 13.18 shows how an audio input might be used to create a gate signal, for controlling both modification and synthesis. In a similar way to a noise gate (described in §11.2, p.341), the amplitude envelope of the input sound is compared to a threshold by

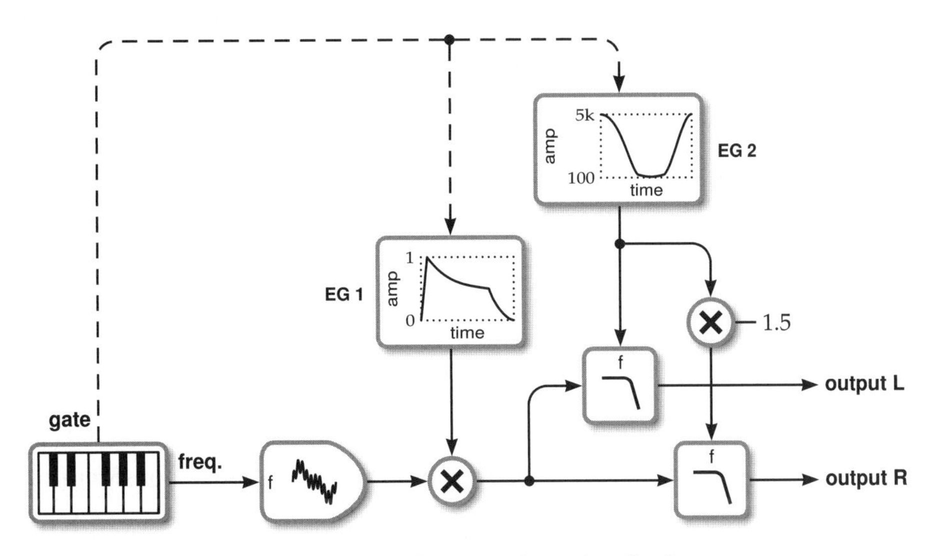

Figure 13.17 Stereo subtractive filtering

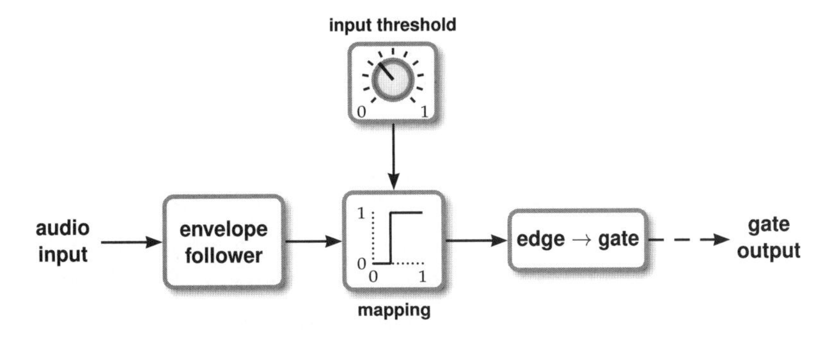

Figure 13.18 Basic audio input to gate conversion

use of a mapping function. If the amplitude passes the threshold then the output of the mapping block will increase from 0 to 1. The "edge → gate" block detects transitions between 0 and 1 (and vice versa) and creates suitable note-on and note-off events. A basic example of this block is described in algorithm 13.1, where the value of variable *lastinput* is maintained between calls to the function, and initially has a value of 0.

This type of form is used in sample replacement, where the gate signal causes the playback of a stored sound to replace a less desirable one. For example, if a kick drum track in a multitrack recording is found to be inadequate, it can be used to trigger prerecorded samples of a better quality. This is often easier than setting up the entire drum kit again. Sample techniques are discussed further in Chapter 15.

Algorithm 13.1 – Edge → gate function

```
input : input signal in
output: output signal out

if in != lastinput then
    if in == 1 then
        out = note-on
    else
        out = note-off
    lastinput = in
```

When using figure 13.18 in practice, there are a number of important considerations:

- The audio input to gate conversion needs to be tuned to react appropriately to the particular input chosen. Not only must the threshold be adjusted, but the envelope follower as well. A peak level method is a reasonable choice (see §8.3, p.245) and it might be necessary to adjust the window length. The aim is to react quickly to an onset in the input, but to ignore fluctuations in amplitude in the body of the note. Missing a note event, or multiple output triggers for one event are possible problems. Filtering the input for a specific frequency range can help.
- It will often be the case that multiple input note events will occur in quick succession, so there might be overlap between the end of one triggered sound and the next. If the triggered sampler or synthesizer is monophonic then there might be an audible discontinuity unless the transition is carefully managed. The alternative is that a polyphonic system is used where each triggering event causes a separate sound to be generated. Synthesis control is discussed in more detail in §23.2 (p.644).
- Different notes in the input might have different amplitude. If keeping this variation is desirable then the envelope follower could be used as a source of amplitude information to multiply by the output of the triggered synthesizer. It is necessary to find the peak amplitude for the input, which is likely to occur at some point shortly after the threshold is reached, and that peak value should be applied to the whole of the output sound.
- Another way of creating variation in the output is to add randomised variations for each output event, such as slightly different samples or variations in filtering, to mimic the natural variations found when playing an acoustic instrument.
- The form in the figure does not distinguish between different pitches or different types of input (such as the difference between a snare and a kick drum). More sophisticated analysis is required if the triggered results are to match those variations.

Figure 13.19 illustrates a development of figure 13.18 to create an envelope reshaping effect. The diagram has some similarities to the noise gate in figure 11.11 (p.348). The delay is chosen to compensate for any processing delay in the upper (sidechain) path. Values are converted from decibels using equation 5.3 (p.113). Decibel values (rather than linear gain units) are used for the threshold and the amplitude range of the envelope generator, as they relate appropriately to the way in which humans perceive amplitude.

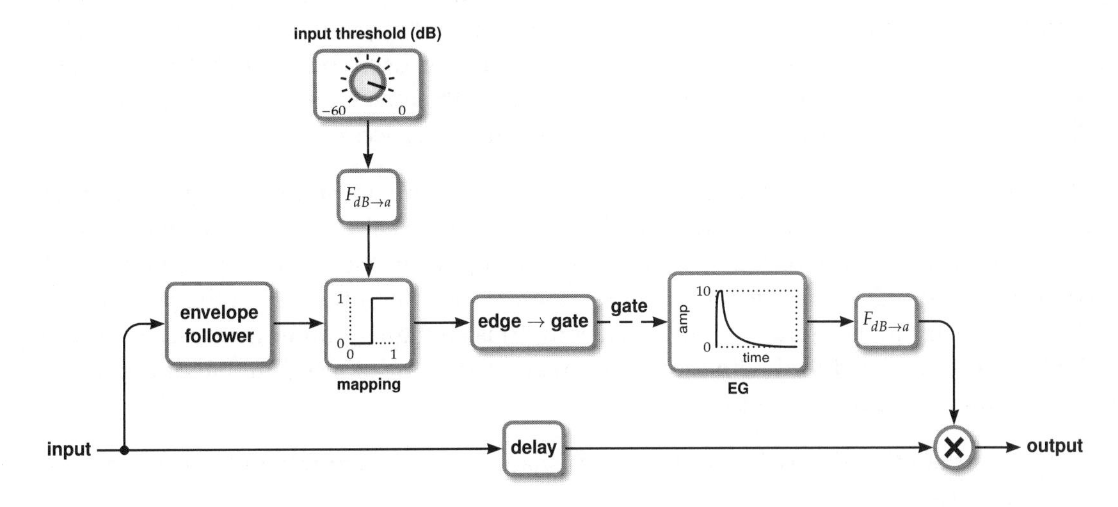

Figure 13.19 Envelope reshaping

The threshold is compared to the input amplitude envelope level. Passing the threshold causes the generation of a gate signal for the envelope generator. Both the length of time and the amplitude range of the envelope can be adjusted to suit different situations. In the figure the envelope shape and range boosts the amplitude of the input signal briefly at the start of the sound by 10dB (a linear gain factor of about 3.16) before returning to 0dB (a linear gain of 1). This can be used to add additional attack emphasis to the input signal. Some alternative envelope ideas include:

- A swell later in the sound, rather than a boost at the start, in order to reshape a sustain or decay portion.
- A complex pattern of tremolo-like variations that change over time, but will be synchronised with the start of the note.
- A negative decibel gain range to allow attenuation, such as softening the attack portion or reducing the length of sound events.

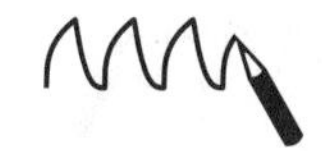

13.3 Tremolo and Vibrato in Synthesis

The most common examples of low-rate cyclical variations in synthesis are tremolo (periodic amplitude variation) and vibrato (periodic frequency variation). The techniques are similar to those seen in Chapter 9. A low rate oscillator is often called an *LFO* (Low Frequency Oscillator) when used in synthesis.

Figure 13.20 shows an example of using a low frequency oscillator to produce tremolo. Oscillator 1 produces a low rate signal, scaled by the depth parameter and then offset by adding 0.5 such that the result is between 0 and 1. This is used to modulate the amplitude of oscillator 2, whose output is subject to the effect of the envelope generator. Figure 13.21 illustrates some typical signals at different points in the process.

The frequency of an oscillator can be modulated over time to produce vibrato as shown in figure 13.22. Oscillator 1 produces a low rate signal, scaled by a depth parameter in semitones and then converted to a frequency multiplier in the same way as figure 13.16 (p.414). Figure 13.23 illustrates some typical signals at different points in the process. Notice how the frequency (and thus the cycle length) is changing, rather than the amplitude. Subtle effects are produced with low depths (say 1 semitone or less), but larger depths can be used for more extreme effects.

As well as changing the oscillator waveform shape there are a number of ways of extending figures 13.20 and 13.22:

- Any synthesis parameter can be varied in a similar way, rather than the techniques being restricted to amplitude and fundamental frequency modulation.
- Using very low modulation rates and a more complex waveform shape can achieve interesting repeating patterns. For example, with a rate of 0.1Hz the modulation pattern will repeat every 10 seconds, producing a slowly evolving result.
- High modulation rates can be used. This is explored further in Chapter 20.
- The gate signal might be used to reset the phase of the modulating oscillator to zero at the start of the sound, such that the same part of the cycle occurs in the same place for each sound event. It is not always the case that this synchronisation is desirable; for example when simulating an electronic instrument where there is a free-running modulating effect, or where a complex pattern is designed to cause an evolution of character over many notes rather than being reset to the start each time.
- The depth might be controlled by an envelope. This allows the effect to be introduced over time, for example, rather than being present from the start of the sound. In some cases it might also be interesting to vary the oscillator rate over time, as well as the depth.

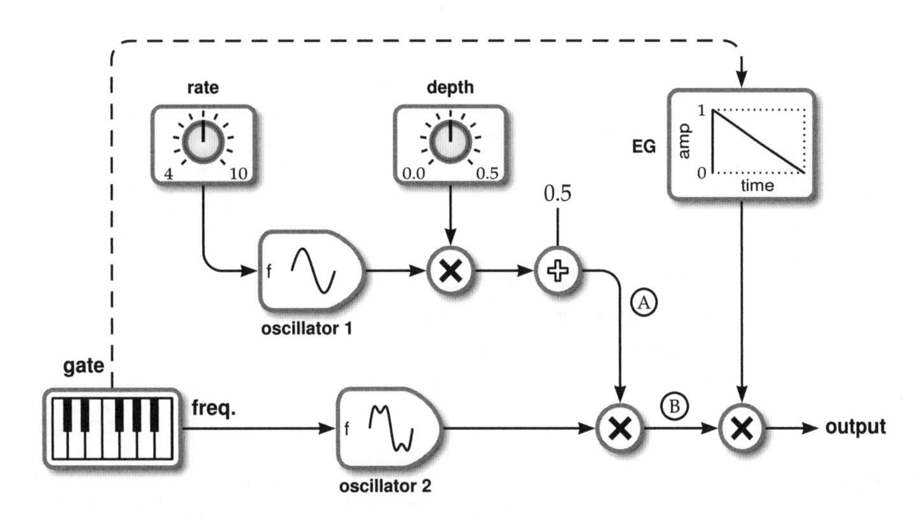

Figure 13.20 Tremolo

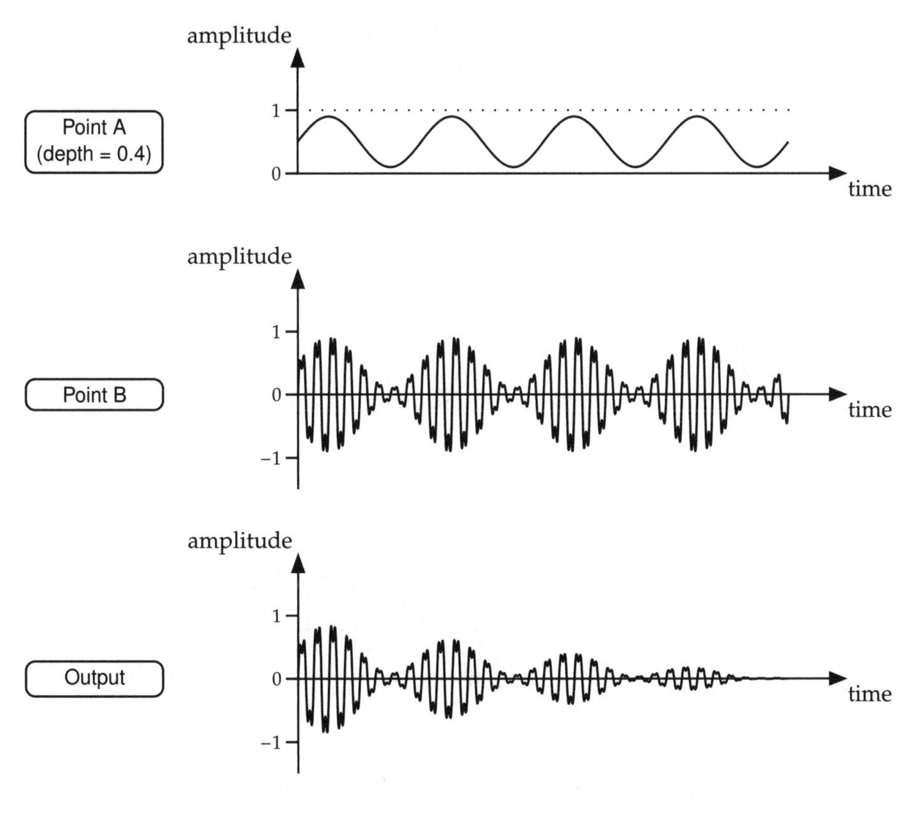

Figure 13.21 Example results for figure 13.20

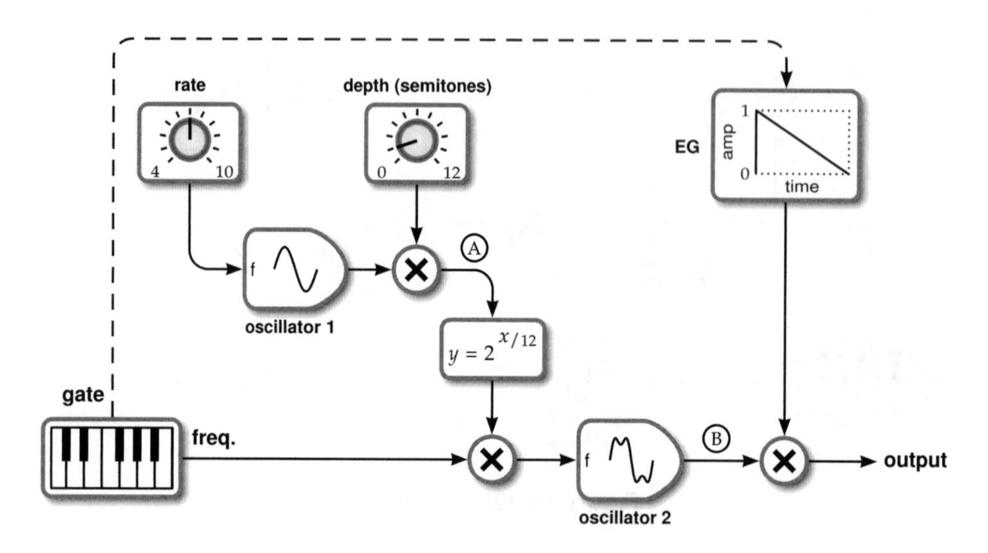

Figure 13.22 Vibrato

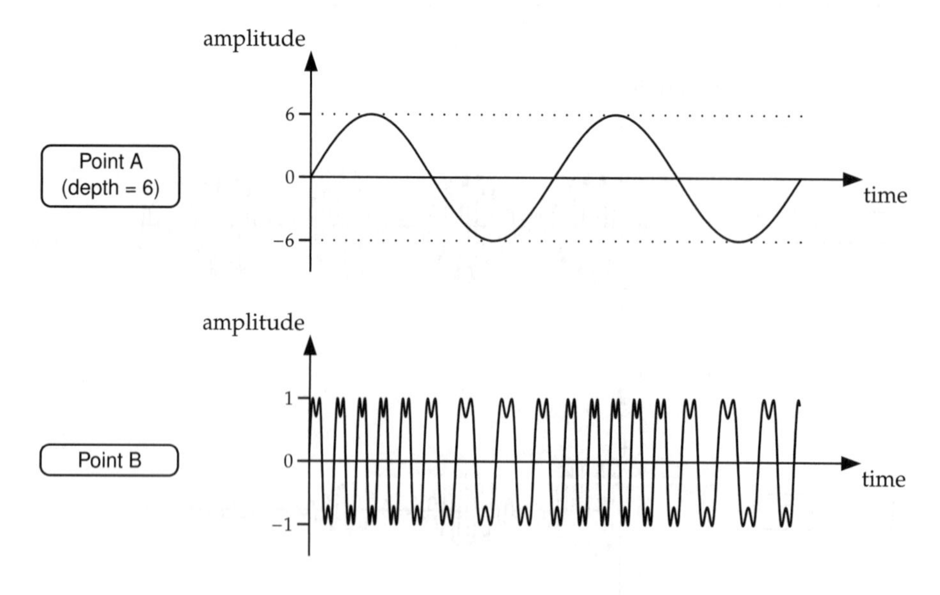

Figure 13.23 Example results for figure 13.22

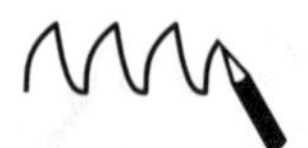

13.4 Developing Processes and Learning More

The synthesizers described in this chapter principally use standard blocks that are found in audio programming libraries and environments. The low-level design of oscillators and envelope generators is discussed in more detail in Chapter 14. Noise generators, which have a related role to oscillators, are considered in Chapter 18. There is also further detail on suitable techniques for organising and controlling synthesis in Chapter 23.

The synthesis forms in this chapter achieve the basic requirements for sound generation. However, to create more interesting tonal characters requires more sophisticated approaches; for example, reshaping waveforms over time (discussed in Chapters 14 and 15), summing and blending multiple amplitude-weighted oscillations (Chapters 16 and 19), more complex filtering schemes (Chapters 17 and 18), advanced modulation techniques (Chapter 20), physical modelling (Chapter 21), or synthesis from granular (non-continuous) forms (Chapter 22). To select a synthesis technique to achieve a particular result requires an appreciation of the different options that are available, as each one has different tonal capabilities, flexibility, and efficiency. It is worth experimenting with different techniques, therefore.

The following book provides further information on a wide range of synthesis techniques and their control:

> Russ, Martin. 2013. *Sound Synthesis and Sampling (Third Edition).*
> Burlington, MA: Focal Press.

Synthesizer techniques draw on many of the concepts and methods explored in detail in previous chapters. The chapters that follow assume familiarity with those ideas.

Developing Processes and Learning More

14

Signal Generators and Shaping

14.1 Introduction

Signal generators are fundamental to a wide range of audio processes. The main types of signal generator in this book are:

- Oscillators that produce a continuous repeating waveform output.
- Noise generators that produce a continuous irregular waveform output.
- Envelope generators that produce a non-repeating output.

All three are related in terms of their construction, as they must all produce a varying output value over a particular length of time. One relationship that is discussed later in this chapter is that an envelope generator can be modified to become an oscillator. This is achieved by controlling whether the process wraps around to the start of the waveform when the end of the shape is reached. This chapter focuses particularly on the design of oscillators and envelope generators, while Chapter 18 describes noise generators and their applications.

The way that an oscillator shape is perceived depends on the fundamental frequency used. At very low frequencies, such as those used for modulation in Chapter 9, the audible effect can relate closely to the visual shape. At higher frequencies, such as when creating a pitched tone for synthesis, there is a more complex relationship between visual form and audible effect, as the relationships between the frequency partials that compose the shape are important. This chapter describes designs that are applicable to all generation frequencies.

Three fundamental signal generation methods are covered in this chapter:

- Equation-based methods, where a mathematical equation can describe the output shape. Such an equation might use trigonometric functions or line segments, for example.
- Breakpoint methods, where a shape is defined by an arbitrary number of time and amplitude coordinate pairs. The generator interpolates output values along the segments between the breakpoints.
- Wavetable methods, where a sampled shape is stored in a buffer with regular spacing between the data points.

Each type of method has different benefits and limitations, which are considered in the following sections.

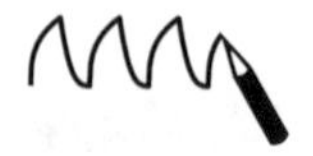

14.2 Equation-Based Methods

14.2.1 Basic Concepts

Equation-based methods are used most commonly in creating oscillators (which will be the focus of this section) rather than envelope generators (where breakpoint methods are more common). Equations describe the relationship between variables. For an oscillator, the relationship between a position in time and an output amplitude value is the concern.

To generate a signal in a digital system requires the production of a series of output values at the sample rate (equally spaced in time). The rate at which the generator moves along the waveform shape determines the length of the output cycle. Consider the single cycle of a sine wave in figure 14.1. If the sample rate is 44.1kHz then there are 44100 samples per second. If the required cycle length is 1 second and the cycle is 2π radians long, then the phase value for the oscillator must take 44100 steps to get from 0 to 2π. Similarly, if the required cycle length is 0.5 seconds, it must take 22050 steps to get from 0 to 2π. Therefore, if T is the cycle length in seconds, and f_S is the sample rate:

$$\text{phase steps per cycle} = T \times f_S \qquad \boxed{14.1}$$

From this result it is possible to work out the size of each step (or *phase increment*, $\Delta\phi$) in radians:

$$\text{phase increment} = \Delta\phi = \frac{\text{radians per cycle}}{\text{steps per cycle}} = \frac{2\pi}{T \times f_S} \qquad \boxed{14.2}$$

For an oscillator it is more appropriate to express this in terms of frequency. As $F = 1/T$:

$$\Delta\phi = \frac{2\pi F}{f_S} \qquad \boxed{14.3}$$

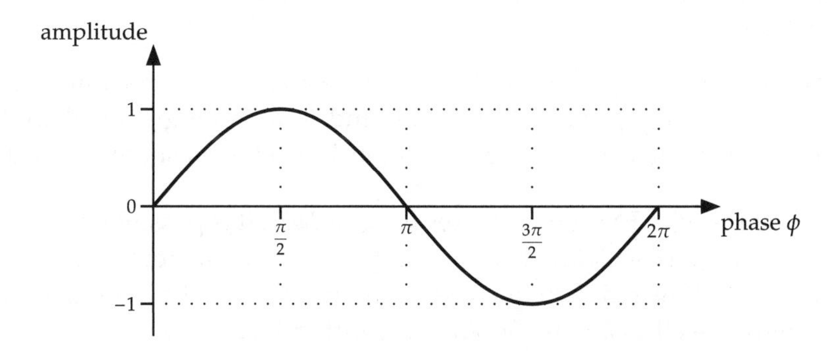

Figure 14.1 Sine wave

Figure 14.2 shows how successive phase positions are chosen. The current phase position starts at 0, and increases by $\Delta\phi$ once per sample, until it is at least 2π. At that point it is wrapped around to the beginning again by subtracting 2π, such that the phase value is in the same position that it would have been on the next cycle and so continuing the oscillation. Maintaining the phase within the 0 to 2π range (rather than constantly increasing) makes the process of defining equations easier.

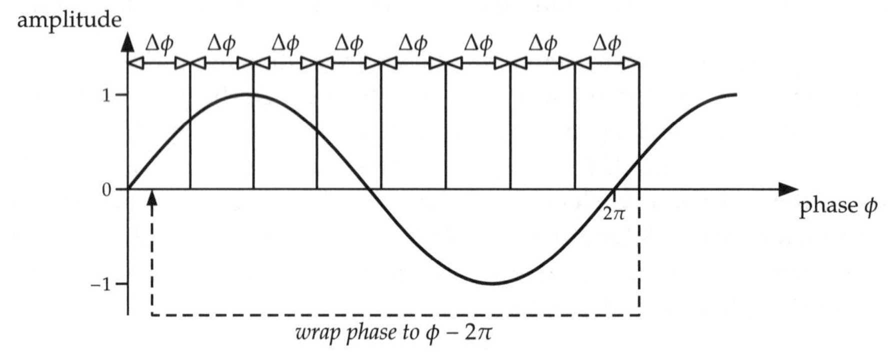

Figure 14.2 Stepping and wrapping phase position

These ideas can be used to create an oscillator function as described in algorithm 14.1. The features are as follows:

- The function is called once per output value (at the sample rate).
- It is assumed that the value of *phase* is maintained between calls to the function, and initially has a value of 0.
- Function *genfunction()* will be defined later. Its role is to return the waveform amplitude value corresponding to a particular phase position.
- For each output sample the *phase* is increased by the phase increment ($\Delta\phi$ from equation 14.3).
- The *phase* value is wrapped around if it is at least 2π, by subtracting 2π. As shown in figure 14.2, usually *phase* will wrap around to a value greater than 0, which is necessary to maintain a correct phase relationship between successive values.

In some cases, such as with FM synthesis (see §20.3, p.567), it is possible to have a negative frequency value fed to an oscillator. This means that the phase increment is also a negative value (equation 14.3). If negative frequencies are to be allowed it is necessary to wrap the phase around zero as well as 2π, as shown in algorithm 14.2.

Algorithm 14.1 – Oscillator function 1

```
input : frequency F
output: output signal out

out = genfunction(phase)
phase = phase + 2πF / samplerate
while phase >= 2π do
    phase = phase − 2π
```

Algorithm 14.2 – Oscillator function 2

```
input : frequency F
output: output signal out

out = genfunction(phase)
phase = phase + 2πF / samplerate
while phase >= 2π do
    phase = phase − 2π
while phase < 0 do
    phase = phase + 2π
```

14.2.2 Example Equations

Figure 14.3 shows the equations for some standard oscillator shapes. The *genfunction()* that is called from the oscillator algorithms will implement these. Algorithm 14.3 demonstrates how the square wave equation translates into code. Because the main oscillator function ensures that *phase* is within the range 0 to 2π, the test in algorithm 14.3 is whether it is less than π or not.

Algorithm 14.3 – Square wave *genfunction()*

```
input : phase value
output: output signal out

if phase < π then
    out = 1
else
    out = −1
```

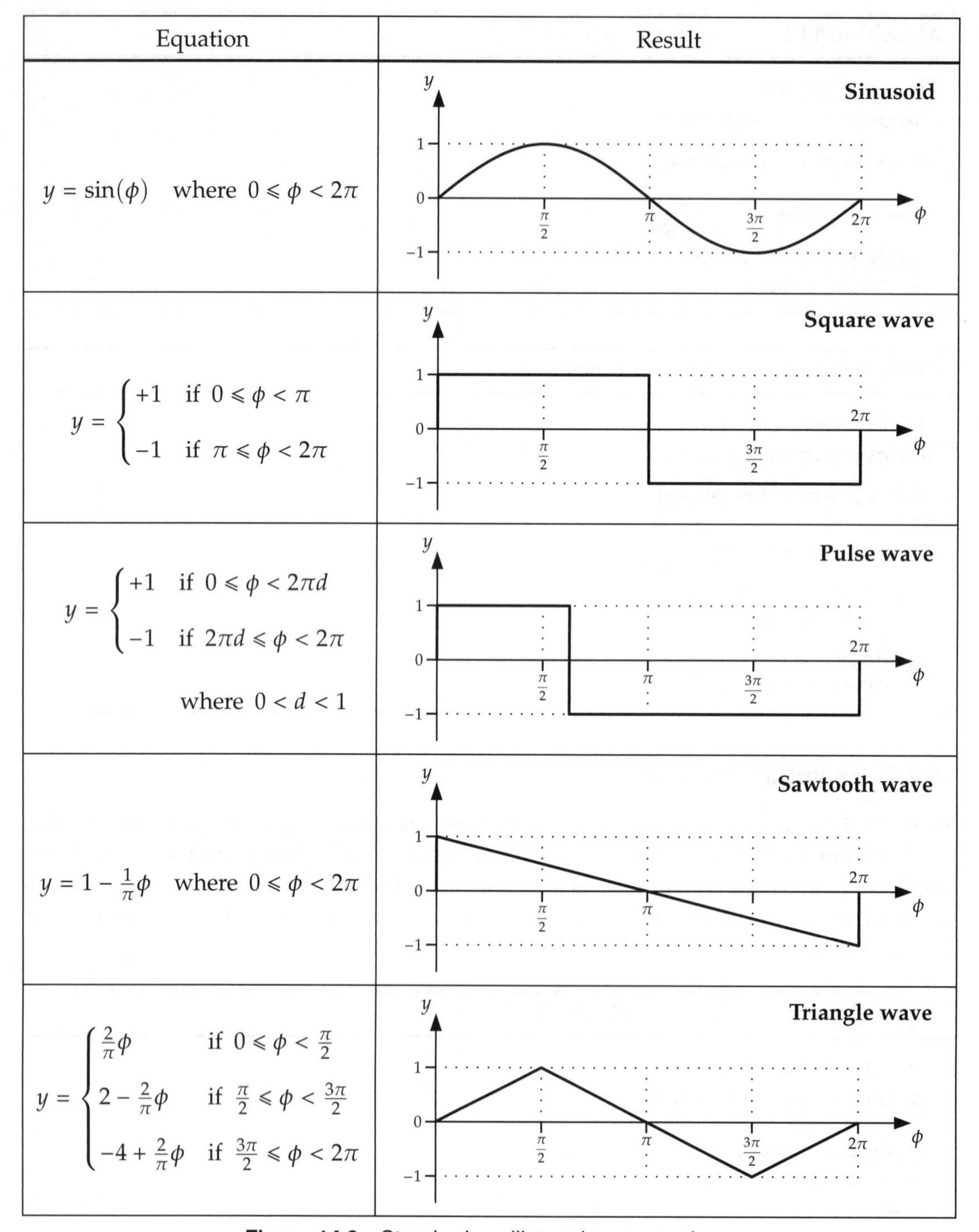

Figure 14.3 Standard oscillator shape equations

Note the following features for the shapes in figure 14.3:

- The pulse wave has a *duty cycle* parameter (d) with a value between 0 and 1. This corresponds to the proportion of the output cycle that has a value of +1, and allows the tonal character (harmonic amplitude balance) to be changed (as shown in figure 4.10, p.82). When $d = 0.5$ a pulse wave is the same as a square wave.
- Sometimes it is useful to be able to invert the shape of an oscillator. For example, a sawtooth wave can be generated as a ramp-up instead of a ramp-down shape. This can be useful at low oscillation rates for controlling parameters where an increasing ramp value followed by a sudden return to the lowest value is needed. To achieve this either the output of the oscillator, or the equation itself, is multiplied by −1 (so the sawtooth equation would become $y = -1 + \frac{1}{\pi}\phi$).

Equation-based methods are not restricted to standard shapes. Figure 14.4 illustrates some examples of how alternative shapes can be created:

- Example 1 combines a sinusoidal shape with a line. This might be used to create a tremolo modulation (see §9.2.1, p.270) that has a pulse effect on half the cycle, rather than constantly varying throughout.
- Example 2 shows how the combination of multiple line segments can be used to create more complex shapes. Working out the equations becomes more difficult as the quantity of lines increases, however. An alternative is the more general breakpoint methods described in §14.3.
- Examples 3 to 5 demonstrate how shapes can be generated from different mathematical functions. Note that the equations often require appropriate multiplying factors to ensure that the peaks of the oscillation are between −1 and +1, as is standard for an oscillator. Example 4 relates to sinusoidal additive methods, which are explored further in Chapter 16.

14.3 Breakpoint Methods

14.3.1 Basic Concepts

It is often useful to describe functions used in envelope generators and oscillators as a series of line segments between *breakpoints*, as shown in figure 14.5. Each segment has three characteristics:

- The amplitude target value at the end.
- The length of time to reach that value (which can be zero to create a vertical line).
- The segment shape (such as straight lines or curves).

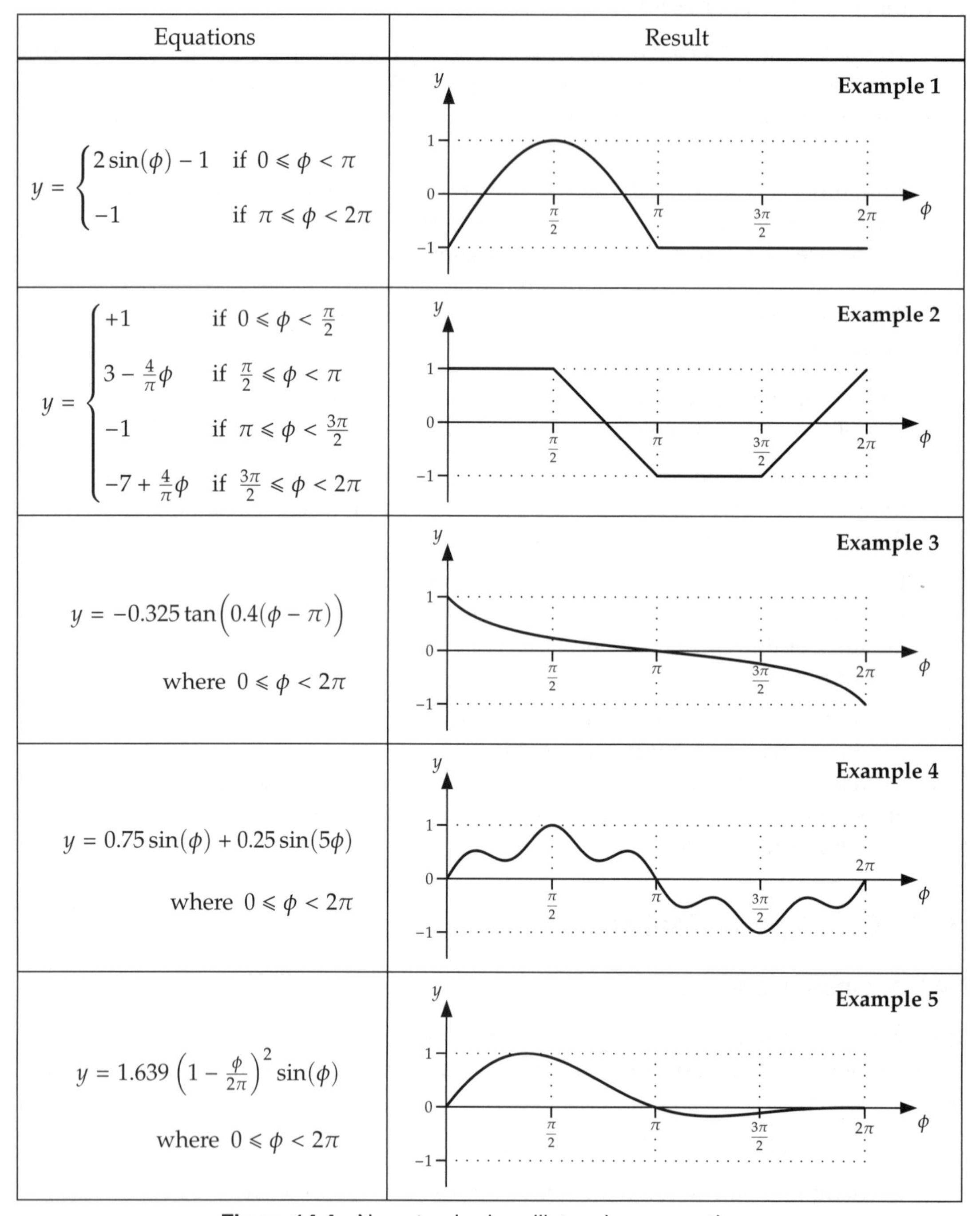

Figure 14.4 Non-standard oscillator shape equations

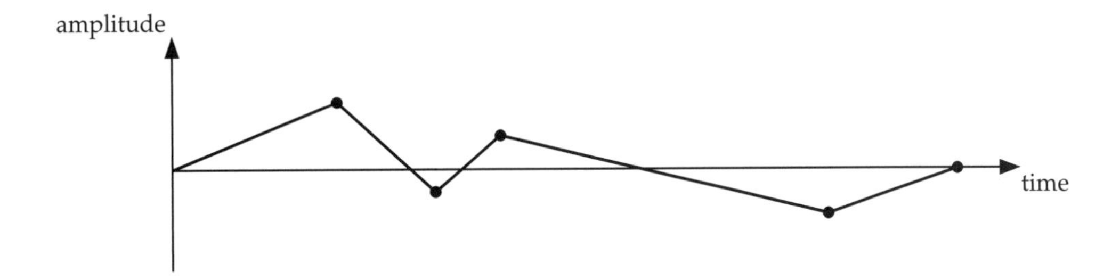

Figure 14.5 Example set of breakpoints joined by line segments

The use of breakpoints has a number of benefits:

- The breakpoints can be irregularly spaced. For example, there might be a concentration of points in one area to achieve a complex variation, but more widely spaced elsewhere.
- It is not necessary to specify all the values between the breakpoints. These are produced automatically by the generator process (such as an oscillator or envelope generator). This also reduces the amount of data to be stored.
- The breakpoints are easy to edit (numerically or graphically). Moving one point repositions all the intermediate values between breakpoints. If every intermediate value in the shape is stored in a data table (see §14.4, p.444), then it is necessary to change many values to achieve a similar repositioning.
- The representation is easily extended. Once the basic algorithm has been created it is possible to add more breakpoints, create new segment shaping functions, and vary the shaping function parameters without much difficulty.
- Breakpoints might be easier to specify than equations (described in §14.2), particularly when the shape is composed of multiple line segments. This is not universally true, such as when adding several sinusoidal functions together (which is clearer in equation form).

Creating the values in between breakpoints is called interpolation (described in §8.2, p.237).

14.3.2 Generating a Single Linear Segment

Figure 14.6 illustrates a segment that starts at *lastvalue* and ends at *targetvalue*, a difference of *diff*. When generating the segment, the current position between the start and end of the line is called *currentfrac*, with values between 0 and 1.

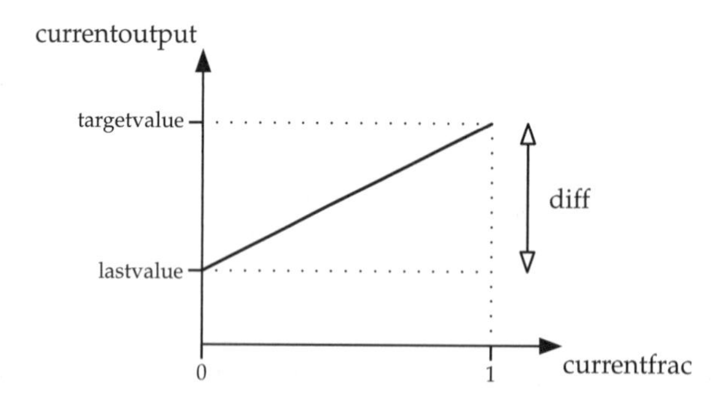

Figure 14.6 Single linear segment

Algorithm 14.4 is the function that is called to initialise the segment generation. This has the following features:

- When the program first starts *currentoutput*, *currentfrac*, *fracincrement*, *lastvalue*, and *diff* will be initialised to 0. Those variable values are maintained between calls to the functions.
- The target value and duration of the segment (in seconds) are provided as input values to the initialisation function.
- If *duration* is not more than 0 then *currentfrac* is set to the end of the line. Otherwise *currentfrac* is set to the start of the line, and *fracincrement* is set to the amount *currentfrac* should increase on each sample.
- The segment starts from the current output value of the generator by setting *lastvalue* to *currentoutput*. This allows a new segment to be initialised at any time, even if the previous segment has not completed and avoids the need to specify both ends of the segment.
- The difference in values could be either positive or negative depending on whether *targetvalue* is greater than *lastvalue* or not.

Once the variables have been initialised it is possible to call the main function (algorithm 14.5). The main function is called once per output sample. The underlying linear interpolation method is the same as that described in §8.2.3 (p.241). The output value will continue to ramp until the end of the segment is reached and the output then holds the *targetvalue* indefinitely. The initialisation function might be called again at any point to set a new target value and segment duration.

Algorithm 14.4 – Single segment generator initialisation function

input : targetvalue and duration

if duration <= 0 **then**
  currentfrac = 1
  fracincrement = 0
else
  currentfrac = 0
  fracincrement = $\frac{1}{\text{duration} * \text{samplerate}}$

lastvalue = currentoutput
diff = targetvalue − lastvalue

Algorithm 14.5 – Single segment generator main function

output: output signal out

currentfrac = currentfrac + fracincrement

if currentfrac > 1 **then**
  currentfrac = 1
  fracincrement = 0

currentoutput = lastvalue + (diff ∗ currentfrac)
out = currentoutput

A single segment generator is not particularly useful for creating oscillators or interesting amplitude envelopes, but it is useful for smoothing value changes over time. For example:

- Control interface values (such as amplitude gain values, delay times, and so on) can jump in value as they are varied by the user (as described in §23.1.3, p.637). This can produce audible effects from the process that is being controlled. By passing the control input through a single segment generator it is possible to create smoother variations for the controlled process. Every time the control value changes, the initialisation function is called with the new target value and a suitable smoothing time (which might only need to be 30ms).
- Sometimes it is desirable to create slow pitch glides between notes (*portamento*) rather than jumping immediately between notes. By passing input note values through the single segment generator, it is possible to control the sliding effect. The duration value will often be chosen by the user and can be as long as desired for the musical context.

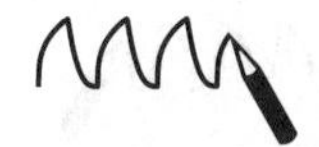

Whether a linear variation is appropriate depends on the type of parameter being considered. For example, with a portamento a steady change in pitch is achieved if the value being smoothed is a note number. If it is a frequency value then the pitch change is non-linear. Methods for reshaping the segment are described later.

14.3.3 Generating Multiple Segments

While the single linear segment generator is useful, there are a number of developments that can be incorporated, to make it easier to use the breakpoint method in general cases:

- It is useful to be able to have any number of breakpoints. This allows the creation of shapes as complex as the user wants.
- Allowing segment shapes that are not linear provides additional flexibility, and can make the generator easier to configure; for example, to achieve a curved path without having to approximate it with many short linear segments.
- The algorithm could support oscillation (by looping), as well as envelope generation once from start to finish.

There are a number of steps required to construct a suitable algorithm. Firstly, two arrays are needed, to hold the breakpoint data:

- The *targetvalue* array contains the breakpoint amplitude values.
- The *duration* array contains the corresponding lengths of time (in seconds) to reach the target values.

Each array contains N values corresponding to the number of breakpoints, which are indexed from 0 to N−1. There are two conditions that must be checked when preparing the array data, such that the algorithm will work properly:

- The *duration* values must not be negative (but can be 0).
- At least one *duration* value must be greater than 0.

Figure 14.7 illustrates some ordered sets of target values and corresponding durations to achieve amplitude envelope and oscillation shapes. The durations depend on the rate of change required (for an envelope generator) or the fundamental frequency (for an oscillator). With an oscillator, the durations are chosen as a fraction of the total cycle length, which is related to the desired fundamental frequency with $T = 1/F$. Negative frequencies are not possible as negative durations are not allowed, so an oscillator using this technique is not suitable for FM synthesis (§20.3, p.567).

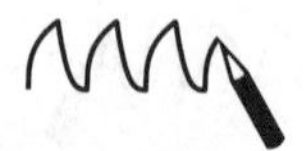

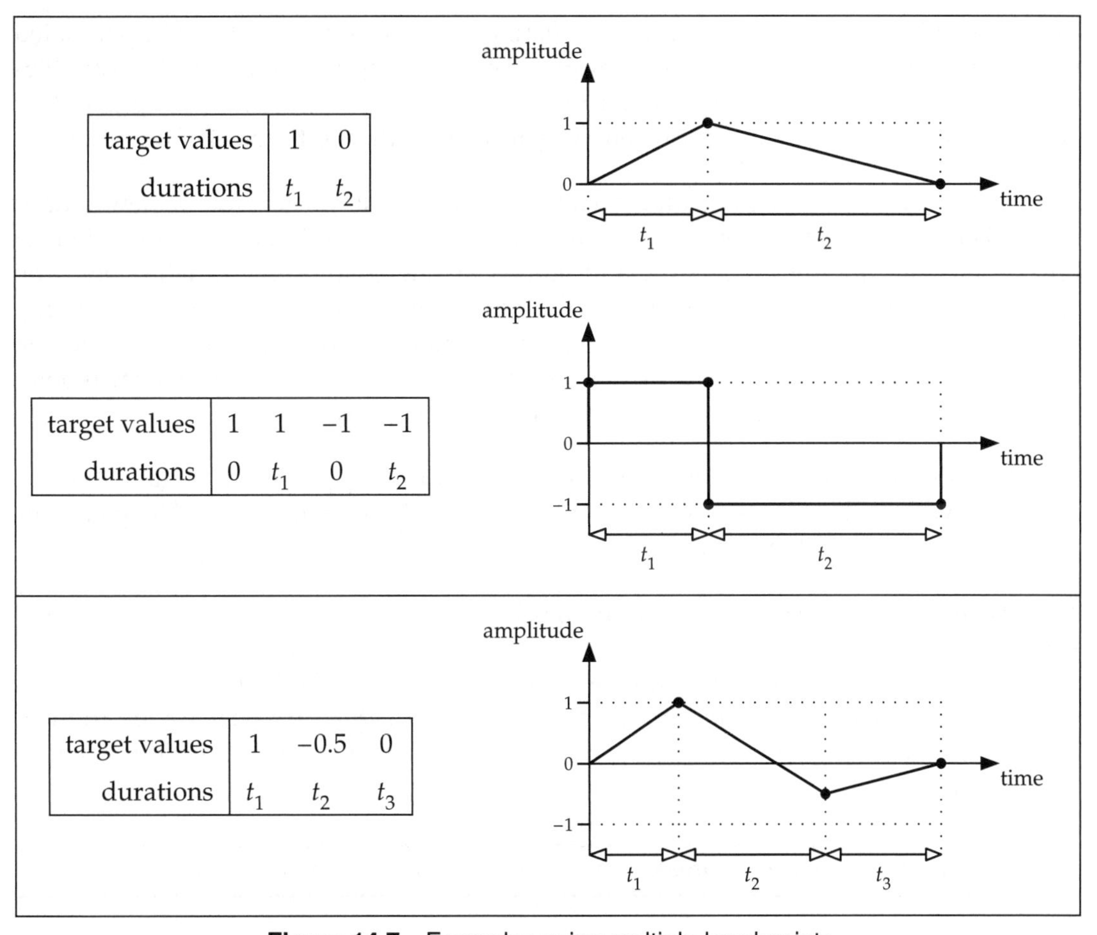

Figure 14.7 Examples using multiple breakpoints

There are a number of variables whose values must be retained between calls to the functions. All will be reset to 0 at the start of the program:

- *currentoutput* is the most recent output value from the generator.
- *currentfrac* is the distance along the current segment (between 0 and 1).
- *fracincrement* is the amount that *currentfrac* increases each sample.
- *currentindex* is the current index position in the arrays.
- *lastindex* is the index of the previous breakpoint.
- *lastvalue* is the value at the start of the current segment.
- *diff* is the difference in values between the end and start of the current segment.

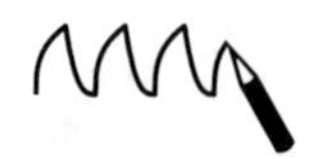

In order to initiate the generator, the *targetvalue* and *duration* arrays must first be populated (and durations checked as described before). The next step is to initialise the variables ready for the main processing function to occur using algorithm 14.6. For a standard envelope generator this will occur when the gate signal indicates the start of the envelope.

Algorithm 14.7 is the function that is called every sample to generate a new output value. The process is fairly sophisticated in order to work with different combinations of breakpoints, and for both oscillating and non-oscillating conditions. Variables *overshoot* and *shapedval* are local to the function. The *oscillating* flag is used to control whether the function shape repeats over and over. In the non-oscillating mode, when the last breakpoint is reached, the output is held at the value associated with that breakpoint indefinitely (or until new breakpoint instructions are received).

Sometimes it is useful to be able to make the generator output jump to (and hold) a particular value. That can be achieved with algorithm 14.8, which causes the generator main function to output the required value.

The *shapingfunction()* that is called from algorithm 14.7 takes a value between 0 and 1, and applies appropriate mapping (to a result range of 0 to 1) to create the desired segment shape. Some example shaping functions are illustrated in figure 14.8. The $y = x$ example is the same as replacing *shapingfunction(currentfrac)* with *currentfrac* in the code and produces linear interpolation over the length of the segment. The other shaping functions produce different types of curved results.

Algorithm 14.6 – Multiple breakpoints generator initialisation function

```
currentindex = 0

// deal with any initial zero-length segments
while duration[currentindex] == 0 do
    currentoutput = targetvalue[currentindex]
    currentindex = currentindex + 1

// configure variables ready for main part of processing
lastvalue = currentoutput
lastindex = currentindex
currentfrac = 0
```

$$\text{fracincrement} = \frac{1}{\text{duration[currentindex]} * \text{samplerate}}$$

```
diff = targetvalue[currentindex] − lastvalue
```

Algorithm 14.7 – Multiple breakpoints generator main function

```
output: output signal out

currentfrac = currentfrac + fracincrement            // advance current position

if currentfrac > 1 then
    // segment is complete
    overshoot = (currentfrac − 1) * duration[currentindex]
    currentindex = currentindex + 1

    if currentindex == N and oscillating then
        // all segments completed but going back to the first one
        currentindex = 0

    while currentindex < N and overshoot > duration[currentindex] do
        // passing short duration segments
        overshoot = overshoot − duration[currentindex]
        lastindex = currentindex
        currentindex = currentindex + 1

        if currentindex == N and oscillating then
            currentindex = 0

    if currentindex == N and not oscillating then
        // all segments completed and holding the last value
        lastvalue = targetvalue[N − 1]
        currentfrac = 0
        fracincrement = 0
        diff = 0

    if currentindex < N then
        // prepare for the next full segment
        currentfrac = overshoot / duration[currentindex]
        fracincrement = 1 / (duration[currentindex] * samplerate)
        lastvalue = targetvalue[lastindex]
        diff = targetvalue[currentindex] − lastvalue
        lastindex = currentindex
```

(continued on the next page)

Algorithm 14.7 – Multiple breakpoints generator main function

(continued from the previous page)

```
// calculate output value
if diff >= 0 then
| shapedval = shapingfunction(currentfrac)
else
└ shapedval = 1 − shapingfunction(1 − currentfrac)
currentoutput = lastvalue + (diff ∗ shapedval)
out = currentoutput
```

Algorithm 14.8 – Multiple breakpoints generator jump function

```
input : new output value
currentoutput = value
lastvalue = value
currentfrac = 0
fracincrement = 0
diff = 0
```

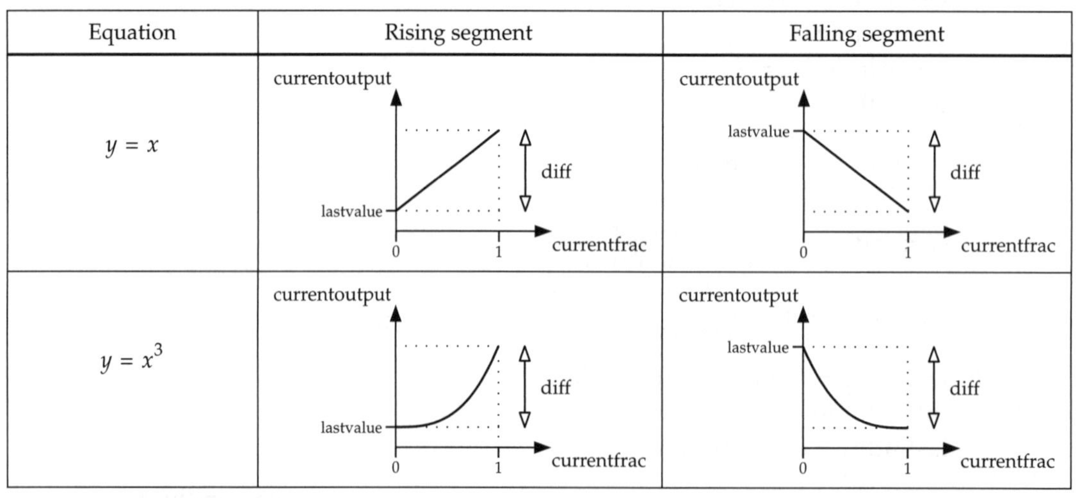

Figure 14.8 Example shaping functions (continued on the next page)

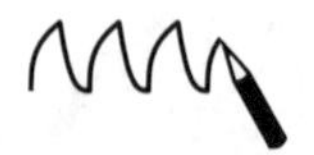

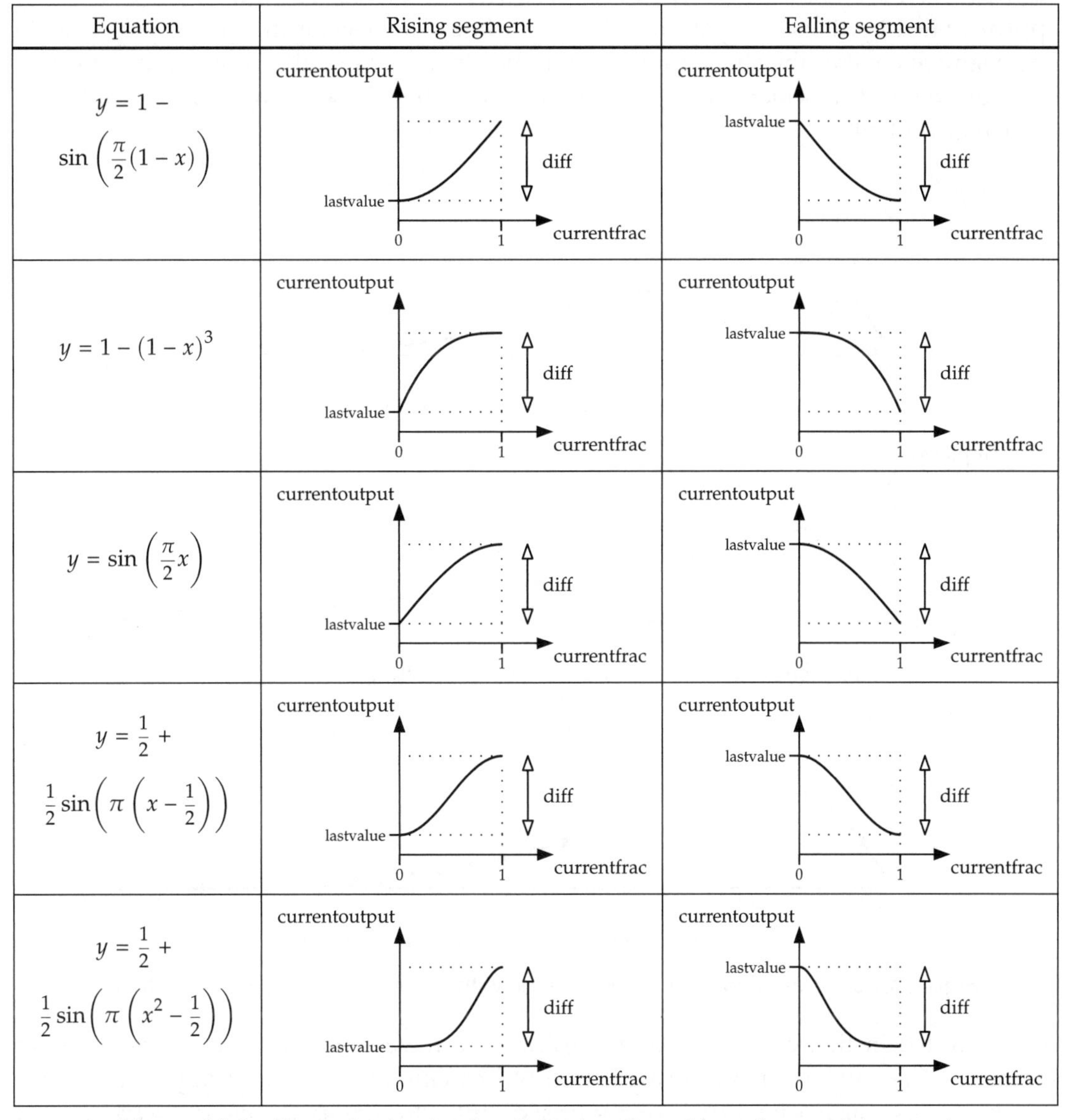

Figure 14.8 Example shaping functions (continued from the previous page)

Curved segments can be useful for achieving naturalistic variations, which might be similar to the amplitude envelopes found in §3.2.2 (p.51). Sometimes a shape produced with a small set of curves can only be accurately achieved with many more straight line segments. Figure 14.9 shows how an envelope with four curved segments is not closely approximated by the same quantity of straight lines. Increasing the quantity of straight line segments makes the shape more similar, but less easy to edit. How many segments are required and of which shapes depends on whether those changes are audible in a particular context.

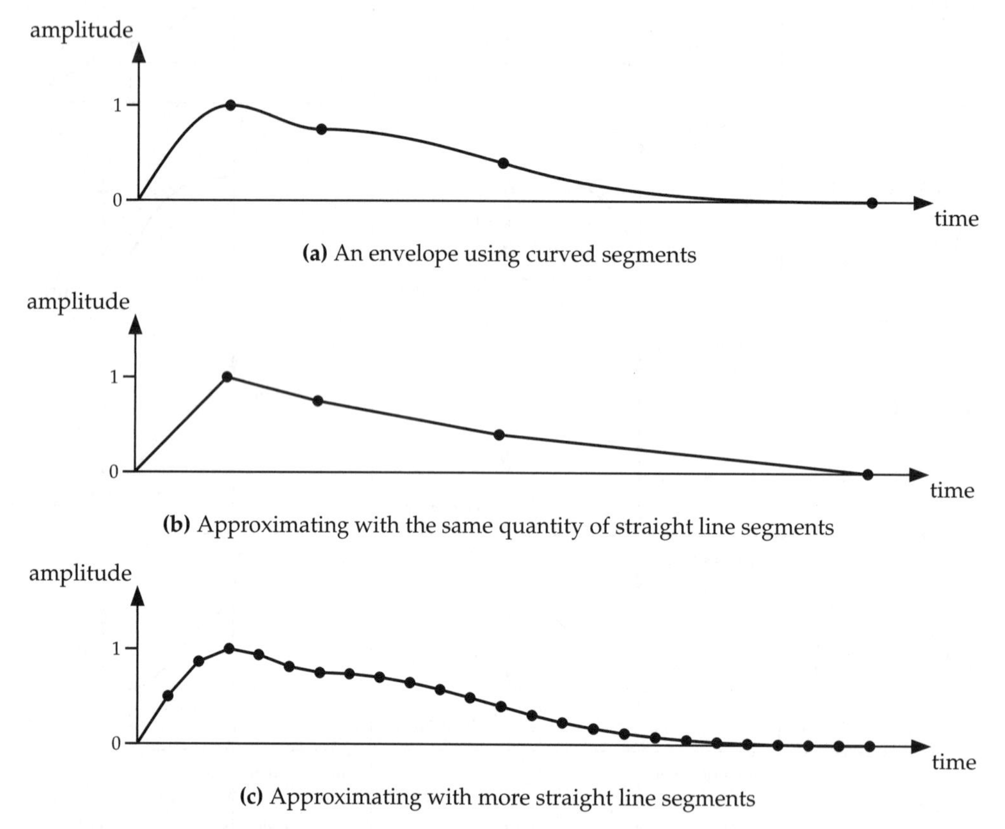

(a) An envelope using curved segments

(b) Approximating with the same quantity of straight line segments

(c) Approximating with more straight line segments

Figure 14.9 Achieving an envelope shape with curved and straight line methods

As illustrated in figure 14.9 it is often desirable to have different shaping for different segments. This can be achieved in algorithm 14.7 by employing a third array that contains the shape type for reaching each of the breakpoints. In that case *shapingfunction()* must also take *currentindex* as an argument and check that *currentindex* is N−1 or less.

It is also possible to construct shaping functions with variable parameters to allow more continuous control over shape. For example, equation $y = x^k$ can take values of parameter k other than 1 and 3 (which are included in figure 14.8).

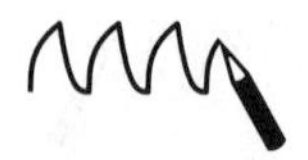

Alternatively it is possible to blend the results of two functions to create an intermediate shaping effect. For example:

$$y = (1 - c)F_1(x) + cF_2(x) \tag{14.4}$$

where $F_1(x)$ and $F_2(x)$ are different equation functions and c is a value between 0 and 1.

Some envelopes using breakpoints include a sustain effect, where the envelope reaches a value that is held until a gate note-off event occurs. At that point the release envelope is played. An example of this is shown in figure 14.10. The simplest way of achieving the sustain and release effect is to have two sets of envelope instructions; one set that describes from the start of the sound to the sustain, and a second that describes the release. These are sent to the initialisation function (algorithm 14.6) on note-on and note-off events respectively. After the first envelope completes, the output of the generator will produce the final breakpoint value continuously. When the note-off event occurs, the second envelope will replace the previous instructions and finish the note.

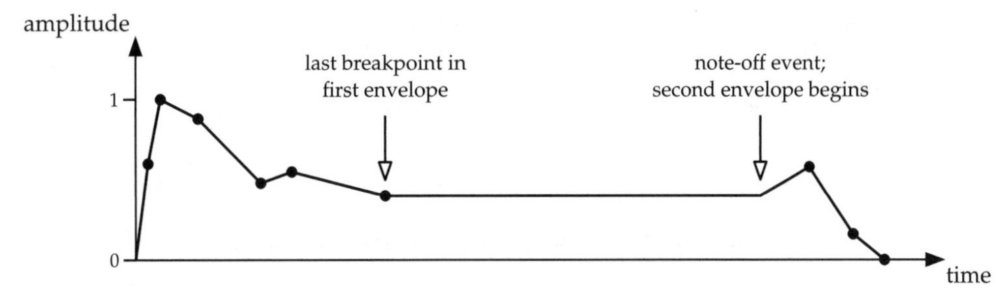

Figure 14.10 Sustain and release amplitude envelope effect

It is possible to call the initialisation function with new breakpoint data even if the envelope has not reached the sustain point, as the generator will continue from the *currentoutput* value towards the next breakpoint. In terms of the timing inside the process implementation, the technique is to complete the current output sample (algorithm 14.7), repopulate the *targetvalue* and *duration* arrays, and then reinitialise (algorithm 14.6) before starting to generate the next output sample.

A limitation with the sustain effect is that the development of the envelope stalls at that point. Sometimes it is desirable to have an envelope that continues to develop indefinitely until the note-off event causes the release envelope. One method is to combine an oscillator and envelope generator as shown in figure 13.15 (p.413). An alternative is to have a looping effect internal to the envelope generator, which is a variation on the oscillation mode.

In the multiple breakpoints generator main function (algorithm 14.7), the value 0 becomes L for the following lines, to achieve a loop back to another breakpoint:

if currentindex == N **and** oscillating **then**
└ currentindex = 0

→

if currentindex == N **and** oscillating **then**
└ currentindex = L

Note that this occurs twice in the algorithm. For a standard oscillator effect, L will be 0. For a looping envelope generator, it can be a breakpoint part way through the envelope. Figure 14.11 illustrates two envelopes. When the first envelope reaches its sixth (and last) breakpoint, it loops back such that the next target is the fourth breakpoint (*targetvalue[3]*, *duration[3]*, with the *oscillating* flag enabled). A condition of this technique is that L is in the range 0 to N−1, and that at least one of the breakpoint durations between L and the end of the envelope is non-zero. When the note-off event occurs, a second envelope is employed to provide the final part of the envelope (with the *oscillating* flag disabled).

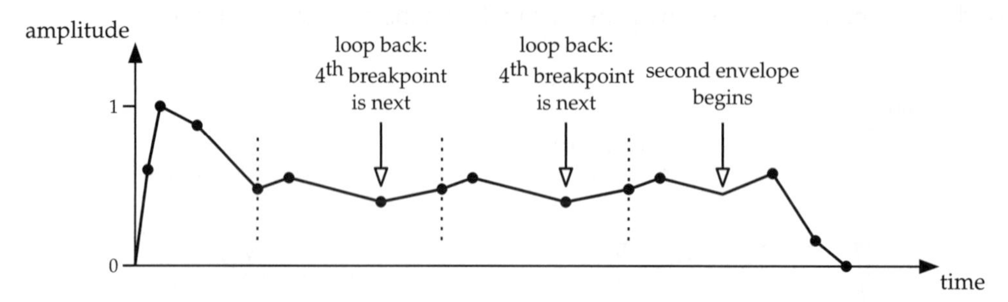

Figure 14.11 Looping amplitude envelope effect

The initialisation function causes the process state to be reset such that the next target is the first breakpoint in the current data. This is suitable for most envelope generation situations. If the technique is being used to produce an audio rate oscillator, however, it is often desirable to change the fundamental frequency without having to reset the generator (which would cause clicks in the output). It is possible to vary the scaling of the *duration* array values (and so the fundamental frequency) without needing to change the quantity of breakpoints or target values, and so a re-initialisation is not necessary. That is, replace *duration[currentindex]* in the algorithms with *(scalefactor* ∗ *duration[currentindex])*. If the *duration* array values sum to a total of 1, then a *scalefactor* of $1/F$ will achieve a fundamental frequency of F.

14.3.4 Mapping with Multiple Breakpoints

Previous algorithms have assumed that breakpoints are being used to generate an output that varies over time in an envelope generator or oscillator. Sometimes it is useful to be able to find the output value at a particular position in time within a set of breakpoints.

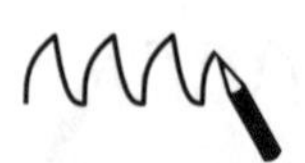

This can be used for mapping, such as creating a shaping transfer function suitable for distortion (Chapter 7), control mapping (Chapter 24), or waveshaping (§14.5.3, p.452).

Algorithm 14.9 illustrates a mapping function for use with multiple breakpoints. The *targetvalue* and *duration* arrays are the same as in §14.3.3 and the number of segments is N. Because breakpoint segments do not specify the starting value (at time 0) for the shape, that must be set in *firstpointvalue*. Variables *mapindex, last, mapfrac, mapdiff,* and *shapedval* are local to the function. The input value *readposition* should be within the total duration specified by the breakpoints. The total duration might be normalised to 1 to allow *readposition* to be a value between 0 and 1 for convenience.

Algorithm 14.9 – Multiple breakpoints mapping function

```
input : readposition
output: output value out

if readposition < 0 then
    readposition = 0

if N > 0 then
    last = firstpointvalue
    mapindex = 0

    while mapindex < N and readposition > duration[mapindex] do
        readposition = readposition − duration[mapindex]
        last = targetvalue[mapindex]
        mapindex = mapindex + 1

    if mapindex == N then
        out = targetvalue[N − 1]
    else
        mapfrac = readposition / duration[mapindex]

        mapdiff = targetvalue[mapindex] − last

        if mapdiff >= 0 then
            shapedval = shapingfunction(mapfrac)
        else
            shapedval = 1 − shapingfunction(1 − mapfrac)

        out = last + (mapdiff ∗ shapedval)
else
    out = 0
```

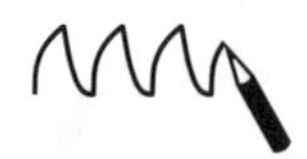

14.4 Wavetable Methods

14.4.1 Creating a Wavetable

Equation and breakpoint-based signal generator techniques use little computer memory, and the results can be specified with a modest number of control values. However, there are situations where such techniques are less desirable:

- It takes computing power to generate values using equations. Whether this is significant depends on the number of signal generators being used and the complexity of the equations. In relative terms, a function such as *sin()* can take significantly more computation than precalculating the values and reading them from memory.
- It is often desirable to record a waveform from another sound source and use it in an oscillator. This can sometimes be a more direct route to achieving the desired tonality, compared to constructing a shape with breakpoints or equations.

A possible solution is to use *wavetables*. A wavetable is a block of memory (a buffer or array) in which a signal is stored as a series of discrete values. If the calculation of values can be performed in advance (when the values are stored in the table), then the output generation process is reduced to reading the values out of the table, which is usually an efficient operation. The techniques for storing and retrieving data from buffers are described in Chapter 8.

Figure 14.12 illustrates an example of a single waveform cycle stored in a wavetable. The wavetable in the figure is small, with only 100 storage locations, in order to make the digitisation of the waveform clearer. Where possible, a wavetable will have a length of thousands of samples, in order to store the waveform with high precision.

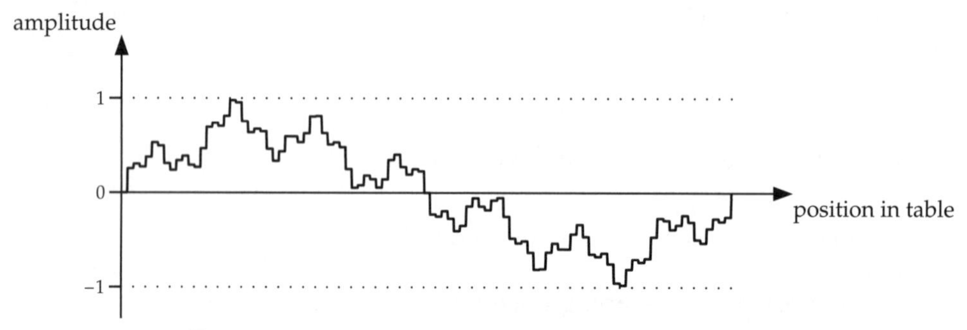

Figure 14.12 A waveform cycle stored in a wavetable

The method for writing data values into a wavetable depends on the source. If the contents of the table are to be created from an equation then algorithm 14.10 is used. In the algorithm, *genfunction()* works in the same way as described in §14.2 (p.425). Array *table*

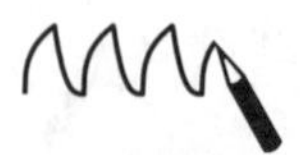

is a buffer of size N whose index values are 0 to N−1. It is necessary to choose the value of N in advance:

- The larger the table size, the more accurately a waveform can be represented.
- Traditionally table sizes are selected as a power of 2 (such as 1024, 2048, 4096, 8192, and 16384). This reflects how digital memory is organised, but using these sizes is not essential with a general purpose programming language.
- The larger the table size, the more memory is required. This was more of a problem historically when memory capacities were smaller.

Algorithm 14.10 – Wavetable writing function

for writeposition = 0 **to** N−1 **do**

$$\text{table[writeposition]} = \text{genfunction}\left(\text{writeposition} \ast \frac{2\pi}{\text{N}}\right)$$

If a wavetable is to be populated with data from a sampled source such as an instrument recording, then the length of the table will be determined by the number of samples for a single cycle at the recorded sample rate. Starting with equation 8.1 (p.220) and knowing that $F = 1/T$, if the sample rate is 96kHz and the fundamental frequency is 100Hz:

$$\text{N} = T \times f_S = \frac{f_S}{F} = \frac{96000}{100} = 960 \ \text{samples} \tag{14.5}$$

These data values could be copied from a recording and written into the table. If data is taken from a source with a high fundamental frequency there will be fewer samples in one cycle than at a lower frequency. If the original source has a high fundamental frequency and the data is replayed at a low frequency, then the result might lack high harmonic detail. There can also be tonal differences across the pitch range of a source.

Filling the table with a single cycle of a waveform will allow an oscillator to be created. However, other forms of data can also be stored in a table, such as an envelope shape, or a transfer function.

14.4.2 Using a Wavetable

Having filled the wavetable with data values it is possible to create signal generators. To create an oscillator requires a similar arrangement to that in §14.2.1 (p.425). Figure 14.13 illustrates how the read position will step along the wavetable and wrap around to the beginning of the table when it reaches the end. Clearly this is very similar to the scheme seen for phase increments in figure 14.2 (p.426). In this case, the step size is called the

sample increment (Δi). Its value is determined by the following equation, where the desired frequency is F, N is the size of the wavetable, and f_S is the sample rate:

$$\Delta i = \frac{\mathrm{N} \times F}{f_S} \tag{14.6}$$

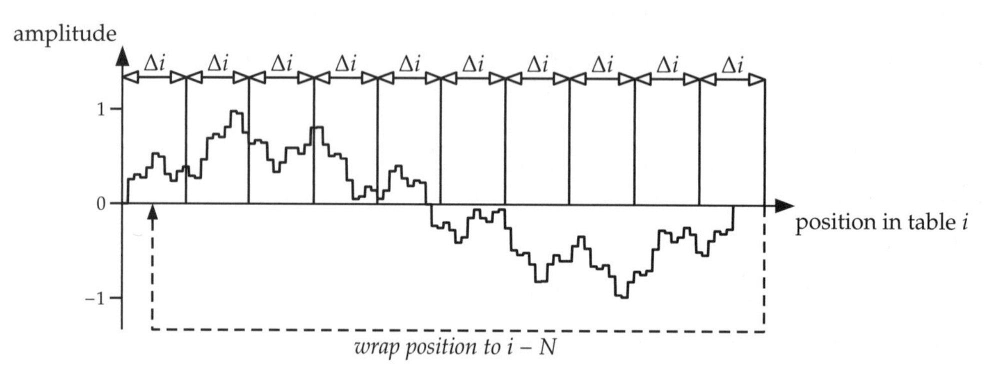

Figure 14.13 Stepping and wrapping wavetable read position

Equation 14.6 has strong similarities to equation 14.3 (p.425). The equations in §14.2 can take any phase value (within the range of 0 to 2π), whereas the values in a wavetable can only be accessed at discrete positions (numbered 0, 1, 2, 3, 4, and so on). Consider a wavetable of length 100 with index positions numbered 0 to 99, and a sample increment of 11 (Δi, calculated with equation 14.6), then the first positions accessed are as follows:

0	11	22	33	44	55	66	77	88	99	10	21	32 ...

In practical circumstances, the sample increment (Δi) is unlikely to be an integer. For example, with an Δi value of 5.5, then the positions accessed should be:

0	5.5	11	16.5	22	27.5	33	38.5	44	49.5	55	60.5	66 ...

Because memory locations 5.5, 16.5, 27.5 (and so on) do not exist, an appropriate interpolation method must be used in order to calculate an appropriate output value (as discussed in §8.2, p.237). The more sophisticated the implementation method, the more computation will be required, however less unintentional waveform distortion (table lookup noise) will be produced. It is necessary to wrap around the ends of the wavetable buffer when interpolating.

Algorithm 14.11 describes a wavetable oscillator with the following features:

- The function is called once per output value (at the sample rate).
- *table* is the memory array that is accessed with indices 0 to N−1.

- *readposition* is the index position that has been reached in the table. It is assumed that the value of *readposition* is maintained between calls to the function, and initially has a value of 0.
- *readposition* can be a value with a fractional part. The *interpolate()* function uses one of the methods described in §8.2 (p.237) to access a value at *readposition* in the wavetable.
- *readposition* must remain within the boundaries of the array and so is wrapped at the edges of the wavetable.

It is possible to produce a non-oscillating result with a wavetable, for purposes of envelope generation. For a standard envelope generator result, a gate signal will indicate the start of the generation process. The value of variable *readposition* will be set to 0, then the function in algorithm 14.12 will be called once per output value (at the sample rate). It is assumed that the value of *readposition* is maintained between calls to the function. The output continues until the end of the stored data (after time T, where $T > 0$). At that point the final value in the wavetable is output indefinitely, or until *readposition* is reset to 0 again. The table could be populated from equations, or by storing the amplitude envelope of a real sound using an envelope follower (see §8.3, p.245).

Another use for a wavetable is for producing transfer function mappings suitable for distortion (Chapter 7), control mapping (Chapter 24), or waveshaping (§14.5.3, p.452). In these cases, an input value needs to be mapped to a position in the wavetable (also known as a *lookup table* for this purpose). In algorithms 14.13 and 14.14 the input range (of 0 to 1, and −1 to +1, respectively) is mapped to a read position 0 to N−1. It is important that the input values do not exceed the maximum input range, or *readposition* will be outside the boundaries of the table.

A further extension to the idea of wavetables is storing and replaying many waveform cycles or a whole sound. This is known as sampling, and is discussed in Chapter 15.

14.4.3 Efficiency and Control

Accessing values from a wavetable is often computationally-efficient compared to calculating values with mathematical functions. For example, when producing the results from a sinusoidal harmonic additive synthesizer (described in Chapter 16) with 100 oscillators it is necessary to compute 100 sinusoidal functions, multiply each by their associated amplitude gain value, and sum the results together for every output sample. If the sum of partials is to remain constant, a wavetable technique allows precalculation and storage of the resulting waveform. The wavetable oscillator calculates a table position and reads from the table, which is efficient.

Algorithm 14.11 – Wavetable oscillator function

input : frequency F
output: output signal out

out = interpolate(table, readposition)

$$\text{readposition} = \text{readposition} + \frac{N * F}{\text{samplerate}}$$

while readposition >= N **do**
  readposition = readposition − N

while readposition < 0 **do**
  readposition = readposition + N

Algorithm 14.12 – Wavetable non-oscillating function

output: output signal out

if readposition < N−1 **then**

$$\text{readposition} = \text{readposition} + \frac{\text{N} - 1}{T * \text{samplerate}}$$

if readposition > N−1 **then**
  readposition = N−1

out = interpolate(table, readposition)

Algorithm 14.13 – Lookup table reading function 1

input : input signal in (maximum 0 to 1)
output: output signal out

readposition = in ∗ (N − 1)
out = interpolate(table, readposition)

Algorithm 14.14 – Lookup table reading function 2

input : input signal in (maximum −1 to +1)
output: output signal out

readposition = 0.5 ∗ (in + 1) ∗ (N − 1)
out = interpolate(table, readposition)

Additive synthesis does, however, have a significant control advantage over synthesis with a fixed waveform in a wavetable, in that the frequencies and amplitude weightings of the partials can change independently over time. This allows complex and inharmonic sound development. A static precalculated wavetable oscillator generally requires additional synthesis methods to create a tonally sophisticated result.

It is possible to combine the efficiency of wavetable methods with other synthesis techniques. In the additive synthesis example, the individual oscillators might be based on a wavetable containing a sinusoidal cycle for efficiency, rather than calculating the *sin()* function directly, while maintaining the separation between the oscillators for control purposes. The contents of a wavetable does not have to be as simple as a sinusoid, however. The output of wavetable oscillators based on complex waveforms can be combined dynamically using techniques such as those described in Chapter 19.

14.5 Modifying and Shaping Oscillation

14.5.1 Bandlimiting and Aliasing

Oscillators produce a repeating waveform and therefore a set of amplitude-weighted harmonic partials (as described in §3.1.2, p.41). The fundamental frequency of oscillation and the harmonic composition of the chosen waveform shape will determine the frequency range of the result. The Nyquist frequency in a digital system determines the highest frequency that can be supported without aliasing occurring (§2.2.2, p.28). There is the possibility that an oscillator will generate frequencies above the Nyquist frequency and so produce unexpected tonal results.

Figure 14.14 illustrates average spectrum plots of a triangle wave oscillator (using the equation in figure 14.3, p.428) with two different fundamental frequencies. The Nyquist frequency is 22.05kHz. At 250Hz only a small number of aliased partials are visible close to the Nyquist frequency, and they have low amplitude due to the rapid roll-off of harmonic amplitudes in the triangle wave (see §4.2.2, p.79). However the quantity of aliased partials with significant amplitude increases when the fundamental frequency is 2.5kHz; all partials from the 9th harmonic (22.5kHz) onwards are aliased to lower frequencies. Some of these partials alias to less than 0Hz, where again they are wrapped around (and so on). Once the output has been generated there is no general way of filtering to remove the aliased partials. Avoiding these effects requires an *antialiased* (or bandlimited) oscillator.

A number of options are possible in this situation:

- The effect could be ignored. This is possible if the oscillator is only being used at low fundamental frequencies, such as for low-rate cyclical modulation (Chapter 9). Similarly, if the chosen waveform has little amplitude in the upper harmonics then the aliased partials might not be audible.

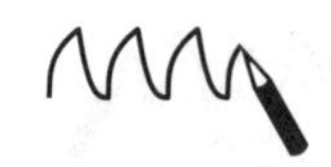

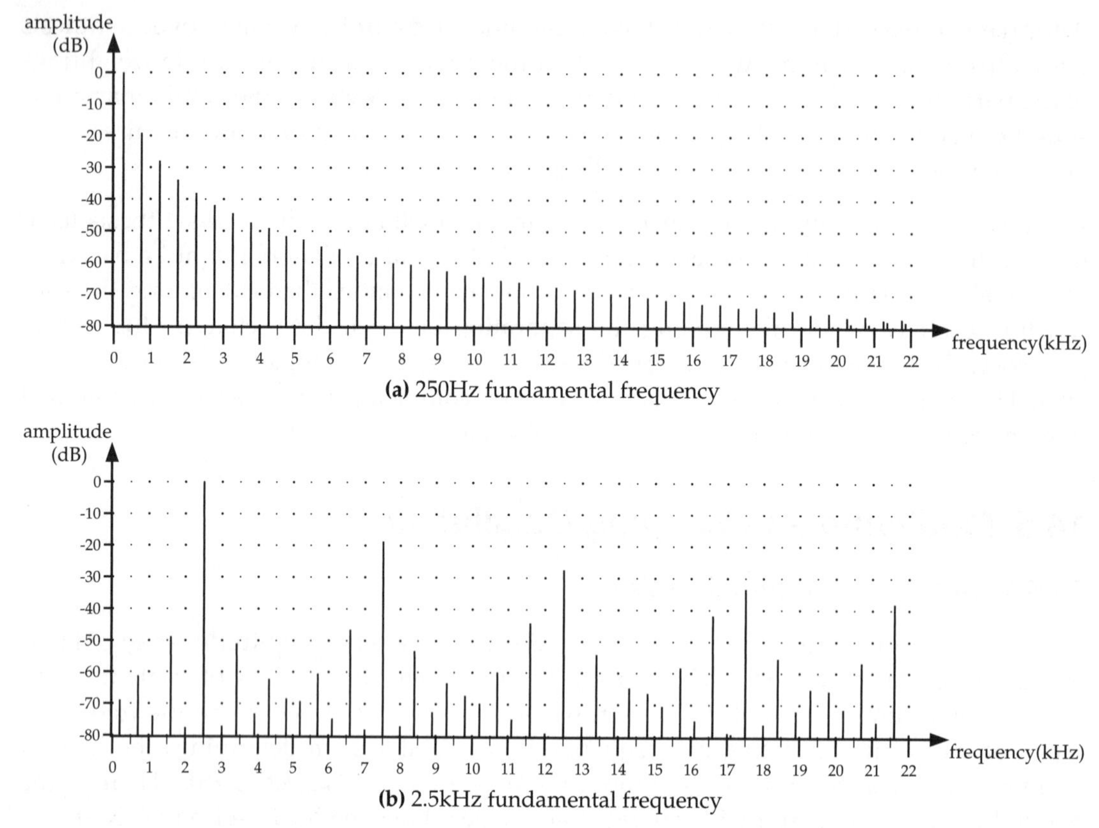

Figure 14.14 Triangle oscillator average spectrum plots (44.1kHz sample rate)

- Occasionally the effect of aliasing might actually be desirable in creating a different tonal character. For example, inharmonic clashing effects might be created deliberately. However, at fundamental frequencies that are the sample rate divided by an integer, the aliased partials are coincident with non-aliased partials, producing a harmonic effect.

- If the composition in terms of partial amplitudes is known, then aliasing can be avoided by employing sinusoidal additive synthesis (Chapter 16). In this case individual sinusoidal oscillators can produce particular partials, and it is possible to calculate whether a partial's frequency is above the Nyquist frequency and so make its amplitude zero. Whether this is a computationally-efficient technique for avoiding aliasing depends on the number of partials being synthesized.

- Rather than changing the oscillator it can sometimes be possible to increase the sample rate and so the Nyquist frequency. When the oscillation is generated at a higher sample rate the aliasing will occur at a higher frequency. The higher the

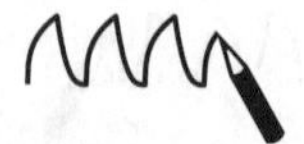

sample rate, the less the chance of aliasing appearing in the audible range. This idea is discussed further in §23.1.3 (p.637).

- It is possible to store multiple wavetables for use with different fundamental frequencies. For example, a wavetable used at low fundamental frequencies can have a wide range of frequency partials. However, a wavetable to be used at high fundamental frequencies would be a heavily lowpass filtered version of the same data to reduce the amplitude of higher harmonics, and so the amount of aliasing. With some sources it is possible to record different pitches and so have different wavetables for each one.
- Algorithms exist for generating bandlimited versions of simple waveforms such as sawtooth and square wave. The complexities of doing so are beyond the scope of this book.

14.5.2 Developing Oscillator Character

Standard oscillators produce a consistent repeating harmonic output due to the nature of their construction. Even if random values are stored into a wavetable oscillator, the output will not be a true noise generator (as described in Chapter 18) as the values will repeat every cycle. For purposes of adding interest to the sound it is often desirable to be able to change the oscillation shape. Shape control parameters might be mapped from a user input, such as a key velocity or pitch value. Alternatively they might be controlled from envelope generators, or be cyclically modulated (as described in Chapters 9 and 20). There are a number of ways of shaping the oscillation:

- The first consideration is whether it is possible to change the generator process. For example, an equation might be constructed to include a parameter to control the shape. Figure 14.15 illustrates an equation with a shaping parameter (c). Similarly the duty cycle (d) parameter can be controlled for the pulse wave in figure 14.3 (p.428). Breakpoint-based methods have control points that can be moved to reshape the output, and so modify the results tonally. The difficulty with any direct waveform modifications is that a simple relationship does not usually exist between the visual appearance and the tonal results.
- Ideas related to changing the generator process are reshaping the output with transfer function-based distortion (Chapter 7) and waveshaping (as described in §14.5.3 below). These can sometimes be easier to achieve than changing the generator, such as when using a sampled wavetable.
- Filtering is a key tool in changing tonal character of oscillator outputs, and one that is moderately straightforward to control. The more complex the filtering the further the tonality can be from the original sound character. These ideas are developed further in subtractive synthesis (Chapter 17).

- Blending oscillator outputs is a way of constructing a more sophisticated character. This is explored further in Chapters 16 and 19. Blending can produce inharmonic results with harmonic output oscillators through use of non-integer fundamental frequency relationships.

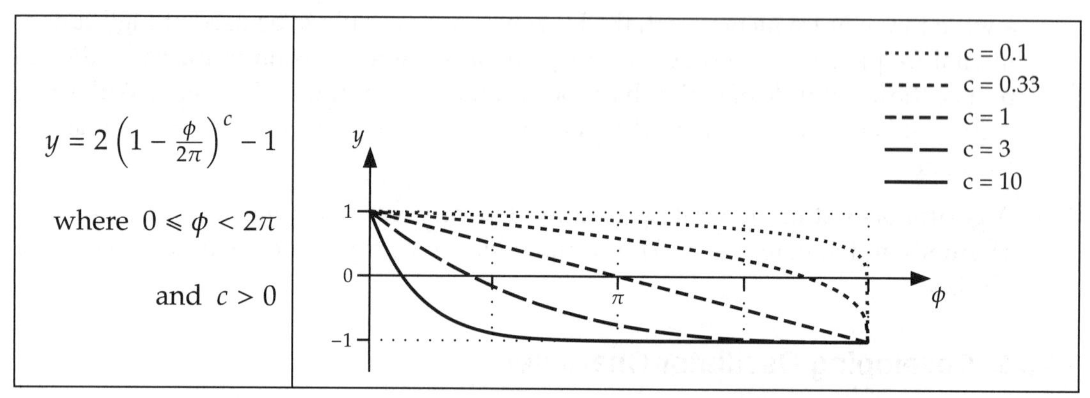

Figure 14.15 Oscillator equation with shape variation parameter

14.5.3 Waveshaping

Chapter 7 described how a waveform can be reshaped with clipping and shaping transfer functions to change the tonality of the result. Such techniques can be extended further to achieve a more general synthesis style known as *waveshaping*. In the soft clipping distortion cases described in §7.2.1 (p.200), the input is assumed to be an arbitrary musical signal, and the transfer function is a fairly simple shape which is always increasing in value from (−1,−1) to (1,1). Waveshaping synthesis provides control of both the input waveform and the shaping transfer function. The shaping function is often considerably more complex than those used for soft clipping distortion.

Figure 14.16 illustrates some example shaping transfer function equations, and the results of applying them to a sinusoidal input. The sinusoidal input is generated by an oscillator (peak amplitude ±1) and then fed into the equation as variable x. Example 1 is a straight through case where the output is the same as the input. Example 2 is a soft clipping function similar to those seen in §7.2.1 (p.200). Example 3 both reshapes and doubles the fundamental frequency of the input. Example 4 is an equation known as a *Chebyshev polynomial*, which in this case is designed to produce the 5th harmonic of a sinusoidal input.

While the examples in figure 14.16 are a useful illustration of what can be achieved with particular equations and a particular input, more general methods are desirable for synthesising with waveshaping. Figure 14.17 illustrates the basic form required. The oscillator produces an output in the range −1 to +1 that is fed to a shaping function that maps input

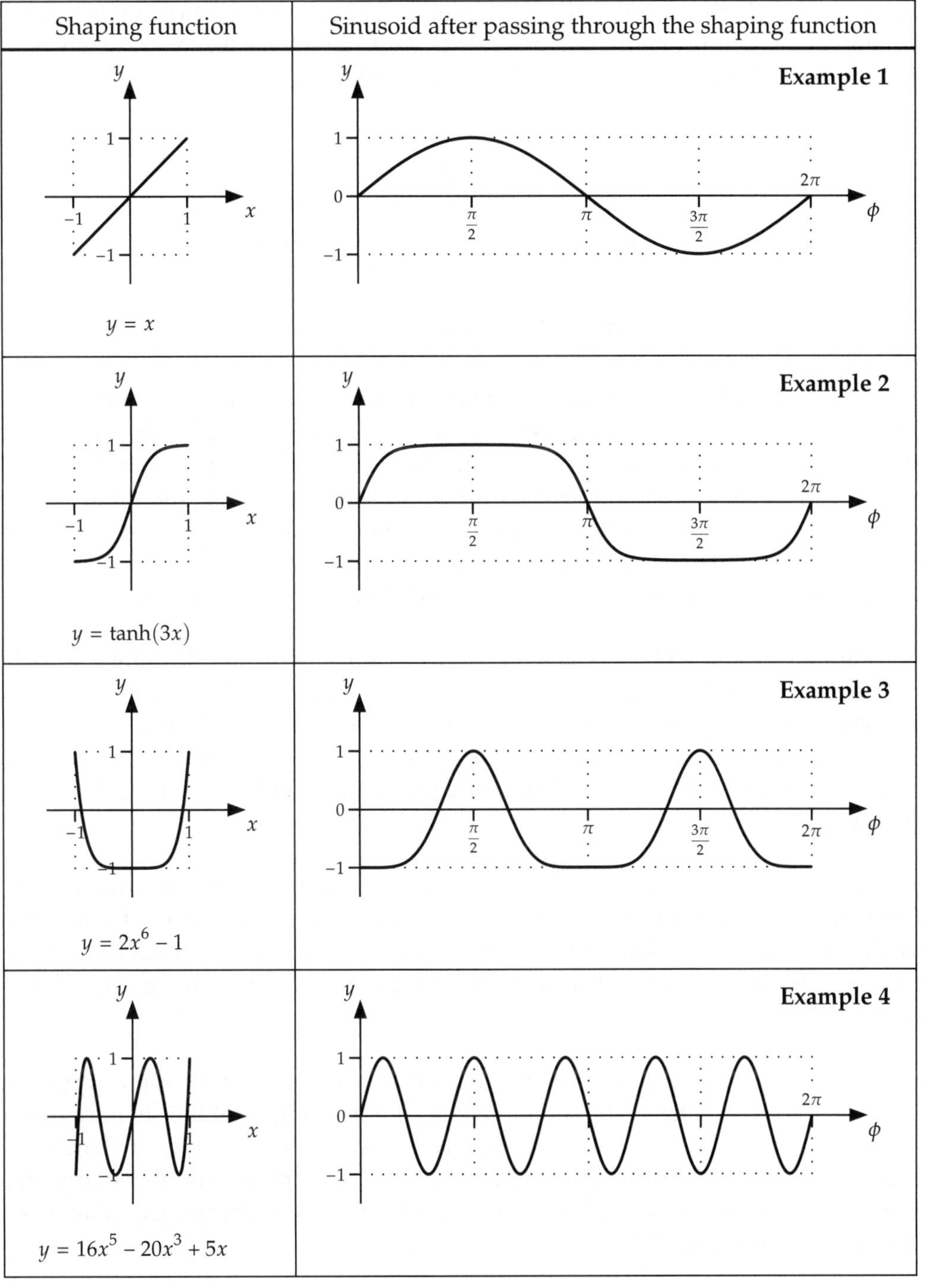

Figure 14.16 Example equations for reshaping a sinusoidal input

to output values. Typically the shaping function will be a wavetable (lookup table), which internally converts from an input range of −1 to +1, to a range of 0 to N−1 (where N is the size of the wavetable) as described by algorithm 14.14 (p.448).

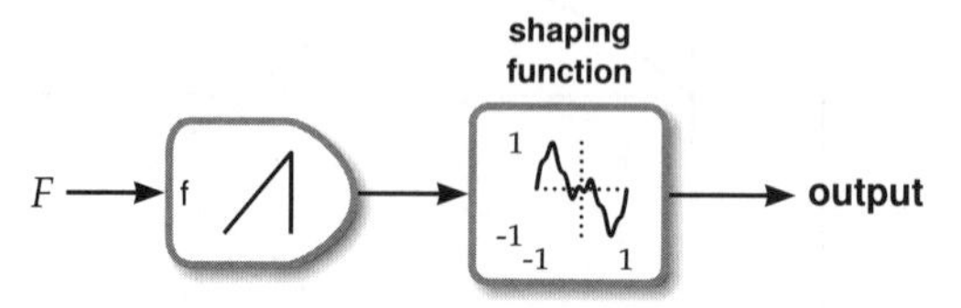

Figure 14.17 Basic waveshaping

The arrangement in figure 14.17 can be varied in a number of ways to produce different results. For example, the shaping function wavetable can be filled using an equation, or with a sampled waveform. The oscillator waveform shape can be changed, or the oscillator output could be multiplied by a scaling factor to change the range of values reaching the shaping function. Quite tonally sophisticated sounds can be produced with waveshaping methods with a modest amount of computation. However, there is not necessarily a simple relationship between the parameters and the tonal results.

When the oscillator waveform shape is a linear ramp (as shown in figure 14.17), the waveform that is produced has the same appearance as the shaping function. However, it is possible to modify the shape of the oscillation and so re-shape the resulting output. This technique is sometimes called *phase distortion*. Figure 14.18 illustrates how changing the oscillation shape at the shaping function input in figure 14.17 will change the shape of the output.

What this technique achieves is the ability to warp the output waveform away from the original shaping function shape to create new timbres. If the variation of the oscillator waveform from a ramp is fairly subtle, then the result retains similar tonal characteristics to the original. If the waveform is very different from the ramp shape, then the sonic character will be as well.

Figure 14.19 illustrates a synthesizer that blends between two oscillator waveforms, in order to vary the character of the sound produced at the output of the shaping function. Envelope generator 1 allows that blend to change over time. The rate of change of the blend envelope will affect the rate of timbral change. For example, a rapid variation might be used at the start of a sound. Blending is not the only way of changing oscillator shape, as described in §14.5.2 (p.451).

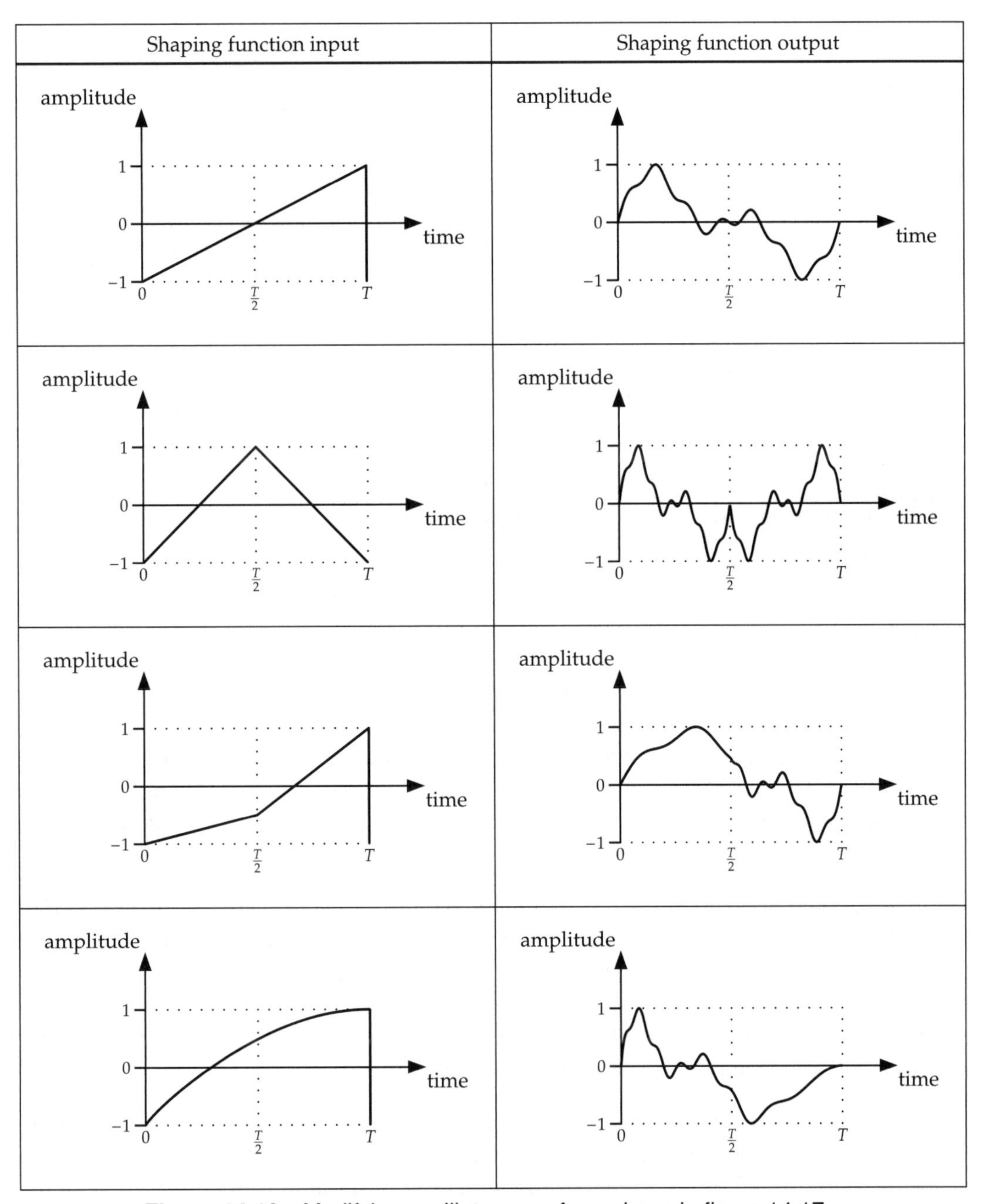

Figure 14.18 Modifying oscillator waveform shape in figure 14.17

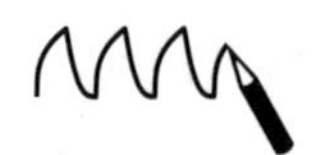

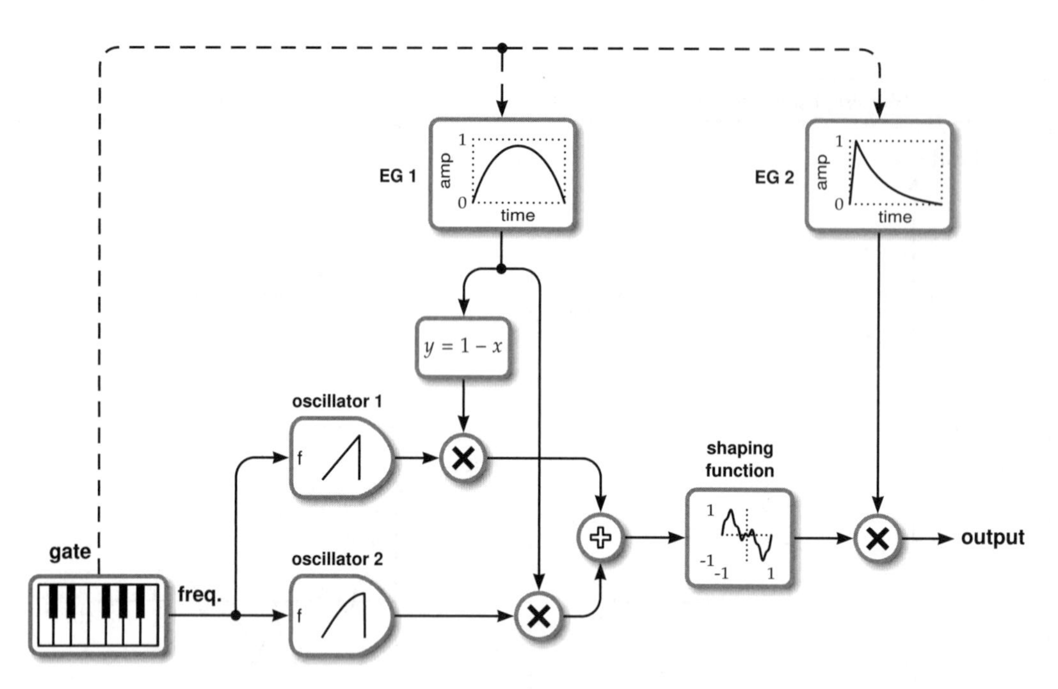

Figure 14.19 Variable oscillator waveform waveshaping

Figure 14.20 achieves waveshaping by scaling the amplitude of the oscillator output (with envelope generator 1) before it reaches the shaping function. The oscillation is around a central value of zero, which corresponds to the middle of the shaping function. As the output value from envelope generator 1 becomes larger, more of the shaping function will be used in producing the output. Figure 14.21 illustrates how the oscillation relates to the position in the shaping function.

Figure 14.22 shows examples of varying the amplitude of the sinusoidal oscillation in figure 14.20 with different envelope generator output values. The shaping function has been chosen such that the rapid shape variations are towards the extremities. This means that low oscillator amplitudes (controlled by envelope generator 1) will produce a less complex output than large amplitudes. In this particular example the oscillator waveform is a sinusoid, which avoids the discontinuities in a ramp (sawtooth) shape.

An additional feature that can be incorporated is to use key velocity from the keyboard in figure 14.20 as part of the tonal control. By use of scaling and offset to a suitable range, it could be multiplied by the signal at the input to the shaping function. With a shaping function such as that shown in the figures, increasing key velocity would lead to increasing tonal complexity.

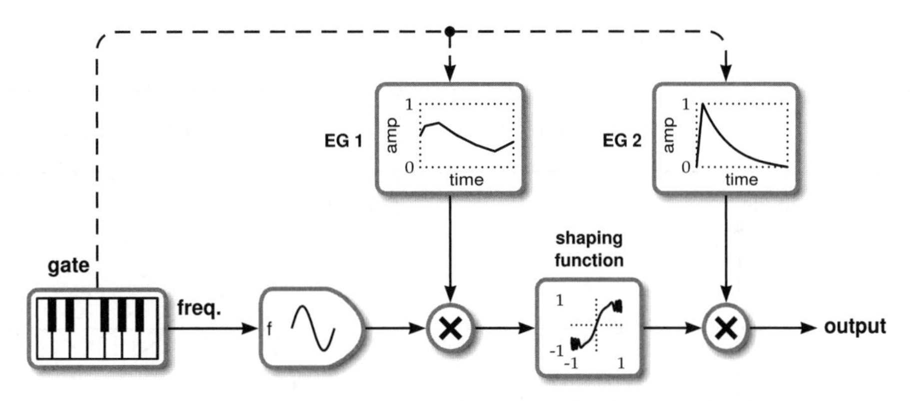

Figure 14.20 Variable oscillator amplitude waveshaping

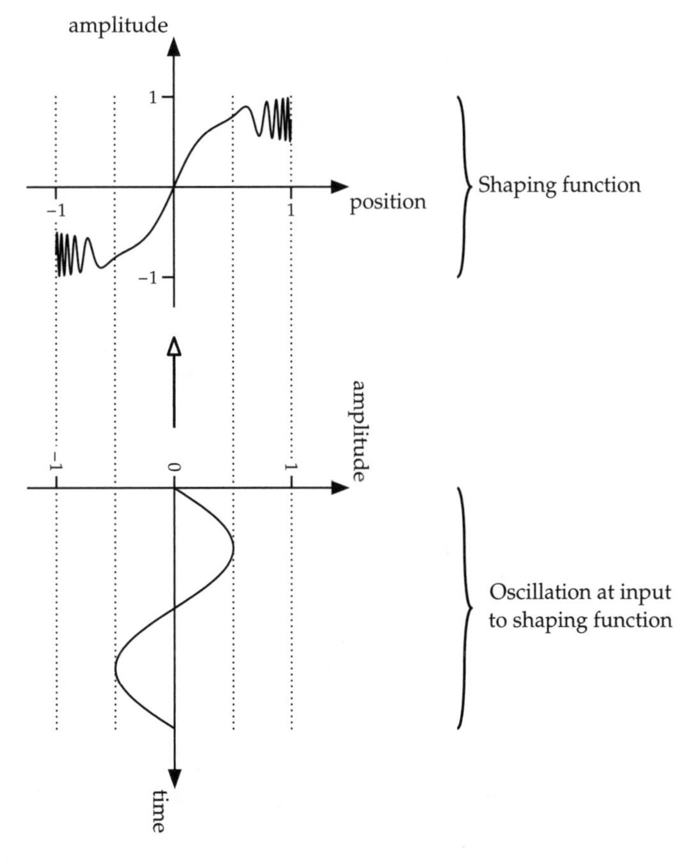

Figure 14.21 Oscillator amplitude relationship to shaping function

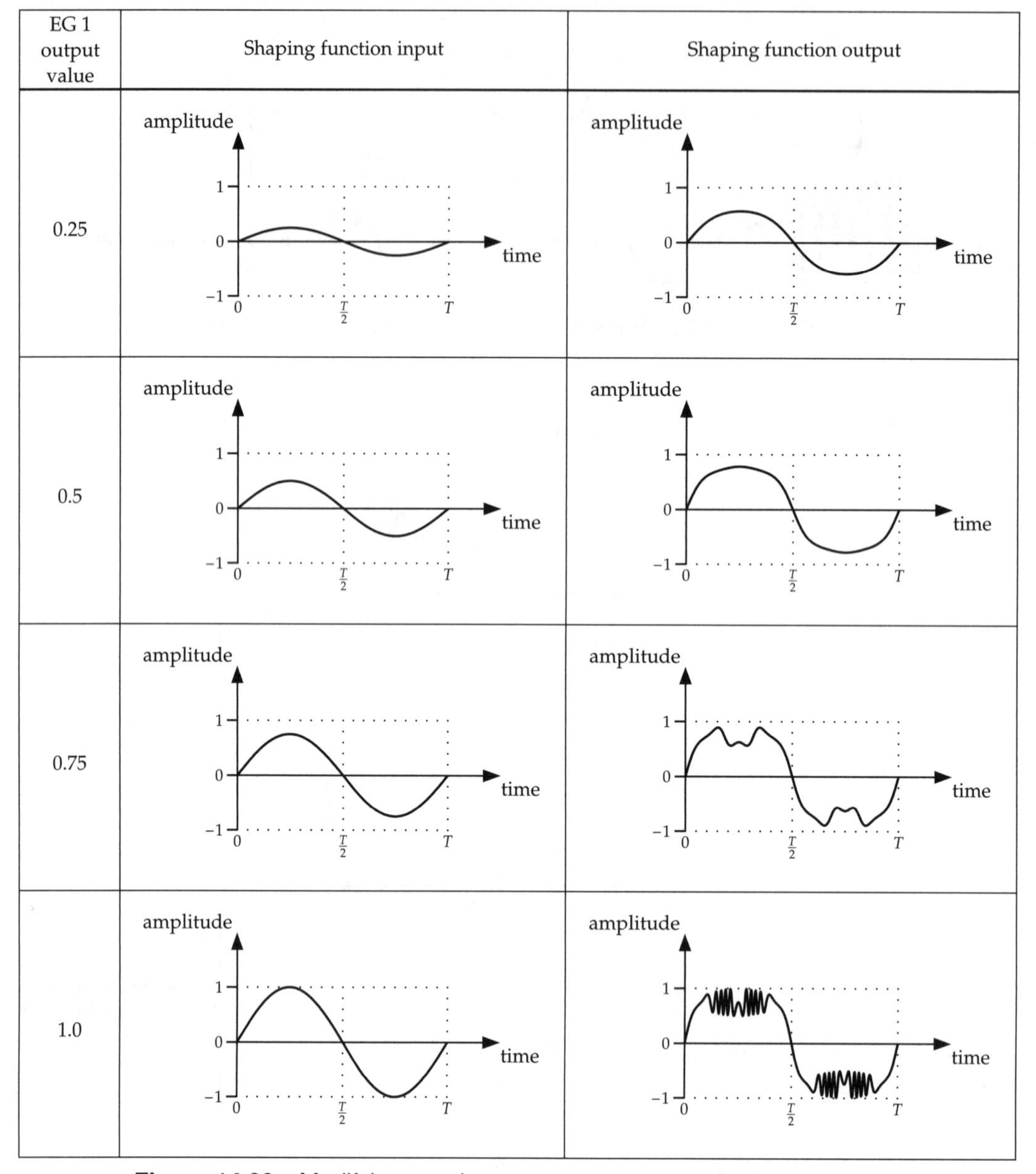

Figure 14.22 Modifying envelope generator 1 output in figure 14.20

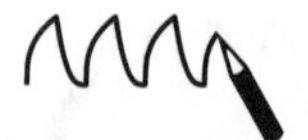

An issue with the variable oscillator amplitude technique is that the output of the shaping function is likely to vary in peak amplitude as the output of envelope generator 1 changes, as well as causing a tonal variation. It might be appropriate to apply a normalisation function in some cases, such that the amplitude effect is mainly determined by envelope generator 2.

14.6 Developing Processes and Learning More

Oscillators, envelope generators, and wavetables are a standard part of audio programming libraries and environments, as they are key building blocks in many types of synthesis. In many cases it is possible to use these standard objects when creating synthesizers without needing to worry about their underlying implementations. However, there are a number of reasons why a deeper understanding can be necessary for development. When using preprogrammed objects it is important to understand their limitations, such as whether oscillators are antialiased (discussed in §14.5.1, p.449), the available shapes of breakpoint envelope segments, and whether an envelope generator can produce a complex release envelope when it receives a note-off gate event. There is also the question of how to modify the underlying data, such as how to specify new oscillator waveform shapes, and the configuration and use of lookup tables for waveshaping.

In some cases, the limitations of standard objects necessitate implementation from scratch. The algorithms described in this chapter are sometimes quite complex compared to others in this book. However, if a specific feature is required then that might be the only option. The following books discuss these topics further:

> Boulanger, Richard, and Victor Lazzarini, eds. 2011. *The Audio Programming Book*. Cambridge, MA: The MIT Press.
>
> Pirkle, Will. 2015. *Designing Software Synthesizer Plug-Ins in C++: For RackAFX, VST3, and Audio Units*. Burlington, MA: Focal Press.

Waveshaping is an efficient way of achieving varying timbre with a small amount of computation. Simple arrangements often produce a distinctive character that is recognisably from that synthesis technique, but it does not necessarily lend itself to imitation of a particular class of acoustic instrument (as is the case with physical modelling, described in Chapter 21). The ability to achieve the desired tonality depends on having a shaping function with the required characteristics that can be accessed from the input oscillator. This might be an arbitrary waveform from a sampled source, for example. However, a carefully constructed shape such as that shown in figure 14.21 provides progressive variation of tonality with input signal amplitude.

The following sources provide some more advanced material that relates to this chapter, which can be used for further study:

Arfib, Daniel. 1979. "Digital Synthesis of Complex Spectra by Means of Multiplication of Nonlinear Distorted Sine Waves." *Journal of the Audio Engineering Society* 27:10:757–768.

Le Brun, Marc. 1979. "Digital Waveshaping Synthesis." *Journal of the Audio Engineering Society* 27:4:250–266.

Moore, F. Richard. 1977. "Table Lookup Noise for Sinusoidal Digital Oscillators." *Computer Music Journal* 1:2:26–29.

Roads, C. 1979. "A Tutorial on Non-Linear Distortion or Waveshaping Synthesis." *Computer Music Journal* 3:2:29–34.

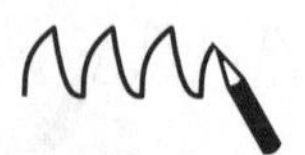

15

Sample-Based Synthesis Methods

15.1 Basic Concepts

15.1.1 Using Sampled Sound

Wavetable oscillators are usually associated with the generation of sound from a single cycle of a waveform (as discussed in §14.4, p.444). *Sample-based synthesis* extends the idea of wavetable oscillators to the storage and replay of longer audio data, such as a whole note, or many sound events (a drum pattern lasting for four bars, for example). Longer segments of sound have development in character over time, which leads to particular considerations and control techniques as described in this chapter.

The word "sample" is used in two different ways:

- To describe an individual data point. For example, each sample value in a 96kHz audio file is separated from the one that follows by $1/96000^{\text{th}}$ of a second.
- To describe a longer stored sound, such as a recording of a complete instrument note. For example, a 7 second piano sample at 96kHz is represented by 672000 data values.

This can lead to confusion if the context is not clear. In this chapter, the main concern is with manipulation and playback of longer segments of sound in the time domain, called sample-based synthesis or sampling. The main advantage of using the replay of recorded samples for generating sound is that the audible results can be identical to the original sound. The basic process of storing and retrieving audio data is described in §8.1.2 (p.221). Recording a sound captures an accurate image of the source under particular playing conditions (pitch, length, sound character). When it is replayed it sounds just like the original source. Sampling is relatively easy compared to creating imitative results with many other synthesis techniques.

The limitation of basic sample-based techniques is a lack of flexibility in sound character variation. Synthesis techniques often have parameters that can be used to modify low-level aspects of the generation process to achieve subtle tonal change. For example, additive synthesis (Chapter 16) allows particular partial amplitude envelopes and frequencies to be modified. Similarly, waveguide physical modelling (Chapter 21) allows the size and shape of a drum head to be modified in a naturalistic manner. The manipulations applied to samples detailed later in this chapter are generally at a larger scale.

Samples do not have to be used for imitation of the original sound source. It is possible to use the recorded material as the starting point for developing different sound characters. Playing a sound slowly can be used to create a substantially different character, as described in §15.3.1 (p.473). It is also possible to use process techniques found in other synthesis forms such as filtering (Chapter 17) or blending (Chapter 19) to achieve tonal variations.

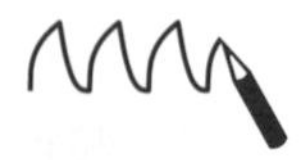

15.1.2 Recording, Editing, and Organising Samples

Samples must be recorded under appropriate conditions and edited to have properties that suit their replay. Some typical considerations are as follows:

- When recording an acoustic source, unwanted background sounds (hiss, rumble, clicks, and so on) are usually avoided, as they will be very apparent if a sound is replayed in isolation. If the sample is changed (such as to a different pitch) then the background will also be affected in the same way. Similar issues can occur with recordings that include reverberation.
- The sound will be trimmed. For example, silence can be removed before the start of a recorded instrument note, such that the sound begins immediately when playback starts. The length of a drum pattern or musical phrase that is to be looped needs to be chosen for synchronisation, such as being exactly two bars long such that the timing is consistent.
- Samples that are used in combination require consistency. For example, if two spoken word samples are to be played one after another the join will be more apparent if they are very different average amplitudes or tonalities. If a sampled piano has one sample per note, then the amplitude, length, and tonality of the notes would need to be consistent.

The recording and editing of samples depends on the situation. There are cases where, for example, background sounds are an intentional part of the character for artistic purposes. Similarly, a recording without reverberation might be useful for placing the sound in a different sonic context, but occasionally reverberation might be a desirable part of the character.

When imitating an instrument that can produce multiple pitches, one method is to record and store a sample for each required pitch, with different versions for each pitch relating to progressive changes in playing style (such as force of excitation). This is sometimes called *multi-sampling*. After editing, the samples can then be associated with performance control values as illustrated in figure 15.1. Depending on the note number chosen and the key velocity (assuming a piano-style keyboard controller), a sample of suitable pitch and tonality is selected and played back. Different samples can be cross-faded depending on key velocity to achieve a continuous variation (cross-fading is discussed in §19.4, p.553).

Recording and editing the samples for an 88 key piano with several distinguishable levels of key force requires a considerable amount of effort, in order to achieve consistency of performance character. An instrument such as a snare drum does not produce different pitches, although it can produce a number of different tonalities with varying stick force and striking position. These ideas also apply to sound sources other than acoustic instruments.

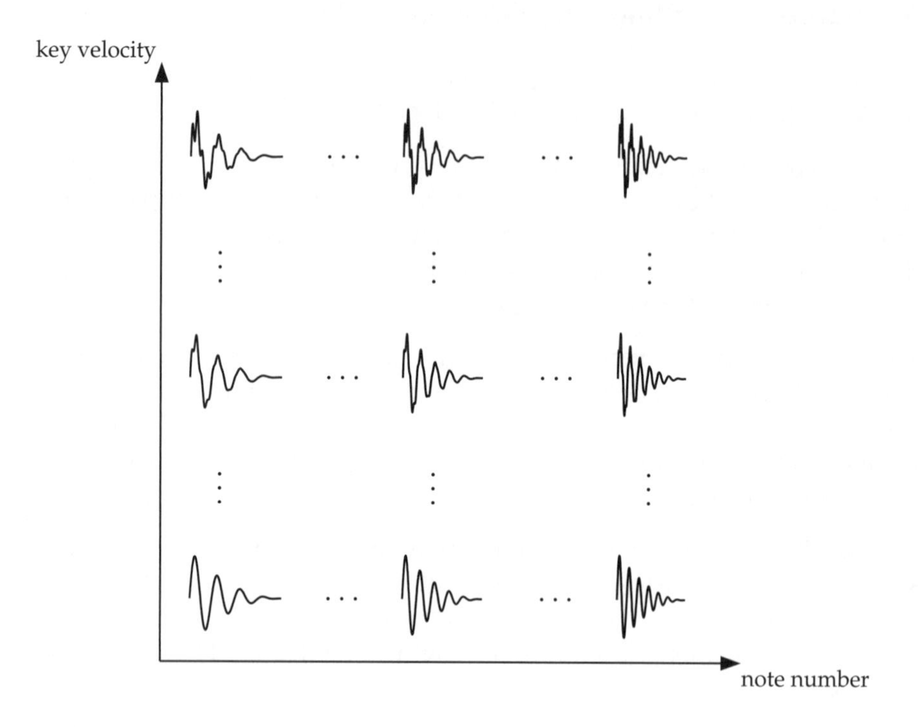

Figure 15.1 Choosing from multiple samples when imitating an instrument

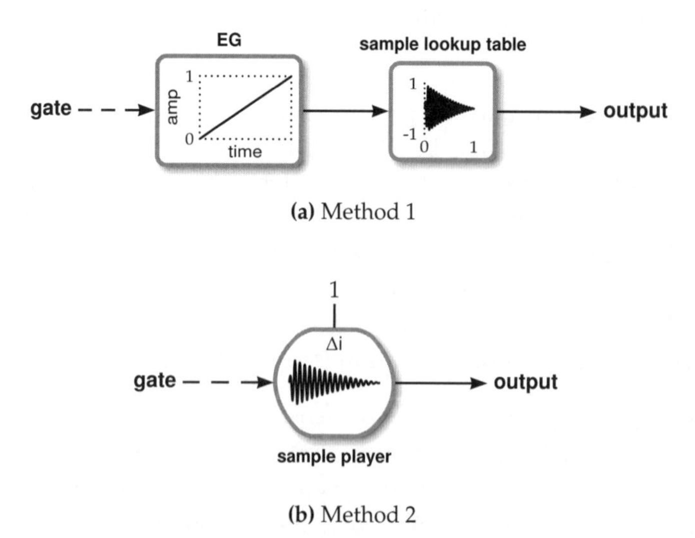

Figure 15.2 Sample playback basic forms

An alternative to individual samples for every pitch and playing condition is to modify a smaller set of samples to have different characteristics (such as a change of pitch, length, or tonality). This might save on the amount of recording and editing to be performed, and has the additional benefit of being able to create outputs for which recording samples is not possible or practical. Some of the issues with this are explored later in the chapter.

15.1.3 Sample Playback

Sample playback involves reading stored audio data with a changing read position over time. Figure 15.2a shows how this can be done with an envelope generator and a lookup table. The envelope generator produces a value that ramps from 0 to 1 over the same duration as the sound stored in the lookup table (N samples in length or N/f_S seconds where f_S is the sample rate). This index value is used to retrieve a value from the lookup table, which uses algorithm 14.13 (p.448). The result will sound the same as the original recording. Modifying the configuration of the envelope generator will change the character of the result, as described later.

The alternative is a dedicated *sample player* as shown in figure 15.2b. This encapsulates the functionality of the envelope generation and lookup table into a single unit. As well as having a gate input in the same manner as an envelope generator, it has a sample increment (Δi) input that controls the speed of progress through the sample. Algorithm 15.1 is a sample player function.

Algorithm 15.1 – Sample player function

input : sample increment Δi
output: output signal out

if readposition < 0 **or** readposition > (N−1) **then**
  out = 0
else
  out = interpolate(table, readposition)
  readposition = readposition + Δi

The features of the algorithm are as follows:

- The function is called once per output value (at the sample rate).
- *readposition* is the index position that has been reached in the table. It is assumed that the value of *readposition* is maintained between calls to the function. It initially has a dummy value (such as −1). When a gate signal indicates the start of the envelope, *readposition* will be set to 0 (external to the function) to cause the generation process to begin next time the function is called.

- *table* is the memory array (buffer) containing the sampled sound, which is accessed with indices 0 to N−1. *readposition* can be a value with a fractional part. The *interpolate()* function uses one of the methods described in §8.2 (p.237) to access a value at *readposition* in the table.
- In figure 15.2b sample increment Δi has a value of 1, so each time the function is called the *readposition* increases by 1 sample. This means that the *readposition* moves forward at the same speed as the sample was originally recorded. Different values of sample increment will be discussed later.

Multiple sample players can be used in parallel with outputs added together to produce polyphonic results. These can be controlled independently and produce overlapping outputs. For example, one might play kick drum samples while another plays snare drum. These would typically be triggered from different input note numbers.

15.2 Position Control and Concatenation

15.2.1 Position Control and Looping

Playing a recording once from start to end is a suitable way of recreating a sound event. In a range of circumstances, however, it is useful to be able to extend and reshape the progression of sound over time. One method for achieving this is to loop the sample by jumping to a different position in the buffer before resuming output generation. Figure 15.3 shows a simple 4 second drum loop. The sample is played from beginning to end, and when the playback position reaches the end of the sample it returns to the start (as indicated by the arrow). This process repeats for as long as the pattern is required.

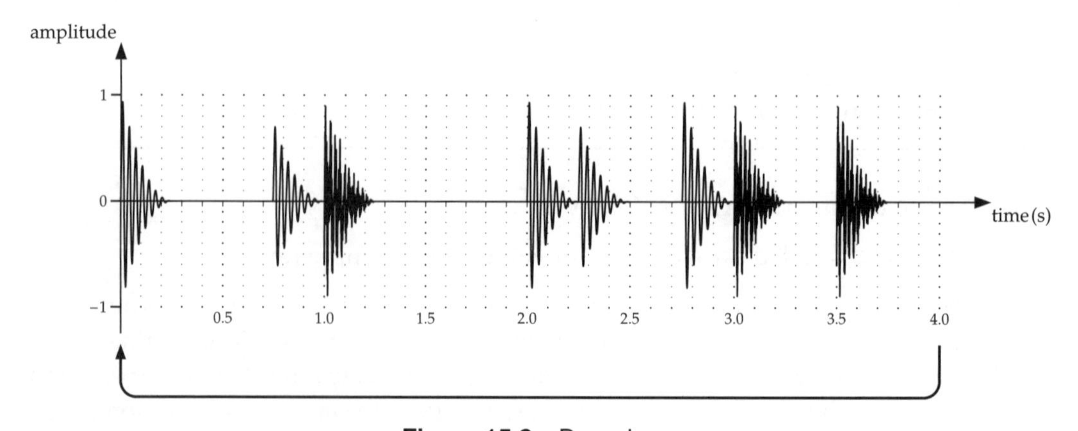

Figure 15.3 Drum loop

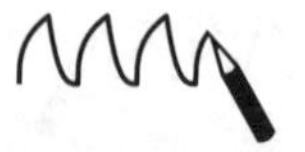

Figure 15.4 illustrates an example of how a 2 second drum loop could be achieved by reordering parts of a 4 second sample. The process begins by playing from 0 to 0.5 seconds, followed by 3 to 4 seconds, followed by 2 to 2.5 seconds, and then returning to the start. Clearly many different patterns can be achieved in this way. The idea of segmenting a sample for purposes of reordering can also be used as a prelude to applying different modifications to the individual parts, such as varying gain, or applying filtering or distortion. These ideas enable quite creative use of what might otherwise be a fairly plain loop.

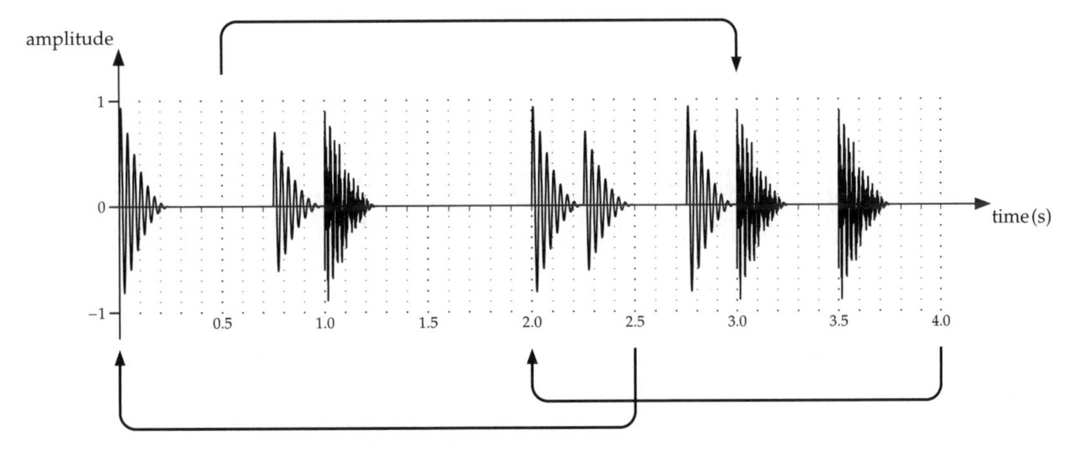

Figure 15.4 Drum loop with reordering

Figure 15.5 demonstrates how looping a steady sustain portion within a single note event can be used to extend the sound. In this example the sound is played up to the section covered by the loop, which occurs a total of 11 times, followed by the final part of the sound. The number of loops used depends on the desired result.

Figure 15.6 shows the opposite effect to figure 15.5. This is useful as a recorded sound might be longer than required. Rather than the position jumping back to loop a section it jumps forward to remove a section and so shorten the sound. The jump is to the start of the final release such that the sound ends in the same way as before.

There is the potential for a discontinuity to be created when the playback position is jumped between different parts of a recording, leading to a click in the output. This is avoided in figures 15.3 and 15.4, as the jumps occur from the silent parts between sound events, to the start of the next event. In figures 15.5 and 15.6 the jump occurs between suitable points in the waveform cycle to create a continuation of the shape after the jump. These issues are explored further in §15.2.3.

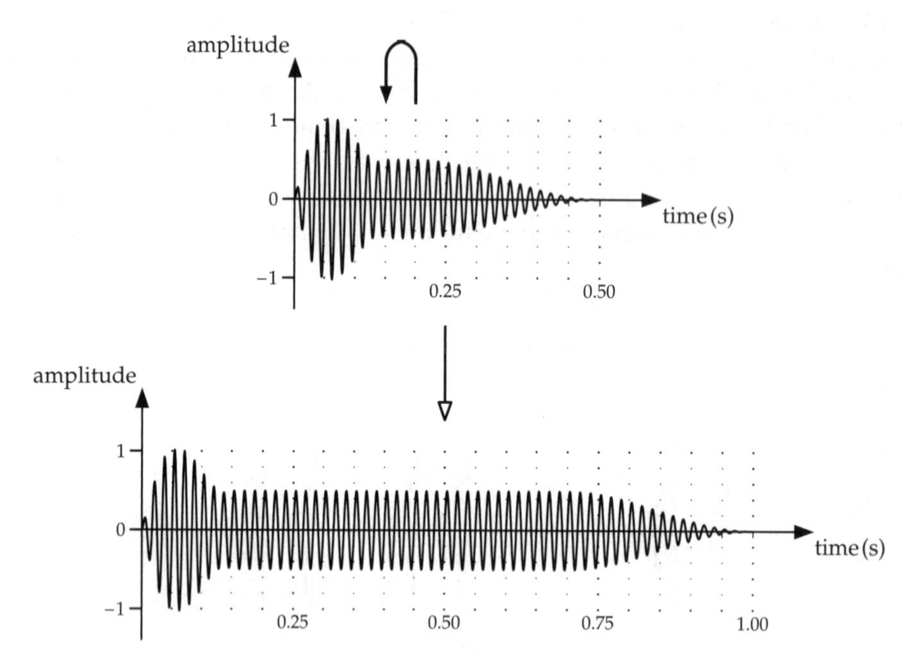

Figure 15.5 Sustain looping within a single note event

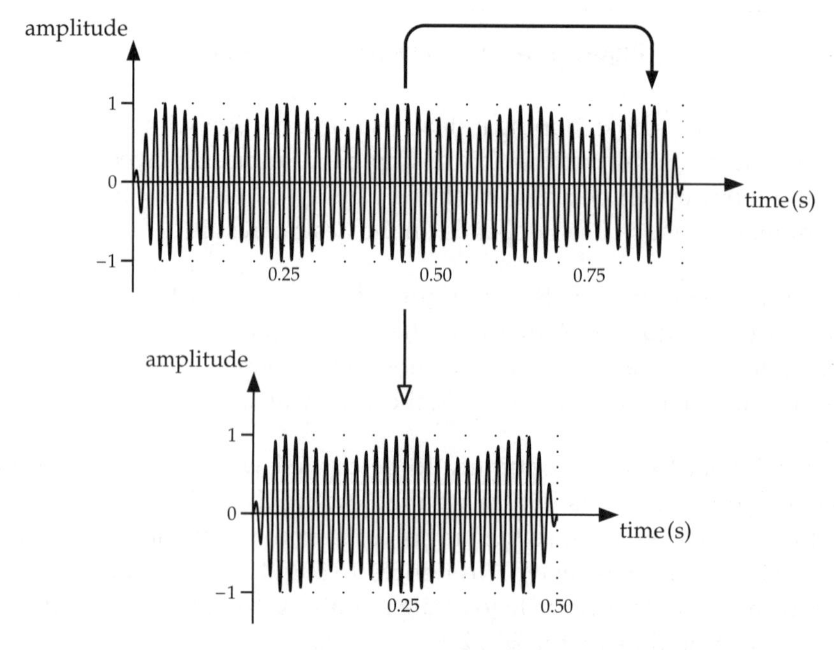

Figure 15.6 Reducing the duration of a single note event

15.2.2 Concatenation

As well as jumping the playback position and looping within a single sample, it is common to concatenate multiple samples or portions of samples. A simple technique is to concatenate prerecorded samples containing short musical patterns (commonly called loops) in order to compose a longer musical piece. Such arrangements of samples can be built up in parallel to construct multi-part arrangements, as shown in figure 15.7. Multiple parts must be generated in parallel and the outputs of the sample players mixed, such that all parts are audible simultaneously. The positioning of loops in this manner is usually possible graphically with Digital Audio Workstation (DAW) software.

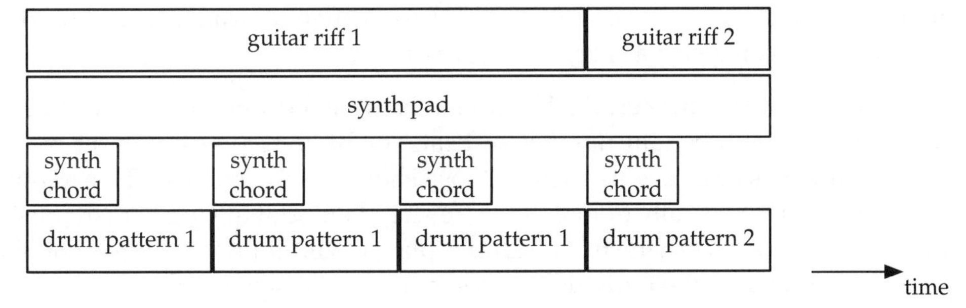

Figure 15.7 Arranging loop samples

Sometimes samples of spoken words are concatenated for use in computer-controlled information services. For example (where | indicates the edge of a sample):

- |You have |six| new messages|.
- |The next train to arrive at platform |two| will be the |ten|twenty-two| service to |Swindon|.
- |The number that you require is |zero|one|seven|nine|three| |five|zero|· · ·

In each of those examples, a section of the phrase could be easily replaced to convey different information. For example, a very long telephone number can be created by only recording samples for the numbers 0 to 9, and then replaying as many numbers as required in sequence. This is far more practical than recording every possible telephone number in its entirety.

To produce natural-sounding results it is necessary to record and edit the samples carefully such that the spacing and pitch variation are appropriate for the position in the sentence. The major limitation is that it is necessary to record every word that might be used with the appropriate tonality to fit the sentences being produced. More general vocal synthesis methods exist that can produce any word, one of which is described in §17.3 (p.509).

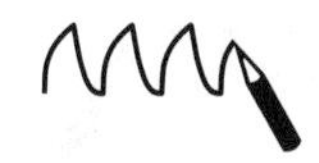

15.2.3 Process Considerations

There are unlimited ways in which samples can be edited, looped, reordered, and concatenated. These are some of the possible mechanisms for controlling this behaviour:

- In many cases, the user will manually choose the positions in a particular sample to associate with particular behaviour; for example, the portion of a note that will be sustained as shown in figure 15.5.
- Performance control data can be associated with particular behaviours; for example, looping the sound in figure 15.5 while a key is depressed, and then completing the sound when it is released. Similarly the choice of different drum samples or looping patterns can be controlled as part of performance.
- A rhythmical pattern of a certain duration in bars can be automatically divided into sections (slices) of a certain number of beats, or by detecting the onset of events (if the sample has clear events such as those shown in figure 15.4). This allows the sections to be automatically or manually reordered without having to mark positions individually to or from which the sample player will jump. It is also possible to spread out or overlap the individual slices in time to change the tempo.

To achieve a change of playback position means changing the value of variable *readposition* before the next call to the function in algorithm 15.1 (p.465). Whether this change of position causes an unwanted audible discontinuity depends on the transition in output values. There are a number of circumstances where problems can occur.

Moving the playback position between two points in a sample means that a join occurs between the audio data values before and after the jump. The join can relate to two different points in the waveform cycle if not appropriately chosen, as shown in figure 15.8a. The discontinuity in amplitude value and the variation in cycle length are audible as an inconsistency. In order to find more suitable positions for points where a jump occurs, it is useful to provide the user with an automated process that finds *zero crossings* (where the waveform passes through the time axis).

Algorithm 15.2 is a function to find the next waveform rising zero crossing (from negative to positive values) beyond the chosen *position* in a buffer *table*. The *position* must be in the range 0 to N−1 to match the range of the buffer. It interpolates and returns a new position value. The function can be used to find the nearest zero crossings when jumping the buffer position. This makes it much easier to produce a good join. Because waveforms are often complex (such as having multiple zero crossing points per cycle and changing shape over time) it is still necessary to manually vary the positions within the zones of interest, and then allow the function to find a close crossing point.

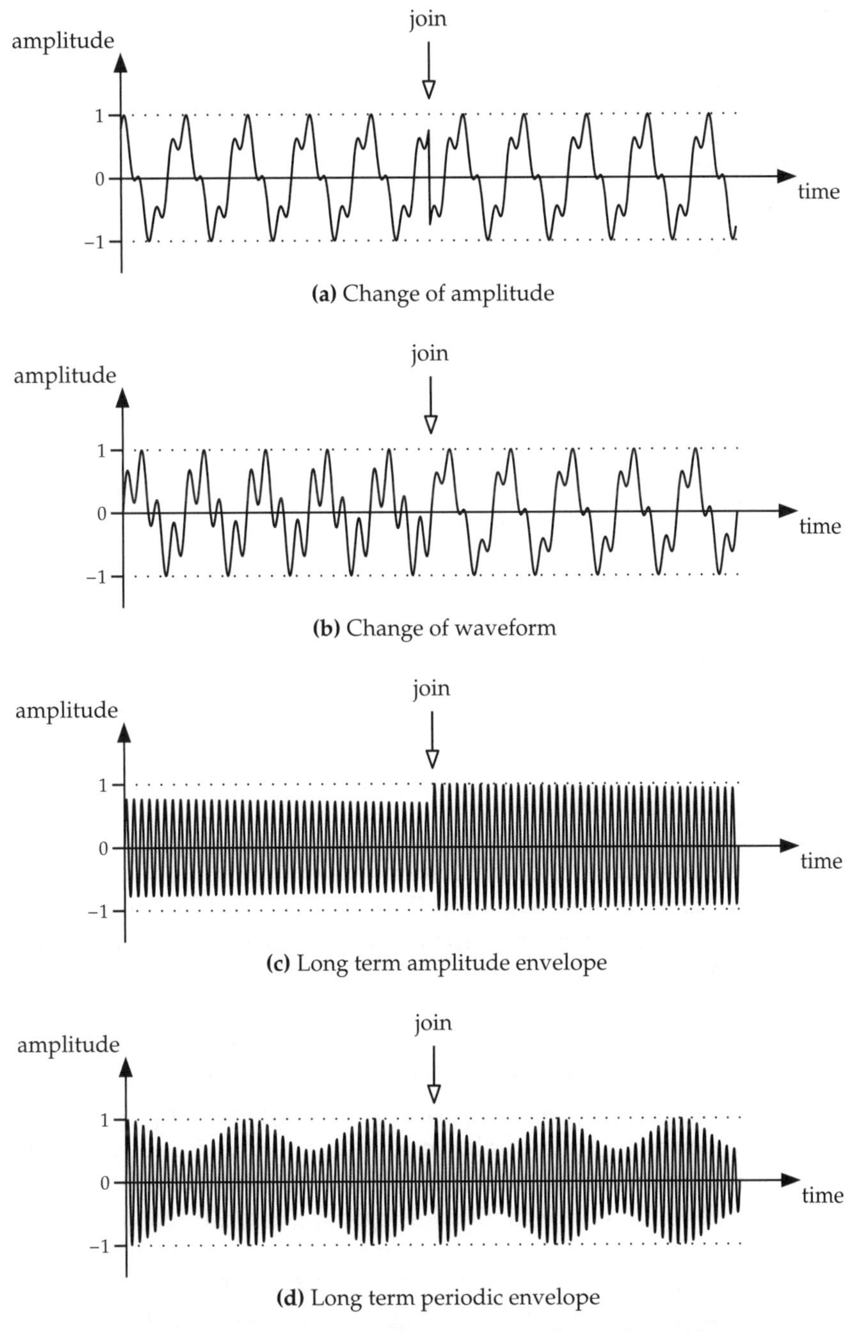

(a) Change of amplitude

(b) Change of waveform

(c) Long term amplitude envelope

(d) Long term periodic envelope

Figure 15.8 Issues with changing playback position

Algorithm 15.2 – Rising zero crossing finding function

```
input  : starting location position
output: zero crossing position out

firstposition = position
lastvalue = interpolate(table, position)
out = −1

while out < 0 and position < (N−1) do
    position = position + 1
    nextvalue = interpolate(table, position)

    if lastvalue <= 0 and nextvalue >= 0 then
        // a rising zero crossing or a flat-line at zero

        diff = nextvalue − lastvalue
        if diff > 0 then
            position = position − nextvalue/diff        // estimate crossing position

        out = position

    lastvalue = nextvalue

if out < 0 then
    out = firstposition
```

A different technique to address the problems of audible joins is to cross-fade between the two parts of the sample over the join. This can be appropriate for smoothing in circumstances where matching zero crossings is not sufficient. Cross-fading is described further in §19.4 (p.553).

Figure 15.8b is a more subtle type of problem, where the join is at a zero crossing, but the waveform shapes are substantially different either side. Because many sounds have a changing tonal character over time, it is possible for a change in position to result in a change of tonality. When creating a sustain loop like figure 15.5, it is often helpful to place the beginning and end points of the loop fairly close together, such that the tonality does not change significantly over its length. Similar logic applies to pitch variations.

Even if the waveform is compatible at the join, it is not necessarily the case that the overall amplitude envelope will be so, as shown in figure 15.8c. For example, if a sound has a decaying amplitude over time, then a loop over a portion of that decay might show this effect. Figure 15.8d shows a related effect, where there might be a periodic variation such

as a tremolo or vibrato. In that case it is desirable for the position change or loop to relate to an integer number of modulation cycles (as was the case in figure 15.6).

15.3 Manipulating Sample Data Values

The techniques described in §15.2 change the sample player output by jumping to a different part of a sample, or a different sample, but still outputting the data values in their original stored form and with a sample increment of 1. This section considers how the sample data values can be manipulated to change the character of the result in terms of pitch, duration, tonality, and amplitude.

15.3.1 Sample Increment Effects

The sample increment used with a sample player can be varied to achieve a different playback speed, and so a change of pitch. Figure 15.9 illustrates how pitch can be controlled with a keyboard input. When the chosen note number is 60 (middle C) the sample increment is 1 and the sample plays back at the original recorded pitch. With a note number of 61, the sample increment is $2^{1/12} \approx 1.059463$ and the sample playback is a semitone higher than recorded (utilising equation 2.2, p.21). With a note number of 58, the sample increment is $2^{-2/12} \approx 0.890899$ and the sample playback is two semitones lower than recorded. The value 60 in the equation in the figure can be varied to suit the required control arrangement and the original pitch of the sample.

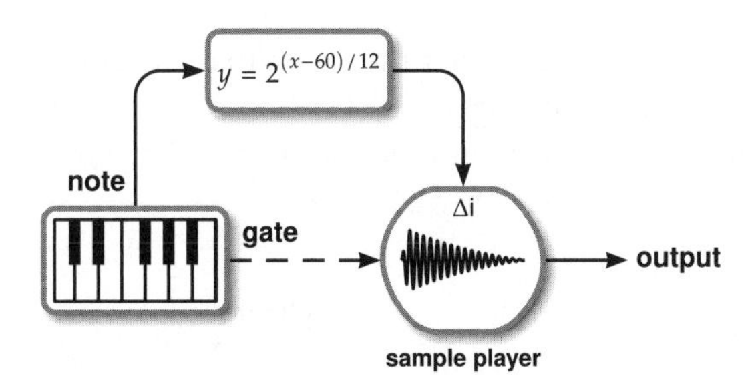

Figure 15.9 Pitch control with a keyboard

It is also possible to use negative sample increment values to reverse the sample playback. For example, a sample increment of $-2^{-12/12} = -0.5$ will cause the sound to be played an octave lower than recorded and in reverse. It is necessary to choose a suitable starting position, such as the end of the sound, before using a negative sample increment. Using negative sample increments can also be used when creating a loop that alternates between playing forwards and backwards, which can help in creating a transparent join in some circumstances.

Changing the sample increment has three principal effects:

- Changing pitch.
- Changing length, and speed of development over time.
- Changing tonality.

The pitch effect is fairly straightforward. Figure 15.10 shows an example of how increasing the sample increment from 1 to 2 for a constant tone means that the sample playback progresses at twice the speed, the cycle length is halved, and so the pitch increases by an octave.

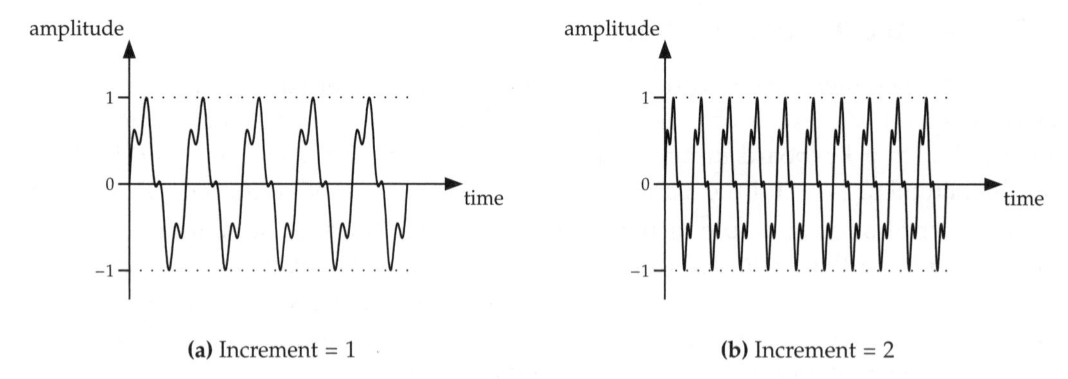

(a) Increment = 1 **(b)** Increment = 2

Figure 15.10 Sample increment effect on pitch

If the sample increment changes, then the time taken to progress from the beginning to the end of the sample will also change. Figure 15.11 shows how an increment of 2 will halve the length of the sample compared to an increment of 1. Similarly, an increment between 0 and 1 will extend the length of the sample.

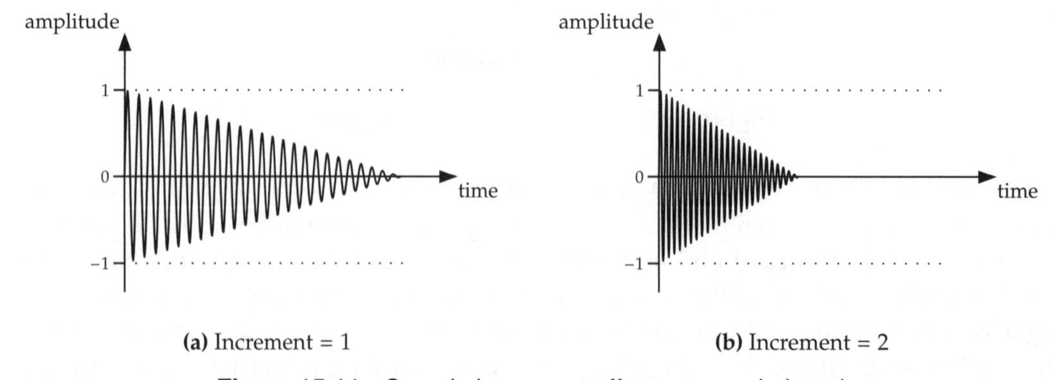

(a) Increment = 1 **(b)** Increment = 2

Figure 15.11 Sample increment effect on sample length

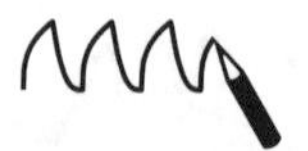

Not only does the overall length of the sample change with the sample increment, but also the speed of progress of features within the sound. Figure 15.12 illustrates how a number of aspects can be affected by the change of sample increment. Moving from an increment of 1 to 2 means that the length of the attack and the length of modulation cycles (such as tremolo or vibrato) will be halved. How rapidly the underlying waveform changes is also scaled in the same way, such as the transition in waveform shape that is visible in the figure.

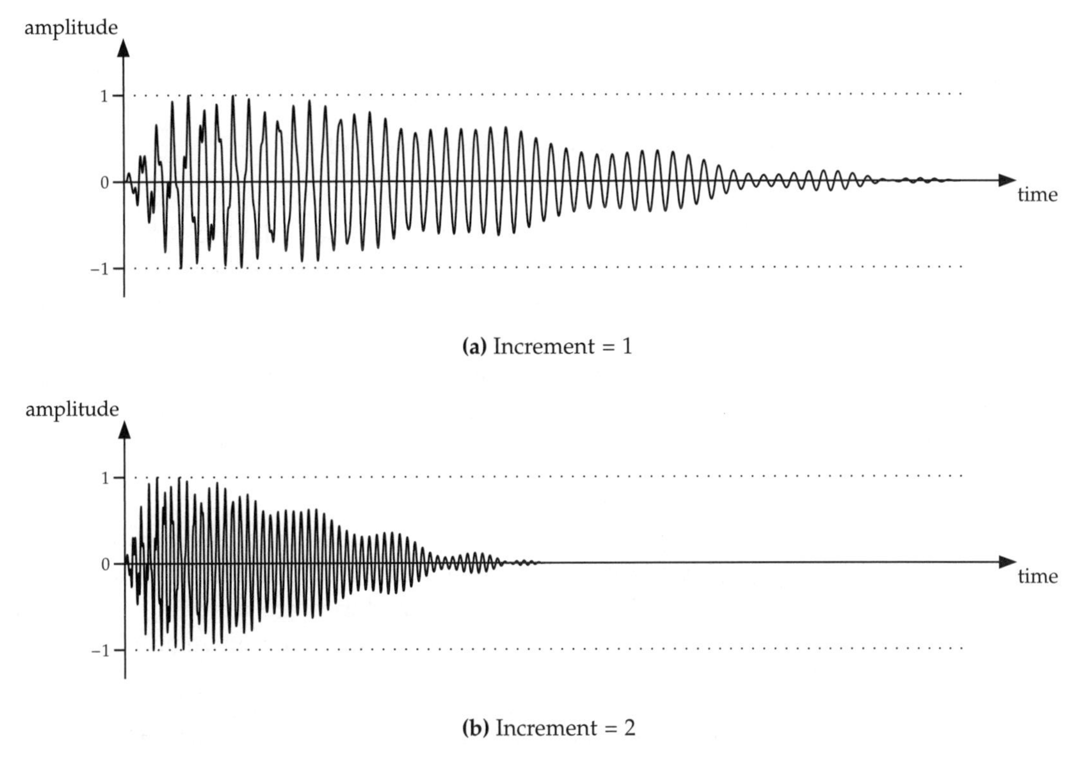

Figure 15.12 Sample increment effect on feature progression

If the length of waveform cycles changes then the frequencies of the partials also change. This can be explored by considering results in the frequency domain. Figure 15.13 illustrates a simple synthesizer whose oscillator produces a waveform with 40 equal-amplitude harmonics, which is passed through a parallel pair of bandpass filters. Figures 15.14a and 15.14b show average spectrum plots for that synthesizer with the oscillator set to fundamental frequencies of 200Hz and 400Hz respectively. In both cases there are peaks corresponding to the centre frequencies of the filters (800Hz and 3.2kHz). The spectral envelope remains consistent with varying fundamental frequency F, as the bandpass filters have fixed parameters.

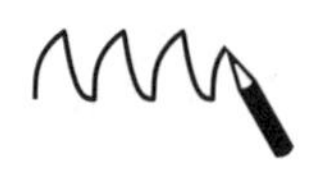

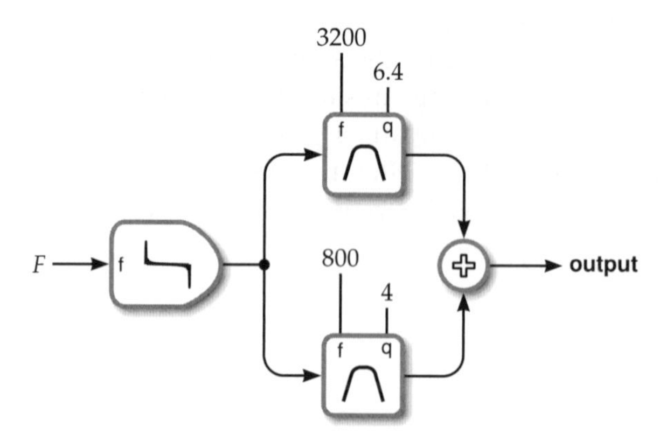

Figure 15.13 Example subtractive synthesizer

Storing the 400Hz sound of figure 15.14b as a sample and then playing it back with a sample increment of 0.5 produces the result in figure 15.14c. Halving the playback speed produces a fundamental frequency of 200Hz. All the partials are halved in frequency, maintaining the harmonic relationship to the fundamental. Likewise storing the 200Hz sound of figure 15.14a as a sample and then playing it back with a sample increment of 2 produces the result in figure 15.14d, producing a fundamental frequency of 400Hz. Comparing the plots it is apparent that the spectral envelope has been compressed or stretched in frequency at the same time as the pitch has changed.

Figure 15.14 demonstrates that playing back a sample with a different sample increment is not the same as changing the fundamental frequency in the synthesizer in figure 15.13. Tonal differences will be heard because the spectral envelopes are different. It is also important to note that the same potential for aliasing exists as for wavetable methods (as described in §14.5.1, p.449).

The context determines whether it is significant that multiple sound characteristics are affected by changes to the sample increment. For example:

- If the intention is to produce a small change in pitch (such as one semitone), then changes in tonality and development over time might not be obvious.
- It might be desirable for artistic purposes to use significant sample increment variations, in order to deliberately change tonality and development over time compared to the original sample character.
- However, if the desired change in pitch is not small, the sound character is supposed to remain consistent, and using multiple samples recorded at different pitches is not appropriate, then a different method might be employed (such as those described in Chapters 12 and 22). With human vocal sounds the spectral envelope is very

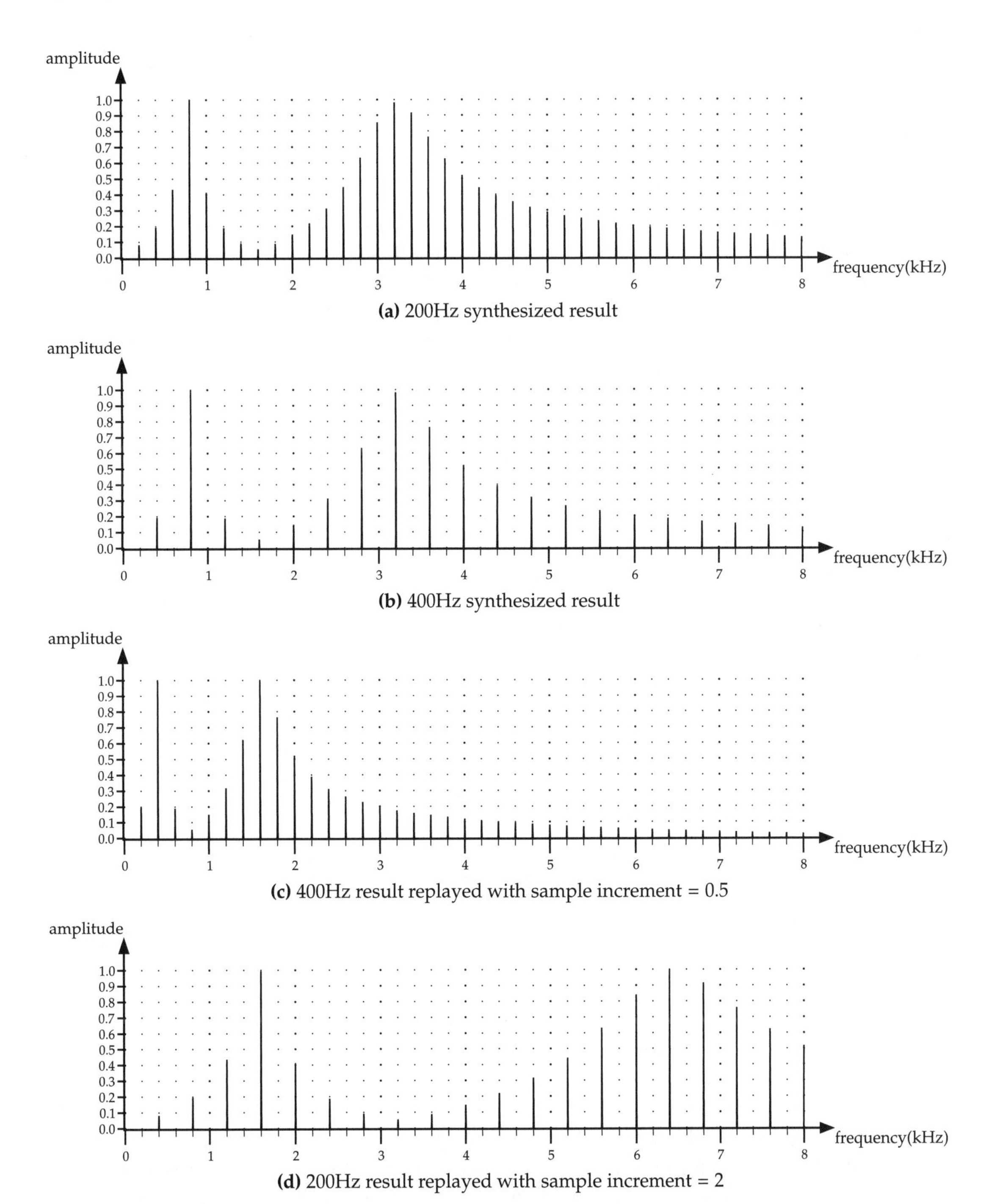

(a) 200Hz synthesized result

(b) 400Hz synthesized result

(c) 400Hz result replayed with sample increment = 0.5

(d) 200Hz result replayed with sample increment = 2

Figure 15.14 Sample increment variation effects in the frequency domain

important in determining what phoneme is being spoken or sung, so the character can appear unusual unless the spectral envelope is maintained.

15.3.2 Further Methods

Figure 15.15 combines the ideas of figure 15.9 (p.473) and figure 13.22 (p.420) to allow vibrato to be added to a sample, as well as achieving controllable pitch. The vibrato envelope allows the depth of modulation to be controlled over the length of the note. The envelope duration will need to be adjusted in order to match the sample length. Because changing the sample increment also affects the length of the result, an equation such as the following could be used, where d_{EG} is the envelope generator duration, d_S is the original recording duration, and n is the current note number:

$$d_{EG} = \frac{d_S}{2^{(n-60)/12}} \tag{15.1}$$

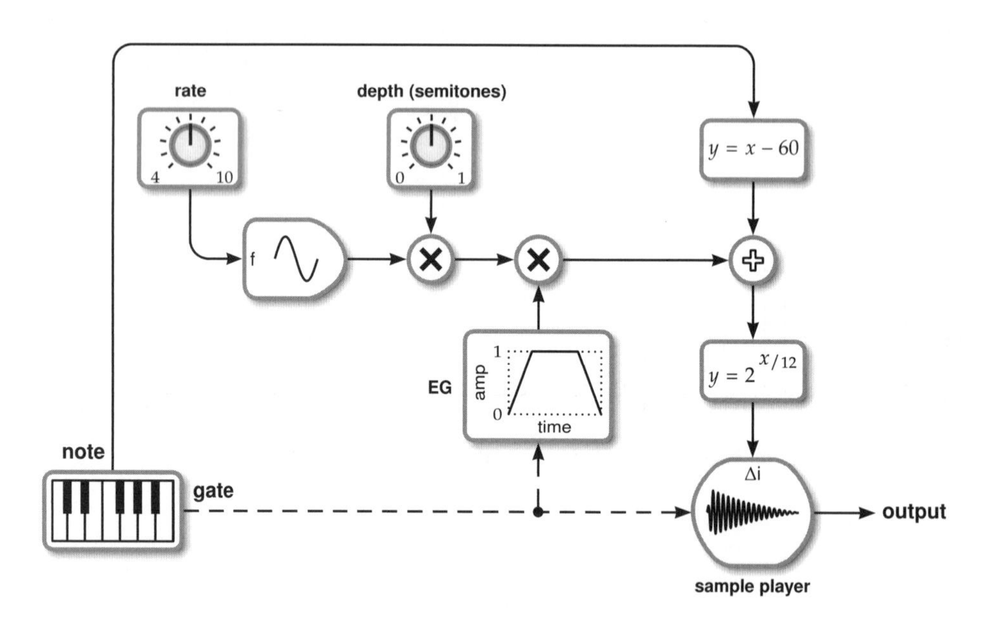

Figure 15.15 Envelope-controlled vibrato

Recorded samples often have their own amplitude envelope, such as a percussive shape for a snare drum sample. Figure 15.16 shows how an envelope generator might be used to allow reshaping of the amplitude envelope. This can produce some similar results to the process in figure 13.19 (p.417). A flat envelope at a value of 1 in the envelope generator means that the output is the same as the original sample.

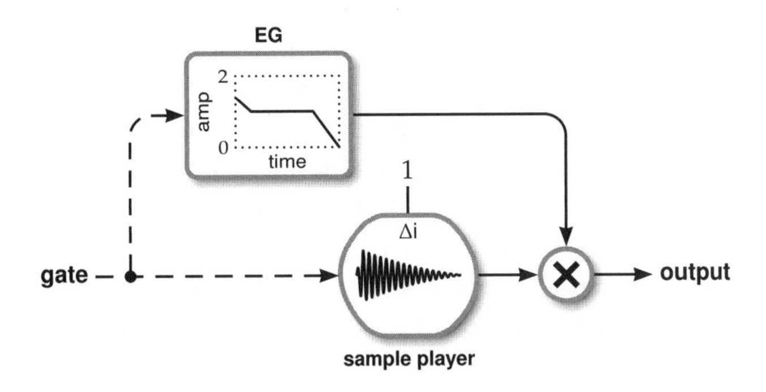

Figure 15.16 Amplitude envelope reshaping

Some possible uses are as follows:

- Interesting variations can be applied to the amplitude envelope, such as boosting or reducing certain parts, or adding complex variations on top of the original envelope. The duration can be reduced compared to the original stored sample by reducing the envelope to zero earlier than the end of the sample length.
- One advantage of applying envelope changes during playback (rather than editing the sample in a waveform editor) is that variations can be applied as part of performance. For example, key velocity might be used to change the envelope shape applied to the sample player output by adapting the method in figure 24.9 (p.664).
- It is possible to select the onset of a longer sound, by use of an envelope that rises from 0 to 1 and back to 0 over a short length of time. This can be useful for creating short percussive sounds. Using different starting positions in the sample player (rather than always starting at the beginning of the sample) provides a wider range of possibilities for selection. This idea is extended in Chapter 22 to a more general technique called granular synthesis.

15.4 Developing Processes and Learning More

Sample-based synthesis is a key technique in imitation of other sound sources, which is something that many people want to achieve. The technological limitation historically was a lack of sufficient memory or other storage, but this is rarely a problem now. A significant challenge in achieving imitative sample-based synthesis is suitable preparation of the source material such that the results are convincing; for example, recording and editing instrument sounds, or choosing suitable looping points.

Time domain playback of samples is computationally-efficient and uses a small set of standard blocks. If multiple samples have been suitably prepared (say, one per note of an instrument) and the control mechanism is suitable for imitating the instrument of interest, then the results can be very convincing when using a sample increment of 1. There is great potential for achieving new sound characters using sample increments other than 1, if the intention is not imitation, due to the combined effects on pitch, length, and tonality. Similarly, there are many musical opportunities in breaking samples into sections and playing them back at different increments, in different orders, and with different processing treatments. Further discussion of sampling techniques can be found in this book:

> Russ, Martin. 2013. *Sound Synthesis and Sampling (Third Edition).* Burlington, MA: Focal Press.

There are other ways of approaching the manipulation of recorded samples, either for convincing imitation, or in terms of using the data for the creation of new sound characters. The playback of samples is closely related to the use of single cycle wavetables described in §14.4 (p.444). A single cycle of a waveform is a snapshot of a longer tonal variation that is found with most sound sources, but can provide very useful source material in a wide variety of synthesis forms. Granular synthesis (as described in Chapter 22) provides techniques for sophisticated manipulation of small segments of sound, which builds on the ideas in this chapter. Alternatively, a frequency domain approach (Chapter 12) allows independent control over the dimensions of time, frequency, and amplitude, which can be a very powerful alternative to time domain methods.

16

Additive Synthesis

16.1 Basic Concepts

16.1.1 Additive Synthesis Characteristics

Additive synthesis is based on the idea of summing individual amplitude-weighted sinusoidal partials at different frequencies to create sounds. Chapters 3 and 4 described how time and frequency domain analysis can be used to discover the internal construction of sounds in terms of sinusoidal partials. Additive synthesis allows the features seen in analysis to be directly synthesized. This has a number of advantages:

- Because the sinusoidal partial is a very simple element, additive synthesis allows great precision of sound construction. For example, the amplitude of a particular harmonic can be changed without affecting any others.
- It is possible to specify the time-varying characteristics of individual partials using envelope generators. This allows very sophisticated control that is not available when generating a complex waveform from a single wavetable oscillator (as per §14.4, p.444) where the different partials have a fixed relationship to each other.
- As well as synthesizing partials to match an existing sound, it is possible to subsequently edit the characteristics in a very precise way that is not easily achievable with time domain sampling methods (Chapter 15). For example, it is possible to remove certain partials, or change a particular inharmonic partial in amplitude and frequency, and so change the tonal character in a subtle manner. Similarly, hybrid sounds can be created by combining particular subsets of partials from two sounds, without having to mix all of the partials.

Interesting sounds often have a large number of frequency partials over a wide frequency range, as illustrated in Chapter 4. Sound character is not only determined by large amplitude harmonic and inharmonic features, but also by the effects of smaller amplitude and inconsistent elements. For example, a noisy onset to a percussive sound might briefly have many hundreds of partials. This has a number of consequences:

- It is necessary to appreciate that the combination of partials results in a particular sound character, rather than individual partials having unique or independent tonal roles. The combination of such elements as harmonics, inharmonics, and the overall spectral envelope must be considered.
- In terms of controlling the sound, it is not practical for the synthesizer user to specify the behaviour of hundreds or thousands of partials on an individual basis. A number of approaches might be taken:
    - The technique could be used principally for less complex sounds.

  - The synthesizer might be constructed in such a way that the characteristics of many partials are controlled by high-level parameters and the individual partial parameters are automatically derived from those settings.
  - The parameters might be determined through automated analysis and synthesizer configuration.
  - Additive synthesis might be combined with other techniques, such as the use of noise generators (Chapter 18) to use the particular advantages of different techniques for different parts of the sound.
- The synthesis of individual partials implies individual sinusoidal oscillators, each with suitable envelope control over frequency and amplitude. Therefore the computational complexity increases with the number of partials being synthesized. This becomes less of an issue as available computational power increases. However, other synthesis techniques can produce sophisticated results with less computation, if not with the same direct control over individual partials.

Although pure additive synthesis concerns the summation of individual sinusoidal oscillations, some of the ideas considered in this chapter can also be applied to groups of partials, as described in Chapter 19.

16.1.2 Frequency Separation

The separation between partials in terms of frequency is important to perception, which has consequences for additive synthesis. Figure 16.1 illustrates a simultaneous pair of sinusoidal partials at frequencies f_1 and f_2, and with amplitudes a_1 and a_2 respectively. Two common scenarios are where the partials are harmonic or inharmonic relative to a fundamental frequency. For example:

- If f_1 = 200Hz and f_2 = 300Hz, then they are both harmonics of 100Hz.
- If f_1 = 237.2Hz and f_2 = 751.5Hz, then they are inharmonic.

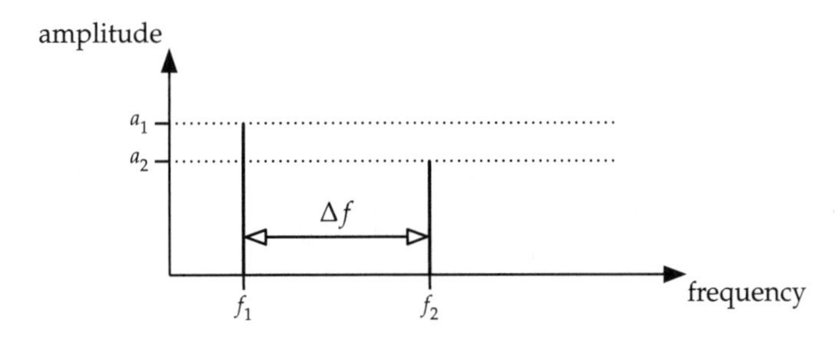

Figure 16.1 Two sinusoidal partials

An additional complication is that the difference in frequency between two partials ($\Delta f = f_2 - f_1$) relates to the perception of *beating* and *roughness*. There are three key areas of interest:

- When Δf is less than about 15 to 20Hz, there is an audible pulsing or beating sensation, and the principal perceived frequency appears to be between that of the two partials. The beats are audible at a frequency of Δf; for example, 204Hz and 207Hz cause beats of 3Hz. A related but weaker effect can also be heard with frequencies that are close to harmonic multiples (such as 200Hz and 403Hz).

  The reason why two partials with close frequencies cause a beating effect is apparent when considering how the partials sum together in the time domain (figure 16.2). The relative phase of the partials at different points is important. The waveform peaks and troughs sum and cancel by different amounts at different points in time.

- As Δf increases beyond 20 to 30Hz, the beating sensation diminishes and becomes one of roughness or dissonance.

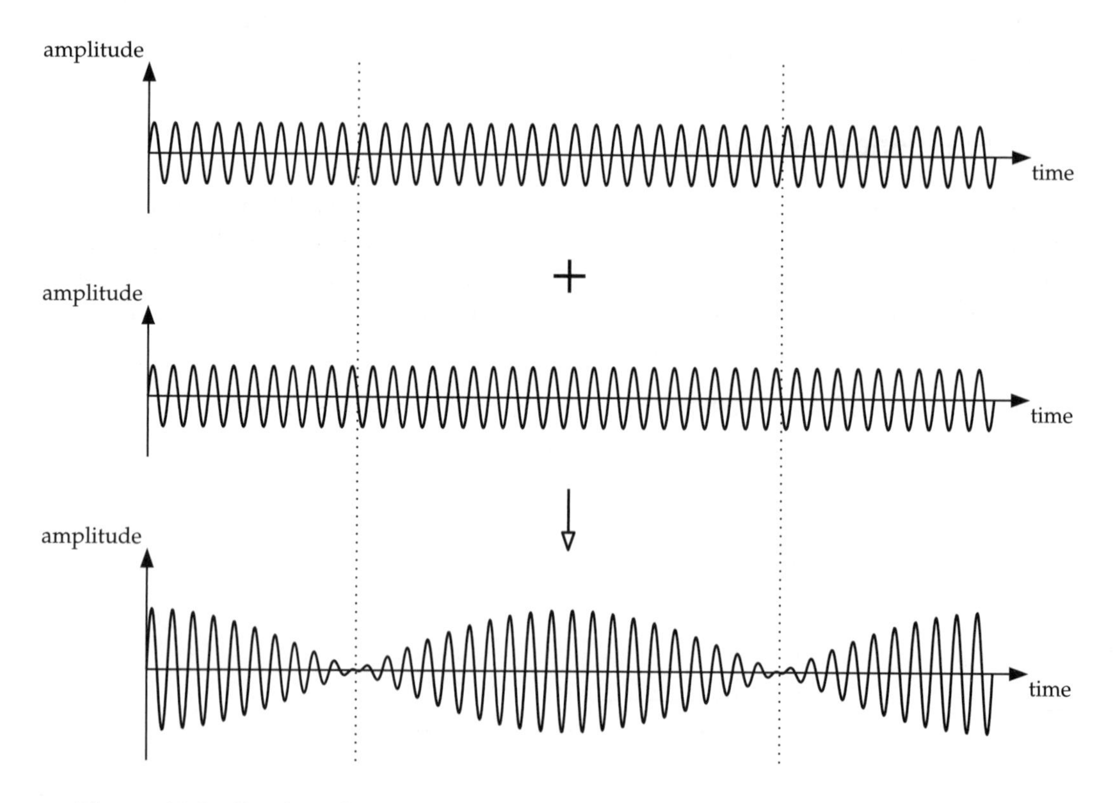

Figure 16.2 Beating effect with two summed partials with slightly different frequencies

- As Δf increases further, the roughness effect becomes weaker until it disappears at what is called the *critical bandwidth*. The critical bandwidth changes with frequency, but is often of the order of a few semitones.

The relative amplitude of the neighbouring partials is important. If the amplitudes are similar then the interaction is clearer than if one is much weaker than the other. These ideas need to be kept in mind when configuring additive synthesis with sinusoidal partials.

16.2 Synthesis with Control over Individual Partials

16.2.1 Synthesizer Form

Figure 16.3 shows a general additive synthesizer, which allows individual sinusoidal partials to be specified in terms of frequency and amplitude variation over time. The features are as follows:

- Although only three parallel paths are shown, any number is possible depending on the required result. All the paths are summed together to create the output. The purpose of this arrangement is to allow different envelopes for each parallel path. If the same variation is required in each case, then it is more efficient in terms of computation and configuration to have global methods. For example, if the same amplitude envelope is required for all paths, then that can be achieved with a single envelope generator output multiplied by the summed output signal.
- Multiplying factors m_1 to m_N determine the base frequencies of the different paths relative to the frequency from the keyboard. The factors can be any positive real number values. The multiplying factors ensure a consistent relative frequency relationship, which means that harmonic and inharmonic patterns are maintained as the input frequency changes. If a situation exists where that is not required, then the input frequency multiplier could be removed and replaced with a fixed value input to the path instead.
- The frequency envelope generators allow variation from the base frequency with multiplication within the range f_{li} to f_{ui}. For example, if the range is 1 to 2, that allows variation between the base frequency and an octave above. A smaller range might be specified for subtle variations, or a different range for each path. The envelope shapes in the figure produce gently decreasing frequencies over time, which can sometimes be heard in struck drum sounds. If variation of frequency over time is not required, then a flat line at a multiplier value of 1 is used. Alternatively, the frequency envelope generators and associated multipliers could be removed, saving computation and configuration effort.

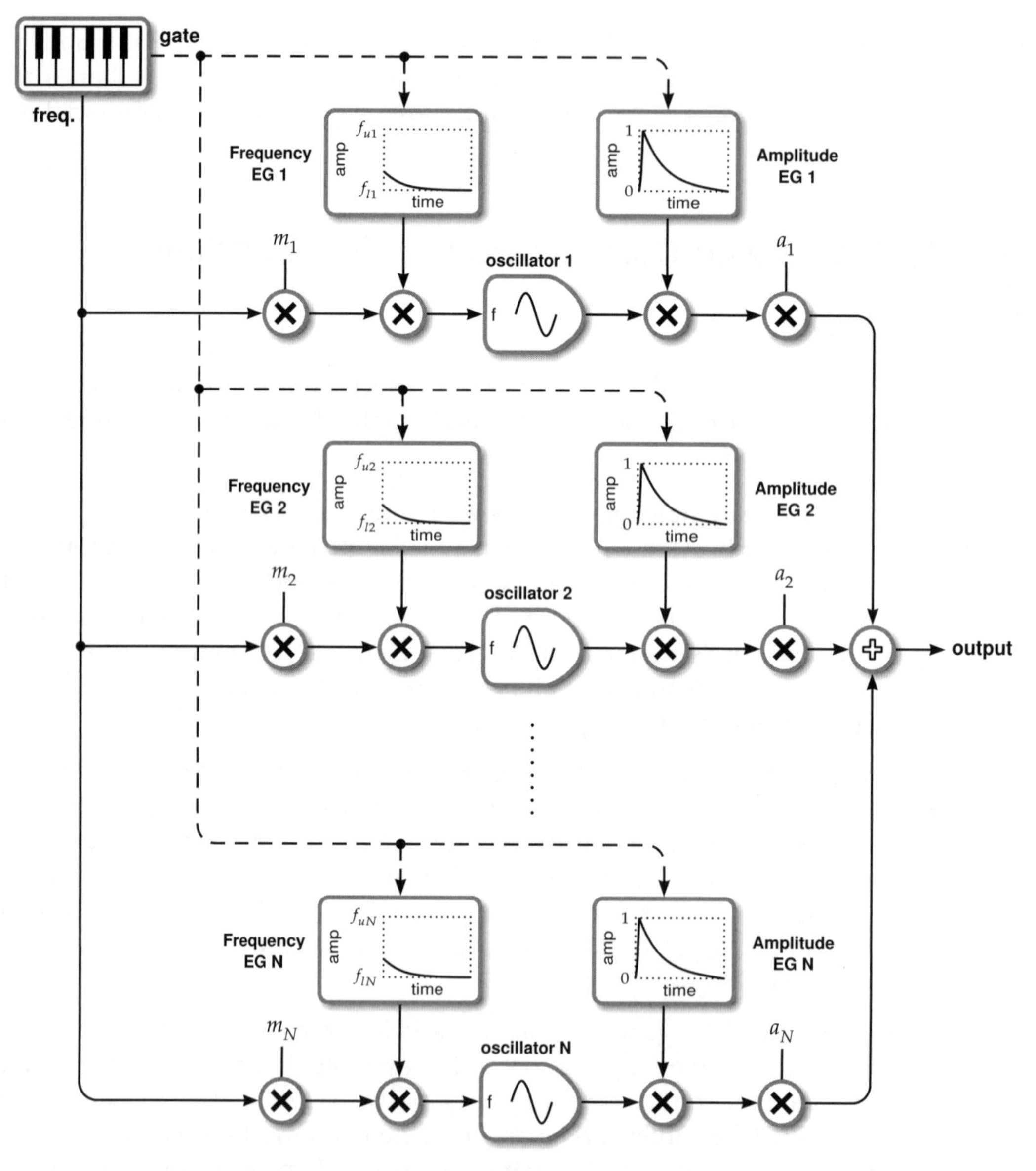

Figure 16.3 Additive synthesizer with control over individual partials

- The amplitude envelope generators and gains a_1 to a_N determine the variation over time and relative levels of the different partials. The envelope shapes in the figure produce percussive amplitude variations. Although amplitude gain is specified in linear units in the figure, in some cases it is more useful to use decibels. This would require a suitable translation to linear units (using equation 5.3, p.113).
- Different partials exist for different lengths of time in many acoustic sounds. It is useful if the control interface allows the overall time length represented by an envelope to be changed with a single parameter. That makes it easier to configure the synthesizer than if all the individual control points must be moved manually.

It might be more appropriate to specify a frequency variation in terms of semitones rather than frequency multiples. In that case the envelope generator output would need to be mapped through the equation $y = 2^{x/12}$ (as per equation 2.2, p.21). Alternatively, it might be desirable to specify a frequency variation in terms of hertz that is added on to the base frequency rather than using multiplication.

The form in figure 16.3 could be extended with further features. For example:

- An overall amplitude envelope generator could be incorporated, whose output is multiplied by the summed output signal. This can simplify configuration for some sounds.
- A static or enveloped stereo pan effect could be included in each parallel path, summing the left and right outputs separately. This allows different parts of the sound to have different positions and spatially spread the frequency spectrum. This is different from applying a pan to the summed output, where all partials would have the same spatial position. Figure 19.5 (p.551) demonstrates this idea for more complex oscillations.
- An individual delay in each path could be used to introduce different partials at different points in the synthesized sound. For complex evolving sounds this can be easier to configure and modify than having envelopes where there are stretches of zero amplitude followed by an increase later.

The following parts describe different ways to configure the synthesizer in figure 16.3.

16.2.2 Configuration from Theory

It is possible to use additive synthesis to construct synthesized sounds to a set of rules. A typical method is to use Fourier series mathematical techniques, which determines the amplitudes of harmonics that compose a waveform. This assumes a repeating (harmonic) waveform shape.

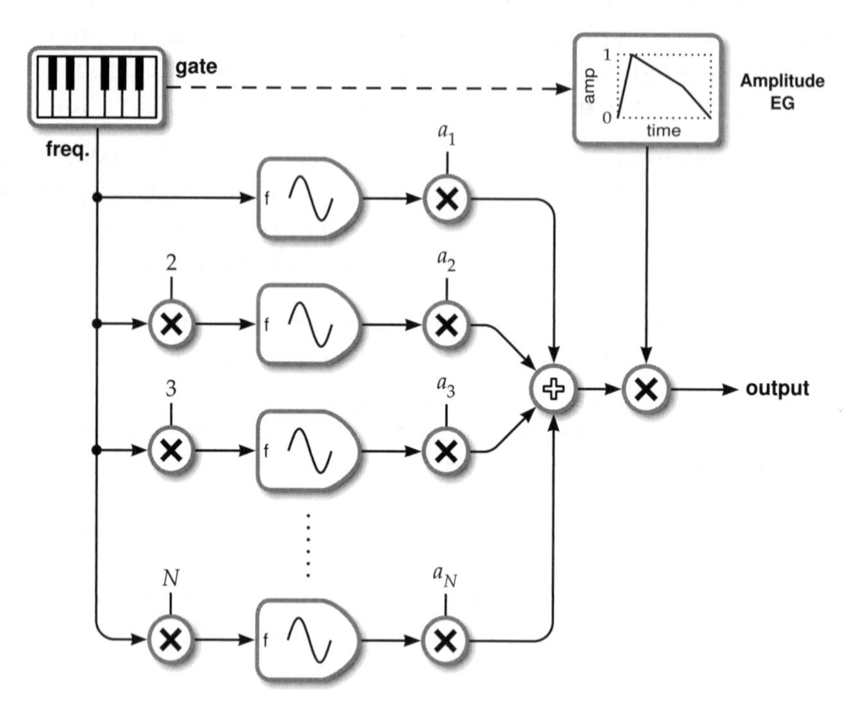

Figure 16.4 Simple harmonic additive form

Waveform	a_1	a_2	a_3	a_4	a_5	a_6	a_7	a_8	a_9	a_{10}	General form a_i
sine	1	0	0	0	0	0	0	0	0	0	
sawtooth	1	$\frac{1}{2}$	$\frac{1}{3}$	$\frac{1}{4}$	$\frac{1}{5}$	$\frac{1}{6}$	$\frac{1}{7}$	$\frac{1}{8}$	$\frac{1}{9}$	$\frac{1}{10}$	$\frac{1}{i}$
square	1	0	$\frac{1}{3}$	0	$\frac{1}{5}$	0	$\frac{1}{7}$	0	$\frac{1}{9}$	0	$\frac{1}{i}$ for odd i
triangle	1	0	$-\frac{1}{9}$	0	$\frac{1}{25}$	0	$-\frac{1}{49}$	0	$\frac{1}{81}$	0	$\frac{1}{i^2}$ for odd i alternately + and −

Table 16.1 First ten harmonic amplitudes for common waveforms

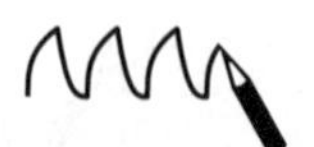

To synthesize a simple series of harmonics with particular amplitudes, the form in figure 16.3 can be simplified to the arrangement in figure 16.4. The individual frequency and amplitude envelope generators have been removed, and the frequency multiplying factors m_1 to m_N are integers to produce harmonics. This means that the variable parameters are the quantity of parallel paths, and the amplitude factors a_1 to a_N. The first ten harmonic amplitudes for common waveforms are shown in table 16.1. The amplitude weights have been normalised such that the fundamental frequency partial has an amplitude of 1.

Correct amplitude weightings achieve the appropriate tonal character when constructing a particular waveform in this manner. However, using appropriate phase is necessary for the visual shape to also appear correct in the time domain:

- The amplitude values in table 16.1 assume that sine waves (rather than cosine) are used.
- The table differs from the description in §4.2.2 (p.79), in that the amplitudes of the triangle wave harmonics are alternately positive and negative. Negative amplitudes are equivalent to a fixed phase shift, which is information that does not appear on a frequency domain amplitude plot, but does affect the time domain shape.
- The oscillators in figure 16.4 are assumed to be synchronised such that all are at zero phase at the start of the fundamental cycle.
- When generating the sawtooth shape, multiplying the output (or all the amplitude weights) by -1 will change the direction of the slope without changing the sound character:

Figure 16.5 shows how a sawtooth wave is built up using the information in table 16.1. The more harmonics are used, the closer the shape becomes to the target shape. If only a few harmonics are used, the lack of high frequencies produces a fairly dull sound. If there were an infinite number of harmonics, the shape would match the target. However, to avoid aliasing and save computation, partials above the maximum frequency supported by the system are not synthesized (frequency f_B in figure 2.15, p.34). For example, if the system cannot reproduce frequency partials above 20kHz, the maximum harmonic of a 880Hz tone that will be possible is the 22nd at a frequency of 19.36kHz.

With a fixed combination of frequencies and amplitudes, it is more computationally-efficient to synthesize using a line-segment or wavetable technique, as described in Chapter 14. However, those techniques can be prone to producing frequency partials above the Nyquist frequency $f_S/2$ and so generate aliasing distortion (as described in §14.5.1, p.449).

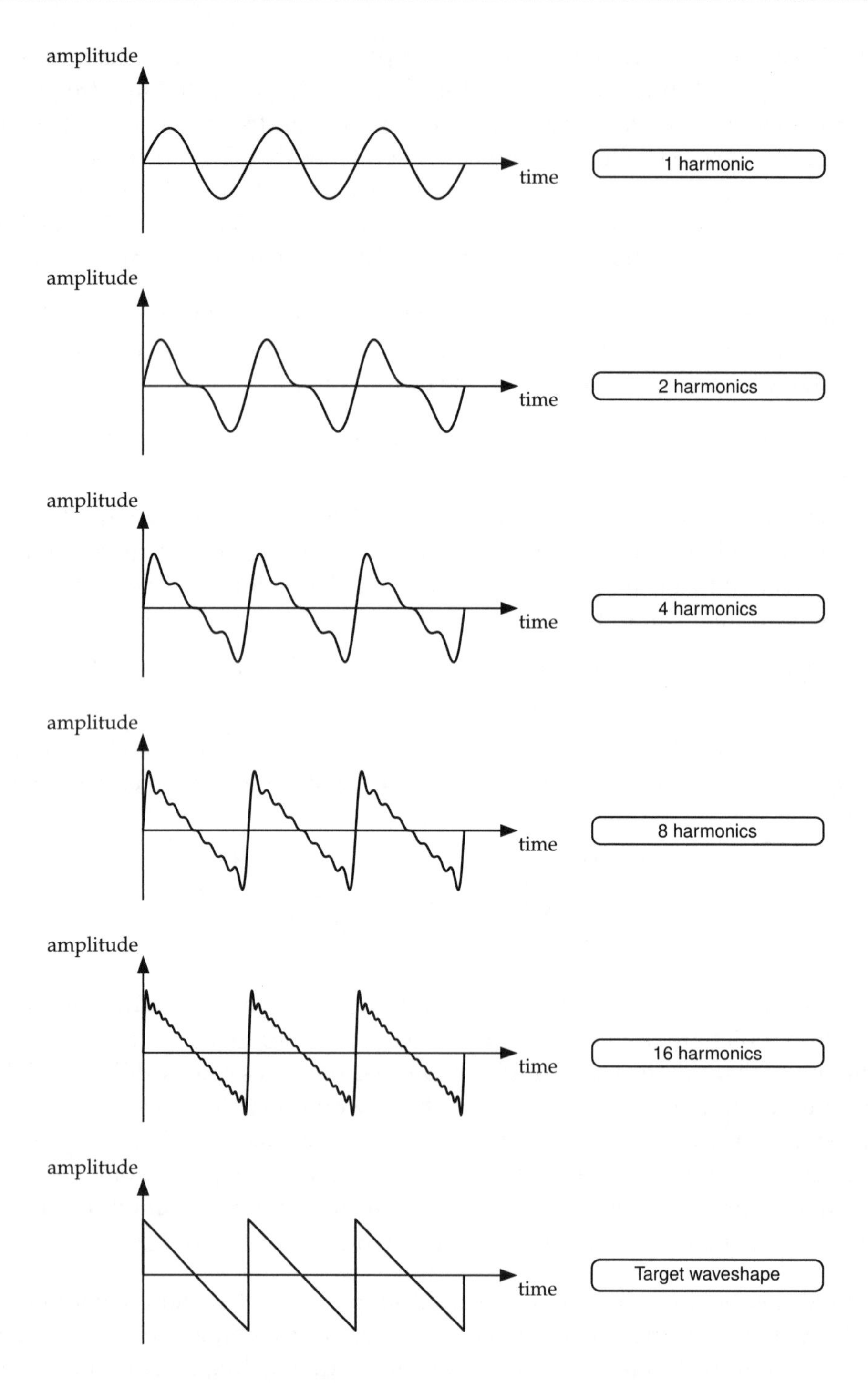

Figure 16.5 Sawtooth wave construction from harmonics

Additive synthesis can be programmed to include tests to prevent the generation of those frequencies, such as setting an oscillator output amplitude to zero when the fundamental frequency is too high. Additive techniques also have the benefit of being able to change parameters over time for individual partials, as described in later examples.

Another approach is to configure the additive synthesizer using the theoretical behaviour of acoustic instruments, or published data gathered by researchers who have analysed real instrument examples. Such sources describe the principal modes of vibration, which are the frequencies that are supported by a resonating object, such as a metal bar, string, column of air, or wooden plate. When expressed as frequency multiples, these values can be used as factors m_1 to m_N in figure 16.3 (p.486). Information on the relative amplitude balance of different partials and their behaviour over time is also required.

16.2.3 Configuration from Sound Analysis

The analysis of existing sounds is a good way of finding suitable parameters with which to configure an additive synthesizer. This technique has the potential to copy key characteristics, and then allow variations to create different pitches, related tonal characters, or results that are a hybrid between two or more sources. The information about individual partials might be derived automatically using frequency domain partial tracking techniques (described in §12.3, p.382) or manual methods of finding and applying the information.

Figure 16.6 illustrates the basic process of resynthesizing a sound based on frequency domain feature analysis. This process is particularly suited to additive synthesis as there is a direct mapping from frequency domain features to the parameters needed to configure the form in figure 16.3 (p.486). However, many other forms of synthesis can also use this method with a suitable mapping from frequency domain features to the synthesis parameters needed to recreate them.

The process of manual configuration starts with choosing a suitable existing sound to be a template. A sound where a very large number of partials contribute strongly to the tonal character is difficult to model with individual sinusoids using a manual configuration technique, and so would probably be avoided. The second stage is suitable use of frequency domain analysis methods, as described in Chapter 4. Average spectrum plots give useful information about frequencies and amplitudes of the partials, and spectrogram and three-dimensional spectrum plots give an indication of the lengths of time and shapes of the amplitude and frequency variations. A typical method is as follows:

- The first step is to determine the frequencies of the partials with greatest amplitude. These can then be normalised by dividing by the fundamental frequency (assuming that the sound has a pitch) or by the frequency of the first partial, to calculate a suitable set of multiplying factors m_1 to m_N.

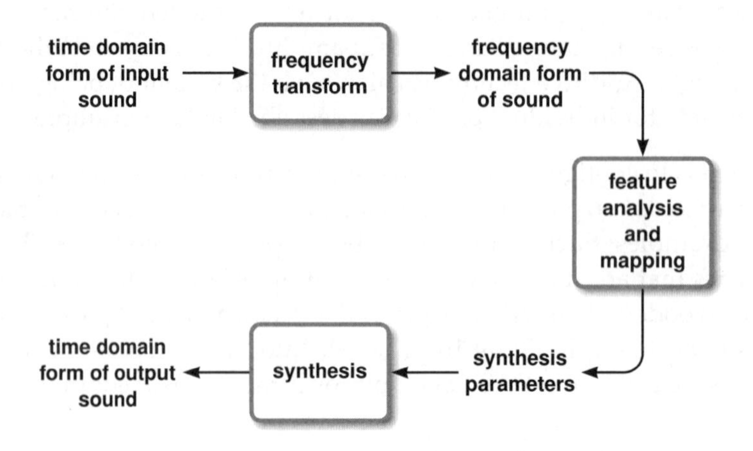

Figure 16.6 Resynthesis process

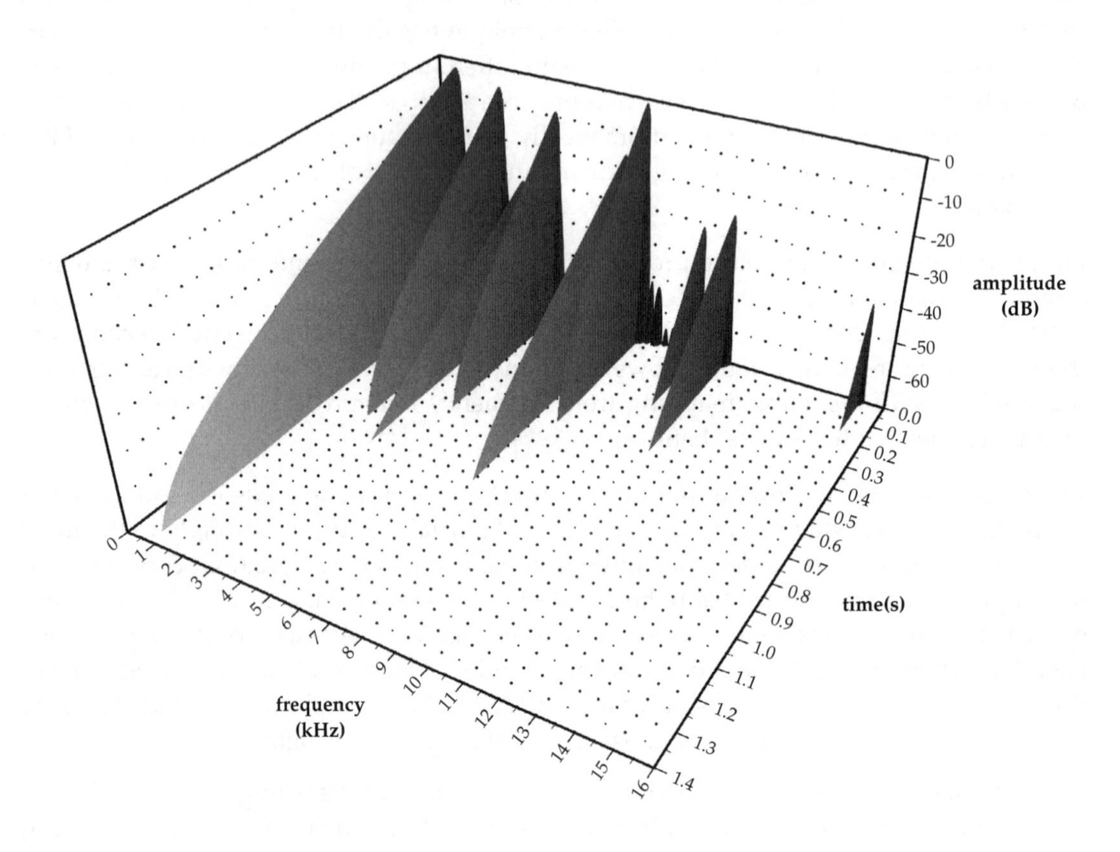

Figure 16.7 Synthesized glockenspiel 3D spectrum plot

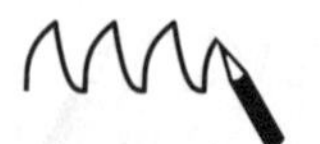

- Average spectrum plots can be used to find a reasonable balance for gain factors a_1 to a_N.
- The next step is to establish the length and general shape of the amplitude envelopes for the different partials (and frequency envelopes if they are varying). The type of sound source being considered will indicate something about the shapes involved. For example, a percussive sound is likely to tend towards exponential decay in amplitude, which will appear somewhat linear on a decibel scale.
- Attention needs to be paid to the onset portion where there is often particular envelope shaping and additional partials that are important to the human auditory system as an indicator of the type of excitation.

Having initially configured the additive synthesizer with parameters based on analysis it is likely that further adjustments will be required. It is necessary to determine how many of the original partials are needed to achieve a convincing tonality. Sometimes low amplitude partials are important to achieving the correct onset character. Assuming that the same fundamental frequency is being used, it is possible to compare the tonal characters and frequency domain analyses of the synthesized result and the original sound to find discrepancies.

Figure 16.7 illustrates a glockenspiel sound synthesized with ten partials. The pitch of the original sound was G5 (a fundamental frequency of 783.99Hz) and the main parameters are as follows:

Frequency multipliers m_i	1.0	3.083	3.929	4.19	5.677	8.89	9.729	12.422	13.65	19.432
Amplitude gains $a_{i\,(\mathrm{dB})}$	−2.7	−4.9	−38.1	−30.8	−7.9	−16.1	0	−29.7	−25.1	−38.1
Envelope lengths t_i (s)	1.4	0.75	0.7	1.1	0.6	0.9	0.5	0.4	0.6	0.25

The amplitude envelopes have a rapid attack of about 5ms and a somewhat exponential decay. The decibel amplitude gains in the table above would have to be translated into linear units (using equation 5.3, p.113) to be used in figure 16.3 (p.486). Frequency envelopes are not used. The tonality is convincing for at least an octave above the original analysis pitch. This technique can also be used with harmonic sounds, as well as those with more complex amplitude or frequency envelopes.

The limitation for this type of sinusoidal additive synthesis is generally the quality of the analysis tools available, and the time taken to configure all the significant partials individually as their number increases. One option is to combine the sinusoidal additive approach with another technique, such as summing with amplitude-enveloped filtered bands of noise (Chapter 18). For example, the additive method could be used to produce

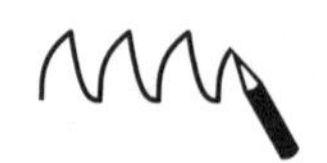

consistent long-term vibrational modes, and the noise source to provide a wide spectrum of dense partials in the onset. Once the characteristics of a source sound have been appropriately duplicated in the additive synthesizer, it is possible to create related tonal characters by changing parameters, such as emphasising certain harmonics or adding additional inharmonics.

16.2.4 Abstract Configuration

It is possible to configure an additive synthesizer using understanding of the important features of sounds, in order to create a specific effect. This requires an appreciation of how patterns of partials contribute to the overall sound character (such as harmonics, inharmonics, spectral envelope, and amplitude variations). The particular strength of additive synthesis is the ability to create very specific relationships between partials and individual amplitude and frequency envelopes, but manual configuration generally means that a modest number of partials will be used. Other synthesis techniques might be more appropriate if the sound does not need that type of construction.

Figure 16.8 shows the result of synthesising three partials, each of which have individual frequency and amplitude envelopes. The result is unlike the examples seen previously, as each partial has a different frequency trajectory. It might be used as a gentle sound effect in a science fiction film. The main parameters are as follows:

Frequency multipliers m_i	1.0	1.5	2.0
Amplitude gains $a_{i\,(\text{dB})}$	0	0	0
Envelope lengths t_i (s)	2.0	1.75	1.5

The key determinants of the sound character are the frequency and amplitude envelopes, which are apparent in the spectrogram plot. The partials start at 440Hz, 660Hz, and 880Hz, rise to twice their values, and then fall back to the original positions. The additive synthesizer allows complete independence of the partials, which allows a constantly changing relationship in terms of frequency and amplitude.

Figure 16.9 shows an additive synthesis example where 30 harmonic partials each have their own amplitude envelope. The balance of shapes and amplitudes is used to achieve a tonal character that is constantly changing over the length of the sound event; different harmonics have prominence at different times so that the tonality is never static.

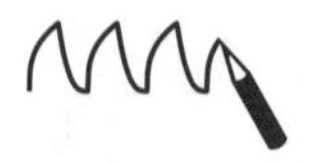

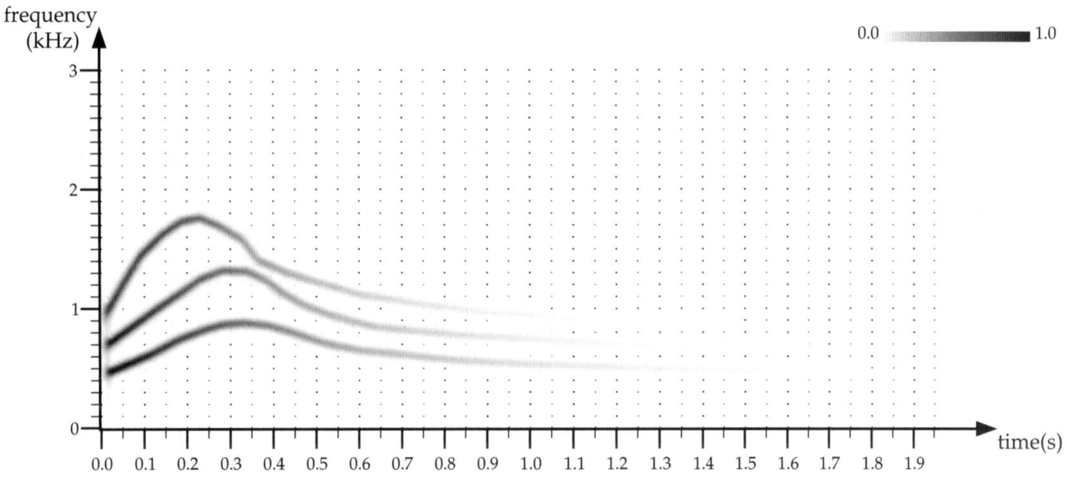

Figure 16.8 Additive synthesis with varying frequencies and amplitudes (spectrogram plot)

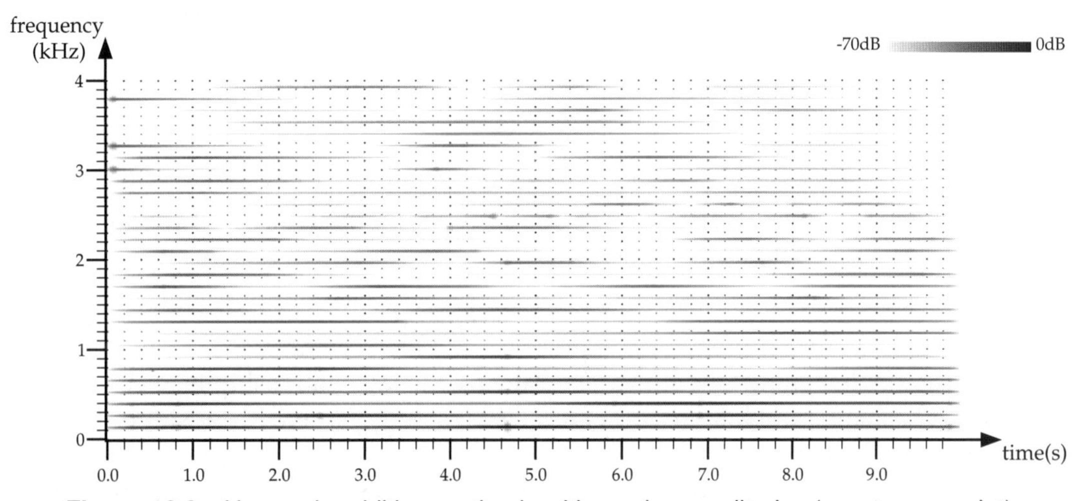

Figure 16.9 Harmonic additive synthesis with varying amplitudes (spectrogram plot)

16.3 Synthesis with Mapped Control over Multiple Partials

A significant advantage of the additive synthesizer is the ability to specify the behaviour of individual partials with great precision. This becomes a more difficult configuration problem as the number of synthesized partials increases. One option is to create control arrangements that allow many partials to be configured simultaneously with modest numbers of parameters. This can reduce the amount of manual configuration required, but naturally reduces flexibility compared to manually specifying the parameter values for each partial.

In order to optimise a control scheme for multiple partials, it is most practical to target a particular sound character, such as an inharmonic percussive sound, or a harmonic sound with continuous excitation, or a sound that evolves over a long period of time. Starting with the additive synthesizer in figure 16.3 (p.486), the idea is to map from master control values to the individual partial parameters using a mathematical formula; that is, to achieve a particular frequency, amplitude, or time relationship between the partials from a small number of controls.

The parallel paths in figure 16.3 are likely to be implemented as an array of objects in a computer program, inside which the array index can be found by a suitable function call. The code or patch will be the same for all parallel instances, but will change behaviour depending on the index. In the following description, the index will be called i and will have values between 1 and N, where N is the number of partials. The most simple example of configuration based on index is achieving a harmonic frequency relationship, where the frequency multipliers are determined by this equation:

$$m_i = i \tag{16.1}$$

The idea is that the values of m_1 to m_N are calculated automatically as 1, 2, 3 ... N. This is very useful if there are, say, 100 partials to be configured. Extending this example, it is possible to add a frequency stretch effect:

$$m_i = i + (i-1)\,k_{\text{fstretch}} \tag{16.2}$$

This allows a single parameter value to vary the frequency relationship between partials for different harmonic and inharmonic effects. When k_{fstretch} is zero, the result is the same as equation 16.1. Positive integer values of k_{fstretch} produce harmonic relationships. Values of k_{fstretch} greater than zero stretch the partials out, whereas values less than zero and more than -1 squash the partials together.

Some example results are given in the following table:

$k_{fstretch}$	m_1	m_2	m_3	m_4	m_5	m_6	m_7	m_8	m_9	m_{10}
−0.9	1	1.1	1.2	1.3	1.4	1.5	1.6	1.7	1.8	1.9
0	1	2	3	4	5	6	7	8	9	10
0.67	1	2.67	4.34	6.01	7.68	9.35	11.02	12.69	14.36	16.03
1	1	3	5	7	9	11	13	15	17	19
2.374	1	4.374	7.748	11.122	14.496	17.87	21.244	24.618	27.992	31.366

As well as controlling frequency relationships, it is also desirable to be able to specify a spectral envelope with a small number of parameters. For example, the following equation can be used to calculate amplitude gains that follow a trend with the increasing index value:

$$a_{i\,(\mathrm{dB})} = (i-1)\,k_{\mathrm{arolloff}} \tag{16.3}$$

Parameter $k_{arolloff}$ controls the change in amplitude gain (in decibels) as index i increases. For example, if $k_{arolloff}$ is −2dB, then the amplitude gains are as follows (in decibels and converted to linear gains):

i	1	2	3	4	5	6	7	8	9	10
$a_{i\,(dB)}$	0	−2	−4	−6	−8	−10	−12	−14	−16	−18
a_i	1.000	0.794	0.631	0.501	0.398	0.316	0.251	0.200	0.158	0.126

Equation 16.3 gives a simple single-parameter control over the slope of the spectral envelope. This can be extended to include a periodic variation in amplitude to create a more sophisticated variation with index, such as the following:

$$a_{i\,(\mathrm{dB})} = (i-1)\,k_{\mathrm{arolloff}} + 0.5\,k_{\mathrm{avar}}\left[\cos\left(\frac{2\pi(i-1)}{k_{\mathrm{avarlen}}}\right) - 1\right] \tag{16.4}$$

This equation adds two parameters, which are the size of variation in decibels called k_{avar} and the number of index positions over which one cycle of cosine variation occurs called $k_{avarlen}$. The cosine function takes an argument in radians. Figure 16.10 illustrates the effect of equation 16.4 with $k_{arolloff} = -1$, $k_{avar} = 8$, and $k_{avarlen} = 10$.

Equation 16.4 enables a fair amount of tonal variation from only three parameters. It is possible to devise more complex mathematical schemes for controlling the values of both a_i and m_i depending upon the desired control style. It might also be desirable to apply envelope control to the equation parameters to achieve variation over time in the relationships between partials.

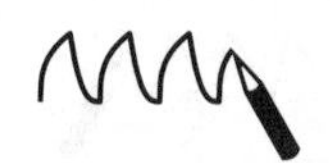

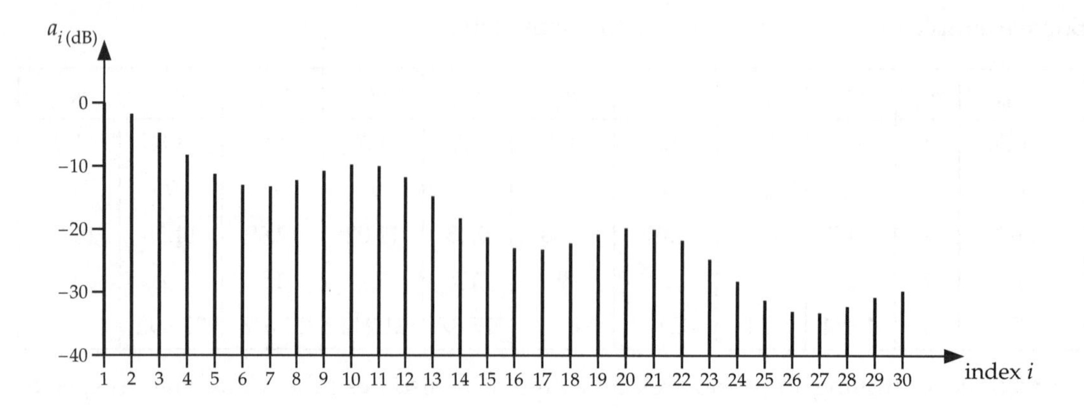

Figure 16.10 Amplitude gain variation based on equation 16.4

It is also desirable to be able to control the behaviour of the envelope generators in a global way. For example, if a percussive sound is being produced, all the partials might have amplitude envelopes with a similar brief attack followed by a somewhat exponential decay. It can be useful for the user to control a limited number of shape and duration parameters, and automatically calculate individual envelopes for each partial based on their index. For example, this equation might be used to calculate amplitude envelope decay times:

$$t_{di} = t_{d1} \, i^{k_{\text{drolloff}}} \tag{16.5}$$

Value t_{d1} is the decay time for the first partial. Subsequent partials have shorter decay times depending on the value of k_{drolloff}, which takes values less than or equal to zero. For example, if t_{d1} is 2 seconds:

k_{drolloff}	t_{d1}	t_{d2}	t_{d3}	t_{d4}	t_{d5}	t_{d6}	t_{d7}	t_{d8}	t_{d9}	t_{d10}
0	2.000	2.000	2.000	2.000	2.000	2.000	2.000	2.000	2.000	2.000
−0.1	2.000	1.866	1.792	1.741	1.703	1.672	1.646	1.625	1.605	1.589
−0.8	2.000	1.149	0.830	0.660	0.552	0.477	0.422	0.379	0.345	0.317

An alternative to using equations to specify the relationship between partial index and parameter values is to use graphical control. Figure 16.11 illustrates a mapping that could be created with a graphical editor. Values for individual partials are automatically read from the plot. Most parameters can be specified in this manner, such as amplitude gains, frequency deviation from harmonic multiples, decay times, and so on. As an alternative to using individual envelope generators in figure 16.3 (p.486), it is also possible to specify

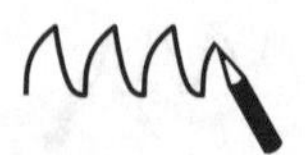

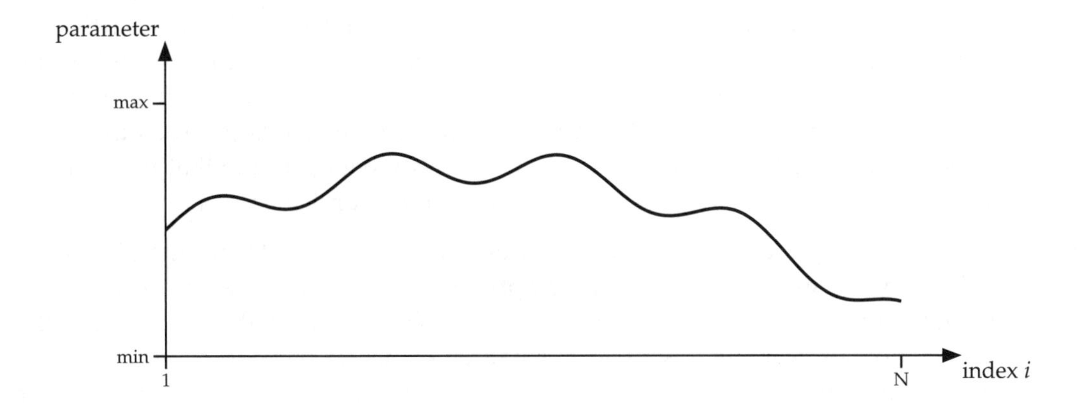

Figure 16.11 Index to parameter mapping

different parameter profiles for the start and end of the sound graphically and cross-fade the value for each partial over the length of the sound. Cross-fading in synthesis is described in more detail in §19.4 (p.553).

One other method of simplifying control over multiple partials is to create group controls. Partials might be grouped into a number of sets, such as odds/evens, harmonics/inharmonics, low/medium/high frequency partials, main/additional tone, and so on. Each set could then have a single numerical parameter or envelope applied to all partials in the set, or a value to cross-fade between the sets. For example, a single amplitude envelope generator might control the gain for all the odd harmonics. It might be desirable, however, to still control the balance within the group by use of different static gain values (a_i).

16.4 Developing Processes and Learning More

Sinusoidal additive synthesis uses a straightforward structure with a close relationship to the results of frequency domain analysis techniques. The synthesizer in figure 16.3 (p.486) uses standard blocks that are found in audio programming libraries and environments. The potential is great for synthesizing a huge range of sounds, either similar or dissimilar to acoustic sources. However, the practical limitations require careful consideration:

- The number of simultaneous partials that is possible is tied closely to the available computational power. Synthesising 10000 individual partials, using a sinusoidal oscillator and two envelope generators for each parallel path, requires vastly more computation than the creation of a similar number of partials when starting with a noise generator (as described in Chapter 18) and using subtractive synthesis techniques (Chapter 17).

- Few synthesis techniques have such a direct relationship to individual partials as additive synthesis, allowing enormously precise manipulation of the sound in the frequency domain. However, strategies are required to achieve effective multiple partial parameter mapping as the number of partials increases (such as those described in §16.3, p.496). There is a danger of control being so fine that it is hard to keep track of how small changes relate to the overall sound character.

The control and configuration strategy is important for all synthesis techniques, but sinusoidal additive synthesis requires particular emphasis in those areas. There is the potential for a very large number of low-level parameters. Controlling the partials must relate to the key frequency domain features described in Chapter 4, such as harmonics, inharmonics, bands of noisy partials, the spectral envelope and changing character over time. Other synthesis techniques focus more on those higher level aspects at the expense of the direct control of individual partials.

The concept of summing oscillations to achieve a more complex result is common to most synthesis techniques. This idea is explored in more detail in Chapter 19, which considers blending methods. Further discussion of additive synthesis and related ideas can be found in these books:

Cook, Perry R. 2002. *Real Sound Synthesis for Interactive Applications.* Natick, MA: A K Peters.

Russ, Martin. 2013. *Sound Synthesis and Sampling (Third Edition).* Burlington, MA: Focal Press.

The following source provides some more advanced material that relates to this chapter, which can be used for further study:

Kleczkowski, Piotr. 1989. "Group Additive Synthesis." *Computer Music Journal* 13:1:12–20.

17

Subtractive Synthesis

17.1 Basic Concepts

There is often a simple relationship between filter parameters and aural effect, which makes filtering a key technique in both modification and synthesis. Basic filters such as lowpass, highpass, and bandpass will significantly attenuate partials outside their passbands, resulting in a reshaped spectral envelope (as described in Chapter 6). When filtering is the principal tonal modification technique in a synthesizer, it is called *subtractive synthesis*.

Figure 17.1 shows an example of how filtering a source sound can affect appearance in the time and frequency domains. Subtractive synthesis combines the generation of a sound with many partials, and filtering the results to change its tonality. Generation of signals with many partials can be moderately simple (as described in Chapters 14 and 18). The filtering in subtractive synthesis is often used to achieve amplitude changes to many partials at once, which can be efficient and can produce very characteristic tonal qualities.

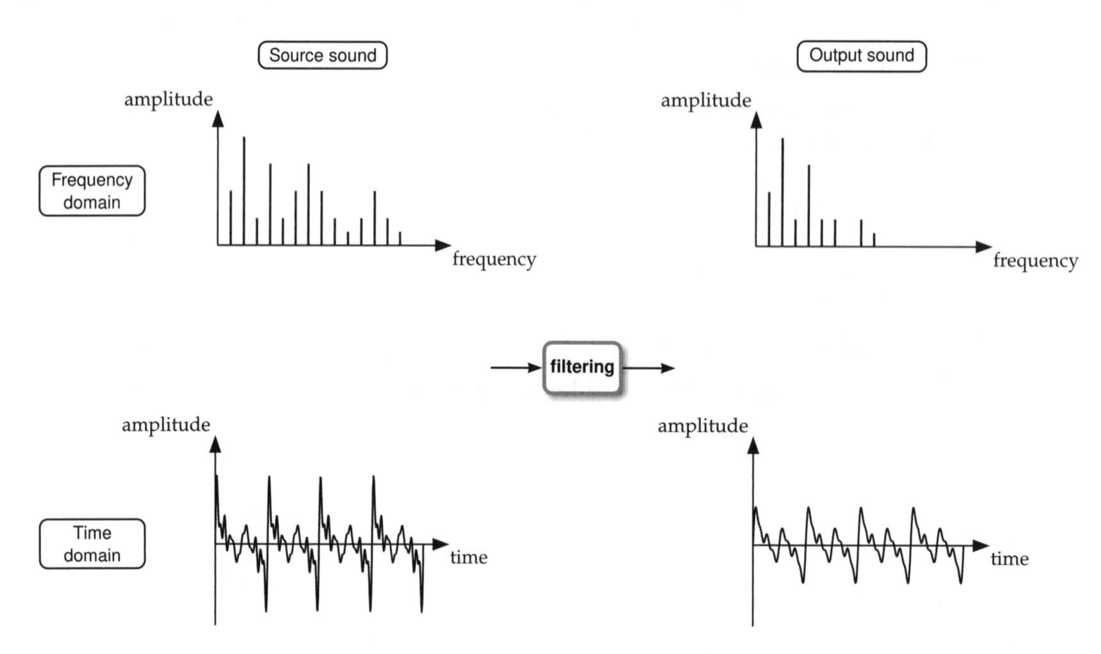

Figure 17.1 Filtering in time and frequency domains

Subtractive synthesis is a *source-filter form* where both the nature of the source signal and the filtering stage contribute to the resulting sound character. For example, with vocal synthesis (described in §17.3, p.509) the difference between pitched/normal speech and whispering/breathy speech can be achieved by changing a harmonic source for one dominated by noise, while keeping the filtering the same. It is also possible to change the filtering stage while keeping the source the same, such as changing the modal frequencies

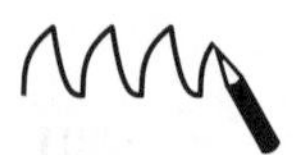

in a synthesizer with highly resonant filters (described in §17.4, p.517). The source-filter separation has some similarities to typical acoustic situations where there is a source of energy that is applied to a resonant body, such as those described in Chapter 21.

The choice of whether to take an additive or a subtractive approach to synthesis depends on the target sound and amount of processing effort required. Sinusoidal additive synthesis provides precision of control over individual partials (Chapter 16), but that can be less easy to manage if the result will be composed of many partials. Subtractive synthesis can take a rich source sound and modify many partials at once with filtering, but if the target is very dissimilar from the source then complex filtering will be required. It might be appropriate to blend different waveforms (as described in Chapter 19) to achieve a suitable source sound to make the subtractive technique more effective.

17.2 Common Subtractive Methods

This section describes some common methods that are used to create interest and evolving character over time through the use of varying filter parameters. These types of subtractive synthesis can be achieved with moderate Q values. Because a filter can affect many source partials at once it can be used to sculpt the spectral envelope. Quite dramatic tonal changes can be achieved with a relatively small number of elements. Suitably strong filtering with variation in parameters can lead to "bubbling" characters and similar sounds. However, more subtlety is required if the goal is to create the spectral envelopes that are associated with acoustic sounds.

17.2.1 Source Selection

There are a number of key features that relate to the selection of a suitable source sound for subtractive synthesis:

- The source must contain the partials that are required in the filtered output. Different waveforms have different frequency partials and different emphasis in the frequency spectrum. This in turn will affect the parameters for the filters that follow, as they must work with the spectral form of the source. For example, if the desired output is to have odd and even harmonics, then a sawtooth wave is a more appropriate source than a square wave (§4.2.2, p.79). However, starting with an over-dense spectrum (many more partials than eventually required) might require quite complex filtering to attenuate many partials.
- Because the filtering will significantly attenuate partials, the source will have more high amplitude partials over a wider frequency range than will be required eventually. The source will therefore often be more harsh, more dense, or more bright than the final output.

- The tonality of the source will not necessarily be disguised by the filtering. This means that some care is required in selection. Standard waveforms such as sawtooth, triangle, and square waves not only have particular patterns in terms of the frequencies of partials, but also particular amplitude roll-offs with frequency. Unless filtering is sophisticated, distinctive aspects of the character of the source will always be audible.

A typical analogue hardware approach to subtractive synthesis is to use a source waveform based on line segments (such as sawtooth, triangle, pulse, and square shapes) that include partials over a wide frequency range. Such waveforms can be generated with simple electronic circuits, so choosing those types of waveforms in a digital system will help to create sound characters similar to early synthesizers. Therefore, to move away from those types of tonalities requires the use of different or more sophisticated sources, such as wavetables which use single cycles extracted from sampled sounds, or a blend of waveforms.

Subtractive synthesis often uses parameters that vary over time to provide interest and tonal development. The emphasis in subtractive methods is on the filter variations, but it is also valid to consider how the source might vary over time. A simple way of achieving this is to cross-fade between two oscillators over the length of the sound event, as described in §19.4 (p.553). Subtractive methods can also be applied to the results of other forms of synthesis.

17.2.2 Filtering Methods

Figure 17.2 illustrates an example single filter subtractive synthesizer. A line segment oscillation waveform is used, with a lowpass filter controlled by an envelope generator to modify the tonal character over time. There are a number of aspects that affect the result:

- The source waveform.
- The filter type (such as a bandpass instead of a lowpass filter).
- The shape of the filter envelope.
- The range of the filter envelope.
- The amplitude envelope.

The form in the figure can be used to achieve a subtle tonal variation over time, such as might be associated with an acoustic source. A common approach, however, is to create more synthetic sounds by aggressive use of filtering, particularly compared to the sort of filter-based modification that is often found in mixing consoles.

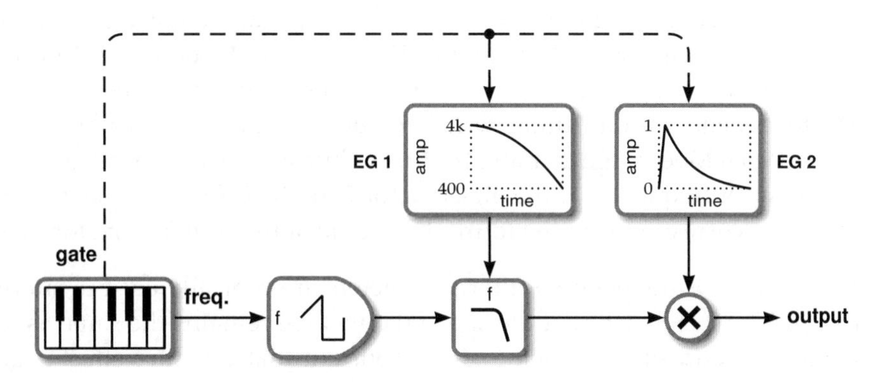

Figure 17.2 Single filter subtractive synthesizer

Some key elements to this are as follows:

- Different filters of the same general type (say, lowpass) can have different low-level designs and therefore different time and frequency responses (as described in §6.4, p.164). The configuration in terms of resonance (*Q*) settings can also be important. The amount of roll-off can be different between different designs. The roll-off can be increased by having more than one filter of the same type in series configured with the same parameters (§6.3.1, p.155). This can lead to a stronger tonal change.
- The range of the filter envelope determines how much movement occurs. A large frequency variation will normally lead to a large tonal variation.
- The rate of variation in the filter envelope shape is important. A long term drift in value is not perceived in the same way as a rapid rise or fall over a wide frequency range. Rather than the envelope shape shown in figure 17.2, the shape might be something like the examples shown in figure 17.3 to achieve a more dramatic effect.

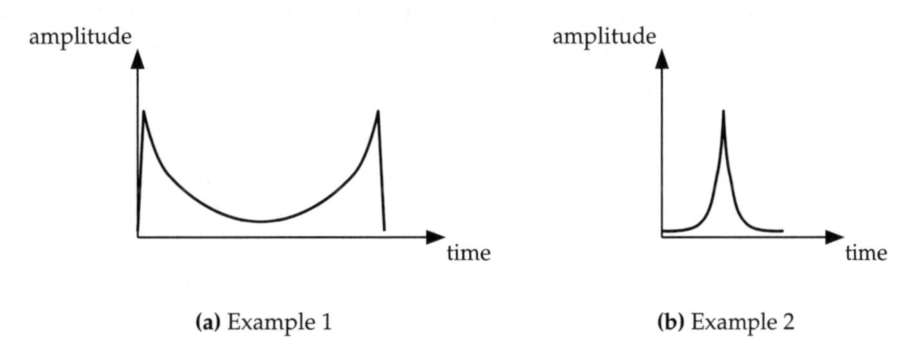

(a) Example 1 **(b)** Example 2

Figure 17.3 Filter cutoff/centre frequency envelopes

Whether filter parameters are linked to the oscillator fundamental frequency (or not) affects the character of the result. While figure 17.2 has an independent cutoff frequency envelope, figure 17.4 illustrates how the offset and depth of cutoff frequency variation can be made to depend on the fundamental frequency (sometimes called *tracking* the frequency). The envelope range is initially 0 to 1, but is scaled and offset by suitable multiples of the input frequency. If the offset factor is set to 4, for example, then 0 on the envelope generator corresponds to the fourth harmonic of the source waveform.

Fundamental frequency-independent filter parameters are typically used in simple vocal synthesis (see §17.3, p.509) such that the spectral envelope remains the same as the pitch changes. For speech and singing sounds it is important that the filter effect is generally unchanging for a particular phoneme (a part of speech such as "ah"). The effect is different if there is tracking of fundamental frequency, as the same filtering will be applied to the same part of the source spectrum (such as particular harmonics) as the frequency changes. This achieves a different type of tonal consistency. An appropriate method is chosen to suit the circumstances.

Figure 17.5 illustrates how the filter frequency variation can depend on a combination of an overall envelope with an oscillation superimposed upon it. This develops from the methods shown in figure 9.15 (p.277) and figure 13.15 (p.413). The rate for oscillator 2 might be very low to provide a slowly evolving character over a long period of time, or faster to provide "wobbling" effects. The gate signal might be used to reset the phase of the modulating oscillator to zero at the start of the sound, such that the same part of the cycle occurs in the same place for each sound event.

Envelope generator 1 controls the depth of oscillation. Envelope generator 2 provides the main filter envelope that offsets the oscillation signal to a suitable frequency, as well as providing its own variation. The advantage of using an oscillator is that, if a sound event is long, the sound can have a constantly changing character without it being necessary to specify a main envelope shape with a large set of variation cycles within it. Envelope generator 2 is useful for producing such effects as a rapid change only at the start of the sound event, rather than it repeating with every oscillator cycle.

The sound in the spectrogram plot in figure 17.6 was created with the form in figure 17.5. A high roll-off resonant lowpass filter was used. The result is a synthetic sound unlike an acoustic instrument, with a constantly changing tonality including a repetitive element. Figure 17.5 could be extended by using the ideas in figure 17.4 to link the range of frequency variation to the fundamental frequency. The oscillator rate might also be determined by an envelope, if required.

The previous examples have considered a single filtering element, but it is possible to use multiple elements to achieve a more complex result. One technique is to use a parallel bandpass filter arrangement such as that shown in figure 6.20 (p.157) to replace the single

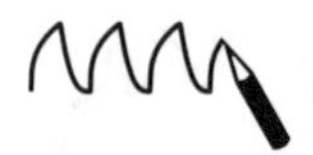

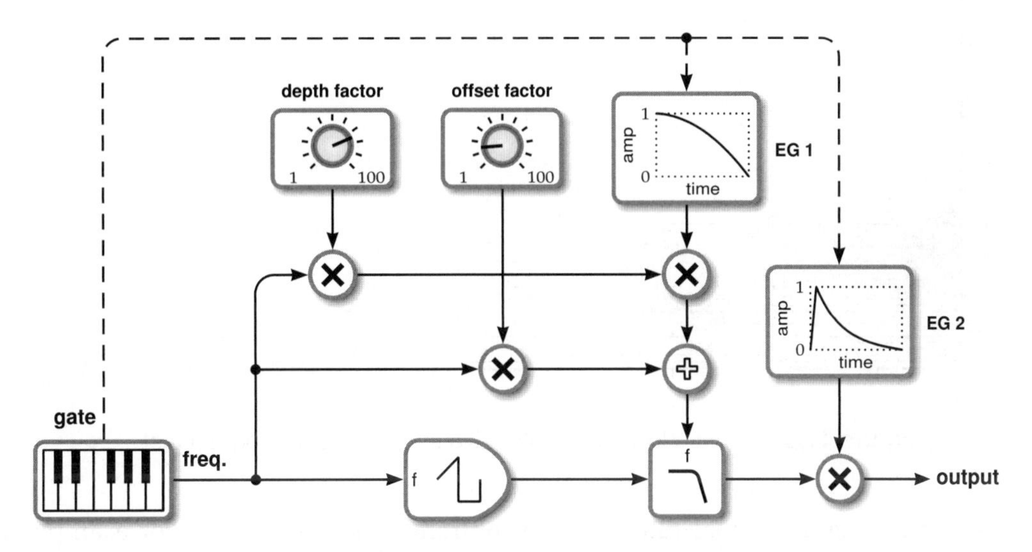

Figure 17.4 Single filter subtractive synthesizer with tracking of keyboard frequency

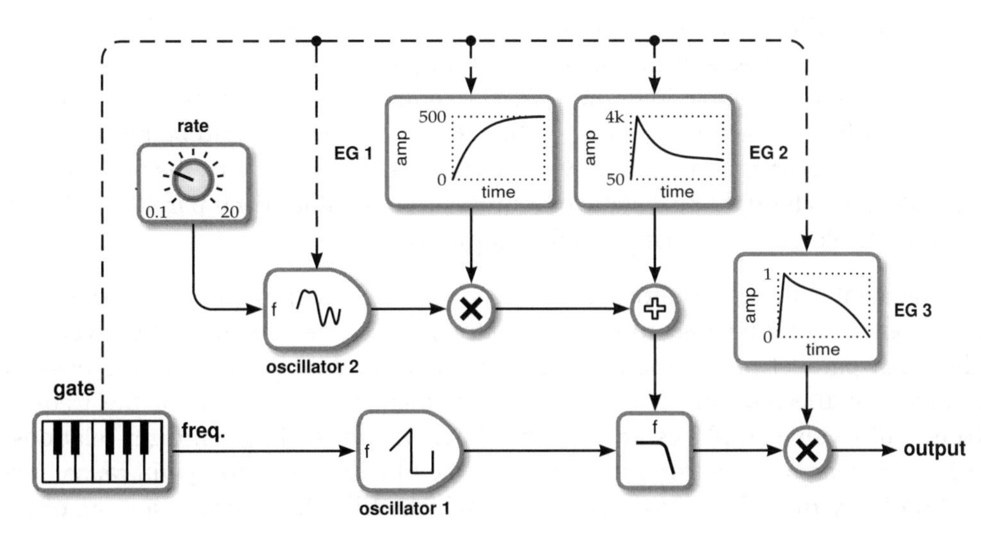

Figure 17.5 Single filter subtractive synthesizer with oscillator modulation

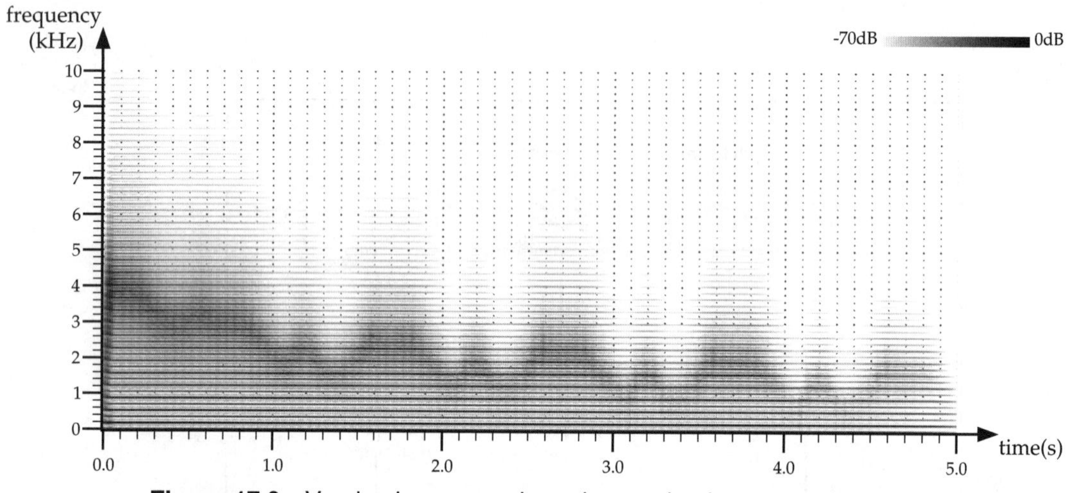

Figure 17.6 Varying lowpass subtractive synthesis spectrogram plot

lowpass filter. The individual filters can be controlled independently. For example, a spectral envelope for shaping an acoustic sound might be created by using either static parameter values, or those appropriately mapped from the input frequency (described further in Chapter 24). Alternatively, individual envelopes might be applied to individual filter parameters to create patterns of emphasis that evolve over time. Centre frequency, Q, and amplitude gain parameters could all be varied.

As the number of filters and envelopes increases, there are greater possibilities for sophistication, but also an increase in parameters to configure. One option is to link parameters for N filters together as shown in figure 17.7. The centre frequencies are determined by the f_c input multiplied by factors m_1 to m_N. The filter frequency f_c could be produced from an envelope generator as shown in previous examples. For simplicity, the filters have the same Q value, which might be a static or a time-varying value. Each parallel path has its own amplitude weighting a_1 to a_N into the output mix.

The arrangement in the figure allows different shapes of frequency emphasis to be created. If the frequency multipliers m_1 to m_N are relatively close and the amplitude weightings vary between parallel paths, then the cluster can form a single undulating passband. Alternatively, if the multipliers are spread out, then different areas of the frequency spectrum will receive emphasis at the same time, such as a simple integer relationship (m_1 = 1, m_2 = 2, m_3 = 3, and so on). Increasing the filter roll-off and Q will cause greater attenuation away from the centre frequencies, which will often produce a more obvious effect.

The complexity of the filtering can be adjusted to suit the desired result. For example, a mix of lowpass and bandpass filters might be used to achieve different types of spectral

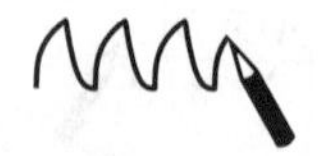

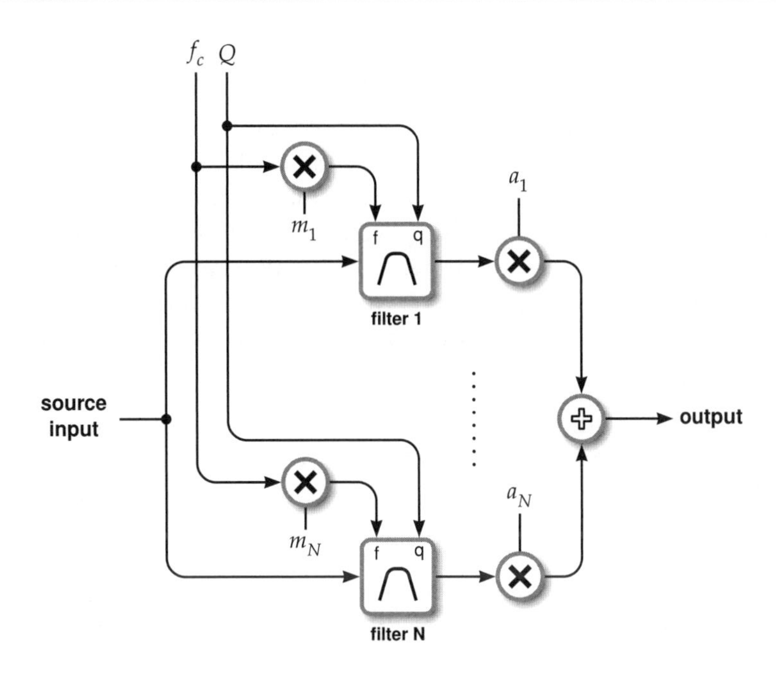

Figure 17.7 Parallel filtering with linked parameters

emphasis. A varying filter section might be used in series with a fixed parameter filter arrangement that applies an overall tonal characteristic. A broad static region of emphasis might be combined with narrow regions of varying frequency, and so on.

17.3 Vocal Synthesis

17.3.1 Introduction

The human voice can be modelled with subtractive synthesis techniques. This allows great flexibility of control, particularly compared to sample-based voice generation methods (described in §15.2.2, p.469), but it is difficult to achieve a naturalistic tonality. There are some key characteristics that need to be incorporated:

- There are two principal types of sound in the vocal tract. *Unvoiced* sound relates to noise effects caused by air turbulence as air passes through constrictions in the vocal tract, which results in sounds such as "ss" and "ff". *Voiced* sound relates to a pitched oscillation produced by vibration of the vocal folds, which results in sounds such as "oo" and "ee". Unvoiced and voiced elements can be combined to produce sounds such as "zz". To synthesize the voice with a subtractive system, an amount of pitched harmonic oscillation is combined with an amount of sound produced with a noise generator (see Chapter 18).

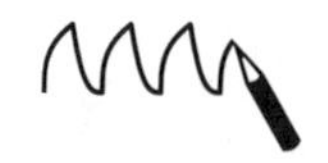

- The human vocal tract acts much like a set of filters, which modify the source sound to achieve particular tonal characters. The resonances of the vocal tract produce *formants* (regions of emphasis in the spectral envelope) whose relative positioning, bandwidth, and amplitude are associated with particular *phonemes* (vocal sounds, parts of speech). Humans recognise a particular part of speech from the spectral envelope largely independently of the pitch of the underlying oscillation. This means that the formants (and so the synthesizer filter configuration) are fairly consistent for a particular phoneme. This is because with a sound such as "ah", muscles hold the resonant cavities in the vocal tract in a fixed position as the rate of vibration of the vocal folds varies.
- To produce a word, multiple phonemes are generated in sequence with suitable transitions in source waveform and vocal tract movement. In a subtractive synthesizer this implies that there must be enveloped movements in parameters to particular preset positions over time.

Figure 17.8 illustrates average spectrum plots of four vowel sounds that are sung at the same pitch by the same person. They have different spectral envelopes, with particular formant peaks that result from the filtering effect of the vocal tract.

17.3.2 Voiced Source Sound Generation

Figure 17.9 illustrates a simplified single cycle of the air flow through the vocal folds when producing voiced sound. The opening in the vocal folds is called the glottis, and so it is called glottal flow. The shape is important to the character of the result, but it also varies with the type of vocal sound being produced. A large number of harmonic partials are produced. The shorter the closing phase relative to the opening phase, and the more abruptly the closing phase reaches the closed phase, the more high frequency emphasis will be produced.

There are a number of ways of achieving this kind of shape, such as the following:

- Using a crude approximation such as a sawtooth wave, or other similar linear segment-based shape. This provides a large number of harmonic partials, which can then be filtered to achieve a result more similar to that associated with the vocal fold vibration. The filtering must be applied carefully to avoid a rather buzzy result.
- Drawing the shape in a suitable graphical wavetable editor and using a wavetable oscillator.
- Using equations to describe the shape. This has the advantage of providing control over the shaping parameters and so an ability to continuously change the shape to achieve the desired source character for different types of vocal sound.

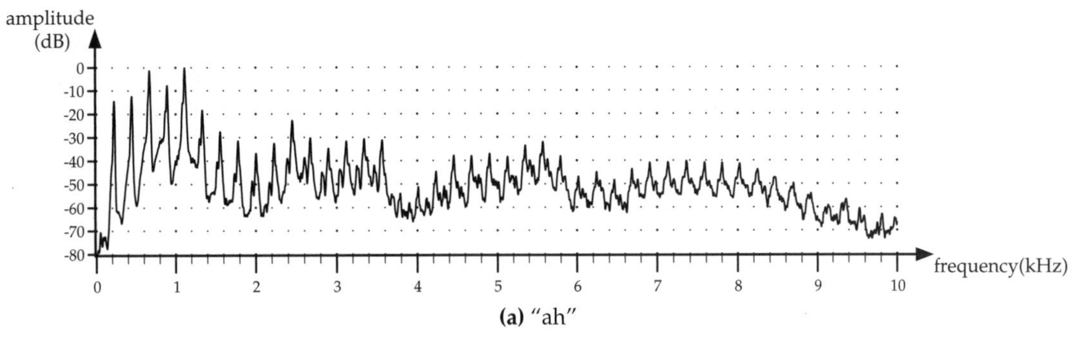

(a) "ah"

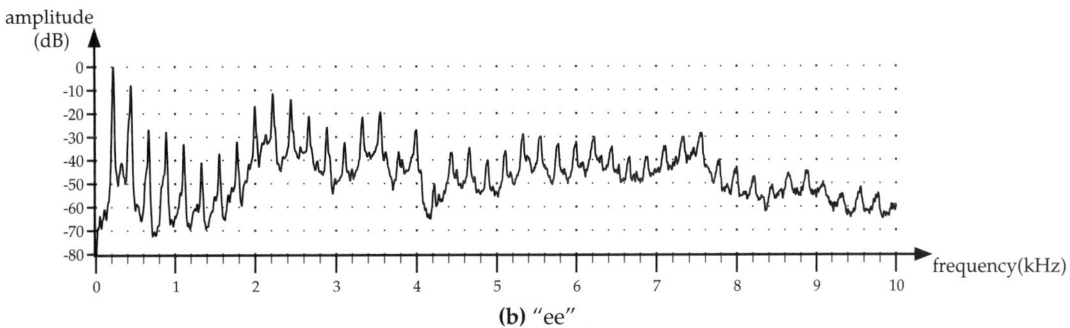

(b) "ee"

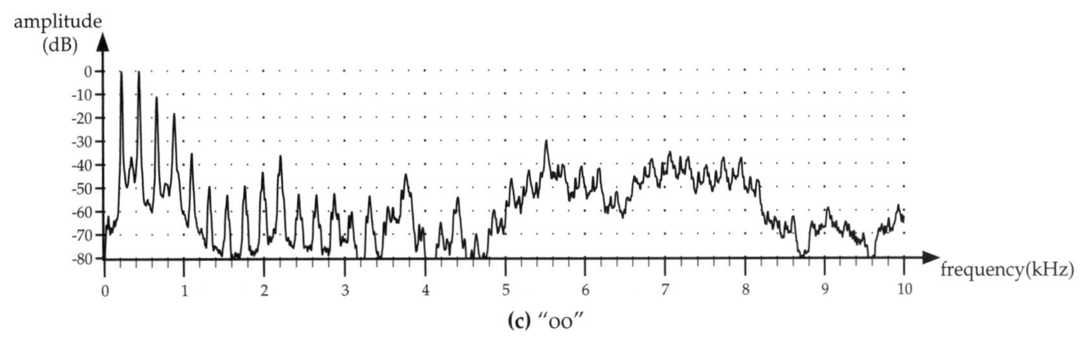

(c) "oo"

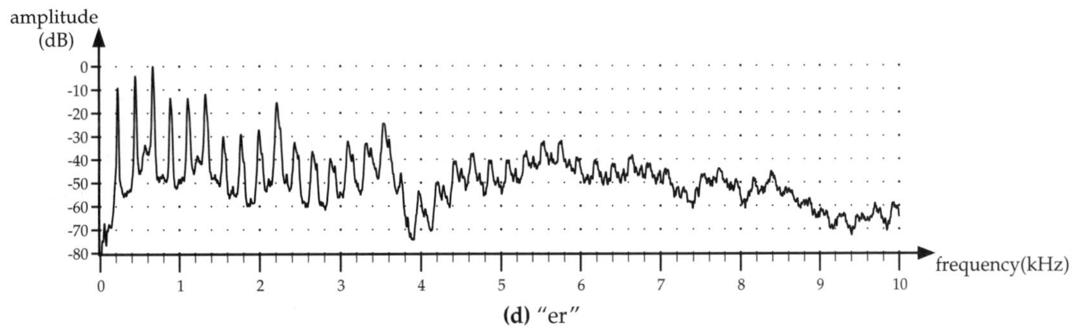

(d) "er"

Figure 17.8 Vocal sound average spectrum plots

The Liljencrants-Fant (LF) model is a set of equations for creating a glottal source oscillation. Rather than recreating the shape in figure 17.9, it creates the derivative (rate-of-change) function shown in figure 17.10. The reason for producing this alternative shape is that it includes the effect of lip radiation. The equations to generate the LF model glottal flow derivative function are as follows:

$$y = \begin{cases} k_0 \, e^{\alpha x} \sin(\omega_g x) & \text{if} \quad 0 \leqslant x < t_e \\ k_1 \left(e^{-(x-t_e)/t_a} - e^{-(1-t_e)/t_a} \right) & \text{if} \quad t_e \leqslant x \leqslant 1 \end{cases}$$

where

$$k_0 = \frac{-1}{e^{\alpha t_e} \sin(\omega_g t_e)} \qquad k_1 = \frac{-1}{1 - e^{-(1-t_e)/t_a}}$$

$$t_e = (1 + r_k)\, t_p \qquad \omega_g = \frac{\pi}{t_p}$$

17.1

The equations achieve the required shape while also allowing it to be varied in a subtle manner to reflect the different waveform shapes produced by the vocal folds at different times. The sine function takes an argument in radians. It is necessary to specify a number of variables in order that the other values can be calculated:

- e is the base of natural logarithms defined as approximately 2.71828183.
- t_p is the proportion of a cycle taken to reach the end of the opening phase. A typical value is 0.5.
- t_e is the point on the derivative function where it sharply changes direction (figure 17.10). This corresponds to the point at the end of the closing phase of the glottal flow where it starts curving towards zero (figure 17.9), which is called the return phase.
- r_k is multiplied by t_p in the calculation of t_e. The smaller the value of r_k, the shorter the closing phase relative to the opening phase. Larger values relate to more fundamental frequency emphasis. A typical value of r_k is 0.3.
- t_a determines the abruptness of the return phase (after the main part of the closing phase). A low value will produce more high frequency emphasis. It has an influence on whether the result is buzzy or dull, or somewhere in between. A typical value is 0.02.

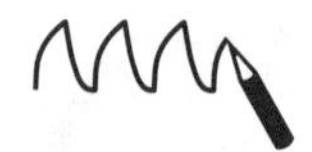

- α affects how the function shape is skewed to the right. It is calculated mathematically such that the integral (area under the curve) of the whole derivative function is zero. This ensures that the glottal flow in figure 17.9 ends at zero. Using $t_p = 0.5$ and $t_a = 0.02$, these are some example values of α as the value of r_k (and thus t_e) is varied:

r_k	t_e	α
0.2	0.60	7.0282
0.3	0.65	4.0211
0.4	0.70	2.3837
0.5	0.75	1.3889

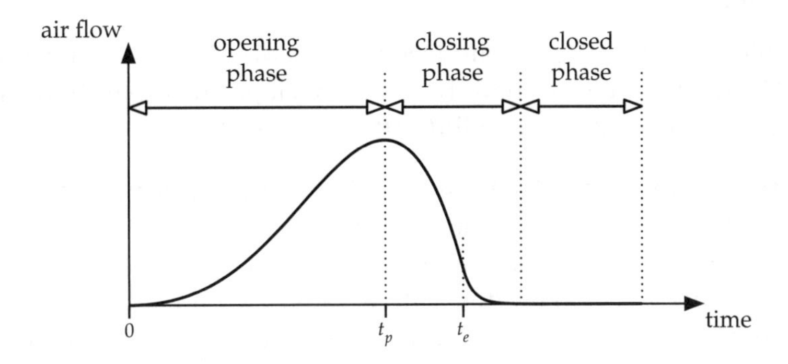

Figure 17.9 Simplified glottal flow

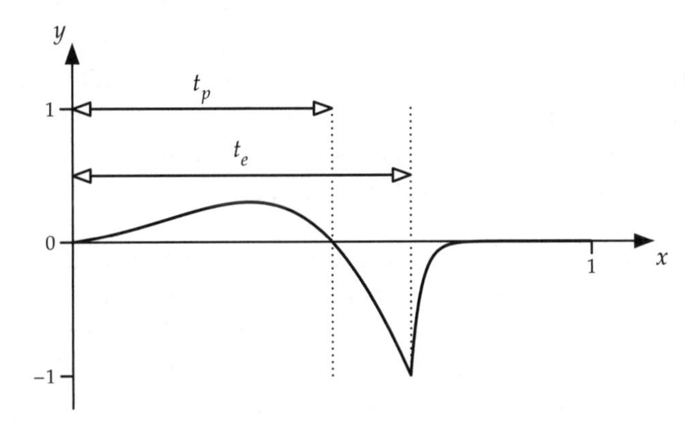

Figure 17.10 Glottal flow derivative function

The LF model is not an exact representation of the vocal fold oscillation, but it is a well known form. In practical terms, it is possible to start with values such as those above, and vary them somewhat while listening to the output from the filter stage, in order to achieve the best sound character for a particular phoneme.

There are a number of ways of enhancing the source character:

- If the vocal sound is for musical purposes, then a fairly constant fundamental frequency is appropriate. In speech synthesis, however, there is often a variation in pitch over the length of a word to produce a more naturalistic result (rather than a monotone).
- Adding a small amount of filtered noise to simulate breath noise (see §18.3.4, p.537) can make the results more convincing. Alternatively, whispering/breathy voice characters can be achieved by having more dominant noise and a reduced harmonic component.
- The application of subtle vibrato (see §13.3, p.418) is suitable for musical applications. The depth of effect might have an envelope such that the vibrato is applied once the sound is established (a little after the onset).

All the description above has been about achieving as realistic a source character as possible. Another approach is to use a radically different type of source, such as playing back an instrument sample or using a non-vocal wavetable oscillator. If the filtering is voice-like (as described below) but the source is not, then it is possible to achieve hybrid type sounds that have some tonal aspects of both. This can be musically interesting.

17.3.3 Formant Filtering

The filtering for a vocal synthesizer needs to recreate the spectral envelope associated with particular phonemes. The technique focuses on the position, bandwidth, and amplitude of the principal formants. These can be created by bandpass filters applied to the source signal. Connecting the filters in series has some similarities to the nature of the human vocal tract. However, a parallel arrangement is easier to configure (due to the independence of the filter paths) and is sufficient for the desired aims.

Figure 17.11 illustrates a suitable vocal filtering arrangement with N parallel paths. Synthesising between three and five formants is necessary to achieve a fair approximation of many phonemes. The lowpass output filter is in series with the parallel paths to provide overall control of bandwidth. Reducing the cutoff frequency (f_{co}) has some similarities to the effect of closing the lips. This effect can be heard when a human produces a constant vocal sound such as "ee" and slowly closes and opens their lips while keeping the rest of the vocal tract in the same position. Value a_0 is used to control the overall amplitude.

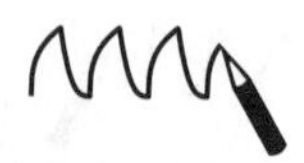

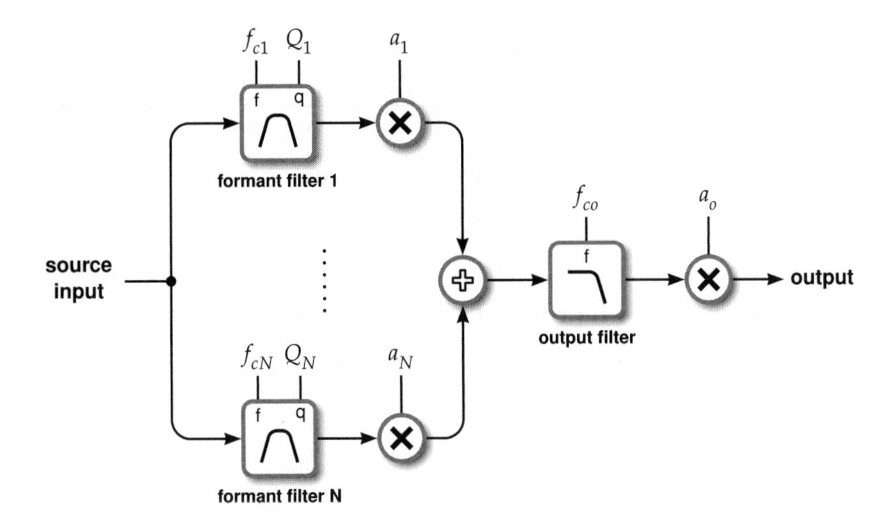

Figure 17.11 Vocal filtering

It is difficult to be precise about the parameter values necessary to achieve particular phonemes for the following reasons:

- There is variation in the implementation of the model components. The source waveform can be achieved in different ways with different amounts of emphasis at different frequencies. Secondly, the filter designs will affect their frequency responses (such as the roll-off outside the passband).
- Humans produce a fairly wide variety of tonalities that are classed as the same phoneme. Age, gender, physical build, and accent all lead to variations in terms of formants. For example, a smaller vocal tract will commonly produce higher frequency formants. While formants are generally consistent for one person and one phoneme, there can be subtle variations with pitch and stress.

Table 17.1 gives an idea of the types of parameters that can be appropriate for some voiced sounds using a fundamental frequency around 100Hz to 200Hz and a male voice. Bandpass filter Q values might be quite large (for example, around 20). Given the issues described above, it is likely that a certain amount of variation will be needed to tailor the values for a particular implementation.

Figure 17.12 shows spectrogram plots of some synthesized vocal sounds. Plots 17.12a to 17.12c show sounds generated with constant parameter values (to achieve an unchanging sound character). These resemble sustained versions of the sounds "w", "ah" and "ee". Notice how there are different regions of frequency emphasis (the spectral envelope) that a human uses to recognise the phoneme.

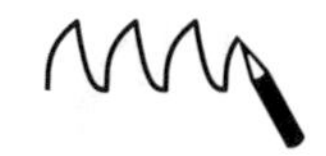

Phoneme	f_{c1}	a_1	f_{c2}	a_2	f_{c3}	a_3	f_{c4}	a_4	f_{co}
"w"	322	1.76	785	0.14	2581	0.06	3500	0.10	192
"ah"	660	1.76	1230	0.83	2525	0.96	—	—	4568
"ee"	341	1.63	2495	0.83	3121	1.54	4078	0.32	5000
"oo"	334	1.76	909	0.72	2530	0.13	3500	0.10	989
"er"	497	1.56	1398	1.09	1903	0.35	3101	0.25	3500

Table 17.1 Example vocal filtering parameters

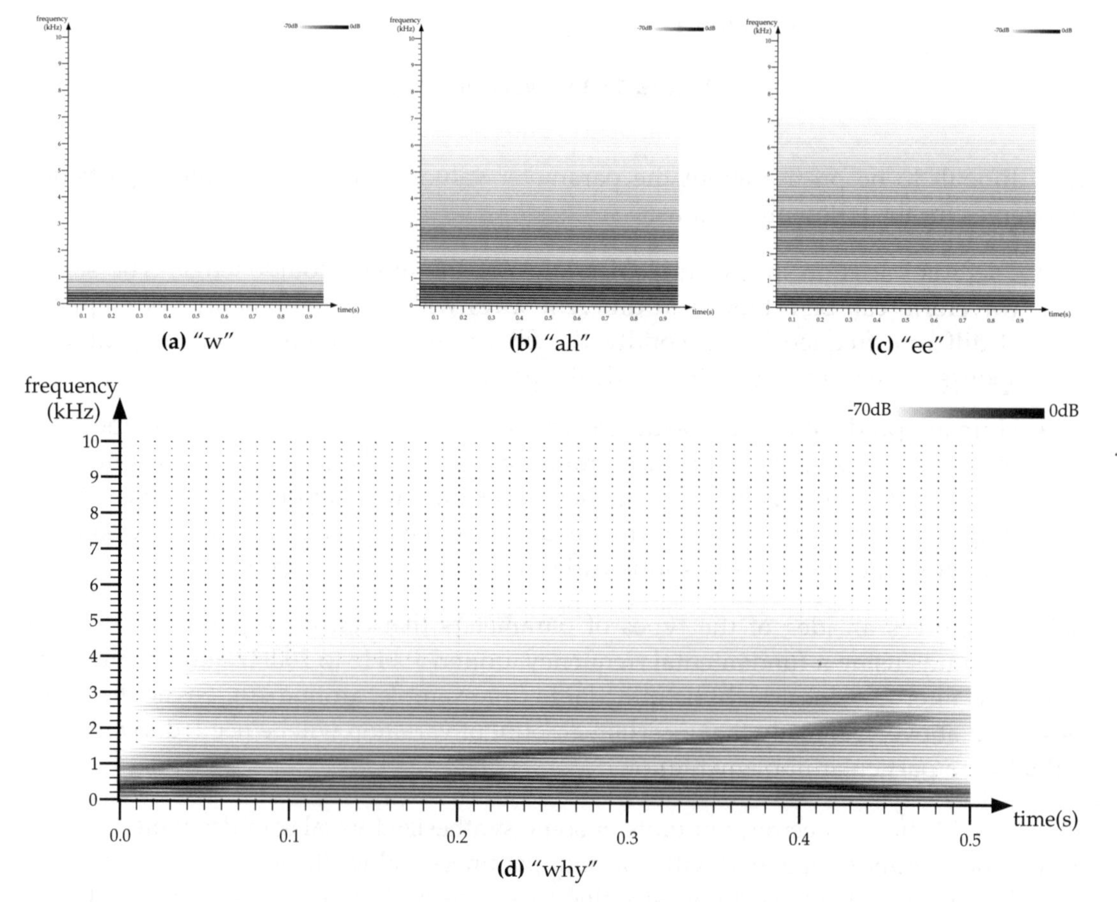

Figure 17.12 Synthesized vocal sounds

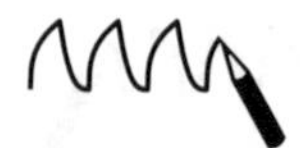

Figure 17.12d shows an effect where the formants are changing over time, which is equivalent to muscles moving the vocal tract. This is achieved by taking the three sets of parameters that produce the static sounds in plots 17.12a to 17.12c, and gradually cross-fading (interpolating) from one set of values to the next (from "w" to "ah" to "ee") to achieve the word "why". That is, parameters f_{ci}, Q_i, a_i, and f_{co} will all be interpolated between values at the three preset points. Cross-fading between pairs of parameter values is described in §19.4 (p.553). An overall amplitude envelope applied to value a_0 is also useful for achieving a natural rise and fall over the length of a word.

Both the rate and shape of the transition between the parameter settings are important to achieving a naturalistic result. Figure 17.13 shows two different interpolation paths between the sounds "ah" and "ee", combining to form a sound similar to the word "eye". Shape A moves towards the "ee" sound more rapidly than shape B, which spends longer with a sound character more similar to "ah".

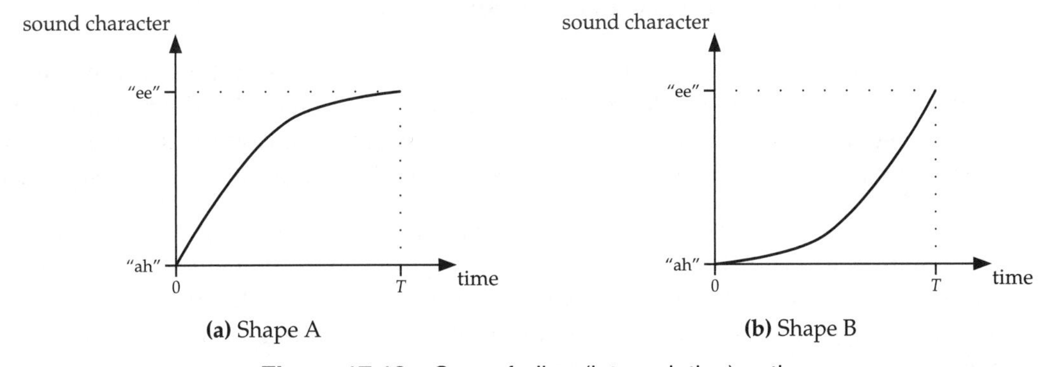

Figure 17.13 Cross-fading (interpolation) paths

It is important that frequency f_{ci} relates to the same formant in the two end-points of a transition. For example, if the values for formant 3 were swapped with formant 1 for one of the phonemes in table 17.1, then transitions between that phoneme and another might sound unnatural.

17.4 High Resonance Methods

A filter that is designed to be resonant (and is suitably configured) can produce a ringing output. Figure 17.14 illustrates an example result when a 15ms long wideband oscillation at 250Hz is the input to a bandpass filter configured with a centre frequency of 500Hz and a Q of 600. The output has an exponential decay that is far longer than the input.

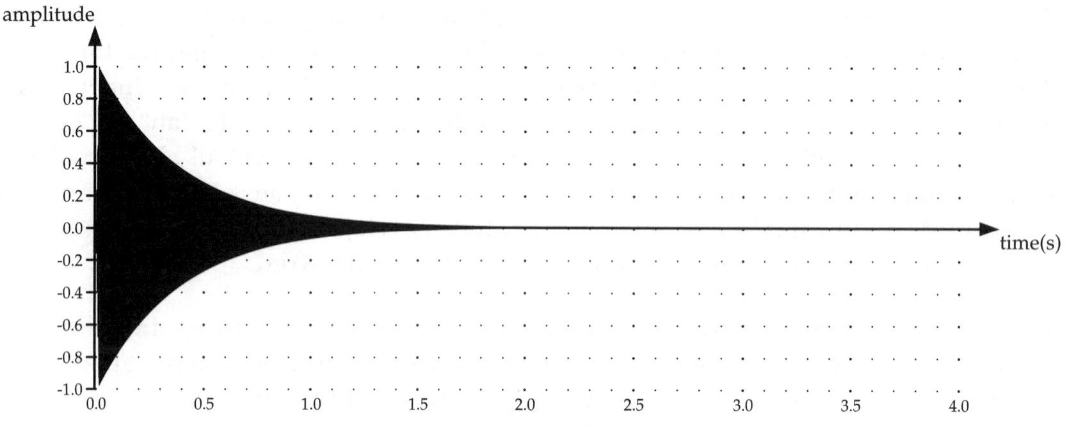

Figure 17.14 Resonant filter result in the time domain

There are some important features with this arrangement:

- The value of Q is far larger than is commonly used for subtle tonal modification with filters. Generally, the larger the value of Q the longer the filter output will take to decay. A large value of Q also relates to a narrow bandwidth, so the range of frequencies associated with the output becomes smaller around the centre frequency.
- Because the filter is tuned to a narrow frequency range, its output will be much more significant when the input has frequency partials that coincide with that range. Those partials might be harmonics of an input oscillation, for example. Sharp envelope edges can also achieve a wide frequency range to stimulate the resonant response.
- The amount of output amplitude depends on the design of the filter being used. In figure 17.14 the amplitude has been normalised to a peak of ± 1. Some filter designs produce significant gain at the resonant frequency with high Q values (such as that shown in figure 6.46, p.177), but in other cases it is necessary to apply additional gain after the filter.

The response of the filter configured with high resonance has significant similarities to the behaviour of resonant physical objects when excited; for example, striking the body of a guitar while muting the strings, or striking a bell. In both these cases a brief, impulsive input provides a wide range of frequency partials that stimulate the vibrational modes of the object, causing it to ring and decay in a somewhat exponential manner. The difference from the single filter example in figure 17.14 is that a physical object often has many resonant frequencies. These are apparent in frequency domain plots as strong harmonics and inharmonics such as those seen in figure 4.28 (p.94).

There is more than one approach to creating vibrational modes in synthesis. Additive synthesis can use many sinusoidal oscillators each with an envelope generator to control the amplitude behaviour over time (see figure 16.3, p.486). An advantage of a subtractive synthesis approach is that natural exponential decays can be created automatically from resonant filters. The additive approach allows more unusual envelope shapes, but requires more configuration. Another alternative is physical modelling (Chapter 21) where the physical processes of sound generation are simulated to create naturalistic vibrations automatically. Physical modelling shares the source-filter approach with subtractive synthesis, but can be more complex in terms of implementation.

Figure 17.15 shows an example arrangement for high resonance subtractive synthesis with N bandpass filters. Large values of Q are employed (typically 100 or more). Two different ways of configuring the frequencies are:

- Fixed values; for example, to simulate the resonances of a guitar or violin body (the wood and air inside) that do not depend on pitch.
- Values related to a fundamental frequency using a similar arrangement to that shown in figure 17.7 (p.509). This enables the creation of resonators such as bells and strings.

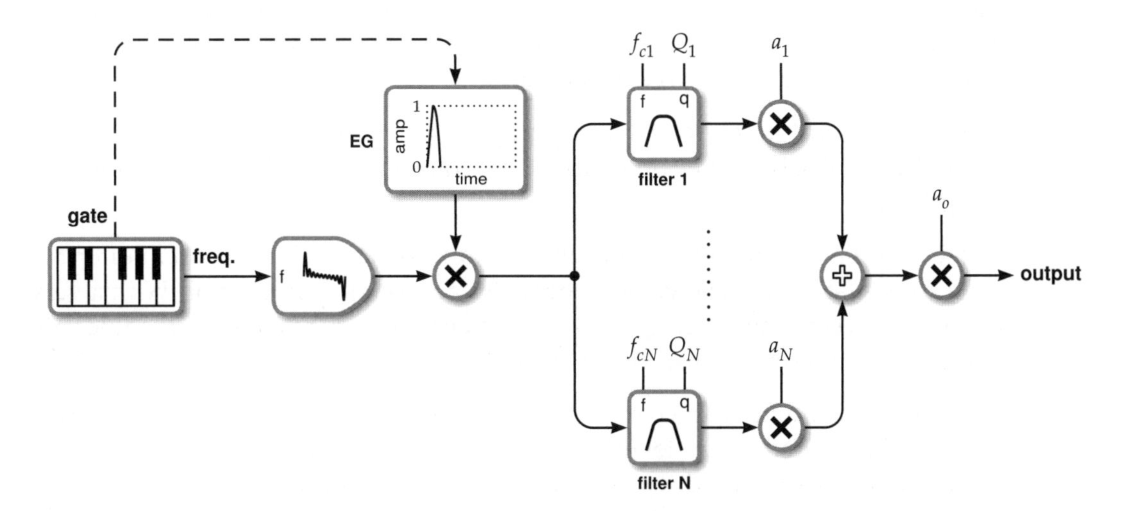

Figure 17.15 High resonance subtractive synthesizer

The envelope generator creates the excitation envelope. This might produce a brief input to the filters equivalent to plucking, striking, or similar inputs. Alternatively, it might produce a longer envelope equivalent to a continuous excitation input such as bowing or rubbing. The filters then resonate in response to that input.

In §17.2 (p.503), the wide bandwidth of the filters caused the amplitude of many source partials to be modified, and so the overall spectral envelope. In the high resonance case, both the source and filtering affect whether particular partials (harmonics and inharmonics) have significant duration in the output. With a very brief envelope, the majority of the output is due to the filter resonances. These can be tuned relative to the keyboard frequency to achieve a pitched effect. With a more sustained envelope the partials of the source contribute to the output over a longer length of time. For example, if a bowed pitched input is fed into filters with fixed centre frequencies to simulate a violin body, the pitched effect comes from the source.

A typical configuration process is as follows:

- An oscillator waveform is chosen with a wide frequency range in order to cause resonance in all the filters. A sawtooth or similar waveform might be used as an approximation to the effect of a bowed input. Alternatively such sources as a wavetable oscillator containing a single cycle extracted from a sample (see §14.4, p.444) or a noise generator (see Chapter 18) might be used. As the configuration of the rest of the synthesizer develops, it is often necessary to return to the source section to adjust the overall character.
- A suitable length and shape of amplitude envelope for the envelope generator are chosen to reflect the type of input (such as brief with sharp edges for percussive results, or a long swell for bowed excitation).
- Frequency relationships can be established by analysing existing sounds (see §16.2.3, p.491) or by suitable harmonic or inharmonic frequency calculation mechanisms (see §16.3, p.496).
- A suitable starting point is with gain values a_1 to a_N set to a value of 1, and uniformly high Q values (say 500). The value a_0 provides an overall gain control. With a very brief source envelope and high Q values, it can be necessary to use considerable gain to bring the output up to a reasonable level.
- It is then necessary to tune the parameters for the desired effect. Q values are varied to achieve the desired decay lengths for the different frequencies. The balance of frequency emphasis is varied with the source waveform, the amplitude gain values, and the shape and duration of the envelope.
- The tonal character produced can depend on the input note range chosen. It might be necessary to map parameter values from the control input frequency to maintain a consistent character if a wide range is desired. Control mapping is described further in Chapter 24.

Under some circumstances, an alternative to using a set of parallel bandpass filters is to use a suitably configured comb filter (see Chapter 6). This can also provide resonant behaviour, but is limited to integer-spaced passbands. Further examples of subtractive synthesis with high Q values are described in §18.3.4 (p.537).

17.5 Developing Processes and Learning More

The subtractive synthesis designs in §17.2 (p.503) are able to produce interesting and controllable results with a small number of parts. Starting with an interesting waveform and then reshaping the tonality with filters can be quite an intuitive and direct way of manipulating sound character. Subtractive synthesis is often found in analogue synthesizers, as the necessary oscillators, filters, and envelope generators can be produced with relatively simple circuits.

There are many possibilities for variation in character within a subtractive scheme. A wide variety of waveform shapes can be used as the starting point, using simple line segments, noise, or wavetables, for example. Chapters 14 and 18 describe the generation of suitable waveforms. It is worth investigating how varying the waveform will change the balance of frequency partial amplitudes, and thus the material available to be filtered.

Increasing the sophistication of filtering through use of series and parallel schemes is the most typical way of creating a more interesting tonal shaping effect. It is also worth trying different filter designs, as they can have noticeable variation in tonal characteristics. Such differences can be apparent in different situations, such as when using multiple filters in series, or with high Q values, or when envelope-controlled filter frequencies are changing rapidly. The synthesizers described in this chapter all use standard blocks that are found in audio programming libraries and environments, but it can be worth looking for other oscillator and filter objects to extend the capabilities of the chosen system, or implementing them from scratch. The following books describe a number of different designs:

> Pirkle, Will. 2013. *Designing Audio Effect Plug-Ins in C++: With Digital Audio Signal Processing Theory*. Burlington, MA: Focal Press.
>
> Pirkle, Will. 2015. *Designing Software Synthesizer Plug-Ins in C++: For RackAFX, VST3, and Audio Units*. Burlington, MA: Focal Press.

Further discussion of subtractive synthesis and related ideas can be found in these books:

> Cook, Perry R. 2002. *Real Sound Synthesis for Interactive Applications*. Natick, MA: A K Peters.
>
> Russ, Martin. 2013. *Sound Synthesis and Sampling (Third Edition)*. Burlington, MA: Focal Press.

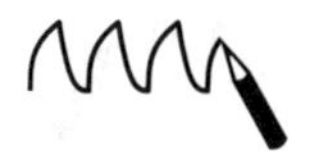

The following sources provide some more advanced material that relates to this chapter, which can be used for further study:

Fant, G., J. Liljencrants, and Q. Lin. 1985. "A Four-Parameter Model of Glottal Flow." *STL-QPSR* 26:4:1–13.

Fant, G. 1995. "The LF-Model Revisited. Transformations and Frequency Domain Analysis." *STL-QPSR* 36:2–3:119–156.

Plumpe, Michael D., Thomas F. Quatieri, and Douglas A. Reynolds. 1999. "Modeling of the Glottal Flow Derivative Waveform with Application to Speaker Identification." *IEEE Transactions on Speech and Audio Processing* 7:5:569–586.

Välimäki, Vesa, and Antti Huovilainen. 2006. "Oscillator and Filter Algorithms for Virtual Analog Synthesis." *Computer Music Journal* 30:2:19–31.

18

Noise in Synthesis

18.1 Consistent and Inconsistent Signals

Most audio synthesis is developed from a view of sound as a combination of sinusoidal frequency partials. There are a number of reasons for this:

- The conventional analysis techniques for determining the constitution of sounds are based on Fourier Transform methods, which produce results related to sinusoidal partials, as described in Chapter 4. These methods are well understood, and are suitable not only for analysis, but are also related to frequency domain modification techniques (Chapter 12) and sinusoidal additive synthesis (Chapter 16).
- Many sounds used in music have a pitch, which is associated with harmonic oscillation (as described in Chapter 3) and basic oscillators produce a harmonic output. The relative amplitude weightings of the associated harmonic sinusoidal partials are important to the tonal qualities of the sound.
- Sinusoidal oscillation is the purest form of vibration found in nature. For example, the chime bar sound simplifies towards a more sinusoidal tone over time, as shown in figure 4.28 (p.94).

Figure 18.1 shows a simple oscillator whose waveform consists of two partials, one at twice the frequency of the other and half the amplitude. The oscillator produces the same waveform shape for every cycle at 100Hz (every 0.01 seconds) and the result is harmonic. The spectrogram plot shows how the partials have consistent frequencies and amplitudes.

Figure 18.2 shows a sum of two of the oscillators seen in figure 18.1, but with an inharmonic relationship between the oscillation frequencies. Even though the time domain signal does not repeat in a clear regular fashion, the two oscillations are consistent and the result has a consistent character.

Sinusoidal frequency partials are not the only type of elements in sounds, however. Many sounds contain *noise*, such as those described in §3.2.8 (p.68). Noise is visibly irregular over short lengths of time when viewed in the time domain. In the frequency domain, noise is found as a cluster or broad band of inconsistent partials. It is apparent from the spectrogram plots in §4.3.3 (p.94) that many acoustic sounds display noisy features.

Sound signals are often between the extremes of highly consistent and inconsistent vibration. A sound might start with inconsistent vibration and become more consistent over the length of the event (like the chime bar shown in figures 3.11 and 3.12, p.50). Similarly, a sound might be composed of noisy elements as well as harmonic and inharmonic elements (such as breath noise in a wind instrument, or snare sound combined with a vibrating drum head in a snare drum).

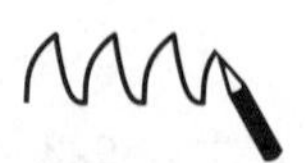

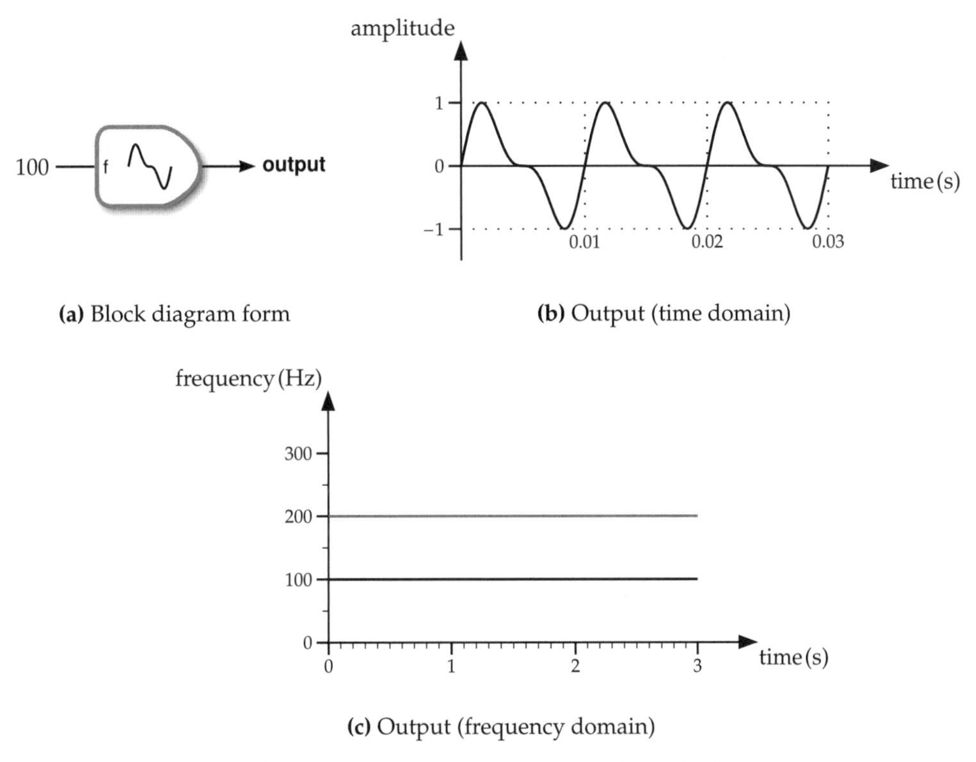

(a) Block diagram form

(b) Output (time domain)

(c) Output (frequency domain)

Figure 18.1 Consistent harmonic oscillation

The inconsistent values produced by a *noise generator* can be used to create audible irregularities in synthesized sounds, particularly at lower generation rates. However, if the output values are produced at the sample rate, the result has a consistent tonal character, which might be used as the basis for creating breath-like noise, or hissing sounds, for example. There are many types of noise and inconsistency, so it is necessary to configure the generation and shaping process appropriately for a particular sonic situation.

18.2 Noise in the Time Domain

18.2.1 Generation and Shaping

Noise is associated with inconsistency, and therefore is related to randomness. Basic noise generation occurs when every output sample is a new random value between −1 and +1 with no relationship between one value and the next. In this case all amplitude values between −1 and +1 are likely to occur equally often, which is called a *uniform distribution*. This property is illustrated in the *probability density function* in figure 18.3a, which shows constant probability density for all values (x).

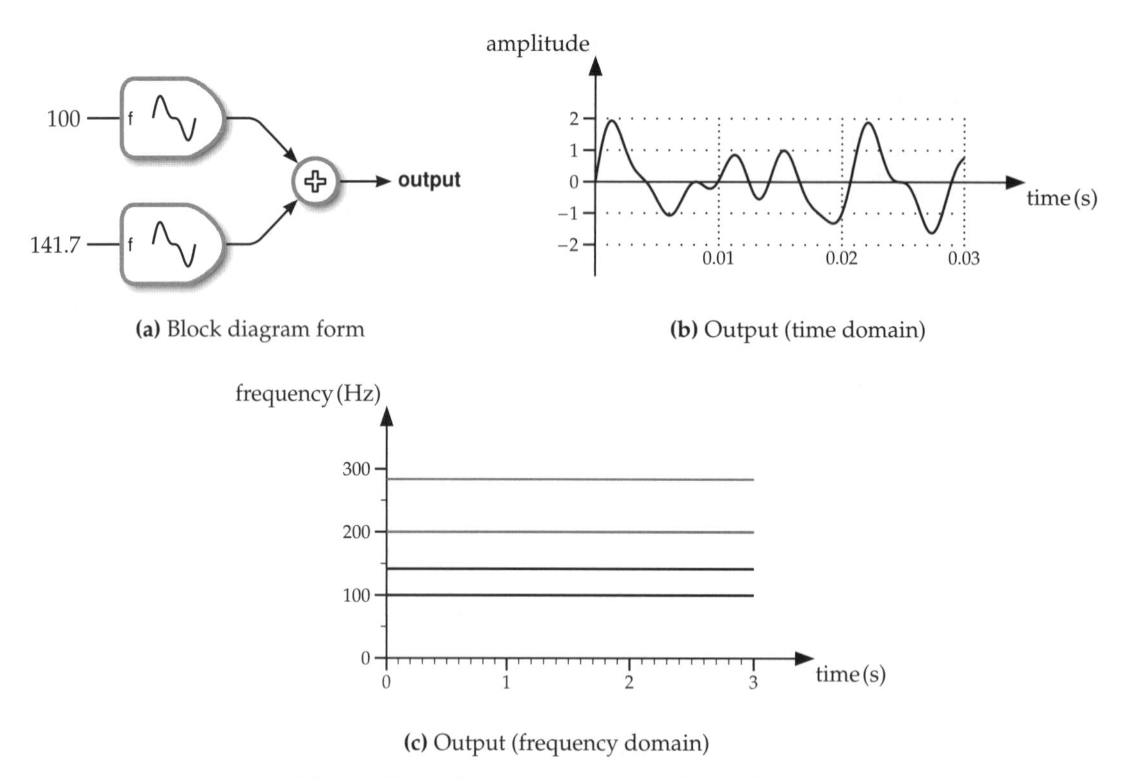

(a) Block diagram form

(b) Output (time domain)

(c) Output (frequency domain)

Figure 18.2 Consistent inharmonic oscillation

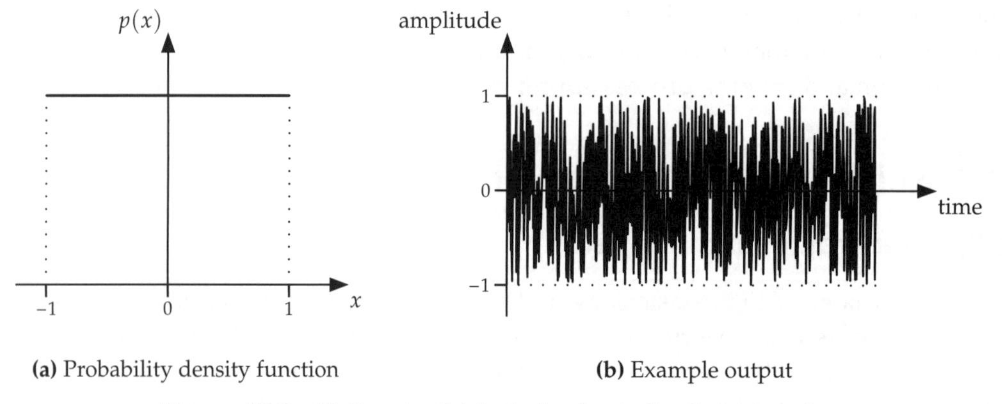

(a) Probability density function

(b) Example output

Figure 18.3 Uniformly distributed noise in the time domain

In practical cases (and over a finite length of time) the output will not be precisely uniform, but it will tend that way. Figure 18.3b shows an example of uniformly distributed noise in the time domain.

All common programming languages have a means of generating uniformly distributed random numbers. In many cases, the output values from these functions will be between 0 and a maximum value. If x_{max} is that maximum, then the values can be scaled and offset into the normal range for an oscillator (−1 to +1) with the following equation:

$$x_{out} = 2\left(\frac{x_{in}}{x_{max}}\right) - 1 \tag{18.1}$$

Digital random number generators are usually *pseudo-random*, as they generate sequences of numbers algorithmically that appear for most purposes to be completely random, but in fact follow a predictable sequence and after a very long time repeat themselves. When generating noise for audio purposes, a good pseudo-random number generator will be sufficiently random.

A uniform distribution of random values is easy to imagine, but not always most appropriate. Other distributions exist, such as the *Gaussian* (or normal) distribution, which is found in many natural physical phenomena. It has a bell-shaped probability density function, as shown in figure 18.4a. This means that values close to zero are most likely, and the likelihood of values occurring decreases away from zero. Figure 18.4b shows an example of Gaussian noise in the time domain. There are more values close to zero and fewer at the extremes than with the uniformly distributed noise.

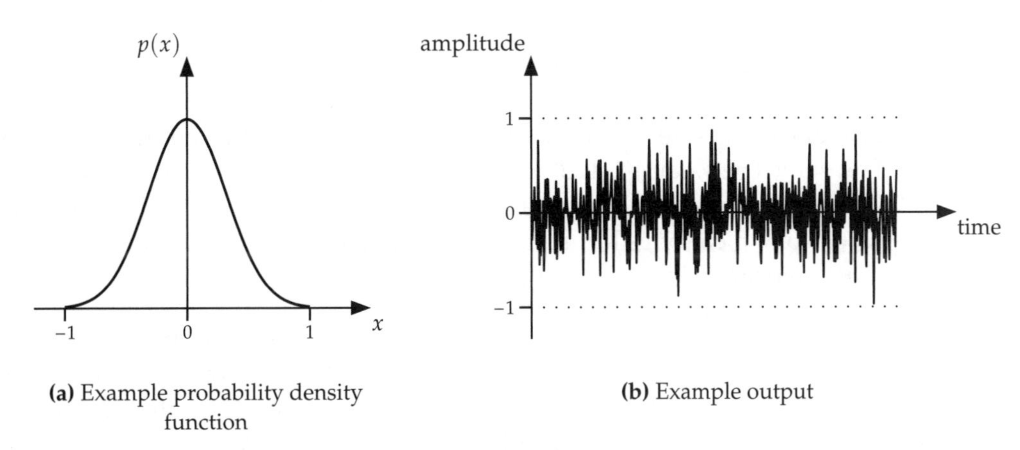

(a) Example probability density function

(b) Example output

Figure 18.4 Gaussian noise in the time domain

It is desirable to create different shapes of probability density function, in order to achieve a variation in random values that suits a particular application. One way of doing this is to generate N random values with a uniform distribution random number generator, and average them (add them together, and divide by N). This is performed for every output sample. When N is 2, the density function is triangular. When N is 3 or more then it is bell shaped, where the sides become steeper and the central part more narrow as the value of N increases. When N is 12, the result is close to a Gaussian distribution.

There are many algorithms for generating particular distributions of random values. A practical alternative is to use a mapping function, as illustrated in figure 18.5. The noise generator produces a uniform distribution of random values between −1 and +1. The mapping function repositions the output values and so the probability density function becomes non-uniform. Figure 18.6a shows a mapping function that will result in values close to zero becoming more likely (which is also the effect of the Gaussian distribution). The mapping function in figure 18.6b will result in values at −1 and +1 more often than those in between, and so a tendency to jump between the high and low values (but still with a random variation). The benefit of the mapping method is that it is possible to create arbitrary probability density functions that have characteristics suitable for particular applications, but with little computation. A graphical interface could be used for designing the shape that is used for mapping.

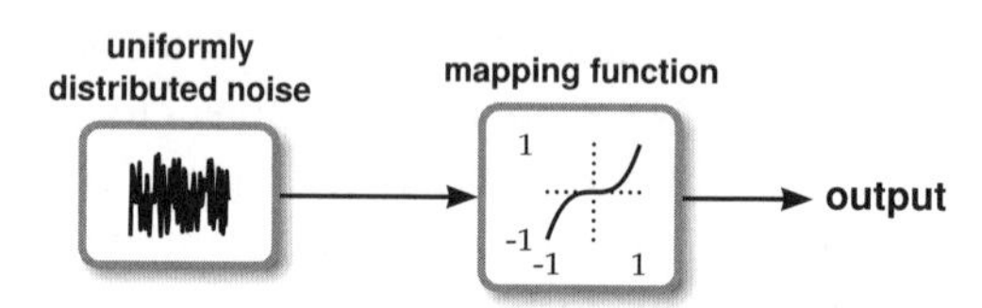

Figure 18.5 Mapping generated noise values

As well as particular probability density functions, there are other characteristics that can be achieved algorithmically. For example, if random numbers are to be used to select songs on a music player, it is desirable that there are no repeats until all the songs have been played. The values between −1 and +1 from a uniform distribution generator could be mapped to the number of songs available (and converted to an integer). The algorithm would keep a record of which songs have already been played and generate a new random number each time a repeat is chosen.

Another example of the use of historical information is a small random change being repeatedly added to the previous output value. This can achieve inconsistent movement through a parameter range, without large jumps from one generated value to the next. This might be applied to a synthesizer control parameter to add tonal variation over time that has both inconsistency and progressive aspects.

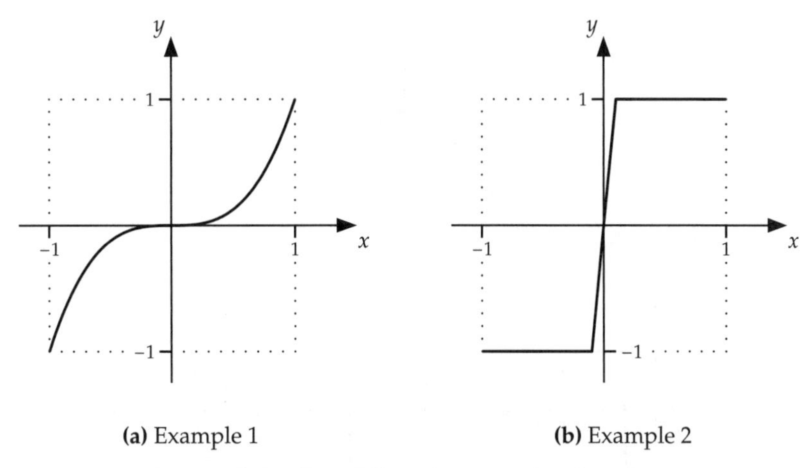

(a) Example 1 (b) Example 2

Figure 18.6 Example noise mapping functions

18.2.2 Rate-Controlled Random Value Generation

With a basic noise generator, a new random value is produced for every sample at the sample rate. There are cases, however, where random values are generated at lower rates. This is useful for creating slow variations, such as where a parameter value should gradually change or meander in a randomised fashion. Figure 18.7a shows the block diagram form of a noise generator that produces values at frequency f (a new random value every $1/f$ seconds). Unlike a normal oscillator, the output is not repeating at f, but rather the output is changing to a new random value at that rate.

Figures 18.7b to 18.7d illustrate how the output of the rate-controlled noise generator might move between the random values. In some cases, jumping between values without interpolation is sufficient, such as where each random value step is associated with an individual sonic event. In other cases, interpolating smooth transitions between the random values is desirable, in order to reduce the effect of a new random value causing an audible jump. Interpolation methods are described in §8.2 (p.237).

18.2.3 Inconsistent Oscillation

Figure 18.8 is an example of how noise generators can be used to mitigate the rather clinical and uniform sound character of simple synthesizers. The low rate noise generators add random variations to the fundamental frequency and output amplitude of the main oscillator. Although the effects are similar to tremolo and vibrato (as described in §13.3, p.418), they are not using periodic modulating waves and so do not achieve quite the same perceptual result.

(a) Block diagram

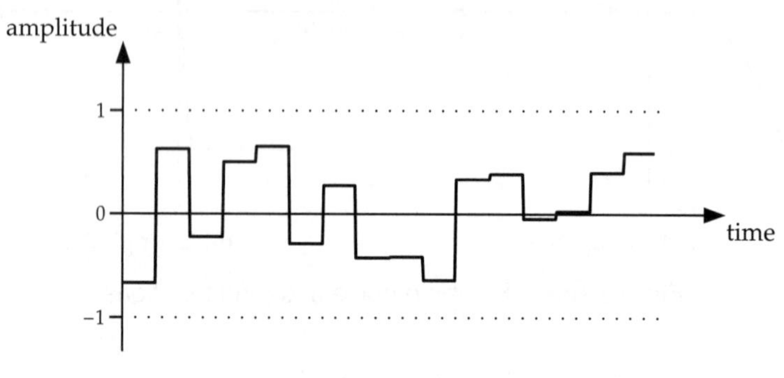

(b) No interpolation

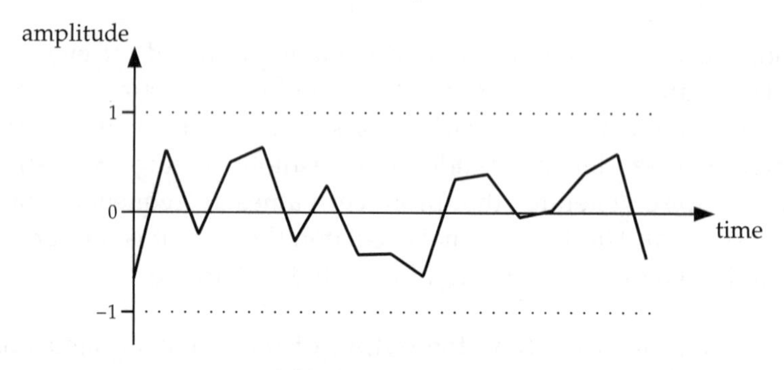

(c) Linear interpolation

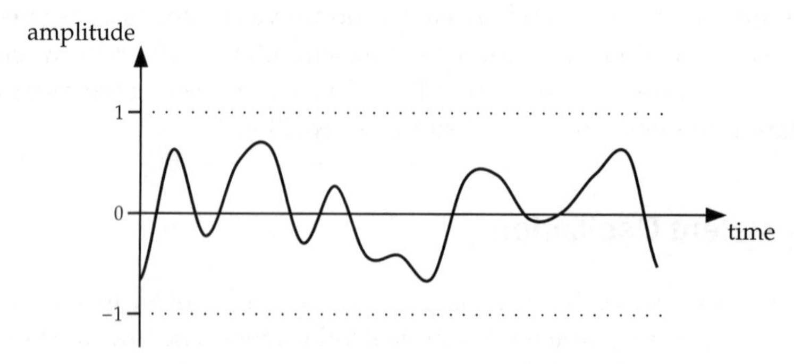

(d) Hermite cubic polynomial interpolation

Figure 18.7 Rate-controlled random value generation

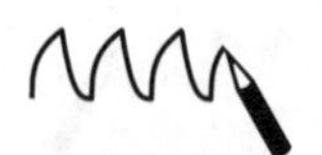

The frequency variation depth is in hertz, and so will have greatest effect at low fundamental frequencies where it is a larger proportion of the sum. Alternatively, it could be made proportional to the frequency produced by the keyboard, in a similar way to figure 13.22 (p.420).

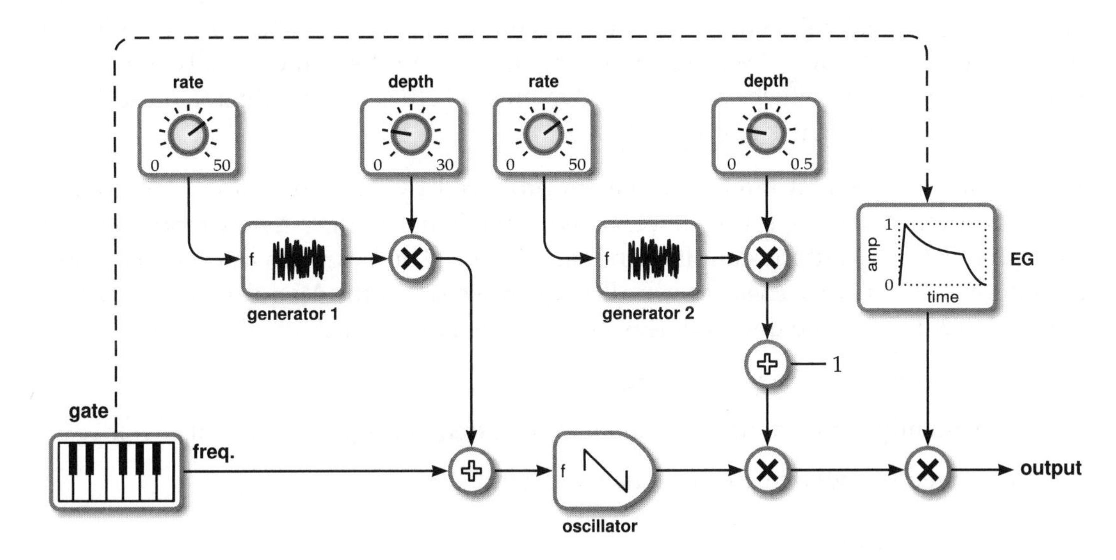

Figure 18.8 Inconsistent oscillation synthesizer

It is not necessary to use both amplitude and frequency modulation effects simultaneously, and quite subtle amounts of modulation might be employed. It is possible to create results that have some similarities to an old or damaged analogue audio system. Typically the noise generators will have a bell-like probability density function such that large output variations are less frequent than small ones. It is also appropriate to use interpolation to achieve smooth variations in value.

Randomised variations can be applied to synthesis parameters other than fundamental frequency and oscillator amplitude. Acoustic sound sources often display inconsistencies in their behaviour and adding some random variations can help to simulate this. Variations in value can either occur throughout the sound event (as is the case in figure 18.8), or the random value can be chosen at the start of the event and kept constant for the duration, depending on the type of variation that is being simulated. Inconsistencies between multiple instruments in an ensemble are also considered in §9.2.5 (p.283) and §19.2 (p.546).

18.3 Noise in the Frequency Domain

18.3.1 Spectral Envelopes

The variation of amplitude values produced by a noise generator in the time domain is useful for understanding low-rate effects, such as how the inconsistent oscillation synthesizer in figure 18.8 will behave. It does not, however, indicate what is happening in the frequency domain. It is desirable to understand how to shape the tonality of noise at higher generation rates, which can be related to musical effects such as breath noise or the inconsistent onset of a struck instrument.

The uniformly distributed random numbers produced by common programming languages have a theoretical spectral envelope as shown in figure 18.9. A new random value is produced for every output sample at the sample rate. This is known as *white noise*, and has uniformly distributed energy over all frequencies up to the Nyquist frequency $f_S/2$ (see §2.2.2, p.28). There are three key features of white noise, which are that it has:

- The widest possible frequency range.
- A consistently high amplitude with increasing frequency (a flat spectral envelope).
- A consistently high density of partials per hertz.

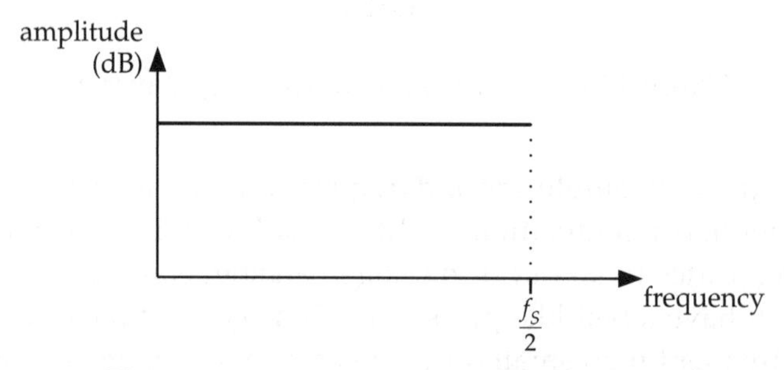

Figure 18.9 White noise spectral envelope

It is the nature of randomness that in practical cases, over short lengths of time, the spectrum plot is not as completely uniform as in figure 18.9, but it tends that way on average over the long term.

White noise has a very distinctive tonal character. The three features above are not typical of acoustic sounds, so it is necessary to modify the characteristics of white noise if it is desirable to simulate acoustic sources. It might be imagined that mapping the amplitude values in the time domain as shown in figure 18.5 (p.528) would change the spectral envelope shape, but it does not. The probability density function describes the likelihood of different amplitude values occurring in the output, not the nature of the frequency spectrum.

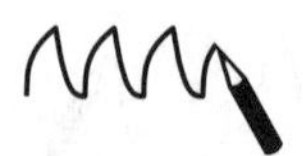

When noise is generated with a non-uniform spectral envelope it is known as coloured noise. A well-known example is *pink noise* (sometimes called $1/f$ noise), where each octave increase in frequency (doubling of frequency) results in a decrease in amplitude of 3dB. Figure 18.10 illustrates how the spectral envelope of pink noise is a straight line when both frequency and amplitude axes are logarithmic.

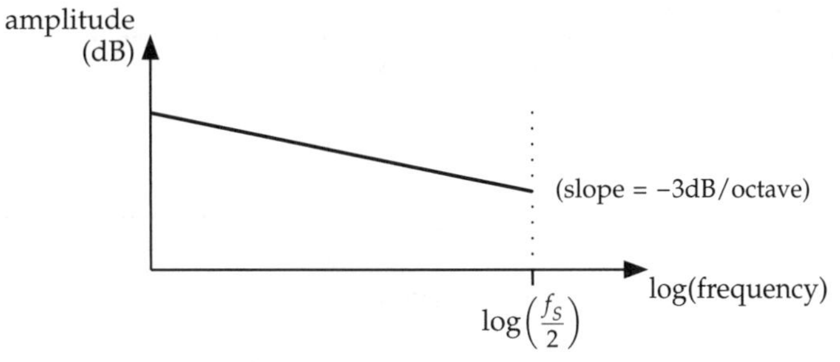

Figure 18.10 Pink noise spectral envelope

Pink noise has quite a gentle roll-off in amplitude with frequency, and produces less high frequency emphasis than a white noise generator. The balance of amplitude against frequency in pink noise produces equal power per octave. Like white noise, pink noise has a very wide frequency range and a consistently high density of frequency partials. Generating pink noise is not a trivial process, and there are a number of algorithms to achieve it. Many audio programming libraries and environments include a pink noise generator.

18.3.2 Rate Control and Modulation

Various algorithms exist for producing different colours of noise with particular spectral envelopes. While these can be useful for particular cases, it is more important to understand the mechanisms that can modify a raw noise source (such as a white noise generator) such that particular tonal characteristics emerge. The first such method is to generate new random values at rates less than once per sample at the sample rate. This can be used to create partials with a smaller frequency range than found with basic white or pink noise.

Figure 18.11 shows two examples of noise generated at a rate of 1kHz (rather than at the sample rate). As was shown in figure 18.7 (p.530), the transitions between the random values must be considered. At low rates in the time domain, the type of interpolation affects the way in which a parameter jumps or glides between the random values. In the frequency domain, it is apparent that without interpolation there are more prominent partials above the generation frequency than with Hermite cubic polynomial interpolation. This has an effect on the perceived frequency balance and the tonal result. The non-interpolated result in the figure has a very artificial character.

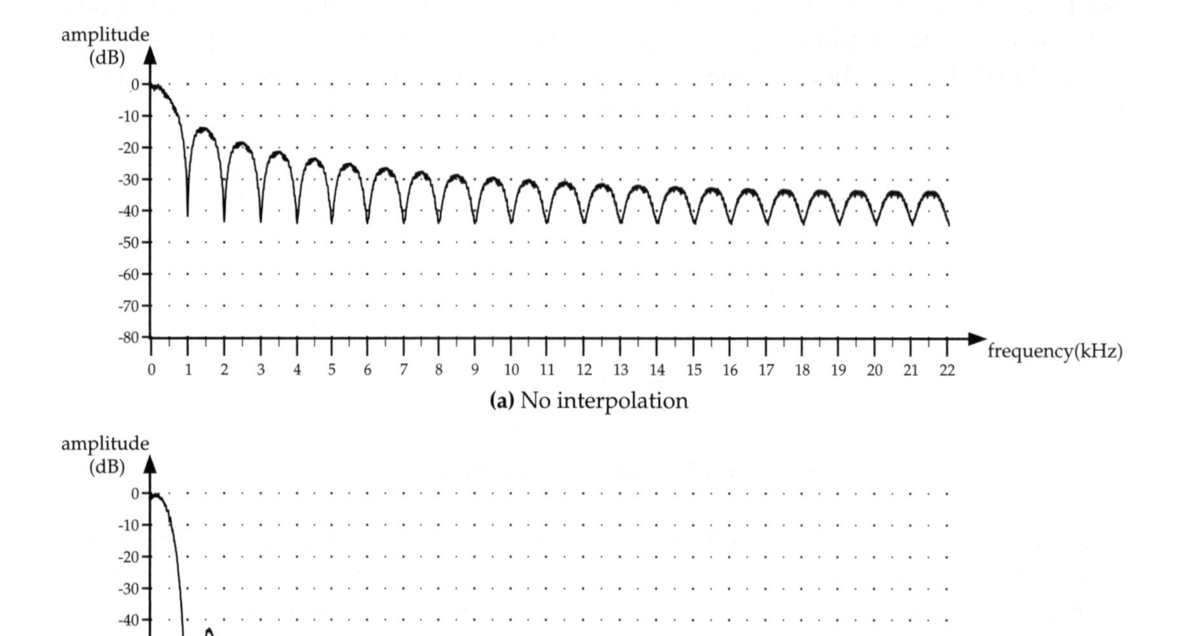

Figure 18.11 Uniform noise generation at a rate of 1kHz (average spectrum plots)

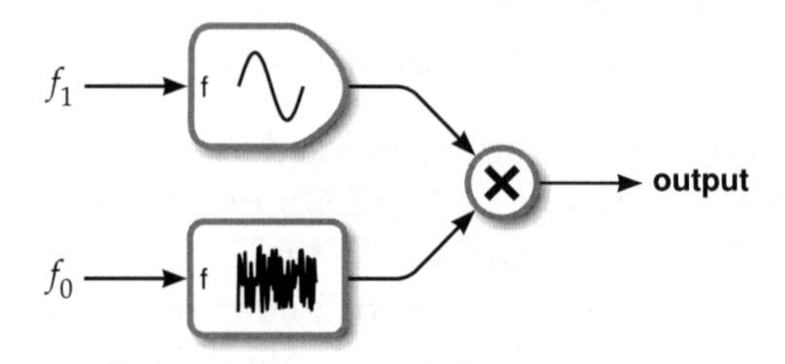

Figure 18.12 Modulated noise generator

It is possible to create a band of noise partials centred at a particular frequency, by taking the rate-controlled noise generator and using amplitude modulation as shown in figure 18.12. The average spectrum plot in figure 18.13 is the result of modulating the interpolated result in figure 18.11b by a sinusoid at frequency 3kHz. Amplitude modulation is discussed in more detail in §20.2 (p.561).

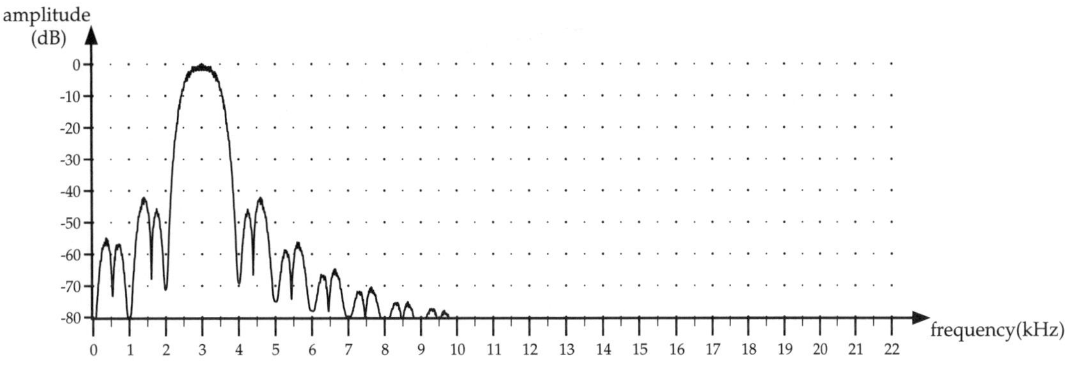

Figure 18.13 Modulated noise generator average spectrum (f_0 = 1kHz, f_1 = 3kHz)

18.3.3 Filtering

A standard way of shaping the spectral envelope of noise is to use subtractive synthesis, which uses filtering to modify the tonality of a signal generator output (see Chapter 17). In general, filtering must be quite aggressive in order to radically change the perceived character of white noise, as the density and consistently high amplitude of the partials requires significant attenuation to cause a particular frequency region to become isolated. For example, consider the plots in figure 18.14 where a lowpass filter with a roll-off of 12dB per octave and a cutoff of 1kHz has been applied to full bandwidth white noise. With a single filter stage, there is significant amplitude at high frequencies after the filter. If five identical stages are used in series, then the roll-off is more significant.

Filtering noise changes the balance of frequency emphasis. The location of frequency emphasis can often be related to pitch-like sensations, even though noise is not a simple set of harmonic partials (normally associated with a pitched result). Consider the spectrogram plot in figure 18.15, which illustrates full bandwidth white noise passed through a bandpass filter with a centre frequency increasing linearly over time. The Q of the filter is 10 and the filter roll-off is fairly gentle, meaning that there are many partials present in the result. However, the changing frequency emphasis produces a rising pitch effect.

The strength of the sensation of pitch in filtered noise relates to the bandwidth of partials with significant amplitude. Increasing the Q on a bandpass filter results in a smaller bandwidth, and the sensation of pitch becomes stronger. As the bandwidth becomes

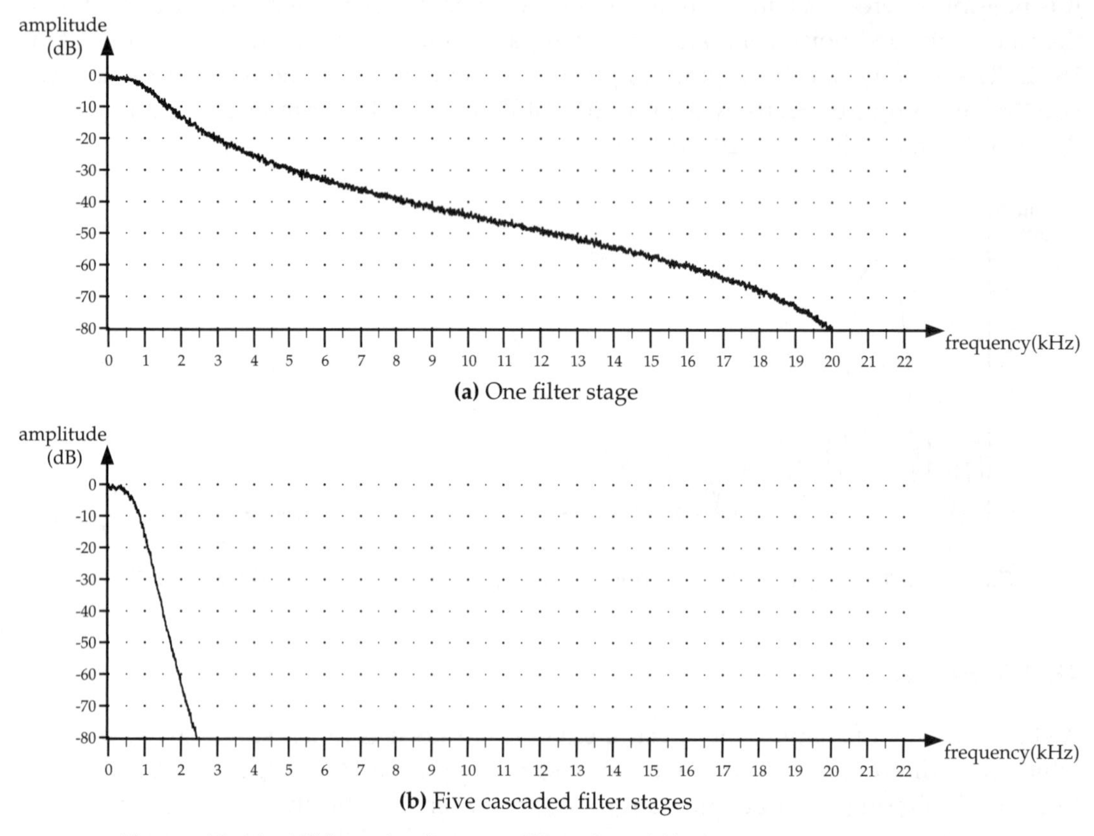

Figure 18.14 White noise lowpass filtered at 1kHz (average spectrum plots)

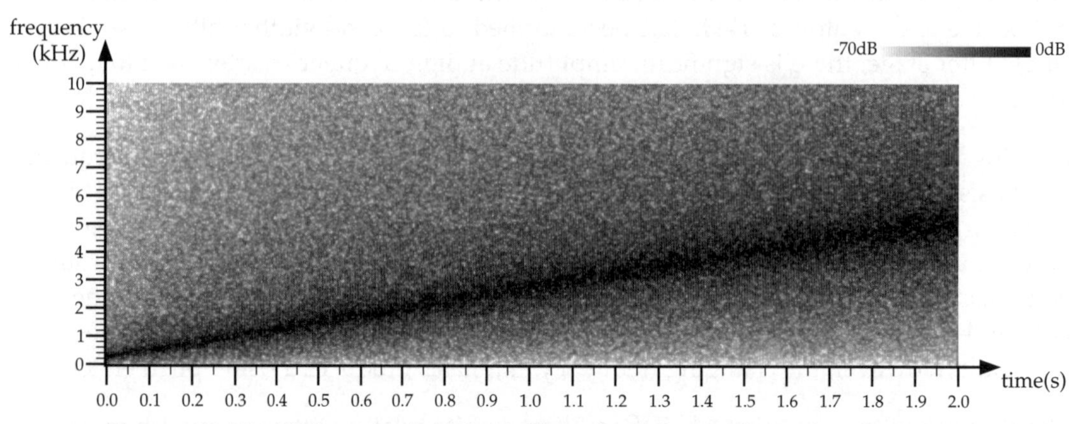

Figure 18.15 White noise bandpass filtered with increasing centre frequency (spectrogram plot)

smaller, the output is closer to that of a single sinusoidal partial, which has a clear pitch. Similarly, as the bandwidth of filtered noise increases, the sensation of pitch becomes more vague.

At moderate bandwidths filtered noise is not necessarily perceived as having a pitch. However, the **relative** difference between lower and higher frequency emphasis can still be audible. This effect is found in acoustic instruments, such as different sized crash cymbals, where a smaller cymbal will be perceived as having emphasis at a higher frequency. However, identifying the particular musical pitch that is being sounded will not be possible. The lack of clarity in pitch is useful, as a performer does not want to have to select particular cymbals for a particular piece of music in order to be in the right key.

It is apparent from spectrogram plots of acoustic instrument sounds (such as those in §4.3.3, p.94) that the shaping of noise in synthesized sounds will need to be quite sophisticated if it is to appear natural. With subtractive synthesis, multiple filters are required to achieve a suitably tailored spectral envelope. It is also necessary to think about the density of partials, as the consistent spread found in white or pink noise is not typical for acoustic sources. For example, there might be more clustering of partials at low frequencies than high frequencies. Precise control of this characteristic can require many filters. Because acoustic instrument sounds change over time, it is also necessary to have suitable enveloped control over parameters to mimic that behaviour.

18.3.4 Applications

Figure 18.16 shows a flexible subtractive synthesizer that uses a parallel set of N bandpass filters to shape the spectral envelope of a suitable noise source. A typical use for this form is creating blown instrument or breathy sounds. The noise source is assumed to be white, but other types might be used to provide different shaping of the source spectrum. Two filters are shown, but any number can be specified as necessary for the required sound. The centre frequencies of the bandpass filters are multiples of the frequency provided by the keyboard. The values of m_1 to m_N do not have to be integers. The filter outputs are weighted by amplitude gain values. The sum is passed through a global lowpass filter and an amplitude envelope is applied, for final overall character control.

There is a single overall envelope for the Q values of the bandpass filters, one for the lowpass filter cutoff, and one for the amplitude envelope. The ranges on the envelope generators will depend on the type of sound being produced. The very wide Q range shown in the figure is suitable for creating very narrow bandwidths and ringing in resonant bandpass filters. In other cases, a lower Q range is used for more gentle shaping of the spectrum.

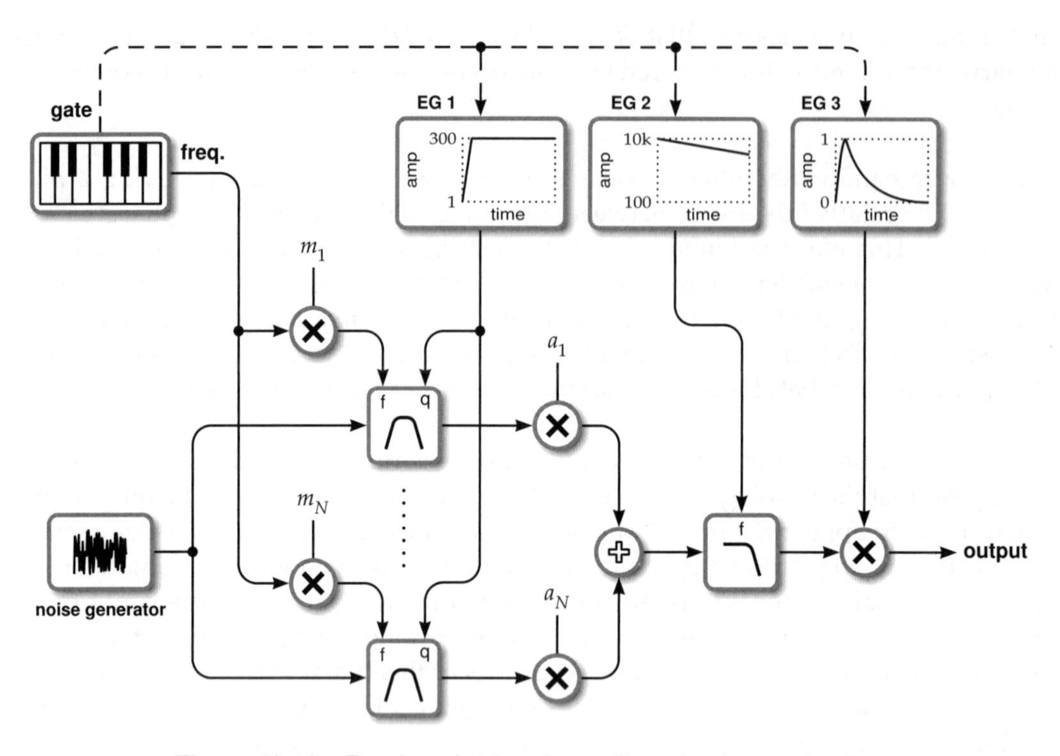

Figure 18.16 Enveloped Q bandpass filtered noise synthesizer

There are options in terms of the types of filters used. Quite an effective choice is a bandpass filter type with a large roll-off (such as two cascaded filters with the same centre frequency, as described in §6.3.1, p.155) and a lowpass filter that has a fairly gentle roll-off (such as 6dB per octave). This achieves more aggressive shaping of the regions of emphasis, but more subtle control for the overall frequency range. The narrower the bandwidth of partials that appears in the output, the more likely it is that greater amplitude gain will be required, to compensate for the amount of attenuation that has occurred, compared to the original input. This might be achieved by increasing the values of a_1 to a_N, or by adding an additional overall gain stage at the end of the process.

Figure 18.17 illustrates a blown bottle type of result produced by the form in figure 18.16. This is achieved with a single filter path (consisting of two cascaded bandpass filters), with a gentle swell in Q and gain envelopes, and a fixed lowpass filter envelope (with a 10kHz cutoff frequency). The Q range is moderately high (say, 20 to 40) and is adjusted to give a balance between pitched tone and breathy character. Changing the Q over time can dynamically vary the breathiness in a naturalistic manner. The spectrogram shows a high amplitude region at the frequency determined by the keyboard ($m_1 = 1$), and a spread of noisy partials around it.

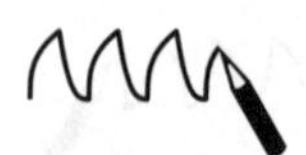

Figure 4.17 (p.87) illustrated how a bell-like sound is often associated with a combination of near-harmonics and strong inharmonics. Figure 18.18 illustrates a synthesized bell-like sound using the filtered noise technique. Five bandpass filter paths are configured, with frequency multipliers relative to the keyboard frequency of 1, 2.24, 3, 4.41, and 11.19. The gains are adjusted to achieve the desired balance of tone. The maximum Q value is very large (say 200 to 300), and has a rapid rise in the envelope at the start of the sound from low values up to that maximum. This achieves the initial striking effect as the filters have a wide bandwidth at the start (simulating broadband energy input), which then rapidly decreases as the sound settles to the principal resonant modes of the instrument. The attack portion of the sound is less convincing without this rapid change. The amplitude envelope is a classic percussive shape (rapid attack, gentle somewhat exponential decay). The lowpass filter has a constant cutoff frequency of 10kHz.

The output from a bandpass filter with a high Q value is not a single perfectly consistent sinusoidal partial, as the noise input has variation when considered at very narrow bandwidths. This results in some inconsistency in the sound character. As well as inharmonic sounds, it is also possible to create harmonic frequency relationships using the form in figure 18.16, such as organ type sounds that have some slight variation in character over time due to the noise input.

As well as synthesis with high Q values, more obviously noisy sounds can be produced. Figure 18.19 illustrates an example of synthesising breath-like noise through a wind instrument. With an instrument such as a clarinet, the air column resonances shape the tone of the noise, and the emphasis will increase with the frequency of the selected note. Four parallel bandpass filters have been used to create the form in the figure, with a constant Q value of 8 and a constant lowpass filter cutoff at 10kHz. The number, position, and gain of filters employed can be changed to achieve the desired character; there is no single arrangement that is correct in all situations.

While the synthesizer in figure 18.16 can produce a fair range of sound characters, it has certain restrictions in order to simplify configuration. There is a single Q envelope for all filters, the frequency and amplitude multipliers are fixed values, and the centre frequencies track linearly with the frequency chosen on the keyboard. The form could be extended by having more complex frequency mappings (or frequency envelopes), and individual Q and amplitude envelopes for each filter.

The windy weather synthesizer in figure 18.20 is an example of how noise generators can be combined:

- The upper noise generator produces ramped values that change slowly (a frequency of 0.1Hz means a new target value for the ramp every 10 seconds). The middle generator produces a result that changes slightly faster.

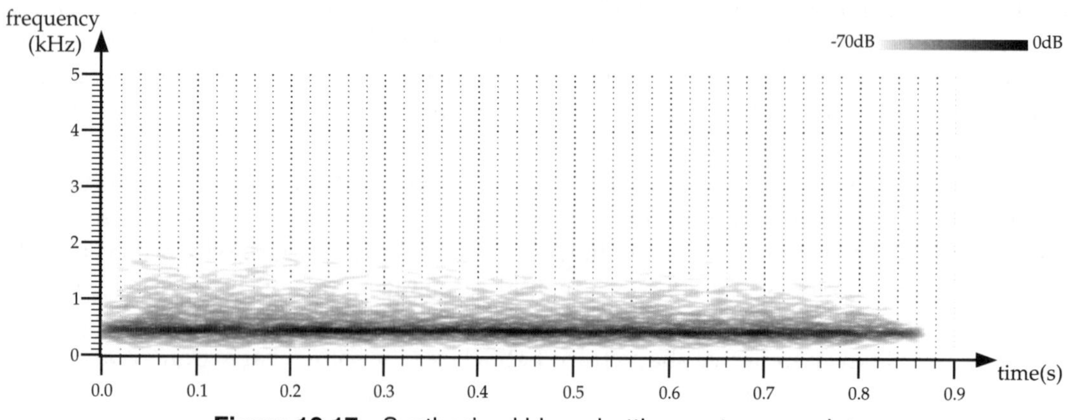

Figure 18.17 Synthesized blown bottle spectrogram plot

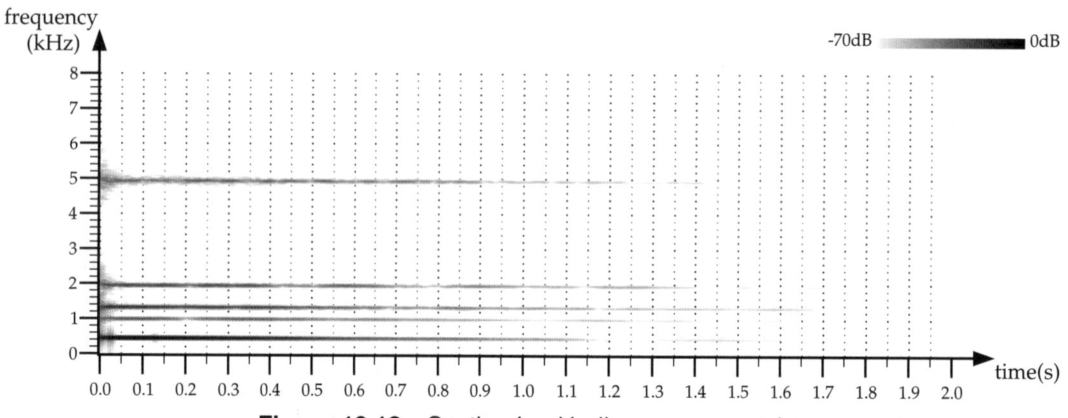

Figure 18.18 Synthesized bell spectrogram plot

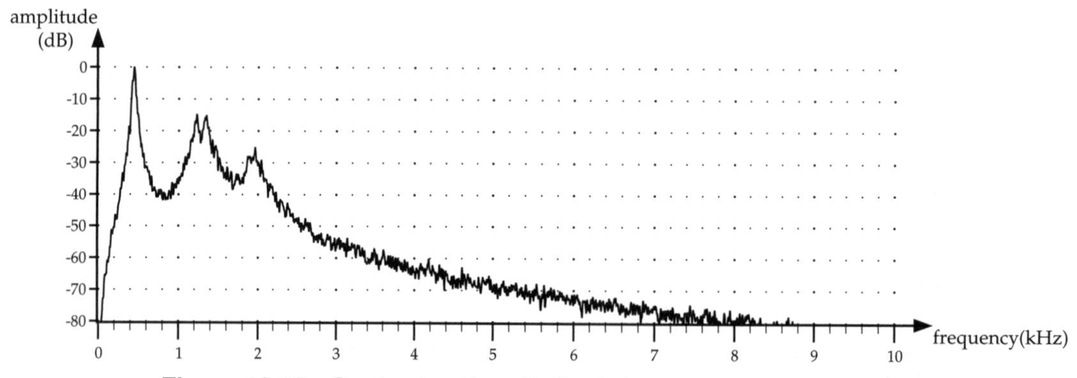

Figure 18.19 Synthesized breath-like noise average spectrum plot

- Values a_1, a_2, and a_3 scale and offset the values produced by the noise generators to a suitable range of values for the filter C centre frequency. This produces changing frequency emphasis over time.
- The three filters shape the white noise.
- Value a_4 couples the frequency and amplitude variations. This means that as the frequency increases, so does the amplitude of the result. That is, as the wind blows harder it becomes both higher in pitch and louder.

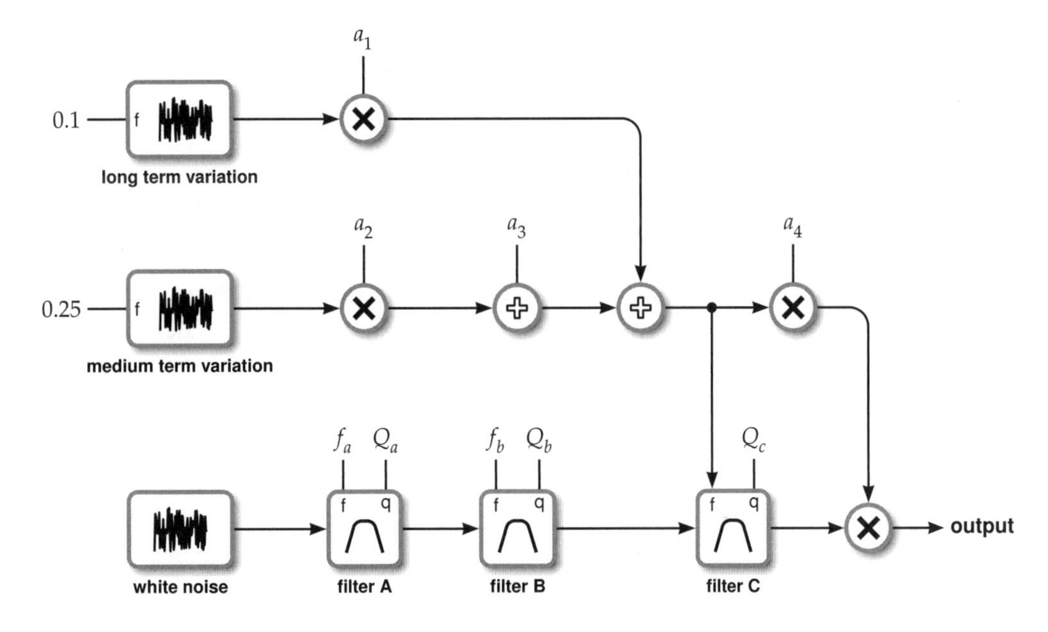

Figure 18.20 Windy weather synthesizer

The appropriate parameter values depend on the type of filters used, but some typical values are as follows:

$$a_1 = 100 \quad a_2 = 100 \quad a_3 = 450 \quad a_4 = 0.005$$
$$f_a = 2000 \quad Q_a = 1 \quad f_b = 500 \quad Q_b = 1 \quad Q_c = 10$$

Those values can be changed to achieve different types of effect. The main aim is to get a combination of noisy hissing/rushing and pitched whistling/howling effects.

18.4 Developing Processes and Learning More

The consistency and accuracy of the elements used to construct digital synthesizer processes can lead to somewhat plain or clinical-sounding results. Many physical and non-digital sound sources display both sonic complexity and impure oscillation, which are often desirable characteristics in synthesized sounds. Complexity can be achieved by extending synthesis processes, such as adding more elements and more varying aspects within the design. Impurity might be achieved by additional processing (such as distorting the output, as described in Chapter 7), or using noise generators to add inconsistency to the sound generation process itself.

The noise generators that are provided as standard in audio programming libraries and environments are a useful starting point for incorporation into synthesis structures. However, in their raw form the output from those generators often sounds very artificial. The use of rate control, interpolation, modulation, or filtering is usually essential. As described previously in this chapter, the noise often needs to be reshaped significantly to adapt the character to the intended application.

The use of noise can be quite subtle, such as a small amount of breath noise in a wind instrument sound, or slight variations in a filter cutoff frequency for each new note event. It can also be used as a more substantial component of the result, such as part of a snare drum sound, or in the applications described in §18.3.4 (p.537). The following book describes some ways of using noise in synthesis:

Cook, Perry R. 2002. *Real Sound Synthesis for Interactive Applications*.
Natick, MA: A K Peters.

19

Blending Synthesized Sounds

19.1 Basic Concepts

Some synthesis techniques can be repeatedly extended to add additional complexity and tonal variation; for example, adding more sinusoidal oscillators to an additive synthesizer (Chapter 16), or more filters to a subtractive synthesizer (Chapter 17). Rather than considering how the underlying synthesis forms might be extended, it is often the case that *blending* the output of multiple synthesis sections in parallel (also known as stacking or layering) can produce increased tonal sophistication with modest effort. The sections might be very similar (such as a number of wavetable oscillators), or they might be quite different (such as a filtered noise generator, a sample playback form, and a sinusoidal additive form).

The emphasis in a blending arrangement is on taking existing synthesis structures that are configured to produce musically useful results, and then combining them to create a hybrid character; for example, blending a flute sound and a trumpet sound, or blending multiple organ sounds to produce a more powerful-sounding combination. This chapter describes some typical blending techniques in the time domain. It is also possible to perform such operations in the frequency domain (as described in §12.3.4, p.389) in cases where it is desirable to consider individual frequency partials rather than larger composite forms.

The most common use of blending is to achieve a thicker, bigger, or broader tonal character. The general result of blending is greater density, spread, or interaction of partials. Such techniques are often used with monophonic analogue hardware synthesizers, as a way of maximising the tonal impact of limited circuitry, as an alternative to, say, creating a duophonic system with half the circuitry dedicated to each note. These methods are equally applicable to digital synthesis.

Figure 19.1 illustrates the general structure used for blending. The input parameters will often be supplied by a keyboard or other control device. A suitable set of parameters for each synthesis section is derived from the control inputs. If each synthesis section is the same, then it will be necessary to have different parameters for each one, in order that the outputs are different; if the outputs of the parallel paths are the same, then the parallelism is not of benefit. The blend is an amplitude-weighted summation such that the characteristics of the sound sources can be flexibly combined.

The results of blending sound sources depend on the frequency partials that compose them. There is a close association between blending and additive synthesis (described in Chapter 16). Interactions between partials can occur that do not exist when they are separate signals. Figure 19.2 illustrates two examples of what can happen when sounds with multiple partials are mixed.

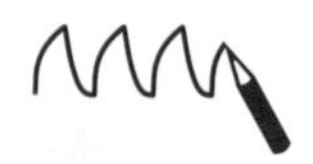

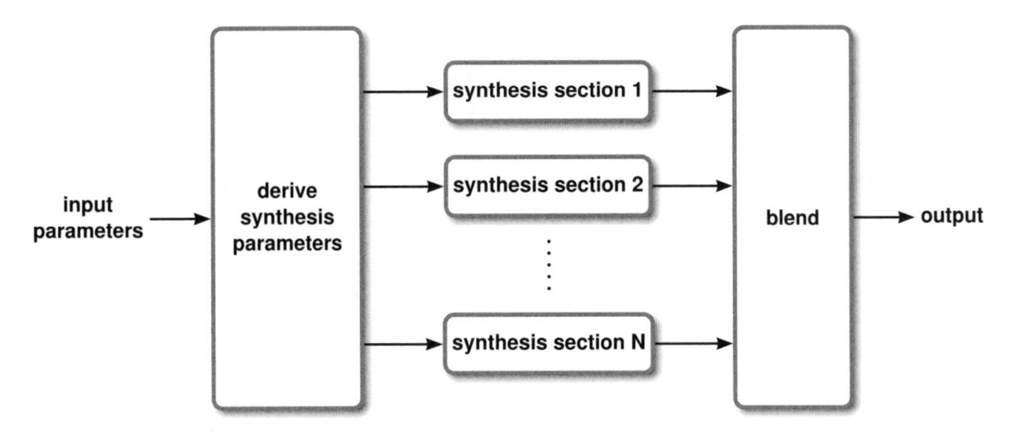

Figure 19.1 General blend structure

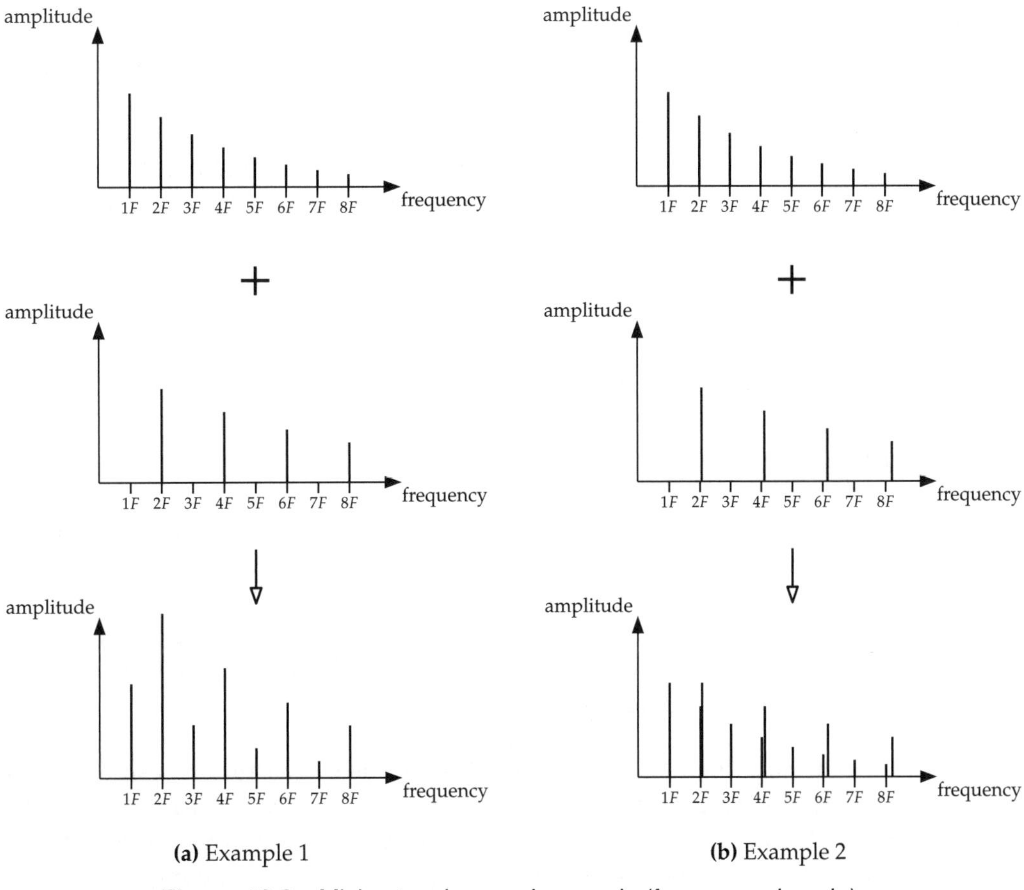

Figure 19.2 Mixing two harmonic sounds (frequency domain)

In figure 19.2a both sounds are harmonic, and the second sound is at a fundamental frequency twice that of the first ($2F$). This means that the partials of the two sounds are coincident for $2F$, $4F$, $6F$, and $8F$, and the mixed result is still harmonic (but with a new pattern of harmonic amplitudes).

In figure 19.2b both sounds are harmonic on their own, but inharmonic when mixed. The sounds have fundamental frequencies of F and $2.05F$. For example, if F is 100Hz then:

harmonics of F (Hz)	100	200	300	400	500	600	700	800	900
harmonics of $2.05F$ (Hz)		205		410		615		820	

Each harmonic of the second sound has a different frequency offset from the neighbouring harmonic of the first. Pairs of partials will interact as described in §16.1.2 (p.483), producing beats, roughness, or clearer separation.

The subtlety of blending effects depends on the configuration. For example, when acoustic instruments are played in unison there are very subtle differences in timing, tuning, and tonality. Similarly an instrument with unison strings for one note, such as a piano or a four course (eight string) mandolin, will display slight differences in tuning between the strings. These can be simulated with subtle differences in parameter values in the synthesized blend. Alternatively a larger variation between parameters can produce a more obvious blend. This might be through having different tonal characters in different synthesis paths, or by more radical changes in parameters such as large pitch differences.

19.2 Fixed Parameter Blends

19.2.1 Static Blend

Figure 19.3 illustrates a basic blend form with static parameter values (apart from the overall amplitude envelope). Multiplying factors m_1 to m_N determine the fundamental frequencies of the oscillators relative to the keyboard frequency. The oscillator waveforms W_1 to W_N could all be the same, or could be different. The amplitude gains a_1 to a_N determine the relative levels of the different oscillations. The number of oscillators used depends on the type of effect being achieved.

A standard oscillator (as described in Chapter 14) produces a harmonic result. A simple use of the static blend form is to produce inharmonic sounds, using harmonic oscillators and non-integer relationships between factors m_1 to m_N. This might be a useful source sound for subtractive synthesis, for example (Chapter 17). The following text describes how it is possible to configure the factors to achieve other musical and tonal relationships.

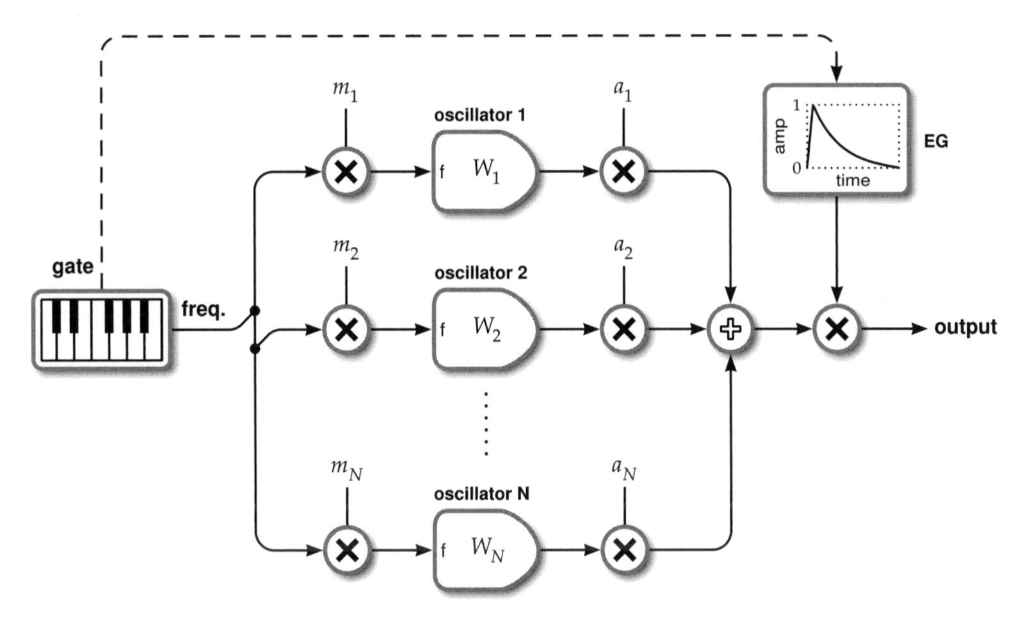

Figure 19.3 Static blend form

Intervals and Chords

Intervals and chords can be achieved with figure 19.3 by calculating frequency multipliers m_1 to m_N with $2^{s/12}$, where s is the number of semitones difference from the base frequency (as per equation 2.2, p.21). Some basic intervals and chords in terms of semitone differences are described in table 13.2 (p.401).

The following multiplier values will produce a chord of the root note, fourth, and fifth intervals in a three oscillator blend:

$m_1 = 2^{0/12} = 1.0$	$m_2 = 2^{5/12} \approx 1.335$	$m_3 = 2^{7/12} \approx 1.498$

To produce a simple chordal effect, all the oscillators use the same waveform and the amplitude gains a_1 to a_3 are the same, to achieve an equal balance between the notes.

Pressing a single key on a pipe organ can cause multiple pipes to sound simultaneously. A common configuration is to use pipes at octave intervals above and below the starting pitch. To simulate this the frequency multipliers might be:

$m_1 = 0.25$	$m_2 = 0.5$	$m_3 = 1$	$m_4 = 2$	$m_5 = 4$

Non-octave stops are also found on some pipe organs, such as frequency multipliers 3, 5, and 6. Different ranks of pipes can produce different tonal characters. Thus, there might be different waveforms for different oscillators in a simulation, as well as different amplitude weightings. The idea can be extended beyond standard pipe organ arrangements to frequency multipliers that are not simple intervals or integer multiples, to add some inharmonic character.

Chorus and Thickening

Unison effects are found in both electronic and acoustic sound sources. For example:

- Different oscillators in an analogue hardware synthesizer can produce slightly different oscillation frequencies for the same control input. Sometimes this is intentional, but it can also be due to miscalibration, or natural variations between circuit component values. When the oscillator outputs are mixed, slight differences in pitch and tonality are apparent.
- With unison strings on a mandolin or piano there will usually be very slight differences in pitch between the strings. Similar results occur with multiple instruments producing the same note in unison, such as violins in an orchestra or voices in a choir.

These chorus-type effects produce a thickening of the sound character. In a modifier process this is typically achieved by taking a single source signal and using varying delay paths, as described in §9.2.5 (p.283). In a synthesizer, however, it is possible to create multiple sound sources and give them each a different fundamental frequency by use of multiplying factors m_1 to m_N in figure 19.3. Synthesising with oscillators that have deliberate deviations from concert pitch is usually called *detuning*.

To appreciate the range of values required for this effect, note the following:

$$\text{Multiplier for 1 semitone pitch increase} = 2^{1/12} \approx 1.05946$$
$$\text{Multiplier for 1 semitone pitch decrease} = 2^{-1/12} \approx 0.94387$$

To achieve unison or chorus results similar to those found with acoustic instruments requires a pitch deviation that is considerably smaller than 1 semitone. A better starting point is a tenth of a semitone (10 cents) or less:

$$\text{Multiplier for 0.1 semitone pitch increase} = 2^{0.1/12} \approx 1.00579$$
$$\text{Multiplier for 0.1 semitone pitch decrease} = 2^{-0.1/12} \approx 0.99424$$

The blend produces pulsing or beating effects with this amount of detuning. For example, this might be a suitable set of multiplier values:

$m_1 = 0.9875$	$m_2 = 0.9954$	$m_3 = 1$	$m_4 = 1.0018$	$m_5 = 1.0027$	$m_6 = 1.0049$

The multiplier values above will usually produce quite a significant effect, which is useful for creating synthetic sounds. However, the values still are too far from 1.0 to be acoustically natural. The pulsing or beating rate depends on the difference in frequency between the partials, as described in §16.1.2 (p.483). As the multipliers get closer to 1, the variations occur over a longer period of time and the effect is more subtle.

The more partials with significant amplitude in the oscillator waveforms, the more possibilities exist for audible interaction between them. The waveforms might be the same for all oscillators, or different ones might be used to achieve interesting hybrids. The amplitude gain values are adjusted to achieve the desired blend of tonality.

The idea of subtle deviations from a multiplier of 1 can be combined with the octave intervals associated with a pipe organ seen previously. Harmonics of oscillations at octaves below and above the principal pitch will coincide, and so subtle deviations will still have the same effect. Some example values are:

$m_1 = 0.5030$	$m_2 = 0.9981$	$m_3 = 1$	$m_4 = 1.0056$	$m_5 = 1.9943$	$m_6 = 2.0033$

19.2.2 Enhancements to Static Blend

Figure 19.4 illustrates a more complex arrangement that can be used in the parallel paths in figure 19.3, which includes modulation of the input frequency with a noise generator. As with figure 18.8 (p.531), the idea is to achieve an inconsistent oscillator frequency and so simulate analogue circuits. The first difference from figure 18.8 is that there are multiple oscillators that can interact, not just one. The second difference is that the variation is multiplied by the frequency produced by the keyboard input rather than added to it. This allows variable m_i to have the same role as in previous examples (such as interval and chorus effects). When modulation depth m_{di} is 0, then the arrangement is effectively the same as figure 19.3.

The values of f_{di} and m_{di} will be small, in order to produce subtle deviations in oscillator frequency over time. For example, f_{di} might be 2Hz or less and m_{di} might be 0.01 or less. Different noise generators and parameters are used for different parallel paths in order to achieve different variations for each one. Instead of using a noise generator, a standard oscillator might be used instead to achieve greater regularity in variation.

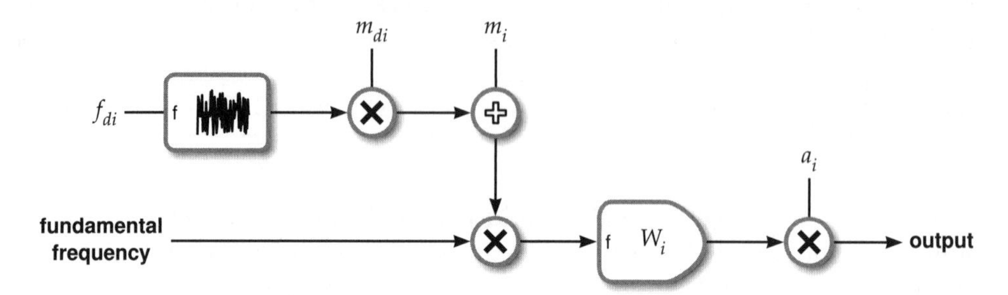

Figure 19.4 Randomised drift modulation

Another enhancement that can be made is to substitute a more sophisticated synthesis form for the single oscillator used in each parallel path in figure 19.3. For example:

- The oscillators might be replaced by waveguide strings, as described in §21.2 (p.584). To simulate a piano unison, three waveguide strings with very slight inharmonicity and very slightly different frequency multipliers might be used. Typically the range of pitch variation in a piano unison will be around ±1 cent or a little less. Therefore, the range of frequency multipliers will be between 0.99942 and 1.00058.
- The oscillators might be replaced by large synthesis structures to allow combination of quite complex sounds. For example, each path might have its own sample playback form (as described in Chapter 15), additive synthesizer (Chapter 16) or subtractive synthesizer (Chapter 17) with multiple parameters to shape the tonal character.

19.3 Envelope-Controlled Blends

The blends described in section 19.2 have fairly consistent tonal character, unless the oscillators are replaced by larger synthesis structures that create variations over time internally. Envelope generators can be added to the blending arrangement to create a varying blend character, as shown in figure 19.5. The figure includes envelope-controlled filter cutoff, amplitude, and pan position. Key points to note are:

- Although only two parallel paths are shown, any number is possible depending on the required result. Additional left and right outputs are summed with those illustrated in the block diagram, just before the output amplitude envelope is applied.
- The parallel paths are configured with different envelopes such that the blend develops in interesting ways through the sound. As the number of paths increases it can become a time-consuming arrangement to configure, because there are three envelopes for each path.

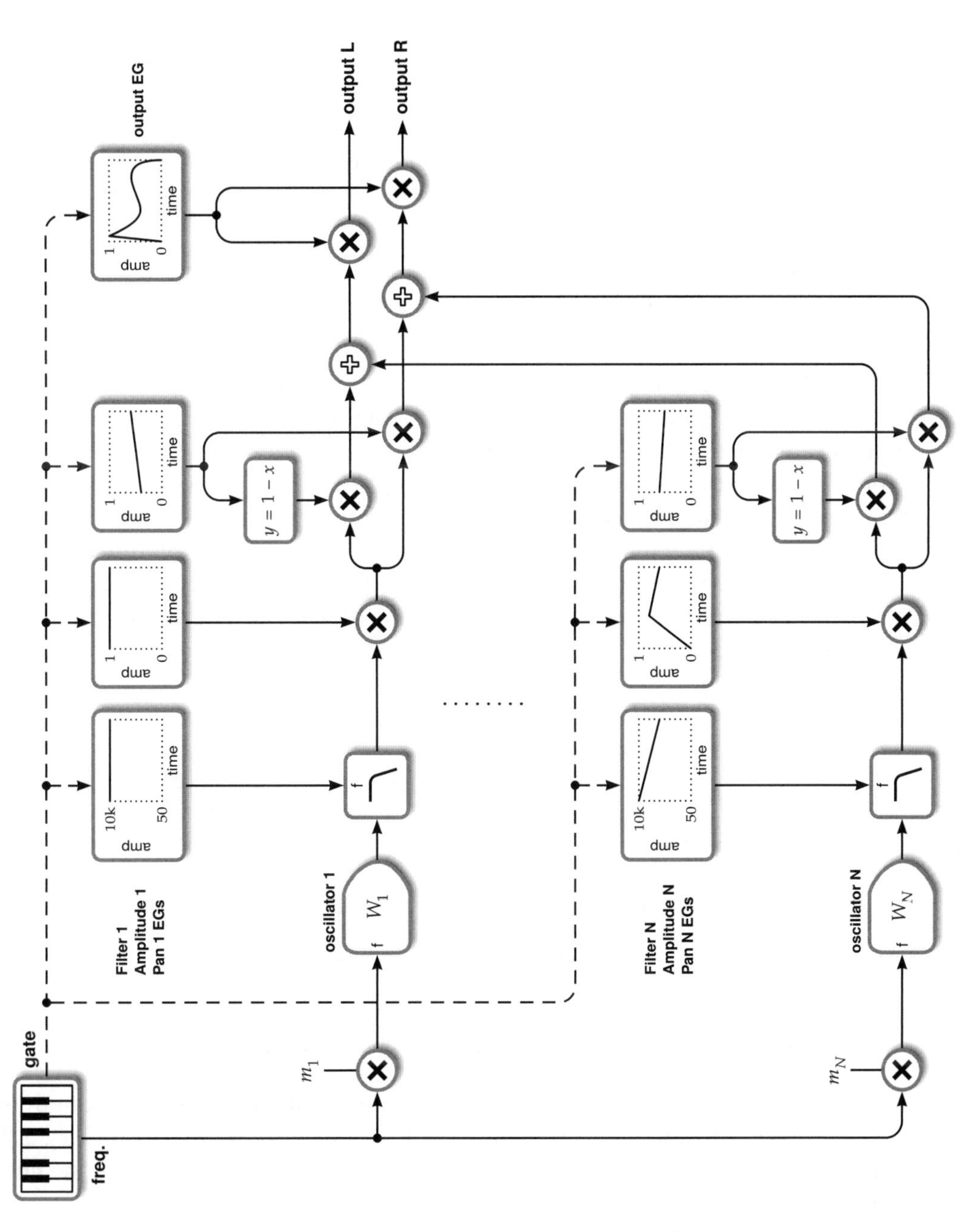

Figure 19.5 Envelope-controlled blend form

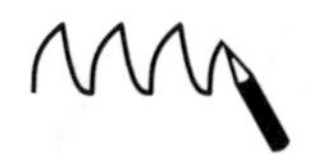

- Frequency multiplying factors m_1 to m_N are used in the same manner as described in section 19.2.
- The signal source in the block diagram is shown as a single oscillator per path. In more sophisticated arrangements this can be a larger synthesis or sample playback form. There needs to be a certain amount of compatibility between the tonal characters produced by the different paths and their pitch relationships, or the output will sound like multiple separate sounds playing at the same time rather than a composite character.
- The filter envelope can be used to limit the frequency range of a certain path or provide a changing tonality over time. The lowpass filter could be replaced with a different type of filter, or a more sophisticated filtering arrangement.
- The amplitude envelope generators provide the ability to emphasise different paths at different times. For example, one waveform might be used primarily in the onset, and others in the main body of the sound. This is useful when the source in each path is complex rather than a single oscillator. If samples of four different acoustic instruments are played simultaneously in their entirety they are likely to be perceived as separate, particularly if all the onset portions are audible. The amplitude envelopes can also be used to make a feature of a particular path, such as a brief swell or sharp decay at a key point within the sound. Figure 19.6 illustrates an example set of three amplitude envelopes; one emphasising the onset portion, one for the body of the sound, and one to provide a pulsing feature.

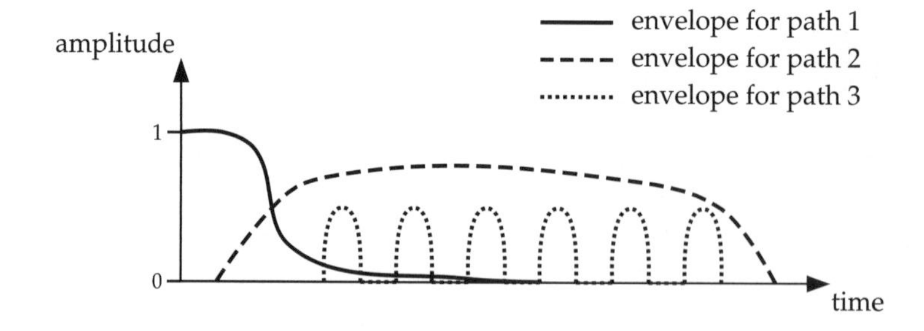

Figure 19.6 Set of three amplitude envelopes to create a blend

- The pan envelope allows different parts of the sound to move in the stereo soundfield over time. It uses a simple linear panning effect as seen in figure 5.32 (p.122). Like the filter and amplitude envelopes this can add interest where otherwise the effect might be static.
- Including an output amplitude envelope generator helps with creating an overall characteristic. If it were not present, then it would be necessary to adjust the amplitude envelopes for the individual paths to sum to the required shape.

19.4 Cross-Fading

19.4.1 Two Signal Cross-Fade

Section 19.3 described the use of individual envelopes to control the amplitudes of different signal paths in a blend. This allows a particular path to be controlled without affecting the others, such that a certain aspect of a blend can be changed in isolation. There are times, however, when it is useful to change the relative balance of different signals with a single control. A common requirement is cross-fading, where the amplitude of one signal increases as another decreases. The difficulty in achieving this with separate envelope generators is how to align the features of one envelope precisely with another, particularly when the shapes are complex.

Figure 19.7 illustrates how an envelope generator can be used to produce a cross-fade between two input signals (A and B). The technique is the same as figure 5.51c (p.135). When the envelope output is 0 then the output is signal A, when it is 1 then the output is signal B, and in between a varying mix of the two is produced. The effect is described by the following equation (where a_x is the envelope output):

$$\text{output} = a_x B + (1 - a_x)\, A \qquad \boxed{19.1}$$

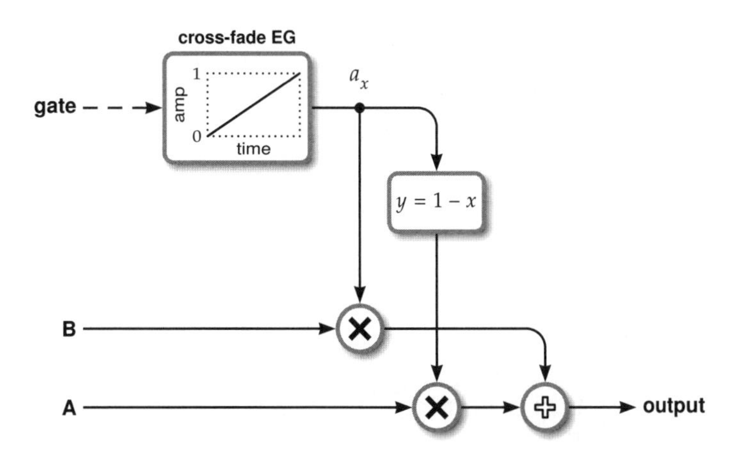

Figure 19.7 Two signal cross-fade

Some example cross-fade envelopes are illustrated in figure 19.8. Example 1 is a linear ramp from 0 to 1 producing a linear cross-fade from signal A to signal B over the length of the note. Example 2 has faster progress than example 1 to begin with, and then slows over time. This can be useful where signal A is used principally for the onset of the sound, and signal B is more important to the main body of the sound. However, it is not necessary to always treat signal A as the starting sound and signal B as the end, as demonstrated in

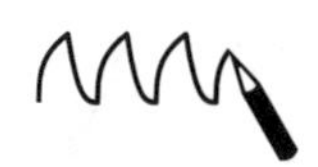

example 3. In cross-fade envelopes a horizontal segment will result in a constant mix for a length of time, and a vertical segment will result in a jump in character.

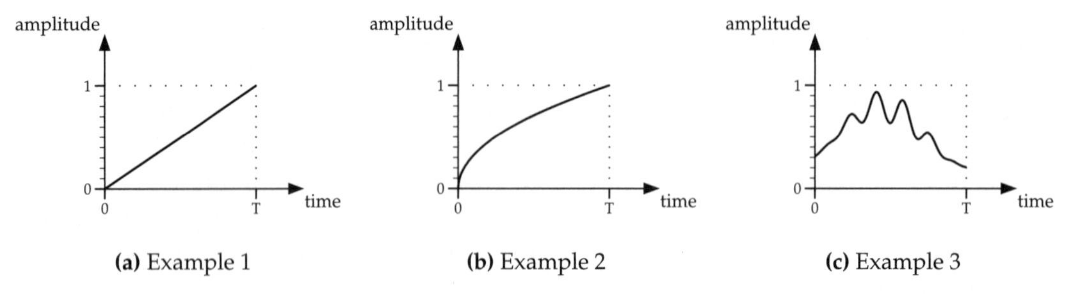

(a) Example 1 **(b)** Example 2 **(c)** Example 3

Figure 19.8 Cross-fade envelopes

Achieving compatibility between blended signals requires some consideration of their relative phases. There is a danger of subtraction occurring when two signals are mixed (as seen previously in figure 3.9, p.48). Figure 19.9 illustrates two cross-faded signals, where the phase relationship between the two affects the amplitude envelope of the result.

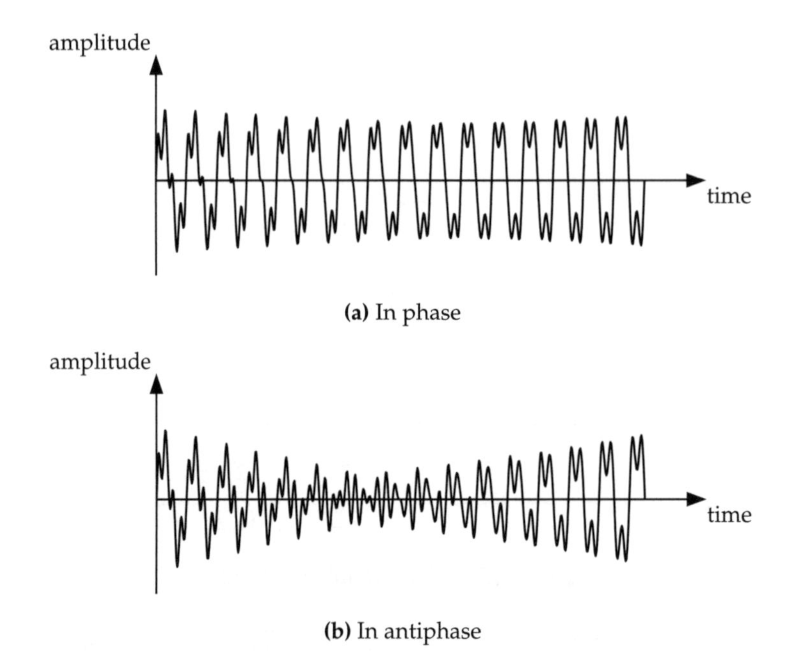

(a) In phase

(b) In antiphase

Figure 19.9 Cross-fading between harmonic sounds

A triggered envelope generator is one way of controlling the cross-fade. Alternatively, a manual performance control might be used to vary the result over time. This would need to be mapped suitably to a range of 0 to 1 (as described in Chapter 24). Another technique

is to combine the envelope generator with a low rate cyclical modulation (similar to the form in figure 13.15, p.413).

Rather than being audio signals, A and B might be parameter values; for example, they might be frequency multiplying factors or filter centre frequencies. A single envelope could fade between multiple pairs of values, replacing the manual blend control in figure 5.52 (p.136).

19.4.2 Four Signal Cross-Fade

The principle of a cross-fade can be extended to four signals (A to D) as shown in figure 19.10. This is often called *vector synthesis*. The envelope generator produces values between 0 and 1 which vary over time. This is passed to a mapping block which contains a two-dimensional path. The position input from the envelope generator determines the current position between the start of the path (position 0) and end (position 1). The direction from start to end is indicated by the arrow. A particular position on the path

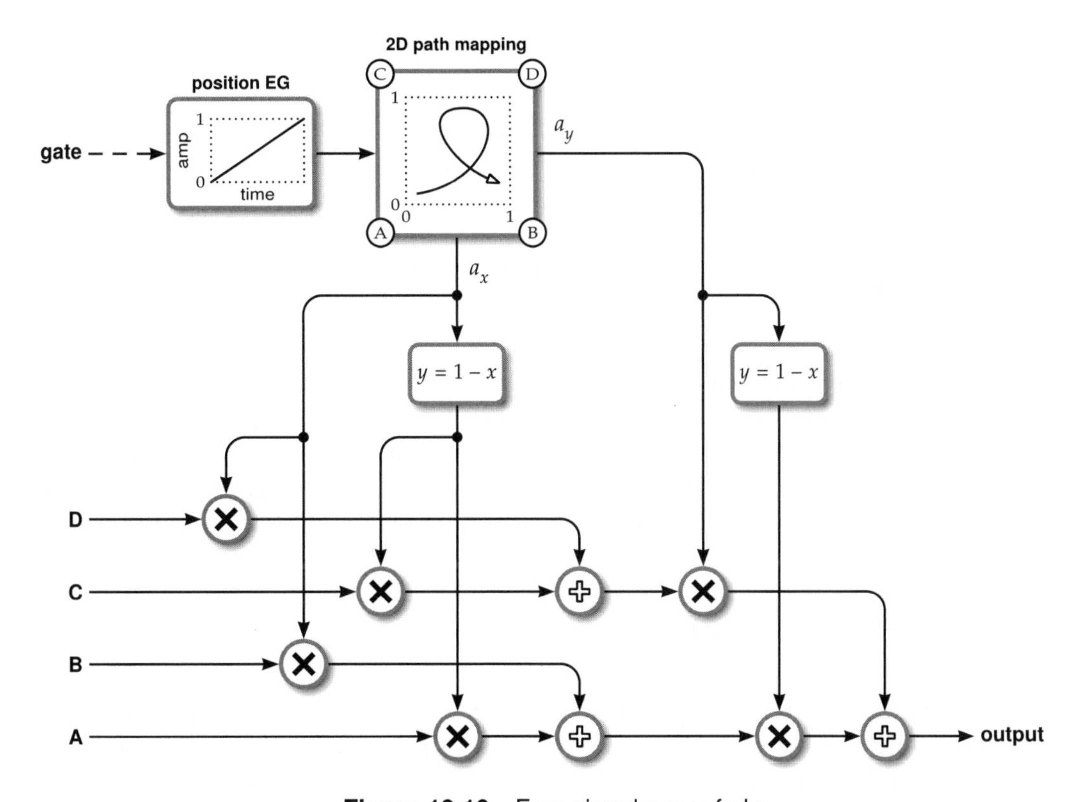

Figure 19.10 Four signal cross-fade

corresponds to a coordinate, which is variables a_x (horizontal position) and a_y (vertical position) each with values between 0 and 1. The values of a_x and a_y control the output blend, which corresponds to the following equation:

$$\text{output} = a_y\left(a_x D + (1 - a_x) C\right) + (1 - a_y)\left(a_x B + (1 - a_x) A\right) \tag{19.2}$$

The mapping block in the diagram is labelled with A, B, C, and D in the corners to indicate which corner corresponds to which signal:

- The output is a single input signal when the current point is in a corner:

  A at (0,0) B at (1,0) C at (0,1) D at (1,1)

- The output is a mix between two signals when the current point is along one edge of the square.
- The output is a mix of all four signals when the current point is in the middle of the square.

If the path follows the edge of the plane with straight lines A to C, then C to D, then D to B, it can be used to achieve a sequence of tonal characters blending between each other a pair at a time. Alternatively it might follow a more complex meandering route through the centre of the plane. There are certain limitations with this four-way style. For example, a mix that contains only signals A and B is possible, but a mix of only A and D is not. Therefore it is necessary to assign appropriate signals to the four inputs to achieve the required transitions.

Configuring the position envelope shape in figure 19.10 is similar to figure 19.7. If there is a linear ramp such as figure 19.8a, then there will be steady progress along the two-dimensional path from start to end. If an envelope such as figure 19.8b is used, then progress will initially be rapid, but slow down over time. If the envelope has a downward slope, then the current point will travel backwards towards the start of the path.

19.4.3 Eight Signal Cross-Fade

A three-dimensional control has the advantage of allowing an eight signal cross-fade, using the arrangement shown in figure 19.11. There are now eight corners corresponding to signals A to G. The idea is very similar to the four signal method in figure 19.10, but the position envelope generator now drives a block which produces three variables; a_x, a_y,

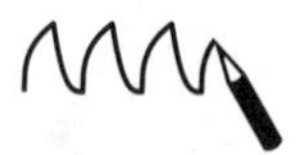

and a_z (with values between 0 and 1). These are used in the following equation to control the output blend:

$$\text{output} = a_z\left[a_y\left(a_xH + (1-a_x)G\right) + (1-a_y)\left(a_xF + (1-a_x)E\right)\right] + (1-a_z)\left[a_y\left(a_xD + (1-a_x)C\right) + (1-a_y)\left(a_xB + (1-a_x)A\right)\right] \tag{19.3}$$

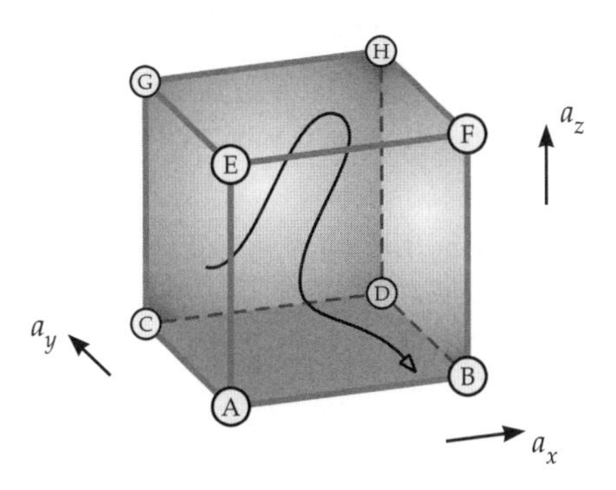

Figure 19.11 Eight signal cross-fade arrangement

It is possible to produce an output which is a single input signal (at a corner), a mix of two signals (on an edge), four signals (on a side) or eight signals (in the body of the cube). The position envelope generator works in the same way as before by producing a value between 0 and 1 corresponding to the position along the length of the three-dimensional path.

Although the arrangement in figure 19.11 has great potential, it depends on having a suitable control mechanism in order to accurately position data points. Historically, three-dimensional graphical controls have been less common than two-dimensional controls in computer audio systems. An alternative to graphical systems is to use sensor hardware to achieve performance control in three physical dimensions.

19.5 Developing Processes and Learning More

Blending is a simple idea in terms of creating more interesting sounds from existing synthesis sections, without necessarily having to reconfigure or extend the underlying forms. The required process elements are standard in audio programming libraries and environments. There are some parallels with instruments like the piano (with multiple closely-tuned strings) and the pipe organ (where multiple pipes of different octaves and

types can be played together). In the digital domain there are a wider range of combinations that are possible, and the blend can be quite complex in terms of the varying balance of different parallel paths over time.

It is worth experimenting with blending to examine the effectiveness of different sound combinations. A significant consideration is the tonal compatibility of the different paths. If the intention is that the result sounds as if it is from a single instrument source, then consideration of the parts that prevent that impression is required. For example, if the onset parts of two blended sounds cause them to be perceptually differentiated, then attenuating one of the sounds at the start is appropriate. Alternatively if a strong chorus-like separation is required, then it is desirable to emphasise the differences in tuning and tonality.

The following book describes some different ways of using blending techniques (referred to as stacking and layering):

Russ, Martin. 2013. *Sound Synthesis and Sampling (Third Edition).* Burlington, MA: Focal Press.

20

Modulation for Synthesis

20.1 Introduction

Modulation is the process of varying one part of a signal, using another signal, over a length of time. The focus in Chapter 9 was on periodic variation of modifier parameters at low modulation rates. In this chapter, there are two significant extensions to the ideas seen previously:

- Using modulation to create new sounds, as well as to modify those that already exist.
- Using modulation of parameters at rates above 20Hz.

Synthesis techniques based on modulation have the ability to create sounds with significant complexity in the frequency domain using a modest number of process elements. This has two implications:

- If those component parts are efficient, it is possible to produce sophisticated sounds with little computational effort. Historically, this has been a great advantage.
- The number of control parameters is often related to the quantity of process elements in a synthesizer. A large number of parameters can be necessary to create a sophisticated tonal character with sinusoidal additive synthesis (Chapter 16). A modulation technique producing a similar number of frequency partials typically has a smaller number of parameters to manage. However, as will be shown later, the relationship between those parameters and the tonal results can be more complex.

While modulation synthesis methods can be used for creating naturalistic characters, they are often very effective in producing synthetic tonalities. Similarly to many other synthesis techniques, modulation methods aim to produce particular patterns of harmonics, inharmonics, envelope effects, and so forth. Synthesizer parameters that might be modulated include amplitude, fundamental frequency, pulse wave duty cycle, and filter cutoff. These subsequently have effects on the amplitudes, frequencies, and phases of individual frequency partials.

Figure 20.1 shows the general form of periodic modulation used in synthesis. As described in Chapter 9, the modulating oscillator produces a cyclical pattern of shape W, at rate f_d, and a ± 1 peak amplitude. This is multiplied by the deviation (or depth) a_d and offset by a_o, such that the modulating signal varies between $(a_o + a_d)$ and $(a_o - a_d)$. This signal is then applied to a parameter of the synthesizer. The modulating signal in figure 20.1 has a sinusoidal wave shape, but the choice depends on the application.

The effects of particular shapes, rates, depths, and offsets depend on what is being modulated. In particular, at the high modulation rates considered in this chapter, the results are more complex than those discussed in Chapter 9.

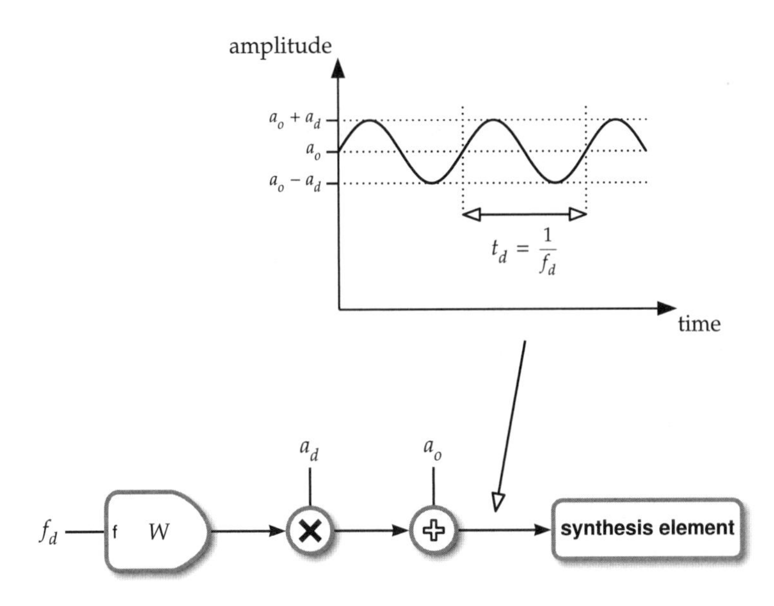

Figure 20.1 General periodic modulation form

20.2 Amplitude Modulation

20.2.1 Basic Principles

Amplitude Modulation (AM) is a periodic variation in the amplitude of one signal produced by another signal. At low modulation rates (typically below 20Hz), AM is called tremolo (as described in §9.2.1, p.270). In synthesis, AM can involve a much wider range of frequencies than are normally associated with tremolo. As the modulating frequency increases, the simple pulsing disappears and additional frequency partials become audible.

Figure 20.2 illustrates the simple AM block diagram form with two sinusoidal oscillators. The oscillator with frequency f_d is called the *modulator*, and that with frequency f_c is the *carrier*. This arrangement is a development from the general form in figure 20.1. The result in the frequency domain is shown in figure 20.3. Although there are only two sinusoidal oscillators, there are three output partials:

- One at carrier frequency f_c with peak amplitude a_o.
- One at frequency $(f_c + f_d)$ with peak amplitude $a_d/2$.
- One at frequency $(f_c - f_d)$ with peak amplitude $a_d/2$.

The sum and difference frequencies are known as *sideband partials*. If $a_o = 0$, then the partial at frequency f_c is not present in the output. In that circumstance the process is often called *ring modulation*.

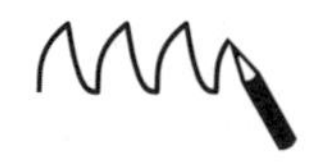

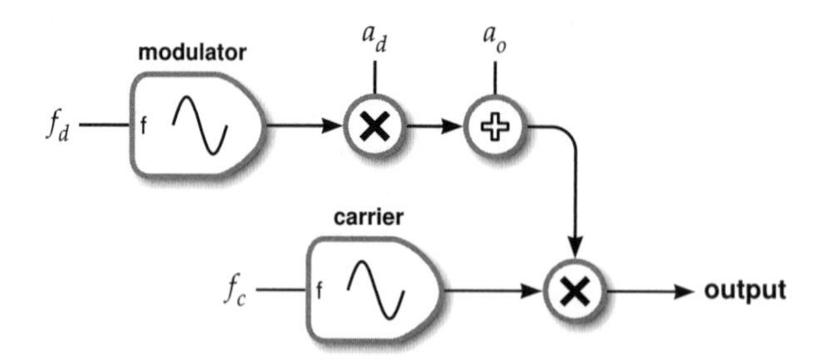

Figure 20.2 Simple AM

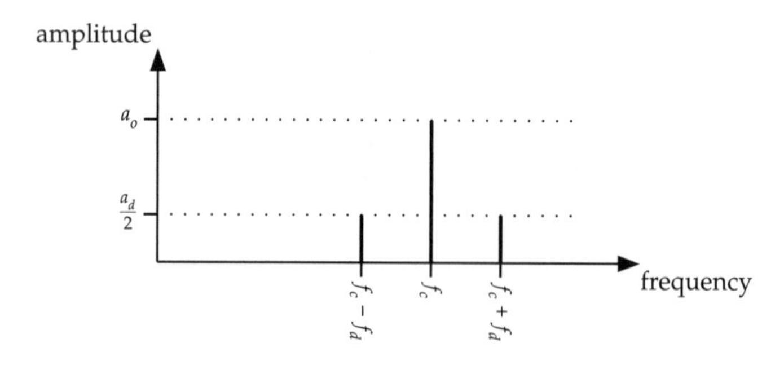

Figure 20.3 Simple AM frequency plot

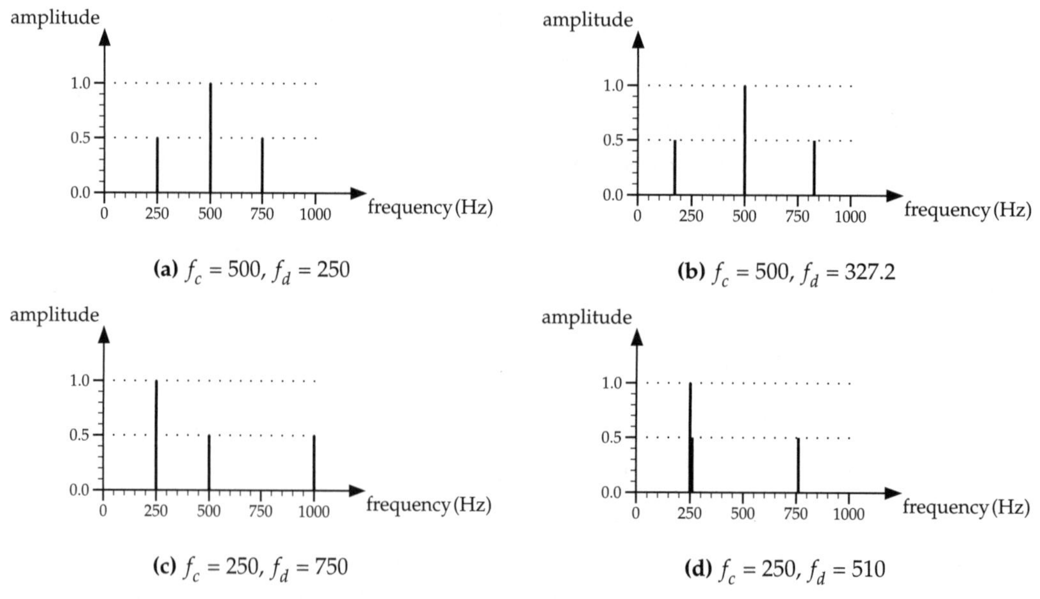

Figure 20.4 Example results for simple AM

Example results for simple AM are shown in figure 20.4. A value of 1 has been chosen for both a_d and a_0 in all cases:

- In figure 20.4a, the carrier and modulator frequencies are related such that the result is harmonic (with a fundamental frequency of 250Hz). Generally any simple integer ratio relationship between f_c and f_d (known as a *rational number*) will result in a harmonic spectrum where the partials are related by integer multipliers to a common frequency. In figure 20.4a, the $f_c : f_d$ ratio is 2:1, but other ratios also produce harmonic results such as 5:2, 4:1, and 4:3.
- Figure 20.4b has a frequency relationship that is deliberately not a simple integer ratio. The result is inharmonic, as is apparent from the pattern of frequencies in the plot.
- In figure 20.4c, the value of f_d is larger than f_c, which means that $(f_c - f_d)$ is a negative number (−500Hz). This reflects (wraps around) to become a positive frequency. A negative frequency means a negative phase increment for an oscillator (see equation 14.3, p.425), so the frequency is the same but the progress through the wave is reversed. In the case of figure 20.4c, the frequencies are still related as a rational number, and the result is harmonic with first, second, and fourth harmonics due to the choice of frequencies.
- Figure 20.4d also produces a negative frequency (−260Hz), which is reflected to a positive frequency of 260Hz. This is close to the carrier frequency (250Hz) and so interaction between the two partials occurs. The result is a rapid pulsing effect (as described in §16.1.2, p.483). If the value of f_d were 500Hz, it would line up exactly with the carrier partial at 250Hz. Such coincident partials can lead to summation or subtraction depending upon their relative phases.

The simple AM form of figure 20.2 can be extended to N carrier and M modulator oscillators as shown in figure 20.5. The result is that each of the carrier partials will have sum and difference partials for each modulator partial. Value a_0 controls the gain of all the carrier partials. Value a_{ci} controls the amplitude of carrier i **and** its sidebands. Value a_{dj} controls the amplitude of the sideband partials for modulator j (associated with modulation frequency f_{dj}) for all the carriers.

As an example, consider a situation with two carrier and three modulator partials:

f_{c1}	a_{c1}	f_{c2}	a_{c2}	f_{d1}	a_{d1}	f_{d2}	a_{d2}	f_{d3}	a_{d3}
500	1.0	1000	0.5	50	1.0	100	0.5	150	0.25

The result is illustrated in figure 20.6 with $a_0 = 1$. Note that each carrier partial (at 500Hz and 1000Hz) has gained sidebands at sum and difference frequencies related to each of the modulator partial frequencies. The a_{dj} values control the pattern of amplitudes either

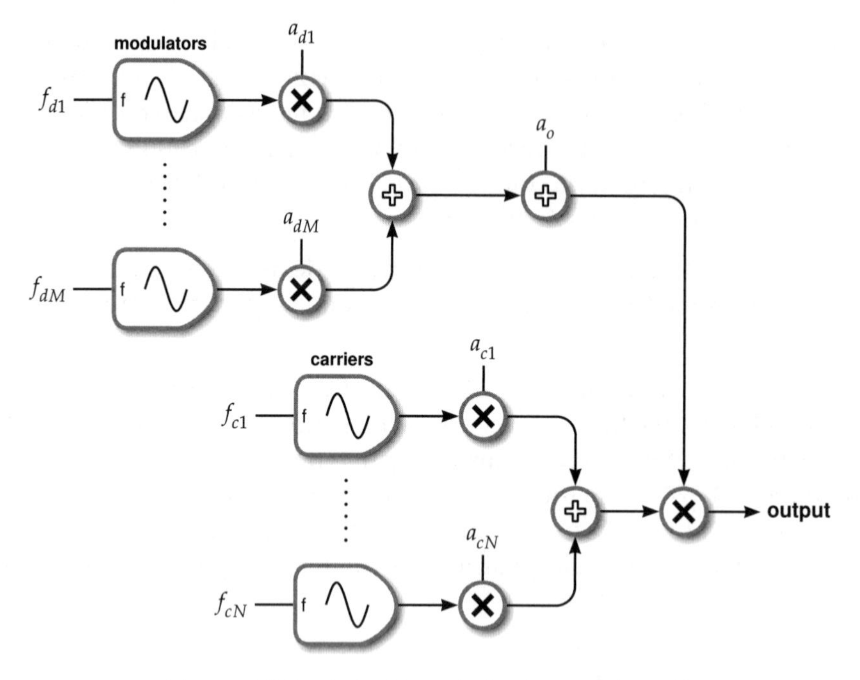

Figure 20.5 AM with multiple sinusoidal oscillators

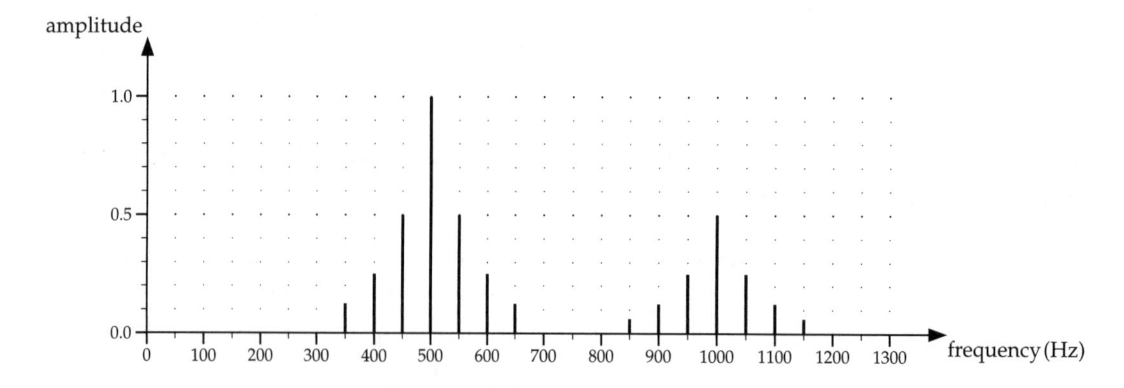

Figure 20.6 Example results for figure 20.5

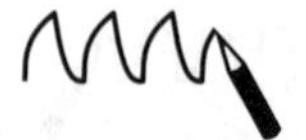

side of the carrier partials. The fact that a_{c2} is half the value of a_{c1} means that all associated partials are proportionally lower.

Amplitude modulation normally results in more partials in the output than are produced by the oscillators at the start of the process. In the example above, 5 sinusoidal oscillators produce 14 partials in the output. A complex oscillation can be considered as a weighted sum of sinusoidal oscillations. It is therefore possible to replace a parallel sum of oscillations in figure 20.5 with a single oscillator if desired. Whatever the quantity of partials, the properties found with two sinusoidal oscillators in the simple AM form remain true. That is, harmonic relationships will result from simple integer frequency ratios, negative frequencies will reflect to positive frequencies, and pulsing will result from partials that are close in frequency.

20.2.2 Practical Examples

Figure 20.7 applies AM as a modification process, rather than as a synthesizer. The carrier oscillator in figure 20.2 (p.562) has been replaced by a general input signal. The input might be a separately synthesized sound, or it might be a recorded input, for example. If the input has many partials it can be regarded as being similar to the sum of sinusoidal oscillations in figure 20.5. Each input partial gains sum and difference partials at a separation of f_d. Parameter a_d controls the amplitude of the additional partials, and a_o the amplitude of the original sound.

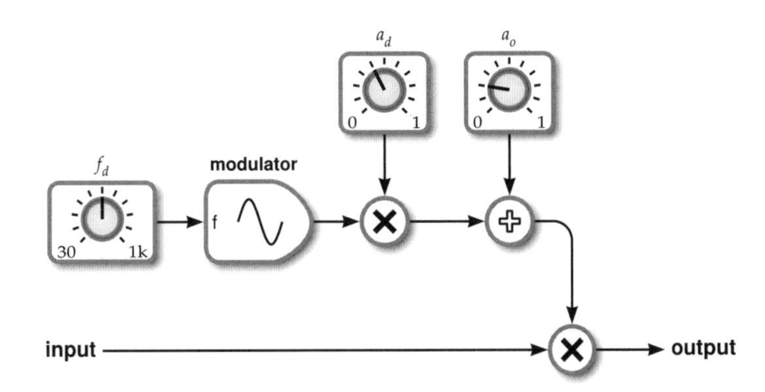

Figure 20.7 AM using a general input signal

The relationship between frequency f_d and the frequency partials in the input signal is important to the tonal character. If the input is fairly complex and changing over time it is unlikely that a fixed value of f_d will be a simple integer ratio relative to the input partials. A common result, therefore, is a clashing inharmonic sound character. For example, a normal voice input can have strong inharmonic elements added by this process, producing

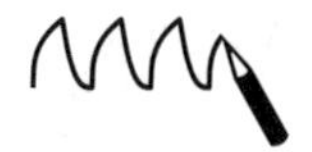

robot voices associated with old science fiction broadcasts and films. It is also interesting to try this effect on instruments such as guitars and drums as a way of creating a harsh inharmonic character.

Figure 20.8 illustrates an AM synthesizer controlled by a keyboard input. The carrier and modulator both produce harmonic waveforms with multiple partials. As with the previous examples, a_d and a_o control the balance of modulator-generated partials and the carrier respectively. The multiplying factors m_d and m_c are used to determine the frequency relationship between the oscillators and the keyboard output. The ratio of the multipliers determines the tonal character. An integer ratio of multipliers will achieve harmonic results, as all the sideband partials generated for all the carrier partials will be located at harmonic positions. Interesting pulsing and inharmonic effects can be achieved by moving away from integer multipliers.

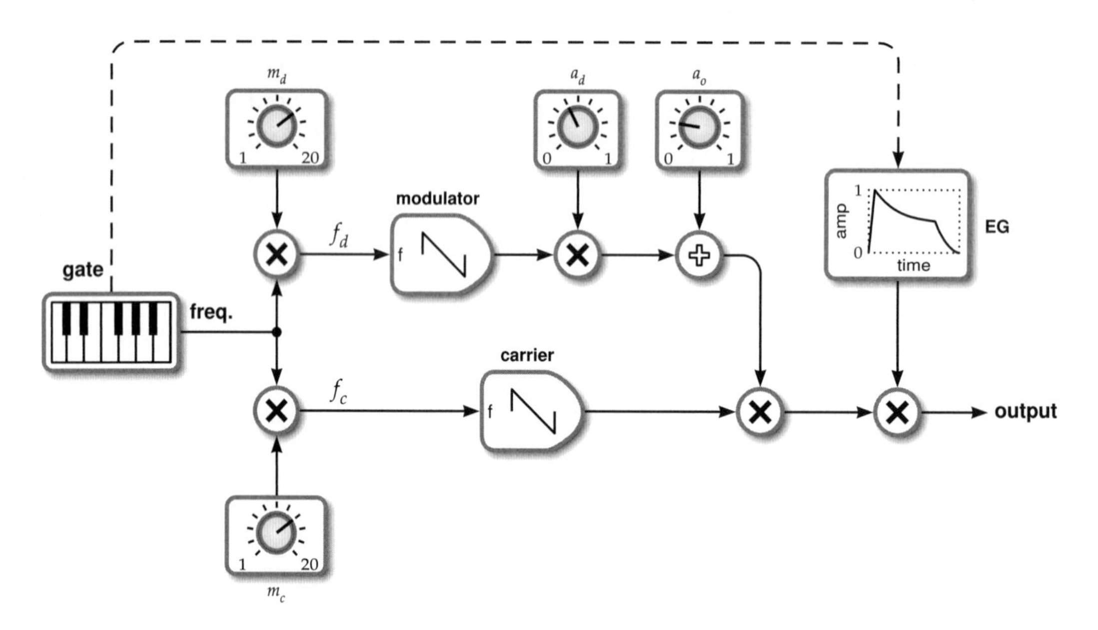

Figure 20.8 Keyboard-controlled AM

There are a number of ways of changing and extending the synthesizer:

- Different combinations of waveforms can be used for the oscillators.
- Envelope control can be used for parameter a_d to create varying amplitude sideband partials over time.
- Multiple parallel AM sections can be employed to construct a more sophisticated composite character, using the blending techniques described in Chapter 19.

20.3 Frequency Modulation

20.3.1 Basic Principles

Frequency Modulation (FM) is a periodic variation in the frequency of one signal produced by another signal. FM is called vibrato at low modulation rates (typically below 20Hz). As the modulating frequency increases, the perceived result changes from one where the rise and fall is audible, to a complex pattern of higher frequency partials. FM generally produces more complex results than AM for similar computational effort.

Figure 20.9 illustrates the simple FM block diagram form with two sinusoidal oscillators. As with AM, the oscillators are called the modulator and the carrier. This time the frequency of the carrier oscillator is varying, rather than its amplitude. Variable I is called the *modulation index*. I is multiplied by f_d to create a gain value that determines how much modulating oscillator output is added to the principal carrier frequency f_c. Value If_d is, therefore, the peak frequency deviation. The modulating oscillator has no effect when $I = 0$, as the input to the second oscillator is just f_c.

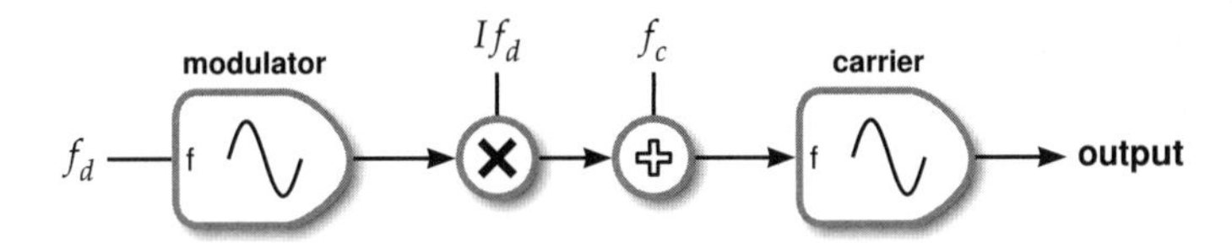

Figure 20.9 Simple FM

The simple FM form can produce a very large number of partials in the output signal, despite having only two sinusoidal oscillators and three parameters (I, f_d, and f_c). The output is:

- One partial at carrier frequency f_c with peak amplitude $J_0(I)$.
- Pairs of sideband partials either side of the carrier partial at frequencies $(f_c + nf_d)$ and $(f_c - nf_d)$ with peak amplitude $J_n(I)$, where n is an integer with values 1, 2, 3, 4, and so on.

Like simple AM, this produces a partial at the carrier frequency f_c, and a pair of partials either side of the carrier frequency at f_d away. However, there are also pairs $2f_d$ away from the carrier, $3f_d$ away, $4f_d$ away and so on. The amplitudes of the output partials are controlled by a function $J_n(I)$, which is called a *Bessel function of the first kind*. The Bessel functions depend on modulation index I, so as I changes, the amplitudes of the partials will vary.

The first 11 Bessel functions are shown in figure 20.10. As the value of I changes, the amplitudes of the output partials will vary according to the lines in the figure:

- The amplitude at frequency f_c is J_0.
- The amplitude at frequencies $(f_c + f_d)$ and $(f_c - f_d)$ is J_1.
- The amplitude at frequencies $(f_c + 2f_d)$ and $(f_c - 2f_d)$ is J_2.
- The amplitude at frequencies $(f_c + 3f_d)$ and $(f_c - 3f_d)$ is J_3.

  (and so on)

The FM synthesis technique is distinctive not only for producing a large number of output partials from two sinusoidal oscillators, but also because control over the amplitude weightings of the partials is achieved through a single parameter (I). The difficulty is in understanding the configuration of I, f_d, and f_c to achieve the desired tonal result.

Figure 20.11 shows the frequency domain output for different values of modulation index I. Note that negative values of $J_n(I)$ are shown as a positive amplitude on a conventional frequency domain plot, as phase is not included. Varying the modulation index allows patterns of amplitude to be produced as the different Bessel functions rise and fall at different times for different sideband partials. This allows the creation of a wide range of tonal characters.

There are a number of significant properties of the simple FM arrangement:

- When I is 0, only the carrier frequency partial exists in the output. As I increases, an increasing number of Bessel functions have significant amplitude causing the bandwidth of sideband partials to increase.
- Modulation frequency f_d controls the spacing between sideband partials and so the amount of spread around the carrier frequency. Larger values of f_d and I mean more amplitude further away from f_c.
- The relationship between f_c and f_d has similarities to that seen with AM (figure 20.4, p.562). Simple integer ratio relationships (rational numbers) produce a harmonic spectrum. Away from those simple integer ratios the result is inharmonic. Negative frequency partials can be produced, which reflect (wrap around) to become positive frequencies.
- The large number of partials that can be produced with FM increases the likelihood of interaction between partials when they are close together. This can produce pulsing effects, or summation, or subtraction. The Bessel functions can have positive or negative amplitude values, which is also important when considering the way in which two partials will combine.

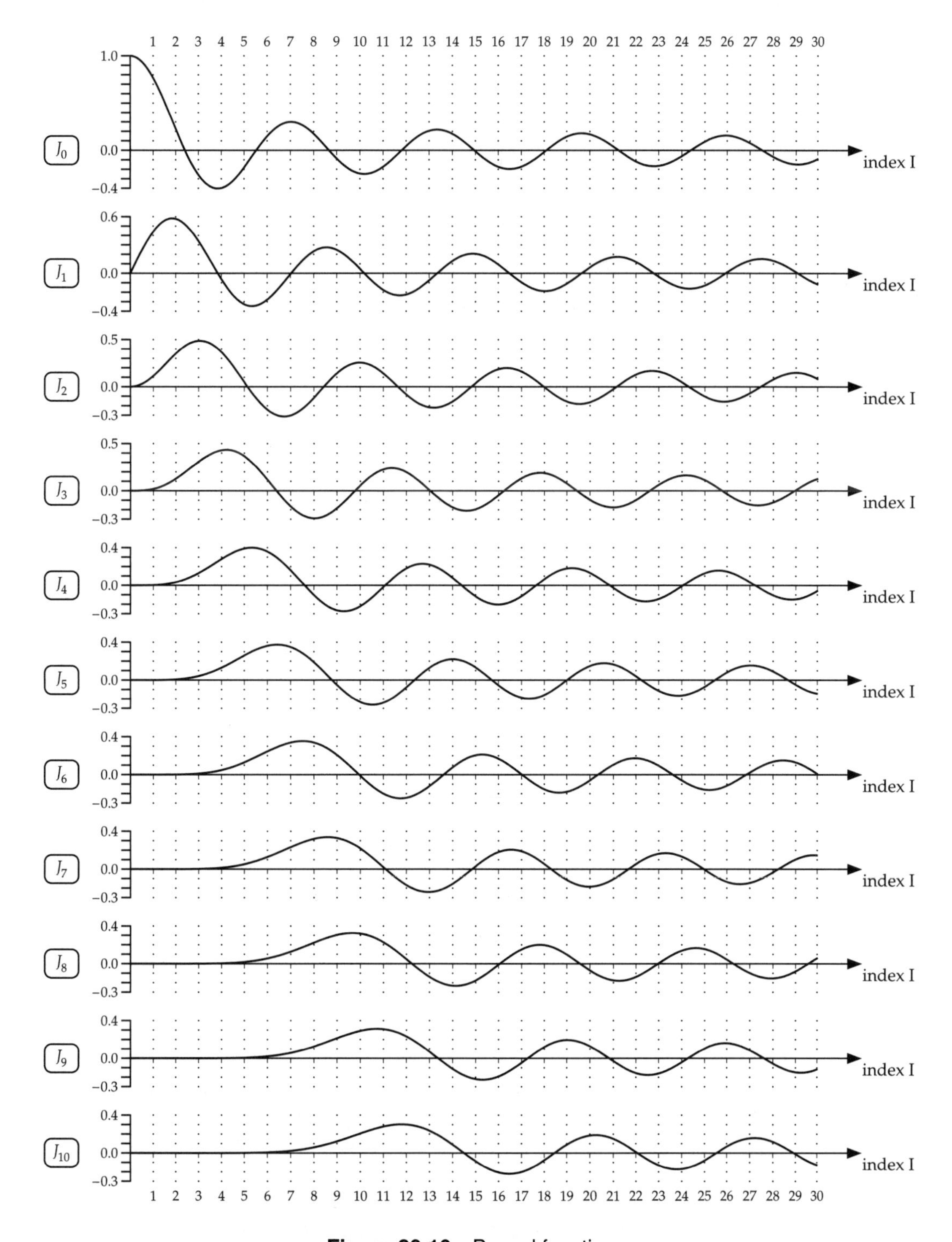

Figure 20.10 Bessel functions

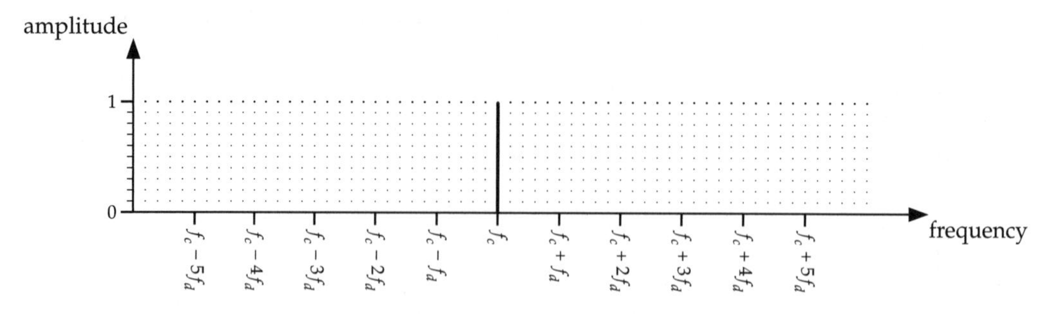

(a) Modulation index I = 0

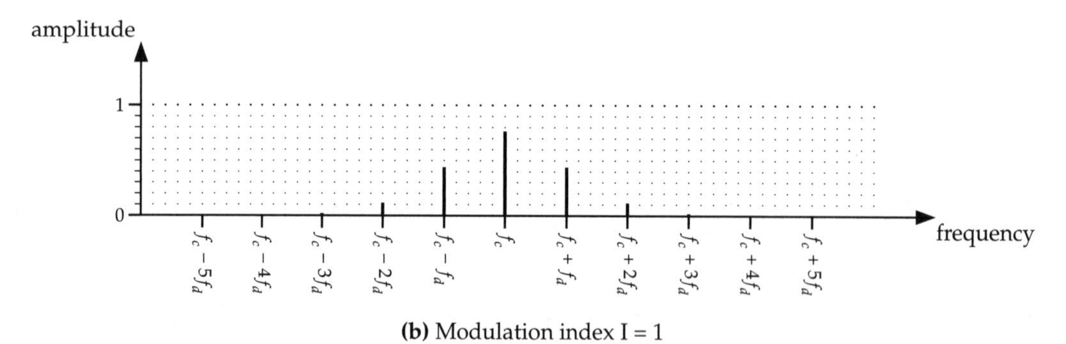

(b) Modulation index I = 1

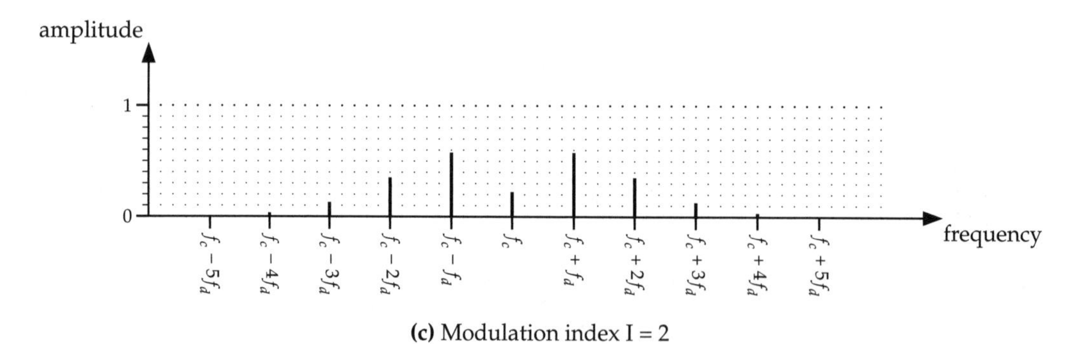

(c) Modulation index I = 2

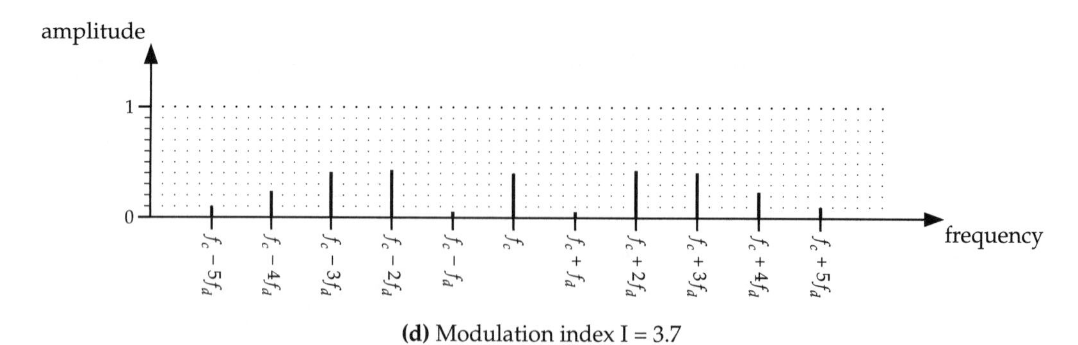

(d) Modulation index I = 3.7

Figure 20.11 Example simple FM output spectra

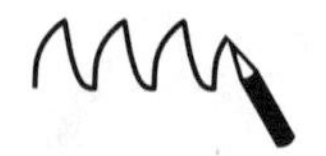

- Small changes in the modulation index I will normally result in modest changes in tonal character, as the Bessel functions vary smoothly. Varying the index over time can therefore create interesting variations in timbre. Starting at a low value of modulation index (say, 2) and moving towards 0 causes the spectrum to simplify towards the carrier partial alone. Larger changes in I will cause significant tonal variation as the Bessel functions alternately increase and decrease in oscillating patterns. From the perspective of trying to achieve effective control, the difficulty is that there is not a simple relationship between modulation index and tonal variation.
- The frequency and amplitude pattern of sideband partials around the carrier and the shape of the Bessel functions means that there is often a distinctive tonal character to FM synthesized sounds and characteristic results when parameters change.

20.3.2 Parallel FM

Figure 20.12 illustrates a practical FM synthesizer that uses parallel pairs of sinusoidal oscillators. Two parallel sections are shown, but any number can be used depending on the required result. All the parallel paths are summed together to create the output. Each section is fundamentally the same as figure 20.9 (p.567), but there are a number of additions to increase the usability of the arrangement:

- The modulator and carrier frequencies (f_{di} and f_{ci}, where i is between 1 and N) are related to the output frequency from the keyboard by multiplying factors m_{di} and m_{ci}. This means that the frequencies will track with the keyboard note. The multipliers achieve particular frequency partial relationships as described previously. If it is not desirable for frequencies to change with the keyboard output for a particular sound then the multipliers could be replaced with fixed values.
- Each section has an envelope generator that is used to control the modulation index, with a user specified range of I_{li} to I_{ui}. Not all synthesis configurations will require a changing modulation index, so either a flat envelope could be used, or the envelope generator could be replaced by a fixed value in those cases.
- The amplitude envelope generators and amplitude gains a_i determine the variation over time and overall balance of amplitude between the different FM sections.

There are significant similarities between the parallel simple FM arrangement and the forms found in figure 16.3 (p.486) for additive synthesis and figure 19.5 (p.551) for blend-based synthesis. In a similar way to those techniques, the aim is to construct a composite sound from independent synthesis paths whose partials are summed together. The partials can interact as described in §16.1.2 (p.483) and §19.1 (p.544). The independent paths allow different parts of the sound to develop at different times, or for some parts to last longer than others (such as a transient element that is only present at the start of the sound). Similarly, the timbral change can be quite different for different parallel sections.

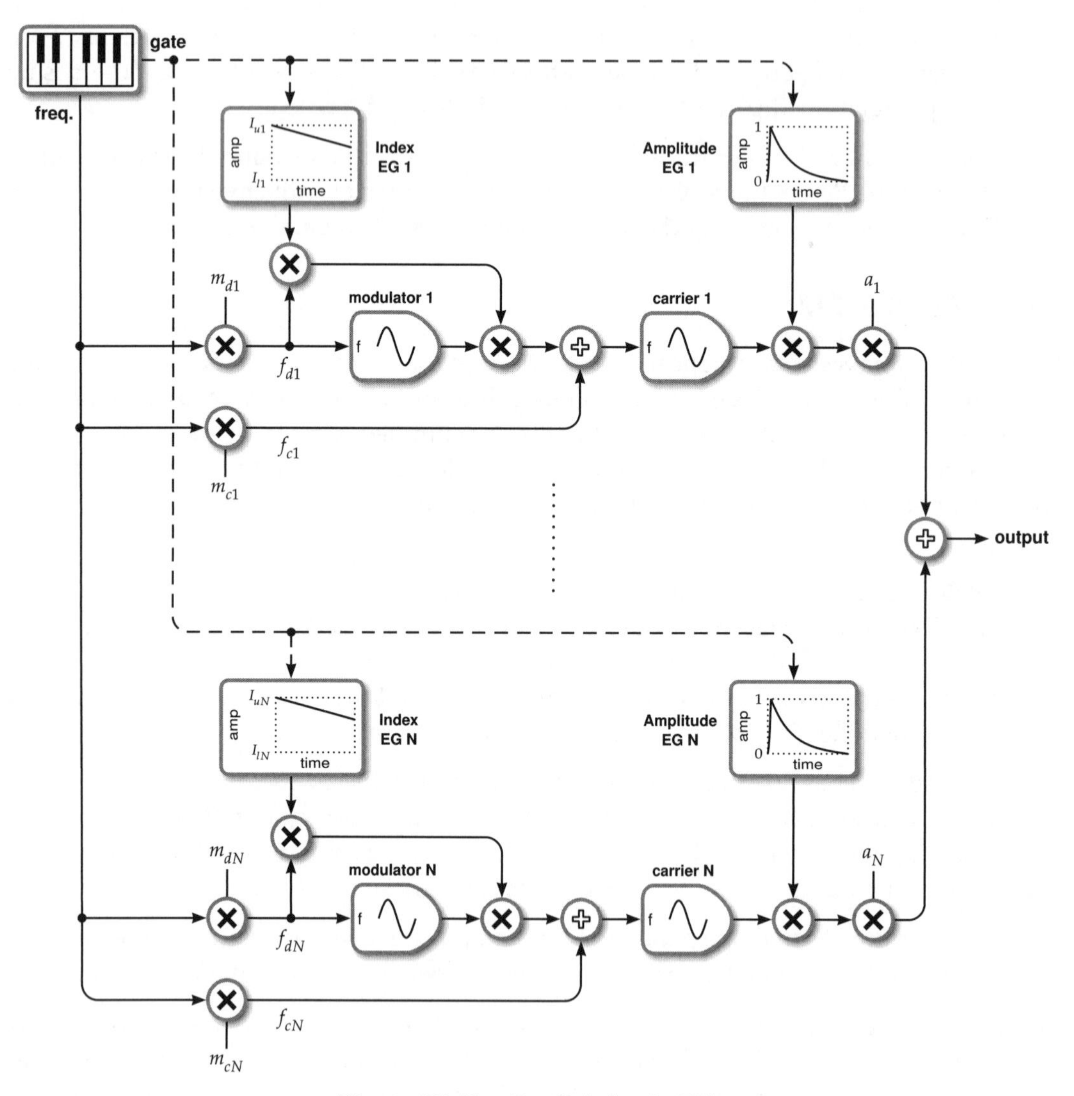

Figure 20.12 Parallel simple FM

Using a single modulator and carrier pair, sound characters such as the following can be created:

sound character	m_{d1}	m_{c1}	I_{l1}	I_{u1}	index envelope	amplitude envelope
bell-like	7.072	1	0	2	gradually decreasing	percussive
brass-like	1	1	0	2.5	rapid increase and moderate decrease to lower level	attack, decay, sustain, release
clarinet-like	4	1	0	1.2	gentle swell	gentle swell

Although labelled to indicate their general character, none of the above settings produce convincingly natural tones. They are a guide to the type of configuration that is needed. FM as a synthesis method is powerful in terms of achieving rich, often distinctively synthetic sounds. To avoid the results becoming sound effects with huge timbral variation, a certain amount of subtlety is required in the use of modulation index variation and the relationships between the frequency multiplying factors.

One of the benefits of the parallel form is in creating a blend of similar signals in parallel, but with slight variations in frequency multipliers to create broader or thicker tones. For example, using non-varying modulation index values and five parallel FM sections:

sound character	m_{d1}	m_{c1}	I_1	m_{d2}	m_{c2}	I_2	m_{d3}	m_{c3}	I_3	m_{d4}	m_{c4}	I_4	m_{d5}	m_{c5}	I_5
close to harmonic	1	0.502	3	1	1.003	3	1	1.998	3	1	1	3	1	2.005	3
somewhat inharmonic	3.45	1	1	3.482	1	1	3.5	0.999	1	3.515	1	2	3.527	1	2

The "close to harmonic" configuration in the above table might be used to create an interesting evolving sound by using long amplitude envelopes. Those envelopes could swell at different times to create a changing character. The "somewhat inharmonic" configuration might be used to create a more percussive sound with amplitude envelopes with a rapid onset and exponential decay.

20.3.3 Multiple Modulator FM Arrangements

The parallel simple FM arrangement in figure 20.12 has the advantage of independence of control for the different parallel sections. This makes parameter configuration fairly comprehensible, as each can be configured in turn and then combined at the end. However, there are other ways of arranging patterns of oscillators to achieve frequency modulation.

The limitation in practical terms is an ability to understand how to choose parameter values to achieve the desired tonal character as the complexity increases.

Figure 20.13 illustrates multiple modulators driving a single carrier oscillator. The number of modulating oscillators can be varied; it does not have to be three. The result is not the same as each modulator having its own carrier oscillator (as in figure 20.12). Figure 20.14 has a simple FM pair of oscillators, which in turn is modulated by a third oscillator in series. This arrangement can be extended by adding further series modulators in a similar manner, if required. In a practical configuration the values of f_{di} and f_c are likely to be the frequency from a keyboard multiplied by suitable factors.

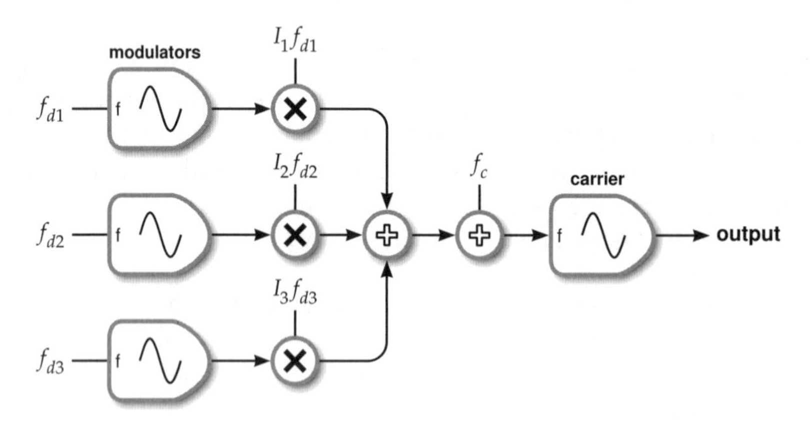

Figure 20.13 Parallel multiple modulator, single carrier FM

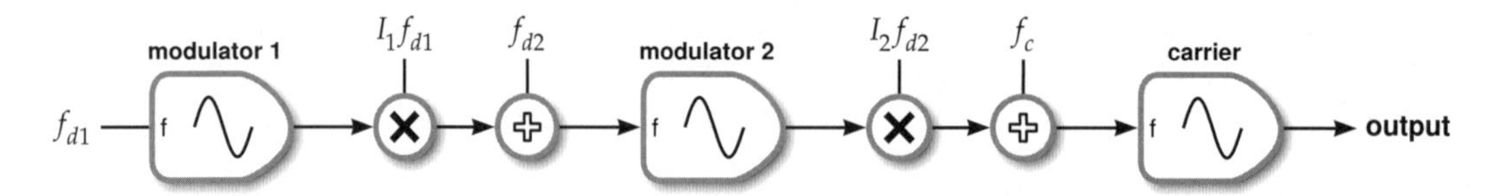

Figure 20.14 Series multiple modulator, single carrier FM

In both the parallel and series multiple-modulator arrangements, the carrier oscillator receives an input signal that is more complex than a single sinusoid (which was the case in previous examples). In practical terms, these extensions lead to a multiplication of the number of partials produced by the synthesizer and so a potentially more rich and complex result. In essence, the sideband partials found in simple FM gain their own sideband partials.

The parallel multiple modulator form with three modulators has a fairly comprehensible response to parameter variations, where simple integer relationships between the frequencies and a keyboard input frequency will tend to produce harmonic results. In the series

form, modulators 1 and 2 can produce many more partials than the three oscillators in the parallel form, given a sufficient value for modulation index I_1. Therefore the input to the carrier oscillator will be more complex. This can make it hard to manage unless the parameters are chosen carefully. Simple integer frequency relationships and low values of modulation index are a reasonable place to start configuration. This might be followed by subtle enveloped variations in modulation index.

20.4 Further Modulation Methods

Although modulation of amplitude and frequency are the most well known methods for purposes of synthesis, the principles can be applied to other types of parameters. Figure 20.15 illustrates three example modulation methods. The differences in the types of parameters being modulated affects the tonal character of the result. The method is fundamentally the same in each case, where a modulating oscillator with fundamental frequency f_d whose output is scaled by depth a_d and offset by a_o is applied to a synthesis parameter. The values of a_d and a_o must be chosen to achieve an appropriate range of values, such as frequency values for the lowpass filter and values between 0 and 1 for the cross-fade and duty cycle methods.

At low modulation rates and depths, the effects can be gentle tonal variations over time. At higher rates (considerably above 20Hz) similar principles apply to those described previously in this chapter:

- The relationship between f_d and f_c is similar to that used for AM and FM. A simple integer ratio will normally lead to a harmonic result. Slight deviations from an integer ratio will produce pulsing/phasing effects. Where the frequencies are further away from simple integer relationships there is more likely to be an inharmonic or dissonant result.
- The filter modulation method (figure 20.15a) is very similar to the design in figure 9.15 (p.277) where low modulation rates are used. The cross-fade modulation method (figure 20.15b) uses the idea seen in figure 9.5 (p.269). In both cases changing the main oscillator waveform, or the modulation parameters will enable the tonal character to be changed.
- The Pulse-Width Modulation (PWM) method uses a variation in the duty cycle ("d" input to the oscillator). The duty cycle is the proportion of the output cycle that has a value of +1 in the pulse wave (as described in §14.2.2, p.427). One feature of PWM is its ability to create quite strong interval/chordal type sound characters where frequency offsets of a number of semitones are also close to integer frequency relationships. For example, when f_c is 300Hz, chordal sounds are heard when f_d is 133.63Hz (14 semitones below, 4:9 ratio), or 224.75Hz (5 semitones below, 3:4 ratio).

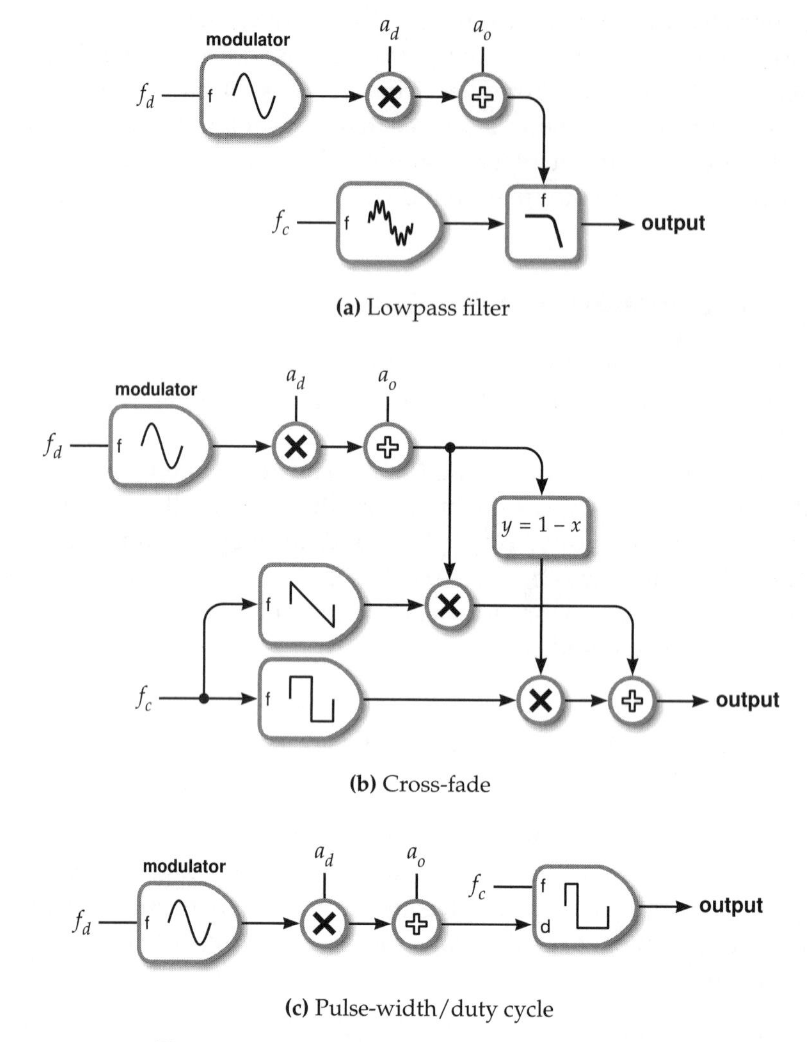

(a) Lowpass filter

(b) Cross-fade

(c) Pulse-width/duty cycle

Figure 20.15 Alternative modulation examples

Similar principles can be applied to other audio process parameters. There is also scope for more complex synthesis arrangements involving enveloped controls, multiple parallel sections, and so on (similar to those described in §20.3.2, p.571 for FM synthesis). These methods might also be combined with subtractive synthesis (Chapter 17) for further tonal shaping.

20.5 Developing Processes and Learning More

Modulation-based synthesis uses standard blocks that are found in audio programming libraries and environments. It is, however, necessary to check that the process element being modulated has the required capabilities:

- In FM synthesis (such as figure 20.9, p.567), there is the potential for the carrier oscillator to be modulated with negative frequency values. This means that the oscillator algorithm must allow negative phase increments. The carrier oscillator must also be able to cope with very large fundamental frequencies; for example when the three parameters I, f_d, and f_c are all large values. Algorithm 14.2 (p.427) is designed to handle these issues.
- When modulating a process element control parameter, such as filter cutoff frequency (figure 20.15a) or duty cycle (figure 20.15c), there is an assumption that the underlying algorithms can cope with high modulation rates. If the designer has assumed that these will only be updated slowly and infrequently, then they might only be processed at control rates rather than audio rates (as described in §23.1.2, p.633), which will affect the tonality of the result.

The tonality of modulation-based synthesis can be changed in subtle ways by small details, such as the relative phase of oscillators and the sample rate. It might make a difference if the phase of oscillators is set to zero on the start of each sound event, or if a cosine rather than a sine oscillator is chosen. The interaction between coincident partials is a consideration, which can happen when partials with negative frequencies are reflected to become positive frequencies that align with other partials, for example. The relative phases of those partials will affect whether there is summation or subtraction of amplitude. These issues mean that slightly different results can occur on different systems, even if the parameter values would suggest that they should be the same.

FM synthesis had an advantage historically of producing a wide range of sound characters (of significant complexity in the frequency domain) with modest computation. The requirement for low computation is less significant than it used to be, which makes other features of the technique more pertinent.

The non-linear relationship between control parameters and the spectral results makes FM a less intuitive synthesis method than subtractive synthesis (Chapter 17). It also makes it harder to achieve direct manipulation of individual partials, which is possible with sinusoidal additive synthesis (Chapter 16). However, the tonal characters that are often achieved with FM synthesis and other modulation techniques sets them apart from other techniques, which is why they are worth using. Such characters are often the result of the particular parameter relationships described in this chapter.

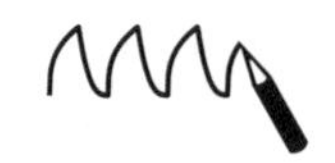

Further discussion of modulation-based synthesis and FM in particular can be found in these books:

Pirkle, Will. 2015. *Designing Software Synthesizer Plug-Ins in C++: For RackAFX, VST3, and Audio Units.* Burlington, MA: Focal Press.

Russ, Martin. 2013. *Sound Synthesis and Sampling (Third Edition).* Burlington, MA: Focal Press.

The following source provides some more advanced material that relates to this chapter, which can be used for further study:

Chowning, John M. 1973. "The Synthesis of Complex Audio Spectra by Means of Frequency Modulation." *Journal of the Audio Engineering Society* 21:7:526–534.

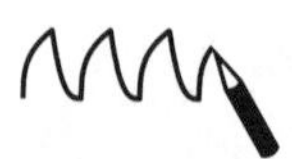

21

Waveguide Physical Models

21.1 Introduction

21.1.1 Basic Concepts

The synthesis techniques described in previous chapters are mainly concerned with creating particular time domain and frequency domain features, or recreating the output of a particular sound source. For example, additive, subtractive, AM, and FM techniques are used to create particular harmonics, inharmonics, spectral envelope characteristics, and amplitude envelopes. Such techniques can produce a very wide range of different sounds, but the synthesis parameters might not be closely related to the physics of the instrument being modelled, making naturalistic changes harder to achieve.

The alternative is to create a model of a sound-producing object from physical principles. A *physical model* of a clarinet can be constructed in software and then the virtual instrument can generate sound by being "blown". This allows the properties of the clarinet (such as the design of the mouthpiece, the material of the body, and the amount of breath pressure applied) to be changed to produce different results.

The physical model approach is likely to result in a form that generates a limited range of tonal characters (much like an acoustic instrument). For example, a clarinet physical model is usually quite different from a drum model. The advantage is that the model can display behaviour that is similar to that found in the physical world. Under-blowing a modelled clarinet might produce a breathy sound lacking tone, and over-blowing might produce a squeak or no sound at all. This can result in a very interesting and naturalistic synthesizer.

Like sampling, creating convincing recreations of acoustic sound sources is a common use of physical models. Physical models normally take more computation than sampling and are more complex. However, a recorded sample represents a single set of performance conditions. To construct a complete realistic sampled instrument usually requires recording many samples and then editing and blending the sounds such that a continuum of character is available to the performer. A single physical model can produce an entire instrument with naturalistic dynamic control over the sound character.

While physical models are principally associated with imitative synthesis, the techniques also provide opportunities to create instruments that do not exist in the real world, by extending or modifying the model structures. For example, once a wind instrument mouthpiece has been created, it might be coupled to a drum head. Strangely shaped resonators might be synthesized that are impossible to construct from materials available in the real world. Similarly, a virtual wooden instrument might change shape and size during performance. This provides interesting possibilities for creating new sounds.

21.1.2 Structure of a Physical Model

The most common way of describing the basic behaviour of a sound-producing object, such as a musical instrument, is in terms of *excitation* and *resonance*:

- An exciter provides the raw energy or vibration to the instrument, such as a drum stick, piano hammer, violin bow, guitar plectrum, or air flow against a clarinet reed.
- A resonator is stimulated by the excitation and extends, amplifies, and shapes the tone of the subsequent vibration, such as a drum head, piano string, xylophone bar, wooden violin body, or an air column in a clarinet. There might be multiple resonators in a single instrument that are coupled together, such as a string on an acoustic guitar, its wooden body, and the air inside the body.

Using a different exciter without changing the rest of the instrument will change the resulting sound. For example, a bowed violin sounds different from one that is plucked. A particular exciter can often be varied in its physical form or application, such as in terms of the size, shape, material, or force of application. For example, striking a cymbal with a brush will produce a different amplitude and frequency balance compared to using a metal bar. In a more subtle way, the way in which breath is applied to a flute mouthpiece, or plucking a guitar string with a pick rather than a finger, can change the tonal character of the result.

A resonator might be varied in terms of size, shape, or material. For example, a drum head might be made of plastic or animal skin, and the thickness might be uniform, or vary between the centre and rim. If the excitation remains the same, a change of resonator will affect the tonal result, even if only one of its characteristics is changed. For example, striking plastic, metal, and wooden bars with the same beater will produce different results, even if they are all the same size. Similarly, changing the size and thickness of a cymbal has an effect on the tonality and frequency emphasis, even if the general shape and material remains the same.

Many exciters produce an impulsive input, a buzzing sound with a large number of harmonics, wideband noise, or spectrally-rich content in general. A resonator will then filter components from that input. For example, striking a chime bar has the effect of injecting wideband energy, which the bar turns into a somewhat exponentially decaying tonal output (as seen in §3.2.1, p.49). This source-filter arrangement has similarities to the subtractive synthesis techniques seen in Chapter 17.

Acoustic instrument behaviour is often described in terms of *resonant modes*. The modal frequencies are those that a resonator supports strongly, and so those that are likely to dominate in the output sound. These are seen in frequency spectrum plots such as those in Chapter 4. The wideband excitation is reduced to a smaller number of partials in resonance. It can be seen when analysing an instrument like a struck chime bar that

the process is not instantaneous. When the excitation is continuous (such as bowing or blowing), there is not such a clear separation between excitation and resonance as seen with a struck instrument.

The relationship between exciters and resonators can be quite complex. There is a coupling between the parts of the instrument through which energy is transferred, ultimately producing audible air pressure variations:

- Striking a cymbal with a drumstick is a simple relationship. There is a brief input of energy and then the single resonator reacts to that input.
- In a wind instrument (such as a clarinet or saxophone) blowing into the mouthpiece excites the reed, which causes air resonance in the tube of the instrument, which in turn causes the reed vibration to become more regular. That is, there is a feedback path from the air column to the reed.
- With an acoustic guitar, a plucked excitation causes the first resonator (the string) to vibrate. The string vibration is passed to the body of the instrument (the wooden plates and the air inside) which resonates, amplifying and shaping the tone. The body resonating will also change the way in which the string vibrates (a feedback path).

There are many ways that the exciter-resonator coupling forms could be constructed, or extended, to mirror the principal characteristics of the sound source of interest. This is a useful start in creating a physical model.

21.1.3 Waveguides

A physical model of an acoustic sound source can be realised in different ways. The most accurate and potentially most realistic results are achieved through a mathematical model of the physics of the sound source. An approach that is more accessible to those without a strong mathematical background is to consider how the component parts of a sound source might be represented as an analogous system of linked excitations, delays, and filters. This is what is called a digital *waveguide* synthesis physical model.

There is some danger of the analogy between waveguide synthesis techniques and the actual physics of an acoustic sound source being stretched too far. However, if the synthesizer is constructed with due consideration to the physical acoustic inspiration, the results can be remarkably natural. In some cases they can produce an interesting and complex sonic result from modest computation.

Waveguide physical models are based on the idea of a *travelling wave* propagating on an enclosed path. As was described in Chapter 10, a sound wave will travel at a finite speed through a medium (such as air, or metal, or wood) until it reaches a boundary, at which point the wave is likely to be partly reflected and partly absorbed. Figure 21.1 illustrates the idea of travelling waves on a plucked string. In this case there is a plucked excitation, at which point two waves travel in opposite directions along the string. When those waves reach boundaries (such as the termination produced by the nut, a fret, or the bridge) some of the energy is absorbed (or transferred into a second resonator, such as the body of an acoustic guitar), and some is reflected back down the string towards the other end as inverted waves. The waves cross over and continue until they reach a boundary again, where they are partly absorbed and partly reflected again. This continues until all the energy is dissipated.

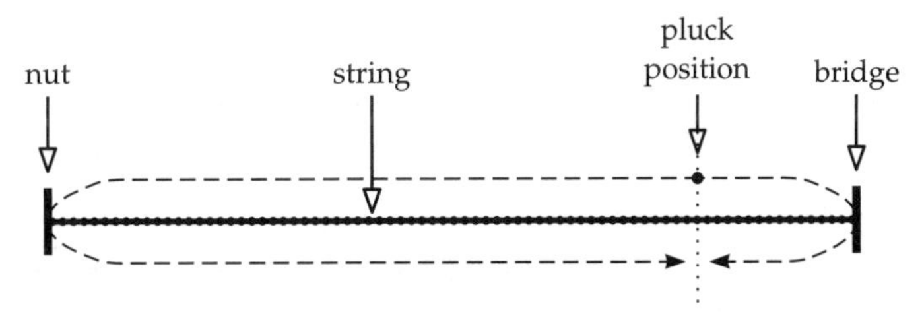

Figure 21.1 Travelling waves on a plucked string

All travelling waves experience delays (which reflect the dimensions of the instrument and the speed of propagation), filtering (different absorption at different frequencies) and reflections. A waveguide resonator simulates a travelling wave effect using a repeated cycle of delays and filtering. By tailoring the delays and filtering in different ways, different resonant effects can be produced.

The waveguide approach achieves a repeated cycle of delays and filtering with a feedback loop. The desired result is a resonant decay that is not too rapid, but neither should the system be unstable (where the output becomes larger and larger until it reaches the limits of the system). The problems are similar to those when creating recirculating reverberation effects (described in §10.4, p.323). When testing values for parameters that affect stability, it is worth keeping sound output at low amplitude, in case the output suddenly increases in level.

A simple oscillator-based synthesizer form (such as that in figure 13.8, p.407) will display consistency of output over a wide fundamental frequency range. A particular physical model, however, is likely to achieve its best tonal effect and consistency over a modest note range, once configured. Real instruments also have limitations in those respects. Limiting the performance note range in the model can also make it easier to optimise results with suitable mappings from note number to parameter values.

The following sections describe different waveguide physical models. Recreating the precise nuances of an acoustic musical instrument is complex, but modelling the general characteristics is less difficult.

21.2 Waveguide Plucked String

21.2.1 Simplest Plucked String

A simple physical model is the plucked string form illustrated in figure 21.2. This type of instrument is very similar to the well-known *Karplus-Strong* algorithm. It produces a reasonable approximation to the required sound with a small number of component parts.

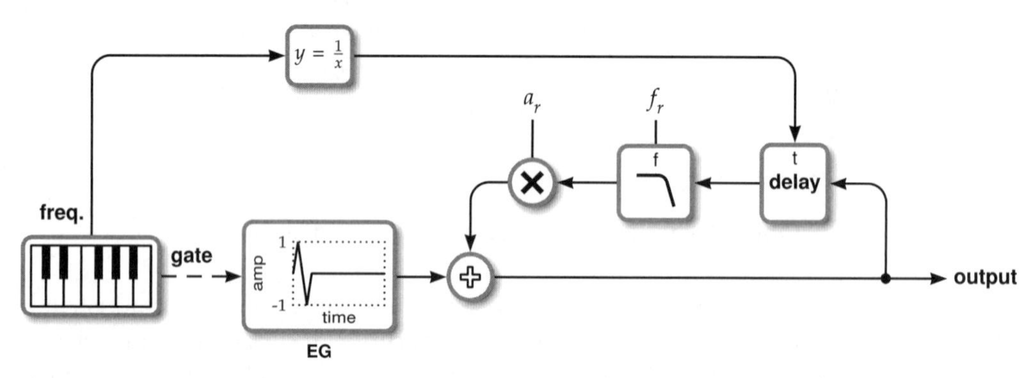

Figure 21.2 Simplified waveguide plucked string form

The excitation is produced by the envelope generator. This is a **single** cycle of a triangular waveform (not a repeating oscillation), which simulates the effect of plucking a string. The length of the excitation cycle affects the character of the result. Typically the cycle length will be somewhere between 1ms and 10ms, where shorter lengths tend to produce greater high frequency emphasis, and longer lengths produce a warmer, softer sound. This relates to the type of object used to pluck the string; a fingernail or plectrum produces a more impulse-like excitation than a softer object such as a fingertip. Other types of excitation will be described in more detail later.

The excitation passes through to the output. The feedback loop is a simplified waveguide, which forms the resonator. It represents the effects applied to the travelling wave as it progresses along the string, is reflected, and returns to the point of excitation. In reality, there are two travelling waves emanating from the plucking point on a string (one heading towards the bridge and one heading towards the stopped fret or nut on the neck, as shown in figure 21.1), but this bidirectional situation can be simplified to a single feedback loop.

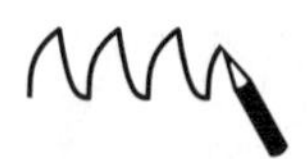

There are three elements in the loop; a delay to represent the time for the wave to travel along the string, a lowpass filter to represent the frequency-dependent losses in the string (principally more attenuation at higher frequencies), and a multiplier to represent general absorption (with values of a_r between 0 and 1). When the wave is delayed, filtered, and attenuated, it passes through to the output, and then around the loop again. Therefore, a new output wave will be produced at a regularity determined by the delay time. In order to achieve a particular repetition frequency, the delay time T is related to the fundamental frequency by $T = 1/F$. The filter will also impart a slight delay (as discussed in §6.4, p.164), which will require a compensating offset in the equation that calculates the delay time.

There are similarities between this form and the recirculating echo effect in figure 10.25 (p.315). The principal difference is that the delay times are much shorter than an echo, such that the periodic repetition is an audible pitch. For example, a 1kHz fundamental frequency requires a delay time of 1ms. The delay will be implemented as described in §8.1.4 (p.232). The delay in samples will be calculated as follows, where f_S is the sample rate, F is the fundamental frequency, and d_c is the number of samples necessary to compensate for any filter delay:

$$\text{delay in samples} = \frac{f_S}{F} - d_c \tag{21.1}$$

As the required fundamental frequency increases, the delay value decreases. If the delay is truncated to a whole number of samples, then significant pitching errors can occur at high fundamental frequencies, as illustrated in figure 21.3. It is necessary, therefore, to use an interpolated fractional delay to achieve correct pitching. Interpolation methods are described in §8.2 (p.237).

Figure 21.4 shows the output of the system just after the excitation has occurred, and at a point further into the sound. The first cycle of the output wave is the same as the triangular input excitation (which is 4ms long in this case). Subsequent cycles are the versions that have passed through the delay, filter, and multiplier blocks and returned to the input of the delay. The distance between each cycle is T seconds (the cycle length is about 9.09ms in this case, in order to achieve a fundamental frequency of 110Hz).

The waveform gradually becomes smoother over time as the filter attenuates the high frequencies. This means that the tonal character is gradually changing throughout the sound. The filter and multiplier combine to remove amplitude from the wave on each cycle, which causes an exponential decay. The rapid attack at the start of the sound and the exponential decay are an appropriate simulation for a plucked string, as described in §3.2.2 (p.51).

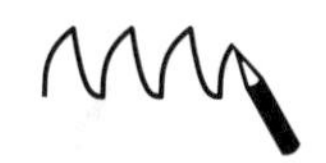

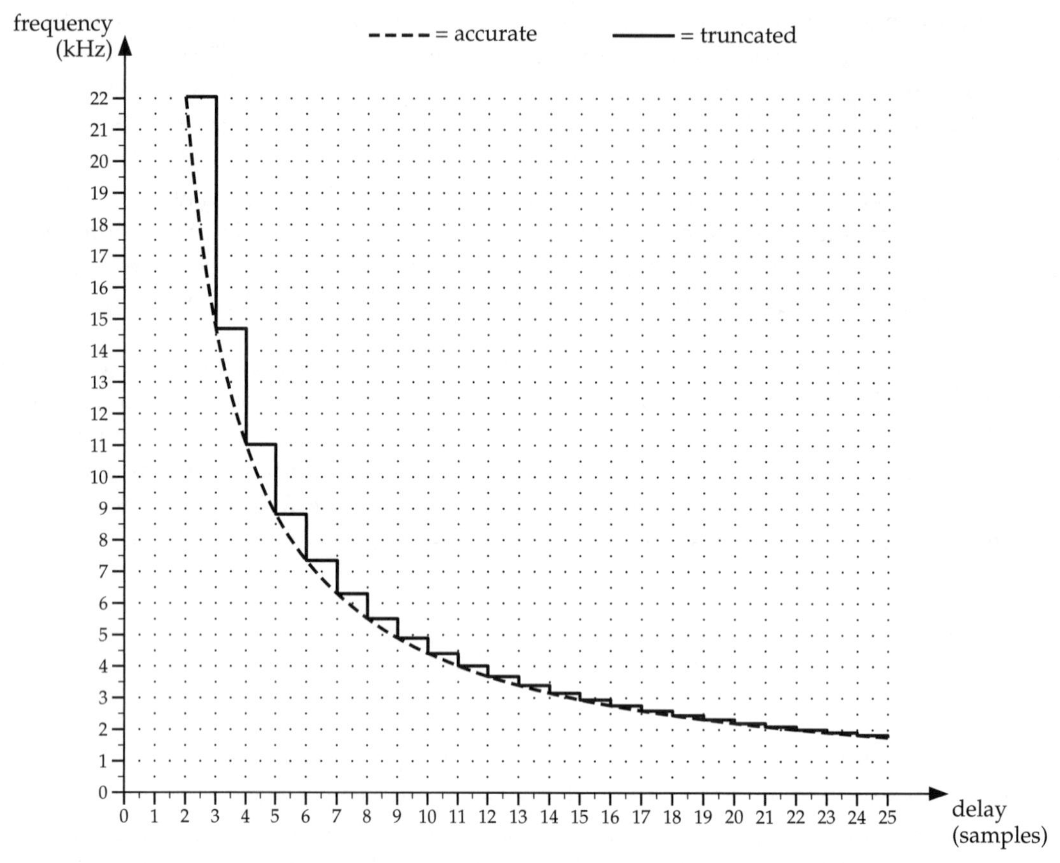

Figure 21.3 Comparison between frequency produced with accurate delay and with truncated delay values (samples stored at 44.1kHz)

The feedback parameters a_r and f_r have to be chosen carefully to ensure a stable system (such that the output does not become larger and larger). The exact values depend on the filter design used (and so the amount of amplitude lost at different frequencies as the signal passes through the filter). Typical values for f_r might be between 1 and 2kHz, and a_r is likely to be between 0.9 and 1.0.

The values of a_r and f_r also depend on the fundamental frequency chosen. With short delay times the recirculating feedback will cause much more rapid decay than with longer delay times, as the signal passes around the loop being filtered and attenuated more frequently. The values of a_r and f_r could be derived using suitable mappings from the note number or fundamental frequency, in order to achieve consistency of decay time and tonality across the note range of interest.

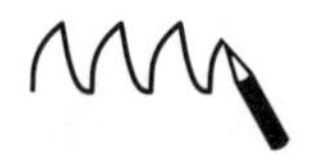

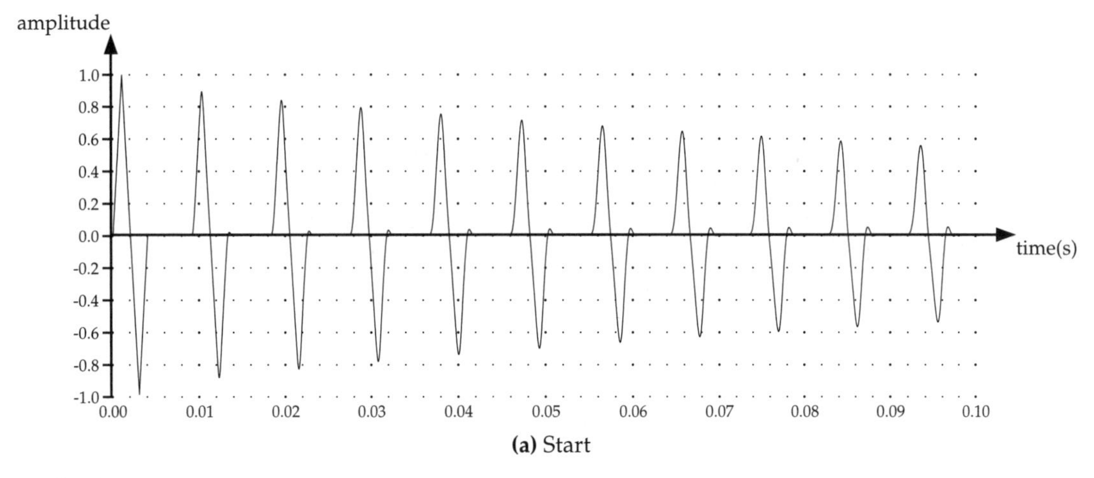

(a) Start

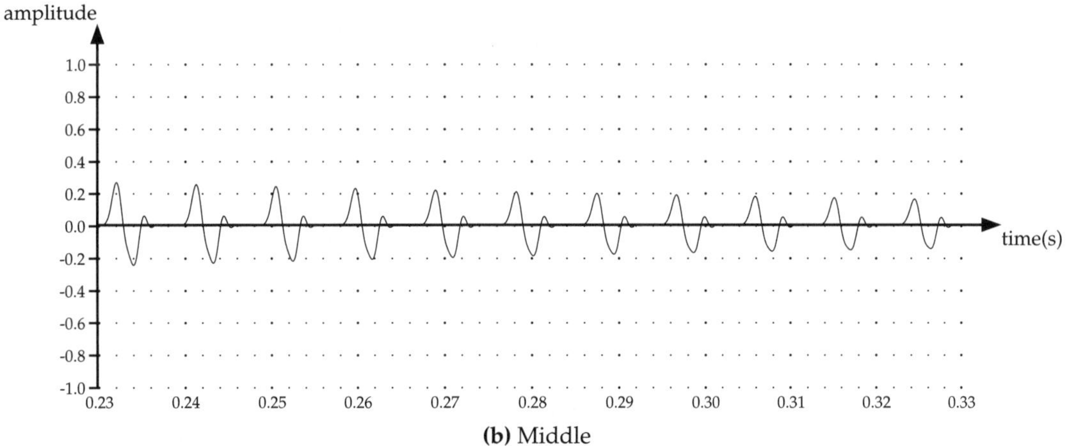

(b) Middle

Figure 21.4 Simple waveguide plucked string output waveform

Different designs of lowpass filter have different frequency responses (as shown in §6.4.2, p.171), which affects the frequency balance over time. For example, a lowpass filter with a gentle roll-off (modest attenuation with increasing frequency) will allow high frequencies to persist in the output for longer than one with a higher roll-off. It is also possible to use a bandpass filter in place of the lowpass filter to achieve a change of tonality. In that case the bandpass centre frequency is the same as the fundamental frequency, and a moderately low Q value is used.

The tonal character of the result is surprisingly natural for such a simple system. Many other synthesis techniques would use envelope generators to explicitly create a similar tonal change and exponential decay over time. However, there are a number of ways in which the effect can be improved, as described in the following sections.

21.2.2 Body Resonances

Figure 21.5 extends the model in figure 21.2 (p.584) by adding parallel bandpass filters to the output. These represent a second resonator block (after the string) to create the tonal shaping effect of the body of the instrument. The filters allow emphasis at particular frequency ranges and can improve realism. The output is now a weighted sum of the sound of the string, and the resonances of the body of the instrument applied to that string effect. Balancing the control parameters depends on the desired tonal character. This form is related to source-filter subtractive synthesis methods (described in Chapter 17).

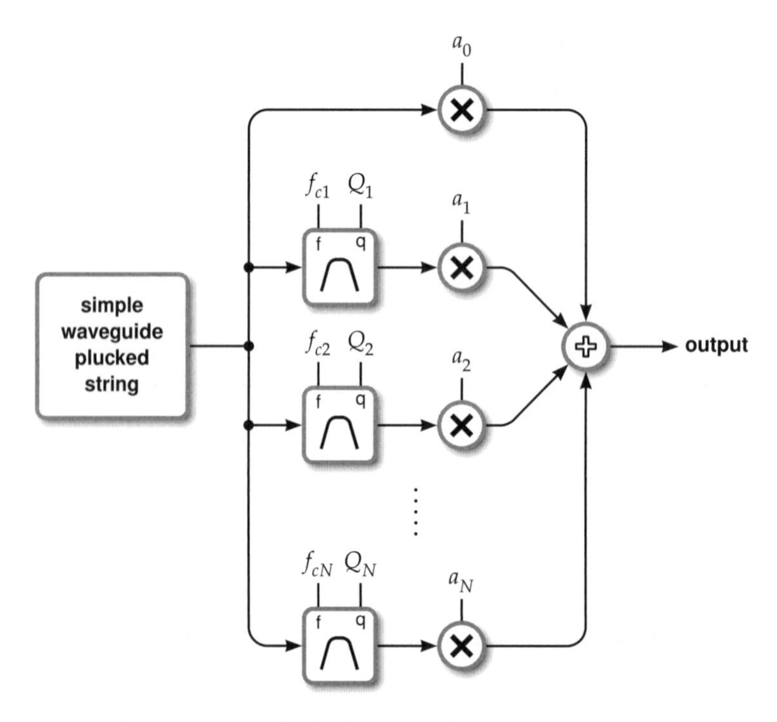

Figure 21.5 Plucked string with body resonances

21.2.3 Modifying the Excitation

The physical model excitation is a wideband input that stimulates the resonant modes of the waveguide resonator. The balance of frequency emphasis in the excitation will affect the resulting output partial amplitudes, and so the tonal character of the result. There are a number of ways of producing a suitable excitation. While different types of plucked character are of interest (such as that from a finger, or a plectrum), it is also interesting to produce others, such as struck and brushed characters. One of the advantages of physical models over sample-based synthesis is the ability to change the excitation of the instrument easily and achieve changes in output tonality.

Figure 21.6a is an extended version of the envelope generator excitation method seen in figure 21.2 (p.584). A short duration waveform cycle produces a signal with a wide frequency range. The shape, duration, and filter cutoff parameters all affect the balance of amplitude at different frequencies. Any desired shape of excitation can be used; it does not have to be triangular. This could be a subtle change (such as changing from a triangle to a square shape) or a much more complex waveform. The lowpass filter allows the harshness of the excitation to be controlled by attenuating high frequencies. Alternatively, more complex filtering might be employed. Finally, the output gain multiplier allows variation in excitation amplitude, whose value could be mapped from key velocity (as described in §24.1.3, p.661).

Figure 21.6b replaces the single cycle of a waveform with a burst of noise generator output. Noise generators produce a wide range of frequency partials (as described in Chapter 18) that can excite the resonant modes. The envelope is assumed to have a short duration (a few milliseconds) as the purpose is to stimulate the waveguide resonator into oscillation rather than drive the output continuously. Filtering and gain control are again used to shape the tone and amplitude of the excitation.

Figure 21.6c extends the idea of figure 21.6b by replaying a stored sample (as described in §15.1.3, p.465). The envelope generator can be used to isolate the onset of a longer sound, and so the length of the envelope depends on the length of the onset in the sample.

In figure 21.6d the synthesized or sampled excitation is replaced with a microphone input, which allows any sound source to be used to excite sympathetic vibrations. The noise gate rejects background noise and prevents unintentional output (noise gates are described in §11.2, p.341). An alternative to a normal microphone is a contact microphone, which is designed to pick up vibrations from a surface. That surface could then be struck by different types of beater, or rubbed to achieve a variation in tonal character.

Figure 21.7 extends figure 21.2 (p.584) by using a form similar to figure 21.6a and adding a comb filter (§6.4.4, p.183) between the lowpass filter and resonator waveguide. The purpose is to simulate the effect of having two travelling waves on a real string that propagate in opposite directions from the plucking position (one towards the neck and one towards the bridge) which are reflected and then summed together. By varying delay time t_p, the apparent plucking position on the string can be changed, which changes the tonal character. The length of the comb filter delay is of a similar order to the waveguide delay, but about 0 to 10ms is often enough to get a good range of effect.

As described in §21.2.1, a waveguide plucked string model with fixed parameter values will not produce a consistent decay time and tonal character across all fundamental frequencies. To achieve this will require all the excitation and waveguide resonator parameters to be determined by suitable mapping functions from the fundamental frequency. The nature of these depends on the chosen type of excitation and filter design.

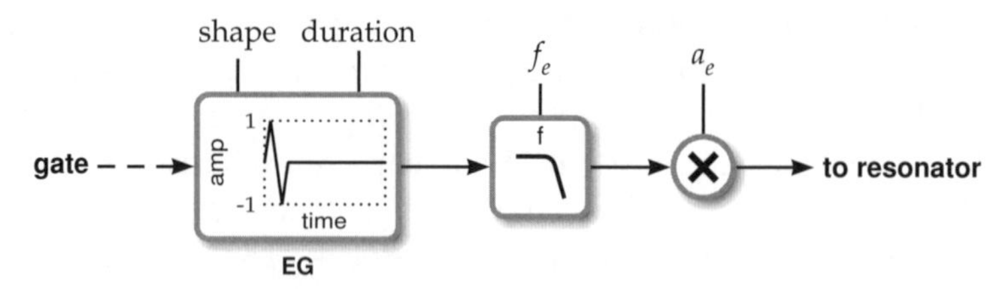

(a) Excitation with character control

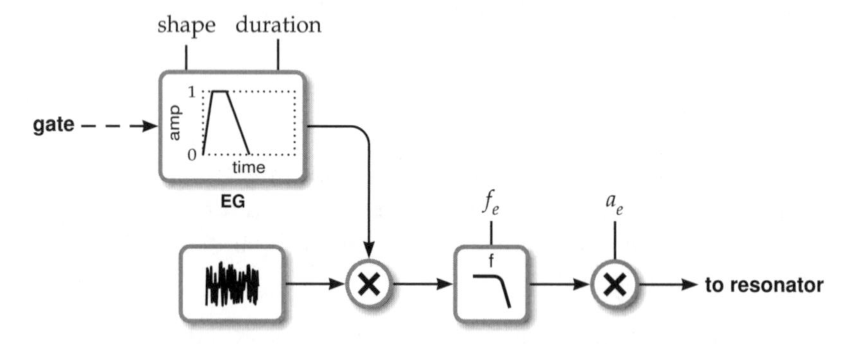

(b) Enveloped noise generator

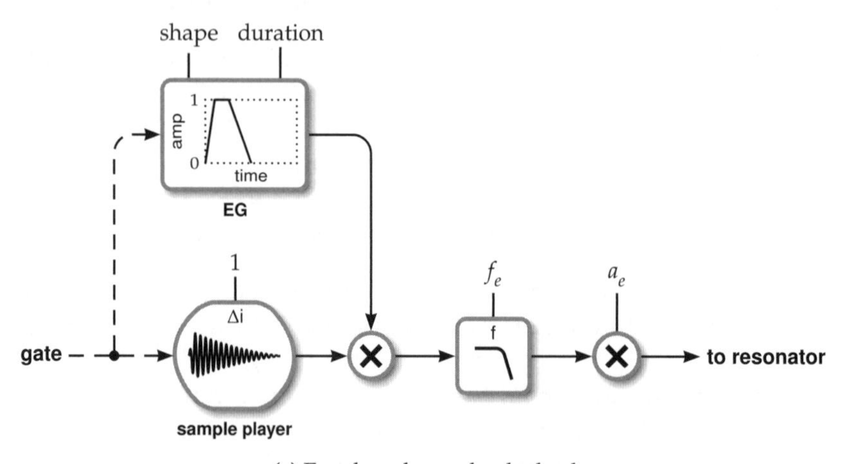

(c) Enveloped sample playback

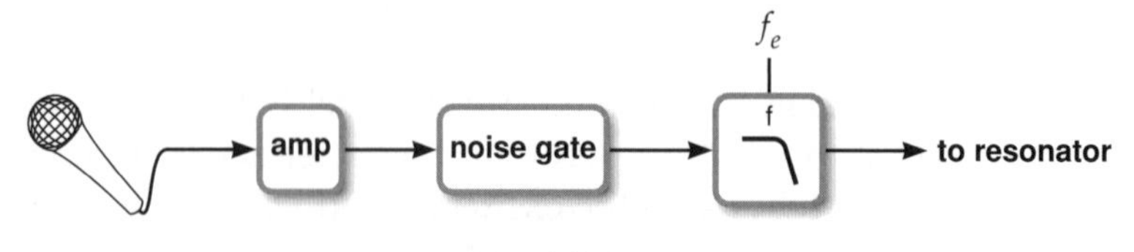

(d) Live input

Figure 21.6 Excitation methods

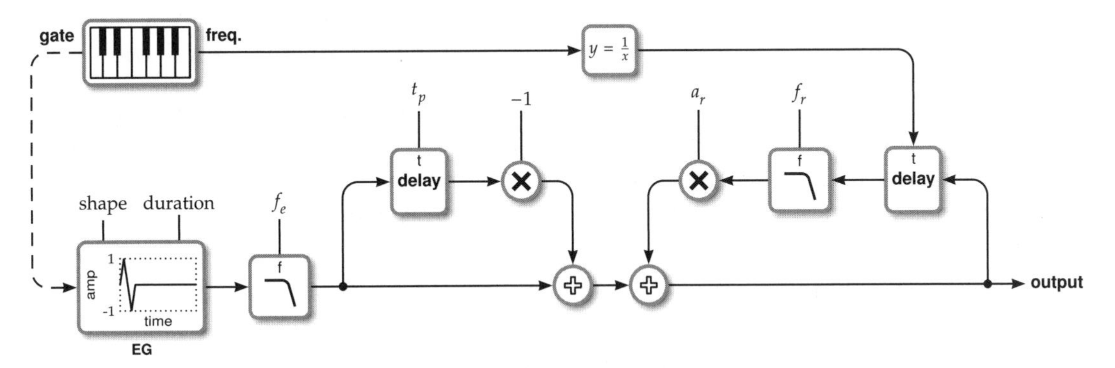

Figure 21.7 Plucked string with excitation position control

Figure 21.8a illustrates the major blocks that have been introduced so far in the waveguide plucked string model. This combines the elements seen in figure 21.7 with the body resonances in figure 21.5. It is possible to reorder the blocks in figure 21.8a as shown in figure 21.8b. Because the different parts are linear and time-invariant, the waveguide, delays, and filtering can occur in a different order without changing the result. This is known as *commuted synthesis*, and allows the possibility of exciting the plucked string model in a different way. As the plucked excitation is somewhat impulsive in nature, the excitation followed by the body resonances is much like a body impulse response. Impulse responses are described in detail in Chapter 10.

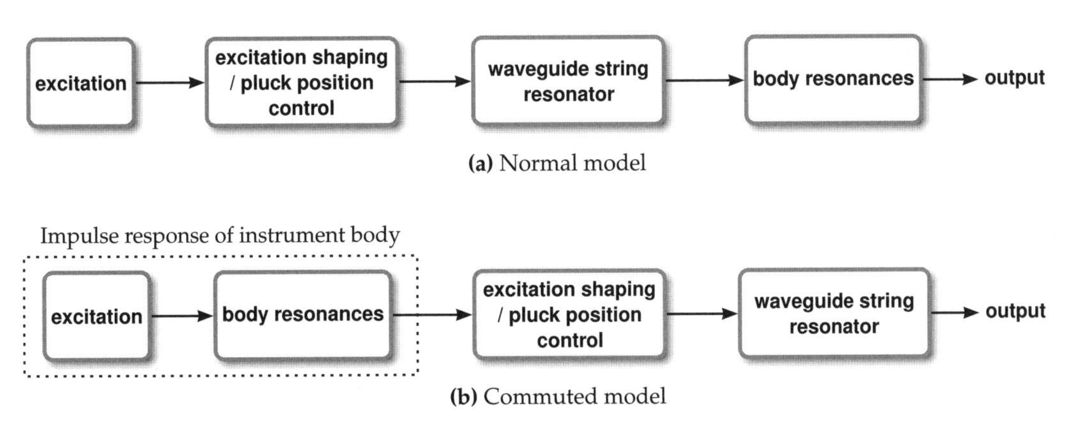

Figure 21.8 Ordering of blocks in the plucked string model

The input section of figure 21.8b can be realised with a sample player loaded with a suitable impulse response. The impulse response needs to include both the excitation and the resonance of an instrument body, such as a recording of sharply tapping the body of a guitar or a violin. The waveguide string resonator part creates different pitches in the same

way as before. This differs from normal sample-based techniques as it is not a complete pitched sound event that is being played back, but just the excited body resonance.

There are a number of ways of developing the basic commuted model. Filtering can be used to adjust the tonal character of the impulse response, and so the resulting tonality. There is the option to play back the sample at a different rate for different results. It is also possible to substitute impulse responses that are not derived from instrument bodies, such as objects hitting metal or plastic surfaces. This allows the creation of hybrid instruments with unusual sonic properties.

21.2.4 Modifying the Waveguide Filtering

The delay block in the waveguide string resonator will delay all frequency partials by the same length of time. This means that all frequencies will be propagated along the virtual string at the same rate. The cyclical repetition is the same for all frequencies, and so a harmonic output is produced. However, in the real world this is not always the case. For example, a thick and stiff piano string will produce a less harmonic result than a thin guitar string.

The waveguide string resonator in figure 21.9 is the same as seen in previous examples, but has an additional allpass filter between the delay and the lowpass filter. The allpass filter has a flat frequency response in terms of amplitude gain, but a non-flat phase response. This means that different frequency partials are delayed by different amounts, which will result in different repetition rates for different frequency partials, and so a somewhat inharmonic result. A second order allpass filter (as described in §6.4.4, p.183) enables a good range of results to be produced.

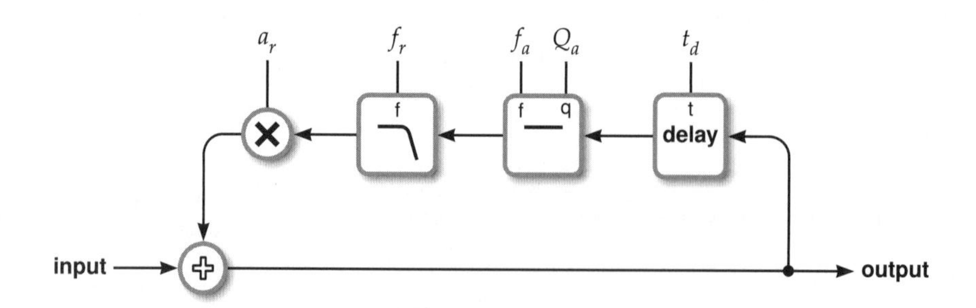

Figure 21.9 Waveguide resonator with allpass filter

Parameters a_r and f_r have the same roles as in previous examples. The principal delay time for the waveguide is t_d, which is normally related to the required fundamental frequency by $t_d = 1/F$. The values of f_a and Q_a are varied to achieve the desired variation of delay with frequency. Figure 6.68 (p.193) illustrates how the response varies with the Q value.

For subtle inharmonicity, the aim is a gradual increase in delay with frequency (higher values of f_a, medium values of Q_a). As the value of f_a decreases and becomes closer to the fundamental frequency, the delay variation can produce more severe effects on lower harmonics, which could be used for creating drum-like sounds, for example.

Because the allpass filter adds a delay that varies with frequency, there is a tendency to move the tuning of the waveguide away from the desired pitch. An appropriate solution is to subtract a compensation value from t_d before it is applied to the main delay. Once again, all the parameters should be mapped carefully in order that the different aspects of the sound (tuning, tonality, decay time) remain suitably consistent as the fundamental frequency changes.

21.3 Waveguides for Percussion

21.3.1 Banded Waveguides

The techniques described in §21.2 use a single waveguide resonator feedback loop. It is possible to extend the idea in parallel. One way of doing this is to create copies of a complete waveguide string instrument model, and use slightly different parameters for each. For example, to achieve a piano unison, three separate parallel waveguide strings with very slight inharmonicity and very slightly different frequency multipliers might be used. Blending of parallel synthesis paths is discussed in more detail in Chapter 19.

A development of the idea of parallel strings is the *banded* waveguide form in figure 21.10. In this form particular resonant modes sum together to achieve an overall character. This relates to the idea of additive synthesis (§16.2.3, p.491) and high resonance subtractive synthesis (§17.4, p.517) where the generation of a combination of harmonic and inharmonic modes is used to simulate sound sources such as tuned percussion instruments. In an additive synthesizer it is necessary to create individual amplitude envelopes for the different modes such that they decay at different rates. With the banded waveguide form the tonal variation and somewhat exponential decay occur as part of the process without needing those individual envelopes, much like the high resonance subtractive methods. The waveguide method is useful for creating percussive results (although less flexible for other types of sound).

The waveguide resonators in the block diagram have some modifications compared to the plucked string form in figure 21.2 (p.584). The important one is that the filter is now a bandpass rather than a lowpass type. The centre frequency is the same as that used to derive the delay time, such that the filter attenuates frequencies away from the principal resonant mode. The component parts of the waveguide have been arranged such that the excitation has to pass through the filter to reach the output. However, each loop still has the same three operations of delay, filtering, and attenuation.

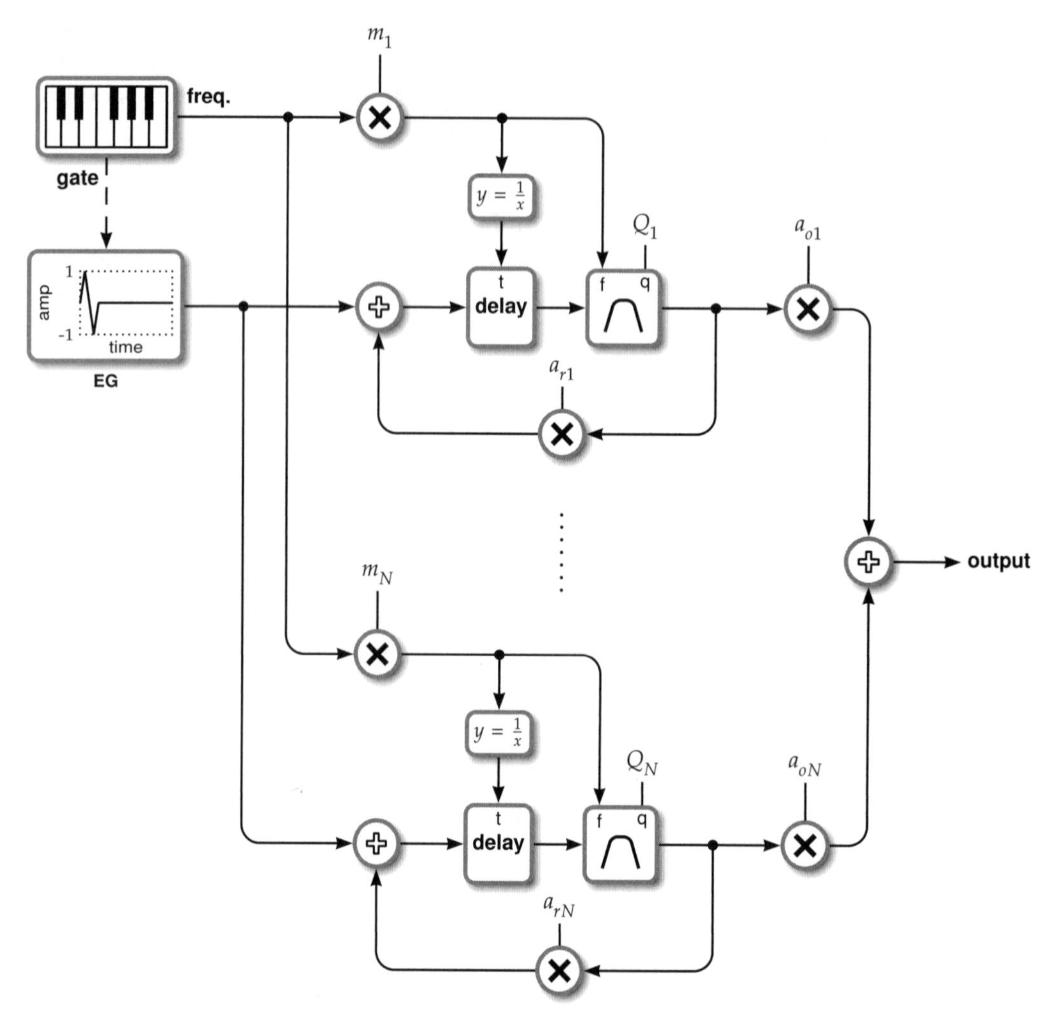

Figure 21.10 Banded waveguide form

A parallel path is used for each required resonant mode. Multiplying factors m_1 to m_N determine the frequencies relative to the input. These might have values derived from a frequency domain analysis of a percussive sound. Filter Q values of about 1 to 3 are often sufficient to attenuate partials away from the modal frequencies. Feedback loop gain values a_{r1} to a_{rN} are likely to be between 0.9 and 1.0, and are often very close to 1.0 to achieve long resonant decay. Different modes can be configured to decay at different rates. Gains a_{o1} to a_{oN} have values between 0 and 1, and are used to balance the amplitudes of the different modes in the output. Although a simple excitation is used in the block diagram, it could be replaced with a more sophisticated form such as those in figure 21.6 (p.590).

The spectrogram plot in figure 21.11 illustrates a sound produced by a banded waveguide synthesizer with 6 parallel paths that sounds like a tuned percussion instrument. There are a wide range of frequency partials at the start of the sound that reduce to particular modal frequencies over time. The frequencies have been chosen to produce an inharmonic result and the resonant modes decay at different rates, as shown in the plot.

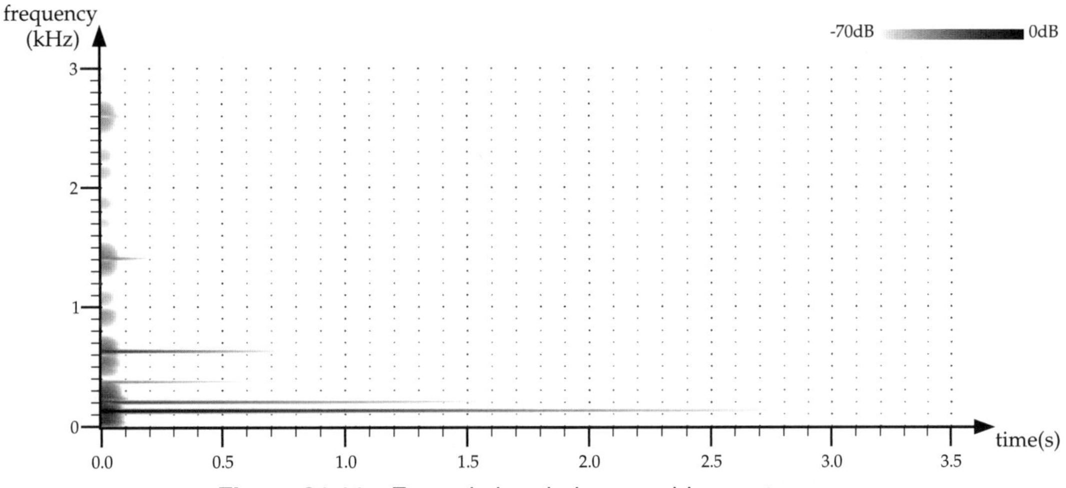

Figure 21.11 Example banded waveguide spectrogram

21.3.2 Waveguide Mesh Drum

Striking a drum head has some similarities to plucking a string. There is a brief excitation that causes waves to be propagated in the resonator. Travelling waves repeatedly cross the surface, reflecting from the boundary at the rim of the drum, losing energy (at different rates for different frequencies) until they decay away to nothing. As with the string, the model must have delay, filtering, and gain control elements. The principal difference from the string is that the drum head is a surface. To model this requires the ability to create a two-dimensional waveguide form.

Figure 21.12 shows the basic component parts of a waveguide drum physical model. The excitation can be achieved with the methods shown in figure 21.6 (p.590). The body of the instrument can be modelled with a parallel filter stage in much the same way as in figure 21.5 (p.588).

Figure 21.12 Waveguide drum

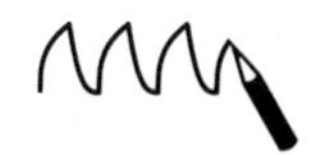

Figure 21.13 illustrates an example waveguide drum head resonator. In this particular case, it is a square mesh of drum surface elements (DSEs) that each model a piece of the drum head. These are surrounded by drum edge elements (DEEs) that model the effect of the travelling waves reaching the edge of the drum and being reflected. A square eight-by-eight mesh has been used, but the form can be extended to different shapes and sizes, which will have different resonant properties. Each DSE has four edges (top T, bottom B, left L, and right R), with an input (I) and an output (O) for each edge. These allow a wave on the drum head to move in two dimensions. At the edges, the DEEs only have an input and output, to achieve a reflection for the neighbouring DSE.

Figure 21.14 shows an example DEE. The gain factor a_{DEE} controls the amount of reflection at the edge of the drum. This will generally be between -0.9 and -1. The multiplier is negative because waves reflect with inverted phase at the edge of the drum. The same value will be used in all DEEs to achieve consistent behaviour around the edge. As values become closer to -1 there is greater ringing in the resonant decay.

Figure 21.15 shows an example DSE. The inputs for the four sides are on the left, and the outputs are on the right, to make the diagram easier to understand. Each path has a delay that corresponds to the time taken for a wave to cross the surface element. The results are summed at the junction and distributed to the outputs (minus the input from the relevant direction in each case). The lowpass filters can be used to control the roll-off of high frequency resonance in the head. A first order (or one pole) lowpass filter is appropriate (as described in §6.4.2, p.171).

There are two parameters for the DSE; the delay time t_{DSE} and the filter cutoff f_{DSE}. Increasing the value of t_{DSE} causes the pitch of the drum to decrease. Increasing the value of f_{DSE} causes the result to sound brighter and reduces the damping of the resonant decay. The two parameters are the same for all the delays and filters in every DSE to achieve a consistent surface character across the entire mesh.

In terms of construction and configuration, the following points are relevant:

- Controlling excitation is similar to that for the plucked string. The excitation cycle length is again likely to be in the region of 1ms to 10ms, and the excitation filter cutoff f_e can be used to control the high frequency content. The excitation technique employed reflects the type of object used to strike the drum head.
- The excitation is applied to the drum head at one of the inputs to one of the DSEs (adding it to the signal arriving from the neighbouring element). The point at which the excitation is applied affects the tonal result. As with a real drum, exciting the mesh towards the edge produces more high frequency emphasis in the result than excitation closer to the middle.

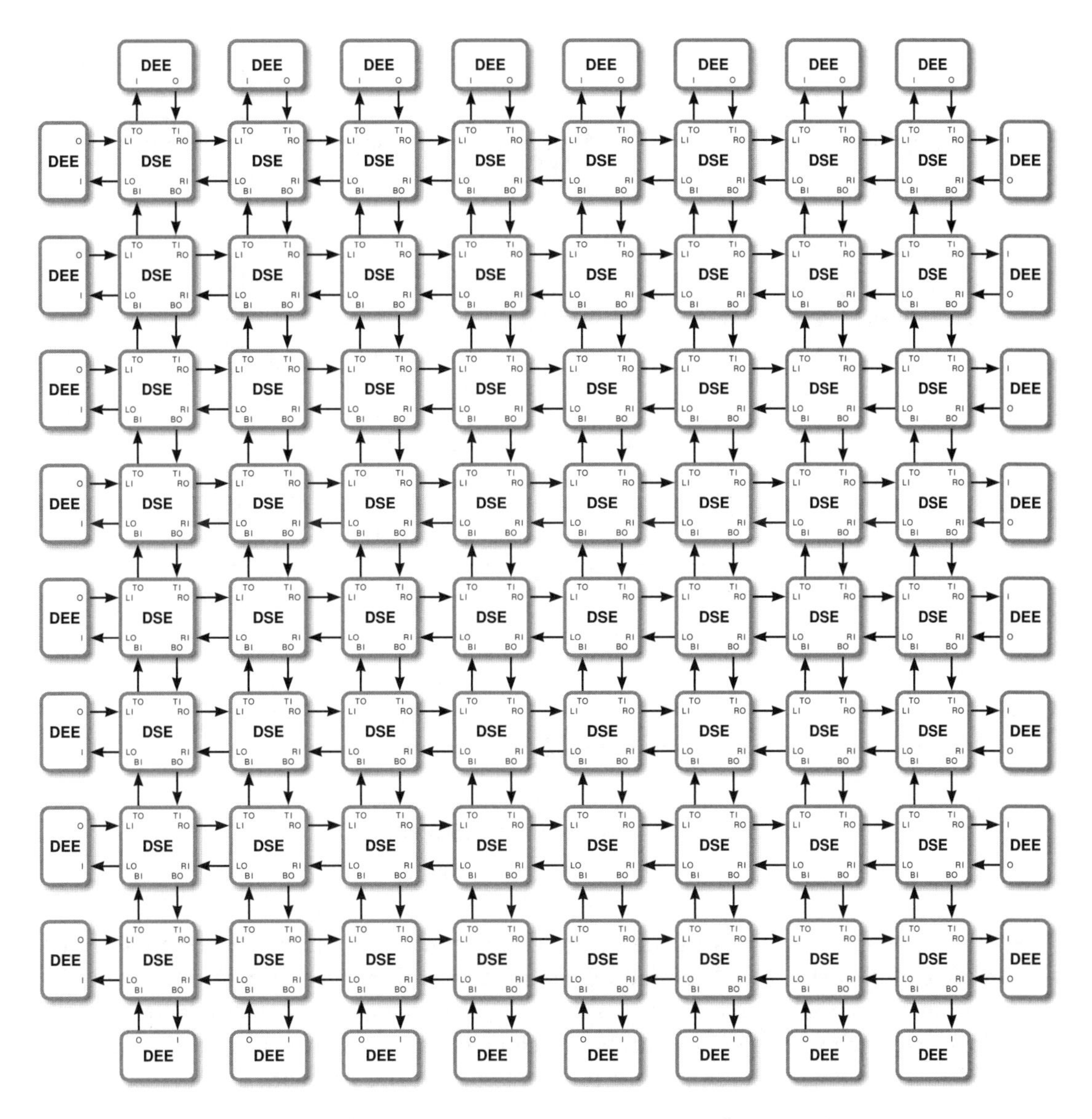

Figure 21.13 Waveguide square mesh drum head

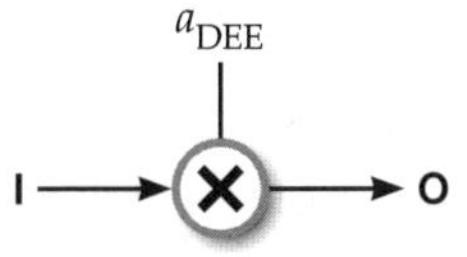

Figure 21.14 Drum edge element (DEE)

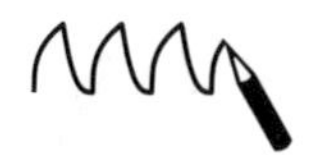

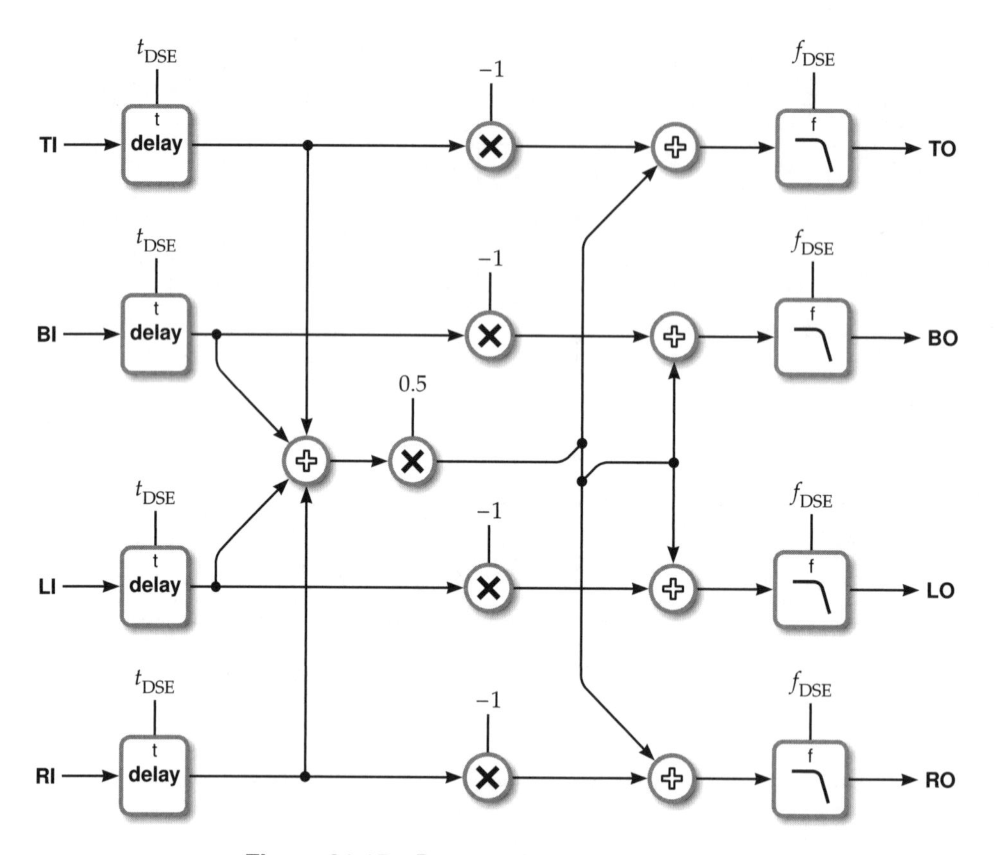

Figure 21.15 Drum surface element (DSE)

- The number of elements in the mesh is important. As the mesh becomes larger, more complex shapes can be modelled (such as with curved edges). However, the amount of computation increases, and the delay time t_{DSE} must decrease to maintain the same pitch with a larger number of elements across the surface. For the square eight-by-eight mesh the delay time is often less than 1ms. As with the plucked string, an interpolated fractional delay will often be used to achieve precise pitch control at short delay times. It is difficult to be precise about the relationship between the delay time and perceived pitch, so it is best tuned by ear.

- The surface filter cutoff f_{DSE} and edge factor a_{DEE} are tuned to reduce unpleasant high frequency resonances and achieve a relatively long decay for the chosen delay time and excitation. f_{DSE} will typically be a few kilohertz and a_{DEE} will be close to −1. Both have to be modified with care to avoid both unstable feedback, and an over-damped sound.

- The output from the drum head can be taken from one of the DSE outputs. As with the excitation position, moving the output position will cause a change in tonality, much like moving a microphone to different points over the drum head. An alternative method is to take several DSE outputs and mix them together in the desired proportions to create a composite tonal character.
- The design can suffer from a DC offset build up (at 0Hz). This is visible in a spectrum plot as a very low frequency element that remains present after the drum tone has ended. The solution is to place highpass filters in series with the lowpass filters in each of the 4 outputs of the DSEs to act as DC blockers. A first order highpass filter is appropriate, with a cutoff frequency of, say, 1Hz.
- The filters in the drum body resonator provide an opportunity to further tune the character of the resulting sound.

The model can be extended further to add additional drum-like characteristics:

- The resonance of the body in a real drum (which relates to the shell and the air cavity inside) will have an effect on the vibration of the drum head. It is possible to add a feedback from the output of the drum body back to the input to the drum head and add it to the excitation. This will have a multiplier in the feedback path with a small positive or negative gain value that is adjusted for the desired tonal and decay effect.
- Some drums exhibit a pitch variation immediately after they are struck, which reflects variation in the tension of the drum head. This can be simulated by causing the delay time t_{DSE} to increase a little over the first 100ms of the sound (and so create a slight decrease in pitch), using an envelope that is triggered at the same time as the excitation.

The model allows a pleasing range of drum tones to be produced, such as tom-tom and timpani. The results have a natural inharmonicity (like a real drum) due to the complex relationships between the delay times as the waves move across the mesh in two dimensions. There is a fairly clear relationship between the controlling parameters and the resulting tonality. There is also a logical relationship between the model and the physics of a real drum, in terms of dimensions and delay times, excitation position, and so on.

21.4 Waveguide Wind Instrument

21.4.1 Basic Wind Instrument

With the plucked string and drum models, the excitation is a brief injection of energy that causes the main resonator (string or drum head) to vibrate for a significant length of time. Some instruments use a continuous excitation rather than a brief one. An example of this

is breath into a wind instrument. There are two differences between this and the plucked and struck examples:

- The excitation is a continuous positive air pressure level that causes an oscillation in the mouthpiece and body of the instrument.
- The resonance occurs for as long as the breath excitation continues, and then stops afterwards. With the plucked and struck examples, the gradually decaying resonance continues for some time after the end of the excitation.

These features are achieved through a close relationship between the mouthpiece and the resonating air in the tube of the wind instrument. The breath input causes a vibration in the mouthpiece (such as a reed vibrating), which in turn causes resonance in the tube of the instrument. The tube air resonance also feeds back to the mouthpiece, causing the vibration to become more regular.

Figure 21.16 illustrates an example waveguide wind instrument. As with plucked string and struck drum examples, there is no need for an oscillator block at the input nor an envelope generator signal to be multiplied into the output. Rather than a brief excitation as seen previously, there is a breath pressure envelope that has a high amplitude for the duration of the note. The shape of the envelope can be varied to control such aspects as the rapidity of the attack or variations in the sustaining portion. The envelope generator might be triggered by a keyboard as shown in the figure, or it might be replaced with a level derived from a continuous control input, such as a breath sensor or an expression pedal.

The next major part after the input is the mouthpiece. The mouthpiece model has a non-linear effect, which can be similar to that of a vibrating clarinet reed, for example. It works in conjunction with the tube resonator to create an oscillating result from the non-oscillating breath pressure input. The signal is modified by scaling, applying an offset, clipping, and shaping. The clipping and shaping functions work in the same way as those used in a soft clipping distortion process (figure 7.7, p.203).

The tube resonator section simulates the effect of travelling waves in the tube connected to the mouthpiece in terms of delay and filtering. The delay time is derived from the chosen fundamental frequency. There is a feedback path from the tube to the input of the mouthpiece, which has similarities to the effect in real instruments. The highpass filter at the output of the synthesizer attenuates DC offsets (0Hz) that can occur in the process.

There are a number of parameters that need to be configured to achieve an output:

- Parameter a_b controls the overall excitation level, where a value of 1 is a suitable starting point. Changing the value will affect the tonality of the output. Too low a value will mean that there is no oscillation.

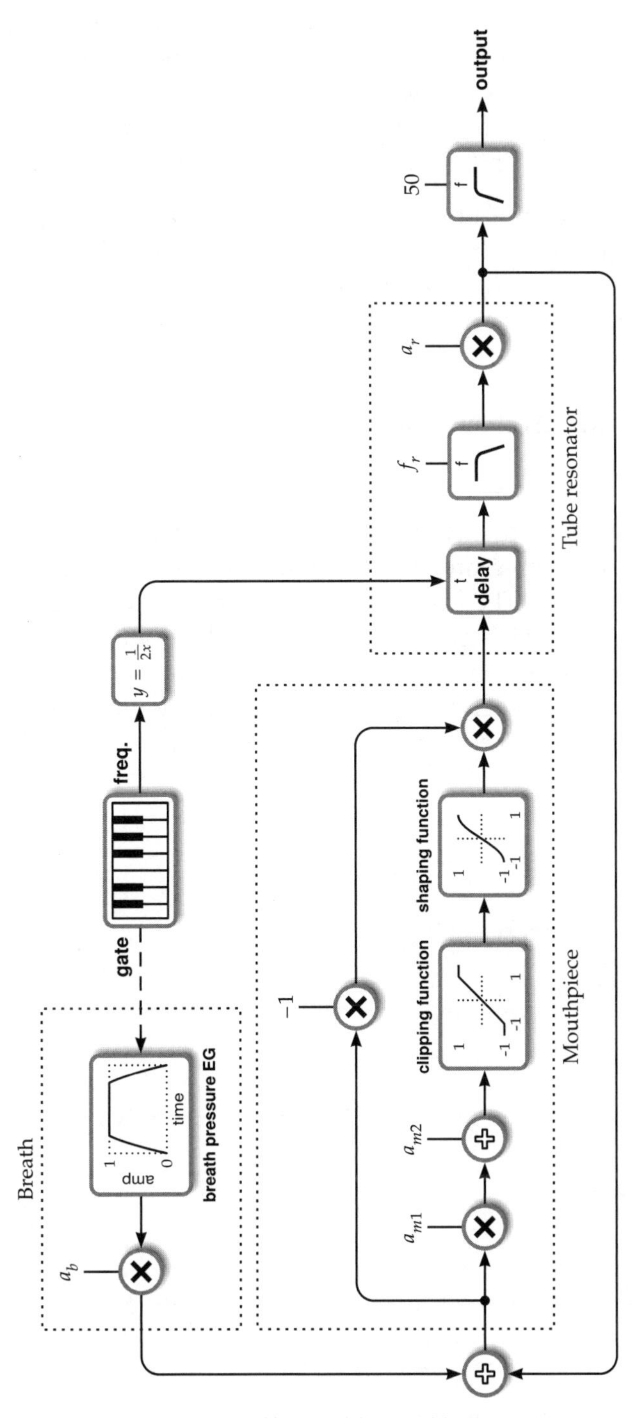

Figure 21.16 Waveguide wind instrument

- The variables a_{m1} and a_{m2} have values in the range 0 to 1, and are adjusted to achieve the required tonal character. These have to be balanced carefully such that the right part of the clipping and shaping functions is used. Starting at values of 0.5 for both factors and then varying from there is sensible. The shaping function can be a simple sinusoidal shape ($y = \sin(0.5\pi x)$) or any function between $(-1, -1)$ and $(1, 1)$.
- Parameters f_r and a_r affect the tone and the stability of the output. Starting at values of 3kHz and 1 respectively is sensible. The values are adjusted until the tone is not too dull and the output is not unstable, but it depends on the design of filter used. A one pole lowpass filter is appropriate (as described in §6.4.2, p.171).

21.4.2 Breath Input Improvements

There are a number of ways of making the waveguide wind instrument more usable, more flexible, and more tonally convincing. The breath input stage in figure 21.16 is an envelope generator to simulate air pressure, and a scaling control. This can be replaced with the form shown in figure 21.17. The first addition is a tremolo breath pressure variation of the same form as seen in figure 9.8 (p.271). It is controlled by rate f_t (typically about 4 to 7Hz for natural-sounding effects) and depth a_t (between 0 and 1). The tremolo oscillation is multiplied by the envelope such that the effect increases with air pressure, which gives a fairly natural result. Tremolo can often make the simulation of wind instrument sounds more convincing.

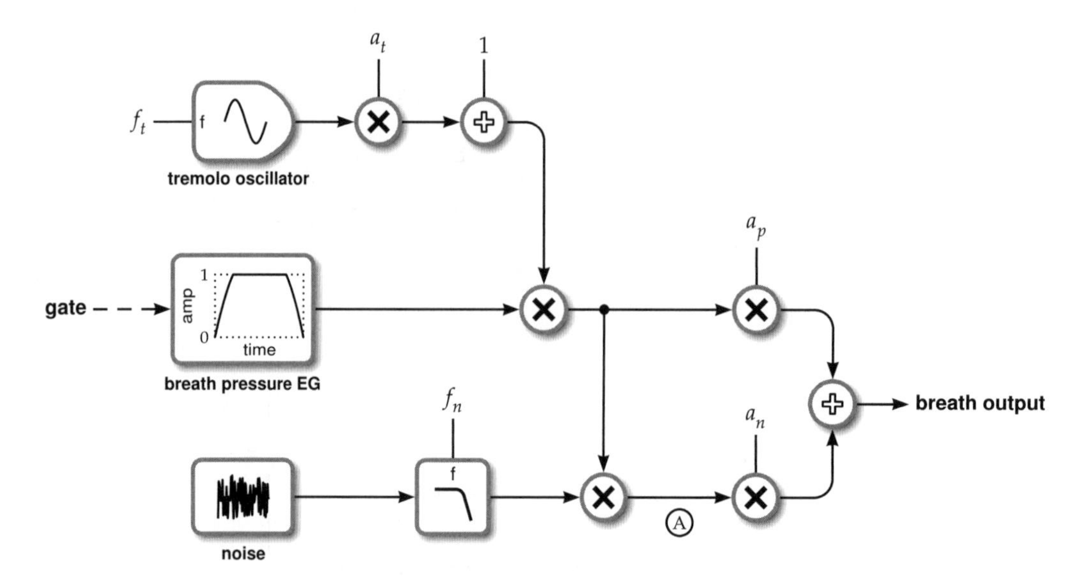

Figure 21.17 Improved breath input stage

The lower path in the figure is a noise generator whose output is shaped by the lowpass filter at cutoff frequency f_n (to attenuate harsh high frequencies) and a depth control a_n. To achieve a convincing breath noise effect, the cutoff might be in the region of 1 to 4kHz, and the depth will be quite low (such as 0 to 0.3). It is scaled by the air pressure level. The breath noise character will be modified by any filtering that occurs later in the synthesizer, so the parameters have to be adjusted in conjunction with those.

Parameter a_p has a similar role to a_b in figure 21.16. Parameters a_p and a_n control the balance of breath pressure and breath noise fed to the mouthpiece. These are adjusted to achieve the required tonality. Subtle amounts of noise can add to the realism of the wind excitation effect, where larger amounts produce more clearly breathy results. More complex filtering can be used to shape the tone of the breath noise and make it more realistic (such as parallel bandpass filters). Techniques for shaping noise are described in Chapter 18. Another variation is to mix some of the noise signal at point A in the figure directly into the final synthesizer output, as if it is emerging directly from the excitation end of the instrument rather than through the tube.

21.4.3 Filtering and Tuning Improvements

A simple way of adding additional tonal control to the wind instrument model is to add filtering to the final output stage, such as a form similar to the parallel filters in figure 21.5 (p.588). This allows the tone to be changed without affecting the configuration of other synthesizer parameters. A more sophisticated technique is to change the filtering inside the tube resonator, such as adding a parallel bandpass filter as shown in figure 21.18. Changing this filtering is similar to changing the body of the instrument, and so is more in keeping with the idea of modelling the instrument than attaching tonal shaping to the output.

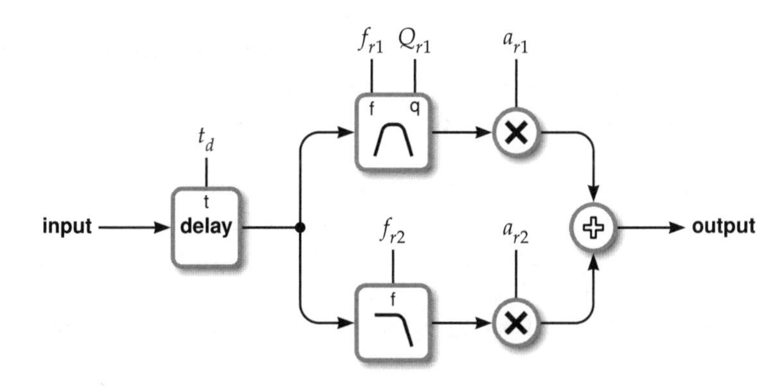

Figure 21.18 Improved tube resonator stage

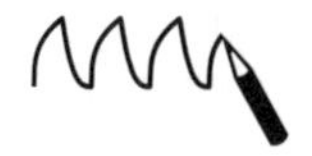

Careful manipulation of the improved tube resonator parameters allows different characters of instrument to be achieved. The cutoff/centre frequency parameters of the two filters might be fixed, or they might be derived from the fundamental frequency through multiplying by suitable factors. This latter method can often be used to achieve more consistent tonality as the fundamental frequency changes. As with the other parameters, the values require some experimentation to achieve pleasing results.

The pitch of the output oscillation is not only affected by the delay block, but also by the configuration of the filters in the tube resonator. Tuning the wind synthesizer requires a more sophisticated mapping from the required note number or fundamental frequency to the delay time. This is often done as the last step in creating the synthesizer, when the desired tonal character has already been achieved.

21.5 Bowed Waveguides

Like the blown wind instrument model considered in section 21.4, a bowed instrument also has a continuous excitation. The interaction between bow and resonator is quite complex and is often called a stick-and-slip friction effect. To take a bowed string as an example, at times the bow will stick to the string, which will drag it in the same direction. When the tension in the string exceeds the static friction force from the bow, the string will slip in the opposite direction to the bow movement. The stick-and-slip effect repeats, producing an excitation into the string.

Figure 21.19 illustrates a simplified waveguide-based simulation of a bowed instrument. The envelope generator produces the bow input. As with the wind instrument model, there is a non-oscillating input level that causes an oscillation to be set up in the waveguide instrument. The bow input is multiplied by gain parameter a_{b1}, from which the current output of the resonator is subtracted. This represents the difference in velocity between the bow and the bowed object. The result then passes into the main part of the model where the friction between the bow and instrument is simulated. Parameter a_{b2} controls how much of the result of that part passes into the resonator. When a_{b2} is zero the resonator will ring freely, as if the bow has been removed.

Configuring the parameters depends on the nature of the resonator section. The main delay element needs to be inline between the resonator input and output to get an appropriate delay in the bowing loop. The technique in the figure works quite well with the banded waveguide form in §21.3.1 (p.593) as the resonator. Achieving a good bowed string effect can be more difficult, for which there are more sophisticated arrangements in the literature.

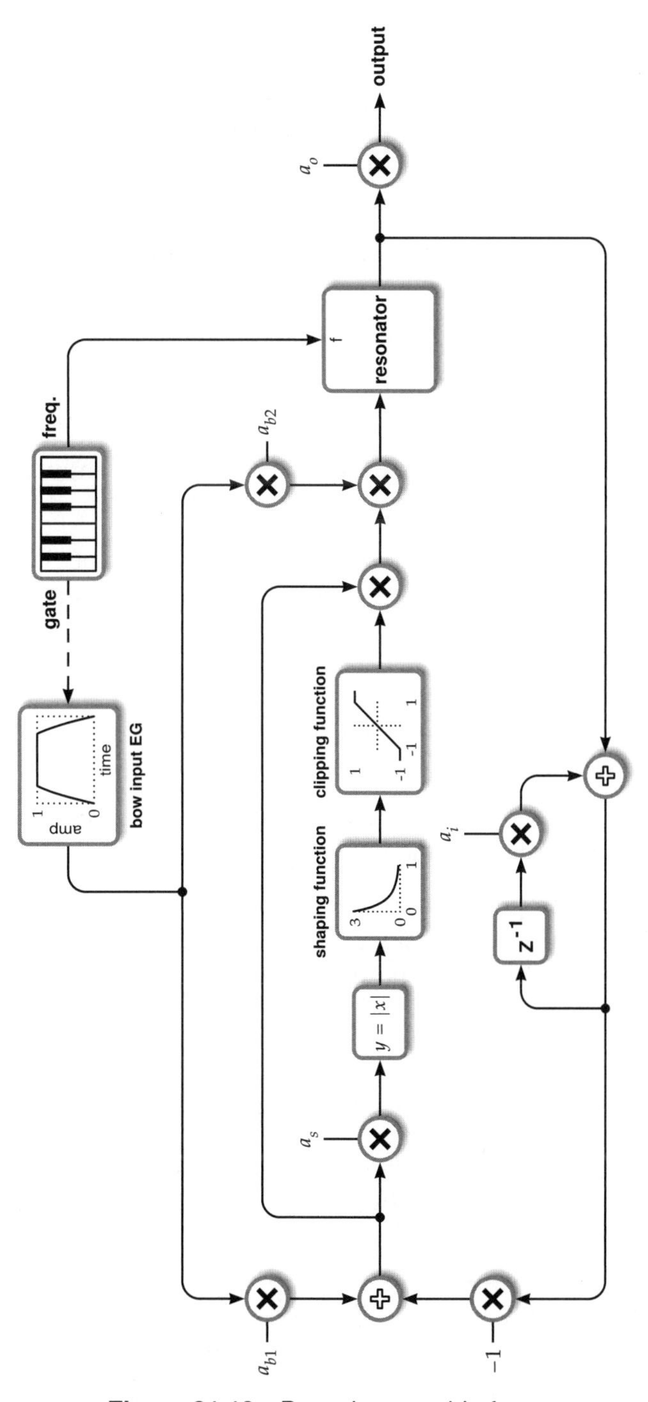

Figure 21.19 Bowed waveguide form

The first step is to make a plucked or struck input produce a pleasant effect from the resonator. Following this, the parameters in figure 21.19 can be configured:

- The block marked z^{-1} is a unit sample delay, so parameter a_i controls how much of the previous sample value at the output of the adder is added to the path from the resonator output (which is a type of integrator, as described in §6.4.1, p.164). Values between 0 and 1 are used for a_i, and a typical value is around 0.8.
- Parameter a_{b1} is used to balance the amount of bow input against the amount of signal fed back from the resonator. Typically, this will have a value around 0.1.
- The central portion achieves the friction simulation:
  - $y = |x|$ means taking the absolute value of the input. In other words, it removes the negative sign if present.
  - The shaping function causes the slip effect as the input becomes larger. A possible equation to achieve this is $y = (x + 0.75)^{-4}$.
  - The hard clipping function prevents values from exceeding ±1. This achieves the stick effect at lower input values to the shaping function.
  - Parameter a_s controls the balance of stick and slip. A typical value might be around 5.
- Parameter a_{b2} is used to control the amount of signal reaching the resonator. Typically, this will have a value between 0 and 0.1.
- The output gain parameter a_o is used to boost the output amplitude, as the amplitude values in the main part of the model will tend to be quite low.

It is necessary to vary the parameter values to achieve a good tonality and consistent output when bowing, such as consistent results for different fundamental frequencies. With a banded waveguide it might be necessary to adjust the outputs from different bands to prevent one mode dominating.

21.6 Developing Processes and Learning More

Waveguide physical models use a wider range of processing elements than are found in typical waveshaping, additive, subtractive, and modulation-based synthesis (as described in Chapters 14, 16, 17, and 20). However, the required elements should normally be part of a standard audio programming library or environment. Most prominent is the delay block, which is used more often with modifiers (such as the echo and reverberation processes described in Chapter 10) than synthesis. As described in §21.2.1 (p.584), the total delay in a waveguide feedback loop must be adjusted carefully to achieve the required pitch. This requires a fractional delay implementation (as discussed in §8.2, p.237), as well

as awareness of how different filter designs will have different group delay characteristics (§6.4, p.164).

In techniques such as additive and subtractive synthesis an oscillator produces the source waveform, and envelope generators are used to impose a tonal and amplitude variation over time. With the techniques in this chapter, those are generally achieved through the waveguide feedback loop. Balancing the control parameters is crucial to the implementation of a controlled resonant decay, which in turn is affected by the choice of process elements (such as the design of filters employed). The characteristics of pitch, amplitude envelope, and tonality are linked to the same parameters within the feedback loop. Therefore, configuration can be less straightforward compared to synthesis techniques that are controlled by parameters that affect those dimensions more separately.

In terms of parameter configuration, there is often a mid-point to be found between too little resonance and an unstable feedback loop. The difficulty is similar to that found with recirculating reverberators in §10.4 (p.323), which have similarities in their form. Waveguide feedback loops also share the need to consider the order of computation, as addressed by algorithm 10.2 (p.317, corresponding to figure 10.25, p.315).

Optimising the configuration with suitable mappings from keyboard frequency or note number to parameters is mentioned a number of times in this chapter. One way of achieving this is the use of lookup tables that store suitable parameter values for particular note numbers, which are optimised by hand to achieve the desired character across the range of interest. If a limited pitch range is acceptable, it makes optimising the synthesis parameters less time consuming.

The amount of computation required to achieve useful results varies between the different models described in this chapter. A simple plucked string form is efficient, whereas a mesh drum head can require much more computation. Whether this is significant depends on the available processing power and the requirements for control characteristics that relate to physical form. Another synthesis technique might be more efficient to achieve a comparable audible result, but will have different control characteristics.

Further discussion of physical models can be found in this book:

Cook, Perry R. 2002. *Real Sound Synthesis for Interactive Applications.* Natick, MA: A K Peters.

The following sources provide some more advanced material that relates to this chapter, which can be used for further study:

Essl, Georg, Stefania Serafin, Perry R. Cook, and Julius O. Smith. 2004. "Theory of Banded Waveguides." *Computer Music Journal* 28:1:37–50.

Jaffe, David A., and Julius O. Smith. 1983. "Extensions of the Karplus-Strong Plucked-String Algorithm." *Computer Music Journal* 7:2:56–69.

Karjalainen, Matti, Vesa Välimäki, and Tero Tolonen. 1998. "Plucked-String Models: From the Karplus-Strong Algorithm to Digital Waveguides and Beyond." *Computer Music Journal* 22:3:17–32.

Karplus, Kevin, and Alex Strong. 1983. "Digital Synthesis of Plucked-String and Drum Timbres." *Computer Music Journal* 7:2:43–55.

22

Granular Synthesis

22.1 Sound from Grains

22.1.1 Introduction

A continuous signal is used in many types of synthesis as the basis for sound generation, such as periodic oscillators (Chapter 14) or noise generators (Chapter 18). These signals are then shaped by the application of amplitude envelopes to form finite length sonic events. For example, figure 13.8 (p.407) has an oscillator that produces a continuous signal, with an envelope multiplied by the output to achieve a changing amplitude over the length of the sound.

An alternative technique is *granular synthesis*, which constructs sounds from short duration sound events called *grains*. The accumulation of grains into a *stream* can be used to create tonal characters that are difficult to achieve by other means. The particle-based construction might be heard in the result, if the individual grains remain apparent. However, the techniques can also be used to achieve smooth continuous sounds where the grains blend together.

Acoustic examples of granular sounds are rainfall, gravel being tipped out of a bag, a large number of people using mechanical typewriters, and an audience clapping. The overall character in all these cases is a composite of individual short grains of sound, each of which has a slightly different character from the others. Granular synthesis incorporates two significant features; the construction of long sounds from much shorter ones, and inconsistencies between different grains in terms of their sound character.

Each grain in a granular stream is typically about 1ms to 100ms in length (although longer grains are possible, as described later). Because grains can overlap in time, there are likely to be tens, hundreds, or thousands of grains per second. With the shorter durations, a single grain will sound like a brief click, and it is too short for a listener to perceive the nature of its composition when played on its own. However, when many grains are produced in quick succession, then the internal makeup of the grain **does** affect the overall perceived sound character.

22.1.2 Granular Stream Generation

Figure 22.1 illustrates a pair of grains, and the key parameters that describe them. All parameters can have an effect on the resulting sound character. Every grain can be different from the others. Because there are a large number of grains in one sound, and a number of parameters to describe each grain, it is not practical to specify each one individually. High-level organisation is required, such as global fixed values or enveloped effects, which are used to describe how the grains change over time. This might incorporate some randomised variations.

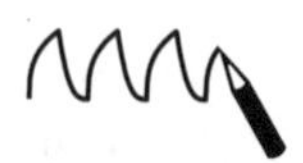

waveform (from choice of source sound, starting position in the sound and sample increment; or synthesis parameters)

amplitude

peak amplitude

amplitude envelope shape

1

0

−1

time

duration

inter-onset time (and thus onset rate and density of grains)

Figure 22.1 Basic grain generation parameters

Grains might be created using another synthesizer (such as a set of oscillators with an amplitude envelope applied, or a physical model). Alternatively, grains can be extracted from a recorded sound, which is selected because part of its character has similarities to the desired result. The grains might be small pieces of a longer sound, as shown in figure 22.2a. They might be from different places within the source sound, or overlapping, or the same every time. Alternatively, the source sound might be short and the whole sound could be a grain, as in figure 22.2b.

Figure 22.3 shows how a granular synthesizer might be constructed. It is necessary to use a parallel form such that grains can overlap in time by being generated simultaneously. A clock internal to the parameter generator indicates when it is time to start a new grain. This clock will be configured with the inter-onset time t (in seconds), or an onset rate r (in hertz) where:

$$t = \frac{1}{r} \tag{22.1}$$

In order to start a new grain, the switch is set to a grain generator that is not currently in use, the required parameter values are set, and the onset of a new grain is triggered. Parameters will remain the same for the duration of the grain, so the parameter generator does not need to keep track of those settings. When a generator has finished producing a grain it becomes available to generate another. Each grain is likely to be produced with different parameter values.

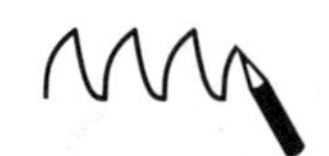

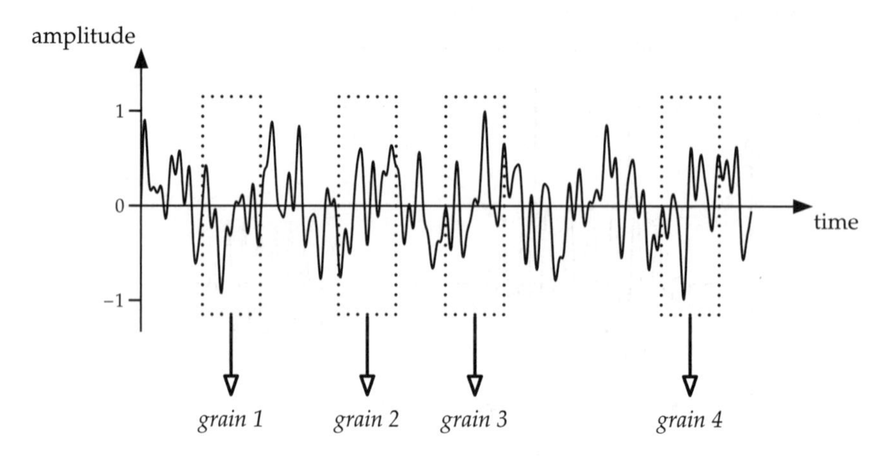

(a) Extracting from a long sound

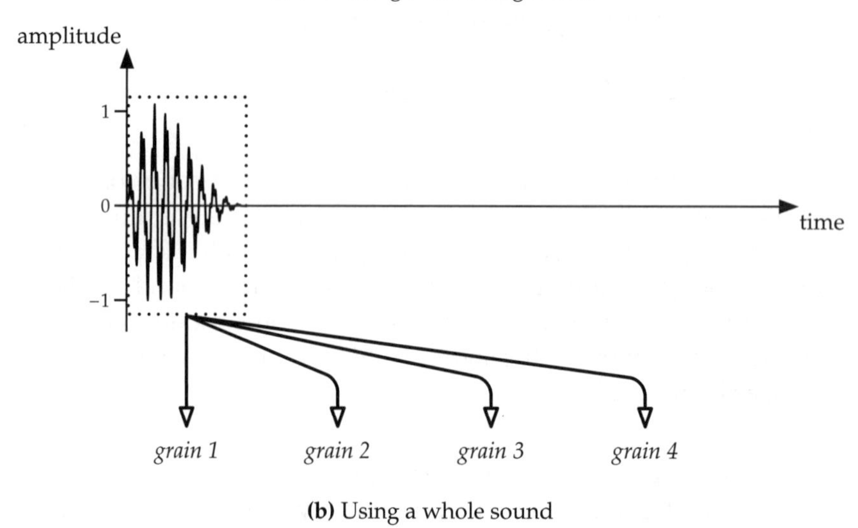

(b) Using a whole sound

Figure 22.2 Examples of grain extraction

Figure 22.4 illustrates an example grain generator that uses a sound stored in a lookup table. The playback mechanism is similar to that described in §15.1.3 (p.465) for sample playback and uses lookup table methods described in §14.4 (p.444). The duration value is the same for both envelope generators, which is the length of the grain. Values p_l and p_u are the chosen starting and finishing positions in the wave lookup table to extract the desired section of the sound. These will be values between 0 and 1, which is the range of the lookup table input, corresponding to the start and end of the stored sound.

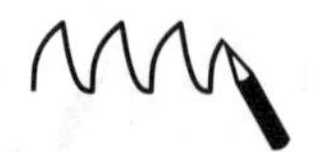

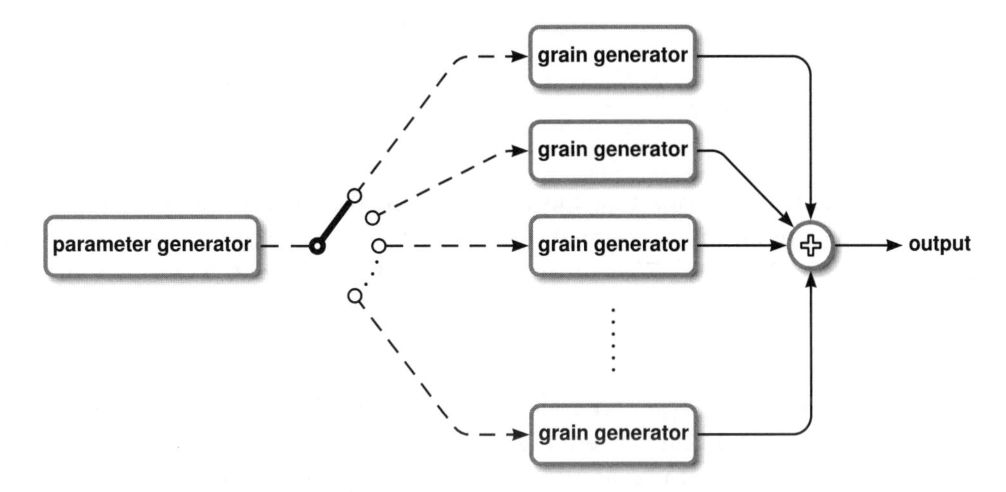

Figure 22.3 Basic granular synthesizer form

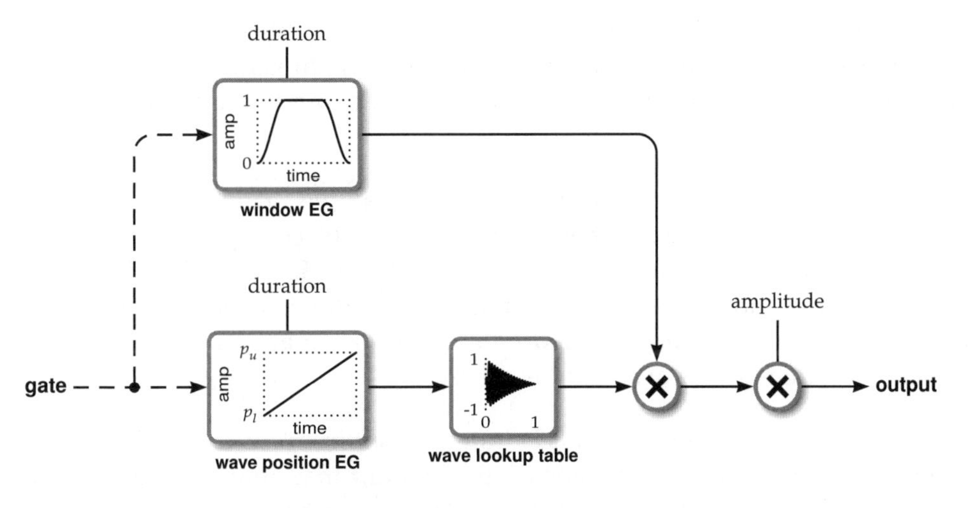

Figure 22.4 Example grain generator

The following calculations can be used (where positions and durations are in seconds):

$$p_l = \frac{\text{starting position}}{\text{stored sound duration}} \tag{22.2}$$

$$p_u = p_l + \frac{(\text{sample increment}) \times (\text{grain duration})}{\text{stored sound duration}} \tag{22.3}$$

A sample increment of 1 means that the waveform in the lookup table is played at its original speed. Changing the increment will affect the playback of a grain in the same way as described in §15.3.1 (p.473). For example, an increment of 0.5 will play the grain at half speed. Negative increments will reverse the playback direction compared to the original source sound.

In the cases when the grain is a complete sound (figure 22.2b) it will have a complete amplitude envelope. The amplitude envelope typically will smoothly rise and fall at the edges. However, when the grains are small pieces of a longer sound (figure 22.2a) it is likely that the amplitude envelope will have sharp jumps as it starts and ends. These can lead to harsh artefacts in the synthesized granular sound.

To avoid the edges of a grain extracted from a longer sound causing artefacts, the grain's amplitude envelope needs to be smoothed at the edges. This is achieved by multiplying the grain by a window function, which has values that tend towards 1 in the centre and taper to 0 at the edges (as shown in figure 22.4). Window functions are described in more detail in Appendix B. A typical choice for granular synthesis is the Tukey window function, which has a convenient shaping parameter (α). In general, the value of α will be chosen by ear to remove any undesirable harshness, but without compromising the underlying character.

It is possible to extend the grain generator. For example, it might incorporate some filtering after the lookup table, whose parameters could change from grain to grain. Similarly there might be a pan position control (§5.5.2, p.121) such that different grains are positioned differently in the stereo soundfield. The grain generator does not have to be based on playback of a sound stored in a lookup table; any synthesizer that can be configured to produce grains of sound can be used.

The number of grain generator instances must be sufficient to cope with the number of simultaneous grains, which depends on the amount that grains overlap in time. As grains might be generated at a high rate, the process of parameter generation, switching, and grain generation will be mainly automatic. Programming the synthesizer, therefore, is about controlling the high-level process operation, such as specifying envelopes that determine how the onset rate and grain duration change over time.

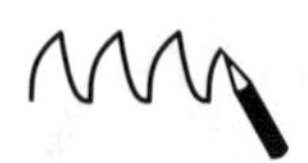

22.1.3 Lookup Table Sources

Two common sources for the lookup table in figure 22.4 are a prerecorded sound or a continuous audio input. The prerecorded sound could be from a sampled source or synthesized for the purpose. This has the advantage of making the whole of the data accessible from the beginning of the sound event, such that it is possible to jump to different positions, play the sound backwards from the end and so on, without delay. Parameter envelopes can be triggered from a gate input such that the tonality evolves in the same way for each sound event.

Using a continuous audio input allows the granular process to be used as a modifier (sometimes called a *granulator*), such that it can be used as an effect. This requires a somewhat different approach to that described previously, as the source is constantly changing. For example, it is not possible to jump to the end of the input sound and work backwards, unless the whole of the input has occurred. If a trigger for parameter envelopes is required then it might require a method such as that described in §13.2.3 (p.414).

With a continuous audio input, a long circular buffer (as described in §8.1.3, p.225) stores the incoming signal. It is necessary to wrap around both ends of the buffer when reading and writing values. Each grain generator will be configured to use a portion of the input buffer by the parameter generator. If the sample increment is less than or equal to 1 (including negative values), then a grain can start at the current write position in the input buffer if required, as the read pointer position will not overtake the write pointer. If a sample increment greater than 1 is required then it is necessary to start reading at an earlier position in the buffer to avoid that problem. The input will have reached the current write position plus the grain duration by the end of the grain.

A typical extension to the continuous audio input method is to incorporate a feedback loop to allow recirculation of results, which can be used to produce a continuation of the output with recursive granulation. An example arrangement is shown in figure 22.5, which uses a recirculating technique (as described in §10.3.2, p.315).

22.1.4 Parameter Relationships

Granular techniques can produce a wide range of sound characters. The relationships between the parameters and the result can be complex. With a long inter-onset time and a long grain played at its original speed, the result is a fairly clear sequence of sound instances; for example, the sound of a water drop falling on a surface at half second intervals. However, as the onset rate increases it becomes a frequency that can be audible in the output (such as 100Hz) in addition to the frequency partials within the source sound.

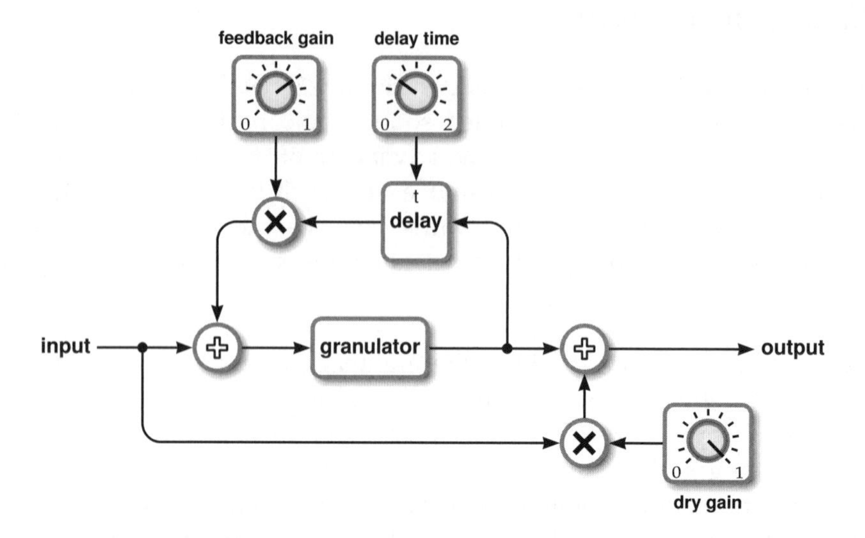

Figure 22.5 Granular technique with continuous audio input and feedback

The example grain stream illustrated in figure 22.6 shows that there are periodicities in both the grain onsets and the underlying waveform. When the onset rate is an audible frequency and the duration is short enough that there is little or no overlap between the grains, a type of amplitude modulation synthesis is produced (as described in Chapter 20), where the modulation rate is the grain onset rate. The result is that perceived pitch can depend not only on the source sound, but also on how the granular process modulates the underlying waveform.

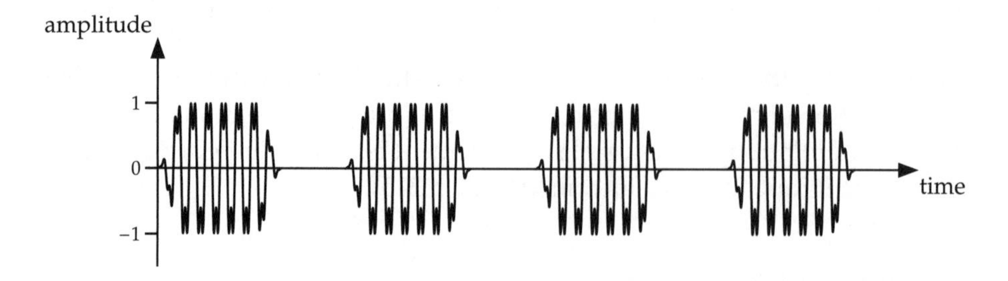

Figure 22.6 Grain stream with regular (periodic) grains

It is also the case that the tonal character is not determined purely by the choice of source sound and position within that sound from which grains are extracted. The grain duration, the shaping provided by the chosen window function, and the onset rate (and so the overlap of grains of a particular duration) are important. With long overlapping grains the output is continuous, whereas with short grains with gaps in between it is not,

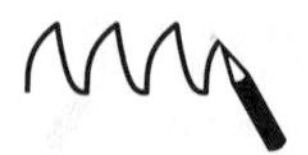

which affects the type of tonality produced. However, the character can also be affected by having a sharp-edged grain envelope, or a high onset rate. Experimentation is required to appreciate the relationships between these parameters and the result.

As a means of aiding control over granular synthesis, it can sometimes be desirable to link parameters together such that they are more correlated, rather than acting independently. For example, grain duration might decrease as underlying waveform fundamental frequency increases.

22.2 Granular Synthesis Techniques

22.2.1 Fixed Parameters

The most straightforward type of granular synthesis uses a fixed sound source (such as a stored sample, or a consistently synthesized tone) and fixed generation parameters to determine the characteristics of a stream of grains. In the case of a stored sound, the starting position in the sound is not changing. The grain onset rate (and so the inter-onset time) is also constant, and so the density of grains is fixed.

Figure 22.7 illustrates how a grain stream might be generated. The horizontal axis shows the passage of time. The vertical axis shows the time domain form of a source sound. The angled lines in the body of the plot indicate individual grains. The vertical range of each line shows how much of the source sound is used to create the grain, and the horizontal range shows the duration of the grain in the output. The lines are at a 45° angle in the figure, which indicates that the output is at the same playback speed as the original sound (a sample increment of 1). Lines at different angles would indicate different sample increments. The figure shows the generation of grains at a fixed onset rate, and a grain duration that is less than the inter-onset time, which means that there is a gap between the grains.

Figure 22.8 shows an example time domain output produced by non-overlapping stream generation. The source waveform is a continuous synthesized tone in this particular case. Each grain has been shaped by the window function.

Figure 22.9 shows a stream of grains, again with no overlap, but where the source waveform is a recorded sample. With a sufficiently long grain, there can be a fairly significant change in waveform over its length. Some of the natural envelope of the section of the sound still exists, but has been further shaped by the window function. One technique is to use a long sample and move the starting position for the grain to find an interesting portion of the sound, and then use the other parameters (onset rate, duration, sample increment, window shape) to modify the character.

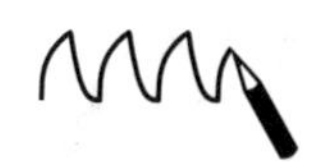

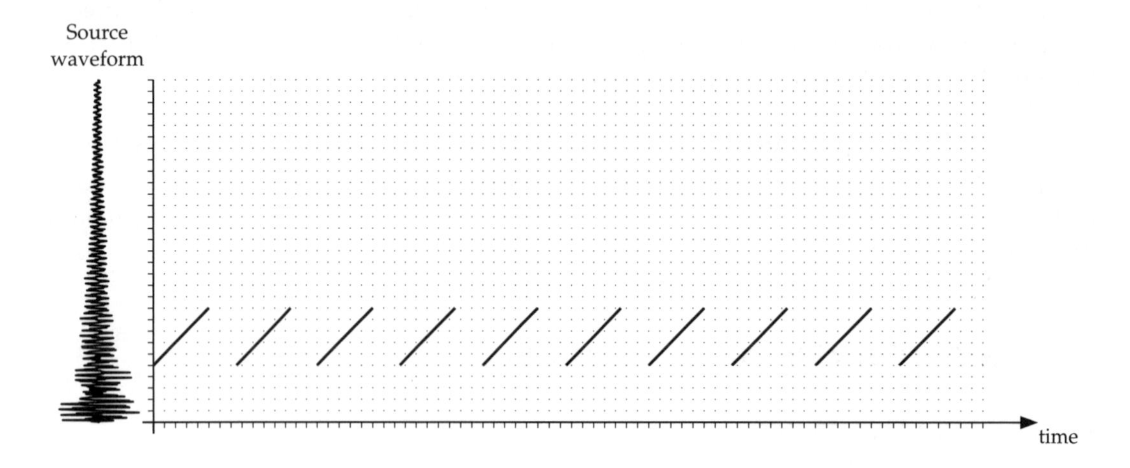

Figure 22.7 Stream generation with non-overlapping grains

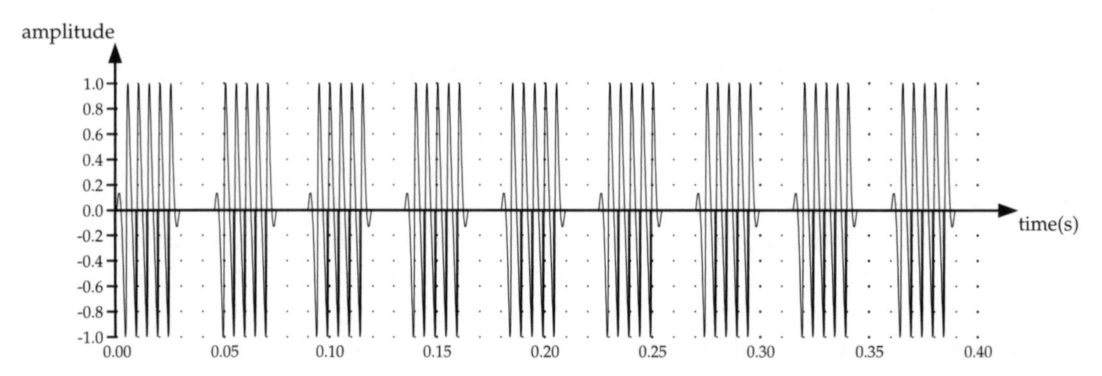

Figure 22.8 Non-overlapping grain stream using a continuous synthesized tone

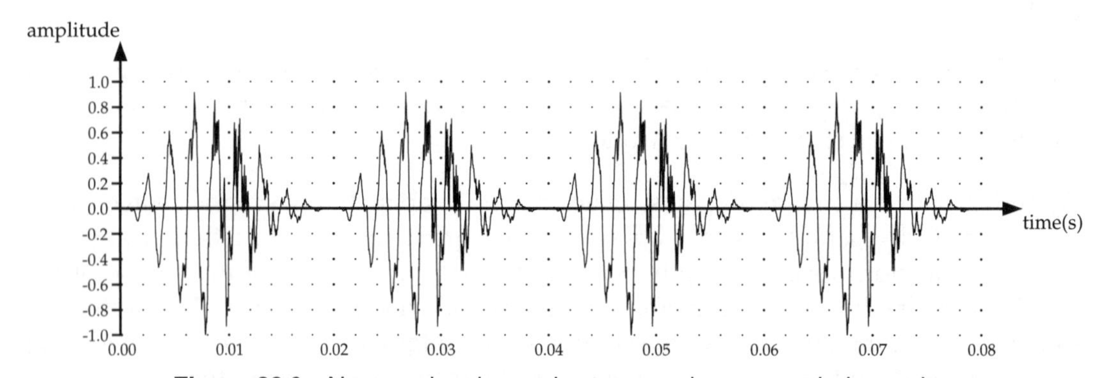

Figure 22.9 Non-overlapping grain stream using a recorded sample

As well as using a part of a longer sound to create a grain, it is possible to use a complete sound as the grain, as shown in figure 22.10. The figure shows how the grain is from the beginning to the end of the source waveform, rather than a section from the middle (as in figure 22.7). This might be a short sound such as a handclap, or a water droplet falling on a surface, or any other short sound that might be used in multiple to create a longer output stream.

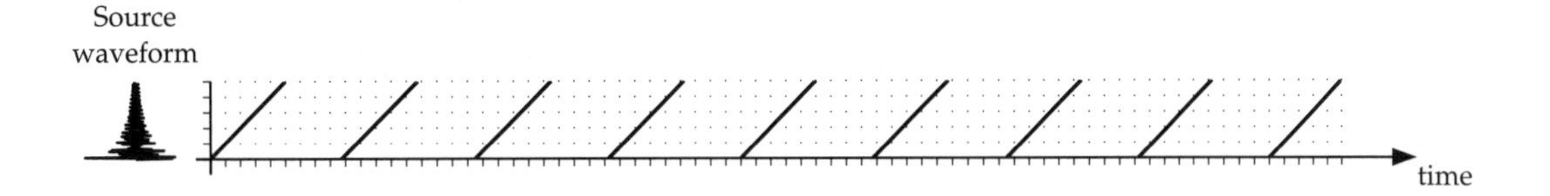

Figure 22.10 Stream generation with a complete sound and non-overlapping grains

If the Tukey window function is used, then the value of α could be 0 if a complete sound is used as a grain. This will help preserve any transient portion at the beginning of the source sound. Figure 22.11 illustrates a stream of non-overlapping complete sounds.

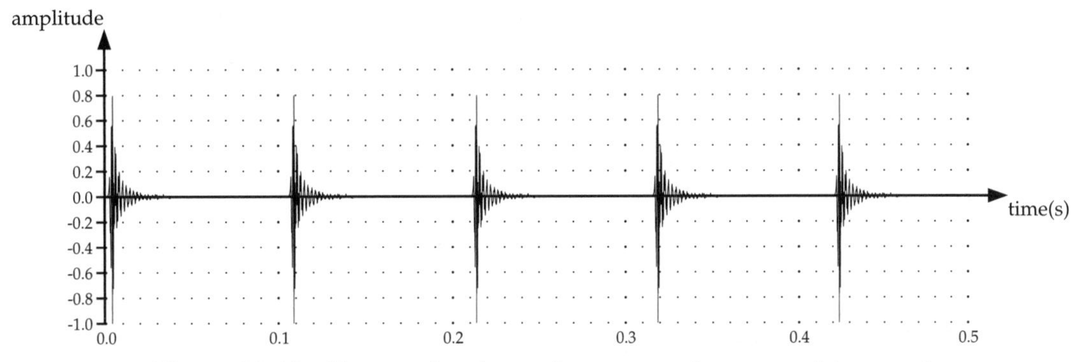

Figure 22.11 Non-overlapping grain stream using a complete sound

Figure 22.12 illustrates grain stream generation where the inter-onset time is less than the grain duration. The overlapped grains are added together and produce an output without gaps between the grains, as shown in the time domain plot in figure 22.13. The source waveform is the same constant synthesized tone as for figure 22.8.

With a constant time between grain onsets, there is a periodic repetition of the waveform. At low grain onset rates and short durations (such as 20Hz and 20ms respectively) the particulate nature of the stream tends to be apparent. However, the more complex amplitude modulation effects described in §22.1.4 (p.615) can occur at higher rates.

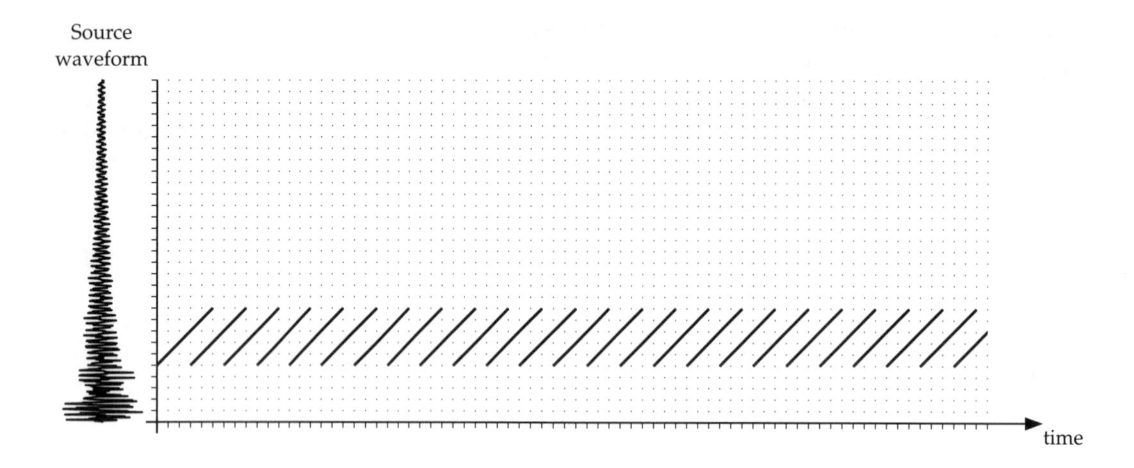

Figure 22.12 Stream generation with overlapping grains

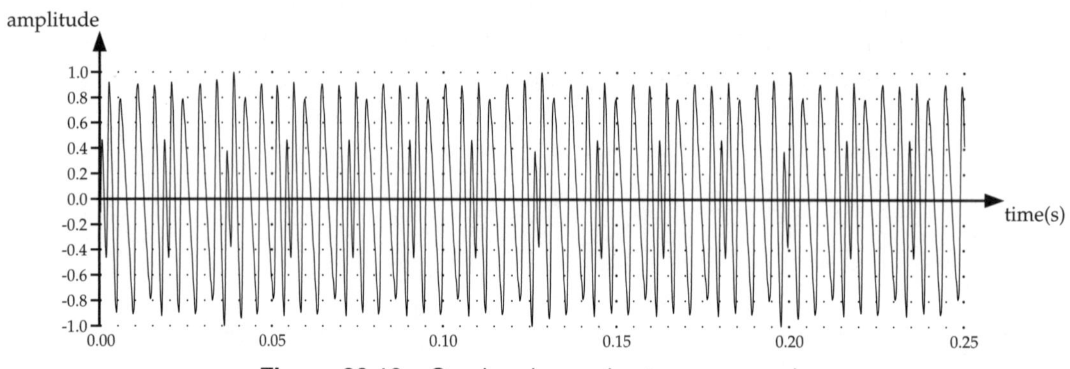

Figure 22.13 Overlapping grain stream example

22.2.2 Envelope Control

Granular synthesis with fixed parameters (as described in §22.2.1) produces an unchanging tonal character. More interesting sounds can be achieved by changing the parameters over time, such that different grains will have different characteristics. Note, however, that each grain will normally have static configuration for its entire duration; the change is from grain to grain.

Figure 22.14 illustrates two envelopes applied to a grain stream. An amplitude envelope is applied over the length of the sound, such that the sound event has a finite length. The amplitude effect has been indicated by a colour scale from white to black, and is a simple rise and fall over the length of the plot. The second envelope has been applied to the onset rate, such that the time between grain onsets changes. In the figure the onset rate

(and so the density of grains) increases from the start to the middle of the sound, and then decreases towards the end. Other grain parameters, such as the starting position in the source sound, the duration, and the sample increment remain constant throughout the sound.

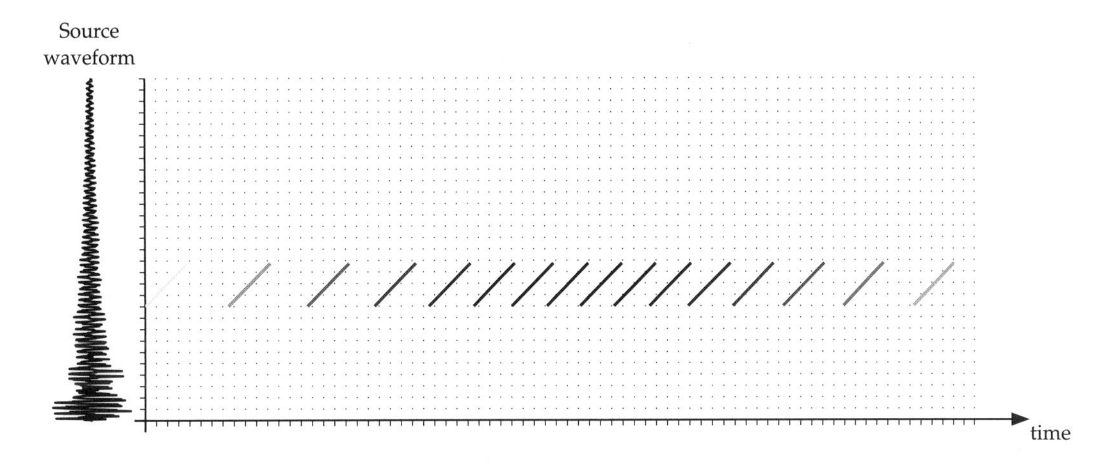

Figure 22.14 Stream generation with envelopes example 1

With relatively small variations in parameters such as onset rate and duration, the variation in tonality will similarly be fairly subtle. With more significant changes in parameters, results with sound effect characteristics are produced, as the tonality varies more substantially. When onset rates significantly less than 100Hz are used in conjunction with shorter durations (say, less than 30ms), the results become more clearly grainy, or like mechanical vibrations. Higher onset rates can produce a less grainy or a pitched result. Choosing the source sound is important; it is useful if it provides a range of sound character along its length, such that the starting position for grains can be varied to find different tonalities. Recorded samples of natural sound events (such as instruments or speech) are useful material.

Figure 22.15 illustrates the use of an envelope to move the starting position of grains through the source waveform from beginning to end over the length of the sound event. Rather than picking out a particular section of the source sound, the whole of the sound will be processed. The result follows the original progression of source sound character. This effect will also occur if the source of sound is a continuous audio input, as described in §22.1.3 (p.615), for which the current position in the sound is constantly changing.

In figure 22.15, the lines indicating the individual grains are not at a 45° angle as in previous examples. In this particular case the sample increment is 0.5 so the grains are played at half the original speed. However, the starting position increases at the same pace as the original sound. With careful choice of parameters this will achieve a pitch

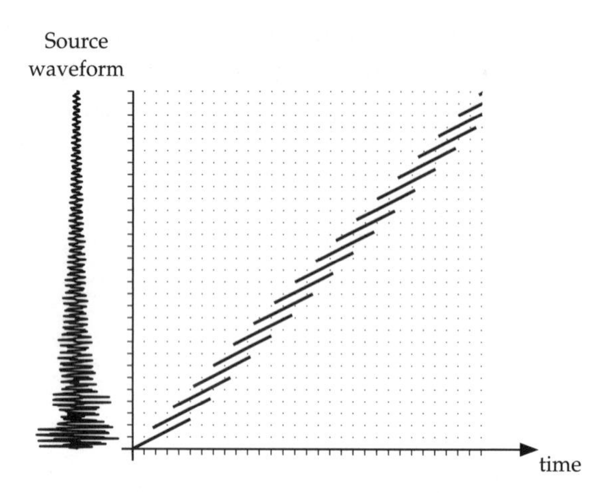

Figure 22.15 Stream generation with envelopes example 2

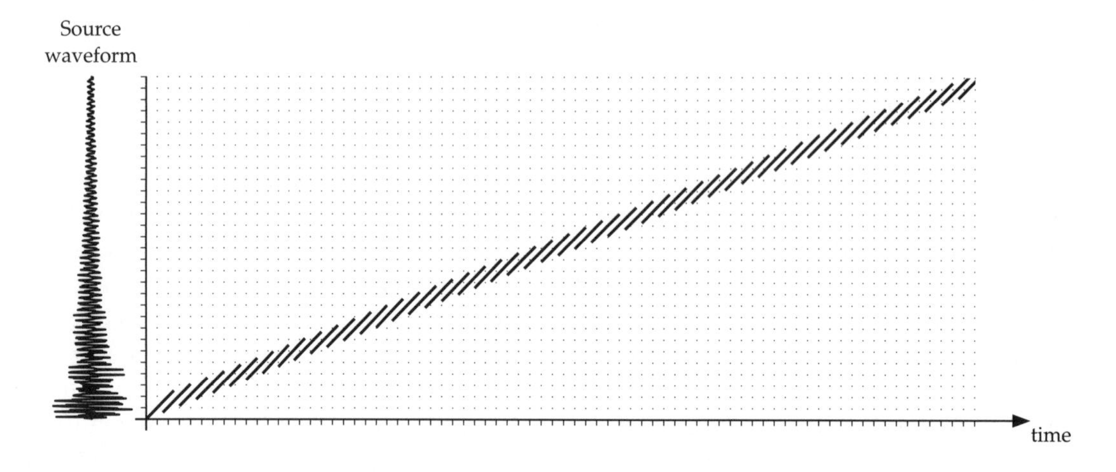

Figure 22.16 Stream generation with envelopes example 3

an octave below the original source sound while maintaining the original length. It is necessary to adjust the parameters to minimise the "bubbling" and chorusing effects that can be produced. For example, an onset rate of about 20Hz to 30Hz and durations of about 60ms to 75ms are a reasonable starting point. Pitch changes do not have to be as radical as an octave shift. A very slight pitch change might be combined with slight delay, filtering, and possibly spatial position changes to produce voice doubling or a similar effect.

With a stored sound it is possible to change the length without changing the pitch. Figure 22.16 shows the starting position moving through the source sound at a slower pace than

the original sound, such that the output can be longer than the original. However, the sample increment of the grains is 1 so the pitch remains the same as it was. By changing the starting position envelope it is also possible to create a sound that is shorter than the original.

The processes illustrated in figures 22.15 and 22.16 have differences from the effects described in Chapter 15 as the pitch and length can be changed independently. The latency (processing delay) with granular methods can be quite small, but the results are not necessarily as smooth as those produced by frequency domain methods (which are described in §12.3, p.382).

22.2.3 Random Variations

The techniques described in §22.2.1 and §22.2.2 assume that the parameter values are fixed, or follow particular envelope shapes. By introducing randomised variation to the parameters they can vary around the envelope positions. This can reduce the sensation of mechanistic grain generation. Subtle randomisation can produce naturalistic variations in tonal character, but larger variations can also be used.

Figure 22.17 illustrates stream generation with three parameters that include a random component; inter-onset time, starting position in the source sound, and amplitude. There is also an envelope that steadily increases the starting position in the source sound. Figure 22.18 shows a method for combining an envelope and a random variation produced by a noise generator, in order to produce values for a parameter. The envelope is added to a random variation of a chosen rate and depth. The combined effect is then scaled to an appropriate range for the parameter in question. The scaling allows the range of effect to be changed easily without having to change the envelope and noise generator depths.

With short grain durations (less than 100ms), the randomisation can add fuzziness to the tonal character. With complete sounds forming the grain, then randomisation can be used to add some more naturalistic qualities to a stream. For example, if a raindrop sample forms the grain, subtle randomised variation to (otherwise fairly fixed) parameters such as onset rate, amplitude, and tonal character (such as with a lowpass filter control) can be applied. The effect then becomes a more convincing dribble of water from a tap, where each drop sounds slightly different from the others. Similarly, with a vocal sample as input, using durations of a similar length to a phoneme or syllable can produce interesting stuttering effects with random variations.

Including randomisation adds another aspect to parameter control. All together the parameters of granular synthesis provide considerable scope for sound generation, but it can take some time to explore the possibilities.

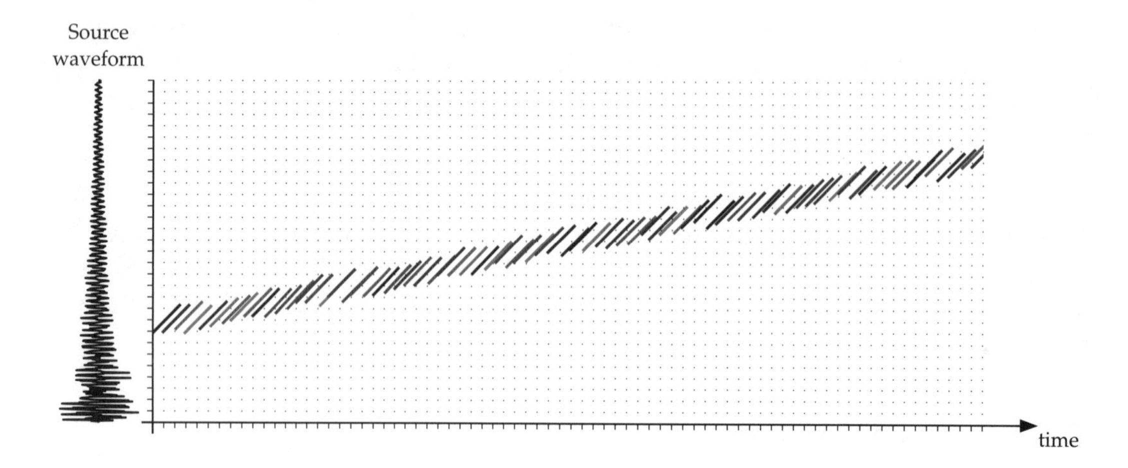

Figure 22.17 Stream generation with an envelope and randomisation

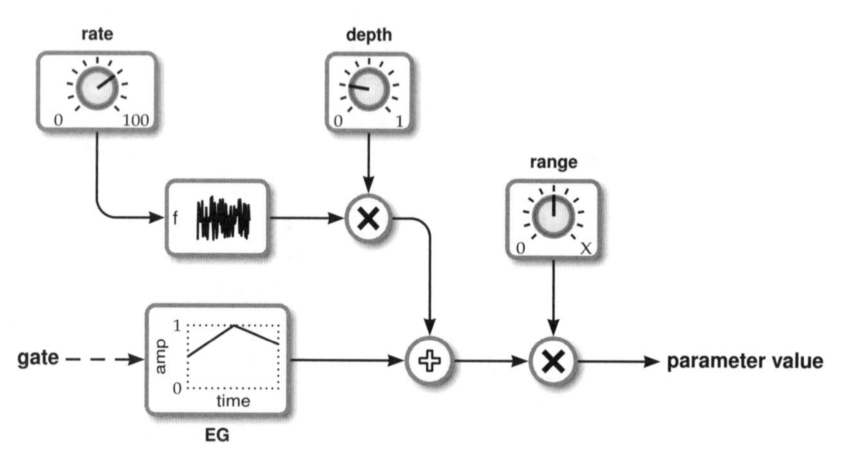

Figure 22.18 Envelope and randomisation combination

22.2.4 Parallel Streams

With a single grain stream, there is one parameter generator, which manages its set of grain generators (as shown in figure 22.3, p.613). This method can produce many different types of sound, but works less well with cases where there is a natural parallelism in the composition of the sound character. For example, it is difficult to make a single stream of handclaps sound like audience applause. Increasing the density of grains through greater onset rate tends to make the result sound like a rattling mechanical device. In the acoustic world, audience applause is actually created by a number of grain streams

playing together (individuals clapping), which is something that can be simulated with a parallel arrangement.

Figure 22.19 illustrates multiple grain streams being generated in parallel that are added together at the output. Each requires its own parameter generator and associated grain generators.

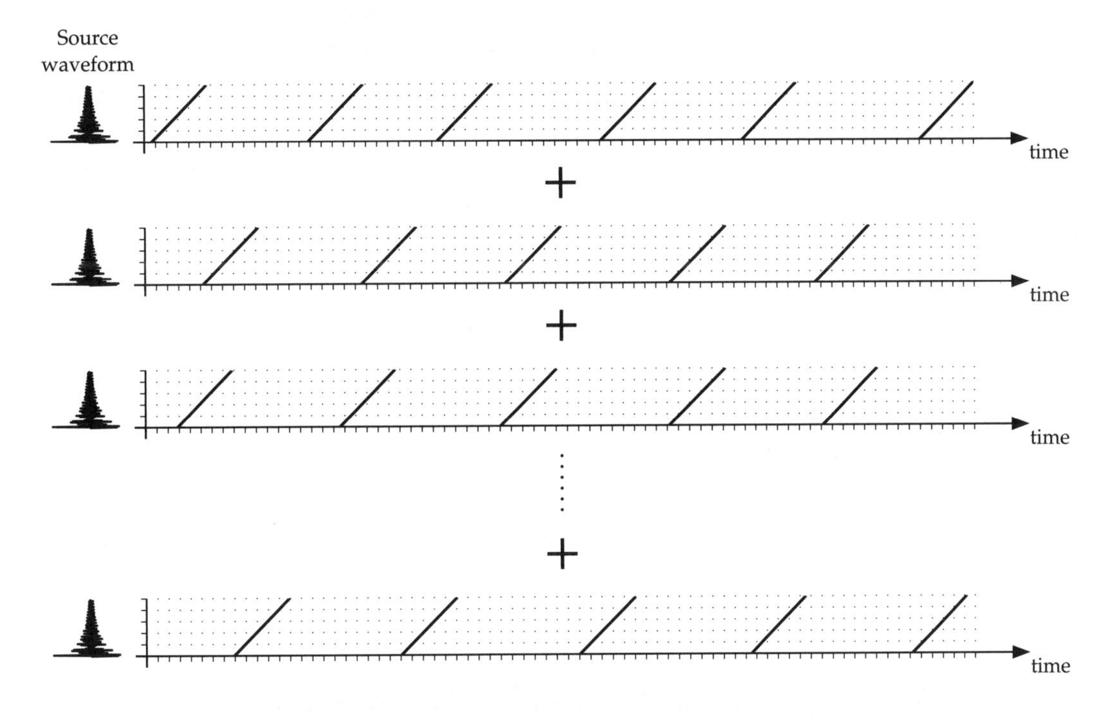

Figure 22.19 Parallel stream generation

A convincing audience applause effect can be achieved with the following configuration:

- Each stream represents one person clapping. Generally individuals clap at a fairly regular rate, although there is some subtle variation. The grains are a complete handclap sound.
- The streams are not synchronised. That is, all individuals clap at their own speed and usually without claps lining up between individuals. Of course, there are cases where audiences clap in near-synchrony, such as clapping to the beat in a song as it is performed. With applause, however, that is not usually the case.
- Different individuals are associated with slightly different sounds, which depend on the size of their hands and how they bring them together, and their position in the room.

Incorporating the following features can increase the realism:

- Using a different clap sound for each stream prevents the streams being too highly correlated, to avoid phasing effects and too much timbral similarity.
- Each stream can have a slightly different acoustic treatment, such as different pan positions and slightly different reverberation effects.
- Small random variations in amplitude or lowpass filter cutoff frequency can be applied to each grain, to simulate natural variations between claps.

The overall result is a very complex pattern of grains, but with individual streams having consistency that can be heard within the output. More streams and more complex relationships between the parameters of the different streams produces a more convincing effect. There are other sounds that can be developed with a similar approach, such as the sound of multiple people walking across a hall together, or parallel dribbles of rainwater falling from a roof onto a path.

Parallel techniques can also be applied in other situations. For example:

- Musical chords or vocal harmonies can be created from a single input source by use of parallel granular streams that each have a different pitch change. This can use the techniques described in §22.2.2 (p.620).
- A composite result might be achieved through use of different source sounds for different streams, or control parameters that are chosen to create different (but complementary) textures or regions of frequency emphasis. The blend might change over time. This has similarities to the ideas described in Chapter 19.

22.3 Developing Processes and Learning More

Granular synthesis has requirements that are notably different from the other synthesis forms described in this book. The implementation must address the issue of generating large numbers of grains in parallel (as per the form in figure 22.3, p.613). At high onset rates, the ability to generate grains with consistency in timing is important to the tonality of the result. It will depend on the underlying programming library or environment as to whether it is possible to generate parallel events in large quantities with audio rate timing accuracy, or whether such techniques are limited to control rates (the differences are described in §23.1.2, p.633).

As well as a need to trigger parallel sound events, it is also necessary to be able to select the grains from the source in the desired manner and apply a window function, such as using the technique shown in figure 22.4 (p.613). This assumes that parameter values can be calculated as required (such as with the form in figure 22.18, p.624, and with equations 22.2 and 22.3, p.614) and buffers can be accessed with those values. In less flexible libraries

and environments, it might require some adaptations or low-level programming to make all the granular techniques possible.

The techniques described in this chapter require different configuration approaches to other synthesis techniques, due to the nature of a granular stream. The configuration style depends on what is chosen for the granular parameters (as shown in figure 22.1, p.611). For example:

- Complete samples of acoustic sound sources used as grains that are replayed at low onset rates can easily be viewed as a collection of sound instances being strung together in a pattern, such as a dripping tap, or someone clapping. Variations in such parameters as the onset rate, amplitude, and processing of the grains (such as filtering or sample increment) have clear relationships to the results.
- At high onset rates with short grains, the parallels with amplitude modulation synthesis are significant (as described in §22.1.4, p.615). This implies a different approach to configuration, with consideration of the frequency relationships between grain onset rate and the underlying waveform.

Granular synthesis provides opportunities to approach sound creation in a different kind of way to the continuous oscillation techniques of, say, additive or subtractive synthesis (discussed in Chapters 16 and 17). This leads to distinctive sound characters (particularly at moderate onset rates) that are hard to create with other synthesis forms. It requires some experimentation to become comfortable with the parameter controls, however.

Further discussion of granular synthesis and related techniques can be found in these books:

Cook, Perry R. 2002. *Real Sound Synthesis for Interactive Applications.* Natick, MA: A K Peters.

Roads, Curtis. 2001. *Microsound.* Cambridge, MA: The MIT Press.

The following sources provide some more advanced material that relates to this chapter, which can be used for further study:

Jones, Douglas L., and Thomas W. Parks. 1988. "Generation and Combination of Grains for Music Synthesis." *Computer Music Journal* 12:2:27–34.

Roads, Curtis. 1988. "Introduction to Granular Synthesis." *Computer Music Journal* 12:2:11–13.

Truax, Barry. 1988. "Real-Time Granular Synthesis with a Digital Signal Processor." *Computer Music Journal* 12:2:14–26.

Part IV
Control

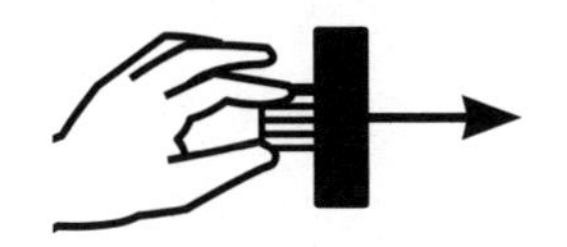

23

Process Organisation and Control

23.1 Components of Organisation and Control

23.1.1 Introduction

The usability of an audio process does not only depend on the underlying process form, such as how a flanger or an additive synthesizer is constructed. The process also requires a suitable practical framework in which it can operate. Firstly, there must be sufficient processing capacity within the system for the chosen application and suitable data management. For example, parallel process paths are required for multichannel modifiers and polyphonic synthesizers. However, there are more subtle ways in which a system is designed in order to achieve the required results. For example:

- Mapping a tonal parameter value from a control input in such a way that equal steps in input result in equal perceptual steps in sound character.
- Controlling the transitions between synthesized notes in a manner that achieves a convincing instrument-like effect.
- Linking a hardware control to multiple underlying parameters in such a way that all desired combinations of values can be achieved.

Figure 23.1 illustrates two methods of amplitude control for a simple synthesizer. In figure 23.1a the oscillator frequency and amplitude gain are provided by separate control inputs. For practical purposes, the amplitude gain control might be a breath sensor, a foot-controlled expression pedal, or another source of continuously-variable values. This arrangement resembles an acoustic instrument such as a clarinet, where there is continuous control over amplitude through breath control, and the fingers select the notes. The main advantage of this form is the ability to create a wide variety of envelope shapes whose features can be varied during performance and be different for every sound event. These features might include unusually-shaped tremolo modulations or a sudden swell at the end of the note.

Figure 23.1b is a synthesizer arrangement with automatic amplitude variation. There is an overall amplitude envelope generator, and oscillator 2 provides a tremolo effect, with parameters f_d, a_d, and a_o as described in §9.2.1 (p.270). The preconfiguration of behaviour means that the synthesizer is easy to play, and consistent between sound events. It can also be scaled up to a polyphonic arrangement, where controlling the amplitude of each note individually is difficult for one person. However, the continuous and direct control of gain in figure 23.1a has been taken away, which will change the audible result.

There are many possible combinations of manual and automated parameter variations to achieve different styles of control for modifiers and synthesizers; for example, whether control values are produced from a hardware device controlled by a person, or replayed from a sequencer. There is no universal control arrangement. Suitable design choices need

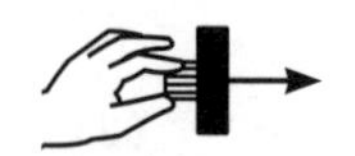

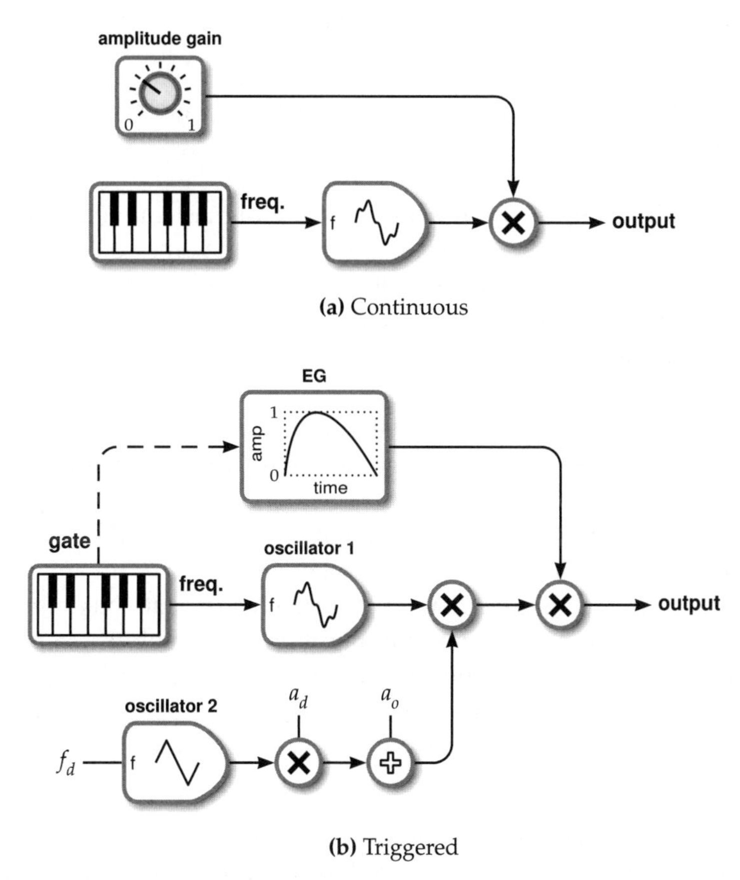

Figure 23.1 Amplitude control in a synthesizer

to be made based on optimising the control relationships for a particular situation. It is important to recognise that those design choices always have implications for the audible results that are achieved.

23.1.2 Process Segmentation

Data flow within a digital audio system occurs at different rates depending upon the production and consumption of that data. Sometimes the rates are chosen by the audio process designer, and sometimes they are imposed from elsewhere, such as by an operating system, host program, or hardware interface. Some typical examples of data rates are as follows:

- The rate at which audio samples are received from, or sent to, a digital audio interface.

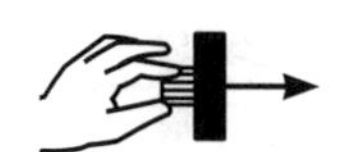

- The rate at which a graphical display is refreshed to show the current peak amplitude level.
- The rate at which new values are received from a hardware rotary control when it is being varied.

As a general rule, audio samples are processed at the highest rate (such as 44.1kHz, or 96kHz), which is the *audio rate* (or audio sample rate). Most other data flows are at rates that are at a considerably lower frequency, which can be broadly categorised as *control rate* values. There are often more than two processing rates within a system, but generally they divide into those categories.

Figure 23.2 represents a typical process model that includes a split between components at control and audio rates. The benefits of segmenting the process include the following:

- It is more efficient to process data at different rates than always at the highest rate. There is no point in updating a visual display at 96kHz as it cannot be refreshed at that rate, nor can changes be visually perceived that fast. Neither is it desirable for unnecessary processing to occur that might impact the ability to perform a more sophisticated task at the audio rate. It is often the case that an audio process can be duplicated (in terms of the number of channels, or number of simultaneous notes) or used at higher audio sample rates, which causes inefficiencies to become more significant.
- It is possible to locate particular computational tasks within the most appropriate segment, which aids in the design and implementation of the processing. Ultimately, this can help achieve efficiency and maintainability.
- Segmentation is the first step towards the use of *parallel threads* in the process. For example, it is desirable to separate the processing of control inputs and visual output from the audio, such that changing a control on a graphical interface does not cause the audio thread to stall.

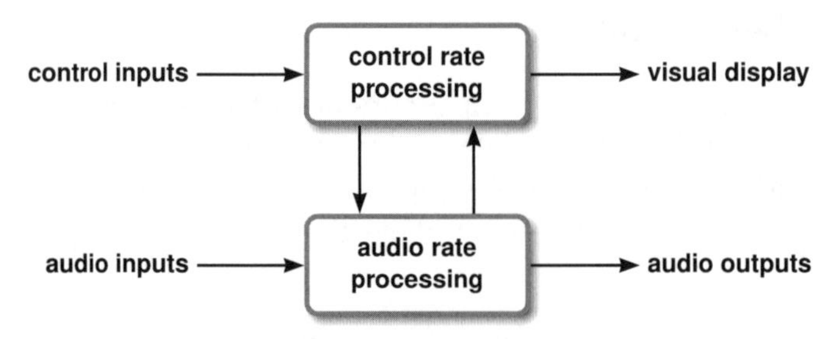

Figure 23.2 A typical process model

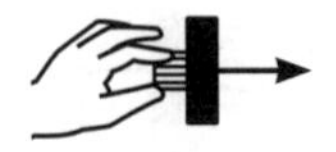

The rate at which certain elements of a process are computed depends on the situation. For example, a manual parameter control is normally processed at the control rate, but if it is replaced with a modulation effect (as described in Chapter 9) then it is appropriate to update the parameter at the audio rate. This can have consequences for the subsequent process elements. If the parameter being modulated is a filter cutoff frequency, then the filter algorithm must allow its parameters to be updated at the higher rate. Similarly, synthesized sound events are often triggered at a low rate (such as from a keyboard input), but in a granular process (Chapter 22) sound events must be created at high rates with accurate timing. Without audio rate processing, the tonality will not be as anticipated.

Many audio processes are used in parallel, which requires a duplication of signal paths such that they can be processed independently. In some cases, the parallel processes will be controlled separately, as illustrated in figure 23.3a. For example, the filter settings for different channels on a mixer will often be different. Sometimes parallel paths will have common controls (figure 23.3b) such as a master amplitude gain applied to a multichannel output. It is also possible to have a mix of different types of control, such as a polyphonic synthesizer where there is some common configuration, and some that is specific to the note being played on a particular synthesis voice (as described in §23.2.2, p.645).

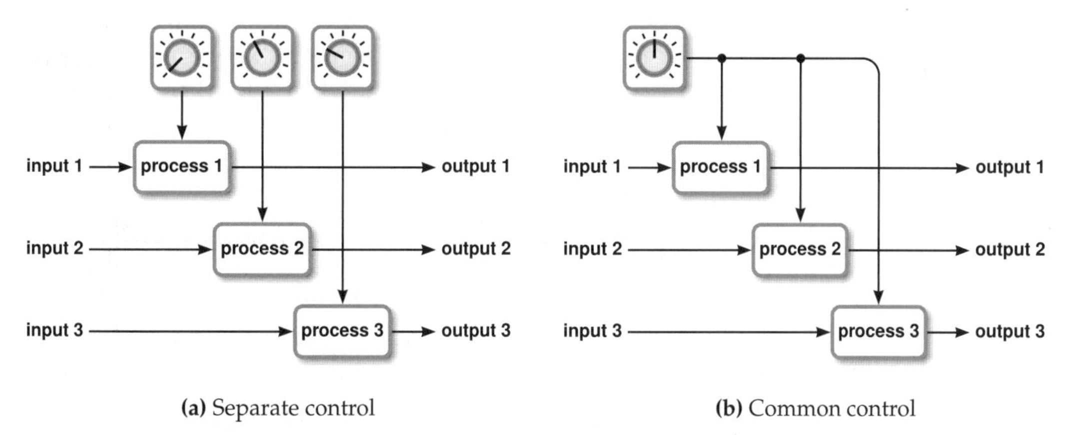

(a) Separate control **(b)** Common control

Figure 23.3 Parallel process paths and their configuration

As audio processes become more sophisticated, they tend to have more parameters to control their operation, which can quickly become difficult to manage. A typical solution is to abstract control into layers. Figure 23.4 shows an example of a two layer control arrangement. The upper layer has a small number of parameters (to provide sufficient control for most situations), whereas the lower layer provides many parameters (to change the fine details of the process operation). In the figure there is one upper layer control that maps to multiple lower layer parameters (a *one-to-many* mapping), one that maps directly to a single lower layer parameter (a *one-to-one* mapping), and one lower layer parameter that is not represented at the upper layer.

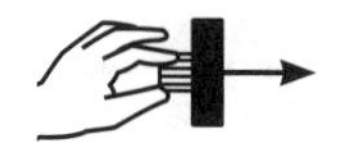

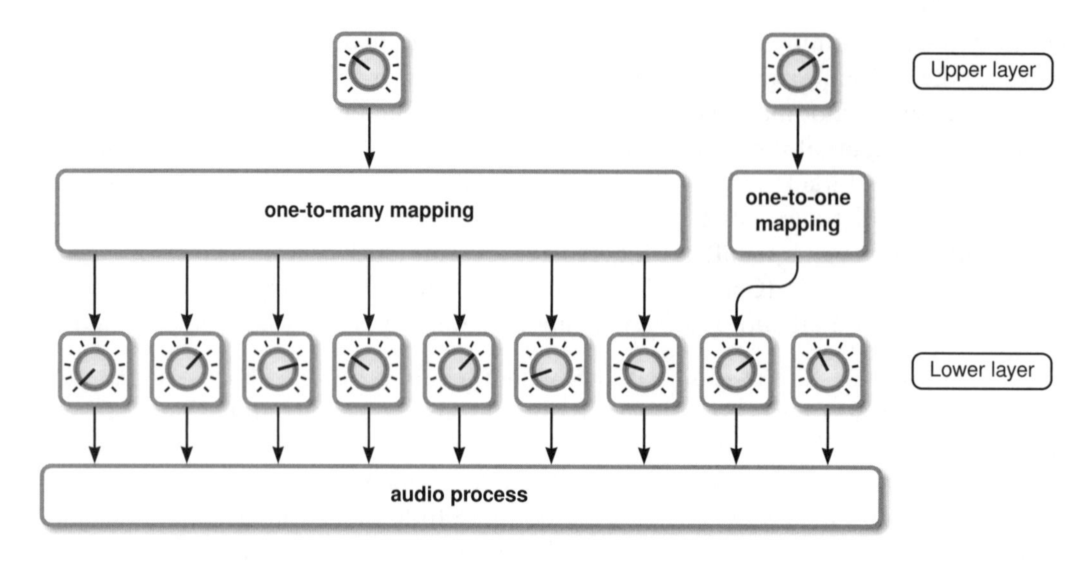

Figure 23.4 Different control layers

A form similar to that in the figure can be used to optimise a control arrangement. This is not only because controlling every parameter individually might be overwhelming for some users, but also because the lower layer parameters might be hard to use, due to an unintuitive or inconsistent control law. Some example uses of multiple layers are as follows:

- A reverberation process (such as those described in §10.4, p.323) can have many parameters. A typical user will not want to change all the delay times, filter frequencies, and gain parameters individually in order to achieve a change of character. The user would normally be provided with a parameter such as "room size" that maps to multiple underlying parameters in order to achieve a progressive variation in character with one control.
- Some mixing consoles allow faders to be grouped such that moving a single control causes the level of all the faders to vary, while maintaining the relative level balance within the group.
- In musical performance, it is often useful for a synthesizer's character to be varied with relatively few controls. For example, a foot-controlled expression pedal might be used to change multiple parameters of the underlying synthesis form, leaving the hands free to play a keyboard. It could be very difficult to vary all the individual lower layer parameters individually in that situation. Multiple layers also allow optimisation of control, by mapping a linear change of input control to a non-linear variation in a frequency parameter, for example.

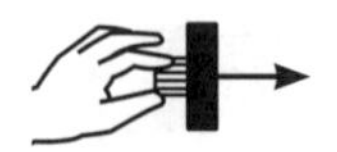

- Different users can require different amounts of control. A novice might only wish to use a subset of controls that are most important. However, the expert might be provided with an option to reveal the lower layer of controls for more fine tuning when necessary. Presets in the interface might also be used to set parameters to common values, from which the user might make smaller changes.

23.1.3 Processing at Different Rates

Having established that there is a need to process data at different rates, it is necessary to consider how this is managed. Generally control data is processed through two mechanisms:

- A control event can trigger a part of the process or update the underlying process state, such as a callback function that only runs when a control change occurs. For example, a button press might cause a modifier to be bypassed for subsequent input samples, or a note-on gate signal might cause envelope generation to begin.
- Alternatively control values can be read and written at regular intervals. For example, the value produced by a hardware input might be read (polled), or a meter updated, at a set rate.

Regular control rate activity can be achieved as part of the audio processing loop. Audio rate sample data is often processed in blocks, as described in §8.1.2 (p.221). Inside the process, a form similar to that in algorithm 23.1 might be used. It is possible to perform some control rate operations once per buffer, and audio rate operations within the inner loop. At an audio sample rate of 44.1kHz and with a buffer size of 512, once per buffer processing will occur at a rate of approximately 86Hz. This might be adequate for reading the values of generally static controls and configuring some process elements, or updating a visual display. However, the regularity will vary with sample rate and buffer size, and might not be sufficiently rapid to avoid audible effects.

Algorithm 23.1 – Processing function 1

input : buffer of N audio rate input samples
output: buffer of N audio rate output samples

```
// perform operations that occur once per block
...
```

for currentposition = 0 **to** N−1 **do**

```
    // perform operations that occur for every sample in the buffer
    ...
```

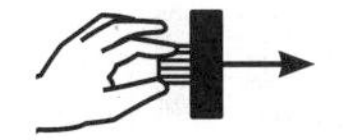

As an alternative to the previous method, algorithm 23.2 uses a counter to determine how often control rate operations occur. The value of variable *controlcount* is maintained between calls to the function, and initially has a value of 0. Knowing the audio sample rate (f_S) and equation 8.1 (p.220) it is possible to calculate the number of samples (C) to achieve the desired regularity of control rate operations:

$$\text{Number of samples equivalent to } T \text{ seconds} = T \times f_S$$

$$\text{Number of samples equivalent to } F \text{ hertz} = \frac{f_S}{F} \qquad (23.1)$$

Algorithm 23.2 – Processing function 2

input : buffer of N audio rate input samples
output: buffer of N audio rate output samples

```
for currentposition = 0 to N−1 do
    controlcount = controlcount + 1
    if controlcount == C then
        // perform operations that occur every C samples
        ...
        controlcount = 0

    // perform operations that occur for every sample in the buffer
    ...
```

There is no rate of control data processing that is perfect for all circumstances. Control values might change regularly or irregularly, and frequently or infrequently. It is inefficient to communicate and process irregular and infrequent data at a regular high rate. The latest value read from a control input might be compared to the previous value, such that further communication and processing will only occur if necessary. However, in some circumstances control data processing must be at a sufficiently high rate to act on rapidly changing values, in which case a control rate of 1kHz or more can be appropriate.

The difference between the control rate and audio rate can produce audible effects. Figure 23.5 illustrates a changing amplitude gain control value, which is read at a rate considerably less than the audio sample rate. It causes jumps in the output signal that can be audible as clicks. The effect of stepped changes is sometimes called "zipper noise". When a control value is used to change a delay time, the consequence can be that the output moves to a very different waveform shape as well as a different amplitude. In a recirculating effect (such as those described in §10.3, p.313 and §10.4, p.323) the audible artefacts of control changes can be repeated, making the effect even worse.

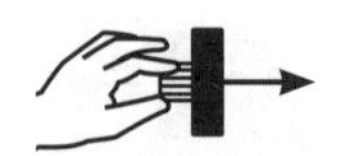

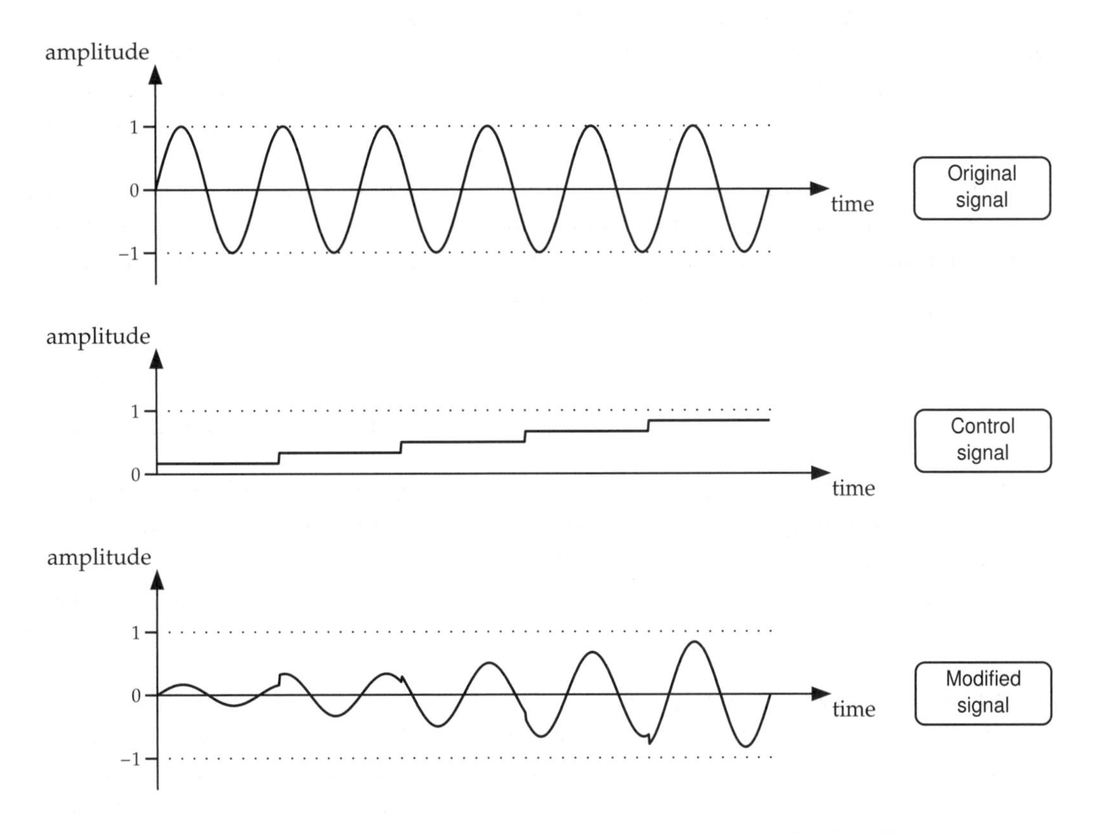

Figure 23.5 Changing control values used for amplitude gain

A logical conclusion might be that a higher control rate should be used to make the control steps smaller and the resulting changes less audible. However, in many practical cases the rate at which values are read from the original source (such as an on-screen graphical control, or a hardware fader) cannot be changed by the audio process. It is also the case that the amplitude resolution of a control might be relatively coarse, and so an increased control rate might not reduce the size of the steps.

A suitable alternative is to use a single segment envelope generator (as described in §14.3.2, p.431) to smooth the transitions between control values at the audio rate before use in the relevant part of the process. The generator initialisation function is called when a change in control value is detected and the target is updated. The duration is chosen to reduce the audible artefacts without making the transitions too slow. A 30ms transition is reasonable for a manually updated amplitude gain control. If the same technique is applied to transitions in delay time, then sliding pitch effects can often be heard rather than clicks; whether this is desirable depends on the application.

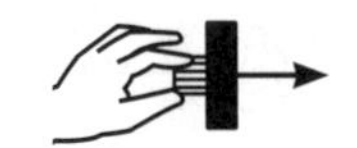

As described in §2.2.4 (p.35) and §14.5.1 (p.449), some processes benefit from having a higher Nyquist frequency to reduce aliasing effects. However, it is not always possible or desirable to increase the sample rate used in the majority of the system. The alternative is to operate internally at a sample rate that is higher than that used at the main input and output of the process. This is achieved by upsampling to a higher rate, performing the main part of the process, and then downsampling to the original rate before the output. The sample rate conversion algorithms that achieve this are beyond the scope of this book, but are sometimes included in audio programming libraries and environments.

Figure 23.6 illustrates two results of a hard clipping modification (as described in §7.1.2, p.196) applied to a sinusoidal input, when processed at different sample rates. The first plot is without sample rate conversion, in which aliased partials are apparent. Sample rate conversion (upsampling, processing, then downsampling) was used in creating the second plot, which achieves a visibly improved result. Whether the additional computation to achieve this is justified depends on the context and severity of the aliasing.

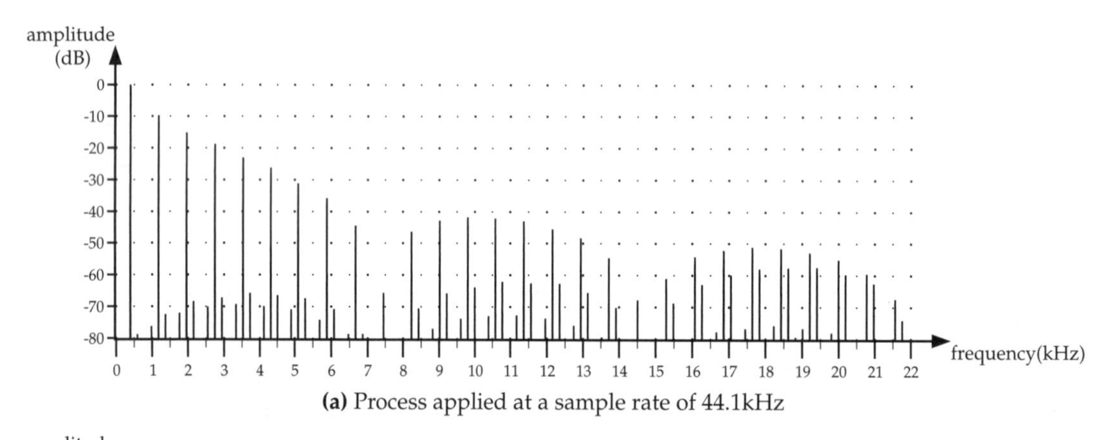

(a) Process applied at a sample rate of 44.1kHz

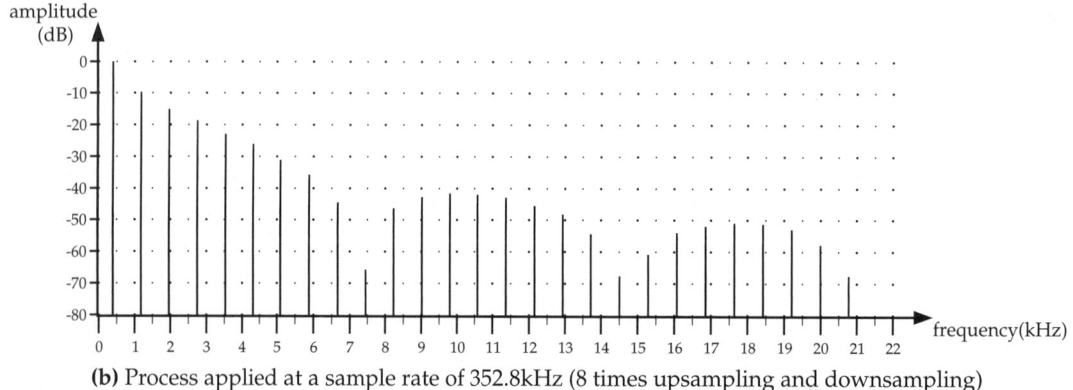

(b) Process applied at a sample rate of 352.8kHz (8 times upsampling and downsampling)

Figure 23.6 Average spectrum plots for a 392Hz sinusoid hard clipped

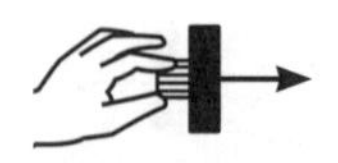

23.1.4 Control Inputs and Mapping

Musical digital audio processes are typically associated with particular hardware controls. Graphical representations of those controls are also found in software interfaces. The prototypical musical hardware systems are:

- The mixing console; with faders, rotary controls, buttons, and switches.
- The piano-style keyboard; with key velocity sensing, and continuous controls such as modulation and pitch-bend wheels.

Those two styles have a strong influence on how audio processes are usually controlled. There are many other forms of control sensing, such as force, 2D or 3D position, acceleration, and orientation. Graphical controls manipulated with a mouse or similar device provide further options. There is no perfect control style that is appropriate in all circumstances. Some example considerations are as follows:

- Whether control values are provided constantly (such as the output from an orientation sensor) or upon particular events (such as a velocity value when a piano-style key is first depressed).
- The nature of quantization (such as semitone-spaced note numbers from a piano-style keyboard) and whether the control magnitude resolution is sufficient (such as whether a range of integer values from 0 to 127 provides small enough steps along the range of a controlled parameter).
- Whether the physical style suits the controlled parameter, such as a centre-sprung pitch-bend wheel, or a non-contact continuous distance sensor.

Changing the control style affects the audible results even if the underlying process remains the same. A continuously variable frequency control produces different results to one limited to semitone steps. A continuous breath sensor controlling amplitude gain allows more performance control than a fixed envelope generator for the same purpose. A foot-controlled parameter allows both hands to be used for other tasks, which is different from the situation where all parameters are hand-controlled.

Figure 23.7 illustrates a typical control path from input to controlled process. The conditioning/analysis block takes outputs from the control device and produces values suitable for the subsequent stages; for example, smoothing the data if the values are inconsistent, or analysing control gestures for complex sensor data. The mapping block is to achieve an effective relationship between the input and controlled process parameters. This includes producing an appropriate parameter value range, preventing regions of control where it is difficult to achieve the desired value and regions that have little effect, and achieving the desired results efficiently (rather than with many time-consuming adjustments).

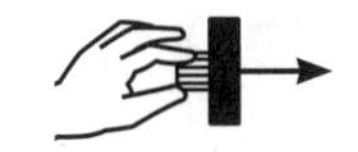

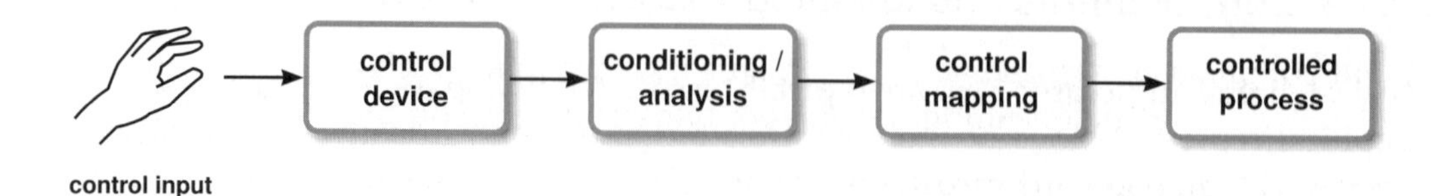

Figure 23.7 Typical control path

In some cases, there is a linear relationship between control input magnitude and device output magnitude. Physical rotary and slider controls exist that have a linear control law (although non-linear taper controls are also common). In other cases, there is a non-linear response by the control device to an input.

Figure 23.8 shows a comparison between a linear control device response and a possible non-linear response. In the linear case, equal steps in control input magnitude lead to equal steps in device output. The non-linear example is not specific to a particular control device, but might be an electronic drum pad sensor response, for example. If the pad is struck very softly then there is no output at all, as the input is below the lowest response threshold of the sensor. When the magnitude of input becomes greater, the sensor starts responding and the curve rises rapidly to a region where it responds approximately (but not completely) linearly. Above that region is an area where the response flattens out. That is, if a pad is struck very hard, or extremely hard, the response is fairly similar in output, as the sensor is less sensitive to variations at those input magnitudes.

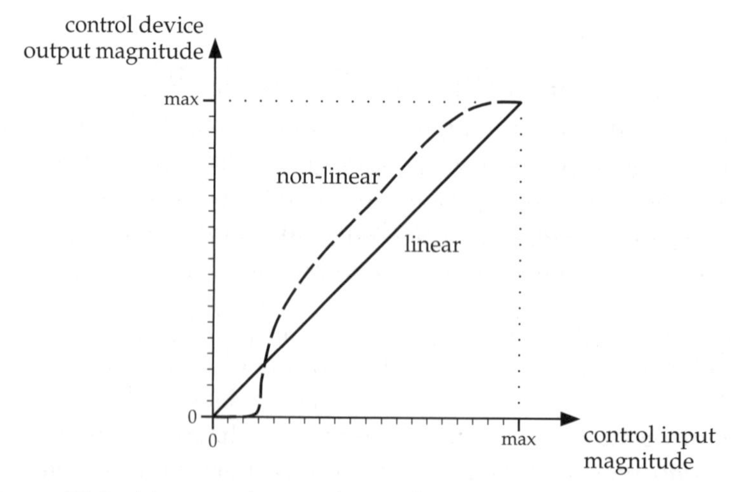

Figure 23.8 Linear and example non-linear control device responses

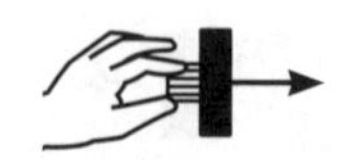

The non-linear response in figure 23.8 might not be what is required. For example, it might be desirable to have greater variation in output for higher values, and more subtle control over low output magnitudes. The control mapping block in figure 23.7 can be used to reshape the response before it reaches the controlled process, as described in Chapter 24.

As regards the controlled process itself, it is clear from previous chapters that parameters are often controlled in a non-linear way. For example:

- A centre frequency control for a bandpass filter (described in §6.2.2, p.149) should often relate to perceived pitch rather than linear frequency to maximise its usability.
- A linear change in a cross-fading parameter (described in §19.4, p.553) will not necessarily lead to a linear variation in perceived character.
- Parameters in frequency modulation synthesis (described in §20.3, p.567) can have a complex relationship to tonal character. As such, a more indirect and non-linear control mapping might be necessary if it is to be made easier to use.

As illustrated in figure 23.4 (p.636), it is not necessarily the case that users will control each underlying process parameter directly and separately. Multiple process parameters can be controlled from a single parameter at a higher level. Sometimes the role of a control will change, such as where it might be assigned different roles on a digital mixer control surface depending on the current task.

Constraining the range of process parameters can aid usability in performance. For example, a small number of semitones mapped from a pitch-bend wheel might be more useful for a particular piece than a range of two octaves. A modest range of flanger depth from an expression pedal could be used to achieve a subtle variation, which would be harder if the control mapping covered a wide range that allows extreme results. A frequency control might be dedicated to mid-range rather than all audible frequencies, in order to make it easier to tune precisely without the physical movement needing to be very small.

The following are three common parameter control arrangements:

- Parameters that are fixed at the configuration or editing stage.
- Parameters that are varied by a signal generator to a configured pattern; for example, mixer control automation, or low-rate modulation by an oscillator.
- Parameters that vary as part of performance; for example, cross-fading between two sources with a fader, or varying the harshness of a synthesized sound with key velocity. Performance parameters can also vary the behaviour of signal generators such as envelope attack time, or oscillator rate.

Each control arrangement requires a suitable consideration of the different parts of figure 23.7.

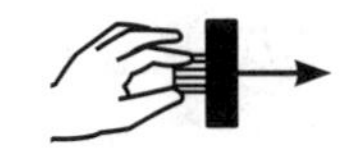

23.2 Controlling Synthesis

23.2.1 Introduction

Synthesizers generally have a more event-driven control form than most modifiers. Synthesis is often associated with a piano-style keyboard, where depressing a key (a note-on event) and releasing it (a note-off event) determine the progression of the sound. These events are conveyed in the gate signal in block diagrams. In a more continuously-controlled parameter scheme, such as the amplitude gain control in figure 23.1a (p.633), the boundaries are less clear; for example, whether it is a new note if the frequency changes, or if the amplitude becomes zero and then increases again, or whether neither relate to a conventional note event.

It is necessary to make decisions about how a process will react to control inputs, in order that the audible results have the required development over time. Figure 23.9 illustrates how choices about synchronisation of process elements to note-on events produce differences in the consistency of the results. The main amplitude envelope in the figure is triggered at each note-on event. One oscillator is used for the underlying waveform, and another for tremolo modulation. In the unsynchronised case, the oscillators are free-running and the result depends on where in the oscillator cycle the note-on occurs. In the synchronised case, the oscillators are reset to zero phase at the start of the note, producing consistent results every time.

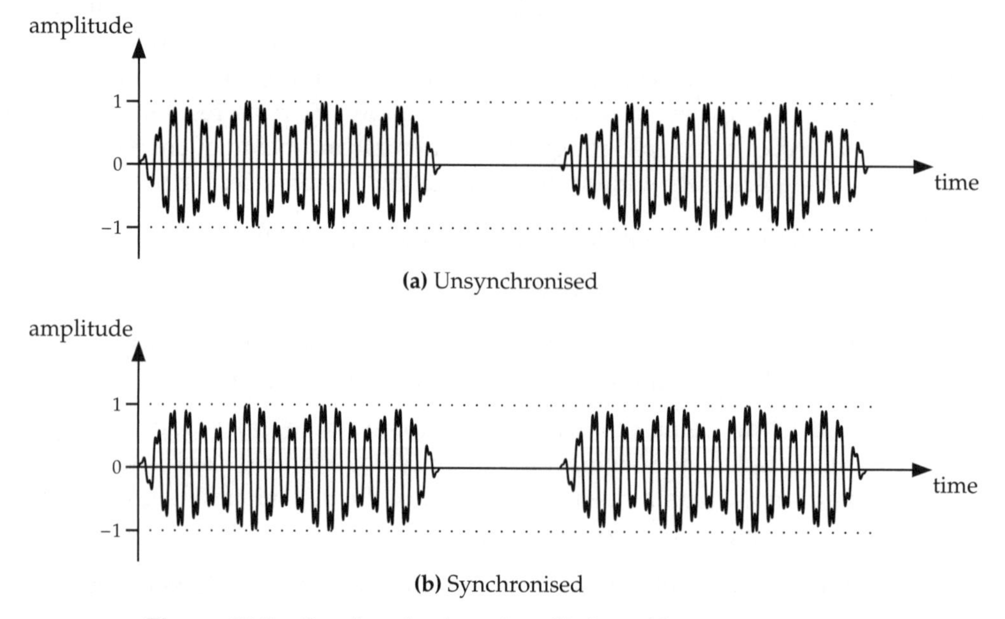

Figure 23.9 Synchronisation of oscillation with two note events

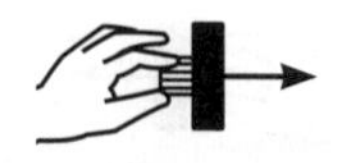

Whether parameters should be set to particular values by control events depends on the context. For example, it might be desirable for a filter variation to change slowly over time, possibly synchronised to a global tempo, rather than being reset at each note. On the other hand, it might be desirable that a filter variation is the same for each note to achieve consistent onset behaviour.

Control events can be used to drive other types of behaviour. The note-on event might cause parameters to be configured slightly differently for each note using small random variations (which is related to noise generation, as described in §18.2, p.525). This enables the simulation of subtle variations that occur when playing acoustic instruments; for example, choosing randomly from a set of similar but slightly different sounds when playing back recorded snare drum samples, and using small random variations in amplitude gain around the standard value. These are chosen at the start of the sound and applied throughout. Similar ideas can be applied to any synthesis parameter to aid in making the results less mechanistic.

As well as using random processes, the extent of the mappings from available control inputs has an influence on parameter variation in performance. If the control input is simply a switch that indicates when the sound should start, then it cannot express subtle variations. If key velocity is available, however, then it can be mapped to subtle variations in tonality.

Note events are not necessarily cleanly separated, which means that it is necessary to consider the transitions between them. For example:

- Sounds might be generated independently in parallel, such as playing two different notes on a piano. This requires synthesis using independent *voices* (or instances) that are unsynchronised such that sound events are able to begin and end at different times.
- A sound might repeat before the previous sound has ended; for example, striking a gong twice in quick succession. The second sound does not necessarily terminate the first and cause the sound to start afresh, but might add to the existing vibration.
- A change of pitch does not necessarily mean a completely independent event. For example, a legato pitch change on a clarinet might continue the existing amplitude level rather than requiring an onset of the same character as if the sound started from silence.

23.2.2 Polyphonic Methods

In many cases it is desirable to be able to synthesize multiple sounds in parallel with different control characteristics for each, which is called *polyphonic synthesis*. The most common example is playing a chord on a piano-style keyboard where each note can not

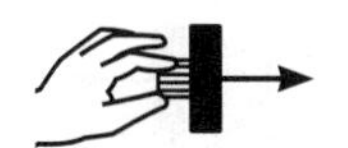

only have a different pitch, but potentially start and end at different times and have different amplitude and tonal characteristics depending on the velocity with which the key is depressed. However, a similar type of parallel processing is also used in cases such as granular synthesis (Chapter 22) that require independently-configured and generated synthesis voices.

Achieving a parallel form is quite simple in some cases. Figure 23.10 shows how separate synthesizers could be dedicated to different parts of a drum kit. The input data is automatically routed (with the switch) to the relevant synthesizer depending on control data such as note numbers. Parallel paths are required such that the different sounds can be generated simultaneously. The use of separate voices allows individual control of the behaviour of each (such as amplitude and tonality depending on the input values) without affecting the others.

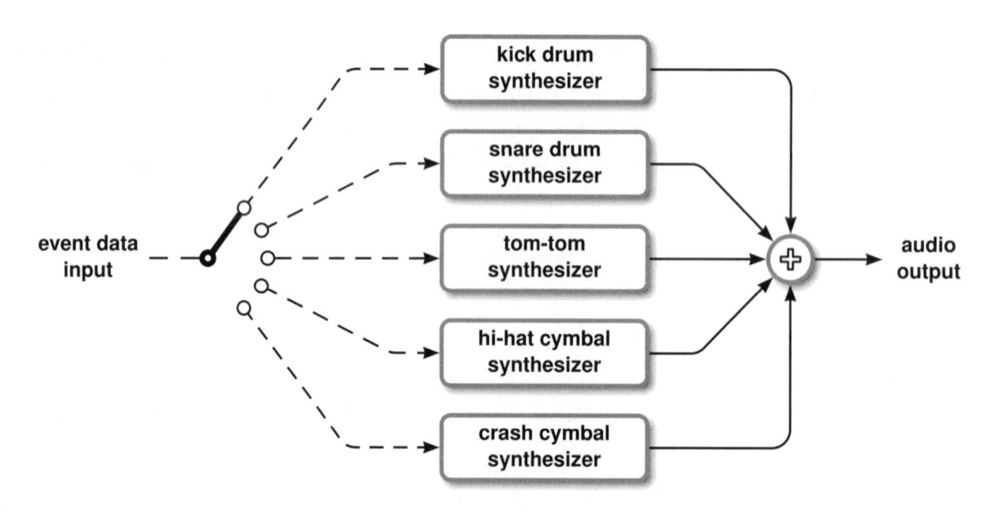

Figure 23.10 Drum kit synthesis arrangement

The form in figure 23.10 is less practical in cases where there are potentially many simultaneous sound events and pitches to be managed. Figure 23.11 shows a general arrangement that is commonly used in polyphonic synthesis. All synthesis voices are the same design, which is appropriate when a single instrument can produce multiple notes with different pitches simultaneously, like a piano or glockenspiel. This is also a suitable arrangement for granular synthesis. There must be sufficient voices to cope with the maximum number of simultaneous sound events that are required. For efficiency, unused voices will not process audio samples, so the amount of computation will vary with the number that are active.

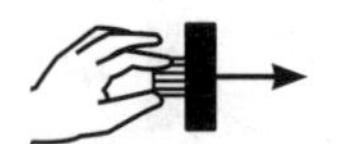

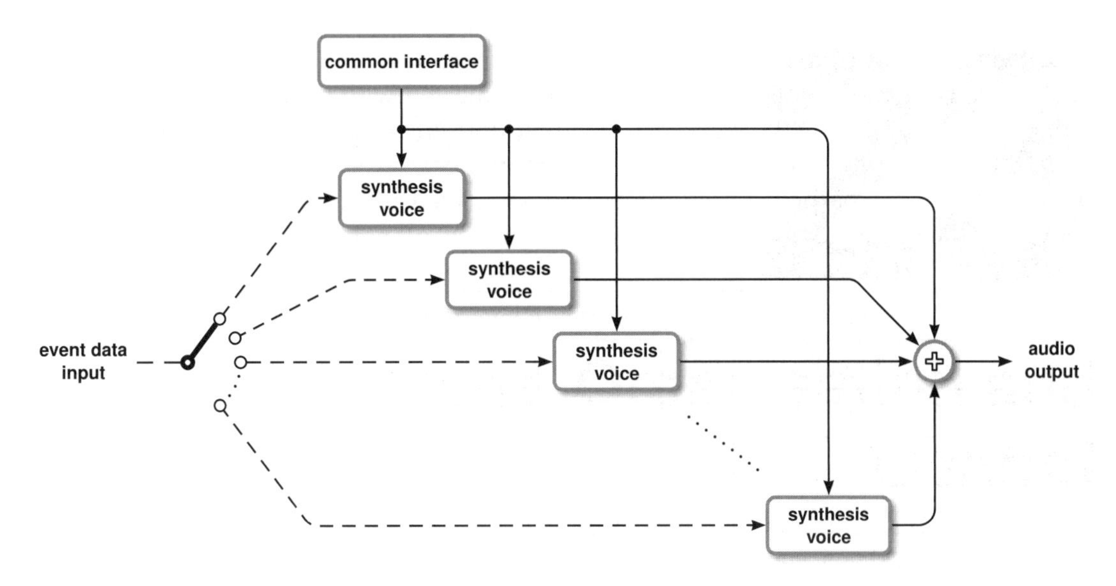

Figure 23.11 Polyphonic synthesis arrangement

Although voices are separate synthesizer copies, they share a common interface that avoids the need to set up each one separately. For example, the shape of a filter envelope and its Q value might be common to all voices. There might also be other global sources of values, such as a pitch-bend wheel, expression pedal, or master vibrato oscillator that affect all results. The event data input is separate to the common interface, and is routed to individual voices to configure characteristics that are specific to that path (such as pitch, amplitude, and tonality). Typically, event data will be information such as the note number and velocity associated with depressing a particular key on a piano-style keyboard.

For practical purposes, the management of the synthesizer must be automatic. One method is to have a voice dedicated to each available note number. With a piano simulation, there would thus be 88 voices with this scheme (corresponding to the number of piano keys). This is a suitable method in some cases, but has two weaknesses:

- It is more efficient to have a quantity of voices corresponding to the maximum number of simultaneous sound generators required for a particular context. For example, there might be a maximum of 16 sound events that occur at the same time, which correspond to a subset of the 128 note numbers in table 13.1 (p.400). If there were 128 voices then most would be idle for the majority of the time.
- Simultaneous sound events do not necessarily always relate to different note numbers. Similarly, in granular synthesis voices are not associated with individual note numbers, but with events that are distinguished by generation time.

To address these issues, a typical scheme is to use each voice as a resource that can be allocated (or assigned) to **any** sound event, if not currently in use. Table 23.1 illustrates an example sequence of events. Unused voices are indicated with a blank slot. When a key is depressed on a piano-style keyboard, the first unused voice (in a set of 8) is allocated to synthesize a sound associated with that note number. When the note ends, the voice associated with that particular note number becomes available for reuse, such as the fourth note using the voice previously associated with the second note.

Event	Note numbers allocated to voices							
Initial condition								
First note starts	**60**							
Second note starts	60	**65**						
Third note starts	60	65	**67**					
Second note ends	60		67					
Fourth note starts	60	**62**	67					
Fifth note starts	60	62	67	**48**				
First note ends		62	67	48				
Fifth note ends		62	67					
Fourth note ends			67					
Third note ends								

Table 23.1 Example polyphonic voice allocation sequence

As well as using note numbers, this style of polyphonic voice management can be used for other cases. With a granular synthesizer a voice is allocated when a new grain is required, and becomes available again when the grain has completed. The quantity of voices required depends on the density of overlapping grains that are being generated by the synthesizer.

Knowing when a sound event has ended is necessary for determining when the associated voice no longer requires processing and is available for reuse. Figure 23.12 shows two example amplitude envelopes. The first case illustrates where the length of the sound is known at the start, such as when simulating a tom-tom (assuming no after-onset damping mechanism) or in a granular synthesizer (where the grain has a known duration). The second case is a traditional sustaining envelope that waits for a note-off before beginning the release portion of the envelope.

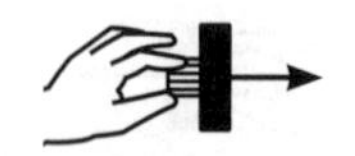

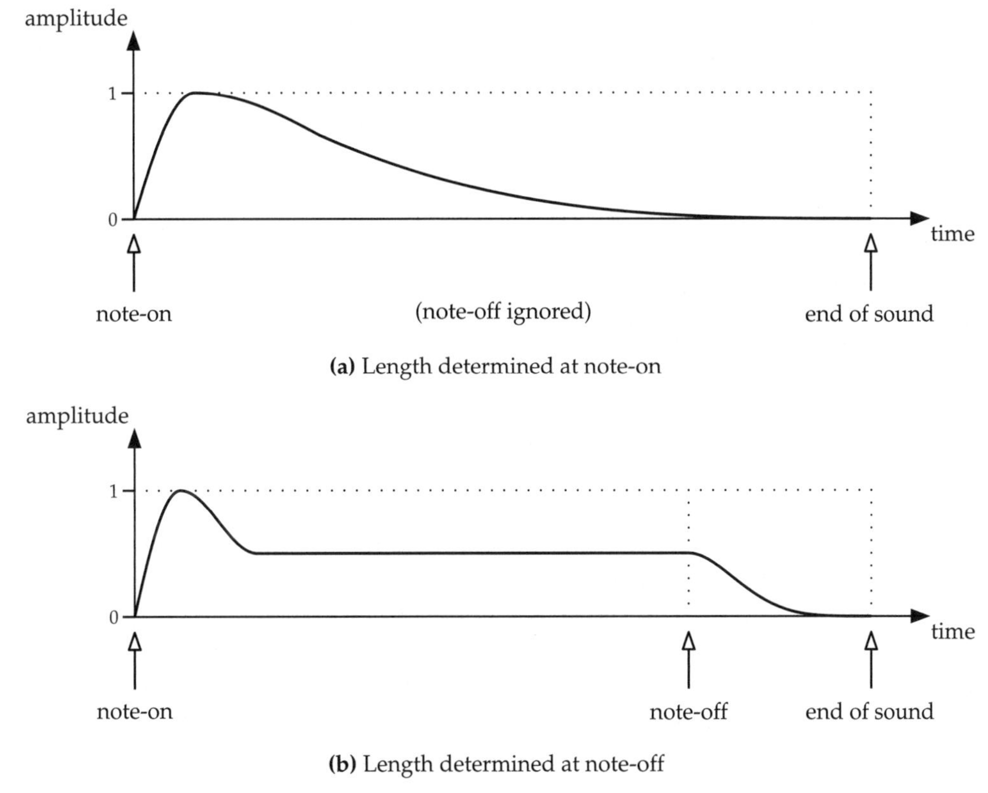

Figure 23.12 Methods for controlling sound event length

Three mechanisms that might be used for determining voice activity are as follows:

- Use the point at which the main amplitude envelope returns to a value of zero to determine when the voice is no longer active. Many traditional synthesis forms have a clear rise and fall of amplitude envelope. However, there can be issues with this approach if it is not easy to determine the overall amplitude envelope, or if it includes a zero value at a point before the end of the envelope.
- Use knowledge of the synthesizer and control mechanism to determine when the sound will end; for example, if a release segment will last a certain duration after the note-off event, or a grain has a particular length.
- Use data relating to the internal operation of particular synthesis elements, to indicate when activity is complete; for example, augmenting a sample playback routine to generate an event when it has reached the end of the sound. Similarly, if a counter is creating a set of control events in sequence, the end of the count could be used as a termination point.

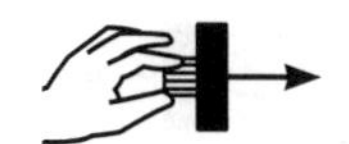

A performer might only instigate a small number of sound events at any one time, but there might be many more active voices. Many sounds continue after the performer ceases contact with the instrument. Acoustic examples include the xylophone, harp, and cymbals. More rapid playing and longer release times produce a greater quantity of overlapping sounds.

A strategy is required for when the **same** note number is used several times in quick succession and the release time is significant (which causes overlaps). One option is to use multiple voices for the same note, where the sounds are independent and the note-off events are received by the voices sequentially. An alternative is to reuse a voice that is active with the same note number, which has similarities to the effect where a piano key is played with rapid repetition. The underlying synthesis form might allow a build-up of excitation (such as a waveguide form described in Chapter 21). In other synthesis designs it might be necessary for a suitable transition to be considered, as described for monophonic methods in §23.2.3.

When resources are limited there is the potential for the control input to demand more voices than are available. One option in this situation is to ignore new note-on events while all voices are allocated. Another is to *steal* one of the existing voices for the new event, such as the one with the lowest amplitude, or the longest-running, or a voice that is in the release phase. None of these options are necessarily satisfactory. Providing a larger number of voices is often the best option, although that implies greater resource usage. An alternative design is to allocate more voices dynamically when required rather than having a fixed pool.

23.2.3 Monophonic Methods

Synthesis restricted to a single sound at once is called *monophonic* operation. Two reasons for using monophonic techniques are as follows:

- The intention can be to simulate an instrument that principally has monophonic characteristics, such as an oboe, the human voice, a trumpet, or a monophonic analogue synthesizer. There are also cases where an instrument that can produce multiple notes at once has monophonic aspects, such as playing different notes on a single guitar string.
- The transitions between notes in a monophonic synthesis situation have a different character to polyphonic synthesis with independent voices. The different character from a monophonically-controlled synthesizer can sometimes be desirable musically.

Monophonic control might be imposed by the input device, such as an infra-red distance sensor that produces a single value at once. Alternatively, there can be a polyphonic control source (such as a piano-style keyboard) whose values are interpreted to achieve monophonic control.

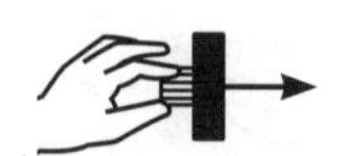

The principal issue with monophonic synthesis is achieving appropriate transitions when notes overlap. One type of overlap occurs when a note-off event has occurred, but the sound has not completed its release before the next note-on event. Alternatively, multiple keys might be held down at the same time on a piano-style keyboard controller, either due to legato playing or more explicitly. A suitable scheme is required to decide what happens each time a note-on or note-off event occurs.

Figure 23.13 shows three ways in which a monophonic note change could be related to an amplitude transition. In the first case the previous event ends abruptly when the new note is chosen, and a complete new onset is used. The second and third cases recognise that a note is already playing and create a legato transition, either with or without an amplitude variation. The designer must choose a transition that suits the context.

The first issue to solve is that a transition makes it likely that a jump in parameter values will occur (such as amplitude, frequency, or delay time). This will lead to an unwanted click in many cases, unless the variation in values is smoothed. It is sensible to use a single segment envelope generator (as described in §14.3.2, p.431) to achieve this. Fairly quick transitions can remove clicks, but slower transitions can be used for deliberate effect. For example, a slow transition in fundamental frequency will be heard as a portamento.

The second issue is how to prioritise multiple concurrent notes, such as when several keys are pressed together on a piano-style keyboard. Table 23.2 shows an example sequence of events and the resulting choice of note number. In the example the note priority scheme always outputs the most recent note number (last note priority). Therefore a new note-on event overrides a previous event. When the most recent note is released, the output reverts to the most recent note of those that remain pressed. This requires the algorithm to keep a record of note numbers and the order in which they are selected.

A number of other possibilities exist for a monophonic note priority scheme, such as always choosing the highest number, or the lowest number, or the earliest of the notes selected. The method implemented depends on the required control style. It is also necessary to consider how the events relate to the control of the underlying synthesis form. For example:

- The amplitude release segment is only likely to occur when the **final** note-off occurs, otherwise a release could happen when notes are still held.
- A change of note number in the output might cause an amplitude and tonal effect as well as a pitch effect. However, when a change of input does not cause a change of output (such as when the second note ends in the table), it might not be desirable to have an audible effect.
- The first note-on might cause a different sound development from those when notes are already held.

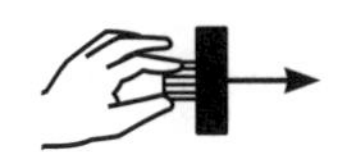

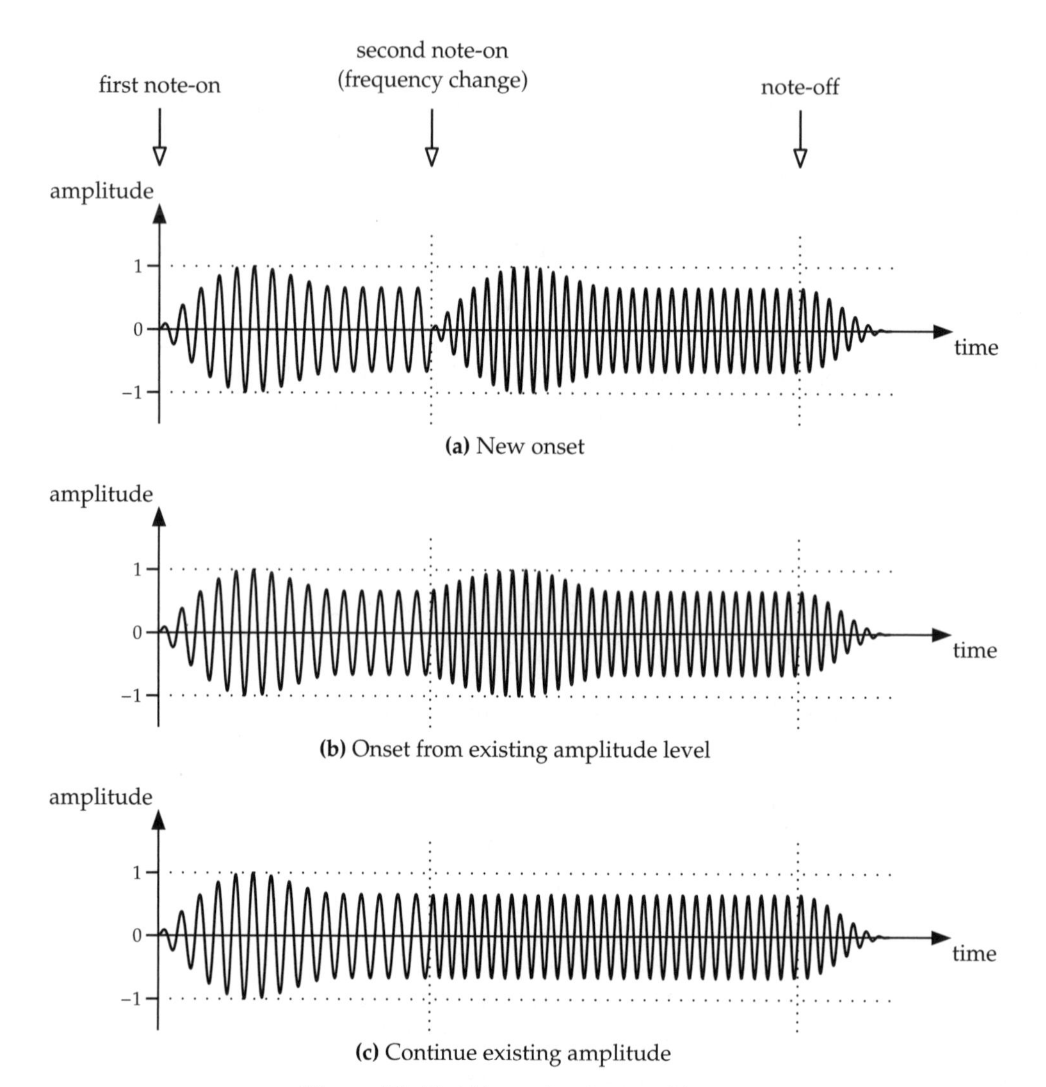

Figure 23.13 Monophonic transitions

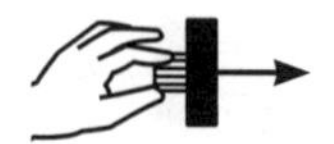

Event	Current notes held			Note number used
Initial condition				
First note starts	60			60
Second note starts	60	64		64
Third note starts	60	64	67	67
Second note ends	60		67	67
Fourth note starts	60	62	67	62
Fourth note ends	60		67	67
Third note ends	60			60
First note ends				

Table 23.2 Example monophonic note priority sequence

23.3 Developing Processes and Learning More

Implementing a process organisation commonly relies on a suitable supporting structure from an audio programming library or environment. There can be significant differences in the approaches taken to such things as control and audio rates, control parameter styles and user interaction, and monophonic and polyphonic note management. It is necessary to experiment with the available functions and objects, and examine existing examples in order to appreciate how to achieve the desired results. It might be the case that certain methods are beyond the standard capabilities of the chosen platform, and can only be achieved by extending the low-level coding.

The choices made in terms of organisation and control will not only affect the limits of the overall system that is created, but also the approach that the user or performer will take, which has artistic implications. There is no universally correct approach, as demonstrated in some of the examples in §23.2. It is not necessarily the case that larger parameter ranges and greater flexibility always lead to better results. Limitations can cause a synthesizer performer to explore the maximum capabilities within the provided timbre space, much like an acoustic instrument performer works within limitations of pitch range, tonal variation, and maximum simultaneous notes.

Further discussion of some of the topics considered in this chapter can be found in these books:

Miranda, Eduardo R., and Marcelo M. Wanderley. 2006. *New Digital Musical Instruments: Control and Interaction Beyond the Keyboard.* Middleton, WI: A-R Editions.

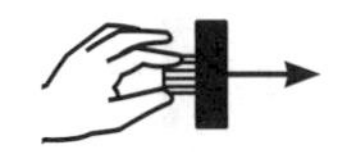

Pressing, Jeff. 1992. *Synthesizer Performance and Real-Time Techniques.* Oxford: Oxford University Press.

Russ, Martin. 2013. *Sound Synthesis and Sampling (Third Edition).* Burlington, MA: Focal Press.

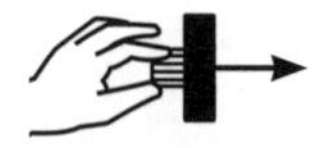

24

Control Mapping

24.1 Frequency and Amplitude

Control mapping is used to achieve an effective relationship between input values and process parameters, as described in §23.1.4 (p.641). There is no universal solution that is appropriate for all circumstances, but the general principles can be adapted to suit the particular task at hand. This section suggests some appropriate mappings for improving the effectiveness of frequency and amplitude control, which are parameters that appear often in audio processes.

24.1.1 Frequency Control

Humans perceive frequency on a logarithmic scale, and so an exponential change will lead to a linear perceived effect, as discussed in §2.1.2 (p.19). Therefore, linear control of frequency is not generally appropriate.

Figure 24.1 illustrates an example control situation where it is possible to manually sweep the cutoff frequency of a lowpass filter from 30Hz to 4kHz. Different applications will require different frequency ranges. The rotary control produces an output value that corresponds linearly to the control position, and the mapping block maps that value through a suitable function (in a similar way to the transfer functions in Chapter 7). The shape used in the mapping block can be varied to achieve different control characteristics. An input control range of 0 to 1 has been chosen to make the mapping easier to understand.

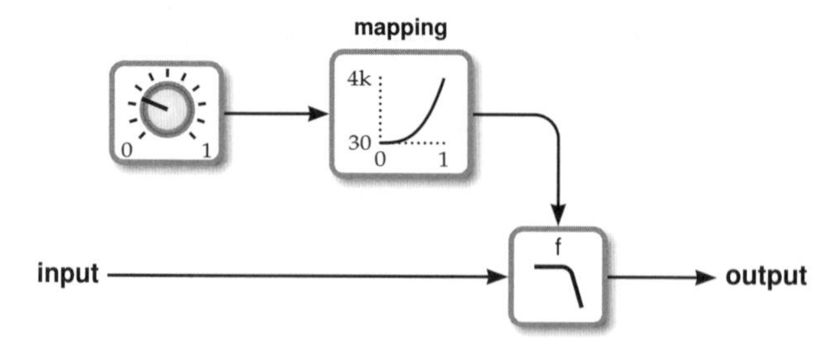

Figure 24.1 Filter frequency control

Figure 24.2 illustrates some possible functions to use in the mapping block. The equation for figure 24.2a achieves a linear mapping of the input x (a range of 0 to 1) to the output y (a range of 30Hz to 4000Hz). The left-hand plot shows the straight line relationship between x and y. The fundamental frequencies of notes A4 to A7 are marked, showing that an octave change corresponds to different amounts of control variation in different parts of the input range. This effect is made clearer in the right-hand plot, where equation 13.2 (p.401) has been used to change the vertical axis from frequency values to notes. It is then apparent that an input change of 0 to 0.1 relates to a range of almost 4 octaves.

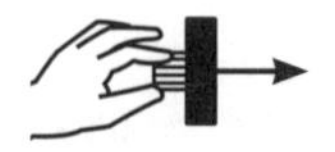

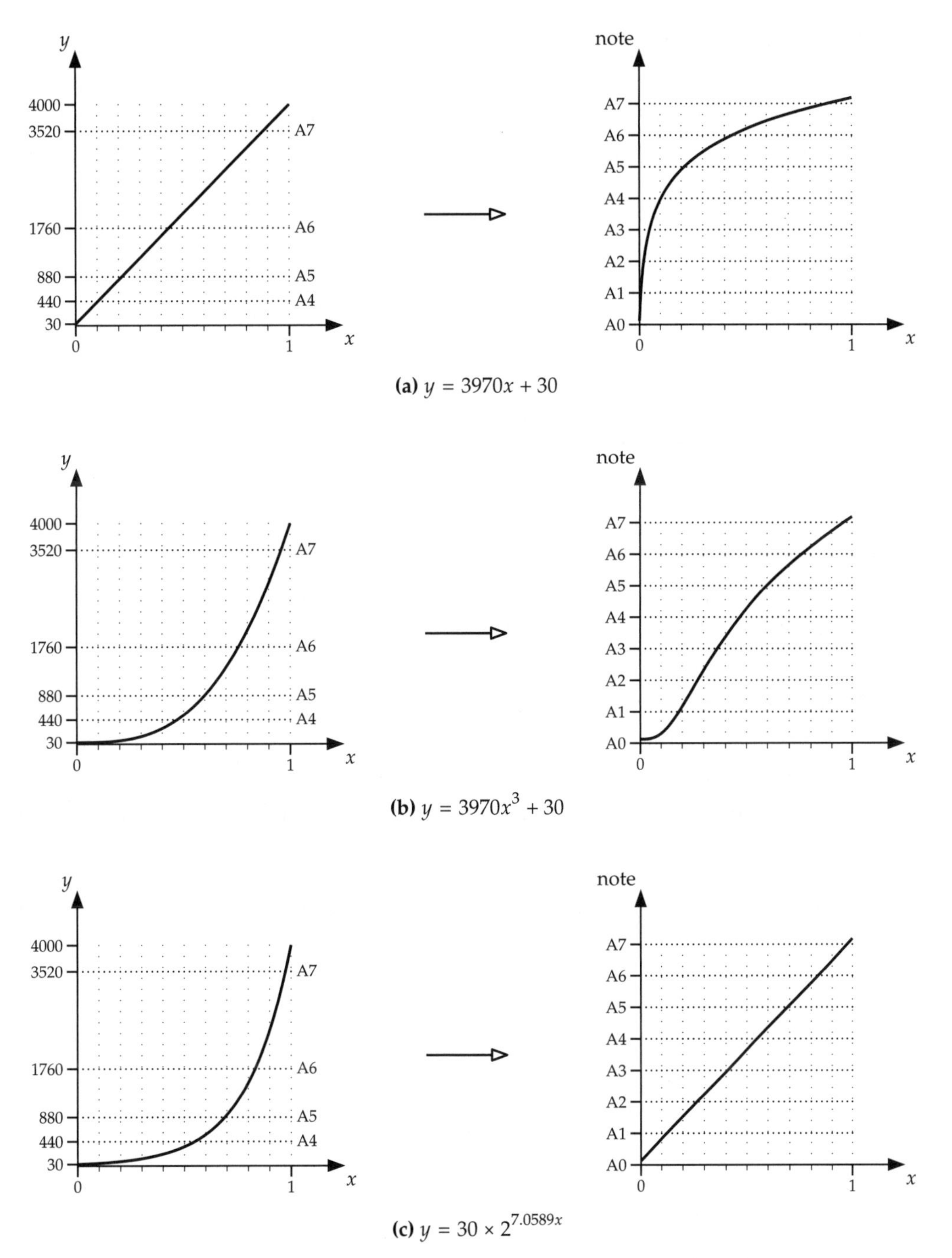

(a) $y = 3970x + 30$

(b) $y = 3970x^3 + 30$

(c) $y = 30 \times 2^{7.0589x}$

Figure 24.2 Example frequency control mapping functions

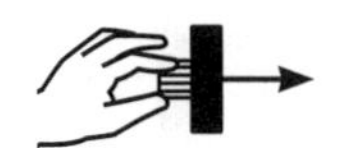

A non-linear mapping is desirable such that more of the input control range is dedicated to low frequencies. Figure 24.2b substitutes x^3 for x in the linear mapping equation, resulting in a more even distribution of input control values to different octaves. Figure 24.2c illustrates a mapping that gives a perfectly linear response in terms of notes (perceived frequency), but is more complex to achieve than the simple x^3 effect. The equation is derived as follows:

$$y = f_l \times 2^{kx} \quad \text{where} \quad \begin{aligned} k &= \log_2\left(\frac{f_u}{f_l}\right) \quad \text{and} \quad f_l > 0 \\ f_l &= \text{lower frequency} = 30 \\ f_u &= \text{upper frequency} = 4000 \end{aligned} \tag{24.1}$$

This has similarities to equation 13.1 (p.401). An alternative method is to linearly map the input control values to a particular note number range (as listed in table 13.1, p.400), and use equation 13.1 to convert the result to a frequency.

It is often desirable to control the filter parameter Q such that low values have more control range dedicated to them. As with frequency, there is no standardised mapping, but equation 24.1 can be adapted for this purpose. For example, $y = 0.125 \times 2^{7x}$ will map an input range of 0 to 1 to an output Q range of 0.125 to 16.

24.1.2 Amplitude Gain Control

Figure 24.3 shows an amplitude attenuator including a mapping block. The gain values applied to the multiplier are between 0 and 1. Figure 24.4 illustrates some possible functions to use in the mapping block. The equations are plotted on the left, and the equivalent plot with decibel gain vertical axis on the right. Values are converted to decibels with equation 5.2 (p.113). As described in §5.3.3 (p.109), a straight-through mapping (figure 24.4a) dedicates too much of the range to high gains and not enough to low gains. The right-hand plot gives an indication of how the control variation might be perceived.

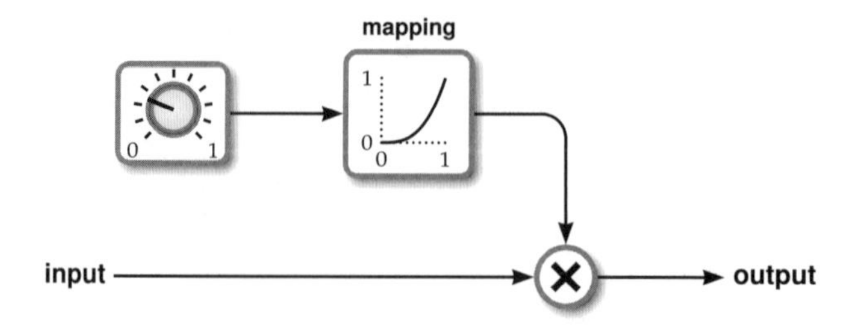

Figure 24.3 Amplitude attenuator

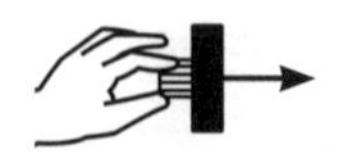

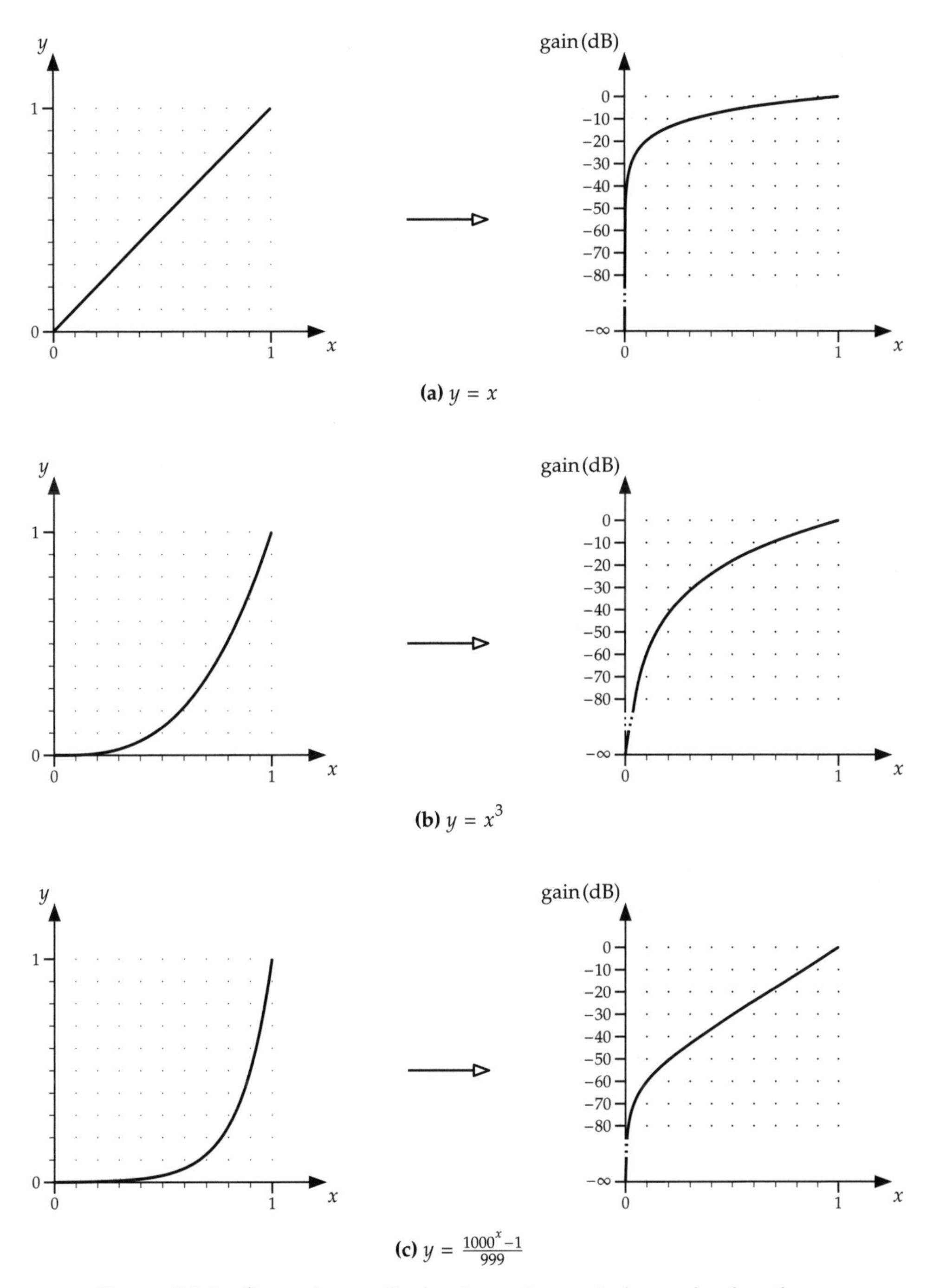

Figure 24.4 Example amplitude attenuator control mapping functions

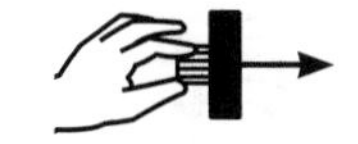

For an application such as a mixer fader, it is necessary to map the bottom of the range to a gain of 0 ($-\infty$dB), such that it is possible to completely silence the output. An infinite range means that it is not possible to create a completely linear gain effect in decibels, but rather the designer must choose how much of the control range is dedicated to different regions. The cubic mapping in figure 24.4b is a simple way of achieving a more useful distribution of decibel gains across the range of the control than the linear mapping.

Figure 24.4c provides a fairly linear effect in decibels for much of the range, with a rapid curve towards a gain of $-\infty$dB for low input control values. The mapping is based on the following equation:

$$y = \frac{k^x - 1}{k - 1} \qquad \boxed{24.2}$$

The constant value k is used to control the gradient of the decibel gain plot line, where k values of 10, 100, 1000, and 10000 correspond to increasing gradient. The choice of mapping depends on the desired relationship between control input and audible result.

When a single control has a wide output range it can be difficult to make small changes, as a small physical movement can cause a large change in output. If reducing the overall range of the control is not a suitable solution, then one alternative is to split the control into coarse and fine adjustments. Figure 24.5 illustrates an amplitude gain arrangement where the range of the fine adjustment is considerably less than that of the coarse. The diagram in the figure allows a gain range from 0dB (both controls to minimum) to +75dB (both controls to maximum), which is suitable for a microphone preamplifier. The controls achieve a linear variation in decibels through use of function $F_{dB \to a}$ (which corresponds to equation 5.3, p.113).

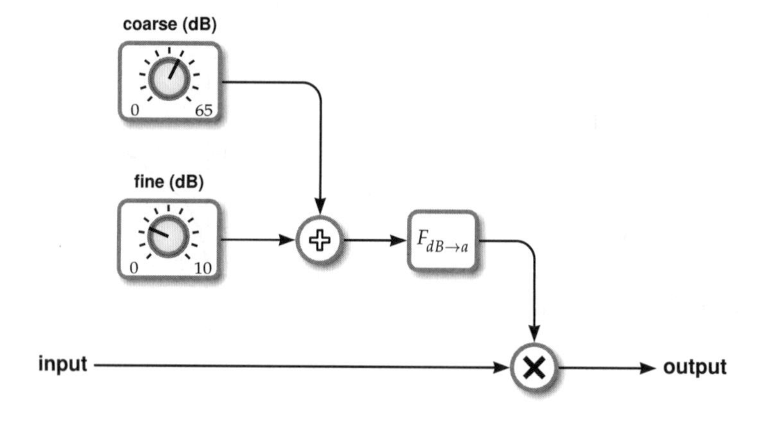

Figure 24.5 Dual amplitude gain control

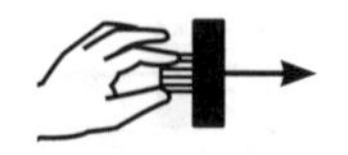

24.1.3 Key Velocity to Amplitude Gain

The simple synthesizer in figure 24.6 illustrates a control arrangement where amplitude gain is mapped from key velocity, which is useful for expressive performance control. In many systems key velocity has a range of 0 to 127, reflecting the range associated with the MIDI protocol. Velocity information is provided at the note-on event, reflecting how quickly the key was depressed. This information only occurs once per note (rather than being continuous). For simplicity in these examples, any velocity information associated with note-off will be ignored.

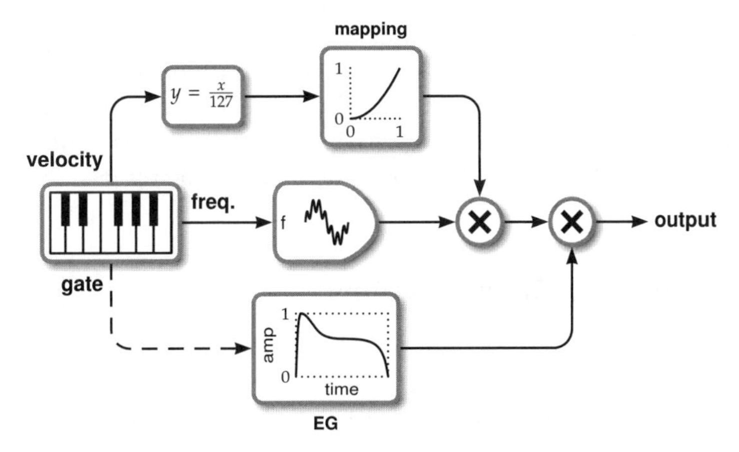

Figure 24.6 Velocity to amplitude gain control

The velocity value is scaled down to a more convenient range of 0 to 1 before the mapping block in the diagram. As with figure 24.3, it is common to use a mapping where more of the control range is dedicated to low gain values than a linear mapping. For example, the cubic mapping in figure 24.4b is suitable for expressive control. However, not all performance situations require the same type of control characteristic. Effective control is not necessarily about linearising the perceived response relative to the input, but rather associating certain amounts of the input range with achieving a particular output range.

The cubic mapping can be generalised to the following equation:

$$y = x^k \qquad \boxed{24.3}$$

The constant k controls the curvature of the function, where $k = 1$ is linear. As the value of k increases, more of the control range is dedicated to low gain values, such that increasingly high velocities are required to achieve significant gain. This variable allows the "feel" of the keyboard (or other input device) to be changed in a continuous manner relative to the nature of the input sensor and desired performance style. Low values of k are typical (say 1 to 4), and non-integer values can be used.

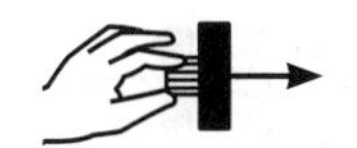

Figure 24.7 shows three further velocity to amplitude gain mapping functions. Figure 24.7a has the effect of reducing expressiveness compared to a linear mapping (figure 24.4a) or cubic mapping (figure 24.4b). The curvature means that output gains tend to be higher values. This can be useful if the performer wishes to have a more consistent gain, but with some variation at lower velocities. Varying the exponent allows the curvature of the function to be controlled:

$$y = 1 - (1 - x)^k \tag{24.4}$$

Figure 24.7b develops the idea of figure 24.7a further by mapping such that gain values around 0.5 dominate for middle velocities, but with some variation possible at low and high input values. Figure 24.7c has the characteristic that middle values produce variation (unlike figure 24.7b), but low and high velocities tend to produce more consistent results. This again produces a different feel to the keyboard response. The mapping is derived from one of the equations in figure 7.8 (p.204). Different shapes could be achieved by replacing the number 100 with a different value, and replacing 99 with the new value minus 1.

24.1.4 Further Mapping Considerations

The mappings described so far are only a selection of the possibilities. Different input devices will have different characteristics, as described in §23.1.4 (p.641). The particular performance situation will also require variation in mapping such that there are no unusual jumps in the output. Using equations for mapping functions has some advantages:

- The mapping is relatively easy to create when there is no graphical interface.
- The implementation can have very precise properties such that the result is exactly as required (like figure 24.2c, p.657).
- The shape can often be changed in a continuous manner using suitable variables in the equation.

Alternatively, in a graphical environment the potential exists to specify a shape visually, particularly for unusual shapes, which can be easier and more flexible than manipulating an equation.

Another way of controlling mapping behaviour is to blend between different shapes. This can be achieved by combining equations in a single mapping block using this form:

$$y = (1 - c)F_1(x) + cF_2(x) \tag{24.5}$$

where $F_1(x)$ and $F_2(x)$ are different equation functions and c is a value between 0 and 1. Alternatively, the same result can be achieved by blending the output of two mapping blocks as shown in figure 24.8. This simple arrangement is similar to figure 5.51 (p.135).

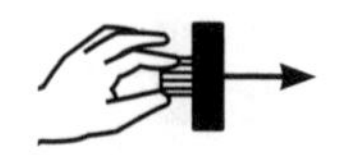

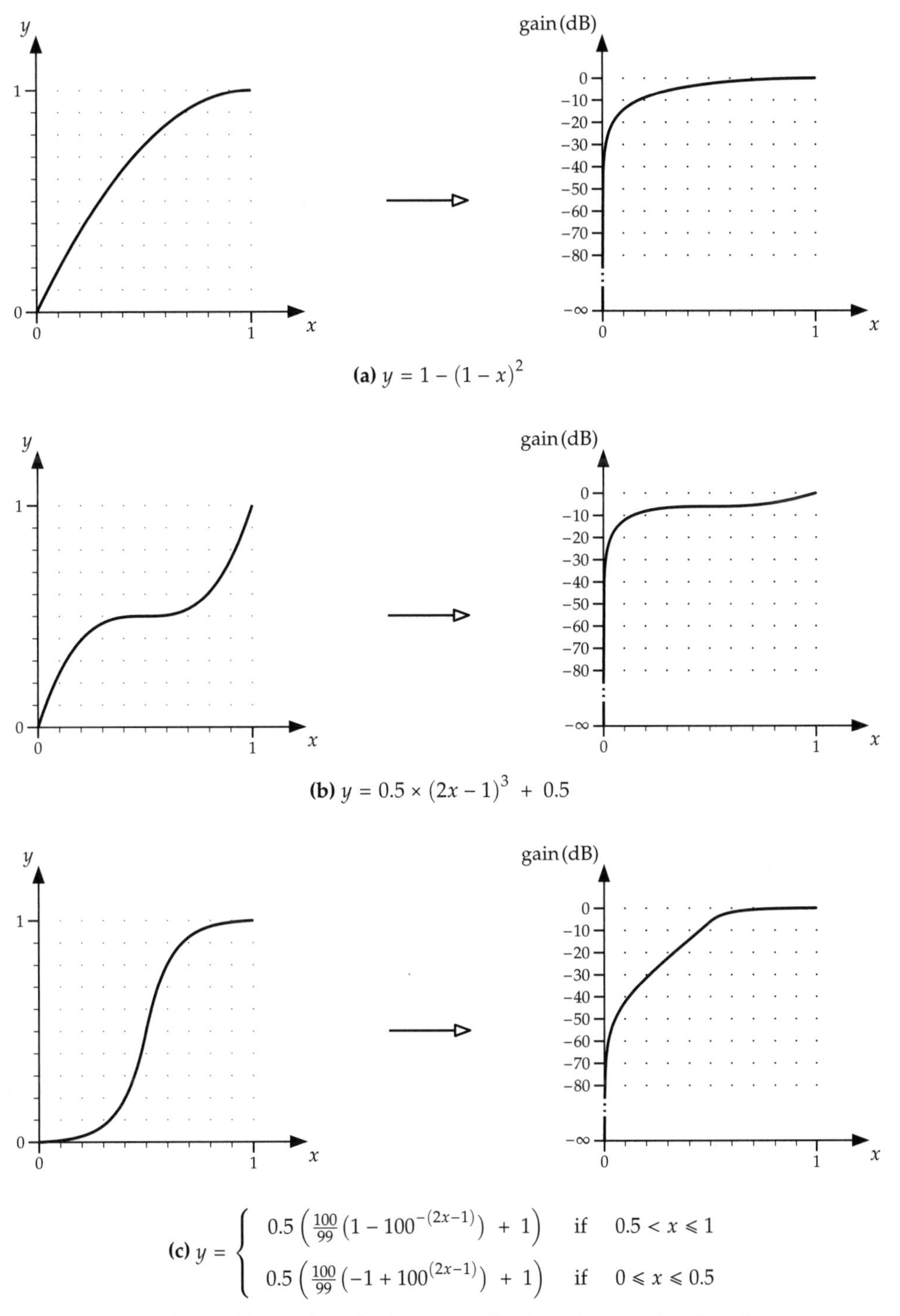

(a) $y = 1 - (1 - x)^2$

(b) $y = 0.5 \times (2x - 1)^3 + 0.5$

(c) $y = \begin{cases} 0.5\left(\frac{100}{99}\left(1 - 100^{-(2x-1)}\right) + 1\right) & \text{if} \quad 0.5 < x \leqslant 1 \\ 0.5\left(\frac{100}{99}\left(-1 + 100^{(2x-1)}\right) + 1\right) & \text{if} \quad 0 \leqslant x \leqslant 0.5 \end{cases}$

Figure 24.7 Example velocity to amplitude gain mapping functions

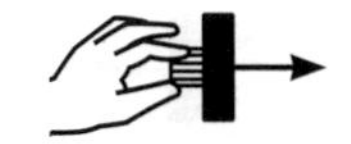

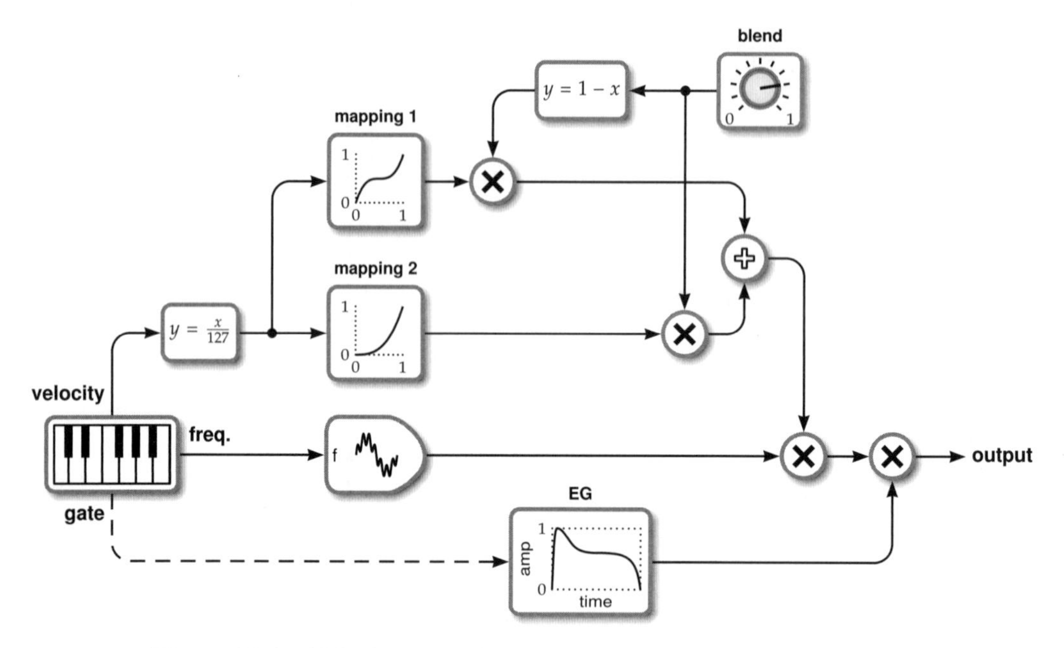

Figure 24.8 Velocity to amplitude gain control with mapping blend

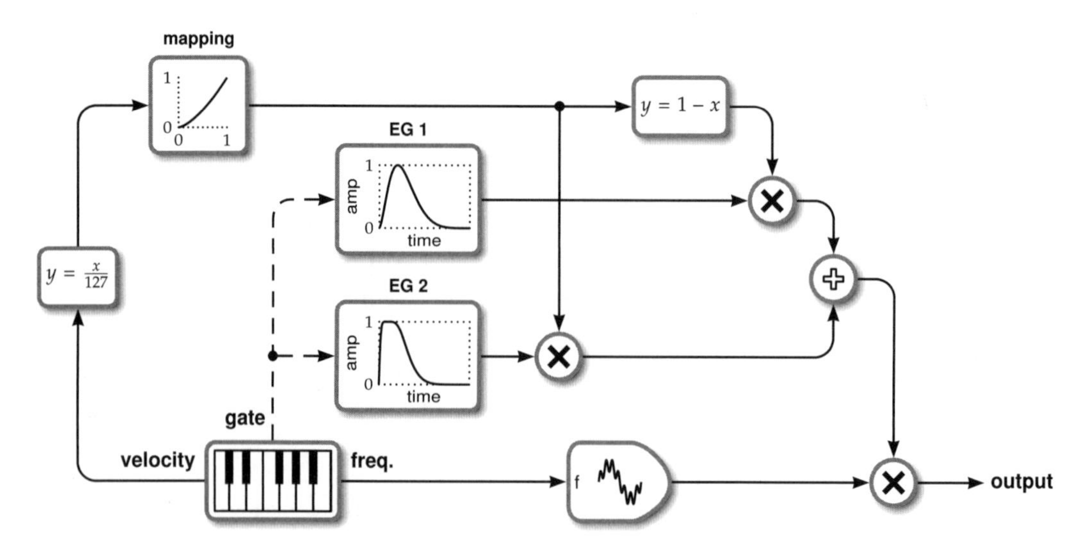

Figure 24.9 Velocity mapped to envelope blend

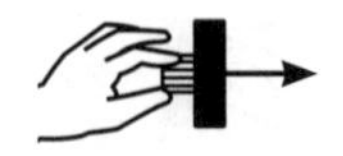

24.2 More Sophisticated Techniques

24.2.1 Mapping to Varying Parameters

In some cases, a parameter value varies over time and it is desirable to control the nature of that variation dynamically. Figure 24.9 illustrates the use of mapped key velocity to control the blend between two amplitude envelopes. Using the envelope shapes shown in the diagram means that increasing velocity produces an increasingly rapid attack.

It is important that the two envelope shapes used in figure 24.9 are sufficiently compatible, such that they produce the expected result when blended. Figure 24.10 shows pairs of envelope shapes and the result of an equal blend of the two (corresponding to a mapped value of 0.5). The equal blend envelope in figure 24.10a has an attack shape part way between the two end points. Figure 24.10b shows the result when two dissimilar envelopes are blended. In this case, rather than a blend between an early peak and a late peak being a single peak half way between the two, the result is a double peak of half the amplitude.

The technique for blending the envelopes in figure 24.9 is a very simple weighted average. If a more sophisticated result is required, then it is necessary to use velocity to control the envelope generation process. For example, if the desire is to relate the velocity to the position of an envelope peak, then a sensible method is to use it to control the position of a breakpoint in the envelope generator. Breakpoint methods are described in §14.3 (p.429).

Figure 24.11 illustrates the use of an *aftertouch* control value to affect modulation depth. While key velocity information is only provided at the note-on event, aftertouch is continuously variable over time. Aftertouch reflects the amount of pressure applied to a key **after** it is depressed. In the figure this allows the performer to choose how much tremolo depth occurs at different times, achieving expressive control. Tremolo is described in §9.2.1 (p.270).

Like key velocity, aftertouch is assumed to have a range of 0 to 127. The mapping function is configured in both range and shape to achieve subtle control over modulation depth, particularly at lower control values, such that the tremolo effect is not overpowering. Not all keyboards have an aftertouch capability, but other continuous control sources could be used in a similar way, such as a foot-controlled expression pedal.

Figures 24.9 and 24.11 show how control mapping can be used in conjunction with oscillators or envelope generators to vary the effect on amplitude gain. The same ideas can be used in other situations; for example, to control an envelope generator shape or duration related to excitation of a waveguide physical model (figure 21.6, p.590), or the depth of oscillator modulation of a filter frequency (figure 17.5, p.507).

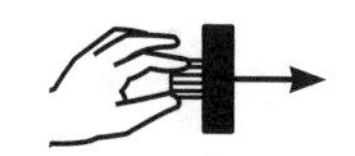

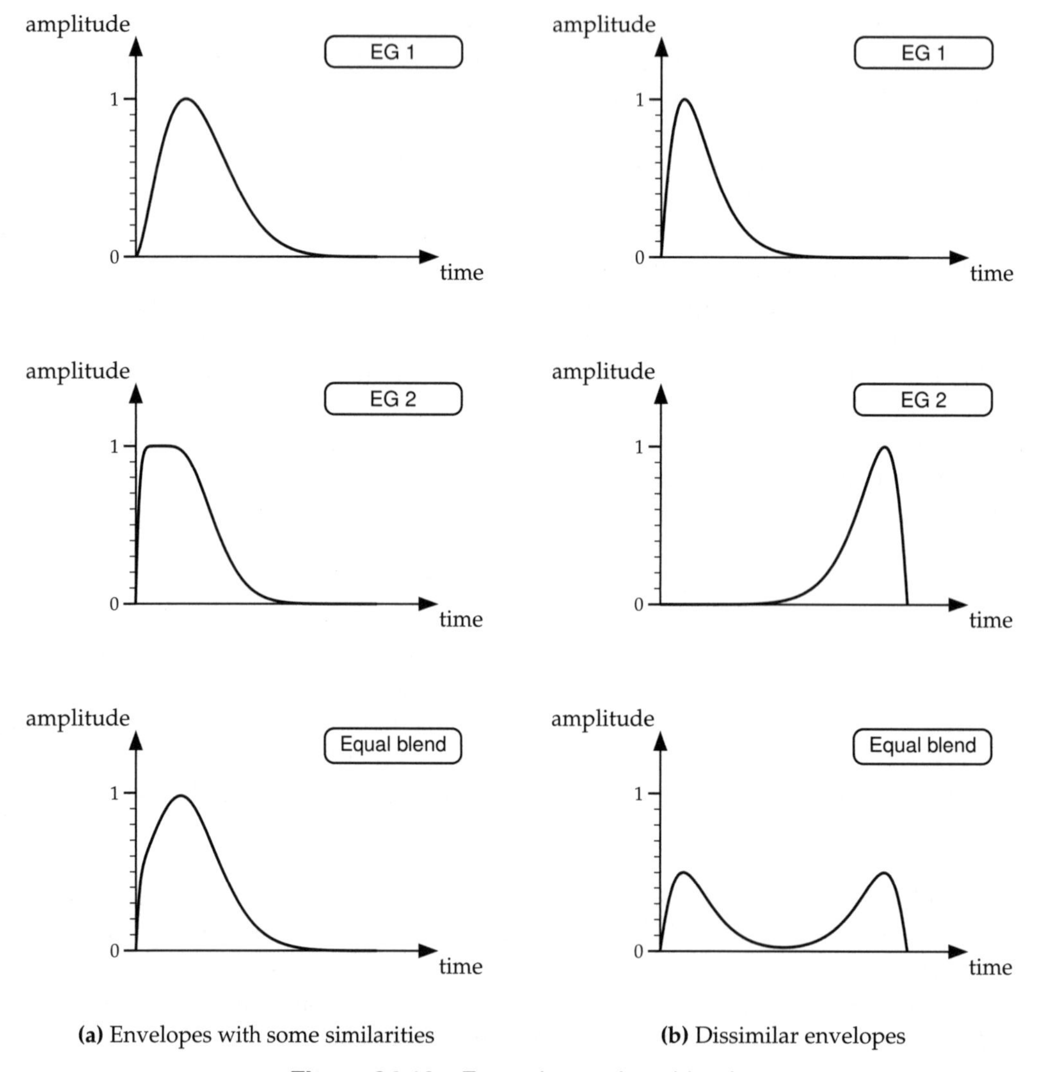

(a) Envelopes with some similarities

(b) Dissimilar envelopes

Figure 24.10 Example envelope blends

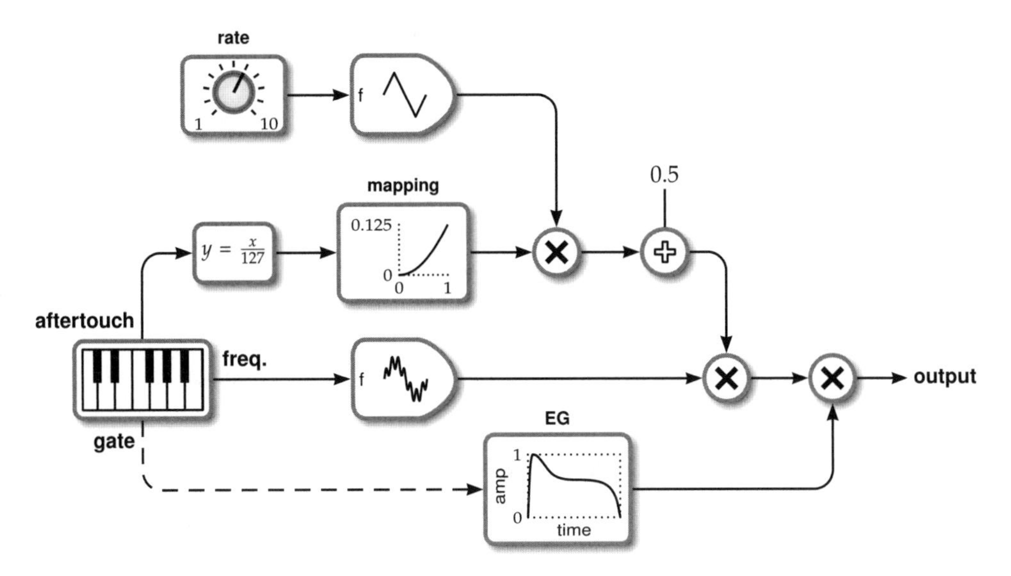

Figure 24.11 Aftertouch mapped to modulation depth

24.2.2 Mapping to Multiple Parameters

As audio processes become more sophisticated they tend to have more parameters to control their operation. It is often desirable for a single control input to affect multiple underlying parameters with a one-to-many mapping (as described in §23.1.2, p.633). Figure 10.21 (p.308) shows how multiple time values can be derived from an input value for purposes of controlling an echo effect. Similarly, parallel synthesizer forms such as figure 16.3 (p.486) derive multiple frequency values from a single input.

Mapping an input to multiple parameters does not necessarily have to be a simple linear mapping, nor do all the controlled parameters have to be of the same type. Figure 24.12 illustrates a simple recirculating echo effect with the feedback gain mapped from the delay time parameter. If the two parameters are independently controlled (as shown in figure 10.25, p.315), then decreasing the time between echoes also decreases the overall length of decaying output effect, as the recirculation and attenuation occurs at shorter intervals. The mapping in figure 24.12 compensates for this effect. Constant k will be a value between 0 and 1 (such as 0.3), and could also be user-controlled.

Figure 24.13 illustrates using the note number in a synthesizer for controlling both oscillator frequency and output pan position. This has some similarities to the effect in a piano where hammers strike strings in different physical positions, creating a spatial effect. As described in §13.1.3 (p.399), note numbers are between 0 and 127, and function $F_{n \to f}$ converts a note number to a frequency value. Note number or fundamental frequency can

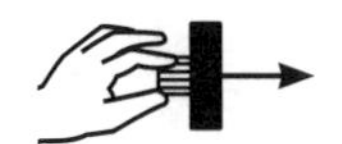

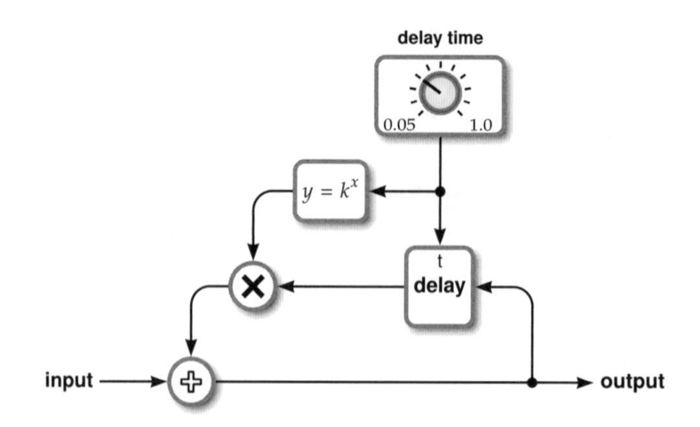

Figure 24.12 Echo effect

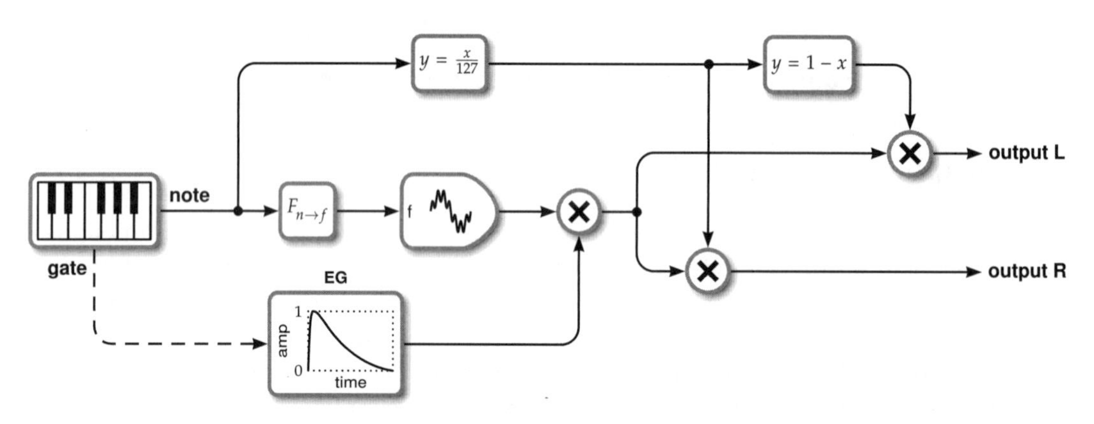

Figure 24.13 Note mapped to pan position

also be mapped to other parts of synthesis forms, in order that parameters vary with the chosen pitch. This technique is sometimes called tracking, and an example is illustrated in figure 17.4 (p.507).

Figure 24.14 is an example of how a single parameter (key velocity) can be used to create a changing tonal blend in a synthesizer. The form has some similarities to figure 19.3 (p.547), but rather than the character being the same for every note, it will depend on the way in which the keyboard is played. This also achieves a performance interaction that is often more expressive than trying to modify individual parameter controls with one hand while playing notes with the other. The velocity is used to control detuning of one oscillator, amplitude gain of two oscillators, and a lowpass filter cutoff after the parallel paths are mixed.

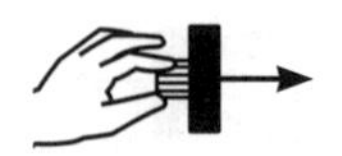

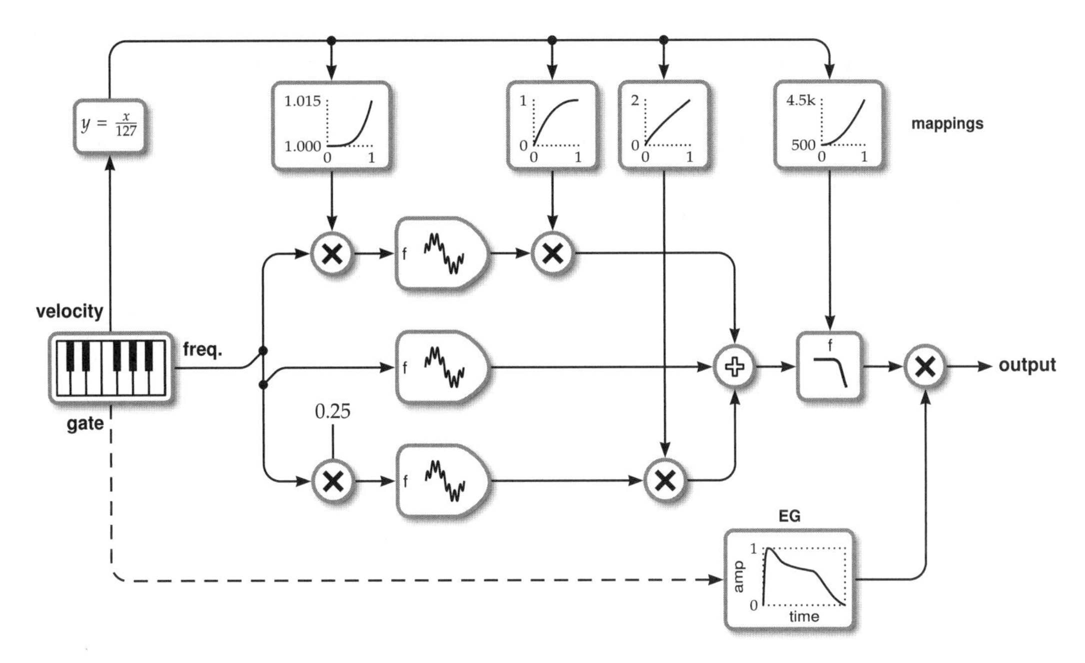

Figure 24.14 Multiple velocity mappings

The configuration shown in the diagram can produce moderately subtle variation. The mapping ranges and function shapes can be adjusted to achieve the desired artistic performance requirements. For example, a wider detuning range could be used, or the gain of one path could decrease as others increase.

As an audio process becomes larger, it can be useful for the user to be able to control many parameters together. A synthesizer with three envelopes is easy to control, but a synthesizer with 30 envelopes is more time consuming to configure. It might, for example, be desirable to change the attack time of all envelopes together, while still maintaining differences in the shapes of the individual envelopes. Similar ideas are explored in §16.3 (p.496).

24.3 Developing Processes and Learning More

The effectiveness of control mappings is an important consideration when using a professional audio product. Processes that are difficult to control cause annoyance, even if their other characteristics are good; for example, if it is hard to adjust certain parameters to the required values, or if the range of a control is insufficient to achieve the desired result. It takes effort to create mappings that are efficient and effective, and some developers in the past have neglected this stage when finishing an audio process.

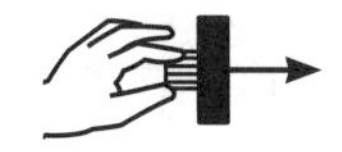

A good way of appreciating the importance of appropriate control mappings is to spend time using recording studio hardware and software. It is often only when trying to achieve a specific result that the limitations of these become apparent. Examples include whether a particular gain control is sufficiently fine to make slight adjustments, or if it appears to jump past the required value; and whether a particular equaliser (EQ) allows all filter bands to be clustered at low frequencies, or if there are limits on ranges. Encountering such issues can help remind the audio process engineer of the importance of this area in designing effective processes.

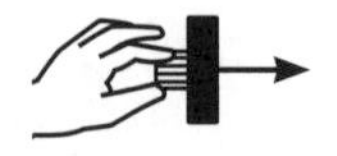

Next Steps

From Design to Implementation

This book describes audio process designs that can be implemented in a wide range of programming languages and environments. It is useful to approach learning about this subject and developing software by utilising a range of different tools:

- Examining the nature of sounds in audio analysis software is very enlightening. It helps in understanding the time domain and frequency domain characteristics of a sound that will be modified, or one whose characteristics will be copied and synthesized, as well as the results of an audio process.
- Using commercial applications such as Digital Audio Workstation (DAW) software and plugins helps in appreciating typical results for a modifier or synthesizer. It is also useful for finding the common ranges of user interface parameters.
- It is not necessarily most productive to start with a complex implementation style, such as using a conventional text-based general purpose programming language. It can be very helpful to develop a prototype in an environment that provides complete audio process elements (sometimes known as unit generators, or objects). The standard elements might be restrictive compared to the intended final product, but it is useful to concentrate on the general concepts and audible results initially.
- Most audio software implementations build on existing libraries, toolkits, and objects. The ability to progressively replace or enhance existing elements, rather than having to create everything from scratch, is particularly useful.

Software choices are influenced by the available hardware and operating system, personal programming experience, and the type of process being considered. It is worth initially starting with low cost or free software, as a way of learning about the features that are important, and relative strengths and weaknesses. That helps in choosing wisely if a more expensive option is the next step.

From Individual Parts to Larger Systems

This book generally presents fairly small and contained examples, which aids the learning process. When constructing a more sophisticated modifier or synthesizer process there are a number of important considerations:

- The effectiveness of an audio process is as much about the control style as the underlying modification or synthesis. It is important to establish what the user expects in terms of the quantity of controls and how they map to the underlying processing. While it is undesirable to be too restrictive, too much variation and flexibility also makes it hard to use a process. The interfaces to commercial products give a good indication of what a typical user might require.
- Sophistication is more than just complexity. A very large process can still produce an uninspiring result if not carefully managed. More sophisticated synthesizers might be distinguished by subtle variations with control inputs (such as the key velocity or note number), a continually-developing sound character over time, and subtle tonal features (such as low amplitude contrasting sound elements). A modifier might have filtering that achieves a subtle variation in emphasis across the frequency range, respond slightly differently as the input amplitude level changes, or produce a subtle stereo effect.
- More highly developed audio processes produce results that are more naturalistic, or fit a particular application or context more suitably. For example, an acoustic environment effect might produce an accurate impression of listening in a certain room, or a synthesizer output could precisely match the character of a particular instrument. Simpler process designs tend to produce more plain results, and it requires additional sophistication to avoid this.
- There are certain expectations about how an audio process should react in practical situations. For example, a reverberation process should not normally have control ranges that allow it to become unstable. Similarly, playing a monophonic synthesizer from a piano-style keyboard should normally produce smooth transitions between notes. Suitable management of the process and its control is required to achieve the expected results. Creating a good sounding result in limited test cases is not necessarily sufficient to indicate satisfactory performance in all contexts, so a more comprehensive scheme is likely to be required.

The development of audio processes is often iterative, where the design is expanded in stages and the parameters are repeatedly modified to push the resulting character towards the desired target. It is usually easier to use a progressive construction approach than to start with a large complex structure and try to fix all the issues at the same time. Thankfully many audio processes lend themselves to a gradual expansion, such as adding further parallel stages, or series stages that build on each other.

From Foundations to Deeper Understanding

The audio process designs in this book are built on decades of work by many dedicated researchers and engineers. This book discusses the major process forms, but there is much more to discover. There are different approaches to the same topics to be found in different books, such as:

- Considering the application of audio processes in the context of studio and recording practice, or electronic music.
- Explaining the implementation of audio processes with reference to a particular programming language or environment.
- Exploring the mathematical and theoretical ideas that underpin the process designs.

Individual audio processes and techniques are described in great detail in journal, conference, and other research papers. These are a valuable source of information both in terms of depth of discussion, and in ideas and techniques that are outside the mainstream. Publishing papers is an opportunity for researchers to explain new experimental techniques and results.

There are other sources of information that complement those described above. Software and equipment user guides are useful for understanding how commercial products are organised and controlled. These indicate what might typically be expected in terms of the quantity and style of user parameters. User guides can often be downloaded from manufacturers' websites. Specialist magazines have a useful role in explaining how to use audio processes, as well as product reviews that describe positive and negative features. There are many forms of information online such as university teaching materials, guides to technique on manufacturers' websites, and discussion forums. However, it is always important to critically consider the source of information before placing trust in it.

There is much to be gained from using an audio process in a real situation, such as playing or recording a piece of music. Understanding the effectiveness of controls, the features of a technique, and the annoying limitations, is often achieved much more quickly in a practical situation than in a basic testing environment.

There is an exciting future for audio processes, as ongoing advances in computational power make ever more sophisticated implementations possible in real-time. This will provide many new tonal and musical possibilities. The principles and techniques described in this book are a suitable starting point for understanding and developing whatever comes next.

APPENDICES

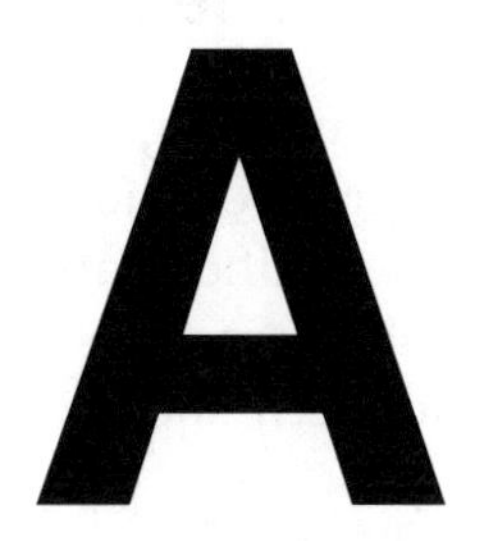

Mathematics for Audio Processes

A.1 The Need for Mathematics

Given enough words, many scientific concepts can be explained fairly well in prose. There are times, however, when a mathematical expression can explain the nature of a scientific relationship more accurately and succinctly. To understand and implement audio processes it is necessary to understand some basic mathematical notation, forms, and techniques.

This appendix is a refresher for those who have been taught mathematics in the past, and might also address some gaps in understanding. To keep it short, this appendix only covers areas that are relevant to the book. It does not cover the topics in extensive detail, so it might be necessary to examine a book about mathematics if more information is required on some parts.

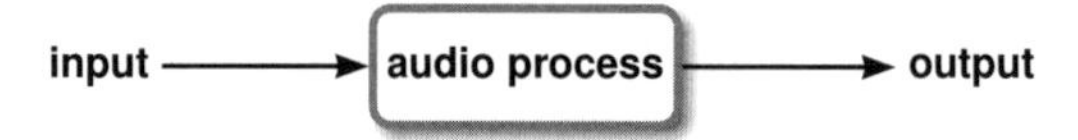

In simple terms, an audio process controls the relationship between an input and an output. For example, an audio process can specify:

- The output produced when a guitar signal is the input to a distortion effect.
- The output produced when an oscillator has a particular input frequency value.
- The output produced when a key velocity is mapped to a particular synthesizer control parameter.

In many cases, these relationships can be described precisely and concisely using a mathematical equation. As an example, the following equation describes a simple amplifier process:

$$y = 2.5x \qquad \text{where} \quad -1 \leqslant x \leqslant 1 \tag{A.1}$$

The equation can be described in words like this: *The input value is called x, which is multiplied by* 2.5 *to produce the output value called y. The input is a value greater than or equal to* −1, *and less than or equal to* +1. Therefore the output values are going to be between −2.5 (which is −1 × 2.5) and +2.5 (which is 1 × 2.5). The power of mathematics is in explaining those ideas in the smallest amount of space. However, the notation and conventions must be understood in order to make sense of mathematical representations. Being able to interpret a mathematical form is necessary for implementing it in a computer program, for example.

A.2 Variables, Simple Equations, Subscripts, Superscripts

Variables

The purpose of variables such as

$$x \quad y \quad t \quad a_2 \quad \rho \text{ and } \phi$$

is to represent changeable quantities. This is a concept that is used in both mathematics and computer programming. The power of the variable is that it can assume different values but always have the same name. This is useful when considering audio processes, as values are often changing. For example:

- The position of a fader on a mixing console.
- The instantaneous value of an audio signal fed to a filter.
- The key number being pressed on a piano-style keyboard.

In general, a variable name can be chosen to be whatever is logical or convenient at the time. However, there are certain conventions that exist in the naming of variables in mathematics. Some of the conventions that are used in this book are as follows:

- A general input is called x and produces an output called y.
- Angles and phase values are called ϕ (phi), and are measured in radians (where π radians = 180 degrees).
- A set quantity of items is represented by the letter N.
- A counter value is represented by i.
- A time variable is t, and frequency is f.

One of the differences between variable names in traditional computer programs (or computer algorithms) and mathematics, is that programs often use long variable names whereas mathematical forms are often very short. This is because:

- A computer program is often a very long complicated piece of text, which means that it is important to have useful descriptive variable names. When the programmer returns to a piece of code after a gap of several months and jumps to a line in the middle of the file that says this:

  $$\text{samplecount} = \text{framecount} * \text{framesize} + \text{offset}$$

  it is a lot easier to comprehend than this:

  $$\text{i} = \text{c} * \text{s} + \text{o}$$

ⓘ

- A mathematical equation, on the other hand, is trying to express a relationship in the smallest amount of space, and so conventionally uses single letters for variables. If an equation is accompanied with descriptive text then it will still be apparent what is going on.

The values of input variables are often important to ensure that the results of a calculation are within the expected boundaries. For example, consider this equation:

$$y = \frac{1}{1-x} \qquad \text{where} \quad 0 \leqslant x < 1 \tag{A.2}$$

The right-hand side says that x will be greater than or equal to 0, and less than 1. If x were set equal to 1, then the fraction would require dividing by zero to calculate the result. Dividing by zero can cause odd behaviour, warnings, or errors in some programming languages. At the other end, when x is 0 then y is 1. If x were set to a value less than 0, then y values less than 1 will be produced, which the person who wrote the equation might be trying to avoid. When implementing equations in software, it is necessary to ensure that the variable values are within the required boundaries.

An equation with multiple cases corresponding to different subdomains (sets of input values) is implemented with *if* statements in conventional programming languages. For example:

$$y = \begin{cases} x & \text{if} \quad x > 0 \\ 2x+1 & \text{if} \quad x \leqslant 0 \end{cases} \tag{A.3}$$

The equation might be implemented using an algorithmic form like this:

```
if invalue > 0 then
 └ outvalue = invalue

if invalue <= 0 then
 └ outvalue = 2 * invalue + 1
```

However, for equations with complementary subdomains such as those above, an *if-then-else* construct can be used:

```
if invalue > 0 then
 | outvalue = invalue
else
 └ outvalue = 2 * invalue + 1
```

Manipulating Simple Equations

It is important to be able to rearrange a simple equation in order to change the subject. Remember to do the same thing to both sides when rearranging. Here is an example equation used in audio processes:

$$f = \frac{1}{t} \quad \text{where } f = \text{frequency, and } t = \text{cycle length (time)}$$

$$\text{therefore} \quad t = \frac{1}{f} \quad \text{(multiply both sides by } t\text{, then divide both sides by } f\text{)} \tag{A.4}$$

Similarly, with three variables:

$$d = st \quad \text{where } d = \text{distance, } s = \text{speed, and } t = \text{time}$$

$$\text{therefore} \quad t = \frac{d}{s} \quad \text{and} \quad s = \frac{d}{t} \tag{A.5}$$

It is also necessary to understand how one side of an equation can be rearranged, or broken down into individual operations. Consider the following equation:

$$y = 1000 - 950x \tag{A.6}$$

Examining this equation piece by piece:

- Multiplication and division occur before subtraction and addition, unless something is used to indicate the order of calculation (such as brackets). Using brackets to make the precedence of multiplication over subtraction more explicit, equation A.6 is the same as:

$$y = 1000 - (950 \times x) \tag{A.7}$$

  But equation A.6 is **not** the same as $y = (1000 - 950) \times x$.

- It is also possible to turn the subtraction into an addition, like this:

$$y = 1000 + (-950 \times x) \tag{A.8}$$

- The two halves of the addition can be reversed and the result is the same:

$$y = (-950 \times x) + 1000 \tag{A.9}$$

It is important to understand the order in which operations occur when implementing an equation in software or representing it in a block diagram. Because x is the input, then the multiplication by −950 is the first thing that happens when describing the equation as a block diagram:

$x \rightarrow [\times\ -950] \rightarrow [+\ 1000] \rightarrow y$ $\quad (y = 1000 - 950x)$

Now try this problem:

Problem 1

Draw a block diagram using multiplication and addition blocks, for the following equation: $y = 1 - x$

Answers to problems are at the end of the appendix.

Subscripts

One way of making mathematical variables easier to understand is to use subscripts. Consecutive letters could be used to represent the amplitudes of a set of oscillators (without subscripts), like this:

$$a \quad b \quad c \quad d \quad e \quad f$$

A better method, however, is to use a subscript, which shows that a group of variables are related, like this:

$$a_1 \quad a_2 \quad a_3 \quad a_4 \quad a_5 \quad a_6$$

This also leads onto a neat piece of shorthand, which is to use a variable as a subscript to another variable. For example, a_i means *any of the variables called a, where i is a counter through the variables in the set*. The following form might be used to represent the amplitudes of a set of 10 oscillators as variables:

$$\text{Amplitude of oscillators} = a_i \qquad \text{where} \quad i = 1, 2, 3, \ldots 10 \qquad \text{A.10}$$

The above form neatly expresses the idea of there being 10 numbers, with variable names a_1 to a_{10} that control the amplitude of some oscillators. In terms of conventional programming languages, the use of subscripts as shown above is similar to the use of an array index, which might be a counter in a *for* loop (or something similar).

As well as providing a grouping effect, subscripts also help to improve the clarity of equations. To understand this, it is worth remembering that it is conventional that two variables next to each other in an equation are multiplied:

$$y = mx \qquad \text{is the same as} \qquad y = m \times x \tag{A.11}$$

Therefore, if variable names in a mathematical equation are longer than one character, it can become confusing. In the following equation it is not clear if there are two variables called i and n, or one called in:

$$\text{Is} \qquad y = in + x \qquad \text{the same as} \qquad y = (i \times n) + x \quad ? \tag{A.12}$$

A subscript can reduce confusion by providing a place to put extra information. For example, the following sort of form might be used where two input parameter values are summed:

$$y = p_{\text{in1}} + p_{\text{in2}} \tag{A.13}$$

Superscripts

Superscripts indicate when a variable should be raised to a power. In simple cases this will be a positive integer. For example:

$$y = x^3 \qquad \text{is the same as} \qquad y = x \times x \times x \tag{A.14}$$

However, powers (also called exponents) can be real (non-integer) numbers, including negative numbers. For example:

$$4^{-3.2} \approx 0.01184 \tag{A.15}$$

The following is an example of an equation using powers. It converts from a note number n, to a fundamental frequency f:

$$f = 440 \times 2^{(n-69)/12} \qquad \text{where} \quad 0 \leqslant n \leqslant 127 \tag{A.16}$$

It is important to calculate all the parts in the right order. The mathematical order of operations requires calculating an exponent before a multiplication. Inside the exponent the brackets take precedence over the division. Therefore, to perform the calculation 69 is subtracted from the note number n, then the result is divided by 12, then 2 is raised to the power that has just been calculated, then the result is multiplied by 440. On a modern calculator, it is often possible to calculate the entire equation in one go. However, it is easy for the calculation to occur in the wrong order if the calculator is not used correctly.

Problem 2

To three decimal places, calculate the fundamental frequencies for the following note numbers (using equation A.16):

a) $n = 60$ (middle C)
b) $n = 61$ (C♯ a semitone above middle C)
c) $n = 60.5$ (half way between C and C♯)

A.3 Repeated Summation

Because one of the purposes of mathematics is to express a relationship in a concise manner, methods exist for expressing repetitive actions. The summation symbol Σ (sigma) is used to express repeated addition of related variables. For example, if there are 10 channel signals called s_1 to s_{10} that are mixed together onto the bus of a mixing console, it could be expressed mathematically as follows:

$$s_{bus} = s_1 + s_2 + s_3 + s_4 + s_5 + s_6 + s_7 + s_8 + s_9 + s_{10} \tag{A.17}$$

Alternatively, a more elegant form is as follows:

$$s_{bus} = \sum_{i=1}^{10} s_i \tag{A.18}$$

The above equation uses an integer counter i that counts from 1 to 10. For each value of i, the value of s_i is added into the total. Therefore, equations A.17 and A.18 are equivalent.

Extending the example, imagine that each channel's signal is multiplied by an amplitude gain value before being added to the total. This is quite common with a mixing console, as there is often a fader to control each channel's overall gain level. The long version of the equation therefore becomes this:

$$s_{bus} = a_1 s_1 + a_2 s_2 + a_3 s_3 + a_4 s_4 + a_5 s_5 + a_6 s_6 + a_7 s_7 + a_8 s_8 + a_9 s_9 + a_{10} s_{10} \tag{A.19}$$

where a_i is the amplitude gain value for channel i. Again, a more elegant form is as follows:

$$s_{bus} = \sum_{i=1}^{10} a_i s_i \tag{A.20}$$

Equations using repeated summation are often associated with digital filters, which usually take a number of input sample values from a digital audio stream, multiply each by a coefficient value, and then add the results together to produce the output. An equation to

calculate the mean average of a set of values can be considered a type of filter. The mean average effect can be defined as *a process that adds together a set of N values, and then divides the result by N*. This can be expressed mathematically as follows:

$$y = \frac{1}{N}\sum_{i=1}^{N} x_i \tag{A.21}$$

For example, if N was 3, then the equation would add together the values x_1, x_2, and x_3 and then divide the result by 3 (as multiplying by $1/N$ is the same as dividing by N).

Problem 3

To three decimal places, calculate the result of the following equation with the values shown below:

$$y = \sum_{i=1}^{4} a_i^2 x_i$$

$a_1 = 0.1 \quad a_2 = 0.2 \quad a_3 = 0.4 \quad a_4 = 0.8$

$x_1 = 0.5 \quad x_2 = 0.5 \quad x_3 = -0.5 \quad x_4 = -0.5$

A.4 Linear Mapping

A variable in an audio process can have the wrong range for a particular task. Sometimes the problem can be fixed at source, such as changing the range of values produced by a software control. However, values might be provided by a piece of external hardware, or by a software library function that cannot be changed. To deal with this situation requires mapping values, which relates to scaling (multiplication) and applying an offset (addition).

Example 1

Imagine that a control input has a range of 0 to 127, but the range of a parameter that needs to be controlled is different. For example, it might be desirable to control a synthesizer brightness input that takes values between 0 and 1:

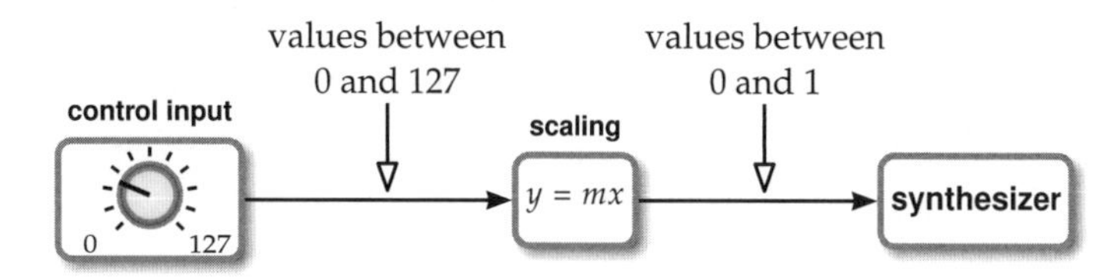

As can be seen in the diagram, the way of converting from a control producing values 0 to 127, to an input that requires 0 to 1, is to use the equation $y = mx$ (where x is the input, y is the output, and m is the scaling multiplier value). The answer to the problem is to divide all the input values by 127, by using a multiplier of $1/127$:

$$y = \frac{1}{127}x \tag{A.22}$$

Putting example input values into the equation demonstrates that it works:

- When $x = 0$, $y = 0$
- When $x = 63.5$, $y = 0.5$
- When $x = 127$, $y = 1$

Because this is a linear scaling effect, all the input values between 0 and 127 will be scaled proportionally, such that they are positioned appropriately in the range 0 to 1.

Example 2

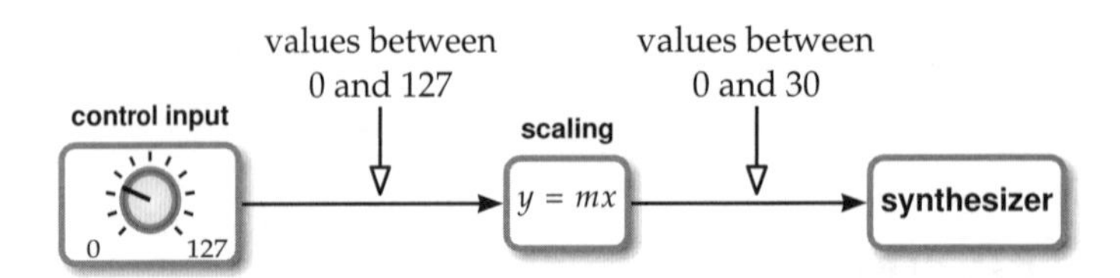

Imagine that the arrangement is the same as in the previous example, but this time the synthesizer parameter being controlled is a tremolo frequency input that has a range of 0Hz to 30Hz. The input is still 0 to 127, but the output is going to be 0 to 30. One way of working out the answer is as follows:

- Scaling from a range of 0 to 127, down to a range of 0 to 1, means dividing by 127.
- Scaling from a range of 0 to 1, up to a range of 0 to 30, means multiplying by 30.
- Therefore, if the two operations are combined, it is the same as going from 0 to 127, to a range of 0 to 30.

That is:

$$y = \left(\frac{1}{127}x \times 30\right) \quad \text{which is the same as} \quad y = \frac{30}{127}x \tag{A.23}$$

Putting example input values into the equation demonstrates that it works:

- When $x = 0$, $y = 0$
- When $x = 63.5$, $y = 15$
- When $x = 127$, $y = 30$

Example 3

Scaling (multiplication) is not always sufficient to achieve the desired range of output values. Sometimes it is also necessary to add an offset to the range. The mapping equation then becomes this:

$$y = mx + c \tag{A.24}$$

where x is the input variable, m is the scaling multiplier, c is a constant offset and y is the output. The values of m and c are calculated as follows:

$$m = \frac{\text{(difference between output range values)}}{\text{(difference between input range values)}} \tag{A.25}$$

$$c = y - mx$$

The standard sine wave function has a range between −1 and +1. Consider how it might be mapped to a range of 50 to 100:

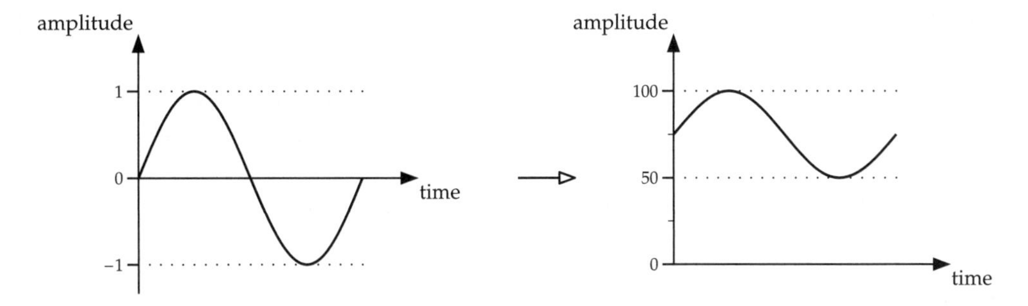

The plot on the left is the input value varying over time. The plot on the right is the output after the scaling and offset have occurred. Using equation A.25 it is possible to calculate values for m and c:

$$m = \frac{100 - 50}{1 - (-1)} = \frac{50}{2} = 25 \tag{A.26}$$

$$c = 100 - (25 \times 1) = 75$$

Notice that c is calculated with example point $y = 100$ and $x = 1$, as the output value 100 occurs when the input value is 1. Therefore, using equation A.24 the mapping equation becomes this:

$$y = 25x + 75 \tag{A.27}$$

The equation means that there is a middle value of 75, which has $25x$ added to it to create the deviation from the middle value. Given that the input is varying between −1 and +1, then the value of $25x$ is between −25 and +25. This fits with what is seen in the plot on the right; 75 – 25 at the bottom of the wave and 75 + 25 at the top.

Example 4

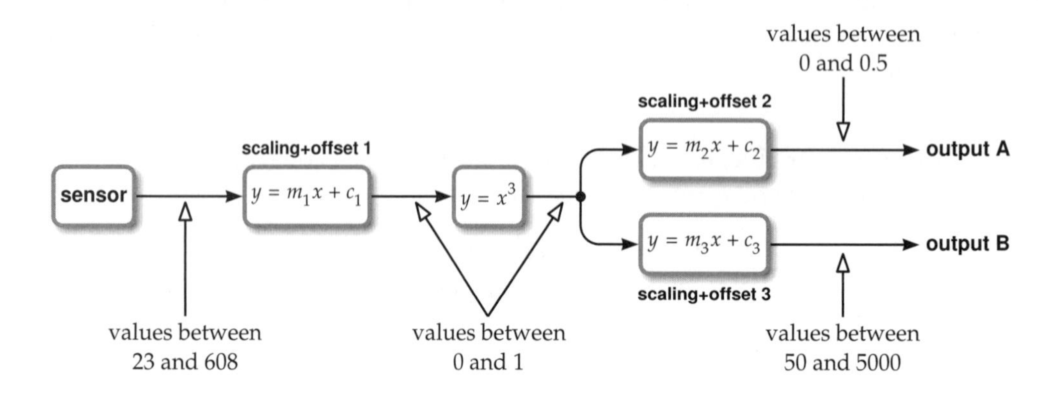

Not all input signals have simple ranges like 0 to 127 or −1 to +1. In the diagram above, a hardware sensor produces a range of 23 to 608. A multi-stage mapping process is illustrated. The first stage maps to a range of 0 to 1. The next step is a non-linear mapping of $y = x^3$. Such non-linear mappings are often used to produce an effective control characteristic, and are easier to specify with an input range of 0 to 1 (as described in Chapter 24). The signal is then split and mapped two different ways such that multiple parameters can be controlled from the same input. In this case, the plan is to produce ranges of 0 to 0.5 for an amplitude gain parameter and 50 to 5000 for a filter cutoff frequency.

Using equation A.25, it is possible to calculate m and c values for the three equations in order to achieve the desired ranges:

$$m_1 = \frac{1-0}{608-23} = \frac{1}{585} \qquad m_2 = \frac{0.5-0}{1-0} = 0.5 \qquad m_3 = \frac{5000-50}{1-0} = 4950$$

$$c_1 = 0 - \frac{23}{585} \qquad c_2 = 0 - 0.5 \times 0 \qquad c_3 = 50 - 4950 \times 0$$

$$y = \frac{x}{585} - \frac{23}{585} = \frac{1}{585}(x-23) \qquad y = 0.5x \qquad y = 4950x + 50 \tag{A.28}$$

Putting example input values into the equations demonstrates that they work:

$$y = \frac{1}{585}(x-23) \qquad y = 0.5x \qquad y = 4950x + 50$$

When $x = 23,\ y = 0$ When $x = 0,\ y = 0$ When $x = 0,\ y = 50$
When $x = 608,\ y = 1$ When $x = 1,\ y = 0.5$ When $x = 1,\ y = 5000$

ⓘ

Problem 4

Using equations A.24 and A.25, work out the equations to scale and offset the following:

a) From a range of 0 to 1, to a range of 0 to 56
b) From a range of 0 to 1, to a range of 0.1 to 0.7
c) From a range of −1 to +1, to a range of 0 to 1
d) From a range of −1 to +1, to a range of 0.8 to 1.0
e) From a range of 0 to 127, to a range of −80 to 0
f) From a range of 0 to 127, to a range of 0 to −80

Test the solutions with the input ranges before looking at the answers.

A.5 Straight Lines

The equation $y = mx + c$ described in section A.4 is an example of a straight line equation. Constant m is usually called the *slope* or *gradient* and c is the y-intercept (the value of y when x is zero). Straight lines are used in a number of audio processes. As an example, imagine creating an amplitude envelope for a synthesizer, where the amplitude rises at the start of the sound, and then tails away over time, as shown in the diagram below.

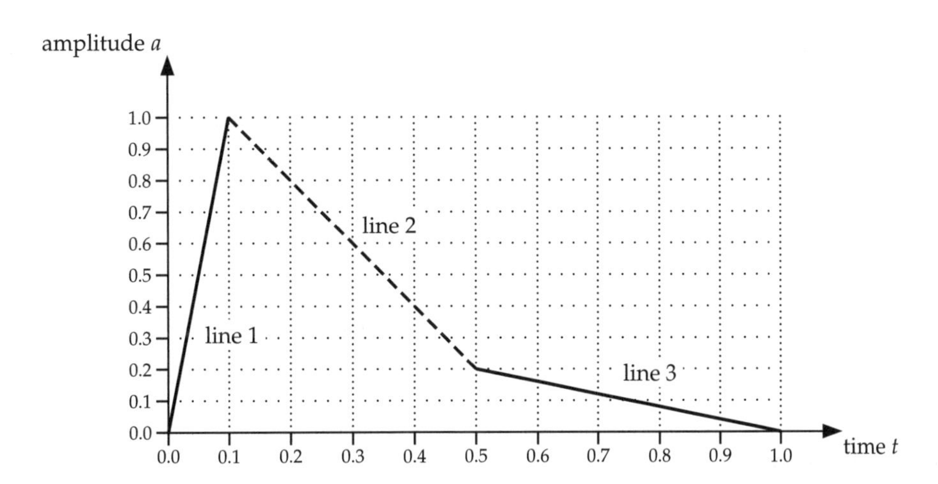

A mathematical form is required to relate time (variable t) to the amplitude of the output (variable a), such that at any point in time, it is possible to automatically calculate the

output. For example, to be able to find the value of a when $t = 0.265$. The first problem is that there are three lines, not one. That means that there are three parts to the equation:

$$a = \begin{cases} m_1 t + c_1 & \text{if} \quad 0.0 \leqslant t \leqslant 0.1 \\ m_2 t + c_2 & \text{if} \quad 0.1 < t \leqslant 0.5 \\ m_3 t + c_3 & \text{if} \quad 0.5 < t \leqslant 1.0 \end{cases} \tag{A.29}$$

The equation is split into three parts depending on the value of variable t. Calculating the values of m_i and c_i for the three parts requires use of equations A.24 and A.25 again. The "difference between output range values" is the difference between the ending and starting values on the amplitude axis for a particular line. Similarly the "difference between input range values" is the difference between the ending and starting values on the time axis. Considering line 2:

$$\begin{aligned} m_2 &= \frac{0.2 - 1}{0.5 - 0.1} = \frac{-0.8}{0.4} = -2 \\ c_2 &= 1 - (-2 \times 0.1) = 1.2 \end{aligned} \tag{A.30}$$

Notice that the change in amplitude is negative for a positive change in time, resulting in a negative value for m_2. This will also be the case for line 3, but not line 1. The equation for line 2 is $a = -2t + 1.2$. It is now worth checking that the ends of the line are in the right places:

- When $t = 0.1$, $a = (-2 \times 0.1) + 1.2 = 1$
- When $t = 0.5$, $a = (-2 \times 0.5) + 1.2 = 0.2$

It is also possible to choose any time value in range and find the corresponding output value:

- When $t = 0.3$, $a = (-2 \times 0.3) + 1.2 = 0.6$
- When $t = 0.45$, $a = (-2 \times 0.45) + 1.2 = 0.3$

Comparing these to the graph shows that the results are correct.

Problem 5

Using equations A.24 and A.25:

a) Work out the equation for line 1.

b) Work out the equation for line 3.

ⓘ

A.6 Logarithmic and Exponential Functions

Logarithmic Functions

The following graph shows part of the base-10 logarithmic function $y = \log_{10}(x)$:

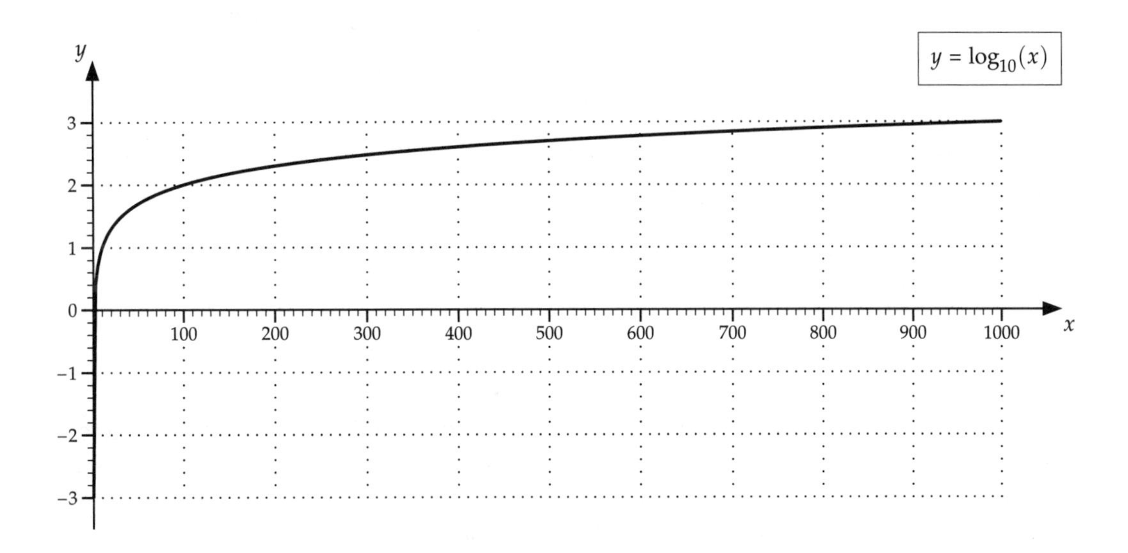

The $\log_{10}(x)$ function causes input values that are spaced by a factor of 10 to become linearly spaced in the output. For example:

x	0.001	0.01	0.1	1	10	100	1000
$\log_{10}(x)$	−3	−2	−1	0	1	2	3

Notice that, for small values of x, a small change in input value leads to a significant change in output value y. However, with larger values, an increasingly large change in x is required to produce the same amount of change in y. For example, when x increases from a value of 0.001 to 0.01, y increases from −3 to −2 (an increase of 1). The same sized change in y also results when x increases from 100 to 1000.

ⓘ

One way of showing this effect more clearly is to use a logarithmic scale on the x axis of the graph as follows:

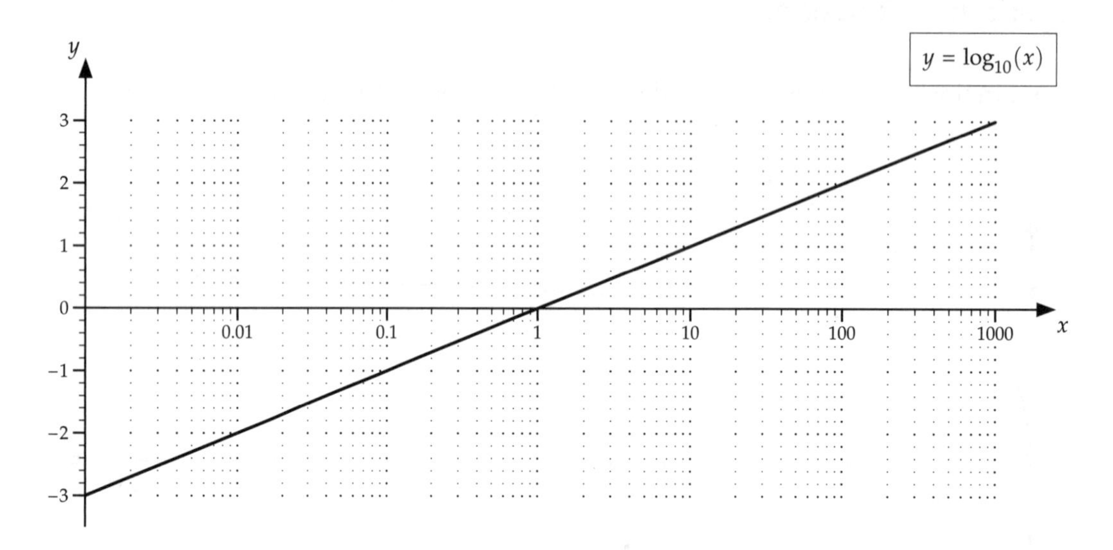

With a logarithmic axis scale, the major marks along the x axis are spaced by a factor of 10, so when the $\log_{10}(x)$ function is plotted, it appears to be a straight line. Comparing the table and the two graphs, it is apparent that they are showing the same function. On a logarithmic axis, there are also minor marks along the x axis between the major marks. If all the points on the axis are labelled, then a section of it looks like this:

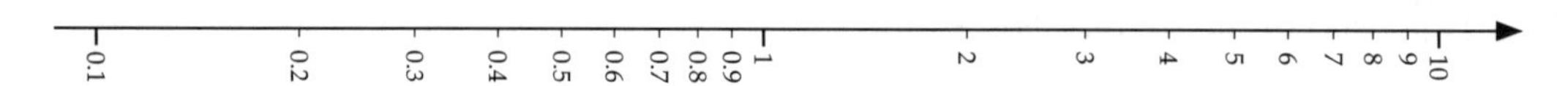

The $\log_{10}(x)$ function is most commonly used in audio processes as part of the equation for converting from a linear value of gain, to gain in decibels (dB) as follows:

$$\text{gain}_{\text{dB}} = 20\log_{10}(\text{gain}) \qquad \text{where} \qquad \text{gain} = \frac{\text{output amplitude}}{\text{input amplitude}} \tag{A.31}$$

For example, if an amplifier produces a signal with an output amplitude twice that of the input amplitude, then it has a linear gain of 2, and so:

$$\text{gain}_{\text{dB}} = 20\log_{10}(2) \approx 6.02\text{dB} \tag{A.32}$$

Here are some other values of linear and decibel gain:

gain	1/8	1/4	1/2	1	2	4	8
gain_{dB}	−18.06	−12.04	−6.02	0	6.02	12.04	18.06

Each time the linear gain doubles, the gain in decibels increases by approximately 6.02dB. The reason for using the decibel scale in audio processes is that it relates well to the way in which amplitude is perceived by the human auditory system. For example, increasing an amplifier's linear gain from 1/4 to 1/2 is perceived as being a similar variation to the change from a gain of 4 to 8 (even though that is a much larger change in linear gain).

Problem 6

Convert the following linear gain values to values in decibels using equation A.31:

a) gain = 10
b) gain = 100
c) gain = 1000

Exponential Functions

Exponential functions have the opposite characteristics to logarithmic functions:

	input	output
logarithmic	x increases by a multiplying factor	y increases by equal linear steps
exponential	x increases by equal linear steps	y increases by a multiplying factor

Typical exponential functions have the form $y = k^x$. For positive integer values of x this means that k multiplied by itself a number of times (e.g. $k^3 = k \times k \times k$). However, values can also be calculated for non-integer and negative values of x.

The following graphs show the functions $y = 10^x$ and $y = 2^x$:

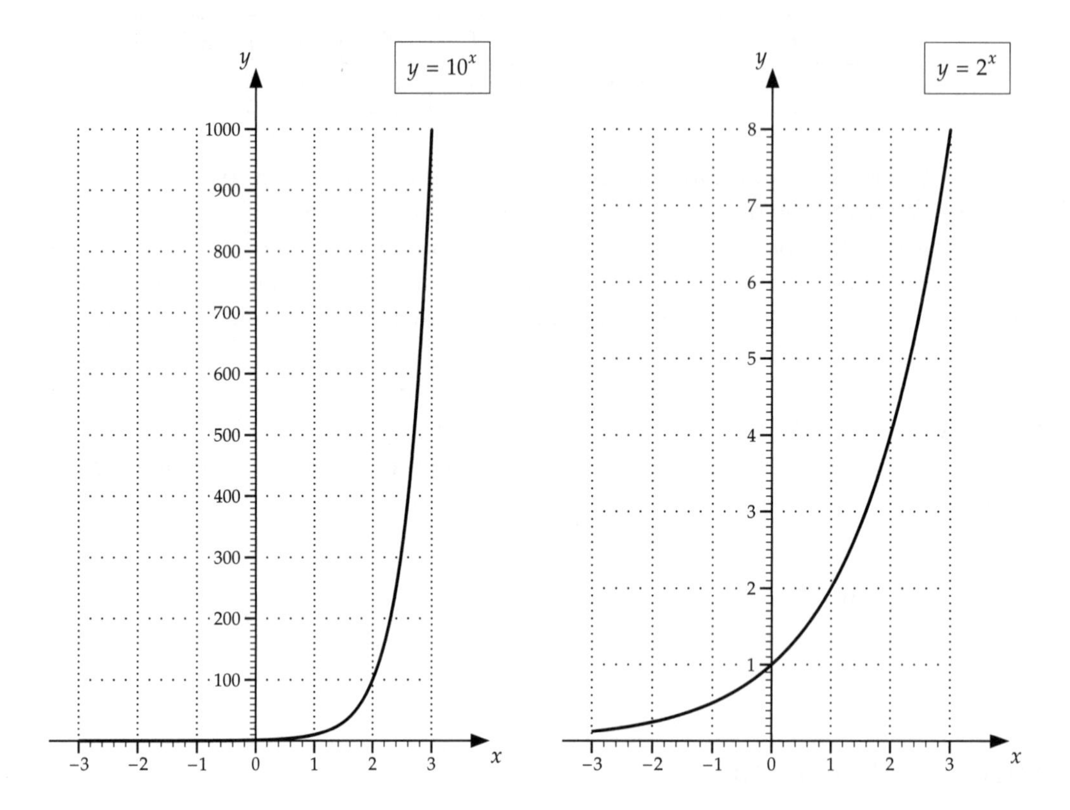

In the graphs above, equally spaced values of x produce values of y that are spaced by a factor of 10 and 2 (respectively):

x	−3	−2	−1	0	1	2	3
10^x	0.001	0.01	0.1	1	10	100	1000
2^x	0.125	0.25	0.5	1	2	4	8

When x increases by 1, then the value of y is multiplied by 10 (in the $y = 10^x$ case) or 2 (in the $y = 2^x$ case).

Plotting $y = 10^x$ with a logarithmic y axis produces a straight line effect and makes the effect clearer:

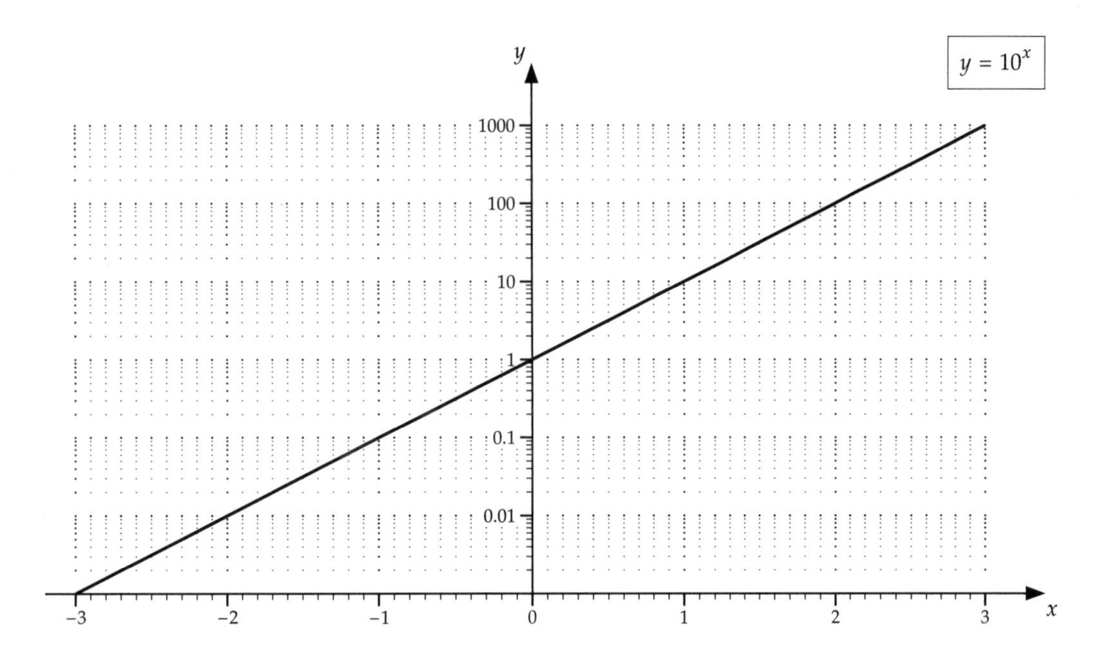

The exponential functions are working in the opposite way to the logarithmic function seen previously:

- $a = 10^b$ is the inverse of $b = \log_{10}(a)$
- $a = 2^b$ is the inverse of $b = \log_2(a)$ where $\log_2(a) = \dfrac{\log_{10}(a)}{\log_{10}(2)}$

Exponential functions, like logarithmic functions, are of interest in audio processes as they relate to physical phenomena. A common example is the perception of pitch. A doubling of the fundamental frequency of a simple harmonic tone produces the sensation of an octave increase. For example, harmonic oscillations with the following fundamental frequencies are perceived as equidistant in pitch:

27.5	55	110	220	440	880	1760

An exponential function can be used to calculate fundamental frequencies. If a note has fundamental frequency f_1, it is possible to calculate the frequency of another note (f_2) that is s semitones away, with the following equation:

$$f_2 = f_1 \times 2^{s/12} \tag{A.33}$$

Equation A.33 is a more general form of equation A.16 (p.683). As an example of its use, middle C has a fundamental frequency of approximately 261.626Hz. A note 2 semitones above middle C would have a fundamental frequency calculated as follows:

$$f_2 = 261.626 \times 2^{2/12} \approx 293.665\text{Hz} \tag{A.34}$$

Similarly, for a note 2 semitones **below** middle C:

$$f_2 = 261.626 \times 2^{-2/12} \approx 233.082\text{Hz} \tag{A.35}$$

So far, when considering the equation $y = k^x$, $k = 10$ and $k = 2$ have been examined. In those examples increasing values of x produce exponentially increasing values of y. However, if k has a value between 0 and 1, then increasing values of x produce an exponentially **decreasing** value of y. For example, consider the graph for the equation $y = 0.7^x$:

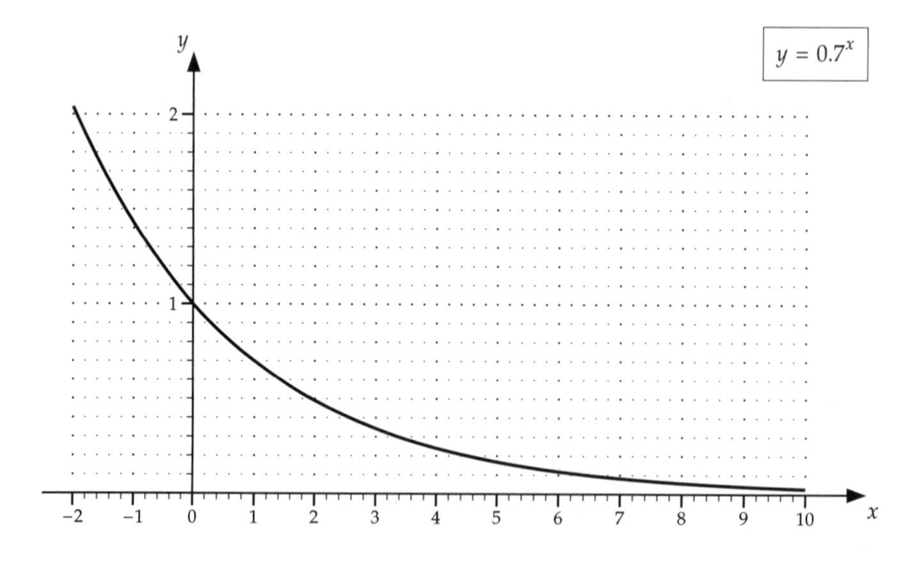

On the above graph, each time x increases by 1, the output is multiplied by 0.7, achieving a curved decay shape. A similar effect is found in many physical systems. For example, when a xylophone bar is struck, after the initial onset the amplitude envelope of the sound has a somewhat exponential decay.

Problem 7

A xylophone bar currently produces a sound with an amplitude of 0.5, and is reduced to 0.4 times its previous amplitude for each second of time. To the nearest whole second, how many seconds will it take before the amplitude is less than 0.001?

A.7 Mapping and Shaping Functions

It is often the case in audio processes that there is a need to explicitly define the mapping from input to output values. A number of these appear in this book, such as:

- Scaling and offset, and the straight line equation $y = mx + c$.
- Logarithmic and exponential functions.
- Trigonometric functions such as $y = \sin(x)$.

There are any number of ways of mapping input to output values. Often the designer of a system will create a function shape that achieves a particular effect. For example, for purposes of creating:

- A compressor transfer function.
- A distortion or waveshaping function.
- A particular mapping from key velocity to synthesizer amplitude.

It is useful to understand what is going on in graphical terms, as well as in terms of equations. Here is a slightly more unusual function than those seen previously:

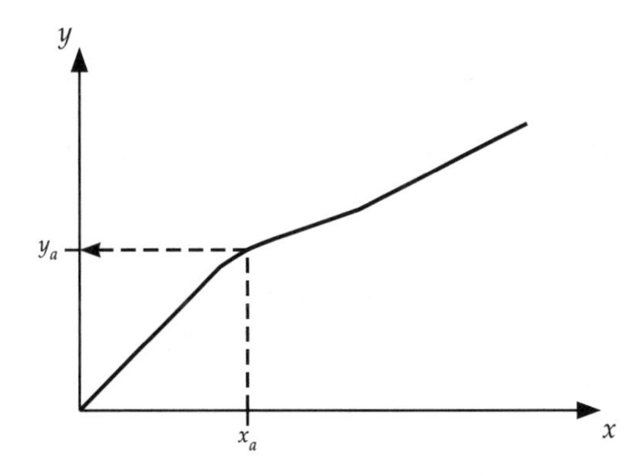

Notice how each value of x is mapped through the line to a particular value of y (such as value x_a to y_a). The mathematical relationship between x and y changes over the length of the function line. This is generally known as a *mapping*, *shaping* or *transfer* function.

A.8 Units, Prefixes, and Symbols

It is important to be familiar with the notation used to specify different quantities in audio processes. Note that capitalisation is often important. The following are some common units:

Quantity	Unit	Symbol
computer storage	byte	B
electric potential (voltage)	volt	V
frequency	hertz	Hz
length	metre	m
time	second	s

Prefixes allow a quantity to be specified without an unnecessary number of zeros. For example, 10MHz is a more compact representation than 10000000Hz. These are some common prefixes and their associated multiplying factors that are used in audio processes:

Prefix	Symbol	Multiplying factor		Example
micro	μ	$0.000001 = 1/1000000$	10^{-6}	$1\mu s$ = 1 millionth of a second
milli	m	$0.001 = 1/1000$	10^{-3}	10mm = 0.01m
kilo	k	1000	10^{3}	20kHz = 20000Hz
mega	M	1000000	10^{6}	5.53MHz = 5530000Hz
giga	G	1000000000	10^{9}	4GHz = 4000MHz

One of the difficulties in dealing with prefixes relates to moving between them (with the right number of zeros in the result). For example:

- one tenth of a second = 0.1s = 100ms = $100000\mu s$ = 100×10^{-3}s
- one tenth of a millisecond = 0.1ms = 0.0001s = $100\mu s$ = 100×10^{-6}s
- 0.0527s = 52.7ms = $52700\mu s$

Getting such results right is a matter of carefully multiplying or dividing by 1000 to move the decimal point. It is very easy to get the wrong number of zeros without sufficient care. Be careful with computer file and memory storage sizes, as the prefixes are sometimes used differently in those cases.

Problem 8

Here are some conversions to attempt:

a) What is 1.767m in mm?
b) What is 0.00473s in μs?
c) What is 172645μs in ms?
d) What is 6.45×10^4 Hz in kHz?

A.9 Accuracy

When dealing with numerical values, particularly those with many decimal places, it is sometimes unclear as to the importance of the less significant digits. It is **not** the case that it is always appropriate to round after a particular digit. The following examples demonstrate the importance of accuracy in numerical values.

Example 1: Performing Calculations

When calculating values, the general rule is this:

Maintain as much accuracy as possible until the end of the calculation, and **then** decide how accurate the answer needs to be.

When using a calculator and working through a calculation by hand, it is important to retain decimal places (for example, by storing values in memory) rather than using a rounded value. Here is an example of the consequences of rounding:

Question: Calculate the value of frequency f (to two decimal places) using the following equation, where control parameter $p = 0.0791$

$$f = \frac{2}{p^2}$$

- Answer 1: Maintaining decimal places:

$$p^2 = 0.00625681 \qquad \text{therefore} \qquad f \approx 319.65\text{Hz} \tag{A.36}$$

- Answer 2: Rounding the value of p^2:

$$p^2 \approx 0.0063 \qquad \text{therefore} \qquad f \approx 317.46\text{Hz} \tag{A.37}$$

ⓘ

Note the following:

- In the above example, rounding the value of p^2 at the fourth decimal place half way through the calculation has led to a difference of 2.19Hz between the answers. That kind of error could produce an audible difference under some circumstances.
- At the **end** of the calculation, the frequency has been rounded to two decimal places. For a frequency value that will often be sufficient. If, however, the frequency is to be used for a subsequent calculation, then it might be necessary to have more accuracy.

Example 2: Accuracy in Measurement

Examine the following oscillating waveform:

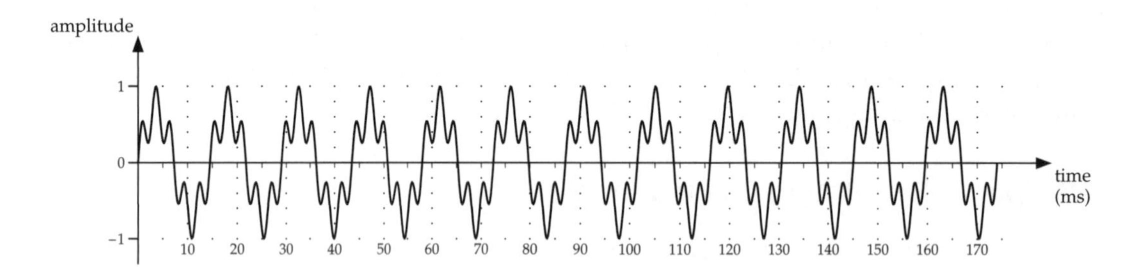

The task is to find the length in time of one cycle of the waveform from the above plot, and subsequently the fundamental frequency:

- If only the first cycle is used, then the cycle length can be said to be approximately 15ms (0.015s). This produces a fundamental frequency as follows:

$$f = \frac{1}{t} = \frac{1}{0.015} \approx 66.67\text{Hz} \qquad \boxed{\text{A.38}}$$

- However, examining the first 10 cycles, it is apparent that 10 cycles lasts 145ms. Therefore, a single cycle length is actually 14.5ms (0.0145s):

$$f = \frac{1}{t} = \frac{1}{0.0145} \approx 68.97\text{Hz} \qquad \boxed{\text{A.39}}$$

The difference in frequency from the two measurements would be audible, and shows that it is necessary to be more accurate than the nearest millisecond in order to calculate a frequency. Again, depending on the context, it might be necessary to be even more accurate than that. Note that the problem was not with the number of decimal places presented in the final result, but with the accuracy of the original measurement. For example, writing the frequency for equation A.38 as 66.66666667Hz does not improve the result and suggests more measurement precision than is actually present.

Example 3: Accuracy in Amplitude

Consider the result of adding sine waves together with the following frequencies and amplitudes:

frequency (Hz)	100	200	300	400	500	600	700	800
amplitude	1/2	1/2	1/3	1/4	1/5	1/6	1/7	1/8

For greatest accuracy, the amplitudes would be achieved by dividing by the number on the denominator of the fractions. If, however, the fractions are converted to decimal numbers and used as multipliers, then the number of decimal places becomes important. For example:

required amplitude	1/2	1/2	1/3	1/4	1/5	1/6	1/7	1/8
to 3 decimal places	0.500	0.500	0.333	0.250	0.200	0.167	0.143	0.125
to 1 decimal place	0.5	0.5	0.3	0.3	0.2	0.2	0.1	0.1

Plotting the sum of sine waves it is apparent that there are differences in the shape of the waveform, which will be audible:

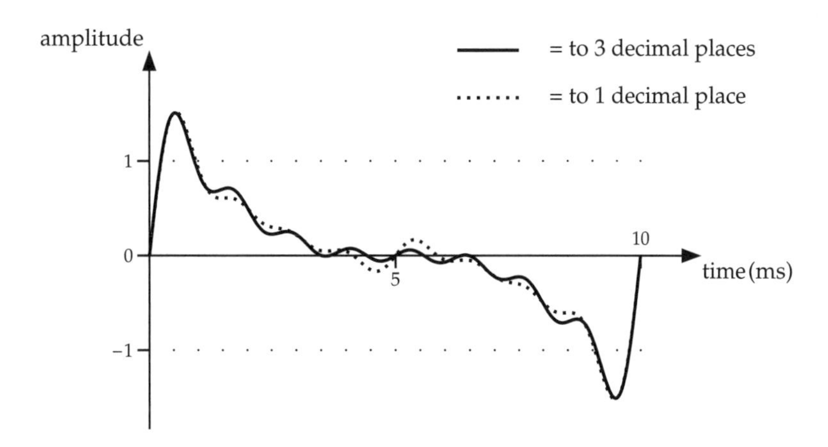

It is better to be cautious and use more decimal places in values, rather than round to a small number of digits.

Example 4: Significance of Numerical Variations

Audio process control parameters do not necessarily have linear perceptual effects. It is sometimes necessary to consider where on the range of a parameter a value falls, and therefore the significance of a particular numerical variation. For example:

- Using equation A.33 (p.695), it can be shown that the following pairs of fundamental frequencies are a semitone apart:

  50Hz — 52.97Hz   1000Hz — 1059.46Hz

  Due to the exponential scale of note fundamental frequencies, differences of 2.97Hz and 59.46Hz are equally perceptually significant at different points on the frequency scale. That means that the number of significant figures is important. The 0.46 in 1059.46Hz is less perceptually significant than the 0.97 in 52.97Hz.

- Using equation A.31 (p.692), it is possible to convert from linear to decibel amplitude gain values. For example:

  $$20\log_{10}(1.01) \approx 0.0864\text{dB} \qquad 20\log_{10}(1000.01) \approx 60.0001\text{dB}$$

  $$20\log_{10}(1.02) \approx 0.1720\text{dB} \qquad 20\log_{10}(1000.02) \approx 60.0002\text{dB}$$

  This shows that the same sized linear change has a very different change in decibels, depending upon the position on the scale.

A.10 Answers to Problems

Problem 1 (p.682)

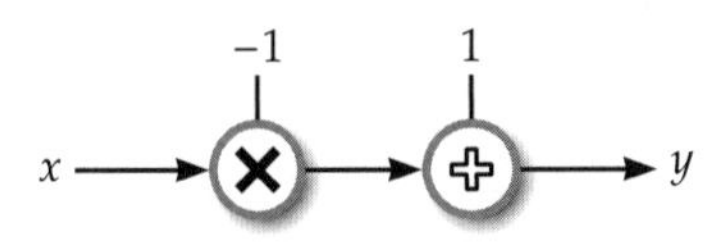

Problem 2 (p.684)

a) $f \approx 261.626$

b) $f \approx 277.183$

c) $f \approx 269.292$

Were the answers rounded to the correct number of decimal places?

Problem 3 (p.685)

$y = -0.375$

Problem 4 (p.689)

a) $y = 56x$

b) $y = 0.6x + 0.1$

c) $y = 0.5x + 0.5$

d) $y = 0.1x + 0.9$

e) $y = \frac{80}{127}x - 80$

f) $y = -\frac{80}{127}x$

Problem 5 (p.690)

a) $a = 10t$

b) $a = -0.4t + 0.4$

Problem 6 (p.693)

a) $\text{gain}_{\text{dB}} = 20\text{dB}$

b) $\text{gain}_{\text{dB}} = 40\text{dB}$

c) $\text{gain}_{\text{dB}} = 60\text{dB}$

Was the third answer predictable after the first two?

Problem 7 (p.697)

If a is amplitude and t is time, the equation for the amplitude of the sound is $a = 0.5 \times 0.4^t$

- When $t = 6$, $a \approx 0.00205$
- When $t = 6.5$, $a \approx 0.00130$
- When $t = 7$, $a \approx 0.00082$

Therefore the answer is 7 seconds.

Problem 8 (p.699)

a) 1767mm

b) 4730μs

c) 172.645ms

d) 64.5kHz

(i)

B

Windowing and Window Functions

B.1 Introduction

The process of extracting a segment of audio from a longer time domain waveform is found in a number of audio processes such as Short Time Fourier Transform (STFT) frequency domain methods (Chapter 12) and granular synthesis (Chapter 22). The purpose of the extraction is such that the segment can be used in isolation. The length of the segment and its position within the source waveform will usually be determined by the configuration of the audio process. It is often impossible to ensure synchrony between the point of extraction and the oscillation of the waveform. It is likely, therefore, that the sample values at the ends of the segment will have non-zero amplitude, as shown in figure B.1.

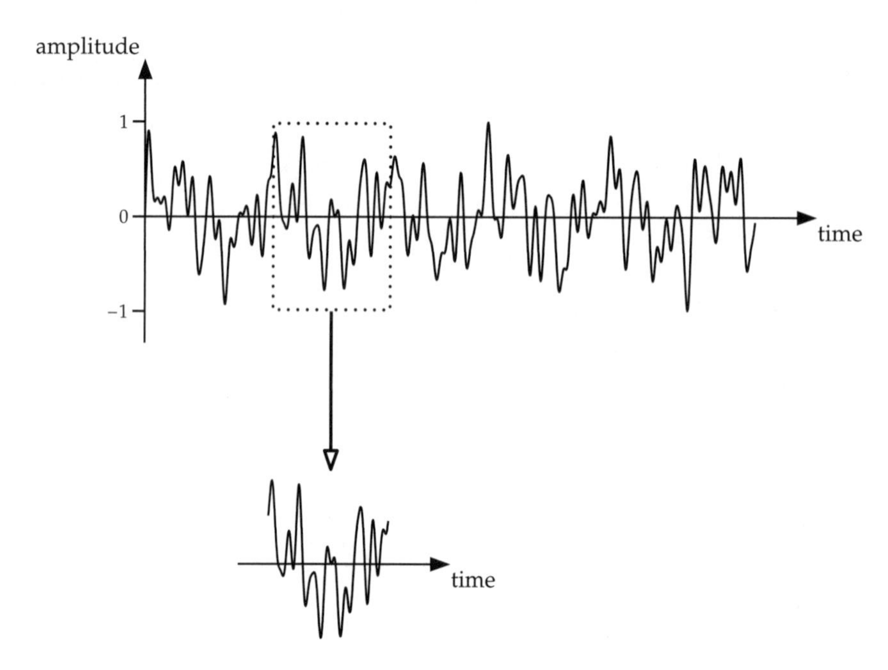

Figure B.1 Extracting an audio segment

The discontinuities at the ends of the segment will affect the subsequent results of the audio process. For example, if the segment is played back there will be a click heard at each end. With granular synthesis, such segments are played back in large numbers in quick succession, so the discontinuities will significantly affect the tonal character of the result.

The process of extracting an audio segment in the manner shown in figure B.1 is called applying a *rectangular window function* (also known as a square window). It is worth examining what happens when rectangular windowed segments are transformed into

the frequency domain. Figure B.2a is an average spectrum plot of a waveform purely composed of harmonics where the fundamental frequency has been chosen such that an integer number of cycles exactly fits within the length of the window. There are no discontinuities at the ends of the segment, and the frequency domain plot shows crisp lines at the partial positions.

Figure B.2b uses exactly the same window length and analysis settings as figure B.2a, but the fundamental frequency has been chosen such that the cycles are cut-off at the edges of the window. The frequency domain analysis process has included these discontinuities in the result, producing fairly high amplitude values between the harmonic partial peaks (known as *leakage*). The segment extraction situation that results in figure B.2b is far more likely in practical circumstances than figure B.2a. Therefore, a better windowing technique is required, in order to improve the consistency and clarity of frequency domain analysis results.

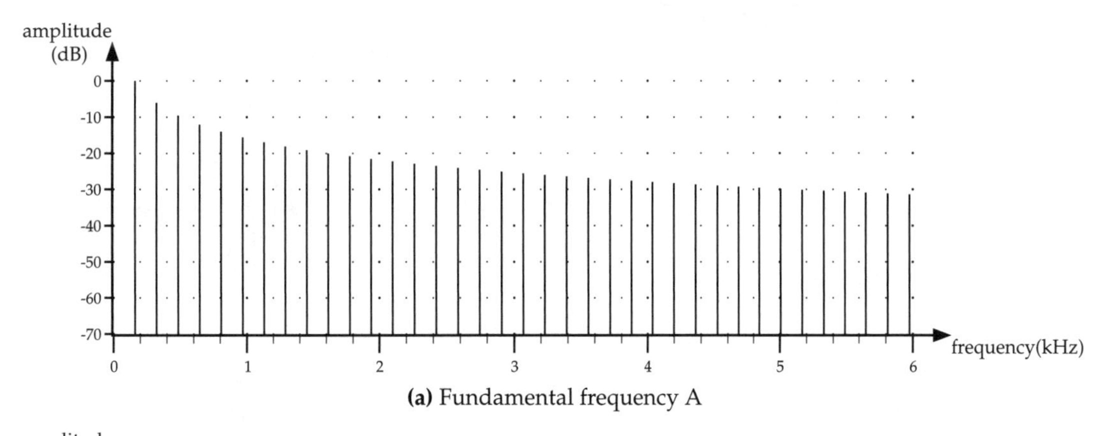

(a) Fundamental frequency A

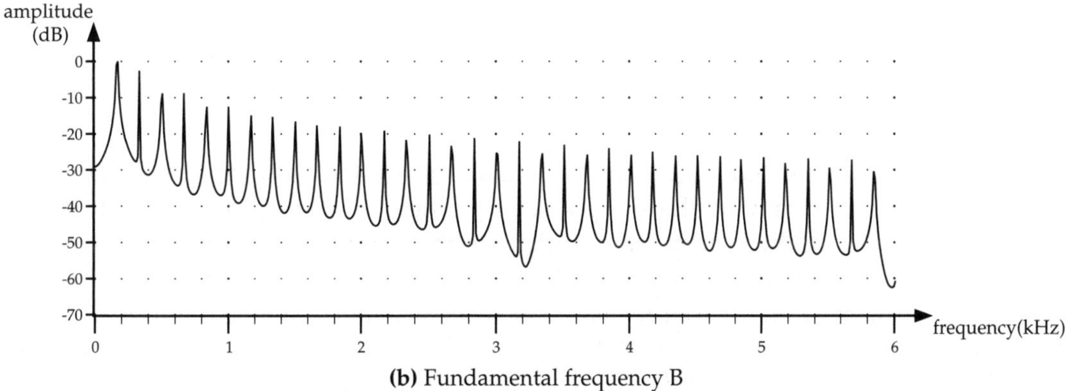

(b) Fundamental frequency B

Figure B.2 Rectangular window function effects on harmonic sounds (average spectrum plots)

To reduce the effects related to discontinuities, it is normal to apply a non-rectangular window function to the audio segment. This process is shown in figure B.3. The window function is an envelope with values between 0 and 1. The window function is applied to the audio segment by multiplying each sample by the function value at the corresponding position in time. A rectangular window function is a flat line at value 1. Non-rectangular functions have large values in the centre, but taper towards 0 at the ends such that the discontinuities are attenuated (as shown in the figure).

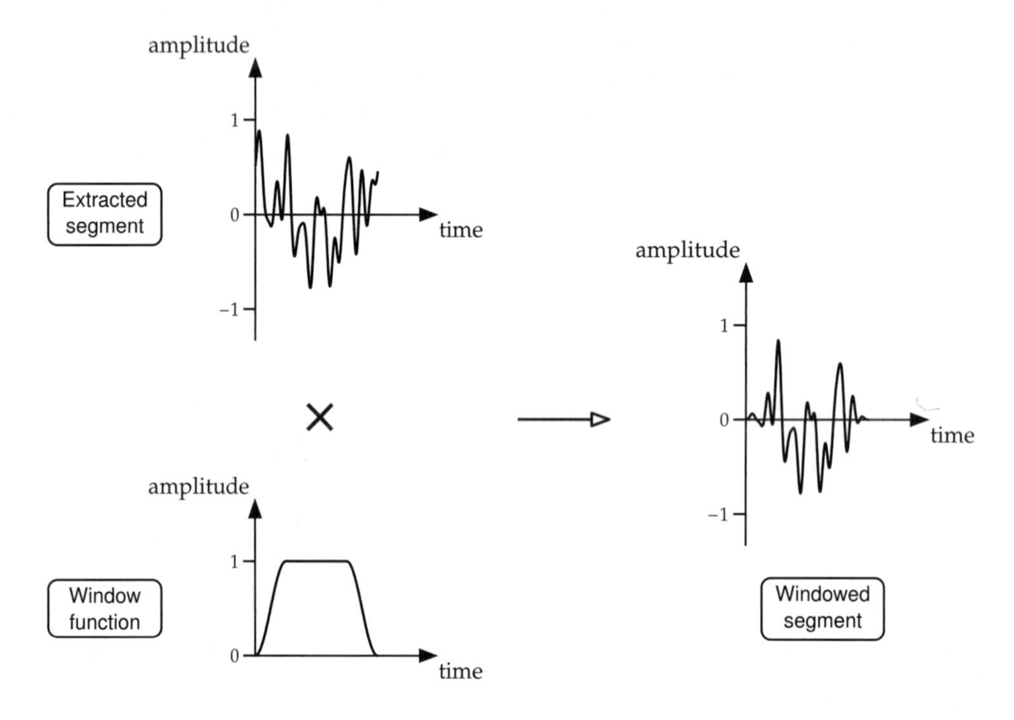

Figure B.3 Application of a window function to an audio segment

In terms of a time domain effect, it is apparent that a non-rectangular window function has the desired effect of removing the sharp discontinuities. However, there are side effects of this process. Firstly, the average amplitude over the segment has been reduced, due to the attenuation of some parts. Secondly, the waveform is not quite the same shape that it was originally. That means that the signal has been changed and so might well sound different when played back, or look different in analysis. There is a compromise between smoothing the discontinuities and preserving the character of the sound.

Figure B.4 shows average spectrum plots of exactly the same two signals as figure B.2, using the same window length and analysis settings, except that a Blackman-Harris window function has been applied (illustrated later in figure B.7, p.712). The consistency between

the two plots is much improved compared to the two rectangular window function plots. Changing the fundamental frequency does not have the dramatic effect that it did before. However there is a side effect in terms of the width of the main lobes (the partial peaks) where the Blackman-Harris window function does not produce the same narrow partial peaks that exist in figure B.2a.

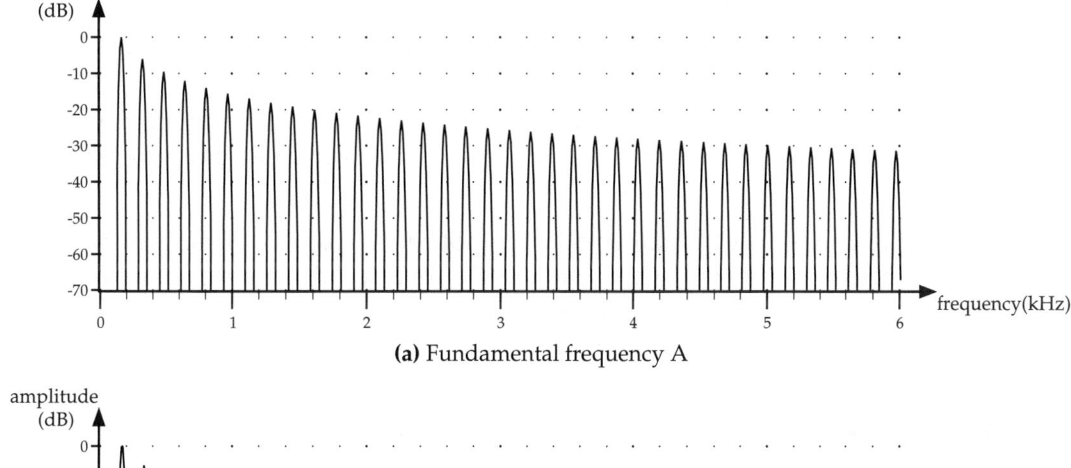

(a) Fundamental frequency A

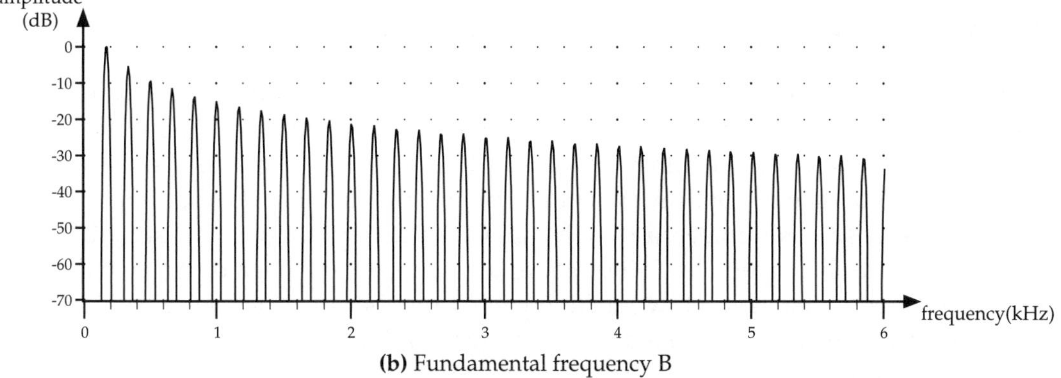

(b) Fundamental frequency B

Figure B.4 Blackman-Harris window function effects on harmonic sounds (average spectrum plots)

In general, non-rectangular window functions are applied to achieve consistency of results, despite the side effects. Adjusting other analysis parameters can often be used to tailor the results as required. All the frequency domain plots in the main part of this book have been produced with non-rectangular window functions. There are a number of factors that should be considered when selecting a particular window function:

- Some window functions (such as those described in §B.2) are used more commonly than others. This is not because they are perfect in all respects. Rather, selecting a common function can be appropriate where results from different analyses are to be compared, for example.

- A more scientific approach to selection is to consider the relative performance benefits of the window functions. Metrics exist that relate to the results of applying the window in the frequency domain, and so its ability to aid in the process of detecting frequency partials. If there was a perfect solution to this, then only one window function would exist. In practice, the functions have different trade-offs such as their ability to produce a narrow peak where partials exist and low sidelobes (leakage either side of the peaks).
- Some window functions provide control parameters for tailoring the effect to a particular circumstance, such as the Tukey window in figure B.8 (p.713). Similarly the overall shape might be more suited to one application than another, depending on how the edges should be tapered and the centre portion of the audio segment preserved.
- Window functions vary in mathematical complexity in terms of their generation. A simple function such as the Hann window (figure B.5, p.712) might suffice for cases where a basic windowing effect is required, but it might be necessary to explore more sophisticated functions where a particular frequency domain result is required.

B.2 Some Common Window Functions

There are a considerable number of window functions in common use. This section describes some frequently used functions and their relative benefits. The functions have been normalised to an x axis range of 0 to 1. This makes it easy to scale the window function to fit a particular application. For example, if the function is to be applied to 1000 sample value positions numbered 0 to 999 in a granular synthesizer (Chapter 22), then dividing the sample position by 999 provides a value for x between 0 and 1. That value can then be used to find a window function value from the equations described later. The resulting y value will be multiplied by the corresponding sample value to produce the windowing effect.

An additional complication occurs when generating a window function for use with Fast Fourier Transform (FFT) and related methods (Chapter 12). In those cases, it is necessary that the window function extends one sample further than the window size. For example, if the window size is 512, with sample positions numbered 0 to 511, then the current position will be divided by 512 (rather than 511) to produce a value of x between 0 and $^{511}/_{512}$. This is due to the underlying nature of the DFT technique and the way that the data being examined is assumed to have periodic extension.

The window values can be calculated from the mathematical equations described below when needed for the current position in the window. Alternatively, if the size of the window is known in advance (say 512 samples) it is possible to calculate the window function values for all of those sample positions and store them in a lookup table. If the

window function is to be applied repeatedly without changing size, then the lookup table method is more efficient.

The *Hann* (or Hanning) window function (figure B.5) is a commonly available choice in software applications. As well as having reasonable performance for such tasks as frequency domain transformation (Chapter 12), it is also relatively simple in mathematical terms. Mathematically it is produced as follows, where the cosine function takes an argument in radians:

$$y = 0.5\left(1 - \cos(2\pi x)\right) \quad \text{where} \quad 0 \leqslant x \leqslant 1 \tag{B.1}$$

The *Hamming* window function (figure B.6) is also commonly available in software applications. It is a subtle modification of the Hann function form to achieve slightly improved nearest sidelobe performance in such applications as frequency domain transformation. Note, however, that the outermost values are slightly above zero. The mathematical form of the Hamming window is as follows:

$$y = 0.54 - 0.46\cos(2\pi x) \quad \text{where} \quad 0 \leqslant x \leqslant 1 \tag{B.2}$$

Blackman and related window functions (figure B.7) use the following mathematical form:

$$y = a_0 - a_1\cos(2\pi x) + a_2\cos(4\pi x) - a_3\cos(6\pi x) \quad \text{where} \quad 0 \leqslant x \leqslant 1 \tag{B.3}$$

A number of different values have been developed for coefficients a_0 to a_3. Some of the most common are as follows:

window name	a_0	a_1	a_2	a_3
Blackman	0.42	0.5	0.08	0
exact Blackman	0.42659071	0.49656062	0.07684867	0
Blackman-Harris (minimum 4-term)	0.35875	0.48829	0.14128	0.01168

The *Blackman-Harris* window function is preferable to the simpler Hann and Hamming techniques in terms of sidelobe effects in such applications as frequency domain transformation, but produces a wider main lobe (width of partial peaks).

ⓘ

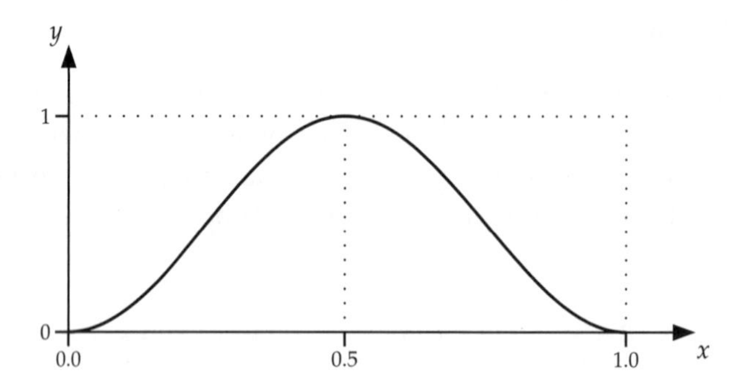

Figure B.5 Hann (Hanning) window function

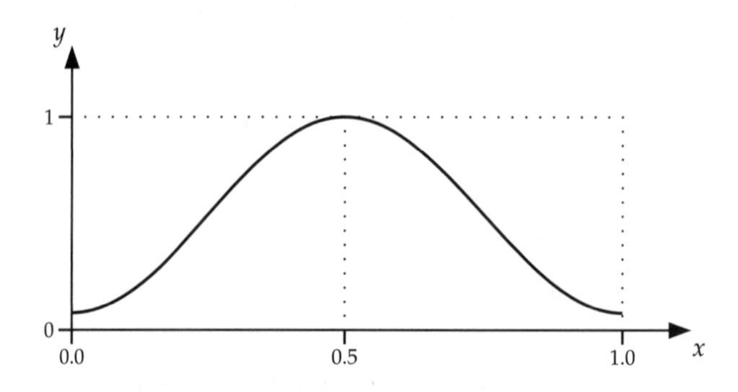

Figure B.6 Hamming window function

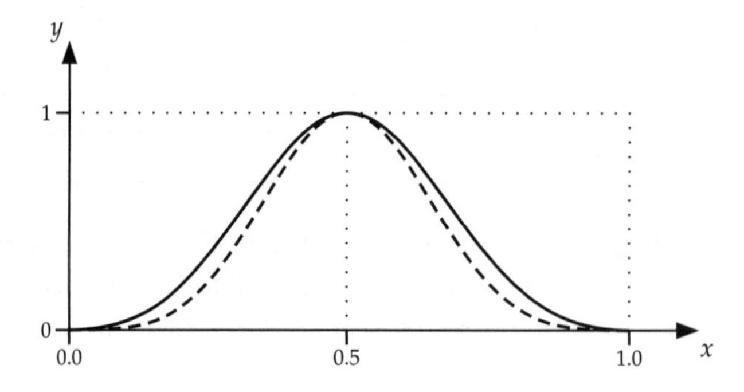

Figure B.7 Blackman (solid line) and Blackman-Harris (dashed line) window functions

The *Tukey* (or cosine-tapered) window function shown in figure B.8 has a flat region in the centre and tapered ends. An advantage of this function for applications such as granular synthesis (Chapter 22), is the flexibility provided by the shaping parameter α (which takes a value between 0 and 1). When α is 0 the window is rectangular and so the original envelope shape of the signal is preserved. When α is 1 the window is the same shape as the Hann window function (figure B.5). In between it is possible to preserve the original wave in the centre portion, while tapering at the edges to attenuate discontinuities. The equations to create the Tukey function are as follows:

$$y = \begin{cases} 0.5\left(1 + \cos\left[\pi\left(\frac{2x}{\alpha} - 1\right)\right]\right) & \text{if} \quad 0 \leqslant x < 0.5\alpha \\ 1 & \text{if} \quad 0.5\alpha \leqslant x \leqslant (1 - 0.5\alpha) \\ 0.5\left(1 + \cos\left[\pi\left(\frac{2x-2}{\alpha} + 1\right)\right]\right) & \text{if} \quad (1 - 0.5\alpha) < x \leqslant 1 \end{cases} \tag{B.4}$$

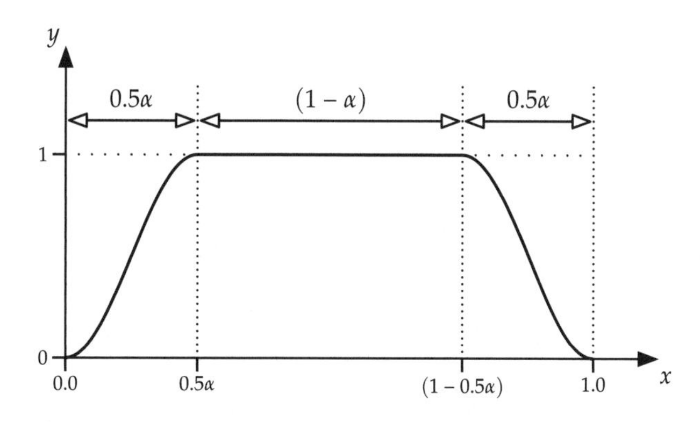

Figure B.8 Tukey window function

B.3 Learning More

The following source provides some more advanced material that relates to this chapter, which can be used for further study:

Harris, Fredric J. 1978. "On the Use of Windows for Harmonic Analysis with the Discrete Fourier Transform." *Proceedings of the IEEE* 66:1:51–83.

Block Diagram Techniques

C.1 Detail and Clarity

Block diagrams are a powerful tool for describing audio processes. The intention is to express the flow of control and audio signal data through process blocks such that it is easy to translate into an implementation (such as a computer program).

One difficulty in creating and using block diagrams is in choosing an appropriate amount of visual detail. For example:

- An oscillator block representation should include the waveform used (figure C.1a), as it is important for explaining the nature of the process. If the shape is very complex, however, then a small visual representation might not be sufficient for knowing how to implement the oscillator. In that case, an additional table of harmonic amplitudes, or a larger plot of the shape might be necessary.
- A visual indication of the shape produced by an envelope generator is helpful for the reader in determining the general character of the result (figure C.1b). However, it is very hard to specify all the finer details of shape and response to control inputs within the representation.
- A block that delays an audio signal by a particular length of time (figure C.1c) could utilise a graphical icon instead of a text label, but it would not convey any additional information. The process is clear from the name, and the underlying technique is too complex to represent graphically.

A key aspect of good block diagrams is clarity, such that the reader does not have to spend additional time interpreting the process. Figure C.2a shows a computer producing an audio signal that passes through two hardware audio processes, and then the computer records the result. However, without arrows on the connections, it is not apparent whether the flow is clockwise or anti-clockwise. Depending on the signal and parameter configuration, this could significantly affect the results.

Some authors use a junction to indicate signals being combined, such as the example in figure C.3a. The problem is that it is hard to distinguish between combination and splitting with that diagram style. For example, it might be assumed that $d = a + b + c$, but if signal c is looping back into another part of the diagram then it could be that $c = a + b$ and $d = c$. It is important to be clear about the type of combination that is occurring, such as whether it is addition or multiplication. Figure C.3b resolves these questions.

In figure C.4a, it is not clear if the output is $(5 - 4)$ or $(4 - 5)$, and in figure C.5a it is not clear if the output is $2/3$ or $3/2$. Rather than using subtraction and division blocks, it is clearer to use addition and multiplication (figures C.4b and C.5b), as the ordering is not important to the final result. That is because mathematically $(a + b) \equiv (b + a)$ and $(a \times b) \equiv (b \times a)$.

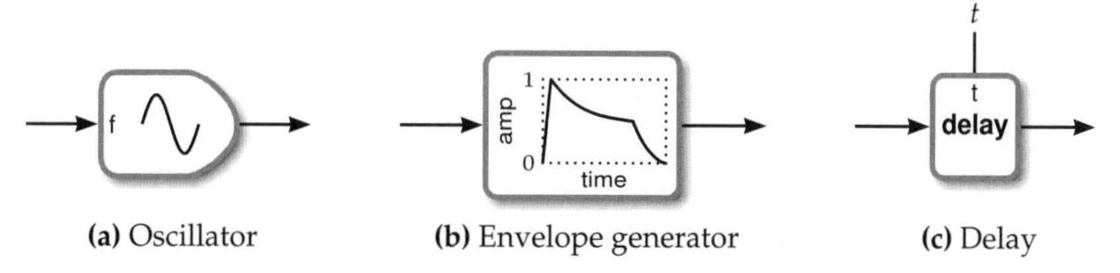

(a) Oscillator **(b)** Envelope generator **(c)** Delay

Figure C.1 Example blocks

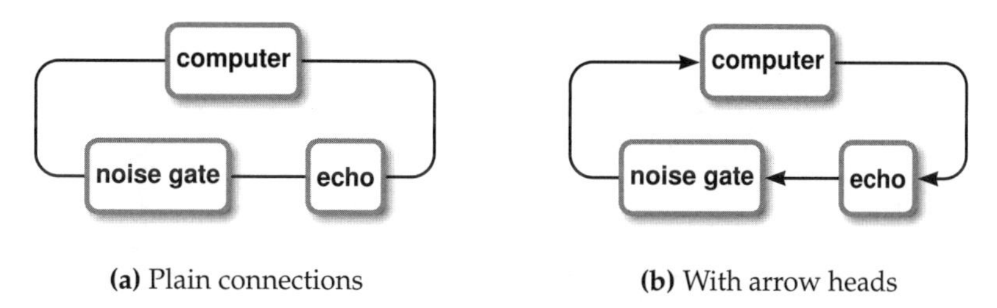

(a) Plain connections **(b)** With arrow heads

Figure C.2 Clarity in flow

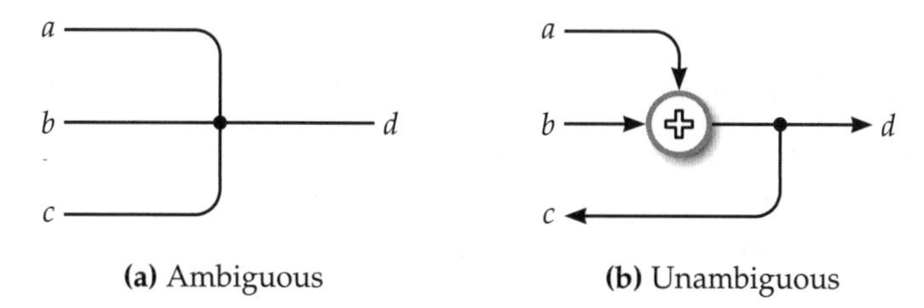

(a) Ambiguous **(b)** Unambiguous

Figure C.3 Clarity where signals are combined and split

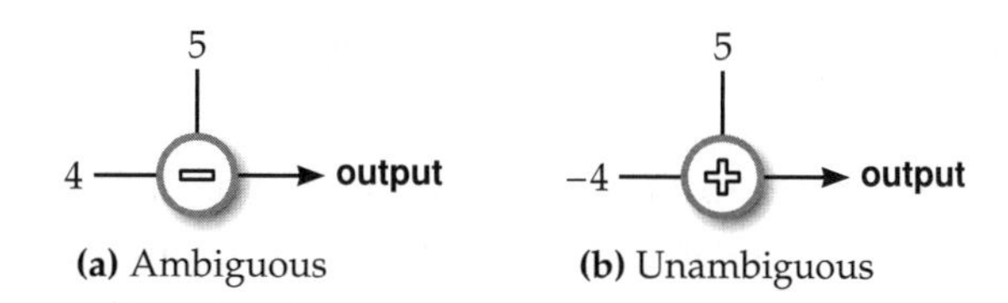

(a) Ambiguous **(b)** Unambiguous

Figure C.4 Clarity where values are subtracted

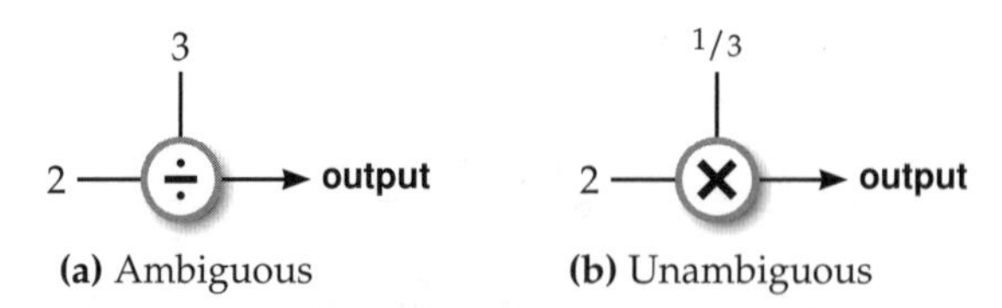

(a) Ambiguous **(b)** Unambiguous

Figure C.5 Clarity where values are divided

With mathematical forms it can be neater to use a block containing an equation rather than expressing the process as discrete mathematical elements. An example is shown in figure C.6.

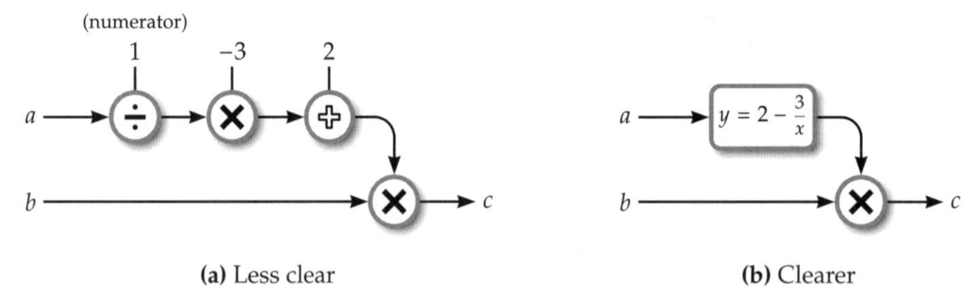

(a) Less clear **(b)** Clearer

Figure C.6 Clarity through use of an equation

C.2 Relating Diagrams and Programming Forms

Taking the block diagram forms in this book and implementing them in a graphical audio programming environment is generally straightforward. Blocks such as filters, oscillators, and envelope generators are usually standard process objects. There might, however, be some issues to consider:

- Implementation details can be hidden from the user; for example, whether varying a lowpass filter cutoff will always update the underlying filter coefficients within one audio sample period, or whether those values will be updated at a lower control rate for efficiency. Similarly, whether an oscillator implementation has the potential to produce partials above the Nyquist frequency, or whether an antialiasing algorithm is being used.
- Different packages have different representations of data, and different policies for dealing with them; for example, whether control data values are sent at regular intervals, or only when values are changed. In some cases, control values and audio sample values are interchangeable, but sometimes there is a requirement for them to be processed in different ways. There might also be policies on whether connections

are updated in a particular order, or whether some parts of the process are prioritised over others.

Conventional text-based general purpose programming languages (utilising a library of audio functions) can have similar issues to graphical audio programming environments. It is also necessary for the programmer to consider how to translate the flow in the diagram into suitably sequenced lines of code. Figure C.7 shows two process blocks in series. Each process block might be an oscillator, filter, or mapping function, for example.

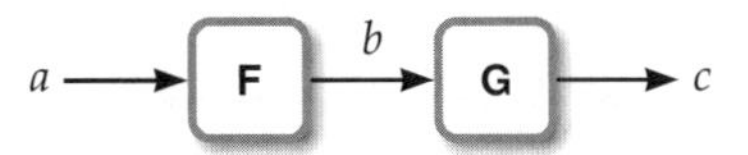

Figure C.7 Blocks in combination example 1

In a text-based programming language, the blocks will typically be processed by calls to functions (or methods). For example:

```
b = F(a)
c = G(b)
```

The ordering of the lines of code is vital to ensuring that the input signal flows through the two blocks in the order shown in the diagram. With a more complex form, such as that in figure C.8, it is important to consider each path from input to output as well as the order of computation.

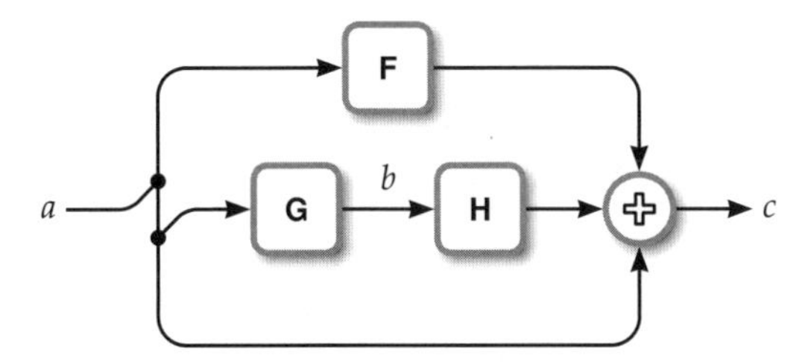

Figure C.8 Blocks in combination example 2

The code for the block diagram is as follows:

```
b = G(a)
c = F(a) + H(b) + a
```

Processes with feedback paths present a challenge of working out the order of computation. In figure C.9, generating output variable *c* depends on knowing both *a* and *b*, but computing the value of *b* requires knowing the value of *c*. If block F is a delay element, then it will usually be possible to read a delayed (old) value from the buffer into variable *b* before having to write a newly computed value (*c*) into the buffer as the last step in the algorithm.

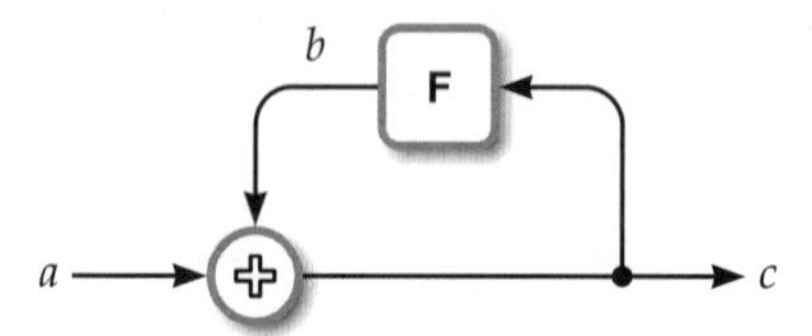

Figure C.9 Blocks in combination example 3

Alternatively, it might be appropriate to use the output value computed for the previous sample as the input to the process block:

```
b = F(lastvalue)
c = a + b
lastvalue = c
```

The value of *lastvalue* must be maintained for the next computation cycle. It is necessary to study the nature of the process to determine the best approach.

Index

E

F

G

X

Z